Nineteenth-Century Literature Criticism

Guide to Gale Literary Criticism Series

For criticism on	Consult these Gale series
Authors now living or who died after December 31, 1999	*CONTEMPORARY LITERARY CRITICISM (CLC)*
Authors who died between 1900 and 1999	*TWENTIETH-CENTURY LITERARY CRITICISM (TCLC)*
Authors who died between 1800 and 1899	*NINETEENTH-CENTURY LITERATURE CRITICISM (NCLC)*
Authors who died between 1400 and 1799	*LITERATURE CRITICISM FROM 1400 TO 1800 (LC)* *SHAKESPEAREAN CRITICISM (SC)*
Authors who died before 1400	*CLASSICAL AND MEDIEVAL LITERATURE CRITICISM (CMLC)*
Authors of books for children and young adults	*CHILDREN'S LITERATURE REVIEW (CLR)*
Dramatists	*DRAMA CRITICISM (DC)*
Poets	*POETRY CRITICISM (PC)*
Short story writers	*SHORT STORY CRITICISM (SSC)*
Black writers of the past two hundred years	*BLACK LITERATURE CRITICISM (BLC)* *BLACK LITERATURE CRITICISM SUPPLEMENT (BLCS)*
Hispanic writers of the late nineteenth and twentieth centuries	*HISPANIC LITERATURE CRITICISM (HLC)* *HISPANIC LITERATURE CRITICISM SUPPLEMENT (HLCS)*
Native North American writers and orators of the eighteenth, nineteenth, and twentieth centuries	*NATIVE NORTH AMERICAN LITERATURE (NNAL)*
Major authors from the Renaissance to the present	*WORLD LITERATURE CRITICISM, 1500 TO THE PRESENT (WLC)* *WORLD LITERATURE CRITICISM SUPPLEMENT (WLCS)*

ISSN 0732-1864

Volume 95

Nineteenth-Century Literature Criticism

Excerpts from Criticism of the
Works of Novelists, Philosophers, and Other
Creative Writers Who Died between 1800
and 1899, from the First Published Critical
Appraisals to Current Evaluations

Juliet Byington
Editor

GALE GROUP

Detroit
New York
San Francisco
London
Boston
Woodbridge, CT

STAFF

Lynn M. Spampinato, Janet Witalec, *Managing Editors, Literature Product*
Kathy D. Darrow, *Product Liaison*
Juliet Byington, *Editor*
Mark W. Scott, *Publisher, Literature Product*

Russel Whitaker, *Associate Editor*
Jessica Menzo, *Assistant Editor*
Jenny Cromie, Mary Ruby, *Technical Training Specialists*
Deborah J. Morad, Kathleen Lopez Nolan, *Managing Editors, Literature Content*
Susan M. Trosky, *Director, Literature Content*

Maria L. Franklin, *Permissions Manager*
Edna Hedblad, *Permissions Specialist*
Kim Davis, *Permissions Assistant*

Victoria B. Cariappa, *Research Manager*
Tracie A. Richardson, *Project Coordinator*
Andrew Guy Malonis, Barbara McNeil, Gary J. Oudersluys, Maureen Richards, Cheryl L. Warnock, *Research Specialists*
Tamara C. Nott, *Research Associate*
Ron Morelli, *Research Assistant*

Dorothy Maki, *Manufacturing Manager*
Stacy L. Melson, *Buyer*

Mary Beth Trimper, *Composition and Prepress Manager*
Carolyn Roney, *Composition Specialist*

Randy Bassett, *Image Database Supervisor*
Robert Duncan, *Imaging Specialist*
Michael Logusz, *Graphic Artist*
Pamela A. Reed, *Imaging Coordinator*
Kelly A. Quin, *Imaging Editor*

Library of Congress Catalog Card Number
ISBN 0-7876-4550-8
ISSN 0732-1864
Printed in the United States of America

10 9 8 7 6 5 4 3 2 1

Contents

Preface vii

Acknowledgments xi

Preface

Since its inception in 1981, *Nineteeth-Century Literature Criticism* (*NCLC*) has been a valuable resource for students and librarians seeking critical commentary on writers of this transitional period in world history. Designated an "Outstanding Reference Source" by the American Library Association with the publication of is first volume, *NCLC* has since been purchased by over 6,000 school, public, and university libraries. The series has covered more than 300 authors representing 29 nationalities and over 17,000 titles. No other reference source has surveyed the critical reaction to nineteenth-century authors and literature as thoroughly as *NCLC*.

Scope of the Series

NCLC is designed to introduce students and advanced readers to the authors of the nineteenth century and to the most significant interpretations of these authors' works. The great poets, novelists, short story writers, playwrights, and philosophers of this period are frequently studied in high school and college literature courses. By organizing and reprinting commentary written on these authors, *NCLC* helps students develop valuable insight into literary history, promotes a better understanding of the texts, and sparks ideas for papers and assignments. Each entry in *NCLC* presents a comprehensive survey of an author's career or an individual work of literature and provides the user with a multiplicity of interpretations and assessments. Such variety allows students to pursue their own interests; furthermore, it fosters an awareness that literature is dynamic and responsive to many different opinions.

Every fourth volume of *NCLC* is devoted to literary topics that cannot be covered under the author approach used in the rest of the series. Such topics include literary movements, prominent themes in nineteenth-century literature, literary reaction to political and historical events, significant eras in literary history, prominent literary anniversaries, and the literatures of cultures that are often overlooked by English-speaking readers.

NCLC continues the survey of criticism of world literature begun by Gale's *Contemporary Literary Criticism* (*CLC*) and *Twentieth-Century Literary Criticism* (*TCLC*).

Organization of the Book

An *NCLC* entry consists of the following elements:

- The **Author Heading** cites the name under which the author most commonly wrote, followed by birth and death dates. Also located here are any name variations under which an author wrote, including transliterated forms for authors whose native languages use nonroman alphabets. If the author wrote consistently under a pseudonym, the pseudonym will be listed in the author heading and the author's actual name given in parenthesis on the first line of the biographical and critical information. Uncertain birth or death dates are indicated by question marks. Single-work entries are preceded by a heading that consists of the most common form of the title in English translation (if applicable) and the original date of composition.

- The **Introduction** contains background information that introduces the reader to the author, work, or topic that is the subject of the entry.

- A **Portrait of the Author** is included when available.

- The list of **Principal Works** is ordered chronologically by date of first publication and lists the most important works by the author. The genre and publication date of each work is given. In the case of foreign authors whose works have been translated into English, the list will focus primarily on twentieth-century translations, selecting those works most commonly considered the best by critics. Unless otherwise indicated, dramas are dated by first performance, not first publication. Lists of **Representative Works** by different authors appear with topic entries.

- Reprinted **Criticism** is arranged chronologically in each entry to provide a useful perspective on changes in critical evaluation over time. The critic's name and the date of composition or publication of the critical work are given at the beginning of each piece of criticism. Unsigned criticism is preceded by the title of the source in which it appeared. All titles by the author featured in the text are printed in boldface type. Footnotes are reprinted at the end of each essay or excerpt. In the case of excerpted criticism, only those footnotes that pertain to the excerpted texts are included. Criticism in topic entries is arranged chronologically under a variety of subheadings to facilitate the study of different aspects of the topic.

- A complete **Bibliographical Citation** of the original essay or book precedes each piece of criticism.

- Critical essays are prefaced by brief **Annotations** explicating each piece.

- An annotated bibliography of **Further Reading** appears at the end of each entry and suggests resources for additional study. In some cases, significant essays for which the editors could not obtain reprint rights are included here. Boxed material following the further reading list provides references to other biographical and critical sources on the author in series published by Gale.

Indexes

Each volume of *NCLC* contains a **Cumulative Author Index** listing all authors who have appeared in a wide variety of reference sources published by the Gale Group, including *NCLC*. A complete list of these sources is found facing the first page of the Author Index. The index also includes birth and death dates and cross references between pseudonyms and actual names.

A **Cumulative Nationality Index** lists all authors featured in *NCLC* by nationality, followed by the number of the *NCLC* volume in which their entry appears.

A **Cumulative Topic Index** lists the literary themes and topics treated in the series as well as in *Classical and Medieval Literature Criticism, Literature Criticism from 1400 to 1800, Twentieth-Century Literary Criticism,* and the *Contemporary Literary Criticism* Yearbook, which was discontinued in 1998.

An alphabetical **Title Index** accompanies each volume of *NCLC*, with the exception of the Topics volumes. Listings of titles by authors covered in the given volume are followed by the author's name and the corresponding page numbers where the titles are discussed. English translations of foreign titles and variations of titles are cross-referenced to the title under which a work was originally published. Titles of novels, dramas, nonfiction books, and poetry, short story, or essay collections are printed in italics, while individual poems, short stories, and essays are printed in roman type within quotation marks.

In response to numerous suggestions from librarians, Gale also produces an annual paperbound edition of the *NCLC* cumulative title index. This annual cumulation, which alphabetically lists all titles reviewed in the series, is available to all customers. Additional copies of this index are available upon request. Librarians and patrons will welcome this separate index; it saves shelf space, is easy to use, and is recyclable upon receipt of the next edition.

Citing *Nineteenth-Century Literature Criticism*

When writing papers, students who quote directly from any volume in the Literary Criticism Series may use the following general format to footnote reprinted criticism. The first example pertains to material drawn from periodicals, the second to material reprinted from books.

Kim McQuaid, "William Apes, Pequot: An Indian Reformer in the Jackson Era," *The New England Quarterly,* 50 (December 1977): 605-25; excerpted and reprinted in *Nineteenth-Century Literature Criticism,* vol. 73, ed. Janet Witalec (Farmington Hills, Mich.: The Gale Group, 1999), 3-4.

Richard Harter Fogle, *The Imagery of Keats and Shelley: A Comparative Study* (Archon Books, 1949), 211-51; excerpted and reprinted in *Nineteenth-Century Literature Criticism,* vol. 73, ed. Janet Witalec (Farmington Hills, Mich.: The Gale Group, 1999), 157-69.

Suggestions are Welcome

Readers who wish to suggest new features, topics, or authors to appear in future volumes, or who have other suggestions or comments are cordially invited to call, write, or fax the Managing Editor:

Managing Editor, Literary Criticism Series
The Gale Group
27500 Drake Road
Farmington Hills, MI 48331-3535
1-800-347-4253 (GALE)
Fax: 248-699-8054

Acknowledgments

The editors wish to thank the copyright holders of the excerpted criticism included in this volume and the permissions managers of many book and magazine publishing companies for assisting us in securing reproduction rights. We are also grateful to the staffs of the Detroit Public Library, the Library of Congress, the University of Detroit Mercy Library, Wayne State University Purdy/Kresge Library Complex, and the University of Michigan Libraries for making their resources available to us. Following is a list of the copyright holders who have granted us permission to reproduce material in this volume of *NCLC*. Every effort has been made to trace copyright, but if omissions have been made, please let us know.

COPYRIGHTED EXCERPTS IN *NCLC*, VOLUME 95, WERE REPRODUCED FROM THE FOLLOWING PERIODICALS:

American Literary History, v. 8, Summer, 1996 for "The Aesthetic of Dispossession: Washington Irving and Ideologies of (De)Colonization in the Early Republic" by Laura J. Murray. Reproduced by permission of the publisher and the author.—*American Transcendental Quarterly,* v. 14, Spring, 1972. Copyright 1972 by Kenneth Walter Cameron./v. 44, Fall, 1979; v. 2, March, 1988. Copyright 1979, 1988 by the University of Rhode Island. All reproduced by permission.—*CEA Critic,* v. 33, 1971 for "Freudianism, American Romanticism, and 'Young Goodman Brown'" by Harry M. Campbell. Reproduced by permission of the publisher and the author.—*CLA Journal,* v. 42, 1999. Copyright, 1999 by The College Language Association. Used by permission of The College Language Association.—*ESQ: A Journal of the American Renaissance,* v. 62, Winter, 1971 for "Hawthorne Interprets 'Young Goodman Brown'" by Robert Emmet Whelan, Jr.; v. 26, 1980 for "The Sources of Ambiguity in Hawthorne's 'Young Goodman Brown': A Structuralist Approach" by Harold F. Mosher, Jr.; v. 40, 1994 for "Recovering 'Rip Van Winkle': A Corrective Reading" by Hugh J. Dawson; v. 40, 1994 for "Goodman Brown and the Puritan Catechism" by Benjamin Franklin, V. All reproduced by permission of the publisher and the authors./v. 31, 1963 for "'Young Goodman Brown': Hawthorne's Intent" by Frank Davidson. Reproduced by permission of the publisher.—*Essex Institute Historical Collections,* v. 104, October, 1968; v. 110, October, 1974. Copyright © 1968, 1974 by The Essex Institute Historical Collections. Both reproduced by permission.—*Folk Music Journal,* v. 5, 1986 for "A Reappraisal of Percy's Editing," by Zinnia Knapman. Reproduced by permission of the publisher and the author.—*Forum,* v. 17, Spring, 1979 for "The Young Thomas Percy," by Cleanth Brooks. Reproduced by permission of the Estate of Cleanth Brooks.—*Hemingway Review,* v. 17, Spring, 1998. Copyright © 1998 by The Ernest Hemingway Foundation. Reproduced by permission.—*Jane Austen: New Perspectives,* v. 3, 1983, for "Feminist Irony and the Priceless Heroine of *Mansfield Park*" by Margaret Kirkham; v. 3, 1983, for "Jane Austen's Dangerous Charm" by Nina Auerbach. Copyright © 1983 by Holmes & Meier Publishers, Inc. All rights reserved. Both reproduced by permission of the publisher.—*Journal of American Studies,* v. 31, 1997 for "'An Avenue to Some Degree of Profit and Reputation': *The Sketch Book* as Washington Irving's Entrée and Undoing" by Alice Hiller. Reprinted with permission of Cambridge University Press and the author.—*Journal of English and Germanic Philology,* v. 74, July, 1975. Copyright 1975 by the Board of Trustees of the University of Illinois. Used with permission of the University of Illinois Press.—*Journal of Narrative Technique,* v. 12, Fall, 1982. Reproduced by permission.—*The Kentucky Review,* v. 3, 1982 for "Thomas Percy: The Dilemma of a Scholar-Cleric," by Bertram H. Davis. Reproduced by permission of the author.—*Literature and Psychology,* v. 29, 1979. Copyright © by Editor 1979. Reproduced by permission of *Literature and Psychology: A Psychoanalytic and Cultural Criticism.*—*Modern Language Quarterly,* v. 44, June, 1983. Duke University Press, 1983. Copyright © 1983 by Duke University Press, Durham, NC. Reproduced by permission.—*The Nathaniel Hawthorne Journal,* 1978 for "'Young Goodman Brown': Hawthorne's Condemnation of Conformity" by Terence J. Matheson. Copyright © 1984 by Bruccoli Clark Publishers, Inc. Reproduced by permission of the author.—*New England Quarterly,* v. 69, March, 1996 for "Hawthorne's 'Young Goodman Brown': Early Nineteenth-Century and Puritan Constructions of Gender" by James C. Keil. Copyright 1996 by *The New England Quarterly.* Reproduced by permission of the publisher and the author./v. 43, September, 1970 for "The Forest of Goodman Brown's Night: A Reading of Hawthorne's 'Young Goodman Brown'" by Reginald Cook. Copyright 1970 by *The New England Quarterly.* Reproduced by permission of the publisher.—*Nineteenth-Century Literature,* v. 23, March, 1969 for "'Young Goodman Brown' and Hawthorne's Theory of Mimesis" by Taylor Stoehr; v. 48, June, 1993 for "A Subdued Gaiety: The Comedy of *Mansfield Park*" by Pam Perkins. © 1969, 1993 by The Regents of the University of California. Both reproduced by permission of the publisher and the authors.—*Novel: A Forum on Fiction,* v. 17, Spring, 1984. Copyright NOVEL Corp. © 1984. Reproduced with permission.—*Philological Quarterly,* v. 65, Spring, 1986. Copyright © 1986 by The University of Iowa. Reproduced by permission of the author.—*Representations,* v. 7, Summer, 1984 for "The Boundaries of Mansfield Park," by Ruth Bernard Yeazell. Copyright © 1984 by The Regents of the University of California. Reproduced by permission of the publisher and the author.—*SEL Studies in English Literature, 1500-1900,* v. 27, Au-

COPYRIGHTED EXCERPTS IN *NCLC*, VOLUME 95, WERE REPRODUCED FROM THE FOLLOWING BOOKS:

PHOTOGRAPHS AND ILLUSTRATIONS APPEARING IN *NCLC*, VOLUME 95, WERE RECEIVED FROM THE FOLLOWING SOURCES:

Mansfield Park

Jane Austen

The following entry presents criticism of Austen's novel, *Mansfield Park* (1814). For information on Austen's complete career, see *NCLC,* Volume 1; for information on *Pride and Prejudice,* see *NCLC,* Volume 13; for information on *Emma,* see *NCLC,* Volume 19; for information on *Persuasion,* see *NCLC,* Volume 33; for information on *Northanger Abbey,* see *NCLC,* Volume 51; and for information on *Sense and Sensibility,* see *NCLC,* Volume 81.

INTRODUCTION

A novel of manners set among privileged British society in the early nineteenth century, *Mansfield Park* chronicles the growth of its heroine, Fanny Price, a timid girl sent to live on her uncle's country estate. Distinguished from Austen's other works for its omniscient narrative, moral didacticism, and lackluster protagonist, critics have nevertheless considered *Mansfield Park* the author's most ambitious, if aesthetically flawed, novel. Set in the relatively isolated world of the English landed gentry, *Mansfield Park,* a comedy outwardly concerned with marriages of social advantage, is additionally thought by critics to reflect not only Austen's superb narrative craftsmanship, but also her brilliant sensitivity to the human concerns of love, virtue, and family.

PLOT AND MAJOR CHARACTERS

The novel begins as Fanny Price, a girl of ten years, is conveyed to Mansfield Park, the estate of her aunt, Lady Bertram. Fanny's mother, who has eight other children and a military husband no longer fit for service, does not have the means to care for all of her offspring, and sends Fanny off to grow up among her cousins Tom, Edmund, Maria, and Julia. While the eldest son, Tom, and the two girls ignore their ignorant, poor relation, the shy and reserved Fanny finds a friend and companion in Edmund. Some five years later, Fanny's uncle, Sir Thomas Bertram, departs for Antigua with Tom. Meanwhile, Maria falls in love with the rich but dull-witted Mr. Rushworth and accepts his offer of marriage. Time passes as it always had, until the arrival of charming Henry Crawford and his beautiful sister Mary. Henry becomes the new rector, and the object of Maria and Julia's interest, while Mary draws the attention of Edmund and Tom, who has since returned from the Caribbean. Tom, at the suggestion of his friend Mr. Yates, decides to stage a play, *Lovers's Vows,* at Mansfield Park. Fanny and Edmund initially resist the idea, but

soon give in. The return of Sir Thomas, however, brings an end to the play and the inappropriate behavior it encouraged. Henry Crawford departs for Bath to the grave disappointment of Maria—her hopes of marrying him instead of Mr. Rushworth now dashed. After returning and attending a ball held in her honor, Henry falls in love with Fanny. Unimpressed with Henry's inconsistency and flirtatiousness, Fanny flatly refuses his proposal of marriage, despite the encouragement of both her uncle and Edmund, now a clergyman who is himself enthralled with Mary Crawford. Incensed at her refusal of such a advantageous match, Sir Thomas sends Fanny to visit with her family in Portsmouth. Hoping that her family will embrace her, Fanny is disappointed at their disinterest and the poverty of their circumstances. In the meantime, Henry follows Fanny to Portsmouth to convince her to reconsider his proposal. Softened by the seeming earnestness of his love, she nevertheless doubts his character and continues to refuse his proposal. He leaves, and soon Fanny learns that Maria, now married to Mr. Rushworth, has run off with Henry. Fanny is called back to a Mansfield Park in disorder, where Maria has been banished, Tom has become seriously ill, and Julia has agreed to marry Mr. Yates. Amid this turmoil, Sir Thomas forgives Fanny for her lack of interest in the immoral Henry. Shortly after Fanny's return, Tom recovers and the now disgraced Maria ends her affair with Henry. Meanwhile, in an effort to separate his family from the Crawfords, Edmund cuts ties with Mary. The tale closes as Edmund finally realizes his love for virtuous Fanny. He and Fanny marry and settle near the family estate.

MAJOR THEMES

Critics of *Mansfield Park* almost invariably focus on its heroine Fanny Price, who is generally thought to be a static figure, the embodiment of Christian virtue firmly placed within the context of nineteenth-century British aristocratic life. Fanny's morally upright behavior in *Mansfield Park* is also said to contrast sharply with the inauthentic and superficial expressions of the other characters in the novel. Others have noted that Austen treats her heroine with the same degree of irony as those of her previous novels, and indeed satirizes the idealized, conduct-book view of woman as the paragon of domestic virtue. Some critics have also interpreted Fanny as the heroine of a *Bildungsroman,* or novel of education, arguing that Austen presents a psychologically complex feminine figure who develops substantially over the course of the novel. In addition to a sometimes contentious thematic focus on

Fanny, critics frequently comment on the subject of marriage, which appears prominently in *Mansfield Park* as it does in all of Austen's novels. Marriage, the sanctity of the family, and the bonds of filial responsibility and love, scholars observe, all exist as principal motifs in the work.

CRITICAL RECEPTION

While *Mansfield Park,* like the remainder of Austen's mature works, has been generally well-received, modern scholars have almost universally labeled the novel Austen's most difficult. As such, the work has elicited a great deal of interest from various quarters, including a range of feminist and cultural critics. A number of commentators have concentrated on the ideological component of *Mansfield Park* and its contrast with Austen's somewhat lighter early novels. Among the most influential appraisals has been that of Marxist critic Edward Said, who has found in the work a deeply imperialist sensibility. Said's comments have also spawned a political understanding of the novel that probes its representation of cultural exclusion. Other assessments of *Mansfield Park* have concentrated on Fanny Price and Lionel Trilling's famous remark that, 'no one, I believe, has ever found it possible to like the heroine of *Mansfield Park.*' Indeed, some critics have viewed Fanny as essentially a morally perfect individual, lacking in dynamic tension. In contrast, many have found this notion reductive. Overall, *Mansfield Park* has not enjoyed the same degree of popularity as Austen's other novels, largely due to issues related to the characterization of Fanny. Still, the work has been considered a complex and rich production of one of the nineteenth century's most insightful novelists.

PRINCIPAL WORKS

Sense and Sensibility (novel) 1811

Pride and Prejudice (novel) 1813

Mansfield Park (novel) 1814

Emma (novel) 1816

Northanger Abbey: And Persuasion (novels) 1818

Lady Susan (novel) 1871

The Watsons (unfinished novel) 1871

Love and Friendship and Other Early Works, Now first printed from the Original MS (juvenilia) 1922

[Sanditon] Fragments of a Novel (unfinished novel) 1925

Jane Austen's Letters to her Sister Cassandra and Others, edited by R. W. Chapman (letters) 1932

Volume the First (juvenilia) 1933

Volume the Third (juvenilia) 1951

Volume the Second (juvenilia) 1963

CRITICISM

Marilyn Butler (essay date 1975)

SOURCE: "*Mansfield Park*: Ideology and Execution," in *New Casebooks: Mansfield Park and Persuasion,* edited by Judy Simons, Macmillan Press Ltd., 1997, pp. 19-36.

[*In the following excerpt originally published in 1975, Butler explores the ideological conflicts—particularly between Fanny Price's Christianity and the Crawford's materialism—in* Mansfield Park.]

With the possible exception of **Sense and Sensibility, Mansfield Park** is the most visibly ideological of Jane Austen's novels, and as such has a central position in any examination of Jane Austen's philosophy as expressed in her art. It is all the more revealing because here she has progressed far beyond the technical immaturity of the period when **Sense and Sensibility** was conceived, to a position where she can exploit to the full the artistic possibilities of the conservative case; and, at the same time, come face to face with the difficulties it presents. By far the most imaginative and accomplished of received anti-Jacobin novels, **Mansfield Park** reveals all the inherent problems of the genre.

The superb draughtsmanship of the opening chapters of **Mansfield Park** makes it easy to forget that they present a set of themes which are entirely commonplace in the period. Its beginning must have encouraged contemporaries to believe that here was yet another novel by a female about female education.[1] Mrs West's novels, from *The Advantages of Education* (1793) on, had hammered the theme. Mrs Inchbald had dealt with it more elegantly and idiosyncratically in *A Simple Story,* and Fanny Burney had made it a very substantial subsidiary interest in *Camilla.* Since the turn of the century it had retained its place as perhaps the most popular of all themes of women novelists, notable examples being Mrs Opie's *Adeline Mowbray* (1804) and Hannah More's *Coelebs* (1808). Maria Edgeworth, whose literary career was dedicated to the proposition that early education makes the man, had recently given it more extended treatment than ever before in *Patronage* (1814). The last-named novel has indeed innumerable incidental resemblances to **Mansfield Park,** which appeared later in the same year,[2] for not only is its virtuous and well-brought-up heroine, Caroline Percy, compared with her foils, the fashionable Arabella and Georgiana Falconer, who strongly resemble the Bertram girls; but one of the most important sequences concerns the performance of a play, in which Georgiana Falconer displays herself, and Caroline Percy virtuously refuses to take part.

The reader of 1814 thus knew broadly where he, or perhaps more typically she, stood. The novel of female education criticised superficial qualities, particularly accomplishments, which were too narrowly aimed at giving a girl a higher price in the marriage-market: accomplishments and mercenary marriages tended to be coupled together. The debate was linked to, indeed was the female aspect of, that common eighteenth-century topic of educationalists, the inferiority of 'wit' or 'cleverness' to judgement. Hence the relevance of showing that the Bertram girls' education had been spent not only on their appearance and accomplishments, but also on superficial information designed to make them appear clever and well-informed in company—'. . . the Roman emperors as low as Severus; besides a great deal of the Heathen Mythology, and all the Metals, Semi-Metals, Planets, and distinguished philosophers' (pp. 18-19).

The structure of **Mansfield Park** is as severely built round the contrast between the girls' education and its consequences as the see-saw structure of *A Simple Story* or *Patronage,* though Jane Austen's artistry does much to soften the outlines of the antithesis. (Technically she is now a world away from **Sense and Sensibility,** where the parallels were so much laboured.) The first part of **Mansfield Park,** until Sir Thomas's return facilitates Maria's marriage, is about the entry into life of the two Bertram sisters: their education, their values, and, especially, their inability to resist the worldly baits proffered by the Crawfords. In the second, slightly longer part, Fanny, the exemplary heroine, encounters in her turn the temptation of Henry's love, and Mary's friendship,[3] and prevails. Her endurance sets right the wrongs done at Mansfield by the older girls, just as in the second part of *A Simple Story* Miss Milner's daughter restores the family which was shattered by her mother's lapse from virtue.[4]

Maria Bertram especially is a girl according to the female moralist's common formula. Having demonstrated her vanity and superficiality in adolescence, she grows up with the typical ambition of marrying for money. 'Being now in her twenty-first year, Maria Bertram was beginning to think matrimony a duty; and as marriage with Mr Rushworth would give her the enjoyment of a larger income than her father's, as well as ensure her the house in town, which was now a prime object, it became, by the same rule of moral obligation, her duty to marry Mr Rushworth if she could' (pp. 38-9). This 'duty' is one of the few Maria acknowledges, for as their father's daughter neither she nor her sister Julia feels any obligation. They are not fond of Sir Thomas Bertram, whose role as parent has hitherto been a negative one, and accordingly they feel nothing but a sense of release when he departs for Antigua. 'They were relieved by it from all restraint; and without aiming at one gratification that would probably have been forbidden by Sir Thomas, they felt themselves immediately at their own disposal, and to have every indulgence within their reach' (p. 32).

But, though the Bertram girls resemble other novelists' shallow females, the ideal figure set up in opposition to them is slightly more distinctive. In characterising her heroine, Fanny, Jane Austen illustrates her ideological disagreement with Maria Edgeworth. Caroline Percy of *Patronage,* like Belinda, Leonora, and other Edgeworth model characters, is essentially a rationalist. Fanny Price is

a Christian. The clue lies in those characteristics in which the Bertram girls are deficient—'It is not very wonderful that with all their promising talents and early information, they should be entirely deficient in less common acquirements of self-knowledge, generosity, and humility' (p. 19). Immediately afterwards, Fanny, in conversation with Edmund, is shown to have the qualities her cousins lack. Humility is obviously an appropriate virtue for the Christian heroine; but equally important in Jane Austen's canon is, as always, the impulse towards self-knowledge. Fanny's sense as a Christian of her own frailty, her liability to error, and her need of guidance outside herself, is the opposite of the Bertram girls' complacent self-sufficiency. For Jane Austen 'vanity', the characteristic of the fashionables, is a quality with a distinctly theological colouring. It means both an unduly high opinion of oneself, and a pursuit of worldly goals, 'vanities'. Such an error arises from an inability to place oneself in a larger moral universe, a context in which the self, and the self's short-term gratifications, become insignificant. As an ideal this is wholly different from the Edgeworthian belief in individual self-realisation, leading to greater—not less—personal independence.

The entrance of the Crawfords soon extends and enriches the didactic case. The Crawfords are sophisticated, fully aware disciples of a worldly creed to which the Bertram girls merely veer unconsciously, on account of the vacuum left in their education. Mary Crawford has actually been instructed, by her social circle in general, the marriage of her uncle and aunt in particular, in a wholly sceptical modern philosophy. Her doctrine includes the notion that there are no values but material ones, and that the gratification of the self is the only conceivable goal. Mary's comments about marriage, uttered to her sister Mrs Grant in the first scenes in which we meet her, are obviously meant to be compared with Maria Bertram's reflections about Mr Rushworth. Where Maria is confused as to her values, and barely half aware of the moral implications of what she is doing, Mary sounds, and is, knowingly cynical. 'Everybody should marry as soon as they can do it to advantage . . . Everybody is taken in at one period or other . . . It is of all transactions the one in which people expect most from others, and are least honest themselves' (pp. 43-6). Even more clearly, Henry Crawford's amoral determination to make the Bertram girls fall in love with him compares with their vague, complacent, and far less formulated readiness to be fallen in love with. The Crawfords, who know precisely what they are doing, are infinitely more dangerous than the Bertrams. More than that, the Bertrams are peculiarly vulnerable to be made the Crawfords' dupes, since their attitudes to life already half incline them to throw off restraint and pursue the self-gratification which the Crawfords' creed allows. It is dangerous to be exposed to worldliness without the worldly-wisdom which goes with it.

The triple contrast, of three kinds of education, three kinds of moral attitude, is maintained in every early scene. The cynical Crawfords, planning their pleasures with cold selfishness; the Bertram girls, equally selfish but more naïve; Fanny, who alone after a few days retains enough insight and objectivity to see that Henry Crawford is still plain. Whatever the topic of dialogue, the moral landscape of the various characters is what really receives attention. Mary, for instance, brings up the question of whether Fanny is 'out' or 'not out', so that Jane Austen can contrast two widely diverging ideals of young womanhood. Edmund considers whether, out or not out, young women act with any real modesty; Mary, whether they act in accordance with convention (p. 50). Similarly, when Mary borrows Fanny's horse, the thoughts and actions of three principals, Edmund, Fanny, and Mary, can be examined in turn. Edmund, who has always been considerate of Fanny, is now seduced by his physical delight in Mary into forgetting her. Fanny, after detecting her own jealousy, and struggling with motives of which she is suspicious,[5] can at least display some genuinely objective concern for the horse. Mary correctly ascribes her own behaviour to selfishness, so gaily that she proves the vice has little meaning for her.

Mansfield Park is the first Austen novel to be conceived as well as executed after the appearance of Maria Edgeworth's social comedies.[6] Jane Austen had deployed lesser characters in a stylised pattern around her heroine before, but she had not exploited in any sustained way the typical Edgeworth intellectual comedy. The brilliant dialogue in *Pride and Prejudice* is the natural culmination of a technique Jane Austen had used since *Catharine*: it gives the reader and heroine simultaneously an objective insight into character. In the first part of *Mansfield Park* a new element is added: the subject-matter of a conversation becomes as important as the insight it offers into character, because conversation becomes the occasion for the clash of distinct systems of value. Three key topics recur, all of them often found in anti-Jacobin novels of the 1790s. The first is Nature, and is illustrated by contrasting the attitudes of different characters towards living in the country. All late-eighteenth-century moralists of whatever colouring prefer the country to the town,[7] but Jane Austen's Fanny does so as a typical conservative: because she associates it with a community, in which individuals have well-defined duties towards the group, and because physically it reminds her of the wider ordered universe to which the lesser community belongs. Urban life, on the other hand, has given Mary selfish values: she betrays her egotism when she laughs at the farmers who will not let her have a wagon to move her harp, and her materialism when she comments that in London money buys anything. The second issue that will recur in conversation in the novel, though sometimes allusively in association with Nature, is religion; the third is marriage. All three come to the fore in the sequence that provides an ideological key to the book, the visit to Sotherton.

The Crawfords' indifferent and even destructive attitude to the country emerges when the visit to Sotherton is first projected, for they go there as improvers. Essentially their feelings are negative about the external scene they propose to deal with. Utility is not a criterion which concerns them.[8]

Nor do they respond to the sentimental connotations of a feature of landscape, the link with the past provided by Sotherton's heavy, ancient avenue of trees. It is actually Mary who first voices the idea that change must temporarily at least mean disequilibrium: she remembers the time when her uncle improved his cottage at Twickenham as a period of anarchy. But she is restless for novelty, and improvements are fashionable; in the arbitrary name of fashion she urges Mr Rushworth to employ a landscape artist such as Repton. It does not occur to her, as it does to Fanny, to regret the destruction of the trees, since she is scarcely aware of inanimate nature, or the wider physical universe beyond herself and the few people she cares for. Sotherton itself is, or ought to be, a Burkean symbol of human lives led among natural surroundings, man contiguous with nature and continuous with his own past. Fanny finds it both these things, when she sees the grounds and begins to walk around the house. But Mary is bored and even hostile (p. 85).

In interpreting the meaning of the house within its grounds, and the chapel within the house, the two minds are joined by a third, Mrs Rushworth's. She has learnt her speech parrot-fashion from the housekeeper, and her interest is far more in the grandeur of the outward appurtenances than in the quality of the life lived. Her casual remarks about the chapel—that the seat-covers were once less tasteful than they are now, and that it was her husband who discontinued the religious services—show clearly enough how superficial her values are. '"Every generation has its improvements",' remarks Mary: and between Rushworth senior, who gutted the house in the interests of modernity, and Rushworth junior, who with Henry Crawford's help proposes to do the same for the grounds, there is morally little to choose.

The scene in the chapel, where Mary is offensive about clergymen, brings out for the first time in full the gulf between the Crawfords and religious orthodoxy. In discussing the suspension of chapel services, Mary thinks only of the immediate convenience to individuals who might have had to attend; while Fanny and Edmund have two concerns—the well-being of the individual, *sub specie aeternitatis,* and the social validity of established forms of worship:

> 'It is a pity', cried Fanny, 'that the custom should have been discontinued. It was a valuable part of former times. There is something in a chapel and chaplain so much in character with a great house, with one's ideas of what such a household should be! A whole family assembling regularly for the purpose of prayer, is fine!'

Mary in her individualism cannot even begin to apprehend the social value Fanny sees in religion:

> 'At any rate, it is safer to leave people to their own devices on such subjects. Every body likes to go their own way—to choose their own manner and time of devotion. The obligation of attendance, the formality, the restraint, the length of time—altogether it is a formidable thing, and what nobody likes. . . .'

Such an argument demands to be answered in terms of the individual, and Edmund does answer it:

> '. . . We must all feel *at times* the difficulty of fixing our thoughts as we could wish; but if you are supposing it a frequent thing, that is to say, a weakness grown into a habit from neglect, what could be expected from the *private* devotions of such persons? Do you think the minds which are suffered, which are indulged in wanderings in a chapel, would be more collected in a closet?'

> (pp. 86-7)

The double function which Fanny and Edmund see religion as serving is important in the novel, and is developed more fully in subsequent conversations between Fanny, Edmund and Mary. In the wilderness Edmund speaks of the social role of the country clergyman, his influence by example and precept on the minds of his parishioners (pp. 92-3). Later, when Fanny discusses Dr Grant with Mary, it is she who raises the more private, spiritual aspect:

> 'I cannot but suppose that whatever there may be to wish otherwise in Dr Grant, would have been in greater danger of becoming worse in a more active and worldly profession, where he would have had less time and obligation—where he might have escaped that knowledge of himself, the *frequency,* at least, of that knowledge which it is impossible he should escape as he is now.'

> (pp. 111-12)

Mary is clearly equally indifferent both to the social aspect of religion ('duty' and 'morals'), and to its spiritual demand of self-knowledge, since she accepts no reality outside her own sensations. But to Fanny and Edmund the two meanings of religion are interdependent, and 'knowledge of the self' and knowledge of a reality outside the self cannot be disassociated from one another.[9]

The theme of marriage is first glanced at in the chapel when Julia spitefully refers to Maria's coming marriage to Mr Rushworth. In the hollow sham of a chapel the full emptiness of the proposed ceremony is felt. Afterwards, in the strangely diagrammatic sequence in the wilderness, we see sketched out the shadowy future, or at least tendency, of the various sexual relationships which are developing in the novel. Edmund and Mary walk up and down, supposedly for a finite time, and within the wilderness; but Edmund, not for the first or last time, forgets his promise to Fanny and strays further than he meant. Henry and Maria arrive with Mr Rushworth at the gate, and while he (their future dupe) is away fetching the key, they escape through the palisade into the liberty of the park. Julia, who acts with the same impatience of restraint as they, and to the same end, is less guilty because she is not escaping from an acknowledged fiancé in the company of a desired lover. And so on. In any other novel such a miming of future events would seem an intolerable contrivance; but, extreme though it is, in **Mansfield Park** it does not seem illegitimate. The action of the novel is so entirely bound up with the value-systems of the various characters that they are always to a greater or lesser extent illustrating, acting out, their beliefs.

The sequence in the grounds, with Fanny still and alone on the seat, the others walking about, is especially expressive in terms of their relative roles. The worldly characters are the real subject of the first half, and Jane Austen is ingenious in letting them occupy the centre of the stage while Fanny as yet remains in the wings. Her consciousness is deliberately left slightly childish and unformed. Instinctively she tries to tell right from wrong, but as yet she lacks the ability; by contrast the Bertram sisters have the decision that comes with greater assurance and maturity, but they have no moral discrimination. Fanny's turn to act is to come, but her role of wondering observer of her cousins' doings is in itself expressive, suggesting as it does the virtuous person's struggle towards judgement and knowledge that is being neglected by the active characters. She has the role which often carries so much prestige in eighteenth-century literature, that of the thoughtful bystander. Like Gibbon's 'philosopher', she strives to interpret, to make some sense out of the superficial chaos of events. However unformed her opinion and inarticulate her expression of it, her anxious vigil on the bench in the park is enough in itself to remind the reader of a long tradition of men who have been wise in retirement, whose ascendancy lay in detachment from the actors and the common scene.

The conclusions Jane Austen tries to direct her reader's attention to are encouraged by Fanny's demeanour, yet not dictated by her at all. Jane Austen is not interested in impressions conveyed by subjective identification with a heroine. While Sterne or Mackenzie induce the reader to act the part of the man of feeling,[10] she casts the reader as a moral arbiter. If there must be identification, it is with Fanny's role, not with her individual responses, which (at least as they affect Edmund) are depicted with ironic detachment. Meanwhile the reader's judgements are guided by other, more objective means. References to familiar issues are no doubt among the most important. But equally interesting, and in actual practice more original, is the extremely detailed presentation of what, after all, Jane Austen wants us to value. For the first time she gives her external world a solidity and scale which eventually belittles individual characters.

Although the scene at Sotherton is stylised, it is also very natural—in its setting, as far as concerns the house and grounds, and in the sense it conveys of the day as a rather unsuccessful outing, an occasion felt in mixed and on the whole uncomfortable ways by the many people involved. The result of this curious blend of stylisation and naturalism is to give flesh to the conservative case as no one else had done except Burke. As in the *Reflections on the French Revolution,* with its reiterated references to hearths, homes and families, so in the scene at Sotherton society takes on visible shapes.[11] The house and grounds are old, impressive, handsome, but under the rule of the Rushworths hollow, without the core of belief (symbolised by the chapel) which could give meaning to so much pompous grandeur. The cynical Crawfords have appeared, like Satan in the Garden of Eden, hostile to the old ethos of the place and bent on destruction. Every detail of what they say and do suggests their self-willed lawlessness: Mary, irrationally challenging the dimensions of the wilderness because she happens to feel tired; Henry, defying the restraint imposed by the limits of the ground and the locked gate. Yet the Crawfords' encroachment at Sotherton, dangerous though it seems, remains in the end curiously ineffective—for, like Burke, Jane Austen not only locates the enemy but diminishes him. In the Bertram sisters and in Henry there is an odd, wilful capacity for self-destruction. They are more likely to reject a momentary restraint than to attack restraints systematically. In escaping into the park, Henry, Maria, and Julia go off in a different direction from their supposed objective, the avenue of oaks; which accordingly survives the threat they originally offered it. Sotherton, although an empty shell, remains intact. By the end of the story it is only individuals, Maria and to a lesser extent Henry, who have destroyed themselves. A little through direct description, more through our sense of the weariness of the characters, we retain an impression of the heaviness, the largeness, but also the age and endurance of Sotherton, which is an important part of the moral framework for what follows.

Although some of its meaning has become obscured by purely historical difficulties of interpretation, the play-sequence remains the most masterly part of **Mansfield Park.** Unlike the account of Sotherton, where the naturalism and the scheme sometimes jar, it is equally fine on its many levels. Best of all is the presentation of that distinctive technique of the first volume of **Mansfield Park,** the serial treatment of several consciousnesses. At the beginning of volume i, chapter xii, for example, we enter successively the minds of Mary Crawford, the Bertram sisters, Henry Crawford, and Fanny. The next chapter, the thirteenth, takes us into and out of the consciousness of Mr Yates; through the views of all the characters involved, first directly in dialogue and then in reported speech; to the silencing of Edmund when Mary joins in, and the happy concurrence of Mrs Norris. There is no other comparable sequence of a Jane Austen novel so independent of the heroine. It is as though the movement of the sentimental period, towards distinguishing the central character by special insight into his inner life, has been put into reverse. The characters in this part of **Mansfield Park** each have their speeches, their scenes, like characters in a drama.

This, since it is a play they are rehearsing, is wholly appropriate. But what amuses Jane Austen—and even amuses Fanny—is that each actor continues to be selfishly absorbed by personal feelings, in spite of the corporate activity they are engaged in. Fanny is 'not unamused to observe the selfishness which, more or less disguised, seemed to govern them all' (p. 131). Many of the actors—Mr Yates, Tom, and Mr Rushworth, for example—clearly think in terms of the effect they will make in acting their own parts. Maria and Henry, though not motivated by the vanity of the actor, are bent on self-gratification of an even more culpable kind. Mary, and even Edmund, focus intently upon the significance to them of their own scenes. Apparently comic dialogues, in which plays and parts are argued over—and the selfishness of the actors revealed—have simultaneously a serious level of meaning. Not one of the actors, not even Edmund, has a proper sense of what it is as a whole that they are doing. When issues of propriety arise, even the more intelligent of them persist in looking at their own speeches: Mary admits that some of hers should be cut, Edmund is embarrassed by his. Only Fanny, the detached bystander, reads the play through and reacts to it as a whole.

Fanny's most important function here is that she alone perceives something pitiful and wrong in solipsism. 'Fanny saw and pitied much of this in Julia; but there was no outward fellowship between them. Julia made no communication, and Fanny took no liberties. They were two solitary sufferers, or connected only by Fanny's consciousness' (p. 163). As at Sotherton, she never directs the reader's opinions in detail: her watchfulness gives the necessary clue. When it comes to discussion of the general issue, to act or not to act, she can seem maddeningly inarticulate. Her general opinion about the play is the bald conclusion, 'everything of consequence was against it'. Pressed to take part herself, she is merely depicted showing the outward signs of confusion and distress (p. 146). Later, when she is alone in the East room, the reader has his first real insight into her attempts to sift right from wrong. But these do not in fact throw much light on the general issue. What is important about Fanny's cogitations is that they involve scrupulous self-examination, the critical mental process that everyone else in the novel neglects.

For a general judgement of the play-acting, therefore, the reader must not rely on Fanny's articulation but on an independent understanding of the issue, informed as at Sotherton by a subtle network of allusion. The reader's efforts to understand are expected to parallel Fanny's, but to be more mature, more experienced about the world and its pitfalls. There seems to be no doubt, for example, that Jane Austen takes as read our familiarity with the common contemporary arguments against amateur acting, even though no one in the novel alludes to them plainly. By 1814 the increasingly strong Evangelical movement had sufficiently publicised the link between upper-class immorality and its rage for private theatricals.[12] A common and important leading objection is that play-acting tempts girls especially into an unseemly kind of personal display. In his *Enquiry into the Duties of the Female Sex,* 1797, which Jane Austen read with approval in 1805, Thomas Gisborne declares that acting is 'almost certain to prove injurious to the female sex'.[13] Even granted that the chosen play 'will be in its language and conduct always irreprehensible' (a condition certainly not met by *Lovers' Vows*), Gisborne believes that acting will harm a young woman through encouraging vanity and destroying diffidence 'by the unrestrained familiarity with the other sex, which inevitably results from being joined with them in the drama'.[14] Fanny's principal doubts seem to relate to the women's parts of Amelia and Agatha (p. 137). Unquestionably Jane Austen expects us to see the play as a step in Maria Bertram's road to ruin.

For the four principals, Maria and Henry, Mary and Edmund, the play represents an elaborate exercise in 'encouraging vanity' and 'destroying diffidence'. Unlike Mr Rushworth or Mr Yates, not one is vain in the trivial sense of seeking self-display; but all are after the kind of worldly 'vanity' that concerns Jane Austen in **Mansfield Park,** since all equate the pretended stage love-making with real love-making. *Lovers' Vows* gives them a licence for what would normally be entirely improper. Their scenes together permit physical contact between the sexes (as when Henry holds Maria's hand) and a bold freedom of speech altogether outside the constraint imposed by social norms. Lionel Trilling has ingeniously but anachronistically suggested that Jane Austen objects to the insincerity involved in acting a role.[15] This is surely near the opposite of the truth. In touching one another or making love to one another on the stage these four are not adopting a pose, but are, on the contrary, expressing their real feelings. The impropriety lies in the fact that they are *not* acting, but are finding an indirect means to gratify desires which are illicit, and should have been contained. The unbridled passions revealed by the play-acting are part of the uninhibited selfishness which it has been the purpose of the sequence to bring out. The point is underlined by the casting, for the actors play exaggerated versions of themselves. Mr Rushworth plays Count Cassel, a foolish and rejected suitor. Mary plays the forward and free-thinking Amelia. Edmund plays a lovelorn clergyman. Maria plays a fallen woman. The stage roles of all these imply not insincerity, but liberation.

The imagined free world which comes into being on stage is a comprehensible entity, the clearest image in all Jane Austen's novels of what she is opposed to. And meanwhile the 'real' world of Mansfield, which is suddenly neglected and at risk, also begins to take on solidity. As at Sotherton, the most eager disciples of the dangerous activity—there it was improving, here play-acting—are those who should be the guardians of the place. Tom is the play's producer, while Mrs Norris happily (and economically) presides over the physical damage caused to Sir Thomas's property. Yet at Mansfield Park, as at Sotherton, the really dangerous figures are the Crawfords: a fact which we see fully only if, like Fanny, we look at the play as a whole.

Ideologically, the choice of play is crucial. Kotzebue's *Lovers' Vows* counterpoints what the rehearsals have revealed of the actors' selfishness and reckless quest for self-gratification, since its message is the goodness of man, the legitimacy of his claims to quality, and the sanctity of his instincts as a guide to conduct. It is, in fact, the dangerous foreign reading-matter which so often appears in anti-Jacobin novels, though wonderfully naturalised. Nor could any literate reader of the period be unaware of

the connotation of the play. Quite apart from its successful runs at Covent Garden, Bath, the Haymarket, and Drury Lane between 1798 and 1802, the name of Kotzebue, by far the most popular, or notorious, of German playwrights in England at this period, was quite enough to indicate what *Lovers' Vows* was likely to be about.[16] He was the most sanguine of optimists about the beauty and innocence of human nature left to follow its own instincts. One of his heroines[17] marries her brother and has children by him, until her happiness is unnecessarily destroyed by the revelations of a meddlesome priest. Another innately virtuous victim of prejudice is the pregnant nun sentenced to death by an alliance of king and priestly hierarchy (in *The Virgin of the Sun*); she is made touchingly innocent, and her persecutors either cowardly or bigoted. This play was not well known in England, but Sheridan scored a tremendous success with the less controversial sequel, *Pizarro*, in 1799. A third Kotzebue play as often seen as *Lovers' Vows*, and even more notorious, was *The Stranger*, in which the heroine is a guilty runaway wife, who is (rightly, the play makes clear) forgiven and reinstated by her husband. There could thus be no doubt in the minds of Jane Austen and most of her readers that the name of Kotzebue was synonymous with everything most sinister in German literature of the period. A sanguine believer in the fundamental goodness and innocence of human nature, the apostle of intuition over convention, indeed of sexual liberty over every type of restraint, he is a one-sided propagandist for every position which the anti-Jacobin novelist abhors.[18] Unless the modern reader feels, like Fanny, the anarchic connotation of the whole play—rather than, like Edmund and Mary, the daring of individual speeches—he is in no position to understand its significance in relation to Mansfield Park and its owner, Sir Thomas.

Like other plays in the Kotzebue canon, *Lovers' Vows* attacks the conventions by which marriage upholds existing rank, and exalts instead the liaison based on feeling. In the main action Baron Wildenhaim, who has endured years of loneliness and remorse since refusing to marry the peasant girl whom he seduced, is persuaded to think more rightly by their illegitimate son, Frederick. In the subplot the Baron's daughter, Amelia, persuades the clergyman, Anhalt, to overlook the fact that she is a woman—by convention passive—and a noble—by convention debarred from marrying a bourgeois; her argument is that in defiance of convention they should obey their impulse.[19] Thus Frederick and Amelia are the two characters in the play who expound Kotzebue's message of freedom in sexual matters, and defiance of traditional restraints. They are played by the Crawfords, who thus again in their play-acting adopt not an assumed role but a real one. During the rehearsals they have often seemed almost diffident. It is only in relation to their parts in the play that they are revealed once more as the advocates of social and moral anarchy.

The affront felt by Sir Thomas has puzzled some observers more than it should. He returns home to find some material damage to his house, and his study in confusion. After discovering this, he steps out on to the stage for an irresistibly comic moment, his startled confrontation with the ranting Mr Yates. Because our insight into the scene is through Tom's eyes, we interpret it as Tom does—in the spirit of pure comedy—and are liable to miss the underlying point of the meeting. The head of the house, upholder in the novel of family, of rank, and of the existing order, is confronted at the heart of his own terrain by a mouthing puppet who represents a grotesque inversion of himself: the dignified baronet meets the 'Baron' whose play-function is to abandon his dignity and to legitimise his mistress. Sir Thomas and Baron Wildenhaim are the heads of their respective worlds, and the sudden meeting emphasises their significant relationship. In the future, the fact that Sir Thomas both resembles and differs from the Baron appears even more ironically, for he is called upon to deal with Maria's real-life lapse from virtue. At the time it is sufficient that a character who is central to the play's ethos makes a direct challenge to the house and its owner. Even the Crawfords, who have abstained from general discussion of the propriety of acting, know immediately that this father will not permit the play to go on. They retreat, as at Sotherton. And, though, as at Sotherton, they appear at first to have done little harm, this time they have made more significant inroads than ever before into the fabric of the Bertram family. The individuals who have sampled what the play means, who have thrown off restraint, are the more likely to do the same again. Much later, after Maria's flight with Henry, Tom describes the 'dangerous intimacy of his unjustifiable theatre' as an ancillary cause of his sister's fall (p. 462).

But this is not the story of the whole book. After the climax created by Sir Thomas's return early in the second volume, a major change occurs. The cast narrows dramatically: Maria and Mr Rushworth, Julia, Mr Yates, and Tom depart, leaving a much quieter world, and a smaller scene. From being a bystander, Fanny becomes the active heroine. Henry turns his attention from the Bertram sisters to her, and the rest of the book requires her to make a positive stand: to discern the true nature of evil, to choose the future course of her life, and, through a period of total loneliness, like a true Christian, to endure.

Notes

[All references to the novel are given in parentheses in the text. Ed.]

1. See Marilyn Butler, *Jane Austen and the War of Ideas* (Oxford, 1975), pp. 54-5.

2. *Patronage* was published in December 1813, although 1814 appears on the title page; *Mansfield Park* about five months later (it was advertised in the *Morning Chronicle* on 23 and 24 May). *Mansfield Park* was finished in the summer of 1813, and was not influenced by *Patronage*.

3. For the frequent reappearance of the lover and the sentimental friend as tempters, see Mrs West's novels and Jane Austen's *Catharine* and *Northanger Abbey*.

4. See Butler, *War of Ideas,* p. 54.

5. As usual in Jane Austen, an awareness that one is influenced by ulterior motives is a sign of grace, not weakness. See the discussion of Elinor in Butler, *War of Ideas,* pp. 199-200.

6. But cf. Mrs Q. D. Leavis, 'A Critical Theory of Jane Austen's Writings', *Scrunity,* X (1942) and XII (1942).

7. See Butler, *War of Ideas,* pp. 97-8 and 110. The Rousseauist of course preferred the country for very different reasons, because it enabled him to be morally independent and left him free to cultivate the self.

8. Cf. Henry's later cavalier dismissal of the farmyard at Thornton Lacey, *Mansfield Park,* p. 242.

9. The question of Fanny's religion is generally dealt with indirectly, for reasons of taste. The nearest suggestion to a religious *experience* is the occasion when she contemplates the stars and reflects that there would be less evil and sorrow in the world if 'people were carried more out of themselves by contemplating such a scene' (p. 113).

10. See Butler, *War of Ideas,* p. 19.

11. For a more detailed discussion of Jane Austen's handling of her two great houses in *Mansfield Park,* and the implicit parallel with Burke, cf. Alistair M. Duckworth, *The Improvement of the Estate* (Baltimore, MD, 1971), pp. 46 ff.; and Avrom Fleishman, *A Reading of Mansfield Park* (Minneapolis, 1967), p. 23.

12. David Spring, 'Aristocracy, Social Structure and Religion in the Early Victorian Period', *Victorian Studies,* VI (1962-3), 263-80. Some critics see special significance in the fact that by acting the Bertrams are aping the aristocratic friends of the Hon. Mr Yates—himself a typically profligate representative of his class. The case against acting as given within the novel is an example of Jane Austen's Tory preference for the sober *mores* of the gentry against those of the Whig aristocracy. See D. J. Greene, 'Jane Austen and the Peerage', *PMLA,* LXIII (1953), 1017-31, and Fleishman, *A Reading of Mansfield Park,* p. 29.

13. Quoted by Frank W. Bradbook, *Jane Austen and her Predecessors* (Cambridge, 1966), p. 36. Cf. *Jane Austen's Letters* (Oxford, 1979), ed. R. W. Chapman, p. 169. In two of the best known novels of the same year as *Mansfield Park,* Fanny Burney's *The Wanderer* and Maria Edgeworth's *Patronage,* the heroine also has scruples about acting for reasons similar to those given by Gisborne.

14. Quoted by Bradbrook, *Jane Austen and her Predecessors,* p. 39.

15. Lionel Trilling, 'Mansfield Park', *The Opposing Self* (New York, 1955), pp. 218-19.

16. For an allusion to the plot of *Lovers' Vows* which assumes that the public still knows it well in 1812, see

Butler, *War of Ideas,* p. 93. Information about performances of the play is given in Walter Sellier's unpublished German thesis, 'Kotzebue in England' (Leipzig, 1901), pp. 19-20.

17. In *Adelaide von Wulfingen,* trans. B. Thompson, London, 1801.

18. For discussion of the relationship of Jane Austen's novel with Kotzebue's play, cf. E. M. Butler, 'Mansfield Park and Lovers' Vows', *Modern Language Review* [*MLR*] (July 1933), and the reply by H. Winifred Husbands, *MLR* (April 1934); and William Reitzel, 'Mansfield Park and *Lovers' Vows', Review of English Studies* (October, 1933). On the whole critics have concentrated on whether the reader of *Mansfield Park* is expected by Jane Austen to know the roles of individual characters in *Lovers' Vows*. I believe, and have tried to show, that some passages in the novel are enriched by our perceiving a connection between play characters and novel characters, yet it seems to me that Austen does not *rely* on our knowing so much. What she does expect (more reasonably) is that we will have a general impression of the ideology of the play.

19. For a summary of the play's attack on rank, see Crane Brinton, *The Political Ideas of the English Romanticists* (London, 1926), p. 39: 'Society—cultivated society—is always wrong. The individual who has courage to act against it is always right.'

John Halperin (essay date 1983)

SOURCE: "The Novelist as Heroine in *Mansfield Park*: A Study in Autobiography," in *Modern Language Quarterly,* Vol. 44, No. 2, June, 1983, pp. 136-56.

[*In the following essay, Halperin contends that* Mansfield Park *is Austen's most autobiographical novel, and considers the work's affinity with Austen's other novels.*]

Mansfield Park is Jane Austen's *Vanity Fair.* Almost everyone in it is selfish—self-absorbed, self-indulgent, and vain. This helps make it her most unpleasant novel—and her most controversial. For years critics have exercised themselves trying to explain, justify, expound, or attack its moral slant. Misreadings of the book by otherwise sensible men and women are legion: *Mansfield Park* "continually and essentially holds up the vicious as admirable," says Kingsley Amis.[1] Commentators complacently discuss the expulsion of wit and scourging of irony in *Mansfield Park,* pronounce Fanny Price a failure, and conclude that the novel as a whole must be one too. The book is supposed somehow to be "different"—not at all, really, Jane Austen's sort of thing, and thus requiring a good deal of explanation.

This is nonsense. *Mansfield Park* is very much of a piece with her other books, and in fact it is one of the best of

them. It is also, as we shall see, one of her most autobiographical volumes. No doubt because of its apparent complexity, more has been written about it than any of the other works.

Like **Pride and Prejudice,** which preceded it into print by only a year, *Mansfield Park* (1814) is largely about true and false values, right and wrong ways of looking at things—how to live, in short. "Selfishness must always be forgiven you know, because there is no hope of a cure," declares Mary Crawford.[2] In this, as in everything else she says and does, Mary (as well as her brother Henry) is wrong. Like Becky Sharp (and Milton's Satan), she is more lively and amusing than many of her fellow players. But, as in Thackeray's novel (and Milton's poem), the author's moral perspective on false values never wavers. "Miss Crawford, in spite of some amiable sensations, and much personal kindness, had still been Miss Crawford, still shewn a mind led astray and bewildered, and without any suspicion of being so; darkened, yet fancying itself light" (p. 367), the narrator remarks late in the story; Edmund observes of Mary, ultimately, that she lacks "the most valuable knowledge we could any of us acquire—the knowledge of ourselves" (p. 459). "Her mind was entirely self-engrossed" (p. 358), the narrator says of Mary. It is indicative that when Fanny remarks to Mary, "One cannot fix one's eyes on the commonest natural production without finding food for a rambling fancy," Mary should reply, "To say the truth . . . I see no wonder in [nature] equal to seeing myself in it" (pp. 209-10). Henry Crawford is described as subject to "the freaks of a cold-blooded vanity" (p. 467); "entangled by his own vanity" (p. 468); a victim of "the temptation of immediate pleasure"; and "unused to make any sacrifice to right" (p. 467). Dr. Grant's great fault, it is obvious, is lack of self-knowledge. Everyone at Mansfield is, to quote a well-known passage in the novel, "shut up, or wholly occupied each with the person . . . dependant on them . . . for every thing" (p. 449).

Of course vice is alluring: it is supposed to be. But we perceive Mary as odious throughout. She and her brother may be more interesting than Fanny Price and Edmund Bertram—more fun at a dinner party—but we know that immorality can be more seductive and fascinating than virtue. And certainly it is easier, often enough, to mock propriety than attempt to understand it, as Stuart Tave has said in what is perhaps the best essay on *Mansfield Park*.[3] He goes on to remind us that what the Crawfords really represent is "liveliness without life" (p. 165); they are foils to the less "lively," but more virtuous, protagonists. That virtue may be duller than vice need not require us to be vicious. Jane Austen hints at something like this in the final chapter, when the narrator comments that "the public punishment of disgrace . . . is . . . not one of the barriers, which society gives to virtue. In this world, the penalty is less equal than could be wished . . ." (p. 468).

Mansfield Park is not nearly so complicated a book as many have thought. Fanny Price, looking on and listening, "not unamused to observe the selfishness which, more or

Jane Austen, 1775-1817.

less disguised, seemed to govern them all, and wondering how it would end" (p. 131), stands in for Jane Austen here. True, the light and bright and sparkling Elizabeth Bennet has gone away. Too much time has passed; the novelist cannot possibly be the same person. Her view of things inevitably is different from what it was in the relatively cheerful 1790s, when *Pride and Prejudice* (then called "First Impressions") was initially drafted. But Fanny Price is as much a part of Jane Austen's personality as Elizabeth Bennet; and it is this, perhaps, that many critics have not wanted to see or admit. A few have recognized that *Mansfield Park* is no "sport" among the books. "Can we doubt that [Fanny's] is Jane Austen's own position, that even when the self is alone and unsupported by human example of approval, it must still imperatively act in accordance with what is 'right,' must still support what is valid in its moral inheritance?" Alistair M. Duckworth asks.[4] "There can be no stability of life, no certainty of conduct, without principles of action, a matter of continual importance to Dr. Johnson as to Jane Austen," Tave reminds us (p. 178). It is always Fanny who sees what the others are up to when they themselves do not understand their own actions. It is she who has the strength of character here—dull or not. "The novel . . . is designed to vindicate Fanny Price and the values for which she stands," as Bernard J. Paris rightly says.[5] Fanny's "judgment may be quite . . . safely trusted" (p. 147), Edmund declares.

We need not love her in order to see that her moral perspective is the most strictly focused one in *Mansfield Park.* "If you are against me, I ought to distrust myself" (p. 155), Edmund remarks to Fanny over the business of the theatricals. Indeed he should. Later he tells his father: "Fanny is the only one who has judged rightly throughout, who has been consistent" (p. 187).

Those who believe that "there is no clearly discernible irony hedging off what [the characters] say from what their author is apparently saying"[6] are surely wrong. And because so many readers have felt this way, the point here about the consistency and clarity of the novel's moral slant must be all the more emphatically made. Nor is *Mansfield Park* in any way a falling-off from the high standard set by preceding works. Newman, incidentally, is known to have read this book once a year "to preserve his style."[7]

Fanny's moral focus is so consistently before us because it is that of Jane Austen. Let us consider the autobiographical resonances of a novel so often said to be uncharacteristic of its author.

Fanny Price has a sailor brother who, after some impatient delay, is promoted through family connections—and who brings her a present of jewelry from abroad. Jane Austen's younger brother Charles is the apparent model here; and he actually brought back for his sister, from one of his ocean journeys in 1801, a topaz cross on a gold chain. Like Charles Austen, William Price loves to dance. William tends to write long, chatty letters to Fanny; both of Jane Austen's sailor brothers, Charles and Francis, wrote to her, but not as often as she would have liked—there may be some wish fulfillment here. "I cannot rate so very highly the love or good nature of a brother, who will not give himself the trouble of writing any thing worth reading, to his sisters, when they are separated" (p. 64), Fanny declares. William is also more generous about distributing his prize money to his relations than either of Jane Austen's sailor brothers ever was: the unspoken reproach may be inferred. Much is said in this book about the advantages "for a lad who, before he was twenty, had gone through . . . bodily hardships, and given . . . proofs of mind" (p. 236). *Mansfield Park* extols the virtue "of heroism, of usefulness, of exertion, of endurance" (p. 236). In the course of the book the names of several of Francis Austen's ships are used in passing (e.g., the *Endymion,* the *Elephant,* the *Cleopatra*). The novelist wrote to her brother to ask his permission to use these names; he replied that she was welcome to do so, though he thought this might endanger her anonymity as a novelist.[8] Mr. Price's description of exactly how the *Thrush* lies in harbor at Spithead (p. 380) is so technical and nautically exact that we may be certain it was drafted for Jane Austen by her brother Francis, who was staying at Chawton when this section of *Mansfield Park* was written.

Between the sisters (Maria and Julia) there is sibling rivalry in love matters more spectacular than in any of the earlier works (with the possible exception of the youthful "Three Sisters"). *Sense and Sensibility, Pride and Prejudice,* and *Persuasion* bristle with rivalry between sisters. The love between siblings, *Mansfield Park* pointedly reminds us, which is "sometimes almost every thing, is at others worse than nothing" (p. 235). Jane Austen was two years younger than her sister Cassandra; and though the contrary is generally believed, the fact is that they did not always get along. A careful reading of some of the surviving letters Jane wrote to her elder sister makes this plain enough. Indeed, the sisters had a disagreement over the ending of this very novel, as we shall see.

Also we have one mother here (Lady Bertram) who is selfishly heartless, and uninterested in her children—and in everything that does not directly concern herself; and another (Mrs. Price) who virtually ignores a grown-up daughter. Can this be a coincidence? While there may be little of Jane Austen's mother in Lady Bertram, the fact remains that in refusing to "go into public with her daughters" and being "too indolent even to accept a mother's gratification in witnessing their success and enjoyment at the expense of any personal trouble" (p. 35), Lady Bertram undoubtedly recapitulates the reclusive side of Mrs. Austen, who became disinclined while still a healthy woman to leave home for any reason. Of Lady Bertram it is said: "Every thing that a considerate parent *ought* to feel was advanced for her use; and every thing that an affectionate mother *must* feel in promoting her children's enjoyment, was attributed to her nature" (p. 285)—falsely, of course, for she feels nothing. The phrasing here is vivid and probably reflects an aspect of Jane Austen's view of her mother. Lady Bertram's "playing at being frightened" (p. 427) in emergencies may represent Mrs. Austen's lifelong hypochondria, which always infuriated her novelist-daughter. The mortification of Fanny at her mother's indifference to her is described by Jane Austen with equally striking vividness: "She had probably alienated Love by the helplessness and fretfulness of a fearful temper, or been unreasonable in wanting a larger share than any one among so many could deserve" (p. 371). The last part of this statement sounds distinctly personal; the Austens, like the Prices, were a large family, and probably there was not enough time for a busy mother laden with household cares to tend to all the needs and desires of a younger daughter. Mrs. Price's "heart and her time were . . . quite full; she had neither leisure nor affection to bestow on Fanny. Her daughters never had been much to her. She was fond of her sons . . . her time was given chiefly to her house and her servants" (p. 389). The Austens had six boys and two girls, and throughout her early and middle years Mrs. Austen would have been chiefly concerned with household management. Nor can there be any doubt that she doted on her sons. In *Mansfield Park* Fanny reflects bitterly that her mother had "no curiosity to know her better, no desire of her friendship, and no inclination for her company" (p. 390). Should we still fail to get the point, the novel makes it plain for us: "Mothers certainly have not yet got quite the right way of managing their daughters . . . To be neglected before one's time, must be very vexatious . . . [it

is] entirely the mother's fault" (pp. 50-51). Probably Jane Austen was "neglected before [her] time" by her mother; it may go far to explain her hostile nature as an adolescent, her lifelong penchant for satire, and the number of silly and insipid mothers who populate her books. Other instances of her impatience with and resentment of her mother abound in more obvious ways in the novelist's letters; mother and daughter even fought over household expenses. These feelings are articulated here in sublimated ways, but without much artifice. Surely it is indicative that Mrs. Austen, who enjoyed the Dashwood sisters and admired Elizabeth Bennet, is on record as detesting Fanny Price.[9]

And it should be equally clear, though critics have not noticed this, that Fanny's aunt Norris is a highly unflattering likeness of Mrs. Leigh Perrot, the woman who married Jane Austen's mother's brother. Mrs. Norris is a tightfisted aunt who torments a saintly niece—and steals. Mrs. Leigh Perrot was accused of, tried for, and eventually acquitted of stealing some lace from a shop in Bath. There is some evidence to suggest a strain of kleptomania in her, though no particular offense was ever positively proven.[10] In any case, she was no favorite with her husband's family during Jane Austen's lifetime. The Austen ladies were furious, after the death of the novelist's father and during subsequent years, over the prosperous Leigh Perrots' refusal to help any member of the family except the already comfortable James Austen, Jane's eldest brother. Since James Leigh Perrot was both a blood relative and perceived as affectionate and likable, his wife was blamed by the Austens, and considered parsimonious. Jane Austen would never know this, but after her husband's death in 1817 Mrs. Leigh Perrot dealt more generously with the Austen family than he ever had done. That Mrs. Norris is a malicious portrait of the resented aunt of the Austens is obvious. Mrs. Norris on two occasions steals baize from Mansfield Park, eventually winding up with the whole curtain bought for the theatricals secreted away in her own house. After the ball at Mansfield she makes off with "all the supernumerary jellies" (p. 283). As for her impoverished nieces in Portsmouth—Mrs. Price's verdict on her sister undoubtedly reflects the feelings of Mrs. Leigh Perrot's nieces at Bath, Southampton, and Chawton: "Aunt Norris lives too far off, to think of such little people as you" (p. 387), Mrs. Price tells one of her daughters.

Other aspects of autobiography are patent here. Into every one of her novels Jane Austen tosses at least one ball, much in the manner in which Trollope would introduce a fox hunt into virtually every tale. What interests a writer will find its way into the fiction. Fanny's enjoyment of dancing reflects that of the novelist years earlier, as Jane Austen's youthful letters amply testify: "The ball . . . such an evening of pleasure before her! . . . she began to dress for it with much of the happy flutter which belongs to a ball" (p. 270). Afterwards, creeping up to bed, Fanny is still "feverish with hopes and fears, soup and negus, sore-footed and fatigued, restless and agitated, yet feeling, in spite of every thing, that a ball was indeed delightful" (p. 281).

Like Jane Austen, Fanny becomes a subscriber to a circulating library—"amazed at being any thing *in propria persona,* amazed . . . to be a renter, a chuser of books!" (p. 398). Like the novelist herself, Fanny abhors "improvements" made by gardeners and architects—it is indicative that Henry Crawford is said to be "a capital improver" (p. 244)—who tear up avenues of trees, remove walks, and fabricate ruins to re-create the "natural" through a synthetic impression. *Sense and Sensibility* and *Northanger Abbey* argue in the same vein.

In this connection, *Mansfield Park* betrays Jane Austen's love of nature, her dislike of urban life, and her growing neurasthenia and distaste for "society." "We do not look in great cities for our best morality" (p. 93), Edmund declares; it might be one of the novel's epigraphs. Even the quality of sunshine is said to be "a totally different thing in a town and in the country." In Portsmouth, "its power was only . . . a stifling, sickly glare, serving but to bring forward stains and dirt that might otherwise have slept. There was neither health nor gaiety in sun-shine in a town" (p. 439). Fanny in Portsmouth—losing, as she observes, the glories of a garden in spring—sits "in a blaze of oppressive heat, in a cloud of moving dust" (p. 439). In the country it is a different matter altogether:

> Fanny spoke her feelings. "Here's harmony!" said she, "here's repose! Here's what may leave all painting and all music behind, and what poetry only can attempt to describe. Here's what may tranquillize every care, and lift the heart to rapture! When I look out on such a night as this, I feel as if there could be neither wickedness nor sorrow in the world; and there certainly would be less of both if the sublimity of Nature were more attended to, and people were carried more out of themselves by contemplating such a scene."
>
> (p. 113)

Thus Fanny at Mansfield. The emphasis here is on the tranquilizing of care; in the city, care is stimulated rather than tranquilized. When Fanny returns home to Mansfield from Portsmouth, "Her eye fell every where on lawns and plantations of the freshest green; and the trees, though not fully clothed, were in that delightful state, when farther beauty is known to be at hand, and when, while much is actually given to the sight, more yet remains for the imagination" (pp. 446-47). Here is another indication that Jane Austen preferred nature untouched by "improvers," who left little to the "imagination."

Fanny's love of nature is underscored by her hatred of noise and disorder; and the Portsmouth chapters of *Mansfield Park* show Jane Austen's chronic neurasthenia growing to greater proportions—undoubtedly stimulated by her hatred of Godmersham, her brother Edward's house, where we know she spent several traumatic months in 1813 revising the novel. Her letters of the time show that she grew impatient to be gone from the place, where a continuous stream of visitors and an oversupply of children, as in the Price household in Portsmouth, provided a constant uproar and made life miserable for anyone who valued peace and quiet. In Portsmouth the Price boys run around and slam doors until Fanny's "temples ache" (p. 381); she is said to be "almost stunned" by the noise (p. 382). "The living in incessant noise was to a frame and temper, delicate and nervous like Fanny's, an evil which no superadded elegance or harmony could have entirely atoned for. It was the greatest misery of all" (p. 391). Here, certainly, is the neurasthenic novelist at Godmersham. It is no accident that Fanny at Portsmouth, subjected to "closeness and noise . . . confinement, bad air, bad smells" (p. 432), thinks (p. 431) of Cowper's line, "With what intense desire she wants her home" (*Tirocinium; or, A Review of Schools,* 565). The "ceaseless tumult of her present abode," where "every body was noisy, every voice was loud," where "the doors were in constant banging, the stairs were never at rest, nothing was done without a clatter, nobody sat still, and nobody could command attention when they spoke" (p. 392), must describe Jane Austen's life at Godmersham in 1813, unheard and "want[ing] her home." The accounts of the effects on a sensitive nature of noise and chaos cannot be wholly invented. *Mansfield Park* gives us a magnificent picture of Jane Austen's personality in her late thirties. In this way it may be seen less as a "sport" among the novels than a most characteristic and revealing performance.

Other elements of autobiography should be mentioned. There may well be a carry-over of the Bigg Wither affair in the story of Fanny Price and Henry Crawford. In 1802 Jane Austen had been put under considerable pressure by her family to accept a proposal of marriage from Harris Bigg Wither, a young man then preparing to take orders. His sisters were close friends of the Austen girls; the families were neighbors in Hampshire. Jane Austen's refusal of Harris Bigg Wither elicited from her family some surprise and resentment—as does Fanny's of Henry Crawford. Sir Thomas petulantly declares, "The advantage or disadvantage of your family—of your parents—your brothers and sisters—never seems to have had a moment's share in your thoughts" (p. 318), and he refers to Fanny's behavior in this crisis as "a wild fit of folly, throwing away . . . such an opportunity of being settled in life, eligibly, honourably, nobly settled, as will, probably, never occur to you again" (p. 319). Something like this may well have been said to the novelist by a member of her family when she turned down Harris Bigg Wither, seen by the Austens and their connections as a respectable, pleasant, prosperous man who, among other things, would have provided the novelist with a large house in her beloved Hampshire and a comfortable income at a time when she had nothing of her own, no means whatever of "being settled in life," that state so single-mindedly pursued by most of Jane Austen's heroines. Certainly we cannot know if her mother or aunt or a brother or anyone else spoke to her in this vein. But it is clear, from evidence recently come to light, that Jane's sister tried to persuade her to alter the ending of *Mansfield Park* to allow Henry Crawford to marry Fanny Price. Apparently feeling that Fanny should indeed be well "settled in life," Cassandra argued the matter gamely; Jane stood firm, and would not allow it.[11] Probably Cassandra's influence is responsible for the assertion late in the novel, by way of mitigation, that if Crawford had "been satisfied with the conquest of one amiable woman's affections" and "persevered," Fanny must have given way to him eventually (p. 467). In the event Fanny of course is seen to be right in her resistance to Crawford. Her judgment never misleads her; and "for the purity of her intentions she could answer" (p. 324). She understands "how wretched, and how unpardonable, how hopeless and how wicked it was, to marry without affection" (p. 324). The sorely tempted novelist may well have felt something like this during that awful, unforgettable night at Many-down, in the course of which Harris Bigg Wither proposed marriage and she accepted him—only to change her mind the next morning, leaving the house in haste, tears, and embarrassment. After all, as Fanny declares, a woman is not *required* to love a man, "let him be ever so generally agreeable. Let him have all the perfections in the world . . . a man [need not] be acceptable to every woman he may happen to like himself" (p. 353). This is as passionate a defense as we are likely to find anywhere of Jane Austen's rejections of the half-dozen or so men who, during her lifetime, offered her marriage. Harris Bigg Wither, according to a family chronicler, turns out to have been a mean-tempered, frail recluse with a stammer.[12] Fanny Price, no less than her author, may be pardoned, even in an age of mercenary marriages, for eluding a match she found repugnant.

The marriage question is of course at the center of *Mansfield Park,* as it often is in the other books. "There certainly are not so many men of large fortune in the world, as there are pretty women to deserve them" (p. 3), the narrator complains in the opening paragraph. And yet marriage as an institution is attacked here with special vehemence—perhaps in part because of the personal applications involved. Maria is said to be "prepared for matrimony by an hatred of home, restraint, and tranquillity; by the misery of disappointed affection, and contempt of the man she was to marry" (p. 202). Mary Crawford tells Mrs. Grant, "Every body is taken in . . . in marriage . . . it is, of all transactions, the one in which people expect most from others, and are least honest themselves . . . it is a manuvring business" (p. 46). Jane Austen undoubtedly felt "taken in" by men on several occasions—in the mid-1790s by Tom Lefroy, her first youthful suitor, who was packed off to Ireland (later to become Chief Justice there) when things between the impecunious young people began to look serious to their families; by the mysterious clergyman who courted her in Devon in 1801 and who, after being virtually accepted by the novelist, disappeared (he may have died, but this is unclear); by several others who proposed to her and, after being refused, found solace elsewhere with what seemed to the novelist spectacular celerity, in the manner of Mr. Collins; and perhaps as well by Harris Bigg Wither, who on one evening appeared to be someone she might like to marry and by the next morning, after much reflection, turned out to be someone quite different after all.

None of this need diminish the role of marriage in giving a woman consequence. *Mansfield Park* provides a series of glimpses into the novelist's resentful perspective during the years leading up to her literary success and recognition. The most usual complaint is lack of personal consequence among others—which must have been especially galling to an intelligent and sensitive woman in her thirties who had had her chances to marry, after all, but had found marriage a "manuvring business" and had eschewed it, thus having to give precedence, as a matter of form when in company, to married women, no matter how ignorant. We can see Jane Austen's irritation over matters such as these in *Emma,* where the insipid Mrs. Elton is given precedence over the intelligent, unmarried Emma Woodhouse merely because the silly woman happens to have a husband. The novelist's distress and impatience are evident in Fanny's feeling that she "can never be important to any one" (p. 26); in her having known, according to the narrator of *Mansfield Park,* "the pains of tyranny, of ridicule, and neglect" because "her motives had been often misunderstood, her feelings disregarded, and her comprehension under-valued" (p. 152); in Mrs. Norris's declaration to Fanny that "wherever you are, you must be the lowest and last" (p. 221); in Fanny's being "totally unused to have her pleasure consulted" (p. 280) on any matter; and in the description of her—it is Henry Crawford's—as "dependent, helpless, friendless, neglected, forgotten" (p. 297). The novelist was the only member of the large Austen family who, before her books began to appear (nothing in print until 1811), had not a single penny of private income. In all of this about Fanny there must be a touch of Jane Austen's own sensibility, though outwardly Fanny is not much like her author. But the word *neglect* echoes and reechoes through the book like a refrain. And as we have seen, Fanny's values are almost always the novelist's.

"To be in the centre of such a [family] circle, loved by so many . . . to feel affection without fear or restraint, to feel herself the equal of those who surrounded her, to be at peace" (p. 370)—these are the things Fanny cherishes, as Jane Austen surely did. Away from Chawton—in "society," among strangers—the novelist could not be secure of them. "A well-disposed young woman, who did not marry for love, was in general but the more attached to her own family" (p. 201), *Mansfield Park* tells us. Outside the family circle she was more likely to lack consequence, certainly; and to be "neglected before one's time" is "very vexatious," as we know. Thus Fanny's sexual jealousy of all the acknowledged beauties in the book: the sight of Mary Crawford, for example, fills her "full of jealousy and agitation" (p. 159). The "necessity of self-denial and humility" (p. 463), "the advantages of early hardship and discipline," and "the consciousness of being born to struggle and endure" (p. 473)[13] are insisted upon instead; and it is precisely these qualities which Maria Bertram and Mary Crawford, so successful with men, conspicuously lack.

Another characteristic and recognizable touch here is the double vision we encounter on questions of security, comfort, and luxury. Although it is better to have these things than not to have them, it is also seen to be ridiculous to measure all life, to tote people up, purely on the basis of wealth. The attack on materialism goes on from the previous books, but it is tempered in *Mansfield Park* by some sober thought. "A large income is the best recipé for happiness I ever heard of" (p. 213), Mary declares. "It is every body's duty to do as well for themselves as they can" (p. 289). And: "Varnish and gilding hide many stains" (p. 434). Still, the moral price paid for personal comfort must not be too high; the price Mary pays is too high, and the result is loss of happiness. Jane Austen attacks the subversive side of Mary with special emphasis. "A poor honourable is no catch" (p. 394), she makes Mary say; and Fanny comments that Mary "had only learnt to think nothing of consequence but money" (p. 436). Mary's friend Mrs. Fraser "could not do otherwise than accept [her husband], for he was rich, and she had nothing" (p. 361). This is marriage as merely a steppingstone to luxury. "Every thing is to be got with money" (p. 58), says Mary: it is one of the bitterest comments in the novel. Almost everyone in *Mansfield Park* is rated by others on the basis of how much he or she has, or can get. Fanny alone seems immune to most of these influences: "she likes to go her own way . . . she does not like to be dictated to . . . she certainly has a little spirit of secrecy, and independence," as even Mrs. Norris sees (p. 323). Throughout her life Jane Austen fiercely protected her own independence—no doubt wishing wistfully at times that she had less need of doing so.

We may see something of the Austen sisters in the amusing account of the Owen sisters, about whom Mary comments: "Their father is a clergyman and their brother is a clergyman, and they are all clergymen together" (p. 289).

And the malicious, heartless side of Jane Austen surely is in evidence when, after telling us that Lady Bertram has little to write letters about until the near-fatal illness of her elder son, the novelist comments acidly that "Lady Bertram's hour of good luck came" (p. 425) and Tom's ordeal "was of a nature to promise occupation for the pen for many days to come" (p. 426). This is Jane Austen herself—the Jane Austen of the letters—speaking, and not Lady Bertram. William Price, ravenous for promotion, is portrayed as impatiently looking forward to the death of the officer immediately superior to him in the *Thrush*. And the novelist is certainly hard on poor Dr. Grant at the end of the book. "To complete the picture of good" facing Edmund and Fanny, the narrator comments, "the acquisition of Mansfield living by the death of Dr. Grant" (due to overeating) "occurred just after they had been married long enough to begin to want an increase of income" (p. 473). There is little irony here.

Many have a fixed image of Jane Austen. People are fond of saying, for example, that Elizabeth Bennet is their idea of what the novelist must have been like. If one accepts this proposition, he is unlikely to think that Fanny Price (or Catherine Morland, or Emma Woodhouse, or Anne Elliot) is a "typical" Jane Austen heroine, or at all like her creator. But none of the heroines is in fact any more or less "typical" than any of the others; each of the novels is equally "typical" of Jane Austen, since she wrote them all. She was a woman of many moods, like the rest of us. The hopeful, more playful mood in which *Pride and Prejudice* was first drafted was quite different from that in which, fifteen years or so later, *Mansfield Park* was written. Neither novel is more or less "typical" of Jane Austen than the other, though published just a year apart. One is a product of the novelist's early twenties, the other of her late thirties; and that, in addition to some understanding of how barren and disappointing the novelist's middle years were, may explain a great deal. Each book is equally a Jane Austen performance.

The personality of the novelist may be glimpsed again when we consider briefly two of the most controversial aspects of *Mansfield Park* and attempt to view them in a more autobiographical light. These are the "ordination" theme and the question of the theatricals (and "acting" in general). In fact there need be little confusion about either of these matters. Jane Austen treats them with clarity and precision—and in a highly characteristic way.

Though obviously the novel, in its final form, turned out not to be primarily about "ordination" after all, despite Jane Austen's characterization of it in these terms in a letter written before the novel had been completed or revised,[14] attitudes toward the church, both as an institution and a profession, are central to the story.

We should never forget that Jane Austen was the daughter of a clergyman and the sister (as it turned out) of two others. She grew up in a household in which it was taken for granted that the profession of clergyman was an important and useful one—one which society could not do without, especially in times of moral laxness. She herself was always a believing Christian, though rarely an aggressive one.

One critic, arguing that the Christianity of *Mansfield Park* is ardent, sees Fanny as the very embodiment of Christianity itself.[15] While it may be tempting for others (once again) to take the side of the vivacious and irreverent Miss Crawford, who makes fun of clergymen, against Edmund and Fanny, who are sometimes pompous and didactic on the subject of religion, one cannot for a moment suspect Jane Austen in *Mansfield Park* of any real animus against the church. Mary Crawford's famous pronouncement, "A clergyman is nothing" (p. 92; in terms of social distinction, she means), touches off a debate in the novel on the merits of the profession. (Jane Austen's cousin and sister-in-law Eliza de Feuillide is supposed to have said something of the sort to James Austen many years earlier, when he proposed to her. She married instead his younger brother Henry, then a banker.)

Mary: "A clergyman has nothing to do but to be slovenly and selfish—read the newspaper, watch the weather, and quarrel with his wife. His curate does all the work, and the business of his own life is to dine."

Edmund: "It is impossible that your own observation can have given you much knowledge of the clergy. You can have been personally acquainted with very few of a set of men you condemn so conclusively."

Mary: "I speak what appears to me the general opinion; and where an opinion is general, it is usually correct."

Edmund: "Where any one body of educated men, of whatever denomination, are condemned indiscriminately, there must be a deficiency of information, or . . . of something else" (p. 110).

Edmund rightly surmises that Mary has got her "information" from the example and the dinner-table conversation of the worldly Dr. Grant. Certainly Jane Austen has no defense for *his* sort of clergyman—or any pity either, as we have seen. But the novel does take up the cudgels for the profession. Edmund declares that "it is not in fine preaching only that a good clergyman will be useful in his parish and his neighbourhood"; his "private character" and "general conduct" provide an example for his neighbors (p. 93). It is for this reason that Edmund plans to live in Thornton Lacey rather than permit a curate to do "all the work." Human nature "needs more lessons than a weekly sermon can convey," as Sir Thomas puts it (p. 248). If the clergyman "does not live among his parishioners and prove himself by constant attention their well-wisher and friend, he does very little either for their good or his own" (p. 248). A man of social consequence himself, Sir Thomas is not blind to the importance of the profession and encourages Edmund in his clerical career. The assertion of self-improvement when a clergyman does his proper duty is also taken up by Fanny, who makes a little speech on the subject.

> "A man—a sensible man like Dr. Grant, cannot be in the habit of teaching others their duty every week, cannot go to church twice every Sunday and preach such very good sermons in so good a manner as he does, without being the better for it himself. It must make him think, and I have no doubt that he oftener endeavours to restrain himself than he would if he had been any thing but a clergyman."
>
> (p. 112)

The question, then, turns not so much on "ordination" as on attitudes toward the profession of clergyman. It is no surprise that the immoral characters in the novel have no use for the church, while the virtuous ones—dull or not—defend it, with Jane Austen's unwavering blessing.

Although the question of the theatricals has been endlessly debated, it is a much simpler matter than many readers have thought. Again a knowledge of the novelist's life is of use here. For Jane Austen there is inherently nothing wrong with putting on plays or acting in them. From the time she was a young girl, she loved the drama. Early on she relished the family theatricals at Steventon, and later the professional theater in London. All her life she was a dedicated theatergoer—sometimes attending the theater every night when she was in the metropolis. As she makes Charles Musgrove declare in *Persuasion,* "We all like a play."[16] The point here is that putting on theatricals at Mansfield Park is not in itself an evil thing. In this particular instance the occasion is used in selfish ways by several people; the situation of some of the principal characters simply makes it wrong to put on a play like *Lovers' Vows.* For these reasons, rather than any generic ones, the theatricals can be condemned. That is to say, an activity that may be perfectly acceptable in life may be used thematically in fiction for negative purposes. As Edmund says (later) of the time of the theatricals, "we were all wrong together" (p. 349).

There were at least four adaptations of Kotzebue's *Natural Son* (originally published in Germany in 1791). In England it appeared under the title of *Lovers' Vows,* and had a great vogue between 1798 and 1802. (Interior evidence, as Chapman says, suggests that the characters in *Mansfield Park* are using Elizabeth Inchbald's text of the play.) *Lovers' Vows* was reprinted again and again; in 1799, for example, a twelfth edition was announced (the characters in Jane Austen's novel would appear to be using the fifth edition).[17] Between 1798 and 1802 *Lovers' Vows* had successful runs at Covent Garden, Bath, the Haymarket, and Drury Lane. Nathaniel Hawthorne saw a production of it in Salem, Massachusetts, in 1820;[18] it was still popular in the 1830s.

Between 1801 and 1805 *Lovers' Vows* was performed six times at the Theatre Royal in Bath; since Jane Austen lived in Bath during much of this time, it is very likely indeed that she saw it performed there. The point is that the play's concern with adultery, elopement, and an abandoned wife, its attack on the conventions of contemporary marriage, and its exaltation of feeling and impulse render it spectacularly inappropriate to the characters in *Mansfield Park* as they are placed at the time rehearsals of *Lovers' Vows* are going forward. Clearly it is dangerous for Maria to play a fallen—or falling—woman, illicitly seduced. Rushworth is cast as a foolish suitor, Mary as a free-thinking "modern" girl (Hazlitt remarked that the role of Amelia in this play was about as far as any contemporary actress was prepared to go; no wonder Edmund is horrified), and Yates as an advocate of elopement. Slated to portray a lovelorn clergyman, Edmund argues that "the man who chooses the profession" of clergyman "is, perhaps, one of the last who would wish to represent it on the stage" (p. 145)—especially when the character is presented unsympathetically. Surely a main ground of Jane Austen's disapproval is that the actors are playing exaggerated versions of themselves rather than really "acting"—to which in fact she had no objection. In *Persuasion,* on several occasions, fashionable evening parties are pronounced to be less interesting and instructive experiences than nights spent at the theater, where—unlike real life—hypocrisy and insincerity are confined to the stage. Those who prefer parties to plays are that novel's most insipid characters. "*I* wanted better acting. There was no Actor worthy naming," Jane Austen grumbled,[19] in the year before *Mansfield Park*'s publication, after seeing a revival of Garrick and Colman's *Clandestine Marriage* (1766) in London. Of another play in town she would comment later: "Acting seldom satisfies me."[20] No other serious reason for her disapprobation of the theatricals can exist—except, perhaps, the alteration of the house in the absence of its master. Indeed, the theme of "My father's house" is resonant.

Surely Fanny's private opinion of the goings-on once again is that of the novelist. Reading through the play, Fanny is astonished "that it could be chosen in the present instance," for she thinks that its "situation" and its "language" are unfit for "a private Theatre," for "home representation" (p. 137). This is undoubtedly true; and anyone who reads both *Mansfield Park* and *Lovers' Vows* will immediately understand the grounds of objection. As an interested follower of the fortunes of the Prince Regent and his wife, Jane Austen knew of the extraordinary condition of manners and morals at the Saxon court within the House of Brunswick in these days; inevitably she would have been suspicious of any play emanating from Germany. Needless to say, there is no blanket condemnation in *Mansfield Park* of the theater or of acting. Indeed, the novel refers enthusiastically to "a love of the theatre" and "an itch for acting . . . among young people" as being "general" and beyond reproach (p. 121). It is only this play, in these circumstances, that is objectionable. Otherwise, it is clear, Edmund would feel differently. "Nobody loves a play better than you do, or can have gone much farther to see one," Julia reminds him (p. 124). Tom Bertram "can conceive no greater harm or danger to any of us in conversing in the elegant written language of some respectable author than in chattering in words of our own"—sentiments with which, quite clearly, the novelist would concur. Tom goes on to remind the family that Sir Thomas has always been fond of promoting "the exercise of talent in young people . . . for any thing of the acting, spouting, reciting kind . . . he has always a decided taste. I am sure he encouraged it in us as boys" (p. 126)—as Jane Austen's father encouraged such activities at Steventon. Indeed, the tradition of family readings in the evening persisted long after his death. It is indicative that Sir Thomas, upon his unexpected return to the house, does not condemn the theatricals outright, but merely inquires *which play* is being rehearsed; and that Fanny, so stunned by the choice of *Lovers' Vows*, always takes great pleasure in hearing "*good* reading," to which "she had been long used" (p. 337)—like Marianne Dashwood in *Sense and Sensibility.* The fact that Henry Crawford reads well and is also a villain hardly constitutes grounds for arguing that Jane Austen hated acting and actors. Being glib and articulate, Henry reads skillfully. What is called into question by his suspect glibness—his capital acting, his good reading, his propensity for "fine" preaching (before fashionable London congregations)—is his *professional* (clerical) commitment. Mary Crawford is a brilliant conversationalist, while Fanny is not; does this mean that Jane Austen preferred dull conversation to lively? We are supposed as readers to retain our moral judgment despite any number of provocations to waver. Certainly Jane Austen's perspective never wavers.

One should see *Mansfield Park* not so much as a falling-off from *Pride and Prejudice* as simply a book in a different vein. They are different works and tell different stories by different means. Neither is any more "characteristic" of Jane Austen than the other: she is, once again, equally the author of both.

The botched ending of *Mansfield Park* is also characteristic of its author—a final piece of autobiography. Once again, in working out the conclusion of a novel, Jane Austen "uses summary rather than dramatic scene."[21] She cannot bear, it seems, to show us her characters' happiness. That goes on offstage; her interest is chiefly in their struggles.

In the last chapter of *Mansfield Park* we have, for the fourth time in four novels, a noisy authorial intrusion into the story, another retreat into cold third-person summary, and a happy resolution glimpsed only from afar. The narrative becomes pictorial rather than scenic, to use James's terminology. "Let other pens dwell on guilt and misery. I quit such odious subjects as soon as I can, impatient to restore every body, not greatly in fault themselves, to tolerable comfort, and to have done with all the rest" (p. 461). It may be tempting to see this as irony—as, that is, a burlesque of the novel in less capable hands (a genre to which Jane Austen often had recourse throughout her life)—this time the focus being the diet of poetic justice indiscriminately handed round at the end. But Jane Austen's "impatience" ("impatient" clearly is the key word in the passage just quoted) to have done with her story, once she has got everybody where she wants them, shows up too often in her fiction to be easily passed over. As in the other novels, she cannot bring herself to write the final love scene. Darcy and Elizabeth, Edward and Elinor, Henry and Catherine, all come to a final understanding out of our hearing; so will Emma and Mr. Knightley. And so here: "I . . . intreat every body to believe that exactly at the time when it was quite natural that it should be so, and not a week earlier, Edmund did cease to care about Miss Crawford, and became as anxious to marry Fanny, as Fanny herself could desire" (p. 470). We have been waiting all through the novel for this to happen; when it finally does, we are not allowed to see it, or Fanny's joy, at firsthand. (One thinks of Emma's response to Mr. Knightley in the garden: "What did she say?—Just what she ought, of course. A lady always does.")[22] Jane Austen somewhat self-consciously offers a reason why she has written such an ending: "Let no one presume to give the feelings of a young woman on receiving the assurance of that affection of which she has scarcely allowed herself to entertain a hope" (p. 471). Why not? Is it because the novelist never played such a scene herself or had these "feelings"—and thus forbears to write about them? She always disliked trying to describe things of which she had no direct knowledge (nowhere in her books is there a scene between two men alone). On the other hand, there was the Bigg Wither affair. That, of course, had a different conclusion. Surely by now, at age thirty-eight, Jane Austen realized that she herself would never play such a scene as Fanny plays opposite Edmund. Perhaps, then, it was too painful for her to write. In any case, she was always more interested in her characters' distress than in their fulfillment. This is true even in **Persuasion,** where, after two drafts of the last chapter, Jane Austen came up with only half a love scene; a careful reading demonstrates that much of the climactic action and dialogue either takes place out of our sight and hearing or fails to get itself written at all.

The mood of **Mansfield Park** is more somber than that of the first three novels (though **Sense and Sensibility** runs it a close race). Now middle-aged and disappointed, Jane Austen was finding it harder to be sunny. Her anger, for example, embraces Maria Bertram, who is not forgiven at the end of **Mansfield Park,** as Lydia Bennet was in **Pride and Prejudice** for a similar offense (of course Maria is much the guiltier of the two). The passage of time, the novelist tells us at the end of **Mansfield Park,** often undermines and revises "the plans and decisions of mortals, for their own instruction, and their neighbours' entertainment" (p. 472). No longer is detachment from the spectacle of life—seeing others as "entertainment" for oneself—treated ironically, as it was in the character of Mr. Bennet. For Jane Austen, detachment had become by 1814 less a peril to be avoided than a state of existence with which to become reconciled. Here we may see creeping in the darker shadows of the later trio of novels.

"There is nothing like employment, active, indispensable employment, for relieving sorrow. Employment . . . may dispel melancholy" (p. 443), **Mansfield Park** tells us. And so Jane Austen found "employment" in writing, and she kept on writing in order to "dispel melancholy."

Notes

1. "What Became of Jane Austen? [*Mansfield Park*]," originally published in *The Spectator,* no. 6745 (October 4, 1957), 339-40; quoted here from *Jane Austen: A Collection of Critical Essays,* ed. Ian Watt (Englewood Cliffs, N.J.: Prentice-Hall, 1963), pp. 141-42.

2. *The Novels of Jane Austen,* ed. R. W. Chapman, 3rd ed., III (London: Oxford University Press, 1934), 68.

3. "A Proper Lively Time with Fanny Price," *Some Words of Jane Austen* (Chicago and London: University of Chicago Press, 1973), pp. 158-204; see especially pp. 182, 164-65, 194, and 175.

4. *The Improvement of the Estate: A Study of Jane Austen's Novels* (Baltimore and London: Johns Hopkins Press, 1971), p. 76.

5. *Character and Conflict in Jane Austen's Novels: A Psychological Approach* (Detroit: Wayne State University Press, 1978), p. 22.

6. Darrel Mansell, *The Novels of Jane Austen: An Interpretation* (New York: Harper & Row, 1973), p. 110.

7. Reported by Park Honan, *Matthew Arnold: A Life* (New York: McGraw-Hill, 1981), p. 60.

8. Jane Austen to Francis Austen, 3 July and 25 September 1813, in *Jane Austen's Letters to Her Sister Cassandra and Others,* ed. R. W. Chapman, 2nd ed. (London: Oxford University Press, 1952), pp. 317 and 340.

9. Mrs. Austen found Fanny "insipid." See "Opinions of *Mansfield Park* collected and transcribed by Jane Austen," in *Jane Austen: The Critical Heritage,* ed. B. C. Southam (London: Routledge & Kegan Paul, 1968), p. 49.

10. On Mrs. Leigh Perrot's trial for shoplifting and other possible offenses committed by her, see Sidney Ives, *The Trial of Mrs. Leigh Perrot* (Boston: privately printed, 1980), *passim.* In a private note to the present writer, Mr. Ives quotes Alexander Dyce as saying that Mrs. Leigh Perrot "had an invincible propensity to theft" and the Austen family knew it. Still, she was never convicted of anything. Jane Austen, who did not like her aunt, was being malicious.

11. The information comes from some correspondence recently discovered at Castle Howard. See Elizabeth Jenkins, "Address" to the General Meeting of the Jane Austen Society (*Report for the Year 1980*), p. 26.

12. Reginald F. Bigg Wither, *Materials for a History of the Wither Family* (Winchester: privately printed, 1907).

13. Despite her avowed dislike of Jane Austen's novels, Charlotte Brontë seems to have remembered this section of *Mansfield Park* well enough when she came to write the scene in *Jane Eyre* (chap. 27) in the course of which the heroine reminds Rochester, "We were born to strive and endure."

14. To Cassandra Austen, 29 January 1813 (*Letters,* p. 298).

15. See Marilyn Butler, *Jane Austen and the War of Ideas* (Oxford: Clarendon Press, 1975), p. 243.

16. *Novels,* V, 223.

17. See Chapman's note on *Lovers' Vows* in *Novels,* III, 474.

18. Reported by Arlin Turner, *Nathaniel Hawthorne: A Biography* (New York and Oxford: Oxford University Press, 1980), p. 26.

19. To Francis Austen, 25 September 1813 (*Letters,* p. 338).

20. To Anna Austen Lefroy, 29 November 1814 (*Letters,* p. 415).

21. John Odmark, *An Understanding of Jane Austen's Novels: Character, Value, and Ironic Perspective* (Totowa, N.J.: Barnes & Noble, 1981), p. 102.

22. *Novels,* IV, 431.

Nina Auerbach (essay date 1983)

SOURCE: "Jane Austen's Dangerous Charm: Feeling as One Ought about Fanny Price," in *Jane Austen: New Perspectives,* edited by Janet Todd, Holmes & Meier Publishers, Inc., 1983, pp. 208-23.

[*In the following essay, Auerbach considers Fanny Price as a version of the Romantic monster.*]

Alone among masters of fiction, Jane Austen commands the woman's art of making herself loved. She knows how to enchant us with conversational sparkle, to charm our assent with a glow of description, to entice our smiles with the coquette's practiced glee. No major novelist is such an adept at charming. Samuel Richardson, her greatest predecessor, disdained gentlemanly amenities in his revelations of the mind's interminable, intractable mixture of motives when it engages itself in duels of love; George Eliot, her mightiest successor, rejected charm as an opiate distracting us from the harsh realities her knobby, convoluted books explore. These majestic truth tellers could not write winningly if they tried, for they are too dismally aware of the dark side of enchantment; while even in her harshest revelations, Jane Austen is a maestro at pleasing.

Yet, from the cacophony of marriages with which it begins, to the depressed union which ends it, *Mansfield Park* is unlikable. When so knowing a charmer abrades her reader, her withdrawal from our pleasure must be deliberate. She herself studied the gradations of liking *Mansfield Park* inspired, something she had not troubled to do with her earlier books, as we know from her meticulously compiled **"Opinions of *Mansfield Park"*:** "My Mother—not liked it so well as **P. & P.**—Thought Fanny insipid.— Enjoyed Mrs. Norris.— . . . Miss Burdett—Did not like it so well as **P. & P.** Mrs. James Tilson—Liked it better than **P. & P.,**"[1] and so on. We do not know whether these carefully measured dollops of liking amused Jane Austen or annoyed her, but we do know that she was intrigued by the degree to which her unlikable novel was liked. Her apparent withdrawal from the reader's fellowship suggests a departure from the community and the conventions of realistic fiction toward a Romantic and a dissonant perspective. If we examine this difficult novel, with its particularly unaccommodating heroine, in relation to contemporaneous genres beyond the boundaries of realism, we may better understand Jane Austen's withdrawal from a commonality of delight.

The silent, stubborn Fanny Price appeals less than any of Austen's heroines. Perhaps because of this, she captivates more critics than they. "Nobody, I believe, has ever found it possible to like the heroine of *Mansfield Park,*"[2] Lionel Trilling intoned in 1955, and few would contradict this epitaph today. Yet Trilling goes on to apotheosize this literary wallflower, transfiguring her into a culturally fraught emblem who bears on her scant shoulders all the aches of modern secularism. Such later interpreters as Avrom Fleishman[3] similarly embrace Fanny as emblem if not woman,

wan transmitter of intricate cultural ideals. It seems that once a heroine is divested of the power to please, she is granted an import beyond her apparently modest sphere, for, unlike Jane Austen's other, more immediately appealing heroines, Fanny has been said to possess our entire spiritual history as it shapes itself through her in historical time. Elizabeth and Emma live for readers as personal presences, but never as the Romantic, the Victorian, or the Modern *Zeitgeist*. Failing to charm, Fanny is allowed in compensation to embody worlds.

But readers who have been trained to respect the culturally fraught Fanny still shy away from her as a character. Living in uncomfortable intimacy with her as we do when we read the novel, we recall Kingsley Amis's taunt that an evening with Fanny and her clergyman husband "would not be lightly undertaken."[4] We may understand our heritage through Fanny Price, but ought we to want to dine with her? The question is important because, for theorists like George Levine, the more bravely realism departs from the commonality of fellowship, the more radically it tilts toward a monstrosity that undermines the realistic community itself.[5] In the very staunchness of her virtue Fanny Price seems to me to invoke the monsters that deny the charmed circle of realistic fiction. Though she uses the word "ought" with unyielding authority, she evokes uncertainty and unease. Though we learn more about her life, and participate more intimately in her consciousness, than we do with Jane Austen's other heroines, the bothering question remains: How ought we to feel about Fanny Price?

Mansfield Park tilts away from commonality in part because it breaks the code established by Jane Austen's other novels. Few of us could read *Pride and Prejudice, Persuasion,* or even *Emma,* without liking the heroines enough to "travel with them," in Wayne Booth's charming phrase.[6] *Mansfield Park* embodies a wryer literary perception, one especially congenial to Jane Austen's poetic contemporaries: the creator of Fanny Price assumes that one may live with a character one doesn't like. One motive power of Romantic poetry is the fascination of the uncongenial. In "Resolution and Independence," Wordsworth can be possessed by a deformed and virtually nonhuman leech-gatherer, although the poet is too remote from the old man to absorb a word of his exhortation; an unkempt sinner, Coleridge's Ancient Mariner, can snatch our imagination from a wedding, that great congenial sacrament of human community. These gnarled figures lure us out of fellowship to adopt the perspective of the monstrous and the marginal.

Fanny captures our imaginations in this same Romantic way, by welcoming the reader into her solitary animosity against the intricacies of the normal: "Fanny was again left to her solitude, and with no increase of pleasant feelings, for she was sorry for almost all that she had seen and heard, astonished at Miss Bertram, and angry with Mr. Crawford."[7] The compelling, blighting power of Fanny's spectatorship at Sotherton is characteristic: morality dissolves into angry and unpleasant feelings whose intensity is an alternative to community. For while Fanny's Romanticism suggests itself in her isolating sensibility, her stylized effusions to nature, she is most Romantic in that, like Wordsworth's leech-gatherer or Coleridge's Mariner, there is something horrible about her, something that deprives the imagination of its appetite for ordinary life and compels it toward the deformed, the dispossessed.

This elevation of one's private bad feelings into a power alternate to social life associates Fanny not merely with early Romantic outcasts, but with such dashingly misanthropic hero-villains as Byron's Childe Harold, Mary Shelley's Frankenstein, and Maturin's Melmoth. Their flamboyant willfulness may seem utterly alien to this frail, clinging, and seemingly passive girl who annoys above all by her shyness, but like them, she is magnetically unconvivial, a spoiler of ceremonies. During the excursion to Sotherton, the rehearsals of *Lovers' Vows,* the game of Speculation, her baleful solitude overwhelms the company, perhaps because it expresses and exudes their own buried rancor. In families ranging from Sir Thomas Bertram's stately authoritarianism to the casual disorder of her father's house, Fanny exists like Frankenstein as a silent, censorious pall. Her denying spirit defines itself best in assertive negatives: "No, indeed, I cannot act" (p. 168).

Fanny's credo resonates beyond her particular disapproval of staging *Lovers' Vows,* for, even when the play is not in question, Fanny refuses to act. Instead, and consistently, she counteracts; a creed which seems a high-minded elevation of her own honesty against the dangerous deceit of role-playing is also resistance to the comic, collective rhythms of realistic fiction itself. The joyless exercises of her delicate body tacitly condemn not only acting, but activity in general; Mary Crawford's elation at horseback riding is as antagonistic to Fanny as is her flair for acting. At Sotherton, Fanny stations herself beside the dangerous ha-ha as a still bulwark against the mutual serpentine pursuit of the other characters; playing Speculation, she alone will not take the initiative that will advance the game. Fanny's refusal to act is a criticism not just of art, but of life as well. Her timidly resolute denial of acting includes activity and play, those impulses of comedy which bring us together in ceremonial motions where fellowship seems all. Her refusals are her counter charm against the corporate and genial charm with which Jane Austen's comedies win love.

Fanny's role as counteractive genius and spirit of anti-play is anomalous in a romantic heroine, but not in a hero-villain. Like Frankenstein and his monster, those spirits of solitude, Fanny is a killjoy, a blighter of ceremonies and divider of families. It is precisely this opposition to the traditional patterns of romantic comedy that lends her her disturbing strength. Her misery amid the bustle of the play is the stigma of her power:

> She was full of jealousy and agitation. Miss Crawford came with looks of gaiety which seemed an insult, with friendly expressions towards herself which she could hardly answer calmly. Every body around her was gay and busy, prosperous and important, each had their object of interest, their part, their dress, their favourite scene, their friends and confederates, all were finding employment in consultations and comparisons, or diversion in the playful conceits they suggested. She alone was sad and insignificant; she had no share in any thing; she might go or stay, she might be in the midst of their noise, or retreat from it to the solitude of the East room, without being seen or missed.

> (p. 180)

But though she is stricken in the midst of play, unable and unwilling to act, Fanny never retreats from activity. Finally, her "jealousy and agitation" seem to take concrete shape in the angry intruder, Sir Thomas Bertram, who lends authority to Fanny's bad feelings and ends the play. Sir Thomas's interruption seems only the culmination of Fanny's silent, withering power over performance, for before he appears she has already drawn control to her watching self. Backstage, she alone is in possession of each actor's secret grievance; watching and prompting from her isolation, she alone knows everybody's lines. A center of fierce inactivity, Fanny broods jealously over the play until she masters both its script and the secret designs of its actors, at which point Sir Thomas's return vindicates her silent obstructive power. Fanny abdicates from stardom to assume a more potent control over the action: she appropriates to her solitude the controlling omniscience of the rapt audience.

As her novel's sole and constant watcher, the controlling spirit of anti-play, Fanny relinquishes performing heroinism to become the jealous reader, whose solitary imagination resurrects the action and keeps it alive. In her own delicately assertive phrase, "I was quiet, but I was not blind" (p. 358). As quietly seeing spectator of others' activities, Fanny plays a role as ambiguous as the reader's own: like Fanny, we vivify the action by our imaginative participation in it, while we hold as well the power to obstruct it by our censure. The anomalous position of the watcher more than justifies Mary Crawford's perplexed question: "Pray, is she out, or is she not?" (p. 81). Withholding herself from play, Fanny ingests the play of everyone she silently sees. As omniscient spectator of all private and public performances, Fanny remains "out" of the action, while her knowledge seeps into its subtlest permutations. Our discomfort at her, then, may incorporate our discomfort at our own silent voyeurism; as a portrait of the reader as a young woman, she is our unflattering if indelible reflection. Her fierce spectatorship forces our reluctant identification.

As omniscient watcher and anti-comic spirit linked in uncomfortable community to the solitary reader, Fanny possesses a subtler power than we find in brighter and livelier heroines of fiction. That dynamic misreader Emma Woodhouse is forced by her own misconstructions into the limited position of actor in the comedy she is trying to control from without, while Fanny's role as omniscient outsider thrives on her continued abstention. In her role as controlling, anti-comic watcher, Fanny moves beyond the sphere of traditional heroinism to associate herself with a host of dashing British villains. Like them, this denying girl will not, perhaps cannot, eat; her abstinence makes her a spectral presence at the communal feast. Reunited with her family at Portsmouth, instead of feasting with them, as any of Dickens' or Charlotte Brontë's waifs would gladly do, she is repelled by the very suggestion of food, by "the teaboard never thoroughly cleaned, the cups and saucers wiped in streaks, the milk a mixture of motes floating in thin blue, and the bread and butter growing every minute more greasy than even Rebecca's hands had first produced it" (p. 428). Family food induces only a strangely modern nausea. Fanny's revulsion against food, along with her psychic feasting on the activities of others, crystallizes her somewhat sinister position as outsider who strangely and silently moves into the interior. Her starved incapacity to eat familial food is suggestive of that winsome predator the vampire, an equally solitary and melancholy figure who haunts British literature in his dual role as dark abstainer from a comic dailiness of which he is secretly in possession. Like Fanny, the vampire cannot eat the common nourishment of daily life, but he feasts secretly upon human vitality in the dark.

In adopting the role of traditional literary villains, Fanny infects our imaginations in a way that no merely virtuous heroine could do. Her hungry exclusion seems unappeasable and triumphant. Insofar as she draws sustenance from her role as omniscient outsider at family, excursion, wedding, play, or feast, she stands with some venerable monsters in the English canon. Not only does she share the role of Mary Shelley's creature, that gloomy exile from family whose vocation is to control families and destroy them, but there is a shadow on her even of the melancholy Grendel in the Anglo-Saxon epic *Beowulf*. An exile from common feasting, Grendel peers jealously through the window of a lighted banquet hall. He defines his identity as outsider by appropriating the interior; he invades the lighted hall and begins to eat the eaters. At the end of *Mansfield Park,* Fanny too has won a somewhat predatory victory, moving from outsider in to guiding spirit of the humbled Bertram family. Fanny's cannibalistic invasion of the lighted, spacious estate of Mansfield is genteel and purely symbolic, but, like the primitive Grendel, she replaces common and convivial feasting with a solitary and subtler hunger that possesses its object. In this evocation of an earlier literary tradition, Fanny is Jane Austen's most Romantic heroine, for she is part of a literature newly awakened to ancient forms and fascinated by the monstrous and marginal. In the subtle streak of perversity that still disturbs readers today, she shows us the monsters within Jane Austen's realism, ineffable presences who allow the novels to participate in the darker moods of their age.[8]

Fanny's jealous hunger, which can be assuaged only by private, psychic feasting, isolates her in comedy while it associates her with such venerable predators as the An-

cient Mariner, the vampire, the Byronic hero-villain, and, in a far-off echo, *Beowulf*'s Grendel. Her initiation is not that of the usual heroine, whose marriage reconciles us to the choreography of comedy; instead, like the hero-villain, she proclaims her uniqueness through possessive spectatorship. The implications of Fanny's refusal to act are more richly glossed in Romantic poetry and fiction than in early nineteenth-century realism, but Romantic criticism also illuminates the complex genesis of a Fanny Price: her stubborn creed, "I cannot act," recalls some problematic characters of Shakespeare, in whom such critics as Coleridge and Hazlitt discovered new significance.

Like *Mansfield Park,* Shakespearean drama characteristically pivots upon the performance of a play within a play; like Jane Austen, Shakespeare increasingly pushes to center stage the character who refuses to act. Thus, in his early *A Midsummer Night's Dream,* all the rustics lumber through their parts in the thoroughly comic "Pyramus and Thisbe," but by the time we reach *Twelfth Night,* the play is marred: the austere Malvolio is made to perform in a cruel drama not of his making, posturing for the delectation of the raucous plotters just as he thinks he is being most sincere. This humiliation of an upright, if unlikable, character by the cruelty of play anticipates the complex tone of *Mansfield Park,* though Fanny's sharper eye for traps forbids her seduction by the players.

Malvolio abandons his part in outrage, bellowing as he exits, "I'll be revenged on the whole pack of you!" Perhaps in his revenge he returns as Hamlet, our most famous star who refuses to act. Like Fanny, Hamlet casts himself as a jealous and melancholy death's head in a gay, if false, company. His stern creed—"Madam, I know not seems"— epitomizes, like hers, refusal to act. Nonactive in the complex political drama of his family life, Hamlet likewise takes no part in the microcosmic play within the play, though, like Fanny, he hovers hungrily around its periphery, knowing all the parts. His avid spectatorship ultimately upstages the actors and spoils the performance, replacing communal play with rage and slaughter; at the end of her novel, Fanny too reigns at Mansfield in consequence of a family havoc begun at the ruin of the play.

Of course, Fanny is not Hamlet, nor was she meant to be. She is not a doomed prince, but a pauper, a woman, and a survivor; she neither rages nor soliloquizes, revealing her power and her plans only haltingly and indirectly. Still, in her complex relation to the play which epitomizes her novel's action, Fanny has more in common with Hamlet than she does with the helpless women he excoriates when they cross his path. For Hamlet is Shakespeare's supreme anti-actor and counteractor, the avid and omniscient spectator of the game, who fascinates us as Fanny does because he expresses his virtue by the characteristics of conventional villainy. Jane Austen's contemporaries were obsessed by this troubling sort of hero: Samuel Taylor Coleridge reconceived Hamlet as a paragon of nonactivity, deifying for the modern age a character too pure to act, whose doom and calling are the destruction of play. Fanny

Price may be one feminized expression of this new, Romantic fascination with Hamlet as a modern type. As Jane Austen's Hamlet, scourge and minister of a corrupted world, the perfection of the character who won't play, Fanny Price in her unyielding opposition, her longing for a purified and contracted world, gains majesty if not charm. She is as sternly denying as Hamlet, banishing in turn her cousins Maria and Julia, her parents, and the rakish, witty Crawfords from her own finer sphere. These multiple banishments align her with one type of Romantic hero, while denying her the warmth readers want in a heroine. Confronted with so richly disturbing a figure, we would insult her to sentimentalize her when *Mansfield Park* itself does not. For, as we shall see, Fanny's anti-human qualities are stressed in the text of the novel as well as in its contexts. In her progress toward power, her charmlessness only increases her efficacy as Mansfield's scourge and minister.

"Nobody falls in love with Fanny Price," Tony Tanner warns us (p. 8). We have seen that few readers have done so; Jane Austen further confounds our emotions by making clear that none of the characters within the novel falls in love with her either, though most heroines exist to win love. She wins neither the affection nor the interest of her parents, though they are not always unresponsive; the charm of a Henry Crawford evokes an answering charm in them, but when Fanny's penitential visit to Portsmouth is over at last, her parents seem as relieved to see her leave as she is to go. Kinship is equally unappetizing to all.

Within Mansfield, the gracious adoptive family to which Fanny returns with such ardor, she wins love in proportion to her cousins' shame, receiving emotional interest they failed to earn. Fanny, despised by all, is embraced as a last resource when Sir Thomas's natural children disgrace themselves in turn. Jane Austen is coolly explicit about the cannibalistic undercurrents of this, and perhaps of all, requited love:

> My Fanny indeed at this very time, I have the satisfaction of knowing, must have been happy in spite of every thing. She must have been a happy creature in spite of all that she felt or thought she felt, for the distress of those around her . . . and happy as all this must make her, she would still have been happy without any of it, for Edmund was no longer the dupe of Miss Crawford.
>
> It is true, that Edmund was very far from happy himself. He was suffering from disappointment and regret, grieving over what was, and wishing for what could never be. She knew it was so, and was sorry; but it was with a sorrow so founded on satisfaction, so tending to ease, and so much in harmony with every dearest sensation, that there are few who might not have been glad to exchange their greatest gaiety for it.
>
> (p. 446)

In this redemption from her usual depression, Fanny's only available happy ending is the predator's comedy; surely there is deliberate irony in Jane Austen's pitiless repetition of "happy" amid this household of collapsed hopes. Never in the canon is the happy ending so reliant

upon the wounds and disappointments of others; though we leave Fanny ministering avidly to these wounds, they will never heal. The love she wins from her adoptive family is not a free tribute to her beauty, her character, or her judgment, but the last tender impulse of a stricken household.

The love of her two suitors, Henry and Edmund, is similarly undermined. Everything about Henry Crawford, that mobile and consummate actor, calls his sincerity into question. He stages his love scenes before select audiences, all carefully chosen to put the greatest possible pressure on Fanny, only to humiliate her flamboyantly by his elopement with Maria once she has begun to respond. As Fanny and we know, his passion for her repeats more grandly his pattern of behavior with her silly cousins, so that only the most sentimentally credulous reader could find this new performance credible. The watcher Fanny knows his love is play, and thus by definition the medium of her humiliation; but in exposing the ardor of the romantic hero as a sadistic game, Jane Austen undermines the reader's own impulse to fall in love with Fanny by undermining love itself.

Readers of *Sense and Sensibility, Pride and Prejudice,* and *Emma* expect Edmund Bertram, Fanny's proper husband and sober soulmate, to redress the balance; the probity of this good suitor's love should define the sham of Henry's. But if for Henry love is another variant of private theatricals, a series of ritual attitudes staged for an audience, Edmund's love is so restrained as to be imperceptible. Like Mr. Knightley, he is exemplary as Fanny's tender mentor, proud of his pupil's right feelings and right attitudes, but he has none of Mr. Knightley's life as an incipient lover. Sexual jealousy fuels the latter's sternly protective manner and his indignant disapproval of Frank Churchill, while Edmund hints of no passions beyond what we see, showing not a glimmer of jealousy when Henry Crawford makes demonstrative love to Fanny. Edmund's impeccably clerical conscience interprets his future wife's prospective marriage as a convenience to facilitate his own engagement to Henry's seductive sister. Jane Austen is a sharp observer of men struggling with powerful feelings; like Knightley, Darcy and Wentworth fight to repress, through prudence or anger, a love that proves too strong for them; but she withholds from Edmund Bertram any feelings worth denying. The unlocated and undramatized conversion that leads to his marriage carries as little emotional weight as it could do: "I only intreat every body to believe that exactly at the time when it was quite natural that it should be so, and not a week earlier, Edmund did cease to care about Mary Crawford, and became as anxious to marry Fanny, as Fanny herself could desire" (p. 454).

This clipped, perfunctory summary, together with the fact that no earlier hints have prepared us for an outbreak of passion on Edmund's part, seems deliberately designed to banish love from our thoughts. The final marriage is as stately and inevitable as Edmund's ordination will be; the ritual is performed, though neither love nor guardianship quite joins the marrying couple. The narrator's reiterated appeal to nature—"what could be more natural than the change?"—is a further symptom of the hopelessness of love, for, as we shall see below, nature is a feeble contender in the manipulated world of **Mansfield Park.** Though Edmund marries the woman he ought, the stern hope he husbands is a loveless strength.

A romance from a writer of marriage comedies that so unremittingly denies love to its heroine is a brave novel indeed, particularly when this heroine is ready to love both her emotionally desiccated suitors. If two wooing men cannot manage to love Fanny, with the true suitor proving as hollow as the false, then surely the reader never will. Austerely alone in a community of fictional heroines for whom love is their chief talent and reward, Fanny is further isolated from affection by her radical homelessness. This waiflike attribute may lead us to associate **Mansfield Park** with such Victorian orphan-myths as *Jane Eyre*: Jane, like Fanny, is an unprepossessing orphan, "a discord" in her corrupted foster family, who grows into an iron-willed little savior. But like most of her orphaned analogues in Victorian fiction, Jane is baptized into strength by the recovery of family: it is not her love for Rochester, but her healing interlude with her recovered cousins, the Rivers family, that allows her identity and her destiny to cohere.⁹ The more radical Fanny similarly recovers her family during a romantic crisis, only to discover her total absence of kin. Her ideal home is her utter homelessness. She belongs everywhere she is not: "When she had been coming to Portsmouth, she had loved to call it her home, had been fond of saying that she was going home; the word had been very dear to her; and so it still was, but it must be applied to Mansfield. *That* was now the home. Portsmouth was Portsmouth; Mansfield was home" (pp. 420-21).

The word may be very dear, but the thing eludes her as she eludes it. Victorian orphan-fiction typically begins with the loss of home and ends with its recovery, but here, home is palpable to Fanny only by its absence. Mansfield itself is no true home. The vacuum at its heart is evident not only in the flights of all its members except the supine Lady Bertram, but in the chilling ease with which it can be transformed into a theater. Upon her return, Fanny compels the gutted Mansfield to be her home by an act of will, but in its shrunken regenerate state it bears little resemblance to the place in which she grew up. Fanny's dual returns, to her natural and then to her adoptive origins, prove only the impossibility of self-discovery through return. Thus, though she may resemble later orphan-heroes, Fanny is a more indigestible figure than these wistful waifs, for whom embracing their kin is secular salvation. In the tenacity with which she adheres to an identity validated by no family, home, or love, she denies the vulnerability of the waif for the unlovable toughness of the authentic transplant. Her fragility cloaks the will to live without the traditional sanctions for like. Underlying her pious rigidity is a dispossession so fundamental that, among nineteenth-century English novelists, only the tact of a Jane Austen could dare reveal it in a lady.

Readers are right, then, to find Fanny a relentlessly uncomfortable figure in a domestic romance and to wonder nervously where Jane Austen's comedy went. This uncompromising novel never dissolves its heroine's isolation; she merely passes from the isolation of the outcast to that of the conqueror. Her solitude is rarely alleviated by pathos; instead, she hones it into a spectator's perspective from which she can observe her world and invade it. In this above all, she is closer to the Romantic hero than to the heroine of romance: her solitude is her condition, not a state from which the marriage comedy will save her. In her relentless spectatorship, Fanny may be Jane Austen's domestic answer to Byron's more flamboyant and venturesome Childe Harold, exile from his kind, passing eternally through foreign civilizations in order to create elegies to their ruins. Though Fanny travels only to Sotherton and Portsmouth, her role too is alien and elegiac, as it is at Mansfield itself; like Byron's persona, she is a hero because she is sufficiently detached to see the death of worlds. Fabricating an identity from uprootedness, she conquers the normal world that acts, plays, and marries, through her alienation from it. In the text of her novel, she is a being without kin, but in its context, she exudes a quiet kinship with the strangers and the monsters of her age.

Like other literary monsters, Fanny is a creature without kin who longs for a mate of her own kind. The pain of her difference explains a longing in **Mansfield Park** that is common to much Romantic literature and that, in its obsessed exclusiveness, may look to modern readers unnervingly like incest: the hunger of sibling for sibling, of kin for kind. Seen in its time, the ecstatic, possessive passion Fanny divides between her brother William and her foster brother Edmund, her horror at the Crawfords' attempt to invade her emotions, seem less relevant to the Freudian family romance than to the monster's agonized attempts to alleviate his monstrosity. Mary Shelley's monster asks only that Frankenstein create for him a sister-wife; Bram Stoker's Dracula experiences his triumphant climax when turning his victims into fellow members of the Undead, thus making of them sisters as well as spouses. Fanny yearns similarly in isolation for a brother-mate, repelling the Crawfords above all because they are so different as to constitute virtually another species: "We are so totally unlike . . . we are so very, very different in all our inclinations and ways, that I consider it as quite impossible we should ever be tolerably happy together, even if I *could* like him. There never were two people more dissimilar. We have not one taste in common. We should be miserable" (p. 345).

This rage of self-removal extends itself to Mary Crawford as well, above all perhaps in the emotional spaciousness with which Mary reaches out to Fanny as her "sister."¹⁰ Mary's quest for sisters of gender rather than family, her uncomfortably outspoken championship of abused wives, her sexual initiative, and her unsettling habit of calling things by their names, all suggest the pioneering sensibility of her contemporary, Mary Wollstonecraft; but Fanny cannot endure so universal an embrace, clutching only the shreds of kinship. The novel ends as it ought, with Mary's expulsion into a wider and sadder world, while Fanny, still isolated, clings jealously to her conquered family.

Fanny as Romantic monster does not dispel our discomfort in reading *Mansfield Park,* but may explain some of it. Until recently, critics have limited their recognition of the monsters that underlie Jane Austen's realism to the peripheral figures whose unreason threatens the heroine, while the heroine herself remains solidly human.[11] Yet Fanny excites the same mixture of sympathy and aversion as does Frankenstein's loveless, homeless creature, and the pattern of her adventures is similar to his. Frankenstein's monster begins as a jealous outcast, peering in at family and civic joys. His rage for inclusion makes him the hunted prey of those he envies, and he ends as the conqueror of families. Fanny too is a jealous outcast in the first volume. In the second, she is besieged by the family that excluded her in the form of Henry Crawford's lethal marriage proposal; finally her lair, the chilly East room, is hunted down like Grendel's and invaded by Sir Thomas himself. In the third volume, Fanny, like Mary Shelley's monster, becomes the solitary conqueror of a gutted family. This movement from outcast within a charmed circle to one who is hunted by it and then conqueror of it aligns Jane Austen's most Romantic, least loved heroine with the kin she so wretchedly seeks.

Modern readers may shun Fanny as a static, solitary predator, but in the world of *Mansfield Park* her very consistency and tenacity are bulwarks against a newly opening space that is dangerous in its very fluidity: even Sir Thomas Bertram's solid home is made vulnerable by economic fluctuations in far-off Antigua.[12] Though the large and loveless house that gives it its name has made many readers feel that *Mansfield Park* is Jane Austen's most oppressive novel, its dominant emotional atmosphere induces a certain vertigo, evident in the apparent rocklike solidity, but the true and hopeless elusiveness, of the word "ought." "Ought" tolls constantly, its very sound bringing a knell of absolutism, and nobody uses it with more assurance than the hero and heroine. Fanny can dismiss Henry Crawford simply because "he can feel nothing as he ought," while Edmund freights the word with religious and national authority: "as the clergy are, or are not what they ought to be, so are the rest of the nation" (p. 121). As a barometer of feelings, morals, and institutions, the word seems an immutable touchstone, but in fact it has no objective validation. Its authority in the novel is entirely, and alarmingly, self-generated. The great houses Mansfield and Sotherton scarcely institutionalize the "ought" that resounds in the novel's language; the Portsmouth of the Prices and the London of the Crawfords are equally ignorant of its weight. It has no echo in the world of households and institutions.

Yet this lack of official authority does not prevent the novel's misguided characters from using the word with the same assurance as Fanny and Edmund do. Sir Thomas says of a Fanny who is brewing rebellion, "She appears to feel as she ought" (p. 230); for Mary, the party with which Maria Rushworth inaugurates her miserable marriage finds everything "just as it ought to be" (p. 406); Maria herself avoids only the word in seeing her mercenary marriage as "a duty" (p. 72). Even Edmund, who has transmitted its value to Fanny, abuses the word throughout the novel, beginning with his myopic pressure on Fanny to live with her hated Aunt Norris: "She is choosing a friend and companion exactly where she ought" (p. 60). The incoherence underlying Edmund's authoritative vocabulary tells us that the word recurs anarchically, for there is no objective code to endow it with consistency. Fanny, for example, longs for a loving reunion with her indifferent mother, hoping that "they should soon be what mother and daughter ought to be to each other" (p. 366), but as usual the novel provides no objective image of this "ought": in *Mansfield Park* and throughout Jane Austen's canon, mothers and daughters are at best indifferent and at worst antagonistic, depriving the commanding word of validation. Fanny is repeatedly hymned as the only character who feels consistently as she ought, but in a world where the word changes its meaning so incessantly, her role as a walking "ought" merely isolates her further. Whatever authority Fanny has comes magically from herself alone. Though she can control the inchoate outside world, it is too lacking in definition to claim kinship with her.

For though Fanny possesses a quasi-magical power over the action, she represents less a moral than a shaping principle, assuming the author's prerogatives along with the reader's: the novel's action happens as she wills, and so her emotions become our only standard of right. In its essence, the world of *Mansfield Park* is terrifyingly malleable. Jane Austen detaches herself from her Romantic contemporaries to reveal both inner and outer nature as pitifully ineffectual compared to what can be made. Mrs. Price grows listless toward Fanny because the "instinct of nature was soon satisfied, and Mrs. Price's attachment had no other source" (p. 382). The gap between Mrs. Price and Mrs. Bertram can never heal because "where nature had made so little difference, circumstances [had] made so much" (p. 400). Mary Crawford's nature, like Maria's and Julia's, is similarly helpless against the constructive, or the deconstructive, power of her medium: "For where, Fanny, shall we find a woman whom nature had so richly endowed?—Spoilt, spoilt!—" (p. 441). By contrast, we know that Susan Price will survive, not because of her natural qualities, but because she is "a girl so capable of being made, every thing good" (p. 409). Nature's insufficiency may explain the deadness of Fanny's effusions to stars, trees, and "verdure," for though she laments improvements, Fanny is the most potent of the novel's improving characters. In so malleable and so defective a world, Fanny is polite to the stars, but she turns her most potent attention on the vulnerable, that which is "capable of being made."

In Mary Shelley's *Frankenstein* as well, family, nature, and even the Alps pall before the monster who is capable of being made. The monstrosity of *Mansfield Park* as a whole is one manifestation of its repelled fascination with acting, with education, and with landscape and estate improvements: the novel imagines a fluid world, one with no fixed principles, capable of awesome, endless, and dangerous manipulation. The unconvivial stiffness of its hero and heroine is their triumph: by the end, they are so successfully "made" by each other that he is her creature as completely as she has always been his. The mobility and malleability of *Mansfield Park* is a dark realization of an essentially Romantic vision, of which Fanny Price represents both the horror and the best hope. Only in *Mansfield Park* does Jane Austen force us to experience the discomfort of a Romantic universe presided over by the potent charm of a charmless heroine who was not made to be loved.[13]

Notes

1. Jane Austen, *Minor Works,* ed. R. W. Chapman (1954; reprinted London: Oxford University Press, 1969), p. 432.

2. Lionel Trilling, *"Mansfield Park,"* reprinted in Ian Watt, ed., *Jane Austen: A Collection of Critical Essays* (Englewood Cliffs, N.J.: Prentice-Hall, 1963), p. 128.

3. Avrom Fleishman, *A Reading of Mansfield Park* (1967; reprinted Baltimore: The Johns Hopkins University Press, 1970), pp. 57-69.

4. Kingsley Amis, "Whatever Became of Jane Austen?" (1957), reprinted in Watt, p. 142.

5. "Keeping the monster at bay is one part of the realist enterprise. The other is to keep him, or her, alive," George Levine, *The Realistic Imagination: English Fiction from Frankenstein to Lady Chatterley* (Chicago: University of Chicago Press, 1981), p. 80. Judith Wilt, *Ghosts of the Gothic: Austen, Eliot, and Lawrence* (Princeton: Princeton University Press, 1980), pp. 121-72, provides an eerily suggestive discussion of the terror that infuses Jane Austen's vision of commonality.

6. Wayne Booth, *A Rhetoric of Fiction* (Chicago: University of Chicago Press, 1961), p. 245.

7. Jane Austen, *Mansfield Park* (1814; reprinted Harmondsworth: Penguin, 1966), p. 127. Future references to this edition will appear in the text.

8. George Levine speculates about the monstrous potential of Jane Austen's more inquisitive heroines, though he assumes, overhastily in my opinion, that Fanny's passivity exempts her from monstrosity (p. 41). Sandra M. Gilbert and Susan Gubar are more catholic in their definition: "[Austen's] heroines, it seems, are not born like people, but manufactured like monsters, and also like monsters they seem fated to self-destruct," Gilbert and Gubar, *The Madwoman in the Attic: The Woman Writer and the Nineteenth-Century Literary Imagination* (New Haven: Yale University Press, 1979), p. 129. For more capacious examinations of Jane Austen's dark Romanticism, see Wilt, pp. 121-72, and my "Jane Austen and Romantic Imprisonment," in *Jane Austen in a Social Context,* ed. David Monaghan (London: Macmillan, 1981), pp. 9-27.

9. See Maurianne Adams, *"Jane Eyre:* Woman's Estate," in Arlyn Diamond and Lee R. Edwards, eds., *The Authority of Experience: Essays in Feminist Criticism* (Amherst: University of Massachusetts Press, 1977), pp. 137-59; and Fleishman, p. 72, for more discussion of Fanny as orphan. For a broader discussion of the subversive implications of fictional orphanhood, see my "Incarnations of the Orphan," *ELH* 42 (Fall 1975): 395-419.

10. See Janet Todd, *Women's Friendship in Literature* (New York: Columbia University Press, 1980), pp. 246-74, for a provocative analysis of Fanny's, and Jane Austen's, rejection of female friendship and the radical autonomy it provides.

11. See, for instance, Donald Greene, "Jane Austen's Monsters," in John Halperin, ed., *Jane Austen: Bicentenary Essays* (Cambridge: Cambridge University Press, 1975), pp. 262-78. Amis, in Watt, p. 144, and Julia Prewitt Brown, in *Jane Austen's Novels: Social Change and Literary Form* (Cambridge, Mass.: Harvard University Press, 1979), p. 100, do in passing call Fanny Price a monster, but this appellation seems more a cry of horror than an expression of sustained literary interest.

12. See Fleishman, pp. 36-42.

13. A somewhat shorter version of this paper was presented as the keynote address of the 1980 meeting of the Jane Austen Society. Their kind invitation to speak made me wonder for the first time how I ought to feel about Fanny Price.

Margaret Kirkham (essay date 1983)

SOURCE: "Feminist Irony and the Priceless Heroine of *Mansfield Park,*" in *Jane Austen: New Perspectives,* edited by Janet Todd, Holmes & Meier Publishers, Inc., 1983, pp. 231-47.

[*In the following essay, Kirkham outlines the irony of Fanny Price's characterization in* Mansfield Park *as it subtly mocks the sentimental conduct-book ideal of womanhood.*]

"'I do not quite know what to make of Miss Fanny. I do not understand her.'" So says Henry Crawford (*Mansfield Park,* p. 230).[1] What to make of Miss Fanny is the central moral puzzle Jane Austen presents to her anti-hero. He fails to discover the correct solution. It is also the central puzzle presented to the reader, testing the soundness of his moral attitudes and the quickness of his wits. It may be that the author misjudged what could be expected of her readers, for they have not, by and large, solved the riddle of Miss Price satisfactorily. Even Henry Austen took a bit of time over it (**Letters,** nos. 92-94). He had the advantage of familiarity with contemporary works to which allusion is made, as well as a knowledge of the author's point of view, and yet he found this puzzle a difficult one. No wonder, then, that later readers, lacking his privileged knowledge, have sometimes blundered.

In this essay, I shall try to show that Jane Austen teases us about Miss Fanny. Irony, far from being suspended in **Mansfield Park,** is turned upon the reader. We are given a heroine who, in some respects, looks like an exemplary conduct-book girl, but this is deceptive. Fanny is not a true conduct-book heroine and, insofar as she resembles this ideal—in her timidity, self-abasement, and excessive sensibility, for example—her author mocks her—and us, if we mistake these qualities for virtue. Jane Austen hated "unmixed" characters in general, and "unmixed" heroines in particular, a point on which she disagreed with the Dr. Johnson of *Rambler* 4. Writing to her niece Fanny Knight (the one with a weakness for Evangelical gentlemen), she discusses the opinions of an aptly named Mr. Wildman, who had not found her novels to his taste:

> Do not oblige him to read any more.—Have mercy on him. . . . He and I should not in the least agree of course in our ideas about Heroines: pictures of perfection as you know make me sick and wicked—but there is some very good sense in what he says, and I particularly respect him for wishing to think well of all young Ladies; it shows an amiable and delicate Mind—And he deserves better than to be obliged to read any more of my Works.[2]

If Jane Austen created a conduct-book heroine, it cannot have been without an ironic intention of some kind. A clue to what it was occurs in an unsigned article on the "Female Novelists" published in *New Monthly Review* in 1852: "Then again, in **Mansfield Park,** what a bewitching 'little body' is Fanny Price . . ."[3] This Victorian writer sees in Fanny, not a paragon of virtue, but a little enchantress, and it is important to notice that, when Crawford falls in love, he too sees her in this way. Fanny's apparent saintliness is closely connected with her sexual desirableness, as Crawford shows in Chapter XII of the second volume, where he tells his sister that he is in love. His appreciation of "Fanny's graces of manner and goodness of heart," as well as his recognition of her "being well-principled and religious," is mingled with his dwelling on her "charms" (p. 294), "her beauty of face and figure," her beautifully heightened color, as she attends to the service of that stupid woman, her Aunt Bertram, and the neat arrangement of her hair, with "one little curl falling forward . . . which she now and then shook back" (pp. 296-97).

Crawford is incapable of understanding that the "religious principles" he admires in Fanny are formed, as Providence intended rational beings to form moral principles, out of rational reflection upon experience. His view of her is deeply sentimental, for he sees her as something like the ideal woman of Rousseau's *Émile,* innocent, virtuous, tractable, and crying out for protective love, which her prettiness and gentleness excite in him. By Volume Three, he discovers that she has "some touches of the angel" in her (p. 344). Henry Austen must have seen at that point, if he had not seen it before, that his sister would not allow her heroine to marry Crawford, for Austen's objection to the comparison of young women to angels is so consistently maintained that this blunder of Crawford's could not pass unnoticed. Elizabeth Bennet once says, jokingly and critically, that her sister Jane has angelic characteristics (**Pride and Prejudice,** p. 134); otherwise, from the *Juvenilia* to the mature works, only fools or villains make this analogy. It is pointedly avoided by all the Austen heroes, but used to define the defects of the more complex anti-heroes, notably Willoughby and Crawford, and to define Emma's disillusion with Frank Churchill (**Emma,** p. 479).

The point is of great importance to a right understanding of Fanny Price and **Mansfield Park,** because it directs us to the criticism of the conduct-book ethos which is the essential irony of Miss Price's characterization. It may seem strange to us that physical weakness, or lassitude, should be thought to enhance a girl's sexual attractiveness, nor do we think religiosity alluring, but it was not always so. The conduct-book ideal of young womanhood was deeply sentimental, and the genre included works in which salaciousness was mixed with moral advice.

Two examples, quoted and proscribed by Mary Wollstonecraft in *A Vindication of the Rights of Woman,* are of especial interest. Wollstonecraft berates James Hervey, whose *Meditations and Contemplations,* written between 1745 and 1746, were "still read" in 1792. Hervey told his readers (mostly female) that:

> Never, perhaps, does a fine woman strike more deeply, than when, composed into pious recollection, and possessed with the noblest considerations, she assumes, without knowing it, superior dignity and new graces; so that the beauties of holiness seem to radiate about her, and the bystanders are almost induced to fancy her already worshipping among the kindred angels.

Mary Wollstonecraft could not stand that sort of thing. "Should," she asks, "a grave preacher interlard his discourses with such folleries? . . . Why are girls to be told that they resemble angels: but to sink them below women." Like Jane Austen, she has no patience either with Dr. Fordyce, whose *Sermons to Young Women* (1766) contain a remarkable passage in which the awfulness of abusing young angels is discussed with salacious relish:

> Behold these smiling innocents, whom I have graced with my fairest gifts, and committed to your protection; behold them with love and respect; treat them with tenderness and honour. They are timid and want to be defended. They are frail; oh do not take advantage of their weakness! Let their fears and blushes endear them. Let their confidence in you never be abused. But is it possible, that any of you can be such barbarians, so su-

premely wicked, as to abuse it? Can you find in your hearts to despoil the gentle, trusting creatures of their treasure, or do anything to strip them of their native robe of virtue? Curst be the impious hand that would dare to violate the unblemished form of chastity! Thou wretch! thou ruffian! forbear; nor venture to provoke Heaven's fiercest vengeance.

Mary Wollstonecraft says, not unreasonably:

> I know not any comment that can be made seriously on this curious passage, and I could produce many similar ones; and some, so very sentimental, that I have heard rational men use the word indecent when they mentioned them with disgust.[4]

It will be remembered that it was Fordyce's *Sermons* that Mr. Collins chose, after having turned down a novel, to read aloud to the ladies at Longbourn. Perhaps it was at just such a passage that Lydia Bennet, no angel, but "a stout well-grown girl of fifteen," interrupted his "monotonous solemnity" to tell her mother an interesting bit of gossip about the regiment quartered nearby. At all events, Mr. Collins' approbation of Fordyce is a clear indication that Jane Austen disapproved of him.

There is good reason to think, in the light of her novels and letters, that this was a disapproval founded in sympathy with rational, post-Enlightenment feminism. This is not to suggest that Austen was in agreement with Wollstonecraft on anything more than these fundamental ideas: (a) that women, being possessed of the same "powers of mind" as men, have the same moral status and the same moral accountability; (b) that girls should be educated in a manner appropriate to this view of the female sex; (c) that a "respectable" marriage is an "equal" marriage, in which man and woman are "partners," and must therefore rest on "friendship and esteem," and (d) that literary works in which any other view is endorsed are objectionable. Modern feminists may find these very tame, but around 1800 they were the essential convictions of rational feminism. We need not be put off because Austen is "a moralist" after the Johnsonian fashion; so, in many respects, is Wollstonecraft, especially in the *Vindication,* itself a sort of conduct book. The moral argument upon which Wollstonecraft bases her feminist case derives very largely from Bishop Butler's *Analogy of Religion* (1796) and from Richard Price's *Review of the Central Question in Morals* (1758). Butler was a bishop of the established church, whose views accord to a large extent with Johnson's. Price was a Dissenter and, through his influence upon progressive Dissent, associated not only with Wollstonecraft herself but with many of the radicals of his time. His ambience was thus quite different from Butler's, but the essential character of his view of morals was not, as he himself acknowledges.

So far as late-eighteenth-century feminism went, Butler and Price could both be seen as laying down principles upon which a feminist moralist could found her argument. This is crucial to a right understanding of the relationship between the first well-known English feminist theorist, Mary Wollstonecraft, and the first major woman novelist in English. Thinking of them, as we do, as totally different in their religious and political affiliations, lifestyle, and temperament, we may easily miss what connects them as feminist moralists, whose roots lie in a common tradition of ethical discussion. There is no need to assume that Austen was an undercover Jacobin because she is so close to Wollstonecraft as a feminist moralist.

Austen's implicit demand that men and women be judged, and judge themselves, by the same, somewhat strict, standard in sexual matters, should not be seen as a sign of her commitment to anti-Jacobin fervor. It is no more than the mark of her convinced feminism. Among the radicals, as both Gary Kelly[5] and Marilyn Butler show, feminist feeling went hand in hand with emphasis upon the need for reason and restraint in sexual matters. Butler is impatient with them about it: "In sexual matters, the Jacobins thought and behaved (whatever their opponents claimed) like forerunners of the Evangelicals." Believing in the power of reason to liberate mankind, they renounced the example of "Rousseau, Goethe and Kotzebue . . . when they refused to exploit sexual passion as a powerful natural ally against a moribund society and its repressive conventions." Butler contrasts the English Jacobins unfavorably in this respect with their Continental counterparts, including Madame de Staël.[6]

A feminist point of view is not only compatible with the argumentative style of an eighteenth-century moralist, but may be positively connected with it. Were **Mansfield Park** primarily about political and social questions *other* than feminist ones, the conservative character of the moral argument which it embodies would justify us in supposing it to be fundamentally conservative in outlook, but, if the feminist issues are the central ones, it may be that the orthodox, rather old-fashioned character of the argument indicates feminist radicalism rather than orthodoxy. An example may be useful here. In attacking the education commonly provided for middle-class girls, Mary Wollstonecraft says:

> Though moralists have agreed that the tenor of life seems to prove that *man* is prepared by various circumstances for a future state, they consistently concur in advising *woman* to provide only for the present.[7]

She refers to the belief, best exemplified in Bishop Butler's *Analogy of Religon,* and popularized in many sermons and moralistic works, that the world is so ordered as to teach us moral principle through secular experience. Even without a belief in God, the order of nature, including human nature, of which rational powers are a part, insures that we are rewarded when we act well and punished when we act badly. It was an orthodox belief of established moralists that this was so, but, in applying it to women, Mary Wollstonecraft is able to use it to attack existing practices in education and social custom, which rule out one half of mankind from the benefits of exercise in the moral gymnasium designed to teach moral principles.

In the Austen novels the heroines learn about morals through the application of rational reflection to experience. This is how they are shown to acquire principle. They never learn it from clerical advisers. The process by which they acquire understanding of duty, and of right courses of action, is entirely secular, as Ryle noted.[8] The way in which they are shown as becoming morally accountable may look a little old-fashioned, if we forget that they are young women, not young men. If we remember it, and see it in relation to contemporary feminist discussion, we may see that Jane Austen is sometimes a radical wolf when she pointedly adopts orthodox moralists' sheep's clothing.

It is time to return to Miss Fanny, and to show further that her characterization is to be illuminated by Mary Wollstonecraft. The implication of this must be that either Austen had read Wollstonecraft or that she was familiar with her works through the filtering through of their arguments and examples to other, less controversial writers. I do not mean to argue the case for direct influence here. During the five years she spent in Bath, with its well-stocked bookshops and circulating libraries, by no means confined to fiction,[9] Austen had access to the works of Mary Wollstonecraft. In the absence of direct biographical information, the case must stand upon the probability implied by closeness of point of view and, in some instances, of allusion and vocabulary.

Vindication is not primarily about the political and constitutional rights of women, but about the ideas referred to above as constituting the essence of post-Enlightenment rational feminism. It is largely an attack upon Rousseau, especially the Rousseau of *Émile,* and upon those sentimental moralists and divines who had followed him in denying women the moral status of rational, adult, moral agents. With them are coupled imaginative writers of both sexes, including Madame de Staël, who, by emphasizing the sensibility of women at the expense of their powers of reason, have "Rendered them Objects of Pity, Bordering on Contempt" (p. 173). Wollstonecraft's animus against Rousseau arises from his having made Sophie—his ideal mate for Émile, the ideal man—a different kind of moral creature. Whereas Émile is to enjoy bodily and mental exercise, Sophie is to be confined to bodily weakness and to obedience. This, Rousseau thought, was in accordance with the nature of the two sexes and with their purposes in life. It was for the man to enjoy the advantages of a free, experiential life; it was for the woman to please him, to arouse his sexual passion, to enjoy his protection, and to obey him. All this was anathema to Wollstonecraft and, to Austen, a fit subject of ridicule.

Take first the question of health and strength, which is of particular importance to the characterization of Miss Fanny. Wollstonecraft objects to Rousseau's belief that genuine weakness and the affected exaggeration of weakness are natural to women and a means by which they gain an ambiguous power over men. She quotes with disgust a passage from *Émile* in which it is asserted of women:

> So far from being ashamed of their weakness, they glory in it; their tender muscles make no resistance; they affect to be incapable of lifting the smallest burdens, and would blush to be thought robust and strong.
>
> (p. 174)

Wollstonecraft declares that

> . . . the first care of mothers and fathers who really attend to the education of females should be, if not to strengthen the body, at least not to destroy the constitution by mistaken notions of female excellence; nor should girls ever be allowed to imbibe the pernicious notion that a defect can, by any chemical process of reasoning, become an excellence.
>
> (p. 126)

She then attacks such conduct-book authors as have taken their cue from Rousseau and encouraged girls to cultivate either real or affected weakness and low spirits. Among these she reluctantly places Dr. John Gregory, whose *A Father's Letters to His Daughters* (1774)

> actually recommends dissimulation and advises an innocent girl to give the lie to her feelings, and not dance with spirit, when gaiety of heart would make her feel eloquent without making her gestures immodest. In the name of truth and common sense, why should not one woman acknowledge that she has a better constitution than another?
>
> (pp. 111-12)

Austen did not admire physical weakness or ill-health or ignorance in young women, but a lot of people, including those who ought to have known better, did. The relevance of this to Miss Price is obvious. Austen created in her a heroine whom the unwary might take for something like the Rousseauist ideal of the perfect woman, but she expects her more discerning readers to see through it, and gives them a good many indications that this is not a proper reading. The most important of these is, of course, the category mistake of the anti-hero, but there is a good deal else. The true hero is never shown as encouraging Fanny in her partly self-imposed fragility and timidity, although he is kind to her when he observes her genuine tendency to tire easily. He gets her a horse, encourages her to ride regularly, and tells her to speak up for herself, even to her uncle. But the major comic emphasis, through which Austen shows that she does not admire hypochondria in women, even beautiful ones, comes through the splendid portrait of pampered indolence in Lady Bertram.

Fanny is quite different from her aunt in that she has, both as a child and as a very vulnerable adolescent, experienced both neglect and hardship. Given Mrs. Price's predilection for sons and her slatternly housekeeping, there is little reason to think that the health (whether of body or mind) of her eldest daughter had ever received much attention. At Mansfield, the somnolence of Aunt Bertram, the sadism of Aunt Norris, and the false regard for wealth and status of Sir Thomas Bertram, his elder son, and his daughters, have all combined to ensure that Fanny's mental and physical health are put in jeopardy. She has not a strong constitution, but she was not as a child devoid of normal impulses to active life. She did not enjoy such freedom as Catherine Morland, rolling down green slopes with her brothers, and it is never positively established that she preferred cricket to dolls or nursing dormice, as Catherine did, but Fanny, in her early years at Portsmouth, was important as *play-fellow,* as well as "instructress and nurse" to her brothers and sisters. The single instance of remembered childhood activity which Austen mentions concerns dancing. William recalls how he and Fanny used to dance together as children. It is what prompts him to ask Sir Thomas if his sister is a good dancer, Sir Thomas being forced to reply that he does not know. William says, "I should like to be your partner once more. We used to jump about together many a time, did not we? when the hand organ was in the street?" (p. 250). Fanny's excessive fragility of body and lack of self-confidence are the result of inconsiderate, and sometimes humiliating, treatment by her illiberal, selfish aunts, but it has not quite stamped out of her an impulse to life which is to be seen in her continued love of dancing. At her first ball, "she was quite grieved to be losing even a quarter of an hour . . . sitting most unwillingly among the chaperons . . . while all the other young people were dancing" (pp. 116–17). Later, when a ball is given in her honor, the narrator tells us, "She had hardly ever been in a state so nearly approaching high spirits in her life. Her cousins' former gaiety on the day of a ball was no longer surprising to her; she felt it to be indeed very charming" (p. 273). And she actually practices her steps in the drawing room, when she is sure Aunt Norris won't see. She gets tired later at this ball, partly because she is jealous of Miss Crawford, but it is three o'clock in the morning, and she is up earlier than anyone else, apart from William, next day, in order to see him off.

Fanny Price's feebleness is not a mark of Clarissa Harlowe-like saintliness, as Lionel Trilling thought, nor is it to be dismissed, as Marilyn Butler dismisses it, as "quite incidental." It is essential to the play of anti-Rousseauist, feminist irony upon Miss Price and those who seek to interpret her. Once her cousins leave Mansfield, prolonged ill-treatment is seen to have curious effects. The affectation of fragility, which it took an expensive education to achieve, Fanny lacks, but a genuine fragility now makes her seem something like the Rousseauist ideal, and by this Crawford is, as he puts it, "fairly caught." But, if Fanny's physical frailty amounts to more than it seems, the strength of her mind, despite the physical and emotional deprivation she has endured, is truly formidable. Housed within the "bewitching little body," lurking behind the "soft light eyes," is a clear, critical, rationally judging mind, quite unlike the tractable, childlike mind of the true conduct-book heroine. Wollstonecraft says, "The conduct of an accountable being must be regulated by the operation of its own reason; or on what foundation rests the throne of God?" (*Vindication,* p. 121). Just before Fanny offends her uncle by insisting upon her right to regulate her conduct, by the operation of her own judgment, in a matter of great mo-

ment, he is made to say, though without understanding what it implies, "You have an understanding, which will prevent you from receiving things only in part, and judging partially by the event.—You will take in the whole of the past, you will consider times, persons, and probabilities" (p. 313). He is talking about Aunt Norris's past behavior, but he describes exactly what Fanny does in forming her opinion of Crawford.

The moral and comic climax of **Mansfield Park** occurs at the start of Volume Three, in the East room, when Fanny confronts her august uncle and defies him. Sir Thomas, once he is able to make out that she intends to refuse Crawford, thunders away at her about ingratitude, selfishness, perversity, and sheer obtuseness as to her own interest. He is forced to wonder if she does not show "that independence of spirit, which prevails so much in modern days, even in young women, and which in young women is offensive and disgusting beyond all common offence" (p. 318). Austen expects us to laugh at him, but she does not spare her heroine either. Returning from her walk in the shrubbery, Fanny finds that a fire has already been lighted, on Sir Thomas's orders, in the bleak East room. She does not say, as a creature wholly regulated by reason might have done, "Well, wrongly though he has judged and acted, he has kind and benevolent aspects." She says— and it is truer to life, as well as to the comic spirit—"in soliloquy," "'I must be a brute indeed, if I can be really ungrateful . . . Heaven defend me from being ungrateful!'" (pp. 322–23).

Jane Austen laughs at Fanny when she herself acquiesces, as she often does, in the submissive role in which an unjust domestic "order" has cast her. She exposes, with a more bitter ridicule, the foolishness which has all but stamped out of Fanny her ability to laugh, dance, play, or to act—in any sense. But she does not despair. Reason, and the will of a less insane God than that invoked by such clerics as Fordyce and Mr. Collins or Dr. Grant, will prevail, where men have such sense as Edmund and women such sense as Fanny. "Good sense, like hers, will always act when really called upon" (p. 399), and so it does. Fanny becomes "the daughter that Sir Thomas Bertram wanted," that is, *lacked,* and, together with Edmund, is shown as capable of establishing at the parsonage a more liberal and more securely based domestic order than that of the Great House.

Fanny does not, as some critics, more concerned with mythic elements of plot than sound moral argument, have thought, "inherit" Mansfield Park. She marries the younger son, not the heir (who is pointedly restored to health), and she goes to live at the parsonage, where an enlightened, rational, secular Christianity is likely to be the order of the day. It is, perhaps, unlikely that the next Lady Bertram will waste so many years in a state of semiconsciousness, devoid of mental or physical life, upon a sofa, with a lapdog and a tangled, useless, meaningless bit of needlework, as the former Miss Maria Ward has done. But it is at the parsonage, not the Great House, that there is to occur that "unspeakable gain in private happiness to the liberated half of the species; the difference to them between a life of subjection to the will of others, and a life of rational freedom," of which J. S. Mill was later to write.[10]

In *Mansfield Park,* Austen shows some sympathy with points made in the *Vindication* and anticipates Mill *On the Subjection of Women.* It looks to me as though she may also have profited from a critical reading of Wollstonecraft's two novels. There is no direct evidence that she read them, but Godwin's publication of his *Memoirs of the Author of a Vindication of the Rights of Woman* in 1798 caused a great deal of interest in its subject. The "Advertisement" to *Mary* (1788) tells us that its heroine is "neither a Clarissa, a Lady G. [randison] nor a Sophie." In it, "the mind of a woman who has thinking powers" is to be displayed. Mary, its heroine, had "read Butler's *Analogy,* and some other authors: and these researches made her a Christian from conviction" (p. 23). Austen would not have countenanced the pretentious tone of this, but, in her own ironic way, she shows us that much the same could be said of Fanny. By the time *Maria* was written—it was still unfinished in 1797, when Wollstonecraft died—the author had become a Deist, rather than a Christian, but this does not prevent her from applying Butler's argument about how we learn moral principles in her new work. She says that in most novels "the hero is allowed to be mortal, and to become wise and virtuous as well as happy, by a train of events and circumstances. The heroines, on the contrary, are to be born immaculate . . ." (p. 73).

Both in Wollstonecraft and Austen, the language of law and property as well as the language of capture and captivation are shown as improperly applied to marriage and to decent sexual relationships. *Mansfield Park* opens with the *captivation* by Miss *Ward* of *Hunting*don, of a baronet to whom her uncle, "*the lawyer, himself,* . . . allowed her to be at least three thousand pounds short of any *equitable claim*" (my italics). Wollstonecraft's Maria talks about "the master key of property" (p. 157). Austen, in the Sotherton episode, makes use of the lock and key image in connection with Rushworth and his property. Wollstonecraft's Maria says, "Marriage had bastilled me for life" (p. 155). Maria Bertram, flirting with Crawford while her intended husband has gone off to look for the key to the iron gate, which gives her "a feeling of restraint and hardship," alludes to the starling which Yorick found caged in the Bastille, and which sang incessantly, "I can't get out, I can't get out" (p. 99). She also refers to Sotherton as a prison, "quite a dismal old prison" (p. 53). Wollstonecraft's anti-hero declares "that every woman has her price" (p. 161). Austen borrows, as the name for her heroine, that of Crabbe's in one of *The Parish Register* tales. Crabbe's Fanny Price is a refuser of the captive-captivate game; Austen's is shown as unfit, by her nature, to become a commodity in the marriage market, though capable of paying the price of enduring wrongful abuse and misunderstanding, which secures her "right to choose, like the rest of us."

Jane Austen does not, like Mary Wollstonecraft, present us with an innocent heroine imprisoned in a marriage for which she is not regarded as bearing a responsibility. Austen's Maria chooses her own fate, though neither Sir Thomas nor the moral standards of the society of which he is a pillar are held blameless. Fanny, who avoids an imprisoning marriage, since she enters a partnership based on affection and esteem, does so not because she is "innocent," but because she is what Milton called "a true wayfaring Christian." Hers is not "a fugitive and cloistered virtue, unexercised and unbreathed," but one that has been put to "trial . . . by what is contrary."[11]

Once the irony at work in the characterization of Miss Price is recognized, the way is open to consideration of what is shown as truly valuable in the right ordering of domestic society and in the world beyond it. Jane Austen did not believe that individuals had to create their own morality; she believed that moral law was objectively enshrined in the nature of the world itself. To that extent, she supposes that human beings are required to be obedient to moral laws or principles, but she is perfectly clear that the individual human being has the right, and duty, of determining, by the operation of his or her own reason, what these principles are and how they are to be applied in the personal regulation of conduct. By showing that Sir Thomas's niece and his younger son are better to be relied upon in judging correctly, an implicit criticism of "birthright and habit," which debar women and younger sons from influence, even when their superior abilities are known, is made. It is quite in line with Wollstonecraft's attitude to "the Pernicious Effects which Arise from the Unnatural Distinctions Established in Society" (part of the title of Chapter 9 of *Vindication*). When Mary Crawford says that Edmund ought to have gone into Parliament, he replies, "I believe I must wait till there is an especial assembly for the representation of younger sons who have little to live on" (p. 214). Sir Thomas is a Member of Parliament, as, presumably, his elder son will also be. It is suggested (p. 161) that Mr. Rushworth will also enter the House when Sir Thomas is able to find him a borough. A rotten borough is not specified but would undoubtedly be appropriate. The case for the recognition of the *equality* of women with men is implicitly allied with the case against such unnatural distinctions and inequalities as are inherent in the law of primogeniture and in the unrepresentative character of Parliament.

Mansfield Park is also pointedly concerned with *fraternity.* What ought to be, and sometimes is—as in the relationship between Fanny and her brother William—the paradigm of equal, affectionate relationships between men and women is always held up as an ideal, having implications beyond the literal meaning of "brother" and "sister." Edmund Bertram treats his inferior little cousin as a sister early in Volume One. He does not fall in love with her until the final chapter, in which this is treated cursorily and ironically. This is not because Jane Austen had suddenly and unselfconsciously become interested in incest; it is because the marriage which provides the necessary happy ending of a comic work carries implications about the right relationships between men and women, both in marriage as a social institution and in society at large. As Mill was to say some fifty or more years later:

> The moral regeneration of mankind will only really commence, when the most fundamental of the social relations is placed under the rule of equal justice, and when human beings learn to cultivate their strongest sympathy with an equal in rights and cultivation.

Austen, in *Mansfield Park,* shows that such an ideal is more readily to be found, in contemporary society, between brothers and sisters than husbands and wives, though she seeks a transference to the marriage relationship of the ideal. With William, Fanny experiences a "felicity" which she has never known before, in an "unchecked, equal, fearless intercourse" (p. 234).

It is, however, with liberty, and the moral basis upon which individual liberty must be founded, that *Mansfield Park* is clearest and boldest. Women, in the Midland counties of England, like servants, were not slaves. Even a *wife,* not beloved, had some protection, "in the laws of the land, and the manners of the age." So Catherine Morland had learnt, under the tutelage of Henry Tilney. "Murder was not tolerated . . . and neither poison nor sleeping potions to be procured like rhubarb, from every druggist" (*Northanger Abbey,* p. 200). But what of an indulged wife? And a falsely respected one? In the Midland counties of England, murder might not be necessary where a wife could retain all the advantages of outward respect, rank, precedence, and "respectability," while passing her days in a state of partly self-induced semiconsciousness. Lady Bertram had "been a beauty, and a prosperous beauty, all her life; and beauty and wealth were all that excited her respect" (p. 332). She values herself on her possession of these things and, in the corrupt social order of which she is part, is valued for them. Never shown as going outside, or breathing fresh English air, Lady Bertram represents the slavery to which women who accede to such ideas reduce themselves, with the unwitting connivance of those, like Sir Thomas, who see nothing disgraceful in their condition. Not literally a slave and not suffering from the effects of a literal sleeping potion, what is she as a human being? What is she morally, as a rational, accountable one?

It is well known that in America the movement for women's rights was accelerated by the part women played in the movement for the emancipation of the slaves. As they heard, and put, moral arguments against slavery, they made an analogy between the moral status of a slave and of a woman, especially a married woman. This analogy is made in the *Vindication* and implied in *Mansfield Park.* Wollstonecraft says that a "truly benevolent legislator always endeavours to make it the interest of each individual to be virtuous; and thus private virtue becoming the cement of public happiness, an orderly whole is consolidated by the tendency of all the parts towards a common centre" (p. 257). Women, however, are not taught to be virtuous in

their domestic life and so are not to be trusted in either private or public life. They learn to be subject to propriety, "blind propriety," rather than to regulate their actions in accordance with moral law as "an heir of immortality" ought. She asks, "Is one half of the human species, like the poor African slaves, to be subjected to prejudices that brutalise them, when principles would be a surer guard of virtue?" (p. 257).

In England, agitation against the slave trade had gone on all through the last quarter of the eighteenth century. The arguments against it were rehearsed widely in the early nineteenth century, leading up to the passing of the Act of Abolition, which became effective in 1808. Jane Austen must have been familiar with them and, in a letter of 1813, speaks of having been in love with Thomas Clarkson's writings (*Letters,* p. 292). In 1808, Clarkson published *The Abolition of the African Slave Trade*:

> We have lived in consequence of it to see the day when it has been recorded as a principle of our legislation that commerce itself shall have its moral boundaries. We have lived to see the day when we are likely to be delivered from the contagion of the most barbarous opinions. Those who supported this wicked traffic virtually denied that man was a moral being. They substituted the law of force for the law of reason. But the great Act, now under our consideration, has banished the impious doctrine and restored the rational creature to his moral rights.

It is easy to see here that a woman who rejoiced that the slave trade had been ended might ask whether it had yet been recorded "as a principle of our legislation that commerce itself shall have its moral boundaries"—so far as women were concerned. Was it universally accepted that woman was "a moral being"? Had the rational creature been restored to *her* moral rights?

Clarkson goes over the history of the anti-slavery movement and refers to a particularly famous legal judgment, which established that slavery was illegal in England. This was the Mansfield Judgment, given by the Lord Chief Justice of England in 1772, in a case concerning a black slave, James Somerset, the question being whether, having been brought to England, he could still be held to be "owned" by his master. Arguing that he could not, counsel for the defence, referring to an earlier judgment given in the reign of Queen Elizabeth, said:

> . . . it was resolved that England was too pure an air for slaves to breathe in . . . and I hope my lord the air does not blow worse since—I hope they will never breathe here; for this is my assertion, the moment they put their feet on English ground, that moment they are free.

Lord Mansfield found in favor of Somerset and, by implication, of this view of English air.

In *Mansfield Park* the English patriarch is also the owner of Antiguan plantations and of the slaves who work them.

When he returns to England, his niece puts a question to him about the slave trade (p. 198). We are not told what the question was, nor what answer was given, but, through her title, the making of Sir Thomas a slaveowner abroad, and the unstated question of Miss Fanny, *her* moral status in England is implicitly contrasted, yet also compared, with that of the Antiguan slaves. Since it is often assumed that Jane Austen could not have thought much about anything which did not impinge upon her domestic life and familial relations, or else been said by Dr. Johnson, it may be worth noting that at the house of her brother Edward she met Lord Mansfield's niece on a number of occasions, and that Boswell reported Johnson's view on another slavery case, *Knight* v. *Wedderburn,* as follows: "No man is by nature the property of another. The defendant is therefore by nature free!"[12]

Slaves have masters but cannot truly be said to have a country, since they are neither protected by its laws nor accorded those rights which belong to freeborn citizens. That this was true in England of women is a point made by Wollstonecraft in *Maria,* where the heroine has no redress in "the laws of her country—if women have a country" (p. 159). Austen, not doubting that even such an unpromising feminist as Fanny Price "speaks the tongue that Shakespeare spoke" and, apart, no doubt, from a small difference about Adam and Eve, holds "the faith and morals . . . which Milton held," assumes that enlightened readers will know that she has the same "titles manifold" to British freedom as anyone else. She assures us that the soil at Mansfield is good, especially at the parsonage, and she makes a great point of the wholesomeness of English air, which is frequently associated with health and liberty. At Sotherton, with its prisonlike atmosphere, all the young people share "one impulse, one wish for air and liberty." Fanny's need for fresh English air is stressed again and again, often in ironic contexts. After berating her for not accepting Crawford, Sir Thomas tells her to get some exercise outside, where "the air will do her good," and Henry Crawford says of her, that she "requires constant air and exercise . . . ought never to be long banished from the free air and liberty of the country" (pp. 410-11). Of course, he means the countryside, but does not Austen expect the intelligent, enlightened reader to see a bit further?

Finally, we come to *Lovers' Vows.* It has been thought that, because this play has been attacked in anti-Jacobin circles, Austen's choice of it must be taken as a sign of her reactionary political viewpoint. However, it is quite directly associated with the main feminist themes of this novel. For a start, as its title shows, it is about the sentimental treatment of lovers' promises and is used to point the contrast between the lack of commitment involved in such promises as Baron Wildenhaim made to Agatha before he seduced her, or as Crawford half-makes to Maria, and the binding nature of the marriage contract. *Lovers' Vows* is a work in that tradition of Rousseauist literature which Mary Wollstonecraft objected to as rendering women objects of pity bordering on contempt. Agatha, having endured twenty years of poverty and humiliation

because Wildenhaim broke his promise to her, makes a grateful, tearful acceptance of his eventual offer (following their son's intervention) to marry her. The curtain comes down on the following tableau:

> Anhalt leads on Agatha—The Baron runs and clasps her in his arms—supported by him, she sinks on a chair which Amelia places in the middle of the stage—The Baron kneels by her side, holding her hand.
>
> BARON. Agatha, Agatha, do you know this voice?
>
> AGATHA. Wildenhaim.
>
> BARON. Can you forgive me?
>
> AGATHA. I forgive you *(embracing him).*
>
> FREDERICK *(as he enters).* I hear the voice of my mother!—Ha! mother! father!
>
> (Frederick throws himself on his knees by the other side of his mother—She clasps him in her arms.—Amelia is placed on the side of her father attentively viewing Agatha—Anhalt stands on the side of Frederick with his hands gratefully raised to Heaven.) The curtain slowly drops.

Anyone who doubts whether Jane Austen laughed at this had better reread *Love and Friendship,* but we have good reason to suppose that she thought the "happy ending" morally objectionable, not because the baron was letting his class down by marrying a village girl, nor the honor of his sex by marrying the girl who had lost her virtue through his agency, but because Agatha should have had more respect for herself, and too much contempt for him to have him at any price.

Mansfield Park remains a puzzling novel, partly, I think, because Jane Austen enjoyed puzzles and thought it both amusing and instructive to solve them. She asks a great deal of her readers—sound moral attitudes, derived from rational reflection upon experience; quick-wittedness and ingenuity in making connections; and a belief in the wholesomeness of laughter. It would be possible to make of *Mansfield Park* something like a piece of feminist propaganda, in which regulated hatred predominates, but it would be false. It is a great comic novel, regulated by the sane laughter of an implish, rational feminist. The pricelessness of Miss Price is its heart—and head.

Notes

1. Page references to *Mansfield Park* and to other Austen novels are to R. W. Chapman, ed., *The Novels of Jane Austen* (London: Oxford University Press, 1931-34).

2. R. W. Chapman, ed., *The Letters of Jane Austen* (London: Oxford University Press, 1932).

3. Item 31 in B. C. Southam, ed., *Jane Austen: The Critical Heritage* (London: Routledge & Kegan Paul, 1968).

4. Mary Wollstonecraft, *Vindication of the Rights of Woman,* ed. Miriam Kramnick (Harmondsworth: Penguin, 1973), pp. 192-94.

5. Gary Kelly, *The English Jacobin Novel* (London: Oxford University Press, 1976), p. 8.

6. Marilyn Butler, *Jane Austen and the War of Ideas* (Oxford: The Clarendon Press, 1975), p. 45.

7. Wollstonecraft, p. 118.

8. Gilbert Ryle, "Jane Austen and the Moralists," in B. C. Southam, ed., *Critical Essays.*

9. W. J. Kite, "Libraries in Bath 1618-1964," thesis for a Fellowship of the Library Association, 1966, pt. 2, *passim.*

10. "On the Subjection of Women," in Richard Wollheim, ed., *John Stuart Mill: Three Essays* (Oxford: The Clarendon Press, 1975).

11. *Areopagitica* in *Milton's Prose*, ed. H. W. Wallace (London: Oxford University Press, 1925), p. 290.

12. James Boswell, *The Life of Samuel Johnson,* ed. Croker, p. 562.

Jane McDonnell (essay date 1984)

SOURCE: "'A Little Spirit of Independence': Sexual Politics and the Bildungsroman in *Mansfield Park*," in *Novel: A Forum on Fiction,* Vol. 17, No. 3, Spring, 1984, pp. 197-214.

[*In the following essay, McDonnell evaluates* Mansfield Park *as a Bildungsroman that deals authentically with feminine childhood experience.*]

Mansfield Park has never lacked detractors. Kingsley Amis is typical, if a little intemperate, in calling it an "immoral book" and the character of Fanny Price a "monster of complacency and pride, who under a cloak of cringing self-abasement, dominates and gives meaning to the novel."[1] Others have criticized the book for being too severely moral, for its serious and even pietistic tone which militates against the familiar Austen virtues of liveliness and wit.[2] And even those critics who praise the novel tend to see it as a thesis book, a book where character and action are subordinated to ideology, whether that be the "war of ideas" between Jacobinism and anti-Jacobinism, or the "improvement of the estate" versus the preservation of the estate with its ideals of stability and continuity.[3] Finally, some readers who profess a sympathetic interest in the character of Fanny Price as having more than schematic interest, sometimes do so largely because of a clinical interest in the pathology of the abused child.[4]

It might be supposed that a feminist critic would be the last to take an interest in Fanny Price and her life history. As an image of weakness not strength, of obedience not independence, of passivity not venturesome activity, Fanny perfectly exemplifies ideal femininity in a patriarchal culture, leading Susan Gubar, for example, to see her as paradigmatically a Snow White, immobile in her deathly virtue.[5] Because *Mansfield Park* is "the story of a girl who

triumphs by doing nothing,"[6] the most disturbing aspect of the book would appear to be Austen's endorsement of Fanny's weakness as a covert form of strength, leading to her unjustified recognition and redemption at the end.

Yet the novel does provide interesting issues for the feminist critic. As Austen's only subjective portrait of a vulnerable child growing to maturity, and also as a critical account of the failures of a patriarchal society to foster individuality in a woman, it commands our interest. The novel deals with crucial questions of female identity precisely because it shows us in Fanny that extreme "femininity" which is marked by sensitivity to the feelings and opinions of others, and a strong need for acceptance, approval, security and love. Like *The Mill on the Floss,* for example, *Mansfield Park* is a dramatic enactment of the social and cultural pathology that produces extreme dependency in women—making Fanny's later moment of rebellion against Sir Thomas all the more remarkable.

Furthermore, as an extended portrait of childhood, education, crisis and identity, *Mansfield Park* really asks to be called an early Bildungsroman. Like those later female Bildungsromane, *Jane Eyre* and *The Mill on the Floss,* Austen's novel involves a relatively long period of time to trace patterns of "growth" from an abused childhood to an assertion of independence in a crisis that involves both family and cultural ideals. And in *Mansfield Park,* as in *Jane Eyre,* an analogy is drawn between the dependency of the child (as orphan or virtual orphan) and the dependent position of women in general. Thus the novel uses the Bildungsroman theme of childhood and youth spent in a hostile setting to focus on questions of sexual politics as well.

We know that *Mansfield Park* was admired by Victorian readers,[7] and indeed it shares a number of qualities (unusual to Austen) with later Victorian fiction and especially with the Bildungsroman. I have already mentioned the use of the child's experience, especially the abandoned or abused child. Other distinctive "Victorian" features of the novel include the focus on suffering, and in particular suffering as a "morally improving" experience for a woman; the religious tone, language and preoccupations of the book, so often noted by critics; the strict distinctions between masculine behavior, authority and power (with Sir Thomas as the failed ideal) and femininity as submissiveness and obedience to male authority; and of course Fanny as a "Romantic" heroine of sensibility much affected by the beauty of landscape.[8]

These "Victorian" qualities of the book are in fact the very qualities most often labelled unsatisfactory and disturbing in the novel. But how does the emerging Bildungsroman pattern fit with the eighteenth-century inheritance of the novel? Specifically, how does the novel deal with questions of female identity—accommodating both the new "experiential" conception of self (Fanny as suffering heroine), with the older "ethical" conception of self (Fanny as moral exemplar) deriving from the Education novel and other sources? In answering these questions perhaps we can also suggest answers to that central question: how can a submissive and passive heroine be the protagonist of a Bildungsroman?

In this essay, I will examine the distinctive features of *Mansfield Park* which associate it with later female Bildungsromane: the emphasis on childhood, the treatment of the mental history of the protagonist, the contrast between provincial life (Portsmouth) and sophisticated society (Mansfield Park and London), the conflict of the heroine with her elders, the "two suitor" convention, and finally, and most importantly, the questions of female "identity" raised by the book. I will also argue that *Mansfield Park* incorporates and ultimately rejects the typical older plot for a woman, what we might call the "erotic text" whereby a woman is identified with her sexuality—and in doing so makes possible the Bildungsroman emphasis on subjectivity and mental history. I will argue that much of the interest (and difficulty) in the book arises from this conflict between conventional fictional femininity as seen in the eighteenth-century "erotic text" and the newer, more subjective self appropriate to the "ambitious text," the Bildungsroman.

Nancy K. Miller makes a useful distinction between what she calls the "erotic" and the "ambitious" texts.[9] Taking Freud's distinction between erotic and ambitious wishes found in daydreams (from his 1908 essay "The Relation of the Poet to Daydreaming"), Miller applies it to women's fiction, arguing that many plots of women's fiction have been labelled as "implausible" because they "reject the narrative logic of the dominant discourse," which is the ambitious text, taking instead "female erotics" to structure their plots. In other words she finds that the "ambitious text" is the repressed content of this fiction, not the dominant one as it is in men's fiction.

Certainly we can say that most plots about male experience are "ambitious texts" and have to do with the impulse to power. They are stories of conflict and struggle leading to achievement and independence (as in the epic, quest romance, or Bildungsroman), or stories of conflict and struggle leading to a tragic death (as in tragedy). The Bildungsroman especially, could be characterized as an ambitious text. As a semiautobiographical, apprenticeship-to-life story, it deals significantly with the mental history, self-determination, and identity of the protagonist. In other words, it is pre-eminently the fictional form which celebrates subjectivity, autonomy and self-definition. As the story of a young person, making a choice of life, it values initiative and industry, separation and individuation, achieved through conflict and struggle with family and society.[10]

Thus the Bildungsroman, in most critical definitions and in many dominant examples, seems to reflect male experience and male gender identity (as well as nineteenth- and twentieth-century conceptions of "self"), and as such it raises many troubling questions for the woman writer and

for the feminist critic. If the form itself follows our cultural notions of so-called "normative development," notions based not on some abstract ideal of human development, but on male development seen as typical, then how useful can it be for the woman writer writing the life history of a woman character? We know, of course, that, especially in 1814, women writers did *not* stress their resemblance to men and pattern the woman's life history after a narrative that involves worldly ambitions, career choices, a crisis of religion, conflict with the father, etc. (issues which come up again and again in male Bildungsromane especially in the nineteenth century). And yet in a sense that is what two male writers, Defoe in *Moll Flanders* and Cleland in *Fanny Hill,* did for their women characters. All of this seems to raise serious doubts about the appropriate use of the term to characterize women's fiction and especially a novel like *Mansfield Park.*

Furthermore we know that the woman writer of the early nineteenth century inherited a well-developed tradition of the "feminocentric" novel, novels by male writers in which women are identified with their sexuality. These are clearly "erotic texts" in which women enact a sexual destiny, and they testify, as Nancy Miller writes in *The Heroine's Text,* not to the "power of the female imagination," but to the "power of the female in the male imagination."[11] This heroine's text in eighteenth-century English and French fiction by male authors is usually either the "drama of the preservation of virtue" (what Miller calls the Euphoric text) or the "tragedy of the single misstep" leading to compromise and ruin (what she calls the Dysphoric text).

Thus we can assume a strong, even coercive tradition, inherited by Austen, of female sexual destiny portrayed in fiction, of "erotic education thematized as social initiation."[12] Fiction about women before Austen was largely made up of stories where the very facts of the woman's biological and spiritual existence put her in jeopardy, where the heroine no matter what else she may have been, was forced to live in the world primarily as a sexual being, and where there was little room for the Bildungsroman issues of "self-definition" or the exploration of a mental history.

Clearly, the erotic text, the text where the woman is identical with her sexual nature, is the text inherited by Jane Austen. The real question for Austen, of course, is how to show female subjectivity, even feminine mastery, in a world dominated by the mercantile considerations of marriage—where the tragedy of the single misstep, or the drama of the preservation of virtue or the marriage market story define the possible lives for women. All of Austen's novels deal with this subject, and *Mansfield Park* confronts it in one of its rawest—or purest—forms.

Furthermore, Mansfield Park, the place itself, establishes a clear sense of the sexual politics of the book. This country estate is a place where right rule is vested in the father, Sir Thomas; where the eldest son, Tom, is the favored child, being groomed to inherit the estate; where the wife of Sir

Thomas, Lady Bertram, is reduced to the indolence and extreme helplessness of a well-married woman in a patriarchal society, someone whose function in life has long ago been completed by marriage and the production of a male offspring; where Maria and Julia Bertram are the well-reared daughters according to patriarchal values—that is, they are trained in the arts of the marriage market, but are empty-headed and restive under these conditions of constraint.[13]

Of course, Fanny Price herself is in many ways perfect femininity in a patriarchal society. Introduced as a child, a poor cousin, into this wealthy Bertram family, she perfectly exemplifies the submissive ideal for a woman: gentle, modest, sweet-tempered and obedient, she makes herself useful as a virtual servant to the family. Kind and thoughtful to her selfish Aunt Bertram, submissive to her manipulative Aunt Norris, obedient to her rather distant and fearful uncle Sir Thomas, she perfectly fulfills the standard of behavior expected of women. In Sir Thomas's words, "she appears to feel as she ought."

In discussing *Mansfield Park* as a Bildungsroman, it seems crucial to note at the beginning that the novel is unique to Austen's fiction and new to women's fiction in general in that it deals extensively and realistically with childhood experience.[14] When Fanny is introduced as a poor cousin to be raised by the wealthy Bertram family, she is just ten years old—"Exceedingly timid and shy, and shrinking from notice," "ashamed of herself," but of an "obliging, yielding temper." Austen's portrayal of her sudden uprooting is deeply sympathetic, juxtaposed as it is with the Bertram family's consciousness of their superiority in doing the poor child a favor.

> . . . the little girl who was spoken of in the drawing-room when she left it at night, as seeming so desirably sensible of her peculiar good fortune, ended every day's sorrows by sobbing herself to sleep.
>
> . . . her consciousness of misery was therefore increased by the idea of its being a wicked thing for her not to be happy.
>
> . . . her feelings were very acute, and too little understood to be properly attended to.[15]

The great interest of this portrayal lies in the contrast between social expectation (Fanny is being given all the advantages of education and training in a wealthy family, thereby greatly increasing her prospects in life) with the simple feelings of a child—who, after all, has been taken from her home and is being turned into an object of charity. Furthermore, we also see that Fanny is beginning to "internalize" the social expectations and to see her grief and loneliness as unacceptable; she is beginning to censure her natural feelings as a form of ingratitude. Thus immediately in the novel, there is established this contrast between social role and feeling, her place in a "text" devised by others and her own internal history.

In noting this emphasis on feeling and childhood experience I do not wish to suggest that Austen shows us "de-velopment" in any modern sense of the term. On the contrary, the first two-thirds of the novel is a series of set pieces—the visit to Sotherton, the play rehearsals, the return of Sir Thomas, and the visit of William—designed to show, not Fanny's development, but rather her "deeper feelings" and "higher species of self command," qualities which enable her to judge the mistakes of other characters.

The novel does not show us Fanny's development in the sense of her changing over a period of time; nevertheless, it does show us the connections between her personality and her circumstances. The passages just quoted demonstrate a very new subject and one that is distinctively appropriate to the Bildungsroman—that is, the psychological portrait of an abused child. The very qualities which most readers find so distressing in Fanny as the novel proceeds—her shrinking temperament, her passive, subservient nature, her very "goodness"—are those qualities which are established at the beginning of the novel as the psychological result of profound neglect.

Fanny's goodness has been extensively and convincingly studied by both Avron Fleishman and Bernard Paris as the defensive strategy of a terrified child and as an example of the Adlerian "feminine" personality type whose submission is really a form of hostility and self-protection.[16]

> Here is the goodness of a terrified child who dreads total rejection if she does not conform in every way to the will of those in power. It is rigid, desperate, compulsive. Fanny is not actively loving or benevolent; she is obedient, submissive, driven by her fears and her shoulds. Her goodness provides, moreover, the only outlet for her repressed aggressive impulses.[17]

Paris is certainly convincing in ascribing Fanny's goodness to her utter vulnerability, in seeing it as the defensive strategy of someone who can gain acceptance only "by being useful, by being good, and by attaching herself to a stronger and more favoured member of the family."[18] As a poor relation with no rights to Mansfield Park, Fanny must earn a place for herself by all the arts of "gratitude."[19]

The compensations for this emotionally impoverished life are what you would expect to find in a Bildungsroman. Fanny is given books and friendship by her older cousin, Edmund, who becomes a kind of life-long tutor to her:

> . . . his attentions were . . . of the highest importance in assisting the improvement of her mind, and extending its pleasures. He knew her to be clever, to have a quick apprehension as well as good sense, and a fondness for reading, which, properly directed, must be an education in itself.
>
> (22)

Thus Fanny's mental history is one of the important themes of the book and it continues for some time: she reads biography, poetry, Crabbe's Tales and Lord Macartney on China. She takes out a subscription to a lending library and she is moved by nature as none of the other characters seems to be. She even seems particularly well versed in Hannah More, who had written *Coelebs in Search of a Wife,* and also *Strictures on the Modern System of Female Education,* which was a major influence on the contemporary education of women:

> . . . she displays, only too obviously, the "thinking" mind that Hannah More and others were praising as the sign of a cultivated intellect. Some of her remarks, indeed, are painfully, and . . . deliberately, similar to passages from the *Strictures* and similar works. Her speech on memory during her conversation with Mary Crawford in the garden of the Mansfield parsonage is all too clearly an example of the sort of philosophizing on the "secret springs" of the mind that Miss More approves in the remarks on the purposes of the study of history. . . .[20]

It is often pointed out that Fanny's education is an education in the "self-knowledge, generosity, and humility" so lacking in her cousins Maria and Julia—who are merely trained in the drawing-room accomplishments of music, drawing, and superficial facts about "the Roman emperors as low as Severus; besides a great deal of the Heathen Mythology, and all the Metals, Semi-Metals, Planets, and distinguished philosophers" (18-19). And much work has been done pointing out the similarities between this novel and earlier or contemporary novels about female education, which also contrasted this superficial marriage-market training so prevalent at the time with the sounder principles of a Christian discipline—Mrs. West's *The Advantages of Education,* Elizabeth Inchbald's *A Simple Story,* or Fanny Burney's *The Wanderer.*[21]

But how is Fanny's story *different* from all those education novels or conduct books showing the inferiority of wit and cleverness to judgment, or of worldly accomplishments to Christian humility? *Mansfield Park* certainly inherits qualities from all those earlier formula stories concerning the "orphan," the "young woman from the provinces" or the "young woman's entrance into the world." (For example, Mary Crawford, new to the neighborhood, is very eager to know if Fanny is "out" or not out, to know whether or not she has been introduced to the world—in order to place her accurately in the right "text" and to decide accordingly how she must be treated.) I think the answer lies in the fact that *Mansfield Park* places emphasis on the educative process itself. The usual structure of the earlier education novel simply contrasted the character of judgment with the character of wit and cleverness. *Mansfield Park* does this certainly, but it goes one step farther and links judgment with feeling. Fanny's story thus is based more on "feeling" than on "knowing"—and in this is different from the typical Austen novel where the suspense is epistemological, and leads to the heroine's enlightenment or change of mind.

Avron Fleishman, who was the first critic (and to my knowledge the only one) to discuss the novel as Bildungsroman, makes this point:

> . . . to see its central position in English fiction we must recognize it as a Bildungsroman—or, more evoca-

tively, a story of the "young man (or girl) from the provinces." The most important treatments of this theme in the eighteenth century—the novels of Fielding and Smollett—mix moral education with picaresque adventure in such a way that their heroes cannot be said to be educated at all . . . Fanny is the first young person . . . who learns enough of the world to win through to success by moral effort . . . in itself an educative process.[22]

Comparing Fanny with Jane Eyre in her "sustained exercise of moral will" and in her desire to live according to her own "ideal conception of herself," Fleishman also contrasts her story with the more typical Austen plot—that of Elizabeth Bennet who, he says, "merely changes her mind."

I think it is this emphasis on psychological complexity, on the *feelings* of a character who seems to function in the novel as moral exemplar (placed there simply to judge the faults of others as she stays clear of any involvement), which has caused so much dissatisfaction with the novel. In other words, we don't know if we are being asked to respond to Fanny as moral exemplar or as suffering heroine. A good passage of this kind of "psychological complexity" appearing in the midst of a passage ostensibly showing Fanny as judge comes during the play rehearsals. Fanny, of course, has been critical of the home theatricals all along and of the intrigues which they encourage, and when she is pressed to take part in them, she is horrified. In a very telling passage, however, she begins to question her own judgment:

> Was she right in refusing what was so warmly asked, so strongly wished for? what might be so essential to a scheme on which some of those to whom she owed the greatest complaisance, had set their hearts? Was it not ill-nature—selfishness—and a fear of exposing herself? . . . It would be so horrible to her to act, that she was inclined to suspect the truth and purity of her own scruples, and as she looked around her, the claims of her cousins to being obliged, were strengthened by the sight of present upon present that she had received from them . . . and she grew bewildered as to the amount of the debt which all these kind remembrances produced.

> (153)

Fanny judges the theatricals to be wrong, yet she begins to wonder if her judgment itself is flawed—if it might be based on the "fear of exposing herself," rather than on real conviction. She begins to wonder if her convictions themselves are merely the reflex actions of timidity, and to be a convincing "cover" for fear. This is real insight, it seems to me. But immediately afterwards, we see Fanny doubting herself only from the old habits of "gratitude" and self-denial. The false claims coming from gifts received from her cousins are confused with any real debt she might owe them.

To sum up, Fanny makes a judgment (she opposes the theatricals and any involvement in them): she bases this judgment on feeling—and then she goes on to doubt this judgment precisely because it was based on feeling. This spells out something significant about Fanny. Nowhere does Austen show more clearly the confounding of the two conceptions of character in Fanny—what we might call the "experiential" and the "ethical," or following Bernard Paris, the "mimetic" and the "thematic."[23]

Other critics of the novel have noted this discrepancy. Identifying these two incongruous roles in Fanny—the exemplary heroine and the suffering heroine—Marilyn Butler relates them to the conflict between the conservative, anti-Jacobin ideology of the novel (with its emphasis on the old values of class, social order and religion) and the expectations of the novel form itself (with its emphasis on the individual). She writes:

> The fault lies in the incongruity of subjective, heroine-centered writing to the theme in hand; or perhaps it is more proper to say that it lies in the incongruity of the old absolutes to the novel, a form which historically is individualistic and morally relative . . . the failure lies not so much in the ideas, as in the attempt to use the inward life of the heroine as a vehicle for them.[24]

She argues that, "since Fanny is the representative of orthodoxy, the individuality of her consciousness must be to a large extent denied."[25]

This does seem to be what happens in the novel. But the very discrepancy tells us something significant about women's fiction and female identity, and perhaps especially about the woman's Bildungsroman as it was developed later in the nineteenth century. *The Mill on the Floss,* to take one important example, also involves this same conflict between the subjective and the ethical conceptions of character in its protagonist—and points, as *Mansfield Park* does, not just to a major conflict in the novel, but also to a paradox at the heart of female identity. The conflict between ideology and feeling—or between responsibility to others and commitment to self, between an ethical concern for others and the demands of the growing consciousness—is squarely at the heart of much writing about women, and of our conceptions of female identity. Both Maggie Tulliver and Fanny Price are controlled by the "ideology" of the feminine—by what they think they ought to be as women—and as such they are representatives of an orthodoxy which succeeds in killing one of them.

Perhaps this is one reason why the novel treats the suffering of the child Fanny so sympathetically—as itself a moral education. If women must sacrifice self in the service of others, then that sacrifice itself has come to be seen as "enriching" the self. Like most nineteenth-century female Bildungsromane (once again, *Jane Eyre* and *The Mill on the Floss* spring to mind, as well as *Villette*) this novel both glorifies and deplores suffering. Suffering is on the one hand deplorable and without justification; it is on the other hand valuable as a superior education. Simply, Austen claims that Fanny's strength of character comes from being shut out from all the normal gratifications of a child's life—even from parental love and approval, earned respect and unearned love. We are invited to feel sympathy and indignation at the treatment of the child Fanny; but it is because of that treatment that she rightfully grows up to "inherit the estate," to be preferred before all other female characters in the book.

But none of this answers the questions of why Austen should *choose* to write about such a child growing to womanhood—about someone who, after all, presents almost insuperable problems of dramatic sympathy, as goodness and unjustified suffering always does. I think the answer lies in the fact that her story is a virtual parable of the life of a woman in a patriarchal society—and the Bildungsroman pattern, which in a sense is a story of origins tracing everything back to childhood, provides the perfect outlines for such a story. The "deep structure" of this story, furthermore, and of the nineteenth-century female Bildungsroman in general, is the Cinderella story.[26] Thus is *Mansfield Park* we find the prototypical "persecuted heroine" who has lost her mother, is abused by her stepmother (both Aunt Norris and Lady Bertram) and by her stepsisters (Maria and Julia) and who is forced to live as a servant in her "own" household. We also find the "magical" help of the fairy tale, not literally in supernatural rescue, but rather in Edmund's sponsorship of her. Like Cinderella, Fanny is "discovered" at a feast (the ball), and she furnishes "proof of identity" (the cross and chain worn to the ball act as symbolic devices showing Fanny as ultimately chosen by and belonging to Edmund). Edmund, of course, is the prince who eventually rescues her, giving her the recognition of true merit and elevation of status at the end. We can even argue that the stepsisters in the tale mutilate themselves, not literally by cutting off their toes to fit the slipper, but by eloping and violating the code of behavior for a woman and therefore effectively exiling themselves from society.[27]

This almost religious pattern of disguise and discovery,[28] of losing self and finding self, of outsider becoming insider[29] in Fanny's life history, seems to bear some deep affinity with the life of a woman in a patriarchal society. One is tempted to say that the conditions of being a woman in a patriarchal society are so desperate that only the "deep structure" of this universalized wish fable will rescue her. Thus in showing us Fanny first as a child, in emphasizing her suffering and, at the same time, showing her as exemplary, Austen is telling us something important about the female "self."

Perhaps it is only during the "crisis" in Fanny's life—during the courtship of Henry Crawford—that Fanny moves out of her exemplary role in a fully satisfactory way and that her suffering comes to have deeper meaning. In these scenes, she becomes a heroine in her own right and her inner conflict as well as her conflict with her elders begins to have more than schematic value. In the rest of this essay I will deal with the Henry Crawford courtship (and with the two suitor convention involving Henry and Edmund), as well as with the Portsmouth episode,

Fanny Price (Frances O'Connor) and Henry Crawford (Alessandro Nivola) dancing in Patricia Rozema's 1999 adaptation of Mansfield Park.

which of course occurs in the midst of that courtship. Furthermore, I will discuss the way this latter part of the book deals not only with crucial questions of female identity (as the first part does), but does so by playing off the "erotic" text against the "ambitious" text in such a way that we can begin to see the real appropriateness of the Bildungsroman pattern to the sexual politics of the book.

In the first part of the book, Fanny often functions as observer of the erotic texts of others. She watches Maria decide to accept Rushworth, Mary Crawford pursue Edmund, and Maria and Julia compete for Henry Crawford. However, after she appears at the ball and Henry Crawford takes it into his head to make her fall in love with him—and then begins rapidly to fall in love with her—at this point Fanny herself becomes the heroine of an erotic text.

In the ballroom scene Fanny is viewed explicitly as the creation of a man—Sir Thomas who has rescued her from a life of oblivion:

> Sir Thomas himself was watching her progress down
> the dance with much complacency; he was proud of his

niece, and without attributing all her personal beauty, as Mrs. Norris seemed to do, to her transplantation to Mansfield, he was pleased with himself for having supplied every thing else;—education and manners she owed to him.

(276)

Austen is evoking here all the old standards of the erotic text: whatever meaning the woman possesses has been conferred on her by a man. Defined as a male creation, Fanny is the product of Sir Thomas' beneficence and Edmund's tutelage, as soon she will be of Henry's recognition. She is the perfect "subdued heroine" who has repressed all indications of individuality and selfhood and accepted fully (so it seems) the character and personality others have assigned to her.

Susan Gubar discusses some of the many myths that show the female as creation, art object, poem or blank page to be inscribed by a male creator: ". . . if the creator is a man, the creation itself is the female, who, like Pygmalion's ivory girl, has no name or identity or voice of her own."[30] Perhaps this will help us to see more clearly why

Fanny Price has been such a cipher, such a nonentity throughout her story so far. Now, in the ballroom scene, where Henry Crawford decides to fall in love with her, it is clear that what makes Fanny so attractive to this most "eligible" suitor is her extreme passivity. In Henry's own words, she is attractive because of her "goodness of heart," her "gentleness," "modesty," "patience and forbearance."

Here is Henry explaining to his sister why he has fallen in love with Fanny:

> "Had you seen her this morning, Mary," he continued, "attending with such ineffable sweetness and patience, to all the demands of her aunt's stupidity, working with her, and for her, her colour beautifully heightened as she leant over the work, then returning to her seat to finish a note which she was previously engaged in writing for that stupid woman's service, and all this with such unpretending gentleness, so much as if it were a matter of course that she was not to have a moment at her own command. . . ."
>
> (296)

In other words, Henry has fallen in love with Fanny's virtues. It is Fanny's perfect goodness and submissiveness that have won her the love of this rather shallow and selfish man—who, of course, clearly sees the advantages of a compliant woman. In this world, female virtue is one of the arts of attraction; its major purpose is to win the love of a suitable man, who then "gets her heart for his own use," as Henry himself puts it.

Of course, everything points to the suitability of this match. As Sir Thomas says, "Here is a young man wishing to pay his addresses to you with every thing to recommend him; not merely situation in life, fortune, and character, but with more than common agreeableness, with address and conversation pleasing to everybody" (315-16). If Fanny were to marry him, she would be fulfilling the major function of marriage in an acquisitive society—she would be strengthening the ties between the two families of friends and she would be acquiring a status and identity she had not had before.

But of course Fanny refuses Henry Crawford. Furthermore her refusal, predictably, is misunderstood, and it is misunderstood in a way that reveals a lot about women's place in this world. The rejection is at first interpreted as a becoming modesty, a coy statement of the opposite from what she intends. "It shows a discretion highly to be commended," says Sir Thomas. And even her beloved Edmund argues with her: "Let him succeed at last, Fanny, let him succeed at last. You have proved yourself upright and disinterested, prove yourself grateful and tenderhearted" (347). Since Fanny has spent her whole life proving herself upright and disinterested, as well as grateful and tenderhearted, Edmund's remark rings with a particular irony. The novel is beginning to call in question the whole ethos of female dependence and gratitude.

Thus it is highly significant that her simple "no" should be interpreted as part of her beguiling innocence, the state-ment of a young woman who doesn't yet know her own mind, but who can be brought round in time. In other words, here is a serious comedy about male privileged vanity where the woman's refusal, based on her own feelings, is interpreted as itself an art of attraction. We remember Mr. Collins' address to Elizabeth Bennet as a similar case, when he says, "Naturally all elegant females must refuse at first," and Elizabeth replies, "I am not an elegant female. I am a rational creature."

By saying no, what is more, Fanny risks the very worst accusation of a patriarchal society—that of independence of mind. Sir Thomas says to Fanny, "I had thought you peculiarly free from wilfulness of temper, self-conceit, and every tendency to that independence of spirit, which prevails so much in modern days, even in young women, and which in young women is offensive and disgusting beyond all common offences" (318). By persisting in her "unfeminine" refusal, Fanny of course risks losing her sponsorship, the economic and familial support of Sir Thomas, without which she is nothing.

It is especially important here to note that in *Mansfield Park* there is no language, no favorable or neutral language for independence in a woman, no linguistic middleground between modesty and pride, gentleness and wilfulness, self-denial and self-conceit. These same either/or alternatives of self-indulgence versus service can be found in *Jane Eyre, Villette,* and *The Mill on the Floss* also, where once again they express something significant about the female "self" in the Bildungsroman: a woman may remain "good" and be less than adult and fully responsible, or she may become "bad" and risk being unfeminine. In other words the rights of the individual bring her into conflict with morality.

It is at this point in the action that Fanny is sent home to Portsmouth to visit her mother. She is sent by Sir Thomas, who hopes the contrast between Mansfield Park and Portsmouth will itself effect a change of heart in Fanny. But the scene works very differently. In contrasting "provincial" with "sophisticated" society, the scene is very important to the Bildungsroman pattern of the book: it shows us an important moment of insight in Fanny's history. But it also defines for us the sexual politics of the book, showing us that there is no alternative to patriarchal values in "home" and "Mother." It demonstrates how Fanny, sponsored exclusively by men, grows up entirely "male-identified."

Fanny is especially eager to be reunited with her Mother, having received a letter from her "convincing [Fanny] that she should now find a warm and affectionate friend in the 'Mamma' who had certainly shewn no remarkable fondness for her formerly" (371). The original rejection by her mother had certainly been the first trauma of Fanny's life, from which she had never recovered, and now she hopes desperately for a reconciliation.

But in returning home Fanny is disappointed in all her expectations, and especially in the hope of her mother's love and sponsorship:

Her disappointment in her mother was greater; there she had hoped much, and found almost nothing. Every flattering scheme of being of consequence to her soon fell to the ground. Mrs. Price was not unkind—but, instead of gaining on her affection and confidence, and becoming more and more dear, her daughter never met with greater kindness from her, than on the first day of her arrival.

(389)

Because her mother shows no real interest in her, Fanny sadly concludes that "William's concerns must be dearest—they always had been—and he had every right." So she continues to think little of herself, and to place male rights, even to maternal affection, before her own.

The crucial significance of this separation from her mother (and the failure to find a mother substitute in her aunts) is made clear for us by such modern psychological theorists as Nancy Chodorow and Carol Gilligan. Chodorow points out how women's identities are formed through closeness to the mother who tends to experience her daughter "as more like, and continuous, with" herself.[31] Therefore, females grow up tending to discover self through relationship, mutuality, sameness and identification—not through the separation and autonomy we generally associate with male development (and with Bildungsromane as a portrait of male identity).

With the help of Chodorow and Gilligan, we can see how Fanny is an extreme case of "feminine" development. As any discussion of her history would make amply clear, empathy is built into her primary definition of self and she clearly has an unusual capacity for sensitivity to the needs of others. Nevertheless, she does not have that capacity for intimacy and attachment, for relationship, which Chodorow sees as an advantage in the training of girls. In the course of her lifetime, she has formed only two attachments and they are both to men (William and Edmund). In other words, she seems to have few of the advantages and all of the liabilities of this training.

Generally, critics have argued that the absent or weak mother in Austen's novels makes possible the daughter's development.[32] This is clearly what happens in *Emma* or *Pride and Prejudice,* for example—but not in *Mansfield Park.* The failures of Fanny's mother establish the possibility for all future failures in Fanny herself—the major one being that she remains male-identified, never coming to have more than a fleeting sense of her own identity as a woman, and that she seeks the "safe" alternative in marriage with a brother figure.

Nevertheless, Fanny in a sense does escape the confines of the erotic text. And the way she does this is not just through her own resistance to Henry Crawford and to Sir Thomas, but also through the rebellion of another woman: Maria Bertram, having learned a false lesson from acting in the home theatricals, runs away with Henry Crawford, thus releasing Fanny to follow another destiny. By acting in *Lover's Vows,* Maria has learned the false lesson that a

woman, seduced and abandoned by her lover, can later be redeemed and offered a second chance. In other words, the play can be read as one of those eighteenth-century "Dysphoric" texts (the sexual misstep leading to ruin and failure) falsely turned into a "Euphoric" text (the woman rescued and redeemed by marriage with the repentant seducer).

Many explanations have been advanced to explain the importance of the home theatricals to the novel, including the petty intrigues which they foster, the rivalry for parts and jealousy among lovers and family members (Julia and Maria especially), as well as the violation of the codes of fitness or propriety entailed in acting itself. But that they should also violate another possible "text"—the "ambitious" one whereby a woman can choose a husband thoughtfully and independently—has not been discussed. Perhaps the main "impropriety" of the play lies in the fact that, by acting these parts, Maria and Mary are participating in an "erotic" text which effectively destroys independence of judgment and freedom of choice. They are participating in an age-old text that renders them powerless as mere sexual beings. For this is precisely the destiny those two characters proceed to follow in the rest of the book. Maria, shortly after her marriage to Rushworth, runs away with Henry Crawford (her son in the play); Julia follows suit by eloping with Mr. Yates, who had played the seducer in the play; and Mary Crawford, by supporting her brother, becomes an outcast from Mansfield Park and from Edmund's affections. Only Fanny is left—both as daughter and as bride.

The scenes in which all of this happens are very interesting—largely because they happen off-stage and are reported to Fanny at Portsmouth in a series of letters. These passages are striking in the way they demonstrate all the excesses of the erotic text—not only in the letters that Fanny receives, but also in her reactions to them ("the horror of a mind like Fanny's," her "stupefaction," and "feelings of sickness," etc.). The news item recounting the scandal of Maria's elopement shows the prurience of the erotic text:

> Fanny read to herself that "it was with infinite concern the newspaper had to announce to the world, a matrimonial *fracas* in the family of Mr. R. of Wimpole Street; the beautiful Mrs. R. whose name had not long been enrolled in the lists of hymen, and who had promised to become so brilliant a leader in the fashionable world, having quitted her husband's roof in company with the well known and captivating Mr. C. the intimate friend and associate of Mr. R. and it was not known, even to the editor of the newspaper, whither they were gone."

(440)

Maria's life has been reduced to a series of letters—and now to a brief gossip column notice in a newspaper. This is the perfect device for showing her objectification in the erotic text, where she will remain forever imprisoned.

But one question remains: why is Fanny's marriage with Edmund the necessary conclusion to this Bildungsroman?

Many readers have pointed out that Edmund is the "safe" alternative in the two suitors, because he is the sexless brother figure. And a number of critics have pointed out the threat of passion itself to an Austen character, but only recently has the contrast between passion and self-determination been commented upon:

> It seems that passion is antithetical to what these heroines are striving for, in the words of Elizabeth Bennet, as "rational creatures," as women who are seeking to know themselves and control their lives. In the end they marry the men who have helped them most in this struggle, who have been most critical of them and most conscious of their compelling need for honesty.[33]

So Edmund is the less threatening lover to Fanny's precarious and emerging sense of identity. It is significant that Edmund has been Fanny's teacher all along and therefore understands and values her mental and spiritual history as no one else can. He is the only character in **Mansfield Park** to foster her intellectual growth and to esteem her sensitivity and "spirituality."

So Fanny chooses a mentor figure, a loving teacher, who has watched over her mental and spiritual growth. One is reminded of some of Charlotte Brontë's male heroes (M. Paul Emmanuel in *Villette,* for example), or some of Eliot's (Maggie Tulliver's "soulmate," Philip Wakem, or Dorothea Brooke's Casaubon, who reminds her of Milton). Many, perhaps all, nineteenth-century female Bildungsromane seem to use in some way this male mentor figure, whose main attraction comes from his involvement (or supposed involvement) with the heroine's intellectual or spiritual quest.

But why end a Bildungsroman with marriage—even marriage with a mentor figure? The answer lies in the fact that choice of a marriage partner is the only really significant choice that an early nineteenth-century woman could exercise in life and one that had profound implications for her sense of self. Present day readers tend either to take this choice for granted or to see it finally insignificant for questions of "identity," since in choosing the right husband a woman still has no real self-determination. Nevertheless, recent historians of women claim more radical implications for this choice of marriage partner:

> The changes in the institution of marriage were . . . to alter the situation of women permanently because they altered women's self-concept. According to Miriam J. Benkovitz, "emotional and sexual self-awareness was the liberating force in woman's self-awareness, her self-evaluation" in the eighteenth century, and was more important than feminist politics in establishing a sense of identity in many women. The increased freedom of choice in marriage led to an emotional awakening in women that was revolutionary; it was the internal force behind the feminist movement of the early nineteenth century and is perhaps the origin of what we understand to be modern womanhood.[34]

Thus Fanny is left free to follow the ambitious text, and the erotic text has been appropriated, revised, or even subverted by Austen for her own uses. Fanny is rescued, as I said, not just by her own resistance, but by the fall of another woman who can be dispensed with—sacrificed, as it were, to the requirements of the erotic text. The erotic text is the subtext of this Bildungsroman and, in a sense, makes it possible. I would like to conclude with a passage from Nancy Miller's article mentioned earlier:

> Women writers . . . are writers . . . for whom the "ambitious wish" . . . manifests itself as fantasy within another economy. The repressed content . . . [of women's fiction] would be, not erotic impulses but an impulse to power: a fantasy of power that would revise the social grammar in which women are never defined as subjects; a fantasy of power that disdains a sexual exchange in which women can participate only as objects of circulation . . . I am talking, of course, about the power of the weak.[35]

Fanny Price's story, then, is clearly a "fantasy of power that would revise the social grammar in which women are never defined as subjects." It is Austen's revenge on the masculine vision of the submissive ideal for a woman. The novel shows the author's resistance to the ideal of feminine virtue for the purpose of attracting and supporting men, since Fanny's heart is for no one's "use" but her own. This heroine, who has been schooled largely by suffering and deprivation, whose power is "the power of the weak," does nevertheless retain an unseduceable selfhood. True, this "self" as defined in Fanny's story may ultimately be just one that can say no; autonomy may be largely negative, the ability to resist and to hold out for the desired prize, the redemption that comes from finally being chosen by Edmund. Nevertheless, there is a significant sense in which Fanny does preserve her mind from violation, her affections from coercion.

Notes

1. Kingsley Amis, "What Became of Jane Austen?" *Spectator* (4 October 1957), pp. 33-40.

2. See, for example, Marvin Mudrick, *Jane Austen, Irony as Defense and Discovery* (Princeton, N.J.: Princeton University Press, 1952).

3. Marilyn Butler, *Jane Austen and the War of Ideas* (Oxford: Oxford University Press, 1975); Alistair M. Duckworth, *The Improvement of the Estate: a Study of Jane Austen's Novels* (Baltimore, Md.: Johns Hopkins University Press, 1971).

4. Bernard J. Paris, *Character and Conflict in Jane Austen's Novels, a Psychological Approach* (Detroit, Mich.: Wayne State University Press, 1978).

5. Sandra Gilbert and Susan Gubar, *The Madwoman in the Attic: the Woman Writer and the Nineteenth-Century Literary Imagination* (New Haven, Conn.: Yale University Press, 1979), pp. 165 ff.

6. Tony Tanner, ed., Jane Austen, *Mansfield Park* (New York: Penguin Books, 1966), p. 8.

7. See, for example, B. C. Southam, ed., *Jane Austen: Sense and Sensibility, Pride and Prejudice and Mansfield Park, a Casebook* (London: Macmillan, 1976).

8. See especially Julia Prewitt Brown, *Jane Austen's Novels, Social Change and Literary Form* (Cambridge, Mass.: Harvard University Press, 1979). She argues that the novel's emphasis on stability and other conservative eighteenth-century ideals is an aspect of the "Victorian anxieties" of the book in the face of the new secularism, the fear of revolution following the French Revolution, and contemporary threats to the traditions of the gentry.

9. Nancy K. Miller, "Emphasis Added: Plots and Plausibilities in Women's Fiction," *PMLA* 96 (1981): 36-48.

10. My definition of the Bildungsroman derives largely from Jerome H. Buckley's *Season of Youth: the Bildungsroman from Dickens to Golding* (Cambridge, Mass.: Harvard University Press, 1974), although I am aware that more recent feminist critics expand on his definition, contrasting the "novel of apprenticeship" (the kind of nineteenth-century novel dealt with by Buckley) with "the novel of awakening" which is more common in women's fiction, especially in the twentieth century. This is an important contrast made by Elizabeth Abel, Marianne Hirch and Elizabeth Langland, eds., *The Voyage In, Fictions of Female Development* (Hanover and London: University Press of New England, 1983).

11. Nancy K. Miller, *The Heroine's Text; Readings in the French and English Novel, 1722-1782* (New York: Columbia University Press, 1980), p. 153.

12. Miller, p. 153.

13. For a good discussion of the sexual politics of the book (although not in relationship to the Bildungsroman), see Leroy W. Smith, "*Mansfield Park*: The Revolt of the 'Feminine' Woman," in David Monaghan, ed., *Jane Austen in a Social Context* (New York: Barnes & Noble, 1981).

14. Education novels such as Mrs. West's *The Advantages of Education* had dealt with childhood experience—but schematically, to prove the virtue of the heroine, not realistically, as Austen does.

15. *Mansfield Park,* in *The Novels of Jane Austen* ed., R. W. Chapman (Oxford University Press, 1923), 3: 15, 13, 14. All references are to this edition.

16. Avron Fleishman, *A Reading of Mansfield Park: An Essay in Critical Synthesis* (Minneapolis, Minn.: University of Minnesota Press, 1967), p. 45.

17. Paris, p. 49.

18. Paris, p. 48.

19. An interesting parallel between Fanny's circumstances and Jane Austen's own has been spelled out by Janet Todd in *Women's Friendship in Literature* (New York: Columbia University Press, 1980). Todd points out parallels between Edmund and Austen's favourite brother, Henry, who delayed taking orders to gain favor with his cousin, Eliza—who lived in the Austen household for a time and whom he eventually married. She notes obvious parallels between Fanny's jealousy of Mary Crawford and Jane Austen's "distrust of the exotic older cousin who enjoyed the precedence her title gave her, boasted of her resources and captivated Jane Austen's older brother." The Bildungsroman frequently has roots in autobiography, but few readers have stressed the autobiographical sources for this novel.

20. Kenneth Moler, *Jane Austen's Art of Allusion,* (Lincoln, Nebraska: University of Nebraska Press, 1968), p. 124.

21. Butler, *Jane Austen and the War of Ideas* and Robert A. Colby, *Fiction with a Purpose: Major and Minor Nineteenth-Century Novels,* (Bloomington, Ind.: Indiana University Press, 1967).

22. Fleishman, pp. 71-72.

23. Paris, p. 32.

24. Butler, pp. 248-49.

25. Butler, p. 247.

26. This is an argument of Gilbert and Gubar, also, in *The Madwoman in the Attic.*

27. At least Maria does. Julia, who does not commit adultery, doesn't suffer the same exclusion.

28. For this insight, I am indebted to an unpublished manuscript by A. K. Ramanujan.

29. An interesting avenue to explore, perhaps in most women's fiction, would be the use of the outsider or marginal figure as protagonist. See Lee R. Edwards, "The Labors of Psyche: Toward a Theory of Female Heroism," *Critical Inquiry,* 6 (1979): 33-49.

30. Susan Gubar, "The 'Blank Page' and the Issues of Female Creativity," *Critical Inquiry,* 8, no. 2 (Winter 1981), 244.

31. Nancy Chodorow, *The Reproduction of Mothering: Psychoanalysis and the Sociology of Gender* (Berkeley: University of California Press, 1978); Carol Gilligan, *In a Different Voice: Psychological Theory and Women's Development* (Cambridge, Mass.: Harvard University Press, 1982).

32. Cathy N. Davidson and E. M. Broner, eds., *The Lost Tradition: Mother and Daughter in Literature* (New York: Frederick Ungar Publishing Co., 1980).

33. Brown, *Jane Austen's Novels,* pp. 14-15.

34. Brown, pp. 19-20. One might argue that it is Maria and Julia who truly assert themselves, who strike out for freedom of choice in marriage partners, and that it is Fanny who remains the unawakened character, choosing as she does Edmund, the safe "brother" to marry. But the novel goes deeper than their either/or choice of marriage for love or marriage for advancement. After all, we remember that Maria had first chosen to marry Rushworth for advancement, then to elope with Henry for love and that neither is a deeply considered choice. Also the original Fanny, the

mother of the present Fanny Price, had married her sailor for love—and had disappeared into a welter of babies and poverty, with a drunken husband who could not provide for them. Her sister, Lady Bertram, on the other hand, had married for advancement—and disappeared into a life of inanity with her pug. So the novel doesn't simply contrast marriage for love with marriage for advantage—but rather the "conscious" life (the ambitious text) with the "unconscious" life (the erotic text).

35. Miller, "Emphasis Added: Plots and Plausibilities in Women's Fiction," pp. 41-42.

Ruth Bernard Yeazell (essay date 1984)

SOURCE: "The Boundaries of *Mansfield Park,*" in *New Casebooks: Mansfield Park and Persuasion,* edited by Judy Simons, Macmillan Press Ltd., 1997, pp. 67-92.

[*In the following essay originally published in 1984, Yeazell presents an anthropological study of* Mansfield Park, *focusing on the novel's concern with transgressed boundaries, such as the anxiety associated with the taint of spiritual pollution.*]

THE DIRT AT PORTSMOUTH

Immediately before the climax of **Mansfield Park,** in the last chapter of Fanny Price's exile at Portsmouth, comes a passage extraordinary for Jane Austen—extraordinary both in the concreteness of its details and in the sense of revulsion it records:

> She felt that she had, indeed, been three months there: and the sun's rays falling strongly into the parlour, instead of cheering, made her still more melancholy; for sun-shine appeared to her a totally different thing in a town and in the country. Here, its power was only a glare, a stifling, sickly glare, serving but to bring forward stains and dirt that might otherwise have slept. There was neither health nor gaiety in sun-shine in a town. She sat in a blaze of oppressive heat, in a cloud of moving dust; and her eyes could only wander from the walls marked by her father's head, to the table cut and knotched by her brothers, where stood the tea-board never thoroughly cleaned, the cups and saucers wiped in streaks, the milk a mixture of motes floating in thin blue, and the bread and butter growing every minute more greasy than even Rebecca's hands had first produced it. . . .
>
> (p. 439)

The vulgar confusion that Fanny has registered ever since her arrival at Portsmouth is here brought vividly into focus. From the walls marked by the oil of her father's head to the unclean utensils on the table marred by her brothers, the motes in the milk and the greasy bread, Austen's heroine sees her family home as stained and polluted. Fanny may have been too long pampered at Mansfield Park, or Austen may have been tempted to indulge in some con-

ventional disparagement of town life. But neither explanation accounts for the intensity of this consciousness of dirt—nor for its surfacing at this particular moment, as if prescient of the moral revulsion about to come. The passage continues:

> Her father read his newspaper, and her mother lamented over the ragged carpet as usual, while the tea was in preparation—and wished Rebecca would mend it; and Fanny was first roused by his calling out to her, after humphing and considering over a particular paragraph—'What's the name of your great cousins in town, Fan?'
>
> A moment's recollection enabled her to say, 'Rushworth, Sir'.
>
> 'And don't they live in Wimpole Street?'
>
> 'Yes, Sir.'
>
> 'Then, there's the devil to pay among them, that's all.'
>
> (p. 439)

Fanny's disgusted perception of dirt and spoilage among her immediate kin at Portsmouth thus directly anticipates her shocked verdict on the 'too horrible . . . confusion of guilt' among her great cousins in London.[1] The squalor of Mrs Price's housekeeping is inevitably swallowed up in the horror of Mrs Rushworth's adultery, and the scandalised Fanny is soon summoned back to Mansfield and away from the mess on the family table. Guilty confusion commands more attention than the homely Portsmouth kind, especially in a world so insistently moralised as Austen's: distracted by the climactic revelations, the rush back to familiar characters and to moral judgement, the reader, too, tends to forget the dirt. But the sense of pollution recorded here is characteristic of the design of Austen's most troublesome novel.

Dirt, Mary Douglas has suggested, is not so much an idea in itself as a function of the need for order—'a kind of compendium category for all events which blur, smudge, contradict, or otherwise confuse accepted classifications'.[2] If pollution ideas come strongly to the fore whenever the lines of a social system are especially precarious or threatened, as Douglas argues,[3] it is not surprising that in this interval of heightened anxiety and suspense, Fanny Price should see dirt. The sojourn at Portsmouth has been characterised from its beginning by peculiar tension and disquiet. To be at 'home' for the heroine of this novel is in fact to be in exile, displaced from the only ground to which her history has truly attached her. '*That* was now the home. Portsmouth was Portsmouth' (p. 431). No firm period has been fixed for her stay, and in the days before the scandal breaks, the term of her banishment threatens to lengthen indefinitely. The noise and disorder of her father's house have not prompted in Fanny the wish to be mistress of Everingham, as Sir Thomas had hoped, but Henry Crawford's persistent courtship of her at Portsmouth has proved unsettling. Without any serious change of heart, she is nonetheless disarmed by his apparent sincerity and embarrassed by the consciousness of all that distinguishes him from her vulgar relations. To walk upon the High Street with Henry and encounter her father is to bring 'pain upon pain, confusion upon confusion' (p. 401). Between her shame at her family and her wavering assessment of Henry's capacity for change, Fanny Price has never before seemed so subject to confusion, her state of mind so vulnerably suspended. Worried and estranged, she must at the same time wait helplessly for the resolution of Edmund's own unsettled state, the outcome of his protracted, indecisive courtship of Mary. Her anxiety has already been further compounded by the news of Tom's illness when the mail brings yet another alarming letter, a hasty note from Mary Crawford, with its disturbing allusions to a scandal she does not name. The troubled suspense that has marked Fanny's entire stay at Portsmouth culminates in still another day of waiting before Mr Price's newspaper unexpectedly confirms the scandal, and anxiety gives way to 'the shock of conviction' (p. 440).

Fanny's revulsion at the news is vehement and absolute. 'She passed only from feelings of sickness to shuddering of horror. . . .' And the origin of the sickness is the discovery of people dangerously out of place, of accustomed categories blurred and confounded:

> The event was so shocking, that there were moments even when her heart revolted from it as impossible—when she thought it could not be. A woman married only six months ago, a man professing himself devoted, even *engaged,* to another—that other her near relation—the whole family, both families connected as they were by tie upon tie, all friends, all intimate together!—it was too horrible a confusion of guilt, too gross a complication of evil, for human nature, not in a state of utter barbarism, to be capable of—yet her judgment told her it was so.
>
> (p. 441)

As D. A. Miller has noted, 'Fanny's curious disbelief and excessive disgust are inadequately served by the moral terms in which they are accounted for'.[4] 'Too gross a complication of evil' is closer to the 'stains and dirt' in the Prices' parlour than it is to considered judgement. Fanny's revolt from the very event as impossible, her conclusion that 'the greatest blessing to every one of kindred with Mrs Rushworth would be instant annihilation' (p. 442), are only climactic instances of the tendency to organise experience by drawing sharp lines of exclusion. Though Fanny is the principal vehicle of such thinking, the novel as a whole reveals a similar impulse to draw a world divided by clear spatial and ontological boundaries—to envision sunshine as 'a totally different thing in a town and in the country'. Anxiety about transitional states and ambiguous social relations is repeatedly countered in *Mansfield Park* by this categorical sorting of things into the clean and the dirty, the sacred and the profane.

To approach *Mansfield Park* in so anthropological a spirit may well seem perverse. The inhabitants of the Park are hardly the natives of a distant culture, and few fictional languages would ordinarily seem less translatable into the anthropologist's terms than the subtle discriminations of Jane Austen. But the fact remains that modern readers have persistently felt *Mansfield Park* as somehow alien and remote, and that alone of all her novels, it seems to require special pleading. Indeed a latent tendency to think anthropologically, or at least to associate *Mansfield Park* with the 'primitive', can be detected in a number of the novel's critics. Lionel Trilling's attempt to explain 'the great fuss that is made over the amateur theatricals' by allusion to 'a traditional, almost primitive, feeling about dramatic impersonation' represents probably the most familiar case.[5] Trilling's contention that there is something Platonic about the novel's distrust of acting has been much disputed,[6] but he is not alone in reaching for such analogies, nor in responding to what he elsewhere terms the 'archaic ethos' of the text.[7] Even a critic so sensitively attuned to the particulars of cultural history as Alistair Duckworth finds himself supplementing his effective use of Edmund Burke by reference to Lévi-Strauss—suggesting that the feeling for local ground at Mansfield might instructively be compared to the Bororo Indians' profound attachment to the circular arrangement of their huts.[8] The frequent association of Fanny Price with Cinderella, sometimes surrounded by vague allusions to 'archetype' and 'myth', may also arise from the sense that this is the closest of Austen's novels to older forms of story-telling, and that it operates by more primitive laws.[9]

Readings of *Mansfield Park* have repeatedly tried to bring the novel into accord with the rest of Austen's canon and to justify the values that govern it.[10] But even the most acute and learned of such efforts do not quite satisfy—in part, I would suggest, because they must labour under the strain of rationalising what is not finally rational. Stuart Tave's patient attempt to explain the disapproval of the theatricals is a case in point. Arguing that the issue is not the theatricals in themselves, but 'these people in these circumstances', he carefully articulates the 'whole series of objections, increasing in specificity and force' which are levelled against the scheme, all the while evading the deep anxiety conveyed by this very need to spin out one objection after another.[11] Like other gestures of rejection in *Mansfield Park,* the drive to condemn the theatricals still seems greater than the sum of these reasonable parts. What is missing from such a beautifully rationalised account is the fundamental sense of taint and pollution that seems to underlie so many of the novel's moral judgements. When other critics observe that the passion for theatricals spreads to Mansfield like a 'germ', call Mary Crawford's correspondence 'tainted', or allude to the 'fear of contamination' that pervades the novel,[12] they come closer to what is at once deepest and most troubling in *Mansfield Park.* Even those unappreciative readers who disgustedly reject the book as corrupt and repellent are perhaps more directly in sympathy with the novel's own impulses to sort and discard.[13]

THE PURGATION OF MANSFIELD PARK

When Sir Thomas Bertram returns from Antigua to discover that the 'infection' of acting has 'spread' from

Ecclesford to Mansfield (p. 184), he undertakes to combat that infection by energetically cleaning house. The theatre that has been temporarily erected in his billiard room is dismantled, the scene painter dismissed, and 'Sir Thomas was in hopes that another day or two would suffice to wipe away every outward memento of what had been, even to the destruction of every unbound copy of "Lovers' Vows" in the house, for he was burning all that met his eye' (p. 191). It takes just 'another day or two' before Mr Yates, the stranger who has carried the infection to Mansfield, voluntarily quits the house: 'Sir Thomas hoped, in seeing him out of it, to be rid of the worst object connected with the scheme, and the last that must be inevitably reminding him of its existence' (pp. 194-5). By wiping away every sign of the theatricals, even burning the books, Sir Thomas does not merely put an end to his children's acting scheme but ritually purges Mansfield of its dangers. Sir Thomas wants 'a home that shuts out noisy pleasures' (p. 186), and his gesture firmly re-establishes those boundaries that 'shut out', restoring a space that had been profaned.

The risks of play-acting at Mansfield have been intensified from the start by circumstances in which boundaries are already significantly threatened, by states of uncertain passage and transition. 'In a *general* light, private theatricals are open to some objections', Edmund argues, 'but as *we* are circumstanced, I must think it would be highly injudicious, and more than injudicious, to attempt any thing of the kind. It would show great want of feeling on my father's account, absent as he is, and in some degree of constant danger: and it would be imprudent, I think, with regard to Maria, whose situation is a very delicate one, considering every thing, extremely delicate' (p. 125). Note that it is not merely Sir Thomas's absence from home that is at issue, but the fact that his travels expose him to 'constant danger'—that his perilous journey renders him the object of suspense and anxiety. The anxieties prompted by Maria's 'delicate situation' are superficially quite different—the risks she confronts are purely social and psychological, not physical; yet she, too, is embarked on a dangerous passage. Any engagement marks a period of transition, but Maria's social place is further unsettled by the fact that she has been pledged to Mr Rushworth while her father is absent; engaged, yet not quite engaged, she is even more precariously suspended than is customary between her father's domain and that of her future husband. If acting 'is almost certain to prove . . . injurious' to the female sex, as Thomas Gisborne's 1797 *Enquiry* on that sex's duties insisted, then Maria's ambiguous position renders her especially vulnerable. The perils that Gisborne associated with any theatrical performance by a woman—the risks of 'unrestrained familiarity with persons of the other sex, which inevitably results from being joined with them in the drama'[14]—can only be heightened for one who is tempted to flirt with the relative freedom of a committed woman, even while she lacks the very protection that firm commitment affords. With its own shifting identities, its toying with sexual licence and transgression, *Lovers' Vows* is hardly the play to minimise such dangers.

The traditional distrust of the actor's role-playing is never directly articulated in *Mansfield Park,* but the anxiety of boundary-confusion is everywhere felt. Edmund suggests that the theatre has its place, in fact, but there is something more than the love of talent behind his preference for 'good hardened real acting' over the amateur's kind (p. 124): hardened actors presumably have a more calloused sense of their own boundaries, are less in danger of too fluidly surrendering to their dramatised selves. When Mary Crawford realises that she must 'harden' herself by private rehearsals with Fanny before she can dare to speak Amelia's lines (p. 168), what she seeks to avoid is the embarrassing consciousness that her dramatic role may be confused with her real one—an embarrassment all the greater because Amelia's immodest speeches themselves transgress the limits appropriate to her sex. Fanny's reluctant attempt to read the part of Anhalt, in contrast, is accompanied 'with looks and voice so truly feminine, as to be no very good picture of a man' (p. 169). Her utter incapacity to act, especially to act across gender-lines, emblematically confirms her integrity: Fanny can represent no one but herself.

The fuss over the theatricals reaches its comic climax when Sir Thomas enters his billiard room only to find himself upon a stage, unwittingly cast opposite Yates's 'ranting young man'. Trivial as the removal of Sir Thomas's billiard table may seem, the 'general air of confusion in the furniture' (p. 182) that he discovers on his return is the sign of a more profound disturbance, as the uneasy consciousness of his children confirms. While their father has been in danger, they have thoughtlessly invaded and violated his 'own dear room' (p. 181). One violation opens the way to others, and the 'confusion of guilt' in London eventually follows. When Edmund grudgingly agreed to act himself rather than open Mansfield to yet more strangers, on the other hand, he characteristically sought 'to confine the representation within a much smaller circle' (p. 155)—to narrow and tighten the borders. Here as elsewhere in the novel, anxiety manifests itself in a heightened attention to the sanctity of domestic space.

Mansfield Park may be the most openly Christian of Jane Austen's novels,[15] but the Christianity of its saving remnant is a peculiarly domestic religion. The only place of worship we see the characters enter is a household chapel, and the novel's theological debate begins when Fanny laments the discontinued custom of family prayer: 'There is something in a chapel and chaplain so much in character with a great house, with one's ideas of what such a household should be!' (p. 86). Fanny's sense of the sacred is typically rooted in domestic ground, and to her way of thinking, the collective disciplines of large households and of religious practice are naturally linked. As Sir Thomas's later defence of the resident clergy also suggests, religion seems to flourish best in a fixed and local space. Nineteenth-century anthropologists might sharply distinguish the modern, universalist impulses of Christianity from the ancients' worship of family, place, and local gods, but the spiritual emotions with which Fanny and Edmund are associated have much in common with that ancient faith.[16] Of course it is precisely because the current generation at Southerton no longer frequents the household chapel that Fanny has been moved to invoke the older ways; the awareness of change typically prompts the celebration of domestic ritual. Mary Crawford, in contrast, presumably gives voice to the restless, individualistic spirit of Sotherton's contemporary inhabitants when she replies that 'it is safer to leave people to their own devices on such subjects. Every body likes to go their own way . . .' (p. 87). Mary speaks for the modern temper; but Fanny, like the novel as a whole, sets herself against the tide of history—almost, in fact, against the very idea of time and change.

Paul Tillich's suggestion that 'a non-historical interpretation of history, even if arising in Christian countries, must return to paganism in the long run',[17] may help to explain why the Christianity of *Mansfield Park* so oddly resembles the domestic religion of ancient Rome. Commentators on the novel have often been troubled by what seems to them Sir Thomas's decidedly un-Christian response to his daughter Maria's fall. For the crime of adultery with Henry Crawford, Mrs Rushworth is apparently to be exiled from Mansfield Park forever. Though Mrs Norris 'would have had her received at home, and countenanced by them all', Sir Thomas 'would not hear of it'. Mrs Norris characteristically assumes that the problem is Fanny, but Sir Thomas

> very solemnly assured her, that had there been no young woman in question, had there been no young person of either sex belonging to him, to be endangered by the society, or hurt by the character of Mrs Rushworth, he would never have offered so great an insult to the neighbourhood, as to expect it to notice her. As a daughter—he hoped a penitent one—she should be protected by him, and secured in every comfort, and supported by every encouragement to do right, which their relative situations admitted; but farther than *that,* he would not go. Maria had destroyed her own character, and he would not by a vain attempt to restore what never could be restored, be affording sanction to vice, or in seeking to lessen its disgrace, be anywise accessory to introducing such misery in another man's family, as he had known himself.
>
> (pp. 464-5)

As Julia Brown has astutely noted,[18] this has a disquieting resemblance to the paternal conduct recommended by Mr Collins in *Pride and Prejudice,* when that cleric advises Mr Bennet on the elopement of Lydia and Wickham: 'You ought certainly to forgive them as a Christian, but never to admit them in your sight, or allow their names to be mentioned in your hearing.' The idea of permanently banishing one of the Bennet girls seems both menacing and absurd, but the exile of Sir Thomas's child is a sober necessity. Mr Bennet pointedly mocks Mr Collins's 'notion of christian forgiveness', and Elizabeth knows 'what curiosities his letters always were' even before she reads his solemn verdict that 'the death of your daughter would have been a blessing in comparison of this'.[19] But the comedy of Fanny

Price's similarly drastic response to the 'disgrace' of Maria is far less clear: 'it appeared to her, that as far as this world alone was concerned, the greatest blessing to every one of kindred with Mrs Rushworth would be instant annihilation' (p. 442). The qualifying clause makes an orthodox concession, but as far as this world alone is concerned, Fanny's code of honour seems more Roman than Christian.

Of course Maria has committed adultery, not merely fornication; if her punishment is more severe than Lydia Bennet's, so is her crime. A different system of relations governs the later novel: *Mansfield Park* draws its boundaries more tightly than does *Pride and Prejudice,* and the transgressions it postulates are correspondingly more extreme. Indeed in a world dominated by worship of the family, adultery is the greatest of crimes, the most threatening violation of domestic purity.[20] Lydia Bennet can return to Longbourn a bride, her guilt at least papered over by marriage, but Maria Bertram must be exiled from home forever—lest 'a vain attempt to restore what never could be restored' only give further sanction to vice. Though Mary Crawford suggests that Maria might recover partial respectability through a second marriage to her seducer, Edmund indignantly dismisses such an alliance. But if domestic religion requires a strict ban on adultery, the corollary of that rule is a certain bias toward incest:[21] at the end of the novel, Fanny quickly passes from Edmund's 'only sister' (p. 444) to his wife. While Elizabeth Bennet comes to love and win a once-proud stranger, *Mansfield Park* rejects such cheerfully exogamous impulses in favour of an insistent endogamy. Anticipating both Fanny's marriage to Henry and her own to Edmund, the misguided Mary Crawford feels that she and Fanny 'are born to be connected' and will one day be 'sisters' (p. 359). But the novel's design is with Fanny, who has no intention of mingling Crawfords and Bertrams. 'Edmund, you do not know *me*', she silently addresses her absent cousin; 'the families would never be connected, if you did not connect them' (p. 424). Once they learn of the adultery, both Fanny and Edmund take for granted that no further connection between the families is possible. 'That Edmund must be for ever divided from Miss Crawford, did not admit of a doubt with Fanny . . .' (p. 453). As for Edmund, though he formally repudiates Mary only when she attempts to gloss over 'the dreadful crime' (p. 457), he already arrives at their meeting 'regarding it as what was meant to be the last, last interview of friendship, and investing her with all the feelings of shame and wretchedness which Crawford's sister ought to have known . . .' (p. 454).

It is precisely with such feelings of irremediable shame that Lydia Bennet's sister conducts what she imagines is her last interview with Darcy, tainted as she is by 'such a proof of family weakness, such an assurance of the deepest disgrace' as must divide her from her former suitor forever. But the plot of *Pride and Prejudice* operates by more accommodating laws, and the sibling's 'infamy' there works to unite the lovers, not to sever them. Elizabeth's very conviction that she has utterly lost Darcy forces her to recognise the strength of her feeling and prepares for his second proposal: 'never had she so honestly felt that she could have loved him, as now, when all love must be vain.'[22] Darcy's memory of his own sister's narrow escape from Lydia's disgrace, his realisation that his pride has kept him from warning others of the danger, prompt him to acknowledge an implicit kinship in the Bennets' shame—and to demonstrate his honour and his devotion by arranging for Lydia's marriage. Lady Catherine may fear that if her nephew in turn makes a sister-in-law of '*such* a girl', the shades of Pemberley will be 'polluted', but the chief function of her final pronouncements is to render all objections to the lovers' union absurd. In the closing paragraphs of the novel the narrator informs us that Lady Catherine 'condescended' to visit the Darcys at Pemberley 'in spite of that pollution which its woods had received'.[23] Though Lady Bertram is also a figure of comedy, no such irony attends her view of Mansfield's vulnerability to pollution and the need of permanently barring her tainted daughter from the house. 'Guided by Sir Thomas', the narrator assures us, 'she thought justly on all important points'—one of which appears to be that Maria's disgrace can never be 'wiped off' (p. 449).

Modest Feminine Loathings

Fanny Price is the only one of Austen's heroines to have a childhood, and the account of her growing up extends over Austen's longest period of narrated time. Yet the Austen novel that most resembles a *Bildungsroman* proves the novel least open to real development and change.[24] When Fanny first arrives at Mansfield, her cousins make much of her deficient education; while they profess shock that she cannot name the principal rivers in Russia, the obvious irony will be that it is Fanny who has the least to learn. She may gain in assurance as she gets older, and we have Sir Thomas as a witness to her increasing beauty, but in character and judgement she is essentially formed from the start. Edmund receives credit as her mentor, yet theirs is a very different balance of wisdom from that between Henry Tilney and Catherine Morland or between Knightley and Emma. On all the most critical questions, whether of engaging in theatricals or of falling in love, it is Edmund rather than Fanny who must discover his mistakes. As he himself says after the catastrophe of *Lovers' Vows*, 'Fanny is the only one who has judged rightly throughout, who has been consistent' (p. 187). And in nothing is she more consistent than in her attachment to Edmund: Austen's narratives typically turn on the heroine's education in love, yet Fanny's romantic emotions virtually have no history. Her choice of Edmund seems fixed before such matters are ever consciously at issue, and it remains steadfast throughout.[25] Even when she is assiduously wooed by the novel's charming young man, it is not Fanny but Sir Thomas and Edmund who are nearly seduced by the performance. Like the flirtations of Willoughby, Wickham, and Frank Churchill, Henry Crawford's pursuit of the heroine serves as a lesson in proper judgement, but in this case the heroine herself requires no enlightenment.

Only while she is indefinitely suspended from Mansfield does Fanny's firm verdict on Henry's character seem to waver, and the novel as a whole appear to flirt with the possibility of significant change. 'I believe *now* he has changed his mind as to foreseeing the end', Austen wrote of her own brother Henry when he was in the midst of the novel's third volume; 'he said yesterday at least, that he defied anybody to say whether H. C. would be reformed, or would forget Fanny in a fortnight.'[26] Yet this suspense does not yield to new knowledge, but to acts that painfully confirm the old, and the anxieties of time are abruptly concluded by the renewed marking of exclusive space. The report of the adultery may nonetheless come to the reader as something of a shock—but just because such plotting so harshly insists that the promise of change was an illusion. Events do not compel the heroine to grow; they simply drive others to recognise what she has always been.

When Mansfield welcomes Fanny back, it is no longer to the humble east room with its chilly hearth; the wicked aunt is vanquished, the two older girls disgraced, and 'the lowest and last' (p. 221) assumes her rightful place in the house. If Fanny resembles Cinderella, as many have sensed, she is perhaps most Cinderella-like in this—that hers is not so much a story of growing up as a myth of recognition, a fantasy of being at last acknowledged for the princess one truly is. In most versions of the fairy tale, the heroine begins as an only and much-loved child; her rags and ashes are a temporary debasement, signs of the humiliation she is forced to endure when a stepmother and stepsisters invade her father's house. At the crucial moment of transformation, degraded appearances are cast off as dirt, and the heroine reveals herself to be worthy of a prince. Magic may transform rats into coachmen and dirty rags into dresses of gold, but hers is the inherent virtue and loveliness—and the small feet. When the glass slipper fits, even her stepsisters are compelled to recognise Cinderella as the beautiful lady of the ball. Cinderella may have dwelled among ashes, but the dirt has not really touched her; in retrospect, she seems to have been simply waiting to be discovered, her essential purity undefiled. Indeed in a curious footnote to his lengthy discussion of the tale, Bruno Bettelheim laments that by mistranslating the French 'Cendrillon', the English name for the heroine incorrectly associates her with cinders rather than ashes—the latter being a 'very clean powdery substance' and not 'the quite dirty remnants of an incomplete combustion'.[27] Though Bettelheim's etymology contradicts his earlier stress on the importance of dirt in the tale, his insistence that the genuine Cinderella was never really dirty at all suggests how deep are the longings her story addresses.

Like 'Cinderella', *Mansfield Park* associates its heroine with dirt only to deny the force of the association. But unlike the fairy tale, the novel establishes her purity not by an outward, symbolic transformation but by an inner response, the experience of revulsion. Fanny visits her parents' home and finds it unclean—discovers, in effect, that she is not her parents' child. She cannot even stomach the food of this 'home', but must send out, covertly, for chaster fare: 'She was so little equal to Rebecca's puddings, and

Rebecca's hashes, brought to table as they all were, with such accompaniments of half-cleaned plates, and not half-cleaned knives and forks, that she was very often constrained to defer her heartiest meal, till she could send her brothers in the evening for biscuits and buns.' As to whether nature or nurture has prompted such disgust, the text seems unable to decide. 'After being nursed up at Mansfield', the narrator observes on the matter of the puddings and the hashes, 'it was too late in the day to be hardened at Portsmouth' (p. 413). But only a chapter earlier, Fanny had felt a 'thrill of horror' when her father invited Henry Crawford to partake of the family mutton, since '*she* was nice only from natural delicacy, but *he* had been brought up in a school of luxury and epicurism' (pp. 406-7). The structure of the novel has made it impossible to determine whether Fanny could ever have thrived at the family table: though Fanny's Portsmouth origins were reported, her represented history only began at Mansfield, and it was at Mansfield that her appetites and affections were given narrative life. Even mother-love has long been displaced: embracing Mrs Price for the first time, Fanny sees features which she 'loved the more, because they brought her aunt Bertram's before her' (p. 377)!

By returning Fanny to her parents' house only when it is clear that she does not belong there, the narrative elides the most problematic interval in a daughter's history, that anxious period in which she gradually shifts her allegiance from one family to another. Fanny never really has to negotiate the passage that proves so dangerous for Maria Bertram; though she literally journeys back and forth between two houses, the sense of movement is largely an illusion. The transfer of its daughters' loyalties poses a difficult problem for any patriarchy, but the more the family is itself the locus of worship, the more critical is the transition, since to enter a new family is to adopt new gods. In the ancient world a bride did not officially cross the threshold of her husband's dwelling until she had first returned home to participate in a solemn rite of passage, a ceremony in which her father formally separated her from the paternal hearth.[28] The preference for Bertrams over Prices is also partly a spiritual choice, but when Fanny returns to Portsmouth, the anxieties of change are evaded by the foregone conclusion. Mr Price greets his daughter with 'an acknowledgement that he had quite forgot her'—and 'having given her a cordial hug, and observed that she was grown into a woman, and he supposed would be wanting a husband soon, seemed very much inclined to forget her again'. Fanny, for her part, 'shrunk back to her seat, with feelings sadly pained by his language and his smell of spirits' (p. 380). At Mansfield, Fanny had imagined that 'to be at home again, would heal every pain that had since grown out of the separation' (p. 370), yet no sooner is she confronted by the vulgar words and odours of Portsmouth than she automatically imitates Mansfield's gestures of exclusion. For all the naturalistic comedy of the scene, the division between father and daughter is scarcely less abrupt and absolute than in the ancient ritual. In fact this daughter's story has been so arranged that the normal separation on coming of age will never occur, since she was taken

from her parents while still a child and will marry into the very family by which she has been raised. The Portsmouth chapters do not offer a history of the heroine's separation from her family of origin, merely repeated demarcations of a space that already divides them.

Though Sir Thomas deliberately tries to unsettle her, Fanny's instinctive revulsions continue to guard her from contamination. She may temporarily soften in her judgement of Henry Crawford, but she is hardly more tempted by his attractions than by Rebecca's hashes. Indeed the lines drawn by Fanny's delicacy are finally more to be trusted than the boundaries of Mansfield Park itself. The house and its inhabitants prove vulnerable to change and corruption, but the distinctions that should ideally be defined by its borders are grounded more securely in the consciousness of the heroine. If the limits of that consciousness may also occasionally be breached, the offending thought can be immediately swept out—as Fanny hastens to do when she once finds herself entertaining dangerous ideas of Edmund:

> To think of him as Miss Crawford might be justified in thinking, would in her be insanity. To her, he could be nothing under any circumstances—nothing dearer than a friend. Why did such an idea occur to her even enough to be reprobated and forbidden? It ought not to have touched on the confines of her imagination.
>
> (pp. 264-5)

The idea that has thus transgressed—that Edmund might be 'dearer than a friend'—has broken in only under the cover of negation, but the alert mental housekeeper has nonetheless quickly spotted it and rushed to remove it. 'It ought not to have touched on the confines of her imagination': like other spaces, consciousness maintains its own purity by shutting things out.

Those internalised lines in the heroine's consciousness, the limiting confines of her imagination, are most evident when she is contrasted with Mary Crawford, as Fanny's own meditation suggests. With the Crawfords' arrival, there are in effect two marriageable young women for the Bertram brothers, but Fanny believes that only Mary may be 'justified' in thinking herself so. As for Mary, she no sooner arrives at Mansfield than she begins to weigh the relative attractions of the elder and younger sons—and to assess the status of the potential competition:

> 'I begin now to understand you all, except Miss Price', said Miss Crawford, as she was walking with the Mr Bertrams. 'Pray, is she out, or is she not?—I am puzzled.—She dined at the parsonage, with the rest of you, which seemed like being *out*; and yet she says so little, that I can hardly suppose she *is*.'
>
> (p. 48)

Mary's question prompts an extended discussion of the etiquette of 'coming out', as the three young people consciously examine the problematic conventions governing female coming-of-age in their culture. As to the 'outs and the not outs', as Edmund somewhat impatiently terms them (p. 49), there would seem no question where Mary herself stands, having boldly introduced the subject in her very first recorded conversation with the Bertram bachelors. Indeed 'till now', Mary declares, she 'could not have supposed it possible to be mistaken as to a girl's being out or not', since 'manners as well as appearance are . . . so totally different', and the moment many a girl crosses that imaginary threshold she abruptly abandons all previous reserve (p. 49). Tom Bertram offers in evidence his own embarrassments with a certain Miss Anderson, whose stony silence at one meeting had given way to boisterous aggression at the next. Though Mary deplores the awkwardness of such sudden transitions, she confesses herself unable to determine 'where the error lies'. But Edmund responds that 'the error is plain enough . . . such girls are ill brought up. . . . They are always acting upon motives of vanity—and there is no more real modesty in their behaviour *before* they appear in public than afterwards.' If modesty can be thrown off, apparently, it is not 'real': true modesty is a form of consciousness, not merely of behaviour, and the test of its existence is that it does not change. The genuinely modest woman would have no wish to behave immodestly even if she were free to do so—nor would she have any idea how to begin. Mary, however, significantly fails to understand him:

> 'I do not know', replied Miss Crawford hesitatingly. 'Yes, I cannot agree with you there. It is certainly the modestest part of the business. It is much worse to have girls *not out,* give themselves the same airs and take the same liberties as if they were, which I *have* seen done. *That* is worse than any thing—quite disgusting!'

> (p. 50)

By presuming that the only alternative to the girl who abruptly alters her behaviour when she comes out is the girl who acts immodestly from the start, Mary unwittingly reveals that she finds a modest consciousness unimaginable. All she can recognise is the difference in manners and appearance, the distinction between acting with or without restraint. Inner boundaries do not exist for her, and when she insists on returning to the problem of Fanny at the close of the conversation, it is only to settle the question in the most conventionally external of terms: 'Does she go to balls? Does she dine out every where, as well as at my sister's?' The answer to both queries being negative, 'the point' for Miss Crawford 'is clear': 'Miss Price is *not* out' (p. 51).

At the close of Edmund Bertram's last conversation with Mary Crawford, he turns to look back at her as she smilingly calls after him from a London doorway—'but it was a smile', as he later tells Fanny, 'ill-suited to the conversation that had passed, a saucy playful smile, seeming to invite, in order to subdue me . . .' (p. 459). Edmund walks on, and gives no sign. If it is perhaps too much to say that the scene suggests a prostitute soliciting a client, there is no question that Mary's equivocal placement and expression are the final emblems of her impurity, and that the

impulse by which Edmund cuts her seems a momentary instinct of revulsion, an effort to avoid contamination.[29] By her willingness to call seduction and adultery mere 'folly' (p. 454), by her hope that the guilty pair might still join in marriage, even live down the scandal with 'good dinners, and large parties' (p. 457), she has betrayed her tolerance for unclean mixtures, the casual promiscuity of her mind.

What finally condemns Mary Crawford is no deed of her own, but the fact that her 'delicacy' is 'blunted' (p. 456)—which is to say that her consciousness fails to draw sharp lines of revulsion:

> 'She reprobated her brother's folly in being drawn on by a woman whom he had never cared for, to do what must lose him the woman he adored; but still more the folly of—poor Maria, in sacrificing such a situation, plunging into such difficulties, under the idea of being really loved by a man who had long ago made his indifference clear. Guess what I must have felt. To hear the woman whom—no harsher name than folly given!—So voluntarily, so freely, so coolly to canvass it!—No reluctance, no horror, no feminine—shall I say? no modest loathings!'

> (pp. 454-5)

Edmund's broken syntax, his hesitation to 'say', conveys its own modest reluctance. To allude to 'poor Maria's' crime is difficult enough, but the guilt of the adultress seems dwarfed by the failure of Mary Crawford to condemn her. What Edmund most hesitates to name is Mary's lack, that absence of 'modest loathings' which has left her mind 'corrupted, vitiated' (p. 456). Mary is 'spoilt, spoilt!' (p. 455)—or 'at least,' as Edmund conscientiously adds when he describes that last dangerously seductive smile, 'it appeared so to me' (p. 459). How Mary actually looked at him and how Edmund needed to see her cannot in the end be distinguished. Like the narrator's ironic allusion to Edmund's going over the story with Fanny again and again, that detail suggests something of the anxiety that may motivate such a vision, the very uneasiness that prompts one to see and reject the unclean.

HOUSEKEEPING LESSONS

The most notorious crossing of a boundary in *Mansfield Park* occurs at Sotherton, the Rushworths' estate, past an iron gate that blocks a way from the wood into the park beyond. Mr Rushworth, betrothed to Maria Bertram, awkwardly returns to the house for the key to the gate, leaving Maria and Henry Crawford alone with the quietly seated Fanny to await his return. (Mary Crawford and Edmund have already departed for a further walk through the wood.) Subject to the combined effects of Henry Crawford's stimulating flattery and Fanny's silent observation, Maria quickly grows restive. 'If you really wished to be more at large, and could allow yourself to think it not prohibited', Henry obligingly suggests, 'you might with little difficulty pass round the edge of the gate, here, with my assistance.' With an 'I certainly can get out that way, and I will', Maria plunges over and away, beyond the reach of Fanny's cautious protests (p. 99). The ingenious management of the scene has been much admired, as Jane Austen makes her imaginary estate the grounds of a lively allegory about female abandonment and restraint. But it is of course still more difficult to represent prohibitions—or to honour them—without the gates, walls, or ha-has which a Sotherton so readily yields. The true test of virtue in the novel is the internalised boundary, and the true heroine polices even 'the confines of her imagination'.

Such spatial frameworks, in all imaginings, tend to suppress or supplant temporal ordering. Thus the conversation of Mary Crawford with Tom and Edmund Bertram about a young woman's coming-of-age automatically becomes an exchange about the 'outs' and the 'not outs'—the speakers conventionally adopting a language which already translates temporal changes into metaphorical positions in space. This emphasis on space, and the boundaries of spaces, is finally what we mean when we think of *Mansfield Park* as 'primitive'. The parodic *Northanger Abbey* and the unfinished *Sanditon* are also fictions named for a special place, but no other novel of Jane Austen's calls such attention to its boundaries, emphasises so strenuously the line between the in and the out, the acceptable and the unclean. The opportunity of presenting a child's development and adaptation to new experience it vigorously converts into an opportunity for revulsion and drawing distinctions. The most religious of Jane Austen's novels—if that term can be used—is not as Christian as the vocation of its hero would lead one to believe. *Mansfield Park* concentrates not on salvation or final ends, but on place and guarded female consciousness. It lacks a Christian sense of history.

Mansfield Park has been called Jane Austen's 'Victorian' novel,[30] and I would like to suggest that what makes it seem Victorian, paradoxically, is just this archaic strain in its thinking. The domestic religion of the Victorians, the culture's anxious insistence on feminine modesty and even 'loathing', may be more general instances of Mary Douglas's rule that pollution ideas come to the fore whenever the lines of a social system are especially precarious and threatened. Austen's novel is worth comparing in this connection to a representation of a different kind, from the following generation in England. Sarah Stickney Ellis's *The Women of England* is another descriptive work that is filled with prescriptions. Like *Mansfield Park,* it offers 'familiar scenes of domestic life', but without the continuous action and specified group of characters of a novel. It is also professedly Christian, though the author apologises in her preface 'for having written a book on the subject of morals, without having made it strictly religious'.[31] Despite its avowals, that is to say, *The Women of England* is not so much an argument for Christian values as for cleanliness and order in the home and 'retiring shyness' and 'purity of mind' in the housekeeper. Associating 'good household management' with the 'wall of scruples' by which English women are guarded, Ellis characteristically links one form of cleanliness with the other, her language metaphorically identifying female purity and the sharp demarcations of domestic space. Women preserve the sanctity of the home, and that sanctity is above all a matter of boundaries: 'In short, the customs of English society have so constituted women the guardians of the comfort of their homes, that, like the Vestals of old, they cannot allow the lamp they cherish to be extinguished, or to fail for want of oil, without an equal share of degradation attaching to their names.' With a flourish of Podsnappery, she declares that 'in other countries' women 'resort to the opera, or the public festival' and carelessly neglect their homes, those other countries being 'necessarily ignorant' of England's 'science of good household management'.[32]

Ellis explicitly addresses those women who have only one to four servants and 'no pretension to family rank', but the domestic order she celebrates seems hopelessly beyond the reach of Mrs Price and her two servants; Ellis's household ideal is much closer to that 'cheerful orderliness' which Fanny, confronted by the chaos of Portsmouth and Rebecca, nostalgically attributes to Mansfield Park (p. 392). Though she would presumably have no more taste for Rebecca's cooking than does Fanny, Ellis has nothing but scorn for those homemakers who prefer the kitchen to the drawing-room and firmly disapproves of 'the constant bustle of providing for mere animal appetite'. The emphasis of *The Women of England* is on order, both outward and inward: 'Not only must an appearance of outward order and comfort be kept up, but around every domestic scene there must be a strong wall of confidence, which no internal suspicion can undermine, no external enemy break through.' What marks off the sanctity of home from the unclean world beyond is not so much a wall of stone or brick—or a gate of iron—as 'the boundary-line of safety, beyond which no true friend of woman ever tempted her to pass'.[33]

The Women of England has much to say of women's influence, their education, dress, manners, conversation, consideration and kindness, but it is virtually silent on the most obvious concern of all: women's role in childbirth and the rearing of children. The women of England play critical roles in the family—but primarily as sisters, daughters, and wives, rather than as mothers. So unequivocally do the walls of home exclude time, along with the unclean, that married women seem to have become sacred virgins, vestals to whom childbearing is apparently unknown. Nothing violates space like children, unfortunately—as Jane Austen, with her host of nieces and nephews and her relatively cramped quarters, must have been well aware. 'The house seemed to have all the comforts of little Children, dirt & litter', she commented sharply to her sister, after returning from the home of one particularly fertile couple; 'Mr Dyson as usual looked wild, & Mrs Dyson as usual looked big.'[34] And nothing more readily carries the imagination backward and forward in time as childrearing: to introduce children into the world is inevitably to confront the pressures of history. Like *The Women of England,* Austen's novels keep out children, especially from a heroine's future, and this exclusion is particularly apparent in *Mansfield Park.* The house at Mansfield has its 'old nurseries' next to Fanny's attic (p. 9), but there is no evidence that they will ever be put to further use. All the children of the novel, of course, are back at Portsmouth, where Mrs Price was experiencing 'her ninth lying-in' when 'her eldest was a boy of ten years old' (p. 5). Such a brood puts the dirt at Portsmouth in perspective.

'Poor Woman!' as Austen wrote to her sister of a similarly prolific acquaintance, 'how can she be honestly breeding again?' 'Poor Animal', another letter sounds the note of revulsion, 'she will be worn out before she is thirty. . . . I am quite tired of so many Children.'[35] Children remind us that we are 'poor animals' caught in time, and whatever Jane Austen's private feelings about parturition, the form of *Mansfield Park* represents a response to anxieties that were not Austen's alone. Such anxieties are in some measure always with us, but the England of Sarah Ellis felt them with a particular intensity. The 'boundary-line of safety' around the women of England shuts out the 'field of competition' in which the men of England are engaged, that arena in which 'their whole being is becoming swallowed up in efforts and calculations relating to their pecuniary success' and in which 'to slacken in exertion, is altogether to fail'. In Ellis's sterilised version of sexual sacrifice, man needs 'all' of woman's 'sisterly services, and, under the pressure of the present times, he needs them more than ever', for sisterly services foster in him 'that higher tone of feeling, without which he can enjoy nothing beyond a kind of animal existence'.[36] Free of an 'animal existence' and its natural consequences, the relation of sister and brother is a purely structural as opposed to a temporal connection between the sexes—or at least offers the illusion of such a possibility. It is not surprising that the final marriage at Mansfield Park should assume this form. Edmund Bertram brings back to Mansfield 'my only sister—my only comfort now' (p. 444).

Notes

1. Jane Austen, *Mansfield Park,* ed. R. W. Chapman (1934: rpt. London, 1960), pp. 439, 441. All further references to this work will be included parenthetically in the text.

2. Mary Douglas, *Implicit Meanings: Essays in Anthropology* (London, 1975), p. 51. The third chapter of this book, 'Pollution' (pp. 47-59), extends and refines the ideas advanced in Douglas's earlier *Purity and Danger: An Analysis of Concepts of Pollution and Taboo* (London, 1966).

3. *Purity and Danger,* p. 139.

4. D. A. Miller, *Narrative and Its Discontents: Problems of Closure in the Traditional Novel* (Princeton, NJ, 1981), p. 58.

5. Lionel Trilling, *The Opposing Self: Nine Essays in Criticism* (1955: rpt. New York, 1959), p. 218.

6. See in particular David Lodge's verdict—'Jane Austen was neither a Platonist nor a primitive . . .'—in *Language of Fiction: Essays in Criticism and Verbal Analysis of the English Novel* (London, 1966), p. 98;

and Stuart M. Tave's extended discussion of the problem of the theatricals in *Some Words of Jane Austen* (Chicago, 1973), pp. 183-94. Tony Tanner, however, pursues the Platonic comparison in his Introduction to the Penguin edition of the novel (Harmondsworth, 1966), pp. 26-31. It might be noted that those who object to the allusion to Plato are critics especially attuned to the verbal texture of Austen's novels, while those who exploit the connection are more concerned with what might be termed the novels' deep structures.

7. Lionel Trilling, *Sincerity and Authenticity* (1971; rpt. Cambridge, MA, 1974), p. 76.

8. Alistair M. Duckworth, *The Improvement of the Estate: A Study of Jane Austen's Novels* (Baltimore and London, 1971), p. 57.

9. For Fanny as Cinderella, see D. W. Harding, 'Regulated Hatred: An Aspect of the Work of Jane Austen' (1940), rpt. in *Jane Austen: A Collection of Critical Essays,* ed. Ian Watt (Englewood Cliffs, NJ, 1963), pp. 173-9; C. S. Lewis, 'A Note on Jane Austen' (1954), rpt. in Watt, pp. 29-30; and Avrom Fleishman, *A Reading of Mansfield Park: An Essay in Critical Synthesis* (Minneapolis, 1967), pp. 57-69. Both Lewis (p. 29) and Fleishman (pp. 66-8) allude to 'archetypes'. Fleishman's entire chapter, which is called 'The Structure of the Myth', also evokes the work of Lévi-Strauss.

10. In addition to Duckworth, *Improvement of the Estate,* pp. 36-80, and Tave, *Some Words of Jane Austen,* pp. 158-204, I would single out Marilyn Butler's chapter on the novel in *Jane Austen and the War of Ideas* (Oxford, 1975), pp. 219-49.

11. Stuart Tave, *Some Words of Jane Austen,* p. 185.

12. Tony Tanner, Introduction to *Mansfield Park,* p. 27; Thomas R. Edwards, Jr, 'The Difficult Beauty of *Mansfield Park*', *Nineteenth-Century Fiction,* 20 (1965), 59; Julia Prewitt Brown, *Jane Austen's Novels: Social Change and Literary Form* (Cambridge, MA and London, 1979), p. 87.

13. See, for instance, Kingsley Amis's notorious pronouncement that *Mansfield Park* is 'an immoral book' and evidence of Austen's 'corruption' in 'What Became of Jane Austen? [*Mansfield Park*]' (1957), rpt. in Watt, pp. 141-4. See also Marvin Mudrick's more subtle but nonetheless severely critical treatment of the novel's 'inflexible and deadening moral dogma' (p. 180) in *Jane Austen: Irony as Defense and Discovery* (Princeton, NJ, 1952), pp. 155-80. 'What imagination will not quail before the thought of a Saturday night at the Edmund Bertrams, after the prayer-books have been put away?' (p. 179).

14. Thomas Gisborne, *An Enquiry into the Duties of the Female Sex* (London: T. Cadell, Jr and W. Davies, 1797), p. 174: p. 175. Jane Austen seems to have read 'Gisborne', as she called it; in a letter to Cassandra of 30 August [1805] she thanked her sister for

recommending it and pronounced herself 'pleased with it'. See *Jane Austen's Letters to her sister Cassandra and others,* ed. R. W. Chapman, 2nd edn (Oxford, 1979), p. 169. Both Frank W. Bradbrook, *Jane Austen and Her Predecessors* (Cambridge, 1966), p. 36; and Marilyn Butler, *Jane Austen and the War of Ideas,* pp. 231-2, cite Gisborne's comments in connection with *Mansfield Park.*

15. That *Mansfield Park* is the most religious of Austen's novels is widely taken for granted, despite the fact that many commentators no longer interpret her famous letter to Cassandra (29 January [1813]) as announcing that the subject of the novel was to be 'ordination' (*Letters,* p. 298). Several offhand, and frustratingly contradictory allusions to the Evangelicals in her letters have also helped to fuel much controversy over the novel's denominational sympathies. On the 'ordination' debate, see Charles E. Edge, 'Mansfield Park and Ordination', *Nineteenth-Century Fiction,* 16 (1961), 269-74; Joseph W. Donohue, Jr, 'Ordination and the Divided House at Mansfield Park', *English Literary History* 32 (1965), 169-78; and letters to the editor of the *Times Literary Supplement* from Hugh Brogan, Brian Southam, Margaret Kirkham, Denis Donoghue and Mary Lascelles (19 Dec. 1968; 2, 9, 16, and 30 Jan. 1969). For discussions of the novel's relation to Evangelicism, see Avrom Fleishman, *A Reading of Mansfield Park,* pp. 19-40; Marilyn Butler, *Jane Austen and the War of Ideas,* pp. 242-5; and David Monaghan, 'Mansfield Park and Evangelicism: A Reassessment', *Nineteenth-Century Fiction,* 33 (1978), 215-30.

16. See Numa Denis Fustel de Coulanges, *The Ancient City: A Study on the Religion, Laws, and Institutions of Greece and Rome* (1956: rpt. Baltimore and London, 1980): 'For us the house is merely a domicile—a shelter; we leave it, and forget it with little trouble; or, if we are attached to it, this is merely by the force of habit and of recollections; because, for us, religion is not there; our God is the God of the universe, and we find him everywhere. It was entirely different among the ancients; they found their principal divinity within the house . . . Then a man loved his house as he now loves his church' (p. 91). *La Cité antique* first appeared in France in 1864; though the publishers do not say so, the Hopkins edition reprints Willard Small's original English translation of 1873. It is difficult to imagine a nineteenth-century Englishman so casually dismissing the house as 'merely a domicile—a shelter'.

17. Paul Tillich, *The Protestant Era,* trans. James Luther Adams (Chicago, 1948), p. 20.

18. Julia Prewitt Brown, *Jane Austen's Novels,* p. 97.

19. Jane Austen, *Pride and Prejudice,* ed. R. W. Chapman (1932: rpt. London, 1959), p. 364; pp. 296-7.

20. Fustel de Coulanges, *The Ancient City,* p. 89.

21. Ibid., n. 7: 'Though this primitive morality condemned adultery, it did not reprove incest; religion

authorised it. The prohibitions relative to marriage were the reverse of ours. One might marry his sister . . . but it was forbidden, as a principle, to marry a woman of another city.'

22. Jane Austen, *Pride and Prejudice,* pp. 278, 279, 278.

23. Ibid., pp. 357 and 388.

24. Avrom Fleishman misleadingly insists on the need to recognise the novel as a *Bildungsroman.* See *A Reading of Mansfield Park,* pp. 71-3. Cf. A. Walton Litz, *Jane Austen: A Study of Her Artistic Development* (New York, 1965): 'Jane Austen took for the heroine of *Mansfield Park* a girl who is essentially passive and uninteresting, and in so doing she deliberately rejected the principle of growth and change which animates most English fiction' (p. 129). See also Lionel Trilling's resonant remarks in *Sincerity and Authenticity*: 'Mansfield Park ruthlessly rejects the dialectical mode and seeks to impose the categorical constraints the more firmly upon us. It does not confirm our characteristic modern intuition that the enlightened and generous mind can discern right and wrong and good and bad only under the aspect of process and development, of futurity and the interplay and resolution of contradictions. . . . It is antipathetic to the temporality of the dialectical mode; the only moment of judgement it acknowledges is *now*: it is in the exigent present that things are what they really are, not in the unfolding future.' Trilling significantly terms this 'an archaic thought' (pp. 79-80).

25. Only Elinor Dashwood perhaps approaches such steadfast devotion, but in *Sense and Sensibility* Elinor's fixed position is counterbalanced by Marianne's dramatic capacity for emotional error and change.

26. Letter to Cassandra Austen (5 March [1814]), *Letters,* p. 381.

27. Bruno Bettelheim, *The Uses of Enchantment: The Meaning and Importance of Fairy Tales* (New York, 1977), pp. 253-4n. See also his subsequent note (pp. 254-5), which elaborates on the association of Cinderella with Vestal Virgins and once again stresses that ashes are a sign of purity as well as of mourning. For a brief and useful account of the many versions of 'Cinderella', see Iona and Peter Opie, *The Classic Fairy Tales* (1974; rpt. New York and Toronto, 1980), pp. 152-9. The Opies reprint the first English translation of Perrault's tale, published in London in 1729 (pp. 161-6).

28. Fustel de Coulanges, *The Ancient City,* pp. 34-9. 'This paternal fire is her [a daughter's] god. Let a young man of the neighbouring family ask her in marriage, and something more is at stake than to pass from one house to the other. She must abandon the paternal fire, and henceforth invoke that of the husband . . . Was it not quite necessary that the young girl should be initiated into the religion that she was henceforth to follow by some sacred cer-

emony? Was not a sort of ordination or adoption necessary for her to become a priestess of this sacred fire, to which she was not attached by birth?' (pp. 35-6).

29. In *Narrative and Its Discontents,* pp. 85-90, D. A. Miller offers a shrewd analysis of the 'closure practised' (p. 89) on Mary in this scene. Miller notes the partial detachment of the narrator from Edmund and Fanny here, and rightly observes that 'in the narrator's final wrap-up' of Mary's subsequent history, she is allowed to regain some of her earlier complexity (p. 87). That Jane Austen could imagine Edmund departing without even a word or an answering gesture is still something of a problem, however; the awkwardness, even the unimaginability, of the scene remains.

30. See Barbara Bail Collins, 'Jane Austen's Victorian Novel', *Nineteenth-Century Fiction,* 4 (1949), 175-85; and Julia Prewitt Brown, 'The Victorian Anxieties of *Mansfield Park*', in *Jane Austen's Novels,* pp. 80-100.

31. Sarah Stickney Ellis, *The Women of England, Their Social Duties, and Domestic Habits* (New York, 1839), pp. vi-vii. Mrs Ellis was already a poet and novelist when she wrote *The Women of England.* First published in 1839, the work was reprinted frequently during the following decade: the British Museum Catalogue lists a ninth edition, published in London and Paris, in 1850.

32. Ibid. Quotations are from pp. 32, 26, 33, 25.

33. Ibid. Quotations are from pp. 21, 37, 26, 32.

34. Letter to Cassandra Austen (11 Feb. 1801), *Letters,* p. 121.

35. Letter to Cassandra Austen (1 Oct. 1808), and Letter to Fanny Knight (23 March [1817]): *Letters,* pp. 210, 488.

36. Sarah Stickney Ellis, *The Women of England.* Quotations are from pp. 32, 48, 50.

David Kaufmann (essay date 1986)

SOURCE: "Closure in *Mansfield Park* and the Sanctity of the Family," in *Philological Quarterly,* Vol. 65, No. 2, Spring, 1986, pp. 211-29.

[In the following essay, Kaufmann sees Mansfield Park *as primarily concerned with the responsibilities of family, rather than the contractual obligations of marriage.]*

Mansfield Park is, above all, a novel not about the sanctity of marriage, but the sanctity of the family. In many ways it sets the two in opposition to each other. Familial relationships cross the generations, and, by emphasizing filial duty, may be defined as hierarchical; marriage, on the other hand, creates a relationship whose obligations re-

main rooted in the same generation, and thus may be defined as contractual. Responsibility is unevenly distributed in hierarchical relations: the younger generation (or, in some cases, younger syblings) owes the older generation, specifically the parents (and sometimes the elder brother), obedience and respect, while the older generation protects, and therefore retains proprietary control over, the rights and privileges the younger inherits. Responsibility in contractual relations, on the other hand, is based on an exchange of property or interest, so that each party both receives and owes. In one sense, the central theme of *Mansfield Park* concerns the integration of the contractual into the more primary hierarchical relationship.[1]

This thematic concern emerges most clearly during closure, when Austen simultaneously resolves the two strands of the plot, which apparently work in opposition to each other throughout the novel.[2] On the one hand, the conflict centers on who will inherit Mansfield Park: the transference of the property represents the more important transmittal of propriety. Austen presents her position through a method I shall call the reversal and transformation of the generations. On the other hand, the story of the novel clearly remains that of a conventional comedy of manners: Austen carefully prepares Henry Crawford's courtship in such a way that his predetermined failure allows Fanny to win Edmund. This resolution she expected readers to accept, but precisely to this conclusion many critics object. Some have questioned the thematic implications of her closural strategy in general, but in no other novel do critics find fault with the structural correctness of the ending.[3] Only *Mansfield Park,* I think, fails to provide closural satisfaction, and only here does Austen herself permit us to question the rightness of the ending by explicitly providing an alternative.

Thus, to understand why Austen insists on the superiority of the sanctity of the family over the sanctity of marriage, and in some ways opposes the two, we must consider these questions: Why is Austen's closural strategy—indeed the entire plot of the novel—based on a reversal and transformation of the generations? Why is an alternative ending, suggested by Henry Crawford's courting of Fanny, permitted to be nearly successful, only to be ultimately rejected, not so much by Fanny, but by Austen? What is the alternative ending's connection to the reversal and transformation of the generations? And, finally, why are some readers and critics dissatisfied with the ending, despite what I believe were Austen's intentions that the reader accept and approve the novel's close?[4] Austen intended to provide a complementary and not an incongruent relationship with her readers, to use Torgovnick's terms.[5]

Readers have noted a degree of cruelty in the ending: Maria's flight with Henry Crawford and later abandonment, while perhaps thematically justifiable, hardly convinces many readers of its structural necessity; Sir Thomas's banishment of Maria seems, while again morally justifiable, rather harsh, especially considering, given Sir Thomas's recognition of his own failures, how judgmental

Austen makes him appear; Mrs. Norris' self-imposed exile, although a consummation devoutly desired by all, is presented with almost malicious glee; reluctantly, Julia is permitted to reenter Mansfield; finally, the culmination of Fanny's and Edward's joy—a return to Mansfield—can occur only when the innocuous Dr. Grant dies. In the last chapter Austen actively condemns every one who opposed Fanny. In her other novels, by contrast, Austen lets the antagonists' disappointment or their realization of their folly suffice.

Aside from Fanny and those immediately connected with her—William, Susan, and Edward—none of the principals receives much joy. Even Fanny's final happiness grounds itself in illusion: no perceptive reader can accept Austen's claim that ". . . every thing else, within the view and patronage of Mansfield Park, had long been" perfect in her eyes.[6] From her arrival at Mansfield until her temporary return to Portsmouth, Fanny has endured insult, suffered neglect and abuse, and been imposed upon and misjudged, even—sometimes especially—by those who meant most to support and advance her. Austen indulges, apparently, in an unexpected irony towards Fanny in the last sentence, an irony that seems misplaced, given how steadfastly she has maintained Fanny's judgment, despite its often cloying rigidity.

If Austen suddenly adopts an ironic attitude towards Fanny, it is an irony that pervades the final chapter, an irony that Austen turns even upon herself. Thus, Austen is uncharacteristically smug as she opens Chapter 48: she begins the second paragraph with "My Fanny." Where else is Austen so possessive of her heroine? Furthermore, the first paragraph seems to establish the ironic tone: "Let other pens dwell on guilt and misery. I quit such odious subjects as soon as I can, impatient to restore every body, not greatly in fault themselves, to tolerable comfort, and to have done with all the rest" (446). Yet she in fact spends most of the chapter not restoring "tolerable comfort," but dwelling on the "guilt and misery" of "all the rest."

If we examine the relationship of the ending of *Mansfield Park* to the beginning, particularly in terms of our earlier questions, we will see that the apparent irony actually serves to unite the two plot threads into a thematic statement that explains why the sanctity of the family must supercede the sanctity of marriage.

The novel begins with a delineation of the status of members of one generation, and concludes with a reversal, or transformation, of the status of their inheritors in the next. Thus, the ending fulfills the expectations set forth in the beginning of the novel: it is clear from the beginning that Fanny and Edmund will wed, that the Crawfords are only superficially respectable, and that Maria and Julia are vain and thoughtless.[7] That this almost painfully transparent plot more often frustrates than fulfills readers' expectations, although a plot based on the reader's foreknowledge of its conclusion tends toward, and ought to provide, satisfaction, results, I think, from underestimating the impor-

tance Austen placed on two strategies. First, narrative irony frames *Mansfield Park.* That is, the intentional discrepancy between what the narrator says she is going to do in the last chapter, "restore everybody to tolerable comfort," and what she actually does, condemns the folly and illusion of all, including, however gently, Fanny, diminishes the value of the foreknowledge we have been given. The relative absence of this narrative irony throughout the story itself underlines its importance in the ending. However, narrative irony appears in the first chapter, although there Austen masks it, presenting it not through the narrator's voice, but that of the Machiavellian Mrs. Norris: "You are thinking of your sons—but do not you know that of all things upon earth *that* is the least likely to happen; brought up, as they would be, always together like brothers and sisters? It is morally impossible" (44). As it turns out, of course, the marriage of Fanny and Edmund is not only morally possible, but morally necessary. Further on, Mrs. Norris states: "It will be an education for the child said I, only being wih her cousins; if Miss Lee taught her nothing, she would learn to be good and clever from *them*" (47). The reverse is the case; Maria and Julia learn whatever they know about goodness and cleverness from Fanny. Though Austen never mentions their reaction to the marriage of their cousin and brother, surely the elevation of Fanny that results, as well as Crawford's reproach that Maria was "the ruin of all his happiness in Fanny," must have forced them to reflect, with whatever varying degrees of bitterness and insight, on the causes of their respective change of status.

Narrative irony thus reveals the plot; it also reveals the closural strategy by drawing attention to the reversal and transformation of the generations that is as vital to thematic and structural closure as the marriage of Edmund to Fanny. Mrs. Norris functions as the mask for narrative irony in the beginning not only because, lacking both spouse and children, she represents the fragility of the link between the generations, but also because, without a family of her own and dependent on her relations, she ought— and appears—to serve as a voice for the sanctity of family over that of marriage. Yet, as we learn, the greatest deceit of this deceitful woman derives from her attempts to subvert family loyalty and exchange it for devotion to a suitor. The final irony towards Mrs. Norris occurs with her exile from the sanctity of the family, represented by Mansfield Park itself, to an ineffective substitute based on favoritism rather than duty.[8]

The purpose for masking narrative irony in the beginning but not the conclusion becomes clear: at the commencement of the story, the forces that undermine the sanctity of the family in order to promote the sanctity of marriage, and which necessitate both the reversal and transformation of the generations as well as the failure of Crawford's suit in order to preserve the primary sanctity of the family, are equally masked. In the ending, they are exposed, so that Austen need not distance herself further than the narrator's voice to reveal what has occurred thematically.

This returns us to the second strategy Austen uses as a counterweight to her otherwise conventional comedy-of-manners plot, and which serves to frustrate those who, from experience of other plots and foreknowledge of this one, expect no more than a traditional conclusion. For Austen is actually telling two stories, one, the courtship of a young girl, the other, the reversal and transformation of the generations. The two are held apart, only occasionally interweaving, throughout most of the narrative. During closure, however, they are combined, returning the reader to the beginning of the plot. Apparently, though, only one conflict—the courtship—is resolved, while the other is left seemingly unexplained, or, perhaps, unexplainable. It is almost as if Austen starts with two stories, but concludes only one.

Mansfield Park opens with an account of the fate of three sisters, the Misses Ward, and concludes with the history of the next generation, centering on, again, three sisters (in fact, if not legally). That Austen intends us to draw this parallel is clear from the choice of names: Maria Ward's eldest daughter is named Maria; her youngest sister's name is Frances (also called Fanny), and Frances's daughter— also named Fanny—becomes the third, youngest daughter of Maria's family. Oddly, the middle daughter of the first generation, who becomes Mrs. Norris, is never given a first name; the anonymity of Mrs. Norris's first name forms a curious parallel to Julia, who, though physically present, remains in the background throughout much of the novel. Thus, Julia is the *only* one who takes no part, active or passive in the crucial scene, the rehearsals for the play. In light of this and other parallels I will delineate, perhaps more than idle speculation suggests that Mrs. Norris was originally Miss Julia Ward.

What occurs, of course, is a reversal of fortune: Maria Ward marries Sir Thomas Bertram, and is "thereby raised to the rank of a baronet's lady" (41). Her daughter Maria also marries for wealth, with, perhaps, as much love as, though certainly more awareness than, her mother, but ends up disgraced and banished, losing all, including her lover. Mrs. Norris gives up hope of marrying as well, and becomes dependent upon her brother-in-law's generosity for her status, a situation that obviously aggravates her ill-tempered disposition and offends her vanity. Julia, too, in accepting Yates, settles for second-best, and, we may conclude, will be dependent on the good will of her father— and her brothers after him—for whatever status she has. Frances defies the family (as Maria Bertram does) and is banished. Yet her daughter Fanny succeeds in gaining entrance to Mansfield Park and wins the good opinion and rank her mother never had.

There are other reversals as well: part of the difficulty Fanny's mother encounters is a result of the profession of Fanny's father. Lieutenant Price, as a marine, was in a profession "such as no interest could reach" (41). At least, no interest of Sir Thomas could reach Lieutenant Price. Yet William, the second Lieutenant Price, gains the acceptance his father never could. In other words, in the second generation, Sir Thomas takes an interest in William, and admits him to the family, centered at Mansfield Park, despite his profession.

"Interest," a term introduced on the first page, becomes a key for understanding how Austen intends the two plots to converge to resolve the conflict between the sanctity of the family and the sanctity of marriage. Sir Thomas has an *interest* in Fanny, in the sense that he has a right or claim on her loyalty, just as Fanny has an *interest* in Edmund, in the sense that she has a share in him, or participates in his fate. Here, the hierarchical and contractual relationships eventually merge. Further, Crawford attempts to gain an *interest* in Fanny; that is, he wishes to benefit her through the *interest* of personal influence, as well as benefit from her. Finally, Sir Thomas's troubles stem from misapplied *interest,* both familial and financial. In both cases he expects an increase or addition over what is owed, but in both cases fails to actively guard the principal, and so nearly loses that as well as the interest due him. Thus, we may state that the dual obligations imposed by the two types of sanctity, family and marriage, are equally satisfied only when the *interest* of each is properly placed in the hierarchy of relationships, and the *interest* of each converges, or can be manifested simultaneously.[9]

We may note other ways in which Austen reverses the generations: Lady Bertram is passive and indolent, Frances Price is introduced as high-spirited and independent. In the next generation, their eldest daughters have the characteristics not of the mother, but of the aunt. Fanny is passive and certainly lacks initiative. Her most salient characteristic seems the negative one of resistance: she resists participating in the play and she resists Henry Crawford. Maria Bertram, on the other hand, appears more like her Aunt Price—high-spirited and independent. And, like her Aunt Price, her spirit and independence leads to a wrong decision, one which excludes her from the family.

There is a similar, if subtler, reversal for each generation's middle child. Mrs. Norris begins as an accepted advisor, whose machinations the noble Sir Thomas, otherwise so perceptive, fails to see through, and ends in exile with her beloved Maria. Julia, begins, if not actually excluded, at least as the outsider in relation to Maria, but her schemes— culminating in the elopement with Yates—result in her acceptance back into the family. Both middle children are dissatisfied with their inferior status and attempt, through manipulation, to change their positions in the family. Both succeed in changing the estimation of the family—most importantly, the opinion of the head of the family—but both also fail to raise their status significantly.

Something happens to the men between the generations, as well, though the phenomenon is not as complex. The reason is clear: traditionally, women are the preservers and transmitters of the family. Whatever of value is to be maintained or transformed must therefore occur through and by the women, because the traditional role of women before and after, though not during, courtship emphasizes cross-generational relationships. As daughter and mother, and even as wife, the woman fulfills her duty by preserving the primary hierarchical, or vertical, relationships. The man, on the other hand, by establishing a contract, that is marrying, a woman, creates a horizontal, or same-generational relationship. Nevertheless, what occurs to the males also reinforces Austen's concern with what happens between the generations.

Thus, Tom and Edmund are more than the traditional elder and younger brother, the first-born a profligate and the second a man of morals and good sense, although Austen is drawing on a tradition as old as the Bible. The two brothers each inherit one side of their father's personality: Tom receives Sir Thomas's sense of patriarchal privilege—often hastily exercised as poor judgment—and liberality—in both senses of the word—while Edmund receives Sir Thomas's moral rectitude and aristocratic sense of propriety. Both must lose, through suffering, part of that inheritance to gain the rest. Tom's illness teaches him decorum, and Edmund's broken courtship provides him with a more realistic perspective. And, of course, we have already mentioned the difference between Lieutenant Price and his son, based on a reversal of pride.

Significantly, however, neither Mary nor Henry Crawford change in the course of the novel, nor do they alter what they have received from the previous generation. Henry is self-willed, self-seeking and stubborn, much like the Admiral, while Mary has learned from her Aunt Crawford the art of dominating and influencing self-willed, self-seeking, stubborn men, for, in many ways, Edmund is as self-willed and stubborn, if not entirely as self-seeking, as Henry. The Crawfords, then, are like catalysts in a chemical reaction: they change those they come in contact with, but remain themselves unchanged.

The circle of the plot, then, is actually a wheel with those who began on the bottom ending on top, those in the middle spinning around, and the Crawfords the force that pushes the wheel. All that is to happen in the novel is stated in the first chapter, only in reverse. A marriage between Edmund and Fanny is impossible, Fanny is to learn proper behavior from her cousins, and the distinctions of rank are to be maintained. Sir Thomas's judgment and moral guidance maintain the family, yet he is, for a large part of the novel, an absent patriarch, while Mrs. Norris, who begins as a trusted advisor—we must remember that she suggests bringing Fanny to Mansfield—is exposed as a conniving, mean-spirited woman.[10]

Clearly, Austen has carefully planned the transformations, all of which, we should note, involve hierarchical relationships changed through aborted contractual relationships. This brings us to the second question: Why is the failed alternative ending, Henry Crawford's winning Fanny, made so prominent, and in some ways, so desirable, a conclusion, and what is its connection to the reversal and transformation of the generations? Though Edmund never sees his relation to Fanny as anything other than that of an

older brother, we are made painfully aware from the beginning that Fanny sees their relationship as something else, and ought to expect, by all the conventions of domestic comedy, that Edmund will see it, too. In other words, the marriage of Fanny and Edmund is supposed to satisfy the demands of the comedy of manners, yet the basic dissatisfaction with the ending results from just that conclusion and Henry Crawford's failure.

Thus, Henry Crawford's role as the agent of same-generational, contractual relationship reveals Austen's closural strategy. It also provides the essential clue to critical objection to her method of closure. That Henry and Edmund become friends is no coincidence: Henry is what Edmund would be if Edmund were an outsider. That is, both Edmund and Henry have an *interest* in Fanny. Edmund's interest begins as hierarchical—the cousin transformed into the brother—but becomes contractual—brother into husband, while Henry's interest always remains contractual. Henry feebly attempts to transform his contractual interest into a hierarchical one—a marriage between Henry and Fanny will not only include Henry in the Mansfield Park family, or kinship, but extend the Mansfield family by including within it Everingham. However, Henry's failure to fulfill his primary, hierarchical, obligations toward his own dependents, those at Everingham, dooms his courtship, his desire to contract with, and establish an interest in, Fanny. Here, as elsewhere in Austen, a man's property represents him. The house becomes a metonymy for the family.

This last point is crucial: *Mansfield Park,* unlike its predecessor, *Pride and Prejudice,* or its successor, *Emma,* takes place entirely within the family. Furthermore, there is less travel here than in the other two novels. Movement abounds in *Pride and Prejudice,* and although not as much ground is covered in *Emma,* we are quite comfortable in the Hartfield neighborhood. Not so here. Fanny's trip to Portsmouth is jarring and seems, appropriately, out of place. Significantly, Henry Crawford makes his greatest advances in Fanny's heart in Portsmouth, away from the family and Mansfield.

Henry is in reality as irresponsible as Darcy is supposed to be—and appears—away from Pemberley, though we are led to believe he is potentially as caring and protective as Mr. Knightley. Yet Edmund is the young, unpolished version of Mr. Knightley. Here, we might ask why Mr. Knightley's pre-marital guardianship of Emma doesn't bother us, while the transformation of Edmund's similar relationship with Fanny does. After all, the age difference between Mr. Knightley and Emma ought to be a barrier as great as the kinship between Edmund and Fanny. An answer lies in our analysis of the relative positions of the two types of sanctity, family and marriage: Emma and Mr. Knightley are already brother and sister-in-law through the marriage of her sister to his brother. Further, Mr. Knightley's regard for, and interest in, Mr. Woodhouse is almost filial, and certainly no less than Emma's. The primacy of the hierarchical, family relationship is established before the courtship begins, and maintained after the suit is won. Thus, Mr. Knightley accepts and supports the primacy of Mr. Woodhouse's *interest* in Emma, even after she has agreed to marry him.

This, I think, leads us closer to the heart of **Mansfield Park,** and the essence of the problem for those critics who have difficulty with the ending. Mr. Knightley is not of Emma's family; Edmund and Fanny are closely related. While the order of importance of the two relationships must remain inviolate, they must also remain separate from each other, or the sanctity of one becomes subsumed within the other. For this reason, generational reversal and transformation becomes necessary in **Mansfield Park,** but not in **Emma** or **Pride and Prejudice.** In all three, however, closural strategy revolves, simply enough, around the question of family. Even Darcy acknowledges the prior *interest* of Elizabeth's family, though he is bothered by it; his concern for the differences in their families hinders his suit, and Elizabeth, torn by the conflict of interest, accepts Darcy only after they have resolved the problem of her family. Henry Crawford, however, does not acknowledge that the interest of the family is primary, and actually attempts to subvert it, as can be seen from the aborted enactment of *A Lover's Vows.*[11]

Obviously, the play, which is the crucial central scene, is a complete muddling of events in the novel. The family is confused, and a bastard is introduced. Henry must play the bastard because it parallels, or prefigures, his role in the novel. A bastard is illegitimate because he represents a profanation of the hierarchical relationships. His claim on—or *interest* in—the family is contractual, based on the father's same-generational liaison, when it ought to be hierarchical, based on his cross-generational status as son. Further, a bastard's interest in—or claim on—the family must be rejected as illegitimate, for to accept this outsider who ought to be within must break the family, destroy the very essence of the hierarchical relationship that sustains the family. In short, the bastard desanctifies the family. Yet only through a steadfast, inflexible commitment to the primacy of the hierarchical relationship can a viable contractual relationship be created or maintained. That Fanny alone protests this confusion and degradation of the family is not surprising, any more than that she is best described as steadfast and inflexible, for she is unwaveringly loyal to the hierarchical relationships and structure of the family. She can be won only through an *interest* in her duty to Sir Thomas, and she wins Edmund only by refusing to be moved from her *interest* in her duty to the family's head.

The play, then, is the pivotal event of the novel, around which the wheel of the plot turns: as the characters adopted confuse the proper familial roles, so later events will result in a more proper inversion of familial roles. In other words, *Lover's Vows,* in an improper context, foreshadows the correct outcome of the plot—and everyone's schemes. Even the title has significance here, since the vows of a lover, particularly one such as Henry Crawford, are notoriously violated—or bastardized. Also, the instability—if not insincerity—of a lover's vows are to be contrasted with the stability and sincerity of vows of a family member.

Whatever transformations will—and ought—to occur during closure, as indicated by the novel's beginning, are here bastardized. Maria ought to marry someone like Yates, that is, someone willing to acknowledge, eventually, at least, the primacy of the family; instead she is seduced by someone who has no real family (Crawford, we will recall, is an orphan). Furthermore, in the play, Crawford, as bastard, reunites the family; in fact, Crawford, as unacceptable outsider, disrupts the family.[12] Also, the nobleman's daughter marries the priest; nobility and spirituality are united. But Mary Crawford is no more a nobleman's child than her brother. Such a union, therefore, is not an affirmation of family sanctity, but a violation of it. Finally, Julia, like Mrs. Norris, remains in the background, allowing the others to act out her own sense of displacement.

Into this quagmire steps the returning Sir Thomas, the hierarchical, patriarchal head of the family, who, by his very presence, sets things aright, to the consternation of the scheming Mrs. Norris and the glee of the petulant, but equally scheming, Julia.

Thus, Crawford's role, and the failure of his courtship, not only links both plots, but also resolves them. Austen herself was clearly aware of how desirable Henry's success was, aesthetically: "Could he have been satisfied with the conquest of one amiable woman's affections, could he have found sufficient exultation in overcoming the reluctance, in working himself into the esteem and tenderness of Fanny Price, there would have been every probability of success and felicity for him. . . . Had he done as he intended, and as he knew he ought, . . . he might have been deciding his own happy destiny" (451). Although authors occasionally call attention to an alternative ending to set off the real ending, it is not a technique Austen normally uses, certainly not as forcefully as she does here. Henry almost succeeds; his opportunity was real, something that cannot be said of Wickham, Mr. Elton, or even Mr. Elliot. If Henry is more than just a foil for the true suitor, as I believe he is, then we must seek another reason for Austen's rejection of this plausible and satisfying ending.

I suspect that readers dissatisfied with the ending want Henry to succeed; though at first he appears at best as a flirtatious, irresponsible young man, he quickly becomes more sympathetic. While he begins as a self-serving rake, much as his predecessors, such as Willoughby in **Sense and Sensibility** or Wickham in **Pride and Prejudice,** though not as overtly malicious as either, something occurs to him after the return of Sir Thomas. It is almost as though, denied the chance to act the role of the bastard in the play, he decides to abandon the part altogether, to see if he might find a way to establish a legitimate contractual relationship, and thus legally find a place in the familial, hierarchical relationship, a place he has never really had. Granted, his initial motivation is still selfish—Fanny's indifference wounds his pride, and he must recover: "I never was so long in company with a girl in my life—trying to entertain her—and succeed so ill! Never met with a girl who looked so grave on me! I have to try to get the better of this" (240). Yet he soon learns that the only way to gain Fanny's affection is to acknowledge the superior *interest* of the family. Thus, he turns from flattery to duty: he goes to London to convince his uncle, the Admiral, to help Fanny's brother, and, in so doing, affirms, for the only time in the novel, his own hierarchical, cross-generational relationship. Further, he is now willing to acknowledge that the sanctity of the family and kinship takes precedence over the sanctity of marriage, or its precursor, flirtatious courtship: "I will make her very happy, Mary, happier than she has ever yet been herself, or ever seen any body else. I will not take her from Northamptonshire. I shall let Everingham, and rent a place in this neighborhood—perhaps Stanwix Lodge." In his conversation with Mary, he makes other comments that show his realization of Fanny's value results from an awareness of her role in the family. However, his final comment in the chapter where he reveals his love also shows that he has not, and probably will not, completely accept that hierarchical relationships must always have prior *interest* to contractual: "Edmund—True, I believe he is (generally speaking) kind to her; and so is Sir Thomas in his way, but it is the way of a rich, superior, longworded, arbitrary uncle. What can Sir Thomas and Edmund together do, what *do* they do for her happiness, comfort, honour, and dignity in the world to what I *shall* do?" (301) Thus saying, Henry sets himself in opposition to the family, something that Darcy, for all his disdain of Elizabeth's family, never does, and something Mr. Knightley could never think of doing. This is why he fails.

Crawford, like Darcy and Mr. Knightley, is an outsider; he is not a member of the family, but one who attempts to gain access by marrying the most vulnerable daughter. Fanny, Elizabeth, and Emma are all vulnerable not only because they are unengaged, but also because they are primarily occupied with other members of the family, rather than with searching for a mate. If not naive, they certainly make mistakes in judgment or evaluation.

The role of the vulnerable daughter deserves further comment. Clearly, she must be the central character in the conventional comedy of manners. Since her affections are unattached and her hand not engaged, she is the only legal object of attention. However, the vulnerable daughter must not be conquered, for that would mean status and propriety could be disregarded, and would represent the triumph of the illegal and illegitimate relationship. Rather, she must be won by suing for her hand, that is, a proper, legal, contractual relationship must be established. This, of course, is marriage. We must note, though, that marriage is *the* institution that maintains and transmits the family across the generations. Thus, the vulnerable daughter is also the focal point of the hierarchical relationship: since, as we've noted, the women are responsible for the maintenance and transmission of the family and its values, the vulnerable daughter alone, precisely because she *is* vulner-able, that is, unwed and unattached, may cause a breakdown in the family or disrupt the generational transfer through an improper or imprudent marriage. Furthermore, the vulnerable daughter faces a dilemma: if she does not marry at all, the family will dissolve, or, at least, its sanctity will be profaned. So, while she must always support the primary sanctity of the family, she must not allow it to dominate her so much that she refuses to accept the sanctity of marriage. This is the central dilemma of Austen's heroines, and, indeed, of all the heroines in a comedy of manners. Treatment of this problem can be varied and enriched, though, by altering one of the circumstances of the vulnerable daughter. That is, her affection can be initially or permanently attached, as with Fanny and Anne Elliott, respectively. Or, she can be engaged against her will.

However, Crawford differs from Darcy and Mr. Knightley in that Fanny's marriage to him will not result, as Elizabeth's to Darcy or Emma's to Mr. Knightley does, in an elevation of the family's rank. The transformation will be a lowering of status, not a raising of it, since he brings neither a greater title, degree of wealth, or social position.[13] So long as Sir Thomas sees Fanny not as his daughter, but only as his niece and ward, a view he maintains until his own daughters, by adultery and elopement, abnegate their position, there can be no objection to the match, since a marriage between Fanny and Henry represents a rise in status for *her* family. Furthermore, he differs from Mr. Knightley in that Knightley, recognizing the superior claims of family to marriage, accommodates and acquiesces to the daughter's father. Darcy, too, recognizes Mr. Bennet's authority, albeit somewhat reluctantly and condescendingly. Of course, Henry Crawford also applies to Sir Thomas, but he does it backwards: rather than asking the father (in this case, the surrogate father, an important point to which I will return) to approve what has been agreed upon, Crawford wishes Sir Thomas to exercise a type of medieval feudal prerogative, forcing Fanny to marry him. By appealing to the father-figure, before he has won his suit with the vulnerable daughter he asks the father-figure to transfer his rights, and the vulnerable daughter to place the contractual relationship over the hierarchical, something she cannot and will not do. Clearly, if Fanny marries Crawford, he will remove her from the family, at least the family at Mansfield, something Mr. Knightley never intends or proposes. Even Darcy recognizes that Elizabeth must acknowledge her family and remain a part of it.

Not insignificantly, Sir Thomas is the only father of the three who shows any strength. Yet his strength, and willingness to make decisions for his daughters, is actually weakness, for by so doing he is at once attempting to maintain a feudal proprietorship over his daughters and break their primary loyalty to the family in favor of the outsider-suitor. Maria's marriage fails and Julia elopes because Sir Thomas has not instilled in them a proper regard for the sanctity of the family while nevertheless insisting on his rights as executor of the hierarchical relationship.

We must wonder how effective Crawford's suit would have been had he applied to Fanny's real father; part of

Sir Thomas's error is that he assumes a role that is not his, one that is, furthermore, no longer plausible—that of feudal overlord. While undeniably Fanny's patron, he is still only her uncle, not her father, and her father is very much alive. This, I think, is one reason for the journey to Portsmouth: there, Henry comes closest to winning Fanny, and there is where Fanny's real family still lives. It is at Portsmouth that Crawford most resembles Darcy and Knightley, for at Portsmouth Henry is truly attentive of Fanny and, more importantly, her family. She is embarrassed to be seen with her family, and is chagrined that someone with the manners and breeding of Henry Crawford should observe how uncouth and ill-mannered her real family truly is. In this, Fanny resembles both Elizabeth and Emma: Elizabeth acknowledges the justice of Darcy's observations about her family, and has been constantly embarrassed by their boorish behavior; Emma is never blind to her father's almost effeminate eccentricities. Though both, like Fanny, are dutiful, all three are painfully aware of the position in which their families place them. Yet at Portsmouth, Crawford acts as nobly as Darcy and Knightley; he makes no comments, and, in delicate regard for the vulnerable daughter's sensibilities, seems to observe nothing indecorous about the family. This reinforces our earlier remark about transformation of status: while a move from Mansfield to Everingham must be seen as a descent, going from Portsmouth to Everingham *is* an elevation of rank.

However, Austen refuses to allow Crawford's suit and courtship to be anything more than a possible alternative. For her purpose, Crawford cannot be allowed to succeed; his suit must represent an attempt to establish the sanctity of marriage by violating the sanctity of the family. This is why, in the end, he does not do as he ought. His flirtation with Julia and Maria, and seduction of the latter, is meant to prove that Crawford is of the type that accept that to establish a marriage, the family must be broken. This, Austen clearly cannot condone.

That some of her readers might disagree with her manipulation of the plot would probably have shocked Austen, for one of Austen's points, I think, is that only when the family is inadequate, when it places insufficient priority and emphasis on the hierarchical relationships, does the outsider-suitor have a chance of succeeding, of supplanting, rather than supplementing, the hierarchical with the contractual. This is one reason, then, for the reversal of generations in *Mansfield Park*: to maintain—or reestablish—the proper order of the two types of generational relationships, the first must be reinstated and reaffirmed.

Yet the opportunity for a proper marriage exists, provided the outsider, in this case, Crawford, recognizes the hierarchy of sanctities. Crawford at his best recognizes this. Discussing Maddison, one of his tenants, with Fanny, he explains why he must go back to Everingham: "I must make him know . . . that I will be master of my own property. . . . The mischief such a man does on an estate, both as to the credit of his employer, and the welfare of the poor, is inconceivable" (403). In other words, the duty of the

one in authority is first and foremost to his own—his own property and his own people. We may remark that Sir Thomas's will is thwarted and his role as family head subverted when he abandons his family—and Mansfield—to attend to business elsewhere. The patriarch must be true, or disappointed. Henry knows this, for in the same speech he says, "I do not wish to displace him—provided he does not try to displace *me*" (403). Yet, ironically, for most of the novel that is precisely what Henry tries to do—displace another. Consciously, frivolously, or unknowingly, until he starts to court Fanny by acknowledging and acting upon cross-generational relationships, all Henry's activity aims at supplanting first Rushworth, then Sir Thomas, and, finally, Edmund.

Austen includes the alternative to reinforce what ought to be, not to tell us what might have been. Crawford, because he will not—or cannot—respect the prior claim to sanctity of the family, ought not to be allowed to win Fanny. This, too, is why Edmund must win Fanny: his primary concern is always for the hierarchy of sanctity. His choice of profession shows this, and Mary Crawford's difficulty with the clergy stems from the same source as her brother's with the family.

We might go so far as to say the Crawfords represent a world where relationship is primary, whereas Fanny represents a world where property and propriety are primary. Not love, but duty, is the first criterion: Elizabeth falls in love with Darcy when she realizes that he is first of all a man of duty, loyal to his family. Emma's regard and love for Knightley stem from an awareness that he is guided by duty and loyalty to those dependent on him. In each case, the heroine accepts the one who, by recognizing the obligation he has towards his dependents, enters into the family, rather than disrupts it.

We now have the answer to why Austen's closural strategy—indeed the entire plot of the novel—is based on a transformation and reversal of the generations. What *Mansfield Park* is about, indeed, what *Emma* and *Pride and Prejudice* are also about, is transmission and continuation of status from one generation to the next. The essential question may be seen as, how is one to preserve duty, how are the vertical obligations to be maintained, when the children must leave, must, in a sense, abandon that to which they owe loyalty? The answer is simply that the outsider, the suitor, the one who represents the horizontal line of change, must enter into the obligations, accept the primary responsibility of the heroine to the previous generation, rather than to himself. If not, there must be a reversal and transformation of the generations from one to the next to maintain the order of the relationships and preserve property, propriety, and status.

We may conclude, then, with an understanding of why the ending bothers some critics: those who object to the ending do not accept Austen's premise that the sanctity of the family supercedes the sanctity of marriage. And in our confusion and frustration lies an insight to the greatness of the novel: Austen has raised a question that must divide every generation. That many of us find ourselves on the other side of the question from Austen only raises the value of her work, for a novel such as *Mansfield Park* forces us to consider whether we ought not to prefer Fanny, with all her inflexibility, to Crawford, despite all his energy.

Notes

1. See Lewis Hyde, *The Gift: Imagination and the Erotic Life of Property* (New York: Random House, 1983) for a discussion of marriage as an example of gift exchange, as opposed to a commodity exchange. His concept of gifts as objects bestowed and unobtainable by our own efforts exemplifies my idea of duty as a hierarchically defined relationship. Of particular interest is his chapter, "A Female Property." As Hyde notes, "Property . . . is a right of action . . . a thing (or person) becomes a 'property' whenever someone has 'in it' the right of any such action" (94). Austen, perhaps in response to changing conditions, transforms marriage to an outsider into a commodity exchange. A successful suitor must first, therefore, gain admittance to the family circle, that is, be willing to replace commodity exchange with gift exchange. In *Mansfield Park* the kinship is more narrowly defined than in any other novel.

2. Alistair M. Duckworth in *The Improvement of the Estate: A Study of Jane Austen's Novels* (The Johns Hopkins U. Press, 1971) notes that the plot antagonizes readers because it "seems first to be moving in an accommodative direction, but . . . is then . . . wrenched from its natural course" (36). Duckworth thus recognizes that "any attempt to consider the novel as central to Jane Austen's thought" (37) must account for a plot that apparently is twisted to fit a thesis. However, if we see that *Mansfield Park* consists of two inter-related, but distinct, plots, then, although we may still dislike the ending, we cannot be dissatisfied with the novel's structure. Duckworth also calls Fanny "the representative of Jane Austen's own fundamental commitment to an inherited culture" (73), a position with which I strongly agree.

3. One of the strongest criticisms remains Marvin Mudrick's in *Jane Austen: Irony as Defense and Discovery,* (1952; rpt. U. of California Press, 1968).

4. Gene Koppel, in "The Role of Contingency in *Mansfield Park*: The Necessity of an Ambiguous Conclusion," *Southern Review* 15, no. 3 (November 1982): 306-13, argues that "frustration and discontent are an important part—though only a part—of the aesthetic response to *Mansfield Park*," since "a central theme of the novel—the essential contingency of human life—by its very nature *must* frustrate the reader's desire for the conclusion to appear inevitable" (306). While useful in many ways, I find this argument less than convincing for two reasons: first, since Austen, despite her use of irony during closure, satisfies her readers' expectations in her other novels, the claim

she is intentionally confrontational here, remains doubtful without other evidence. Second, the argument that "All—the elements, the balances, and the readers' perceptions of them—are contingent" (311) strikes me as dangerously close to isogesis. All of Austen's novels, particularly *Mansfield Park,* emphasize that proper relationships must be moral and therefore fixed, not contingent.

5. Marianna Torgovnick, *Closure in the Novel* (Princeton U. Press, 1981). Although I don't use Torgovnick's terms in this essay, I am greatly indebted to her analysis of closure, particularly the ending's relation to the rest of the novel and the author's relation to the reader during closure, for the direction of much of my thinking.

6. Jane Austen, *Mansfield Park,* ed. Tony Tanner (Baltimore: Penguin, 1966), p. 457. Subsequent page references are to this edition and are included in the text.

7. For a different, though not contradictory, approach to the relationship of the beginning and ending, see Gene W. Ruoff, "The Sense of a Beginning: *Mansfield Park* and Romantic Narrative," *The Wordsworth Circle* 10, no. 2 (Spring 1979): 174-86.

8. Karen Newman in "Can This Marriage Be Saved: Jane Austen Makes Sense of an Ending," *ELH* 50, no. 4 (Winter 1983): 693-710, recognizes Austen's ironic closural strategy, but forces her interpretation of its purpose. Significantly, her argument ignores *Mansfield Park.*

9. See J. G. A. Pocock, "Burke and the Ancient Constitution," *Politics, Language and Time: Essays on Political Thought and History* (New York: Atheneum, 1971), pp. 210-12 for an insightful discussion of the political application of the term and its meaning for Burke. Burke's use of "interest," and Pocock's analysis thereof form the paradigm of what I have called the hierarchical relationship. Also, Duckworth, ibid, pp. 46-47, discusses the concept of improvement and "veneration of traditional structures" in Burke and its usefulness to Austen.

10. See Peter L. DeRose, "Hardship, Recollection, and Discipline: Three Lessons in *Mansfield Park,*" *Studies in the Novel* 9, no. 3 (Fall 1977): 261-78.

11. For an excellent analysis of the relationship between the play and the novel, see Dvora Zelicovici, "The Inefficacy of *Lover's Vows,*" *ELH* 50, no. 3 (Fall 1983): 531-40.

12. The adulterous liaison between Crawford and Maria is a consequence of a violation of the social contract. In this regard, the introduction to Tony Tanner's *Adultery in the Novel: Contract and Transgression,* (Johns Hopkins U. Press, 1979), provides a thorough background for many of the questions about status and family discussed here.

13. I am using Tzvetan Todorov, *The Poetics of Prose,* trans. Richard Howell (Cornell U. Press), pp. 226-30, for my definition of the term "transformation of status."

C. Knatchbull Bevan (essay date 1987)

SOURCE: "Personal Identity in *Mansfield Park*: Forms, Fictions, Role-Play, and Reality," in *SEL: Studies in English Literature 1500-1900,* Vol. 27, No. 4, Autumn, 1987, pp. 595-608.

[*In the following essay, Bevan discusses acting and fiction-making as inauthentic forms of self-expression in* Mansfield Park.]

Two papers which deal pertinently with acting as a rhetorically crucial theme in **Mansfield Park** are those by Lionel Trilling and Thomas R. Edwards.[1] Of these, Lionel Trilling's seminal essay fails to observe the pervasiveness of the theme of role-play in the novel as a whole. Professor Edwards, though he deals cogently with the whole question of acting and its relationship to emotional reality in **Mansfield Park,** tends to focus his attention almost exclusively on the personal relationships explored and developed through the novel, and to ignore the wider significance of such relationships placed as they are within a broad thematic context of personal identity in its relation to a reality which includes but goes beyond the emotional to embrace phenomena, language, and art.

This paper sets out to examine the importance of acting, and of fiction-making, as themes in **Mansfield Park.** It will be argued that acting is used both as an illustration of, and as a metaphor for, invalid attempts to express and define the self. Such attempts are shown to be invalid because, ultimately, they deny the self they seek to create. They deny, also, important realities of the external world in which the self must exist, substituting for them forms, fictions, and material values. To this false art of life, exemplified at its most extreme by the Crawfords, is opposed a true art of life, consisting in a harmonious relationship between the perceiver and all that is perceived, where the objects of perception are the self, others, natural phenomena, and artefacts. The exemplar of this true art of life is Fanny Price. Her creative tools are two personal qualities, delicacy and associative memory, and these qualities are opposed throughout **Mansfield Park** to the fictions, forms, and role-play by means of which the Crawfords, and others, seek to create their own reality.

At the time of the rehearsals for *Lovers' Vows* Fanny makes a revealing statement. Tom has asked her to act Cottager's wife. She replies: "Indeed you must excuse me. I could not act anything if you were to give me the world. No, indeed, I cannot act" (p. 145). Again, a little later, she explains: "It is not that I am afraid of learning by heart but I really cannot act" (pp. 145-46). This would seem to be a

crucial comment by Fanny upon herself, for we are made strongly aware from the first that Fanny, unlike almost all those by whom she finds herself ignored or patronised at Mansfield, is incapable either of creating fictions or of performing in them. Furthermore, as is so often the case in Jane Austen,[2] the performing arts, acting and music, are opposed negatively, in **Mansfield Park,** to nature and to rational conversation. At one point Fanny, left alone with Edmund at the drawing-room window, turns to the scene outside and observes the brilliant unclouded night and the contrasting colour of the woods. "'Here's harmony!' said she, 'Here's repose! Here's what may leave all painting and all music behind, and what poetry only can attempt to describe'" (p. 113).

Nature provides the truest and best art, all else is imitation. Those who have been taught to "*think* and *feel* on the subject" (italics mine) have been well taught. But having himself acknowledged the value of Nature, Edmund moves towards the fortepiano, away from nature and from rational conversation to performance and the rendering of applause. What he has done is to follow with his person what he has already followed admiringly with his eyes, the appeal of artifice in appearance, whether the appearance in question be an attractively composed woman or musical glee. "She [Mary Crawford] tripped off to the instrument, leaving Edmund looking after her in an ecstasy of admiration of all her many virtues, from her obliging manners down to her light and graceful tread" (p. 112).

That Fanny "cannot act" is seen as the expression of her contact with nature both human and phenomenal. When she first arrives at Mansfield we are told, by the author-commentator, that "Her feelings were very acute." It is a result of her education at Edmund's hands that these "feelings" are developed in the direction of the understanding of herself and others so that they become "sympathetically" acute. It is just this "sympathetic acuteness of feeling," or delicacy that is missing from Fanny's treatment by the Mansfield relations, by all of whom Fanny is viewed less as a person than as one who must fulfil a preordained role. To Mrs. Norris, Fanny is a poor relation who is to be used. To Sir Thomas it is, not altogether improperly, Fanny's household and social roles that matter. To Maria and Julia, Fanny is to be judged by her possessions and her lack of accomplishments, while to Lady Bertram Fanny has one role only, that of helper. What all these attitudes reveal is the absence of a sympathy which arises from feeling and seeks knowledge. Fanny's emotional reality is denied by people who themselves habitually cast others, as they cast themselves, in roles. Role-casting is presented as the polar opposite, and as the inhibitor, of that "sympathetic acuteness of feeling" of which Fanny, as the result of Edmund's educational care, is to become the exemplar. A term used frequently in **Mansfield Park** to describe this quality is "delicacy," and it is in terms of their lack of delicacy that the human incompleteness of other characters is often expressed. Thus Mr. Yates is "without discernment or diffidence, or delicacy, or discretion enough" to understand that Sir Thomas had rather leave the topic of theatricals alone. Henry Crawford's unwelcome perseverance with Fanny's affections is regarded by her as "a want of delicacy and regard for others." Fanny considers that Sir Thomas, "He who had married a daughter to Mr Rushworth," can have no "romantic delicacy" which might enable him to see beyond merely factual information, into her real feelings concerning Crawford. The term "delicacy," then, would seem to connote sympathetic discernment, of the kind demonstrated by Edmund when he finds the child Fanny crying on the stairs, and of the kind shown by Fanny in her constant concern with the workings of the minds and feelings of others, and of herself. It is a measure of Edmund's falling off from excellence, during his pursuit of Mary Crawford, that he allows his prepossession in favor of her brother Henry to blunt the delicacy of his perceptions. Having assured Fanny "you did not love him—nothing could have justified your accepting him," he immediately exhorts her.

> "But (with an affectionate smile), let him succeed at last, Fanny, let him succeed at last. You have proved yourself upright and disinterested, prove yourself grateful and tender-hearted; and then you will be the perfect model of a woman, which I have always believed you born for."
>
> (p. 347)

Edmund is here asking Fanny to dispose her emotional reactions to Henry Crawford much as she is in the habit of disposing her active life in the service of others. But Fanny, in pursuing her life of service, is being emotionally true to herself. She cannot, and herein lies Edmund's lack of delicacy, assume emotional roles, because to do so would mean being untrue to the grounds of feeling within her. She "cannot act."

What Fanny demonstrates, in direct contradistinction to the Crawfords, and to the other role-players and role-imposers, is a state of being grounded in feeling, not in role-play, in actual, not in imagined experience. This state of being consists in a harmonious relationship between the inner and the outer life, and between self and others. Thus she is constantly engaged in the effort to see both herself and others as they really are in terms of motive, feeling, and moral intention, not as she would have them be. When Fanny and Edmund are in conversation, or when Fanny is employed in speculative meditation, one notices frequent evaluations which are themselves the subject of doubt and enquiry. In an early discussion of Mary Crawford (p. 63) moral judgments are qualified by such expressions of doubt as "I think," "I do not know that," "It must be difficult," "I do not pretend to know," "Do not you think." Fanny, whose "own thoughts and reflections were habitually her best companions," tries to exercise them in honest enquiry even when her own pride is under attack as, from a distance, she observes Mary Crawford's competent horsemanship and Edmund's apparently eager attentions. "She saw it, or the imagination supplied what the eye could not reach. She must not wonder at all this; what could be more natural than that Edmund should be making himself

useful, and proving his good-nature by any one?" (p. 67). Fanny's approach to all experience is to question it and, she hopes, to discover meanings. Inferences are recognized for what they are and are qualified by reasonable doubt.

Unlike Fanny, Mary Crawford deals with experience not by trying, through sympathetic feeling, to understand it. Instead she creates out of it fictional anecdotes, and her language is characterized not by doubt and enquiry but by assertion and by a conscious pattern-making designed to delight the listener and to distort the truth. The devotional life of the Rushworth forebears, the wilderness at Sotherton, the Owen girls, the sensation that Fanny's marriage to Crawford is to make in the fashionable world, are all entertaining fictions which satisfy Mary Crawford's urge to create rather than to know. What her brother's plans for radical improvement are to Sotherton, so Mary Crawford's fictional renderings of reality are to reality itself; imposed re-creations. They are not developments of what is in fact there, but falsifications. This disjunction between reality and the Crawford fictions receives expression in the language Mary Crawford uses. Frequently we observe an incompatibility between the syntactic forms she employs and the semantic function these forms actually perform. Most typical of her speech is her use of the attributive clause.[3] Thus when she declares clergymen to be motivated by "indolence and love of ease—a want of all laudable ambition, of taste for good company, or of inclination to take the trouble of being agreeable," the qualities she attributes to clergymen are, clearly, not factual but merely expressions of her own feeling. Underlying the formal syntactic realization here is a function which should appropriately be expressed in a reactive clause. She uses language, in short, to manipulate truth and to falsify it, not, after the fashion of Fanny and Edmund, in order to discover it.

The relationship of Fanny to reality is, then, harmonious, for she is always seen trying to come to terms with it by discovering it. That of the Crawfords is disharmonious, for they are shown always to recreate it and thereby to falsify it.

Fanny's harmonious relationship to reality receives further expression, and rhetorical reinforcement, in frequent accounts of the importance to Fanny of people, places, and possessions, and in the nature of their operation upon her memory. At Sotherton, while Mrs. Rushworth is lecturing Fanny and Mary Crawford on the ancestral pictures, Mary Crawford had, we are told, "only the appearance of civilly listening," while Fanny listened eagerly, "delighted to connect any thing with history already known." Her pleasure at William's visit is thus accounted for:

> All the evil and good of their earliest years could be gone over again, and every former united pain and pleasure retraced with the fondest recollection. An advantage this, a strengthener of love, in which even the conjugal tie is beneath the fraternal. Children of the same family, the same blood, with the same associa-

tions and habits, have some means of enjoyment in their power, which no subsequent connections can supply.

(pp. 234-35)

Earlier, after she has been upset by Tom's insistence that she act, Fanny goes off alone to her east room.

> The comfort of it in her hours of leisure was extreme. She could go there after any thing unpleasant below, and find immediate consolation in some pursuit, or some train of thought at hand.—Her plants, her books—of which she had been a collector, from the first hour of her commanding a shilling—her writing desk, and her works of charity and ingenuity, were all within her reach . . . she could scarcely see an object in that room which had not an interesting remembrance connected with it.—Everything was a friend, or bore her thoughts to a friend.

(pp. 151-52)

The function of memory here is to blend together events, people, possessions, and emotional experience, into a totality of harmonious association. Through memory, Fanny's loved ones and her possessions become a part of the self, inseparable from it. Upon them her self depends, and from them it receives definition. In contrast the Crawfords are, to use a term often employed in *Mansfield Park,* "unfixed," having no attachment to people, places, or things. Thus, "To any thing like permanence of abode, or limitation of society, Henry Crawford had, unluckily, a great dislike" (p. 41). He is "every thing to every body and seemed to find no-one essential to him" (p. 306). That his sister's predicament is identical with his is demonstrated at the time when Fanny and Mary are together in the parsonage shrubbery. Fanny observes:

> "Every time I come into this shrubbery I am more struck with its growth and beauty. Three years ago, this was nothing but a rough hedgerow along the upper side of the field, never thought of as any thing, or capable of becoming any thing; and now it is converted into a walk, and it would be difficult to say whether most valuable as a convenience or an ornament. . . . How wonderful, how very wonderful the operations of time, and the changes of the human mind . . . If any one faculty of our nature may be called *more* wonderful than the rest, I do think it is memory."

(p. 208)

Memory at once locates in time and links in time, links the shrubbery as it was to the shrubbery as it is, and links also the human perceiver to the inanimate objects that are perceived. Mary Crawford, however, who is without fixed location and thus without the associative capability that felt memory provides, "untouched and inattentive, had nothing to say." Shortly afterwards she remarks, "I see no wonder in the shrubbery equal to seeing myself in it." There is surely more to this than a bald revelation of egotism. What her remark reveals, more importantly, is her isolation from the phenomena which, through the action of memory, give people communal roots in experience. To be

free, as Mary Crawford and her brother are, is to be alone. It is an important irony in *Mansfield Park,* perhaps the most important, that it is the Crawfords, who appear to be the most socially adept of all the characters, who are in reality the most alone, whereas Fanny, the most socially isolated, is in other and crucial senses the most fully integrated. The isolating nature of the Crawfords' freedom is revealed in another incident. Mary Crawford expresses surprise at the difficulty of hiring a horse and cart to convey her harp from Northampton to Mansfield. Being unrooted in a community, she cannot see that horses and carts have their necessary function in the seasonal rhythms upon which the Mansfield community must depend (it is the time of the hay harvest), and that the London maxim "every thing is to be got with money" substitutes artificial and material for natural bonds. Again, in the discussion on Sotherton and improvement, Edmund counters Henry Crawford's radical suggestions with the remark "I would rather have an inferior degree of beauty of my own choice, and acquired progressively." Here change, as in Fanny's observations on the shrubbery, is viewed as developmental not radical, progressive not sudden.

What the Crawfords are being shown to lack, and Fanny to possess, are delicacy and seminal memory. Of these two qualities, delicacy, or sympathetically concerned interdependence between people, creates harmony on the personal level. Seminal memory further establishes that harmony, as in the case of Fanny's love for her brother William, and extends it to comprehend both the natural phenomena upon which communities depend, and the possessions which, by association, link past with present feeling into a unified whole. It is these qualities of delicacy and memory which anchor Fanny in the real world. Their absence from the Crawfords' experience unfixes both from necessary links with people, places, and phenomena and, consequently, from any community of felt experience. It is for this reason that, having but slender links with reality, they live by fictions.

But the Crawfords are not fiction-makers only, they are performers also, interpreters, that is to say, of those fictions by which they aim to manipulate reality into the form most appealing to their creative imaginations. In the parsonage shrubbery, Mary Crawford addresses Fanny who has suggested that Mansfield and its environs are perhaps too quiet for Mary. "'I should have thought so *theoretically* myself, but'—and her eyes brightened as she spoke—'take it all in all, I never spent so happy a summer.—But then'—with a more thoughtful air and lowered voice—'there is no saying what it may lead to'" (p. 210). Speech and gesture are here represented in the manner of stage dialogue, with gesture expressed as stage directions. These directions are emphasized by their placing, for when they occur they break, each time, a syntactic unit. This emphasis draws the reader's attention to them and thus to Mary Crawford's communication as an exercise in studied elegance, a means of enabling the speaker to fulfil an assumed role, in this case that of hopeful lover. A similar technique is used a little later with some utterances of

62

Henry Crawford. He is talking of Rushworth and Maria, and his aim is to impress Fanny.

> "Poor Rushworth and his two-and-forty speeches!" continued Crawford. "Nobody can ever forget them. Poor fellow!—I see him now;—his toil and his despair. Well, I am much mistaken if his lovely Maria will ever want him to make two-and-forty speeches to her"—adding, with a momentary seriousness, "She is too good for him—much too good." And then changing his tone again to one of gentle gallantry, and addressing Fanny, he said, "You were Mr. Rushworth's best friend."
>
> (p. 224)

Stage-directions are used again to suggest the staginess of the speaker, whose tonal gestures are shown to be successively manufactured with a view to creating conversational effects, rather than as a means of expressing genuine feeling.

The Crawfords are actors who invent and perform their own dramas as a substitute for the reality of which they have, ultimately owing to a faulty education,[4] been deprived. Jane Austen cleverly reduces the art they practice to triviality in a single episode in volume one, when Mary Crawford is ready to play on her harp to a receptive audience.

> A young woman, pretty, lively, with a harp as elegant as herself; and both placed near a window, cut down to the ground, and opening on a little lawn, surrounded by shrubs in the rich foliage of summer, was enough to catch any man's heart. The season, the scene, the air, were all favourable to tenderness and sentiment. Mrs Grant and her tambour frame were not without their use; it was all in harmony; and as every thing will turn to account when love is once set going, even the sandwich tray, and Dr Grant doing the honours of it, were worth looking at.
>
> (p. 65)

Such conscious patterning in such an emphatically homely context is delightfully absurd. In this comic little arrangement of people and setting, people are indistinguishable in function from place, for both are important only insofar as they contribute to the harmonious visual impact of the scene. Mary Crawford is, with rhetorical appropriateness, first deindividualized, becoming merely "a young woman," and then dehumanized, as elegant as—her harp. The entire description presents an epitome, which is at the same time a *reductio ad absurdum,* of the Crawford world view, in which people exist merely as objects to be disposed to the most agreeable, and convenient, advantage.

The Crawfords, then, are creative artists, actors, and producers. They are creative artists in that they invent the fictions by which, and in which, they choose to live; they are actors in that they exercise their skill in order to present these fictions persuasively, and they are producers in that they aim to regulate the reactions of others to conform with the roles they envisage for them in the Crawford drama. Thus, for Henry Crawford, people, like landscapes,

are assessed on the grounds of their capabilities. Of Fanny we learn that "he was no longer in doubt of the capabilities of her heart" (p. 235).

I have earlier observed how it is that Mary Crawford falsifies reality by manipulating language. Language too has "capabilities," and her use of it must be further considered, for there is more than one feature of her language use that exemplifies what is for her, as for her brother, the primacy of rendition over truth. First there is her use of the modal auxiliary *must.* This she uses, as an attributive intensifier, simultaneously to express prediction, obligation, and, often, logical necessity. Tom *must* be preferred to Edmund; it *must* be the case that almost everybody is taken in when they marry; she *must* "look down upon any thing contented with obscurity when it might rise to distinction." Here, as frequently elsewhere in Mary Crawford's speech, language is chosen and arranged so as to suggest the certain accuracy of the fictions she invents. Her style has other functions, all wittily inventive and falsifying. She may aim to give a comic elegance, and hence an appeal, to the morally unjustifiable. Alternatively she may invest the trivial with a spurious dignity. Two of her aphorisms, both of which have a marked Wildean quality, may be adduced as examples of the first category of linguistic creation. 1. "Selfishness must always be forgiven, you know, because there is no hope of a cure" (p. 68). 2. "I am very strong. Nothing ever fatigues me but doing what I do not like" (p. 68). In both these cases the inventive wit, and the appeal, reside in linguistic falsification. In the first, "selfishness" is given an additional selectional feature (+ disease), and in the second, "fatigue" is given two simultaneous features (+ physical and + boredom), which, in orthodox usage, it may possess only separately depending upon whether the term is used literally or figuratively. The wit lies, in other words, in skilled semantic trickery. It is this that, incidentally, seems to distinguish Mary Crawford's speech from that of Elizabeth Bennet in *Pride and Prejudice.*[5] Unlike Elizabeth, Mary Crawford consistently exploits the falsifying surface of language in order to communicate fictions which, through the choice and organization of the language in which they are presented, give appeal to untruth. But, in the case of Mary Crawford, Jane Austen ensures that although rhetoric aims at concealment within the action, it simultaneously highlights for the reader those truths it aims to hide. The conversation in the shrubbery between Mary and Fanny provides a case in point. Mary begins to elaborate upon the pleasures offered by country residence:

> "I am conscious of being far better reconciled to a country residence than I had ever expected to be. I can even suppose it pleasant to spend *half* the year in the country, under certain circumstances—very pleasant. An elegant, moderate-sized house in the centre of family connections—continual engagements among them—commanding the first society in the neighbourhood—looked-up to perhaps as leading it even more than those of larger fortune, and turning from the cheerful round of such amusements to nothing worse than a tete-a-tete with the person one feels most agreeable in the world."
>
> (p. 210)

In this case, the trivial is dignified by a syntactic arrangement of parallel post-modifying phrases and clauses, which magnifies triviality into dignity through the emphasis of repetition. At the same time the evident contrast between emphasis and moral meaning, form and content, highlights the shallow insignificance of the speaker's views. Edmund's appearance very soon afterwards is used in order to place Mary Crawford's views in negative contrast with Fanny's. To Mary, the name Edmund, signalling that its owner is a younger brother, is pitiful. For Fanny, it is Mr. Bertram that is "cold and nothing-meaning," and Edmund which has "nobleness," being "a name of heroism and renown—of king's, princes, and knights; and seems to breathe the spirit of chivalry and warm affections." The difference between the two young women is located in the kind and quality of association made by each. Fanny's words function in such a way as to draw attention to the large areas of emotional experience that Mary Crawford's judgment excludes. To judge people, as Mary Crawford does, by the standard of social position is, of course, to judge by form. Her language, like her judgments, is formally conceived with a view to appearance, not substance.

To the organic patterning of Fanny's emotional and moral life is contrasted patterning of a purely social and linguistic kind. The contrast may be seen as one between two opposed conceptions of art. In the one, that embodied in Fanny Price, order is created by the sympathetic imagination, controlled by moral principle, which responds to and thereby coheres the animate and inanimate world by which it is confronted and through which it lives. In the other, that embodied in the Crawfords, order is created by an imposition of the will upon reality. The world is, as it were, reshaped, and its real constituents ignored at the wishes of the "improver." Such an aesthetic cannot, and in the case of the Crawfords does not, take into account the emotional life of others, for to view experience with "sympathetic acuteness of feeling" would be to lay one's art of life open to modification by external and unpredictable forces. The creative will would no longer be free. The Crawford art of life is as unreal in the artificiality of its patterning as the invented world of Millamant, whose hair must be pinned up with love letters in verse, never with those in prose.[6] Like Millamant, the Crawfords invent their own alternative to reality, and similarly delightful in its outrageous patterning it often is. But such invention, appropriate though it is to comic art, is inappropriate to life, for comedy demands emotional distance and, with the Crawfords, emotional distance becomes emotional impoverishment, a debility far more crippling than Fanny's merely physical frailty.

The Crawfords' emotional impoverishment is a consequence and an expression of their lack of involvement with people and places, of their unwillingness to "fix" themselves. Their threat to Mansfield lies in their encouragement of these selfsame destructive forces, all of which are shown to exist at Mansfield already, before they arrive. Thus Tom, like Henry Crawford, is unfixed both in place and in his affections. Sir Thomas, after his return, perceives as we have already perceived, that Rushworth is "as ignorant in business as in books, with opinions in general unfixed, and without seeming much aware of it himself" (p. 200). Maria and Julia are likewise unfixed in moral principle and in emotional contact with their family. In consequence they follow the formal constraints and expectations their society imposes without being capable of giving felt consent to these constraints. Thus Julia, at precisely the permitted time in her life, "was quite ready to be fallen in love with" (p. 44). Mr. Rushworth "was from the first struck with the beauty of Miss Bertram, and being inclined to marry, soon fancied himself in love" (p. 38). To Maria, as to Rushworth, marriage is merely a proper step in life's pre-ordained ritual. "Being now in her twenty-first year, Maria Bertram was beginning to think matrimony a duty."

In these cases, formal expectation decrees that feeling be fabricated; there are no emotional realities, only ritual procedures. That this is so is shown to be in great part the fault of Sir Thomas who, man of principle though he be, is damagingly unable to move beyond form to feeling: "and would he only have smiled upon her and called her 'my dear Fanny' while he said it, every former frown or cold address might have been forgotten." His immediate reaction to Rushworth is also revealing. "There was nothing disagreeable in Mr. Rushworth's appearance, and Sir Thomas was liking him already." Even his newly awakened concern over Fanny, after his return from Antigua, seems to arise only from her improved physical looks. Sir Thomas unwittingly begins what the Crawfords deliberately continue when they provide those formal conditions, the theatricals, which function as the sanction for unprincipled conduct. Where forms, not felt principles, are the springs from which behavior arises, then morality becomes dependent upon formal conditions alone.

The Crawfords' preference for fiction-making and for linguistic patterning over enquiry and the search for truth is exemplified in Mrs. Norris, whose foolishness functions as an oblique evaluation of these qualities in the Crawfords. It is through language manipulation, though of a naive kind, that Mrs. Norris creates the world she clearly does not, in reality, inhabit. In Mrs. Norris's case, self-concern masquerades as concern for others. Linguistically, this contrast between role and reality is, typically, given simultaneous expression. Role is projected through hyperbole—*excessively, vast, every thing, prodigious, always* (pp. 53-54). These hyperbolic terms suggest the intense, though notional, activity to which Sotherton inspires Mrs. Norris. Reality is conveyed in the structure of her discourse. Its movement from Sotherton to Mrs. Norris in her parsonage reveals her egocentricity, and its lack of ordered cohesion her foolishness.

It is not, of course, that Jane Austen meant to persuade readers that a life lived according to forms is necessarily less than fully human. At Portsmouth we see a combination of formlessness and egotism that makes Fanny reflect with longing upon the formality of Mansfield life, where "there would have been a consideration of times and seasons, a regulation of subject, a propriety, an attention towards every body which there was not here" (p. 383). It is simply that formal regulations should be informed by conscious moral principle rooted in feeling. Without such moral principle, forms, so the action of *Mansfield Park* demonstrates, may become divorced from feeling, and function as the weapons of pretense and self-seeking in the armory of the emotionally and morally isolated self. Thus it is that the selfishness of the Crawfords, disastrous practically though its consequences are, is primarily significant as a contradiction of true, integrated selfhood. The self, without contact through sympathetic feeling with others, without those roots in place nurtured by memory through association, becomes an empty shell seeking substance through those forms, fictions, and invented patterns which, ironically, display its emptiness.

If this is so, then the Mansfield theatricals must be regarded as thematically central. The point is not that acting itself is morally wrong. Professional actors, whose performances may be considered "good hardened real acting" are in control. For the "hardened" actor the self is forgotten in the role but remains intact to be later resumed. But the Mansfield actors, encouraged by the Crawfords, conflate role and self, so that the role becomes the self. The theatricals are thus an exercise in deracination, cutting away those values which root the characters, morally and emotionally, in their community. In displacing their father's furniture they are devaluing associations, the formative importance of which is made clear in Fanny's reflections on her own possessions in the east room. In allowing her allotted role to give free rein to her desire for Henry Crawford, Maria is moving even further away than her misguided education has already placed her from the harmonious life in which social forms, moral principle, and feeling are conjoined. In compromising his moral principles by agreeing to act, Edmund is allowing appearances to supercede moral realities, as he has already begun to do as a result of his attraction to Mary Crawford. In allowing the desire for display to displace feeling for each other, to displace delicacy, in a word, the entire company is denying harmony. "Every body had a part either too long or too short—nobody would attend as they ought, nobody would remember on which side they were to come in— nobody but the complainer would observe any directions" (p. 165). This harmony, the denial of which the Crawfords exemplify and encourage, is presented throughout *Mansfield Park* as a harmony of nature, not of artifice. It is principle that is the harmonizing force, linking the self to other people, to places, and to possessions.

Much of the importance of the theatricals lies, then, in their figurative relationship to the novel as a whole. In theater, what is required is effective rendition, not personal sincerity or feeling; fiction not fact; role not reality; form or effect, not truth. The Crawfords bring to Mansfield a manner of personal living in which the self is lost in the role, and truth in fiction and rhetoric. The only major character undamaged by them is Fanny Price, and Fanny "cannot act."

Notes

All quotations from *Mansfield Park* are taken from the edition edited by R. W. Chapman (Oxford: Oxford Univ. Press, 1923).

1. Lionel Trilling, *The Opposing Self* (New York: Viking, 1955), pp. 207-30. Thomas R. Edwards, Jr., "The Difficult Beauty of *Mansfield Park;*" *NCF* [*Nineteenth–Century Fiction*] 20 (1965):51-67.

2. See *Pride and Prejudice,* ed. R. W. Chapman (London: Oxford Univ. Press, n.d.), p. 25.

3. See M. A. K. Halliday, "Types of Process" in his *System and Function in Language* (Oxford: Oxford Univ. Press, 1976), pp. 159-73. Halliday distinguishes three clause types, those of *action,* of *mental process* and of *relation.* The attributive clause is a clause of *relation* containing two terms joined usually by the verb *to be,* as in the clause, "*Goldsmith was vain.*" In this attributive clause, as in all attributive clauses, the relation between the two terms, here *Goldsmith* and *vain,* is one of class inclusion. The reactive clause is one of *mental process,* consisting, as in the clause, "Mary Crawford likes music," of *processor* (Mary Crawford), *phenomenon* (music), and a *verb of reaction* (likes).

4. The crucial importance of education as a means of handing down, and thus of maintaining, values whose existence is objective and divinely validated, is implied throughout A. M. Duckworth, *The Improvement of the Estate* (Baltimore: John Hopkins Univ. Press, 1971).

5. See Lionel Trilling, p. 213. Of Mary Crawford, Trilling observes, "Irony is her natural mode, and we are drawn to think of her voice as being as nearly the author's own as Elizabeth Bennet's is."

6. William Congreve, *The Way of the World,* II.ii.

Edward W. Said (essay date 1989)

SOURCE: "Jane Austen and Empire," in *Contemporary Marxist Literary Criticism,* edited by Francis Mulhern, Longman Group, 1992, pp. 97-113.

[*In the following essay originally published in 1989, Said evaluates* Mansfield Park *as a pre-imperialist text.*]

We are on solid ground with V. G. Kiernan when he says that 'empires must have a mould of ideas or conditioned reflexes to flow into, and youthful nations dream of a great place in the world as young men dream of fame and fortunes.'[1] It is, I believe, too simple and reductive a proposition to argue that everything in European and American culture is therefore a preparation for, or a consolidation of, the grand idea of empire that took over those societies during 'the age of empire' after 1870 but, conversely, it will not do to ignore those tendencies found in narrative, or in political theory, or in pictorial technique that enable, encourage, and otherwise assure the readiness of the West during the earlier parts of the nineteenth century to assume and enjoy the experience of empire. Similarly, we must note that if there was cultural resistance to the notion of an imperial mission there was not much support for such resistance in the main departments of cultural thought. Liberal though he was, John Stuart Mill—as a particularly telling case in point—could still say that 'the sacred duties which civilized nations owe to the independence and nationality of each other, are not binding towards those to whom nationality and independence are certain evil, or at best a questionable good.'[2]

Why that should be so, why sacred obligation on one front should not be binding on another, are questions best understood in the terms of a culture well grounded in a set of moral, economic and even metaphysical norms designed to approve a satisfying local, that is European, order in connection with the denial of the right to a similar order abroad. Perhaps such a statement appears preposterous, or extreme. In fact, I think, it formulates the connection between a certain kind of European well-being and cultural identity on the one hand, and, on the other, the subjugation of imperial realms overseas in too fastidious and circumspect a fashion. Part of the difficulty today in accepting any sort of connection at all is that we tend to collapse the whole complicated matter into an unacceptably simple causal relationship, which in turn produces a rhetoric of blame and consequent defensiveness. But I am *not* saying that the major thing about early nineteenth century European culture was that it *caused* late nineteenth century imperialism, and I am not therefore implying that all the problems of the contemporary non-European, formerly colonial, world should be blamed on Europe. I am saying, however, that European culture often, if not always, characterized itself in such a way as simultaneously to validate its own preferences while also advocating those preferences in conjunction with distant imperial rule. Mill certainly did: he always recommended that India not be given independence. When for a variety of reasons imperial rule occupied Europe with much greater intensity after 1880, this schizophrenic practice became a useful habit.

The first thing to be done now is more or less to jettison the simple causal mode of thinking through the relationship between Europe and the non-European world. This also requires some lessening of the hold on our thought of the equally simple sequence of temporal consecutiveness. We must not admit any notion, for instance, of the sort that proposes to show that Wordsworth, Jane Austen and Hazlitt because they wrote before 1857 actually caused the establishment of formal British government rule over India. What we should try to discern instead is a counterpoint between overt patterns in British writing about Britain and representation of what exists in the world beyond the British Isles. The inherent mode for this counterpoint therefore is not temporal, but spatial. How do writers in the period before the great age of explicit and programmatic colonial expansion in the late nineteenth century—

the scramble for Africa say—situate and see themselves and their work in the larger world? We will find some striking but careful strategies employed, most of them deriving from expected sources—the positive ideas of home, of a nation and its language, of proper order, good behaviour, moral values.

But positive ideas of this sort do more than validate 'our' world. They also tend to devalue other worlds and, perhaps more significantly from a retrospective point of view, they do not prevent or inhibit or provide a resistance to horrendously unattractive imperialist practices. No, we are right to say that cultural forms like the novel or the opera do not cause people to go out and imperialize; perhaps Carlyle did not drive Rhodes directly, and he certainly cannot be 'blamed' for the problems of today's South Africa. But the genuinely troubling issue is how little the great humanistic ideas, institutions, and monuments, which we still celebrate as having the power ahistorically to command our approving attention, how little they stand in the way of an accelerating imperial process during the nineteenth century. Are we not entitled to ask therefore how this body of humanistic ideas coexisted so comfortably with imperialism, and why until the resistance to imperialism *in the imperial domain,* among Africans, Asians, Latin Americans, developed, there was little significant opposition or deterrence to empire at home? May we suspect that what had been the customary way of distinguishing 'our' home and order from 'theirs' grew into a harsh political rule for accumulating more of 'them' to rule, study and subordinate? Do we not have in the great humane ideas and values promulgated by mainstream European culture precisely that 'mould of ideas and conditioned reflexes' of which V. G. Kiernan speaks, into which the whole business of empire would later flow?

The extent to which these ideas are actually invested in distinctions between real places has been the subject of Raymond Williams's richest book, *The Country and the City.* His argument concerning the interplay between the rural and the urban in England admits of the most extraordinary transformations, from the pastoral populism of Langland, through Ben Jonson's country-house poems, the picture of Dickens's London, right up to visions of the metropolis in twentieth-century literature. And while he does tackle the export of England into the colonies Williams does so, in my opinion, less centrally, less expansively than the practice actually warrants. Near the end of *The Country and the City,* Williams suggests that 'from at least the mid-nineteenth century, and with important instances earlier, there was this large context [the relationship between England and the colonies, and its effects on the English imagination which, Williams correctly says, 'have gone deeper than can easily be traced'] within which every idea and every image was consciously and unconsciously affected.' He goes on quickly to list 'the idea of emigration to the colonies' as one such image prevailing in various novels by Dickens, the Brontës, Gaskell, and he quite rightly shows that 'new rural societies', all of them colonial, enter the imaginative metropolitan economy of

English literature via Kipling, early Orwell, Somerset Maugham. After 1880 there comes a 'dramatic extension of landscape and social relations': this corresponds more or less exactly with the great age of empire.[3]

It is dangerous to disagree with Williams. Yet I would venture to say that if one began to look for something like an imperial map of the world in English literature it would turn up with amazing centrality and frequency well before the middle of the nineteenth century. And not only turn up with an inert regularity that might suggest something taken for granted, but—much more interestingly—threaded through, forming a vital part of the texture of linguistic and cultural practice. For there were established English interests in America, the Caribbean and Asia from the seventeenth century on, and even a quick inventory will reveal poets, philosophers, historians, dramatists, novelists, travel writers, chroniclers, and fabulists for whom these interests were to be traced, cared for, prized, and regarded with a continuing concern. A similar argument could be made for France, Spain and Portugal, not only as overseas powers in their own right, but as competitors with the British. How then can we examine these interests at work in England *before* the age of empire that officially occurred during the last third of the nineteenth century?

We would do well to follow Williams's lead, and look at that period of crisis following upon wide-scale land enclosure at the end of the eighteenth century. Not only are old organic communities dissolved, and new ones forged under the impulse of parliamentary activity, industrialization, and demographic dislocation, but, I would suggest, there occurs a new process of relocating England (and in France, France) within a much larger circle of the world map. During the first half of the eighteenth century, Anglo-French competition in India was intense; in the second half there were numerous violent encounters between them in the Levant, the Caribbean and of course in Europe itself. Much of what we read today as major pre-Romantic literature in France and England contains a constant stream of references to the overseas dominions: one thinks not only of various encyclopaedists, the Abbé Reynal, de Brosses, and Volney, but also of Edmund Burke, Beckford, Gibbon, and William Jones.

In 1902 J. A. Hobson described imperialism as the expansion of nationality, implying that the process was understandable mainly by considering *expansion* to be the more important of the two terms, since 'nationality' was a fixed quantity.[4] For Hobson's purposes nationality was in fact fully formed, whereas a century before it was in the process of *being formed,* not only at home, but abroad as well. Between France and Britain in the late eighteenth century there were two contests: the battle for strategic gains in such places as India, the Nile delta and the Caribbean islands, and the battle for a triumphant nationality. Both battles place 'Englishness' in contrast with 'the French', and no matter how intimate and closeted such factors as the supposed English or French 'essence' appear to be, they were almost always thought of as being (as op-

posed to already) made, and being fought out with the other great competitor. Thackeray's Becky Sharp, for example, is as much an upstart as she is because of her half-French heritage. Earlier, the upright abolitionist posture of Wilberforce and his allies developed partly out of a desire to make life harder for French hegemony in the Antilles.[5]

These considerations, I think, suddenly provide a fascinatingly expanded dimension to *Mansfield Park,* by common acknowledgement the most explicit in its ideological and moral affirmation of all Austen's novels. Williams once again is in general dead right: Austen's novels all express an 'attainable quality of life', in money and property acquired, moral discriminations made, the right choices put in place, the correct 'improvement' implemented, the finely nuanced language affirmed and classified. Yet, Williams continues,

> What [Cobbett] names, riding past on the road, are classes. Jane Austen, from inside the houses, can never see that, for all the intricacy of her social description. All her discrimination is, understandably, internal and exclusive. She is concerned with the conduct of people who, in the complications of improvement, are repeatedly trying to make themselves into a class. But where only one class is seen, no classes are seen.[6]

As a general description of how by the effect of her novels Austen manages to elevate certain 'moral discriminations' into 'an independent value', this is excellent. Where *Mansfield Park* is concerned, however, a good deal more needs to be said and in what follows I should like to be understood as providing greater explicitness and width to Williams's fundamentally correct survey. Perhaps then Austen, and indeed, pre-imperialist novels generally, will appear to be more implicated in the rationale for imperialist expansion than at first sight they have been.

After Lukács and Proust, we have become so accustomed to regarding the novel's plot and structure as constituted mainly by temporality that we have overlooked the fundamental role of space, geography and location. For it is not only Joyce's very young Stephen Dedalus who sees himself in a widening spiral at home, in Ireland, in the world, but every other young protagonist before him as well. Indeed we can say without exaggeration that *Mansfield Park* is very precisely about a whole series of both small and large dislocations in space that must occur before, at the end of the novel, Fanny Price, the niece, becomes the mistress of Mansfield Park. And that place itself is precisely located by Austen at the centre of an arc of interests and concerns, spanning the hemisphere, two major seas, and four continents.

As in all of Austen's novels, the central group that finally emerges with marriage and property 'ordained' is not based principally upon blood. What her novel enacts is the disaffiliation (in the literal sense) of some members of a family, and the affiliation between others and one or two chosen and tested outsiders: in other words, blood relationships are not enough for the responsibilities of continuity, hierarchy, authority. Thus Fanny Price—the poor niece, the orphaned child from the outlying port city of Portsmouth, the neglected, demure and upright wallflower—gradually acquires a status commensurate with, and even superior to, her more fortunate relatives. In this pattern of affiliation and of assumption of authority, Fanny Price is relatively passive. She resists the misdemeanours and the importunings of others, and very occasionally she ventures actions on her own: all in all, though, one has the impression that Austen has designs for her that Fanny herself can scarcely comprehend, just as throughout the novel Fanny is thought of by everyone as 'comfort' and 'acquisition' despite herself. Thus, like Kim O'Hara, Fanny is both device and instrument in a larger pattern, as well as novelistic character.

Fanny, like Kim, requires direction, requires the patronage and outside authority that her own impoverished experience cannot provide. Her conscious connections are to some people and to some places, but as the novel reveals there are *other* connections of which she has faint glimmerings that nevertheless demand her presence and service. What she comes into is a novel that has opened with an intricate set of moves all of which taken together demand sorting-out, adjustment and rearrangement. Sir Thomas Bertram has been captivated by one Ward sister, the others have not done well, and so 'an absolute breach' opens up; their 'circles were so distinct', the distances between them were so great that they have been out of touch for eleven years (*MP,* p. 42);[7] fallen on hard times, the Prices seek out the Bertrams. Gradually, and even though she is not the eldest, Fanny becomes the new focus of attention as she is sent to Mansfield Park, there to begin her new life. Similarly, the Bertrams have given up London (the result of Lady Bertram's 'little ill health and a great deal of indolence') and come to reside entirely in the country.

What sustains this life materially is the Bertram estate in Antigua, which is not doing well. Austen takes considerable pains to show us two apparently disparate but actually convergent processes; the growth of Fanny's importance to the Bertrams' economy, including Antigua, and Fanny's own steadfastness in the face of numerous challenges, threats and surprises. In both processes, however, Austen's imagination works with a steel-like rigour through a mode that we might call geographical and spatial clarification. Fanny's ignorance, when as a frightened ten-year-old she arrives at Mansfield, is signified by her inability to 'put the map of Europe together' (*MP,* p. 54), and for much of the first half of the novel the action is concerned with a whole range of things whose common denominator, misused or misunderstood, is space. Not only is Sir Thomas in Antigua to make things better there and at home, but at Mansfield Park Fanny, Edmund, and her Aunt Norris negotiate where she is to live, read and work, where fires are to be lit, the friends and cousins concern themselves with the improvement of the estates, and the importance of chapels (of religious authority) to domesticity is debated and envisioned. When, as a device for stirring things up, the Crawfords (the tinge of France

that hangs over their background is significant) suggest a play, Fanny's discomfiture is polarizingly acute. She cannot participate, although with all its confusion of roles and purposes, the play, Kotzebue's *Lovers' Vows,* is prepared for anyway.

We are to surmise, I think, that while Sir Thomas is away tending his colonial garden, a number of inevitable mismeasurements (associated explicitly with feminine 'lawlessness') will occur. Not only are these apparent in innocent strolls through a park, in which people lose and catch sight of each other unexpectedly, but most clearly in the various flirtations and engagements between the young men and women left without true parental authority, Lady Bertram being too indifferent, Mrs Norris unsuitable. There is sparring, there is innuendo, there is a perilous taking on of roles: all of this of course is crystallized in preparations for the play, in which something dangerously close to libertinage is about to be (but never is) enacted. Fanny, whose earlier sense of alienation, distance and fear all derive from her first uprooting, has now assumed a sort of surrogate consciousness of what is right and how far is too much. Yet she has no power to implement her uneasy awareness, and until Sir Thomas suddenly returns from 'abroad' the rudderless drift continues.

When he does appear, preparations for the play are immediately stopped, and in a passage remarkable for its executive dispatch, Austen narrates the reestablishment of Sir Thomas's local rule:

> It was a busy morning with him. Conversation with any of them occupied but a small part of it. He had to reinstate himself in all the wonted concerns of his Mansfield life, to see his steward and his bailiff—to examine and compute—and, in the intervals of business, to walk into his stables and his gardens, and nearest plantations; but active and methodical, he had not only done all this before he resumed his seat as master of the house at dinner, he had also set the carpenter to work in pulling down what had been so lately put up in the billiard room, and given the scene painter his dismissal, long enough to justify the pleasing belief of his being then at least as far off as Northampton. The scene painter was gone, having spoilt only the floor of one room, ruined all the coachman's sponges, and made five of the underservants idle and dissatisfied; and Sir Thomas was in hopes that another day or two would suffice to wipe away every outward memento of what had been, even to the destruction of every unbound copy of 'Lovers' Vows' in the house, for he was burning all that met his eye.
>
> (*MP,* p. 206)

The force of this paragraph is unmistakable. This is not only a Crusoe setting things in order: it is also an early Protestant eliminating all traces of frivolous behaviour. There is nothing, however, in *Mansfield Park* that would contradict us were we to assume that Sir Thomas does exactly the same things—on a larger scale—in Antigua. Whatever was wrong there, and the internal evidence garnered by Warren Roberts suggests that economic depression, slavery, and competition with France were at issue[8]—Sir Thomas was able to fix, thereby maintaining his control over his colonial domain. Thus more clearly than anywhere else in her fiction Austen synchronizes domestic with international authority, making it plain that the values associated with such higher things as ordination, law and propriety must be grounded firmly in actual rule over and possession of territory. What she sees more clearly than most of her readers is that to hold and rule Mansfield Park is to hold and rule an imperial estate in association with it. What assures the one, in its domestic tranquillity and attractive harmony, is the prosperity and discipline of the other.

Before both can be fully secured, however, Fanny must become more actively involved. For this, I believe, Austen designed the second part of the book, which contains not only the failure of the Edmund-Mary Crawford romance as well as the disgraceful profligacy of Lydia and Henry Crawford, but Fanny Price's rediscovery and rejection of her Portsmouth home, the injury and incapacitation of Tom (the eldest) Bertram, the launching of William Price's naval career. This entire ensemble of relationships and events is finally capped with Edmund's marriage to Fanny, whose place in Lady Bertram's household is taken by Susan Price, her sister. I do not think it is an exaggeration to interpret the concluding sections of *Mansfield Park* as the coronation of an arguably *unnatural* (or at the very least, illogical) principle at the heart of a desired English order. The audacity of Austen's vision is disguised a little by her voice, which despite its occasional archness is understated and notably modest. But we should not misconstrue the limited references to the outside world, her lightly stressed allusions to work, process and class, her apparent ability to abstract (in Raymond Williams's phrase) 'an everyday uncompromising morality which is in the end separable from its social basis'. For in fact Austen is far less diffident, far more severe than that.

The clues are to be found in Fanny, or rather in how rigorously we wish to consider Fanny. True, her visit home upsets the aesthetic and emotional balance she had become accustomed to at Mansfield Park, and true, she had begun to take for granted the wonderful luxuries there as something she cannot live without. These things, in other words, are fairly routine and natural consequences of getting used to a new place. But Austen is talking about two other matters we must not mistake. One is Fanny's newly enlarged sense of what it means to be at home; this is not merely a matter of expanded space.

> Fanny was almost stunned. The smallness of the house, and thinness of the walls, brought every thing so close to her, that, added to the fatigue of her journey, and all her recent agitation, she hardly knew how to bear it. *Within* the room all was tranquil enough, for Susan having disappeared with the others, there were soon only her father and herself remaining; and he taking out a newspaper—the customary loan of a neighbour, applied himself to studying it, without seeming to recollect her existence. The solitary candle was held between himself and the paper, without any reference to her possible convenience; but she had nothing to do, and was glad to have the light screened from her aching head, as she sat in bewildered, broken, sorrowful contemplation.
>
> She was at home. But alas! it was not such a home, she had not such a welcome, as—she checked herself; she was unreasonable . . . A day or two might shew the difference. *She* only was to blame. Yet she thought it would not have been so at Mansfield. No, in her uncle's house there would have been a consideration of times and seasons, a regulation of subject, a propriety, an attention towards every body which there was not here.

(*MP,* pp. 375-6)

In too small a space you cannot see clearly, you cannot think clearly, you cannot have regulation or attention of the proper sort. The fineness of Austen's detail ('the solitary candle was held between himself and the paper, without any reference to her possible convenience') renders very precisely the dangers of unsociability, of lonely insularity, of diminished awareness that are rectified in larger and better administered spaces.

That such spaces are not available by direct descent, by legal title, by propinquity, contiguity or adjacence (Mansfield Park and Portsmouth are after all separated by many hours' journey) is precisely Austen's point. To earn the right to Mansfield Park you must first leave home as a kind of indentured servant, or to put the case in extreme terms, as a kind of transported commodity; this clearly is the fate of Fanny and William, but it also contains the promise for them of future wealth. I think Austen saw what Fanny does as a domestic or small-scale movement in space that corresponds to the longer, more openly colonial movements of Sir Thomas, her mentor, the man whose estate she inherits. The two movements depend on each other.

The second matter about which Austen speaks, albeit indirectly, is a little more complex, and raises an interesting theoretical issue. To speak about Austen's awareness of empire is obviously to speak about something very different, very much more alluded to almost casually, than Conrad's or Kipling's awareness of empire. Nevertheless, we must concede that Antigua and Sir Thomas's trip there play a definitive role in *Mansfield Park,* a role which, I have been saying, is both incidental, because referred to only in passing, and absolutely important, because although taken for granted it is crucial to the action in many ways. How then are we to assess the few references to Antigua, and as exactly as possible what are we to make of them interpretively?

My contention is that Austen genuinely presages Kipling and Conrad, and that far from being a novelist only dedicated to the portrayal and elucidation of domestic manners, Austen by that very odd combination of casualness and stress reveals herself to be *assuming* (just as Fanny assumes, in both senses of the word) the importance of empire to the situation at home. Let me go further. Since

Austen refers to and uses Antigua as she does in *Mansfield Park,* there needs to be a commensurate effort on the part of her readers to understand concretely the historical valences in the reference. To put it differently, we should try to understand *what* she referred to, why she gave it the role she did, and why, in a certain sense, she did not avoid the choice, keeping in mind that she might *not* have made use of Antigua. Let us now proceed to calibrate the signifying power of the references to Antigua in *Mansfield Park*; how do *they* occupy the place they do, what are they doing there?

According to Austen, no matter how isolated and insulated the English *place* is (e.g. Mansfield Park), it requires overseas sustenance. Sir Thomas's property in the Caribbean would have had to be a sugar plantation maintained by slave labour (not abolished until the 1830s): these are not dead historical facts but, as Austen certainly knew, the results of evident historical processes. Before the Anglo-French competition to which I referred earlier, there is for Britain the major distinguishing characteristic between its empire and all earlier ones (the Spanish and Portuguese principally, but also the Roman). That was that earlier empires were bent, as Conrad puts it, on loot, the transport of treasure from the colonies to Europe, with very little attention to development, organization, system; Britain and, to a lesser degree, France were deeply concerned with how to make the empire a long-term profitable and, above all, an on-going concern. In this enterprise the two countries competed, nowhere with more observable results than in the slave colonies of the Caribbean, where the transport of slaves, the functioning of large sugar plantations dedicated exclusively to sugar production, the whole question of sugar markets which raised problems of protectionism, monopolies, and price: all these were more or less constantly, competitively at issue.

Far from being something 'out there', British colonial possessions in the Antilles and Leeward Islands were during the last years of the eighteenth century and the first third of the nineteenth a crucial setting for Anglo-French colonial competition. Not only was the export of revolutionary ideas from France there to be registered, but there was a steady decline in British Caribbean profits: the French sugar plantations were producing more sugar at less cost. By the end of the century, however, the slave rebellions generated in and out of Haiti were incapacitating France and spurring British interests to more intervention, and greater power locally. Yet compared with their prominence for the home market during the eighteenth century, the British Caribbean sugar plantations of the nineteenth century were more vulnerable to such countervailing forces as the discovery of alternative sugar supplies in Brazil and Mauritius, the emergence of a European beet-sugar industry, and the gradual dominance of free trade (as opposed to monopolistic) ideology and practice.

In *Mansfield Park*—and I speak here both of its formal characteristics as well as its contents—a number of all these currents converge. The most important of course is

the complete subordination of colony to metropolis. Sir Thomas is absent from Mansfield Park, and is never seen as *present* in Antigua, which requires at most a half dozen references in the novel, all of them granting the island the merest token importance to what takes place in England. There is a passage from John Stuart Mill's *Principles of Political Economy* which catches the spirit of Austen's use of Antigua:

> These are hardly to be looked upon as countries, carrying on an exchange of commodities with other countries, but more properly as outlying agricultural or manufacturing estates belonging to a larger community. Our West Indian colonies, for example, cannot be regarded as countries with a productive capital of their own . . . [but are, rather,] the place where England finds it convenient to carry on the production of sugar, coffee and a few other tropical commodities. All the capital employed is English capital; almost all the industry is carried on for English uses; there is little production of anything except for staple commodities, and these are sent to England, not to be exchanged for things exported to the colony and consumed by its inhabitants, but to be sold in England for the benefit of the proprietors there. The trade with the West Indies is hardly to be considered an external trade, but more resembles the traffic between town and country.[9]

To some extent Antigua is like London or Portsmouth, a less desirable urban setting than the country estate at Mansfield Park. Unlike them, however, it is a place producing goods, sugar, to be consumed by all people (by the early nineteenth century every Britisher used sugar), although owned and maintained by a small group of aristocrats and gentry. The Bertrams and the other characters in *Mansfield Park* constitute one sub-group within the minority, and for them the island is wealth, which Austen regards as being converted to propriety, order, and at the end of the novel, comfort, an added good. But why 'added'? Because Austen tells us pointedly in the final chapters, she wants to 'restore every body, not greatly in fault themselves, to tolerable comfort, and to have done with all the rest' (*MP*, p. 446).

This can be interpreted to mean, first, that the novel has done enough in the way of destabilizing the lives of 'everybody', and must now set them at rest: actually Austen does say this explicitly as a bit of metafictional impatience. Second, it can mean what Austen implicitly suggests, that everybody may now be finally permitted to realize what it means to be properly at home, and at rest, without the need to wander about or to come and go. Certainly this does not include young William, who, we are right to assume, will continue to roam the seas in the British navy on whatever missions, commercial and political, may still be required. Such matters draw from Austen only a last brief gesture (a passing remark about William's 'continuing good conduct and rising fame'). As for those finally resident in Mansfield Park itself, more in the way of domesticated advantages is given to these now fully acclimatized souls, and to none more than to Sir Thomas. He understands for the first time what has been missing in his education of his children, and he understands it in the terms paradoxically provided for him by unnamed outside forces so to speak, the wealth of Antigua and the imported example of Fanny Price. Note here how the curious alternation of outside and inside follows the pattern identified by Mill of the outside *becoming* the inside by use and to use Austen's word, 'disposition':

> Here [in his deficiency of training, of allowing Mrs Norris too great a role, of letting his children dissemble and repress feeling] had been grievous mismanagement; but, bad as it was, he gradually grew to feel that it had not been the most direful mistake in his plan of education. Some thing must have been wanting *within,* or time would have worn away much of its ill effect. He feared that principle, active principle, had been wanting, that they had never been properly taught to govern their inclinations and tempers, by that sense of duty which can alone suffice. They had been instructed theoretically in their religion, but never required to bring it into daily practice; to be distinguished for elegance and accomplishments—the authorized object of their youth—could have had no useful influence that way, no moral effect on the mind. He had meant them to be good, but his cares had been directed to the understanding and manners, not the disposition; and of the necessity of self-denial and humility, he feared they had never heard from any lips that could profit them.
>
> (*MP*, p. 448)

What was wanting *within* was in fact supplied by the wealth derived from a West Indian plantation and a poor provincial relative, both brought in to Mansfield Park and set to work. Yet on their own, neither the one nor the other could have sufficed; they require each other and then, more important, they need executive disposition, which in turn helps to reform the rest of the Bertram circle. All of this Austen leaves to her reader to supply in the way of literal explicitation.

And that is what reading her necessarily entails. But all these things having to do with the outside brought in, seem to me unmistakably *there* in the suggestiveness of her allusive and abstract language. A 'principle wanting within' is, I believe, intended to evoke for us memories of Sir Thomas's absences in Antigua, or the sentimental and near-whimsical vagary on the part of the three variously deficient Ward sisters by which a niece is displaced from one household to another. But that the Bertrams did become better if not altogether good, that some sense of duty was imparted to them, that they learned to govern their inclinations and tempers, and brought religion into daily practice, directed disposition: all of this did occur because outside (or rather outlying) factors were lodged properly inward, became native to Mansfield Park, Fanny, the niece, its final spiritual mistress, Edmund, the second son, its master.

An additional benefit is that Mrs Norris is dislodged from the place: this is described as 'the great supplementary comfort of Sir Thomas's life' (*MP*, p. 450). For once the principles have been interiorized, the comforts follow:

Fanny is settled for the time being at Thornton Lacey 'with every attention to her comfort'; her home later becomes 'the home of affection and comfort'; Susan is brought in 'first as a comfort to Fanny, then as an auxiliary, and at last as her substitute' (*MP*, p. 456), when the new import takes Fanny's place by Lady Bertram's side. Clearly the pattern established at the outset of the novel continues, only now it has what the novel has intended to give it all along, an internalized and retrospectively guaranteed rationale. This is the rationale that Raymond Williams describes as 'an everyday, uncompromising morality which is in the end separable from its social basis and which, in other hands, can be turned against it.'

I have tried to show that the morality in fact is not separable from its social basis, because right up to the last sentence of the novel Austen is always affirming and repeating a geographical process involving trade, production, and consumption that pre-dates, underlies, and guarantees the morality. Most critics have tended to forget or overlook that process, which has seemed less important to the morality than in devising her novel Austen herself seemed to think it was. But interpreting Jane Austen depends on *who* does the interpreting, *when* it is done, and no less important, from *where* it is done. If with feminists, with great Marxist critics sensitive to history and class like Williams, with historical and stylistic critics, we have been sensitized to the issues their interests raise, we should now proceed to regard geography—which is after all of significance to *Mansfield Park*—as not a neutral fact (any more than class and gender are neutral facts) but as a politically charged one too, a fact beseeching the considerable attention and elucidation its massive proportions require. The question is thus not only how to understand and with what to connect Austen's morality and its social basis, but *what* to read of it.

Take the casual references to Antigua, the ease with which Sir Thomas's needs in England are met by a Caribbean sojourn, the uninflected, unreflective citations of Antigua (or the Mediterranean, or India, which is where Lady Bertram in a fit of distracted impatience requires that William should go 'that I may have a shawl. I think I will have two shawls'—*MP*, p. 308). They stand for something significant 'out there' that frames the genuinely important action *here,* but not for something too significant. Yet these signs of 'abroad' include, even as they repress, a complex and rich history, which has since achieved a status that the Bertrams, the Prices and Austen herself would not, could not recognize. To call this status 'the Third World' begins to deal with its realities, but it by no means exhausts its history with regard to politics or cultural activities.

There are first some prefigurations of a later English history as registered in fiction to be taken stock of. The Bertram's usable colony in *Mansfield Park* can be read proleptically as resulting in Charles Gould's San Tome mine in *Nostromo,* or as the Wilcoxes' Anglo-Imperial Rubber Company in Forster's *Howards End,* or indeed as any of these distant but convenient treasure spots in *Great Expec-*

tations, or in Jean Rhys's *Wide Sargasso Sea,* or *Heart of Darkness,* resources to be visited, talked about, described or appreciated—for domestic reasons, for local metropolitan benefits. Thus Sir Thomas's Antigua already acquires a slightly greater density than the discrete, almost reticent appearances it makes in the pages of *Mansfield Park.* And already our reading of the novel begins to distend and open up at those points where ironically Austen was most economical and her critics most (dare one say it?) negligent. Her 'Antigua' is therefore not just a slight but definite way of marking the outer limits of what Williams calls domestic improvements, or as a quick allusion to the mercantile venturesomeness of acquiring overseas dominions as a source for local fortunes, or one reference among many attesting to a historical sensibility suffused not just with manners and curtsies but with contests of ideas, struggles with Napoleonic France, awareness of seismic economic and social change. Not just those things, but also strikingly early anticipation of the official age of Empire, which Kipling, Conrad and all the others will realize a full three-quarters of a century later.

Second, we must see 'Antigua' as a reference for Austen held in its precise place in her moral geography, and in her prose, by a series of historical changes that her novel rides like a vessel sitting on a mighty sea. The Bertrams could not have been possible without the slave trade, sugar, and the colonial planter class; as a social type Sir Thomas would have been familiar to eighteenth- and early nineteenth-century readers who knew the powerful influence of the class in domestic British politics, in plays (like Cumberland's *The West Indian*), and in numerous other public ways. As the old system of protected monopoly gradually disappeared, and as a new class of settler-planter displaced the old absentee system, the West Indian interest lost its dominance: cotton manufacture, open trade, abolition reduced the power and prestige of people like the Bertrams whose frequency of sojourn in the Caribbean decreased appreciably.

Thus in *Mansfield Park* Sir Thomas's infrequent trips to Antigua as an absentee plantation-owner *precisely* reflect the diminishment of his class's power, a reduction immediately, directly conveyed in the title of Lowell Ragatz's classic *The Fall of the Planter Class in the British Caribbean, 1763-1833* (published in 1928). But we must go further and ask whether what is hidden or allusive in Austen—the reasons for Sir Thomas's rare voyages—are made sufficiently explicit in Ragatz? Does the aesthetic silence or discretion of a great novel in 1814 receive adequate explication in a major work of historical research written a full century later? If so, can we assume that the process of interpretation is thereby fulfilled, or must we go on to reason that it will continue as newer material comes to light?

Consider that for all his learning Ragatz still finds it in himself to speak of 'the Negro race' as having the following characteristics: 'he stole, he lied, he was simple, suspicious, inefficient, irresponsible, lazy, superstitious, and loose in his sexual relations.'[10] Such 'history' as this therefore gave way (as Austen gave way to Ragatz) to the revisionary work of Caribbean historians like Eric Williams and C. L. R. James, works in which slavery and empire are seen directly to have fostered the rise and consolidation of *capitalism* well beyond the old plantation monopolies, as well as a powerful ideological system whose original connection to actual economic interests may have passed, but whose effects continued for decades.

> The political and moral ideas of the age are to be examined in the very closest relation to the economic development . . . An outworn interest, whose bankruptcy smells to heaven in historical perspective, can exercise an obstructionist and disruptive effect which can only be explained by the powerful services it had preciously rendered and the entrenchment previously gained . . . The ideas built on these interests continue long after the interests have been destroyed and work their old mischief, which is all the more mischievous because the interests to which they correspond no longer exist.[11]

Thus Eric Williams in *Capitalism and Slavery* (1961). The question of interpretation, and indeed of writing itself, is tied to the question of interests, which we have seen are at work in aesthetic as well as historical work, then and now. We cannot easily say that since *Mansfield Park* is a novel, its affiliations with a particularly sordid history are irrelevant or transcended, not only because it is irresponsible to say that, but because we know too much to say so without bad faith. Having read *Mansfield Park* as part of the structure of an expanding imperialist venture, it would be difficult simply to restore it to the canon of 'great literary masterpieces'—to which it most certainly belongs—and leave it at that. Rather, I think, the novel points the way to Conrad, and to theorists of empire like Froude and Seeley, and in the process opens up a broad expanse of domestic imperialist culture without which the subsequent acquisition of territory would not have been possible.

Notes

1. V. G. Kiernan, *Marxism and Imperialism* (London: Edward Arnold, 1974), p. 100.

2. J. S. Mill, *Disquisitions and Discussions,* vol. III (London: Longmans Green, Reader & Dyer, 1875), pp. 167-8.

3. Raymond Williams, *The Country and the City* (London: Chatto and Windus, 1973), p. 281.

4. J. A. Hobson, *Imperialism* (1902; repr. Ann Arbor, U Michigan Press, 1972), p. 6.

5. This is most memorably discussed in C. L. R. James, *The Black Jacobins: Toussaint L'Ouverture and the San Domingo Revolution* (1938; repr. New York, 1963; London: Allison and Busby, 1980), especially ch. II, 'The Owners'.

6. Williams, *The Country and the City,* p. 117.

7. Jane Austen, *Mansfield Park,* ed. Tony Tanner (1814; repr. Harmondsworth: Penguin, 1966). All references to this edition of the novel are indicated parenthetically after the citation as *MP.* The best account of the

novel is in Tony Tanner's *Jane Austen* (Cambridge, Mass. and London: Macmillan, 1986).

8. Warren Roberts, *Jane Austen and the French Revolution* (London: Macmillan, 1979), pp. 97-8. See also Avrom Fleishman, *A Reading of Mansfield Park: An Essay in Critical Synthesis* (Minneapolis: U Minnesota Press, 1967), pp. 36-9, and *passim.*

9. J. S. Mill, *Principles of Political Economy,* vol. III, ed. J. M. Robson (Toronto: U Toronto Press, 1965), p. 693. The passage is quoted in Sidney W. Mintz, *Sweetness and Power: The Place of Sugar in Modern History* (New York: Sifton, 1985), p. 42.

10. Lowell Joseph Ragatz, *The Fall of the Planter Class in the British Caribbean, 1763-1833; A Study in Social and Economic History* (1928; repr. New York: Octagon, 1963), p. 27.

11. Eric Williams, *Capitalism and Slavery* (New York, 1961), p. 211.

Pam Perkins (essay date 1993)

SOURCE: "A Subdued Gaiety: The Comedy of *Mansfield Park,*" in *Nineteenth-Century Literature,* Vol. 48, No. 1, June, 1993, pp. 1-25.

[*In the following essay, Perkins examines* Mansfield Park *for its juxtaposition of two traditions of literary comedy—the sentimental humor of feminine development and Restoration wit.*]

At the beginning of *Shirley,* Charlotte Brontë warns readers fresh from the Gothic thrills of *Jane Eyre* not to expect anything like her earlier work. What they are about to read, she informs them, is mere lenten fare, "something unromantic as Monday morning." Aggrieved Jane Austen fans, finding *Mansfield Park* rather heavy going after the "light, bright, and sparkling" *Pride and Prejudice,* might think that Austen would have been well-advised to include a similar disclaimer in her subdued follow-up to a popular success. Numerous hostile readers have caricatured the book as a rather dour morality tale about dull people, the ugly duckling of the Austen canon. The darkest, most sombre of the six mature works, it has prompted vociferous and sometimes acrimonious critical debate, with opinions about it ranging from open dislike to respectful admiration.[1] While the novel has undergone a considerable shift in reputation since the beginning of the twentieth century, when most readers reacted to it with some distaste,[2] even today a number of critics who admire its artistic achievement continue to dislike it. It is a novel that "has always been more respected than loved," as Marilyn Butler admits in her introduction to a recent edition of the book.[3]

The objections of *Mansfield Park* are easy to summarize: readers complain that it lacks the sparkling comedy of the other novels and that the mundane, "Monday morning" virtues of its hero and heroine are bland or even unattractive. Both Edmund and Fanny are, in the most favorable light, quiet and rather dull; their goodness might shine in daily life, but it is certainly not calculated to appeal to readers looking for the wit or charm of *Pride and Prejudice* and *Emma.* Most readers, even while admitting that the book is a tour de force, continue to prefer the more charming type of good writing that provides us with the wittiness of an Elizabeth Bennet or Emma Woodhouse. Yet the interest of *Mansfield Park* does not lie only in Austen's ability to transform rather dull and undemonstrative goodness into great art. The book might not be as funny as its predecessors, but that does not mean that Austen has suddenly adopted a blandly humorless moral stance at the expense of any interest in comedy. On the contrary, the novel displays a considerable interest in comedy as a literary genre, or, more specifically, in exploring the relative virtues and limitations of two major styles of comic writing. A notoriously difficult word to define, "comedy" has never meant only writing that evokes laughter; in its broadest literary sense it describes any movement from despair to happiness. Eighteenth- and early-nineteenth-century literary theory consistently makes a distinction between "laughing" comedy—such as we find in *Pride and Prejudice*—and the rather solemn but uplifting "sentimental" comedy, the latter being intended not to make an audience laugh but rather to show virtuous protagonists acting nobly in the face of adversity and eventually triumphing over impending personal disasters.[4] It is possible, among the many ways of looking at Fanny and Mary, to see them as being drawn from these two standard but very different types of literary comedy. Fanny is a Burneyesque heroine; her roots lie in the domestic and often sentimental comedy of female development that reached the height of its popularity in the last quarter of the eighteenth century.[5] Mary, on the other hand, looks back to a much older mode of comic expression; she, somewhat like Austen's earlier antiheroine, Lady Susan, has her roots in the witty, amoral temptresses of the Restoration and early-eighteenth-century "laughing" comedy. In juxtaposing her two heroines, Austen is setting the values and weaknesses of two very different types of comic writing against one another and, in doing so, playfully exposing the limitations of each.

Of course, Fanny is usually seen as a relentlessly unfunny heroine rather than as the representative of any comic tradition. Yet she is, very clearly, a figure drawn in the pattern of the rather naïve, often sentimental young heroines of domestic comedy. Critics do not often note this indebtedness, perhaps because the burlesque of Marianne Dashwood's sensibility has made them wary of identifying places in which Austen treats sentiment favorably.[6] Nevertheless, Fanny has far more in common with Marianne than she does with Mary. Like Marianne, she is a strong believer in the enduring nature of a first love. Unlike the far more cynical—or realistic—narrator, who assures us on several occasions that Fanny would have eventually fallen in love with Henry had he persisted and had Mary married Edmund, Fanny is convinced of the undying nature of her own love. Moreover, the alternative conclusion to *Mansfield Park* provided by the narrator is couched in

MANSFIELD PARK:

A NOVEL.

BY JANE AUSTEN,

AUTHOR OF

" SENSE AND SENSIBILITY," " EMMA," &c.

LONDON:

RICHARD BENTLEY, NEW BURLINGTON STREET,

(SUCCESSOR TO HENRY COLBURN):

BELL AND BRADFUTE, EDINBURGH;

CUMMING, DUBLIN; AND

GALIGNANI, PARIS.

1833.

terms remarkably similar to the conclusion of *Sense and Sensibility.* Marianne, we are told, "voluntarily" became "the reward of all" Colonel Brandon's patience;[7] likewise, the narrator tells us that had Henry persevered, "Fanny must have been his reward—and a reward very voluntarily bestowed" (*Mansfield Park,* p. 467). Fanny is a far more complex—even if less likeable—character than Marianne, but in their strength of romantic feeling the two women are remarkably alike.

There are other similarities as well. Fanny and Marianne are both atypical Austen heroines in that they prefer landscape to people; that the narrator endorses Fanny's love of nature and pokes fun at Marianne's does not make their tastes dissimilar. Fanny might not go so far as to share Marianne's notorious love of dead leaves, but she does mourn the probable loss of an avenue of trees that she has never seen. One might recall Elinor's thankfulness that Marianne did not hear of the loss of walnut trees at Norland (see *Sense,* p. 226). Of course, there are some differences in their attitudes. Marianne, as innumerable readers have pointed out, learns her love of nature from the pre-Romantic poets whom she admires so extravagantly, while Fanny, although fond of Cowper and Crabbe, seems to derive ideas from moralists such as Hannah More, Thomas

Gisborne, and Edmund Burke as well.[8] However, this difference merely points to the reason that Fanny's love of nature is more completely endorsed than Marianne's—Austen is demonstrating that far from being a thoughtlessly and selfishly sentimental pose, as conservative novelists of her day tended to assert, love of nature can also be grounded in a responsible, Christian morality. The distinction does not make Fanny's love of nature less Romantic or deeply rooted than Marianne's; it merely shows Austen adding a new depth and complexity to the conventional role of the sentimental heroine.

Mary, on the other hand, is anything but sentimental; Avrom Fleishman states unequivocally that "her closest literary relations are with the witty, vamp-like heroines of Restoration comedy."[9] While Fanny worries incessantly about proper behavior, Mary creates for herself a comic world in which nothing is taken seriously except the ability to amuse and be amused. Her principles do not stand up to Fanny's careful scrutiny, but her cheerful wit makes her an attractive character despite her inability to live up to the standards affirmed by the concluding vision of Mansfield. In many ways she is also a character in the style of other witty heroines from the Romantic period, such as Robert Bage's Miss Fluart, Edgeworth's Lady Delacour, and Byron's Lady Adeline. All are attractive, self-confident women who are more concerned with making themselves agreeable than they are with abstruse moral problems. Significantly, they are all verbally dextrous; Miss Fluart and Lady Delacour can quash anybody with an epigram, while Lady Adeline is an accomplished amateur poet. One of the most important attributes of the conventional wit is, of course, her mastery of language. The domestic heroine, in contrast, tends to be silent, expressing herself most effectively through nonverbal signals.[10] Notably, at the end of *Mansfield Park,* Mary's last attempt to win Edmund is through silence—she invites him back not with her characteristic wit, which has ultimately failed her so badly, but with a smile. Although any interpretation of the scene must be tentative, as it is presented from Edmund's obviously biased perspective, it is quite possible to read it as Mary's attempt to co-opt the silent charm of her rival once her verbal skills have become useless.[11]

The verbal styles of the two heroines are one of the most important marks of the opposing traditions from which they are drawn, and are so dissimilar that one could argue that Austen was subtly exaggerating to make a point. Fanny is a notoriously silent heroine—Tony Tanner calls his chapter on *Mansfield Park* "The Quiet Thing"—who epitomizes the intelligent silence praised by conservative novelists and conduct writers.[12] Yet at times Fanny speaks as well as observes, and especially at the beginning of the novel she does so in a manner that is almost comically evocative of the moral guide-books that Burney's heroines live by and exemplify. One of the first speeches we hear from the adult Fanny has a stilted, exclamatory style, which gives an initial impression of her as being dull and pedantic. Reminded by Edmund of her first riding lessons, she responds not with a casual comment but with a formal speech:

Yes, dear old grey poney. Ah! cousin, when I remember how much I used to dread riding, what terrors it gave me to hear it talked of as likely to do me good;— (Oh! how I have trembled at my uncle's opening his lips if horses were talked of) and then think of the kind pains you took to reason and persuade me out of my fears, and convince me that I should like it after a little while, and feel how right you proved to be, I am inclined to hope you may always prophesy as well.

(Mansfield Park, p. 27)

Jane Austen could write better dialogue than that. The style is unnaturally stiff and affected, particularly given the context in which the speech appears. Fanny has just learned that she might have to go live with Mrs. Norris, and given her emotional turmoil, one might be a little surprised at her ability not only to dwell on memories of her "poney," but also to take such care to balance her phrasing. As Kenneth Moler observes,

Fanny is often made to talk in a manner that seconds artificial and out of place in the real-life conversations in which her speeches occur. Her rhetoric sounds stilted and excessively "literary," and she often seems to be echoing uncomfortably closely literature—particularly educational and didactic literature—with which an early-nineteenth-century audience would have been familiar.

("The Two Voices," p. 173)

This speech makes it a little difficult to respond entirely favorably to her earnestness, especially since we know that Austen was capable of creating morally upright heroines who do not talk like Hannah More. Neither Anne Elliot nor Elinor Dashwood ever sound quite so pompous.

Fanny's verbal stiffness is even more pronounced when she is put in direct contrast with Mary. The comic—as opposed to the didactic—side of Austen's juxtaposition of both sets of conventions is at its height in the scene when the two heroines sit together in the Parsonage shrubbery. Fanny's idea of light conversation is to muse on the past, present, and future of the shrubbery in which they are sitting, then to segue into a lecture on the nature of memory. When she eventually notices that her companion is "untouched and inattentive," she does make an attempt to shift the conversation, but can only hit upon another subject for a lecture:

The evergreen!—How beautiful, how welcome, how wonderful the evergreen!—When one thinks of it, how astonishing a variety of nature!—In some countries we know the tree that sheds its leaf is the variety, but that does not make it less amazing, that the same soil and the same sun should nurture plants differing in the first rule and law of their existence.

(p. 290)

Not only is the tone inappropriate to casual conversation, but also, as Moler points out, the thoughts are commonplace. Fanny may be displaying a genuine love of nature, but she is doing so in a manner that is, at best, unconvinc-

ing because it is couched as a moral lecture. At worst it arouses suspicions—though ultimately unjust ones—that her love of nature is learned from books and repeated by rote rather than from observation. As such it would differ little from the rote knowledge of history and geography that the narrator condemns at the beginning of the novel. This is not to say that Fanny fakes her Romantic impulses and love of nature; it merely means that initially, at least, she is so dependent upon verbal patterns learned from earlier literature that she is unable to express them with any real feeling, much less communicate them to her companions.

The limitations of the convention of the silently pure heroine, who speaks only when she has some morally irreproachable reflection to make, and the very real appeal of the less morally sound conventions embodied by Mary are further suggested later in the scene, when Mary finally participates in the conversation. Her contribution, like Fanny's, is a quotation. However, she is able to use it to lighten the oppressive dialogue with a genuinely amusing witticism:

"To say the truth," replied Miss Crawford, "I am something like the famous Doge at the court of Lewis XIV; and may declare that I see no wonder in this shrubbery equal to seeing myself in it."

(pp. 209-10)

The reference is to an anecdote in Voltaire's *Louis XIV,* indicating that even though Mary's conversation is frivolous, her reading is not. Voltaire himself was a questionable author in the reactionary England of 1814, but history was an unexceptionable pursuit for young ladies. Despite the eminently proper nature of Mary's reading, however, she does not become pedantic, but rather illustrates the ability of "a lively mind" to seize upon "whatever may contribute to its own amusement or that of others" (p. 64). While Fanny's observations undoubtedly have more moral weight, she is unable to adapt them to ordinary social interaction and so is left with principles that can guide her in large matters but that merely seem comically ponderous in smaller ones. In contrast, Mary takes even a matter of instruction and makes it entertaining. As we learn later in the novel, this practice is far from being entirely admirable, but Austen makes no attempt to hide the fact that it is much more immediately appealing than Fanny's rather solemn good principles.

Books are important not only because of the ways in which they shape conversation; Austen also links her heroines to their respective literary traditions by associating them with certain books or authors. It is entirely appropriate that the witty, cynical Miss Crawford should quote Voltaire on nature while Fanny quotes Cowper and More. Similarly, in choosing a play, Mary's tastes, "though politely kept back" (p. 130), incline toward comedies such as *The Rivals* and *The School for Scandal* rather than Shakespeare. Fanny, in contrast, is enthralled against her will when Henry reads *Henry VIII* to her. This type of association is made even more subtly in the chapel at Sotherton. The narrator tells us that Fanny is disappointed by the chapel because she had expected something more "fitted up for the purpose of devotion" (p. 85), but the reasons that Fanny herself gives for her dissatisfaction seem to arise more from her taste for romance than from her piety:

> "I am disappointed," said she, in a low voice, to Edmund. "This is not my idea of a chapel. There is nothing awful here, nothing melancholy, nothing grand. Here are no aisles, no arches, no inscriptions, no banners. No banners, cousin, to be 'blown by the night wind of Heaven.' No signs that a 'Scottish monarch sleeps below.'"
>
> (pp. 85-86)[13]

Since Sotherton is a comfortably modernized Elizabethan manor, not a Gothic castle, Fanny's disappointment is no less unreasonable than Catherine Morland's dismay at the good roads leading up to and the modern comforts in Northanger Abbey. Like Catherine's, Fanny's ideas of the world are based on books, not experience; her expectations of a chapel owe as much to Scott as they do to her sense of religious fitness. In that way she is not entirely different from Mary, whose concept of a chapel seems also to derive from literature, although of a very different sort. Her imaginary belles "with their heads full of something very different" from piety evoke early-eighteenth-century comedy at the expense of frivolous ladies of fashion.[14] The choice offered by the two heroines is not simply the easy, obvious one of piety versus cynical amusement, but is also a choice between Romantic and eighteenth-century tastes in literature.

Of course, Fanny and Mary are not simple literary stereotypes; they are complex, realistic characters whose conflicting behavior and principles are not reducible to preexisting sets of literary rules. Jane Austen is not writing about a one-dimensional conflict, something that she avoids even in the far more schematic *Sense and Sensibility.* Yet she is constructing a work of fiction, not writing biography or social history, and in doing so she inevitably draws upon familiar literary types and motifs in order to make her work satisfying and intelligible to an audience conditioned by its previous experience of fiction of that type. A more serious objection to a reading of the novel that sees Austen playing with comic conventions by juxtaposing figures drawn from two different traditions is that the grouping of a sweet heroine and a witty friend is itself a convention, going back in English literature at least as far as *Much Ado About Nothing.* Closer to Austen's time, and drawing only from work that we know she read, we can find such examples of paired heroines as Bage's Miss Campinet and Miss Fluart, Edgeworth's Belinda and Lady Delacour, and Burney's Camilla and Mrs. Arlbery.[15] Austen herself provides an exemplary use of this convention in Jane and Elizabeth Bennet—except that she goes against what seems to have been the prevailing taste of her day and (like Shakespeare) makes the wit the main character and the sweet friend the confidante.

Yet even if Austen is drawing upon this convention of paired heroines in *Mansfield Park,* she is doing so in a

manner that distorts it almost out of recognition. For one thing, her paired heroines dislike one another; or if dislike is too strong a word for Mary's reaction to Fanny (Mary genuinely welcomes the idea of Fanny as a sister-in-law), there is no doubt that Mary values her supposed friend more for her connection to Edmund than for her intrinsic personal worth. In addition, and more subtly, Austen makes it very clear that the two women do not complement each other, as do Jane and Elizabeth and other examples of this convention, but rather clash sharply. Jane and Elizabeth have the same principles and ideas; their differing temperaments merely lead them to be more or less generous in deciding whether or not others' behavior lives up to those principles. In contrast, Fanny and Mary have radically opposed principles as well as temperaments. Austen might be playing upon readers' expectations by evoking comparisons with conventional comedy that offers a proper moral exemplar in the main character and amusement from her confidante, but here she twists that convention dramatically and in the process forces us to confront questions of morality in responding to both women.

These moral issues are vital in differentiating the two heroines and the comic traditions they represent. Although Austen amuses us by juxtaposing the incompatible comic styles of Fanny and Mary, there is also a didactic impulse behind her play with the conventions of comic literature; she is making a very serious point that takes precedence over any delight in technical virtuosity or unease about the limitations of traditional comic form. As a descendant of Restoration and early-eighteenth-century wits, Mary is a character who makes amusement and social advancement the bases upon which she lives her life. Her refusal to be guided by the moral standards that Mansfield comes to represent is not as blatant as the amorality of the heroines of Restoration drama, but it is no less real. For example, her sense of marriage as a financial, not spiritual, union is deep and unquestioned. Discussing a friend's unhappy marriage, she observes,

> it was a most desirable match for Janet at the time. We were all delighted. She could not do otherwise than accept him, for he was rich, and she had nothing; but he turns out ill-tempered, and *exigeant*; and wants a young woman, a beautiful young woman of five-and-twenty, to be as steady as himself . . . [and yet] She took three days to consider of his proposals; and during those three days asked the advice of every body connected with her, whose opinion was worth having. . . . This seems as if nothing were a security for matrimonial comfort!
>
> (p. 361)

"Matrimonial comfort," Mary seems to assume, ought to be guaranteed by the husband's wealth, by the wife's cool indifference to her suitor's personality (after the marriage, Janet is surprised to discover her husband's staidness), and by society's approbation of the match. Notably, it does not even occur to Mary that Janet ought to have considered affection and a similarity of tastes in choosing a husband. There is no doubt, however, that Mary is at fault in overlooking these matters as a foundation for matrimony; Austen makes it clear through the opposing views of Fanny and Edmund that in her world, unlike that of much Restoration comedy, there are very real values that transcend those of amusing oneself and advancing socially. When Edmund meets Janet Fraser, he tells Fanny that

> she is a cold-hearted, vain woman, who has married entirely from convenience, and though evidently unhappy in her marriage, places her disappointment, not to faults of judgment or temper, or disproportion of age, but to her being after all, less affluent than many of her acquaintance, especially than her sister, Lady Stornaway, and is the determined supporter of every thing mercenary and ambitious, provided it be only mercenary and ambitious enough.
>
> (p. 421)

Edmund's explanation of why Mrs. Fraser is unhappy matches exactly Mary's reasons for thinking that she ought to be happy, highlighting the complete lack of contact between her standards and those of Mansfield, and suggesting the ultimate emptiness of her inability to see beyond her own cool cynicism. Moreover, Austen is careful to show that, like the amoral heroines she is modeled upon, Mary is profoundly indifferent to others' feelings. Though professing to like Fanny, she encourages Henry's plans to amuse himself by making Fanny "think as I think, be interested in all my possessions and pleasures, try to keep me longer at Mansfield, and feel when I go away that she shall be never happy again" (p. 231). Even Henry, whom she truly loves, is not exempt from being used in her search to amuse herself. She shows no more regard for his feelings than for Maria's in her desire to bring the pair together in London to see what will happen.[16]

The fact that Mary comes so close to winning her desires, and has won so much sympathy from readers, is thus a subtle comment not just on the dangers of *her* charm but, more importantly, on that of the comic tradition in which she is drawn. The harshness of Mary's repudiation at the end of the novel can be read as a tacit admission of the strength of the amoral charm of the type of comedy that she represents, rather than as a reflection of the seriousness of her moral lapse. Her absolute dismissal from any participation in the happy ending is a punishment completely disproportionate to the moral seriousness of her "crime." Although she merely refuses to call the elopement of Henry and Maria anything worse than "folly," she is as a result rejected with horror by Fanny, Edmund, and even the narrator as a completely abandoned woman. In contrast, Maria, who actually does elope, is made into more an object of pity than of horror. Her atonement for her error frequently wins some sympathy because of the grimness of the life she faces with Mrs. Norris;[17] Mary, on the other hand, makes her final and decisive move into her place as antiheroine when she refuses to treat shocking behavior by others as an irredeemable catastrophe. Admittedly, it is difficult for us as twentieth-century readers to comprehend the full extent to which Maria's elopement would horrify her family and friends, but even so, it seems rather unreasonable to withhold from Mary, whose loss of the man she genuinely loves is precipitated more by light speech than light morals, the pity granted Maria.

Despite this unequivocal repudiation of Mary, *Mansfield Park* is not simply a moral study wholeheartedly endorsing the type of comic expression represented by Fanny over the more seductive but less wholesome conventions embodied by Mary. Certainly, if we allow ourselves to think of the novel in those terms, we have to admit as a concomitant that it is a dismal failure. Few heroines have attracted such intensely vituperative commentary as Fanny, and even her defenders tend to apologize for her. Tony Tanner has observed that "nobody has ever fallen in love with Fanny Price," but he understates the intensity of the reaction against her. Long before feminist readings began to attack her passivity and prudery, a number of critics were making it quite clear that they found her distasteful. The objections began early. Among the opinions Austen collected on *Mansfield Park* are a number of complaints about Fanny (admittedly, there are a number of readers who praise her as well), including one from Mrs. Austen, who thought her "insipid" (see *Minor Works,* pp. 431-35). Reginald Farrer, writing early this century, declared that Henry Crawford had had a "lucky miss," since "fiction holds no heroine more repulsive in her cast-iron self-righteousness and steely rigidity of prejudice" than Fanny.[18] Most recently, Nina Auerbach has argued that Fanny is the archetypal outsider who becomes monster-like in her isolation.[19] Auerbach's argument is notable for its attempt to explain our dislike and to justify it as a necessary element of the book, but it nonetheless takes for granted that Fanny is a completely unlikable figure who therefore cannot represent a straightforward alternative to the values offered by Mary.

If Austen were trying to create a moral study in which Mary Crawford's amoral charm is shown to be hollow by Fanny's quiet piety, then she has failed miserably for a sizable proportion of her audience. Yet one can certainly raise questions as to whether or not that is actually what Austen is doing. As Martin Price shrewdly observes, a large part of the appeal of *Mansfield Park* lies in our willingness to laugh at Fanny's relentless self-castigation and at her naive assumption that morality must be purchased at the cost of pleasure. He argues convincingly that Austen might endorse the morality, but not the "inflexible solemnity" with which Fanny pursues it.[20] Certainly a study of the narrator's comments forces one at least to wonder whether Fanny is being as unproblematically endorsed as many critics—including both those who like and those who dislike her—assume. The famous concluding reference to "my Fanny" (p. 461), for example, might certainly be taken to imply affection for the character, as many critics have argued, but one does not have to assume as a concomitant of that affection an uncritical admiration of all of Fanny's attitudes throughout the book. In fact, the reference leads into a rather condescendingly amused account of Fanny's feelings, rather than an endorsement of them:

> My Fanny indeed at this very time [after the double elopement of Julia and Maria, Tom's near-fatal illness, and the collapse of Edmund's marriage plans], I have the satisfaction of knowing, must have been happy in spite of every thing. She must have been a happy creature in spite of all that she felt or thought she felt, for the distress of those around her. . . . Edmund was very far from happy himself. He was suffering from disappointment and regret, grieving over what was, and wishing for what could never be. She knew it was so, and was sorry; but it was with a sorrow so founded on satisfaction, so tending to ease, and so much in harmony with every dearest sensation, that there are few who might not have been glad to exchange their greatest gaiety for it.
>
> (p. 461)

Austen's notoriously slippery irony is at work here. In this seeming pleasure in Fanny's happiness, we are being told not only that she lacks self-awareness (she only "thought she felt" for her grieving relatives) but also that the narrator, unlike Fanny herself, is fully aware of the incongruity of a "sorrow" that is built on "satisfaction" and produces "ease." This confusion of emotions is perfectly understandable in a shy and repressed eighteen-year-old, but it is hardly the mark of the paragon of morality that Fanny is often made out to be.

As Mary Lascelles points out, in an argument often overlooked by those who see the narrative as a straightforward endorsement of Fanny, the narrative voice in *Mansfield Park* is unusually flexible, molding its tone to suit the sensibilities of the characters who dominate a given episode.[21] As such, it cannot be a simple reflection of Fanny's personality, and in fact, at times it approaches Mary's voice far more closely than Fanny's. The witticisms at the expense of various characters have a savagery that goes far beyond anything of which Fanny is capable. For example, we are told that Maria was "prepared for matrimony by an hatred of home, restraint, and tranquillity; by the misery of disappointed affection, and contempt of the man she was to marry" (p. 202); similarly, the narrator observes that Sir Thomas's reflections that "he had sacrificed the right to the expedient, and been governed by motives of selfishness and worldly wisdom . . . were reflections that required some time to soften; but time will do almost every thing" (pp. 461-62). Fanny would certainly applaud the morals implied by such statements, but the sardonically cynical manner in which they are expressed would shock her.

It is clear that despite readings of *Mansfield Park* that make the book into Tory apologetics, it is difficult to see it as an unproblematic endorsement of Fanny's quiet virtues. Austen is not simply writing a Burneyesque account of female development through trials, however much the book is indebted to the conventions of that tradition. David Monaghan observes that Fanny's "unadorned virtue" might be admirable, but unless she can attract attention and emulation it is useless to anybody but her. Only through gaining some of the social graces that Mary so effortlessly commands can she win the attention and respect she deserves.[22] Neither woman is perfect; each needs to learn something from the other. Fanny triumphs because she learns her lesson faster than Mary, who fails to appreciate until too late the importance to her of the "domestic happiness" she learned to value at Mansfield. Austen is, very subtly, undermining the convention that modesty and moral virtue alone are sufficient to gain respect and happiness. As Monaghan points out, even though Fanny's principles remain static throughout the book, nobody except Edmund pays them or her any attention until she starts participating in the society around her and attempting to co-opt some of Mary's charm to further her own ends.

There are other reasons for us to be suspicious of readings that make Fanny into a perfect moral exemplar. Not only is Fanny's "perfection" problematic, but also the heroine who improved others around her by her shining example was, as we know, a figure Austen poked fun at in her Juvenilia and continued to dislike all of her life. "Pictures of perfection as you know make me sick & wicked," she wrote to her niece Fanny Knight a few months before she died.[23] In her burlesque **"Plan of a Novel,"** probably written in 1816 in response to James Stanier Clarke's well-meant but silly suggestions for her future work, she mocks the convention at greater length:

> Heroine a faultless Character herself—, perfectly good, with much tenderness & sentiment, & not the least Wit—very highly accomplished, understanding modern Languages & (generally speaking) everything that the most accomplished young Women learn, but particularly excelling in Music—her favourite pursuit—& playing equally well on the Piano Forte & Harp—& singing in the first stile. Her Person, quite beautiful—dark eyes & plump cheeks. . . . The heroine's friendship to be sought after by a young Woman in the same Neighbourhood, of Talents & Shrewdness, with light eyes & a fair skin, but having a considerable degree of Wit, Heroine shall shrink from the acquaintance.
>
> (*Minor Works,* pp. 428-29)

One can see that this mocking catalog of conventions is not much exaggerated by looking at any of a number of novels from the time.[24] Susan Ferrier's very popular *Marriage* (1818), which Austen could not possibly have known, might almost be taken as the model for her sketch. The heroine, Mary, dances and draws with natural talent; her singing is in "a style full of simplicity and feeling," and "in the modern languages she was perfectly skilled."[25] Though not strictly a beauty, she is "an elegant interesting looking girl" (p. 163). Her friendship is sought by her beautiful, good-natured, and intelligent cousin Emily, but Mary, though grateful for Emily's interest, is constantly shocked by her outspoken wit. Though far from dull, in outline *Marriage* reveals its extreme reliance upon a familiar pattern for the female novel.[26]

Clearly, Austen was well aware of the conventions of the novel centered around a young moral exemplar, and just as clearly, her treatment of Fanny mocks and undermines rather than upholds those conventions. Almost all of the elements of the description of the heroine in the burlesque **"Plan"**—and the serious description of Mary in the otherwise comic *Marriage*—are present in one way or another in *Mansfield Park,* but are employed in reference to characters other than Fanny. The Bertram daughters are conventionally accomplished young women whose schooling, as Austen points out, provides them formal instruction in just about every field except "self-knowledge, generosity, and humility" (p. 19).[27] By pointedly reminding us that the polite education of heroines does not include any moral instruction, and by making the unaccomplished Fanny the only female character with a sense of morality, Austen calls attention to the artificiality of the convention that young women, by the age of sixteen or seventeen, can be skilled in music, history, languages, art, and literature, and still have had time for the serious reflection necessary to be morally self-aware. Only in her suspicion of Mary's wit does Fanny fit the conventional depiction of the moral heroine, and even then she is right at least partly for the wrong reasons. As Austen makes quite clear, sexual jealousy, as well as moral indignation, fuels Fanny's rejection of Mary.

By drawing upon two different traditions of literary comedy, Austen manages to suggest the limitations and appeal of both. Mary's charm might be dangerous and amoral, but its attractiveness is very real. On the other hand, Fanny's virtues, wholesome as they undoubtedly are, not only seem rather dryly unappealing without some leaven of charm, but also fall far short of the inhuman standards of perfection normally expected of a moral heroine. Far from offering the simple alternative of moral heroism to Mary's amorality, Fanny herself implies some of the limitations of the conventions that lie behind her characterization. The novel is thus not merely an attack on one form of conventional comedy and an endorsement of another; if it were, it would be only a slightly more complicated but otherwise unproblematic example of the conventional Burneyesque comedy of female development. The tensions produced by juxtaposing and questioning both sets of conventions make *Mansfield Park* into a far more complex and innovative work than are the models it takes as a point of departure. These tensions are most clearly visible not in our more-or-less uneasy responses to the two heroines, however, but in the notoriously troublesome conclusion of the novel, which catapults the reader from quiet country life into an almost shockingly melodramatic mixture of adultery, elopements, and broken hearts.

Mansfield Park is not alone among Austen's novels in having a troublesome conclusion; *Sense and Sensibility* has proved just as difficult to deal with, and understanding the reasons for that trouble might help one in dealing with *Mansfield Park.* As Tony Tanner has complained, in *Sense and Sensibility* Austen seems more concerned with providing a conventionally happy ending than she is with maintaining consistency of action or character. In a comedy heroines get married, and since Marianne is a heroine, her character and energy are ruthlessly "sacrificed to the

overriding geometry" of the conventional happy ending, which requires that she be married to Brandon (*Jane Austen,* p. 100). This strict observance of conventions, Tanner claims, distorts the novel, leaving only "devitalised symmetry" and falsely avoiding the tragedy implicit in the movement of the book as a whole (p. 101).[28] If, as Tanner believes, *Sense and Sensibility* privileges symmetry over logic, one must also argue that the conventions demanding such symmetry cripple Austen's work.

This hobbling by the demands of conventions becomes even more critical in *Mansfield Park,* when Austen is dealing with two very different conventional patterns. According to one, the wits should triumph, winning their true loves as a reward for amusing us. In her introduction to *Mansfield Park* Butler makes this point, suggesting that Austen keeps us aware of an "alternative sphere," a world embodied by *Lovers' Vows,* in which Mary "might have succeeded in luring Edmund back, might have won him over, married him, taken him to live in Sloane Street. . . . In [this] world, Maria would have been forgiven" (p. xxvii). By the standards of Fanny's plot, however, what ought to happen is precisely what does. Fanny has been in love with Edmund from the very first pages of the novel; she is the Cinderella heroine and therefore ought to get her heart's desire, while Edmund is the mentor-hero who has left Fanny's mind "in so great a degree formed by his care" (p. 470) that Austen tells us it is natural that he should love her. Moreover, we ought to be accustomed to seeing goodness triumph over the hollow charms of wit, if we are at all familiar with the sentimental fiction of the day, and the fair heroine triumph over the dark. Yet however appropriate the ending is according to these criteria, many readers remain unsatisfied with it. As Austen subtly undermines the conventions of domestic heroism, we are left uncomfortable with a conclusion that unequivocally rewards them. Moreover, by first sketching a plausible alternative ending, in which Fanny reforms and "very voluntarily" marries the "villain," and then baldly rejecting that conclusion, Austen stresses the arbitrariness of the resolution that she actually provides and forces readers out of any uncritical contentment with her allotment of conventional rewards and punishments. Contrary to the assumption of some critics that the conclusion shows a failure of artistry—Paul Pickrel states that it is so badly done that it reveals Austen to be "tired and in uncertain control"[29]—the resolution of *Mansfield Park* actually shows Austen following the logic of the method that she has employed throughout the book. If neither conventional form of comic writing is entirely satisfactory on its own, neither of the two "appropriate" endings can be either.

Critics who blame Austen for rushing over the process of Edmund's falling out of love with Mary and in love with Fanny are therefore missing an important part of her irony. Her famous refusal to "dwell on guilt and misery" (p. 461) is not the sign of a tired writer taking the easy way out, but the politely obliging response of a writer who knows her readers expect a happy ending and is willing to provide it, whatever the strains on probability. As Auerbach has observed about Austen's conclusions in general, the author's "apparent conformity to the norms of her silliest readers frees her to laugh at us all" (*Romantic Imprisonment*, p. xvii); her adherence to conventions is a joke at the expense of both the conventions themselves and the readers who insist that they be observed. Admittedly, in *Mansfield Park* the joke turns sour. Henry and Mary are left in a limbo of useless regrets; Maria and Mrs. Norris are sent into permanent exile and self-torment; Tom is sobered only by a narrow escape from death; Julia is tied to the foolish Mr. Yates for life; and Sir Thomas and Edmund have their worlds temporarily shattered. Even the harmless gourmand Dr. Grant is killed off by apoplexy so that Fanny and Edmund can return to the Mansfield parsonage.[30] Yet this ruthlessness is used to highlight the artificiality of the happy ending. Marianne at least marries a suitor who has loved her from first sight, and only after she has had half the book to get used to the idea of Willoughby's perfidy. Fanny's and Mary's reversals in fortune come with breathtaking rapidity, and only because Tom's illness, Henry's weakness, Maria's discontent, and Mary's folly all happen to converge. Austen is quite willing to provide us with a happy ending that meets at least one set of conventional requirements, but only at the price of straining our credulity to its limits.

The idea that Austen is parodying conventions with her conclusions is a familiar one,[31] but it has not been applied carefully to *Mansfield Park.* Henrietta Ten Harmsel, in fact, says bluntly that the conclusion of the novel does not work because of Austen's uncritical lapse into Richardsonian didacticism (pp. 100-102). Lloyd Brown, in an otherwise perceptive discussion of the ending, errs in the opposite direction and concludes that not only is it logically consistent with the rest of the book but also that it privileges realistic experience over conventional expectations. Austen, he says, is describing

> everyday experiences in which moral conventions are ignored, both by the individual and his society. Instead, society builds its own set of traditions and these are contrasted here, as they are in *Sense and Sensibility,* with the conventional morality to which they are ideally expected to adhere.

(p. 233)

Yet the swiftness and ruthlessness of the punishments doled out hardly support the idea that Austen is writing a *realistic* ending to mock the foolish expectations of conventionalism. On the contrary, through the extreme and arbitrary disposal of characters in order to provide Fanny's happy ending, Austen criticizes conventionalism by giving us a ruthlessly conventional ending without any attempt to naturalize it or increase its probability. Austen provides us with the happy ending that we expect—even demand—but we still are not happy. Conventions of her genre demand that characters be neatly accounted for and disposed of, so Austen redirects Edmund's love, silences Mary, and exalts Fanny, treating the characters like puppets and destroying the illusion of them as autonomous beings that she has la-

bored throughout the novel to create. Her form demands neatness, symmetry, and restriction, so she provides it, but only after stressing precisely how artificial such restriction is and how much we lose by flattening out the complex characters so that they can live happily ever after. Ultimately, what we have in her comic fiction is a subtle commentary on the artificiality of such comedy.[32]

Austen is clearly aware of the ways in which established conventions limit her work, and while ultimately she chooses to provide her readers with the conventional entertainment they want, she mockingly stresses that what they are getting is a product of literature rather than either a faithful or an idealized representation of the world in which they live. Dour and moralistic Fanny might be, but *Mansfield Park* itself is no humorless sermon. The book is highly critical of misread or overused literary conventions, yet this criticism is expressed in a manner that reflects a fundamental belief in the value of comedy as a literary mode. Throughout her career Austen suggests that traditional conventions of comic writing have become badly inadequate, but in her mature work, particularly *Mansfield Park,* she is not content merely to demonstrate that inadequacy. Instead she attempts to find a way to work beyond it, exploring and, more importantly, demonstrating the ways in which she can reanimate the conventions of her genre—ironically enough, by poking fun at them. As the continuous arguments over what *Mansfield Park* is *really* about indicate, Austen has managed to shape a most unconventional and challenging novel out of the numerous conventional elements she is drawing upon, demonstrating the continuing importance of comedy as a mode in her work. Even though it lacks the sparkle of *Pride and Prejudice* and its tone is often subdued, in its structure *Mansfield Park* retains all of the playful mockery characteristic of Austen's comic vision.

Notes

1. For the best presentations of the conservative argument, see Alistair M. Duckworth, *The Improvement of the Estate: A Study of Jane Austen's Novels* (Baltimore: Johns Hopkins Univ. Press, 1971); Marilyn Butler, *Jane Austen and the War of Ideas* (Oxford: Clarendon Press, 1975); and Tony Tanner, *Jane Austen* (Cambridge, Mass.: Harvard Univ. Press, 1986). Both Duckorth and Tanner see *Mansfield Park* as Austen's masterpiece; Butler, arguing for the brilliance of the first half, nonetheless agrees with Q. D. Leavis in ranking it second to *Emma* overall. More troubled readings of *Mansfield Park* are provided by many critics, including Marvin Mudrick, *Jane Austen: Irony as Defense and Discovery* (Princeton: Princeton Univ. Press, 1952); Sandra M. Gilbert and Susan Gubar, *The Madwoman in the Attic: The Woman Writer and the Nineteenth-Century Literary Imagination* (New Haven: Yale Univ. Press, 1979); Katrin R. Burlin, "'At the Crossroads': Sister Authors and the Sister Arts," in *Fetter'd or Free? British Women Novelists, 1670-1815,* ed. Mary Anne Schofield and Cecilia Macheski (Athens: Ohio Univ. Press, 1986),

pp. 60-84; and Claudia L. Johnson, *Jane Austen: Women, Politics, and the Novel* (Chicago: Univ. of Chicago Press, 1986).

2. The shift in critical opinion started with Lionel Trilling's enormously influential essay on *Mansfield Park* in *The Opposing Self: New Essays in Criticism* (New York: Viking Press, 1955); reprinted in *Jane Austen: A Collection of Critical Essays,* ed. Ian Watt (Englewood Cliffs, N.J.: Prentice-Hall, 1963), pp. 124-40.

3. "Introduction" in *Mansfield Park* (New York: Oxford Univ. Press, 1990), p. vii.

4. Austen's contemporaries Leigh Hunt and William Hazlitt both wrote essays called "On Wit and Humour," which discuss these varied aspects of comedy; see Stuart M. Tave, *The Amiable Humorist: A Study in the Comic Theory and Criticism of the Eighteenth and Early Nineteenth Centuries* (Chicago: Univ. of Chicago Press, 1960), for a very detailed twentieth-century study of eighteenth-century comic theories.

5. For an account of the rise in popularity of the novel of female development, see the chapter "Reformed Heroines" in Jane Spencer's *The Rise of the Woman Novelist: From Aphra Behn to Jane Austen* (Oxford: Basil Blackwell, 1986).

6. Calling Fanny sentimental does not necessarily mean that she possesses undue sensibility in any case. As Janet Todd points out in her *Sensibility: An Introduction* (London: Methuen, 1986), "sensibility" and "sentiment" were not always synonymous during the eighteenth century. She argues that Sterne's use of the word "sentimental" helped to push the use of the two words closer together, but states that even though "after Sterne's novels, [the word "sentiment"] frequently takes the meaning of refined and tender emotion . . . the denotation of moral reflection also continues" (p. 7). Fanny, who is both emotional and moralistic, is clearly sentimental in this eighteenth-century sense of the word.

7. Jane Austen, *Sense and Sensibility,* vol. 1 of *The Novels of Jane Austen,* ed. R. W. Chapman, 3d ed., 6 vols. (Oxford: Oxford Univ. Press, 1933), p. 378. All further references to Austen's works are from this edition and are included in the text.

8. Kenneth L. Moler first pointed out that Fanny's most rhapsodic descriptions of nature are in fact near-quotations from Hannah More (see *Jane Austen's Art of Allusion* [Lincoln: Univ. of Nebraska Press, 1968], pp. 111-25; and "The Two Voices of Fanny Price," in *Jane Austen: Bicentennary Essays,* ed. John Halperin [Cambridge: Cambridge Univ. Press, 1975], pp. 172-79). Duckworth traces Fanny's ideas on nature to Cowper and Burke (pp. 44-47).

9. *A Reading of "Mansfield Park": An Essay in Critical Synthesis* (Minneapolis: Univ. of Minnesota Press, 1967), p. 31.

10. Sometimes, however, silence can backfire even for these heroines. Burney's Evelina initially bores her future husband because he reads her silence as inanity rather than maidenly reserve. More seriously, Camilla, the third Burney heroine, nearly loses her lover when, acting upon the advice of her father and an older woman friend, she attempts to win him through coded behavior rather than a direct admission of love.

11. Ruth Bernard Yeazell interprets this scene very differently, arguing that Mary's "equivocal" smile is among the "final emblems of her impurity." To support this interpretation, however, she must admit that Mary's actual appearance cannot be distinguished from "how Edmund needed to see her" (see "The Boundaries of Mansfield Park," in *Representations,* 7 (1984), 145-46).

12. John Gregory instructs his daughters that modesty will "naturally dispose you to be rather silent in company, especially in a large one.—People of sense and discernment will never mistake such silence for dullness. One may take a share in conversation without uttering a syllable" ("Conduct and Behavior," in *A Father's Legacy to His Daughters* [Dublin, 1774], pp. 13-14). Similarly, Hannah More's Lucilla Stanley, the ideal wife in *Coelebs in Search of a Wife,* is "rather silent . . . yet it was evidently not the silence of reserve or inattention, but of delicate propriety" (More, *Works,* vol. II [Philadelphia: J. J. Woodward, 1830], p. 370). For a discussion of Fanny's debts to the conservative ideals of femininity, see Linda C. Hunt, "A Woman's Portion: Jane Austen and the Female Character," in *Fetter'd or Free?,* pp. 8-28.

13. The quotations are from Scott's *Lay of the Last Minstrel,* II, x and xii. The chapel described is the one in which the wizard Michael Scott is buried with his magic book, and the whole passage is thoroughly Gothic, making the quotations even more inappropriate as choices to illustrate Fanny's piety.

14. See, for example, a letter to *The Spectator,* 53 (1 May 1711), which describes the tactics of a young lady in church who was "resolved to bring down my Looks, and fix my Devotion on her self" (*The Spectator,* ed. Donald F. Bond, 5 vols. [Oxford: Clarendon Press, 1965], I, 227).

15. The latter two are themselves variations on the convention, since in those cases the sweet heroine is an ingenue, and the wit a somewhat older woman of the world who half-protests, half-endangers her. Another interesting variation on this form occurs in Inchbald's *Simple Story* (1791), in which the two heroines are of different generations—the wit is the erring mother and the sweet one her impeccable daughter.

16. One can argue, as does Mudrick (pp. 165-67), that Austen betrays Mary and that the character who wishes for Tom's death and entices Edmund with a "prostitute's" smile is not the one we have seen else-

where in the book. Yet until the end of the novel, Mary's self-interest is never in direct conflict with conventional morality, so she is never forced to betray her true amorality. At most, one can say that Austen reveals Mary's basis in comic convention more nakedly at the end of the book than she does elsewhere.

17. A number of critics, including Leavis, Mudrick, Brown, and Johnson, have suggested that Sir Thomas's treatment of Maria is unreasonably punitive, comparing it to Mr. Collins's recommendation in *Pride and Prejudice* that Mr. Bennet forgive Lydia and Wickham "as a christian" but never "admit them in your sight, or allow their names to be mentioned in your hearing" (p. 364). In fact, Mr. Bennet, like Sir Thomas, initially refuses to allow Lydia to visit Longbourn, relenting only when Elizabeth pleads with him to do so. Moreover, Sir Thomas "secured" Maria in "every comfort," acting far more generously than Mr. Bennet was able to do. Finally, Maria's elopement as a married woman is far more disastrous than Lydia's, which could be rectified by a quick wedding. Julia's elopement is a closer parallel to Lydia's, and she is quickly received back in Mansfield. By our standards Sir Thomas is unpleasantly harsh, but by the standards of his day, by which we must measure him, he was behaving in a relatively enlightened manner, far from the most unchristian behavior recommended by Mr. Collins.

18. Reginald Farrer, "Jane Austen's *Gran Rifiuto*" (1917), in *"Sense and Sensibility," "Pride and Prejudice," and "Mansfield Park": A Casebook,* ed. B. C. Southam (London: Macmillan, 1976), pp. 210-11.

19. See *Romantic Imprisonment: Women and Other Glorified Outcasts* (New York: Columbia Univ. Press, 1985), pp. 28-29.

20. See Martin Price, *Forms of Life: Character and Moral Imagination in the Novel* (New Haven: Yale Univ. Press, 1983), pp. 84-87.

21. See *Jane Austen and Her Art* (Oxford: Oxford Univ. Press, 1939), pp. 102-3.

22. David Monaghan, *Jane Austen: Structure and Social Vision* (London: Macmillan, 1980), p. 95.

23. *Jane Austen's Letters to Her Sister Cassandra and Others,* ed. R. W. Chapman (London: Oxford Univ. Press, 1952), pp. 486-87. Austen also complained that Anne Elliot "is almost too good for me" (p. 487). Perhaps significantly, she never made any comments about Fanny's excessive goodness. Margaret Kirkham also argues that Austen is poking fun at the conduct book heroine through Fanny, but concludes that Fanny transcends this model, ultimately undermining those "pictures of perfection" (see "Feminist Irony and the Priceless Heroine of *Mansfield Park*," in *Jane Austen: New Perspectives,* ed. Janet Todd [New York: Holmes and Meier, 1983], pp. 231-47).

24. One can turn also to conduct books, which preached impossible standards of female perfection. In 1779,

for example, Vicesimus Knox holds up for our emulation a young lady who reads Greek, Latin, French, and Italian; has a thorough knowledge of English poetry and history; plays harpsichord and dances; and, though not particularly interested in sciences, gains "a superficial knowledge of astronomy, of the solar system, of experimental philosophy, and of geography, mathematical, physical, and political. This little was necessary for rational conversation" (quoted in Vivian Jones, ed., *Women in the Eighteenth Century: Constructions of Femininity* [London: Routledge, 1990], pp. 107-8).

25. Susan Ferrier, *Marriage,* ed. Herbert Foltinek (Oxford: Oxford Univ. Press, 1986), p. 159.

26. Examples of this pattern in late-eighteenth- and early-nineteenth-century fiction could easily be multiplied. *Camilla* (1796) and *Belinda* (1801) both feature beautiful, accomplished, and impeccably moral heroines who are befriended, somewhat to their dismay, by charming wits. Mary Brunton's *Self-Control* (1810-11), which Austen mocked in her letters, features a perfect heroine who sacrifices everything to filial duty, also like the heroine of the "Plan."

27. The child (usually a girl) whose mind has been "improved" at the cost of her morals is also a convention in the literature of the time; compare Edgeworth's description of a young woman in her novella *The Good French Governess*: "Isabella was about fourteen; her countenance was intelligent, but rather too expressive of confidence in her own capacity, for she had, from her infancy, been taught to believe that she was a genius. Her memory had been too much cultivated; she had learned languages with facility, and had been taught to set a very high value upon her knowledge of history and chronology. Her temper had been hurt by flattery, yet she was capable of feeling all the generous passions" (in *Moral Tales,* vol. 1 of *Tales and Novels,* 10 vols. [London: George Routledge and Sons, 1893], p. 284).

28. Julia Prewitt Brown sharply debates Tanner's conclusion that a truly courageous novelist would have let Marianne die, following the inexorable logic of the plot. However, she sees the ending of *Sense and Sensibility* as it stands as unhappy, implicitly agreeing with Tanner that the conventional marry-and-live-happily-ever-after ending cannot work in this novel (see Brown, *Jane Austen's Novels: Social Change and Literary Form* [Cambridge, Mass.: Harvard Univ. Press, 1979], pp. 62-63).

29. "'The Watsons' and the Other Jane Austen," *ELH,* 55 (1988), 459.

30. One of Austen's most overlooked ironies is that even though Fanny's values ultimately shape Mansfield, she does not become its mistress, as a number of critics have asserted. Susan has replaced her at the house, and as sister-in-law of the future Sir Thomas and mistress of the parsonage, she actually inherits the position of her old nemesis Mrs. Norris rather

than that of Lady Bertram. The despised poor relation ousts not the mistress of the house, but, perhaps even more fittingly, her chief oppressor.

31. See, in addition to Auerbach's comments, Henrietta Ten Harmsel, *Jane Austen: A Study in Fictional Conventions* (The Hague: Mouton, 1964), p. 27; and Lloyd W. Brown, *Bits of Ivory: Narrative Techniques in Jane Austen's Fiction* (Baton Rouge: Louisiana State Univ. Press, 1973), pp. 222-35. Gilbert and Gubar also discuss her conclusions in some detail, but see in them an angry protest against restrictions rather than amused mockery of them.

32. D. A. Miller argues that any attempt to impose closure upon a novel involves reduction and oversimplification of the elements that have made the story "narratable" up to that point, but suggests that it is Fanny and Edmund, not the narrator, who simplify Mary and her discourse in order to fulfill the demands of comic form and provide closure. Even though Miller is arguing a thesis very different from mine, his view supports my contention that we cannot see the ending as an uncritical rejection of Mary and her conventions by the narrator (see *Narrative and Its Discontents: Problems of Closure in the Traditional Novel* (Princeton: Princeton Univ. Press, 1981), pp. 87-89).

John Wiltshire (essay date 1997)

SOURCE: *"Mansfield Park, Emma, Persuasion,"* in *The Cambridge Companion to Jane Austen,* edited by Edward Copeland and Juliet McMaster, Cambridge University Press, 1997, pp. 58-83.

[*In the following excerpt, Wiltshire probes the psychological focus and narrative technique of* Mansfield Park.]

Mansfield Park was published only a year after *Pride and Prejudice,* but moving from one novel to the other the reader is keenly aware of a change of tone and atmosphere. Partly it is that *Mansfield Park* is evidently the work of an older, maturer, woman. The narrator is not an intrusive presence, by any means, but one who, while an insider of the world she depicts, can also see beyond it. 'Poor woman! she probably thought change of air might agree with many of her children', she remarks of the beleaguered Mrs. Price at the conclusion of chapter 1 ([*Mansfield Park* hereafter] *MP* 11). It is a voice with a range of sympathy beyond the social commonwealth of rich families that is the milieu of *Mansfield Park.*

Almost everyone in this novel is wealthy. Sir Thomas Bertram is a Member of Parliament with a large estate and property in the West Indies; Henry Crawford also has an estate, and enough income easily to afford to have it totally 'improved' as soon as he comes of age. His sister Mary has twenty thousand. Mr. Rushworth has a park five miles round and a Tudor mansion. Told that Henry Craw-

ford has 'four thousand a year', Mrs. Rushworth senior seems to feel that this is just enough to get by: 'Very well.—Those who have not more, must be satisfied with what they have' (118). These are 'young people of fortune', far better off than those in any other Austen novel, and untroubled, despite Sir Thomas' need to see to his Antigua estates, by any sense of financial insecurity. Only Mrs. Norris is obsessed with saving, a neurotic compensation for her inferior family position whose other manifestation is her remorseless bullying of her even poorer niece, Fanny Price. In part the novel is a study in the assumptions and manners of the very rich, in the manners of 'society', as the initial conversation between the Crawfords and the Bertrams, about 'coming out' (48-51), indicates. Spoilt, full of self-consequence, good-looking, healthy, the Bertrams do not need to be proud like Lady Catherine de Bourgh or Sir Walter Elliot. Their vanity is in such good order that they can appear free of it. Lordly, careless, insouciant, and selfish, Tom Bertram at least has some sense of humour.

In *Pride and Prejudice,* the great estate of Pemberley is viewed by a visitor and outsider, and Elizabeth Bennet gives it all the awe and respect of one who can say only that she is 'a gentleman's daughter'. But in *Mansfield Park,* the reader is, so to speak, a resident, shown what it is like to live from day to day in such a place. The spaciousness of the house is an important factor in the lives and events that the novel traces, and much of Austen's narrational skill in the brilliant first volume consists in the manipulation and interweaving of a large number of characters and destinies within one locale that is also a group of distinct spaces. For Fanny, the novel's uprooted heroine, '[t]he grandeur of the house astonished, but could not console her. The rooms were too large for her to move in with ease. Whatever she touched she expected to injure, and she crept about in constant terror of something or other' (14-15). Just taken away from her mother and her family, Fanny projects onto the furniture her own sense of the potential injuriousness of this space, felt to be both empty and hostile. Mansfield is not, on the whole, a glamorous or idyllic home (until it becomes such in Fanny's eyes at the end of the novel). Harassed and disregarded, Fanny gradually constructs a substitutively maternal space where she can be happy; furnishing the East room with discarded bric-à-brac and carelessly donated gifts, she makes a fragile 'nest of comforts' that is an emotional as well as physical improvisation. But this room which Fanny thinks of as 'her own', that she has made her own, is always actually marked as the room of a dependent, a transient, by the absence of a fire in the grate.

Jane Austen's ability to make the setting integral to her development of character can be illustrated too, by the early scene where the youthful Fanny is waiting for Mary Crawford to return with the mare that she has borrowed. She is scolded out of the house by Mrs. Norris and discerns the party of Edmund, Mary, and the groomsmen across the valley. 'The sound of merriment ascended even to her' (67): the phrasing subtly makes Fanny's geographical distance from the group a simultaneous index of her emotional isolation. 'After a few minutes, they stopt entirely, Edmund was close to her, he was speaking to her, he was evidently directing her management of the bridle, he had hold of her hand; she saw it, or the imagination supplied what the eye could not reach' (67); and the rhythm supplies the undercurrent of Fanny's jealousy. Not 'see' but 'reach'. How that suggests the distance across which Fanny's eyes are straining!

From one point of view, Fanny Price is an interesting psychological study in the manners and attitudes of a radically insecure and traumatized personality. The impatience that one inevitably feels with some of her more censorious or prim judgments may be moderated by the careful history of displacement Austen has provided for her, her years of unremitting intimidation by Mrs. Norris, and her youthful dependence on an Edmund whose kindness comes along with a good deal of tutorly instruction. Her disapproving attitude towards Mary is always complicated by its jealous colouring as well as an even more disqualifying trait, envy. Fanny's moral attitudes in general are overdetermined—part the result of Edmund's coaching, part the result of her own nature and insecurities—and so it is a great simplification to see her as modelling a 'conduct book', a Christian, or an evangelical heroine. Does she refuse to act in *Lovers' Vows* out of fear of acting, or out of disapproval of the play? She certainly offers her timidity as her excuse, thereby displaying that timidity rather than moral righteousness.

Mansfield Park is a novel in the mode of the omniscient narrator, and for the first and only time in her novels, Jane Austen continuously allows the narrative to move freely in and out of the consciousnesses of a whole range of characters. In *Pride and Prejudice,* there are moments, especially early in the novel, when Darcy's and Charlotte Lucas' thoughts are presented. In *Persuasion,* the reader is shown at one crucial moment Captain Wentworth's stillburning anger against Anne. But in *Mansfield Park* the independence of the narrator from any one controlling consciousness is a structural principle. This text at various times represents the thinking processes or picks up the internal speech-cadences of Maria Bertram, Edmund Bertram, Sir Thomas, Mary Crawford, and several others, besides Fanny Price. When Sir Thomas overhears Mr. Yates in full ranting flight on the improvised stage at Mansfield the narrative borrows his point of view at the beginning of the paragraph, and, to heighten the comic effect, Tom Bertram's at the close (182-3).

Perhaps most significantly, this novel presents whole scenes and dialogues from which the heroine is absent. The scenes at the Parsonage between Mary and Henry Crawford (and sometimes with Mrs. Grant) are quite freestanding. They depict the relationship between the Crawfords at first without reference to Fanny. Thus the novel is structured with two different centres or foci of interest. In the mode of 'free indirect speech', Mary's thoughts about her prospects on entering a new place and about older

brothers, for example, are allowed to enter the text without authorial commentary. Following from these gay and brilliant introductory scenes (volume 1, chapters 4 and 5) the narrator naturally keeps the reader in touch with Mary Crawford's private thoughts—she has been given the representational treatment of a major figure, and her projects accordingly draw from one a certain sympathetic attention. It is not the fact that Mary is vivacious, while the supposed heroine Fanny is timid and nervous, that makes for this novel's moral complications: it is that the rival figures are each accorded an almost equivalent narrative stature until Fanny's removal to Portsmouth in the last volume.

The reporting of Mary's thoughts moves fluidly between the medium of indirect speech, the dramatic representation of her behaviour, and direct commentary on both. Different modes, or rather dimensions or aspects, of presentation throughout the novel tend to suggest different moral agendas. When Sir Thomas Bertram interviews Maria and asks her whether she wants to press on with the engagement to Rushworth (200-1) his thoughts are outlined like an internal monologue without quotation marks. The reader is expected to see through the self-deceptions and convenient blindnesses of his reasonings, but to retain the vestigial sympathy one conventionally has for a figure whose thought-processes, whose capacity to reflect, one has intimately followed. (This is one of the reasons why Sir Thomas, for all his failures—and he never fails in his kindness to his wife—is a fundamentally respectable figure.) The caustic comments that follow—'Such and such-like were the reasonings of Sir Thomas'—are an abrupt shift of address, and require a change of attitude from the reader from participatory leniency to dismissive contempt. These abutments of aspect (not always as abrupt as here) are one source of the novel's scintillating life, but they sometimes cause ethical anxiety in the reader that is not entirely resolved.

The presentation of Mary and Henry Crawford, freestanding, but doubled through the perspective of the heroine, is the major instance of this challenge. Mary has lived in London and has a range of social skills that are apparently worldly and sophisticated, but viewed from Fanny's position, she often seems sadly maladroit. One complication of her tone—her 'sweet peculiarity of manner' as Edmund describes it—is a tincture of disillusionment that is not quite as cynical as she imagines. The sketch of Mary's years at the Admiral's house that emerges from her allusions, however witty and professedly unconcerned, indicates a history that invites sympathy for a damaged life. When she is married, she tells Mrs. Grant, she will be a staunch defender of the marriage state, and adds 'I wish my friends in general would be so too. It would save me many a heart-ache' (47). Her disrespectful description of her uncle's household—'of *Rears* and *Vices,* I saw enough'—is witty, but the crudity of the wit laughs off an enormity she feels but has no way of approaching directly. (Her assessment is not in doubt: the narrator has said previously that the Admiral was a man of 'vicious habits'.)

'In short, it is not a favourite profession of mine. It has never worn an amiable form to *me*' (60). The remarks scandalize Fanny and Edmund, but their intensity, which is replicated whenever Mary brings up the topic of life at the Admiral's, betrays an unhappy experience that is clearly formative. Mary's history, brought up in the charge of her aunt and uncle, mirrors Fanny's, and one might justly suppose that the traumatic effects of her adoptive home on one personality are as relevant to the author's purpose as they are on the other. In other words, though Mary's worldliness is viewed critically (through the eyes of Fanny and Edmund especially) it is also readable as a coping strategy, a sign of an insecurity much less manifest than Fanny's, but nonetheless, critical.

The complications of feeling and judgment these different dimensions of narration give rise to can be exemplified by the famous scene when Mrs. Norris turns on Fanny and accuses her of being 'a very obstinate, ungrateful girl . . . very ungrateful indeed, considering who and what she is' (147). The setting is the drawing room, where Tom, Maria, Henry Crawford, and Mr. Yates are at a table with the play in front of them, while Lady Bertram on her sofa, Edmund, Fanny, and Mrs. Norris are grouped nearer the fire. The separation is political. Mary Crawford's predicament and nervousness (she wants Edmund to act the Anhalt role but does not know how to approach the question) is defined by her movement between one and the other set of people within the room. She shifts from group to group, in response to different promptings, her freedom a sign not of independence but of her need to attach herself, to find a centre for her emotional life—almost, one might say, to find a home. When Edmund snubs her, she 'was silenced; and with some feelings of resentment and mortification', the reader is told, 'moved her chair' towards Mrs. Norris at the tea-table.

The reader's main focus is on Fanny, who is the target of Tom's plans, so that the little drama of Mary's manoeuvres interweaves it only as a subsidary theme. The climax is Tom's repeated 'attack' on Fanny and Mrs. Norris' angry speech. Mary's immediate response is 'I do not like my situation; this *place* is too hot for me' and her moving of her chair once again to the opposite side of the table. Mary's action, the completion of her series of movements, is sympathetically described as she continues to talk to Fanny and to try 'to raise her spirits, in spite of being out of spirits herself'. But in a moment one's admiration for her courage and kindness becomes undermined: 'By a look to her brother, she prevented any farther entreaty from the theatrical board, and the really good feelings by which she was almost purely governed, were rapidly restoring her to all the little she had lost in Edmund's favour' (147). This odd sentence, beginning with Mary's (or the narrator's) point of view and ending with Edmund's, seems to attribute to him an unwarranted insight into Mary's motives, and the upshot is a carping note all-too-consonant with the suspiciousness of Fanny. The dramas of the two young women have been presented contrapuntally, but at this point where their projects actually clash the task of

keeping sympathy for both figures alive in the narrative proves just too much. This episode presents a miniature version of the narrative knot that Austen cuts in the last section of the novel by removing Fanny to Portsmouth and allowing only her consciousness to preside.

'By a look to her brother': the reader's responses to Mary Crawford are also complicated by the fact that the dialogues between Mary and Henry emphasize their mutual rapport. They seem to have a family style, teasing, humorous, generous, that contrasts with the absence of anything like wit or style among the Bertrams. One never sees Julia and Maria, who are said to get on well, for example, in conversation, and Tom only speaks to Edmund in order crudely to make clear who is boss. Henry, as Mary declares, 'loves me, consults me, confides in me' (59). Henry's regard for Mary invites the reader to see his flirtations with Maria and Julia in a light that is perhaps a shade different from the youthful Fanny's abhorrence. (Mary's resolve to keep her affections under control also cannot but make one despise Maria's sulky disregard of consequences.) Thus the Crawfords' worldliness is accompanied by a complicating un-Bertramesque mutuality, kindness, and adulthood. They exemplify that 'fraternal' tie (235) the narrator celebrates explicitly in reference to Fanny and William.

Henry Crawford is as marked as his sister by the arrangements in his uncle's household. Fatherless and allowed a free rein by the Admiral, Henry does not require the approval of others to feel justified in what he does: in fact he rather relishes opposition than the reverse, which perhaps explains his persistence in the courtship of the anything but graciously reluctant Fanny. Henry's pursuit of his sexual objects, in this instance Maria, is accompanied by contempt for those objects. Austen implies that he has picked up such attitudes from his uncle. But she also succeeds in suggesting how his spoilt and liberal upbringing can result in fascination when the beloved offers the challenge, but also the comfort, of inflexible resistance. '"I could so wholly and absolutely confide in her," said he; "and *that* is what I want"' (294).

Henry's courtship of Fanny is accompanied by conversations in which he discusses it with Mary, and his love for Fanny by her endorsement, or, perhaps, collusion. The dual focus is most brilliantly exploited in chapters 11 and 12 of the second volume. For many chapters, the novel has seen events mainly from the standpoint of Fanny Price. It is her view of Henry's flirtations that has been given, her mistrust, resentment, and reluctance have been highlighted, even while it is counterpointed and ironically at odds with the excitements and delights of the Crawfords. After the ball, which Sir Thomas has organized from the hardly conscious wish to promote Fanny's chances with Henry, Edmund goes away to be ordained. In chapter 11, Fanny's state of mind is described, but then the narrative shifts its focus on to Mary at the Parsonage. It is now she whose thoughts are filled with anxiety and self-mistrust, and who now contends 'with one disagreeable emotion entirely new to her—jealousy' (286). The positions of the two young women have been reversed as Mary tries to extract some reassurance of her power over Edmund from the unbending Miss Price.

In chapter 12, Henry returns and announces, to Mary's astonishment, that he intends to marry Fanny Price. The genius of this almost entirely dramatic scene is that it gives full recognition to the excitement, gaiety, and exhilaration of the two figures who challenge the narrative and moral status of the hero and heroine. The reader's responses are not inhibited by reservations from the narrator. What also makes it so telling is that it is not merely a scene of mutual delight and congratulation, but that it touches once more on the painful family history that has made these two, and their needs, what they are. Henry, even while he acknowledges the grossness of his uncle, says of him 'Few fathers would have let me have my way half so much.' In the midst of her delight, with her mind racing ahead to what this means for her own prospects, Mary is stopped and sounds a sombre note: 'Henry, I think so highly of Fanny Price, that if I could suppose the next Mrs. Crawford would have half the reason which my poor ill used aunt had to abhor the very name, I would prevent the marriage, if possible' (296). The gravity of this declaration suggests once again the unhappy psychological background that leads Mary, in this very dialogue, to fantasize a reconstituted family—cousins and brother and sister—together in Northamptonshire, a fantasy that ironically duplicates some of Fanny's own longings.

It is not only psychological depth and narrative orchestration that make *Mansfield Park* a milestone in the English novel. The novelist imagines the physical world in which her figures move to have a palpable presence, an effective bearing on their lives. At one point in *Pride and Prejudice,* the narrator remarks casually on 'the shrubbery where this conversation passed' ([*Pride and Prejudice* hereafter] *PP* 86). Settings are never neutral backgrounds in *Mansfield Park,* and the gardens at Sotherton, famously, are made to play an integral, even determinative part in the action. It is not only that one can read them in allegorical terms, as the punning exchange of Henry and Maria about her 'prospects' invites one to do. It is rather as if emotional pressures and urgencies were felt, and conveyed to the reader, in spatial terms, as when Maria declares so intensely 'I cannot get out, as the starling said' (*MP* 99). As the figures move, disperse, and reassemble within the various venues Sotherton and Mansfield and Portsmouth offer them, one is made vividly conscious not only of the opportunities and inhibitions of these spaces, but of their being at issue—contested over, claimed, and owned. Maria's disregard of the locked gate is to be echoed in Tom's overturning the arrangements of his father's rooms: both express their egotistical drives as the usurpation of territory. Fanny seeks to keep Edmund at the window looking at the stars, Mary lures him indoors with her music. Characters and their bodies are imagined precisely within settings that are drawn into the narrative and act as provocations to conversation and action.

This capacity to dramatize space and to make the human drama inseparable from its physical location reaches its peak in the scenes at Portsmouth. As Edward Said observes [in *Culture and Imperialism* (London: Vintage, 1994)], for example, the 'solitary candle' that Fanny's father holds 'between himself and the paper, without any reference to her possible convenience' (382) 'renders very precisely the dangers of unsociability, of lonely insularity, of diminished awareness that are rectified in larger and better administered spaces'. It is this evening that Fanny remembers three months later when her depression is deepened by the sun that brings its glare to illuminate the dirt and disorder of her parents' parlour. When she returns to Mansfield with Edmund in early spring an affiliation between emotional state, narrative purpose, and landscape setting—the trees in 'that delightful state . . . while much is actually given to the sight, more yet remains for the imagination' (446-7)—suggests the possibilities that are to be explored further in *Emma* and *Persuasion.*

FURTHER READING

Anderson, Misty G. "'The Different Sorts of Friendship': Desire in *Mansfield Park*." In *Jane Austen and Discourses of Feminism,* edited by Devoney Looser, pp. 167-83. New York: St. Martin's Press, 1995.

> Discerns evidence of homoerotic desire in *Mansfield Park.*

Cleere, Eileen. "Reinventing Nieces: *Mansfield Park* and the Economics of Endogomy." In *Novel* 28, No. 2 (Winter 1995): 113-30.

> Sees the extended family as the "primary source of middle-class empowerment" proposed in *Mansfield Park.*

Cohen, Paula Marantz. "Stabilizing the Family System at Mansfield Park." In *ELH* 54, No. 3 (Fall 1987): 669-93.

> Analyzes Austen's representation of a nuclear family model in *Mansfield Park,* viewing it as one of "perfect equilibrium."

Crick, Brian. "Jane Austen on the 'Relative Situation': What Became of Mrs. Norris's 'Morally Impossible' in *Mansfield Park*." In *The Critical Review* 39 (1999): 77-106.

> Focuses on the central importance of marriage and family life in *Mansfield Park.*

De Rose, Peter L. "Hardship, Recollection, and Discipline: Three Lessons in *Mansfield Park*." In *Studies in the Novel* 9 (1977): 261-78.

> Comments on moral lessons in *Mansfield Park,* arguing that the didactic component of the novel does not interfere with Austen's creation of a sympathetic character in Fanny Price.

Dunn, Allen. "The Ethics of *Mansfield Park*: MacIntyre, Said, and Social Context." In *Soundings* 78, Nos. 3-4 (Fall-Winter 1995): 483-500.

Argues against reductive assessments of morality in *Mansfield Park,* proposing instead a view of ethical behavior embedded in its social contexts but free from the simplifications of conservative or Marxist readings.

Easton, Fraser. "The Political Economy of *Mansfield Park*: Fanny Price and the Atlantic Working Class." In *Textual Practice* 12, No. 3 (Winter 1998): 459-88.

Claims that *Mansfield Park* presents an attack on the social ramifications of economic modernization associated with capitalism and the exploitation of labor.

Flavin, Louise. "*Mansfield Park*: Free Indirect Discourse and the Psychological Novel." In *Studies in the Novel* 19, No. 2 (Summer 1987): 137-59.

Considers Austen's use of narrative technique and fictional layering to explore the psychological states of anxiety, guilt, and jealousy in *Mansfield Park.*

Fraiman, Susan. "Jane Austen and Edward Said: Gender, Culture, and Imperialism." In *Critical Inquiry* 21, No. 4 (Summer 1995): 805-21.

Objects to Edward Said's characterization in *Culture and Imperialism* of the author of *Mansfield Park* as a flatly conservative figure.

Gardiner, Ellen. "Privacy, Privilege, and 'Poaching' in *Mansfield Park*." In *Jane Austen and Discourses of Feminism,* edited by Devoney Looser, pp. 151-65. New York: St. Martin's Press, 1995.

Studies Fanny Price's achievement of critical authority in *Mansfield Park.*

Gillis, Christina Marsden. "Garden, Sermon, and Novel in *Mansfield Park*: Exercises in Legibility." In *Novel: A Forum on Fiction* 18, No. 2 (Winter 1985): 117-25.

Explores the interaction between landscape, text, the observer, and the observed in *Mansfield Park.*

Gillooly, Eileen. "Rehabilitating Mary Crawford: *Mansfield Park* and the Relief of 'Throwing Ridicule.'" In *Feminist Nightmares: Women at Odds—Feminism and the Problem of Sisterhood,* edited by Susan Ostrov Weisser and Jennifer Fleischner, pp. 328-42. New York: New York University Press, 1994.

Perceives Mary Crawford as the narrative counterpart to Fanny Price and a symbolic threat to phallocentrism in *Mansfield Park.*

Hudson, Glenda A. "Incestuous Relationships: Mansfield Park Revisited." In *Eighteenth-Century Fiction* 4, No. 1 (October 1991): 53-68.

Sees the incestuous marriage of first cousins Fanny and Edmund in *Mansfield Park* as an important element of Austen's theme of marriage based upon familial and fraternal bonds.

Kelly, Gary. "Reading Aloud in *Mansfield Park*." In *Nineteenth-Century Fiction* 37, No. 1 (June 1982): 29-49.

Notes the association between reading, eloquence, and morality in *Mansfield Park.*

Kilroy, G. J. F. "*Mansfield Park* in Two Volumes." In *English: The Journal of the English Association* 34, No. 149 (Summer 1985): 115-29.

Traces structural parallels between the two parts of *Mansfield Park.*

Lenta, Margaret. "Androgyny and Authority in *Mansfield Park*." In *Studies in the Novel* 15, No. 3 (Fall 1983): 169-82.

Highlights Austen's belief in intellectual equality between the sexes as expressed in *Mansfield Park.*

Lew, Joseph. "'That Abominable Traffic': *Mansfield Park* and the Dynamics of Slavery." In *History, Gender & Eighteenth-Century Literature,* edited by Beth Fowkes Tobin, pp. 271-300. Athens: The University of Georgia Press, 1994.

Observes Austen's participation via *Mansfield Park* in the nineteenth-century debates over slavery and the political rights of women.

Litvak, Joseph. "The Infection of Acting: Theatricals and Theatricality in *Mansfield Park*." In *ELH* 53, No. 2 (Summer 1986): 331-55.

Considers the subversive theatrical subtext in Austen's otherwise morally conservative novel.

Marshall, David. "True Acting and the Language of Real Feeling: *Mansfield Park*." In *Yale Journal of Criticism* 3, No. 1 (Fall 1989): 87-106.

Concentrates on Fanny Price's ability to express authentic emotions through acting in *Mansfield Park.*

McKenzie, Alan T. "The Derivation and Distribution of 'Consequence' in *Mansfield Park*." In *Nineteenth-Century Fiction* 40, No. 3 (December 1985): 281-96.

Examines *Mansfield Park*'s concern with the responsibilities and actions of individuals of social "consequence."

Murray, Douglas. "Spectatorship in *Mansfield Park*: Looking and Overlooking." In *Nineteenth-Century Literature* 52, No. 1 (June 1997): 1-26.

Discusses the framing, exclusion, and concealment of visual aesthetic experiences in *Mansfield Park.*

Skinner, John. "Exploring Space: The Constellations of *Mansfield Park*." In *Eighteenth-Century Fiction* 4, No. 2 (January 1992): 125-48.

Probes the tensions between different kinds of space—public, intimate, diegetic, and hermeneutic—in *Mansfield Park.*

Smith, Johanna M. "'My Only Sister Now': Incest in *Mansfield Park*." In *Studies in the Novel* 19, No. 1 (Spring 1987): 1-15.

Suggests that the incestuous marriage in *Mansfield Park* reveals the novel's representation of constrictive familial bonds.

Smith, Peter. "*Mansfield Park* and the World Stage." In *Cambridge Quarterly* 23, No. 3 (1994): 203-29.

Investigates motifs of improvement and memory as they relate to slavery, morality, and society in *Mansfield Park*.

Steffes, Michael. "Slavery and *Mansfield Park*: The Historical and Biographical Context." In *English Language Notes* 34, No. 2 (1996): 23-41.

Places Austen's apparent tolerance of slavery in *Mansfield Park* within its historical context.

Sutherland, Kathryn. "*Jane Eyre*'s Literary History: The Case for *Mansfield Park*." In *ELH* 59, No. 2 (Summer 1992): 409-40.

Juxtaposes *Mansfield Park* and Charlotte Brontë's *Jane Eyre* as culturally conservative and radical feminine texts, respectively.

Trickett, Rachel. "*Mansfield Park*." In *The Wordsworth Circle* 17, No. 2 (Spring 1986): 87-95.

Enumerates Austen's departures in *Mansfield Park* from the theme and form of her other novels, praising the imaginative quality of this work.

Waldron, Mary. "The Frailties of Fanny: *Mansfield Park* and the Evangelical Movement." In *Eighteenth-Century Fiction* 6, No. 3 (April 1994): 259-81.

Contends that *Mansfield Park* presents an oblique challenge to the moral precepts of Anglican Evangelicalism.

Additional coverage of Austen's life and career is contained in the following sources published by the Gale Group: *Authors & Artists for Young Adults,* **Vol. 19;** *Concise Dictionary of British Literary Biography, 1789-1832;* *Dictionary of Literary Biography,* **Vol. 116;** *DISCovering Authors; DISCovering Authors: British; DISCovering Authors Modules: Most-Studied Authors, Novelists;* **and** *World Literature Criticism.*

"Young Goodman Brown"

Nathaniel Hawthorne

The following entry presents criticism of Hawthorne's short story "Young Goodman Brown" (1835). For information on Hawthorne's complete career, see *NCLC*, Volume 2; for information on *The Scarlet Letter,* see *NCLC*, Volume 10; for information on *The Blithedale Romance,* see *NCLC*, Volume 17; for information on the "Marble Faun," see *NCLC*, Volume 23; for information on *The House of Seven Gables,* see *NCLC*, Volume 39; for information on "The Minister's Black Veil," see *NCLC*, Volume 79.

INTRODUCTION

One of the most frequently studied short stories in American literature, Hawthorne's "Young Goodman Brown" has been a favorite of readers and critics alike. Hawthorne's masterful depiction of a young Puritan's discovery that evil lurks in all men, a theme he would later develop more fully in his novels, has led critics to deem him a pioneer of psychological fiction. Additionally, his masterful use of symbolism and allegory, especially in the figure of Brown's beribboned bride Faith, has recieved intense critical scrutiny. Of this ambiguous story, the American novelist Herman Melville, a friend and admirer of Hawthorne, wrote, "Who in the name of thunder would anticipate any marvel in a piece entitled 'Young Goodman Brown'? You would of course suppose that it was a simple little tale, intended as a supplement to 'Goody Two-Shoes.' Whereas it is deep as Dante."

BIOGRAPHICAL INFORMATION

Hawthorne graduated from Bowdoin College in Maine in 1821 and returned to his mother's home in Salem, Massachusetts, with the intention of becoming an author. The next decade of his life, which marked his apprenticeship as a writer, was characterized by hard work, lack of recognition—both critical and monetary—and loneliness. As he wrote, he admitted to feeling like "the obscurest man of letters in America," but he focused on developing his literary ability and in 1828 published his first novel, *Fanshawe*. Realizing that the novel was a mistake, he destroyed as many copies as he could locate; during this period he also prepared and then burned the first of several collections of short fiction that failed to find a publisher. "Young Goodman Brown" was written during this low point in Hawthorne's career, in 1828 or 1829. It first appeared in *New-England Magazine* in April, 1835, and was later included in *Mosses from an Old Manse,* a collection of short stories Hawthorne published in 1846 and revised in 1854. Like so much of his other short fiction, "Young Goodman Brown" attests to Hawthorne's symbolic habit of mind and to his interest in the past, myth, and human psychology. Yet by the time he included "Young Goodman Brown" in *Mosses,* Hawthorne already viewed his early tales as somewhat antiquated and obscure. He wrote in a letter to James T. Fields in 1854, "Upon my honor, I am not quite sure that I entirely comprehend my own meanings in some of these blasted allegories." Though he would eventually write more short fiction, Hawthorne's interest turned to novel writing, where he eventually resolved the tension between the past and the present still evident in the stories in *Mosses.*

PLOT AND MAJOR CHARACTERS

Set in seventeenth century Puritan Salem, Massachusetts, "Young Goodman Brown" is recounted by an omniscient narrator who intentionally casts doubt over all the events he relates. As the story opens, Goodman Brown, a young, newly married Puritan, says goodbye to Faith, his wife of only three months, and is about to embark upon a mysterious overnight journey. Faith begs him not to go, but Brown says that he has a task that must be finished before sunrise. He walks down the main street of Salem and into the forest; as he proceeds deeper, he meets an old man who is actually the Devil in disguise. The old man looks a little like Brown and carries a walking stick shaped like a black snake. He invites Brown to walk on with him and to take the stick to make his journey easier. Although neither frightened nor surprised at meeting the Devil, Brown is reluctant to join him and mentions that his ancestors would never have gone on such a walk. To Brown's astonishment, the Devil explains that he is well acquainted with Brown's ancestors and that he helped Brown's father and grandfather punish religious dissenters and massacre Indians. Along the way, they also meet Goody Cloyse, Brown's childhood religious instructor, who clearly knows the Devil. In spite of her pious nature and respected position in Salem, Goody Cloyse turns out to be a witch. Brown realizes from their conversation that a meeting (a Black Mass) will take place that night in the forest. Further on, he sees that the minister and deacon from Salem village are also on their way to the Black Mass. As he finds himself full of doubts about good and evil and his Puritain beliefs, only the thought of his wife, Faith, sustains him. When Brown begins to pray, he hears Faith's voice, and soon discovers that she is about to be initiated into the

Devil's party. At a crude altar in the forest, the Devil's congregation, a mixture of Salem's upstanding citizens as well as its corrupt, immoral denizens, sing their songs of worship. Brown cries out to Faith to resist the Devil, but then instantly finds himself alone again in the forest. He returns to town the next morning, turning away from everyone he meets, including Faith, believing that he now knows their true hypocritical nature. He never finds out whether he dreamed his experience in the forest or if it really took place, but from that time on, Brown is a lonely, distrustful man who rejects his wife and his religion. When the time comes for him to die, many years later, the narrator explains that "his dying hour was gloom."

MAJOR THEMES

As many critics have pointed out, in "Young Goodman Brown" Hawthorne is interested in exploring the psychological and social effects of guilty knowledge, whether or not that knowledge is founded on fact. At the outset of the story, Brown is self-confident and secure in the knowledge that the world around him is as he believes it to be. He particularly cherishes the knowledge that his wife, Faith, is innocent and good—an angel on earth. Believing that his place in heaven is assured by his wife's goodness, Brown disregards the consequences of making and keeping an appointment with the Devil. Hawthorne presents Brown's ordeal in the forest as his first brush with evil, but it is significant, leading him to reject his previous conviction in the prevailing power of good. His discovery that the people he admires and believes to be good Christians are actually hypocrites sets the tone for the rest of his life. Though he himself resists the Devil, he allows his newfound awareness of sin to fester and rejects what he believes to be a community of sinners. Hawthorne portrays Brown as the greatest sinner of all because he has turned away from the rest of humanity and has so easily given up his faith. Sin is an inescapable part of human nature, Hawthorne shows, and Brown's forest experience is symbolic of the spiritual journey from innocence to experience that is a part of emotional maturity. Because Brown cannot accept what he has learned, both his emotional and physical development is arrested and he stagnates spiritually until he dies. Additionally, there are parallels between "Young Goodman Brown" and the witchcraft hysteria that occurred in Salem in 1692, in which one of Hawthorne's ancestors played a significant role. The ambiguous narrator and the similarities in setting invite comparison between the historical events and Hawthorne's portrayal of evil lurking in every corner. "Young Goodman Brown" questions Puritan culture and the issues of conformity that led to the witchcraft hysteria by demonstrating how questionable, or spectral, evidence can so completely effect the course of an individual's life.

CRITICAL RECEPTION

"Young Goodman Brown" ranks foremost among Hawthorne's short stories in both popular appeal and critical respect. Readers are drawn by Hawthorne's superb storytelling technique and by the theological, moral, psychological, social, and historical dimensions he develops in the tale. The story has also had its critics: in the nineteenth century, Edgar Allan Poe wrote that the allegorical elements in the story detract from its natural form, and Henry James posited that the presentation of the forest experience as a dream constituted Hawthorne's taking the easy way out of a narrative dilemma. More recently, critics such as Frank Davidson and Leo B. Levy have explored Hawthorne's handling of Brown's emotional crisis in the story. Going even further in this direction, Edward Jayne and Michael Tritt have written extensive Freudian readings of the tale, focusing on Brown's arrested psychological development and projection of guilt. The historical context of the story continues to attract critical interest, as well, with scholars delving into the Puritan belief system and seventeenth-century American cultural values for clues to interpreting "Young Goodman Brown." Twentieth-century critics have also become increasingly interested in the narrative technique Hawthorne uses in "Young Goodman Brown" with such commentators as Harold Mosher, among others, discussing the storytelling aspect of the tale. The ambiguous sybmolism and the allegorical nature of "Young Goodman Brown" ensure continued interest and vigorous critical attention

---

PRINCIPAL WORKS

Fanshawe: A Tale (novel) 1828

Twice-Told Tales (sketches and short stories) 1837

Twice-Told Tales (second series) (sketches and short stories) 1842

Mosses from an Old Manse (sketches and short stories) 1846

The Scarlet Letter: A Romance (novel) 1850

The House of the Seven Gables (novel) 1851

The Snow Image and Other Tales (short stories) 1851

The Blithedale Romance (novel) 1852

Life of Franklin Pierce (biography) 1852

A Wonder-Book for Girls and Boys (short stories) 1852

Tanglewood Tales for Girls and Boys; Being a Second Wonder-Book (short stories) 1853

The Marble Faun; or, The Romance of Monte Beni (novel) 1860; published in England as *Transformation; or, The Romance of Monte Beni,* 1860

Our Old Home (essays) 1863

Passages from the American Notebooks of Nathaniel Hawthorne (journal) 1868

Passages from the English Notebooks of Nathaniel Hawthorne (journal) 1870

Passages from the French and Italian Notebooks of Nathaniel Hawthorne (journal) 1872

Septimius Felton; or, The Elixer of Life (unfinished novel) 1872

The Dolliver Romance and Other Pieces (unfinished novel) 1876

Doctor Grimshawe's Secret: A Romance (unfinished novel) 1883

CRITICISM

Frank Davidson (essay date 1963)

SOURCE: "'Young Goodman Brown': Hawthorne's Intent," in *ESQ: A Journal of the American Renaissance,* Vol. 31, Part 2, 1963, pp. 68-71.

[*In the following essay, Davidson argues that Hawthorne's purpose in "Young Goodman Brown" was to demonstrate the power of an "evil thought" to corrupt psychologically and ultimately to lead an individual to "an evil deed."*]

One considers the number and variety of attempts made to clarify the meaning of **"Young Goodman Brown"**[1] and wonders whether there is perhaps some simpler explanation of the story than has been made. May it have been the author's purpose to have the reader realize keenly the transforming power and the paralyzing deceptiveness of an evil thought, which once entertained, starts into action subtle psychological processes against which one may make resolves but which, begun, proceed with increasing strength to demoniacal frenzy and the perpetration of an evil deed?

About the period of the publication of the story (1835), the author was displaying considerable interest in the relation of the "evil in every human heart" to evil thought and evil deed. In 1836, for example, he set down among themes for stories, the observation that evil may remain latent in the heart through a lifetime or may, through circumstance, be suddenly activated;[2] that a man may "flatter himself with the idea that he would not be guilty of some certain wickedness,—as, for instance, to yield to the personal temptations of the Devil,—yet to find ultimately, that he was at that very time committing that same wickedness."[3] Not later than 1836 he wrote **"Fancy's Show-Box,"** in which he stated that "It is not until the crime is accomplished that Guilt clinches its gripe upon the guilty heart, and claims it for its own" and expresses the hope "that all the dreadful consequences of sin will not be incurred, unless the *act* have set its seal upon the thought."[4]

The over-all pattern Hawthorne employs in **"Goodman Brown"** is similar to that used by Shakespeare in the first two acts of *Macbeth.* Confused by the suggestion of evil lodged in his mind by the witches, Macbeth soliloquizes:

> My *thought*, whose murder yet is but fantastical, / Shakes so my single state of man that function / Is smothered in surmise, and nothing is / But what is not
>
> (I.iii.139-142).

Conflict follows between conscience and evil desire. He cannot put out of mind the prophecy that he will be king; neither is he willing to transform it to fact by murder; he wavers between but, despite his resolves to the contrary, moves toward the evil until his will is out of his control. Circumstances buttress the desire, as do outside persuasion and ocular illusion. The conflict ends as he announces, "I have done the *deed*" (italics added). Remorse and bitterness immediately ensue.[5]

In *Macbeth* and **"Young Goodman Brown"** the evil thought moves quickly to consummation; its course is a single night. Witchcraft is associated with events of both, as are deceptions of eye or ear or both and strange disorders in the natural world including "lamentings heard i' the air." The evil, however, to which Brown succumbs is more inclusive and profound than is murder; it is a cynical skepticism based in the conviction, falsely arrived at, that the nature and destiny of man are evil.

The theme Hawthorne is primarily interested in in **"Young Goodman Brown,"** is what he omits in *The Scarlet Letter*—the evil thought in its progress toward the guilty deed of which that work recounts only the consequences. Of the eighteen pages of the story as it appears in *The Complete Works,* the author allots one to the farewell between Brown and his wife, Faith: her plea that he not leave her on this particular night, his chiding her for doubt (the critical motive of the story), and his "Amen" to her "God bless you." The final page is about the goodman's mental state after his harrowing experiences of the night. The sixteen pages intervening are the account of Brown's journey into the dark forest. In those pages Hawthorne traces the visible course Brown pursues, part way with a guide, and simultaneously the invisible inner journey from the time he entertains the evil thought to the moment when he pleads with Faith to "resist the wicked one." The goodman's experiences he presents in four scenes, each closing with a halt in the travel, each successive one mounting in intensity beyond the preceding.

In the first the goodman enters the forest and meets the devil, with whom he has previously made tryst. When urged to mend his pace he comes to a full stop, resolved, now that he has kept his appointment, to return home. On his companion's suggesting, however, that they walk on, reasoning as they go, he "unconsciously" resumes his walk.

As they proceed he states his scruples against continuing the journey, but he continues: he would not violate family decorum or the respect he has for the traditional piety of his native region. These defenses his companion crushes with what seems to be some timely truth that comes as a surprise to Brown: the devil claims long and close acquaintance with the father and the grandfather,[6] in whose image, it seems, he appears; and he has had an active part in the government of New England. Instead of coming to the rescue of his family and community, the goodman counters with another scruple, the awe in which he holds his minister. This meeting with ridicule, which "nettles" him, he pleads his love for his wife, who, he says, would be heart-broken if she knew his errand. With a sympathetic gesture concerning Faith and a placating suggestion that the goodman go his own way, the companion attempts to allay the resentment he has stirred. He quickly and deftly nullifies his seeming concession by casually directing Brown's attention to what purports to be the figure of Goody Cloyse on the path ahead. Brown conceals himself lest she see the company he is in but keeps watch. Her presence in the forest and her ease in conversing with the devil (as much an ocular deception as what seemed the movement of the snake carved on the devil's staff, for she disappears with mysterious suddenness),[7] astonishes Brown and moves him deeply, for in his childhood she had been his religious counselor. Taking advantage of Brown's discomfiture, the companion urges more "speed," and, as they move along, discourses "so aptly that his arguments seemed rather to spring up in the bosom of the auditor [Brown] than to be suggested by himself." But when Brown sees twigs and little boughs of a freshly-plucked maple stick wither and dry up at the touch of his companion's hand, he "sat himself down on the stump of a tree and refused to go any farther."[8] So end the first and second phases of the journey of the irresolute goodman. Trust in family virtue, trust in the religious tradition of his community, trust in the sincerity and goodness of his childhood instructor have been subverted, and the devil's thought seems to have become one with his own.

His companion is so assured now of no deviation in him that he tosses him his maple staff and quickly vanishes. Ironically, Brown congratulates himself on his own exhibition of strength, rests complacently a few moments in the promise of meeting his minister next day with a clear conscience, of looking into the deacon's eyes unshrinkingly, and of spending the remainder of the passing night with Faith. His rosy contemplation is interrupted, however, by the sound of horses' hoofs. Then follow aural deceptions of the presence of deacon and minister on the forest path. Their conversation, penetrating his covert, convinces him they are bound to the same destination as he. He does not see them, though he makes an effort to do so, nor do they hinder his view of "the strip of bright sky athwart which they must have passed." The shock he sustains causes him to "catch hold of a tree for support, being ready to sink down on the ground, faint and overburdened with the heavy sickness of his heart" and to entertain doubt as to whether there is a heaven above him. Then, sight of the blue arch of the sky brings momentary assurance, and he makes one more resolve, that, with "heaven above and Faith below [he] will yet stand firm against the devil." But even as he lifts his hands to pray,[9] a cloud suddenly hides the stars; strange cries that seem to involve Faith mingle with the noises of wind in the trees, though he "doubted whether he had heard aught but the murmur of the old forest." Another deception, optical and tactual, follows, as he watches a pink ribbon, emblem of Faith, flutter down and lodge on a branch, from which he seizes it. Actual? We hear no more of it until he reaches home and sees it deco-

rating the head of his wife. Deluded fancy, however, convinces him his last bastion has crumbled. Grief, rage, and terror master him, and any shred of resistance he might yet possess fades. Confident now "[t]here is no good on earth; and sin . . . but a name," he invokes the devil and, like Northumberland on hearing of the death of his son, invites the chaos of total disorder and darkness.

The tempo quickens. He sets forth again, this time at such speed as to appear "to fly along the forest path" until he reaches the scene of the witches' rendezvous. There he seems to hear a familiar tune, often sung at the village meetinghouse, but it trails off into "sounds of the benighted wilderness"; he think he recognizes in the congregation assembled a score of the "church members of Salem village," though his sight, says the narrator, may have suffered from "gleams of light flashing over the obscure field."[10] Near the baptismal font he meets Faith, and the two stand, the only pair, so it seems, "who were yet hesitating on the verge of wickedness in this dark world." He cries to her to look to heaven and resist.[11] All, however, is but the deception of a mind seduced by evil; for, "hardly had he spoken when he found himself amid calm night and solitude," staggering against a rock that felt chill and damp, his cheek sprinkled "with the coldest dew" from a twig that a moment before had seemed to be on fire.

The brief conclusion speaks of the immediate and the lasting effects on Goodman Brown of his night's adventure with an evil thought that got out of control. The story opens on a note of doubt spoken facetiously by Brown; it closes with his own doubt's expansion into cynical disbelief of any good in man. "Blessed are all simple emotions, be they dark or bright!" Hawthorne wrote of Giovanni in **"Rappaccini's Daughter"**; "It is the lurid intermixture of the two that produces the illuminating blaze of the infernal regions."

Notes

1. F. N. Cherry, "The Sources of Hawthorne's 'Young Goodman Brown,'" *AL* [*American Literature*], V (Jan., 1934), 342-348, states that the "chief interest . . . of the story lies in the graphic portrayal of a witches' Sabbath" and introduces in partial support of this view some details Hawthorne probably found in Cervantes' *El Coloquio de los Perros*. In interpreting the story the critic assumes that the characters whom Brown saw or heard in the forest practiced witchcraft. Richard Fogle, "Ambiguity and Clarity in Hawthorne's 'Young Goodman Brown,'" *NEQ* [*The New England Quarterly*], XVIII (Dec., 1945), 448-465, treats what he considers ambiguities in the story and analyzes the near-flawless art that harmonizes them with the story. Thomas E. Connolly, "'Young Goodman Brown,' an Attack on Puritanic Calvinism," *AL*, XXVIII (Nov., 1956), 370-375, examines the story as satire. D. C. McKeithan, "Hawthorne's 'Young Goodman Brown': an Interpretation," *MLN*, LXVII (Feb., 1952), 95-96, states, correctly I believe, that the story is that of a "man [everyman]

whose sin led him to consider all other people sinful." Mark Van Doren, *The Best of Hawthorne* (N.Y., 1951), presents some similarities between the story and *The Scarlet Letter* and perceptively points out the failure of both Brown and Dimmesdale to understand "the presence of evil inside the imagination," and how, "when Brown is made aware of it . . . it becomes a monster with which he cannot cope . . . a monster of his own making." (p. 416)

2. *The Complete Works of Nathaniel Hawthorne,* Wayside ed., 13 vols. (Boston, n. d.), IX, 43. Subsequent references to Hawthorne's Works are to this edition.

3. *Ibid.,* IX, 38.

4. *Ibid.,* I, 256, 257. Italics added. This relationship of evil thought to evil deed may have been suggested by Isabella in her plea for Angelo (*Measure for Measure,* V.i.446-451).

5. Cf. the first 679 lines of *The Rape of Lucrece* for another example of the pattern. Of Tarquin, Shakespeare says that "some untimely thought did instigate / His all too timeless speed" (11. 43-44). Later Tarquin reviews his conflict (11. 498-504) from his conceiving the thought to the moment before the commission of the deed: the strife within his soul, his consciousness of the consequences of his act, his wavering, his loss of self-control. The last three acts of *Othello* exemplify an extended and complex form of this pattern.

6. Brown's companion is perhaps telling the truth here for a purpose; Brown later thinks he has a vision of his father beckoning him toward the devil's baptismal font. Cf. Banquo's observation on the "instruments of darkness" sometimes telling truths "to win us to our harm" (*Macbeth,* I.iii.122-126).

7. Cf. *Macbeth,* II.i.33-34: "Is this a dagger that I see before me, / The handle toward my hand?" And Banquo, after the first meeting with the witches questioned, "Were such things here as we do speak about?" (I.iii.83)

8. Cf. *Macbeth,* I.vii.31: "We will proceed no further in this business."

9. Cf. *Macbeth,* II.ii.28-31.

10. Throughout the story Hawthorne employs a device that is common to all his fiction—a sly casting of doubt on any experience he records as fact which is, on the face of it preternatural, supernatural, or highly unusual. This device has, I think, caused some critics to find ambiguities in his work where, perhaps, none exists.

11. Brown, of course, "had no power to retreat one step, nor to resist, even in thought . . ." (Hawthorne, *Works,* II, 102).

James W. Mathews (essay date 1965)

SOURCE: "Antinomianism in 'Young Goodman Brown,'" in *Studies in Short Fiction,* Vol. 3, No. 1, Fall, 1965, pp. 73-75.

[*In the following essay, Mathews suggests that Brown's passivity—the result of his antinomianist belief that he is saved regardless of his personal actions—leads him into error and doom.*]

Almost everyone commenting on Nathaniel Hawthorne's **"Young Goodman Brown"** has noted that its general theme is the loss of personal faith. On the specific application of certain symbols, however, there has been a good deal of disagreement. Some time ago Thomas E. Connolly re-asserted the paramount allegorical significance of the character Faith and justifiably concluded that "this story is Hawthorne's criticism of the teachings of Puritanic-Calvinism,"[1] though he limited the object of Hawthorne's criticism to predestination. Giving further scrutiny to Faith can establish a more specific probability of meaning, which converts to theological terms Hawthorne's ubiquitous thesis that the most serious personal evil is retreat from reality and responsibility.

A doctrine of one group of Calvinists during the time depicted in the story was Antinomianism,[2] which insisted that salvation was of faith, not of works. If good works existed, they came only as a secondary by-product of the mysterious divine grace; personal volition was de-emphasized, if not completely eliminated. Grace itself was contingent on the degree of the individual's faith; and a strong faith, which usually resulted in an emotional experience, was evidence enough of one's predestined salvation. According to Perry Miller, one question inherent in Antinomianism was "since the recipient of grace is assured of salvation without ever doing anything to deserve it, should he not surrender to the intoxication of certainty and give no further thought to his behavior?"[3] Extreme Antinomians among the High Calvinists believed that "if a man was elected and predestined to salvation, no power in heaven or on earth could prevent it; and hence, no matter what the moral conduct of a man might be, his salvation was sure if he was one of the elect; the wicked actions of such a man were not sinful, and he had no occasion to confess his sins or break them off by repentance."[4]

"Young Goodman Brown" depicts a man who is so confident in his recent union with faith that he walks superciliously into the devil's own revival without any fear whatsoever. Hawthorne tells us nothing of Goodman Brown's earlier life and acts. Though Brown seems to enjoy a good reputation, there is no reference to his good works. Unlike Everyman, he does not produce them as a last-minute testimony to his worthiness. Only his faith exists, deluding him into passivity. Faith's admonition to "put off your journey until sunrise and sleep in your own bed tonight"[5] suggests that the influence of Faith over Brown is essentially negative. The insubstantiality of Brown's religious faith manifests itself in the pink ribbons of his wife's cap; their texture is aery and their color the pastel of infancy.

Brown is aware that his secret nocturnal journey is for an "evil purpose." He does not enter the forest ignorantly or under duress. He is prepared to witness evil and perhaps partake. But as an Antinomian, he would believe that no evil is charged against those with faith: "I'll cling to her skirts and follow her to heaven," he cries. He is quick to exonerate himself and brand the others faithless despite his own deliberate act of keeping the evil rendezvous. He has his Faith, and the devil leads him into false confidence early when he says: "I would not for twenty old women like the one hobbling before us that Faith should come to any harm." Faith is secure at home and is Brown's supposed mystical shield against whatever may menace him. In explaining to the devil why he is late, he says that "Faith kept me back a while." Faith, thus, is temporary protection, functioning only in isolation. Her own apprehension over Brown's leaving points to her lack of remote spiritual control over her husband.

Since Brown is confident that the faith of his ancestors has protected them from the devil, he feels that he too will turn back in time or at least avoid permanent harm. As evidence of the righteousness of his people and of his righteousness, he stresses the theoretical side of religion with the practical as secondary: "We are a people of prayer, and good works to boot, and abide no such wickedness." Then amid suggestions that his own ancestors have been prone to evil notwithstanding their faith, Brown indignantly asks whether such is "any reason why I should quit my dear Faith" and join their company. Further, he asserts, "with heaven above and Faith below, I will yet stand firm against the devil." The poignant irony in Brown's show of certainty is that he lost the protection of Faith the very moment he left the confines of their cottage. Soon he hears the "voice of a young woman, uttering lamentations, yet with an uncertain sorrow, and entreating for some favor, which, perhaps, it would grieve her to obtain; and all the unseen multitude, both saints and sinners, seemed to encourage her onward." Faith is now not only a symbol of Brown's tottering assurance; she also reflects the lost hope of all who have suffered the Antinomian delusion of the abstract.

When Brown identifies this voice as that of his wife, he declares that "Faith is gone" and he becomes "maddened with despair." Now, he thinks, "there is no good on earth"; and in the sudden divestment of his old theology, his negative conclusion is understandable. Faith, who has appeared invulnerable at home removed from any encounter with sin, has become one of the devil's disciples. And as Faith is, Brown is. They stand together: ". . . the wretched man beheld his Faith, and the wife her husband, trembling before that unhallowed altar." Brown concurs with the devil's declaration that "evil is the nature of mankind." To a relativist and not a dogmatist, this recognition would be taken in stride. But the inverted Brown retreats. With one

final, desperate attempt to preserve his heretofore comfortable doctrine of assurance, he urges Faith to "look up to heaven, and resist the wicked one." Here he voices the passive Antinomian means of salvation: the union of faith below and grace from above.

Though he does not see whether Faith follows his advice or not, Brown has evidence enough that passive faith is ineffectual. Hence his silent disdain of his "pious" forebears and contemporaries; in his condemnation of them he circumstantially accuses himself. He thereafter becomes "a stern, a sad, a darkly meditative, a distrustful, if not a desperate man," and he dies in "gloom." After his experience he becomes as passively cynical as he has been passively trusting. He knows that Faith has been false; but what he never fathoms is that her weakness (and the repulsive grossness of all mankind) is the result of his own theological error and is exaggerated by his continuous passivity.

Notes

1. "Hawthorne's 'Young Goodman Brown': An Attack on Puritanic Calvinism," *American Literature,* XXVIII (November 1956), 375.

2. That Hawthorne was aware of the furor caused by Antinomians in Massachusetts is evident in his highly ironic sketch of Mrs. Hutchinson. See *The Works of Nathaniel Hawthorne,* George Parsons Lathrop, ed. (Boston, 1883), XII, 217-226.

3. *The New England Mind: The Seventeenth Century* (Cambridge, Mass., 1954), p. 369.

4. J. Macbride Sterrett in *Encyclopaedia of Religion and Ethics,* James Hastings, ed. (New York, 1928), I, 582.

5. All quotations from "Young Goodman Brown" are from *Works,* II, 89-106.

B. Bernard Cohen (essay date 1968)

SOURCE: "Deodat Lawson's *Christ's Fidelity* and Hawthorne's 'Young Goodman Brown,'" in *Essex Institute Historical Collections,* Vol. 104, No. 4, October, 1968, pp. 349-70.

[*In the following essay, Cohen contends that Deodat Lawson's* Christ's Fidelity, *a work about the Salem witchcraft trials in 1692, inspired Hawthorne to write "Young Goodman Brown."*]

Despite much praise and many fine words expended on Hawthorne's **"Young Goodman Brown,"** interpretations of this well-wrought tale have varied as widely as the critics and their personal biases. The abundant ambiguities present in the story yield opportunity to all: those who would see Hawthorne as confirming Calvinism's central doctrine of man's innate depravity, others who view him as rejecting the same tenet, some who would apply a latter-day symbolism involving phallic pine trees and sexual guilt, and still others who would by expert juggling of old ideas in new semantic dress convey the impression that an original interpretation is being offered.[1]

After such great argument it is refreshing and heartening to see an admirable article by Professor David Levin, in which he sanely urges that we "try to read the story in terms that were available to Hawthorne."[2] Professor Levin cogently argues that belief in the validity of spectral evidence, as it was acceptable to the magistrates, offered the rationale on which Hawthorne constructed **"Young Goodman Brown,"** and that any attempt to interpret the story must take this factor into account. If heeded, this plea that we consider the tale in its historical context will prevent us from wandering in an hypothetical forest as variously populated as was that which Brown entered on the fateful night.

Even before Professor Levin's essay, others had explored Hawthorne's interest in the Salem history that underlies **"Young Goodman Brown."** Hawthorne's concern about the role of Judge Hathorne in the witchcraft delusion of 1692 has long been recognized by biographers and critics, and the autobiographical expression of his guilt feelings in the Custom House essay is frequently cited. Further evidence of his ancestral burden appears in such works as **"The Hollow of the Three Hills," "Alice Doane's Appeal,"** and **"Main Street."**

It is also generally understood that Hawthorne during his long years of apprenticeship read widely in old state papers, legal records, musty sermons, and other colonial relics. Here he often encountered significant names linked with Judge Hathorne, and he made use of them in his fiction. G. Harrison Orians and Tremaine McDowell were among the first to point out that some of the characters appearing in **"Young Goodman Brown"** represent actual citizens of Salem who had been accused as witches before Hathorne.[3] In a later study Professor Arlin Turner disclosed the names of two additional colonial worthies who are prominent figures in the story, and, in extension of the investigation, attributed much of the basic material to Cotton Mather's *Wonders of the Invisible World.*[4]

Unnoticed among these autobiographical and historical stimulants to Hawthorne's imagination is a book that was in his personal library—Deodat Lawson's *Christ's Fidelity.* This slender volume was dedicated to Judge Hathorne, among others, and across from his ancestor's name on the dedicatory page Nathaniel Hawthorne affixed his own signature.[5] The contents include a sermon delivered in Salem Village on 24 March 1692, when John Hathorne conducted a vigorous interrogation of accused witches.[6] In an appendix Lawson related his own observations of the witchcraft phenomena and other "Remarks [which] were afterwards, (at my Request) Revised and Corrected by some who Sate Judges on the Bench . . ."[7]

A careful examination of Hawthorne's copy of *Christ's Fidelity* reveals how the volume, so intimately linked with

the grim judge who hovered always on the threshold of his descendant's consciousness, may have provided the imaginative impetus to the creation of **"Young Goodman Brown."** The details in the Appendix of Lawson's book and the theology contained in his jeremiad gave Hawthorne the psychological basis for, and the artistic approaches to, his story. In effect, **"Young Goodman Brown"** is an imaginative and ironic rejoinder to Lawson's version of the witchcraft phenomena.[8]

I

Undoubtedly wide and random reading contributed to **"Young Goodman Brown,"** but emotional attachment may have made indelible some of the details found in Lawson's Appendix to the 1704 volume. This enumerates matters of record which could have suggested to Hawthorne the psychological basis of his story with its dreamlike atmosphere so suitable to the mental aberrations involved in spectral experiences. Above all, some details cited by Lawson may have provided Hawthorne the master psychological and structural symbol of his story: the pink ribbons.

Basic to the psychological structure of **"Young Goodman Brown"** is the problem of what constitutes reality. The crucial question may be phrased thus: Do the events in the historical and fictional Salem Village actually occur, or does the imagination or heart, no matter how distorted, create its own vision of reality? Accepting as truth the existence of supernatural agents capable of intervening in human activities, Lawson and Cotton Mather consider the seemingly unreal witchcraft occurrences as reality and attribute them to the power of Satan. For Hawthorne the events have reality only as they exist in an aberrant human mind which conjures up its own spectres and doubts. Utilizing recorded data from Puritan history, Hawthorne offers us a psychological version of reality as it might be created in the mind of any man.

The witchcraft experiences recounted by Lawson in his Appendix stress the power of evil spirits to alter reality. For instance, the testimony of Joseph Ring describes the phenomenon of forced transport to witches' meetings. To Lawson and the officials of Salem Village, Ring's adventure is the work of evil spirits and hence evidence against witches. To Hawthorne, transport represents an excellent example of the mind's distortion of reality and serves as the fundamental motif of the journey in his story.

As a faithful recorder of contemporary events, Lawson inscribes the following account of Ring's testimony:

> A Person who has been frequently *Transported* to and fro by the Devils, for the space of near *Two Years* . . . did depose upon *Oath,* that . . . he was many times *Bodily* Transported, to places where the Witches were gathered together, and that he there saw *Feasting* and *Dancing* . . . [and] *he did* take his Oath, that he did with his *Bodily* Eyes, see some of the *Accused* at those Witch-meetings several times; . . . he also proved by

sundry Persons that at those times of Transport, he was *Bodily* absent from his Abode, and could no where be found, but being met with by some on the Road at a distance from his home; was suddenly conveyed away from them.[9]

This passage helps explain the feeling of compulsion which Brown expresses when Faith tries to prevent his departure from Salem Village. In the same account there are also hints of Brown's evasive actions: the hide-and-seek played by Brown with Goody Cloyse, as well as his shifting aside from the woodland path to avoid a direct encounter with the minister and Deacon Gookin. Brown's later frenzied rush through the dark forest to the rendezvous reflects the hypnotic force of the trance-like experience of transport. Neither Ring, the case history, nor Brown, the fictional character, actually had such experiences. Both perceived them only in their imaginations, but both undoubtedly believed in them.

Other details in Lawson's Appendix may have added to the atmosphere of delusion which Hawthorne created in his story. The situation in which Deacon Gookin and the minister force Brown—or so he believes—to come to the baptismal font reflects the records kept by Lawson.[10] There are also vivid descriptions of the sacramental rites of witches, as in this passage:

> They were also Accused to hold and Administer Diabolical Sacraments, *viz.,* a *Mock-Baptism,* and a *Devil-Supper,* at which *Cursed* Imitations of the Sacred Institutions of our *Blessed Lord,* they used Forms of Words to be trembled at, in the very Rehearsing. . . . At their Cursed Supper, they were said to have *Red* Bread, and *Red* Drink, and when they pressed an Afflicted person to Eat and Drink thereof, she turned away her Head, and Spit at it, and said, *I will not Eat, I will not Drink, it is Blood, that is not the Bread of Life, that is not the Water of Life, and I will have none of yours.*[11]

Here Hawthorne may have obtained the artistic and psychological clue to the magnificent rendering of lights, shadows, colors, and sounds filtering through Brown's consciousness.

To this climactic scene Lawson could have contributed other details. For example, the appearance of the ghost of Brown's father and mother may be an echo of Lawson's interest in testimony that ghosts of his own wife and daughter had appeared to the afflicted (pp. 98-100). In this detail Hawthorne, of course, saw an opportunity to place a supernatural vision within the framework of an experience of transport which already demonstrated dislocation of reality. For Brown, this mental distortion leads to family discord and distrust—a reflection of Lawson's reports of children accusing their parents of witchcraft (pp. 118-119). Even the devil-minister's powerful pronunciamento on the supremacy and universality of evil finds a parallel in Lawson: "They affirmed that many of those Wretched Souls, had been Baptized . . . and as to the manner of Administration, the *Great Officer of Hell* . . . said over them, *Thou art mine, and I have Full Power over thee,* and there-

upon they Engaged and Covenanted to Renounce God, Christ, their *Sacred Baptism,* and the whole way of *Gospel Salvation,* and to use their utmost Endeavours, to *Oppose* the Kingdom of CHRIST, and to set up and *Advance* the Kingdom of Satan."[12] The words uttered in this rite become for Brown the reality of a lifetime after he returns to the village.

Each of the parallels cited thus far suggests that reality in Hawthorne's story is not derived from the power of evil spirits but from Brown's fancied construction of events. In each detail which Hawthorne took from his source or sources, the real and unreal, the familiar and unfamiliar, the natural and supernatural become inextricably mingled in the deluded consciousness of Brown. In fact, since the same problem of the nature of reality is implicit in the many case histories cited by Lawson, Hawthorne's reading of the Appendix may have inspired him to focus on the psychological distortions within one mind representative of many in Salem Village. In this sense, Brown's fearful single journey symbolizes the frightful experience of an entire community.

Although the story is told by an omniscient author, some of whose comments and judgements are quite clear, Hawthorne did limit himself almost exclusively to the consciousness of his central character. Within this consciousness so uncertain of actuality, the experience of transport can indeed begin with a confrontation of a man (as devil image) who resembles Brown's grandfather. Thus to Brown the sacraments so customary in his everyday religion become part of a Satanic meeting. Thus people familiar and close to him are participants in his vision of the distortion of God's ordinances. Thus even witch spectres and the ghosts of dead people mingle in the surrealistic experience stirred by his own fancy.

Since Hawthorne concentrated on the inner experiences of this single representative consciousness, he attempted to render an atmosphere suitable to the central mind of the story. That atmosphere blurs any true comprehension of reality, creates constant tension between the trappings of everyday life and spectres, and ultimately conveys a set of dream-like experiences. Hawthorne's basic method is to create in the forest those shifting lights and shadows and strange images and sounds which lurk at the threshold between the imagined and the actual stimuli of vision and hearing, and which, as critics have pointed out, are powerfully rendered in the story. It is an atmosphere adapted to the psychological distortions going on in Salem Village—distortions which a Lawson or a Mather could not understand as well as Hawthorne did.

Because it has not been fully understood that Hawthorne created ambiguities of atmosphere and plot detail in **"Young Goodman Brown"** in order to capture in fiction the hallucinatory nature of transport, much quibbling has occurred about whether the experiences of Brown were reality or dream. Hawthorne never explicitly says that the sequence of events during the forest journey is a dream.

After he poses the choice, he does refer twice to these oc-currences as a dream. However, it is more important to re-alize that from the details included in Lawson's book Haw-thorne chose to create not necessarily a dream but a dream-like or visionary atmosphere appropriate to his psychological interpretation of historical events. Essen-tially interested in mental and emotional conflicts and ab-errations, Hawthorne uses the ingredients of the dream to convey psychological states. The dream-like quality of the story serves beautifully to portray the mingling of the real and unreal, the consequent blurrings of actuality, and the creation of a new kind of reality which encompasses dis-trust and loss of faith in man and even God. Thus neither Ring nor Brown literally dreamed his journey; in Haw-thorne's view each underwent a profound psychological experience which may have seemed like a dream.

The most important factor in the portrayal of Brown's wa-vering consciousness is Faith's pink ribbons. Some ac-counts in Lawson's Appendix help explain their prominent function in the psychological and narrative structure of the story. As Professor Levin has pointed out, Faith's pink rib-bons are related to spectral evidence, which was a baffling and agonizing problem during the witchcraft trials. Strangely enough, the two seemingly disparate elements— the spectral evidence which was used to convict and hang nineteen people, and the innocent pink ribbon which in her husband's eyes condemned a simple housewife—are inex-tricable.

As Lawson's sermon, which will be discussed, shows, the spectral aspect of the witchcraft hysteria goes back to the Puritan's theological belief in a titanic Satan of chameleon nature. During the disturbances of 1692, this image of the devil became so frightfully enlarged that legal and minis-terial authorities found it hard to define the limitations of Satan's spectral powers. Could a witch, while being corpo-really present to some observers, yet venture outside his own person and, visible only to the afflicted in a "shape" or "spectre," impose torments on another individual who might recognize and accuse the witch? Did the appearance of such a "spectre" afford a reasonable presumption that the person from whom it emanated was indeed a witch? Judge Stoughton insisted that the devil could appear in the shape of a guilty person but could not assume the shape of an innocent person. Thus it followed that to him anyone whose spectre appeared to the afflicted was presumed guilty of being in league with Satan.[13] On this point there was great dispute. Even Mather's attempt in *Wonders* to settle the issue was equivocal.[14] In Lawson's sermon, de-livered before *Wonders* was compiled, the ex-minister of Salem Village avoided facing the problem directly, yet at the same time he justified the actions of the judges, who did condemn on merely spectral evidence. In addition, he presented in his Appendix many examples of spectral ex-periences as if they were history or fact[15]—the kinds of ex-periences which Hawthorne, as we have seen, may have borrowed for his story.

To corroborate the allegations of the afflicted, the magis-trates sought physical evidence of spectral actions. In the

testimony during the examinations of witches there is em-phasis on visible marks imprinted on the sufferers; for ex-ample, the teeth marks of George Burroughs were said to have been found on the body of one of his victims. In the accounts of Lawson and Mather, one also finds concrete, physical objects cited as evidence of a spectral visitation. It is from this kind of experience that Hawthorne derived the artistic symbol of the pink ribbons.

As "an Eye and Ear Witness, of most of those Amazing things, so far as they came within the Notice of Humane Senses" (p. 93), Lawson records two anecdotes which help us to understand the appearance of the pink ribbons in **"Young Goodman Brown."** Since the spectres of Salem obeyed the immutable laws of poltergeists the world over, they were often invisible themselves but contrived to leave tangible tokens of their immaterial presence. Lawson de-scribes one such incident:

> A iron Spindle of a woollen Wheel, being taken very strangely out of an House at *Salem* Village, was used by a Spectre, as an Instrument of Torture to a Sufferer, not being discernable to the Standers by; until it was by the said Sufferer snatched out of the Spectres Hand, and then it did immediately appear to the Persons present to be really the same iron Spindle.[16]

Certainly to persons already inclined to accept as fact the existence of a world of infernal spirits, this concrete evi-dence must have been extremely convincing!

Lawson's own amazement and credulity can be read even more plainly between the lines of an entry which he placed in the climactic portion of the first section of the Appen-dix:

> A young Woman that was afflicted at a fearful rate, had a Spectre appeared to her, with a white Sheet wrapped about it, not visible to the Standers by, until this Suf-ferer (*violently* striving in her Fit) snatched at, took hold, and tore off a Corner of that Sheet; her Father be-ing by her, endeavoured to lay hold upon it with her, that she might retain what she had gotten; but at the passing-away of the Spectre, he had such a violent Twitch of his Hand, as if it would have been torn off; immediately thereupon appeared in the Sufferers Hand, the Corner of a Sheet, *a real Cloth, visible* to the Spec-tators which (*as it is said*) remains still to be seen.[17]

Hawthorne's choice of the pink ribbon as the familiar physical evidence which leads to Brown's condemnation of Faith and his own wild plunge into the forest of doubt certainly could have been based on this incident of the sheet.[18] Like all the details taken from Lawson and other sources, those involving the spindle and the sheet fuse the familiar tangible item with the bizarre, unfamiliar spectres. Just as the spindle and the sheet confirmed the reality of spectres for the credulous people of Salem, so Hawthorne employs the pink ribbon to support Brown's widening sus-picions in the haunted forest created by his mind.

Like Brown's experiences of transport and Satanic bap-tism, which have counterparts in the records kept by Lawson, his vision of the ribbon on the branch of a tree in the Puritan forest relates to the problem of reality. Was the ribbon there? Did he seize it in his hand? Or did the waverings of his mind created by the ambiguous and fearful mingling of the familiar and unfamiliar lead him to imagine that the ribbon fell? In the context of all the witchcraft details cited thus far, the descent of the ribbon is perhaps the most important distortion of reality in Brown's mind.[19]

The ribbons, which are both real and spectral, and hence emphasize the psychological basis of the story, contribute a great deal to the structure of **"Young Goodman Brown."** The tale consists of three parts. There is a frame: (1) departure from home and Faith, and (2) return to Faith and Salem Village. In the latter section of the frame the permanent results of the night away from home are concisely depicted. Not only are these parts relatively short and almost exactly equal, but they are the clearest sections of the story; that is, the details narrated and the effects summarized by Hawthorne are vivid and effective. Within this frame is the source of the changes in Brown observable by the end of the story: the forest journey, which is one of the longest temptation scenes Hawthorne ever wrote. This long sequence of temptation divides into two parts, each with smaller components. The first shows the erosions of Brown's trust in his forbears and in his respected contemporaries: his ancestors, plus Goody Cloyse, Deacon Gookin, and the minister. Between this part and the next comes his loss of belief in Faith. The next section of temptation plunges Brown deeper into the forest in his progress to the witch meeting, where Faith seems to appear and where Brown's doubts envelop all humanity.

In the opening part, the ribbons, referred to three times, are identified with Faith. Brown's last glimpse of Faith emphasizes both the ribbons and a human response in her to his departure: ". . . he looked back and saw the head of Faith still peeping after him with a melancholy air, in spite of her pink ribbons."

In the long temptation sequence, where Hawthorne is concerned chiefly with Brown's consciousness, Faith never really appears clearly as a human being. However, the ribbon, the prime spectral evidence of her guilt, descends between the two parts of the Satanic temptations. In effect, Hawthorne builds up the distortions in Brown's mind so that the ribbon, so pointedly emphasized at first, can become spectral assurance for Brown. In the baptismal scene the ribbon does not appear, but a spectre of Faith is present, or so Brown believes. Since he has already accepted the falling ribbon as evidence of Faith's venture into witchcraft, it is not surprising that the appearance of her spectre completes the process of conviction in his credulous mind.

In the final portion of the tale the real ribbons, as depicted in the early half of the frame, return. However, the spectre of the ribbon and of Faith in the forest have contributed immeasurably to the new version of reality which Brown brings home with him. Although in the cases of the spindle and the sheet the victims of spectres were left with tangible evidence of the visitations, Brown does not hold the ribbon in his hand, even though he was supposed to have seized it. The ribbons are still in Faith's cap as she welcomes him on his return. This fact makes Brown's experience even more spectral than the cases cited by Lawson.

In this analysis of the structure, the ribbons emphasize the nature of Brown's psychological experience and at the same time provide important links in the construction of the story. The ribbons are a token of Hawthorne's ability to convert his source materials into literary art.

II

Without fully realizing the impact which his sermon might have on the congregation in Salem Village, Lawson in effect provided theological explanation for the spectral nature of witchcraft. Although this sermon of 1692 does not contain the kinds of vivid case histories in the Appendix, Hawthorne may have seen in it the essential allegorical and dramatic conflict between faith and Satan which is central to Brown's spectral delusions. In addition, he ironically deploys Lawson's theological position in the narrative and psychological structure of his story by balancing Lawson's emphasis on prayer against Brown's growing doubt, and Lawson's faith in sermons against Brown's reactions to them in the story.

In his address Lawson had to face crucial problems: why should a God-fearing community suddenly be enveloped by supernatural phenomena upsetting the family, community, and religious security of the people? And how can individuals noted for their godliness become agents or victims of Satan? Lawson's answer, supported by countless Biblical passages and by the arguments of covenant theology, places all the responsibility for witchcraft on Satan's malignity and powers of seduction. God, Lawson argues, is testing the faith of the village by granting Satan freedom to spread evil. Thus Satan is God's agent used to serve His own "most Holy Designs . . . by the Trying of his People and the *Judicial Blinding,* and hardening of *Obstinate* and *Impenitent* Sinners unto their Eternal Destruction" (p. 43).

Such an attempt to explain witchcraft phenomena on theological grounds led Lawson into the ironical position of emphasizing the dominion of Satan as much as the supreme power of God, if not more so. Like his contemporary clergymen, he thinks in black and white categories: Satan versus God or each member of the Trinity, Satan versus man, the accused versus the afflicted, breaking the covenant versus faith, the kingdom of darkness versus the kingdom of light. Yet at the same time he acknowledges Satan's power to blur the splendor of God and to impersonate an angel of light. In attributing all to the seduction of Satan, Lawson had to stress the frightful dangers of the Devil's cunning, and therefore at least one third of the sermon is devoted to this power. Even when Lawson turns to God, Satan is ever present as the opposing force in the struggle, and when in the last part of the sermon he offers advice to his former parishioners the image of a terrifying devil is kept vividly before them.

Early in his discourse Lawson comprehensively portrays the powers of Satan:

> He is a *Spirit,* and hence strikes at the *spiritual* part the most *Excellent* (Constituent) part of man. Primarily disturbing, and interrupting the *Animal* and *Vital* Spirits, he maliciously *Operates* upon, the more *Common Powers* of the *Soul,* by strange and frightful *Representations* to the Fancy, or Imagination, and by violent *Tortures* of the body, often threatning to extinguish life; as hath been observ'd, in those that are afflicted amongst us. And not only so, but he vents his malice; in *Diabolical Operations,* on the more sublime and distinguishing *faculties,* of the *Rational Soul,* raising *Mists* of Darkness, and ignorance, in the *Understanding* . . . Stirring up, the *innate Rebellion* of the will, though he cannot *force* it unto sin. Introducing Universal *Ataxy,* and *inordinancy,* in the Passions, both Love and *Hatred,* the *Cardinal* or *Radical* affections, with all other that accompany or flow from them . . .
>
> (pp. 18-19).

This discussion of Satan's powers as they operate in terms of the Puritan concept of man could have suggested to Hawthorne the process of emotional and spiritual disintegration stimulated in Brown's mind.

In a passage which may have been marked by Hawthorne, Lawson stresses the methods employed by Satan to undermine the "Rational Soul" and to stir up emotions:

> . . . when he useth *Mankind,* he seemeth to bring in what he intends, in a way of *Familiar Converse* with us Mortals, that he may not be suspected at the bottom of all. Hence he Contracts and Indents with Witches and Wizzards . . . [and] he will use their *Bodies* and *Minds, Shapes,* and Representations, to *Affright* and *Afflict* others, at his pleasure, for the propagation of his *Infernal Kingdom,* and accomplishing his Devised *Mischiefs,* to the *Souls, Bodies,* and *Lives* of the *Children* of men; yea, of the *Children* of GOD too, so far as permitted and is possible.
>
> (pp. 28-29).

In such operations Satan is adept at assuming the form of an angel of light "endeavouring to look so like the *true Saints,* and Ministers of Christ, that it were possible, he *would deceive the very Elect . . . by his Subtilty*" (p. 31). This power of Satan accounts for the grim uncertainties of spectral evidence.

Because of these powers and methods employed by Satan, Lawson is acutely aware of the potentialities for discord and distrust. In his Introduction he had stressed God's giving Satan freedom to range and "to introduce as Criminal" God-fearing people who may become "the Instruments *of his* [Satan's] *malice, against their Friends and Neighbours.*" In the sermon itself during a plea for humility, he emphasizes the conflict between the kingdoms of Satan and Christ and sees the people of Salem in the middle of

the struggle. In the same passage (marked, perhaps, by Hawthorne) he describes the possibility of Satan's dividing Christ's kingdom "*against* itself, that being thereby weakened, he may the better take Opportunity to set up his own *Accursed Powers* and Dominions" (pp. 63-64).

Sensing such a danger, Lawson feels it his duty to warn the Salemites against spreading the blight and turning brother against brother by "*giving way unto Sinful and unruly Passions, such as Envy, Malice, or Hatred of our Neighbours and Brethren.* These Devil-like, corrupted Passions, are *Contrary Unto,* and do endanger the letting in *Satan,* and his *Temptations . . .*" (p. 71).

Despite such admonitions, however, Lawson, envisioning the "roaring Lyon Satan" as the great and all-but-omnipotent enemy, rallies his hearers to a supreme effort to defeat the Devil, a kind of New England crusade. In the most belligerent passage in the sermon even the printed words seem to shout: "I am this day Commanded to Call and Cry an Alarm unto you, ARM; ARM; ARM; handle your Arms, see that you are fixed and in a readiness, as Faithful Soldiers under the Captain of our Salvation, that by the Shield of FAITH, *Ye* and *We* all may *Resist* the Fiery Darts of the Wicked" (p. 81). Here is the basic irony of Lawson's position: his vigorous urging of warfare against evil would encourage the very emotional responses which he warns against. In seeking the destruction of Satan, he sounds the war cry against the witches and hence stimulates further hate and distrust.

As counterbalance to Satan's malevolence, the positive forces offered by Lawson to support the people in their tribulations seem somewhat colorless and ineffective. The sources of faith, the church and God, are portrayed in rather conventional terms. The church he compares to a woman "shining with utmost brightness, of the *Faith* and *Order* of the Gospel" (p. 29). God is described as the real power—albeit the unleasher—behind the surge of witchcraft and the supreme party to the true convenant. The Christian virtues which Lawson would have the people of Salem Village embrace anew during these dark hours are those already familiar to them: fidelity to the covenant, self-examination under the eyes of God, and humility before Him. For the afflicted—but not for the accused—he urges "True Spiritual Sympathy," the compassion central to Christianity. And above all there is the duty, and the inspiration, of prayer: "Again, Let us be Faithful in Prayer. The life of Prayer, lies in the Exercise of *Faith* therein. It is to the Prayer of Faith that the promise of *Answer* is made . . . Besides, it is said the Prayer of Faith, *shall save the sick . . . Faith* in Prayer engageth the Glorious Intercessor on our behalf . . . *Faith* in CHRIST Exercised in Prayer, is the token of God's Covenant, with his Elect under the Gospel . . ." (p. 83).

The godly or Christian side of Lawson's argument is well summed up in a passage which reminds us of Brown's desire to cling to Faith's skirts: ". . . we should take the faster hold of GOD by Faith, and cleave closer to him, that

Satan may not, by any of his Devices or Operations, draw us from our steadfastness of Hope, and Dependance on the God of our Salvation" (p. 54).

In this way Lawson tried to balance the two "mighty opposites" of a perplexing theological problem. In his attempt to justify God's unleashing of Satan, Lawson may have had a neat theological argument, but his psychological insight was sadly deficient. What he did not realize was that his vivid depiction of the powers of Satan might outweigh his emphasis on faith and Christian virtues. Bound by his covenant theology, he did not realize that he could not call for restraint of distrust and hatred, while at the same time urging even greater militancy against those in league with Satan.

The fallacy inherent in Lawson's theological argument may have suggested to Hawthorne the allegorical and dramatic conflict—the clinging to Faith during the temptation of the devil-figures—which is so significant in the structure of **"Young Goodman Brown,"** especially in the long middle section. Instead of using theological or Biblical arguments, Hawthorne visualizes the opposing forces as human beings struggling within Brown's mind, and at the same time he allows them to assume a symbolical meaning which points up the dichotomy of Lawson's thesis.

On one side in Brown's vision is the fresh image of a youthful wife, Faith, to whose skirts Brown hopes to cling during a flight heavenward after the one compulsive experience in the dark wilderness. The pink ribbons, as we have seen, are the important structural device which identifies Faith early in the story, becomes the spectral evidence promoting Brown's doubt, and ultimately leads him to the delusion of condemning her. While this image of a youthful woman is very real, it also operates symbolically in terms of faith—of Brown's loss of faith.

The other side of Lawson's theological argument is conveyed in Brown's mind through the devil images in human form, both old and distrustful of man. In portraying the first, who resembles Brown's grandfather, Hawthorne skillfully endows the mortal shape with attributes of supernatural power: the old man's snakelike staff and his powers to summon the spectres of people familiar and dear to Brown. As a background for the New England minister who is the second devil figure, Hawthorne creates a surrealistic mélange of visions and sounds which reflect Brown's mind. In this latter setting, full of ocular deceptions, the devil image is quite direct and blunt in his condemnation of human nature. This directness, as compared to the deviousness and sophistry of the first devil figure, indicates the degree to which Brown's mind has disintegrated. Softened by the subtleties of the first devil and of spectral experiences, he is now ready to absorb the message from whose destructive impact he will never recover.

During the psychological and symbolical conflict the balance of power is on the side of Satan, not faith. Actually the wife Faith does not struggle with the images of Satan; it is Brown who is torn between visions of Faith and the seductions of the devil. The preponderant power of the devil is indicated in the structure of the story. Satan does not appear in the brief opening part, although the premonitions expressed there do prefigure the emotional conflicts to come. However, in the long middle section the devil conjured by Brown literally and figuratively consumes and distorts Brown's mind and emotions. The third part demonstrates the horrible effects of Satan's triumph over Brown and over Faith. No matter how desperately he had tried to cling to Faith's skirts, Brown is irrevocably pulled away from her, and he becomes a thrall of the devil.

In this, Brown's progress toward a hell of his own making, Hawthorne shows his understanding of the psychology of the witchcraft delusion. Versed in theology but not in human behavior, Lawson erected well-worn safeguards against the onslaught of Satan. To him the conflict between Faith and Satan was explained in theological terms; to him faith would be triumphant. On the other hand, Hawthorne saw the same conflict as a psychological struggle within Brown. In narrative form Hawthorne attempted to indicate how Lawson's emphasis on Satan's powers could have an effect on the Goodman Browns of Salem Village—and of the world—which would be exactly opposite to that intended. By giving concrete and human form to *Fidelity* and to *Satan's Malignity* warring in the mind of Brown, and by artistically recreating the psychology of spectral conflict, Hawthorne expressed his disapproval of Lawson's theological position.

The fallacy of Lawson's dogma enters the psychological and narrative structure of Hawthorne's story in another way: the ironic motif emphasizing Lawson's injunction to prayer and trust in heaven as a mainstay. In every division of the story there are references to prayer. At the beginning, Brown, attempting to quell Faith's fears about his sojourn and about her being alone, tells her to pray: "'Say thy prayers, dear Faith, and go to bed at dusk, and no harm will come to thee.'"

Such confidence in prayer, like his feeling that Faith is "'a blessed angel on earth,'" becomes a part of the psychological struggle during the experience of transport. After the first devil-tempter tries to undermine his ancestors, Brown says, "'We are a people of prayer, and good works to boot, and abide no such wickedness.'" When the shape of Goody Cloyse appears, she is described as mumbling indistinct words, "a prayer, doubtless." Because of his prayerful gesture of looking up to heaven, Brown does not actually see the devil-figure give his staff to Goody Cloyse. Shortly after, when Brown thinks that he hears the voices of Deacon Gookin and the minister, their spectres are described as passing "through the forest, where no church had ever been gathered or solitary Christian prayed." To counter the impact of this experience and the "heavy sickness of his heart," Brown looks up to the sky again, but in the turmoil of doubt he wonders "whether there really was a heaven above him." However, seeing the blue arch and the brightening stars, he says, "'With heaven above and

Faith below, I will yet stand firm against the Devil!'" But, as he lifts "his hands to pray," a cloud covers the stars. In these references to prayer before the ribbon falls, the struggle in Brown's mind between faith and the seductions of the devil clearly echoes Lawson's ineffectual emphasis on prayer as a solution to the witchcraft problem of Salem Village.

When the spectral ribbon moves him to strong doubt, Brown comes to the witch meeting, where he finds people who, "Sabbath after Sabbath, looked devoutly heavenward." In the sermon which he now hears, the devil underscores the hypocrisy of the people present: "'There . . . are all whom ye have reverenced from youth. Ye deemed them holier than yourselves, and shrank from your own sin, contrasting it with their lives of righteousness and prayerful aspirations heavenward. Yet here are they all in my worshipping assembly.'" A few moments later, just before he emerges from the state of transport, Brown urges the spectre of Faith to "'look up to heaven, and resist the wicked one.'" This last reference to the saving force of heaven and prayer is ironical because Brown has already succumbed to the spectral temptations summoned by his own imagination. As soon as he returns to the village he demonstrates that he has adopted the devil's concepts of hypocritical piety and of the universal evil of man. In this way Hawthorne reverses Lawson's faith in prayer.

Hawthorne's distrust of Lawson's belief in prayer is clearly depicted in the final section. When Brown hears the holy words of Deacon Gookin's prayer through an open window, he asks, "'What God doth the wizzard pray to?'" And when his own family kneels down "at prayer," he scowls, mutters to himself, gazes sternly at Faith, and turns away. With such severity Hawthorne underlines the psychological damage done to Brown in the forest, as well as his new version of reality which no longer includes prayer, faith in covenant theology, faith in man, or even faith in God.

Just as Hawthorne makes ironic rejoinder to Lawson in regard to prayer, he also emphasizes the paradox of the theological argument by the placement of sermons or references to them in the structure of his story. Not until the first devil image begins to operate upon Brown does the sermon become prominent. To this "shape" of evil, Brown objects, "'But were I to go on with thee, how should I meet the eye of that good old man, our minister, at Salem Village? Oh, his voice would make me tremble both Sabbath day and lecture day.'" This statement, ironically foreshadowing Brown's attitude toward the minister in the last section, is made after Brown loses faith in Goody Cloyse, who had taught him his catechism, and before the voices of Deacon Gookin and the minister are heard on the forest path. After he thinks that he has evidence of their fall, Brown's confused mind seems to hear a sermon delivered by a Satanic minister who is described as follows: "With reverence be it spoken, the figure bore no slight similitude, both in garb and manner, to some grave divine of the New England churches." In the witchcraft documents, including

Lawson's Appendix, this divine can be literally identified as George Burroughs, who, among other misdeeds alleged, was said to have administered the sacraments at fiendish orgies. However, if this figure is identified with Lawson, or with any minister supporting his theology, then one may interpret the sermon in the wilderness—which is a naked, almost sensuous pronouncement of the supremacy of evil—as representing that aspect of Lawson's theology which magnified the powers and dominion of evil in order to arouse the faithful to destroy it. The net effect of Hawthorne's irony is to make Lawson the devil's spokesman who under the guise of fidelity to Christ is actually leading people to distrust and loss of faith.

This climactic sermon is balanced by another reference to a sermon. So profound is the spectral baptismal experience that Brown can no longer listen to the supposedly true word of his minister, whose voice formerly inspired his reverence. On his return to the village—the final structural frame—Brown is unable to accept the opposite side of Lawson's theological coin: the injunction to exercise positive Christian virtues. He shrinks from the gentle blessing of the old clergyman, and "When the minister spoke from the pulpit with power and fervid eloquence, and, with his hand on the open Bible, of the sacred truths of our religion, and of saint-like lives and triumphant deaths, and of future bliss or misery unutterable, then did Goodman Brown turn pale, dreading lest the roof should thunder down upon the gray blasphemer and his hearers."

Brown has heard two sermons, one during the forest scene which reflects his deluded vision and one after his return home. These parallel Lawson's theology (faith versus Satan's malignity), but instead of a divine victory, Hawthorne stresses Satan's triumph. Instead of having the faith he once had in his minister, in prayer, and in God, Brown has irrevocably converted himself to Satanic hatred and suspicion.

III

Whereas Adam and Eve may have experienced a *felix culpa* from which a regeneration of positive virtues might spring, Brown has suffered a complete fall from faith.[20] Temptation has conquered him, not in a mythical Garden of Eden but in a spectral New England forest. Relying on materials from the American past, materials intimately connected with his own family, Hawthorne gave us a memorable portrayal of the psychological erosion of one Goodman Brown of Salem Village in 1692. In a dramatic and detailed temptation scene which artistically renders the states of Brown's mind, Hawthorne used Lawson's *Christ's Fidelity* and other sources for the names of actual people, details from recorded experiences, and the theological arguments current in that historic time. But his Brown is not just a Salemite or a completely destroyed Adam, because Hawthorne with his keen understanding of human nature realized that the inner struggle between faith and doubt transcends Salem Village. With the artist's genius for insight and technique, Hawthorne thus created a new and timeless drama about the distortions of the human mind.

Notes

1. For a very able listing of seven "different" interpretations of the theme of the story, see D. M. McKeithan, "Hawthorne's 'Young Goodman Brown': An Interpretation," *MLN*, LXVII (Feb. 1952), 93-96. (The reader can, I believe, easily note considerable overlapping, with differences more apparent in terminology than in substance.) To these should be added the following: Thomas E. Connolly, "Hawthorne's 'Young Goodman Brown': An Attack on Puritanic Calvinism," *AL* [*American Literature*], XXVIII (Nov. 1956), 370-375; Thomas F. Walsh, Jr., "The Bedeviling of Young Goodman Brown," *MLQ* [*Modern Language Quarterly*], XIX (Dec. 1958), 331-336; Paul W. Miller, "Hawthorne's 'Young Goodman Brown': Cynicism or Meliorism?," *NCF* [*Nineteenth-Century Literature* (formerly *Nineteenth-Century Fiction*)], XIV (Dec. 1959), 255-264; Roy R. Male, *Hawthorne's Tragic Vision* (Austin, Texas, 1957), pp. 76-80; Daniel G. Hoffman, *Form and Fable in American Fiction* (New York, 1961), pp. 149-168; and E. Arthur Robinson, "The Vision of Goodman Brown: A Source and Interpretation," *AL*, XXXV (May 1963), 218-225. Two other important works deal with the story: F. O. Matthiessen, *American Renaissance* (New York, 1941), pp. 283-285; and R. H. Fogle, *Hawthorne's Fiction: The Light and the Dark* (Norman, Oklahoma, 1952), pp. 15-32.

2. "Shadows of Doubt: Specter Evidence in Hawthorne's 'Young Goodman Brown'," *AL*, XXXIV (Nov. 1962), 344-352. For a dissenting view, see Paul J. Hurley, "Young Goodman Brown's 'Heart of Darkness'," *AL*, XXXVII (Jan. 1966), 410-419. It is partly my purpose to expand and reinforce Professor Levin's position, and to give some indication of the artistry with which Hawthorne shaped the original materials.

3. Orians, "New England Witchcraft in Fiction," *AL*, II (March 1930), 54-71; McDowell, "Nathaniel Hawthorne and the Witches of Colonial Salem," *N&Q* [*Notes & Queries*], CLXVI (March 3, 1934), 152. Goody Cloyse, Goody Cory, and Martha Carrier are the witches mentioned. Orians cites Mather's *Wonders of the Invisible World* as a source of the description of the witches' Sabbath.

4. "Hawthorne's Literary Borrowings," *PMLA*, LI (June 1936), 545-546, 552. Turner adds Goodman Brown and Deacon Gookin to the cast of characters drawn from history and identifies other details in the story—such as the experience of transport, the respectable nature of the participants in the perverted sacraments, and the allusion to child murder—as elements possibly drawn from Mather's *Wonders*. Both Orians (p. 65) and Turner describe as an almost exact quote from *Wonders* the auctorial comment in "Young Goodman Brown" that Martha Carrier had received the devil's promise that she would be queen of Hell.

5. This volume, now in the collection of the Houghton Library, contains fulsome information on its title page: "Christ's Fidelity, the only Shield against Satan's Malignity. Asserted in a Sermon Deliver'd at Salem-Village the 24th of March, 1692. Being Lecture-day there, and a time of Publick Examination of some Suspected for Witchcraft. By Deodat Lawson, Minister of the Gospel. The Second Edition. Printed at Boston in New England, and Reprinted in London, by R. Tookey, for the Author . . . 1704." Although there is no date of acquisition in the signed volume, the evidence presented in this essay indicates that Hawthorne had the book in his library or at least had read *Christ's Fidelity* before he wrote "Young Goodman Brown." In fact, Hawthorne may be responsible for the markings in the volume. These appear on pp. 28-29, 62, 63-64, 69, 73, 93, 109, 112, 115. They consist of occasional underlining of words in Lawson's text; a few "X" marks; and lines drawn vertically in either the right or left margins. In some instances both margins have vertical lines, and the passages are boxed in by horizontal lines. On page 69, the word *appropriate* is written beside a boxed passage. The context deals with repentance, and the annotated passage tells of a condemned witch who speaks to the Reverend Mr. Simmes about the truth of his sermon which she had heard him deliver twenty-four years ago. The subject of the sermon was "Your sin will find you out . . ." This passage could have some relevance to *The Scarlet Letter.*

I am indebted to the Houghton Library for permission to examine Hawthorne's copy of Lawson's book and to quote from it in connection with the present study. In addition, I should like to acknowledge my gratitude to Professor Norman Holmes Pearson, whose investigations into Hawthorne's personal library originally led me to the volume.

6. Deodat Lawson had succeeded George Burroughs as minister of Salem Village and had served there from 1683 until 1688. His tenure was marred by factionalism and discord, chiefly about financial arrangements, with the result that early in 1687 a committee composed of Major Gedney, John Hathorne, William Brown, and the elders of the Salem church was appointed to arbitrate the troublesome matters. Although the committee report appears to have sustained Lawson's position and warned his parishioners against prejudice and animosity, his ministry evidently continued to be an uneasy one, for in May 1688 he removed to Boston, and shortly afterward the Salemites began negotiations with the Reverend Samuel Parris to settle among them. The record of Lawson's service in Salem Village has been published by the Danvers Historical Society in its *Historical Collections,* XIII (1925), 103-118; and XIV (1926), 66-75.

It is not surprising that with such close links to the prominent figures involved in the witchcraft hysteria, Lawson, then minister of the Scituate church, should have been invited to return to Salem in March 1692 to deliver a lecture-day sermon. He was perhaps the more eager to appraise the local situation because it was alleged that his first wife and daughter, both of whom had died during his residence in Salem, had been murdered by a witch. During his visit from the 19th of March to the 5th of April, he carefully noted down all that he observed, and on his return to Boston he published his account in *A Brief and True Narrative,* which, identifying individuals by name or initials, became the first printed report on the witchcraft phenomena. This *Narrative* was included by Cotton Mather in his *Wonders of the Invisible World,* published in October 1692, and it has been reprinted by George L. Burr in *Narratives of the Witchcraft Cases,* 1648-1706 (New York, 1914), pp. 147-164.

7. Preface to the Appendix, *Christ's Fidelity,* p. 94. This Appendix in the 1704 edition incorporates most of the material in the earlier *Narrative,* but it has been rearranged, the identifications have been dropped, and additional data have been added. This version has been reprinted as "Deodat Lawson's Narrative" at the conclusion of C. W. Upham, *Salem Witchcraft* (Boston, 1867), II, 525-537. All references in this essay are to the 1704 edition owned by Hawthorne.

8. It is not my intention to displace Mather's *Wonders* as a possible source but to focus on an important volume which complements Mather's work. In footnotes I shall indicate parallels between *Wonders* and *Christ's Fidelity.*

9. Lawson, p. 113. This testimony is also reported by Cotton Mather, who identifies the deponent as Joseph Ring. See *Wonders of the Invisible World* (Mount Vernon, New York, n. d.), p. 120.

10. This passage follows the account of Joseph Ring: "The *Afflicted Persons* related that the Spectres of several Eminent Persons had been brought in amongst the rest, but as the Sufferers said the Devil could not hurt them in their *Shapes,* but two *Witches* seemed to take them by each hand, and lead them or force them to come in." (pp. 113-114). I have found no parallel account in Mather.

11. P. 111. See also pp. 117-118, where Lawson again discusses the administration of the sacrament. *Cf. Wonders,* pp. 107, 128, and 130. Lawson's accounts are frequently more vivid than those of Mather.

12. P. 118. *Cf. Wonders,* p. 124. The Mather version is pallid.

13. Stoughton's view, which is implicit in Lawson's narrative, inevitably caused an epidemic of suspicion in Salem Village. This phenomenon may be reflected in the direction which Brown's distrust takes throughout the story—moving from specific people who had previously been among the innocent in his mind, to all men.

14. This issue has been covered by Perry Miller in *The New England Mind: From Colony to Province* (Boston, 1961), pp. 191-208. He makes clear the fact

that Mather's *Wonders,* written at the behest of Stoughton, was a stumbling apologia for the judges, an attempt to convince both Mather himself and the public that no defendant had been convicted solely on spectral evidence.

15. Lawson's prefatory address to the 1704 edition indicates that this new printing was occasioned, at least in part, by a desire to justify the actions of the judges. It is distinctly defensive in tone: ". . . I have given way to the Publishing of them [these Amazing things]; that I may satisfy such as are not resolved to the Contrary; that there may be (and are) such Operations of the Powers of Darkness on the Bodies and Minds of Mankind; by Divine Permission; and that those who Sate Judges in those Cases, may by the serious Consideration, of the formidable Aspect and perplexed Circumstances, of that Afflictive Providence; be in some measure excused; or at least be less Censured, for passing Sentence on several Persons, as being the Instruments of Satan in those Diabolical Operations, when they were involved in such a Dark and Dismal Scene of Providence, in which Satan did seem to Spin a finer Thred of Spiritual Wickedness, than in the ordinary methods of Witchcraft; hence the Judges, desiring to bear due Testimony, against such Diabolical Practices, were inclined to admit the validity of such a sort of Evidence, as was not so clearly and directly demonstrable to Human Senses, as in other Cases is required, or else they could not discover the Mysteries of Witchcraft . . ." (p. 93).

It is suggested by some authorities that Lawson himself came under some obloquy because of his association with the witchcraft proceedings, for he is referred to in contemporary records as "the unhappy Deodat Lawson," and mention is made of his having returned to England in disgrace. See Burr, p. 150.

16. Pp. 102-103. See *Wonders,* pp. 69, 131.

17. Pp. 108-109. See *Wonders,* p. 132. On p. 69 of *Wonders* Mather also reports a suggestive detail not recorded by Lawson, an incident in which money stolen by "wicked Spectres" was later, before spectators, dropped out of the air into the hands of the sufferers.

18. In the first three references and in the final one to the ribbons, Hawthorne uses the plural form. In the forest scene, however, he refers to *a* ribbon. This distinction between *ribbons* and *ribbon* suggests a part for the whole, just as the small piece of sheet in Lawson's account represents the entire sheet. In my discussion I shall follow Hawthorne's practice of alluding to the spectral ribbon in the singular.

19. To complement the pink ribbon and the other details cited, we should refer to the passage which seems to represent Brown's loss of the feeling of transport: "He staggered against the rock, and felt it chill and damp; while a hanging twig, that had been all on fire, besprinkled his cheek with the coldest dew." The parallels are clear: the real rock versus that

which had contained the spectral font; the real twig versus the one which, like everything else in the spectral vision, had seemed to be on fire. All quotations from "Young Goodman Brown" are in the Riverside Edition, ed. George P. Lathrop (Boston, 1883).

20. For a fuller explanation of Brown's fall, see my essay "*Paradise Lost* and 'Young Goodman Brown'," *E. I. Historical Collections,* XCIV (July 1958), 282-296.

Taylor Stoehr (essay date 1969)

SOURCE: "'Young Goodman Brown' and Hawthorne's Theory of Mimesis," in *Nineteenth-Century Fiction,* Vol. 23, No. 4, March, 1969, pp. 393-412.

[*In the following essay, Stoehr examines "Young Goodman Brown" in light of Hawthorne's ideas on the relationship between spiritual and natural truth, and the dangers implicit in confusing the two.*]

The tellers of tales—in America, writers like Poe, Hawthorne, Melville, and later Mark Twain—construct their fictions around some single and striking figure of speech, at once abstract and concrete, an idea embodied in an action, object, circumstance, or the like, so that it becomes, as it were, a trope of life. The tale's main "effect"—to use Poe's term for it—reduces again and again to some bizarre image: a house collapsing with the death of its owner, a woman dying with the removal of her birthmark, a stutterer whose speech is act, a package of limburger cheese mistaken for the putrescence of a corpse, a chandelier of human torches, a "Pygmalion" figurehead for a ship, a "writer" who would "prefer not," a burglar-alarm system with a will of its own. This is in contrast with authors like James, who write a different genre, the short story, and who are concerned with character, situation, life or a slice of it. The teller of the tale carefully leads up to or surrounds his central conception with a series of events which may sometimes look like a realistic plot, but which differ in that they comprise something like a closed system, the elements interconnected and interdefined (like a perfectly logical language), and all organized by the dominant image. If there is often a good deal of ornament along the way, it is neither naturalistic nor gratuitous. Detail is not offered for its own sake, nor in the interests of verisimilitude, but is part and parcel of the "effect." Generally in Poe and Twain the end of the tale is the final clicking into place of the essential cog, for the sake of which everything else exists—the revelation of the secret, the discovery of the truth, the magic word, the punch line, the gimmick or nub or snapper. In Hawthorne and Melville it is the reader's job to discover the key; then, as in the analysis of dreams, the fantastic filigree of secondary elaboration collapses to a single symbolic image, the dream-thought or hidden content.

Clearly this is not realism, nor is the purpose of these writers to hold the mirror up to nature. And yet it would not be fair to say that their tales have nothing to do with life or reality or truth. What sort of an imagination is it, and what sort of a vision of the world does it imply, when an author is continually blowing up fictional balloons only to pop them or to invite the reader to reduce them to a neat little bang?

The comparison to dreams may be helpful at this point, for these writers used the analogy themselves. Poe addressed himself "to the dreamers and those who put their faith in dreams as in the only realities." Hawthorne said he chose Brook Farm as the scene of *The Blithedale Romance* because, "being certainly the most romantic episode of his own life,—essentially a day-dream and yet a fact," it thus offered "an available foothold between fiction and reality," and Melville approvingly described his reading of *Mosses from an Old Manse* as being spun "round about in a web of dreams." Twain too finally came to rest on similar insubstantial ground, for example in *The Mysterious Stranger,* where Satan pronounces the final truth toward which everything in that gloomy story (and much in Twain's development as an author) has been heading: "*Life itself is only a vision, a dream. . . . Nothing exists save empty space—and you!* . . . And you are not you—you have no body, no blood, no bones, you are but a *thought.* I myself have no existence; I am but a dream—your dream, creature of your imagination." We are reminded of Ishmael on the mast-head, White-Jacket in the water, or Pierre, who did not see "that all the great books in the world are but the mutilated shadowings-forth of invisible and eternally unembodied images in the soul; so that they are but the mirrors, distortedly reflecting to us our own things."

Already we will be noting differences in the views of our authors, but we may begin in general by saying of them that the solipsistic bent is in none of them a genuinely philosophical attitude. It is instead a particular artistic stance, in its most extreme version a promotion of fiction to a rank of reality above life, and a conception of experience as predominantly verbal, or at least gaining its significance from expression in language rather than from acting-out in life. It is not so much that these writers can believe in nothing but the reality of their own fantasies—though Poe often pretends to such a view and Twain bitterly toys with it at the end of his career—but rather that the sense that they are able to make of the world automatically frames itself in fantasy, and that this is by virtue of some very specialized uses of language to render experience. It should be emphasized that "dreams, visions, fiction," a triad of equivalencies found in *The Mysterious Stranger,* are terms closely related, if not synonymous, in all four writers; accordingly the correspondences of dream and reality are to a great extent problems of verbal imagination, referential language, and literary mimesis. "To dream" is to use language about life and the world in special ways.

In brief, these special uses of language may be stated as follows: for Poe, a kind of word-magic built chiefly on metonymies, in which words are treated as if they were naturally or supernaturally rather than conventionally and arbitrarily attached to their referents; for Hawthorne, a heavily metaphorical style, in which whatever is described seems always on the verge of turning into its metaphorical description, and in which one often cannot tell the difference between the imaginary and the real; for Melville, a similar ambiguity, based on irony rather than metaphor, words turned against themselves, until reference disappears at the other end of Poe's blind alley; for Twain, a hyperbolic use of language, in which most expressions turn out to be heightened and distorted inventions, exaggerations, even lies, about the ordinary world.

The center or kernel of Poe's tales is frequently a visual pun taken literally and in deadly earnest—as Hop-frog puts the torch to the human chandelier, or Dupin finds "The Purloined Letter" in plain sight on the thief's letter rack. In Hawthorne some metaphor, such as "Life figures itself to me as a festal or funeral procession" ("The Procession of Life"), is allowed to flower into or to cap with one all-encompassing emblem a series of similar images. Melville focuses on bits of human speech—or the lack of it, in "Billy Budd"—and reiterates until all meanings have been canvassed, and *none* are left. Twain in his turn tells the tall tale, built on a succession of whoppers, and reserving some monstrously inflated absurdity to ring down the curtain.

Poe and Twain typically end their tales with a sort of explosion—it is the dreaded revelation in Poe, when, as in "Morella," the name calls the thing named into being, and the narrator's consciousness goes blank in horror (this blankness or blotting out is the familiar abyss or maelstrom in Poe—"the end"); in Twain, it is the deflation of the hyperbolic balloon, when the last great puff of hot air from the narrator, who has gone *too* far this time, leaves the audience collapsing with laughter. In both cases, the end of the fictional structure is likely to come with a sudden neatness; the last words fall into place and, with a shock, we are back in our own reality again, where we become aware that we are holding our breath, or our sides.

Some of Hawthorne's tales go this way also, emphasizing the literal boundaries of fiction, the beginning and the end. More often, however, and especially in his best pieces, Hawthorne (like Melville) puts the confrontation between the imaginary and the real directly into his plots, as the focus of interest rather than as the means to an effect. One might even say—and this will be a large part of our concern in what follows—that a tale like **"Young Goodman Brown"** is *about* the relations of fiction and reality, a study of the true-to-life, a sketch for a theory of mimesis.

The structure of events in Hawthorne's tales is not linearly, that is to say temporally, conceived as in Poe's, where disaster awaits at the end, but rather cyclically or spatially, as befits thematic rather than anecdotal organization; and of course the built-in predispositions of emblematic art lend themselves to such a method. Hawthorne's

tales sometimes have plots, but when they do they are mere pretexts for the configurations which he wants to present. Most of his tales exist for the sake of a single scene or image, and the reverberations he can make it echo with. One thinks of **"The Minister's Black Veil," "The Bosom Serpent," "The Wedding Knell," "The Birthmark,"** and so on. In some cases, as for example the processional **"My Kinsman, Major Molineux,"** the crucial image is reserved for the climax, but more usually it is present from the beginning, an emblem which Hawthorne can constantly refer to as a source of moral comment and fanciful speculation. The emblematic moment recurs again and again in different guises and contexts. Very often it builds to some physical confrontation of the characters, standing in different moral planes, for example the deathbed scene in **"The Minister's Black Veil"** or the final coming-true of the prediction of **"The Prophetic Pictures."** This is the methodology of Hawthorne's novels as well, which are rather like collections of tales strung together as series of tableaux showing the characters in a variety of physical and moral postures *vis à vis* one another. One almost wants to say that nothing else happens *in the novels*; all the action takes place behind the scenes and in the wings.

The central images on which Hawthorne bases his tales are easy to isolate and study; many of them are precisely formulated in the *American Notebooks*, for example:

> A man to swallow a small snake—and it to be a symbol of cherished sin.

> **("The Bosom Serpent")**

> The semblance of a human face to be found on the side of a mountain, or in the fracture of a small stone, by a *lusus naturae*. The face is an object of curiosity for years or centuries, and by and by a boy is born, whose features gradually assume the aspect of that portrait. At some critical juncture, the resemblance is found to be perfect. A prophecy may be connected.

> **("The Great Stone Face")**

> To make one's own reflection in a mirror the subject of a story.

> **("Monsieur du Miroir")**

> . . . An essay on the misery of being always under a mask. A veil may be needful, but never a mask.

> **("The Minister's Black Veil")**

Here as in Poe we see a fondness for the bizarre or grotesque image, but unlike Poe, Hawthorne usually conceives his emblem as having a moral, as embodying some truth, and in the actual working out of the tale he invariably directs it to some meaning for ordinary life. One need only compare the morals pointed at the ends of **"Drowne's Wooden Image"** or **"The Prophetic Pictures"** or **"Edward Randolph's Portrait"** with the more simply fantastic treatment of the same sort of idea in Poe's "The Oval Portrait" to see the difference in intention—all the more strongly highlighted in this case by a similarity in both design and effect. Pursuing the comparison a bit further, it is

surprising to discover the number of entries in Hawthorne's *American Notebooks* which suggest or actually
parallel tales developed by Poe. Had he had access to
them, there are several entries that would have made Poe
hesitate, in his review of *Twice-told Tales,* before accusing
Hawthorne of transcendentalist symbol-hunting and (what
is more ironic) unconscious plagiarism. Here are some examples which show how far toward the purely fantastic
Hawthorne might have gone, had he not been committed
to the "metaphor run-mad," as Poe called his rival's technique:

> To make literal pictures of figurative expressions;—for
> instance, he burst into tears—a man suddenly turned
> into a shower of briny drops. An explosion of laugh-
> ter—a man blowing up, and his fragments flying about
> on all sides. He cast his eyes upon the ground—a man
> standing eyeless, with his eyes on the ground, staring
> up at him in wonderment &c &c &c.
>
> (Cf. Poe's "A Predicament")
>
> Questions as to unsettled points of History, and Myster-
> ies of Nature, to be asked of a mesmerized person.
>
> (Cf. Poe's "Mesmeric Revelation")
>
> The strange incident in the court of Charles IX (*sic,* for
> VI), of France: he and five other maskers being attired
> in coats of linen covered with pitch and bestuck with
> flax to represent hairy savages. They entered the hall
> dancing, the five being fastened together, and the king
> in front. By accident the five were set on fire with a
> torch. Two were burned to death on the spot, two after-
> wards died, one fled to the buttery, and jumped into a
> vessel of water. It might be represented as the fate of a
> squad of dissolute men.
>
> (Cf. Poe's "Hop-Frog"; Hawthorne had this idea from
> Froissart's *Chronicles* in 1838 and Poe probably from
> a secondary source when he later developed the
> anecdote.)

There are dozens more of these grotesque ideas recorded
in the *American Notebooks,* the majority of which never
found their way into Hawthorne's tales. Of those that finally did grow to full treatment, most of them have a
moral already pointed in the first conception, and if they
do not originally have moral significance, are given it in
their fictional elaborations. This, of course, was what Poe
found offensive and "transcendental" in Hawthorne. Probably he would have been all the more vexed to find that
the image or emblem ordinarily occurred first to Hawthorne, and was then pressed for some symbolic meaning
or significance. Often one sees him groping unsuccessfully
for a meaning in the notebooks—"A person to catch fire-
flies, and try to kindle his household fire with them. It
would be symbolical of something"—and it was precisely
this difficulty of finding a meaning adequate to his symbols that, in his last years, proved Hawthorne's stumbling
block (see Davidson's editions of *Dr. Grimshawe's Secret*
and the other unfinished manuscripts). The central struggle
of his art is to maintain a tension between the terms of his
symbols, to enliven dead metaphors, to force his daydreams into a certain relation with everyday life without

giving up their essential strangeness. Hawthorne's typical
stance may further be distinguished from Poe's in that the
narrative point of view of a moral tale is outside the tale
itself, whereas in the tale of pure fantasy the teller is not
only part of the tale, but, in Poe at any rate, peculiarly
identical with it. The usual Poe narrators—men like the
morbid husband of Ligeia—become the characters in Hawthorne—like Ethan Brand or Young Goodman Brown or
Rev. Hooper. (Rappaccini and Hawthorne's other evil scientists are like Poe's Dupin, or like Poe the poet-critic of
"The Philosophy of Composition"; and it is interesting
that the ratiocinative figure in Poe is rarely the narrator
unless Poe is speaking in his own voice—the women are
generally the abstruse and metaphysical ones.) Hawthorne
maintains a certain essayistic distance from his characters
and their stories. He presents his tales as purported translations, parts of an unpublished book, stories told him by
others, imagined historical events, and so forth, and his
prose is full of little reminders of the narrator's essential
uninvolvement: "It only remains to say . . . ," "the historian of the sect affirms . . . ," "at that moment, if report
be trust-worthy. . . ."

Hawthorne's narrative stance is different from Poe's because Hawthorne wants to bridge the gap between imagination and reality while Poe prefers to fall in. The former's
emblems are *of* something, have bearing on life, while the
latter's are grotesque climaxes marking the boundary-line
of fantasy and its sharp division from the ordinary world,
which, so far as his tales are concerned, might as well not
exist. In Poe there is no distinction between the expressions of language and what those expressions express. All
reality but that of language is denied, and Poe is like his
character in "The Power of Words" who speaks the stars
into existence. Whereas Hawthorne does not deny extra-
linguistic reality, he does assign it a peculiar status in his
view of things. He does not believe "in dreams as the only
realities," as Poe does, but he says—or allows his narrator
in *Blithedale* to say—that their "airiest fragments impal-
pable as they may be, will possess a value that lurks not in
the most ponderous realities of any practicable scheme."
The contrast between dream and reality is what interests
Hawthorne. The world, he writes in **"The Old Manse,"** is
"tormented by visions that seem real to it now, but would
assume their true aspect and character were all things once
set right by an interval of sound repose." His advice to the
world, to "take an age-long nap," is fancy carried to Hawthorne's most annoying extreme of whimsy, but serious
analyses of the relations between dream and reality occur
in tale after tale. In these, Hawthorne sometimes trusts the
dream, sometimes the reality, sometimes cannot decide between them. Perhaps he is more often found on the side of
the dreamer than that of the realist—Clifford rather than
Judge Pyncheon, Owen Warland rather than Robert Dan-
forth, Violet and Peony rather than their father—and moreover, the whole evidence of his choice of subject matter
and method—the preponderance of tales over essays,
fables over sketches—attests his nearness to Poe's stance
as a pure fantast. But while Poe wants to blot out reality

and allow fantasy to fill the consciousness, Hawthorne is more interested in exploring the relations between the two.

. . . . .

Probably the most interesting of Hawthorne's tales, seen in this light, is **"Young Goodman Brown."** The core of the plot is a pun—not taken with perverse literalness as it would be in Poe, but preserved as a pun and pressed to its full ambiguity in the course of the tale. Young Goodman Brown, an ordinary young and good man, has a sweet and doting wife whose name is Faith. By the end of the narrative, Brown has grown old, is no longer good in any ordinary way, and has lost his Faith, that is, his religious faith, his faith in his fellowmen, his faith in his wife. The story opens with Brown taking leave of his wife for an overnight trip. She begs him to remain, says she fears that bad dreams will visit her in his absence, but he tells her to say her prayers and no harm will come to her. He himself, as it turns out, is off to a Witches' Sabbath, a gathering of the devil's own in the forest, where tonight several converts are to be admitted to the communion. On his way he meets the devil, who looks very like Brown's own father. Disconcerted by his companion and his "serpent" staff, Brown hesitates, finally refuses to go on to the meeting, even though he has meanwhile discovered that he is to be in the company of all the most valued of his religious guides and counselors—Goody Cloyse, Deacon Gookin, and even the village pastor himself. Apparently everyone he respects is a hypocrite, actually a partaker of the devil's sacrament. Still reluctant, he is next astonished to hear what seems to be the voice of his own wife as she prepares to join with Satan's revellers in the distant clearing, and, as a token of her apparent defection, a pink ribbon which she wore "fluttered lightly down through the air."

> "My Faith is gone!" cried he, after one stupified moment. "There is no good on earth; and sin is but a name. Come, devil; for to thee is this world given."

Brown now proceeds to the clearing where the whole town appears to be gathered, including his wife. Even yet there seems to be one more chance for Brown and his Faith. They approach Satan's altar where they are to pledge themselves to him. Satan welcomes them:

> "Depending upon one another's hearts, ye had still hoped that virtue were not all a dream. Now are ye undeceived. Evil is the nature of mankind. Evil must be your only happiness. Welcome again, my children, to the communion of your race."

At the last moment Brown calls out to his Faith: "'look up to heaven, and resist the wicked one.'" Immediately his surroundings change, take on their ordinary appearance, and he is alone. Apparently he is saved. He does not know whether his wife has saved herself too or not. Indeed, it seems equally possible that he has merely "fallen asleep in the forest and only dreamed a wild dream of a witch-meeting." Yet, dream or no, the experience produces a profound change in Brown. Although his wife greets him with unsuspecting joy the next morning, his faith is gone.

He now mistrusts all men, his life becomes a succession of suspicions and secret judgments, and "his dying hour was gloom."

Even this bare outline of the tale presents us with some interesting puzzles. If, as seems apparent, Brown does look up to heaven at the last moment, with the consequence that the whole evil scene disappears and he is left alone in the woods, is not this circumstance an indication that he has preserved his faith after all, by refusing the devil's communion? How then are we to explain his later behavior? Alternatively perhaps we are to take the whole episode as a dream. Hawthorne has a plan in the *American Notebooks* for a tale to be composed like a dream:

> To write a dream, which shall resemble the real course of a dream, with all its inconsistency, its strange transformations, which are all taken as a matter of course, its eccentricities and aimlessness—with nevertheless a leading idea running through the whole. Up to this old age of the world, no such thing ever has been written.

But if **"Young Goodman Brown"** is an outgrowth of this idea, it has surely changed considerably. Among other things we are missing the "eccentricities and aimlessness," although we have the "matter of course." Further, **"Young Goodman Brown,"** if it has a dream in it, must also have a reality, and there are no very clear boundaries marking the one off from the other. Where does it begin? And what does it mean?

If we do take Brown's experience as a dream, we must then regard his loss of his faith, both wife and virtue, as a kind of wish—at least we may say that *he* imagines the loss, and thus far chooses it. He similarly imagines the worst of all mankind, and by so imagining these horrors, he wakes into the condition of believing them. If the reader has trouble distinguishing the boundary between dream and reality here, all the more is Brown unable to discern it, for his dream becomes his waking life—what he imagines comes true for him.

The ambiguity of Brown's experience, both chosen and forced upon him, imaginary and real, is worth dwelling on, for it is at the center of the problem of faith as Hawthorne conceives it. So far as we know, Brown himself never questions the reality of his adventure in the woods. And, if we suppose with him that it all really happened, I think we have to admit that Brown has good reason for his loss of faith—at least in his fellowman—since everyone except himself seems to be in the devil's service. Supposing, however, that it was only a dream, then we must judge Brown harshly, as having chosen his loss, just as Ethan Brand seems to choose his fate in that tale. But Hawthorne seems to leave the question in the air; he will not say for sure, nor give us any certain evidence, that Brown's experience was either dream or reality. Nor is it somewhere in-between the two (whatever that could mean); in a way it is both. To make this clear, we must return again to the text.

The language of Hawthorne's tales is particularly abundant with expressions of *apparent circumstance*: "as if," "as though," "it appeared that," "it seemed that," "it might have been," "it must have been," "doubtless," "perhaps," "were such a thing possible," "he fancied that," "as it were," "some affirm that," and so forth. There are at least thirty such expressions in this tale, not counting subtler versions. Going hand in hand with these is the vocabulary of surfaces—faces, facades, visages, countenances, aspects, images, tokens, types, symbols, and the like—all quite appropriate to the presentation of fantasy and dream-vision. In most writers we expect such expressions to signal statements and descriptions which we are not to take literally but rather metaphorically. Moreover, in a case like Hawthorne's, where the tales are so thoroughly permeated with "as if" and "as though" constructions, we are tempted to take the whole as allegorical, a highly organized saying of one thing to mean another. In Hawthorne, however, this is not quite the effect. His emblematic technique is less allegorical than "hypothetical," less a matter of systematically reading other meanings into the literal statement than a matter of withholding judgment on all apparent meanings, which are nonetheless offered as possibilities.

In proposing the term "hypothetical" to characterize Hawthorne's method, I wish to emphasize that it must be taken here in the loosest sense. Hawthorne does not present a hypothesis which he expects in any way to be verified or verifiable, as, for example, a writer of utopian fiction like Bellamy or a Chicago realist like Henry Blake Fuller might. In most of Hawthorne's tales—certainly in "Young Goodman Brown"—the statements put forth are not to be regarded as either true or false, or even possibly so, except in the broadest meaning of "truth-to-life." We are not to imagine that what happened to Goodman Brown really happened to someone, or will, although much of the account Hawthorne gives could stand just as it is, had there been such a person with such a history. Nor are we asked to "suspend our disbelief" in reading the tale—not at least in any strict sense of that expression. In reading Hawthorne, as a matter of fact, we are constantly to bear in mind that it is only a fiction we are engrossed in. We take the story as neither true nor false, not by agreeing to leave such questions in abeyance, but by recognizing (and in Hawthorne, even concentrating on) the fact that such questions do not apply in the ordinary way. As with certain other kinds of imaginative accounts—for instance daydreams or jokes—we are required to put an "as if" construction on everything, to begin the experience with a silent "Supposing that . . ." which determines our attitude toward what we read. Again as in daydreams, jokes, and so forth, it is obvious that our attitude of "supposing" is quite different from an attitude of "believing" or even "pretending to believe." Imagine believing or pretending to believe in "Young Goodman Brown"! This does not mean that we do not take such fiction seriously, for certainly we do; but only that our serious reaction to it is different from what it would be in the case of non-fiction. One does not write letters to the *Times* protesting the outrages committed in a tale (unless one happens to be a literary critic); one does not pass the hat for the relief of fictional orphans. Like as not, one takes thought rather than action.

Obviously there is much more to say about the logical implications and psychological effects of fiction as opposed to non-fiction. We have gone far enough, however, to see that **"Young Goodman Brown,"** with its insistence on its own "as-ifness," is a rather special sort of tale, peculiarly about itself, about the nature of belief in imagined realities, and about the status of such realities. What happened to Young Goodman Brown in the woods is, first and foremost, a part of a fiction invented by Hawthorne. Brown of course cannot know this; that would be a twist for a modern novelist or playwright. Brown *can* know that his experience is in direct contradiction to his everyday sense of things, and that one or the other of them must be false—if they are to be regarded as matters of truth and falsity at all. This is just his difficulty. Logically, either Satan is right when he says, "ye had still hoped that virtue were not all a dream. Now are ye undeceived. Evil is the nature of mankind," or else Brown *had* "fallen asleep in the forest and only dreamed a wild dream of a witch-meeting." But how is Brown to decide which of the two accounts to trust? Remembering always that this is a *logical* question only if the accounts *are* true or false, let us go on to see what criteria or means of deciding are open to him. Perhaps he has some subtle moral sense, some faculty of intuition that could tell him. Hawthorne sometimes seemed to believe in such a faculty, as in this passage from the *American Notebooks*:

> A person, while awake and in the business of life, to think highly of another, and place perfect confidence in him, but to be troubled with dreams in which this seeming friend appears to act the part of a most deadly enemy. Finally it is discovered that the dream-character is the true one. The explanation would be—the soul's instinctive perception.

Such an "explanation" might fit **"Young Goodman Brown."** Assuming for the moment that it does, we should observe that it is not necessarily the apparent dream that is to be distrusted; distrust itself, to put it another way, is likely to lead to mistakes about reality:

> Distrust to be thus exemplified [another entry in the *Notebooks* reads]: Various good and desirable things to be presented to a young man, and offered to his acceptance—as a friend, a wife, a fortune; but he to refuse them all, suspecting that it is merely a delusion. Yet all to be real, and he to be told so, when too late.

Back again with a character who needs "to be told" which is dream, which reality, we see Hawthorne here identifying the lack or loss of faith with a sort of suspicious pessimism—rather like that which Young Goodman Brown is said to arrive at as a consequence of his loss of faith. Perhaps instead it *constitutes* that loss.

Let us look at one more striking example of the sort of dilemma posed in these entries and in **"Young Goodman**

Brown"—a situation in **"Rappaccini's Daughter"** that is so instructive an illustration of the problem that we must quote from it at some length. The hero, Giovanni, has fallen in love with the beautiful but deadly Beatrice. He has discovered that Beatrice is so imbued with the poisons of her father's garden that her very breath is fatal. At first unbelieving, he exclaims, "It is a dream . . . surely it is a dream," but

> he could not quite forget the bouquet that withered in her grasp, and the insect that perished amid the sunny air, by no ostensible agency save the fragrance of her breath. These incidents, however, dissolving in the pure light of her character, had no longer the efficacy of facts, but were acknowledged as mistaken fantasies, by whatever testimony of the senses they might appear to be substantiated. There is something truer and more real than what we can see with the eyes and touch with the finger. On such better evidence had Giovanni founded his confidence in Beatrice, though rather by the necessary force of her high attributes than by any deep and generous faith on his part. But now his spirit was incapable of sustaining itself at the height to which the earthly enthusiasm had exalted it; he fell down, grovelling among earthly doubts, and defiled therewith the pure whiteness of Beatrice's image.

As it turns out, so far as the reader can tell, Giovanni was quite right to be suspicious of Beatrice. Although he is certainly cruel to her, and although his attempt to achieve earthly happiness with her by administering powerful antidotes to the poison in her system is unquestionably fatal to her, yet surely he made no mistake about her potent infirmity. Yet Hawthorne says, "had Giovanni known how to estimate" Beatrice's virtues properly, they "would have assured him that all this ugly mystery was but an earthly illusion." If we ask what difference that could have made, considering the realistic circumstances, the only answer that presents itself—and it is surely a curious one—is that Hawthorne could have invented some sort of loophole for his hero, if only his hero had had the "high faith" worthy of such a miracle. This may sound like the literary critic grasping at straws, but I believe that it is somehow Hawthorne's point—that after all, it is only a story, that the characters might have acted differently, the outcome might have been whatever they wanted, had they only realized it.

Both here and in **"Young Goodman Brown,"** Hawthorne seems to throw the blame on his characters, while at the same time he gives them no possible means of saving themselves. He undermines his condemnation of them by telling their dreams as realistically as he does their actual experiences, so that even the reader can see little difference between the two. Were the author not on hand to put us right, by dropping an "as if" here and there, or, in **"Rappaccini's Daughter,"** by explicitly telling us what to think, would we know that Brown and Giovanni are to be condemned for their tragic losses—any more than Brown and Giovanni know it themselves? Hawthorne's technique puts us in nearly the same position as his characters, except that we are given some additional hints as to how we should come to terms with *our* dream, the tale we are reading.

For us it is a case of "supposing," which we are to take seriously but not literally. We are to learn from it, as another of Hawthorne's notebook characters who never made it into fiction:

> A person to look back on a long life ill-spent, and to picture forth a beautiful life which he would live if he could be permitted to begin his life over again. Finally to discover that he had only been dreaming of old age,—that he was really young, and could live such a life as he had pictured.

For this character, as for his readers, the typical Hawthorne illusion turns out well enough, but the Young Goodman Browns have no kindly author looking out for their interests, allowing them to "discover" that all is a dream. One feels that Hawthorne would have preferred to have all his tales come out so luckily for their characters. He worried over the unrelieved gloominess of *The Scarlet Letter* and wanted to include a few lighter pieces with it. Persuaded to separate publication by Fields, he followed it with an attempt at a book with more sunshine in it, *The House of the Seven Gables,* and if one reads through the complete works, the surprising thing is how many dreary cheerful things he did write—often for children. But at his best he invariably sees things at their worst. For a man who is always complaining about his characters' lack of faith, Hawthorne himself is singularly dubious about the possibilities of life and human nature. To quote the *Notebooks* one last time, he frequently seems to be in the following situation:

> A person to be writing a tale, and to find that it shapes itself against his intentions; that the characters act otherwise than he thought; that unforeseen events occur; and a catastrophe comes which he strives in vain to avert. It might shadow forth his own fate,—he having made himself one of the personages.

One suspects that Hawthorne had his own experience in mind here. In any case, it is certainly related to the experience of Young Goodman Brown, whose dream turns into his reality merely by virtue of his belief in it. If Brown "strives" at all, it is certainly "in vain" to avert *his* catastrophe; ditto his creator.

. . . . .

Hawthorne's tales are attempts to find meanings adequate to the emblems of life with which he fills his notebooks. In this respect he may be said to be rather like his Concord neighbor Thoreau, taking the measure of worldly facts, reading them as signs, and worrying a transcendental meaning out of them. But even in *The Seven Gables* Hawthorne's beans come up with scarlet blossoms, and his pond is a Maule's well. Thoreau uses language to create a world in which his spirit can breathe, which is neither entirely factual, past, and dead, nor entirely fanciful and unattainable. To borrow the rather Thoreauvian pun with which Hawthorne concludes one of his tales, he tries to "look beyond the shadowy scope of time, and living once for all in eternity, . . . find the perfect future in the present." But Hawthorne, like the protagonist of **"The Birthmark"** so enjoined, cannot live up to such advice, or, as almost seems to come to the same thing for him, his characters cannot live up to it. Looking into the hearts of his Giovannis and Young Goodman Browns, Hawthorne finds no warrant for the faith he seeks. His "supposings" for them regularly issue in disaster.

Hawthorne's tales do tell us that things need not be what they seem, that there is always another, better world possible to faith. But contrariwise, the means to this faith is itself through fiction and related activities of the imagination, dreams and visions. As he also says in **"The Birthmark,"** *à propos* of Aylmer's dream: "Truth often finds its way to the mind close muffled in robes of sleep, and then speaks with uncompromising directness of matters in regard to which we practise an unconscious self-deception during our waking moments." This, especially in the context of Aylmer's experiment, is a gloomy version of something Emerson says in *Nature,* "that a dream may let us deeper into the secret of nature than a hundred concerted experiments." Hawthorne's position is in some wise an Emersonian or Thoreauvian optimism, but without the grace to find his faith supported by the dreams which he and his characters are assailed by. Not that their dreams don't come true, but that they turn out nightmares, like Aylmer's or Young Goodman Brown's.

While exploring the problem of faith through his characters, Hawthorne does not hesitate to probe the question of his own disappointment in them. He seems to recognize that if the fault is somehow in his characters, it is no less in himself, in his very decision to explore and experiment with their moral natures. Here we come at last to the perennial crux in Hawthorne, what in one way or another keeps him from being a transcendentalist—the unpardonable sin. Among the speeches of Satan to Brown and his wife, as they are welcomed to the communion, is the following:

> "This night it shall be granted you to know their secret deeds. . . . By the sympathy of your human hearts for sin ye shall scent out all the places—whether in church, bedchamber, street, field, or forest—where crime has been committed, and shall exult to behold the whole earth one stain of guilt, one mighty blood spot. Far more than this. It shall be yours to penetrate, in every bosom, the deep mystery of sin, the fountain of all wicked arts, and which inexhaustibly supplies more evil impulses than human power—than my power at its utmost—can make manifest in deeds."

Despite his refusal to join the devil's communion, Brown comes out of his experience—be it dream or reality—with precisely the power here promised him. The knowledge of good and evil (mainly evil) which he thereby gains is a curse. In it consists his loss of faith—in all senses of the word—for he now *sees* the sin in his wife and in his fellowmen, and he believes that the world is the devil's. The exercise of this power of secret knowledge is what, in the *Notebooks* and later in **"Ethan Brand,"** Hawthorne calls

the "Unpardonable Sin"—"a want of love and reverence for the Human Soul; in consequence of which, the investigator pried into its dark depths, not with a hope or purpose of making it better, but from a cold philosophical curiosity."

Although Hawthorne uses the phrase "cold *philosophical* curiosity," it should be noted that the unpardonable sin, breaking the "magnetic chain of humanity," is not the exclusive propensity of the calculating scientists in Hawthorne; the artists too are liable to pry too deeply into the "mystery of sin" in others, with the result that they are as much responsible for that sin as the sinners themselves. So the painter of **"The Prophetic Pictures"** asks himself, "Was not his own the form in which that destiny had embodied itself, and he a chief agent of the coming evil which he had foreshadowed?" And yet, how can the painter help seeing what he sees, foretelling what his power of vision reveals?

The difference between Hawthorne's artists and his scientists is that while the former, men like the painter of **"The Prophetic Pictures"** or Holgrave in *The House of the Seven Gables,* have the ability to transcend the here and now through a kind of artistic clairvoyance, the latter, like Aylmer, Rappaccini, and Chillingworth, are meddlers with time and space, Dupin-like reasoners who, since they can never get beyond the alchemical confines of their methodology, end up destroying the subjects of their experiments. As Aylmer discovers in **"The Birthmark,"** ". . . our great creative Mother, while she amuses us with apparently working in the broadest sunshine, is yet severely careful to keep her own secrets, and, in spite of her pretended openness, shows us nothing but results. She permits us, indeed, to mar, but seldom to mend, and, like a jealous patentee, on no account to make." The artists are also tempted to *act* on their special knowledge of "the mystery of sin," the "dark depths" of the human soul, but the best of them characteristically refuse to go so far, or, if they do allow themselves *even* the painter's mimetic act, they are by so much the less possessors of the "high faith" that is the ultimate value in Hawthorne.

What disturbs Hawthorne most, and in fact gives rise to his conception of the unpardonable sin, is that his artists, like his scientists, may after all be guilty of attempting to "make" reality, and consequently, by virtue of their insight into the recesses of the human heart and their power to portray what they see with Pygmalion-like verisimilitude, they may actually call into being what would otherwise lie dormant, may sacrilegiously "commit" the sins they "imagine" in others. Obviously this fear has special import for Hawthorne's own situation. As Melville said in his review of *Mosses from an Old Manse,* one cannot finish reading **"Young Goodman Brown"** ". . . without addressing the author in his own words—'It shall be yours to penetrate, in every bosom, the deep mystery of sin.'" But this is a question for a more psychoanalytic reading of him than I am now attempting.

One might extract from Emerson a fuller view of language to help explain how Hawthorne gets out of his mimetic dilemma, in so far as he does get out.

> Words [Emerson says] are signs of natural facts. The use of natural history is to give us aid in supernatural history; the use of the outer creation, to give us language for the beings and changes of the inward creation.
>
> It is not words only that are emblematic; it is things which are emblematic. Every natural fact is a symbol of some spiritual fact.
>
> The world is emblematic. Parts of speech are metaphors, because the whole of nature is a metaphor of the human mind. The laws of moral nature answer to those of matter as face to face in a glass.
>
> In like manner, the memorable words of history and the proverbs of nations consist usually of a natural fact, selected as a picture or parable of a moral truth.

By this account, truth-to-life is a necessary result of the proper use of language. The emblematic writer like Hawthorne cannot help but be in touch with reality. This is not a matter of mere factual or literal description; on the contrary, Emerson tells us we must "rise above the ground line of familiar facts," to figurative language, images, and metaphors.

As the *American Notebooks* amply testify, Hawthorne believed with Emerson that "Every natural fact is a symbol of some spiritual fact," and that "The laws of moral nature answer to those of matter as face to face in a glass." It is only a little step further to a thorough reversal of the Realist's theory of mimesis; holding the mirror up to nature becomes, in Romantics like Hawthorne, not a means of seeing nature, but a means of seeing, reflexively, back into the seer himself, which is the point of the passage from *Pierre* cited at the beginning of this study. To quote Emerson again,

> These are not the dreams of a few poets, here and there, but man is an analogist, and studies relations in all objects. He is placed in the centre of beings, and a ray of relation passes from every other being to him. And neither can man be understood without these objects, nor these objects without man.

The ordinary Realist, a writer of short stories, wants to "reproduce" reality, or some aspect of it, in language. Words are thus conceived and valued as indicators of things, referring to the various "facts" of life and nature, and the writer is advised, for example by Henry James (though it was not exactly his practice), to take notes on his experience, the better to render it later in fiction. Ordinary Realism is premised on the view, whether tenable or not, that the writer can "match up" the things in his fiction to the things of life, through the agency of words, which act as neutral conductors, like the "half-tone dots" of a newspaper photograph. By contrast, in Hawthorne's mimesis with its dependence on emblematic language, what is "imitated" is not nature at all, but the supernatural—

"moral law," "spiritual fact," "the beings and changes of the inward creation"—and these by means of natural emblems. In Emerson, this is one way of defining faith itself, "man's power to connect his thought with its proper symbol, and so to utter it." "[P]icturesque language," he says, "is at once a commanding certificate that he who employs it is a man in alliance with truth and God." For him it is the essence of faith to find the natural world only a metaphor for the spiritual: he can act in this world enlivened by imagination; there is a universe for him. Belief, desire, and act are amalgamated, and one creates reality as one goes along: I make things happen, and thus *prove* my existence *and* the existence of what happens.

But for Hawthorne these "creative imitations" of the spirit are always accompanied by the admonition *not* to take them as reality, not to act upon them as upon evidence or fact. The products of the imagination, though they may comprise the highest truths of all, are only "supposed" truths, "as ifs" which crumble at the touch or disappear in the daylight, as Hawthorne coyly warned the reader of *Twice-Told Tales.* This is not regarded as a disadvantage so much as a safeguard, nor is he so sure of its invariable efficacy. As we have seen, his emblems carry a somber meaning, one which produces in him a nagging sense of guilt, as if he were to blame (and who else?) for the truths he divines. He keeps reminding us of the danger of taking the symbolic burden of an emblem literally, like Ahab in *Moby-Dick,* and thus destroying oneself in pursuit of an illusion—which for Melville too is tantamount to calling it magically into life. Less concerned with faith than with its loss, Hawthorne offers the following analysis: once we treat a spiritual truth as a natural truth, as something to act on, it immediately becomes a chimera breathing real fire; *active* belief is fatal to desire, and we are left with only half of faith, if not doubt then horror. His refuge was a theory of mimesis, or the rudiments of one: fictions, and their truths, are not matters of truth or falsity at all. For him, faith depends on remaining *out* of doubt, on maintaining the aesthetic distance.

Richard C. Carpenter (essay date 1969)

SOURCE: "Hawthorne's Polar Explorations: 'Young Goodman Brown' and 'My Kinsman, Major Molineux,'" in *Nineteenth-Century Fiction,* Vol. 24, No. 1, June, 1969, pp. 45-56.

[*In the following essay, Carpenter considers "Young Goodman Brown" and "My Kinsman, Major Molineux" as companion pieces, with the first tale treating corruption brought on by isolation, and the second by society.*]

The misadventures of Young Goodman Brown and Major Molineux's youthful cousin Robin have in recent years been as extensively interpreted as any of Hawthorne's shorter works. Since both tales are ambiguous and puzzling in the characteristic fashion of the best Hawthorne stories, it is not surprising that they have elicited attention from a variety of critical perspectives. Their imagery, symbols, cultural milieus, historical backgrounds, psychoanalytic implications, and mythic patterns have all been so thoroughly examined that we know as much about the individual tales as we can rightly expect from the application of the critical intelligence. Nevertheless, all this critical acumen and industry has allowed one curious lacuna to remain. Although alone among Hawthorne's tales these two are so closely parallel in form and manner as to be properly considered companion-pieces, there has been no investigation of this fact. Passing comments there are aplenty, but curiosity apparently has stopped there.

It may be that the close similarities in structures, characterization, theme, and imagery have been considered too apparent and obvious even to the casual reader, or it may be that these parallels have been assigned to coincidence. But the obvious in Hawthorne, as in James, is often only a surface which disguises, like Poe's purloined letter, matter of more than passing moment. The meaning of the scarlet letter and the golden bowl is quite obvious, but no serious reader would stop his consideration at the mere fact of adultery. Coincidence, on the other hand, while possible, is hardly likely. Whether or not Hawthorne was consciously aware (as I feel he must have been) of similarities in stories published only three years apart, his return to the same structure and themes more reasonably implies a proclivity of the artistic imagination than it does a happenstance. Painfully aware of the few thin strings on which he had to play, Hawthorne appears usually to have striven to make his works as different as he could. The parallels between **"Young Goodman Brown"** and **"My Kinsman, Major Molineux"** imply a powerful impulse to explore a basic problem more than once. One may charge the artist with a tendency to repeat himself—the greatest artists always do—but not with coincidence, because the artist is the victim not of chance but of obsession.

It would therefore appear reasonable to investigate the parallelism in these two tales and to determine the significant ways in which each diverges from the common foundation on which they both rest. Possibly these stories form a kind of test-case or laboratory experiment in which Hawthorne was able to try out his reagents in the same systematic way on what appeared to be distinct psychic substances, discovering in the process in what ways their elements were really the same. Or to shift an over-scientific metaphor to something closer to the creative process, perhaps by writing the same story as a twice-told tale, Hawthorne performed a kind of exploration of the boundaries of his moral universe—moving from the center to the verges and back again.

. . . . .

The first evidence of parallelism, reconstructing the exploration as best we can, is the plot, a series of events sufficiently alike to lend themselves to a single synopsis:

A youth, identified obscurely by a generic and symbolic name, sets out from the security of home and family on a journey which promises to bring him to a new way of life. Untested and naive, he sees this adventure as difficult yet filled with opportunity. He goes somewhat unwillingly, and thinks on occasion of the home he has left behind, but is persistent in his search. Early in his journey he meets an elderly gentleman whose emblem is a staff and who seems to know more about the youth than he knows himself. Darkness falls as he goes on; his way becomes confused; from various quarters he hears demoniac laughter; he is half-convinced that he is subject to hallucinations. People and objects appear and disappear in phantasmagoric fashion; he is confronted at a climactic point by a devilish apparition; he becomes increasingly excited as he nears his goal and bursts out in demoniacal laughter himself. Watching a profane rite, lurid against a surrounding darkness, he very nearly becomes a participant, but comes to his senses to find the vision dissipated and the natural order restored. He apparently has been profoundly affected by this experience; the remainder of his life will be completely altered by the events of this one night.

In these days of Northrop Frye and Joseph Campbell, such a plot is inevitably seen as a type of quest, and commentators have not been remiss in pointing this out. What might nevertheless strike an attention not too jaded with mythic analysis is the fact that *both* these stories exemplify with unexampled clarity the typical quest-pattern, much less "attenuated" or "displaced," as Mr. Frye would say, than is usual in fiction, and unique in Hawthorne's work, where the mere shadow of such a pattern is rare indeed. Nowhere else, so far as I can determine, did Hawthorne write even one story that can be so neatly assimilated to the main circumstances of the journey of the hero as Campbell has outlined it for us:

> The mythological hero, setting forth from his hut or castle, voluntarily proceeds to the threshold of adventure where he encounters a shadow presence which guards the passage. He defeats or conciliates this power and goes into the kingdom of the dark. Beyond the threshold he journeys through a world of unfamiliar yet strangely intimate forces, some of which severely threaten him and some of which give magical aid. When he arrives at the nadir of the mythological round, he undergoes a supreme ordeal and gains his reward, represented by his recognition by the father-creator. He returns to the world but the transcendental powers must remain behind.[1]

Not all of this fits precisely, of course. (It does not fit Campbell's examples precisely either.) But it does apply to several aspects of each story. Brown, for instance, meets the "shadow presence" in the form of his grandfather—really the devil taking on the form most suited to the occasion; he "conciliates," or agrees with this "presence" that he will go into "the kingdom of the dark."[2] The forest through which he journeys is at once unfamiliar and seems related to himself, even a projection of his own spiritual state. He is both severely threatened and aided on his evil journey by the voices he hears from the cloud overhead and the discovery of Faith's pink ribbon, an ironic emblem, fluttering down from the sky and catching in the branches of a tree. His supreme ordeal is in the very depths of the forest, where he recognizes and is recognized by the Devil, who is in this situation his "father-creator," for Brown is to become a demon like those he sees at the blasphemous rite—a child of Satan. He resists this fate at the crucial moment, in effect returning to the world, because the "transcendental powers" disappear. Yet Brown has been drawn into the orbit of evil by his experience, and he never recovers from it.

Robin, whose other name must be Molineux, although Hawthorne goes to some pains to conceal this fact from us,[3] meets a kind of "shadow presence," in the person of an elderly gentleman who represents the society of the town and who refuses to answer Robin's questions: he is a guardian of the town's secret. Robin neither conciliates nor defeats this guardian but is not deterred in his search. The forces which aid and threaten Robin are, on the other hand, more explicit than those Brown encounters: an innkeeper, a saucy wench, and the watchman all hinder his quest, while a friendly stranger, "a gentleman in his prime, of open, intelligent, cheerful, and altogether prepossessing countenance," gives him help and advice. Robin is, in similar fashion to Brown, involved in "a world of unfamiliar yet strangely intimate forces," because he is in the dark about the fate being prepared for his kinsman, so that he is continually bewildered and frustrated while the townspeople are all aware of his search and his problem. His crucial moment comes as he sees Major Molineux dragged in the cart, tarred and feathered. As the psychoanalytic critics point out, it is here that he encounters and recognizes the father-figure for whom he has been searching. He joins in the demoniac laughter of the crowd; the vision sweeps out of sight, leaving "a silent street behind"; and Robin, wondering if he has been dreaming, is encouraged by his mentor to stay in the town, to profit from his experience.

The basic structure of this quest-myth is supplemented by the machinery typical of such journeys. The setting in both tales is made preternatural and foreboding by a feeling of disorientation. It is plain enough that Brown, venturing ever deeper into the wilderness, should find his surroundings sinister and confusing. But the same is true for Robin, who is traversing the streets of a little provincial capital. His is an "evening of ambiguity and weariness" like Brown's, and the byways of Boston are nearly as labyrinthine as the depths of Brown's woods or the streets of the town through which K. makes his confused way in *The Castle*. In the fashion characteristic of quests, the hero must be drawn out of his accustomed track in order to become psychologically prepared for the totally new experience which awaits him.

A sense of the phantasmagoric accompanies the spatial dislocation felt by each hero. The Devil's staff, as Goodman Brown sees it, "bore the likeness of a great black snake, so curiously wrought that it might almost be seen to twist and wriggle itself like a living serpent." Like the apparition of Goody Cloyse and the Devil himself, the ap-

YOUNG GOODMAN BROWN.

YOUNG Goodman Brown came forth at sunset into the street of Salem village; but put his head back, after crossing the threshold, to exchange a parting kiss with his young wife. And Faith, as the wife was aptly named, thrust her own pretty head into the street, letting the wind play with the pink ribbons of her cap while she called to Goodman Brown.

"Dearest heart," whispered she, softly and rather sadly, when her lips were close to his ear, "prithee put off your journey until sunrise and sleep in your own bed to-night. A lone woman is troubled with such dreams and such thoughts that she's afeard of herself sometimes. Pray tarry with me this night, dear husband, of all nights in the year."

"My love and my Faith," replied young Goodman Brown, "of all nights in the year, this one night must I tarry away from thee. My journey, as thou callest it, forth and back again, must needs be done 'twixt now and sunrise. What, my sweet, pretty wife, dost thou doubt me already, and we but three months married?"

"Then God bless you!" said Faith, with the pink ribbons; "and may you find all well when you come back."

"Amen!" cried Goodman Brown. "Say thy
(87)

pearance of the staff "must have been an ocular deception, assisted by the uncertain light." Brown hears the minister and Deacon Gookin but can see nothing; disembodied accents are "talking . . . strangely in the empty air." From overhead comes to his ears the "confused and doubtful sound of voices" out of a cloud which hurries "across the zenith" and hides the "brightening stars," although there is no wind stirring. Yet "so indistinct [are] the sounds" that he doubts whether he hears "aught but the murmur of the old forest, whispering without a wind."[4] Throughout the rest of the tale, Hawthorne continues to emphasize this kind of ambiguity, as he similarly provides the reader with a sense of the unreal in Robin Molineux's surroundings. Robin's disoriented sense is that of sight instead of Brown's hallucinations of hearing; the effect of dream, even of nightmare, is much the same. "Strange things we travellers see" repeats Robin, observing without understanding their meaning the preparations for tarring and feathering his kinsman, the figures hurrying along the deserted streets, the man with two faces, "as if two individual devils, a fiend of fire and a fiend of darkness, had united themselves to form this infernal visage." Almost falling asleep, he confuses his memories of home with this place where he now sits in weariness and frustration, and asks, most significantly, "Am I here, or there?" And when the horrid procession appears, Robin has become ready to respond to its dionysiac frenzy, in part at least because he has lost his common-sense perspective.

Both Brown and Robin have talismans: the staff which the Devil gives Brown and Robin's cudgel; they both undergo their adventures literally at night, as well as undergoing a "night-journey"; they observe and very nearly participate in what can only be called a *rite,* and that rite is in both cases lurid with fire against a predominant darkness; both youths come back to themselves with a start after the crisis, as if they had been in a trance or dreaming. In more than coincidental fashion Young Goodman Brown and Robin Molineux are much the same type of man involved in the same basic experience of the quest for knowledge of good and evil.

. . . . .

Quests, to be sure, though archetypally the same, take many different forms: Ahab, Peer Gynt, and Sir Galahad are classic heroes of quests, but the themes and tones of their stories are in each case radically different. Quests run the gamut from philosophical tragedy to satire to light-hearted comedy; indeed if we accept the suggestion of Northrop Frye, the quest-myth is the basic pattern of which romance, tragedy, irony, and comedy are "episodes,"[5] and it should not surprise us to find elements of the quest in any work where we wish to seek it out. Nevertheless, the differences among works built on this fundamental pattern are also important and instructive.

With **"My Kinsman, Major Molineux"** and **"Young Goodman Brown"** these differences—or perhaps *modulations* would be the better word—appear in the type of adventure on which the heroes are embarked, in the specific nature of the setting, and in the character of the hero himself and the characters whom he encounters. Goodman Brown's journey is into the wilderness while Robin's is into the city. There is a kind of parallelism here, as we have indicated, in the labyrinthine and disorienting nature of Robin's city. Yet it is a much more solid place than Brown's forest. The figures Brown sees are so insubstantial as to disappear in the wink of an eye; the voices he hears may be nothing but the product of his fevered imagination; the Satanic ritual and its communicants leave not a trace behind when Brown calls upon Faith to "look up to heaven, and resist the wicked one." While both tales have a dreamlike quality, Robin's world is altogether more substantial than Brown's. Essentially Brown is living in solipsism, the projection of his own tortured doubt and loss of faith. His quest is into the depths of his soul, given symbolic realization in the figures he thinks he sees and hears in the wilderness, whereas Robin's is into society. Labyrinthine though the city is, distorted and portentous as it seems to be, the city does exist, with its taverns, barbershops, churches, and crowds of people walking its streets. While it is possible to think, as Hawthorne half-encourages us to do, that Brown really has dreamed all that has happened to him, it is much more difficult to think this with Robin. When Brown comes to himself nothing remains

but "calm night and solitude," the once burning twig "besprinkles" his cheek "with the coldest dew"; when Robin recovers, the town is still around him and the kindly stranger urges him to stay where he may rise in the world without the help of his kinsman.

Evil in **"Young Goodman Brown"** is concentrated in the Devil, who first appears in the guise of Brown's grandfather and then in his own dark shape as he presides over the Witches' Sabbath in the depths of the forest. Robin encounters him, however, or the evil of which he is the manifestation, in several characters: the hem-ing gentleman with his indifference and his threats; the girl with the scarlet petticoat and her sexual invitation; the sleepy watchman; the man with two faces, closest to the Devil in his role as a Lord of Misrule presiding over the ruin of Major Molineux. Each of these is evil in a special way; one critic has suggested that not only is the two-faced man symbolic of the Devil, but the other characters can be seen as assistant tempters: pride, lust, avarice (in the innkeeper), and sloth.[6] Whether we consider them this way or not, they are clearly something quite different from the radically metaphysical, the unfocused essence of evil sought by Goodman Brown. Robin is exposed not to the singular evil of the human soul so much as to the multiple evils of a social cosmos.

The characters of Brown and of Robin are also distinct, even though neither is highly individualized. Brown is a young Puritan husband—that is all we know—but Robin is described as a rustic properly prepared for his encounter with the city, clad in durable garments, with "vigorous shoulders, curly hair, well-shaped features, and bright, cheerful eyes." Of particular interest is the emblematic staff with which Brown is equipped, a really supernatural instrument fashioned by the Devil from a maple branch plucked by the wayside, contrasted to Robin's "heavy cudgel formed of an oak sapling, and retaining a part of the hardened root"—a serviceable weapon in his forest home but useless here in the city. Several times Robin wishes he could use the cudgel to get some satisfaction from his tormentors, but in these surroundings his heavy club has no value. What he needs is something like the long, polished cane which the hem-ing gentleman strikes down before himself at every step. For Brown, who is an archetypal Everyman, the Devil's staff is a magic instrument to help him on his way toward evil; for Robin cudgel and staff are means of contending, at this time unsuccessfully, but later with probable success, against a world where one must know the "right" things to do. Like a young Madison Avenue executive, Robin needs to find out the mores of the society into which he is moving. It is a corrupt world, but apparently at the end he has discovered how to come to terms with it.

Other modulations imply this same point: the symbol of femininity in **"Young Goodman Brown"** is a pink ribbon, whereas in Robin's story it is a scarlet petticoat belonging to a young harlot; laughter in Brown's forest is despairing, demoniac, whereas the laughter Robin hears is mocking, derisive, contemptuous; the assembly Brown sees in the forest has undergone a change in aspect because of their spiritual alteration, the mob Robin watches seems fiendish because of their costumes and actions; when Brown turns to religion for help he asks Faith to look to heaven, Robin sees the Bible illuminated by a single ray of moonlight, a symbol, so he conjectures, of nature worshipping in "the house that man had builded." Brown's environment is not only the solitary forest, but the solitary spirit; Robin's is the world of men.

. . . . .

The reasons why Hawthorne wrote stories with so many similarities but provided them with such striking divergences must necessarily remain conjectural, yet I believe that although we cannot determine reasons some conclusions concerning results may be tentatively drawn. The first of these is that **"Young Goodman Brown"** differs from **"My Kinsman, Major Molineux"** in some of the ways that tragedy differs from comedy. Brown seems to suffer from a degree of *hubris,* despite his hesitancy about embarking on his journey; he acts from that peculiar combination of free will and predestination that often guides tragic protagonists; he suffers a kind of spiritual death tantamount to the physical death that overtakes most tragic heroes, although it might be noted that Oedipus, the prototypal tragic hero, suffers in much the same way in *Oedipus Tyrannus.*

Robin, on the other hand, has many of the characteristics of the stock comic figure of the country bumpkin, from his sturdy homemade clothes to his cudgel to his self-assurance.[7] Naive and blundering, he prides himself on his "shrewdness," which Hawthorne underlines with heavy irony by mentioning it again and again. He is both importunate and gullible: he tugs at the coat of the man with the cane and is threatened with the stocks for his rudeness; he thinks that the innkeeper's "superfluous civility" is due to a recognition of Robin's family resemblance to the Major; he allows himself to believe, or half-believe, that the pretty whore is the Major's housekeeper and almost falls into her toils. Despite his encounters with sinister people and frightening events, the best responses he can make are "Mercy me!" and "Strange things we travellers see!" In addition to Robin's character as bumpkin, the story itself observes some of the conventions of comedy: the youthful hero (or *eiron*) blocked in his search for fortune by absurd circumstances; the helpful confidant who assists the hero in his cause; the implication of his being rewarded with romance, or sex at least, as well as fortune, since the saucy eye and silvery laughter of the pretty wench are at his elbow in the climactic scene; an "assembly scene" at this climax where everyone Robin has encountered reappears; the expulsion of a scapegoat figure from the society, to the accompaniment of much raucous laughter.

Although it would be plainly a distortion to make these stories out to be a tragedy and a comedy respectively, it is clear that Hawthorne was using these orientations to create two different stories from what is basically a single plot

and that consequently we see what appear to be two different possible outcomes to the same essential situation. Everyman may, by going deeper and deeper into the wilderness of the self, discover such evil there that he ever after must project it upon the world about him—Hawthorne's theme of the tragedy of moral isolation, the withdrawal "from the chain of human sympathies," the soul seeing its sin in a hall of mirrors where the thronging terrors it perceives are only itself infinitely multiplied. Or Everyman may find himself in a society—a world of interrelated people—whom he has difficulty recognizing because of his concern with himself, until he eventually comes to a sudden revelation of his innocence, which appears absurd in these circumstances, and falls from that innocence into sophistication, an event so excruciatingly comic that he can do nothing but laugh in concert with those around him.

But although the outcomes are different, at the same time this pushing of the comic to the extreme leaves it but a hairsbreadth from tragedy so that *two* stories become in effect *one.* The tragic and comic constitute, in fact, a kind of cyclical process rather than actual antinomies; as in the universe of contemporary physics, if you go far enough in one direction, you will end up where you started. By using the archetype of the quest, Hawthorne takes us on alternate routes that turn out to have practically the same destination. In the one, man comes to grief through his own self-regard, his willful isolation; in the other he comes to grief—this time without quite realizing what is happening to him—by being absorbed into the ways of thought and feeling of a corrupt world, laughing with the mob at his previous innocence, and at the spectacle of his kinsman—the term is significant—shamed and tormented by an assemblage of demons: "On they went, like fiends that throng in mockery around some dead potentate, mighty no more, but majestic still in his agony. On they went, in counterfeited pomp, in senseless uproar, in frenzied merriment, trampling all on an old man's heart."

Thus Hawthorne, exploring the limits of his moral universe, saw man's quest as the same, regardless of its specific form. None of his protagonists is more of an *isolato* than Brown; as cut off from humankind as are Ethan Brand and Roger Chillingworth, they still live in a web of human relationships. And no protagonist seems likely to rise in the social world in the way Robin indubitably will. Yet, ironically, they both are fallen. By telling us the same story and framing it so differently, Hawthorne has shown us, as in a paradigm, the themes with which he was to deal in most of his work. The ritualistic form of the quest serves him especially well in bringing his underlying idea to the fore. Probably the reason why he did not continue to provide his tales with such a clear-cut metaphor is that he intuitively (or artistically) recognized its limitations. In later work, and in other tales written about the same time as **"Young Goodman Brown"** and **"My Kinsman, Major Molineux,"** he would turn the physical search into an intellectual or spiritual odyssey, keeping the theme but not the metaphor. Occasionally, as in **"Roger Malvin's**

Burial" or **"Ethan Brand,"** a portion of the tale takes us on a quest, but the main drift is in the direction of a spiritual journey. Aylmer, Owen Warland, Giovanni Guasconti, Arthur Dimmesdale, Donatello—all are engaged in one or another kind of spiritual journey that may be taken to be the equivalent of Brown's and Robin's "actual" quests. But, with the exception of **"The Celestial Railroad,"** which is a special kind of satiric allegory, none of Hawthorne's other works so plainly employs the unadorned archetypal pattern of the journey from innocence into destructive knowledge.

Significantly enough, Hawthorne did not continue to find the journey into the corrupting world as imaginatively effective as that into spiritual isolation. The comic, while it appears more frequently in his work than one might think from reading some contemporary critics, is not Hawthorne's dominant mode. Even in **"My Kinsman, Major Molineux"** it is ambiguous comedy with no joy in it and a sinister note at the climax. Probably *The House of the Seven Gables* has less ambiguous comedy than any other of his works, a generally sunnier attitude. But even in that novel—if it is a novel—the sinister influence of Maule's curse prevents us from feeling that all is fundamentally harmonious in this social world. Although I have claimed elsewhere that the ending of the novel, with its sudden flood of good fortune, is an integral part of the theme, the implication of the curse is still with us. Comedy is hardly Hawthorne's métier, even if he did try it on a number of occasions.

We may conclude, cautiously and with an awareness of the tenuity of our chain of reasoning, that the parallels of the stories we have been examining, together with the deviations from those parallels, were far from fortuitous in their end result, no matter what unknowable genesis they may have had. By establishing for Hawthorne the topographical frontiers of his moral territory, the polar explorations of these tales served his imagination well. If he had not undertaken such explorations, I venture to say that the assurance and artistry of his later works would certainly have been much different. In **"Young Goodman Brown"** he pursued the idea of isolation as far as was artistically feasible, as he followed the idea of corruption by society as far (for him) as was appropriate in **"My Kinsman, Major Molineux."** He did not need to survey those limits again but could map the intervening territory in all its fascinating contours and complexities. As indeed, he did.

Notes

1. *The Hero With a Thousand Faces* (New York, 1956), pp. 245-246. I have condensed Campbell's summary to some extent.

2. Although Brown's trip has been previously planned and there probably has already been contact between him and the devil, the initial encounter nevertheless has for him the authentic shock of a threshold experience.

3. Several reasons might be given for this secretiveness, among them the desire to preserve the social distance between the rustic Robin and his powerful (or once-powerful) kinsman, while at the same time preserving the blood relationship between them. The most probable explanation, to my way of thinking, is that Robin must be kept an Everyman despite his human and social relationships.

4. Cf. Paul J. Hurley, "Young Goodman Brown's 'Heart of Darkness,'" *American Literature,* XXXVII (January, 1966), 410-419. His thesis is that the events all indicate Brown's hallucination, which he *wills,* rather than that they are ambiguously real or unreal events: "A more acceptable interpretation of the ambiguity of the story is to see in it Hawthorne's suggestion that the incredible incidents in the forest were the product of an ego-induced fantasy, the self-justification of a diseased mind. It seems clear that the incidents were not experienced: they were willed" (p. 419). I substantially agree with this position.

5. *Anatomy of Criticism* (Princeton, 1957), p. 215.

6. Cf. Hyatt H. Waggoner, *Hawthorne: A Critical Study* (Cambridge, Mass., 1955), p. 46n.

7. Cf. Daniel Hoffman, *Form and Fable in American Fiction* (New York, 1961), pp. 113-125.

Reginald Cook (essay date 1970)

SOURCE: "The Forest of Goodman Brown's Night: A Reading of Hawthorne's 'Young Goodman Brown,'" in *New England Quarterly,* Vol. 43, No. 3, September, 1970, pp. 473-81.

[*In the following essay, Cook discusses 'Young Goodman Brown' in terms of Hawthorne's probing of the moral imagination, pointing out that Brown's motives are ambiguous, but that the results of his actions are "clear and frightening."*]

"Thou wouldst not think how ill all's here about my heart . . ."

Hamlet v. 2, 220

I

In a literary epoch when the dominant field of action was the frontier settlement, the forest, and the fort, Hawthorne focussed on the world of moral imagination. His **"Young Goodman Brown"** (1835) is a paradigm of this particular world, and Brown's behavior on a fateful night in his life is the key to this haunting tale. Although the motives for Goodman Brown's behavior are ambiguous, the consequences of his compulsive acts are clear but frightening.

It is truly an enchanted forest into which Goodman Brown enters on his way to keep a tryst. "The magic forest," says Heinrich Zimmer in *The King and the Corpse,* "is always full of adventures. No one can enter it without losing his way. The forest has always been a place of initiation for there the demonic presences, the ancestral spirits, and the forces of nature reveal themselves." Brown is no exception. For in the forest he is made aware of demonic presences, ancestral spirits, and he confronts the forces of nature in their strange and fearful aspects. "The forest is the antithesis of house and heart, village and field boundary, where the household gods hold sway and where human laws and customs prevail," continues the explanatory Zimmer. "It holds the dark forbidden things—secrets, terrors, which threaten the protected life of the ordered world of common day." With one exception this is true of Brown's experience. The seat of darkness upon which the castle of Merlin stands in the forest of ancient myth is transformed in Hawthorne's tale into a Witches' Sabbath where the enchantments of primitive mythology are secularized in the dour Calvinistic scheme of universal human guilt.

"But the chosen one, the elect, who survives its [the enchanted forest's] deadly peril is," as Zimmer says, "reborn and leaves it a changed man." Ironically, Brown's initiation and rebirth represent an inversion of the customary ritual. His survival is physical; forevermore he is spiritually spellbound, the effect of which is both bewilderment and distrustfulness. Sinking into a torpor of unredemptive guilt-consciousness, when he dies no hopeful verse is carved upon his tombstone, "for his dying hour was gloom."

The reader does not fail to see that as Brown goes from the village to the forest he passes from a conscious world to a subconscious one. Upon returning from the extraordinary forest coven to the commonplace village orthodoxy, Brown's traumatic shock leaves him a deeply suspicious man. To a reader indoctrinated in Freudian and Jungian psychology the tale gathers meaning from the modern explorations of the subconscious mind, enkindles the aesthetic sensibility by its reliance on imagination, and appeals to the antirational, which interests us in the surrealistic art of Salvador Dali, Marcel Duchamp, and Joan Miro.

We are introduced to the strange world of young Goodman Brown by its "solidity of specification." The locale is Salem Village; the time shortly after King Philip's War. Since the forest is fifteen minutes from the village, the action is significantly within the ambit of civilized society. Only the forest of the night is strange. The beginning and the end of the tale are real enough but the middle is somnambulistic. At the close Hawthorne inquires: "Had Goodman Brown fallen asleep in the forest and only dreamed a wild dream of a witch meeting?" Not to keep us waiting, Hawthorne begins the next paragraph balefully. "Be it so if you will, but, alas! it was a dream of evil omen for young Goodman Brown." If the author's "be it so if you will" is so much dust in the eyes to keep us off the target, I for one don't mind. Hawthorne's make-believe is more evocative of the heart's truths than many realist's spitting image of actuality.

II

When he leaves his three-months' wedded wife, Faith (an obvious symbol) and her pink ribbons in Salem, Brown's nocturnal journey, it is understood, cannot be postponed. It must be accomplished between sunset and sunrise. Nor is it enticing journeying. The road is dreary and narrow; the forest is gloomy. The real can hardly be distinguished from the illusory. Shadow density is accentuated. Twilight fades into dusk, dusk into gloomy night. It is scary—"as lonely as could be"; and perhaps a devilish Indian stands behind every wayside tree.

Then Brown is joined by a fellow traveler of the same rank, similarly dressed, resembling him in expression but distinguishable. He is, indeed, the Devil. Not Cotton Mather's diabolical "small black man," or Goethe's Mephisto, the tempter, or Henry James's clever Peter Quint, or Gide's *raissoneur*, or Ivan Karamazov's irritating *alter ego*, but certainly God's old Arch-Enemy—an urbane intrigant, who carries for a fetish a twisted staff that resembles a great live black snake. The diabolic fellow traveler knows all about the hereditary taint in Brown's forebears. "They were my good friends," he acknowledges familiarly. He once helped Brown's grandfather lash the Quaker women; he kindled the pitch-pine knot with which Brown's incendiary father ruthlessly set fire to an Indian village in King Philip's War. He has, to say the least, "a very general acquaintance here in New England."

Smooth, wily, taunting, facile in argument, mercurial in mood, now gravely considerate, now irrepressible in laughter, he turns aside Brown's attempts to defend the good works of his family. Subtly the Devil succeeds in infecting Brown with an apprehension of evil in his family, in his friends, in his moral and spiritual advisers, in the worthies of the community, and, not least, in his young wife. Blighting what he touches, and denigrating whomever he mentions in human society, the Devil casts a spell of profound disillusionment on Brown. First he exposes the duplicity of Goody Cloyse, moral instructress of Brown's youth, whose shadowy figure appears on the forest path in the dusk. Stubbornly Brown refuses to succumb to general suspicion on such slight circumstantial evidence. He will still trust in Faith. So the Devil to break him down confronts him with the revered minister of the village and with good old Deacon Gookin. Brown, who has stepped aside from the thread of the narrowing forest path, cannot be sure of the shadowy figures that pass along the way; only their voices are recognizable. Goody Cloyse had mumbled anticipatory remarks about seeing somewhere in the forest at "the meeting" a nice young man (Brown!). The minister and the deacon anticipate seeing a goodly young woman (Faith!) "taken into communion." Even this trying episode is not enough to overwhelm the devil-resistant Brown. He looks heavenward where the stars are "brightening." "'With heaven above and Faith below, I will yet stand firm against the devil!' cried Goodman Brown." And he does for the moment.

Brown's resolution is not shaken until he hears from an ominous dark cloud the "confused and doubtful sound of voices" of both "pious and ungodly" people. One lamenting voice is that of a young woman—apparently Faith— "yet with an uncertain sorrow, and entreating for some favor, which, perhaps, it would grieve her to obtain." This low-pitched, connotative statement is surely a stroke of Hawthorne's art when we consider the emotional plight of a baffled and bereft Brown. Shouting out Faith's name, he is mocked to the echo. Then his resolution breaks and, in his extreme dejection, the dark cloud disappears and a pink ribbon which flutters down compounds his anguish. There is no goodness he thinks; "sin is but a name." He capitulates. "Come, devil; for to thee is this world given." Abandoned, he despairs, and despairing, like Ethan Brand, he laughs hysterically loud and long. Unlike the Devil's laughter, his is not mirthful, but terrible to hear.

Brown runs madly along the wild, dreary, obscure path that takes him deeper into the heart of darkness. The night is now filled with frightful sounds and, among these, as in Moussorgsky's "A Night on Bald Mountain," there is a sound "like a distant church-bell"—the wind. Possessed by the hysteria of despair, Brown tries to outlaugh what he thinks is the scornful derision of the wilderness. In the forest of the night—that is to say, in the blackness of his subconscious despair—"he was himself the chief horror of the scene, and shrank not from its other horrors." Devil-possessed and despairing, he runs through the haunted forest, brandishing his staff, venting horrid blasphemy, outracing the fiend who, by now, has pretty well victimized the bedeviled husbandman.

Goodman Brown's frenzied charge through the forest is halted by a lurid red light in a forest enclosure where a grave and darkclad congregation, their several voices rolling solemnly through the wild night, worship at a Witches' Sabbath. Before the forest-hemmed group rears a pulpit rock, illumined by blazing pine tops, and among the assembled leaders of the Salem community are both the reputable and pious as well as the suspect, dissolute, and criminal. Sinners and Indian priests, heathen and Christian, are distinguishable but united. And leading the impious assembly is one of the grave New England divines.

When the cry for converts is raised, Brown is led forward by Deacon Gookin to the blazing altar where he stands with another proselyte, a veiled woman, none other than Faith. Welcomed to the loathful brotherhood of lechers, poisoners, parricides, and infanticides, the couple is exhorted to be undeceived. "Evil is the nature of mankind," they are told. "Evil must be your only happiness." Before the fiend-light of the unhallowed altar, gazed at by faces "that would be seen next day at the council board of the province, and others which, Sabbath after Sabbath, look devoutly heavenward, and benignantly over the crowded pews, from the holiest pulpits in the land," the husband and wife about to be baptized in "the mystery of sin" look upon each other and shudder. Imploring his wife to resist the devil and look to heaven, Brown breaks the spell.

The telltale disclosure of Brown's illusory nocturnal meeting is a natural fact. First he staggers against a rock which *feels* chill and damp. Then a hanging twig, which a moment before had seemed on fire, "besprinkled his cheek with the coldest dew." The tactile fact disabuses his overwrought imagination. The fiery twig is delusive. Nevertheless the nocturnal meeting will haunt him to his dying day. Next morning he is observed in Salem Village "staring around him like a bewildered man." He shrinks from the good old minister; he challenges as a recusant the old Deacon whom he overhears praying; he interferes in Goody Cloyse's religious exercises by snatching away a child being catechized, "as from the grasp of the fiend himself," and he behaves strangely to Faith who "almost kissed her husband before the whole village."

Young Goodman Brown is not the same man who at sunset the day before entered upon the errand into the wilderness with such grudging compulsion. The "fearful dream" has done its work. Somewhere in this fact and phrase is the heart of Hawthorne's message, it would seem.

III

How shall we riddle this marvellous tale? One of Hawthorne's attributions is an ability to penetrate the surface of conscious perception. In his introduction to *Psychology and Alchemy,* Jung says: "It must be admitted that the archetypal contents of the collective unconscious can often assume grotesque and horrible forms in dreams and fantasies, so that even the most hard-boiled rationalist is not immune from shattering nightmares and haunting fears." In **"Young Goodman Brown"** Hawthorne continues a lonely vigil in the dark surrealistic forest of the American mind. He reveals presciently the turbulence beneath the layers of the Puritan conscience: the form its guilt takes, the contributions of grace and election, the sense of justice, the invocation of mercy. He evokes the depth of the Puritan mind which expresses itself, not only in witches' waxen images pricked with thorns, but in the nocturnal coven and in the black man's book in which are inscribed names in blood from cut fingers. Under the spell of the dark imagination which apprehends tragic realities, Hawthorne never fails to acknowledge the community of human relationship. What Brown discovers is a terrible thing, surely; not that evil co-exists with good in human nature, but that "evil is the nature of mankind." He also finds out what it means to be inducted into a mystery that makes him "more conscious of the secret of others." And he exults as he beholds "the whole earth one stain of guilt, one mighty blood spot." One mighty blood spot! To the exclusion of anything else, guilt prevails, and all things are evermore suspect.

The effect of Brown's discovery is terrible. What he should have recognized as only one of the powerful forces in "the collective unconscious" becomes *the* exclusive force. After the night of the fearful dream, Goodman Brown, of whom there are thousands resembling him as his name, sex, and age imply, is unable to accept as true of himself what is true of all men: that evil is counterbalanced by an essential good.

The dream journey is a remarkable one. The compulsion that drives him is not only inward (he doesn't, for instance, share its motive with anyone else, certainly not with Faith); it is downward. The descent is symbolized by the journey from daylight into night, from consciousness to subconsciousness, from reality to illusion, from physical to psychical, from light to dark. The chief positive factor is Brown's fidelity to the covenant, the consequences of which suggest that fidelity is not a higher virtue than intelligent exercise of will. The effect upon him is negative; he is equal to the obligation of the tryst but he is not equal to its consequences. He is forever turned darkly inward, a distrustful and despairing man.

When Brown returns from the forest, the nature of his change is as arresting as the motive for his compulsive pact with the devil is equivocal. He has been *there,* but exactly why he has had to be there is not clear. In *The Hero with a Thousand Faces,* Joseph Campbell describes the mythic hero. "A hero ventures forth from the world of common day into a region of supernatural wonder," he says; "fabulous forces are there encountered and a decisive victory is won; the hero comes back from this mysterious venture with the power to bestow honors on his fellow men." How little of Campbell's description of the hero can be applied to Hawthorne's protagonist. The world of common day is in the tale; so, too, is the region of supernatural wonders and the fabulous forces. But there is no victory, and so Brown's return from the mysterious venture is without prestigious power to bestow honors. Quite the contrary. An antihero, he rabidly infects his fellow man with the virus of his grim, inexpiable despair of human trust.

IV

What meaning does this tale have for us today? What in the story has survival value beyond the interest a reader has in the effectiveness of Hawthorne's artistic competence? How to account for Brown's malaise is really less relevant than the meaning of his actions. It would appear—and this is, I think, Hawthorne's insight—a case of psychic masochism in which Brown's compulsion is in reality the expression of the desire for self-punishment. Brown appears to do nothing wrong except to go through with a commitment that he might reasonably have rejected in the first place. Yet once having committed himself, he still might have exorcised the inner devil of suspicion. That he fails to do this is *his* particular story and *our* particular revelation. There is no forestalling self-punishment. Neither is it possible to modify the effects inflicted on others—on Faith and the community of Brown's fellowship. And this is similarly applicable to every self-destructive protagonist in literature, whether a Byronic, Melvilleian, Hardyesque, or contemporary fictional character.

The symbolic forest of the night is, in effect, young Goodman Brown's own dark soul where belief turns into doubt, faith into skepticism, and where the people encountered are the adumbrations of his daily familiars and ancestral past. This dream is symbolically true. Significantly, it underscores D. H. Lawrence's contention. "You *must* look through the surface of American art and see the inner diabolism of the symbolic meaning," said Lawrence. "Otherwise it is all mere childishness." The symbolic meaning is to be found in the stresses and conflicts, the compulsions and repressions whose compensations, as Sir Herbert Read says in *The Philosophy of Modern Art,* are found in "the physical horrors of war and persecution." The *Walpurgis Nacht* of Dachau and Buchenwald of the 1940's had its source in the conflict between the Nazis and the Jews for the extension of power in the economic system of twentieth-century Germany.

Hawthorne's tale embodies the effect of tensions applicable in the social life of a nation, a people, and individuals. **"Young Goodman Brown"** focusses on one of these archetypal stresses. The tale is, as we have noted, a paradigm. It focusses on a fearful dream that is part of our subconscious reality. Although Hawthorne's medium is fiction, he is focussing on truth as he understands it. But he has chosen to release this truth as though it were a dream fantasy. The gas ovens of the 1940's and the lurid Witches' Sabbath of the seventeenth century are equally symbolic. So symbolic, in fact, that he who runs may read, but he who runs with most deliberation may read the deepest meaning. Diabolism is quite as apparent in what others do to us by persecution as it is in what we do to ourselves when we fail in acknowledging the moral consequences of our actions.

The important point in Hawthorne's tale is not that Brown's malaise is, or seems, incurable, but that it is definitely symptomatic. Given these traits, tendencies, and impulses and the effect will be comparable. Anyone of us might be susceptible to a similar psychological predicament. The syndrome is complete. What is significant about the tale? The epiphany occurs when the reader released from the narrative's pervasive darkness is struck by Hawthorne's laser. However much Brown fails himself by stubborn will, determined pride, callow gullibility, and obsessively fixated self-centeredness, he does not, even in his frailty, fail us. As Robert Frost says: "So false it is that what we haven't we can't give." This is one of the great paradoxes in the human condition. Brown's negativism challenges us to find a means of establishing positive traits. The opposite of Brown's unendurable world of incertitude is one where the enabling virtues of compassion and pity, love and trust, fidelity, and hope are activated. Brown, one in the gallery of Hawthorne's moody men which includes Brand and Bourne, Warland and Chillingworth, is the psychological victim hung up between damnation and salvation.

In the harrowing world of incertitude in which he lives out his days Brown is psychologically sick with the fear that what he has seen in the illusory forest of the night is so, that all those hallucinatory scenes were in reality peopled by victims of sin familiar to him. When illusions are mistaken for realities the victim is caught in his own trap; is, in effect, self-betrayed. Hawthorne's climactic statement is apposite. "A stern, a sad, a darkly meditative, a distrustful, if not desperate man, did he become from the night of that fearful dream." In the forest of Brown's night only the wrath of God burns brightly. His journey into an awareness of evil brings a consciousness of guilt *without* redemption. Unable to transcend the experience through humility and compassion, he is resigned to desperation. In consequence, he symbolizes the man who is shriveled rather than tempered by the pain and suffering which accompany an encounter with evil. It can never be said of him as it is said in *Meister Eckhart*: "Not till the soul knows all that there is to be known can she pass over to the unknown good."

Hawthorne's insight is startling: that confronting us everywhere is the inescapable universal guilt, like one mighty blood spot as ineradicable as the stains on Lady Macbeth's hands and soul. The effect on Brown—and on us—is haunting. This tale reenacts an *unfortunate* fall. Brown keeps his compact, encounters a demon, and suffers an ordeal, only to be irrevocably transformed by the experience in no soul-cleansing way. "But clear Truth is a thing for salamander giants only to encounter;" says Melville, "how small the chances for the provincials then?" Small, indeed, if the provincial is like Goodman Brown who, when tested by a searing experience, proves equal to the occasion but unequal to its effect, and forever after remains a victim of a corrosive soul-torturing suspicion of general human guilt.

Robert Emmet Whelan, Jr. (essay date 1971)

SOURCE: "Hawthorne Interprets 'Young Goodman Brown,'" in *ESQ: A Journal of the American Renaissance*, Vol. 62, Winter, 1971, pp. 2-4.

[*In the following essay, Whelan argues that, unlike* The Scarlet Letter, *in "Young Goodman Brown" Hawthorne leaves no possibility of redemption for the protagonist at the conclusion of the tale, for Brown's "self-inflicted nightmare" haunts him until his death.*]

Though we have good explications of **"Young Goodman Brown,"**[1] the best and most succinct is Hawthorne's, appearing as a description of Hester Prynne's moral state in the penultimate paragraph of Chapter V of ***The Scarlet Letter***: "Her imagination was somewhat affected, and, had she been of a softer moral and intellectual fibre, would have been still more so, by the strange and solitary anguish of her life. Walking to and fro, with those lonely footsteps . . . it now and then appeared to Hester,—if altogether fancy, it was nevertheless too potent to be resisted,—she felt or fancied, then, that the scarlet letter had endowed her with a new sense. She shuddered to believe, yet could not help believing, that it gave her a sympathetic knowledge of the hidden sin in other hearts. She was terror-stricken by the revelations that were thus made. What were they? Could they be other than the insidious

whispers of the bad angel, who would fain have persuaded the struggling woman, as yet only half his victim, that the outward guise of purity was but a lie, and that, if truth were everywhere to be shown, a scarlet letter would blaze forth on many a bosom besides Hester Prynne's? Or, must she receive those intimations—so obscure, yet so distinct—as truth? In all her miserable experience, there was nothing else so awful and so loathsome as this sense. It perplexed, as well as shocked her, by the irreverent inopportuneness of the occasions that brought it into vivid action. Sometimes the red infamy upon her breast would give a sympathetic throb, as she passed near a venerable minister or magistrate, to whom that age of reverence looked up, as to a mortal man in fellowship with angels. 'What evil thing is at hand?' would Hester say to herself. Lifting her reluctant eyes, there would be nothing human within the scope of view, save the form of this earthly saint! Again, a mystic sisterhood would contumaciously assert itself, as she met the sanctified frown of some matron, who, according to the rumor of all tongues, had kept cold snow within her bosom throughout life. That unsunned snow in the matron's bosom, and the burning shame on Hester Prynne's,—what had the two in common? Or, once more, the electric thrill would give her warning,—'Behold, Hester, here is a companion!'—and, looking up, she would detect the eyes of a young maiden glancing at the scarlet letter, shyly and aside, and quickly averted with a faint, chill crimson in her cheeks; as if her purity were somewhat sullied by that momentary glance. O Fiend, whose talisman was that fatal symbol, wouldst thou leave nothing, whether in youth or age, for this poor sinner to revere?—such loss of faith is ever one of the saddest results of sin. Be it accepted as proof that all was not corrupt in this poor victim of her own frailty, and man's hard law, that Hester Prynne yet struggled to believe that no fellow-mortal was guilty like herself" (V, 111-112).[2]

No such proof, however, can be urged in defense of Young Goodman Brown; for, as a result of his journey into the wilderness of temptation and sin, he comes to believe that all his fellow mortals are guilty like himself. Just before he becomes completely corrupt—just before he is baptized into Evil by Satan—he is surrounded by that nightmare vision which takes all its reality from the diseased activity of his own sinful mind and heart. At this moment he is about to receive in fullest measure that new sense which apparently grants him, as it apparently granted Hester, "a sympathetic knowledge of the hidden sins in other hearts" (V, 111). It is this sixth sense that Satan describes when, pointing to his assembly of worshipers, he addresses these words to Goodman Brown and Faith: "There . . . are all whom ye have reverenced from youth. Ye deemed them holier than yourselves, and shrank from your own sin, contrasting it with their lives of righteousness and prayerful aspirations heavenward. Yet here they are in my worshipping assembly. This night it shall be granted you to know their secret deeds. . . . By the sympathy of your human hearts for sin ye shall scent out all the places—whether in church, bed-chamber, street, field, or forest—

where crime has been committed, and shall exult to behold the whole earth one stain of guilt, one mighty blood spot. Far more than this. It shall be yours to penetrate, in every bosom, the deep mystery of sin, the fountain of all wicked arts, and which inexhaustibly supplies more evil impulses than human power—than my power at its utmost—can make manifest in deeds" (II, 103-104).

Because of his own sins, therefore, Brown's faith has grown too weak to "'look up to heaven, and resist the wicked one'" (II, 105); and this is why Brown receives upon his forehead the mark of baptism that makes him "more conscious of the secret guilt of others, both in deed and thought, than [he] could now be of [his] own" (II, 104). In reality, the only new faculty Brown acquires from his reception into the Devil's communion is the gift of experiencing the deep mystery of sin at work within his own breast. The most pernicious effect of it is that it deceives him into believing that he can now sense the presence of hidden sin in every heart. Having listened too credulously to "the insidious whispers of [his] bad angel," he has interpreted these "intimations [of his own sinful heart]—so obscure, yet so distinct—as truth;" and has thus persuaded himself that "the outward guise of purity [is] but a lie" (V, 111). These obscure intimations, then, are the psychological reality behind Goodman Brown's finding all his fellow townsmen at the witch-meeting in the wilderness.

The early stages of Brown's descent into depravity are rather obviously dramatized by his conversation with the devil, who discourses so aptly "that his arguments seemed rather to spring up in the bosom of his auditor than to be suggested by himself" (II, 95). Naturally enough, the further Goodman Brown travels into the darkness of temptation and sin, the darker become the moral spectacles through which he views his fellow men. Attempting in the manner of most sinners to mitigate his sinfulness by means of self-deceptive rationalization, Brown calls to mind, with his personal devil's help, that neither his grandfather, in his cruelty to the Quakers, nor his father, in his cruelty to the Indians, was exactly an exemplary Christian. Nor is it long before the representatives of church and state—the church deacons, the selectmen, the governor and his council—are seen through the disfiguring lens of Brown's self-inflicted astigmatism. Brown's faith is more seriously threatened when he allows himself to turn this disfiguring lens of cynicism upon the Goody Cloyse who taught him his catechism, and then upon the minister and the deacon of his own church. From doubts about the virtue and sanctity of these pillars of religious faith to actual scepticism about the truth of religious faith itself is an easy step which Hawthorne marks allegorically when he has Brown behold one of Faith's pink ribbons falling from the heavens; for upon beholding this symbol of faith Goodman Brown, "maddened with despair," cries out, "My Faith is gone! . . . There is no good on earth; and sin is but a name. Come, devil; for to thee is this world given" (II, 99). To be brief, when Brown apparently discovers that Goody Cloyse, Deacon Gookin, the minister, and Faith herself are on their way to join the assembly of devil-

worshipers, Hawthorne is merely giving us the allegorical orchestration of the measure to which Brown's sin-tainted imagination steps. Because sin has darkened his heart Brown finds himself left "in the heart of the dark wilderness, still rushing onward with the instinct that guides mortal man to evil" (II, 99). He is "the chief horror of [this] scene" because he is really the only horror.

When we leave Salem with Goodman Brown, neither he nor we are really doing so except in the sense that we depart from the objective world of Salem into the subjective world of Goodman Brown's heart. There Brown's "Faith" in God and his fellow man still dwells. In short, the faith that Brown's wife personifies is contained in the two great commandments—love of God and love of neighbor; and for this reason Hawthorne has Brown address his wife as "'My love and my Faith . . .'" (II, 89). Because holy love still lives as a counsellor in his bosom Faith whispers, "Dearest heart . . . prithee put off your journey until sunrise and sleep in your own bed tonight. . . . Pray tarry with me this night, dear husband, of all nights in the year" (II, 89). Indeed, Goodman Brown, in succumbing to temptation, journeys into the dark wilderness of sin and thereby separates himself from the sunshine of faith and love. Faith's request is the voice of conscience urging Brown to put his temptation behind him. The implication is the same when Hawthorne has Brown explain his late arrival to the devil with: "Faith kept me back a while" (II, 91). When a novice in evil like Brown is about to surrender to temptation, he usually deceives himself into thinking that after this one moral lapse he will repent and sin no more as Brown does when he tells himself that after the work of this one night he will "'cling to [Faith's] skirts and follow her to heaven'" (II, 90). "With this excellent resolve for the future" he feels "justified in making more haste on his present evil purpose" (II, 90). And since Brown's self-deceptive rationalization deepens as he travels further into the forest, his personal devil (with allegorical promptitude) cajolingly says, "Let us walk on, nevertheless, reasoning as we go; and if I convince thee not thou shalt turn back. We are but a little way in the forest yet" (II, 91-92).

Unfortunately Brown never returns from the forest except in terms of the surface story. Yet in spite of his sin-blackened consciousness the life of Salem persists unchanged: the minister meditates his sermon; old Deacon Gookin appears at domestic worship; Goody Cloyse catechizes a little girl; and Faith, with *all* her pink ribbons, anxiously awaits Brown's return. Both she and the faithful remain a reality in Salem; but they have ceased to be realities within the "dream of evil omen" (II, 106) which has become Brown's sole inheritance as a result of his journey into sin. Concerning this Hawthorne leaves us in no doubt; for Goodman Brown shrinks from the minister's blessing "as if to avoid an anathema;" suspects Deacon Gookin of praying to Satan; snatches away the child being instructed by Goody Cloyse "as from the grasp of the fiend himself;" and, looking sadly and sternly into Faith's face, passes her by without a greeting (II, 105). Like Father Hooper, Brown reveals no one's depravity but his own when he looks around him and sees "'on every visage a Black Veil'" (I, 69). And because his fearful dream continues, he lives on "a stern, a sad, a darkly meditative, a distrustful, if not desperate man" (II, 106). On the Sabbath, when the congregation sings a holy psalm, he cannot listen because the anthem of sin rushes "loudly upon his ear and [drowns] all the blessed strain" (II, 106). Brown's self-inflicted nightmare, still raging within him at the moment of his death, makes it allegorically impossible to carve any "hopeful verse" (II, 106) upon his tombstone.

Notes

1. See D. M. McKeithan, "Hawthorne's 'Young Goodman Brown:' An Interpretation," *MLN*, LXVII (February, 1952), 93-96; Thomas F. Walsh, Jr., "The Bedeviling of Young Goodman Brown," *MLQ* [*Modern Language Quarterly*], XIX (December, 1958), 331-336; and Paul J. Hurley, "Young Goodman Brown's 'Heart of Darkness,'" *AL* [*American Literature*], XXXVII (January, 1966), 410-419.

2. Volume and page references to Hawthorne's works are to *The Complete Works of Nathaniel Hawthorne*, ed. George Parsons Lathrop, Riverside ed., 12 vols. (Boston, 1883).

Harry M. Campbell (essay date 1971)

SOURCE: "Freudianism, American Romanticism, and 'Young Goodman Brown,'" in *CEA Critic*, Vol. 33, No. 3, March, 1971, pp. 3-6.

[*In the following essay, Campbell criticizes the trend among Hawthorne critics to interpret "Young Goodman Brown" in Freudian terms, pointing out that this approach tends to oversimplify and narrow the interpretation of the story.*]

Certainly Freudian criticism has made substantial contributions to the understanding of some aspects of American romanticism—in studies of the sexual symbolism in much of Whitman's best poetry, the tortured ambiguities of Melville's *Pierre* and some of his short stories, and the relation between Poe's probable impotence and his creative work, to mention only a few examples that come readily to mind. It has even been said that some of the American Romanticists themselves anticipated Freud in describing the shadowy subliminal origin of some of their images. It seems to me, however, that in the twilight area between the unconscious and the conscious of the Romanticists these vague beginnings of images which then emerged into the conscious and became full images were not pre-Freudian but were far closer to what Jacques Maritain has called creative intuition or the spiritual preconscious, of which, says Maritain, "Plato and the ancient wise men were aware, and the disregard of which in favor of the Freudian unconscious alone is a sign of the dullness of our times." Maritain says that poetic intuition is born in the unconscious but emerges from it, and the poet may be

aware of it, as Bergson would have said, on the edge of the unconscious; but the Freudian unconscious is one "of blood and flesh, instincts, tendencies, complexes, repressed images and desires, traumatic memories, as constituting a closed or autonomous dynamic whole." The Freudian unconscious, then, is *automatic* or *deaf*—"deaf to the intellect, and structured into a world of its own apart from the intellect."[1] If this description seems unfair to Freud, we must remember that even so devoted a psychoanalyst as C. G. Jung, who for several years was a follower of Freud, finally broke with him in 1913, because, in Jung's opinion, Freud's unconscious is limited to the "animal" and does not include the "divine" in man. In other words, the libido for Jung is equivalent to all psychic energy, both "human" and "divine," or, as one critic has said, Jung's libido "is created genetically and is desexualized. . . ."[2]

Freud's position, to say the least, is paradoxical, perhaps even contradictory. He acknowledges his indebtedness to the romantic poets and philosophers who he says discovered the unconscious before him, but at the same time Freud's philosophy is deterministic and he claims to be strictly scientific. With all his interest in literature, it constitutes for him a type of clinical study, and he considers the literary man a neurotic escapist from reality—the escape being relatively harmless unless it becomes involved with religion, which Freud regards as a dangerously harmful illusion.

The real connection, in my opinion, between Freudianism and some types of Romanticism is (1) their overemphasis on the supremacy of the individual—his boundless possibilities for realizing both pleasure and happiness, the Aristotelian distinction between pleasure and happiness becoming somewhat blurred in the process; and (2) the tendency of both Freudianism and certain types of Romanticism to employ extravagant metaphors or symbols. The loose metaphors of the Romantic poets have been analyzed and attacked (sometimes unjustly) by the New Critics. Freud, too, is fundamentally a Romantic poet though writing in prose and concentrating on sexual metaphors or symbols that will hardly bear close logical inspection to describe the hidden motives of human thoughts and actions. The fertility of his poetic imagination applied usually to sex (sometimes to other bodily functions) reminds one of Whitman and may have its origin in ancient Dionysian or phallic rites which Whitman, it will be remembered, named as one of his many "faiths."

Freud, to be sure, does show some imaginative discrimination in the application of his theory to literature, but, perhaps flattered by their adoration of him, he lends his approval to the work of some of the most extreme among his followers—most notably perhaps Albert Mordell and Marie Bonaparte. In *The Erotic Motive in Literature,* for example, Mordell says that the source of much re-explanation of creative genius will be found "in the infantile love life of the authors." And in her *Edgar Poe, Étude Psychoanalytique,* Marie Bonaparte postulates a strong unconscious necrophilia in Poe stemming originally from his infantile sexual desire for his mother. Of course, fixation on his mother was undoubtedly one of the sources of Poe's abnormality; but, since his mother died when he was three years old, it is highly questionable whether infantile sexuality could extend that far back—such was the more reasonable conclusion of Krutch's distinguished psychoanalytical biography on this point.

If, then, there is clearly danger of excess in Freudian criticism of obviously abnormal writers like Poe, how much more caution is needed in applying such criticism to Romantic authors such as Hawthorne and Longfellow, who were not in reality sexually abnormal and for whom sex (even imaginatively) was not of primary importance as it was for Whitman.

My final illustration is concerned with the Freudian analyses of "Young Goodman Brown," specifically those by Roy Male, Daniel G. Hoffman, and Frederick C. Crews. Crews says that Brown's whole forest journey is "a vicarious and lurid sexual adventure" of one whose "sexual attitude is that of a young boy rather than a normal bridegroom," and whose "fantasy experience, like that of Robin Molineux, follows the classic Oedipal pattern."[3] Male says that "almost everything in the forest scene suggests that the communion of sinners is essentially sexual. . . ."[4] Daniel G. Hoffman finds that "phallic and psychosexual associations are made intrinsic to the thematic development of [Hawthorne's] story. . . . Brown's whole experience is described as a penetration of a dark and lonely way through a branched forest. . . . At journey's end is the orgiastic communion amidst the leaping flames."[5] Of the pink ribbons specifically, Male says, ". . . the pink ribbons blend with the serpentine staff in what becomes a fierce orgy of lust" (p. 79).

My objection to these interpretations is that they oversimplify Hawthorne by making him narrowly Freudian (or pre-Freudian). In the first place, there is nothing in the story specifically indicating the sexual blending of the ribbons referred to by Male and carried to a further extreme by Daniel Hoffman and especially by Crews. The ribbons—mentioned several times near the beginning of the story, again just before (and helping to precipitate) the climax, and again at the end (where Faith joyfully greets Brown returning from the forest)—are an important unifying symbol. They operate at the literal level to identify the young and faithful wife. The ribbon falling from the sky in the dark forest indicates that she has succumbed to temptation. Brown's perception of the falling ribbon indicates also that he has ceased to struggle against temptation ("My Faith is gone!"), and he immediately rushes to the Witches' Sabbath.

The apparent realism of the falling ribbon (to which Matthiessen objects, though not on Freudian principles) is only one aspect of the calculated ambiguity which Hawthorne achieves all through the story. His great artistry consists in his keeping the reader in the twilight zone between the fantastic or the supernatural and the realistic,

with a leaning toward the former but with enough of the latter to make his treatment of "the mystery of sin" both complex and convincing. In this twilight zone the effect on the reader soon moves from an association to a fusing of the realistic and the fantastic. The realistic falling ribbon, then, soon (and almost imperceptibly) merges into the supernatural atmosphere of the preparation for the Witches' Sabbath—the same type of fusion that has been in process throughout the story.

Of course, sexual sins are mentioned in the Witches' Sabbath, but so are various other sins. For Hawthorne fornication and adultery were sins, even when (as with the lovers in *The Scarlet Letter*) there were mitigating circumstances. But for Hawthorne, as for Dante, there were far worse sins than the carnal (that of Chillingworth, for example, in *The Scarlet Letter*), and these also are in "Young Goodman Brown." Brown feels "a loathful brotherhood" with the congregation at the Witches' Sabbath "by the sympathy of *all* [italics mine] that was wicked in his heart"; and the Devil says in his sermon to the whole group: "It shall be yours to penetrate, in every bosom, the deep mystery of sin, the fountain of all wicked arts. . . ."

Brown's sin, then, is far worse than deserting his wife. There is no real evidence for believing, as does Crews, that the main theme of "Young Goodman Brown" is "Brown's horror of adulthood, his inability to accept the place of sexuality in married love." As a matter of fact, Brown has been very happily married to Faith, and the thought of this happiness almost persuades him to return to her after he has been disillusioned by discovering the wickedness of his former spiritual teacher Goody Cloyse. As he is resolving to return to Faith, these thoughts go through his mind: "And what calm sleep would be his that very night, which was to have been spent so wickedly, but so purely and sweetly now, in the arms of Faith!" Furthermore, the melancholy of Faith at his departure and her rejoicing at his return indicate that she has been as happy in their marriage as he. The immediate cause of Brown's failure to act on his good resolution to return to Faith is the appearance in the evil forest of two others, Deacon Gookin and the minister, in both of whom Brown has trusted for spiritual guidance, but who were clearly headed for the Witches' Sabbath. Such, in Hawthorne's opinion, are the depths of "the mystery of sin" that even happily married people are often destroyed by it. Even Faith participated in the evil rites but recovered the next day and could have been happy again if Brown could also have recovered.

Crews limits Brown's "fantasy-experience" to "the classic Oedipal pattern . . . conjoined with ambiguous sexual temptation." When the Devil is reciting to Brown the sins of Brown's ancestors, Crews interprets them all as sexual. For example, the constable lashing "the Quaker woman so smartly through the streets of Salem" is, in Crews's opinion, guilty of sadistic "sexual irregularity." Following this pattern, the pitch-pine knot with which Brown's father set fire to an Indian village would have to be a phallic symbol. The "state secrets" of the church deacons, town selectmen, and members of the Great and General Court referred to by the Devil would have to be sexual in implication, for, as Crews tells us, Brown's whole forest experience "serves his private need to make lurid sexual complaints against mankind."

To repeat: The dramatic interweaving of realism with fantasy so that we willingly suspend our disbelief in the fantasy is facilitated by the pink ribbons, which are used both to maintain the realism and to unify the story. Sexual sin is present in this story, because it is part of what Hawthorne considered to be the evil in human nature, but to interpret the ribbons, the serpentine staff, the pine-knot, the constable's whip, and other objects mentioned in the story as specifically sexual symbols is to limit it to a narrowly Freudian allegory. Hawthorne was concerned, indeed almost obsessed, with what he considered to be "the deep mystery of sin, the fountain of all wicked arts," and the power of his work lies in his ability to dramatize his ideas so that they move even those who disagree with him about the nature of man.

Freudian criticism, then, can throw light on those aspects of American Romanticism which are predominantly sexual, at least in implication, but to push such analysis beyond this point is not much more helpful than, though seldom so ridiculous as, the explanation by one Freudian critic that Little Red Riding Hood's red cap is a menstrual symbol and that her whole story is an allegory of the conflict between male and female in which the young virgin outwits the ruthless, sex-hungry "wolf."[6]

Notes

1. Jacques Maritain, *Creative Intuition in Art and Poetry* (New York, 1955), p. 67.

2. Frederick J. Hoffman, *Freudianism and the Literary Mind* (Baton Rouge, Louisiana, 1945), p. 44, quoting Fritz Wittels.

3. Frederick C. Crews, *The Sins of the Fathers* (New York, 1966), pp. 102, 103.

4. Roy R. Male, *Hawthorne's Tragic Vision* (Austin, Texas, 1957), p. 78.

5. Daniel G. Hoffman, *Form and Fable in American Fiction* (New York, 1961), pp. 165-166.

6. Erich Fromm, *The Forgotten Language* (New York, 1957), p. 240.

Fred Erisman (essay date 1972)

SOURCE: "'Young Goodman Brown'—Warning to Idealists," in *American Transcendental Quarterly,* Vol. 14, Spring, 1972, pp. 156-58.

[In the following essay, Erisman suggests that in "Young Goodman Brown" Hawthorne wanted to point out the psychological and social dangers of "excessive innocence."]

Readings of Nathaniel Hawthorne's **"Young Goodman Brown"** (1835) focus almost exclusively upon its dual

evocation of Calvinism and demonism. The Puritanic gloom and the Satanic gleam that permeate the story are so obviously significant, in fact, that one scholar has virtually denied the possibility of any other readings.[1] There is, however, persuasive evidence that Hawthorne had more than Puritans and witches in mind as subjects for his tale. Indeed, his treatment of Young Goodman Brown himself, of the curious nature of faith, and of the effects of the loss of faith, taken in the context of Hawthorne's intellectual development in the years immediately prior to 1835, points to the conclusion that he was making a much broader religious and philosophical comment than is usually recognized.

Hawthorne's presentation of Young Goodman Brown is richly suggestive. Brown is, of course, "Goodman." Although this is a commonplace form of seventeenth-century address,[2] the reader familiar with Hawthorne's multi-leveled technique cannot help hearing echoes of "good man," with its implications of human goodness. Moreover, Brown is *Young* Goodman Brown, with all the idealistic self-reliance of youth. As he says at one point, "I have nothing to do with the governor and council; they have their own ways, and are no rule for a simple husbandman like me."[3] Finally, as "husbandman" connotes, he is very much a married man. Wed to his Faith, he is, literally, a "man of faith," both as husband and as believer. In these qualities Hawthorne gives an important clue to one theme of the tale.

A second clue emerges in the way in which Hawthorne deals with faith. On the one hand, Faith is no more than Brown's literal wife. On the other, however, faith is also what Mark Twain (in *Following the Equator*) has called "believing what you know ain't so"—*i.e.,* an intuitive, non-reasoned belief that is, and must be, taken for granted. As such, it demands total commitment. Faith, in the pure state, cannot be modified or compromised without being destroyed; when its polished ideality meets the bleak reality of experience, it is shattered. Such, too, is Young Goodman Brown's faith. In its original, pristine form, it sustains him: "With heaven above and Faith below," he says, "I will yet stand firm against the devil!" (p. 1038). This faith, however, can be affected by experience. "Depending upon one another's hearts, he had still hoped that virtue were not all a dream," says the sable leader of the witches' Sabbath: "Now are ye undeceived" (p. 1041). In the presence of knowledge, hope (or faith) vanishes. And, when Brown's idealized faith at last disappears, it is replaced by a corroded, bitter, equally all-embracing faith: "'My faith is gone!' cried he [Brown], after one stupefied moment. 'There is no good on earth; and sin is but a name. Come, devil; for to thee is this world given'" (p. 1038). The sullying of Brown's faith, as so often happens with absolutistic, viscerally held faiths, results in an equally absolutistic reversal.

Hawthorne's treatment of the effects of Brown's loss of faith completes the picture. The destruction of his idealized faith destroys Young Goodman Brown. Unlike the true Calvinist, who, as Perry Miller has noted, "emphasized his [man's] irremediable depravity and found in him nothing whatsoever that was good," and who did his best to live with this knowledge, Brown is annihilated.[4] He becomes an embittered, cynical and "distrustful" man, living out a life of suspicion and dying in an hour of gloom (p. 1042). His reaction to the discovery of evil in mankind, far from being that of the sincere (or even insincere) Calvinist, is that of the disillusioned idealist.

The point that Hawthorne is making seems plain. Throughout the tale, he reveals the hazards of excessive innocence; of excessive regard for youth and self; and of excessive reliance upon an idealistic, untested faith. He singles out for criticism, in short, qualities that characterize the Romantic in general, and the Transcendentalist in particular, presenting them in such a way that **"Young Goodman Brown,"** for all its Puritan overtones, can be seen as a cautionary remarking upon the embryonic stages of Transcendentalism.

Although Emerson's *Nature* was not to appear until 1836, Hawthorne by 1835 had had ample opportunity to become aware of the development of Transcendental thought in New England. As his charges at the Salem Athenaeum show, he had already withdrawn the first nine volumes of *The Christian Examiner,* containing contributions by W. E. Channing, George Ripley, Charles Follen, Andrews Norton, C. C. Felton, and William Bourne Oliver Peabody, on subjects so diverse as antinomianism, Goethe, Quakerism, Unitarianism, and the common-sense philosopher Dugald Stewart. Moreover, he had had access to Robert Barclay's *An Apology for the True Christian Divinity* (1775), on Quaker thought; to Coleridge's *Aide to Reflection* (1825), with its crucial distinction between Reason and Understanding, as well as to the poetry of Coleridge, Shelley, and Keats; to *The Koran*; to fourteen of the thirty-seven volumes of Rousseau's *Oeuvres Completes* (1788); to either Schiller's *Kleinere Prosaische Schrifte* (1792-1802) or Thomas Carlyle's *Life of Schiller*; and to Dugald Stewart's *Philosophical Essays*.[5] Although, to be sure, he was at the same time reading Machiavelli and the Mathers, he was obviously being exposed to the works and ideas that contributed to the foundations of Transcendentalism.

Hawthorne's acquaintance with Transcendentalism is customarily dated from his courtship of Sophia Peabody in 1838 and after.[6] It is clear from his library records, however, that, by the time he wrote **"Young Goodman Brown,"** he was generally acquainted with the raw materials from which Transcendentalism sprang. When one considers his later reservations about the absolute validity of Transcendental idealism (as stated, for example, in his sketch of the Giant Transcendentalist in **"The Celestial Railroad"** of 1843, or in his version of the Brook Farm phalanx in **The Blithedale Romance** of 1852), it seems probable that he would respond to the earlier materials as he did to the later—as a dedicated skeptic. This skepticism, explicit in such approximately contemporaneous stories as **"My Kinsman, Major Molineux"** or **"Dr. Heideg-**

ger's Experiment," is implicit in **"Young Goodman Brown."** Although Hawthorne's chief concern throughout the story is certainly the examining of a young man's discovery of evil, he makes that discovery all the more striking by making its effects avoidable. Had Young Goodman Brown been less absolutistic, less dependent upon a romantic faith, and more aware of the frailties of humanity, his fate would have been different. The fledgling philosophical idealists of his own time, Hawthorne seems to say, would do well to benefit from Brown's example.

Notes

1. Richard H. Fogle, "Ambiguity and Clarity in Hawthorne's 'Young Goodman Brown,'" *New England Quarterly,* 18 (1945), 454n.

2. E. Arthur Robinson, "The Vision of Goodman Brown: A Source and Interpretation," *American Literature,* 35 (1963), 218-220.

3. Nathaniel Hawthorne, "Young Goodman Brown," in *The Complete Novels and Selected Tales of Nathaniel Hawthorne,* ed. Norman Holmes Pearson (N.Y.: The Modern Library, 1937), 1035. Further references to this edition will appear in the text.

4. Perry Miller, *The New England Mind: The Seventeenth Century* (Cambridge: Harvard University Press, 1954), 402.

5. For Hawthorne's library charges, see Marion L. Kesselring, "Hawthorne's Reading, 1828-1850," *Bulletin of the New York Public Library,* 53 (1949), 55-71, 121-138, 173-194. For the contents of *The Christian Examiner,* see William Cushing, *Index to the Christian Examiner* (1879), reprinted in *Research Keys to the American Renaissance,* ed. Kenneth Walter Cameron (Hartford, Conn.: Transcendential Books, 1967), 3-82.

6. Randall Stewart, *Nathaniel Hawthorne: A Biography* (New Haven: Yale University Press, 1948), 49ff.

Claudia G. Johnson (essay date 1974)

SOURCE: "'Young Goodman Brown' and Puritan Justification," in *Studies in Short Fiction,* Vol. 11, No. 2, Spring, 1974, pp. 200-03.

[*In the following essay, Johnson discusses "Young Goodman Brown" in light of the Puritan doctrine of justification—the idea that God will "justify" sinners who recognize themselves as such and seek divine help. Johnson argues that Brown's actions are an example of false justification because he never admits to his own sinful nature.*]

Criticism of **"Young Goodman Brown"** has traditionally been divided into speculations about the nature of the hero's journey. Was it a dream? Or was it reality? Newton Arvin is usually cited as representative of the view that Goodman Brown received a true vision of human depravity in the woods, and F. O. Matthiessen is representative of the view that the sins witnessed by young Goodman Brown were creatures of his own making.[1] Almost no modern critic supports Arvin's view, however, so the old argument rarely arises in the old way. Questions about the reality of the story and Brown's relationship to it continue to interest critics, however.[2] A new dimension is given the problem of Goodman Brown's relation to a special kind of reality in the light of what we know and what Hawthorne knew about the Puritan doctrine of justification, a belief which has to be understood in terms of Covenant Theology.[3] The Puritan believed that, since Adam broke the first covenant with God in the Garden of Eden, man labored under the burden of God's wrath. However, God had made a second covenant which gave man hope for some respite from God's wrath during man's life on the earth; at a time of His choosing, God might open the hearts of certain men, allowing them to descend within in order to know themselves. All things on which they had depended and all pride were mortified. Only when they had lost self in this experience would they turn to God who, subsequently, lifted the sinners up and justified them, changing their relationships to God and making their lives on earth a little easier without the burden of God's wrath.

The Puritan minister gave considerable attention not only to what justification was, but to what it was not. He knew that many sinners had convinced themselves that they had made the justifying descent when, in fact, they had not. It was the Puritan minister's duty to urge self-scrutiny in this matter. If the sinner believed that he had been completely helpless in initiating his descent and had been utterly reduced by a "sense" of sin, then he had probably known a "true" descent. If, on the other hand, he thought that he had been in some small way responsible for initiating the descent, if he had been aware of an iota of goodness within himself at the time of descent, or if he had only "known" his sins without "having a sense" of them, then his had been a false or a mock descent. He could not, therefore, expect that he would be justified.

Young Goodman Brown's journey is just such a mock descent in the Puritan tradition. Like the Puritan sinner, he begins what seems to be a journey into an inner inferno. The landscape through which he travels is but a hellish externalization of his own heart. He encounters the fiend, who also rages in his own breast, and fiend worshippers. He hears hell's "awful harmony" of inhuman sounds and perverse hymns. He sees the "lurid" red blaze against the sky. The witches' sabbath is, like Milton's picture of hell, an inverse heaven: the harmonious music of heaven is discord here; the light, unlike that of heaven, "is "as one great Furnace, flam'd yet from those flames / No light, but rather darkness visible. . . ."[4] The once-angelic company is transformed, and the gathering in **"Young Goodman Brown"** is like the gathering of the fiends in Pandemonium around the throne of Satan to discuss the fate of Adam and Eve.

As if he were in the traditional Puritan descent, Goodman Brown's various "props" or "crutches," those things on

which he has depended, fall from under him. The father, the teacher, the state, the community, the church, the concept of womanhood are all challenged during his journey. But Goodman Brown's journey is far from being a genuine justifying descent. The story is, rather, similar to the Puritan minister's detailed description of the false descent, and young Goodman Brown is a paradigm for Hawthorne's negative definition of the unregenerate man whose incomplete experience with hell perverts his vision and warps his life.

Regeneration is only possible if one's sense of his own sin is as profound as that which the Puritans described in the genuine humiliation: the man in the throes of a true descent must feel that he is the most wretched creature on the earth and must know a mortification of pride in particular. To be sure, Goodman Brown knows despair and feels his own rational limitation in coping with the universe, but in no way would this hellish journey to a witches' sabbath be construed by the Puritans as a genuine descent, for Goodman Brown feels the depravity of others but not the full extent of his own.

Although the reader sees Goodman Brown as "the chief horror of the scene" (p. 99) Goodman Brown has no such vision of himself. In his decision to rage toward the witches' sabbath, he sees himself as choosing through pride to out-do the devil: "Let us hear which will laugh loudest. Think not to frighten me with your deviltry. Come witch, come wizard, come Indian powwow, come devil himself, and here comes Goodman Brown. You may as well fear him as he fear you" (ibid.). His descent does not bring him to a vision of his own helplessness and sinfulness. Rather, from motives of despair and revenge, he initially believes that he can willingly choose to combat evil. It is Faith's sinfulness that embitters him, not his own. Furthermore, his return to the village finds him piously snatching little children from the clutches of their teachers as if he, alone, were untainted.

Momentarily he feels, with repugnance, a sense of brotherhood with the community, but that which keeps Goodman Brown in gloom is the vision given those who partake of the devil's baptism: that he would ever be "more conscious of the secret guilt of others, both in deed and thought," than he could ever be of his own (p. 104). This is conclusive evidence that Goodman Brown's descent was not genuine.

The point is not that a vision of dark reality (of either himself or of others) has warped his life. What he has seen is not a true vision of others or himself. His has been a mock journey, a false vision. Though the landscape of his heart was available to him, he never saw the true extent of its terrors. Like the passengers on the Celestial Railroad, he never exposes himself to the landscape and is, thus, never sufficiently humiliated to ascend in love to a new life. The dark vision he saw was not nearly so dark as the one he should have seen but did not see. Like the stock example of the deluded, self-satisfied man of the justification sermon, young Goodman Brown stands as a negative definition of the true regenerative descent.

Notes

1. Newton Arvin, *Hawthorne* Boston: Little, Brown, 1929); F. O. Matthiessen, *American Renaissance* (New York: Oxford University Press, 1941).

2. Richard P. Adams, "Hawthorne's 'Provincial Tales,'" *New England Quarterly,* 30 (March, 1957), 39; Richard Harter Fogle, "Ambiguity and Clarity in Hawthorne's 'Young Goodman Brown,'" *New England Quarterly,* 18 (December, 1943), 448-465; David Levin, "Shadows of Doubt: Spectral Evidence in Hawthorne's 'Young Goodman Brown,'" *American Literature,* 34 (May, 1963), 218-225; Taylor Stoehr, "'Young Goodman Brown' and Hawthorne's Theory of Mimesis," *Nineteenth-Century Fiction,* 23 (March, 1969), 393-409; Thomas F. Walsh, Jr., "The Bedeviling of Young Goodman Brown," *Modern Language Quarterly,* 19 (December, 1958), 331-336. Walsh doesn't believe that the reader can know or has to know whether the experience was real or a dream: rather one gets at the meaning offered to him by examining certain symbolic patterns. David Levin argues that the reader mistakenly supposes that the devil speaks for Hawthorne, whereas, the devil lies and all of his spectral evidence is untrustworthy. Stoehr believes that the whole point of the story is the relationship between fact and fiction. Goodman Brown is damned because he accepts the dream as reality through lack of faith. Fogle and Adams also stress Goodman Brown's dilemma of uncertainty. Adams notes that, "Having refused to look at evil, he is left in a state of moral uncertainty that is worse, in a way, than evil itself."

3. Almost all justification sermons contain some statement about Covenant Theology but succinct statements of the Covenant and justification, with which the American Puritans would agree, appear in John Calvin's *Institutes of the Christian Religion,* Books II, III (Philadelphia, MCMLX). The following is a selection of justification sermons which serve to clarify the doctrine: William Dewsbury, *A Sermon on the Important Doctrine of Regeneration* (Philadelphia, 1740); Giles Firmin, *The Real Christian* (Boston, 1742); Cotton Mather, *The Everlasting Gospel* (Philadelphia, 1767); Samuel Mather, *The Self-Justiciary Convicted* (Boston, 1707); Thomas Shepard, *The Sincere Convert* (Philadelphia, 1664); Gilbert Tennent, *The Duty of Self Examination* (Boston, 1739); Samuel Willard, *A Brief Discourse on Justification* (Boston, 1686).

4. John Milton, *Paradise Lost,* ed. Merritt Y. Hughes (New York: Odyssey Press, 1957), p. 10.

Michael J. Colacurcio (essay date 1974)

SOURCE: "Visible Sanctity and Specter Evidence: The Moral World of Hawthorne's 'Young Goodman Brown,'" in *Essex Institute Historical Collections,* Vol. 110, October, 1974, pp. 259-99.

[*In the following essay, Colacurcio examines "Young Goodman Brown" in the context of Puritan theology, faith, and "spectral evidence" of witchcraft and the devil. Colacurcio suggests that Hawthorne uses his story to demonstrate "that witchcraft 'ended' the Puritan world".*]

Any seriously "complete" interpretation of Hawthorne's **"Young Goodman Brown"** must somehow take account of David Levin's rather exact description of Brown's experience in the actual language of 1692. It may be possible to disagree with his final assertion that the "literal" dimension of **"Young Goodman Brown"** is "social," condemning "that graceless perversion of true Calvinism which, in universal suspicion, actually led a community to the unjust destruction of twenty men and women"; but it seems impossible to deny that "spectral evidence" is, in some sense, the central issue of the tale. The attempt to "answer" him has proved unproductive; and it is now possible to see that all the early readings which argued that Brown's desperate conclusions might not be fully justified by the nature of his evidence were at least implicitly pointing out one central issue: namely, the inadvisability of accepting the Devil's word about the constitution and ordering of the invisible world.[1]

This is not to imply that psychoanalytic, even purely Freudian, acumen is out of place in the criticism of the tale. The author of a casebook on **"Young Goodman Brown,"** though obviously committed to a theological reading, can nevertheless show (with charts) a deliberately contrived and consistently maintained sexual "level" of allegory everywhere in the tale; thus, presumably, are freshmen persuaded that the moralist need be neither discomfited nor disgusted by the "impudent knowingness" of Frederick Crews.

But one need not choose tendentious examples to make the point. A recent study of Hawthorne's tale in relation to a Deodat Lawson pamphlet entitled *Christ's Fidelity* cannot let its criticism rest at this level of probable if curious historic encounter. Anxious lest he be misunderstood to think that Hawthorne's story is to be conceived chiefly as an answer to Lawson, or that Hawthorne writes only about the fixities and definites of a rather parochial (even tribalist) group of misguided religious zealots, the author feels the need to end with a ringing declaration of Hawthorne's psychological generality: "With his genius for insight and technique, Hawthorne thus created a new and timeless drama about the distortions of the human mind." And even Levin himself, whose commitment to the "Defense of Historical Literature" is perfectly unambiguous, ends on a similar note: the important thing about Haw-thorne is the way he worked a "narrow range of types and subjects" to discover a "remarkable range of insights into human experience."[2]

What makes these gestures sympathetic is our perception of how accurately the critics in question have sensed the prejudices of their entrenched academic audience. That audience does not exactly cling to *The Interpretation of Dreams* as part of the canon of Revelation; but it does, very emphatically, believe that literature is more philosophically general than history. And, having substituted psychology for ontology as the first philosophy, its way of being philosophical is to affirm a commitment to abstractions such as "the human mind" or "human experience." If Freud turns out to have given us the ultimate structures, well, so be it. We'd much prefer the softer, not-quite-consistent determination of an Erik Erikson. Better still would be our own random gleanings from our favorite humanist authors, *seriatim* and *ad hoc*. But we can face the truth, so long as it's a General Truth. We are, apparently, willing to take our Platonism wherever we can find it.

Now granting the inevitability of all this, the point is still that "timeless" psychoanalytic readings of **"Young Good-man Brown"** do not circumvent the problems of 1692: even if we choose to say that the devil's forest sideshow is only a fantasy conjured up out of Brown's own sexually troubled psyche (so that he is the victim of his own devil), we are still involved in what Hawthorne always thought of as the "spectral regions" of the "haunted mind." To put the case quite bluntly: not only are the proven Puritan sources of the tale obsessed with the technical implications of spectral evidence, which wracked the official conscience of latter-day Puritanism like almost no other; not only is specter evidence the explicit vehicle of the tale, determining the ultimate psychological meaning as surely as a "red, red rose" determines the aspect under which "my love" can be known; but further, from **"Alice Doane"** straight through his unfinished romances Hawthorne allowed the Puritan language of the "invisible world" to determine his vocabulary and set the limits to his own psychological investigations. In short, it would have taken a singularly obtuse reading of Cotton and Increase Mather (not to mention Deodat Lawson) to have missed either the specific or the general import of their actual problem; or a singularly dilettantish reading to preserve dozens of minute details while ignoring their significance; or a singularly self-involved reading to reduce the whole affair to a version of his own oedipal anxieties.[3]

In fact, Hawthorne's story preserves the central Puritan issue of spectral evidence in an even larger way than Professor Levin has suggested. Significantly, **"Young Good-man Brown"** is not "about" the Salem Village trials any more than **"The Gentle Boy"** is "about" the judicial murder of Quaker protesters in 1659. Although the tale refers to certain non-diabolical personages whose names figure in the records of 1692, there is nothing about witch hunts in the tale: the unhappy Goodman Brown simply lives out

his faithless life in quiet and gloomy desperation; there is no suggestion that he was ever to know the clash of court-room controversy. We can say, if we wish, that the action takes place "near Salem Village, probably in 1692," but there is no need to insist on this sort of pseudo-historicity.[4] Far more significant, as we shall see, is the simple fact that Goodman Brown is a third-generation Puritan. At issue, accordingly, is far more than that one infamous outbreak of "universal suspicion," though Hawthorne's mature reflections in **"Main Street"** (1849) make it clear that the gothic terror of **"Alice Doane's Appeal"** was not mere managed melodrama; that Hawthorne continued to feel real horror when he thought of that outbreak. In **"Young Goodman Brown"** an important habit of the Puritan mind is on trial: even as Hawthorne revises **"Alice Doane's Appeal"** he discovers that the problem of how to tell a witch is distressingly similar to the radically Puritan problem of how to tell a saint.[5]

Although the episode of 1692 stood out like an ugly blot on the historical page, Hawthorne could not view it as an isolated event, separate from the whole character of Puritan moral experience. As with the Quaker persecutions, customary moral assumptions might not always produce their most proper psychological effects; but it was not altogether surprising if occasionally they did. They did, Hawthorne felt, in the actual events of 1692, and they do in the fictional experience of Goodman Brown. His story is, like that of Tobias Pearson, Hawthorne's way of inspecting certain pervasive Puritan attitudes. If Hawthorne would not "localize" his response to 1692, neither would he quite "universalize" it. We will not find him saying (explicitly) with certain modern historians that, since nearly everyone in the seventeenth century believed in witchcraft, there can be nothing peculiar about the episode at Salem Village; nor (implicitly) with certain modern critics that, since all minds are tempted to bad faith and projection, there can be no specifically "Puritan" version of witchcraft. In Hawthorne's rigorous view, Goodman Brown's forest-education enfigures the ultimate breakdown of the Puritan attempt to define the human form of the Kingdom of God: "spectral evidence" turns out to be only the negative test case of the definitive Puritan problem of "visible sanctity."

II

At the beginning of his fateful excursion into the forest, Goodman Brown is a more than tolerably naive young man. We scarcely need to observe his dismay at hearing (and then seeing) communicants and tavern-haunters, saints and sinners, mixed together to sense his initial assumption that the orderly divisions of the Puritan Community embody Moral Reality. More particularly, his initial attitude toward his wife is so naive as to be condescending: "Say thy prayers, dear Faith, and go to bed at dusk, and no harm will come to thee" (II, 89).[6] On the face of things this is too easy; and the reader of **"Fancy's Show Box"** knows that, on the contrary, "In the solitude of a midnight chamber . . . the soul may pollute itself with those crimes we are accustomed to deem altogether carnal" (I, 250). But such naivete is far from his worst trait. Whatever may be the truth about the moral character of Brown's pink-ribboned wife, and whatever may be our own working assumptions about the relation between faith and salvation, we are expected to worry about this Goodman's belief that "after this one night" he can cling to the skirts of Faith and "follow her to heaven" (90). Even before we get any sense of the sorts of self-indulgence that may become available to Goodman Brown, we know that this sort of temporizing with one's eternal salvation is likely to be risky.

Actually, as it turns out, Goodman Brown is already in a state of "bad faith": there has already been some sort of devilish prearrangement concerning his nocturnal outing; he knows at the outset that he is going off to "keep covenant" with the Powers of Darkness. His "excellent resolve for the future" may be temporarily successful in allowing him to feel "justified in making more haste on his present evil purpose" (90), but the rationalization is as transparent to the psychologist as the risk is to the theologian; it is not likely to stand much testing. And, as an external sign of his compromised internal condition, he has *already* begun to be suspicious of others, even those in whose virtue he is most accustomed naively to trust. Accordingly, his wife's understandable plea that he stay with her, to quiet her fears, on this "of all nights of the year," draws a nervously revealing response: "Dost thou doubt me already, and we but three months married?" (89). Now October 31 *is* a good night for Puritans to stay home,[7] and there is not the slightest evidence to suggest that Faith doubts her husband in any way. Brown's attitude is clearly some sort of guilty projection: his own will-to-evil is *already* causing him to begin the transfer of his own moral obliquity to others.

Clearly, then, much more is at stake than simple naivete, or the much-discussed innocence of the archetypal American hero. Studied closely, Brown's situation is not much like that of Robin Molineux.[8] And well before the analyst has much evidence of oedipal anxiety to work on, any decent theologian (Puritan or otherwise) is constrained to conclude that Goodman Brown is deeply involved in that particular sort of bad faith which used to be called "presumption." He is assuming his own final perseverance, even as he deliberately embarks on a journey which he knows is directed diametrically away from the normal pursuit of salvation. The point is not trivial: to understand the "unpardonable" gravity of his initial moral assumptions is to be protected from being more tender-minded about the terrifying results of his experience than Hawthorne's tough and tight-lipped conclusion asks us to be. No especially severe morality is required to see that, from one very significant point of view, Goodman Brown deserves whatever happens.[9]

Given the unflinching and unpardoning outcome, of a story that is already well under way when we first began to hear about it, we ought to find ourselves wondering how Good-

man Brown has got himself *already* so far involved in the "unpardonable sin" of presumption. If everything seems to follow from, or indeed to be contained in, the initial situation of the story, perhaps that initial situation itself deserves very careful attention. We need to proceed with care: on the one hand, it is very easy to distort and make nonsense out of Hawthorne's delicate ethical formulae by going behind the donnée of his initial premises; on the other hand, his stories are often packed with clues about exactly "where," morally speaking, we really are. And **"Young Goodman Brown"** does not leave us entirely without such clues.

If Brown is "but three months married" to Faith, then it is absolutely necessary to regard him as a recent convert to the high mysteries of the Puritan religion; Thomas Connolly is certainly right about this, even if the story is not as purely or consistently "allegorical" as he wants it to be.[10] But evidently the situation is not quite simple, for we swiftly learn that this good man's father and grandfather have been faithful Puritans before him; and that he himself has been duly catechized, in his youth, by the dutiful Goody Cloyse. At the first glance there may seem to be some sort of confusion in the allegory: can Goodman Brown be, at once, a new convert *and* an heir to a redoubtable saintly ancestry and a formidable Christian nurture? The solution to this apparent difficulty, as well as the key to Goodman Brown's presumptuous psychology, lies in the implicit but clear and precise Puritan background of the story, in the subtly emphasized fact that Young Goodman Brown is a *third-generation* Puritan.

Thus even before we encounter any enchantments, we are forced to realize that Hawthorne's reading in Mather's *Magnalia* has been extremely perceptive and that his use of a particular Puritan world is entirely functional; for Goodman Brown is quite evidently the product (victim, as it turns out) of the Half-Way Covenant, that bold compromise by which the Puritans tried to salvage their theory of "visible sanctity," of a church composed of fully professed saints, in the face of changing historical conditions.[11] Externally, at least, Goodman Brown's status is perfectly standard, indeed inevitable: as a third-generation Puritan he would have been spending the years of his minority in the half-way situation defined by the compromise of 1662. Grandson of an original saint, son of a professing member, he has been reared, like virtually everyone else in his generation, in the half-way condition of presumptive but not yet professed or tested sainthood. Obviously he has had something to do with the community of visible saints because the promises of the new covenant are made with "the seed" of saints as well as with the saints themselves; but just as obviously he has not (until very recently) been a full, "communing" member because he had not been capable of that fully voluntary confession of conversion and profession of committed sainthood which alone could redeem the New England Way from the crassest sort of tribalism.

Original sin might well be transmitted by the simple act of physical generation. So also, as the theological plot thickened, might something called "federal grace"; or, less technically, a saint might fairly expect baptism for his seed, and baptism ought to have some gracious significance. But in the last analysis the new birth had to be truly "spiritual" in every sense; thus "sanctifying grace" could come neither biologically nor by infant ritual. And so, as the New England theology gradually clarified itself, that troubled third generation of Puritans simply had to *wait*: in the *expectation* of full, visible sainthood *eventually,* they all attended church, were duly catechized and nurtured, were thoroughly indoctrinated (and threatened) by jeremiads into the proper respect for the ancestral appearances of saintliness. And eventually some, however few, were admitted into that most guarded and holy of holies—full, "communing" membership.[12] Into this ultimate earthly state, Goodman Brown has but newly entered. After years of "preparation" and presumptive but not proven sainthood Goodman Brown has, we must infer, finally received official certification by the public representatives of the Communion of Saints. In an ultimate theological sense, which in his world is by no means trivial, Brown has finally arrived. And this fact can scarcely be unrelated to the terrible ease of his moral premises.

Goodman Brown's assurance is not, one should hasten to stress, orthodox. The expounders of the Puritan system never tired of emphasizing that (despite Calvin's stress on the "comfort" the saint might find in a predestinarian system) one's assurance could never be complete: indeed too great (or, at any rate, too easy) an assurance should certainly mean that one's experience of gracious regeneration was illusory. But Hawthorne was no mere "expounder" of the system, and he seems to have sensed that all such warnings would not alter the basic psychology of the situation. Some modern commentators have held that the Half-Way Covenant inevitably cheapened the concept of sainthood by allowing some recognizable church-status to persons without, so far as they or anyone else could tell, any specifically "Christian experience."[13] Apparently Hawthorne thought otherwise: whenever one declared oneself a saint and had that weighty claim accepted by the community, the basic declaration and the social fact might well tend to loom larger, psychologically, than any attendant (fussy) qualifications about continuing uncertainty, or about the sole importance of God's free grace in the process, or about the continuing need for watchfulness and sanctification; and by providing a formalized schema of waiting or probation out of which many persons never moved, the Half-Way Covenant may well have served to increase this basic psychological tendency. Although the new dispensation served to broaden the base of baptized membership in the Puritan churches, it left the inner circle of full communicants as small as ever, and seemed, if anything, to heighten the significance of that *sanctum sanctorum.*[14]

When one moved, then, from the lamented and berated coolness of half-way membership into the warmth of full communion, the event could have no small significance. And one perfectly likely (though by no means "approved")

meaning of such an experience is implied in the moral posture of Goodman Brown as recent-convert. After all protective distinctions have been made, the doctrine of election, especially in the context of third-generation Puritanism, which Hawthorne so delicately evokes, is likely to mean the sin of presumption. Hawthorne seems to say it all in the first scene when he tells us that "Goodman Brown *felt himself justified.*" To Cotton Mather, no doubt; to Edward Taylor; or to any other approved theorist of latter-day Puritan conversion psychology, Brown would be an example of the bold hypocrite, outrageously presuming on grace: no really converted person ever *would* behave in such a manner. We can view him that way if we choose. To Hawthorne himself, however, he is only the enduring natural man whose naturally self-regarding instincts have been treacherously reinforced by the psychological implications of doctrine.

Now all of this is merely the story's background, implied by the setting and compressed context, and helping us to place the sociologically and doctrinally precise point of Goodman Brown's departure. If the analysis seems somewhat technical, we may well recall that, as early as the sketch of **"Dr. Bullivant,"** Hawthorne had been intensely interested in the mentality of declining Puritanism; and here he associates the experience of Goodman Brown not only with the context of the witchcraft (the most dramatic problem of Puritan third-generation declension) but also with the pervasive moral quality of that mentality.[15] No one can read Hawthorne's known sources without sensing that with the death of the original saints, whose experience in England and in "coming out" to America made their stance of sainthood seem natural and believable, the problem of continuing an order of visible saints became disproportionate, even obsessive. The rest, perhaps, is Hawthorne's own speculation; but surely it is apt. No Arminian critic of Calvinism ever fails to warn that the doctrine of election protects the sovereignty of God only at the risk of human smugness, over-confidence, self-indulgence, antinomianism. The Calvinist doctrine of election looks very much like the traditional sin of presumption.[16] And nowhere, Hawthorne cogently suggests, was the danger greater than in declining New England, in those exasperating days when the Puritan churches turned nearly all their attention to the continuance of churches constituted of God's visible saints. Obviously Goodman Brown's experience is not to be taken as a model of "Augustinian Piety." And even if his career does not represent any sort of statistical Puritan "average," he is a representative, latter-day Puritan nevertheless, following a highly probable moral logic. The general situation is indeed as Roy Harvey Pearce has suggested: "granting the Puritan faith . . . it is inevitable that Young Goodman Brown should have envisaged his loss of faith as he did and as a consequence have been destroyed as a person."[17]

Accordingly, his situation will not bear immediate psycho-analytic translation or complete reduction. *Of course* Goodman Brown will prove anxious about his relation to his father, and to "his father before him"; this is an inevitable fact of Puritan life in the 1670's, 80's, and 90's, where, as Perry Miller has remarked, the spokesmen for the failing Puritan Way "called for such a veneration of progenitors as is hardly to be matched outside China."[18] It is *their* reputed level of piety which has, we are asked to imagine, been repeatedly used to mark the level of Goodman Brown's own declension. In a very real sense it is into the community of *their* putative sanctity that he has so recently been admitted. The perception that the Puritan world "in declension" was bound to be fraught with oedipal anxiety belongs as obviously to the order of history as to the order of psychoanalysis. And the suspicion that in such a world a son, however naive, might be all too likely to make certain diabolical discoveries about his venerable progenitors belongs to the order of common sense. Together these insights add up to something like the figure of Young Goodman Brown, the moral adolescent who, after years of spiritual (as well as sexual) anxiety, has newly achieved what his ancestors defined as "Faith"; and who is now, from the absolutely "inamissable" safety of that position, about to check out the reality of the dark world he has escaped.

III

The moral progress of Young Goodman Brown, from the presumption of his own salvation by Faith, together with a naive but thin confidence in the simple goodness of familiar saints; through a state of melodramatic despair; and on to the enduring suspicion that outside of his own will "there is no good on earth," represents a triumph of compression unequaled in Hawthorne's art. Robin Molineux's "evening of weariness and ambiguity" is, by comparison, tediously drawn out. Here things happen almost too fast, and only with a sense of the special Puritan character of Brown's beginning can we accurately trace his path.

Brown enters the forest convinced that he can always return to the Bosom of Faith; his nice pink-ribboned little wife and his familiar place in a stable and salutary community of saints will always be there. It may be that neither his marriage nor his conversion has, after three months proved quite so enduringly satisfactory or perpetually climactic as could be hoped; but both have provided him with the assurance needed by one who would press beyond the limits of socialized sex or religion. Recalling the typological significance of marital union in **"The Maypole of Merry Mount,"** or of its absence in **"The Man of Adamant,"** we can see the danger of Brown's presumptive confidence. But the full significance of his presumption lies in his feeling that he can now explore the dimension of diabolical evil with impunity. Having joined the ranks of the safe and socially sanctioned he can, he believes, have a little taste of witchcraft, which is simply, as Cotton Mather says, human depravity *par excellence*: without the grace of Faith, "we should every one of us be a *Dog* and a *Witch* too."[19] An intriguing proposition. Now that he is finally sure which side he is on, he can afford to see how the other moral half lives.

The most significant fact about Brown's naive acceptance of the appearance of sanctity in his fellow saints is the swiftness with which it disappears. Based on the normal, approved, social, presumably "real" manifestations of goodness, it is destroyed by extraordinary, private, "spectral" intimations of badness. His ancestors have been "a race of honest men"; Goody Cloyse "taught him his catechism in his youth"; the Minister and the Deacon are pillars of the religious community, sentries who stand guard at the "wall" which surrounds the "garden" of true grace, models of converted holiness whose experiences are the standard by which those of new applicants for communion are judged. All this is evidentially certain: it is visible; it makes the Puritan world go round. But what if these same figures of sanctity are reported, or even "seen" to perform other actions? What if a grandfather is reputed to have had devilish motives in lashing a Quaker woman (half naked) through the streets? or the teacher of catechism is seen to conjure the Devil? or the sternly inhibiting elders are heard to smack their lips over a "goodly young woman" about to be taken into a quite different communion? Surely this contradiction of evidences will prove unsettling to a young man who has the habit of believing the moral world is adequately defined as the mirror-image opposition between the covenants and communions of God and Satan, and that these ultimate differences can be discovered with enough certainty to guarantee the organization of society. Only some very special, as yet undreamed species of faith could rescue him from such a contradiction of evidences.

Ultimately, of course, Goodman Brown passes through a phase of distraught, despairing confusion into a more or less settled state of faithless desolation. But more remarkable, almost, is the equanimity with which he at first accepts the Devil's "revelations." He jokes about the moral secrets of his saintly ancestors: funny he had never heard any such family secrets before; no, on second thought he guesses they *would* keep their forest activities a secret, since we Puritans are "a people of prayer and good works to boot, and abide no such wickedness" (92). With the telling and technical pun on "Boot" (a seventeenth-century nickname for the Devil), the joke is a little funnier to us than it consciously is to Goodman Brown. As yet he does not quite wish to define a universal Puritan hypocrisy as the prayers to God of people who actually serve the Devil. But he is still being rather too easily ironical about his worthy forebears. And if he is, in the next moment, truly amazed to hear the Devil claim such an impressively general acquaintance among the important personages of New England, still he responds less by doubting or discounting the Devil's claim to near-sovereignty than by writing it off as irrelevant to his own moral condition: "Howbeit, I have nothing to do with the council; they have their own ways, and are no rule for a simple husbandman like me" (93). This social deference might be a species of humility; except that Goody Cloyse, with whom his moral connection *has* been direct and important, whose "rule" has been quite literally his own rule, can be dismissed just as easily: "What if a wretched old woman do choose to go to the devil when I thought she was going to heaven; is that any reason why I should quit my dear Faith and go after her?" (96).

Now clearly all of Goodman Brown's responses are still too easy. Even before the Devil has introduced his most convincing, most visible evidence; even when it is all a matter of mere rumor, Goodman Brown has been quite willing to accept the Devil's "doubtful" informations at something like their face value; he believes their truth and merely denies their relevance. At one level, of course, this mental operation is merely an extension of his initial bad faith in relation to his wife; at another, however, it seems to adumbrate the implications of some sort of belief in "limited atonement." Brown's habitual, doctrinally ingrained sense of the relative fewness of the visibly elect is growing more and more keen. Firmly possessed of the distinction between the inner circle of proven saints and all outer circles of the many "others," he seems willing to reduce the circumference of that inmost circle *almost* to its single-point limit. *I* and *my* Faith: it all comes down to that naive center. But since he has already deceived and abandoned his wife (and, in doing so, vitiated his faith through presumption), even this two-term protestation rings false. The Devil really has not very much difficulty with this Easy-Faith of a Young Goodman Brown. "With heaven above and Faith below, I will yet stand firm against the devil!" (98), so our self-assured young man roundly declaims, after consigning the rest of his world to perdition. But a murmur of spectral voices and a flutter of spectral ribbons later and his "Faith is gone." It could hardly have turned out otherwise.

And yet the swiftness and seeming inevitability of Goodman Brown's reduction to despair depend for their believability on more than his naive and presumptuous understanding of faith as a sort of private haven. **"Young Goodman Brown"** is, no less than **"Rappaccini's Daughter,"** a story about Faith and Evidence; and so there is also, just as crucially, the question of his evidences to be considered. Explicitly, of course, Hawthorne raises the question only at the very end of the story, and then in a completely non-technical way: "Had Young Goodman Brown fallen asleep in the forest and only dreamed a wild dream of a witch-meeting"? (105). Was his evidence, therefore, only "subjective," a species of that diseased fantasy to which the nineteenth century universally ascribed the witchcraft "delusions"? As David Levin has amply and carefully shown, however, the evidence or "reality" question is built into the story everywhere in a very precise seventeenth-century way. Not only are we apprised from the outset that Goodman Brown is speaking to the Father of Lies, so that scandalous rumor and innuendo may be even *less* trustworthy than usual, even in a notoriously quarrelsome Puritan small town; but everywhere the persons seen by Brown are referred to as "shapes" or "figures" or "appearances." People appear and disappear in the most magical sorts of ways, and no one is substantial enough to cast a shadow. It is all, quite demonstrably, a technical case of specter evidence. And this is precisely why Hawthorne's seemingly casual answer to the dream-or-not question ("Be it so if you will") is neither a coy evasion nor a profound "ambiguity." It simply does not matter: obviously not in terms of practical consequences,

since the psycho-moral response is certain and terrible, whatever the nature of the stimulus; and not in terms of epistemological assumptions either, since the choice lies (as Levin put it) "between a dream and a reality that is unquestionably spectral."

It is really distressing to see a critic claim that Levin has tried to make all the stories' challenging moral problems go away by blaming everything on "infernal powers"; and that, *really*, Goodman Brown's "'visions' are the product of his suspicion and distrust, not the Devil's wiles." The point is surely that in Hawthorne's psychological schema Brown's suspicion and distrust and the Devil's wiles are not different.[20]

Hawthorne "believed in" the Devil even less than did Spenser, who had long before deliberately conflated Archimago's magic powers with the Red Cross Knight's suppressed desires; and as Hawthorne conned the lesson of Spenser's faith-protagonist, and then defined the problem in **"Alice Doane's Appeal,"** specter evidence became *nothing but* the necessary historical "figure" for guilty, projective dreams or fantasies. "Literally," in the seventeenth century, Brown "sees specters" that *seem* to reveal the diabolical commitment of the persons to whom they belong; but this seeming is highly untrustworthy, and Brown's inferences are illegitimate. "Allegorically," as we interpret Brown's twilight or limit-experiences; as we try, with Hawthorne, to imagine what sort of reality might lie behind the widespread but ultimately superstitious belief that people have detachable specters which may or may not require a pact with the Devil to detach, we can only conclude that specter evidence *is* projective fantasy.[21]

Once again, as so often is the case in a Hawthorne "allegory," history itself provided the "figurative" term: specter evidence was simply there, a given; Hawthorne had merely to imagine what it really (psychologically and morally) meant. And if we really understand this perfectly historical but almost antiallegorical process, we can see how fundamentally wrongheaded is the assumption that Hawthorne merely "used history" as costume or as convenient setting for his timeless themes. Hawthorne's problem in **"Young Goodman Brown"** was not to find an appropriate historical delusion which might validly enfigure Man's persistent tendency to project his own moral uneasiness onto others; it was, rather, to discover the sorts of reality (some of them transient, some of them permanent) which made the belief in specter evidence possible at *any* point in human experience. As is the case with **"The Gentle Boy,"** **"Young Goodman Brown"** is primarily a moment in which there is brought to bear on an actual, complex historical situation all the imaginative sympathy and psychological acumen at the command of the artist. That, I think, we are constrained to call *history as history*. It is good history because the artist in question was one who constantly monitored his own, and speculated about all other mental life.

The doctrine of specters as a specific form of superstition is actually not very complicated, though the story is immeasurably enriched for the reader who is familiar with the witchcraft sources, and who can thus sense the full historic reality of Goodman Brown's problem as a classic case of seventeenth-century religious epistemology. Perhaps we need not linger over all the wonderful ramifications of the problem about whether God would or would not permit Satan to manipulate the spectral form of a person who had *not* entered the Devil's own covenant. The arguments are inexhaustibly fascinating.[22] On the one hand if Satan can do such things, wouldn't this constitute a rather drastic lacuna in the Providential order? If the observance of someone in diabolical settings or activities might or might not really indicate his adherence to the Devil's party, would not appearance and reality have come so far apart as to make the whole moral world illusory? What, more especially, would be the significance of that ever-so-watchful moral surveillance so characteristic of the covenanted community? What could you believe? Whom could you trust? But on the other hand—and Cotton Mather himself said it all—the scripture doctrine is clear: "the Devil has often been transformed into an angel of light." And so, who could assert with assurance that, as some sort of ultimate Faith-test for a special people, a royal priesthood set apart, God would not permit Satan to impersonate saints so as to lead astray, if possible, even the elect? But if the ramifications are teasing, still the crux is simple. To imagine the epistemological heart of Goodman Brown's problem, Hawthorne probably needed no more than a single interrogative suggestion from Increase Mather's *Illustrious Providences*: "Suppose the devil saith, these people are witches, must the just, therefore, condemn them?"[23]

Mather is speaking, literally, of vulgar, "white-magic" sorts of witch-detection (such as the water test), which he condemns as using the Devil's own means to detect the Devil; and Brown is not quite the sort of "judge" Mather probably had in mind. Still, his question covers the matter of spectral activity as well: the appearance of a person's specter is, in precise fact, the devil's ocular claim that the person thus spectrally represented is indeed a member of his own desperate anticovenant. And it is hard to imagine a clearer posing of the question which faces Goodman Brown. Whether we are thinking of the Devil's verbal slanders, or the spectral sounds and sights of the forest, or those famous now-you-see-them, now-you-don't pink ribbons, the case is essentially the same. For granting that the Devil is, from time to time, permitted to impersonate saints without their consent; and granting that in these days of his last desperate assault against the purity of Faith in the New World he would do so if ever he could; then, "literally," there is no evidential difference between the Devil's general and urbane innuendoes about all the Great and Holy of New England and Goodman Brown's actually "seeing" Goody Cloyse, or Deacon Gookin, or his parents, or Faith, with or without her ribbons. Nasty small-town rumor, simplistic tricks of "materialization" such as even Pharaoh's Magi could perform, spectral simulation: in all these instances, Goodman Brown's vaunted "insights" into

Mankind's Total and Unredeemed Depravity depend on a diabolical communication.

Such informations would be scanned. A less technical case did not turn out well for Young Nobleman Hamlet: things were rotten enough in Denmark, one discovers, but man's ghost-bidden (and oedipally anxious) revenge did not exactly accomplish God's Justice. And the case of Brown's direct spiritual ancestor is even more instructive: the instinctive "jealousy" Spenser's Red Cross Knight feels when he beholds the Spectral Una disporting in lewd amours with a Spectral Squire suggests that even the Arch-Magician's specters embody little more than suppressed suspicion or repressed desire.[24] Hawthorne is too sympathetic a moral historian to imply, flatly, that "He who believes in the Devil, already belongs to Him"; but **"Young Goodman Brown"** exists to suggest that any belief, whether literal or allegoric, in the Devil's account of the moral world represents a culpable degree of credulity. If you want the Devil's views, you must go to meet him. But if you do this, you are already on dubious ground at best; you might well expect the worst. And so, Goodman Brown's spectral intimations of Depravity are merely the seamy psychological underside of his initial naivete and (even more) of his initial bad faith.[25]

Probably, if we find such speculations interesting, the Devil is telling the truth when he implicates Brown's ancestors in persecution and sadistic cruelty: these are, after all, the sins of Hawthorne's own fathers, and of the fathers of many others among his historically naive generation; doubtless the Father of Lies is well practiced in the meretricious rhetorical art of universalizing the Half Truth. Probably the Devil exaggerates when he claims that nearly all of the deacons, selectmen, and general court representatives in New England owe him their covenanted allegiance. (Hawthorne would have been, I imagine, less disturbed than some liberal modern historians to learn that, for all the historian can discover, there was indeed some real enough witchcraft at the bottom of the Salem hysteria; but his statistical reservations about the size of Satan's consciously enlisted army would have been as wary as his doctrinal reservations about the Totality of human depravity.) And presumably the Devil's use of the specific "specters" of Goody Cloyse, Deacon Gookin, and Faith is pure deceit: he conjures their shapes without their contractual permission in order to test (destroy, as it lamentably turns out) the naive and compromised faith of Goodman Brown. A cheap trick, perhaps, but not without a certain diabolical cleverness; and not, in this case, ineffective. Young Calvinist Brown may think that Faith is "inamissable," that the final perseverance of the Elect is certain and "indefectable." But Satan evidently knows better: even fully communing Saints can be had. Or, if the Calvinist Fathers of Dort were correct, if the gracious gift of a true faith cannot indeed be lost, then at least there is the diabolical pleasure of hazing the "presumptive" saint whose faith only seemed true and whose salvation was all too easily assumed. In any case, the extreme result of this new communicant's presumptive bad faith is his willingness to accept spectral (whether diabolical or traumatic) intimations of evil as more authoritative than the ordinary social appearances of goodness.

IV

Once we realize how fundamentally Goodman Brown's moral discoveries depend on the spirit (and the place) in which he asks his questions, we are inevitably led to wonder about the validity of the questions themselves. Clearly it is "impertinent" (in Levin's language) to ask whether the people represented to Brown in the forest are "really" evil: questions concerning the nature and extent of human depravity may not, in themselves, lie "beyond the limits of fiction"; but surely the true, ultimate condition of Goody Cloyse is a question whose answer lies beyond the proper limits of *this story,* which is "not about the evil of other people but about Brown's doubt, his discovery of the *possibility* of universal evil."[26] And there is reason to believe, further, that certain forms of the depravity-question are themselves illegitimate. Posed in certain terms, they may be the Devil's own questions.

From Hawthorne's frankly Arminian, though by no means Pelagian, point of view, Goodman Brown is habitually making simple judgments about settled moral realities in a world where only the most flickering sorts of appearances are available as evidence. And he is asking about spiritual "essences" where probably only a process exists. In one very important sense the private evidence of the forest is no more "spectral" than was all the previous communal evidence in favor of the saintliness of the now-exposed hypocrites. Hawthorne repeatedly joked about the separation between his own real and spectral selves; and as the author of **"The Christmas Banquet"** he perfectly agreed with the Emersonian dictum that "souls never touch." Further, he made it unmistakably clear in **"Fancy's Show Box"** (which ought to be read as a gloss on **"Young Goodman Brown,"** revealing Hawthorne's *own* doctrine of depravity) that stains upon the soul are simply not visible. Moral or spiritual status is, accordingly, an invincibly interior and a radically *in*visible quality. Any outward representation of a person's absolutely private moral intentionality, of his voluntary allegiance to God or Satan, of his "state" with reference to the "grace" of "faith" (even if this is not a process of constant, "ambivalent" fluctuation) is a mere simulacrum—a specter.[27] Giving the epistemology of Berkeley or Kant a distinctive moral twist (which Jeremy Taylor could have appreciated better than Emerson), Hawthorne means to suggest that all moral knowledge of others exists in us as phenomena, or idea, or appearance merely; the moral essence, like the Lockean substance or the Kantian *ding an sich,* remains an *ignotum x.* True, for certain fairly important social uses, we must assume that a person's statements and bodily actions correspond to his own intention, that he and not some devil is in control of his bodily form. But this is only a working premise. It should not be taken as an accurate rendition of Reality. Clearly a religious system which would, rejecting the ironic personal lesson and then the powerfully pro-

phetic teaching of Roger Williams, confuse the compromises imposed by the necessities of worldly order based on appearances with the absolute configurations of the invisible moral world would be running a terrible risk.[28]

In a sense, therefore, any answer to questions concerning an individual's absolute moral condition will be in terms of spectral evidence. Probably the truth lies with the Arminians and Pragmatists and Existentialists: man makes himself; he has a moral history but no moral essence, not at birth and not by rebirth; his whole life is a journey which may or may not lead to the goal, and a series of choices in which any one choice may undo the moral import (though not, of course, all the psychological results) of any other. The "sides" in such a world would be impossible to define. But even if there were sides, ineluctably defined by ineffable divine decree, who could ever discover them? Accordingly, Goodman Brown's mental organization (and, by implication, the Puritan ecclesiology) dissolves into moral chaos because in every instance he must choose between the show of social appearance and the specter of diabolical simulation and suggestion. In every case evidence counters evidence, where, Hawthorne implies, only faith can be salutary.

The paradigmatic instance of this dilemma quite properly concerns Brown's wife: the test of faith is Faith. Supposing the worst, let us adopt the improbable view that Hawthorne intends the forest experience of Goodman Brown to have the full authority of a sort of "Melvillean" vision of "blackness," uncomplicated by the epistemological uncertainties inherent in the historical problem of specter evidence or the psychological problem of Brown's bad faith. Even if we should decide that Brown's discoveries are neither the troubled, projective dreams of a man in bad faith nor their literal seventeenth-century equivalent, a show of black magic put on by the Devil for Brown's private "benefit"; that is, even if everything he sees and hears in the forest is unequivocally asserted by Hawthorne himself to be "true"—his ancestors, his moral perceptors and models, and virtually all other New England saints are consciously and voluntarily in league with the Devil; even granting all this, we are still forced by the logic of the tale to make an exception for Faith. Again, grant that it was *her* literal voice from the cloud which obscured Brown's view of, and seemed to obliterate his belief in heaven; that her *real* and not spectral ribbons floated down to crush her husband's spirit; that she was really *there,* with Goodman Brown's parents, physically, transported to an actual blasphemous witch-meeting; still we come to a cardinal uncertainty ("ambiguity," if you will) which cannot be resolved except by faith—either a gracious and charitable decision to believe the best or, alternately, an extreme of pernicious credulity. We know that Goodman Brown's own protracted dalliance ends in revulsion, expressed in his agonized plea that Faith "look up to heaven, and resist the wicked one" (105). This plea, we must presume, constitutes his own last-second refusal to accept an unholy baptism and communion: in spite of his earlier blasphemies, he seems to draw back at the last moral instant. But "whether Faith obeyed" his plea, we, like Goodman Brown can never know with certainty. In the structurally climactic, epistemologically paradigmatic, and (for Goodman Brown) emotionally crucial instance, there is, evidentially, only uncertainty.

Ultimately, evidence fails. Finally, in a way Goodman Brown had little expected and is totally unprepared to accept or even comprehend, everything does depend on Faith. The individual can judge his own moral case. Imperfectly, no doubt, but with some legitimacy; for besides the Searcher of Hearts only he has access to the evidence of his own intentions, which are (according to Jeremy Taylor) related to his words and actions as the soul to the body. In every other case, moral judgment is irreducibly a species of faith. Morally speaking, we can observe specters flirting with the Devil, but (even if such a thing is possible), we cannot observe a soul fix itself in an evil state.

That certain people in a Puritan world might *wish* so to fix themselves, we can easily imagine: the case recorded by Winthrop, of the woman who murdered her child so that she could now be "sure she would be damned," is full of terrible instruction; and doubtless there were many more unrecorded cases of persons for whom "a guilty identity was better than none."[29] Especially in the latter days of Puritanism, when so many people lived out whole lives of spiritual tension in a half-way status, the temptations must have been both strong and various: simply to get the whole business settled; or manfully to accept the highly probable import of one's unremitting sinfulness (and perhaps to enjoy some sense of true significance in this world); or even to join the Devil's party out of sheer rebellion against such singularly infelicitous figures of Covenant authority as Cotton Mather. Thus for every village hag who practiced some crude form of image magic or evil eye to frighten her neighbors into a frenzy of self-destruction, there must have been dozens of more robust souls who saw their appropriate moral hypothesis quite clearly: "If I am the devil's child, I will live then from the devil." But obviously such intentions are reversible: above all else the Puritans tried to obtain repentant confessions from accused witches, to bring them back from the Deviant to the Normative Covenant. This might strain their predestinarian logic, but not perhaps unduly. One could be as wrong about one's reprobation as about one's election: in either theological case, one "consented" but did not, himself, make the really efficacious choice; and in psychological practice, a wild, desperate, overly wilful embracing of unconditional and irrevocable reprobation is probably no easier to protect from doubt or change of mood than the astonished and relieved acceptance of one's election. Certainly Goodman Brown ultimately draws back—from one of the most blasphemous declarations of despair in all literature.

But this is getting slightly ahead of the immediate question, which concerns the relation of faith and evidence to the serious moral judgement of others. The question put so directly and so unavoidably to the theologically ill-

prepared Goodman Brown at the climax of his forest-experience is, quite simply, Hawthorne's version of the faith-question in its human dimension: in the face of the final breakdown of all reliable evidence concerning the hidden but defining essence of moral decisions or continuing "heart" intentions of others, which are you more prepared to believe in, goodness or badness? Much critical ink has been spilled over the angst of Goodman Brown's wracking doubt, his ambivalence, his inability finally to settle his belief one way or the other; and in an ultimate sense, of course, it is true that Brown does not hold a fixed and final conviction that his wife is in league with the devil. But practically there is not much question. Hawthorne did not need the will-to-believe analysis of William James to tell him that theoretical doubts have a way of solving themselves in practice, in accordance with the individual's deepest suspicions: and at this level Brown's ideas are quite clear. He hears an "anthem of sin" when the congregation sings a holy psalm; he scowls while his family prays; he shrinks at midnight from the bosom of Faith; and he dies in an aura which even Puritans recognize as one of inordinate moral gloom.

To be sure, he does not die in precisely the same state of "despair" that sent him raging through the forest, challenging the Devil, burning to meet him on his own ground. At that moment his despair is universal: "there is no good on earth; and sin is but a name." At that moment it includes himself; indeed it applies to himself preeminently: "Come witch, come wizard, come Indian powwow, come devil himself, and here comes Goodman Brown. You may as well fear him as he fear you" (99). At that moment only does the element of hesitancy (or as one recent critic rightly insists, "ambivalence") disappear from his mental state; and as it disappears Brown becomes guilty not only of some sort of cosmic blasphemy but also of that personal and technical sort of "despair" which, in its utter abandonment of the possibility of personal redemption, constitutes the second of traditional Christianity's two unpardonable sins—the other, its obverse, being the presumption with which Brown began. But as we have said, this lurid, melodramatic phase subsides: his call upon Faith to "resist" is, in part, his way of taking back his own overly wilful self-abandonment.[30] And thus, as he was initially not entirely certain he wanted to sneak off into the forest at all, so he is finally not convinced that he himself is a lost soul. Nevertheless neither his crucial refusal of baptism nor his returning ambivalence can now save him from some sort of moral gloom for which there may be no neatly prepared theological name, but which the story exists to define. Indeed Goodman Brown's final (exorcised) state may be his worst of all.

Having begun by assuming that all visible sanctity was real sanctity, and by presuming his own final perseverance in faith; having next despaired of *all* goodness; he ends by doubting the existence of any ultimate goodness but his own. There is, it seems to me, no other way to account for the way Goodman Brown spends the rest of his life. Evidently he clings to the precious knowledge that he, at least, resisted the wicked one's final invitation to diabolical communion; accordingly, the lurid satisfactions of Satan's anti-Covenant are not available to him. But neither are the sweet delights of the Communion of Saints. He knows he resisted the "last, last crime" of witchcraft, but his deepest suspicion seems to be that Faith did not resist. Or if that seems too strong a formulation for sentimental readers, he cannot make his faith in Faith prevail. Without such a prevailing faith, he is left outside the bounds of all communion: his own unbartered soul is the only certain locus of goodness in a world otherwise altogether blasted.[31]

It would be easy enough to praise Young Goodman Brown for his recovery from the blasphemous nihilism of his mid-forest rage against the universe; for his refusal to translate his cosmic paranoia into an Ahabian plan of counterattack. Or, from another point of view, it would even be possible to suggest that if the Devil's proffered community of evil is the only community possible, perhaps he should have accepted membership instead of protecting the insular sacredness of his own separate and too precious soul. Perhaps salvation is not worth having—perhaps it is meaningless—in a universe where depravity has undone so many. But both of these moral prescriptions miss Hawthorne's principal emphasis which, as I read the tale, is on the problem of faith and evidence; on that peculiar kind of "doubt" (in epistemological essence, really a kind of negative faith) which follows from a discrediting of evidences formerly trusted. Brown is damned to stony moral isolation because his "evidential" Puritan biases have led him all unprepared into a terrifying betrayal of Faith. He believes the Devil's spectral suggestions not merely because he is naive, though he is that; and not merely because he is incapable of the sort of evidential subtlety by which John Cotton instructed the very first members of those newly purified New England churches in the art of separating sheep and goats, or by which the Mathers sermonized the court of oyer and terminer on the occult art of the distinguishing of spirits.[32] Brown believes the Devil because, at one level, the projected guilt of a man in bad faith *is* specter evidence and because, even more fundamentally, absolute moral quality is related to outward appearance as a real person is to his specter.

In short, Hawthorne suggests, one had better not raise such ultimate questions at all: to do so is to risk the appearance-and-reality question in its most pernicious form. At best one would be accepting the deceptive appearances of sanctity, as Goodman Brown evidently continued to be accepted at the communion table of a community which never suspected his presumption, despair, blasphemy and his near approach to witchcraft; or as the representative Mr. Smith of **"Fancy's Show Box"** is, in later times, accepted as a paragon in spite of his impressive list of sinful intentions. And at worst, if one is already in bad faith, his penetrating glimpses into the "reality" behind the appearances will be no more than spectral projections of his own guilty wishes; such are the evidences Goodman Brown accepts no less clearly than Leonard Doane or Spenser's Red Cross Knight. The truly naive

will simply accept the smiling light of daytime, church-day appearances; the already compromised will "see" in others (as irrevocable commitment) what already preexists in themselves (as fantasy, wish, desire, or intention). The only alternative would seem to be the acceptance of some ultimate and fundamental equality in a common moral struggle; a healthy skepticism about all moral appearances, firmly wedded to the faith that, whatever men may fantasize, or however they may fall, they generally love the good and hate the evil.

That such standards will suffice for all judgements except perhaps the Last, Roger Williams, Solomon Stoddard, and various Arminians variously tried to suggest, as against the main thrust of the New England Way.[33] What none of them could quite say, but what Hawthorne quite clearly saw the witchcraft "delusion" to prove, is that beyond this sort of moral and epistemological humility lie only varieties of specter evidence. And these, ironically, turn out to be species of perverted faith after all.

For finally, once Goodman Brown's search for evidences has ended in nightmare, his enduring doubt and suspicion prove to be only an abiding "faith" in the probability of evil. Lacking conclusive evidence, he yet suspects—"believes," I think we may say—the worst of Faith. His doubt of goodness is equally a faith in evil. The Judgement of Charity (which the wariest of the Puritans always insisted was the proper rule in estimating the presence of grace and by which they almost undid their basic premises)[34] might construe even Faith's actual presence in the forest in some lenient way; charity ought to be willing to believe that a wife would refuse a Devil at least as soon as a husband would. But bad faith precludes such charity. What determines Brown's practical disbelief in Faith and in all "other" goodness is the subconscious effort of his own dark (if ambivalent) reasons for being in the forest, reinforced no doubt by the violence of his blasphemous nihilism; the total personality, it turns out, is less supple and flexible than the "will." Brown's initial easy-faith in his own election, which makes everything else possible, is based on the evidence of his acceptance (finally!) into a community of professing, visible saints. His final gloomy-faith in the reprobation of the rest of his world is based on the suppression and outward projection of his own continuing fallenness. Goodman Brown believes the Devil's spectral evidence because ultimately it coincides with his own guilty projections; indeed the "levels" of the "allegory" collapse so perfectly that the spectral evidence produced by the Devil's most potent magic becomes indistinguishable from the bad dream of a man in bad faith. Goodman Brown's supposedly "inamissable" faith has, to paraphrase Poe, indeed "flown away." And whether "In a vision, or in none, / Is it therefore the less gone?" The note of finality seems cruel, but so, apparently, are the pitfalls of visible sanctity for a Young Calvinist Saint.

V

Hawthorne will return to the question of faith and evidence, most significantly in **"Rappaccini's Daughter"** at the climax of his second or **"Old Manse"** period. There the "vile empiric" will turn out to be not any scientific experimenter or positivist, but the Brown-like Giovanni Guasconti, who loses his Dantesque Beatrice for many of the same reasons Goodman Brown loses his Spenserian Faith. By then, Hawthorne's fictional arguments will have caught up with contemporaneous religious questions; in the case of **"Rappaccini's Daughter,"** with the "miracles controversy" raging three-sidedly among Calvinists, Unitarians, and Transcendentalists, and with the universal problem of the fate of "historical Christianity" of which that controversy is a part.[35] But in the early and middle 1830's, Hawthorne is not yet writing **"The History of His Own Time."** His outlook is still dominated, and his most serious concerns are still unified, by his wide and perceptive readings in seventeenth-century Puritanism; the subjects of his most penetrating analyses are still Puritans trapped by the moral definitions of their historical world. As with **"The Gentle Boy," "Young Goodman Brown"** unarguably demonstrates that (however we choose to define "history as history") Hawthorne's most powerful early stories grew directly out of an authentic and creative encounter with the Puritan mind.

The neo-Puritan Calvinism of Hawthorne's own nineteenth-century world was, despite its fairly widespread continuance of the structures begun with the Half-Way Covenant of 1662, not obsessively concerned with the attempt to unite the visible church with the invisible. Most local New England religious communities were still divided into "the church" (of converted saints) and "the congregation" (of hopeful, or interested, or habitual service-attenders); often the line divided families in half, or even into more disproportionate fractions; but the explosive potential seemed to be going out of such divisions. Despite the undeniable effect of successive waves of revival enthusiasm which stressed the saving (and normative) importance of a converting "Christian experience," New England seemed to be on its way to learning the lesson summarized so succinctly, much later, by the heroine of Harold Fredric's most Hawthornean novel: "The sheep and the goats are to be separated on Judgment Day, but not the minute sooner. In other words, as long as human life lasts, good, bad and indifferent are all braided up together in every man's nature, and every woman's too."[36] Hawthorne was, no doubt, helping to teach or to reinforce that lesson, along with everyone else involved in any way with "the moral argument against Calvinism." But it was a lesson already pretty well learned in practice, if not a doctrine settled in theory. And it would be doing Hawthorne no essential service to assert this sort of historical "relevance" as one of the chief claims to greatness of **"Young Goodman Brown."**

"Young Goodman Brown" is, nevertheless, a dazzling achievement of the historical imagination, and its greatness cannot be accounted for without close and continuous reference to its insight into the psychology of religion in New England, especially in its most "troubled" period. From one point of view, **"Young Goodman Brown"** may

well be "Freud Anticipated"; from another it unquestionably is "Spenser Applied." But it applies the Spenserian teaching to New England's problems of spectral evidence and visible sanctity as certainly and as precisely as **"The Maypole of Merrymount"** applies the Miltonic doctrines of mythic innocence and historic fall to the problem of America's imaginative (and political) state; or, later, as surely as **"The Celestial Railroad"** would apply Bunyan; or **"Rappaccini's Daughter,"** Dante; or **"Ethan Brand,"** Goethe, to problems which had a specific American context and quiddity. And if **"Young Goodman Brown"** is one of Hawthorne's more stunning anticipations of Freudian themes, it *discovers* these themes in the historical record, not only in the painfully obvious testimony of men who were lewdly tempted at night by the "specter" of the local prostitute, but also in that painfully distressing record of the moral identity crisis which two generations of Saints had inevitably if inadvertently prepared for a third. Granted the "enthusiastic" decision of the 1630's to depart from all previous Reformation practice and require virtual "proof" of sainthood for full membership in Congregations of Visible Saints; and granted the existence of scores of diaries and spiritual autobiographies from the first and second generations of New England saints, documents written "Of Providence, For Posterity," solemnly charging the son "to know and love the great and most high god . . . of his father"; granted these, the piteous and fearful experience of Puritanism's third generation was indeed inevitable.[37] And Hawthorne has enfigured it all, with classic economy and without misplaced romantic sympathy, in the tragic career of Young Goodman Brown.

First of all, Hawthorne has completely elided the sentimental question of "persecuted innocence" which, as Michael Bell has shown, so obsessed the popular romancers who dealt with the episode of 1692. Furthermore, he has gone beyond all naive versions of the question of witchcraft "guilt"—individual or collective, unique or commonplace, original or actual, self-limiting or transmitted—which troubled those of his more professionally historical contemporaries who knew or cared enough to consider the problem, and with which he himself wrestled somewhat clumsily (if honestly) in the beginning and end of **"Alice Doane's Appeal."**[38] In this, though not in every instance, Hawthorne is a writer of *psycho-historical* fiction; as such, and with the full authority of Scott behind him, he has gone straight to the task of creating a doctrinally adequate and dramatically believable version of "how it might have felt" to live in the moral climate of Puritanism's most troubled years. The imaginative insight which lies behind **"Young Goodman Brown"** may stand as a significant part of Hawthorne's reasons for being so "fervently" glad to have been born beyond the temporal limits of the Puritan world. Hawthorne was, to be sure, far from unique in preferring the moral climate of the 1830's to that of the 1690's: perhaps only a minority of his readers (in Boston, or Salem, or Concord at least) really felt that America had declined, even from the best qualities of the noblest figures of the first generation of Puritan Fathers; and, less tendentiously, it would imply no very impressive moral or political virtue to prefer the liberal utterances of William Ellery Channing to the jeremiad rhetoric of *The Spirit of the Pilgrims*. But no one else in Hawthorne's generation was able to dramatize with such compelling clarity, and with so firm a grasp of the psychological implications of doctrine, what the older system might have meant to a representative individual conscience.[39] And beyond this achievement of history as psychological vivification, there is the brilliant hypothesis by which Hawthorne has offered Goodman Brown's representative encounters with the spectral world as a comment on the meaning of witchcraft in the specific context of latter-day Puritan experience.

Except for those who have set out to blacken the Puritans by cliché and oversimplification, most modern commentators are at pains to prove that there is no operable or intelligible connection between New England's Puritanism and its problems with witchcraft. The American Puritans, it has been tediously reiterated, executed fewer witches and gave over the whole enterprise of witch-hunting sooner than enlightened men and practicing Christians elsewhere. The whole accumulated bulk of such arguments, I think, would not have impressed Hawthorne. He heard the argument, at its source, from Charles Upham in 1831; and while he may have appreciated it as a subtler response than that of the romancers (who kept insisting that the persecution of supposed witches was simply the most horrendous form of Puritanism's hysterical intolerance), he seems to have seen that it combined two questions which must be kept distinct. For to establish that, up to a certain point in human history, everybody believed in and, from time to time, hunted witches is not quite to demonstrate that the belief in witchcraft, or the impulse to become a witch, or the need to expose and punish this form of deviancy has had, in all times and all places, precisely the same meaning.[40] Perhaps we could admit, *a priori,* that, deep down at its psychic source, all witchcraft is the same witchcraft—just as, presumably, all oedipal strife or all anal fixation reveals a single, boring morphology. But, obviously, that is not the only sort of "meaning" witchcraft might have. There remains the question of witchcraft as an event in intellectual history: what do various witches, witch-hunters, and skeptical critics have to *say* about the meaning of their actions? Such declarations might be a species of rationalization, either cheap or elegant; but people do put constructions on the most elemental responses; they do strive to find names for and thus make intelligible to themselves even those actions to which they are driven by their most unopposable "drives." And in this sense, New England witchcraft has its own fairly unique meaning.

Certainly the everyone-did-it arguments would have astonished those men who wrote about witchcraft in New England between 1684 and 1705, including those who either attacked or defended the proceedings of 1692. Not one of them could doubt that what was happening was directly connected with New England's existence as a covenanted community of proven saints, a saving remnant against which the powers of darkness were most likely to be arrayed; at very least, what was happening had to do with certain people's *vision* of New England in these terms.[41] In a sense it is our very historical sophistication which is likely to mislead us here: the fact that "such things happened everywhere," and the discovery that, therefore, the Puritans were by our enlightened standards "no worse" than anyone else, is likely to blind us to the unique meanings witchcraft may have had in a (still) fairly unique Puritan world. Hawthorne is not so blinded. His suggestion is that, whatever might be the meaning of witchcraft elsewhere, in New England in 1692 it is not to be considered apart from the larger problem that Puritan Sons were having in trying to keep the outlines of the moral world as clear as they had been in the minds of those Puritan Fathers who first defined the community's project of salvation.

The reader of **"Young Goodman Brown"** needs to keep constantly in mind the first theological premises and the latter-day ecclesiological practices of the Puritan economy of salvation. For the Puritan, salvation "by faith" was in a sense "voluntary," but it was by no means a free option depending critically on the originating impulse of man; rather it was an event which the human will might or might not experience, according to the hidden "Pleasure" (or, for the more rationally inclined, the "Wisdom") of God. But if the "Reason" of the Divine Decrees lay hidden in His mysterious and transcendent essence, the results of those decrees were a good deal more clear; no Puritan could understand *why* he was elected while still a sinner and in spite of his sinfulness, but none was allowed to remain ignorant of what followed if indeed he were so elected; and, in the seventeenth century, at least, it was the rare congregation which permitted the spiritually unsure to relax into a state of settled neutrality on the question of regenerating experience. After all sorts of appropriate distinctions had been made and a range of individual differences allowed for, the Puritan system (defined by 1636 and not *essentially* compromised in 1662) depended radically on the Church's fairly sound ability to determine who was and who was not elect of God. On all necessary occasions the Puritan apologist could, of course, argue that "visible sanctity" meant no more than sanctity insofar as that mysterious quality could ever *be* visible—that is, relatively and not absolutely, with human approximation rather than divine certitude. But in the end, as Hawthorne seemed to know, the defining essence of American Puritanism, socially considered, is its rather confident attempt to locate by profession, institutionalize by Covenant, and monitor by discipline Christian experience as such.[42] No modest ambition this.

Small wonder, then, if such a group begins its witchcraft investigations with sufficient confidence in its ability to identify witches, those actively hostile anti-saints. If a people is accustomed to sift the relatively delicate evidence that constituted the rainbow-like shadings of the conversion experience, from the inconclusively preparatory to the definitively sanctified, surely the distinguishing of witches would prove a simple matter by comparison.

Evidentially speaking, depravity should immediately expose itself by its very lurid and melodramatic colorings. And, once the problem was fairly raised and widely discussed, the Puritan system seemed to depend as essentially on the institutional identification of witches as of saints: not only psychologically or sociologically, as a certain style of normative behavior may seem to require and create an appropriate deviancy in mirror image of itself; but also as a confirmation of the epistemology which underlay orthodoxy and a guarantee of the logic which confirmed identity. If the Mathers (and all others who opposed the heretical innovations of Solomon Stoddard) were correct, the New Englanders were God's Chosen Saints, or they were Nobody. It was precisely *because* they were saints, organized and mobilized as such, that they were now being exposed to a plague of witches. If witch-identity could not be confirmed, then how could their own? And hence the "Several Ministers Consulted" might well call for "speedy and vigorous prosecution" in spite of their own clear warnings about the Devil's undoubted ability to appear "in the Shape of an innocent, yea, and a virtuous Man."[43]

One had always been warned about hypocrites in the Church, and one was moderately well prepared to grant the presence within the holy community of a few people who were simply wrong about their conversion. With less equanimity, perhaps, one could even accustom oneself to the bold reprobate who simulated grace for social advantage. Such cases simply indicated the practical "limits" toward which the theory of visible sanctity could only approximate. But what if it should prove utterly impossible to detect a witch? What if, in a given case, all the available evidence made it impossible to decide whether a given person belonged to God's Covenant or the Devil's Party? Then, presumably, one had reached the inevitable outer limit of one's world, and, if the question of Saint or Witch seemed vital, the reduction to absurdity of one's fundamental premises. Then, presumably, was it time to give over the whole attempt to make church-exclusions based on "visible" moral distinctions and return, in *some* manner, to a more lax Presbyterian system (not to say "free and catholic spirit") of including everyone who was willing to announce his intention to do good and avoid evil. This could mean "Stoddardism," but that was not the only alternative. It had to mean a recognition that Augustine was right after all: there is, on earth, no way to identify the invisible church with the visible. And it also created a strong presumption in favor of Roger Williams' rather than John Cotton's reading of the parable of the wheat and the tares.[44]

In this ultimate context, what **"Young Goodman Brown"** dramatizes is the final failure of all "visible" (or any humanly "outerable") moral evidence. To the explicit destruction of Goodman Brown, and to the implicit confounding of the Puritan system, **"Young Goodman Brown"** takes up where the carefully controlled, even exasperatedly technical definitions of **"Alice Doane's Appeal"** leave off: it lets us watch a representative latter-day

Puritan fail the ultimate test of faith and undergo moral self-destruction precisely when it becomes impossible to tell whether his wife is a saint or a witch.

Brown's enduring suspicion of his whole world, but especially of his wife, gives us a quiet and reduced version of that melodramatic moment of madness Hawthorne describes in **"Main Street,"** when "among the multitude . . . there is horror, fear, and distrust; and friend looks askance at friend, *and the husband at his wife,* and even the mother at her little child." There, as Hawthorne tries to be a fairly "regular historian" of the public frenzy of 1692, the problem is that "in every creature God has made, they suspected a witch, or dreaded an accuser" (III, 471). But here, as we have said, the public frenzy and the courtroom accusation are absent; and accordingly, Hawthorne's approach is more radical. No doubt much of the historical record of 1692 is to be explained in terms of spectral deceits not unlike the ones revealed in **"Alice Doane's Appeal"** and **"Young Goodman Brown,"** but the ultimate question lies deeper. What Hawthorne suggests is that the "real" breakdown of faith in Salem Village and its "enfigured" loss by Goodman Brown are both the result of Puritanism's ecclesiastical positivism, of its definitive attempt to found a church (and beyond it a state) on the premise that visible sanctity can be made to approximate true sanctity. For Hawthorne, such a system could only end in nightmare: it introduced evidence into a system where only faith could be appropriate and salutary.[45]

The witchcraft episode provided the logically necessary (if humanly regrettable) test. When in a spectral epiphany you realized you could not tell a saint from a witch, your logical world, by logical necessity, collapsed. When you realized that the Devil's ability to "transform himself into an Angel of Light" could be used one day, by Increase Mather, as an argument against William Stoughton's injudicious use of spectral evidence; and another day, by his son, as a way to discredit an impressive last-second, gallows-hill protestation by George Burroughs; then someone would surely *see* it had collapsed. Robert Calef may have seen it: his handling of Cotton Mather's behavior at the execution of George Burroughs is extremely skillful and suggestive. And Hawthorne certainly saw it: when a moving profession of faithfulness (such as ordinarily proved necessary and sufficient for admission into Puritanism's Congregational full communion) could be discredited with the same slogan used to warn overly aggressive witch hunters about the insufficient subtlety of their judicial epistemology, then the "dissolution of the world" which Cotton Mather feared had indeed occurred. It is not at all surprising to hear Mather regret ever having to "mention so much as the first letters" of the name of "This G. B." And it is probably no accident that his initials are also those of Goodman Brown.[46] For although **"Alice Doane's Appeal"** depends on the Burroughs episode more directly than does **"Young Goodman Brown,"** still the logical contortions into which the case of George Burroughs forced Cotton Mather are built into the career of Goodman Brown.[47]

VI

In *Grandfather's Chair* Hawthorne offers May 1692 as the end of the "era of the Puritans." The event which marks the break is the death of Old Simon Bradstreet, "the sole representative of [the] departed brotherhood" of original-charter governors; after that "Sir William Phips then arrived in Boston with a new charter from King William and a commission to be governor" (IV, 483). Such indeed are the political realities, and so indeed might the story be divided for children. But in a far more fundamental sense, **"Young Goodman Brown"** shows us that witchcraft "ended" the Puritan world. Its logic of evidence could not stand the test of Faith.

We now know, of course, that it is unhistorical to believe in the idea of a massive popular revulsion against a clerical oligarchy which hurried a well meaning but unsteady populace into a frenzy of suspicion and judicial murder.[48] And yet there may be some reason to believe that the events of 1692 really did accelerate a growing disbelief in human ability to chart the invisible world. To be sure, the new charter forbade New England to use proven sainthood as the sole requirement for provincial citizenship; but it may not be altogether wishful to believe that the discoveries made in 1692 about the diabolical subtleties of spiritual evidence—and about the preeminent human need for Faith as a Judgement in Charity—may have hastened the realization that all temporal separations of sheep and goats are premature. If so, then the Puritans' first religious premise would be as intolerable as their first political premise was intolerant. The statistics concerning the desire for full communion just before and just after the events of 1692 are not available. It is clear, however, that the popularity of Stoddard's practice of open communion continued to grow; and that the hegemony of the Mathers was about to be challenged, from within their own sphere of influence, by persons who believed in the premises underlying a church of visible saints even less than did Stoddard. It is probably more than coincidence that one of the founders of the Brattle Street Church, which admitted all baptized persons to full communion and discontinued the tests for specific Christian experience, had written, in 1692, a fairly cogent letter against the basic assumptions of the witchcraft proceedings; and that he seems to have furnished Calef with his materials for *More Wonders*. And worlds of skeptical faith might fairly be read into Samuel Sewall's recognition of how the truth had eluded his most judicious search in that matter of "doleful witchcraft."[49]

But whatever should turn out to be the case in statistical or other "regular" history, the moral historian's view is clear: in bad faith and with a hopelessly inadequate sense of what True Faith might require, Goodman Brown has come to the end of the Puritan moral world; his inevitable moral collapse stands for the process by which the quest for visible sanctity leads unavoidably into the realm of specter evidence. A more authentic, less institutional form of Puritan piety might yet be "revived," in 1735 or 1740 (or in **"The Minister's Black Veil"**); the political dyna-

mism of Puritanism might be "reawakened," in the various moments which make **"The Legends of the Province House"** bristle with the hostility of Endicott. But the power of "visible sanctity" to organize the American world ended in 1692. And the credibility of the logic by which it proposed to do so disappeared in doubt when Hawthorne's Goodman Brown discovered that only faith could save his Faith from doubt. Without accepting a fundamental change of premises Puritanism could, like Goodman Brown, continue to exist only as "gloom."

Notes

1. Levin's widely reprinted (and variously revised) article originally appeared as "Shadows of Doubt: Specter Evidence in Hawthorne's 'Young Goodman Brown,'" *American Literature* [*AL*], 34 (1962). Levin cites with approval the following predecessors: D. M. McKeithan, "Hawthorne's 'Young Goodman Brown': An Interpretation," *Modern Language Notes,* 67 (1952); Thomas F. Walsh, Jr., "The Bedeviling of Young Goodman Brown," *Modern Language Quarterly* [*MLQ*], 19 (1958); and Paul W. Miller, "Hawthorne's 'Young Goodman Brown': Cynicism or Meliorism?," *Nineteenth-Century Fiction* [*NCF*], 14 (1959). He might, it seems to me, also claim some kinship with Thomas E. Connolly's "Hawthorne's 'Young Goodman Brown': An Attack on Puritanic Calvinism," *AL*, 28 (1956). The most direct "answer" to Levin is Paul J. Hurley, "Young Goodman Brown's 'Heart of Darkness,'" *New England Quarterly* [*NEQ*], 37 (1966); in my opinion, Hurley has misunderstood Levin's fundamental point, obscured the issue Levin was trying to clarify, and set criticism of the tale back a few steps. Evidence of this new confusion is Walter Blair's view that Hurley's attack on Levin comes "from a position much closer to McKeithan's and Walsh's than to those of other critics"; see the Revised Edition of *Eight American Authors,* ed. James Woodress (New York, 1971), p. 127.

   Critics who have grasped and tried to build on Levin's insights include the following: Darrel Abel, "Black Glove and Pink Ribbon: Hawthorne's Metonymic Symbols," *NEQ,* 42 (1969); Michael Bell, *Hawthorne and the Historical Romance of New England* (Princeton, N.J., 1971); Neal Frank Doubleday, *Hawthorne's Early Tales* (Durham, N.C., 1972); and B. Bernard Cohen (see note 2). The essential point, as I shall argue later, is that Levin does *not* trivialize the story by simply blaming everything on supernatural agency; rather, he provides the language to talk about Goodman Brown's epistemological problem, and he shows that "Young Goodman Brown" is about the dynamics of faith rather than the nature and extent of depravity.

2. See Thomas E. Connolly's "Introduction" to *Nathaniel Hawthorne: "Young Goodman Brown"* (Columbus, 1968), pp. 6-8; B. Bernard Cohen's "Deodat Lawson's *Christ's Fidelity* and Hawthorne's 'Young Goodman Brown,'" *Essex Institute Histori-*

cal Collections, 104 (1968), 349; and Levin's "Shadows," p. 352. Levin's conclusion, of course, concedes the least to the anti-historicists; and the essays collected in his *Defense of Historical Literature* (New York, 1967) reveal the full depth and richness of his commitment to historical criticism.

3. Again, the problem with single-minded, "reductive" psychoanalytic readings of the tale (e.g. that of Frederick C. Crews) is that they very probably reverse vehicle and tenor: it seems likely that Hawthorne intended the figure of Goodman Brown to stand for a representative historical mentality and the tale's psychoanalytic suggestions to be applied to a complex historical case. In any event, it will not do to say that the story is about "escapism"; too much of the historicity so carefully wrought into the vehicle is then simply wasted, and all Hawthorne tales begin to collapse into the same tale. See Frederick C. Crews, *The Sins of the Fathers* (New York, 1966), esp. pp. 99-106.

4. See Doubleday, *Early Tales,* p. 202.

5. The present essay—a version of a chapter from a book-length study—was written well before the appearance of Bell's *Historical Romance.* He has, however, anticipated some of my own discussion—not only in trying to build on the insights of Levin, but also in seeing the direct comparability of ADA ["Alice Doane's Appeal"] with YGB ["Young Goodman Brown"] in terms of the theme of specter evidence. And though I quite appreciate what he means when he says that "what is obscured . . . in 'Alice Doane's Appeal' is revealed far more clearly in 'Young Goodman Brown'" (p. 76), I think the matter is not that simple: there is little genuine "confusion" in ADA; the "sensationalism" is entirely controlled and purposeful; and, really, the revised "Alice Doane" probably exists to make a technical statement about what is going on in YGB and how it works.

6. All quotations from the story are from the Riverside Edition of *The Complete Works of Nathaniel Hawthorne* (Boston, Mass., 1883) and will be identified by page number in the text. References to other Hawthorne works are from the same edition and will be identified by volume and page.

7. The story never actually *tells* us what night "of all nights" we are dealing with, but I see no reason to quarrel with the conjecture of Daniel Hoffman; see *Form and Fable in American Fiction* (New York, 1961), p. 150.

8. The most explicit comparison is made, with rather too much self-congratulation about originality, by Richard C. Carpenter in "Hawthorne's Polar Explorations," *NCF,* 24 (1970). The same sorts of similarities are pressed by Crews and, behind him, Melvin W. Askew and Richard P. Adams; see "Hawthorne, the Fall and the Psychology of Maturity," *AL,* 34 (1962), 334-343 and "Hawthorne's *Provincial Tales,*" *NEQ,* 30 (1957), 39-57.

9. The earliest article to stress the idea that what happens to Goodman Brown is the result of his own initial sin is that of McKeithan (see note 1). For a reading of the tale in terms of the twin unpardonable sins of Christian tradition, see the unjustly neglected article by Joseph T. McCullen, "'Young Goodman Brown': Presumption and Despair," *Discourse,* 2 (1959).

10. See his "Introduction" to "*Young Goodman Brown,*" p. 8. This "Introduction" is the third of Connolly's contributions to the Goodman Brown debate: the first is cited in note 1; the second—"How Young Goodman Brown Became Old Badman Brown," *College English* [*CE*], 24 (1962)—is conceived as an answer to Robert W. Cochran's "Hawthorne's Choice: The Veil or the Jaundiced Eye," *CE,* 23 (1962).

11. In my view, Hawthorne's ability to write YGB was as fundamentally dependent on his reading of Books Four and Five of the *Magnalia*—together with Cotton Mather's *Parentator*—as on any of the proven witchcraft sources, including Mather's own *Wonders of the Invisible World.* We know, from Kesselring, that Hawthorne read the *Magnalia* as early as 1827. And we strongly suspect, from the evidence of *Grandfather's Chair* (IV, 511-514), that it was a book he kept rereading, one that made as deep an impression on his mind as did *The Faerie Queene.* We also know that Hawthorne read the *Parentator* very early: he cites it in his early sketch of "Dr. Bullivant" (1831), though a corruption in the Riverside Edition obscures an allusion that is perfectly clear in the original (*Salem Gazette*) version. The impression of these works would have been augmented by a reading of Daniel Neal's *History of New England,* which derives from the *Magnalia,* and Benjamin Trumbull's *History of Connecticut* which, though written much later, rather "parallels" the *Magnalia.* But the *Magnalia* would have been enough: Cotton Mather's diagnosis of and prescriptions for the maladies of the third-generation Puritans would have given Hawthorne all he needed to know about the Half-Way Covenant and its *perceived* effects on the theory and practice of "visible sanctity." There, as Perry Miller has suggested, were all the jeremiad themes collected (if not exactly compressed) into one very troubled and very revealing book.

12. "Revisionist" interpretation of the precise significance of the Half-Way Covenant begins with Chapter Four of Edmund S. Morgan's *Visible Saints* (New York, 1963). After that moment of clarity, things have once again grown confused, but two other books seem essential: for the theology, Norman Pettit, *The Heart Prepared* (New Haven, Conn., 1966), esp. pp. 158-216; and for the sociology and ecclesiology, Robert G. Pope, *The Half-Way Covenant* (Princeton, N.J., 1969).

13. See, for example, Emil Oberholzer, Jr., *Delinquent Saints* (New York, 1956), pp. 7-12. The idea that the arrangements of 1662 cheapened the concept of vis-

ible Puritan sainthood seems to me at least as funda-mental an error as the coordinate idea Morgan set out to answer in *Visible Saints*; namely that the Half-Way Covenant was the prime and unambiguous cause of a real and widespread "declension."

14. This, as I have argued elsewhere, is precisely the representative problem faced by Edward Taylor in *Gods Determinations Touching His Elect*: now that there was *some* place for the doubtful, it took an ex-treme of something or other to declare for the status of "visible saint"; see "*Gods Determinations* Touch-ing Half-Way Membership," *AL*, 39 (1967).

15. The most important fact about the "Bullivant" sketch is precisely that any "literary" effect it may have been intended to have is lost in a welter of carefully qualified generalizations about the where and the when of "declension." It is obvious that somewhere between "Bullivant" and YGB Hawthorne solved his technical problems by substituting representative dra-matic instance for additive sociological generaliza-tion; but it cannot be shown that the locus of his his-torical interest changed very essentially. "Main Street" (1849) would be the other instructive ex-ample: it is at once a prosaic summary of the Puritan themes and situations Hawthorne had worked with in the tales written in the 1830's and preparation for a highly poetic treatment of those same materials in *The Scarlet Letter*. The burden of that sketch is, as Michael Bell has noted, the problem of what the original Puritan ancestors left to their descendants (see *Historical Romance*, pp. 62-64).

16. Although James W. Matthews is rather too casual in his suggestion that "A doctrine of one group of Cal-vinists during the time depicted in the story was An-tinomianism," still his suggestion that Brown's style of reliance on Faith is not quite salutary is well taken; see "Antinomianism in YGB," *Studies in Short Fic-tion*, 3 (1965). Ultimately, this sort of "moral argu-ment against Calvinism" may lie closer to the heart of the story than that stressed by Thomas E. Con-nolly—namely, the argument that Calvinism is really a religion of sin and damnation.

17. "Romance and the Study of History," in *Hawthorne Centenary Essays* (Columbus, Ohio, 1964), p. 233.

18. *The New England Mind: From Colony to Province* (Cambridge, Mass., 1953), p. 135. The last word on the problem of the Puritan "generations" is still far from being uttered. The new demographic studies make the lives of ordinary New Englanders of the third and fourth generations seem less melodramati-cally lurid than one might gather from Miller's evo-cation of their lives as ritualistic schizophrenia—regularly confessing the "declension" revealed in those social "sins" which their developing economy and inherited ethic made it impossible for them to avoid. But even the most reassuringly statistical of the new studies cannot entirely avoid raising "oedi-pal" questions. Only by about 1720 did Puritan sons begin to be significantly free of an original and pow-erful patriarchalism. See, for example, Philip J. Greven, *Four Generations* (Ithaca, N.Y., 1970), espe-cially pp. 261-289.

19. *Memorable Providences, Relating to Witchcrafts and Possessions*, quoted from David Levin, ed., *What Happened in Salem?* (New York, 1960), p. 102. Mather makes it clear that although witchcraft is in-deed the "furthest Effort of our *Original Sin*" (99), still all are "tempted hereunto" (102). In itself it is a kind of despair, since "All the *sure Mercies* of the New Covenant . . . are utterly abdicated" (98). But the *way into* witchcraft often involves presumption: "*Let him that stands, take heed lest he fall*" (102).

20. See Levin, "Shadows," p. 352; and Hurley, "Brown's 'Heart of Darkness,'" p. 411.

21. For a suggestive account of how guilty projection might have worked in the actual, outward world of witch accusations in seventeenth-century New En-gland, see John Demos, "Underlying Themes in the Witchcraft of Seventeenth-Century New England," *American Historical Review*, 75 (1970), 1311-1326.

22. The best way to prepare to read YGB with some-thing approaching adequate historical alertness is to make one's way through G. L. Burr's *Narratives of the Witchcraft Cases* (New York, 1914) and David Levin's *What Happened in Salem?* (see note 19). Hawthorne's historical insight also appears to good advantage if compared to that of modern commenta-tors: see, for example, Miller, *The New England Mind: From Colony to Province*, pp. 194-208; Marion L. Starkey, *The Devil in Massachusetts* (New York, 1949); and, for a revisionist emphasis, Chad-wick Hansen, *Witchcraft at Salem* (New York, 1969).

23. *An Essay for the Recording of Illustrious Providence* (Boston, 1684), p. 200. The extreme suggestiveness of the Increase Mather sentence and its context is not an argument *against* the relevance of other sources, particularly Cotton Mather's *Wonders*. See G. H. Orians, "New England Witchcraft in Fiction," *AL*, 2 (1930); Tremaine McDowell, "Nathaniel Hawthorne and the Witches of Colonial Salem," *Notes and Que-ries*, 166 (1934); Arlin Turner, "Hawthorne's Liter-ary Borrowings," *PMLA*, 51 (1936); and more re-cently, E. Arthur Robinson, "The Vision of 'Young Goodman Brown': A Source and Interpretation," *AL*, 35 (1963). I have already suggested that the *Magna-lia* may be as fundamental an influence on YGB as anything else; and the same would hold for the Red Cross Knight and Archimago episode of *The Faerie Queene*.

24. Evidently "Alice Doane's Appeal" takes up the Spenserian psychology directly: for Red Cross Knight and Leonard Doane alike, spectral deception is ultimately a form of guilty projection. Though the psychological dynamics are a little subtler in YGB they are essentially the same. In fact it is technically true to assert that the Red Cross Knight and

Archimago episode provided the "mythos" for YGB: in both cases a young man who is rather too sure of himself is separated from his one true faith because he believes spectral deceptions which enfigure his own moral obliquity. Book One of *The Faerie Queene* is thus an even more potent influence on YGB than has yet been recognized: see Randall Stewart, "Hawthorne and *The Faerie Queene*," *Philological Quarterly,* 12 (1933), and Herbert A. Leibowitz, "Hawthorne and Spenser: Two Sources," *AL,* 30 (1959).

25. Again Increase Mather's warning seems as much to the point as anything else: "we may not in the least build on the devil's word"; if we do, "the matter is ultimately resolved into a diabolical faith" (*Providences,* p. 200).

26. "Shadows of Doubt," p. 351. As I read Levin's argument, he does not really mean to say that all discussion of the nature and extent of human depravity is beyond the proper limits of all fiction, but only that *this story* is designed in such a way as to reveal that Goodman Brown (and we ourselves) can never really know the moral essence of others. Nor—contra Hurley—does he really deny that, once we *do* get beyond the "literal" level, Brown's experiences are "the product of his own fancy with no reality save that supplied by his depraved imagination" ("Brown's 'Heart of Darkness,'" p. 411).

27. "Fancy's Show Box" provides a useful gloss on YGB not only because it stresses the "spectral" and illusory relation of Mr. Smith's solid-seeming outward life to his inner or intentional life, but also because it stresses the variability of intention. If wicked intentions *do* produce "a stain on the soul," still this terrible doctrine is partly relieved by its counterpart; a reversal of intention blots out the stain: "one truly penitential tear would have washed away each hateful picture, and left the canvas white as snow" (I, 255). Furthermore, the dominant theme of the sketch seems to be the *extreme* fluidity of intention, the psychological impossibility of fixing oneself, once and for all, in a single moral state. For the most part, Hawthorne hypothetically argues (on behalf of Mr. Smith), we really do not know a firm intention from a flitting fantasy. "There is no such thing in man's nature as a settled and full resolve, either for good or evil, except *at the very moment* of execution" (257, my italics). Before an "act," intention is hypothetical; and afterwards as gloating or regretting memory, it is scarcely more substantial: one can continue to "will" a sin after its commission; but one can also repent. What this proves, quite simply, is that Hawthorne himself could not believe in the permanent psychological efficacy of a compact with the devil. Of course, he is an Arminian and not a Calvinist: not believing in predestination, he cannot personally believe in witchcraft as a reprobate's embracing of the inevitable; and he can see no other way to make a will-to-evil fixed and final. To be sure, the will-to-evil exists. Goodman Brown in mid-career *wants* to

fix himself in a depraved condition, and probably he goes as far as it is possible to go. But he pulls back. Doubtless Hawthorne would say that every other character in YGB has been similarly inclined, or had similar intentions, at various times; in the language of the story, they too had been into the forest, but had pulled back at the last second. What damns Goodman Brown, therefore, is something much subtler than a fixed and irreversible will-to-evil. It is his failure to believe that the will-to-evil is no more settled in others than it has been in himself. In short, he not only projects his guilt onto others, but he fixes it there. What has existed in his own soul as forest-temptation and then as forest-intention but never as forest-baptism must, he believes, exist in others as the final reality.

28. As is clear to us from a book like Morgan's *Visible Saints*—and as we are constrained to conclude was clear to Hawthorne from the *Magnalia*—American Puritanism's defining essence is the attempt to conflate the Visible with the Invisible Church, to test religious experience so severely that those who comprised the visible people of God should be only his elected saints. From *within* the premises of Calvinistic predestinarianism, Roger Williams was the first American to protest: after his career of purer-and-purer churches, he finally gave it up; deciding that election was a matter between the individual soul and God, he saw that the reality of election could not be made to guarantee *any* visible, worldly agency, whether magisterial or ecclesiastical. For a full and sympathetic account of his career, his doctrines, and his criticisms of the standard Puritan "Way," see Edmund S. Morgan, *Roger Williams: The Church and the State* (New York, 1967); Morgan's book, in turn, is deeply indebted to Perry Miller's *Roger Williams* (New York, 1953).

29. The formula is one which Frederick Crews applies to Hawthorne himself, in his relation to his hated Puritan "fathers" (see *Sins,* p. 38); but it applies a little more appropriately to Puritan Witches than to our blue-eyed Nathaniel. For Winthrop's account of the child-murderer, see his *Journal* (1790; rpt. New York, 1908), I, 230. Arguments about the undeniable reality and psycho-social meaning of the Salem witchcraft may be found in Hansen's *Witchcraft* (see note 22) and Kai T. Erikson's *Wayward Puritans* (New York, 1966), especially pp. 137-159.

30. For Goodman Brown's refusal of baptism as part of a pattern of contrary motivation, see Walter J. Paulits, "Ambivalence in 'Young Goodman Brown,'" *AL,* 41 (1970).

31. Ever since Richard Harter Fogle wrote that in YGB "Hawthorne wishes to propose, not flatly that man is primarily evil, but instead the gnawing doubt lest this should be the case" ("Ambiguity and Clarity in Hawthorne's 'Young Goodman Brown,'" *NEQ,* 18 [1945], 448), critics have been sensitive to a range of meanings other than a simple affirmation of Calvinist

Total Depravity. The effect of recent criticism is to make Hawthorne's *own* affirmations or denials more and more indirectly related to those of Goodman Brown: what does *Brown* believe? on what evidence? with what justification? My proposal is that though he is not absolutely certain the rest of the world is in league with Satan, his theoretical doubt amounts, practically, to a very strong suspicion. And, more important, that his suspicion is specifically and formally *of others*. Critics (like Connolly) too often assume that Brown's final state is to be described as a belief, or a near-belief, in the Devil's baptismal sermon on *total* depravity; I would suggest that, based on his own refusal of baptism, he is constantly making an exception for himself. However strongly he believes, or doubts, or suspects witchcraft in others, what he remembers about himself is not his mid-forest rage but his witch-meeting refusal.

32. For latter-day Puritan subtlety—not to say double-ness—see *The Return of Several Ministers Consulted*, reprinted in Levin, *What Happened in Salem?*, pp. 110-111. And for an example of the earlier mode of subtlety—on the distinguishing of hypocrites—see the selections Perry Miller has made from John Cotton's *The New Covenant*, in *The Puritans* (New York, 1938), I, 314-318.

33. Williams' solution, as I have already suggested (see note 28), was to suggest that, since true spirituality was so ineluctably "inner," there is really no such thing as a *true* church in this world. Stoddard, like Williams, remained a staunch Calvinist and gave over the project of trying to make ecclesiastical distinctions on his or anyone else's ability to detect the presence of saving grace; but he remained a staunch "theocrat." Treating the Lord's Supper as a "means," and admitting to it therefore all baptized persons of sound belief and upright life, he essentially demystified the idea of membership in a Puritan church (see Miller, *The New England Mind: From Colony to Province*, pp. 227-302). Arminians, of course, disbelieved in the doctrine of "final perseverance," and hence knew that *only* on the last day could the wheat and the tares be distinguished.

34. A very perceptive discussion of the problems raised by the notion of the "Judgement of Charity" is contained in Robert Middlekauff's *The Mathers* (New York, 1971). Especially interesting is the question of the subtleties the doctrine ultimately involved. Richard Mather, a Founding Father, spoke of "rational charity" but, as Middlekauff shrewdly suggests, "he might well have substituted 'suspicious' for rational" (pp. 52-53). A generation later, his son Increase, who knew (in the witchcraft proceedings) that the devil's ability to appear as an angel of light presented profound legal difficulties, also knew more about the difficulties of testing for saving Faith; he was, accordingly, more genuinely "charitable" in his "rational" judgements (pp. 126-133).

35. I have argued the "Rappaccini" case elsewhere: see "A Better Mode of Evidence," *Emerson Society Quarterly*, 54 (1969).

36. The speaker is Sister Soulsby, the female evangelist in *The Damnation of Theron Ware*. The context is the crassly revivalistic Methodism in the long since "burned-over" district of New York; but if the situation strikes us as more vulgarly modern than classically Puritan, still the theological (and the epistemological) problem is the same—the American-Evangelical problem of the distinguishing of Saints.

37. For evidence that the decision to admit to the status of "visible saints" only those tested for "gracious," or "faithful," or specifically "Christian" experience was the result of enthusiastic fervor, see David D. Hall's "Introduction" to *The Antinomian Controversy, 1636-1638* (Middletown, Conn., 1968), pp. 3-20. For a selected analysis of intimidating Puritan autobiographies, see Daniel B. Shea, Jr., *Spiritual Autobiography in Early America* (Princeton, N.J., 1968). The solemn charge quoted is from Thomas Shepard to his son, on the first page of his *Autobiography*. That particular document may stand as typical of the way first-generation Puritans created spiritual trauma and oedipal strife for their descendants; see *Publications of the Colonial Society of Massachusetts*, 27 (1932), 357-392.

38. For the emphasis of the popular romancers, see Bell, *Historical Romance*, pp. 99-100. The obvious analogue of the explicit historical moralizing Hawthorne does in ADA is Charles W. Upham's *Lectures on Witchcraft* (Boston, Mass., 1831).

39. In my view Michael Bell has generally underestimated the differences between Hawthorne and his contemporary writers of historical romance; less in the case of YGB than of other tales, but measurably. See *Historical Romance*, pp. 72-104.

40. The classic formulation of the argument that there was "nothing Puritan" about the Salem witchcraft is G. L. Kittredge's "Witchcraft and the Puritans," the last chapter of his famous *Witchcraft in Old and New England* (Cambridge, Mass., 1929). Though richer in examples, his argument is *in logic* identical with that of Charles Upham's second Salem lecture. In both authors, the argument is just as "tedious"—and, for precise intellectual history, just as "irrelevant"—as Perry Miller has suggested; see *The New England Mind: From Colony to Province*, pp. 191 ff.

41. As Miller formulates the case, "We shall avoid confusing ourselves by an irrelevant intrusion of modern criteria only when we realize that what struck Salem Village was intelligible to everybody concerned—instigators, victims, judges, and clergy—within the logic of the covenant" (*The New England Mind: From Colony to Province*, p. 192). The essence of that covenant, of course, remained the obligation to protect pure churches; and this obligation rested, in turn, on the ability to make a fairly reliable chart of

the invisible, moral world. Clearly Cotton Mather spoke the consensus when he suggested that, after many "abortive" attempts toward the "extirpation of the vine which God has here planted," the devil's growing desperation has led him to make "one attempt more upon us, an attempt more difficult, more surprising, more snarled with unintelligible circumstances than any hitherto encountered, an attempt so critical that if we shall get through, we shall soon enjoy halcyon days with all the vultures of hell trodden under our feet"; see *Wonders of the Invisible World* (Boston, Mass., 1693), p. 7.

42. The formula is one of my own devising, but one may infer it from Mather's *Magnalia*; and I believe it will adequately summarize the findings of Edmund S. Morgan in *Visible Saints*; see especially pp. 1-32.

43. The "Several Ministers" are quoted from Levin, *What Happened in Salem?*, p. 111. The document in question then goes on, as is well known, to "recommend unto the Government, the speedy and vigorous Prosecution of such as have rendered themselves obnoxious, according to the Direction given in the Laws of God, and the wholesome Statutes of the *English* Nation, for the Detection of Witchcrafts." If anyone felt any contradiction, the feeling is not recorded. And indeed, Cotton Mather subsequently makes quite clear (in the book which Perry Miller accuses of having "whitewashed" the whole legal proceedings and having "prostituted" the whole grand notion of the covenant) exactly what was at issue: if there should turn out to be *no way* to discover and prove a witch, then that fact "threatens a sort of disollution upon the world."

44. For Cotton vs Williams on the parable of the wheat and the tares, see Miller, *Williams*, pp. 102-128. Since for the mature Williams, the only *real* church was spiritual and invisible, the field in the parable had to refer to the world: *ex hypotheosi*, there could be no weeds in God's real church, and of course there were sinners and saints in the world. Cotton's problem was far more complicated: after the revival of the 1630's began to wear off, he came to accept (and even in certain contexts to defend) the idea of weedlike hypocrites among the wheatlike saints in the field of the New England Churches; but he never for a moment abandoned the idea of a pure church of visible (and for the most part true) saints as the prime agency of God's Glory in this world.

45. The verdict of Marion L. Starkey seems to echo that of Hawthorne: the witchcraft "had brought a division and a sore sickness of spirit on the people. Husband had 'broken charity' with his wife and wife with husband, mother with child and child with mother" (*The Devil*, p. 248). Starkey even wonders with something like bewilderment how a husband could come to suspect his wife on the strength of such evidence as the Salem trials were able to uncover. Hawthorne obviously felt horror and revulsion at such facts, but he seems to have been too familiar with the supernatu-

ral projects of the Puritans to have been really surprised at any such natural displacements.

46. It is also possible that, at another level of consciousness, Goodman Brown's name may owe something to the story, told in the records of the Plymouth Colony, of John Goodman and Peter Browne. The two mysteriously disappeared from the Community one day at noon. Assumed dead, the two were actually hunting. They got lost, fell asleep, and woke up terrified to hear "two lyons roaring exceedingly, for a long time together." The analogy is not too close; but the "lyons" may have been spectral, and Hawthorne surely knew what Adversary it was who "went about as a roaring lion, seeking whom to devour." For the story, see George F. Willison, *Saints and Strangers* (New York, 1945), pp. 163-165.

47. See *Wonders*, quoted in Burr, *Narratives*, p. 215. The text of 2 Corinthians 11:14 was widely cited during the witchcraft episode. And, as things distressingly turned out, it could be used in opposite ways. Granted: "Satan himself is transformed into an Angel of Light." But whereas Increase Mather used the doctrine to warn the rash about the subtle treacheries of spectral evidence, and so to restrain an overly vigorous prosecution, Cotton Mather evidently used it to "compass" the death of George Burroughs. See, on the one hand, Levin's selection from *Cases of Conscience Concerning Evil Spirits Personating Men* (*What Happened in Salem?*, pp. 117-129); and, on the other, the account given by Robert Calef of the death of George Burroughs (Burr, *Narratives*, pp. 360-361).

48. Starkey retains a hint of the older version: the people suddenly realized that "Their leaders had suffered the devil to guide them. They were turning from such leaders" (*The Devil*, p. 249). Miller's version is less melodramatic: "The onus of error lay heavy upon the land; realization of it slowly but irresistibly ate into the New England conscience. For a long time dismay did not translate itself into a disbelief in witchcraft or into anticlericalism, but it rapidly became an unassuageable grief that the covenanted community should have committed an irreparable evil" (*The New England Mind: From Colony to Province*, p. 208).

49. For the spread of Stoddardism *up to* 1692, see Pope, *Half-Way Covenant*, especially pp. 239-260. For the relation of Stoddardism to the Brattle Street Church, see Morgan, *Visible Saints*, pp. 139-152. Thomas Brattle's letter of 1692 is included in its entirety (along with most of Calef's *More Wonders*) in Burr's *Narratives*. And for Judge Sewall's change of heart, see his *Diary* (Mass. Hist. Soc., 45-47 [1878-1882]), for 19 August 1692 and 15 January 1696/7. And (finally) for a slightly different view of Salem witchcraft and the end of the authentic Puritan world, see Erikson, *Wayward Puritans*, pp. 155-159.

Leo B. Levy (essay date 1975)

SOURCE: "The Problem of Faith in 'Young Goodman Brown,'" in *Journal of English and Germanic Philology*, Vol. 74, No. 3, July, 1975, pp. 375-87.

[*In the following essay, Levy discusses the role of faith in "Young Goodman Brown" and contends that Hawthorne's intent is to depict the sin of falling into despair once faith is gone.*]

Few of Hawthorne's tales have elicited a wider range of interpretations than **"Young Goodman Brown."** The critics have been victimized by the notorious ambiguity of a tale composed of a mixture of allegory and the psychological analysis of consciousness. Many of them find the key to its meaning in a neurotic predisposition to evil; one goes so far as to compare Goodman Brown to Henry James's governess in *The Turn of the Screw*.[1] The psychological aspect is undeniably important, since we cannot be certain whether **"Young Goodman Brown"** is a dream-allegory that takes place in the mind and imagination of the protagonist, an allegory with fixed referents in the external world, or a combination of these that eludes our ordinary understanding of the genre itself. The story is all three: a dream vision, a conventional allegory, and finally an inquiry into the problem of faith that undermines the assumptions upon which the allegory is based.

Whether we think of the central episode of the witches' Sabbath as a dream or an hallucination, or as a nightmarish "real" experience, it must be placed in relationship to elements of the story that are outside Brown's consciousness. His point of view is in the foreground, but it must contend with the point of view of a narrator who is not identified with his perceptions. The narrator's irony and detachment, and his frequent intrusions, are measures of the distance he places between himself and a protagonist he regards with a mixture of condescension and pity. No fewer than three attitudes toward faith emerge from the story: Brown's, the view expressed in the concluding parable, and that which by implication is Hawthorne's. The elusiveness with which the narrative moves into Brown's state of mind and then outward arises from this complex view of faith, and also from the conception of Faith as a double, who "like Beatrice Rappaccini is both pure and poisonous, saint and sinner."[2] She is at once an allegorical idea and the means by which the idea is inverted. Those celebrated pink ribbons on Faith's cap—the objects of an astonishing range of responses by critics of the story—are vital to an understanding of her metamorphosis and of Brown's desperate efforts to recover his faith.

The impression that the story hovers on the borderline between subjective and objective reality derives from Hawthorne's suggestion that Brown's experience is peculiar to him and yet broadly representative. Not until the next to last paragraph are we offered what seems to be a choice between these alternatives: Hawthorne asks, "Had Goodman Brown fallen asleep in the forest and only dreamed a wild dream of a witch-meeting?"[3] His reply—"Be it so if you will; but alas! it was a dream of evil omen for young Goodman Brown"—is often taken to mean that we may read the story either way; but we may wonder why Hawthorne defers this question until the end. The reader may suspect that **"Young Goodman Brown"** is a tale in which reality is entirely subsumed by the consciousness of the protagonist; if so, his suspicion will be heightened when Hawthorne, in the sentence following his question and answer, less tentatively alludes to "the night of that fearful dream." And yet even this statement leaves the issue unresolved. This irresolution is not coyness on Hawthorne's part: if the dream theory were confirmed, it would have the effect of canceling a whole range of intimations that surround the dream but are not part of it. Through the dream metaphor the many hints of Brown's unconscious fascination with evil are communicated, but Hawthorne recognizes that our waking life and the life of dreams are bound up together—that life is like a dream in its revelation of terrifying truths. His point is that the truth conveyed in the dream—that faith may betray us—is also a truth of waking experience.

I

The story begins as a conventional allegory, creating the expectation that the characters will consistently exhibit the abstractions they symbolize. If Hawthorne intends Brown to be a pathological case, that intention is not evident in the early stages. The problem of man's journey into the mystery of evil is presented in the broadest possible terms. Faith Brown, the wife of three months, is simply "Faith," and Goodman Brown is Everyman. The bargain he has struck with Satan is the universal one, reinforced by such signs as the innocence with which he convinces himself that he can turn aside from his covenant and the assurances he offers himself of his good intentions. Initially, he is a naïve and immature young man who fails to understand the gravity of the step he has taken. Though Hawthorne does not provide a transitional development, he drastically alters this picture: the early indications of Brown's immaturity are succeeded by a presumably adult determination to resist his own evil impulses. His continuing willingness to join the community of sinners coexists with a reaction against that willingness. As the task of turning back becomes increasingly difficult, confronting him with one frustration after another, his struggle takes on heroic proportions.

Far from showing himself to be "a prospective convert who is only too willing to be convinced,"[4] Brown displays a mounting resistance to the Devil's enticements. No sooner does he leave Faith than "his heart smote him"; he replies to the Devil's reproach for his lateness at the appointed place, saying "Faith kept me back awhile." As the two travel into the forest the Devil observes the slowness of his companion's pace and ironically offers him his staff, thereby prompting the young man to confess, "I have scruples touching the matter thou wot'st of." He genuinely wishes to escape the Devil's snare: he withstands the revelation that the deacons and selectmen of his village, and the governor himself, have preceded him on this journey; and the discovery that Goody Cloyse, the old woman who had taught him his catechism, is a witch does not affect his determination to turn back: "What if a wretched old woman do choose to go to the Devil when I thought she was going to heaven: is that any reason why I should quit my dear Faith and go after her?" He assures himself that when he returns home he will meet the minister with a clear conscience, "nor shrink from the eye of good old Deacon Gookin"; he will sleep "so purely and sweetly now, in the arms of Faith!" It is not surprising that he is "ready to sink down to the ground, faint and overburdened with heavy sickness of his heart," when he learns that the deacon and the minister are of the Devil's company. Nevertheless, he cries out, "With Heaven above and Faith below, I will yet stand firm against the Devil!"

Beyond this point, Brown calls out three times for Faith to come out to his aid, and not until he sees a pink ribbon from Faith's cap that has fluttered down from the sky and caught on the branch of a tree does he abandon hope, crying "My Faith is gone." As if to reinforce the tangible evidence of Faith's desertion, Hawthorne writes that Brown "seized" and "beheld" the fateful ribbon. He now knows that Faith's voice has been mingled with the other "familiar tones, heard daily at Salem village," but now issuing from the depths of a cloud—from the company of Satan's followers sailing through the air. The most frightful episode of the tale follows: Brown becomes a "demoniac," "the chief horror" in a scene full of horrors—of terrible sounds made up of "the creaking of trees, the howling of wild beasts, and the yell of Indians." Utterly possessed by the Devil, he yields to the conviction that the world is given over to sin. But when silence falls and he enters the clearing where the assembly of the damned is gathered for the performance of its ritual, his hopes rise again because Faith, whom he expects to see, is not there. But she soon stands with him among those who are about to undergo their initiation. They are "the only pair, as it seemed, who were yet hesitating on the verge of wickedness in this dark world." They look at each other in fearful anticipation, and for the last time Brown calls out for help: "Faith! Faith! . . . look up to heaven, and resist the wicked one." But "whether Faith obeyed he knew not." The whole spectacle of the witches' Sabbath vanishes at this instant, and Brown, staggering against the rock that had formed the altar, finds himself alone in the wilderness.

It cannot plausibly be argued that Brown has all along been prone to the despair into which he is then plunged, since after abandoning himself to wickedness and turning himself into an image of the fiend he recovers his composure and calls upon Faith once more. He is alone among Hawthorne's many "demoniacs" in reversing the process of committing himself to evil. Nevertheless, the sequel shows him irrevocably fallen into gloom and despair, condemned to a long life of withdrawal and suspicion. Brown has exhibited a compulsive denial of his compact with the Devil; but when his efforts to recover his former relation-

ship with Faith collapse, he has no recourse except despair. No effort of the conscious will can save him. And yet the story is least of all a study, like **"Roger Malvin's Burial,"** of unconscious motivation. Instead, Hawthorne seems content to emphasize Brown's helplessness. The spiritual test to which he is submitted is conducted on terms that only demonstrate the futility of his attempts to extricate himself. Even if we suppose that he unconsciously chooses to end his dream before Faith can reply, thereby condemning himself to a lifetime of faithlessness, the fact remains that Hawthorne has caught him in a trap as diabolical as anything the Devil might invent.

The psychoanalytically oriented critics interpret Goodman Brown's helplessness in terms of the projective mechanism of the dream or fantasy, which they regard as symptomatic of mental illness.[5] The difficulty of this approach is not the contention that the presence of the Devil and his company and the rites into which Brown is drawn are projections, but that it ignores the conflict and resistance to which Hawthorne gives such explicit and emphatic attention. The projective aspect of Brown's experience is not the whole of it. His submission to evil suggests that the demands of the id have overtaken the ego; his prolonged resistance is a denial of the wishes that are the source of his projections. His conflict originates in the superego, whose task is to punish the ego for its defections and, as the voice of conscience, to repress the satisfactions of the instinctual life. Brown's recovery from the *Walpurgisnacht* episode, in which he gives way completely to the id, is made possible by the activated defense mechanisms of the ego, which cries out to be saved. If we wonder why the witches' Sabbath ends with such breathtaking abruptness, the answer might be that the ego cannot tolerate the threat of destruction that awaits it if the initiation rites take place. The sexually fraught demands of the id are put down, though at a terrible price. In psychoanalytic terms, **"Young Goodman Brown"** is about the defeat of the id by the ego and the superego. The result of this suppression is that Brown, despairing and embittered, belongs neither to the Devil's party nor to the only other life-sustaining cause he knows—that of the Puritan faith and the Puritan community. The withdrawal and gloom that envelop him after his return to the village come about not because he has yielded to the overwhelming vision of evil in the forest, but because he has repressed it. The ego forbids him to accept his evil impulses as his own; hence he projects them upon his wife, whose virtue he now distrusts, and upon the other villagers, in whose goodness he can no longer believe.

But this—or any other psychological interpretation—restricts our understanding of a story that is cast in religious and theological terms. We must move outside the limits of the dream or fantasy, beyond any view of the nature of the forest experience, and examine the ideas that structure that experience. A clue to the basic question raised by the story is provided by Henry James's complaint that "if it meant anything, it would mean too much."[6] James does not identify the specific source of his objection, but the context of his remark makes it clear that he believes that behind **"Young Goodman Brown"** is a kind of extravagance and even irrationality that gives rise to a "magnificent little romance," as he calls it, that cannot be taken seriously (James, p. 81). Evidently he found the image of a man pleading for faith and deprived of it with such arbitrariness baffling. The magical, supernatural, and mysterious connotations accompanying the disappearance of the witches' Sabbath and Brown's "awakening" may well have offended James's sense of fictional propriety as well as his sense of the writer's obligation to describe a moral crisis in rational terms. This development in the story originates in the Gothic idea of an irresistible and omnipresent evil. James, reacting against this vision, insists that the tale "evidently means nothing as regards Hawthorne's own state of mind, his conviction of human depravity and his consequent melancholy" (James, p. 81). However, it was not necessary for Hawthorne to literally subscribe to such a vision in order for his imagination to be powerfully engaged by it. The very excessiveness of his story is the source of its lasting impression upon those who have read it. Behind it is the motive that shapes such tales as **"John Inglefield's Thanksgiving," "The Minister's Black Veil,"** and **"The Christmas Banquet,"** among others, which are intelligible only on the principle that Hawthorne is dramatizing his feeling that once the commitment to evil has been made, its impact must prevail. There is no power strong enough to oppose it. In **"Young Goodman Brown"** the struggle is so unequal that Faith, supposedly the Devil's antagonist, is drawn into the camp of the enemy.

II

Not the least terrifying aspect of the story is the insinuation that Faith has made her own independent covenant with the Devil. There is a faint suggestion that her complicity may be prior to and deeper than Brown's. This "monstrous inversion," as Terence Martin aptly calls it,[7] is as sinister as anything to be found in Hawthorne's writings. This development is anticipated when Faith, imploring her husband not to leave her, says that "a lone woman is troubled with such dreams and such thoughts that she's afeard of herself sometimes," and she urges him to stay with her "this night . . . of all nights in the year." In this way, her bad dreams are linked to his, suggesting that both have prepared themselves for the same experience. However, we know nothing of the circumstances that bring her into the forest except what Brown discovers for himself. When Goody Cloyse tells the Devil that she has heard that "there is a nice young man to be taken into communion tonight," he denies the report, just as he had previously assured Brown that his Faith will not come to any harm. Brown overhears a voice like Deacon Gookin's declare that "there is a goodly young woman to be taken into communion," a statement offered not as something Brown imagines but given by one who does not know that he is listening. When the converts are brought forth, Brown approaches the congregation, "with whom he felt a loathful brotherhood by the sympathy of all that was wicked in his heart." He imagines—or sees—his father beckoning him on and his mother warning him back. Here again Haw-

thorne blurs the distinction between actual participants and projections. However, no such ambiguity attends the identification of "the slender form of a veiled female" brought forth by Goody Cloyse and Martha Carrier to take part in the baptismal rites: "the wretched man beheld his Faith, and the wife her husband, trembling before that unhallowed altar."

There is little agreement among critics about Faith as a character or as an allegorical figure. For some, Faith is allegorically consistent: Neal Frank Doubleday takes it as a sign of Faith's benevolence that when Brown calls upon Faith to "'resist the wicked one' . . . he is released from the witch-meeting."[8] Even those who recognize Faith's dual character argue that she retains her allegorical identity. For Roy R. Male, "almost everything in the forest scene suggests that the communion of sinners is essentially sexual and that Brown qualifies for it by his marriage."[9] And yet Male does not regard Faith's participation in the sexuality of marriage as an indication that she is "evil" in the sense that Brown is; one wonders why the sexual union leaves her free of the stain of original sin. Daniel Hoffman writes that "in one sense, she *is* the forest, and Brown has qualified for admission to the witches' orgy by having carnal knowledge of her."[10] Hoffman, too, absolves Faith of her share in the consequences of carnal knowledge: she "transcends Brown's knowledge of evil with all-encompassing love." In following Brown's corpse to the grave, "Faith remains true to him" (pp. 158, 156). But Hoffman's argument cannot resolve the paradox he himself describes: if "she *is* the forest"—if she too is guilty of carnal knowledge—how can she remain "the Devil's only antagonist in this tale," having "such faith in man that she can transcend the revelation that [Brown] is fallen?" (p. 167). After all, she too has fallen. The Devil's only antagonist, so far as the reader can tell, is Goodman Brown.

This confusion of the fictional character of Faith with the allegorical concept has its roots in the story itself. The basic thrust of the story is that faith is deficient, but the deficiency arises not from the personification of Faith as a woman and a wife but from Hawthorne's handling of the abstraction. He is not suggesting that Faith as an abstraction is susceptible to the human frailties of Everyman but somehow transcends them, even though he creates the correspondences that give rise to this misconception. His position seems to be that faith is a self-consistent principle, however unreliable and unpredictable. There is a submerged, possible unintended, but nonetheless dreadful irony in the manner in which Faith greets Brown on his return to the village, as if she had not been present in the forest and had played no part in the terrible events that take place there. She is as she was at the beginning—except that it is impossible for Brown to see her as she was. The meaning of the story arises from this discrepancy.

Faith's most conspicuous physical characteristic consists of the pink ribbons on her cap. They are the subject of many attempts to sustain an argument about her allegorical significance and to reconcile the two Faiths, one comely, almost lightsome, and the other in complicity with the powers of darkness. The ribbons provide the symbolic continuity between Faith as an ideal of religious fidelity and as a partner in a witches' Sabbath. The most obvious feature of these interpretations is their ingenuity and their diversity. To Thomas E. Connolly the ribbons "seem to be symbolic of [Brown's] initial illusion about the true significance of his faith, his belief that that his faith will lead him to heaven." Elsewhere, Connolly finds that they symbolize "illicit passion and purity." For Paul W. Miller, the ribbons "keep Faith humble and honest, and thus contribute to her ultimate preservation from the Evil One," and for E. Arthur Robinson they are "representative of woman's physical nature" and of Faith's sexual passion. Darrel Abel considers the ribbons "a badge of feminine innocence." For Paul J. Hurley, they represent "the ritualistic trappings of religious observance," and for Hyatt Waggoner they signalize Brown's immature faith. Richard H. Fogle has commented that "as an emblem of heavenly Faith their color gradually deepens into the liquid flame or blood of the baptism into sin."[11] There is no way to choose among views that differ so in their symbolic attributions; how one interprets the ribbons obviously depends upon one's prior understanding of the story.

F. O. Matthiessen observes of the scene in which Brown believes he has visible proof of Faith's betrayal that "only the literal insistence on that damaging pink ribbon obtrudes the labels of a confining allegory, and short-circuits the range of association." He evidently means that the ribbon fails to work symbolically in an otherwise powerful depiction of Brown's inner experience. He contrasts Hawthorne's image of the ribbon to Melville's metaphor of "the ball of free will" held (and dropped) by Ishmael and Queequeg in *Moby-Dick,* remarking that "only by discovering such metaphors can the writer suggest the actual complexity of experience."[12] But when Matthiessen adds that "we are bothered by the ribbon because it is an abstraction pretending to be something else" (p. 285), he fails to recognize that, on the contrary, it is because the ribbon is no more than a tangible object that its effect is "literal" rather than abstract, and for this reason cannot function metaphorically. It is simply a descriptive element, one of the realistic details that gives Faith such physical reality as she has. The ribbons belong to a fictional character described as "sweet," "pretty," and "little," more reminiscent of a genteel girl of Hawthorne's own day than a Puritan woman who might also have worn pink ribbons. She is the cheerful wife, one of Hawthorne's feminine figures, like Phoebe or Hilda, who serves as an emblem of steadfastness in a world of pollution.

David Levin argues that "Brown's sensory perception of the ribbons is no more literal or material than his perception of the Devil, his clutching of the staff, or his hearing of the Devil's statement about the fifteen-minute trip from Boston to the woods near Salem village."[13] Approving this view, Frederick Crews disputes the claim that the "tangible reality" of the pink ribbons is evidence that Faith is "really" in the forest, adding that "Brown shares Othello's fatuous concern for 'ocular proof,' and the proof that is seized upon is no more substantial in one case than in the other."[14] These critics do not perceive that whether we are looking at the story in psychological terms or in terms of evidence that Brown is beset by counterfeit images—spectres of real persons—conjured by the Devil, the literary relationships that give rise to these and other interpretations are still there, on the page and in the text. In this sense, it does not matter which critical perspective we choose to pursue. The ribbons are in fact an explicit link between two conceptions of Faith, connecting sweet little Faith of the village with the woman who stands at the Devil's baptismal font. We can legitimately disagree about the meaning of this duality; the fact remains that in proposing that Faith's significance is the opposite of what he had led the reader to expect, Hawthorne violates the fixed conceptual meaning associated with his character. This breaking of the allegorical mold is more than a technical violation of the genre: it turns the story in an entirely new direction, so that it is deprived of the essential feature of all allegory—the ability to derive an abstract truth from its unfolding.

As we have noted, Hawthorne combines the kind of allegory that depicts the interaction of characters in an external setting—a technique of "realistic" as well as allegorical narrative—with the internalization of the action in the mind of the protagonist, for the purpose of dividing the reader's perception of what is happening. The ambiguity that results has the effect of enriching the story; but when the method is applied to the ribbons, the effect is a kind of teasing. The ribbons intrude themselves upon the symbolic sphere of the story where they do not belong; they have no meaning except as a fanciful joke, a grace note woven into the solemn theme of the tale.[15] However, they have an important dramatic function: as we see them at the beginning and end of the story, the ribbons identify the physical as distinct from the allegorical character of Faith; we have no need to see them in symbolic terms, since Faith as an abstraction is fully defined by her name alone. They are part of her adornment of dress, and they suggest, rather than symbolize, something light and playful, consistent with her anxious simplicity at the beginning and the joyful, almost childish eagerness with which she greets Brown at the end. It is only in the forest scene that the single ribbon becomes disturbing. The critics have seized upon this ribbon no less desperately than Goodman Brown himself in order to establish the continuity of the allegorical theme. But it is by means of the ribbon that Hawthorne disrupts the allegory; all that we see of Faith now is the ornament that warrants her physical presence just when her allegorical presence vanishes. The moment is dramatic in the contrast of the frivolous, fluttering piece of ribbon with the darkness, agony, and doubt that envelop the scene. It is as if Hawthorne were saying, "Yes, it is truly Faith, as you see by this ribbon, who is no longer Faith."

The psychology-oriented critics believe that they solve the problem of the ribbons by saying that they are part of

Goodman Brown's dream, no more or less "real" than the rest of what his diseased mind invents out of its own necessities. This theory cannot tell us when the dream begins: does Brown dream that he bids good-bye to Faith? If so, then he may also be dreaming of his return to the village and of the despair that afflicts him, and even of his long, unhappy life and eventual death. Did he dream that he made a covenant with the Devil? Did he do so before he entered the forest to keep his appointment, waking from one dream only to fall victim to another, after a pointless evening walk? The story is constructed in such a way that questions of this kind cannot be answered; but it does make a distinction between Brown's departure and return and the period between them. We may believe that the interval is a dream, even though we cannot know when it begins. This assumption has much to be said for it; but if we follow it we must conclude that the ribbons are both in and out of the dream, that Brown is dreaming about something he is familiar with in his waking experience. It is little wonder, then, that the sight of the ribbon produces the shock that leads him to connect his dream with reality in such a devastating fashion. In emotional as well as visual terms, the world of the nightmare and the world of the Puritan community are united. This development is reinforced by the bewilderment of Brown's return to the village and its profoundly disorienting consequences. Perhaps it is not until he encounters the minister, Deacon Gookin, and Goody Cloyse, and then sees "the head of Faith, with the pink ribbons, gazing anxiously forth," that his faith is permanently shattered. The breakdown of the beliefs and assumptions that gave order and stability to his life is complete.

III

It is sometimes said that Hawthorne's purpose in **"Young Goodman Brown"** is to demonstrate the unresponsiveness of Puritanic Calvinism to the needs of the believer. However, Hawthorne's equation of the Puritan experience with the devil-worship that is its inversion is a form of dramatic hyperbole that should not be taken literally. The Puritan vision of evil was a dreadful one, and there can be no doubt that Hawthorne means to dramatize its excesses; but this is not the same thing as drawing up an indictment of Puritan faith. Hawthorne knew that witches' Sabbaths and Black Masses were not confined to Puritan New England, and he knew that the possibility of being overwhelmed by the discovery of the power of evil was universal. He reacted strongly against the bigotry, cruelty, and hypocrisy of his New England ancestors, but that reaction does not exhaust the complex judgment he formed of them. Even the Reverend Dimmesdale, that pious hypocrite, has in his possession a larger share of the truth about the human condition—truth that derives from his faith—than the romantic and memorable rebel, Hester Prynne. Hawthorne well knew the variability of the experience of faith among the Puritans. Elsewhere he shows us that it may lead to serenity, to a dehumanizing dogmatism, or to intense suffering of spirit. Faith may also, as in **"Young Goodman Brown,"** mysteriously abandon us.

As a form, allegory is a systematic organization of fixed beliefs; Hawthorne utilizes the form for the purpose of showing that the safety and security implicit in it are illusory. The meaning of the story is that its own simple definitions do not work. Instead, we are shown that there is no necessary connection between our critical need for faith and the responsiveness of faith. This is the larger significance of **"Young Goodman Brown,"** not the comfortable parable that warns us against the sin of despair, which the moralistic tenor of the conclusion would have us believe can be avoided if only we listen attentively enough. The last paragraph turns Brown into an object lesson; but, as is often the case with Hawthorne's tales, a truer meaning is discovered before this point of constriction is reached. In his penetrating analysis of the problem of faith in Hawthorne's fiction, Taylor Stoehr, writing of **"Rappaccini's Daughter"** as well as **"Young Goodman Brown,"** observes that "Hawthorne seems to throw the blame on his characters, while at the same time he gives them no possible means of saving themselves." Stoehr adds that "for a man who is always complaining about his characters' lack of faith, Hawthorne himself is singularly dubious about the possibilities of life and human nature."[16]

For Hawthorne, the loss of faith is always imminent, a danger that increases in proportion to our involvement in a moral reality that is always more unsettling than we like to believe. His concern in **"Young Goodman Brown,"** apart from describing the terrors of the Puritan struggle for faith, is with our inability to foresee the consequences of our choices or to judge the nature of the moral forces that press upon us. We can easily move past the point of return, and, like Goodman Brown, find that it is too late for what we want and need. Brown's last cry for Faith is the most poignant moment of the story, expressing his need to assimilate the experiences through which he has passed, and even his capacity to do so. The silence between dream and waking, or between the actuality of the witches' Sabbath and his ordinary life, is the silence of the void between spiritual need and spiritual sustenance. The reader is not less stunned than Brown himself, since he cannot easily resolve the paradox into which he has been led. He saw Brown at the outset abandon Faith; if that were all that he is meant to see, the tale would be very simple. But now the reader finds that Faith has deserted Brown—a distinction that may seem elusive but is nevertheless the crux upon which everything turns. Faith is originally the "good angel" to whose skirts Goodman Brown resolves to cling hereafter. To suggest that the good angel may turn herself into a demon is an insight that Hawthorne does not often risk, though there is also a hint of the diabolical in the transformations through which he takes Priscilla in *The Blithedale Romance*.[17]

Hawthorne typically pays detailed attention to the costume and dress of his feminine characters as symbolic evidences of the stages through which they move. Except for her ribbons, Faith is pictorially a cipher, an abstraction for which Hawthorne refuses symbolic amplification, perhaps because of his sense of its precarious status. Therefore, Faith (or faith) becomes unresponsive, it disappears, and when it reappears it stands in the midst of all that it dreads. If, awaking at midnight, Goodman Brown shrinks from the bosom of Faith, it is because he has taken the full measure of her duplicity. "Such loss of faith is ever one of the saddest results of sin." Hawthorne says of Hester Prynne, and in *The Scarlet Letter* he castigates "the Fiend" for leaving nothing "for this poor sinner to revere."[18] But in **"Young Goodman Brown"** it is Faith, not Satan or the sinner, whose defection is at issue.

Notes

1. Darrel Abel, "Black Glove and Pink Ribbon: Hawthorne's Metonymic Symbols," *NEQ* [*New England Quarterly*], 42 (1969), 180.

2. Roy R. Male, *Hawthorne's Tragic Vision* (New York, 1964), p. 77.

3. Quotations from "Young Goodman Brown" are from *The Complete Short Stories of Nathaniel Hawthorne* (Garden City, N.Y., 1959), pp. 247-56.

4. David Levin, "Shadows of Doubt: Specter Evidence in Hawthorne's 'Young Goodman Brown,'" *AL* [*American Literature*], 34 (1962), 350.

5. Paul J. Hurley attributes the ambiguity of the story to "Hawthorne's suggestion that the incredible incidents in the forest were the product of an ego-induced fantasy, the self-justification of a diseased mind" ("Young Goodman Brown's 'Heart of Darkness,'" *AL,* 37 [1966], 419). According to Frederick Crews, the Devil's address to Brown and his fellow initiates, itemizing the sexual sins of mankind, "issues from Brown's own horror of sexuality in married love" (*The Sins of the Fathers: Hawthorne's Psychological Themes* [New York, 1966] p. 102). Michael Davitt Bell argues that "if Brown's experience in the woods is real, then this is a tale about the depravity of mankind. . . . But if the experience . . . is dreamed . . . then the story is hardly moral at all. In this case Brown . . . is simply sick" (*Hawthorne and the Historical Romance of New England* [Princeton, N.J., 1971], p. 77).

6. Henry James, *Hawthorne* (1879; rpt., New York, 1956), p. 81.

7. Terence Martin, *Nathaniel Hawthorne* (New York, 1965), p. 93.

8. Neal Frank Doubleday, *Hawthorne's Early Tales: A Critical Study* (Durham, N.C., 1972), pp. 208-209.

9. Male, p. 78.

10. Daniel Hoffman, *Form and Fable in American Fiction* (New York, 1965), p. 158.

11. Thomas E. Connolly, "Hawthorne's 'Young Goodman Brown': An Attack on Puritanic Calvinism," *AL,* 27 (1956), 374; Connolly, "Introduction," *Nathaniel Hawthorne: Young Goodman Brown,* The Merrill Literary Casebook Series, ed. Thomas E. Connolly (Columbus, Ohio, 1968), p. 9; Paul W. Miller, "Haw-

thorne's 'Young Goodman Brown': Cynicism or Meliorism?" *NCF* [*Nineteenth–Century Fiction*], 14 (1959), 260; E. Arthur Robinson, "The Vision of Goodman Brown: A Source and Interpretation," *AL,* 35 (1963), 224; Abel, p. 169; Hurley, "Young Goodman Brown's 'Heart of Darkness,'" p. 416; Hyatt Waggoner, *Hawthorne: A Critical Study* (Cambridge, Mass., 1963), p. 210; Richard H. Fogle, "Ambiguity and Clarity in Hawthorne's 'Young Goodman Brown,'" *NEQ,* 17 (1945), 456.

12. F. O. Matthiessen, *American Renaissance* (New York, 1941), p. 284.

13. Levin, p. 350.

14. Crews, p. 101.

15. Edwin Honig, *Dark Conceit: The Making of Allegory* (New York, 1966). Honig writes of "analogical baiting or teasing of the reader" as a result of an unsuccessful evolving of narrative correspondences, rather than of a deliberate withholding of the symbolic term (p. 125). Commenting on the symbolism of "Young Goodman Brown," Honig says that "the detail of the stick that looks like a serpent—that 'might be seen to twist and wriggle itself'—may be taken on the factual level for 'an ocular deception, assisted by the uncertain light.' On another level, it is vitally relevant to Brown's search for and subsequent disillusionment with the faith of his ancestors" (p. 128). Honig does not discuss the ribbons; it should be noted that Hawthorne specifies the correspondence between the literal and symbolic levels of Satan's staff—it looks like a serpent and hence is associated with other like elements of the story. No such correspondence is supplied for the ribbon.

16. Taylor Stoehr, "'Young Goodman Brown' and Hawthorne's Theory of Mimesis," *NCF,* 23 (1969), 406-407.

17. Leo B. Levy, "*The Blithedale Romance*: Hawthorne's Voyage Through Chaos," *SIR* [*Studies in Romanticism*], 8 (1968), 1-15.

18. *The Scarlet Letter,* The Centenary Edition (Columbus, Ohio, 1962), p. 87.

Terence J. Matheson (essay date 1978)

SOURCE: "'Young Goodman Brown': Hawthorne's Condemnation of Conformity," in *The Nathaniel Hawthorne Journal,* 1978, pp. 137-45.

[*In the following essay, Matheson interprets "Young Goodman Brown" as Hawthorne's condemnation of a society that emphasizes conformity over spiritualism. Matheson argues that Brown's overriding concern for conformity, rather than a moral rejection of evil and sin, keeps him from joining with the Devil.*]

At first glance, it might appear farfetched to see Hawthorne's Goodman Brown as the spiritual ancestor of someone like Sinclair Lewis's Babbitt. Nevertheless, there is considerable evidence that the same preoccupation with social convention, public appearance, and conformity in general that characterized Lewis's twentieth-century protagonist is behind most of the speeches and actions of Hawthorne's seventeenth-century Puritan. Indeed, if Brown does lose the battle with the Devil for his soul, a case can be made that his lack of self-reliance is the most important contributing factor in his damnation.

Virtually everything Brown says and does stems from a concern with preserving his public image in some form or other. This is first seen as he bids farewell to his "aptly-named" and obviously allegorical wife Faith. That Faith is Brown's wife, and hence "his," is symbolically just as important to the story as is her name. For this indicates that whatever can be said about her symbolic role actually applies to some aspect of Brown. They speak in a strangely ritualistic and artificial tone, as if their conversation had been rehearsed, neither Brown nor his wife really meaning what each says to the other. They give the impression of speaking not from conviction, but as if reciting lines from a prepared text. Faith's initial comment, a rather saccharine appeal to put off his journey, might appear well-intentioned enough, even though it has a lackluster ring to it. But when Brown refuses absolutely to cede to her request, brushing her off with an unconvincing speech of his own (he gives no reasons, but merely states dogmatically that he "must" go), rather than press the issue, she concludes with "'God bless you.'"[1] This suggests, among other things, that she had not expected him to change his mind and spoke not from conviction but simply because she believed it was expected of her.

Also important is that Faith seems to know why Brown is leaving her. She is plainly aware that his journey, far from being routine and normal, involves danger and perhaps evil as well. Her reference to "this" night—probably Hallowe'en—"'of all nights in the year'" (p. 74), reveals her awareness that no good Puritan would venture forth from the Christian security of his home on this particular evening, unless he was up to no good. In spite of all this, we see only "melancholy" in Faith's expression (rather than sorrow, frustration, despair, or even anger) when Brown, having paid no attention to her, proceeds on his way.

Had Hawthorne wished us to see sincere efforts to dissuade Brown, surely he would have shown her persisting in her appeal. That she does not leads one to suspect the quality of Brown's religious faith generally.[2] It certainly says a great deal about the kind of man we are dealing with, a man whose faith can provide only token guidance in a predictable and uncompelling manner. Clearly, as Brown does not take his wife's plea seriously—there is no reason why he would, so lacking in vehemence is her appeal—so he does not take faith and all that goes with it any more seriously. Religious faith is to him something "pretty" but lacking in substance or strength, something pleasant to possess but of no importance as a guide to his behavior; in a phrase, it is something to pay lip service to.[3]

Brown's opening reply to Faith, that his journey "'must needs be done'" (p. 74), demonstrates his firm resolve in this matter: despite all that has been said about Brown's naiveté, it is plain that he has a reasonable notion of what he is about to do. He knows his purpose is "evil" and that he is a "'wretch'" to leave her "'on such an errand'" (p. 75); later, we are told his meeting with the Devil is "not wholly unexpected" (p. 76).

Brown then tells Faith, "'Say thy prayers . . . and go to bed at dusk, and no harm will come to thee'" (p. 75), advice which says much about his character. First, if he really believes that personal harm can be avoided so easily, he is more than a little naive. But more important, he assumes that all one need do to guarantee salvation is go through the motions of piety by observing a few simple precepts that pertain to superficial conduct alone. Saying prayers and retiring early are far from the most essential means whereby one attains purity of soul. That Brown believes them to be important indicates a serious deficiency in his moral sense. He is unaware that genuine virtue is an inner quality which bears at best only an incidental relationship to one's seemingly virtuous social and religious behavior.

Leaving Faith, Brown reassures himself that "'after this one night'" of sin he will "'cling to her skirts and follow her to Heaven'" (p. 75), an assumption even more vacuous. No intelligent Puritan would ever have maintained that salvation depended on geographical proximity to another, apparently virtuous person; on a literal level, the state of Faith's soul says nothing about the state of Brown's. But the passage also reveals that Brown thinks he can consciously perform secret acts of evil and return, unscathed, to the fold of true virtue; that by creating only an illusion of piety in the community, while simultaneously doing evil things, he can still be virtuous and get to Heaven. Here, the true core of his morality lies only in keeping up appearances. He does not understand true, inner goodness; his only moral criterion consists in conforming to social postures of which his society approves.

Brown's conversation with the Devil supports the above contention. Here, on several occasions he appears to resist the Devil, and on the surface his resistance seems to speak well of him. However, when his reasons for resistance are examined, it is plain that they do not proceed from a meaningful appreciation of the moral issues involved. For Brown's "scruples," at least initially, are only that neither his father nor grandfather ever "went into the woods on such an errand" (pp. 76-77). What bothers Brown is simply that in continuing along with the Devil, he would be deviating from the "virtuous" behavior that he believes his social superiors upheld. The nonconformity and unconventionality of his journey prompt Brown's hesitation rather than any real awareness that consorting with the Devil is intrinsically sinful.

The Devil dismisses Brown's argument with a brief but revealing account of his forefathers' hypocrisies. Strictly speaking, the Devil's reply is weak and irrelevant. First, there is no proof that what he says is true. But even if it were, the evil acts of a man's ancestors could not justify his pursuit of a present evil course, as Brown will soon conclude. To anyone possessing even a modicum of moral awareness, this would be self-evident. But to Brown, for whom conformity has been the whole of his morality, the Devil's revelation and its personal implications are difficult to refute. That Brown is shocked by the eye-opening information is understandable, but that he cannot penetrate its illogic suggests his own moral shallowness and the paucity of his moral principles.

Brown doggedly proceeds in his resistance and asks how he could "'meet the eye of that good old man, our minister, at Salem village?'" (pp. 77-78). As before, Brown's underlying point is his fear of the consequences of deviating from accepted social mores. What also bothers him is the possibility that he could not conceal his soon-to-be-evil, but true, identity in public, before this admired (and presumably admiring) pillar of society, the minister. In a similar vein, he adds that it would break Faith's heart, were he to cooperate with the "elder traveller." Throughout, he fears only exposure to those whose respect or admiration he craves. To underscore this fact, Hawthorne does not allow Brown to make a strong moral point anywhere in his conversation with the Devil. At no time, for example, does Brown ever touch on the intrinsic immorality of the Black Mass. Nowhere does he say, simply, that he refuses to go on because it is morally wrong to do so. Conspicuous by its absence is any mention by Brown of the evil involved in Devil worship, because Brown has no awareness as to *why* it is evil. His only concern is that to behave in such a manner would be not to conform.

That the Devil recognizes this characteristic and deals with it accordingly is seen in the all-too coincidental appearance of "Goody Cloyse," who may well be a specter conjured up to drive the young conformist to even greater distraction.[4] Significantly, Brown, always conscious of appearances, takes "a cut through the woods" (p. 78) so as not to be seen behaving unconventionally. There, he is provided with evidence that would seem to put Goody clearly in the Devil's camp. In one sense what Brown hears is understandably disconcerting; a naive young man has been convinced of weaknesses and failings in a person he has hitherto respected from childhood. But, however shocking or disillusioning the experience may be, there should not be quite the "world of meaning" (p. 80) for Brown in his simple discovery that a respected member of the community may have an evil side or be a consummate hypocrite. Hawthorne's suggestion that Brown has been shaken to the core reinforces our awareness that his entire morality has been based on the public behavior of members of his society. Furthermore, when these behavioral models fail him, he will be left with nothing, his conscience having virtually atrophied during his social indoctrination.

Brown does appear to come close to the truth in his final exchange with the Devil:

"Friend," said he, stubbornly, "my mind is made up. Not another step will I budge on this errand. What if a wretched old woman do choose to go to the devil, when I thought she was going to Heaven! Is that any reason why I should quit my dear Faith, and go after her?"

(p. 80).

Although this may well represent Brown's closest proximity to the real issue, his speech is deficient, if not in the argument, at least in the manner of its presentation. First, he speaks "stubbornly" rather than from conviction. Secondly, he phrases his point as a question, suggesting doubt of the argument's worth. Surely, Brown's words are not spoken by a man firmly convinced of what he is saying. He does not put his point forcefully (for example, saying "That *is* no reason") but phrases it in an indecisive, interrogative form that seems to invite a rebuttal by the Devil.

At all events, Brown has unwittingly stumbled close enough to the central moral issue to cause the Devil to retreat temporarily, there being no satisfaction for Satan in forcing a person into Hell against his will. He retires, and Brown, flushed with smug triumph, does not think of the moral victory he appears to have won, but basks in un-Christian self-satisfaction, complacent about what an upstanding citizen he is. His thoughts are not of how pleased God would be with him, but only with how pleasant his relationship to society has become. Hawthorne refers to Brown's meditations as "pleasant and praiseworthy" (p. 81), the sarcasm reminding us that his victory has been illusory.

Brown hears footsteps and again hides, having "deemed it advisable to conceal himself within the verge of the forest, conscious of the guilty purpose that had brought him thither, though now so happily turned from it" (p. 81). Again, Brown's appearance in the community remains more important to him than the inner state of his soul. His purity, if genuine, should have produced greater openness on his part, since, if the victory were genuine he would have nothing to hide. That he does conceal himself shows where Brown's deepest concerns still lie. Even at this moment of apparent strength, he is plainly fearful of his social superiors seeing him in a moment of unconventional behavior.

Hawthorne creates much ambiguity surrounding the encounter with "the voice like the deacon's" and "the solemn old tones of the minister" (p. 81) to make us question what Brown thinks he sees. But Brown, trained to emulate his elders as paragons of virtue, is disillusioned by his discovery. He despairs, "doubting whether there really was a Heaven above him," despite "the blue arch, and the stars brightening in it" (p. 82). There is no justification for Brown to reach such extensive and dismal conclusions; that he does so reveals again that he has no inner moral principles to fall back on. Brown reacts as if he has seen God Himself on His way to a Black Mass, and indeed in a way he has, for to the unfortunate conformist his human elders have always been his true gods.

We have seen that the only reason for Brown's reluctance to participate at the Mass is his fear of the social consequences should his participation be discovered; there is no evidence that he would not want to go if he knew he could get away with it. Could he be convinced that everyone else was behaving in a similar manner, the only major obstacle would be removed. It is doubtless for this reason that Brown seems at times to be looking for excuses to attend. Hawthorne's comment that the Devil's arguments in favor of attending seemed "to spring up in the bosom of his auditor" (p. 80); Brown's readiness to believe the worst of his fellows in the light of increasingly flimsy pieces of evidence; Hawthorne's observation of Brown's "instinct that guides mortal man to evil" (p. 83) and his reminder that Brown "was himself the chief horror of the scene" (p. 83): all suggest that Brown has been looking for a way of justifying his participation, by rationalizing that everyone else has done likewise. If so, it is not surprising that Brown's next—and least convincing—vision should involve a cloud that he suspects is bearing all the townspeople to the Mass and sounds of their voices that could easily be "the murmur of the old forest" (p. 82). The vision concludes with the appearance of a pink ribbon out of the sky, presumably linking Faith with the Devil-worshippers. But though the ribbon is by itself no necessary proof of Faith's participation at the Mass, Brown by this point is ready—too ready—to suspect the worst of everyone, and concludes that she "'is gone.'" While this conclusion is flimsy, flimsier still is Brown's second conclusion, that "'There is no good on earth; and sin is but a name. Come, devil! for to thee is this world given'" (p. 83).

Brown reaches this conclusion because, having no concept of moral life as involving a personal relationship with moral values, he can conceive of it only as a social relationship with his community; in short, if others do it, to the conformist Brown it must be "right" or at least permissible. It is significant that he gives in immediately after concluding that *all* the others are on their way. His ensuing, almost eager rush to the Mass is consistent with his earlier conformity, for he is still doing what everyone else does, literally going along with the crowd, and is as oblivious to alternatives as he is to the evil involved; the voice of his conscience is nowhere to be heard. Hawthorne exposes the true weakness of the conformist's morality, by demonstrating how a man, whose every prior act has been based on the behavioral examples set by his society, behaves when he learns (or thinks he has learned) that this society regularly commits acts of evil. Having always conformed, Brown can have nothing but conformity to fall back on. Rather than see that these superiors in the community are not and never were valid models worthy of blind emulation, given the instinctively evil nature of man, and that mere conformity can never be a valid guide of action for this reason, Brown continues to conform to these same models even though he ought to realize that they are no longer worthy. Why he does so is possibly for reasons of security or habit, or because he simply "wants to." Most important, it reveals his ignorance as to how he might otherwise behave. That Brown is conforming when he rushes to the Mass is evident from Hawthorne's many suggestions that he is actually blending into the atmosphere of the evil forest and becoming indistinguishable from it: his laugh is echoed by the forest's laugh, and his cry "was lost to his own ear, by its unison with the cry of the desert" (p. 84). Brown has become one with his surroundings, the perfect mark of the conformist, by adapting his own behavior to that around him, in "awful harmony."

The entire spectacle of the Black Mass may well be presented by the Devil merely to confirm Brown's own belief in the ubiquity of human evil. It is interesting that despite the Devil's detailed catalogue of the vices and sins of Brown's fellows, he says nothing that Brown has not already determined on his own. For example, when Satan concludes that "'Evil is the nature of mankind. Evil must be your only happiness'" (p. 88), he agrees with Brown's earlier conclusion that there was no good on earth and that the world was given over to the Devil. As for Brown's witnessing of Faith at the Mass, he has already concluded that she is on her way there; doubts about his relatives have occurred very early in the tale. It is not really surprising, then, that Brown does see virtually everyone; he has already determined that he would do so. Nor is it surprising, given his conformity that Brown is initially powerless to resist. Appropriately, "the minister and good old Deacon Gookin seized his arms, and led him to the blazing rock" (p. 86); as before, since they are typical of the forces determining his every act, they continue to have dominance over him.

Why, then, does Brown resist the baptism, in a final surge of apparent strength? Surely, we have been given little if any evidence that Brown has enough strength to resist. Indeed, we have every reason to doubt his sincerity and to suspect that, even if he is doing the right thing, it may be for the wrong reasons.[5] If Brown's resistance were meant to be seen as virtuous, surely Hawthorne would have prepared us in some way to believe Brown capable of such an act. Instead, he has made every effort to demean Brown in our eyes, presenting him as utterly lacking in moral sophistication or sensitivity. Brown is not merely a naive, but basically good, man: he is superficial, cunning, and consummately hypocritical. Why then this apparent reversal?

The only answer can be that no reversal has been intended by Hawthorne and that no deviation from what we have seen of Brown's character has taken place. Close examination of the passage immediately preceding Brown's resistance makes this clear: "The husband cast one look at his pale wife, and Faith at him. What polluted wretches would the next glance shew them to each other, shuddering alike *at what they disclosed* and what they saw!" (p. 88, my italics). We have seen before that Brown's public image and resulting social status mean a great deal to him. Significantly, he does not resist the Devil earlier, when the Devil promises Brown that "'It shall be yours to penetrate, in every [other!] bosom, the deep mystery of sin . . .'" (p.

87). What bothers him is the sudden realization that such disclosure is to be mutual. It is only at this point, realizing that others will in turn see *him* as he truly is—a wretch—that he balks, and he resists not in the name of virtue but from the same fear of exposure to the public of his true nature (and the nature of his "faith") that has characterized his every previous action. Still obsessed with the need to protect his public image, even in these bizarre circumstances, Brown resists participation in the loathful brotherhood for the wrong reasons: because he is afraid of revealing himself as he actually is, not because he has seen that such participation is intrinsically evil.

He may also be dimly aware that such resistance would give him a tremendous social advantage over his fellows, for by resisting he becomes himself a pinnacle of apparent virtue, at least in his own eyes. Others may well look up to him, and certainly he will be able to derive great satisfaction from his resistance. Certain events do seem to point to this. Brown was seen before, just after his earlier "victory" over the Devil, as a self-righteous man. Moreover, Hawthorne suggests that this self-righteousness remains with him for the rest of his life, as Brown continues to regard himself as the one pure man in a community of hypocrites. As he shrinks from his wife or shudders at the minister, it is hard not to suspect that he is taking perverse satisfaction from these constant reminders of what a virtuous fellow he is in contrast with other members of his society. If the "goodly procession" of followers at his funeral is any indication, Brown has achieved his goal, having become a respected if not loved member of society. The hollowness of his achievement is, of course, underscored by Hawthorne's brief summary of his joyless life and gloomy death, the latter comment reminding us that he had essentially sold his soul for the social status he enjoyed.

Hawthorne also shows the paradoxical nature of Brown's final relationship to his society. Obsessed by the discovery that his society is unworthy of emulation, he cannot embrace "the sacred truths of our religion" (p. 89) or take succor from the hope offered by "saint-like lives"—true examples of virtue—because there is within his mind no room for such truths to exist, let alone grow. Obsessed with the realization that his society failed to provide adequate moral leadership, he is nonetheless so preoccupied with societal concerns to the exclusion of spiritual ones that any true sense of higher moral purpose is forever beyond him. Brown's relationship to his society, rather than his relationship to God, is still his only concern. Though he turns away from his now-reviled, former social ideals, he can conceive of no higher sphere to which he could turn that would provide him with meaningful, alternative moral knowledge; hence, his despair and gloom and his life-long obsession with his society's hypocrisy.

In a sense, **"Young Goodman Brown"** becomes as much a criticism of a rigid, conformity-ridden society as it is a portrayal of one man's lack of self-reliance. Surely, had the importance of one's public image and the consequent need to assume social postures not been so deeply impressed on Brown, and had more attention been focused on personal virtue and integrity as things of value, Brown would probably have been able to rise above the Devil's temptation to despair. That he could not is an indictment of both Brown and the society he lived in, a community where the importance of conformity has run rampant, with disastrous consequences for all concerned.

Notes

1. Nathaniel Hawthorne, "Young Goodman Brown," in *Mosses from an Old Manse,* volume 10 of *The Centenary Edition of the Works of Nathaniel Hawthorne,* edited by William Charvat et al. (Columbus: Ohio State University Press, 1974), p. 74. Subsequent references to this source are parenthesized in the text.

2. The shallowness and hypocrisy of Brown's "Faith" are again emphasized at the Mass, if one chooses to disregard David Levin's "spectral" theory and assume that she is really present. On the literal level, her participation makes a mockery of her plea to keep Brown at home. See below, fn. 4.

3. Other critics have, of course, made this point before. See, for example, Paul Hurley, "Young Goodman Brown's 'Heart of Darkness,'" AL [*American Literature*], 37 (Jan., 1966), 410-419.

4. For a detailed examination of this possibility, see David Levin, "Shadows of Doubt: Specter Evidence in Hawthorne's 'Young Goodman Brown,'" *AL,* 34 (Nov., 1962), 344-352.

5. Many critics contend that, though Brown may not have emerged the better for his experience at the Black Mass, his resistance to it was still a good act and speaks well of him. In one of the more interesting recent attempts to show how and why Brown has failed, Walter Paulits has argued that Brown has been tricked by the Devil into failing to distinguish between the knowledge offered him of human evil—in itself not intrinsically evil—and the temptation to make evil one's only good, which is evil. Brown presumably sees the evil of the latter and resists accordingly, but ignores the necessity of grasping the former, and spends the rest of his life in doubt and indecision. Still, Paulits feels the basic act of resistance to be one of virtue. See "Ambivalence in 'Young Goodman Brown,'" *AL,* 41 (Jan., 1970), 577-84.

Frank Shuffelton (essay date 1979)

SOURCE: "Nathaniel Hawthorne and the Revival Movement," in *American Transcendental Quarterly,* Vol. 44, Fall, 1979, pp. 311–32.

[*In the following essay, Shuffelton examines "Young Goodman Brown" in the context of New England spiritual revival movements of the 1820s and 1830s, finding some parallels between revival meetings and Brown's experience in the forest.*]

Because the best of Nathaniel Hawthorne's fiction so often incorporates historical materials, a great deal of scholarly attention has been devoted both to these materials and to his use of them. Although this activity is crucial to our understanding of Hawthorne's work, our concern with his artful transformation of his sources can also mislead us about the nature of his imagination and his art. Intensive study of Hawthorne's use of history ironically tends to encourage the stereotype of the recluse writer in a Salem attic by suggesting that his working out of universal human dilemmas in historical terms displaced any interest in the immediate problems of his society. Hawthorne the lonely artist is such an appealing figure that it is easy to forget Samuel Goodrich's industrious editor, the worker at Brook Farm, the customs official, and the campaign biographer; he was enmeshed in the issues of his age even if they did not appear directly in his fictions.[1]

His ability to connect past and present has not been overlooked, but the presence of so many portraits of ancestral Hawthornes has focused critical attention upon the personal nature of the connection at the expense of its social dimension. **"Young Goodman Brown"** for example has stimulated many valuable studies of Hawthorne's use of his sources and of his family's involvement in persecuting Quakers, killing Indians, and hanging witches, and these studies have considerably enriched our understanding of the story.[2] Our understanding can be still richer, however, if we also consider certain intellectual and religious crises of the early 1830's when Hawthorne was writing the story he first published in 1835. The religious revivals of the late 1820's and early 1830's in particular seem to provide a background against which the events of the story take on a more definite shape and a larger dimension of meaning.

At the end of his study of Hawthorne's theology Leonard Fick is forced to conclude, "In the accepted sense of the term, . . . Nathaniel Hawthorne was not a religious man. He attended church only by way of exception, was unalterably opposed to all attempts at proselytizing, and cannot in any sense be considered a sectarian."[3] Nevertheless, he was an interested observer of other men's religion, most notably that of Puritans, Shakers, and Roman Catholics, but also that of the more conventional nineteenth-century Protestants who were his neighbors and acquaintances. If his tales did not usually deal with their religious extravagances directly, stories like **"Earth's Holocaust"** and **"The Celestial Railroad"** provided screens from behind which he could satirize various protestant aberrations. When he looked into that best-seller of the early eighteen-thirties, Frances Trollope's *Domestic Manners of the Americans* (1832), his observant eye might have been caught by her account of an overnight visit to a camp-meeting "in a wild district on the confines of Indiana."[4] Mrs. Trollope's journey into the forest bears an obvious structural similarity to Goodman Brown's withdrawal and return to society, but it is interesting to note that the religious upheaval she sees in the forest is also surprisingly like what Brown encounters.

No alert reader of **"Young Goodman Brown"** can miss the tale's inverted religious imagery: Goodman Brown keeps covenant with his diabolical companion, overhears allusions to a young man and woman who will "be taken into communion" in "tonight's meeting," and thinks he sees residents of his village who have a peculiarly religious signification for him—Goody Cloyse, who taught him his catechism, Deacon Gookin, and his minister.[5] When he approaches the meeting in the forest, he hears "what seemed a hymn . . . a familiar one in the choir of the village meeting-house," and discovers "a numerous congregation" before "a rock bearing some rude natural resemblance either to an altar or a pulpit" (84). Next appears an "apparition" which "bore no slight similitude, both in garb and manner, to some grave divine of the New England churches" (86). At the command "Bring forth the converts!," Brown advances into the dark man's "worshipping assembly," there to receive "the mark of baptism" (86-88). This imagery is usually understood as establishing Goodman Brown's attendance at a witches' sabbath, itself a diabolic inversion of orthodox Christian ritual. But because of its associations with the traditional New England religion of covenants and congregational meetings, this imagery may also invite us to meditate less on witchcraft than on other perversions of conventional religion. Hawthorne's twilight imagery reflects daylight realities even as it portrays the night's darker visions.

Mrs. Trollope set out not as a potential convert but as a good British empiricist, "determined to see with my own eyes, and hear with my own ears, what a camp-meeting really was" (167), but her possible categories for defining camp-meetings seem as rigidly dualistic as Goodman Brown's. On one hand she "had heard it said that being at a camp-meeting was like standing at the gate of heaven, and seeing it open before you," and on the other it "was like finding yourself within the gates of hell" (167). Observing the ambiguous scene, she first chooses for particular description two characters who could almost have been Goodman Brown and Faith together before the dark man:

> . . . a handsome looking youth of eighteen or twenty, kneeled just below the opening through which I looked. His arm was encircling the neck of a young girl who knelt beside him, with her hair hanging dishevelled upon her shoulder, and her features working with the most violent agitation; . . . as if unable to endure in any other attitude the burning eloquence of a tall grim figure in black, who, standing erect in the centre, was uttering with incredible vehemence an oration that seemed to hover between praying and preaching.

> (169)

After strolling about the grounds and noticing "the distorted figures that we saw kneeling, sitting, and lying amongst it, joined to the woeful and convulsive cries" (170), she received a midnight summons to join the whole camp in the central area of the grounds before "a rude platform" for the preacher and surrounded by "Four high frames, constructed in the form of altars, . . . on which burned immense fires of blazing pine-wood" (168). Mrs.

Trollope's friend, the French artist Auguste Jean Jacques Hervieu, visited this camp meeting with her and supplied for *Domestic Manners* an illustration showing three of the four fires, the ministers' platform, and the participants writhing in grotesque postures before it in the half-obscurity of the firelight. The picture reinforces the similarity of this scene to Hawthorne's, where "four blazing pines . . . obscurely discovered shapes and visages of horror on the smoke-wreaths, above the impious assembly" (84).

After an exhoration by a preacher which assured them "of the enormous depravity of man as he comes from the hands of his Maker," the crowd began "to sing a hymn, calling upon the penitents to come forth" (171). Just as the hymn Goodman Brown heard was both "familiar . . . in the choir of the village meeting-house" and a "dreadful anthem" (84, 85-86), the context of this hymn struck Mrs. Trollope as ambivalent:

> . . . the combined voices of such a multitude, heard at dead of night, from the depths of their eternal forests, the many fair young faces turned upward, and looking paler and lovelier as they met the moon-beams, the dark figures of the officials in the middle of the circle, the lurid glare thrown by the altar-fires on the woods beyond, did altogether produce a fine and solemn effect, that I shall not easily forget; but ere I had well enjoyed it, the scene changed and sublimity gave place to horror and disgust.
>
> (171-172)

The would-be converts who next came forward were, she says, "above a hundred persons, nearly all females, . . . uttering howlings and groans, so terrible I shall never cease to shudder when I recall them" (172). After the dark man's company finished their impious hymn but before the call went out for the converts to come forward, Young Goodman Brown, also caught up in the emotional excess of the moment, thought "the unconverted wilderness" itself was in uproar, but Mrs. Trollope, like Hawthorne himself a detached observer, located the source of horror in the disturbed mental states and shocking behavior of the human figures. She heard "Hysterical sobbings, convulsive groans, shrieks and screams the most appalling, burst forth on all sides" and she "felt sick with horror" (172).

She was most repelled by the implicitly sexual undertone of the comforts offered by the preachers who "moved about among them, at once exciting and soothing their agonies."

> I heard the muttered "Sister! dear sister!" I saw the insidious lips approach the cheeks of the unhappy girls; I heard the murmured confessions of the poor victims, and I watched their tormentors, breathing into their ears consolations that tinged the pale cheek with red.
>
> (173)

Mrs. Trollope was not alone in connecting licentiousness and camp-meetings, for charges of sexual misbehavior as a result of revival-inspired emotionalism were a recurring theme in criticisms of the revival movement.[6] It should be noted that the "secret deeds" Hawthorne's dark man promises to reveal to his converts are all either manifestly or latently sexual in nature.

After the "atrocious wickedness of this horrible scene" drove her from the meeting, Mrs. Trollope spent the rest of the night in her carriage, "listening to the ever increasing tumult." Yet in the morning the picture is as different from the night before as Brown's orderly Salem village was from his night in the forest:

> At day-break the horn again sounded, to send them to private devotion; and in about an hour afterwards I saw the whole camp as joyously and eagerly employed in preparing and devouring their most substantial breakfasts as if the night had been passed in dancing; and I marked man a fair but pale face, that I recognized as a demoniac of the night, simpering beside a swain, to whom she carefully administered hot coffee and eggs.
>
> (174)

Mrs. Trollope's ironic, even cynical, view of human nature in America saved her from having to decide whether she has seen the gates of heaven or of hell, but Brown's naivete gave him ground only for suspicion and horror concerning his neighbors. (The English lady's ironies, however, were used to undercut democratic pretensions, whereas Hawthorne's ironic treatment of Brown made democracy possible in the face of seemingly damning truths about human nature.)

The similarities listed here are the most obvious, although by no means the only ones, and the general structural parallel between Mrs. Trollope's account and Hawthorne's story is perhaps as important as any similarity of detail. As Terence Martin has observed, "the motif of withdrawal and return" is basic to Hawthorne's fiction,[7] and in *The Domestic Manners of the Americans* as in **"Young Goodman Brown,"** the narrative carries the reader from the order of everyday life through scenes of drastic emotional and moral upheaval back to a re-establishment of the daily order which now cannot be perceived in quite the same way. But even if we assume Hawthorne to have been thinking of Mrs. Trollope's report of the camp meeting, it is clearly not a source for the story of the same kind as the writings of the Mathers or Deodat Lawson to which other scholars have pointed. Historical documents provided Hawthorne with his facts; his point of view and the attitudes with which he shaped his material came from elsewhere. In this regard Mrs. Trollope's account is merely a curious analogy which points to a larger body of opinion concerning religious enthusiasm, a morbid and perverse enthusiasm from the liberal Unitarian point of view with which Hawthorne must surely have been acquainted.

Mrs. Trollope was not unique in the 1830's in remarking upon the demonic aspects of protestant zeal, for her camp-meeting was only a western instance of a wave of revivals which from 1825 to 1835 swept all parts of the country, but particularly New England and the East.[8] Hawthorne

Nathaniel Hawthorne, 1804-1864.

services, holding inquiry meetings for the spiritually distressed, and, perhaps most important, using the "anxious seat." This was a row of seats or a bench placed at the front of the meeting for the use of those who felt themselves under special conviction of sin. After coming forward to occupy the anxious seat, sinners were prayed for and encouraged to make an immediate decision to accept the offer of salvation. The use of these new measures was accompanied by vigorous rhetoric in preaching and prayer, and elsewhere some of Finney's more enthusiastic disciples invented other stimulating techniques. "Every nerve and muscle was called into requisition," observed one critic of Jedediah Burchard's preaching, adding that as soon as he entered the pulpit, the church "at once became a *theatre*." Luther Myrick was accused of using "Profane language such as you are black as hell, The Devil is in you, Hell hardened, God provoking," and Daniel Nash, "Father Nash," at one time wore a double black veil over his face while participating in revival meetings.[9]

According to William G. McLoughlin, "Finney was convinced from his own experience that the use of anxious seats and anxious meetings was 'undoubtedly philosophical and according to the laws of mind.'"[10] Finney's notions of "the laws of mind," however, were simplistic in a number of important ways, dangerously so from the point of view of a man like Hawthorne who was aware of the complex integrity of the human mind. Finney's new measures were obviously sophisticated techniques for inducing psychological and emotional crisis, but his understanding of how the crisis was to be resolved seemed unsatisfactory. "I understand a change of heart," said Finney, "to be just what we mean by a change of mind . . . the world is divided into two great political parties: the difference between them is that one party choose Satan as the god of this world . . . The other party choose Jehovah for their governor." The grounds of this choice appeared clear enough to Finney, who could see in drinking, smoking, card-playing, dancing, and reading of "Byron, Scott, Shakespeare, and a host of triflers and blasphemers"[11] indubitable signs of diabolic service, but critics not prepared to make these easy assumptions, feared that Finney's dualism was more likely to increase anxiety than to allay it. Albert Dod, an important critic of Finney's *Lectures on the Revivals of Religion,* argued in 1835 that the new measures, particularly the anxious seats, tended to "foster delusion and create false hopes," and "should be deprecated as fraught with almost certain evil."[12]

Dod attacked Finney from the conservative viewpoint of orthodox Calvinism, but attacks couched in somewhat similar language came from the Unitarian left as well. Whereas Dod and the orthodox feared religious "delusions," the Unitarian critics were more concerned with social dissension and with increasingly bitter divisions among the general protestant community. James Walker and others in articles in *The Christian Examiner* began in 1827 to attack the Finney revivals as "extravagances" with a "tendency to create even in well disposed minds a distrust of religion itself."[13] Walker referred to Finney and his

might not ordinarily have interested himself in the traditional camp-meetings, which were primarily southern and western events, but when revivalists employed camp-meeting tactics in Boston's Park Street Church, they provoked lengthy debates among the New England clergy, both Unitarian and orthodox. These debates over the revival movement generated a field of public opinion which suggested categories of image and situation to Hawthorne and which provide for us a context in which **"Young Goodman Brown"** acquires richer meanings. To understand the contemporary background which informs Hawthorne's story, we must look beyond the parallels with Mrs. Trollope's camp-meeting, then, to the positions of the revival movement's leading exponent and those of his most articulate critics.

Charles Grandison Finney began the new wave of revivals in upstate New York, overcame initial resistance from more conservative ministers like Asahel Nettleton and Lyman Beecher who vigorously opposed his coming into New England, and by August of 1831 was preaching in Boston on Beecher's invitation. Revivals were hardly a novelty in New England, but Finney's evangelical techniques were both new and widely debated. His "new measures," as they were called, included holding protracted evenings, employing a "holy band" of assistants to work on would-be converts, praying for individuals by name without their consent, permitting women to pray during associate Nathaniel S. Beman as "incendiaries," who wished to "have the satisfaction of beholding the fires of religious frenzy, which have flashed up in particular places, spread through the land, to use their own expression, 'as fires spread and roar through the parched forests.'"[14] Quoting observers of the New York revivals, Walker criticized the revivalists' "pungent preaching" for its crude or blasphemous language, their praying for the unconverted by name as a libel on the character of good men, and their inquiry meetings as nocturnal excesses designed to stimulate unhealthy emotions. "They are generally, if not always, held in the night. The room is darkened, so that persons can only see to walk and discover each other, and the reign of universal silence is interrupted only by now and then a dolorous groan from different parts of the room."[15]

The result of all this religious frenzy as Walker saw it was "division and estrangement of families, a neglect and contempt of the social duties, the ascendancy of men of coarse and vulgar minds."[16] Little wonder that some men ascribed the revivalists' abuses of decency to "the direct and preternatural agency of the evil one." Although Walker himself as a rational Unitarian put no stock in diabolic intervention, he enjoyed quoting the Calvinists against each other, particularly when they saw Satan standing at their neighbors' backs. Thus he quoted Lyman Beecher," . . . churches must be instructed and prepared to resist the beginnings of evil,—the mask must be torn off from Satan coming among the sons of God, and transforming himself into an angel of light."[17] C. C. Felton, another Unitarian critic, saw the revivalists as "deluded but crafty agitators" who drew "monstrous terrors" from their "exhaustless imaginations." He was particularly critical of revivals got up among the young, for the "ordinary pursuits of sound and wholesome learning have been thrown aside. The buoyant and throbbing joyousness of youth and childhood have been changed to an indescribable sadness and gloom."[18]

The volumes of *The Christian Examiner* containing the attacks on the Finneyite revivals were variously charged from the Salem Atheneum by Hawthorne and his aunt, Mary Manning, and although Aunt Mary would have been the more likely reader, Hawthorne might have found suggestive material in their pages.[19] *The Christian Examiner* articles linked the revivals with both unhealthy, disordered emotionalism and Satanic intrusion upon society. At least one essay discussed the Great Awakening of George Whitefield as an implicit historical analogue to the contemporary wave of revivals, thus pointing to the appropriateness of criticizing the Finneyite movement through historical displacement.[20] Whether or not Hawthorne read *The Examiner,* however, the real question, as with Mrs. Trollope's *Domestic Manners,* is not one of sources, interesting as that is, but of the climate of opinion. Mrs. Trollope's much talked about book presents a widely disseminated portrayal of evangelical religion, and the *Examiner* articles reveal an attitude toward revivals which would have been held by enlightened, rational Christians, even non-sectarian ones like Hawthorne. The revivals were such notorious

events that Hawthorne could not have escaped a knowledge of them, nor could he have overlooked the significance of the language of terror purveyed by the revivalists and their critics.

If **"Young Goodman Brown"** is in some ways similar to Mrs. Trollope's account of a camp-meeting, it also reflects the conditions of a revival meeting; the aberrant behavior of the spiritually distressed in the western forests was also induced in those who attended the revivals of Finney and his disciples in Boston and the East. In Hawthorne's version of the revival meeting, Goodman Brown is caught up in a world as starkly dualistic as Finney's where, whipsawed by its polarities, he is manipulated by a quasi-religious leader into an emotional and ethical crisis. Finney exhorted sinners to grasp their salvation as an act of individual will, and the dark man subtly urges Goodman Brown to choose his own fate. The dark man has his own holy band of assistants to guide Brown down the path to conversion, his own anxious seat before the congregation. Just as Finney continually showed the anxious sinner the depravity of seemingly innocent social customs and of any previous religious professions, so the dark man apparently reveals to Brown the evil of even his Faith and promises to initiate him into "the mystery of sin."

When the diabolic minister tells Goodman Brown and Faith, "Depending upon one another's hearts, ye had still hoped, that virtue were not all a dream; now are ye undeceived!" (88), he puts "virtue," "hope," and "depending upon one another's hearts" into an ontological relationship—they are not necessarily linked by cause and effect, yet they cannot exist apart. To accept the dark man's promised happiness is to accept evil as "the nature of mankind," and it is to accept one's almost solipsistic isolation from humanity, for to reject virtue is to reject the essential communal bonds of hope and trust. The community of evil described by the devil is a community of suspicion and cynicism, and as Goodman Brown turns his back on Salem village in order to venture into dark nature and his darker self, he rejects the society which has nurtured him from the self-willed terrors of the imagination. This perception is for Hawthorne the central truth of the story, and it is simultaneously the old error toward which Puritanism tended and the mistake of the contemporary revivalists. Even defenders of the revival movement recognized as one of its possible evils "a spirit of self-righteousness" in which men reject "fellow Christians" for not conforming to their own private visions of order.[21] This self-righteousness is a fundamental misreading of the "mystery of sin" which repeats in Hawthorne's own century the error of Goodman Brown. The answer is in the old Puritan truth which Thomas Hooker called rational charity—a recognition of hypocrisy in men but a willingness to accept a neighbor's professions of righteousness when supported by apparently good actions.

Unlike Finney's successful converts, Goodman Brown is trapped in the seat of his own guilt and suspicion. Unable to join the dark man's church, he cannot accept the daylight Christianity of his family and neighbors either, and thus living in a self-created twilight, "his dying hour was gloom." A Unitarian critic of revivals like Felton might have predicted as much, for showing man the monstrous terrors of sin does not necessarily enable him to become a more loving husband or virtuous citizen. In a well-known sermon, "Sinners Bound to Change Their Own Hearts," preached in Boston's Park Church in October 1831, Finney used a famous trope illustrating a sinner's rescue by an evangelist:

> Suppose yourself to be standing on the bank of the Falls of Niagara. As you stand upon the verge of the precipice, you behold a man lost in deep reverie, approaching its verge, unconscious of his danger. He approaches nearer, until he actually lifts his foot to take the final step that shall plunge him in destruction. At this moment you lift your warning voice above the roar of the foaming waters and cry out, *Stop.* The voice pierces his ear and breaks the charm that binds him; he turns instantly upon his hell, all pale and aghast, quivering from the verge of death.[22]

Finney thought the dream-walker was successfully awakened, but a more skeptical reading of the passage reveals that he is still "pale and aghast"; if turned from inevitable commitment to destruction, he is still "on the verge of death" and not yet returned to safety. The voice that stops Brown is less clearly providential, but when he awakes, his cheek "besprinkled . . . with the coldest dew" (88), he too is still on the brink, a position from which he is unable to find an easy retreat.

In making Brown's own voice break the binding charm, Hawthorne is surely a better psychologist than Finney was in his illustrative trope. He recognizes the integrity of dreaming and waking consciousness, the singular identity of the conscious and the subconscious, and he knows that dreams are in their own manner the result of the same will that leads to daylight actions. Finney and the revivalists in their eagerness to simplify man's answer to the evangelical call extended their moral dualism to consciousness itself; one either slept or waked, knew the mystery of sin or didn't. Finney's moral and psychological dualism recognized no middle ground, but in **"Young Goodman Brown"** Hawthorne shows us the twilight regions in which our imaginations are most intensely alive and in which we must make our profoundest moral decisions. For Hawthorne our ability to live in this middle world defines our humanity, and we can resolve the anxiety inherent in this situation only by hope and love rather than by willing ourselves toward impossible absolutes.

We should not, however, conclude that the story is about the revivals any more than we should conclude that it is about his own family or about Salem witchcraft. David Levin has reminded us, "By recognizing that Hawthorne built **'Young Goodman Brown'** firmly on his historical knowledge, we perceive that the tale has a social as well as an allegorical and a psychological dimension."[23] If beginning with the tale's historical dimension leads us to a recognition of its social implications, our examination of the story's social context must lead us back to an enriched understanding both of its other dimensions and of the nature of Hawthorne's art. By seeing that the story's meaning has an anchor in a specific social situation in Hawthorne's nineteenth-century present, we understand the balancing power of the specific richness of the story's historical knowledge as detailed by so many scholars. Hawthorne can thus simultaneously comprehend the nature of the past and shed light on the present while avoiding the literary equivalent of historicism and presentism: his past does not determine the present nor his present the past.[24] The tale's fidelity both to the Puritan experience and to the revival experience thus allows it to draw direction-finding lines upon ahistorical truths of the human heart, for the tale is about neither Puritan nor revivalist situations but about the human situation as portrayed in the universal terms of art.

James W. Clark, Jr. is undoubtedly right when he claims Hawthorne saw "that in the shades of the forest existed a storyteller's complex world."[25] Hawthorne's imagination worked upon what he learned from looking within himself, what he learned from his researches into the world that had gone before, and what he learned from looking at the world about him. His best stories like **"Young Goodman Brown"** synthesize from the complete range of his experience in order to substitute the mystery of art for the mystery of sin.[26] If his imagination in his best work most frequently found itself at home in dealing with historical materials, it is an imagination solidly grounded in his present, and no understanding of his fiction can be complete unless it understands both that present and that past.

Notes

1. Although scholars are long past believing in the recluse Hawthorne, most studies of his social interests focus on the last decade and a half of his career, e.g., Lawrence Sargent Hall, *Hawthorne, Critic of Society,* (New Haven: Yale University Press, 1944) and Terence Martin, "Hawthorne's Public Decade and the Values of Home," *American Literature,* 46 (1974), 141–152.

2. For a recent survey of the scholarship, see James W. Clark, Jr., "Hawthorne's Use of Evidence in 'Young Goodman Brown'," *Essex Institute Historical Collections,* 111 (1975), 12. A step beyond the articles in Clark's list is Michael Colacurcio's "Visible Sanctity and Specter Evidence: The Moral World of Hawthorne's 'Young Goodman Brown'," *Essex Institute Historical Collections,* 110 (1974), 259-299, which argues that the issue of specter evidence determines the tale's "ultimate psychological meaning" and that "from 'Alice Doane' straight through his unfinished romances Hawthorne allowed the Puritan language of the 'invisible world' to determine his vocabulary and set the limits to his own psychological investigations," p. 261.

3. Leonard J. Fick, *The Light Beyond, A Study of Hawthorne's Theology* (Westminster, Maryland: Newman, 1955), p. 155.

4. Frances Trollope, *Domestic Manners of the Americans,* ed. Donald Smalley (New York: Knopf, 1949), p. 167. Further quotations from Mrs. Trollope will be identified parenthetically in the text. See Smalley's Introduction, pp. vii-x, for a discussion of the wide circulation of the book. When Hawthorne met Thomas Adolphus Trollope in Florence on 27 June 1858, he referred to him in his note book as "the son, I believe, of Mrs. Trollope, to whom America owes more for her shrewd criticisms than we are ever likely to repay." *The French and Italian Notebooks,* ed. Thomas Woodson (Columbus: Ohio State University Press, 1980), p. 339. This comment, unfortunately, does not establish when Hawthorne read her "criticisms."

5. Nathaniel Hawthorne, *Mosses From an Old Manse,* Centenary Edition (Columbus: Ohio State University Press, 1974), pp. 79, 81. Further quotations from "Young Goodman Brown" will be identified parenthetically in the text.

6. See Charles S. Cole, Jr., *The Social Ideas of the Northern Evangelists, 1826-1860* (New York: Columbia University Press, 1954), p. 93.

7. Martin, "The Method of Hawthorne's Tales," in *Nathaniel Hawthorne,* ed. J. Donald Crowley (New York: McGraw, 1975), p. 17. The essay originally appeared in *Hawthorne Centenary Essays,* ed. Roy Harvey Pearce (Columbus: Ohio State University Press, 1964).

8. On Mrs. Trollope and the revival movement, the anonymous reviewer of *Domestic Manners* in the *American Quarterly Review,* for instance, quarreled with her portrayal of American life, but in a long comment on the camp-meeting chapter he felt forced to agree that she, "unhappily, has too much occasion for sneer and censure. Her description of what may be styled the *maladie du pays* . . . is scarcely exaggerated." He goes on to deplore the "readiness with which the unconscious, the young and timid, fall victims to wild and exaggerated sentiments—startling delusions—gloomy and devastating terrors—the chimeras of a deeply roused imagination" ("Mrs. Trollope and the Americans," *American Quarterly Review,* 12 [1832], p. 122).

9. Quoted by William G. McLoughlin, *Modern Revivalism* (New York: Ronald, 1959), pp. 133-134.

10. McLoughlin, p. 95.

11. Finney quoted in McLoughlin, *Modern Revivalism,* pp. 120, 69-70. This radical distinction was frequently drawn by both sympathizers and opponents of the revivals; e.g. "One of these two positions must be true: either revivals of religion are a work of *evil origin* and a delusion, or else they result from an outpouring of the Spirit of God." *The Christian Spectator,* 4 (1832), p. 26. *The Spectator* supported revivals.

12. William G. McLoughlin, "Introduction" to Charles Grandison Finney, *Lectures on the Revivals of Religion* (Cambridge: Harvard University Press, 1960), p. xxxviii.

13. *The Christian Examiner,* 4 (1827), 242-243.

14. *Examiner,* 4 (1827), 243-244. The charge of spiritual incendiarism was a commonplace.

15. *Examiner,* 4 (1827), 249-256, 257.

16. *Examiner,* 4 (1827), 262.

17. *Examiner,* 6 (1829), 127, 107.

18. *Examiner,* 8 (1830), 112.

19. Marion L. Kesselring, *Hawthorne's Reading, 1828-1850* (New York: New York Public Library, 1949), p. 47. Hawthorne was in Salem when the volumes I quote from were charged, and books he obviously was reading himself were charged on the same dates.

20. *Examiner* 4 (1827), 464-495. Historical analogues were frequently called up. Calvin Colton in his *History and Character of American Revivals of Religion* (London: Frederick Westley and A. H. Davis, 1832) had a chapter showing "The Connexion of American Revivals with the Spirit of the Pilgrim Fathers." *Spirit of the Pilgrims* was also the title of a religious journal generally favorable to the revivals; it began publication in Boston in 1828.

21. William B. Sprague, *Lectures on Revivals of Religion* (New York: D. Appleton, 1833), pp. 181-182.

22. Quoted by McLoughlin, *Modern Revivalism,* p. 71.

23. Levin, "Historical Fact in Fiction and Drama: The Salem Witchcraft Trials," in *In Defence of Historical Literature* (New York: Hill and Wang, 1967), p. 87.

24. Michael D. Bell, *Hawthorne and the Historical Romance of New England* (Princeton: Princeton University Press, 1971) claims that in his later fiction "Hawthorne becomes increasingly concerned with the relation between past and present" while the earlier fiction more simply "attempts to understand the past," p. 194. This is a suggestive distinction, yet Hawthorne even in the 1830's is concerned about the relevance of the past for the present. Consider, for example, a story like "The Gray Champion."

25. Clark, p. 22.

26. The relatively inferior tale, "Earth's Holocaust," may also have some connection to a review in *The Christian Examiner.* In Boston's Hollis Street Church the Reverend John Pierpont preached a sermon entitled "The Burning of the Ephesian Letters" from Acts 19: 19-20—"Many also of them who used curious arts, brought their books together, and burned them before all men; and they counted the price of them, and found it fifty thousand pieces of silver. So mightily

grew the word of God with them." Pierpont's sermon defended temperance and abolitionism under the figure of burning the books. If Hawthorne found an idea here, he, like Pierpont, chose to give it an allegorical instead of an historical setting, and his tale is the poorer for the missing element of his experience. This sermon of December 1833 was published in Boston in 1834 and reviewed by *The Examiner* in 16 (1834), 98-103; unlike the above volumes of *The Examiner,* however, there is no evidence that Hawthorne checked this volume out of the Salem Atheneum.

Edward Jayne (essay date 1979)

SOURCE: "Pray Tarry with Me Young Goodman Brown," *Literature and Psychology,* Vol. 29, No. 3, 1979, pp. 100-13.

[*In the following essay, Jayne presents a psychoanalytic reading of "Young Goodman Brown," asserting that Brown exhibits classic symptoms of paranoia and homosexual tendencies.*]

Hawthorne's almost transparent use of paranoia as an organizing principle has been generally overlooked even in psychoanalytic studies of his fiction. There have been many critical approaches to Hawthorne, but most if not all of them have provided an essentially "normal" response to his paranoid manipulation of experience. It almost seems as if his uncompromising delusional intensity has provoked a variety of normal defenses among those who are sufficiently tantalized to want to deal with it without coming to terms with its fullest implications. By doing so they both accept and deny whatever resonance this manipulation of experience has produced in themselves, as would be demonstrated by their indignation when challenged on these grounds. Nevertheless, once noticed, unmistakable symptoms of paranoia are everywhere to be observed in Hawthorne's fiction, and these can and should be investigated as a pattern of behavior which is consistent enough to justify its independent clinical evaluation. It is Hawthorne's fiction which should be diagnosed, not Hawthorne, his sympathetic audience, nor even his tormented and guilt-ridden characters. Magnificent in its brooding solitude, his fiction literally organizes itself as an intact delusional system which may be tried out for size by its author and readers who are able to share in the nightmarish experience it imposes upon its characters.

One of the most obvious examples of paranoid consciousness in the canon of Hawthorne's works is **"Young Goodman Brown,"** a short story which is fully as relevant to the central tradition of American fiction as it is to the personal circumstances of either Hawthorne or his readers. The story can be explained, I think, both as a remarkable case history of paranoid aberration and as a "negative" example of the wilderness consciousness which has persisted

from Natty Bumppo's exploits to those of the detectives, cowboys and anti-heroes who crowd our media today. The principal difference would be that Young Goodman Brown briefly tests and rejects the adventures to which they dedicate their lifetime endeavors. But in doing so, he successfully exposes the inadequacies he shares with them despite the restraint which supplants material accomplishment with the suspicion and bitterness which he must endure for the greater part of his life. The temporary forest ritual he denies in himself expresses the syndrome he shares with them except to the extent that he is complicated enough to try to reject it.

Briefly recounted, Hawthorne's narrative tells how the sensitive and vulnerable Young Goodman Brown goes into the forest to carry out his overnight assignation with Satan. Faith, his equally vulnerable young bride, pleads with him to "tarry" with her at home, but he feels inexplicably compelled to leave and fulfill his mysterious obligation. Once in the forest he meets Satan, who leads him toward the site where an unexplained midnight ritual is to be conducted. The two of them soon overtake his old nurse, Goody Cloyse, who had taught him his catechism in his childhood. He is shocked to learn that she is on her way to the same ceremony and has been a long-standing friend of Satan on the most intimate of terms. When she accepts Satan's staff to fly like a witch to their destination, Young Goodman Brown decides to profit from Faith's example by refusing to cooperate any further. Abandoned by Satan, who has become impatient with his naiveté, Young Goodman Brown finds himself alone in the dark and listening to voices in the clouds overhead, evidently of other women flying to the same event. One of these sounds as if she is Faith, his young wife, and a red ribbon which descends from the sky seems to be hers. With this discovery he loses his composure and frantically rushes to join in the evil proceedings, spurred on by the voices of two respectable local clergymen riding on horseback to the same destination.

Young Goodman Brown finally stumbles into a clearing illuminated by four burning pines and full of local citizens, many of them from among the most pious and prosperous families he knows. He finds that everybody has gathered and been waiting to perform the ritual baptism of Faith and himself as two new converts into what Satan describes as "the communion of their race." Only one figure, probably his mother, motions him not to participate, but she seems to be lost in the crowd. Satan begins his invocation before a blood-filled basin when Young Goodman Brown suddenly changes his mind and cries to Faith, who stands next to him, to join in resisting "the wicked one." Exactly at this instant the entire gathering disappears, Faith included, and Young Goodman Brown once again finds himself alone in the dark forest. The next day he returns home again entirely disillusioned. He does stay on with Faith to raise a family of children and grandchildren, but he can never determine whether his extraordinary experience had been a dream or not. As a result he remains suspicious and embittered until he finally dies of old age still unreconciled with those about him.

Before the origins of the paranoid syndrome are explored as suggested in the story, it would be useful to list some of the many overt paranoid symptoms which occur throughout its narrative. The cause-and-effect interaction between vulnerability and its projective defenses typical of paranoia is carried out in this story in almost textbook fashion, but a discussion of its more obvious paranoid traits seems necessary before launching into their etiology.[1] Listed, these traits stand as follows:

1. There is a complete and intact delusional system, an elaborate explanation of events which justifies Young Goodman Brown's final hostility against all others.

2. Young Goodman Brown is pitted against a conspiracy so pervasive that everybody, even his trusted bride, is probably involved. It is only his rigid commitment to virtue that prevents him from succumbing to it, and because of his refusal he becomes alienated from the entire town, a "pseudocommunity" of potential enemies.[2]

3. Paranoid "centrality" is gained by Young Goodman Brown because his evil communion is supposed to be celebrated by all of society and because his salvation becomes the principle battlefield, however temporary, in the cosmic struggle between God and Satan.

4. There is supernatural interference by powers too enormous to be resisted except by soliciting one in the struggle against the other. Young Goodman Brown is nothing more than a pawn in the "cold war" between forces he cannot entirely understand.

5. Undue emphasis is put upon the exaggerated Manichaean choice between sin and virtue. Young Goodman Brown stakes his life and happiness upon a clear-cut ethical issue, all-good versus all-bad, and he must remain steadfast in his commitment to "the good" despite evil temptations to which everybody else has very probably succumbed.

6. There is a pronounced tendency toward "premature closure" in the judgment of others. We are never certain whether Young Goodman Brown's experience is real, but following his single evening's ordeal he absolutely and humorlessly commits himself to the perpetual rejection of his family and neighbors.

7. The possibility of compromise is totally excluded. Once Young Goodman Brown has made his choice, his fate is determined and no accommodation can be made for the rest of his life with his relatives and neighbors.

8. There is an excessive emphasis upon the detection of clues to expose the truth to Young Goodman Brown about the conspiracy against him: his wife's hair ribbon, peculiar resemblances, snatches of familiar voices heard in the dark, etc. All of these must be sifted as evidence to be used to save Young Goodman Brown from the fate which would otherwise await him.

9. There is an overcompensatory reduction of sexual roles to simplified stereotypes. Women are divided into pure beings such as Young Goodman Brown's mother and threatening temptresses and/or witches such as Goody Cloyse. Unfortunately, Faith seems willing to join the devil's party, so the temptation she represents would bring about his destruction if he didn't have the will power to withstand it.

10. There is prolonged uncertainty whether events are real or imaginary. Particularly noteworthy are the voices heard in the dark of the clergymen and the women passing by on the cloud overhead. Hearing voices is of course one of the typical symptoms of advanced paranoia, even in a story such as "Young Goodman Brown" in which forest darkness provides a kind of secondary elaboration to justify its occurrence.

11. The story of Young Goodman Brown is told with a disarming candor which emphasizes the truth at one level of interpretation in order to obscure it at another. The narrator is always careful to differentiate uncertainty from the clear-cut truth, and of course a struggle must be understood to occur between satanic deception and the ultimate truth. However, the central issue of the story, Young Goodman Brown's rejection of his role as husband, is kept almost entirely excluded from conscious recognition, as are the more fundamental reasons for his choice through his fear of sex.

12. Finally, there is even a good deal of paranoid imagery to the story. Young Goodman Brown makes his regressive journey along a dark and threatening trail in order to participate in a ghastly ritual dominated by burning pines and a rock basin full of blood. An enormous crowd has gathered to watch his humiliating baptism, but it suddenly disappears to leave him stranded in the darkness. This kind of oneiric intensity effectively puts experience in the service of paranoid hostility through perceptions which confirm one's closest harbored suspicions.

Unmistakably paranoid, then, would be the mood and ambience of the story. The way it unfolds upon itself as a justification of Young Goodman Brown in his struggle against demonic forces offers itself as almost a classic psychiatric case history of paranoid delusional thinking.

But more important than symptoms alone would be the Freudian etiology of paranoia which is actually given its sequential explanation in being traced from its acute to its chronic stages as Young Goodman Brown's story advances from beginning to end. The source of Young Goodman Brown's paranoid circumstances through his unresolved Oedipal fixation is emphasized and reemphasized throughout the story of his ordeal. As maintained by Frederick Crews, the devil is clearly a father figure in the disguise he assumes as Young Goodman Brown's venerable grandfather who has long since been dead.[3] Together, Satan and Young Goodman Brown are described at one point as looking like father and son, and grandfather translates into father exactly as Goody Cloyse, Young Goodman Brown's satanic nurse, translates into bad or licentious mother, the willing mistress of his father's designs. Moreover, the celebration led by the father-figure at the witch's sabbath in the woods would simply consist of Young Goodman Brown's ultimate act of identifying with his father through his marriage with Faith according to patriarchal custom and expectations. They are newly-weds, and, as in the case of all marriages, church and civil rites must be completed by an act of intimacy which would impose upon Young Goodman Brown the role his father had once enjoyed with his mother. Of course it is specified in the story that he and Faith have been married for three months, ample time to have consummated their relationship much earlier, but whether they did or not, the forest ritual at least serves as its symbolic reenactment. Sexual consummation obviously seems to be what is meant by Satan, its patriarchal figure-head, when he refers to "the communion of your race," and all of those who can attend this communion seem to have lost their virginity in a comparable fashion.

Faith makes her conjugal demands explicit at the beginning of the story, "Pray tarry with me this night, of all nights in the year." Why of all nights in the year? Or of all nights in one's life? Chronological displacement would apparently be the answer—from the passage of a single day, when marriage is customarily both sealed and consummated, to a quarter year, the period of time which elapses between solstice and equinox. Whether conscious or unconscious, the effort seems plain to disguise the crisis faced by Young Goodman Brown, for the story's symbolism would be all too obvious if it were explicit that this ceremony takes place on his marriage night. So it becomes important to specify that the two are newly-weds, but with enough of an interim since their marriage to support the symbolic disguise which might let the story be told— exactly the same use of concealment as occurs in dream formation. Nevertheless, it remains obvious, as Crews insists, that sex is the issue and that what happens in the story is the rejection of sex except for the unpleasant necessity of bearing children.

Sexual temptation is also very likely suggested even at the story's beginning when it is said that Faith "thrusts her own pretty head into the street, letting the wind play with the pink ribbons of her cap . . ." If head at all implies maidenhead, as can be the case in Shakespeare's plays, for example, the young wife displays a forwardness which demeans or "thrusts into the street" her chastity. That she does so by projecting her head from the open door of her house also suggests the cookbook (but not invalid) Freudian dream symbolism of houses as bodies and doors as apertures to these bodies. Through displacement, however, her door isn't penetrated inwards, but outwards, and this is done by herself, not Young Goodman Brown, courting shame and disgrace in her effort to induce him to remain with her in their house. Her words "Pray tarry with me" which are spoken at this point confirm the licentious implications of her gesture, and her fluttering pink ribbon, emphasized by its wayward personification as something "played with" by the wind, only begins to prepare Young Goodman Brown for the blood-filled basin he later sees into which one's hands might be dipped in the ritual of

consummation. Young Goodman Brown's immediate departure despite Faith's seductive pleas expresses his preliminary rejection of this temptation, but without his fully understanding the implications of his action. Then when he passes behind the meeting house so their view of each other is obstructed, it seems as if this structure comes between them—as if the symbol of both community and bodily sharing must paradoxically separate the two in much the same way as his journey to consummate their relationship in a witch's sabbath is what in fact destroys it. Thus the first few lines of the story very likely offer a kind of initial epiphany to anticipate Young Goodman Brown's more explicit encounter with the ritual of sex in the forest's clearing. The way Faith is left behind, waving from her doorway, offers complex symbolization which explains his final abandonment of her on moral grounds at the story's end.

The supposedly dangerous temptation of conjugal love is also plain in the rampant symbolism of Satan's invocation at the forest ritual:

> By the sympathy of your human hearts for *sin* ye shall *scent* out all the places—whether in church, *bedchamber,* street, field, or forest—where crime has been committed, and shall exult to behold the whole earth one *stain of guilt,* one mighty *blood spot.* Far more than this. It shall be yours to *penetrate,* in every bosom, the *deep* mystery of sin, the *fountain* of all wicked arts . . ."

[italics added]

Here the satanic image of a body's penetration and its flow of blood is extended even to the feminine personification of earth, of course suggesting Gaeia, the earth goddess from whom humanity and the rest of the gods originally spring. Interestingly, the specific crimes next listed by Satan suggest sex and parenthood:

> . . . how hoary-bearded elders of the church have whispered wanton words to the young maids of their households; how many a woman, eager for the widow's weeds, has given her husband a drink at bedtime and let him sleep his last sleep in her bosom; how beardless youths have made haste to inherit their father's wealth; and how fair maidens—blush not, sweet ones—have dug little graves in the garden, and bidden me, the sole guest, to an infant's funeral.

In other words, if Young Goodman Brown, a "beardless youth," can identify with his father as Satan (i.e. "inherit his father's wealth"), he would have no trouble in consummating his marriage to Faith by breaking the hymen and penetrating "the fountain of all wicked arts"—the drink which would "let him sleep his last sleep in her bosom." Moreover, his infancy would be given its funeral by Faith (his own "fair maiden") in her little garden grave, an overdetermined image of the womb which suggests both the homicidal rejection of adult responsibility by means of infanticide and a regressive fear of growing up, in this case through identification with the infant corpse. Maturity is simple but fearful. Young Goodman Brown need only divert his filial loyalty from his "good" mother, now little more than a half-recognized gesture of restraint, to his "bad" mother, Goody Cloyse ("good" becomes "goody," something entirely different), a witch who has lost her broom and is willing to accept in its place the father figure's serpentine staff. It is this staff, by the way, which Satan repeatedly tries to pass on to Young Goodman Brown as if it were his rightful inheritance, his initiation to the mysteries of adult experience. Once again the symbolism is not only obvious but crucial to the meaning of the story as a whole. Young Goodman Brown's infantile dependence upon a nurturing mother must be successfully displaced to phallic identification with his father in order to benefit from the mature recognition that women are sinners too, individuals with whom sexual companionship is possible. But he cannot complete this transition, and with the result that the parent figures who encourage his efforts to do so are rejected in their personifications as Satan and "Goody Cloyse" (or "delectable cloister"), a clutching and unpleasant witch.

As in the classic Freudian explanation of the origins of homosexuality, Young Goodman Brown's inability to identify with his father is indicated by his unwillingness to accept the ritual consummation of his marriage, and this very probably results from his uncertain sense of masculine identity which arises from his close affinity to his mother.[4] It is no accident that he rejects Satan's obviously phallic staff or that the single individual who tries to dissuade him from going through with consummation is probably his cherished "good" mother. It is she who offers the only resistance to the ceremony which would ritualize his communion, and in doing so she becomes his twisted conscience, the brief visual embodiment of his regressive and infantile strivings. This distinction is important: not his father but his mother dominates his conscience (or superego), and in fact her influence preserves him from excessive intimacy with her young surrogate, his bride, who could only disrupt the unbroken bond between the two of them, mother and son, on the basis of dependency rather than mature compatibility. Because Young Goodman Brown finds it easier to identify with his mother than with his father, he is willing to relinquish his patriarchal obligations as family head and respectable member of the community. He does not become an overt homosexual—this too would be evil, even unspeakable—but his confusion is externalized and brought under control by means of a delusional experience which carries out the double displacement of denial and projection typical of paranoid logic as explained by Freud: "Not that I cannot love Faith; rather, it is she who is involved in a universal plot to destroy my soul." In this manner Young Goodman Brown's insecure sexual identification can be justified by the ever-convenient religious choice between sin and virtue which puts all others at fault, not himself. He can be protected from the discovery of his personal difficulties (as can the reader who empathizes with him) simply by rejecting these others as probable agents of hell. They are plotting against him by trying to deprive him of his virtue, and their designs can only be thwarted through his hostility and vigilance for the

rest of his life, ". . . for his dying hour was gloom." His single night's crisis thus suggests the "acute" stage of paranoia as triggered by unacceptable conjugal demands, and when it is resolved through his relentless struggle against the universal communion of mankind, his affliction has advanced to the so-called "chronic" stage of paranoia. There is modest relief in having at least identified his enemies, if not in having defeated them or successfully dealt with his own genuine problems.

Young Goodman Brown's infantile expectations in marrying Faith are obvious when he says, "I'll cling to her skirts and follow her to heaven," much as might have been demanded of his mother. But "good" Faith reveals "bad" faith (pun intended) when she makes physical demands exceeding those of his mother, as is divulged by her plea for him to "tarry" with her because of her uncontrollable feelings: "A lone woman is troubled with such dreams and such thoughts that she's afeard of herself sometimes." By implication Young Goodman Brown has even more to fear from her than she does herself, and he must somehow find an adequate defense acceptable to his conscience, one which would enable him, true to his name, to be "good" and "man" at the same time. His story tells how this is accomplished in two clearly defined stages: first when he leaves Faith to journey into the world of shadows where her demands might be disguised as satanic ritual, and then when this ritual is abruptly terminated because it is satanic. Of course Young Goodman Brown begs the question by making his renunciation in this manner since it is he himself who raises the issue of sin, but the laws of deduction can be comfortably ignored through the primary process reasoning of delusional intensity which is dictated by his motives. Whether fallacious or not, a doubled withdrawal sequence from his wife—into the woods and out again—is successfully manipulated to be justified by Young Goodman Brown's suspicions and hostility for the rest of his life. Later he and Faith do have children and grandchildren, but their marriage is never really consummated as a union of two kindred souls since Young Goodman Brown cannot rely upon his wife to satisfy his innermost regressive needs. The story of his revelation thus embodies and carries out the denial-projective pattern of paranoid delusions as explained by Freudian theory. There is denial because of his inability to acknowledge the problem that lies within himself, and then there is projection in the moral repudiation of others as if it were they who cause the problem because of their conspiracy to thwart his salvation. Through a sequence of discoveries which obliges this understanding, the narrative of Young Goodman Brown's life shifts from his confused early expectations to a maturity which dispels this confusion, but at the sacrifice of being dominated by gloom and the necessity of ceaseless vigilance against others. As a documentation of this transition, plot itself becomes an elaborate *coitus interruptus* required by the bizarre ethical pretension of being engaged in a unique cosmic struggle against the devil. In the nick of time Young Goodman Brown is able to withdraw from consummating his marriage, and of course for reasons of profound religious significance.

Paradoxically, Young Goodman Brown first rejects his wife's overtures in order to make his symbolic journey into the woods (often public in dream formation) where these overtures might be disguised to be rejected once and for all as the symbolic ritual of consummation. But his reluctant quest is symbolic of both sexual penetration and the regressive withdrawal into his mother's womb. The choice represented by his passage into the thicket is entirely ambiguous and could have anatomical reference either to his mother or wife, and, as it were, with either a comic or tragic outcome. With a comic outcome Satan could serve as an accepted father figure comparable to Prospero, Theseus, Undershaft and others in presenting the hand of his son (if not his daughter) in marriage at the forest clearing. The warning gesture of the mother would not be seen, and the forest's ritual would end with consummation and the universal harmony to be expected of Menandrine comedy, for example with the concluding marriage ceremonies of *A Midsummer Night's Dream* and *As You Like It*. With a tragic outcome, in contrast, the Oedipal love of one's mother would oblige self-destructive aggression against a father figure comparable to Laius, Claudius, etc.—in this instance by engaging in a struggle of almost Miltonic proportions against the invidious powers of the devil. A young woman such as Faith would very likely not be involved, or, if she were, she too would probably be destroyed, like Ophelia, by the almost cosmic release of Oedipal violence to be expected of tragedy. But of course neither comedy nor tragedy takes place. The story of Young Goodman Brown, notable for its brevity, displays little more magnitude than a parable or bad dream, and what does prevail is a nightmarish enactment of the psychosexual ambivalence which obliges perpetual fear and uncertainty. The apparition of his mother gives Young Goodman Brown the courage to reject marriage as the "communion of your race," so he finds himself in limbo between two ego ideals, paternal and maternal, neither of which can be exactly appropriated. There is neither identification with this father through the act of consummation nor with his mother through overt homosexual identification. He consequently finds himself in a closet he doesn't understand and hostile toward the enemy voices which can be heard on the other side of the door. His story tells how and why he makes his decision not to come out of his closet, and once his choice is made his story has for all practical purposes been brought to its conclusion. An abortive transition has been made from a bridegroom's frightened expectancy to the resounding denial of a "stern, a sad, a darkly meditative, a distrustful, if not a desperate man." Nothing is left but gloom as Young Goodman Brown tries to live out his undeclared compact with his mother and no one else, one which falls short of homosexual identification through paranoid denial.

Most of this explication is of course an elaborate reconstruction, and it must be acknowledged that there is no single passage in the story which affords a single global explanation of Young Goodman Brown's problem. However, shades of paranoia, everything fits. Everywhere the story furnishes the necessary fragments of information to be combined and interpreted by anybody who seriously intends to give it the clinical evaluation which it deserves. Typical of paranoid behavior, the story doesn't take pains to spell out its inadequacies for all to recognize, but instead almost reluctantly discloses these in thorough if piecemeal fashion in the process of dealing with them. It is our task as readers and critics to be able to recognize the overall pattern of experience which emerges organized as fiction. Literary convention might somewhat disguise the syndrome for those who insist upon treating literature as being absolutely separate from personal experience, but for the rest of us the resemblance should really be too obvious to be ignored. If a distraught young gentleman, Y. G. Brown, were to walk into a psychiatrist's office and confide that he had recently talked to the devil disguised as his grandfather, that this same devil had tried to steal his soul in a witch's sabbath, and that he knows from the voices he heard that everybody except his mother was involved in the conspiracy, even his bride—the diagnosis, I think, would be plain: a classic case of paranoia, almost too perfect to be true except in fiction.

Again it must be insisted that this doesn't mean that Hawthorne was paranoid or even that Young Goodman Brown, his fictive creation, suffers from this disorder. Often in this paper I have diagnosed his problems as if he were a flesh and blood human being with a personality which is complex enough to be fully evaluated in psychoanalytic terms. In fact he is a fictional character, not a real person, and his personality lacks the flexibility and polydimensional complexity to be expected of real people, even the most tortured victims of paranoia. He certainly exhibits some of the symptoms of paranoia, as I think has been amply demonstrated, but these are in large part dictated by his circumstances which are imposed, after all, by the delusional requirements of his story. It is his story as a whole which enacts the paranoid syndrome, and he himself remains mostly innocent of its delusional excesses despite the extent to which his life is dominated by them. Not he but his author and sympathetic readers resort to a demonic vision in order to reject patriarchal identification, and even these don't exactly commit themselves to such a fundamental decision. The most that can be claimed would be that they make a conscious and/or unconscious use of Young Goodman Brown's example to question, if not challenge, the often oppressive demands which confront them in their own lives. It is their freedom to indulge in this kind of tentative exploration confident that its harmful consequences will be kept pretty much the burden of Young Goodman Brown. So whether he himself projects his fantasies, as maintained by Crews, he certainly exists as the projection of fantasies by others, his audience, and for this reason he cannot be held fully responsible for being paranoid. Moreover, it is to be emphasized that what Young Goodman Brown suspects might well be true in the context of his story. A devil very probably does approach him disguised as his grandfather, and he very probably does allow himself to be led to a witch's sabbath, making paranoid delusion a reality at least as far as he, a fictional character, is concerned. Anybody who is really approached by the devil, as is not uncommon in literature, cannot be diagnosed as being psychotic for thinking so. What he sees he sees, and he must deal with this as best he can under the circumstances. He might live in a paranoid reality, but as a figment of this reality he can hardly be diagnosed as having been its author.[5] The victim of the imagination of others, he is ultimately innocent of the problems which have been bestowed upon him. This is of course the typical complaint of the paranoid individual, but in the case of a fictional character such as Young Goodman Brown it happens to be true, and he himself at least has no complaints about his mistreatment at the hands of his readers.

Does this mean that it is primarily Hawthorne and his readers who must be charged with being paranoid? Not necessarily. These too escape the diagnosis, but for entirely different reasons. To enjoy a work of fiction which manifests paranoid tendencies does not mean that readers and authors are paranoid or even pre-paranoid, for it is possible to benefit from this cathartic use of fiction without otherwise resorting to paranoia in the conduct of one's affairs. Disbelief can be suspended by readers without giving any credence whatsoever to the delusions they might temporarily entertain while engrossed in reading a story. The paranoid syndrome can be utilized on a provisional and "literary" basis, and with a pleasure and flexibility not to be enjoyed by the genuine victim of paranoia. Paranoia can be "tried on" for the occasion, and with the total confidence that it can just as easily be discarded once it has made its accounting of the eternal struggle between good and evil, happiness and despair, etc. To a certain extent it does provide the same battery of defenses to the reader as it does to the genuine paranoid individual, but with this important difference: the reader can always set it aside with the fullest confidence that it is fiction and that his life needn't be dominated by this fiction. Consequently, neither Hawthorne nor his readers, nor in fact his characters, are to be automatically diagnosed as being paranoid, not even for a story laden with as many paranoid symptoms as can be found in **"Young Goodman Brown."** As indicated earlier, what obviously *can* be described as being paranoid is simply the overall action of the story which pits characters against their circumstances in a paranoid fashion, i.e. in such a manner as to cause the paranoid response. It is the story itself which serves as a kind of free-floating multipurpose delusional system, temporary and artificial, one in which a great variety of personal problems can be brought to allopathic focus upon an intense conflict against hostile forces of one sort or another. By exaggerating this conflict and then bringing it to its resolution, a story such as **"Young Goodman Brown"** shares the same purpose as the paranoid delusion in its reduction of anxiety levels, but unlike the paranoid delusion it makes itself accessible to balanced and healthy vicarious involvement. Such a story is organized in the same manner as the paranoid delusion, but for a larger audience and with the benign and "normal" intention of bringing confrontation to its satisfactory resolution. Like Pirandello's six characters in search of an author, it offers itself as an intact delusional system in search of whatever audience might find temporary pleasure in its manipulation of experience—unified, intensified, and, as it were, both purposeful and ethically determined.

The final and perhaps the most interesting question is whether the paranoid dynamics of **"Young Goodman Brown"** are peculiar to this single story or can be found elsewhere in literature. To what extent, if any, can **"Young Goodman Brown"** be taken as a paradigm of literary experience in general? Can it be used as a model to help explain and understand other works of fiction? And, more specifically, does it have any special relevance to the central tradition of American fiction? There doesn't seem to be any problem in making such a comparison with the rest of Hawthorne's works, since the Oedipal interpretations offered by Crews, Simon Lesser and others can easily be extended to take into account the paranoid traits which are obsessively reenacted from the stories of Ethan Brand and Rappacini to those of Hester and Zenobia. The vision of Hawthorne's fiction has enough guilt-ridden consistency (described by Crews as "underlying sameness") to make such an extension pretty much an exercise in belaboring the obvious.

Nor does there seem to be any difficulty in finding parallels with the mature fiction of Melville, especially *Moby Dick,* which was both written under Hawthorne's influence and dedicated to him. In fact, there are bizarre resemblances and implied interactions which can and ought to be explored in greater depth in order to demonstrate the full precariousness of Young Goodman Brown's desperate choice in life. As Leslie Fiedler has amply demonstrated, *Moby Dick* displays considerable evidence of latent homosexual tendencies, suggesting that it exceeds Hawthorne's fiction in its resistance to patriarchal identification, and with hostility intense enough to be brought to its culmination in tragic self-destruction. Ahab's obsessive pursuit of Moby Dick leads to his doubly phallic destruction impaled to it wherever it penetrates the seas. More fortunate is Ishmael, who very probably survives because he can lovingly handle sperm (i.e. the flesh of whale) and consummate his brotherhood with Queequeg to deserve the coffin which symbolically buoys him to the surface when the Pequod is drawn into its thalassic vortex of destruction. If Melville's symbolism has enough schematic consistency for the ocean to symbolize the womb and Moby Dick the phallus, denizen of the womb, Ahab's obsession forces his self-sacrifice to heterosexual demands—exactly the martyrdom repugnant to Young Goodman Brown. In contrast, Ishmael, like Young Goodman Brown, is repelled by this fate—and in fact, one step better, he can reject it by acknowledging the homosexual affinities which presumably afford him the possibility of salvation. Melville thus seems to resolve Young Goodman Brown's paranoid ambivalence through the polar distinction between these two figures, Ahab and Ishmael, whose respective fates demonstrate the inverted *carpe diem* theme that homophobic repression can only bear self-destructive consequences. If a novel could offer itself as an exemplum to a short-story character, the message of *Moby Dick* to Young Goodman Brown would very probably be that he remove himself from his closet by similarly purging himself of the potentially tragic homophobic impediments which still clutter his imagination. But of course such a recommendation would be particularly repulsive to Young Goodman Brown, even more so than the witch's sabbath he declines.

It is obvious that Melville identifies with Ishmael (he begins *Moby Dick* by telling the reader, "Call me Ishmael"), and, interestingly enough, there is a close resemblance between Ahab and Hawthorne as described by Melville in his correspondence with Hawthorne and in his laudatory review "Hawthorne and his Mosses," where his praise is clearly suggestive of the portrait of Ahab in Chapter XVI. Melville likewise describes Hawthorne in one of his letters with almost exactly the same words as he uses to describe Ahab: "There is a grand truth about Nathaniel Hawthorne. He says No! in thunder; but the devil himself cannot make him say yes." This, we recall, is also suggestive of Young Goodman Brown's rejection of Satan at the forest ceremony. In another of his letters to Hawthorne, Melville also consecrates his novel with Ahab's baptism of the harpoon in the name of the devil, "Ego no baptizo te in nomine patris, sed in nomine diaboli!" But in doing so he truncates his sentence, "This is the book's motto (the secret one), Ego non baptiso te in nomine—but make out the rest for yourself," suggesting that Hawthorne, like Ahab (and Young Goodman Brown too), could be expected to know the temptations of the devil. In "Hawthorne and his Mosses" Melville even makes a direct comparison between Hawthorne and **"Young Goodman Brown"** by paraphrasing one of its sentences, "It is yours to penetrate in every bosom the deep mystery of sin."[7] But of course the ability to make such a penetration does not mean it is exercised, so the ambiguity of "penetrate" (either to "perceive" or "thrust into") puts Hawthorne in the same difficult circumstances as Young Goodman Brown, torn between the examples of Ahab and Ishmael. If there is any resemblance at all between Hawthorne and Ahab, or between Ahab and Young Goodman Brown, it might indeed result from comparable biographical and autobiographical intentions (contrary to my earlier precautions in this paper), but Hawthorne would have been far less fervid in his satanic obsession than Ahab—much closer, in fact, to the example he himself proposed in Young Goodman Brown, and even here the resemblance was probably slight. Melville's implied equation nevertheless stands. If Ishmael could have stepped across the boundaries of fiction to suggest that Young Goodman Brown might "tarry" with him, the latter could be expected to have become instantly transmogrified into another Captain Ahab, peg leg and all. "No, in thunder," he too would have cried, but without plunging to tragic destruction into his own ocean's vortex, mother of life itself. Nor could he even have drunk the more modest glass of poison suggested by Hawthorne's Satan. It was his fate to remain torn between the examples of Ahab and Ishmael, unable to deal with the choice except as a devilish temptation. Extravagant these parallels might seem, but they are too persistent to be overlooked.

What relevance is there beyond Melville of the paranoid example offered by Young Goodman Brown to the continuity of the American literary imagination? Are there any other connections besides this one brief and remarkable instance of personal friendship which seems to have been documented and thereby terminated through the agency of fiction? More, I think, than might be immediately recognized, for Young Goodman Brown epitomizes our national rejection of patriarchal responsibility by means of a regressive dedication to frontier conflict which has been insightfully explored by Fiedler and others in their studies of American fiction. Like Young Goodman Brown, the typical frontier hero offers the reader his escape from domestic priorities through a wilderness quest in which Oedipal difficulties can be projected as if these were an external crisis to be brought to its satisfactory resolution. Young Goodman Brown is perhaps unique as a "negative" example since he confronts the wilderness just once, and very briefly, before returning home to the obligations he must fulfill but cannot entirely accept. As opposed to the seasoned frontiersman, he makes what amounts to a one-night stand, and the farthest he penetrates (both bodily and conceptually) is the clearing where ritual hell-fire provides the turning point in his life. For these others much longer journeys can be undertaken precisely because their Oedipal crisis has been better disguised, more effectively rendered as an issue of frontier survival. As a result, story becomes more optimistic as a repetitive-compulsive pursuit of victory against enemies, personal weaknesses, and a variety of bigger forces to be encountered under western skies. Moreover, the charming but vacuous integrity of the frontiersman can be repeatedly proved as he challenges and extends the unique boundaries of our national consciousness exactly as predicted by Frederick Jackson Turner, if in strictly psychosexual terms with the fruits of emotional paucity absorbed through paranoid frontier victory. In popular culture this frontiersman later becomes the detective whose innocent sophistication at last prevails against sinister schemes to make a "fall guy" of him, then an equally innocent Joe Citizen who is caught in the struggle against communism, international conspiracy, or even a berserk CIA, but who is likewise protected from destruction by his almost regressive integrity. Whatever his persona, he resembles Young Goodman Brown in being saved by his innocence from destructive powers he cannot fully understand—powers which in fact embody and epitomize the latent tendencies his readers must reject in themselves through their compensatory dedication to virtue, justice, and cosmic righteousness.

If such a hero seems to be more capable of spectacular accomplishments than Young Goodman Brown, he nevertheless suffers from the same deficiency in self-awareness and personal integration. Equally important, he almost inevitably falls victim to the same inability to form mature emotional attachments with women, and with little talent for coping with this inadequacy except through profligacy or Platonic admiration—or, in extreme cases, through his sublimation of sexual confusion into a compensatory dedication to violence. This is true of Natty Bummpo, Huck

Finn, and all the rest of the pantheon of American heroes in both the high and low media—even Gatsby and Jake Barnes, Rabbit Angstrom and Augie March, Benny Profane and Humbert Humbert. Like Young Goodman Brown, each seems to be dominated by the regressive search for a Faith too elusive to be put (or kept) on her pedestal. Without skirts to cling to or anybody to follow to heaven, they can only pursue an impotent wilderness quest whose unconscious intentions cannot possibly be accomplished, let alone recognized. Excitement usurps the responsibility incurred by patriarchal identification, a substitution that seems entirely justified by the unhappy example of Young Goodman Brown. The emotional deadlock is perhaps broken which reduces Hawthorne's to chronic anger and suspicion, but vestigial paranoid defenses do remain which are just as much an avoidance of Satan's blood covenant. For this reason Young Goodman Brown should be recognized (at least by psychoanalytic critics) as perhaps the most remarkable of the "negative" archetypes which define the American vision. Hundreds of years before its mythic frontier finally closes in upon itself, he tests its perimeter, judges possibilities, and finds it a "dream of evil omen," one which must bring him to his dying hour a distrustful, if not a desperate man.

Notes

1. The paranoid organization of narrative structure is more thoroughly discussed in my articles, "Defense of the Homophobic Imagination," *College English,* vol. 37, no. 1 (Sept., 1975), pp. 62-67a, and "The Dialectics of Paranoid Form," *Genre,* 11 (spring, 1978), pp. 131-157. A roughly comparable application to poetry is made in my earlier article, "Up against the 'Mending Wall': The Psychoanalysis of a Poem by Frost," *College English,* vol. 34, no. 7 (April, 1973), pp. 934-951.

2. Norman Cameron, "The Paranoid Pseudo-Community," *American Journal of Sociology,* 49:32, 1943; "The Paranoid Pseudo-Community Revisited," *American Journal of Sociology,* 64:52, 1959. Also useful as introductory references are Norman Cameron's "Paranoid Conditions and Paranoia," in *American Handbook of Psychiatry,* ed. by Silvano Arieti, vol. I (New York, 1959), pp. 508-539; and *The Paranoid,* by David Swanson, Philip Bohnert, and Jackson Smith (Boston, 1970).

3. *The Sins of the Fathers: Hawthorne's Psychological Themes* (Oxford, 1966), pp. 98-106.

4. Young Goodman Brown's characterization effectively meshes Freud's explanation of homosexuality in *Leonardo da Vinci: A Psychosexual Study of an Infantile Reminiscence* and his explanation of paranoia as repressed homosexuality in his study of Schreber, *Psycho-analytic Notes on an Autobiographical Account of a Case of Paranoia (Dementia Paranoides).* Seldom is the connection quite so plain either in fiction or the personality of genuine victims of paranoia.

5. It would be tempting to suggest that Young Goodman Brown's most natural response to his difficulties would have been to try his hand at fiction, concocting the life and works of Nathaniel Hawthorne.

6. Leslie Fiedler, *Love and Death in the American Novel* (New York, 1960, 1966), pp. 369-388.

7. Herman Melville, "Hawthorne and his Mosses, by a Virginian Spending a July in Vermont," *Literary World,* August 17, August 24, 1850—in *Billy Budd and Other Prose Pieces by Herman Melville,* ed. by Raymond W. Weaver, from *The Works of Herman Melville* (London, 1924), vol. XIII, p. 140. Also ref. Merrell R. Davis and William H. Gilman, *The Letters of Herman Melville* (New Haven, 1960), pp. 124, 125, 133, 140, etc.

Harold F. Mosher, Jr. (essay date 1980)

SOURCE: "The Sources of Ambiguity in Hawthorne's 'Young Goodman Brown': A Structuralist Approach," in *ESQ: A Journal of the American Renaissance,* Vol. 26, No. 1, 1980, pp. 16-25.

[*In the following essay, Mosher uses a structuralist critical approach to focus on contradictions in meaning and on the reader's relationship with the narrator in "Young Goodman Brown".*]

As Jonathan Culler has observed, the structuralist method, based on the linguistic model, should "account for our judgments about meaning and ambiguity, well-formedness and deviance." The structuralist critic studies the conventions of any system that enables its signs to produce meaning or certain effects. He does not primarily study meaning or seek to formulate new interpretations; rather he examines how meaning or effects are achieved.[1] In such analyses, of course, consideration of meaning cannot be ignored. Thus, Claude Lévi-Strauss, by a method that consists of "dividing the syntagmatic sequence into superposable segments, and in proving that they constitute variations on one and the same theme," studies patterns of opposition that produce meaning in myths.[2] A. J. Greimas has developed the "semiotic square" to account for even more complex relations governed by the principles of contradiction and contrariness.[3] Similarly, a structuralist reading of Hawthorne's **"Young Goodman Brown,"** rather than revealing new meaning, concentrates on how the story produces its ambiguities as well as how it suggests an unambiguous meaning. Using Lévi-Strauss' method, I propose to examine the structure of oppositions in the syntagmatic chain, and adapting other structuralist methods suggested by Gérard Genette, Gerald Prince, and Seymour Chatman,[4] I shall study the contradictions of meaning between and within the unmediated and mediated elements of the discourse, essentially involving the reader's relationship with the narrator and the characters.

Certainly the ambiguity that has created so much critical debate, resulting most obviously from the narrator's refusal to answer his own question about Brown's dream, is real. **"Young Goodman Brown"** is not unique in this respect in Hawthorne's *corpus,* sharing at least its moral ambiguity with that in such other major works as **"My Kinsman, Major Molineux"** and *The Scarlet Letter.*[5] In **"Young Goodman Brown,"** Hawthorne, like his admirer Henry James, tries to create in his readers the same moral ambiguity that confronts his characters while suggesting, often very subtly, the implied author's judgments. Contradictions abound, leading in the imperfect reader (the "narratee" in Gerald Prince's terms)[6] to a confusion similar to the one Brown feels, but at the same time much evidence indicates the implied author's condemnation of Brown's final behavior.

In making these conclusions, I am, of course, not alone. Many critics have pointed out that the ambiguities of the story make a judgment about Brown's condemnation of his fellow villagers virtually impossible.[7] On the other hand, while some think that Brown did experience the forest events and is right in his condemnation of the villagers, still others believe that Brown dreamed or imagined the forest events and is wrong in his condemnation. Sheldon W. Liebman's 1975 article on the story, with which I am basically in agreement, provides a succinct classification of the studies subscribing to these three views and then, while recognizing the story's "diverting ambiguities" on unresolvable and relatively unimportant issues, argues that the story is unambiguous, if one attends closely to point of view, in showing Brown to be a victim of his own thoughts.[8] Liebman, however, provides no clear basis for distinguishing the narrator's point of view from Brown's, claiming that by the principle of "dissimulated point of view" the focus shifts "imperceptibly from narrator to character so that the reader sees through the character's eyes even when he thinks he is seeing through the narrator's" (p. 158). Though Liebman is right in pointing out the many verbs indicating Brown's perception of the action after he leaves Faith, his generalization that thenceforth Hawthorne reports subjective action as if it were objectively happening is open to question and is in fact contradicted, as shall be seen, by Liebman himself. One might, for example, agree with Liebman that the adjective "excellent" describing Brown's "resolve" as he hurries into the forest could represent Brown's interest point of view[9] (or it could, as Richard H. Fogle claims,[10] express the narrator's irony), but the following remark about the solitary traveller is evidently the narrator's editorial, identified by its generalizing sense and use of the present tense: "and there is this peculiarity in such a solitude, that the traveller knows not who may be concealed by the innumerable trunks and the thick boughs overhead; so that with lonely footsteps he may yet be passing through an unseen multitude."[11]

A similar claim to Liebman's that the action of the central part of the story is seen exclusively from Brown's point of view is made by Thomas F. Walsh, Jr., who believes, however, that a study of point of view throws no light on the ambiguities.[12] But Walsh mistakenly identifies the narra-

tor's editorial on man's instinct for evil as Brown's thought and then contradicts his claim for the consistency of Brown's point of view by ascribing to "Hawthorne" the judgment of Brown as "the chief horror" (pp. 334-335). Likewise, David Levin identifies the point of view as Brown's in the paragraph describing the baptism preparations where a shift to the narrator's point of view at least temporarily occurs in the description of Brown's and Faith's hesitating on the verge of evil. Levin argues from the assumption of consistency in point of view, but even a Jamesian consistency involves switches from the central consciousness to the narrator.[13] Agreeing with Levin, Darrel Abel compares Brown's sole authority to the governess' in James' *The Turn of the Screw,* "verifiable by no other observer or 'control.'"[14] But *The Turn of the Screw* is told in the first person, not in the third-person selective omniscient mode of **"Young Goodman Brown."** Furthermore, if the action is viewed exclusively from Brown's point of view, we have to accept such contradictions as his revering his father while picturing him in the devil's guise, as E. Arthur Robinson observes.[15] Although in dreams such contradictions can occur, the text does not clearly set off the real world from the dream world. Even if we were to accept the forest episode as the dream, the narrator's voice and focus are still present periodically throughout the discourse and are distinguishable, at least in many places, from Brown's.

To neglect the switches in point of view which can reveal the narrator's presence and interpretation is to ignore what Leo Levy describes as the mixed realistic/objective and allegorical/subjective nature of the tale whose narrator "moves into Brown's state of mind and then outward" elusively.[16] Although many of these critics' conclusions about the tale's meaning are not invalid, often their analyses of Hawthorne's techniques would benefit from more attention to detail. To examine these techniques in greater depth, I plan to analyze not only the story's structure but also its point of view and particularly what Genette calls "paralipses," omissions by the omniscient narrator (p. 212). Agreeing with much recent criticism, I assume that the implied author intends certain ambiguities because he allows his narrator to leave them unresolved, especially the one on the nature of the action in the forest. I shall also argue that the condemnation of Brown is relatively unambiguous. What I propose to study are the methods by which both the ambiguities and the condemnation are conveyed to the reader.

I will begin with probably the greatest source of ambiguity in **"Young Goodman Brown"**—the unmediated or nonnarrated parts, what characters say and think about themselves and each other and what characters do, as recorded by a relatively "absent" narrator. In Chatman's terminology, the narrator may be either "overt"—describing, summarizing, characterizing, judging, generalizing, and commenting on the discourse (pp. 219-253)—or "covert"—reporting characters' words and thoughts in indirect discourse and its variations (pp. 196-219)—or "absent"—reporting characters' words and thoughts in direct discourse and its variations. This last is considered unmediated narration whereas the first two are mediated (pp. 146-194). The story's beginning emphasizes by dramatic (unmediated) interpretation or characterization the moods of Faith, Brown's wife. The message that the narratee receives directly from her speech is that she is "troubled" and "afeared of herself" for this "of all nights in the year," and her parting husband also analyzes directly her mood in his thoughts as "melancholy" and troubled by the warnings of her dreams. Furthermore, Brown characterizes Faith as an "angel," in contrast to himself, whom he dramatically and indirectly characterizes as temporarily belonging to another persuasion, at least until the morrow (pp. 74-75).[17] This portrait of the wife concerned for her husband seems to accord with the vision of Faith joyfully welcoming Brown the next morning on his return, but her concern for her own steadfastness might just as well be indirectly conveyed by these remarks and especially by her caution to Brown, "may you find all well when you come back" (p. 74). These stasis statements not only expose ambiguous traits and moods of existents (characters), but at the same time project by implied prolepsis (flashforward) events in the future of the plot and thus create suspense, another from of uncertainty.[18] Of what is Faith afraid? What will possibly change the next day's situation?

Brown's character traits are even more evidently self-contradictory, paradigmatically, and are presented, at least dramatically, in the syntagmatic pattern of alternating oppositions, typical of the story's plot.[19] Early he characterizes himself as eliciting doubt from Faith, as being a "wretch," and as having "scruples" for this "one night" after which he will follow Faith "to heaven" (p. 75). In contrast, Brown describes himself to the figure in the forest as one of a "race of honest men and good Christians," who "abide no such wickedness" and vows to return to Faith to avoid this "wickedly" spent night and his feeling of guilt (pp. 77, 81). Despite these professions of goodness, Brown continues deeper into the forest, and, confronted with various spectacles of temptation to pursue evil, he embraces the opportunity to follow the call of the wilderness and identifies with the brotherhood of the wicked, having found his true nature, as the witch minister tells him, inherited from his grandfather and father. The last macro-episode or large segment in the syntagmatic chain shows Brown again resisting evil, or what he considers to be evil, in the form of his fellow citizens, including Faith.

The flat characters, who tend to be part of the setting in accordance with Chatman's distinction between bona fide characters and named but unimportant ones (p. 141), are also characterized contradictorily by unmediated or dramatic means. Brown calls Deacon Gookin and the minister "holy" and Goody Cloyse "pious and exemplary" (pp. 82, 78). Again, however, in the typical pattern of alternating contrasts, this portrait of the villagers is contradicted by framing sets of dramatic characterizations, which picture Cloyse's and Brown's ancestors as friends of the devil in the earlier part of the plot and, in the final part, the deacon and minister as involved in "deviltry" and the whole vil-

lage as steeped in sin.[20] Finally, the devil is somewhat less ambiguously characterized, the syntagmatic pattern being a simple two-part opposition between his first appearance in "grave and decent attire" in the person of Brown's grandfather (as is learned later from Goody Cloyse) and his gradual identification as the devil until he is directly named so by Cloyse. By such contradictory dramatic characterizations, the story and discourse involve the narratee in the moral ambiguities confronting Brown.

According to the conventions of most nineteenth-century fiction, the implied reader could usually count on the omniscient reliable narrator to convey overtly through the narratee the "truth" of the narrative, as the implied author intends it. This is not entirely the case in Hawthorne's tale, beginning with the overtly mediated interpretation of Faith, who is "aptly named." The narratee might accept this trait only up to a certain point in the plot; after the cloud, which seems to Brown to contain Faith's voice, has passed overhead, something flutters down, and Brown "beheld a pink ribbon." The mystery is resolved for Brown, who decides on the basis of this ocular evidence that his "Faith is gone" (p. 83). To the narratee caught up in the excitement of this discovery, the evidence of Faith's guilt might also be convincing, but a narratee closer to the implied reader might look more analytically at the point of view and decide that this token of Faith's infidelity is perceived through Brown's interest point of view and therefore is not evidence for a "fact" of the ribbon's existence. The narrator has only reported that "something fluttered lightly down."[21] This more perceptive narratee might take the description of the ribbon as the narrator's report of what Brown thinks he sees; that is, the narrator is reliable in characterizing Faith as "aptly named" and in reporting strictly what happens in Brown's mind, though the narrator does not comment on the "truth" of those thoughts. A sort of paralipsis has occurred.[22]

Thus the contradictions that seem to abound in the narrator's characterizations and judgments of the Salem villagers may turn out not to be his self-contradictions at all when the point of view is scrutinized. For example, Goody Cloyse is judged to be "pious" (p. 78) and an "excellent old Christian" (p. 89); the "good old minister" is characterized as a "venerable saint" (p. 88). When elsewhere these citizens are called "fiend worshippers" (pp. 87, 88), point of view plays an ambiguous role. Although the judgment of Cloyse as "pious" might very well be Brown's, these other characterizations could be either Brown's or the narrator's. Likewise, during the witches' sabbath episode, it is sometimes not clear whether the action is seen through Brown's eyes or the narrator's. By the omnitemporal analeptic (Genette's term for flashback, p. 82) and proleptic description of these very faces' devout and benign looks, the point of view seems to be the narrator's, but if so, he is describing only the appearance of faces, not necessarily character. Even the presence of the governor's wife is qualified by the narrator's dubious "Some affirm" (p. 85). After the narrator asserts the presence of other Salem villagers including "high dames" and "church members of . . . especial sanctity," he leaves their attendance at the ceremony open to question by switching to Brown's "bedazzled" (p. 85) point of view. The physical, metaphysical, and moral confusions continue as the narratee must reconcile the presence of these people at a witches' sabbath with the narrator's characterization of them as "grave, reputable, and pious" (p. 85). Moreover, in this passage, the narrator uses the very terms—"Good old Deacon Gookin" and "venerable saint"—in which he describes the same characters as they appear in Salem the next day (pp. 88-89). Such a contradiction may indicate the narrator's ironic stance or his unreliability, or it may suggest disagreement between his judgment of the villagers' piety and Brown's conception of their wickedness, or an identification of his language with Brown's in reporting Brown's point of view.

In addition to this manipulation of point of view, the narratee is also subjected to other paralipses. Some minor examples include the narrator's hesitant description of the minister of the witches' sabbath as one who "bore no slight similitude . . . to some grave divine" (p. 86) and whose "once angelic nature could yet mourn for our miserable race" (pp. 87-88). The narratee will probably recognize him as the devil in yet another disguise. The narrator also hesitates in this episode to identify the contents of the communion cup as being either "water, reddened by the lurid light" or "blood" or "liquid flame" (p. 88). Earlier the narrator had analyzed Goody Cloyse's mutterings as "a prayer, doubtless" (p. 79), as if he were not sure, just as he is not certain about the dark figure's staff: that it could "almost be seen to twist and wriggle itself like a living serpent" "must have been an ocular deception" (p. 76). It is certainly difficult at this point in the tale for the narratee to decide if the narrator is speaking ironically (describing indirectly or implicitly), implying that the staff is actually a snake, or describing directly what is the "truth"—that the form of the staff and the light were deceptive. As Victor Vitanza points out,[23] from the point in the plot at which Brown passes "a crook of the road" and sees a "figure of a man" (p. 75), the rest of the action might be recuperated, in Jonathan Culler's term, as a delusion, except that the narrator does seem to assert the objective existence of "these two," Brown and the figure (p. 76).

In contrast, these paralipses and apparent contradictions yield to the narrator's consistency in his characterization and judgments of Brown, who is pictured as "evil" (p. 75), a "horror" (p. 83), "frightful" (p. 83), "demoniac" (p. 84), and a "polluted" wretch (p. 88). One of the major ironies of the tale should be mentioned. As opposed to Brown's and the narrator's paraliptic ignorance about the outcome of Faith's indoctrination into the knowledge of evil, the implied reader must observe what apparently is Brown's awareness of evil by the end of the plot when he sees evil or thinks he sees it everywhere, fulfilling the promise of the "sable form." The narratee might be tempted to conclude that Brown's successful quest for evil turns him into evil, as Brown's own identification with the wicked brotherhood and the wilderness attests. At any rate, the result is,

as the narrator characterizes Brown at the end of the story, a "stern, a sad, a darkly meditative, a distrustful, if not a desperate man" (p. 89), suffering the effects of his search. Does the implied author intend the implied reader to conclude that in a tale of conflicting binary oppositions in the characterizations and judgments of all the other characters, where these oppositions do not exist, the "truth" of the fiction lies? One of the narrator's few generalizations would seem to support this conclusion about Brown's evil nature and consequently mistaken opinion about the evil of life (one delusion leads to another): "The fiend in his own shape is less hideous than when he rages in the breast of man" (p. 84).

But before deciding this matter, I want to look at some of the events, in addition to the existents, both narrated and nonnarrated (Chatman's synonyms for mediated and unmediated). Actually the mutterings of Goody Cloyse and the incident of the staff may be considered not only as integrative indices (signs) of character but also as satellites (minor events), or part of the distributive chain of functions (actions).[24] As already noted, the discourse treated them paraliptically. Paralipsis is a mark of this discourse's narrating other events as well and would therefore seem to be, in turn, an indirect dramatic index of the narrator's unreliability or else his manipulation of the narratee, effected by the narrator's inability, on one hand, or his refusal, on the other, to tell what "really" happened. Thus the narrator's discourse is filled with expressions of doubt. For example, when the dark figure gives his staff to Goody Cloyse, the narrator observes that "perhaps, it assumed life, being one of the rods which its owner had formerly lent to the Egyptian Magi" (p. 79). At first, such an indirect authorial identification of the figure with the devil seems clear, but the "perhaps" modifies not only the "fact" of the transformation of the rod into life but also the reason for that transformation. The narrator might be said to be speculating ironically on a popular explanation of the transformation, if, indeed, a transformation occurred. Or again the narrator tells the narratee that the minister and Deacon Gookin "appeared to pass along the road . . . ; but owing doubtless to the depth of the gloom at that particular spot, neither . . . were visible" (p. 81). The narrator ambiguously both asserts the existence of the "hoof tramps and the voices of the riders" and "their figures" and seems to deny their reality with the qualifiers "appeared" and "neither . . . were visible."[25] Although the point of view here is not always the narrator's, it might well be argued that the narrator is attempting to "naturalize" supernatural events by physical or historical explanations to assure the narratee, at least in this second example, that the figures are people who are there but invisible because of the dark, not apparitions or delusions in Brown's mind. But such reassurances are contradicted paradigmatically by the pervading atmosphere of the supernatural: the miracle of Satan's staff and the "haunted" forest, for instance. Of course, one could argue also that the narrator is ironic and only pretending to convince the narratee that the rod assumed living form or that the people are "real," while expecting the implied reader to realize that the narration is indirect and that these are phantoms of evil or appearances only to Brown. Or, again, the position that the point of view is partly Brown's, at least in the vision of the minister and deacon, can also be argued.[26]

Similar to this trait of the narrator's to imply that supernatural appearance might be explained realistically is the "seems" expression. After describing what to Brown is convincing evidence of Faith's guilt in the form of the ribbon, the narrator says that Brown "seemed to fly along the forest-path rather than to walk or run" (p. 83). Here the narrator's incompetence to report what "really" occurred would appear clear because the point of view can only be his. Later he narrates the hesitancy of Faith and Brown before the baptismal font—"there they stood, the only pair, as it seemed, who were yet hesitating on the verge of wickedness" (p. 88)—as if the narrator did not know how many other pairs might also be hesitating.[27] But these expressions of appearance could also be interpreted simply as common exaggerations which the narrator expects the implied reader to detect. By far the most often repeated expression of paralipsis is "as if." The devil, after Goody Cloyse's disappearance, waits "calmly as if nothing had happened" (p. 80). He disappears "as if he had vanished" (p. 80). Sounds are heard, "as if from the depths of the cloud" (p. 82); their echoes mock "as if bewildered wretches were seeking" Faith (p. 83). Again, though, the doubt could be ascribed to the ambiguity of point of view: these observations might be Brown's.

Other paraliptic measures serve the same purpose of confusing the narratee by either contradicting or asserting and denying. As already noted, the narrator will switch point of view without warning. At the witches' sabbath the identifying of the congregation seems to be in the omniscient narrator's register, but this changes to a simple report of what, in an obscure prolepsis, "Some affirm" (p. 85). The same passage continues, "Either the sudden gleam of light . . . bedazzled Goodman Brown, or he recognized a score of the church members" (p. 85). The narrator is not sure exactly whom Brown sees, if anybody. Such uncertainty might, however, again be ascribed to the narrator's "naturalizing" Brown's hallucination. Switching from Brown's view, the narrator then offers his own judgment of the hymn in the short generalization that it expresses what "our nature can conceive of sin" (p. 85; the first person is a sign of the narrator's voice), and concludes in another editorial, "Unfathomable to mere mortals is the lore of fiends" (p. 85). These two generalizations are somewhat self-contradictory in asserting both the common knowledge and the ignorance of sin. Further, the first one seems to contradict a conclusion about the exclusive evil of Brown. But because generalizations, though perhaps inspired by the fictional action, point outside that action, these are not necessarily commenting on this particular congregation. At the same time, however, the generalization about shared evil serves its contradictory purpose of ironically implicating others, including the narratee, in Brown's evil while seeming to place that evil exclusively in the congregation at the witches' sabbath. On the other

hand, the narrator, earlier in the discourse, might seem to be asserting the morality of that congregation. With the same phrase, "In truth" (p. 83), he had used to judge Brown's frightfulness as he ran madly toward evil, the narrator replies to Brown's dramatic characterization of the congregation as a "grave and dark-clad company" by commenting, "In truth, they were such" (p. 84). But this is only a comment on the appearance of the multitude and is not necessarily making a character judgment. In the same episode the narrator might seem to naturalize the supernatural fire by describing it to be like one in a clearing where felled trees burn, but he immediately cancels this reassuring, realistic impression by saying that only the tops of the pines were burning, "like candles at an evening meeting" (p. 84). The narratee is continually made a victim of apparently reliable commentary that subsequently seems to be denied but seldom provides a firm basis for a definitive judgment.

Again, though, the narratee might conclude that these binary oppositions serve to emphasize the unambiguous theme that the narrator is only reporting the conflicting delusions of a fanatic's mind. Evidence for this view might include the description of the tempest that accompanies Brown's apparent conversion. When the cloud first appears hurrying across the sky, the narrator says that "no wind was stirring" (p. 82) and later that the sky was "clear and silent" (p. 83), but when Brown then accepts evil and hurries off to look for it, the narrator reports that the trees creaked and the "wind tolled" (p. 83), becoming a "tempest" (p. 84) swelling in the hymn at the Ceremony. After Brown calls on Faith to abandon wickedness, he finds himself in a calm, as the wind's roar dies away. The narrator might intend us to interpret the wind as an objective correlative of Brown's excited delusion or, less metacritically, as part of his delusion.[28] Of course, the most obvious paralipsis creating ambiguity is the narrator's raising the question addressed directly to the narratee, suggesting that Brown might have just dreamed this action. On one hand, the narrator seems to answer his own question: "it was a dream of evil omen"; but on the other, this assertion is qualified by the preceding clause—"Be it so, if you will" (p. 89)—as if the identification of the experience as a dream depended on the narratee's decision and is therefore a subjective choice and relatively unimportant. According to the narrator, only the consequences of Brown's experience are significant, being "of evil omen" (p. 89), for the rest of his life and his death were "gloom" (p. 90).

The paradigmatic pattern of binary oppositions or contradictions for the existents is also evident in the syntagmatic structure of the plot's narremes or shorter events.[29] In most of the plot, the alternation between the assurance that life in the story is or can be normal, "real," or good and the doubt or suspicion that it is odd, supernatural, or evil is strikingly regular. For instance, the plot begins with a normal leave-taking, but this normalcy is immediately questioned by Faith's warnings. This is followed by Brown's recognition of his extraordinary errand. His prolepsis about following Faith to heaven after this particular night is undermined by the narrator's judgment of his "present evil purpose" (p. 75) and by the appearance in the forest of the suspicious dark figure. This regular alternation continues until the meeting with Goody Cloyse, during which several narremes elicit doubt about the goodness and normalcy of life. A similar span of unsettling narremes occurs after Brown discovers the pink ribbon, but the alternation resumes when Brown believes that the figure of his mother warns him away from the initiation ceremony. The pattern continues to the end of the plot with such reassuring narremes as Faith's and Brown's hesitation before the baptismal font, Brown's warning to Faith, the disappearance of the vision of the witches' sabbath, and the question from the narrator suggesting that Brown had only dreamed this experience. These narremes alternate with Brown's irresistible attraction to the ceremony, the dark form's description of evil pervading the world, the preparation for baptism, Brown's doubt in Faith's refusal of the baptism, his unusual behavior the next morning in Salem, and finally his ensuing darkened life.

Lévi-Strauss has warned that the oversimplification involved in establishing binary oppositions can result in the contrasting items being changed or distorted beyond recognition.[30] To try to avoid this error, I have multiplied the categories to cover different situations: normal, real, and good are opposed to odd, supernatural, and evil. One must also consider that the identification of this paradigmatic pattern of alternation depends on the recognition of the syntagmatic progress of the narremes that fulfill the pattern. Oversimplification results also from the narratee's failure to see the variations within this pattern. There is in Brown an increasing realization of and attraction to evil as the doubting narremes increase somewhat in quantity and, much more significantly, in importance, particularly in the witches' sabbath episode. Another subtle change that the pattern alone does not reveal is that Brown first denies, then accepts the existence of evil in others and eventually recognizes it also in himself. From a patient enduring happenings, Brown becomes an agent causing actions in his search for evil and then returns to being a patient enduring the evil in himself or ineffectively resisting the evil outside himself.[31] Ultimately we might say that the pattern of doubt and assurance and its subtle variations dramatize the insidious self-persuasion in Brown, and possibly in the narratee, of the prevalence of evil in the world. Brown, at any rate, comes to an assurance that the world is evil, not good, and at least one type of narratee might also be encouraged to doubt that it is entirely good, "real," and normal. Furthermore, because of the network of conflicting characterizations, the narrator's paralipses, contradictions, and ambiguous and switching points of view, as well as the pattern of alternating doubt and assurance, the narratee in the end may not be able to decide whether Brown's rejection of the world receives the author's commendation as a refusal of evil or his condemnation as a result of an immersion in the knowledge of evil. I have suggested that close analysis reveals that Brown is responsible for many questionable judgments which an undiscriminating narratee might assign to the narrator, and I have further argued that the narrator's consistently unfavorable judgment of Brown may reveal the implied author's preference for condemning Brown. Whether one accepts this conclusion or prefers, using Wayne Booth's principle of "unstable irony,"[32] the interpretation accepting the story's ultimate ambiguity, the structuralist critic has learned, by studying the story's pattern and the discourse's manipulation of point of view, something about the sources and effects of that ambiguity.

Notes

1. *Structuralist Poetics* (Ithaca: Cornell Univ. Press, 1975), p. 31.

2. *The Raw and the Cooked,* trans. John and Doreen Weightman (New York: Harper and Row, 1969), p. 307.

3. *Du Sens* (Paris: Seuil, 1970).

4. Genetee, "Discourse du récit" in *Figures III* (Paris: Seuil, 1972), pp. 65-273; Prince, "Introduction à l'étude du narrataire," *Poétique,* 14 (1973), 178-196; Chatman, *Story and Discourse* (Ithaca: Cornell Univ. Press, 1978).

5. Regarding this problem of ambiguity, and more specifically its source, Edgar A. Dryden, *Nathaniel Hawthorne: The Poetics of Enchantment* (Ithaca: Cornell Univ. Press, 1977), p. 138, notes that in *"The Scarlet Letter* and *The House of the Seven Gables* it is difficult to distinguish between fiction and history, imagination and perception."

6. Wayne Booth, *The Rhetoric of Fiction* (Chicago: Univ. of Chicago Press, 1961), pp. 70-71, is, of course, responsible for the term "implied author," the real author's other self, invented as the moving principle for the fiction. Gerald Prince, "Introduction," pp. 179-187, makes careful distinctions among types of readers and narratees. See also Chatman, pp. 33; 147-151; 253-262, on narratee, narrator, implied author, and implied reader.

7. Referring to the realistic and the fantastic readings of the story, Charles Child Walcutt, *Man's Changing Mask* (Minneapolis: Univ. of Minnesota Press, 1966), p. 126, remarks that "Hawthorne . . . has interwoven these two possibilities so tightly that it is impossible to show that either one represents the accurate reading of the story."

8. "The Reader in 'Young Goodman Brown,'" *The Nathaniel Hawthorne Journal 1975*, ed. C. E. Frazer Clark, Jr. (Englewood, Colo.: Microcard Editions Books, 1975), pp. 156-169. See Liebman's review of some of the scholarship, p. 157, and also Robert J. Stanton, "Secondary Studies on Hawthorne's 'Young Goodman Brown,' 1845-1975: A Bibliography," *Bulletin of Bibliography,* 33 (1976), 32-44, 52.

9. Chatman, *Story and Discourse,* p. 162, defines interest point of view as the concerns of a character, if not actually his vision or thought.

10. *Hawthorne's Fiction: The Light and the Dark* (Norman: Univ. of Oklahoma Press, 1952), p. 31.

11. Nathaniel Hawthorne, "Young Goodman Brown" in *Mosses from an Old Manse,* ed. William Charvat, Roy Harvey Pearce, and Claude M. Simpson, The Centenary Edition of the Works of Nathaniel Hawthorne, X (Columbus: Ohio State Univ. Press, 1974), p. 75. Further references to this edition will be noted in the text.

12. "The Bedeviling of Young Goodman Brown," *Modern Language Quarterly,* 19 (1958), 331.

13. "Shadows of Doubt: Specter Evidence in Hawthorne's 'Young Goodman Brown,'" *American Literature,* 34 (1962), 350.

14. "Black Glove and Pink Ribbon: Hawthorne's Metonymic Symbols," *New England Quarterly,* 42 (1969), 180.

15. "The Vision of Goodman Brown: A Source and Interpretation," *American Literature,* 35 (1963), 222.

16. "The Problem of Faith in 'Young Goodman Brown,'" *Journal of English and Germanic Philology,* 74 (1975), 375.

17. My terms "indirect" and "direct" correspond to Chatman's implicit (ironic) and explicit commentary respectively, p. 228.

18. For more complete definitions of "stasis statement," "exposing," "projecting," and "events," see Chatman, pp. 32-33. "Prolepsis" is Genette's term, p. 82.

19. I am using "paradigmatic" and "syntagmatic" in the usual Saussurean, structuralist way to mean, respectively, the reserve of meaning (particularly character traits and settings) available for the discourse's use and the sequence of actions occurring "linearly" throughout the story.

20. Joseph T. McCullen, "Young Goodman Brown: Presumption and Despair," *Discourse,* 2 (1959), 149 and 156, n. 13, notices these contradictions but attributes them to Hawthorne's belief in the mixture of good and evil in people. On the other hand, without taking contradictory evidence into consideration, D. M. McKeithan, "Hawthorne's 'Young Goodman Brown': An Interpretation," *Modern Language Notes,* 67 (1952), 96, asserts the goodness of the Salem villagers.

21. P. 83. L. Moffitt Cecil notes the correspondence between Brown's deluding eyesight and his faulty insight as typical of many of Hawthorne's characters in "Hawthorne's Optical Device," *American Quarterly,* 15 (1963), 82-83.

22. Liebman, "The Reader," pp. 161-162, points out many such instances of objective "facts" being actually only perceived by Brown who, for instance, "beheld the figure of a man," "recognized a very pious and exemplary dame," "heard the tramp of horses," "recognized the voices," "sees" a black cloud and a fire, thinks he sees his father and mother, and "beheld" Faith at the meeting. Many critics have, of course, discussed the famous pink ribbons, testing

their reality or symbolic value. Leo Levy, "The Problem of Faith," p. 377, argues for their reality on the basis of the "tangible evidence" that Brown seizes and beholds, but Hawthorne's grammatical constructions typically do not allow such positive identification. What Brown seizes is referred to as "it," whose antecedent is the vague "something" that has fluttered down and which is seen only by Brown as a ribbon. Faith has her ribbons the next day. As for the symbolic significance of the ribbons, the ambiguity of the story has inspired much difference of opinion, as Levy points out, "The Problem," p. 382.

23. "Teaching Roland Barthes' Method of Textual Analysis, with an Example from Hawthorne," unpublished paper given at the Roland Barthes Special Session, Modern Language Association Convention, 1977.

24. Chatman's terminology, pp. 32-33, 53-56, is borrowed and adapted from Roland Barthes' as developed in his seminal article, "Introduction à l'analyse structurale des récits," *Communications,* 8 (1966), 1-27.

25. Taylor Stoehr, "'Young Goodman Brown' and Hawthorne's Theory of Mimesis," *Nineteenth-Century Fiction,* 23 (1969), 402-403, points out Hawthorne's use of these qualifying expressions in his tales and claims that about thirty of them appear in "Young Goodman Brown." The purpose, according to Stoehr, is not to suggest allegorical meanings but rather to suspend "judgment on all apparent meanings, which are nonetheless offered as possibilities" (p. 403). This technique (and I agree) puts the reader in the same ambiguous situation as the characters but "with some additional hints" as to the solutions of the problem (p. 406). Stoehr, however, does not give any specific examples of these hints.

26. Misreadings by critics like Leo B. Levy, "The Problem of Faith," p. 381, who on one hand seems to recognize the possibility of Brown's projection in hearing "a voice like Deacon Gookin's" but on the other claims that Gookin's words are not offered as "something Brown imagines," may very well result from a neglect of point of view. The narrator emphasizes the subjective quality of Brown's perceptions by such qualifying words as "appeared," "without discerning," "were such a thing possible" (p. 81). Similarly, the other extreme of interpretation, like that of Paul J. Hurley, "Young Goodman Brown's 'Heart of Darkness,'" *American Literature,* 37 (1966), 415, which denies the possibility of the narrator's attesting to the objective existence of the minister and the deacon, is equally mistaken in neglecting the ambiguity and the shifting of point of view.

27. Liebman, p. 159, notices other examples of the "seems" expression: the figure's "snakelike staff actually seemed to wriggle in sympathy" and the figure touches Goody Cloyse's neck "with what seemed the serpent's tail." But Liebman claims that the comment about the couple's hesitation is Brown's, not the nar-

rator's (p. 162), while identifying the following comments on the contents of the baptismal font to be "Hawthorne's" (p. 159), a contradiction of his principle of subjective action. As noted before, Liebman does not provide a clear basis for distinguishing between the narrator's and Brown's points of view.

28. Liebman, p. 163, also interprets the tempest as part of Brown's delusion.

29. Richard Harter Fogle, *Hawthorne's Fiction: The Light and the Dark,* rev. ed. (Norman: Univ. of Oklahoma Press, 1964), pp. 25-27, points out other contrasts like those between day and night, town and forest, red and black, serving as symbolic and stylistic balancing, as well as the thematic opposition between appearance and reality.

30. See Culler, p. 15.

31. The relation between patient and happening and agent and action is defined by Chatman, p. 32.

32. See *A Rhetoric of Irony* (Chicago: Univ. of Chicago Press, 1974), p. 240. In unstable irony, "the author—insofar as we can discover him, and he is often very remote indeed—refuses to declare himself, however subtly, *for* any stable proposition."

James L. Williamson (essay date 1981)

SOURCE: "'Young Goodman Brown': Hawthorne's 'Devil in Manuscript,'" in *Studies in Short Fiction,* Vol. 18, No. 2, Spring, 1981, pp. 155-62.

[*In the following essay, Williamson suggests that Hawthorne exhibits a gleeful, mocking narrative persona in "Young Goodman Brown" in order to expose pretensions about life and literature.*]

When Hawthorne commented on the vocation of authorship, he was often drawn to analogies between writing and damnation. ". . . authors," he wrote with tongue-in-cheek in 1821, "are always poor devils, and therefore Satan may take them."[1] The pun is on "devil," which can mean a literary hack; and the meaning is clear: to write conventionally and without integrity is to damn oneself as a writer, even at the cost of popularity and recognition. ". . . America is now wholly given over to a d[amne]d mob of scribbling women," Hawthorne wrote in 1855, "and I should have no chance of success while the public taste is occupied with their trash—and should be ashamed of myself if I did succeed."[2] Yet, going to the devil, in another context, was the highest form of praise Hawthorne could bestow on a fellow author. "The woman writes as if the Devil was in her," he commented upon reading Sara P. Willis's *Ruth Hall,* "and that is the only condition under which a woman ever writes anything worth reading. Generally women write like emasculated men . . . ; but when they throw off the restraints of decency, and come before the public stark naked, as it were,—then their books are

sure to possess character and value."[3] To write as though possessed in this sense meant to penetrate beneath social convention and to speak in an authentic, potent voice. Such a descent could be liberating (for writer and reader), as well as damning in a personal and professional sense. For when Hawthorne described *The Scarlet Letter* as "positively a h[el]l-f[ire]d story," he bestowed upon his Romance his highest praise and severest criticism. A hell-fired story was "powerfully written," but, for that reason, unlikely to "appeal to the broadest class of sympathies," nor to "obtain a very wide popularity."[4] To write as though possessed from this perspective was to contend with social and literary conventions (as the root meaning of "Satan" is "adversary"), and a writer who challenged such conventions could expect to alienate part of the popular reading audience.

The personal cost of going to the devil as a writer was earliest dramatized in the figure of Oberon, the artist hero of **"The Devil in Manuscript,"** a burlesque on the conditions of authorship in America in the 1830's. Published in the *New-England Magazine* seven months following the appearance of **"Young Goodman Brown,"** the sketch provides an excellent gloss on that tale. For Oberon has given himself to the devil; that is, his vocation has been dedicated to creating in fiction "'the character of a fiend, as represented in our traditions and the written records of witchcraft.'" "'You remember,'" he tells his companion, "'how the hellish thing used to suck away the happiness of those who, by a simple concession that seemed almost innocent, subjected themselves to his power. Just so my peace is gone, and all by these accursed manuscripts.'" Just so Goodman Brown's innocent venture into the devil's woods and simple concessions to the devil's arguments will end in his permanent loss of peace and happiness. And just so will Brown come to find himself trapped in a world of uncertainties and spectral appearances. "'I am surrounding myself with shadows,'" laments Oberon, "'which bewilder me, by aping the realities of life. They have drawn me aside from the beaten path of the world, and led me into a strange sort of solitude—a solitude in the midst of men—where nobody wishes for what I do, nor thinks nor feels as I do. The tales have done all this.'" But Oberon, unlike Brown, is finally of the devil's party. His tale concludes not with death and gloom, but with fire and triumph, as the ashes from his burning manuscripts escape from the chimney to set the town ablaze. "'My tales!'" he cries. "'The chimney! The roof! The Fiend has gone forth by night, and startled thousands in fear and wonder from their beds! Here I stand—a triumphant author! Huzza! Huzza! My brain has set the town on fire!'" Oberon's final words affirm the demonic, that is, destructive but liberating aspects of his art as it awakens his neighbors from their accustomed slumbers to "fear and wonder." Although Brown lacks the ironic, cosmopolitan perspective of the artist, and although he fears the wrath of an Old Testament God throughout his life of gloom, he nonetheless suffers the fate of the romantic writer: a damnation that becomes a salvation (however unorthodox). To examine **"Young Goodman Brown"** from this point of view, however, we must turn from Brown for a moment to focus on the speaker of the tale, remembering Hawthorne's analogies between writer and devil, as well as between writing and damnation. As we shall see, the devil figures who appear to Brown in the woods will each bear a certain resemblance to the speaker of the tale, or to those characteristics of the speaker dramatized in his voice. The speaker, that is, will show himself to be of the devil's party, and Brown's experience in the woods will come to represent the experience of art, of reading the tale **"Young Goodman Brown."**[5]

II

At a climactic moment, as he is about to be baptized into the devil's fold, Goodman Brown calls upon Faith to "'Look up to Heaven, and resist the Wicked One!'" Yet in the course of the tale, Brown encounters not one, but three "wicked ones," each with a peculiar character and distinct voice. The first of these devils presents himself as a casual, urbane individual: "simply clad" and "as simple in manner too," but possessing "an indescribable air of one who knew the world, and would not have felt abashed at the governor's dinner-table, or in King William's court. . . ." Adept at the art of understatement, this devil addresses Brown in an amused, patronizing tone as he mimics Brown's own naive pretensions and self-righteousness. Witness the following dialogue:

> "My father never went into the woods on such an errand, [exclaimed Brown] nor his father before him. We have been a race of honest men and good Christians, since the days of the martyrs. And shall I be the first of the name of Brown, that ever took this path, and kept—"
>
> "Such company, thou wouldst say," observed the elder person, interpreting his pause. "Well said, Goodman Brown! I have been as well acquainted with your family as with ever a one among the Puritans; and that's no trifle to say. I helped your grandfather, the constable, when he lashed the Quaker woman so smartly through the streets of Salem. And it was I that brought your father a pitch-pine knot, kindled at my own hearth, to set fire to an Indian village, in King Philip's war. They were my good friends, both; and many a pleasant walk have we had along this path, and returned merrily after midnight. I would fain be friends with you, for their sake"
>
> (X, 76-77).[6]

This devil subverts Brown's sentimental view of his ancestral past in manner as well as matter; for linked with the evidence of those ancestors' sins is a satiric, parodic mode of expression that reduces Brown's arguments to a child's recitations. It will be no accident that the second devil figure Brown witnesses will appear in the form of the old woman who taught him his catechism; but just as telling is the first devil's striking resemblance to both Brown's father and grandfather.[7] In appearance, as well as theme and tone, this devil mocks Brown's words.

The speaker, too, shows these devilish characteristics; for he can be quite condescending and sarcastic toward his bewildered hero. For example, Brown begins his night experience with the following sentiment about Faith: "'Well; she's a blessed angel on earth; and after this one night, I'll cling to her skirts and follow her to Heaven.'" "With this excellent resolve for the future," responds the speaker in a tone that parodies Brown's naive presumptuousness, "Goodman Brown felt himself justified in making more haste on his present evil purpose." And when, deep within the dark woods, Brown sits down and refuses to go on with the devil, the speaker makes the following damning comment:

> The young man sat a few moments, by the road-side, applauding himself greatly, and thinking with how clear a conscience he should meet the minister, in his morning-walk, nor shrink from the eye of good old Deacon Gookin. And what calm sleep would be his, that very night, which was to have been spent so wickedly, but purely and sweetly now, in the arms of Faith! Amidst these pleasant and praiseworthy meditations . . .
>
> (X, 80-81).

Like the urbane devil, the speaker mocks Brown in Brown's own words. The consequence of this technique is a sustained tone of satire in the tale. To cite another example, consider how the speaker describes Brown's initial reactions to the gathering of devils and witches in the woods:

> Either the sudden gleams of light, flashing over the obscure field, bedazzled Goodman Brown, or he recognized a score of the church-members of Salem village, famous for their especial sanctity. . . . But, irreverently consorting with these grave, reputable, and pious people, these elders of the church, these chaste dames and dewy virgins, there were men of dissolute lives and women of spotted fame, wretches given over to all mean and filthy vice, and suspected even of horrid crimes. It was strange to see, that the good shrank not from the wicked, nor were the sinners abashed by the saints
>
> (X, 85).

Here the speaker combines his omniscient point of view that allows him to describe Brown's feelings about events with a viewpoint that imitates Brown's literal process of observation. His "either . . . or" device dramatizes Brown's dilemma as a participant in the events of the tale; but, at the same time, his melodramatic, almost mawkish sentiments are satiric comments on Brown's moral priggishness: his naive desire to see clear-cut divisions in human experience.

The second devilish figure, a boisterous old hag named Goody Cloyse, appears to Brown in the shape of the "very pious and exemplary dame" and "Christian woman," who we are told, "had taught him his catechism." Colloquial in speech, folksy, and something of a gossip (in the nineteenth as well as the seventeenth century meaning of the word) and quarreler, she overflows with a mirthful spirit and mocking wit. The scene in which she appears commences with a pun and verges upon farce as it develops:

> "The devil!" screamed the pious old lady.
>
> "Then Goody Cloyse knows her old friend?" observed the traveller, confronting her, and leaning on his writhing stick.
>
> "Ah, forsooth, and is it your worship, indeed?" cried the good dame. "Yea, truly is it, and in the very image of my old gossip, Goodman Brown, the grandfather of the silly fellow that now is. But—would your worship believe it?—my broomstick hath strangely disappeared, stolen, as I suspect, by that unhanged witch, Goody Cory, and that, too, when I was all anointed with the juice of smallage and cinque-foil and wolfs-bane—"
>
> "Mingled with fine wheat and the fat of a new-born babe," said the shape of old Goodman Brown.
>
> "Ah, your worship knows the receipt," cried the old lady, cackling aloud. "So, as I was saying, being all ready for the meeting, and no horse to ride on, I made up my mind to foot it; for they tell me, there is a nice young man to be taken into communion to-night . . ."
>
> (X, 79).

The old hag's opening exclamation works as an ironic counter to Brown's repeated invocations of "Faith"; indeed, the pervasive tone of her remarks mocks Brown's sentimental expectations of how "pious" older women should conduct themselves, while retaining the childish diction associated with religious persons in their dotage. If the first devil acts as her foil on this occasion, then the speaker participates in the jesting as well, repeatedly referring to her as the "pious old lady" and "good dame" in blatantly ironic contexts and mimicking Brown's point of view when he introduces her as "mumbling some indistinct words, a prayer, doubtless. . . ." Later at the witch meeting, the speaker will become something of a gossip himself. "Some affirm," he tells us as though he were repeating a rumor, "that the lady of the governor was there. At least, there were high dames well known to her. . . ." And, when the shape of Martha Carrier appears, he gives vent to a sudden outburst of devilish spite: "A rampant hag was she!"

Going to the devil, in **"Young Goodman Brown,"** means not just encountering certain unsettling insights into the terrible and the grotesque in human experience, but also confronting a mocking, satiric attitude toward such revelations. The devils who haunt Brown's woods know how to laugh; and there is a kernel of devilish wisdom in the first figure's words to Brown during "a fit of irrepressible mirth": "'Ha!ha!ha!' shouted he, again and again; then composing himself, 'Well, go on, Goodman Brown, go on; but pr'y thee, don't kill me with laughing!'" Could Brown learn to laugh, that is, could he learn to take an ironic view toward his experience in the Salem woods, then he might well begin to exorcise his tormenting devils. He will never be able to dismiss their words, but he might learn to live with them. Perhaps the best commentary on this aspect of the tale is to be found in a passage written two decades later in *The Scarlet Letter.* Commenting on Dimmesdale's vigils before the looking glass, in which "diabolic shapes" grin and mock at the bewildered minister and "spectral thoughts" assume life-like form, the speaker of the Romance points out that, although such fantasies are "the truest and most substantial things" to Dimmesdale, and although their effect is to steal "the pith and substance out of whatever realities" surround him, nevertheless: "Had he once found power to smile, and wear a face of gayety, there would have been no such man!" (I, 145-146). Certainly in both **"Young Goodman Brown"** and *The Scarlet Letter,* the speaker is on hand to show the reader that such laughter is possible; indeed, that an amused, ironic attitude toward the darker aspects of human experience is an accommodation of art to the recognition of the perverse and the demonic.

The third devil figure, who appears to Brown at the witches' meeting, is more grave and formal than his predecessors, though he shares their disposition for mocking wit. "With reverence be it spoken," the speaker tells us, "the figure bore no slight similitude, both in garb and manner, to some grave divine of the New-England churches." And this devil addresses Brown "in a deep and solemn tone, almost sad, with its despairing awfulness, as if his once angelic nature could yet mourn for our miserable race." Nonetheless, the incongruity between dark matter and light, ironic manner is apparent in his sermonic form of speech.[8]

> "There . . . are all whom ye have reverenced from youth. Ye deemed them holier than yourselves, and shrank from your own sin, contrasting it with their lives of righteousness, and prayerful aspirations heavenward. Yet, here are they all, in my worshipping assembly! This night it shall be granted you to know their secret deeds; how hoary-bearded elders of the church have whispered wanton words to the young maids of their households; how many a woman, eager for widow's weeds, has given her husband a drink at bed-time, and let him sleep his last sleep in her bosom; how beardless youths have made haste to inherit their fathers' wealth; and how fair damsels—blush not, sweet ones!—have dug little graves in the garden, and bidden me, the sole guest, to an infant's funeral . . ."
>
> (X, 87).

The speaker, too, affects a reflective, mock-reverential pose. His appeal to "the sacred truths of our religion" at the conclusion of the tale, as well as such asides to the reader as: "With reverence be it spoken . . ." (cited above), express a mock-pious attitude; but the speaker can also affect a graver, moralistic tone. "The fiend in his own shape is less hideous," he tells us as, maddened with despair, Brown rushes through the forest, "than when he rages in the breast of man." Like the devils in the tale, the speaker is something of a chameleon, assuming now an amused, satiric tone of voice, now a graver, moralistic seriousness.

III

The speaker in **"Young Goodman Brown"** bears, then, a striking resemblance to the devil figures in the tale. He shares with them an ironic, parodic mode that ranges from boisterous laughter, to subtle, amused satire, to mock-reverential reflectiveness. In manner, as well as matter, the devils subvert Brown's naive notions; and the speaker is on hand to support their designs. Indeed, the speaker's mocking attitude is directed not just toward Brown, but toward the conventions of Romance as well. "And Faith, as the wife was aptly named . . .," he comments in the opening lines of the tale, countering his allegoric appeal with an amused detachment toward the very process of allegory. "But the only thing about him, that could be fixed upon as remarkable," he tells his reader when introducing the first devil figure, "was his staff, which bore the likeness of a great black snake, so curiously wrought, that it might almost be seen to twist and wriggle itself, like a living serpent. This, of course, must have been an ocular deception, assisted by the uncertain light." Throughout the tale the speaker will present his reader traditional emblems like the serpentine staff, but will do so in a teasing manner. Affecting a naive pose, so that he appears an inquisitive, unsophisticated spectator of events, he mimics Brown's perspective. Yet his commonsense observations have a sarcastic resonance to them, reinforced by such ironic qualifiers as "of course," "doubtless," "in truth," and "perhaps." Like the devil figures in the tale, the speaker feigns a Brown-like innocence as he satirically mocks such credulity.

Brown's complacent faith in saintly ancestors and angelic wives, as well as a moral order that reflects a clear-cut segregation between good and evil, makes him an inviting target for the devils' satire. Behind this attack on Brown lies Hawthorne's own burlesque on certain conventions of authorship in the 1830's: the attitude, for example, that historical romance should suppress those aspects of the past which, in Rufus Choate's words, "chills, shames, disgusts us," while accommodating "the show of things to the desires and needs of the immortal, moral nature,"[9] and, for another example, the cult of "Heaven, Home, and Mother"[10] preached by the scribbling women Hawthorne damned in 1855. For Brown acts as a determined sentimentalist throughout his adventure, fleeing from the unpleasant aspects of his past and his home into pat, reassuring morals whenever he can. The opening scene of the tale dramatizes this pattern well.

"Dearest heart," whispered [Faith], softly and rather sadly, when her lips were close to [Brown's] ear, "pr'y thee, put off your journey until sunrise, and sleep in your own bed to-night. A lone woman is troubled with such dreams and such thoughts, that she's afeard of herself, sometimes. Pray, tarry with me this night, dear husband, of all nights in the year!"

"My love and my Faith," replied young Goodman Brown, "of all nights in the year, this one night must I tarry away from thee. . . . What, my sweet, pretty wife, dost thou doubt me already, and we but three months married!"

"Then, God bless you!" said Faith, with the pink ribbons, "and may you find all well when you come back."

"Amen!" cried Goodman Brown. "Say thy prayers, dear Faith, and go to bed at dusk, and no harm will come to thee"

(X, 74-75).

Though Faith's manner is coy and playful, her words reveal a deeper, more unsettling aspect of her character. A "lone woman," "troubled with such dreams and such thoughts, that she's afeard of herself, sometimes," she seems to want Brown to remain at home to protect her from experiencing facets of herself with which she is uncomfortable. Her parting words to her husband show a troubled resignation and sound more like a challenge than a blessing. Brown's responses show his reluctance to scrutinize his wife's troubled words and puzzling tone. In leaving behind "a blessed angel on earth" for a flirtation with evil in the night woods, Brown seems to hope to evade a problematic moment in his marriage; but in the woods he will be forced to confront unpleasant aspects of his wife and himself as he encounters the dark words and unsettling visions of the devils. Behind these mocking antagonists stands the skeptical figure of the author's persona, mocking such pretensions about life and literature. This "devil in manuscript," like his counterparts in the tale, combines a tragic perspective with a satiric wit, converting "gloom" into demonic delight: the delight of writing "hell-fired" satires like **"Young Goodman Brown."**

Notes

1. From a letter dated 13 March 1821 from Hawthorne to his mother. See Julian Hawthorne, *Nathaniel Hawthorne and His Wife; A Biography* (Boston: Osgood, 1885), I, 108.

2. From a letter dated January, 1855, from Hawthorne to William D. Ticknor. See Caroline Ticknor, *Hawthorne and His Publisher* (Boston: Houghton, Mifflin, 1913), p. 141.

3. *Hawthorne and His Publisher,* p. 142, from a letter from Hawthorne to Ticknor dated February, 1855.

4. From a letter dated 4 February 1850 from Hawthorne to Horatio Bridge. See Bridge, *Personal Recollections of Nathaniel Hawthorne* (New York: Harper, 1893), pp. 111-112.

5. The following studies of "Young Goodman Brown" have most influenced this approach to the tale. Curtis Dahl's "The Devil is a Wise One," *Cithara*, 6 (May 1967), 52-58, makes the well-taken point that the devil can often be a spokesman in Hawthorne's tales for the author's own subtle and paradoxical ideas. R. H. Fogle's two studies of the tale discuss its "light and idealizing" tone, as well as its elements of understatement and parody. See "Ambiguity and Clarity in Hawthorne's 'Young Goodman Brown,'" *New England Quarterly,* 18 (December 1945), 448-465, and "Weird Mockery: An Element of Hawthorne's Style," *Style,* 2 (Fall 1968), 191-202. Sheldon W.

Liebman contributes to the discussion of Hawthorne's narrative mode in "The Reader in 'Young Goodman Brown,'" *Nathaniel Hawthorne Journal 1975* (Englewood, Co.: Microcard Editions, 1975), 156-169. The reader, he finds, is made to be the central character of the story, and Hawthorne's narrative technique works to put him in Brown's place. Indirect but nonetheless important sources for this discussion are Taylor Stoehr's "'Young Goodman Brown' and Hawthorne's Theory of Mimesis," *Nineteenth-Century Fiction,* 23 (March 1969), 393-412, and Darrel Abel's "Black Glove and Pink Ribbon: Hawthorne's Metonymic Symbols," *New England Quarterly,* 42 (June 1969), 163-180. For writers like Hawthorne, writes Stoehr, "correspondences of dream and reality are to a great extent problems of verbal imagination, referential language, and literary mimesis." The tale, from this perspective, is "peculiarly about itself, about the nature of belief in imagined realities, and about the status of such realities."

6. All quotations from Hawthorne's fiction are from *The Centenary Edition of the Works of Nathaniel Hawthorne,* eds. William Charvat et al. (Columbus, Ohio: Ohio State University Press, 1962-). References to longer passages are identified by volume and page numbers.

7. "Still, they might have been taken for father and son," the speaker tells us, referring to the first devil figure and Brown. Later, a witch in the shape of the woman who taught Brown his catechism will compare this devil to "the very image of . . . Goodman Brown, the grandfather of the silly fellow that now is."

8. Fogle makes the following comment on this passage: "The difference between matter and manner is great, considering that the matter is lust, murder most foul, and possibly abortion. There is a ceremonious gallantry, along with an indulgent chiding, in 'fair damsels—blush not, sweet ones.' Girls will be girls, and a very entertaining circumstance it is, too." See "Weird Mockery: An Element of Hawthorne's Style," p. 199.

9. Quoted from extracts of Rufus Choate's 1833 oration, "The Importance of Illustrating New-England History by a Series of Romances Like the Waverly Novels," reprinted in Neal Frank Doubleday's *Hawthorne's Early Tales, A Critical Study* (Durham, N. C.: Duke University Press, 1972), p. 25. See especially Doubleday's discussion of literary theory and Hawthorne's practice in the "Age of Scott," pp. 18-26.

10. See Herbert Ross Brown's discussion of Richardson and the "triumph of the novel" in America in *The Sentimental Novel in America, 1789-1860* (New York: Pageant Books, 1940), pp. 3-51.

Norman H. Hostetler (essay date 1982)

SOURCE: "Narrative Structure and Theme in 'Young Goodman Brown,'" in *Journal of Narrative Technique,* Vol. 12, No. 3, Fall, 1982, pp. 221-28.

[*In the following essay, Hostetler discusses variant critical interpretations of Brown's experience as seen by both Brown and the narrator in "Young Goodman Brown." Hostetler posits that Hawthorne's intersection of these two points of view illustrates "the fatal consequences of psychological misjudgment."*]

One of Nathaniel Hawthorne's major themes concerns conscious awareness of the reality which the mind imposes on external objects. Hawthorne's characters are repeatedly confronted by the need to establish the relationship between their imaginations and the external world.[1] Their ability to make the epistemological distinctions between the products of their mental processes and their sense impressions of the external world frequently governs their ability to develop a sound moral relationship with other people.

"Young Goodman Brown" illustrates especially well the fatal consequences of psychological misjudgment concerning perception and reality.[2] The problem of establishing point of view is central to developing this interpretation. Although Hawthorne's narrator exists outside the story line, the tension between the conflicting interpretations of experience provided by the narrator and Goodman Brown from their different points of view creates the basic ironic tone of the work. From this irony, Hawthorne develops his criticism of Brown's lack of awareness of the controlling power of the mind.

Recognition of this cause for Brown's behavior is essential in order to reconcile the divergent emphases that have been placed on the story. Interpretations have generally concerned themselves with the way in which Brown is deluded rather than with why Brown should make such serious errors in judgment or with why Hawthorne should so sharply and pervasively differentiate the narrator and Brown.[3] Most critics have, of course, recognized that at least a part of Brown's experience is a "dream," "vision," or "hallucination," but they are more concerned with individual choice, often moral or theological (in which case Brown is a deluded individual), or with an introduction to knowledge, usually psychological (in which case Brown's initiation is Everyman's).[4] Brown does destroy himself morally, as the end of the story makes clear, yet as Frederick Crews notes, "the richness of Hawthorne's irony is such that, when Brown turns to a Gulliver-like misanthropy and spends the rest of his days shrinking from wife and neighbors, we cannot quite dismiss his attitude as unfounded."[5] By differentiating the points of view of the narrator and Brown, Hawthorne creates the multiple perspective necessary to validate all these critical emphases.

The narrator's description of events is characterized by the ambiguity that Richard Fogle has pointed out.[6] The "uncertain light" that plays over everything obscures and confuses all appearances so that it is impossible to ascertain anything objective. Fogle, in fact, does not really go far enough in discerning ambiguities, for he restricts himself mostly to the narrator's literal expressions of doubt and alternative possibilities. He accepts as fact that Brown's conductor into the forest "is, of course, the Devil," and that Brown sees there Goody Cloyse, the minister, and Deacon Gookin, among others.[7] But the narrator never once refers to them by their names. They are always described as "figures" or "forms." Apparently, they have taken the shape of the persons whose names they use, although the evidence for this position comes only from the highly unreliable testimony of Goodman Brown and from the specters themselves—whose existence has been established only in relation to Brown's perceptions,[8] and not the narrator's.

Brown, indeed, is the only person to whom ambiguity is an impossibility. He is absolutely certain about these identifications, despite the fact that they become progressively more ambiguous as the journey into the forest continues. The narrator first says only that Brown "beheld the figure of a man" (X, 75) which seems to resemble Brown's father or grandfather. But Brown, whose preceding remark ("What if the devil himself should be at my very elbow!") indicates the tenor of his thoughts, assumes at once that the figure is the devil, although he scruples against calling him such.

In the next instance, the narrator's carefully restricted construction suggests even less validity to Brown's perception. There appears a "female figure on the path, in whom Goodman Brown recognized a very pious and exemplary dame" (X, 78). The extent to which this figure can be identified with Brown's real "moral and spiritual adviser" is uncertain at best, but Brown immediately concludes that what he perceived is unquestionably Goody Cloyse, although as soon as he "cast up his eyes in astonishment," he no longer "beheld" her (X, 79).[9]

The minister and the deacon do not even exist as figures, but merely as disembodied voices—the conversation is supplied only by "the voice like the deacon's" and "the solemn old tones of the minister" (X, 81). With less evidence than before, Brown assumes that he has overheard the real "holy men." Finally, out of the rush and babble of clouds and wind, Brown fancies that he discerns the "familiar tones" of his townspeople, and particularly, "one voice, of a young woman" (X, 82). Yet Brown exhibits no doubt about what he assumes he has perceived passing overhead, crying "Faith!" after his wife.

At this point appears the famous "pink ribbon," which F. O. Matthiessen condemned as too jarringly literal to be accepted into the pattern of Brown's past hallucinations.[10] Fogle rather lamely defends the ribbon as "part and parcel of his dream," like everything else, and, moreover, of only momentary impact.[11] There is a sounder argument for its use, because Matthiessen's assumption of the ribbon's lit-

eral existence is contradicted by the pattern of the expanding gap between the narrator's ambiguity of description and Brown's certainty of identification. From figures to voices to clouds to wind, the objects upon which Brown projected his certainties have become more and more vague and uncertain. This incident extends the pattern, for the narrator says only that "*something* fluttered lightly down through the air, and caught on the branch of a tree" (my italics). Only Goodman Brown "beheld a pink ribbon" (X, 83).[12] Considering the quality of his past perceptions, it would be exceedingly naive to trust his eyesight at this point. The narrator, moreover, has the last word on the subject, his insistence that Faith still wears the ribbon the next morning serving as a final ironic comment on Brown's perception of the "something."[13]

The effect of this divergence of viewpoint is to establish the credibility of the narrator's perceptions and to undermine Brown's. The reader's confidence in the narrator's point of view has been reinforced by the objectivity of the unemotional tone, reflected in the eighteenth-century rhetorical patterns,[14] by the candor that allows him always to present Brown in terms of the latter's current evaluation of himself, and above all by the honesty that results from his refusal to commit himself to a single-minded view of an external reality that he cannot truly know.

The reader, therefore, accepts the narrator as the norm for perception against which to judge Brown, who is beset by emotional vagaries and is blind to his own motivations. Brown's expressed ideas are constantly being undercut by his situation and actions, and yet he is absolutely certain—so certain that it never occurs to him to doubt it—that he knows what constitutes external reality. This fallacious certainty and the unconscious assumption upon which it is based provide for Brown's self-destruction.

Brown's assumption is that an absolute reality actually exists, that it lies in the external world, and that it is finally knowable by man through the perception of his senses. Brown is thus an extreme Lockean in his psychology—he insists on attributing all his mental impressions to external realities which have inscribed themselves on his *tabula rasa*. It never occurs to him that the source of some of his ideas may lie within himself, in his mind and imagination. Yet through the ironic tension between Brown's ideas and the perceptions of the narrator, Hawthorne has been making clear all along that the source of Brown's only significant ideas—that is, those which actually motivate and control his actions—is Brown himself.

Brown goes into the forest in search of the source of evil (or sin, or knowledge, or whatever moral or psychological term one wishes), fully confident of finding that source in some person or place—that is, in something external to himself. Since it will be external to himself, his relation to it will be subject to his own definition, limitation, and control, as suggested by his reiterated belief that he can stop his journey and turn back whenever he wishes. From the beginning, however, Hawthorne has undercut Brown's belief through the narrator's subtle insistence that Brown has carried all his ideas of evil, and therefore all the evil of which he is capable, into the forest with him. Everybody else who enters the forest has done so, too, but Brown's psychology will not permit him to accept the analogy presented to him by his experiences, whether real or imagined. Brown's exploration of the dark forest of the mind is qualitatively indistinguishable from the one that has been experienced implicitly by all other characters in the story (including the narrator), and explicitly by Faith, who has "such dreams and such thoughts, that she's afeard of herself, sometimes" (X, 74). But Brown refuses to recognize that evil and knowledge and their sources are intrinsic parts of all human nature. In this sense, therefore, it is finally irrelevant whether or not Brown's experiences "really" occurred. The crucial point is that Brown asserts certainty when he ought to be raising questions and doubts.

The narrator notes at the very beginning that all of Brown's good intentions are postulated only in the form of future actions—"With this excellent resolve for the future, Goodman Brown felt himself justified in making more haste on his present evil purpose" (X, 75). Brown's "companion" appears to him only after he expresses his idea that "the devil himself" might be present (X, 75). Brown exclaims that he has already penetrated "too far" into the forest, but at the same time he was "unconsciously resuming his walk" (X, 76). The devil's arguments are so apt that they "seemed rather to spring up in the bosom of his auditor, than to be suggested by himself" (X, 80). While "applauding himself greatly" for determining to resist the devil, Brown hears "amidst these pleasant and praise-worthy meditations" the sounds of the minister and the deacon (X, 80-81).

If Brown had any sense of this source of his own perceptions, he might have drawn the correct analogy with the examples of innate depravity and taken his place with Faith in the brotherhood of man. His insistent assumption that all his ideas have a reality external to himself leads him instead to the wrong conclusion. "There is no good on earth; and sin is but a name. Come, devil! for to thee is this world given" (X, 83). This idea obviously fills him with despair, so that he continues to the witches' meeting (or unconsciously permits himself to imagine the experience), but he still has no concept of his own nature, as events at the meeting illustrate. For him, evil is still the province of the devil—that is, the source of it is external to Brown. To that error he adds his Manichaean certainty of the distinctness and absoluteness of good and evil, merely reversing his previous assumption that everybody else is good to the assumption that everybody else is bad.

Once again, however, the narrator has the last word, concluding the first portion of the story with remarks that leave no room for doubt about where the source of evil really lies. Brown rushed into the

> heart of the dark wilderness . . . with the instinct that
> guides mortal man to evil. . . . he was himself the

> chief horror of the scene, and shrank not from its other horrors. . . . In truth, all through the haunted forest, there could be nothing more frightful than the figure of Goodman Brown. . . . The fiend in his own shape is less hideous, than when he rages in the breast of man.
>
> (X, 83-84)

The narrator also leaves no doubt about Brown's relationship to the rest of mankind:

> The verse died heavily away, and was lengthened by a chorus, not of human voices, but of all the sounds of the benighted wilderness, pealing in awful harmony together. Goodman Brown cried out; and his cry was lost *to his own ear,* by its unison with the cry of the desert.
>
> (X, 84—my italics)

Brown does not hear his own cry for the cry around him, but the narrator hears both.

Although he does not accept the idea, Brown has already joined the congregation of evil, "with whom he felt a loathful brotherhood, by the sympathy of all that was wicked in his heart" (X, 86). He does not need the "baptism" to experience evil but to know its nature and the way it relates him to all people. The devil stresses this point by associating the knowledge of the catalogue of "secret deeds" with the ability "to penetrate, in *every* bosom, the deep mystery of sin, the fountain of all wicked arts, and which inexhaustibly supplies more evil impulses than human power—than my power, at its utmost!—can make manifest in deeds" (X, 87—my italics). *Every* bosom would include Brown's.

It would be a mistake, however, to assume that the devil is the real hero, trying his best to awaken Brown to the reality of human nature. Hawthorne's ironic ambiguities are much too complex for that. The devil is still one of Hawthorne's numerous false guides, subtly encouraging people to extend partial truths into erroneous absolutes. Although he admits the source of evil lies in the individual human, he does all in his power to foster its development and expression, as was illustrated earlier by the kinds of assistance he had offered Brown and all his friends and relations. Now he will succeed in securing Brown's damnation by encouraging him to *refuse* the baptism.

Essentially, he plays upon Brown's Manichaean conviction that everybody else is totally committed to evil. If you wish to be fully human, to join "the communion of your race," he in effect tells Brown, you too must commit yourself to evil as "your only happiness" (X, 88). That the devil lies when he says that "evil is *the* nature of mankind" (X, 88—my italics) is established by the narrator, who makes a special point of referring to the religious activities the next morning of "the good old minister" and "that excellent old Christian, tian," Goody Cloyse, as well as to the anxious and joyful Faith (X, 88-89). Part of the irony of the characterizations may well be turned against the characters themselves, in view of their previous night's associations, but, in any case, their holy activities are certainly no less real than the witches' sabbath, and a great deal more plausible, given the total lack of ambiguity in the narrator's descriptions.

But Brown has already thrown the good out with the bad. Rightly convinced that a conscious commitment to the idea of total depravity would be disastrous, he naively accepts the devil's explanation, which is actually only a necessary consequence of Brown's beliefs, that a commitment to the knowledge of the moral community of human beings means the same thing. By so believing, Brown throws out forever any possibility of sympathetic identification with other people, thus cutting himself off from the only way for him to test the validity of his perceptions. His rejection of brotherhood is, therefore, equally a disaster, for it is ironically based on an unconscious commitment to the concept of total depravity. It is this commitment that allows Brown (and Brown alone, as the narrator stresses) to hear only oaths, anathemas, hypocrisy, and anthems of sin, instead of prayers, blessings, preaching, and psalms (X, 89).

The narrator insists on this ironic quality by such devices as his remark that Brown is followed "to his grave" by Faith (X, 89-90), an ironic inversion of Brown's previous belief that he would hereafter cling to Faith's skirts "and follow her to Heaven" (X, 75). Such a commitment would have succeeded, not because Faith was "an angel on earth" as he originally thought, but because he would be accepting humanity.

Thus the narrator carefully works out the culminating irony of the story. In seeking to cut himself off from the evil in the external world, Brown has committed himself to the evil of his own mind, without hope of understanding or correction. Seeking salvation for himself, he has committed himself to the only course that will guarantee his destruction, for only those who believe in the reality of ideas independent of sense impressions can have hope for any future except the grave. And so "his dying hour was gloom" (X, 90).

One of the consequences of being aware of the nature of Brown's obsession is that the critic can no longer safely dismiss Brown at the end of his analysis as merely a deluded or even deranged person. Brown, after all, clearly retains the ability to behave acceptably in his social relationships. But he has lost the ability to transcend the external forms of these relationships and thus has lost the power to create moral relationships. Hawthorne's structure and theme imply that only through moral relationships can one create a positive human existence. Brown's failure in this regard is at once more subtle than is suggested by the references to "depraved imagination" and "distorted mind"[15] and more universal than is suggested by the historical confinement of the problem to seventeenth-century Salem[16] or even to Hawthorne's own mind.[17] Brown's problems with perception and the products of his own imagination are potentially those of every human being. The reader dismisses the possibility of identification with Brown only at

the peril of falling into Brown's obsession—another example of the complex ironies Hawthorne leaves waiting to trap the unwary reader who fails to recognize that it is precisely the contrast between the narrator's and Brown's perceptions that allows one to accept the universality of the experience while denying the validity of Brown's response to it.

Notes

1. David W. Pancost suggests a relationship in Hawthorne's works between the uncertainty of appearances and intuitive sympathy in "Hawthorne's Epistemology and Ontology," *Emerson Society Quarterly,* 19 (1973), 8-13. Nina Baym also notes Hawthorne's position that "the imagination controls what people do and hence is inseparable from actuality" (*The Shape of Hawthorne's Career* [Ithaca: Cornell Univ. Press, 1976], p. 33).

2. In *Mosses From an Old Manse, The Centenary Edition of the Works of Nathaniel Hawthorne,* X (Columbus: Ohio St. Univ. Press, 1974), 74-90. References made in the text will be to the volume and page number of this edition.

3. Some critics do not even recognize the existence of the narrator. For example, Robert E. Morsberger asserts that "nowhere does the author intrude; such moral generalizations as the story contains are spoken by the devil" ("The Woe That Is Madness: Goodman Brown and the Face of the Fire," *Nathaniel Hawthorne Journal,* 3 [1973], 177). Perhaps Morsberger means only the "author," but the narrator generalizes frequently. When he does so, he usually shifts from the past to the present tense (e.g., "The fiend in his own shape *is* less hideous, than when he rages in the breast of man" [X, 84—my italics]). This shift draws attention more sharply to the distinction between the narrator's point of view and Brown's.

4. Compare such authors as F. O. Matthiessen, David Levin, and Paul J. Hurley, who stress the former, with those whose typical concern is for the latter, such as Richard H. Fogle, Daniel Hoffman, Roy R. Male, and Rita K. Gollin: Matthiessen, *American Renaissance: Art and Expression in the Age of Emerson and Whitman* (New York: Oxford Univ. Press, 1941), pp. 282-84; Levin, "Shadows of Doubt: Spectre Evidence in 'Young Goodman Brown,'" *American Literature,* 34 (1962), 340-52; Hurley, "Young Goodman Brown's 'Heart of Darkness,'" *American Literature,* 37 (1966), 409-19; Fogle, *Hawthorne's Fiction: The Light and the Dark,* rev. ed. (Norman: Univ. of Oklahoma Press, 1964), pp. 15-32; Hoffman, *Form and Fable in American Fiction,* corrected ed. (New York: Oxford Univ. Press, 1965), pp. 136-54; Male, *Hawthorne's Tragic Vision* (1957; rpt. New York: Norton, 1964), pp. 76-80; Gollin, *Nathaniel Hawthorne and the Truth of Dreams* (Baton Rouge: Louisiana State Univ. Press, 1979), pp. 124-128 and 134-139. A minority view sees Brown as primarily a

vehicle for Hawthorne's attack on historical Puritanism. In the most detailed of these, Michael J. Colacurcio argues that Brown is representative as a culturally-conditioned victim of the Half-Way Covenant ("Visible Sanctity and Specter Evidence: The Moral World of Hawthorne's 'Young Goodman Brown,'" *Essex Institute Historical Collections,* 110 [1974], 259-99).

5. *The Sins of the Fathers: Hawthorne's Psychological Themes,* (New York: Oxford Univ. Press, 1966), p. 106.

6. *Hawthorne's Fiction,* pp. 15-32. The chief value of Fogle's work, to which I am much indebted, lies in his stylistic and structural exposition of the counterbalanced ambiguity of meaning and clarity of technique.

7. *Hawthorne's Fiction,* pp. 17-18.

8. Levin, "Shadows of Doubt," pp. 347-50. Not being concerned about the functions of the narrator, however, Levin accepts the reality of the devil, who in turn creates all the other spectral aspects of the story. The central question for Brown, as it was for Mather, is determining whether or not the devil had the people's consent to impersonate them (pp. 351-52). Cf. Hurley, who argues that the pervasive ambiguity necessitates the conclusion that none of the characters, including the devil, have any existence except as Brown's visions ("Young Goodman Brown's 'Heart of Darkness,'" pp. 414-15), and Crews, who argues that "Brown is facing embodiments of his own thoughts in the characters he meets in the forest" (*The Sins of the Fathers,* p. 100).

9. To be sure, Brown's preceptor calls her "Goody Cloyse" too, but only after Brown does. Moreover, as the story later makes clear, the reader cannot trust the devil to tell the truth either.

10. *American Renaissance,* p. 284.

11. *Hawthorne's Fiction,* pp. 18-19.

12. Cf. the use of the verb "beheld" in *The Scarlet Letter,* where the narrator specifically argues that the red A that Dimmesdale thought he "beheld" in the sky was primarily a product of his "guilty imagination" (V, 189).

13. Cf. Levin, "Shadows of Doubt," who cites similar evidence to argue that the ribbon is simply another of the devil's spectres (p. 350). Critics who desire a literal alternative can provide one easily enough. For example, if Hoffman is right about the night being Halloween (*Form and Fable,* p. 150), then the something might as well as not be a reddish leaf falling. But the ambiguity seems firmly established without one of the narrator's usual literally expressed alternatives. Crews also notes in passing that "Brown shares Othello's fatuous concern for 'ocular proof'" (*The Sins of the Fathers,* p. 101), a concern that most definitely is not shared by the narrator.

14. Fogle, *Hawthorne's Fiction,* p. 31.

15. Hurley, "Young Goodman Brown's 'Heart of Darkness,'" pp. 411 and 419.

16. Levin, "Shadows of Doubt," pp. 351-52; Colacurcio, "Visible Sanctity and Specter Evidence," pp. 289-90.

17. Crews, *The Sins of the Fathers,* p. 106.

Karen Hollinger (essay date 1982)

SOURCE: "'Young Goodman Brown': Hawthorne's 'Devil in Manuscript':—A Rebuttal," in *Studies in Short Fiction,* Vol. 19, No. 4, Fall, 1982, pp. 381-84.

[*In the following essay, Hollinger presents a rebuttal to James L. Williamson's 1981 essay (see above) on "Young Goodman Brown," arguing that the narrator is not "of the devil's party," but someone who exposes the hypocrisy of Puritan New England society.*]

James L. Williamson's "'Young Goodman Brown': Hawthorne's 'Devil In Manuscript'" identifies Hawthorne's tale as a "hell-fired" satire in which the speaker in the course of his telling the story "shows himself to be of the devil's party" and expresses a "demonic delight" in narrating a satanic tale, a delight that establishes him as the counterpart of the work's other devil figures, yet a close analysis of the narrative perspective in **"Young Goodman Brown"** shows its speaker to maintain a substantial distance from all of the characters in the story, and especially from those associated with the devil's party.[1] Williamson's argument centers on his identifying the speaker's method of telling his tale with the voices of the three major diabolical figures that Goodman Brown meets on his journey, the "traveler with the twisted staff," Goody Cloyse, and the ministerial figure at the witches' meeting, but the speaker's attitude toward these figures is, on the contrary, so distant that Williamson's identification of a similarity in their voices appears extremely doubtful.

The speaker takes special pains to identify the figure with the twisted staff with specific personages: he bears a facial resemblance both to Young Goodman Brown and to Brown's grandfather, and has had intimate dealings not only with Brown's Puritan ancestors, but also with his contemporaries, deacons of the New England churches, members of its Great and General Court, and even the governor,[2] but never does the speaker in this long catalogue of identifications make any connection whatsoever between himself and this diabolical character; he maintains instead a careful distance, refusing even to assign this strange traveler a name, calling him only Brown's "fellow traveler," "the other," "he of the serpent," "the elder person," "the traveler with the twisted staff," "the elder traveler," and finally "the shape of Old Goodman Brown." Clearly, the primary motive for this obfuscation cannot be to hide the satanic character of this figure, for it is all too apparent, but rather to accomplish the speaker's distancing from him. The only connections between the speaker and the "traveler with the twisted staff" are, as

Williamson notes, their mockery of Young Goodman Brown's naïvety and their sarcastic reactions to his blind unrecognition of the evil within man, but Williamson fails to note the crucial difference between them, the very different aims served by their sarcasm and mockery: the "traveler with the twisted staff" hopes to convert Brown entirely to the cause of evil, while the speaker stands apart as an advocate of a balanced recognition of man's capacity for both good and evil. That both men adopt a sarcastic stance toward Brown does not seem evidence enough to connect their identities, and, in fact, the aims of their sarcasm seem to divorce them from each other. Williamson also connects the "traveler with the twisted staff" and the speaker in their "amused" attitude toward Brown, an attitude that leads "the traveler" to a "fit of irrepressible mirth" when Brown expresses his confidence in the righteousness of his ancestors (p. 78), yet this fit of mirth, or of "boisterous laughter" as Williamson calls it,[3] does not seem at all characteristic of the speaker, who may be sarcastic, condescending, and mocking of Brown, but never seems to find his situation in the least mirthful.

The connection that Williamson makes between the speaker and the second diabolical figure in the tale, Goody Cloyse, is also unconvincing in that it is based solely on the notion that Cloyse and the speaker are united in their tendencies to gossip. When Goody Cloyse converses with the "traveler with the twisted staff," she identifies him as "in the very image of my old gossip, Goodman Brown, the grandfather of the silly fellow that now is" (p. 79), the meaning of gossip in this context being ambiguous and open to two interpretations: either a relayer of sensational and personal rumor in the modern sense of the word or an old friend or crony in the archaic sense. Goody Cloyse's use of the personal pronoun "my" would seem to make the archaic usage more likely, but Williamson proposes that the modern meaning is suggested and that the speaker demonstrates similar tendencies to gossip in his description of the witches' meeting.[4] His saying that "some affirm that the lady of the governor was there" and his calling Martha Carrier "a rampant hag" represent, according to Williamson, two instances in which the speaker descends to the level of gossip and shows himself similar in character to Goody Cloyse, but these two phrases can, in fact, be interpreted otherwise to refute this imputation (pp. 87, 86).[5] The indirect reference to the governor's wife can be seen as the speaker's attempt to cast doubt, as he does so often in the narrative, on the certainty that events actually happened as Brown perceived them and to exercise his sarcasm at the expense of Puritan hypocrisy by pretending to doubt that this hypocrisy could extend even to the most respected members of New England society, and the use of the term "rampant hag" in regard to Martha Carrier seems intended not as a piece of village gossip, but to add to the speaker's portrait of the witches' meeting as a union in satanism of both the apparently evil and the seemingly good, the "rampant hag" Martha Carrier and "that pious teacher of the catechism" Goody Cloyse coming together to help the proselytes in evil to the "canopy of fire." But the significant distinguishing features of Goody Cloyse's

voice, as Williamson does note, are her colloquial, folksy speech and her somewhat quarrelsome, yet mirthful attitude toward "his worship," the "traveler with the twisted staff,"[6] yet these qualities of voice, as Williamson does not point out, are in no way duplicated in the tone of the speaker who is never colloquial, quarrelsome, or mirthful.

The third satanic figure, the Puritan divine who leads the congregation of witches and sets out to initiate Young Goodman Brown and Faith into it, is quite rightly identified by Williamson as assuming a "sermonic form of speech," and this tone, according to Williamson, is duplicated in the speaker's mock-reverential tone in such phrases as: "With reverence be it spoken . . ." and "the sacred truths of our religion" and to his moralistic insertions such as: "The fiend in his own shape is less hideous than when he rages in the breast of man" (pp. 86, 89, 84).[7] The difference, however, is between reverence and mock-reverence: the Puritan divine as leader of the witches' meeting uses a tone of reverential sermonizing that is never meant by him as sarcastic mockery, while the speaker's reverential and moralistic phrases seem, on the other hand, to be used for this purpose.

There are indications in the story not only that the speaker's voice is not intended to be associated with that of the diabolical figures, but also that he wishes to remain very distant from them. His initial narrative perspective is that of Young Goodman Brown, who is the first figure introduced, the character through whom Faith's parting words and the meetings with the diabolical figures are perceived, and the comrade with whom the speaker undertakes the journey into the gloomy forest. If the speaker identified with the evil characters in the tale, it would seem at least once he would slip into their consciousness to record their perceptions of events, but this never occurs. The encounters with the "traveler with the twisted staff," Goody Cloyse, the minister and Deacon Gookin, and the experiences of the witches' meeting are all perceived through Brown's consciousness and only his internal reactions to them are described, a particularly telling scene occurring when Brown leaves the "traveler with the twisted staff" to avoid an encounter with Goody Cloyse. The speaker follows Brown into the trees to observe the meeting from this distant perspective rather than remain with his diabolical figures; this abandonment of evil to follow naïve virtue seems further to call into question the possibility of the speaker's identification with this evil. A second scene revealing the speaker's attitude toward evil involves Brown's perception of a dark cloud completely blackening the sky overhead as he moves farther into the forest's gloom, causing him to doubt that there is even a heaven above. At this point, the speaker breaks off from Brown's perspective to insist that "yet there was the blue arch and the stars brightening in it . . . the blue sky was still visible, except directly overhead" (p. 82). The speaker now begins slowly to divorce himself more and more from Brown's perspective as Brown becomes so shocked and disillusioned by his initiation into evil that he is unable to see the good that is also within man, as the blue sky is behind the dark cloud just overhead. To the speaker, Brown's incapacity to view man as both good and evil makes the rest of his life a nightmare and "his dying hour" one of "doom" (p. 90). Far from being of the devil's party, the speaker in **"Young Goodman Brown"** is a member of the party of man believing in his enormous capacity for both good and evil, a capacity that the speaker believes the hypocrisy of Puritan New England made it impossible for Goodman Brown to accept, or even to understand.

Notes

1. James L. Williamson, "'Young Goodman Brown': Hawthorne's Devil in Manuscript," *Studies in Short Fiction,* 18 (Spring 1981), 155-162.

2. Nathaniel Hawthorne, "Young Goodman Brown" in *The Centenary Edition of the Works of Nathaniel Hawthorne,* eds. William Charvat et al. (Columbus, Ohio: Ohio State University Press, 1962), pp. 76-77, 79. All further citations from the tale are to this edition and will be identified parenthetically in the text.

3. Williamson, p. 161.

4. Williamson, p. 159.

5. Williamson, p. 159.

6. Williamson, pp. 158-159.

7. Williamson, p. 160.

Michael Tritt (essay date 1986)

SOURCE: "'Young Goodman Brown' and the Psychology of Projection," in *Studies in Short Fiction,* Vol. 21. No. 1, Winter, 1986, pp. 113-17.

[*In the following essay, Tritt explores "Young Goodman Brown" in terms of the psychological phenomenon of projection, suggesting that Brown projects his own feelings of guilt and sin onto those he sees during his night in the forest.*]

A recent bibliography of Hawthorne criticism suggests that the four hundred or so articles written about **"Young Goodman Brown,"** "cover an intimidating array of responses that pursue every possible interpretive nuance, from esoteric theological dogma to technically precise but scientifically complex psychoanalytic themes."[1] Despite this wealth of illuminating comment, however, there is still much contention about the meaning of the tale. The psychology underlying Goodman Brown's reaction to his forest experience, for example, still remains puzzling. How exactly does Brown regard his devilish[2] behavior in the forest?

The most common reading of the tale asserts Brown's loss of faith, in himself and in his fellows. Critics argue that, as a result of his nighttime experience, Brown comes to believe all men corrupt and inevitably evil. Yet there is another possibility. In my view, Brown's bewilderment, and

subsequent withdrawal, results from his conviction (however misguided) that he yet remains unfallen. In an attempt to *escape* his guilt-consciousness and the concomitant moral anxiety, Brown projects his guilt onto those around him. While many readers of the tale have acknowledged the extent to which Brown's feeling of his own duplicity colours his nighttime vision and subsequent sense of those around him, none has adequately examined this phenomenon of colouring (projection) as it is defined by psychology.

Readers typically assert that the horrors of Brown's dream vision and his criticism of others derive from the projection of Brown's subconscious guilt. Nevertheless, these same readers still conceive of Brown as *self-consciously* guilt-ridden, and thus desperate, at the tale's end. Yet the process of projection classically functions to "defend" the individual from his anxiety. The result is that while guilt persists, it persists only at the *subconscious* level. Brown's desperation at the end of the story is not primarily, then, the result of a guilt-consciousness, but rather originates with a guilt he is unable to recognize and admit. Conceiving of himself as unscathed, Brown obsessively locates the source of his anxieties in those around him.

Through Brown's experience in the forest, he comes to know the duplicity of human nature. His more lurid revelations, however, involve the depths of his own corruption. For an unknown reason (yet one of "evil purpose" [75]) he decides to go into the forest to meet with the "dark figure" there (86). Yet Brown is unable to contain his journey within the limits of his arranged meeting; as one critic aptly puts it, "he becomes a man who leans too far over the edge of a pit."[3] Inevitably, Brown tumbles into "the heart of the dark wilderness . . . with the instinct that guides mortal man to evil" (83). In the process, he becomes "the chief horror of the scene" (83), "giving vent to an inspiration of horrid blasphemy" (84): he is transformed into a "demoniac" (84) who feels a "brotherhood by the sympathy of all that was wicked in his heart" (86) with the "grave and dark-clad company" of "fiend-worshippers" (87).

Many readers agree with Reginald Cook's assertion that "as Brown goes from village to forest he passes from a conscious world to an unconscious one."[4] The forest in this context reflects a world of Brown's sinfulness. Johnson describes "the landscape through which [Brown] travels" as a "hellish externalization of his own heart."[5] Walsh writes of "The Black Man" as an "objectification of the dark side"[6] of Brown's Nature. Crews similarly suggests that the characters Brown meets in the forest are "the embodiment of his own thoughts," and further states that "the accusation that Brown's devil makes against all mankind the more pointedly against faith, clearly issues from Brown's own horror of adulthood. . . ."[7] These critics and others,[8] affirm that Young Goodman Brown enacts a deep-seated guilt-consciousness in his journey to the heart of the wilderness.

Brown returns from that nightmarish journey, but he returns "like a bewildered man" (88). In what way does he seem bewildered? He accepts his vision of evil in the community at large, accusing the members of that community with being the devil worshippers of his nighttime experience. Along with the evil of his neighbors, however, the forest experience depicted his *own* evil. Yet when he spies Goody Cloyse ("that excellent old Christian" [89]) catechising a little girl, Brown "snatched away the child, as from the grasp of the fiend himself" (89). How can we explain this action? If Brown truly conceives of himself as fallen, why would he snatch the child from one "fiend" to yield her to yet another, namely himself?[9] Brown must believe himself untainted, or at least less tainted than various members of his community.

If we further examine the final paragraphs of the tale, we notice a continuing pattern of condemnation.

> "He shrank from the Venerable Saint as if to avoid an anathema."
>
> (88-9)

> "'What God doth the wizard pray to?' quoth Goodman Brown."
>
> (89)

> "Brown looked sternly and sadly into her face, and passed on without a greeting."
>
> (89)

> On the Sabbath-day, when the congregation were singing a holy psalm, he could not listen, because an anthem of sin rushed loudly. . . . When the minister spoke from the pulpit . . . then did Goodman Brown turn pale, dreading, lest the roof should thunder down upon the gray blasphemer. . . . He shrank from the bosom of Faith . . . and gazed sternly at his wife and turned away.
>
> (89)

Brown consistently focuses his attention outwards. There is loathing, but it is manifestly not self-loathing. The congregation, from which *he* is clearly withdrawn, sings an anthem of sin, while it is the minister, speaking from the pulpit, who is the "gray blasphemer." Unlike Hooper, in **"The Minister's Black Veil,"** Brown never glimpses his own image as something fearful and iniquitous.

Brown's focus outward suggests a psychological design, though as Hawthorne describes elsewhere, it is "only . . . such instinctive design as gives no account of itself to the intellect."[10] Brown's compulsive condemnation of others, along with his consistent denial of his own culpability, illustrates a classically defined case of projection.

> A person is projecting when he ascribes to another person a trait or desire of his own that would be painful for his ego to admit. Since the act of projecting is an *unconscious mechanism,* it is not communicated to others *nor is it even recognized* as a projection by the person himself. Projection in the Freudian sense, therefore, represents a misperception or a false perception. The fault or the unsavory desire or trait is still in the

person's unconscious; it is not in the person or object on whom the projection is made.[11]

The "misperception" or "false perception" is manifest in two respects. First, Brown locates his own evil in others. Second, and of greater significance to my argument, Brown believes himself to be without guilt, even though in fact, "the unsavory desire or trait is still in . . . [his] subconscious." Although Brown's lifetime obsession with the guilt of others functions, then, as a "mechanism of defense . . . keeping off dangers" ". . . at all costs,"[12] *inevitably,* the original anxiety remains festering within.

The type of devilish behavior Brown exhibits in the forest would be sinister enough to shake most anyone's moral self-confidence, but for Brown, the Puritan, such devilishness presents an irreparable shock. Reeling from his self-revelation, he "inadvertently . . . create[s] for himself . . . the distorted and fantastic people"[13] who become his neighbors. "Then did Goodman Brown turn pale, dreading, lest the roof should thunder down . . ." (89). Freud suggests that "not infrequently . . . the ego . . . has paid too high a price for the services which these [defense] mechanisms render."[14] Such is the unfortunate example of Goodman Brown, who inevitably pays with a terrible isolation, becoming a "stern, a sad, a darkly meditative, a distrustful . . . man . . ." (89).

Writing of Brown, Frank Davidson describes "the transforming power and the paralyzing deceptiveness of an evil thought which . . . starts into action subtle psychological processes. . . ."[15] The vice-like grip with which such processes grasp Brown is all the more paralyzing, indeed terrifying, because "one cannot flee oneself; flight is no help against internal dangers."[16] The origins of Brown's behavior lie buried beneath his consciousness. As a result, Brown is trapped, an unwary prisoner of forces acting from within, though ironically, in trying to "defend" himself, he feels victimized from without. The universality of such susceptibility to ungovernable forces; the pervasiveness of what Hawthorne elsewhere termed our "unconscious self-deception,"[17] may explain the manifold responses to this most powerful of Hawthorne's tales.

Notes

1. Lea Newman, *A Reader's Guide to the Short Stories of Nathaniel Hawthorne* (Boston: G. K. Hall, 1979).

2. "He was himself the chief horror of the scene." Nathaniel Hawthorne, "Young Goodman Brown," *The Centenary Edition of the Works of Nathaniel Hawthorne* (Ohio: St. University Press, 1974), X, 83. All subsequent references to the tale will be from this edition and noted by parenthesized page number.

3. Thomas F. Walsh Jr., "The Bedevilling of 'Young Goodman Brown,'" *MLQ* [*Modern Language Quarterly*], 19 (1958), 333.

4. Reginald Cook, "The Forest of Goodman Brown's Night: A Reading of Hawthorne's 'Young Goodman Brown,'" *NEQ* [*New England Quarterly*], 43 (1970), 474.

5. Claudia D. Johnson, "'Young Goodman Brown' and Puritan Justification," *SSF [Studies in Short Fiction]* 11 (1974), 202.

6. Walsh, p. 334.

7. Frederick C. Crews, *The Sins of the Fathers* (New York: Oxford, 1966), pp. 100, 102.

8. See, for example, Robert Emmet Whelan Jr., "Hawthorne Interprets 'Young Goodman Brown,'" *ESQ*, 62 (1971), 2-4; Frank Davidson, "'Young Goodman Brown': Hawthorne's Intent," *ESQ*, 31 (1963), 68-71; Dennis Brown, "Literature and Existential Psychoanalysis: 'My Kinsman Major Molineaux' and 'Young Goodman Brown,'" *CRAS*, 4 (1973), 65-73. There is disagreement about the sources of Brown's guilt. A number of Freudian critics (Crews, Male, and Hoffman, for instance) suggest that the source of that guilt is sexual. Though these Freudian critics discuss the unconscious sources of guilt, none examine the process of projection as it might explain Brown's behavior.

9. In the forest scene, the narrator suggests that "The fiend in his own shape is less hideous, than when he rages in the breast of man" (84) (i.e. Brown).

10. Hawthorne, Vol. II, *The House of the Seven Gables*, p. 132.

11. Harold H. Anderson and Gladys L. Anders, Eds., *An Introduction to Projective Techniques and Other Devices For Understanding the Dynamics of Human Behavior* (Englewood Cliffs: Prentice-Hall, 1951), p. 3. (Italics mine).

12. Sigmund Freud, "Analysis Terminable and Interminable," *The Complete Works of Sigmund Freud* (London: The Hogarth Press, 1974), Vol. 23, p. 237.

13. Henry P. Laughlin, *The Ego and Its Defenses* (New York: Appleton-Century Crofts, 1970), p. 233.

14. Freud, p. 237.

15. Frank Davidson, "Young Goodman Brown: Hawthorne's Intent," *ESQ*, 31 (1963), 68.

16. Freud, p. 237.

17. Hawthorne, Vol. X, "The Birthmark," p. 40.

Christopher D. Morris (essay date 1988)

SOURCE: "Deconstructing 'Young Goodman Brown,'" in *American Transcendental Quarterly*, Vol. 2, No. 1, March, 1988, pp. 23-33.

[In the following essay, Morris examines misnaming and misreading in "Young Goodman Brown" in a deconstructive critical approach to the tale.]

Two trends in recent criticism of **"Young Goodman Brown"** form the background to this essay. First, historicist critics, analyzing the story's Calvinist dilemmas, often remark upon the seeming inevitability of its action. Thus Michael Colacurcio concludes that "everything seems to follow from, or indeed to be contained in the initial situation of the story" (391). Jane Eberwein believes that the hero's "exploration of the hitherto concealed recesses of his soul would have come eventually as a test of his new birth" (26). For these and other critics, the story argues some necessity in Brown's confrontation with evil in the forest.[1] It is as if young Goodman Brown's fate was always, already inherent in his marriage to Faith. Second, among commentators who adopt newer critical approaches to the story, there is a growing consensus that its theme concerns reading. Thus James L. Williamson writes that "Brown's experience in the woods will come to represent the experience of art, of reading the tale **'Young Goodman Brown'**" (156). Williamson builds his thesis on Sheldon W. Liebman's argument that the reader is "made to be the central character of the story" (158). These interpretations continue a long-standing tradition of interest in the self-reflexive character both of this story and of Hawthorne's oeuvre.[2]

In this essay I want to extend the direction of these two trends by arguing that the necessity articulated in the story is the inevitability of misreading. In order to arrive at this de Manian sense of the tale, I will examine, first, the problems of character-names, especially as these relate to the narrator. Next I discuss how misnaming is related to the story's subversion of the distinction between proper and common nouns. These two sections raise the possibility of some necessity for the reader, following the narrator, following Brown, to recognize misinterpretations only belatedly, only after having suffered them. In the third section I analyze how the foregoing primary deconstruction of the figures of the tale is repeated in a secondary deconstruction, of the reader's experience in interpretation.[3]

I

In a general way, deconstruction—like **"Young Goodman Brown"** itself—seeks to illuminate unexamined assumptions in interpretation. Hence it will serve as an introduction both to the tale and to this essay's method to discuss certain critical presuppositions with regard to characters' names. Richard Hostetler correctly points to the hidden assumptions in the work of R. H. Fogle and others who accept without qualification the names, used in Brown's forest-journey, for which the narrator provides no verification (222). For example, many commentators call young Goodman Brown's fellow-traveller "the Devil" (or "the devil"—as we shall see, even conventions of capitalization are not unimportant in the tale), but the narrator never does.[4] Several passages in the text may give rise to such an identification, among them the following interchange:

> The traveller put forth his staff and touched her withered neck with what seemed the serpent's tail.
>
> "The devil!" screamed the pious old lady.
>
> "Then Goody Cloyse knows her old friend?" observed the traveller, confronting her and leaning on his writhing stick.

"Ah, forsooth, and is it your worship indeed?" cried the good dame. "Yea, truly it is, and in the very image of my old gossip Goodman Brown, the grandfather of the silly fellow that now is."

(79)

But close inspection of this passage reveals that it affords no incontrovertible basis for identifying Brown's fellow-traveller as the Devil. On the contrary, the fellow-traveller responds to the old lady's startled expletive with a question, not a statement, after which she refers to him as "your worship." (The interchange thus reveals a confusion of two functions of language, the semantic and the poetic, in Jakobson's terminology, an indeterminacy which as we shall later see can subvert other namings too.) The most that can be said of the passage is that a catachresis is expressed: the old lady believes that "it" is "your worship," in the image of someone else. But even if we equated "your worship" with the Devil, we would still need to evaluate both the woman's belief and the fellow-traveller's acquiescence in it: by itself the catachresis cannot establish "true identity"; on the contrary, the trope blocks it.

Similarly, although on their journey Brown and his fellow-traveller use the name Goody Cloyse, the narrator never does so. The closest the narrator comes to concurrence with their sobriquets is in the account of Brown's astonished glance when he beheld "neither Goody Cloyse nor the serpentine staff" (80). Thus the narrator's "confirmation" of this character's name is expressed simultaneously with her disappearance, a paradox which suggests that critical usage of "Goody Cloyse" may unwittingly perpetuate an interpretation that the story itself does not ratify.

As many readers have noted, doubts may also be raised concerning Brown's attribution of identities to the two voices he hears in the forest.[5] Even though he hears only a "voice like the deacon's" and "the solemn old tones of the minister" (81), Brown unquestioningly believes these represent the minister and Deacon Gookin. The fact that one voice uses a noun-of-direct-address in an apparent reply to the other does not resolve the doubt, if only because the story's use of similar-sounding, even identical names for various characters underlines the arbitrariness of signification in the tale: thus, Martha Cory and Martha Carrier are both witches; Goodman Brown is the name of both grandfather and grandson. Thus, young Goodman Brown's attribution of presence to the two voices he overhears must remain, even at this semantic level, only a hypothesis.

Yet the fact that Deacon Gookin, the minister, and Goody Cloyse are mentioned by the narrator later, at the forest-ceremony and in the village, raises the more complex issue of the unexamined assumptions in the use of all those other names that *are* cited by the narrator. For if the judgments of young Goodman Brown, Goody Cloyse, and the fellow-traveller are called into question for hastily attributing names to "figures" whom the narrator regards more neutrally, the narrator's judgments are correspondingly undermined.

James L. Williamson has shown that the diversity of the narrator's styles reflects those of the three putative devil-figures whom Brown encounters on his journey (the fellow-traveller, Goody Cloyse, and the ministerial leader of the forest ceremony): variously sarcastic, gossipy, and sermonic in tone, the speaker's styles implicate the fiction-maker in the morally equivocal, demonic world into which Brown is introduced (161). But other characteristics of the speaker also make his unreliability evident. First, the apparently baffling allusion to the Egyptian magi can be understood only in self-indicting ways: if the narrator "means" his own allusion, then he becomes a genuinely superstitious proponent of the view that Brown's fellow-traveller is more than six thousand years old. Note here that the narrator's claim goes beyond an arguably plausible, Calvinist assertion that the fellow-traveller might represent a contemporary avatar of some principle of evil permanent in history; instead, the narrator seems sufficiently convinced actually to insert this "diabolic" agent into the text of Exodus. But, if on the contrary, the allusion is merely frivolous or hyperbolic, then our faith in the narrator's judgment, allusiveness, and naming elsewhere in the story is shaken. (As we shall see, this essay's argument is that a necessary departure from *faith in naming* may be an important construal of Hawthorne's allegory.)

And there is a disconcerting dimension even to the content of the allusion: in Exodus, Yahweh tells Moses and Aaron that the rod which is thrown down to the ground and changes into a serpent will be the sign of their divine direction. However, the magis of the Pharoah are able to duplicate *exactly the same sign,* thereby at once calling into question the signifiying capacity of Yahweh's sign. For the writer of Exodus, it is only when the serpents of Moses and Aaron eat those of the magi that Divine guidance of the Israelites is "incontrovertibly" established.

To this deliberate subversion of narrative reliability should be added other contradictions. When young Goodman Brown is seized by a fit of demonic laughter, the speaker comments: "The fiend in his own shape is less hideous than when he rages in the breast of man" (84). Again, the alternative interpretations of the passage call the narrator's judgments into question. If, as some argue, the narrator "means" simply to impart a cliche of folk-wisdom, then his own perspecuity in judgment elsewhere may be doubted. But if the narrator "means" what he says, then we must believe that he has in fact seen the "fiend in his own shape." These alternatives for interpretation are equally destablizing: the narrator is thus either a hyperbolic fool or a superstitious fanatic.

Finally, the narrator's attitude toward the historical era that forms the backdrop to his story cannot be decided. Writing in retrospect from approximately the 1750s, the narrator understands the outcome of the witch trials. He alludes, apparently without irony, to Mather's judgment of Martha Carrier. When combined with his concluding, apparently approving references to "the sacred truths of our religion" (89), the reference would seem to establish the narrator as an orthodox Calvinist who evidently approves of church policy and history with regard to heresy. And yet, just as clearly, the history of criticism of the story shows that the tale itself calls such orthodoxy into question. Again the alternatives form a contradiction: the narrator's sincerity presupposes obtuseness to the point of opacity; but to impute cynicism to him would vitiate the story.

In fact, the story recounts a double misinterpretation: first, young Goodman Brown and other characters attribute names to figures in a process to which the reader, following the narrator, demurs. Yet when the narrator subsequently makes similarly definite attributions, and then interpretations, we are led to wonder if he commits the same errors as young Goodman Brown. That which at first establishes the credibility of the narrator—his refusal hastily to attribute presence to mere "figures"—serves by the end of the tale to subvert the authority of narration in general.

This paradox is an instance of what J. Hillis Miller, following de Man, calls "varnishing," that is, an authorial gesture which asserts some putative presence or signified while simultaneously disclosing the untenability of such a center.[6] **"Young Goodman Brown"** dramatizes a seeming necessity for such varnishing: the mistakes of the characters and the narrator are not simply ridiculed from some normative satiric perspective; on the contrary, critics agree that they seem inherent in the opening situation, in the marriage of young Goodman Brown to Faith. To understand how such misinterpretation could come to seem necessary, it will help to examine critical presuppositions with regard to Faith.

Just as most commentators hastily attribute the signification "devil" to the fellow-traveller, so the tradition is nearly universal that Faith means "faith in God." However, it must be conceded that this traditional interpretation is itself an inference, an attribution of an absent signified to a signifier. While everything in the social and historical contexts of Hawthorne's tale makes such interpretation understandable, it is nevertheless an interpretation. Now some sense of the *necessity* for interpretation may begin to emerge here: we protest, rightly, that Faith must be faith *in something,* that faith must have a *referent.* And certainly **"Young Goodman Brown"** sustains such protests to the extent that it depicts a world in which interpretation is, indeed, unavoidable.

As a means of respecting the complexity of this dilemma, let us assume for a moment that Faith means not "faith in God" but "faith in a signified," faith in some unequivocal relation between signifier and signified. Such an assumption does no immediate violence to the tale, since faith in significance would appear to be a precondition of any subsequent theological faith. With this (admittedly erroneous) attribution in mind, we might attempt to paraphrase Hawthorne's allegory in this way:

> We are married to faith in a signified in the sense that discourse is impossible without the presupposition of some presence, some referent for the "figures" we en-

counter in life. Yet at the same time, doubt of the signified is inherent in the very nature of such faith. Therefore, once we "begin on the path" of our necessary misinterpretations, we arrive at a place which calls into question all previous names and identifications. It is at such a point that we see that the "object" of faith may itself be merely a signifier.

(Like all paraphrase, this one is clearly misleading since, as Derrida argues, it strategically serves as a supplement which privileges the ontological status of its "original," the story.) Nevertheless, with such a context in mind, we can return to the story and examine its details from a different vantage point.

II

If all putative signifieds may be only signifiers in their turn, then the distinction between proper and common nouns may be undermined. As J. Hillis Miller has observed: "No name is 'proper.' All names, proper or common, are sobriquets, nicknames, figurative substitutes for proper names that can never be given and that cannot exist" ("Address" 289). **"Young Goodman Brown"** questions the distinction between proper and common nouns most obviously with regard to its titular hero. In what sense is "Goodman" a proper noun? The narrator also refers to him as "the goodman." Of course, the hero's name, like Goody Cloyse, is an instance of the Puritan custom of converting moral attributives into proper names. But Hawthorne's usage has the effect of interrogating the basis of the distinction implied by Puritan tradition. Are these names substantives, attributives, or both? In fact, the very word "goodman" is a blend of both. Thus the uncertainty with regard to proper nouns leads to the even more fundamental one, between substantive and attributive. Such binary oppositions found Western logocentrism: thing and attribute, necessary and accidental, content and form. If "Goodman" may not be a "true name," and may in fact blur the categories of noun and adjective, then what of "young"? The capitalization of the word in the title and in the story's first sentence momentarily seconds the doubt: as part of a title, the word takes on part of a quality of a noun; it partly names the *thing,* the story **"Young Goodman Brown"** (which, however, after all, consists of signifiers). And these doubts are redoubled by the name "Brown," a most quotidian and common attributive redeployed here as a substantive.

That mere capitalization "distinguishes" proper and common nouns reinforces the arbitrariness of the logical and grammatical distinction, and Hawthorne plays with this doubt throughout the story. Thus, we read of "the minister and Deacon Gookin" (81); we reflect on the convention that like the word "young," titles are capitalized "when they are integral parts of names"; yet the signified of "the minister" now becomes problematic: does the phrase refer to a particular person after all? This undecidable is later, symmetrically, repeated when Brown thinks he hears "a voice like the deacon's" (81). Of course, Hawthorne's capitalization is "consistent and correct"; nevertheless, its effect is to call into question the logical and grammatical distinction sustained only apparently and precariously by the convention.

The uncertainty created by the capitalization of the word "Young" in both the title and the story's first sentence is also repeated. At the forest ceremony we read of "Good old Deacon Gookin" but on Brown's return of "Old Deacon Gookin." Again, Hawthorne's practice is correct: the convention for capitalizing sentence-beginnings has created the doubt. Nevertheless, the persistence of the awkwardness and its obvious correlation to the name of the titular hero call into question exactly how we know what "attributes" are "essential." But even to frame the issue this way is to challenge the expectations of binarism and referentiality which readers must bring to the story, if only first to make semantic sense of it.

The most telling undecidable created by conventions of capitalization is evident in the last sentence Brown speaks. Back in his village, overhearing Deacon Gookin, Brown wonders: "What God doth the wizard pray to?" (89). Here the undecidability extends to that most important signifier in the story, that arche or origin of signification. The capital "G" in the word "God" would ostensibly presuppose Christian monotheism. And yet Brown's very question challenges monotheism by implying the existence of multiple gods. This doubt cannot be resolved; capitalization alone is inadequate to secure referentiality. And, even beyond this doubt, we must concede that such uncertainty is in fact created in language and sustained in writing. For it is the narrator who "writes" Brown's question. The narrator must make a choice—capitalization or lower case—but this act of interpretation only perpetuates a misunderstanding which would be always, already inherent in such a question even if spoken and overheard. Thus the narrator cannot escape the undecidability generated by the very necessity to articulate.

That troping is inherent in naming, misinterpretation in the very act of articulating, is apparent in Faith's first words to her husband:

> "Dearest heart," whispered she, softly and rather sadly, when her lips were close to his ear. . . .
>
> (74)

There would be a kind of grim, Custom-House humor about this passage were it not for the fact that Faith's misdirected noun-of-direct-address is but one of so many which come to seem inevitable in the story: heart is no truer a name than "Goodman" is.

We've seen that the narrator's allusion to the magis' rods uncomfortably raised the prospect of a sign which might signify equally divine guidance or its absence. But other signs and their interpretations in the story are also equivocal to the point of undecidability. Two simple examples occur during the discussion of young Goodman Brown's ancestors. The hero protests:

> "And shall I be the first of the name of Brown, that ever took this path, and kept—"
>
> "Such company, thou wouldst say," observed the elder person, interpreting his pause.
>
> (77)

Here the signifier is a pause, literally nothing. Hence, whatever the merit of the fellow-traveller's interpretation, it cannot be confirmed. The point is quickly reinforced by young Goodman Brown himself, as he reacts to the innuendos made against his ancestors:

> "If it be as thou sayest," replied Goodman Brown, "I marvel they never spoke of these matters; or, verily, I marvel not, seeing that the least rumor of the sort would have driven them from New England."
>
> (77)

The silence of Brown's ancestors gives rise to two mutually exclusive interpretations of their characters, that they led lives of probity and that they didn't. Like the magis' rods, the signifiers here (silences) generate not simply ambiguity, but undecidability, since to interpret at all is blindly to fill in a vacancy. And yet, as certainly, such silences cannot remain uninterpreted.

But the most notorious undecidables are Faith's pink ribbons, which have generated extensive critical commentary.[7] The ribbons are mentioned at several points in the tale; however, the most momentous occasion takes place after young Goodman Brown cries out in grief after Faith.

> But something fluttered lightly down through the air, and caught on the branch of a tree. The young man seized it, and beheld a pink ribbon.
>
> "My Faith is gone!" cried he, after one stupefied moment. "There is no good on earth; and sin is but a name. Come, devil! for to thee is this world given."
>
> (83)

This passage suggests the dilemma of interpretation throughout the story: an arbitrary signifier is confronted and an interpretation, necessarily, follows. But the interpretation cannot be sustained from the signifier. (We have no way of knowing that this is Faith's ribbon or, if it is, that it denotes her being "gone" in the sense of having gone over to evil, etc.) Therefore, it is impossible, once more, to "verify" young Goodman Brown's interpretation. On the other hand, we must note that the interpretation is *literally* true, since Faith "has gone" in the sense that she does not here accompany young Goodman Brown. As in the case of the magis' rods, we are left with self-cancelling interpretations. These interpretations are not simply ambiguous; they are undecidable, because each is "potentially correct"; therefore, the necessity to interpret, to choose one interpretation, presupposes misinterpretation.

The recognition that all signifiers are ultimately undecidable, referring not to some presence but, endlessly, to other signifiers, is made clear in the story's climax, in which young Goodman Brown exhorts Faith to resist the wicked one by looking up to heaven. The idea that evil can be resisted by a gesture, by a reference, to something outside a signifier has everywhere been called into question by the tale: Faith is not a signified, a fixed entity whose "possession" could guarantee safety, much less salvation. Like the staffs, like the ribbons, like the silences, faith stands in need of an external signification which always escapes from it. Thus the narrator's final verdict ("We cannot know if Faith obeyed") merely ratifies the story's undecidability.

III

The primary deconstruction showed us that by following young Goodman Brown, the fellow-traveller, and the narrator, the reader repeats the necessary misinterpretations they commit. When we arrive, with Brown, at the forest clearing, we witness with him, belatedly, the secondary deconstruction, the source of the errors necessitated by our own interpretation of the story. This moment occurs in the speech to the assembled characters by "the dark figure" or "the sable form." The antinomian or gnostic content of the philosophy espoused in this speech has received adequate comment. In many ways this speech invites Brown to accede to a Nietzschean "transvaluation of all values." The shock of Brown's recognition, of his resistance and his later reaction to this "ultimate" implication of the loss of signification has also received long and careful scrutiny, in an effort to establish the tale's judgment on Brown's lifelong misanthropy. But before we satisfy our understandable need to interpret the end of Brown's life, we should pause to consider how this Nietzschean conclusion is conveyed to him. We learn through the assumed speech of "the dark figure" or "the sable form." But after we conjure in our minds the picture of some (male? female?) leader (of a "black" mass?), we understand that the words also refer *to the words themselves,* to the dark figures or inky signifiers we have been reading on the page, throughout **"Young Goodman Brown."**

Attendant on this recognition is the retrospective acknowledgment that, in our attempt to interpret the story, we, too, have been making figures, especially personifications. For example, the use of the term "narrator" or "speaker" is precisely such a prosopopoeia—the presupposition of some speaking, human entity narrating a tale, whose voice and judgments ought to be reconciled with the story's action. But of course this has been but a fiction—a fiction *necessary,* it is true, as a precondition to making semantic sense of the tale. Nevertheless, the act of reading has made a young Goodman Brown out of the reader. And like him we may react with misanthropy that we have been gulled, that the betrayal of our faith was inherent in our first act of "suspending disbelief," of extending faith to the storyteller, narrator, or author. In this way the reader may trace the path of his own illusions in Brown's.[8]

Notes

1. For example, B. Bernard Cohen argues that one probable source of the story was *Christ's Fidelity* by Deodat Lawson, whose rigid Calvinism Hawthorne subverted by presenting Brown's experiences as "even more spectral than the cases cited by Lawson" (361). Hawthorne's exaggerations culminate in the scene in which Brown is "irrevocably" pulled away from Faith. Frank Shuffleton sees in the tale Hawthorne's response to contemporary revival movements, especially the "old error [of self-righteousness] toward which Puritanism tended" (319). Michael Bell sees Brown as "a falling-off from the manhood of the first generation" of Puritans and considers such a decline "an inevitable result of the principles of the founders" (80, 81).

2. For example, in arguing that the story recounts the Freudian etiology of paranoia, Edward Jayne asserts that the story itself represents a delusional system similar to Brown's (109). Leo B. Levy anticipates part of my thesis in his claim that "the meaning of the story is that its own simple definitions do not work" (386). And even the historicist critic James W. Clark, Jr., sees Brown as "a willing convert like a new reader of a new author . . . he is reading and believing the devil's new book" (22). For a dissenting view of Williamson's argument, see Karen Hollinger's note.

3. This distinction between primary and secondary deconstructions was first formulated by Paul de Man: "The paradigm for all texts consists of a figure (or a system of figures) and its deconstruction. But since this model cannot be closed off by a final reading, it engenders, in its turn, a supplemental figural superposition which narrates the unreadability of the prior narration. As distinguished from primary deconstruction narratives centered on figures and ultimately always on metaphor, we call such narratives to the second (or third) degree *allegories*" (205). Accordingly, this essay claims no privilege for its own thesis. On the contrary, in keeping with de Man's concept of an allegory, it attempts in passing and in conclusion to uncover the probable sources of its own errors.

4. In addition to Fogle, Hostetler might also have added the following critics who identify the fellow-traveller as the devil, the Devil, or Satan: Cook (475), Jayne (103), Bell (78), Levy (376), and Liebman (160).

5. See Williamson (222) and Liebman (165).

6. Miller first used this term in his essay included in the collection *American Criticism in the Poststructuralist Age* (34); however, the concept is elaborated more fully in *The Ethics of Reading.*

7. Levy summarizes the many conflicting interpretations of Faith's pink ribbons (382-384) and concludes that they should be understood as forming the link between "two conceptions of Faith" (384)—generally, literal and figurative. But Levy, too, presumes when he states that the ribbon Brown seizes was from Faith's cap (377). In addition to the interpretations Levy discusses, Clark interprets them as evidence of

Faith's fall (30); Cohen, as spectral evidence (357); and Liebman, as the last in a series of sensory illusions.

8. A shorter version of this paper was read at the International Conference on the Expressions of Evil in Literature, Philosophy and the Visual Arts, sponsored by West Georgia College, November 6-8, 1987, in Atlanta, Georgia.

Works Cited

Bell, Michael. *Hawthorne and the Historical Romance.* Princeton: Princeton University Press, 1971.

Clark, James W., Jr. "Hawthorne's Use of Evidence in 'Young Goodman Brown.'" *Essex Institute Historical Collections* 111 (1975): 12-34.

Cohen, B. Bernard. "Deodat Lawson's *Christ's Fidelity* and Hawthorne's 'Young Goodman Brown.'" *Essex Historical Collections* 104 (1968), 349-370.

Colacurcio, Michael. *The Province of Piety: Moral History in Hawthorne's Early Tales.* Cambridge: Harvard University Press, 1984.

Cook, Reginald. "The Forest of Goodman Brown's Night: A Reading of Hawthorne's 'Young Goodman Brown.'" *New England Quarterly* 43 (1970): 473-481.

de Man, Paul. *Allegories of Reading: Figural Language in Rousseau, Nietzsche, Rilke, and Proust.* New Haven: Yale University Press, 1979.

Eberwin, Jane. "My Faith is Gone! 'Young Goodman Brown' and Puritan Conversation." *Christianity and Literature* 32 (1982): 23-32.

Hawthorne, Nathaniel. "Young Goodman Brown." *Mosses From an Old Manse.* The Centenary Edition of the Works of Nathaniel Hawthorne. Columbus: Ohio State University Press, 1974.

Hollinger, Karen. "'Young Goodman Brown': Hawthorne's 'Devil in Manuscript': A Rebuttal." *Studies in Short Fiction* 19 (1982): 381-384.

Hostetler, Norman H. "Narrative Structure and Theme in 'Young Goodman Brown.'" *Journal of Narrative Technique* 12 (1982): 221-228.

Jayne, Edward. "Pray Tarry With Me, Young Goodman Brown." *Literature and Psychology* 29 (1979): 100-113.

Levy, Leo B. "The Problem of Faith in 'Young Goodman Brown.'" *Nathaniel Hawthorne Journal 1975.* Englewood, Colorado: Microcard Editions, 1975. 156-169.

Miller, J. Hillis. "The Ethics of Reading: Vast Gaps and Parting Hours." Ed. Ira Konigsberg. *American Criticism in the Poststructuralist Age.* Ann Arbor: Michigan Studies in the Humanities, 1981.

———. *The Ethics of Reading.* New York: Columbia University Press, 1987.

———. "Presidential Address 1986. The Triumph of Theory, the Resistance to Reading, and the Question of the Material Base." *PMLA* 102 (1987): 281-291.

Shuffleton, Frank. "Nathaniel Hawthorne and the Revival Movement." *American Transcendental Quarterly* 44 (1979): 311-323.

Williamson, James L. "'Young Goodman Brown': Hawthorne's Devil in Manuscript." *Studies in Short Fiction* 18 (1981): 155-162.

Joan Elizabeth Easterly (essay date 1991)

SOURCE: "Lachrymal Imagery in Hawthorne's 'Young Goodman Brown,'" in *Studies in Short Fiction*, Vol. 28, No. 3, Summer, 1991, pp. 339-43.

[*In the following essay, Easterly discusses Hawthorne's use of lachrymal, or tear, imagery in "Young Goodman Brown," emphasizing Brown's inability to cry either out of sorrow for others or in repentance for his own sins.*]

> "Faith! Faith!" cried the husband. "Look up to Heaven, and resist the Wicked One!"
>
> Whether Faith obeyed, he knew not. Hardly had he spoken, when he found himself amid calm night and solitude, listening to a roar of the wind, which died heavily away through the forest. He staggered against the rock and felt it chill and damp, while a hanging twig, that had been all on fire, besprinkled his cheek with the coldest dew.

(Hawthorne ["Young Goodman Brown"] 88)

Thus ends the crucial scene in Nathaniel Hawthorne's tale of **"Young Goodman Brown,"** the story of a Puritan lad who leaves his bride of three months to secretly watch a witches' Sabbath in the deep forest outside Salem village. In so doing, he willfully betrays his commitment to his wife, the moral code of his society, and the teachings of his religion. The experience of this one night in the forest changes Goodman Brown for the rest of his life, for it poisons his relationship with his wife, isolates him from his neighbors, and destroys his ability to worship God. Whether dream or reality, one wild night is the turning point of Brown's existence; afterward he is "a stern, a sad, a darkly meditative, a distrustful, if not a desperate man" and, when he dies, "they carved no hopeful verse upon his tombstone" (90).

Literary critics have interpreted the significance of Goodman Brown's experience in many fashions—allegorical, moral, philosophical, and psychological. However, there is an intriguing absence of any reference to the last line of the Sabbath scene to explain Hawthorne's characterization of the young Puritan, despite the fact that Hawthorne signals the importance of the cold drops of dew in a periodic sentence. In essence, Hawthorne here carefully delineates the image of a young man who has faced and failed a critical test of moral and spiritual maturity.

Young Goodman Brown, leaning against the cold rock after the witch-meeting vanishes, is reproached by his creator because he shows no compassion for the weaknesses he sees in others, no remorse for his own sin, and no sorrow for his loss of faith. The one action that would demonstrate such deep and redemptive human feelings does not take place. Goodman Brown does not weep. Therefore, Hawthorne quietly and gently sprinkles "the coldest dew" on his cheek to represent the absence of tears.

This lack of tears, the outward sign of an inward reality, posits the absence of the innate love and humility that would have made possible Brown's moral and spiritual progression. A meticulous artist and a master of symbolism, Hawthorne uses the twig and dewdrops deliberately. Drops of water on a man's cheek can only suggest tears.

The hanging twig that sprinkles the drops of water on Goodman Brown's face calls to mind a picture of the beadle perched on a high stool in the back of a Puritan meeting house, holding two long switches. According to legend, one switch had a feather attached to the end and the other a stone or burr. If a lady fell asleep during the long service, the beadle would awaken her by tickling her face with the feather, but any gentleman inclined to drowse or small boys inclined to mischief knew that the stone hung over their heads like the bait on a long fishing rod and that their recall to propriety would not be so gentle. Likewise, Goodman Brown is awakened to reality from his dream or vision by a "hanging twig" that had been burning during the witch meeting but now scatters cold dew on his cheek. Like the beadle's switch, a twig from on high is the vehicle for bringing to Brown's face the reminder of what would be correct behavior and attitude for a man in this situation. He should be weeping, but he is not.

The clear, cold drops of dew are a direct contrast to the flaming blood-like liquid with which the Satanic figure is about to baptize Faith and Goodman Brown when the young man's cry, "Look up to Heaven, and resist the Wicked One!" (88), interrupts the ceremony. The words—which trigger the disappearance of the witch-meeting—and the immediate sprinkling of dew on Goodman Brown's cheek suggest that the cold water is also a baptism, a sign of salvation, grace, and renewal. This interpretation would then imply that since Brown alone has resisted Satan, he would justly find his life intolerable in Salem, where all of those whom he has revered have betrayed his confidence in their faith. If the drops of water are a sign of blessing, then Goodman Brown's vision would seem to have been a true one, and he is consigned to live in the horror of being the one good man in a village of witches whose true maleficence is cloaked in piety. However, the placement and form of the water drops signify that they are not a reminder of Christian grace. In the story the devil's mark of baptism was to be laid on the communicants' foreheads as a mockery of the Christian sacrament. In contrast, the drops of dew that fall on Brown's cheek do not signify Christian baptism because this rite, by the oldest tradition, involves the forehead and flowing water rather than sprinkled water.

Instead, Hawthorne deliberately and ingenuously uses the image of dewdrops, suggestive of an uncomfortable, chilling dampness from the earth (rather than, for example, raindrops, which are associated with cleansing, warmth, and heaven), to reprove Goodman Brown. The Puritan has just seen the sinfulness of his neighbors and friends clearly exposed, and has become acutely aware of the evil in his own heart as the unholy celebration arouses in him a feeling of "loathful brotherhood" with the fiend worshipers. However, not only does Brown fail to display the pity indicative of a sense of moral maturity in regard to the weakness and depravity of others, he likewise shows no regret for his own wickedness, a response that would start him on the path to spiritual maturity. The spiritual implications of Brown's failure are emphasized by Hawthorne's presenting the young man's dilemma in the context of a witches' meeting, and Brown's assimilation of the Satanic figure's assertion that mankind is predominately wicked indicates his lack of faith in the power of God to overcome evil. On a moral level, Brown's acceptance of others as they are—imperfect and subject to temptation—would have made a mature adulthood and productive and healthy relationships with others possible. But his lack of remorse and compassion, as symbolized by the absence of tears, condemns him to an anguished life that is spiritually and emotionally desiccated. The drops that Hawthorne places on Brown's cheek are of "the coldest dew," devastating in their connotation, for they represent the coldness of a soul that is dying, in contrast to the regenerative warmth of true tears and love.

Young Goodman Brown's inability to cry after the shock of the witches' meeting would be a strong argument for those who typecast the tale as an "initiation story" in which the protagonist fails to achieve adulthood. As psychologists Carol Gilligan and John Murphy state in "Development from Adolescence to Adulthood":

> While formal logic and principles of justice can release adolescent judgment from the binding constraints of a conventional mode of moral reasoning, the choices that arise in adulthood impose a new context for moral decision . . . an expanded ethic that encompasses compassion, tolerance, and respect.
>
> (410)

Using these criteria, Goodman Brown demonstrates none of the characteristics of the adult "expanded ethic." He shows no compassion for the sinfulness he sees in others (and which he shares), no tolerance for others' imperfections, and no respect for their attempts at faithful lives. Compassion is the most important of these characteristics because it could engender the other two emotions, and it is Brown's lack of compassion that Hawthorne wishes to emphasize in the story. Whether one classifies the young man's experience at the witches' Sabbath as a failed initiation into adulthood or as simply the critical moment in his moral and spiritual growth, Hawthorne's portrayal of a young Puritan of immature faith and simplistic morality is rendered more complete by the realization that Brown is a man who does not weep.

Human tears are an emotional response, and Hawthorne's allusion to the lack of tears underscores Brown's emotional barrenness. Critical analyses have hitherto focused primarily on Brown's faulty or immature moral reasoning, arguing that the Puritan fails the test of the Sabbath because he fails to *reason* on a mature moral level, either because of the legalism of Puritan doctrine or because of his refusal to admit his own sinfulness (Frank 209, Folsom 32, Fogle 23, Stubbs 73). Yet Hawthorne clearly indicates that Brown also destroys his chance to progress morally and spiritually because of his inability to respond intuitively to the shock of the experience with mature, positive *emotions* that would have enabled him to deal with the vision of evil in his neighbors as well as with the knowledge of his own wickedness. Goodman Brown does not weep tears of deep sorrow for others because he cannot love or forgive them. He does not weep for his own sins because he lacks a deeply felt faith, which tears of contrition—arising from a broken spirit sensitive to the baseness of sin and to God's loving mercy and grace—would signify.

Hawthorne emphasizes Brown's lack of positive emotions and implies his regression into emotional sterility by the cold, damp forest, which is in dramatic contrast to the description of the witches' meeting, where the trembling Puritan's horror is evoked by the blasphemy of the unholy worship and the loathsome kinship he feels with the congregation. The emotional prose intensifies with the dreadful, confused sounds of the fiends' hymn and the images of blazing fire, blood, and smoke as Brown becomes aware of the power of evil and the sinful nature of everyone whom he respects. When the vision disappears at Brown's anguished cry to Faith, the suddenly changed scenery of the next paragraph deliberately corresponds to young Brown's emotional state. Words like "solitude," "rock," "chill," "damp," and "coldest" suggest the absence or denial of positive feelings, which Brown demonstrates immediately afterward. The townspeople he encounters on his return from the witches' meeting are involved in good works—preparing a sermon, praying, catechizing a child—yet he rejects them, and when his young wife greets him with joy and affection, he spurns her. This heartlessness is the pattern for the rest of Brown's life, and Hawthorne, who was aware of the complexity and mystery of human nature, completes his portrait of a young man whose life is blighted in a single night by revealing in the crucial paragraph through chilly rock and coldest dew that young Goodman Brown's moral and spiritual disaster is also due to an inappropriate emotional response at the critical moment.

In conclusion, Nathaniel Hawthorne, the master of symbolism and suggestion, softly sprinkles cold tears on the cheek of young Goodman Brown. This lachrymal image, so delicately wrought, is the key to interpreting the young

Puritan's failure to achieve moral and spiritual maturity. Brown cannot reconcile the conflict caused by his legalistic evaluation of others, nor can he transcend this moral dilemma by showing compassion and remorse. In final irony, Hawthorne tells us that the man who sheds no tears lives the rest of his life a "sad" man, whose "dying hour was gloom" (90).

Works Cited

Fogle, Richard Harter. *Hawthorne's Fiction: The Light and the Dark.* Norman: U of Oklahoma P, 1964.

Folsom, James K. *Man's Accidents and God's Purpose: Multiplicity in Hawthorne's Fiction.* New Haven: College & UP, 1963.

Frank, Neal. *Hawthorne's Early Tales: A Critical Study.* Durham: Duke UP, 1972.

Gilligan, Carol, and John Michael Murphy. "Development From Adolescence to Adulthood: The Philosopher and the Dilemma of the Fact." *Readings in Developmental Psychology,* 2nd ed. Ed. Judith Krieger Gardner. Boston: Little, 1982. 400-12.

Hawthorne, Nathaniel. "Young Goodman Brown." *Mosses from an Old Manse.* Ohio State UP, 1974. 74-90.

Stubbs, John Caldwell. *The Pursuit of Form: A Study of Hawthorne and the Romance.* Chicago: U of Illinois P, 1970.

Benjamin Franklin V (essay date 1994)

SOURCE: "Goodman Brown and the Puritan Catechism," in *ESQ: A Journal of the American Renaissance,* Vol. 40, No. 1, 1994, pp. 66-88.

[*In the following essay, Franklin examines the influence of Cotton Mather's catechism entitled* Milk for Babes, *which focuses on humankind's innate moral depravity, on Hawthorne's "Young Goodman Brown."*]

If the importance of an artistic creation may be gauged by the amount of critical attention it receives, then Hawthorne's **"Young Goodman Brown"** is surely one of the most significant stories ever written. From Melville's comments in 1850 to the present, this dark tale has engaged many of Hawthorne's best readers and is likely to continue attracting them. I would suggest, however, that while such scholars as Hyatt H. Waggoner, Richard Harter Fogle, Frederick Crews, and other, more recent critics have helped us understand Hawthorne in general and **"Young Goodman Brown"** in particular, they have overlooked a statement by Brown which, when analyzed, helps explain his inability to function satisfactorily in Puritan society.[1]

Soon after permitting his guide, the devil figure, to persuade him to go deeper into the woods than originally agreed, and after first seeing Goody Cloyse, Brown responds to her unexpected presence by saying, "A marvel, truly, that Goody Cloyse should be so far in the wilderness, at night-fall!"[2] But then, after observing and hearing most of what transpires between his guide and her and after she seems magically to leave for a meeting deep in the woods, he exclaims, "That old woman taught me my catechism!" In asserting that "there [is] a world of meaning in this simple comment" (80), the narrator insists that Brown's seemingly innocuous statement reveals something significant about the young man.

In an exhaustive historical examination of Hawthorne's art that encompasses this tale, Michael J. Colacurcio takes Brown's statement at face value, commenting that Brown "has been duly catechized, in his youth, by the dutiful Goody Cloyse." Neal Frank Doubleday, in a study of Hawthorne's early tales, mentions Brown's sentence but does not interpret it. Although Sheldon W. Liebman argues that the reader of the tale must "distinguish between appearance and reality by way of determining what happens in the story and why," he does not subject the sentence or its implications to such a test. Most surprisingly, critics like Melinda M. Ponder who examine the narrator of this story also ignore the sentence, despite the extraordinary claim, implicit in the narrator's remark, that any reader wishing to understand Brown must take it into account.[3]

As best as I can determine, only two critics analyze the sentence: Thomas E. Connolly in 1956 and Robert C. Grayson in 1990. Arguing that during his night in the woods Brown discovers the "full and terrible significance" of his faith and that the story "is Hawthorne's criticism of the teachings of Puritanic-Calvinism," Connolly posits that the "'world of meaning' in Brown's statement is that [Goody Cloyse's] catechism teaches the way to the devil and not the way to heaven."[4] Regrettably, Connolly seems merely to assume the nature of a Puritan catechism without having consulted one.

Grayson focuses much more sharply than Connolly on the importance of a catechism in **"Young Goodman Brown."** He argues that Hawthorne alludes to a specific catechism and that the four references to it in the tale collectively suggest the meaning of Brown's statement. Grayson identifies the catechism as John Cotton's and quotes from two of the answers (the sixth and the eighth) that catechumens, including Brown, would have given to questions asked by a catechist. Apparently on the basis of these answers, he concludes that "by its emphasis on total depravity, [the catechism] soured the milk of human kindness" in Puritans generally and in Brown specifically, so that it "actually undermined trust in mankind and thus did the work of the devil." As a result of studying with Goody Cloyse, Grayson asserts, Brown's "heart has been withered, at least in part, by the catechism."[5] However, only four sets of questions and answers (the fifth through the eighth) in the catechism of sixty-four such sets address the issue of

innate depravity. In the remaining sixty sets, the author offers rules for living and addresses in considerable detail requirements for attaining salvation, the possibility of which children would have acknowledged in their first answer during catechism instruction. Failure to consider the entire text thus causes Grayson to assign greater importance to innate depravity than the catechism calls for, thus distorting the meaning of the catechism and misinterpreting its probable effect on Brown.

In this essay, I confirm Grayson's identification of the catechism to which Hawthorne alludes in his tale. I then examine the entire catechism and apply it to Brown, demonstrating that he never masters its meaning. I also show that the narrator speaks truthfully in his pregnant but elliptical comment about Brown's words.

By the year 1700, the Massachusetts Puritans had used a number of catechisms, including the Westminster Assembly's shorter version. As Grayson shows, Hawthorne consulted books that identify the specific catechism used in Salem Village in the late seventeenth century. Moreover, Marion L. Kesselring's catalogue of books that Hawthorne borrowed from the Salem Athenaeum reveals that before publishing **"Young Goodman Brown"** in the *New-England Magazine* in April 1835, he once withdrew (and his Aunt Mary Manning earlier twice withdrew, apparently for him) the sixth volume of *Collections of the Massachusetts Historical Society*. This volume contains "A Description and History of Salem," in which William Bentley specifies that the Salem Village Puritans of Brown's time used John Cotton's catechism, *Milk for Babes*.[6] Then, on 21 September 1833 and 30 December 1834, Hawthorne withdrew from the Athenaeum Joseph B. Felt's *Annals of Salem*, which records that on 10 September 1660 *Milk for Babes* was selected as the catechism for Salem children.[7] In referring to a catechism in **"Young Goodman Brown,"** therefore, Hawthorne clearly has Cotton's in mind.[8]

Did Hawthorne then read the catechism in order to learn what it says? No evidence exists to indicate that he did. However, Hawthorne's close familiarity with the details of early American history is well known. In some of his tales he even alludes to or cites texts that illuminate the historical material he is presenting, as in **"My Kinsman, Major Molineux"** (Thomas Hutchinson's *History of Massachusetts*), **"The Gentle Boy"** (William Sewel's *History of the Rise, Increase, and Progress of the Christian People Called Quakers*), and **"The May-Pole of Merry Mount"** (Joseph Strutt's *Sports and Pastimes of the People of England*). Further, it seems unlikely that Hawthorne would have his narrator comment so boldly about Brown's allusion to a text if he, Hawthorne, were unaware of what the text says, especially when he knew its author's name and its title. In all probability, he sought out and read Cotton's text before completing **"Young Goodman Brown."**[9]

In his research, Hawthorne would have discovered that *Milk for Babes* addresses innate depravity only after a positive beginning, which raises the possibility of salvation and details the nature of God and humanity's relationship to him:

Q. *What hath GOD done for you?*

A. God hath made me, He keepeth me, and he can save me.

Q. *Who is God?*

A. God is a Spirit of himself, and for himself.

Q. *How many Gods be there?*

A. There is but one God in three Persons, the Father, the Son, and the Holy Ghost.

Q. *How did God make you?*

A. In my first Parents holy and righteous.

Q. *Are you then born holy and righteous?*

A. No, my first Father sinned, and I in him.

Q. *Are you then born a Sinner[?]*

A. I was conceived in sin, and born in iniquity.

Q. *What is your Birth-sin?*

Answ. [*sic*] *Adams* sin imputed to me, and a corrupt nature dwelling in me.

Q. *What is your corrupt nature?*

Ans. [*sic*] My corrupt nature is empty of Grace, bent unto sin, and onely unto sin, and that continually.

Q. *What is sin?*

A. Sin is the transgession of the Law [the Ten Commandments].[10]

At the beginning of each catechism lesson, then, catechumens like Brown would have acknowledged two of the primary tenets of Puritan faith: first, the possibility of salvation; then, humanity's certain sinful nature.

Although the treatment of innate depravity in the catechism is relatively brief, this was only one source of information about human corruption and its implications available to Puritan youth. As part of the Puritan upbringing that implicitly precedes Hawthorne's tale, Brown doubtless would have sat through many sermons that emphasized innate depravity, which his family of churchgoers presumably reinforced, if only by reading and discussing the book of Genesis. Even if he been inattentive during the sermons or if for some reason his family had been derelict in fulfilling their religious obligation to him, the Puritans of Salem Village would have taught him this belief, either directly or indirectly. Theirs was a religious society, after all; people talked about their faith. Young Brown might have encountered reading material conveying the same message about depravity, such as *The New-England Primer,* the reader that offers the verse "In *Adam's* Fall / We Sinned all" to help abecedarians master the letter *A.*

And the same verse, or one expressing a similar sentiment, might have appeared on the hornbook Brown would have used to learn the alphabet, or elsewhere.[11] Because he has been reared and lives in Salem Village in the seventeenth century, Brown cannot have avoided regular exposure to the Puritan belief in innate depravity.

But before leaving the home he shares with his wife, Faith, does he believe—really believe—the gloomy philosophy presented in four sets of questions and answers at the beginning of Cotton's text? Clearly not. He thinks mortals good. How else explain the vow he makes, immediately after leaving home and while still observing his wife, that following his one night away from Faith, "a blessed angel on earth," he will "cling to her skirts and follow her to Heaven" (75)?[12] If he believed in the certainty of depravity and only the possibility of salvation, as the catechism teaches, he would know that even so righteous a person as Faith is corrupt and not necessarily of the elect, appearances notwithstanding. And how else explain his disappointment in Goody Cloyse, the minister, Deacon Gookin, and Faith when he apparently encounters them in the woods? Disappointed—and shocked—he surely is. After seeing his catechist, he says, "What if a wretched old woman do choose to go to the devil, when I thought she was going to Heaven!" (80); after hearing the minister and Deacon Gookin, "With Heaven above, and Faith below, I will yet stand firm against the devil!" (82); and after hearing Faith's voice and seeing her pink ribbon, "My Faith is gone! . . . There is no good on earth; and sin is but a name" (83). He now thinks that he was mistaken about these people he has "reverenced from youth" (87) and, by extension, about all people, especially those of his society. Only at this point does Brown finally comprehend the innate corruption of humanity. (The guilt he apparently feels at leaving Faith for the appointment with his guide seems to stem more from his violating her trust than from any belief in depravity.) As if to prove that he is one with the multitude he now views darkly—and possibly to demonstrate that he at last understands the full, somber reality of one part, if only one small part, of the catechism—Brown goes forward to participate in a fiendish version of the baptismal rite, which he finds the "Shape of Evil" conducting in the woods (88).[13]

Without addressing the catechism directly, Colacurcio, in calling Brown "theologically ill-prepared,"[14] offers one reason why Brown, before leaving home, has such an un-Puritan view of human nature: perhaps he does not comprehend the tenets of his faith, one important source of which is the catechism. Goody Cloyse might share this view. In terming her former student a "silly fellow" (79), she may intend to suggest that although he memorized the catechism answers, his latitudinarian attitude toward her, Faith, and others before he enters the woods signals his inability truly to understand and psychologically assimilate the full significance of *Milk for Babes.* Even if this is not what she means, the historical record indicates that many young people before, during, and after Brown's time have had difficulty mastering the meaning of a catechism.

This problem attracted the attention of several important seventeenth- and early eighteenth-century divines, both American and English. No less a figure than Richard Mather implies that too many people fail to master the meaning of a catechism. In his 1657 farewell sermon, he observes, "[C]omonly they that fall to erro[ur,] [ar]e defective in the knowledg of Catechistical points."[15] At almost precisely the same time that Brown would have been studying the catechism with Goody Cloyse, however, the English cleric Richard Baxter was suggesting that it is more important for children to memorize the words of a catechism than to understand what the words mean, at least initially. He writes: "*Cause your younger Children to learn the words, though they be not yet capable of understanding the matter. . . . A child of five or six years old can learn the* words *of a Catechism or Scripture, before they are capable of understanding them.*"[16] If this attitude prevailed in Salem Village during the time when Goody Cloyse would have been teaching *Milk for Babes,* it might help explain Brown's early inability to embrace the full significance of Cotton's text: there would have been no compelling reason for him to master it; he would have been required only to memorize the words. Yet he would have been expected to understand the catechism as he matured and to begin conducting his life according to its principles. He does neither.

Others also expressed opinions about the common deficiency in understanding a catechism. Cotton Mather, for example, addressed this problem in 1699, only seven years after the probable date of the events in **"Young Goodman Brown."** Clearly, he is less inclined than Baxter to make allowances for children's lack of comprehension:

> Be sure, that they [catechumens] Learn their *Catechism* very perfectly; But then content not your selves with hearing them say by Rote, the *Answers* in their *Catechism*; *Question* them very distinctly over again about every clause in the *Answers*; and bring all to ly so plain before them, that by their saying only, *Yes,* or, *No,* you may perceive that the sense of the Truth is Entred into their Souls.[17]

Three years later, Mather's concern had not abated. He includes the text of Cotton's catechism in one of his own publications and adds to it questions that can be answered affirmatively or negatively, precisely as he prescribed in 1699. He admonishes: "To *Remember,* and not *Understand,* is as *Tedious* as *Useless* a Thing. It is a thing of the first Importance, that our Children do *Understand,* what they *Remember,* of their *Catechism,* and not recite it, like meer *Parrots,* by rote."[18] In 1730, the English hymnographer and catechism writer Isaac Watts argued even more directly:

> [I]f by virtue of a faithful memory persons should retain the words which they have learned in childhood, they will vainly imagine themselves furnished with a set of principles of religion, though they feel no power of them upon conscience in the conduct of life; and all this because these articles do not lie in the heart, or even in the understanding, as a set of principles for practice, but rather in the head or memory as a set of phrases.[19]

In stating that children should not memorize what they cannot comprehend, the Mathers and Watts disagree with Baxter; to them, catechumens must understand a catechism from the outset. If they do not, they will be deluded into thinking themselves morally prepared for life and will therefore think as they should not and comport themselves poorly, as Watts avers. Such is the case with Brown. Clearly, his attitude before leaving for the woods is contrary to the Puritan way of thinking conveyed in *Milk for Babes,* a text he should have mastered. His decidedly non-Puritan faith in the goodness of humanity permits awareness of human corruption, once it comes, to destroy the young man's heart. David Levin, although he does not discuss the catechism, implies something similar in asserting that **"Young Goodman Brown"** is "about Brown's . . . discovery of the *possibility* of universal evil."[20] I would amend Levin's statement by changing the word *possibility* to *certainty.* As a Puritan reared in Salem Village, Brown should not have to make such a discovery as a young adult, years after Goody Cloyse taught him the doctrine of innate depravity during their catechism lessons.

Even had Brown not understood human imperfection from the catechism or other sources as he progressed into adulthood, he should have suspected it because of his own moral shortcomings, his latent desires to violate religious precepts set forth in the catechism and especially the Ten Commandments. To the Puritans, the Commandments were extremely important: they served as a summary of scriptural instruction on proper behavior in every circumstance. In fact, Cotton stresses their significance by devoting twenty-seven sets of questions and answers to them in his catechism.[21] How successfully does Brown obey the Commandments? Either in his dream or in reality, in the woods or after returning to Salem Village, he disobeys all of them to one degree or another.

When Goody Cloyse, in the course of catechistical training, presumably asked young Brown to explain the meaning of the First Commandment, "Thou shalt have no other Gods but me," the proper response would have been, "That we should worship the onely true God, and no other beside him" (*MB* [*Spiritual Milk for Babes*], 2). Similarly, when she asked for Brown's understanding of the Second Commandment, "Thou shalt not make to thy self any graven image, &c.," he would have said, "That we should worship the true God with true worship such as God hath ordained, not such as man hath invented" (*MB,* 2-3). But Brown violates both commandments. He might not worship his guide, the devil figure, but he permits his companion to manipulate him in an almost godlike manner. He obeys his cicerone. And as Brown moves toward the forest altar, he prepares to worship the "dark figure," the "Shape of Evil," who is about to initiate the converts into "the communion of [their] race" (86), which is to say into evil. Only awakening from his dream, if such it is, keeps Brown from worshiping under the direction of this minister, who is hardly the equivalent of a Puritan divine. Brown accepts and embraces for the remainder of his life the man's dark message that converts "shall exult to behold the whole earth one stain of guilt, one mighty blood-spot"—a message that differs from Cotton's at the beginning of the catechism by emphasizing only the negative and by urging mortals "to penetrate, in every bosom, the deep mystery of sin" (87).

In explaining his understanding of the Third Commandment, "Thou shalt not take the name of the Lord thy God in vain, &c.," Brown would have said, "To make use of God, and the good things of God, to his Glory, and our good; not vainly, not unreverently, nor unprofitably" (*MB,* 3). After observing (or dreaming about) people in the woods and then returning home, Brown cannot acknowledge that there are "good things of God" and that he lives among them, flawed as he believes Faith and the others are. Not only does he fail to use the townspeople to glorify God, he also distances himself from them emotionally, revealing his vanity and arrogance, his irreverence and ignorance. Instead of glorifying his creator, Brown cares only about preserving himself from the threat of spiritual contamination. As he finds others "unprofitable" to him, so too does he become to them, although Faith apparently continues loving him for the remainder of his life. In separating himself from his fellow mortals, he violates the Third Commandment.

Following his return to Salem Village, Brown might or might not rest on the Sabbath; certainly, though, this morose young man never frolics then, or at any time. However, disillusioned with humanity and most especially with the church officials, he does not perform the Lord's work or feel close to God, even on Sunday. Therefore, he disobeys the Fourth Commandment, "Remember that thou keep holy the Sabbath day, &c.," which means that "we should rest from labor and much more from play on the Lord's day; that we may draw nigh to God in holy Duties" (*MB,* 3-4).

Brown also violates the Fifth Commandment, "Honour thy Father and thy Mother, that thy dayes may be long in the Land which the Lord thy God giveth thee." When Goody Cloyse asked Brown to define father and mother, he would have replied, "All our Superiors, whether in Family, School, Church, and Common-wealth"; and in detailing what honor he owes these people, he would have said, "Reverence, obedience, and (when I am able) Recompense" (*MB,* 4). Goody Cloyse, the minister, and Deacon Gookin are clearly Brown's religious superiors. Before his night in the woods, Brown had revered these people, but he did not truly obey them in the sense that he did not honor their teachings about human depravity. And after this night, he reveres them no more. To him they are now hypocrites whose apparent goodness veils corruption. In the woods, Brown does honor his father, or what he believes is "the shape of his own dead father" (86). The image of the elder Brown beckons him to the ceremony and Brown obeys. But a woman (the narrator suggests that she might be Brown's mother) warns him not to come forward. He disobeys her. And at the end of the tale, if not at the beginning, Faith is clearly Brown's superior. She obvi-

ously loves her husband, presumably functions more or less normally in her society, and exhibits an enthusiasm for life, whereas Brown, following his night in the woods, loves nobody (except possibly himself), quits functioning as a social being, and necessarily withdraws from life. In rejecting Faith upon returning to Salem Village, Brown humiliates and dishonors her. In fact, of the characters in the tale, Brown honors only the image of his father, the man who apparently conducts the ceremony in the woods, and his guide.

Just as surely as Brown fails to obey the Fifth Commandment, he also violates the Sixth, "Thou shalt do no murther." Religious novitiates indicated their understanding of this commandment by saying it means "[t]hat we should not shorten the life, or health of our selves or others, but preserve both" (*MB,* 4). Brown lives a long life, long enough to see Faith "an aged woman" (90) and to have grandchildren follow his corpse to its grave. But his emotional health, his psychological health, dies during his night in the woods; his long life is essentially a long non-life. The murder Brown commits is spiritual suicide.

If Brown does not violate the Seventh Commandment, it is not for lack of trying. Even Puritan prepubescents must have known what "Thou shalt not commit Adultery" really means; but when asked to define it, they said, "To defile our selves, or others with unclean Lusts." And to indicate that they understood their responsibilities, they stated that their duty was to "[c]hastity, to possess [their] vessels in holiness and honour" (*MB,* 5). Definitions usually clarify, not obfuscate; but even today, adults might use euphemisms as vague and locutions as evasive as these in a similar context. At this late date, though, few would doubt that Brown goes to the woods primarily for sexual reasons.[22] Support for this interpretation emerges in sexual imagery, as when Goody Cloyse says that "there is a nice young man to be taken into communion to-night," or when Deacon Gookin says that "there is a goodly young woman to be taken into communion" (79, 81). Other evidence includes the apparent presence in the woods of the governor's wife and other women, many of them exalted, but all without their husbands. Their companions are "men of dissolute lives and women of spotted fame, wretches given over to all mean and filthy vice, and suspected even of horrid crimes" (85). I would suggest that Brown goes to the woods to participate in an orgy, in clear violation of the Seventh Commandment.

Puritan youth were taught that "Thou shalt not steal," the Eighth Commandment, forbade them "to take away another mans goods, without his leave, or to spend [their] own without benefit to [them]selves or others" (*MB,* 5). In separating himself emotionally from Faith and their children for the remainder of his life, Brown steals from himself and from them the life of normal familial interaction that they might reasonably have anticipated.[23] In similarly subtle ways, he disobeys the Ninth Commandment: "Thou shalt not bear false witness against thy Neighbour." Brown would have explained to Goody Cloyse that bearing false witness means "to lye falsly, to think or speak untruly of our selves or others" (*MB*, 6). He certainly thinks "untruly." Not only does he perceive Faith, Goody Cloyse, the minister, and Deacon Gookin incorrectly, both before and after his night away from home, but in thinking himself superior to them upon returning to Salem Village, he thinks untruly about himself.

Finally, Brown violates the Tenth Commandment, "Thou shalt not covet, *&c.*" This commandment forbids "[l]ust after the things of other men, and want of contentment with our own" (*MB*, 6). Brown is not content. Either he is unhappy with Faith, or he is not yet able to be faithful to her sexually, or both. Surely, when he goes to the woods, he knows what is happening there "this night . . . of all nights in the year" (74), and he wants to participate. Even though he does not frolic with the women he desires, he consummates a physical relationship with more than one of them in his heart. This newlywed defiles himself with what he once would have identified, in explaining the Seventh Commandment to Goody Cloyse, as "unclean Lusts" (*MB*, 5).

The fact that Brown violates, or dreams of violating, the Commandments either in the woods or later in Salem Village suggests that he had urges to disobey them before leaving home.[24] And if so, he should have surmised from observing himself, if not from having studied the catechism with Goody Cloyse or from living in a Puritan society, that people are fundamentally corrupt, precisely as Cotton states in *Milk for Babes*. That Brown fails to honor the Commandments does not make him unique among mortals, however; nor does it mean that he is necessarily destined for eternal damnation. Rather, Cotton relates in the catechism that because of Adam's sin, no human is capable of keeping the Commandments:

> Q. *Have you kept all these Commandements?*
>
> Ans. No, I and all men are sinners.
> (*MB*, 6)

Had Brown understood from childhood that humans, all of whom are depraved, cannot obey the Commandments, that fidelity to God's law is impossible, he would not be so surprised to see, or to think he sees, the several worthies preparing to act in a decidedly non-Christian manner in the woods. But because he did not learn this lesson well, he is surprised; and as a result, he thinks that, in the words of Emily Miller Budick, "evil is our only reality and the devil our only God."[25] For the remainder of his life he retains this view, which destroys him.

After presenting the Ten Commandments, Cotton concludes the catechism by addressing salvation once again. Doing so is structurally appropriate because it reintroduces the hope expressed in the first catechism answer that God "can save me" (*MB*, 1). It is also theologically appropriate, the natural Christian conclusion to a traditional presentation of the gospel, as interpreted by St. Paul in Romans

8.[26] Cotton devotes twenty-eight sets of questions and answers to the possibility of salvation, illustrating its importance. Also, in this section, he requires catechism students to give their longest, most detailed answers, forcing them to address some of the fine points concerning salvation.

In helping Brown with the conclusion to the catechism, Goody Cloyse would have taught him that because all mortals are sinners, only Jesus can save them. But in order to gain salvation, they must look to the Bible, which teaches their need for a savior. Although unworthy of Christ's grace, they may attain it by denying themselves and demonstrating faith in him, by praying to God, by repenting (detesting their sins and asking forgiveness), and by attaining a new life (rejecting their corrupt state and walking before Christ as church members). The faithful of the church have a covenant wherein they give themselves to God, whom they worship, and to the church officials. Baptism and communion, the seals of the covenant, provide for resurrection from the dead on Judgment Day, a time when God will determine the fate of all souls on the basis of works performed in conjunction with the faith that gives them merit in God's sight.[27] Some souls will reside in heaven, some in hell.

Brown fulfills only one of the requirements for attaining salvation, and it is one in which he was necessarily passive. Assuming he was born in the late 1660s to church members, he would have been baptized as an infant. Even had his parents not demonstrated evidence of saving faith and therefore not been recognized as full church members, the Half-Way Covenant of 1662 permitted the newborn Brown to be baptized.[28] But following his night in the woods, Brown apparently does not subject himself to the Bible, or at least not to the New Testament, if his rejection of the imperfect but admirable members of his society and his long, somber life are any indications. In refusing to deny himself, Brown demonstrates a lack of faith in Christ, which makes praying for deliverance irrelevant. He does not repent his sins. While he attains a new life, it is, in its gloominess, the antithesis of the positive new life Cotton requires in the catechism. Since Brown probably no longer remains a member of the church, he cannot properly subject himself to God or the clergy, thus rendering himself ineligible to receive holy communion, one of the seals of the covenant.[29] According to Cotton's teachings, then, Brown's soul will not find eternal residence with God in heaven but will reside forever in hell.

Indeed, Connolly and Grayson state correctly that the Puritan catechism treats the issue of innate depravity, as any text detailing the tenets of Puritanism must. But *Milk for Babes* does so only briefly, at the beginning of the text. As the Bible progresses from the talionic Old Testament to the caritative New Testament, so does Cotton's catechism progress, beginning with the fifth answer, from judgment to hope. Because it is essentially a *vade mecum* for living morally and attaining salvation, it is a hopeful, not a pessimistic, document. Clearly, then, Connolly misstates in claiming that the "catechism teaches the way to the devil and not the way to heaven"; and Grayson errs in proclaiming that "Connolly is right about the deleterious effects of the catechism."[30]

Aware that the Salem Village of Brown's time used *Milk for Babes,* Hawthorne astutely has his narrator state that "there was a world of meaning" in Brown's comment, "That old woman taught me my catechism" (80). Indeed, there is considerable meaning; the narrator does not speak idly—or ironically. Brown incriminates himself as one who has been unable to assimilate into his view of humanity the fundamental beliefs of his faith and of his society, as Cotton expresses them. Before leaving home, Brown thinks mortals close to perfection; an understanding of the catechism would have disabused him of this assumption. But after returning home from his night in the woods, he considers irredeemable these people he has revered. This judgment, too, is flawed. Since Brown never masters the lessons Goody Cloyse tried to teach him, he cannot fit spiritually, emotionally, or psychologically into his own society. As a result, he becomes, like Hawthorne's Wakefield, an "Outcast of the Universe"[31] on whose tombstone "they carved no hopeful verse . . . ; for his dying hour was gloom" (90).

Notes

1. See Herman Melville, "Hawthorne and His Mosses," in *The Piazza Tales and Other Prose Pieces, 1839-1860,* ed. Harrison Hayford et al., vol. 9 of *The Writings of Herman Melville* (Evanston and Chicago: Northwestern Univ. Press and The Newberry Library, 1987), 251-52; Hyatt H. Waggoner, *Hawthorne: A Critical Study,* rev. ed. (Cambridge: Harvard Univ. Press, 1963), 14, 59, 60-61, 119, 209-10, 253; Richard Harter Fogle, *Hawthorne's Fiction: The Light and the Dark,* rev. ed. (Norman: Univ. of Oklahoma Press, 1964), 15-32; and Frederick Crews, *The Sins of the Fathers: Hawthorne's Psychological Themes* (New York: Oxford Univ. Press, 1966; Berkeley and Los Angeles: Univ. of California Press, 1989), 98-106. Crews disavows the psychological underpinnings of his study in the afterword to the reprint edition; see especially 278-79.

2. Nathaniel Hawthorne, "Young Goodman Brown," in *Mosses from an Old Manse,* ed. William Charvat et al., vol. 10 of the Centenary Edition of *The Works of Nathaniel Hawthorne* (Columbus: Ohio State Univ. Press, 1974), 78; hereafter cited parenthetically by page number.

3. Michael J. Colacurcio, *The Province of Piety: Moral History in Hawthorne's Early Tales* (Cambridge: Harvard Univ. Press, 1984), 288; Neal Frank Doubleday, *Hawthorne's Early Tales: A Critical Study* (Durham: Duke Univ. Press, 1972), 205; Sheldon W. Liebman, "The Reader in 'Young Goodman Brown,'" in *The Nathaniel Hawthorne Journal 1975,* ed. C. E. Frazer Clark Jr. (Englewood, CO: Microcard Editions Books, 1975), 157; Melinda M. Ponder, *Haw-*

thorne's Early Narrative Art, vol. 9 of *Studies in American Literature* (Lewiston, NY: Edwin Mellen, 1990), 52-62, 138-39.

4. Thomas E. Connolly, "Hawthorne's 'Young Goodman Brown': An Attack on Puritanic Calvinism," *American Literature* 28 (1956): 375, 373.

5. Robert C. Grayson, "Curdled Milk for Babes: The Role of the Catechism in 'Young Goodman Brown,'" *Nathaniel Hawthorne Review* 16 (Spring 1990): 1, 5, 3.

6. Marion L. Kesselring, *Hawthorne's Reading, 1828-1850: A Transcription and Identification of Titles Recorded in the Charge-Books of the Salem Athenaeum* (New York: New York Public Library, 1949), 56. Grayson mistakenly states that Hawthorne himself withdrew the volume three times ("Curdled Milk for Babes," 3). Also see William Bentley, "A Description and History of Salem," *Collections of the Massachusetts Historical Society* 6 (1799): 260.

7. See Kesselring, *Hawthorne's Reading,* 50; and Joseph B. Felt, *The Annals of Salem, From Its First Settlement* (Salem: W[illiam] and S[tephen] B[radshaw] Ives, 1827), 207. The Salem church had jurisdiction over the Salem Village church until their separation in 1689 (Bentley, "A Description and History of Salem," 266). Therefore, until at least that date the catechism used in Salem, *Milk for Babes,* would also have been used in Salem Village.

8. There are seven extant seventeenth-century editions of John Cotton's *Milk for Babes* in English, as well as a translation into Massachusett by Grindal Rawson:

Milk for Babes (London: J[ane] Coe for Henry Overton, 1646). Wing 6443.

Spiritual Milk for Boston Babes in Either England (Cambridg[e], MA: S[amuel] G[reen] for Hezekiah Usher, 1656). Evans 42.

Spirituall Milk for Boston Babes in Either England (London: Henry Cripps, 1657). Wing 6462A.

Spiritual Milk for Babes (London: Henry Cripps, 1662). Wing 6459A.

Spiritual Milk for Babes (London: Peter Parker, 1668). Wing 6460.

Spiritual Milk for Babes (London: Peter Parker, 1672). "Corrected in Quotations by *L. H.* 1665." Wing 6461.

Spiritual Milk for Boston Babes, in Either England (Boston, 1684). Evans 39225.

Nashauanittue Meninnunk wutch Mukkiesog, trans. Grindal Rawson (Cambridge, MA: Samuel Green for Bartholomew Green, 1691). Evans 550.

Although substantive textual differences exist among the editions in English, they do not affect meaning. Other editions reportedly were published in London in 1648, Cambridge in 1668, and Boston in 1690;

and there might have been other seventeenth-century editions. See Wilberforce Eames, *Early New England Catechisms: A Bibliographical Account of Some Catechisms Published before the Year 1800, For Use in New England* (1898; reprint, New York: Burt Franklin, n.d.), 24-25. In this essay, I follow the established practice of referring to Cotton's catechism as *Milk for Babes.*

9. If *Milk for Babes* were unavailable to Hawthorne under its own title, he would nevertheless have had access to it in numerous eighteenth-century editions of *The New-England Primer.* See Charles F. Heartman, *The New-England Primer Issued Prior to 1830* (New York: Bowker, 1934).

10. John Cotton, *Spiritual Milk for Babes* (London: Peter Parker, 1672), 1-2; hereafter cited parenthetically as *MB,* with page number. In quoting from Cotton's text, I make no effort to reproduce the long *s*; I also do not include the marginal glosses to biblical verses. I base my use of this particular edition on the following reasoning: First, I assume that the tale is set in 1692 (due to the suggestions of witchcraft) and, further, that the protagonist is in his mid-twenties. In a demographic study of Andover, Massachusetts (fewer than fifteen miles from Salem Village), Philip J. Greven Jr. shows that from 1690 to 1694, Andover men married at the average age of 23.5 (see *Four Generations: Population, Land, and Family in Colonial Andover, Massachusetts* [Ithaca: Cornell Univ. Press, 1970], 117). Hawthorne had access to similar demographic data about Andover: in September 1834, only seven months before the publication of "Young Goodman Brown," he withdrew from the Salem Athenaeum Abiel Abbot's *History of Andover from Its Settlement to 1829* (Andover: Flagg and Gould, 1829), which includes, on 185-86, birth and death data from 1652 through 1700 (Kesselring, *Hawthorne's Reading,* 43). Assuming that Salem Village's data would be similar to Andover's, and that Brown married at the average age in 1692 (he and Faith have been married for only three months at the tale's opening), then were he a real person, he would have been born in 1668 or 1669. Because he would have begun catechism lessons around age five, it is likely that Goody Cloyse would have taught him using the 1672 edition of Cotton's text, the one I cite here. (Grayson cites the edition of 1646.)

11. *The New-England Primer Enlarged* (Boston: S[amuel] Kneeland and T[imothy] Green, 1727), 7. Evans 2927. This is the earliest extant text of the *Primer,* which was possibly first published before 1690. For further information, see Paul Leicester Ford, *The New-England Primer: A History of Its Origin and Development* (1897; reprint, n.p.: Columbia Univ., 1962); George Livermore, *The Origin, History and Character of the New England Primer* (1849; reprint, New York: Cha[rle]s Fred[erick] Heartman, 1915); Worthington Chauncey Ford, "The New England Primer," in *Bibliographical Essays: A Tribute to Wil-*

berforce Eames (1924; reprint, New York: Burt Franklin, 1968), 61-65; A. S. W. Rosenbach, *Early American Children's Books* (1933; reprint, New York: Kraus Reprint, 1966); Heartman, *New-England Primer Issued Prior to 1830*; William Sloane, *Children's Books in England and America in the Seventeenth Century* (New York: King's Crown Press/Columbia Univ., 1955), 191-93; Cornelia Meigs, ed., *A Critical History of Children's Literature: A Survey of Children's Books in English from Earliest Times to the Present,* rev. ed. (London: Collier-Macmillan, 1969), 110-19; Daniel A. Cohen, "The Origin and Development of the *New England Primer,*" *Children's Literature* 5 (1976): 52-57; and David H. Watters, "'I Spake as a Child': Authority, Metaphor and *The New-England Primer,*" *Early American Literature* 20 (1985-86): 193-213. No seventeenth-century hornbook is known to exist.

12. If Brown understood the catechism, he would know that a relationship with another person does not influence the ultimate disposition of one's soul. One does not gain salvation by proxy, as it were.

13. Cf. Nathaniel Hawthorne, "The Hollow of the Three Hills," in *Twice-Told Tales,* ed. William Charvat et al., vol. 9 of the Centenary Edition of *The Works of Nathaniel Hawthorne* (Columbus: Ohio State Univ. Press, 1974), 200. Here, in what is possibly Hawthorne's earliest published tale, a "Power of Evil" performs the "impious baptismal rite."

14. Colacurcio, *Province of Piety,* 301.

15. Richard Mather, *A Farewel Exhortation to the Church and People of Dorchester in New-England* (Cambridg[e], MA: Samuel Green, 1657), 6.

16. Richard Baxter, *A Christian Directory; or, A Summ of Practical Theologie, and Cases of Conscience* (London: Robert White for Nevill Simmons, 1673), pt. 2, 582. Baxter argues that learning the words of a catechism without mastering their meaning will make understanding easier when children are capable of comprehending theological concepts. Then, instead of struggling to learn both words and meaning, they can focus on the latter. Also see David D. Hall, *Worlds of Wonder, Days of Judgment: Popular Religious Belief in Early New England* (New York: Alfred A. Knopf, 1989), 37.

17. Cotton Mather, *A Family Well-Ordered; or, An Essay to Render Parents and Children Happy in One Another* (Boston: B[artholomew] Green and J[ohn] Allen for Michael Perry and Benjamin Eliot, 1699), 19-20.

18. Cotton Mather, *Maschil; or, The Faithful Instructor. Offering, Memorials of Christianity in Twenty Six Exercises upon the New-English Catechism* (Boston: B[artholomew] Green and J[ohn] Allen for Samuel Phillips, 1702), 11.

19. Isaac Watts, "A Discourse on the Way of Instruction by Catechisms, and of the Best Method of Compos-

ing Them," in *The Works of the Reverend and Learned Isaac Watts, D. D. Containing, besides His Sermons, and Essays on Miscellaneous Subjects, Several Additional Pieces, Selected from His Manuscripts* (London: J[ohn] Barfield, 1810), 3:214.

20. David Levin, "Shadows of Doubt: Specter Evidence in Hawthorne's 'Young Goodman Brown,'" *American Literature* 34 (1962): 351.

21. Cotton also writes elsewhere about the importance of the Ten Commandments to the Puritans: "[A]ll the sins and good things found in the wlhoe [*sic*] Bible, are to be ranked within the compasse of the ten Commandments." See *A Practical Commentary; or, An Exposition with Observations, Reasons, and Uses upon the First Epistle Generall of John* (London: R[obert] I[bbitson] and E[dward] C[rouch] for Thomas Parkhurst, 1656), 235.

22. For a discussion of sexuality in "Young Goodman Brown," see Crews, *Sins of the Fathers,* 98-106.

23. Unless Faith is pregnant with more than one child before Brown leaves her for the woods, they have sexual intercourse after he returns, and probably more than once. Their "children" follow his body to the grave (90).

24. If Brown actually violates the Commandments, as opposed to merely dreaming about disobeying them, he might be violating civil as well as ecclesiastical law. In 1690 the General Court encouraged ministers to suppress such sins as "*Unbelief, Worldliness, Heresy, Pride, Wrath, Strife, Envy,* and the *Neglect* of communion with God, in both Natural and Instituted *Worship,* and the *Contempt* of the *everlasting Gospel,* with a shameful want of due *Family-Instruction,* which are the *Roots of Bitterness* in the midst of us" (*By the Governour and General Court of the Colony of the Massachusetts Bay* [Cambridge, 1690], [2]).

25. Emily Miller Budick, *Fiction and Historical Consciousness: The American Romance Tradition* (New Haven: Yale Univ. Press, 1989), 91.

26. See, for example, Romans 8:38-39, quoted from the Authorized (King James) Version:

> For I am persuaded, that neither death, nor life, nor angels, nor principalities, nor powers, nor things present, nor things to come,
>
> Nor height, nor depth, nor any other creature, shall be able to separate us from the love of God, which is in Christ Jesus our Lord.

27. Cotton states elsewhere that mortals cannot know, on the basis of their works, if their souls are heaven bound: "Sanctification . . . is no evidence, or witness of our union with Christ" (*A Treatise of the Covenant of Grace, As It Is Dispensed to the Elect Seed, Effectually unto Salvation,* 2nd ed. [London: William Miller, 1662], 43). This belief, of course, does not contradict Cotton's statement in the catechism that God judges souls according to mortals'

works. For discussions of Cotton's attitude toward works, especially in the context of Anne Hutchinson and the Antinomian controversy, see Larzer Ziff, *The Career of John Cotton: Puritanism and the American Experience* (Princeton: Princeton Univ. Press, 1962), 110-12; William K. B. Stoever, *"A Faire and Easie Way to Heaven": Covenant Theology and Antinomianism in Early Massachusetts* (Middletown, CT: Wesleyan Univ. Press, 1978), 54-55; R. T. Kendall, *Calvin and English Calvinism to 1649* (Oxford: Oxford Univ. Press, 1979), 167-83; and Everett Emerson, *John Cotton,* rev. ed. (Boston: Twayne, 1990), 64-67, 85-96.

28. I refer to the fifth proposition in the Half-Way Covenant, which permits children of church members to be baptized:

> Church-members who were admitted in minority, understanding the Doctrine of Faith, and publickly professing their assent thereto; not scandalous in life, and solemnly owning the Covenant before the Church, wherein they give up themselves and their children to the Lord, and subject themselves to the Government of Christ in the Church, their children are to be Baptized."

(Propositions Concerning the Subject of Baptism and Consociation of Churches [Cambridge, MA: S(amuel) G(reen) for Hezekiah Usher, 1662], 19)

29. Colacurcio suggests otherwise. He says, "Goodman Brown evidently continued to be accepted at the communion table" (*Province of Piety,* 303). But following his return to Salem Village, Brown has no reason for wishing to remain in the church. Further, because he can no longer meet church membership requirements, as Cotton presents them, he could conceivably be excommunicated. Following the adoption of the Half-Way Covenant in 1662, Puritan churches continued to excommunicate members "for misconduct or for openly expressed heretical ideas" (Edmund S. Morgan, *Visible Saints: The History of a Puritan Idea* [New York: New York Univ. Press, 1963; Ithaca: Cornell Univ. Press, 1965], 127).

30. Connolly, "Hawthorne's 'Young Goodman Brown,'" 373; Grayson, "Curdled Milk for Babes," 5.

31. Nathaniel Hawthorne, "Wakefield," in *Twice-Told Tales,* 140.

James C. Keil (essay date 1996)

SOURCE: "Hawthorne's 'Young Goodman Brown': Early Nineteenth-Century and Puritan Constructions of Gender," in *New England Quarterly,* Vol. 69, No. 1, March, 1996, pp. 33-55.

[*In the following essay, Keil focuses on the blurring of masculine and feminine spheres in "Young Goodman*

Brown" and suggests that the reader needs to take into account historical as well as psychological implications of gender in the tale.]

Nathaniel Hawthorne's **"Young Goodman Brown"** traditionally has been read as an examination of crises of faith, morality, and/or psychosexuality. Early readings focused on questions of theology and conduct,[1] but since the opening years of the 1950s, a second category of readings has emphasized the psychosexual elements. Roy Male, for example, argued that "the dark night in the forest is essentially a sexual experience, though it is also much more," while Frederick Crews observed that in his dream experience, the young, newly wed, and still oedipal Brown, fleeing from the sexuality of married love, removes himself to a place where he can voyeuristically and vicariously enjoy that which he directly shuns.[2] The third important category of readings attempts to ground the story in the late seventeenth- and early eighteenth-century documents about witchcraft to which Hawthorne had access. Most significant of these considerations are David Levin's contention that the most important topic of **"Young Goodman Brown"** is the theological and epistemological issue of "specter evidence" and Michael Colacurcio's thesis that the historical documents from which Hawthorne worked, especially those involving how you tell a saint from a witch or any other sinner, limit the scope of Hawthorne's investigation into Brown's (or his own) psyche to that made possible by the language and content of the Puritan documents.[3] In all three of these critical categories, the authors generally assume, if they address the matter at all, that Hawthorne is concerned with late seventeenth- and early eighteenth-century issues and events surrounding American Puritan life. We must recognize, however, that—contra the assumptions that some scholars make about Hawthorne as a Puritan historian—Hawthorne could not re-create Puritan history in his historical tales; he could only construct it, basing his construction upon his readings of Puritan documents and the experience that he, as a nineteenth-century, middle-class New Englander, brought to them.

At least one reader suggests that part of the experience Hawthorne brought to the Puritan documents was his familiarity with contemporary documents. Frank Shuffleton has pointed out convincingly that, in the climactic scene of the "witches' sabbath," Hawthorne appeared to have been working not only from Puritan archives but also from Frances Trollope's contemporary observations on the demonic aspects of evangelical tent meetings in *Domestic Manners of the Americans* (1832). Without denying the crises of faith, morality, and psychosexuality that earlier critics had discovered in **"Young Goodman Brown,"** Shuffleton notes that Hawthorne was likely to find those issues in contemporary as well as Puritan documents and events. Moreover, in recognizing that "the story's meaning has an anchor in a specific social situation in Hawthorne's nineteenth-century present, we understand the balancing power of the specific richness of the story's historical knowledge as detailed by so many scholars."[4] If theology,

morality, and psychosexuality were a devilish brew for Hawthorne's Puritan ancestors, they were no less so for Hawthorne and his contemporaries. Hawthorne places the story in the seventeenth century in order to explore the nexus of past and present in New Englanders' attitudes towards these central life experiences.

In addition to the Puritan problems of telling the saintly from the damned and the innocent from the corrupt, **"Young Goodman Brown"** takes as part of its context fundamental changes in gender and gender relations in the growing middle-class world of New England. One aspect of these changes in gender and sexuality with which the story surely is concerned is the nineteenth-century ideology of separate spheres. During the early decades of the nineteenth century, a discourse developed that sought to divide the world into public and private spheres based on gender.[5] Men and women had lived socially, economically, and politically distinct lives in the Puritan period, but what is significant about the new, nineteenth-century gender ideology is that it constructed a "male" world that was even more and decidedly self-consciously distinct from the "female." Men should be the "sole" economic providers of the household, working, increasingly, outside of it, in the public realm. Women should provide all the other needs of the family, laboring (although it was seldom seen as such) only within the house—a structure that during this period became known as the "home" and became identified primarily with women and their children.

Of particular relevance to Hawthorne's story, however, since its concerns are with transgression as much as catechism, is that in the last two decades historians have come to understand that the clear boundaries between male/female, public/private, and work/home were blurred—that these separate spheres, essential to constructions of the middle-class world and heretofore thought rigid barriers, more accurately should be seen as thresholds through which nineteenth-century Americans frequently passed.[6] Moreover, historians have also confirmed that the 1830s was a critical decade of change.[7] **"Young Goodman Brown,"** probably written no earlier than the initial years of the decade and published anonymously in 1835, chronicles Hawthorne's observations about the anxieties caused by such discrepancies between ideology and behavior. Young Goodman Brown, who has come to believe with religious fervor what he has been taught prior to marriage about the separation of spheres, is disoriented by the behavioral expectations he confronts once he has entered that institution. The ideology of separate spheres was not transgressed, Hawthorne seems to suggest in **"Young Goodman Brown,"** without some psychological and moral costs.

I

Michael Colacurcio has advised that readers look for the historical contexts of early Hawthorne stories in the opening paragraphs, and that is precisely where this reading will begin.[8] It is here in the opening paragraphs that we are introduced to both a Puritan setting and another of what Shuffleton has called Hawthorne's contemporary "anchors." The story begins with an explicit presentation of issues of gender, sexuality, and intimacy, all of which take place in the doorway between public and private.

> Young Goodman Brown came forth, at sunset, into the street of Salem village, but put his head back, after crossing the threshold, to exchange a parting kiss with his young wife. And Faith, as the wife was aptly named, thrust her own pretty head into the street, letting the wind play with the pink ribbons of her cap, while she called to Goodman Brown.[9]

In this scene, we learn that the setting of the story is Salem village, the site of many mysterious activities in the minds of Hawthorne's contemporaries, and the time is sunset. The scene takes place in the doorway of the Browns' house, a threshold that both joins and separates not only private and public but, literally in this case, female and male. It is a threshold that both characters violate for reasons of intimacy, although she, as we see, is clearly the more intimate of the two. About the two characters we learn that the man is young, that he is embarking on a nighttime journey, and that, apparently, he is distracted or hurried, since he fails to kiss his wife before leaving the house. Of the woman, we learn that she is married to the young man, is named Faith, is pretty, and, although she modestly wears a cap over her hair, she has adorned it with pink ribbons.

The ambiguity in the description of Faith—is or is not her name a sign of her spirituality or faithfulness? is she modest or immodest?—will recur throughout the story, and this ambiguity is the cause of Brown's great sadness and the subject of much of the scholarship on the story. Here it is important to note that the ambiguity is repeated also in her not waiting for him to return to kiss her, in her thrusting her own head through the doorway and "letting" the breeze animate the ribbons with which she has dressed her cap. Not only is the "letting" ambiguous when combined with the thrusting, "letting" is an activity that itself raises questions about who is in control of the action. Having thrust her head through the doorway in order to give her husband his goodbye kiss, Faith whispers "softly and rather sadly, when her lips were close to his ear,"

> "Dearest heart, . . . pr'y thee, put off your journey until sunrise, and sleep in your own bed to-night. A lone woman is troubled with such dreams and such thoughts, that she's afeard of herself, sometimes. Pray, tarry with me this night, dear husband, of all nights in the year!"
>
> [P. 74]

Surely Hawthorne means for us to think of this story as taking place in Puritan Massachusetts.[10] Certain other factors, however—such as the threshold setting, the description of Faith, the couple's bad dreams, the implication that he has failed to sleep in his own bed on other occasions—suggest a more contemporary setting. John Demos indicates that the early decades of the nineteenth century pro-

duced scads of literature on domestic life, and the "shrill tone of the new advice betrayed deep anxieties about the evolving shape and future prospects of the family."[11] It is of course the Browns' prospects for the future about which they are most concerned. The family was changing in fundamental ways in Hawthorne's lifetime, and many New Englanders were writing and reading about the uncertainty they felt. That domestic literature was supplemented by sexual advice literature that portrayed men as sexually predatory and—a distinct difference from the Puritan construction—women as virtually passionless. Unlike the Puritan ethos, this same nineteenth-century advice literature also threatened disaster if abstinence were not the rule in all aspects of non-procreative sexuality.[12] It is unlikely that Hawthorne was unaware of this new literature on domestic life and human sexuality, but at the very least his story betrays the same profound anxieties about contemporary family and sexual life.

Although much of Brown's anxiety later in the story involves traditional suspicions that women are especially sexual creatures, a failing of which men must beware, Faith herself may better fit an ideal of womanhood popular in the magazine literature of Hawthorne's time. According to Lois Banner, Hawthorne "gave [this ideal] epic representation in the dovelike Hilda of *The Marble Faun* and the manipulated Priscilla of *The Blithedale Romance*." Such a woman was known as the "steel-engraving lady" both for the "process by which she was created" and her own "moral rectitude": "When her pictorial representation is colored, her complexion is white, with a blush of pink in her cheeks."[13] Attending a gala New York City ball in 1822, James Fenimore Cooper encountered the real-life counterparts of this American ideal: "'There is something in the bloom, delicacy, and innocence of one of these young things, that reminds you of the conceptions which poets and painters have taken of the angels.'"[14] The ideal's delicacy and spirituality were important; later in the story, Brown will refer to Faith as a "'blessed angel on earth'" (p. 75). Another characteristic of the ideal is her youth, which "underscored her purity and reflected both the nineteenth-century romanticization of childhood and its tendency to infantilize women, to view them as creatures of childlike disposition."[15] Such characterizations of femininity contrast quite specifically with Puritan constructions of womanhood, which were based on Eve's seduction by the devil and her deception of Adam in the Garden of Eden.[16]

Perhaps as the last in a series of efforts to keep Brown home this night, Faith pleads with her husband not only to stay home but to sleep with her. The young wife's desire for intimacy with her husband could not be more explicit. Brown's reply is no less direct:

> "My love and my Faith, . . . of all nights in the year, this one night must I tarry away from thee. My journey, as thou callest it, forth and back again, must needs be done 'twixt now and sunrise. What, my sweet, pretty wife, dost thou doubt me already, and we but three months married!"
>
> [P. 74]

In this passage Brown has deliberately conflated his wife's name with a belief system. Hawthorne's construction of Brown's speech in this manner, his association of religion with the role of wife, suggests both Puritan and contemporary possibilities. According to Edmund Morgan, for example, Puritans feared that love of spouse could rival and interfere with love of Christ. On the other hand, in Hawthorne's lifetime women, thought to be morally superior to men, were entrusted with preparing children for Christian salvation. Nancy Cott argues that the evangelicals of the early decades "linked moral agency to female character with a supporting link to passionlessness."[17] If Hawthorne's concerns are as much with contemporary as Puritan gender ideology, then having a wife named Faith seems an appropriate characteristic for his main character. However, except for Brown's distrust of Faith, it is at this point in Hawthorne's story that, although the setting seems Puritan and both periods sometimes confuse sex with "going to the devil," the gender relations begin to have more in common with nineteenth-century ideology and behavior than Puritan history.

In Brown's reply to Faith, there is an element of huffy self-importance, as if Brown were giving a prepared speech. Here we find an indication that the events of the forest are not entirely responsible for Brown's becoming a "darkly meditative, a distrustful" man (p. 89); for all his youth and inexperience, Brown is already very serious, and this hyper-seriousness is part of his foolishness. In insisting that he must leave Faith this night, Brown misreads her sexual desire and fear of being alone as anxiety about his marital fidelity. Note the irony of Brown's question: he doesn't realize that it is a sexual life with her that he is running away from when he portrays himself to his young wife ("dost thou doubt me already") as a licentious stud who would take other lovers after only three months of marriage, a self-portrait that suggests nineteenth-century manhood.

In the nineteenth century, with many men away from the home for long periods of time, middle-class Americans needed a gender ideology that sanctified woman's isolation among her children. Whereas men had played important roles in the moral upbringing, education, and socialization of children in former periods, in the early nineteenth century such responsibilities all but evaporated for many middle-class men. At the same time, women's important role in the economic production that sustained the household of the eighteenth century was, at least in the discourse, eliminated. "Having required the bourgeois woman to be both elegant and nonproductive," and leaving her on her own with the children all day, Carroll Smith-Rosenberg asks, "how could the bourgeois man ever trust her virtue or rest securely in the symbols of his class" (i.e., primarily, in his elegant woman and well-kept children)?[18] What was to keep this consumer, rather than producer, of resources from straying—economically, sexually, morally, religiously? The solution was a socially redeemed image of womanhood: woman as Angel of the Home. Middle-class woman's sole province became the production of "home" life, where the values of the culture could be instilled into the items she produced, her children.[19]

Yet Faith both conforms to and violates nineteenth-century ideology. Standing inside the doorway, she is pretty, modest, discreet, and her name suggests her spirituality and her devotion to her husband. At the same time, she is, within the terms of nineteenth-century ideology, aggressive in her sexuality. The reversal of the expected that we see Brown encounter on the threshold of his own home is probably not unprecedented. His language seems to suggest that marriage may have been a rude awakening for him. Brown's discovery of Faith's sexuality may have shattered his conception of the passivity and disinterest that women were supposed to demonstrate about sex, and this knowledge may have threatened the security of his home. The events that take place in the woods may be nothing more than his playing out of his anxious fantasies about Faith's sexuality and the ideology of separate spheres that he demonstrates in his speech and behavior at the entrance of his home.

The story's introduction, then, describes several threshold experiences, not just because it takes place in a doorway (although that too is important to our understanding of the action of the public/private discourse) but because it is this parting of Faith and Brown that defines their future intimacy. That is to say, from now on they will cross this threshold repeatedly. Intercourse is also physically and emotionally a threshold experience, and the act itself is suggested in the opening paragraphs where Faith and Brown repeatedly stick their heads in and out of a doorway graced by her pink ribbons.[20] There is much about the physical act of sex—the orgasms, the levels of intensity, the sleeping in one's own bed—that involves thresholds, but so too does the emotional aspect, particularly the intimacy that may proceed from as well as contribute to the physical experience. Whatever we may think today, coition and orgasm were not the *sine qua non* of human sexuality in the nineteenth century; a wide range of intimate activities constituted sexuality.[21] But notice also how those recurrent pink ribbons may have blurred Brown's whole notion of privacy, (woman's) purity, and the sanctity of the separate woman's sphere. Brown encounters these ribbons adorning the public world everywhere he goes: each time he sees Faith sticking her head out of the doorway, he notices them, and later one floats down out of the forest sky to convince him that "'There is no good on earth'" and to the devil "'is this world given'" (p. 83).[22]

What happens in the woods, then, is also part of this public/private borderland, only here Brown realizes that the divisions are grotesquely blurred, and the sexual theme significantly expands to include the issues of manhood and fatherhood—much to Goodman Brown's chagrin.

II

As we follow our new husband into the woods, we notice that the image of the threshold recurs when Brown looks back at Faith before turning the corner of the meeting-house and, presumably, going out of her sight. Upon entering the woods, he finds that the "dreary road" he has chosen is "darkened by all the gloomiest trees of the forest, which barely stood aside to let the narrow path creep through, and closed immediately behind." The trees seem to cut him off effectively from his life with Faith and from Salem village. He will soon pass a "crook" in the road, which will further isolate him. Or so it would seem. His only emotions at this point are his loneliness—the same emotion his wife is, presumably, experiencing—and his guilt. However, even this guilt and loneliness, we are told on two occasions, may be occurring in the midst of "an unseen multitude" (p. 75). Having left the private sphere for the public as the story begins, Brown now apparently enters another sphere in which the public and private have been completely blurred.

As for Brown's thoughts of his wife and his pangs, if any, about his mission, we read:

> "Poor little Faith!" thought he, for his heart smote him. "What a wretch I am, to leave her on such an errand! . . . Methought, as she spoke, there was trouble in her face, as if a dream had warned her what work is to be done to-night. But no, no! 'twould kill her to think it. Well; she's a blessed angel on earth; and after this one night, I'll cling to her skirts and follow her to Heaven."
>
> [P. 75]

Brown finds it impossible to believe that Faith could imagine her husband so immoral.[23] As we soon learn, however, Faith not only can imagine Brown on such a mission, she herself takes part in one. More interesting, perhaps, is his conviction that later he will "cling to her skirts and follow her to heaven." This vision suggests the strength of Brown's *au courant* identification of his wife as a morally superior "blessed angel." But modern too is Brown's figuring of his wife as a mother to whose skirts he can cling, an image that bears witness to the difficulty Brown has in differentiating love of mother from love of wife, a dilemma with which Hawthorne and his contemporaries were not unfamiliar.

Wife came to replace mother as the moral guardian and disciplinarian of a nineteenth-century, middle-class young man's family. The move from mother's home to wife's, from child's world to man's world should not, then, be all that difficult. Of course, in reality it is far from simple, particularly because the grown son must spend half his life away from mother-wife in the world of men for which his childhood in woman's sphere has not prepared him. Many young men must have found adult life frightening and confusing. T. Walter Herbert believes that Hawthorne did: "Nathaniel maintained a 'childlike' persona because his effort to become a 'man' was complicated by the difficulties of crossing the gap between the maternal/marital sphere and the world beyond."[24]

Faith has referred to what Brown is leaving home for as a "journey," but it is clear that he does not think of it as

such. He first refers to what he is about to do as an "'errand'" and two sentences later as "'work.'" There is also no doubt that Brown is both fleeing Faith and setting out to "go to the devil," as he phrases his errand when talking about Goody Cloyse further on. What is it the devil can offer him that his Faith cannot? When Brown meets up with the devil, the gravely dressed man, mentioning the striking of the clock on Boston's Old South Church, reprimands Brown for being a "'full fifteen minutes'" late (p. 75). In this reference to the clock, the "devil's work" becomes associated with contemporary work—labor of a modern, rational, time-ordered sort—and thus "going to the devil" carries the connotation of "men's business." Here also in this encounter we notice that the devil has been expecting Brown and knows him by name and appearance, as if the two had met before (and we are reminded of Faith's implication that this is not the first night she has spent alone). When to the devil's reprimand Brown replies, "'Faith kept me back a while,'" we realize that he knows the devil well enough to use his wife's first name with him and, further, that he believes the devil will accept the explanation that a woman was interfering with his ability to set to the "errand" or "work" that is to be done (p. 76).

Brown's morality is Manichean, gendered, as is his religious sensibility, which is reminiscent of the Puritans and evangelicals. He has been catechized to believe in the ideology of separate spheres, and his faith brooks no blurring of them. Figuring the world of wife/mother/home as on the side of good, angels, and heaven, Brown constructs the world of men/father/nonhome as siding with evil and the devil. Hence, we meet the devil in the shape of Brown's father and grandfather.

Brown's new traveling companion is described as being "about fifty years old, apparently in the same rank of life as Goodman Brown, and bearing a considerable resemblance to him, though perhaps more in expression than features." So similar are their appearances that "they might have been taken for father and son"; indeed, Goody Cloyse later recognizes the similarity immediately (p. 76). But Brown does not.[25] Within the context of our present concerns, that lack of recognition can be understood as reflecting middle-class fathers' absence from the home. Middle-class mothers and children were not to cross the threshold of the father's soiled workplace (the disaster that could result when masculine space was invaded by the feminine is the subject of Hawthorne's **The Birthmark"**), and so increasingly sons' experiences of what fathers did and who they were were limited to a few hours a day. Advice literature even urged that the son's sexual education be supervised by the mother.[26]

Brown's failure to recognize his father and to see the world as anything other than devil's work might also be attributed to the devil-father's magical power: "the only thing about [the devil-father], that could be fixed upon as remarkable, was his staff, which bore the likeness of a great black snake, so curiously wrought, that it might almost be seen to twist and wriggle itself, like a living serpent" (p. 76). In Brown's immature sensibility, in his underdeveloped sense of fatherhood and manhood, the father has never escaped the expression of his mature sexuality, his erect and animated phallus. It is in Brown's mind the most significant feature about him, in fact the devil-father's only remarkable feature.

The devil-father wishes to speed the pace of their travels and taunts Brown, saying: "'this is a dull pace for the beginning of a journey. Take my staff, if you are so soon weary.'"[27] Instead of accepting the challenge, Brown gives his companion his reasons for refusing to take up the staff: "'having kept covenant by meeting thee here, it is my purpose now to return whence I came. I have scruples, touching the matter thou wot'st of'" (p. 76). That is to say, the son replies to the devil-father's taunt by challenging his moral authority by virtue of the "scruples" he learned in the woman's sphere to which he now would return.

In this passage we also learn why the appearance of the devil-father was not unexpected: the son had previously agreed to the rendezvous. It is nothing other than the sight and offering of that twisting, writhing, serpentine staff, then, that energizes the newlywed's scruples. As he has done more than once since he walked through the door of his home, young Goodman Brown hesitates, pauses, looks back. Even as he unconsciously walks on, urged forward by the devil-father, identified in all his "evil" sexuality as "he of the serpent," the son objects to proceeding any further; again he renounces his "friend's" paternal relationship to him, claiming that *his* "'father never went into the woods on such an errand, nor his father before him.'" The devil-father, smilingly reassuring young Brown that he need not fear being "'the first of the name of Brown, that ever took this path,'" confides that "'I have been as well acquainted with your family as with ever a one among the Puritans. . . . They were my good friends, both. . . . I would fain be friends with you, for their sake'" (pp. 76-77). The devil-father comforts Brown by promising him that he is following in his father's and grandfather's footsteps (which of course he literally is in this scene); he is fulfilling an honorable paternal tradition, and the devil-father would befriend Brown so that the tradition of the fathers might be perpetuated. Of course, the foremost and essential tradition of the fathers of any multi-generational family is the continuity of past, present, and future achieved through the production of a family, through intercourse and sexual intimacy, through the literal blurring of many boundaries between the genders.

When the naive young man insists that none of the patriarchs of his family engaged in "'such wickedness,'" all being men of prayer and good works, the devil-father replies that, wicked or not, such behavior is common among all the patriarchs of the colony (p. 77). In the midst of going about his father's business, Brown next encounters, much to his surprise, a woman intruding upon their forest space; she is not just any woman, this Goody Cloyse, but Brown's religion teacher. Hiding out of her sight, Brown overhears an exchange between his traveling companion and his teacher which begins with the devil-father touching her neck with his staff and the old hag recognizing him as the devil "'in the very image of my old gossip, Goodman Brown, the grandfather of the silly fellow that now is.'" Despite the fact that someone has stolen her broomstick and the old woman must travel on foot, she is determined to get to the meeting because, she says, "'they tell me, there is a nice young man to be taken into communion to-night'" (p. 79). As he had once extended it to Brown, the devil-father now offers his staff to Goody Cloyse to aid her on her journey to the evening's assembly, and she disappears from sight.

Goody Cloyse's interest in things sexual is explicit in this encounter; this and her appearance in the woods break down the supposed barrier between male and female, public and private, work and home, husband and wife.[28] Brown calls it a "'marvel'" to find Cloyse in the woods at night, and the narrator points out that it was Cloyse "who had taught [Brown] his catechism, in youth, and was still his moral and spiritual adviser, jointly with the minister and Deacon Gookin" (p. 78). After witnessing her intimacy with the devil-father, Brown reiterates that "'[t]hat old woman taught me my catechism.'" Hawthorne's narrator emphasizes that "there was a world of meaning in this simple comment" (p. 80). Hawthorne's association of women and ministers with the religious education and spiritual welfare of the community is another characteristic of this part of the story that is more reminiscent of nineteenth-century gender relations than those of the Puritan period.[29] Goody Cloyse's reference to Brown as that "'silly fellow'" indicates some sense on her part, too, that much of his life Brown may have had trouble distinguishing belief from practice. Moreover, Goody Cloyse, in her references to "'that silly fellow'" and the "'nice young man to be taken into communion to-night,'" unwittingly has confused two aspects of Brown's identity: as child/innocent and as man/sexual creature.

As the devil-father and Brown proceed through the forest, the older man breaks off a branch of maple limb and fashions yet another walking staff. When Brown once again refuses to go any further, the devil-father suggests that he rest for a while and, before disappearing, throws the young man his staff. Brown then thinks he hears in the forest the voices of his spiritual patriarchs, his minister and Deacon Gookin, conversing about tonight's meeting. When one of them also stops to "pluck a switch," Brown overhears Deacon Gookin saying that he is looking forward to the impending ceremony, where they will find "'a goodly young woman to be taken into communion'" (p. 81). Shaken, Brown cannot decide whether or not what he is witnessing is real. His doubt is so great that, looking up into the night sky, he cannot make up his mind whether "there really was a Heaven above him" (p. 82).

Brown's belief system, his moral certainty, dependent as it seems to be on the nineteenth-century ideology of separate spheres with which he has been catechized, is quickly shattering in the heavily peopled forest. The voices of additional fellow townspeople fall on his ears, and it is obvious that all are hurrying to a late-night rendezvous. In the heart of this commotion, Brown hears "one voice, of a young woman, uttering lamentations, yet with an uncertain sorrow, and entreating for some favor, which, perhaps, it would grieve her to obtain" and for which the townspeople "both saints and sinners, seemed to encourage her onward" (p. 82). Brown immediately recognizes the woman's voice as Faith's. But how much more ambiguous could Faith's voice be? She both is and is not a sexual creature in this description of her cries. She both is and is not present. Faith's disembodied voice, as well as Goody Cloyse's ability to fly, to travel effortlessly, without labor, may speak to the nature of Brown's gender fantasy. One recent scholar has suggested about the ideology of separate spheres that as it "engenders and demarcates the spaces of work and personal (as opposed to working) life, both labor and women are divested of their corporeality, defined as different rather than extensive with the body."[30] Brown screams Faith's name out into the night, only to have the forest mockingly echo his "cry of grief, rage, and terror." Brown should indeed be terrorized by this experience, for he has built his entire belief system on the moral rectitude of his mother and wife—and on their rightful place nowhere but in the home.

Surely, Goody Cloyse and his Faith have no business in this forest of moral uncertainties. Brown listens in silence for a response to his cries, only to hear "a scream, drowned immediately in a loud murmur of voices, fading into far-off laughter, as the dark cloud swept" by. Something substantial floats down out of the sky, filled as it is with insubstantial voices, and Brown snatches it off of a tree limb. It is one of Faith's pink ribbons. Just as the serpentine staff is Hawthorne's synecdoche for the sexual potential of the father, this pink ribbon is, as earlier implied, his synecdoche for the sexuality of Faith. Brown cries out, "'My Faith is gone!'" It is usually argued that with this outburst, Brown proclaims his lost religious belief, but much more has been lost: his wife Faith is also literally gone; if she is present in the forest, then she cannot, according to his belief system, be who he thought her to be.

Now Brown takes up the devil-father's staff and hurries to the communion. Along the way he encounters a forest "peopled with frightful sounds." And soon the scariest noisemaker in the forest is he: "all through the haunted forest, there could be nothing more frightful than the figure of Goodman Brown" (p. 83). Now deep in the heart of the forest, where no trail remains, Brown encounters "a numerous congregation . . . peopling the heart of the solitary woods" (p. 84). In fact, much of the adult population of Salem village has crowded into this space, both the "grave, reputable, and pious people" and "men of dissolute lives and women of spotted fame, wretches given over to all mean and filthy vice, and suspected even of horrid crimes." Most telling is the narrator's comment that it "was strange to see, that the good shrank not from the wicked, nor were the sinners abashed by the saints" (p.

85). Here in the forest private and public spheres blur into one another; or, perhaps, the difference between public and private is nowhere as certain as Brown once thought it was.

As Goodman Brown feels himself called forth with the rest of the converts, he "could have well-nigh sworn, that the shape of his own dead father beckoned him to advance." Indeed, he meets his spiritual fathers when his village "minister and good old Deacon Gookin seized his arms, and led him to the blazing rock" to be initiated. But this "community of men, as we have seen, includes both men and women. Even his mother seems to appear, if only, in keeping with her role as angel of the home, to throw "out her hand to warn him back" (p. 86). The master of ceremonies, a kind of devil-preacher, then invites his "children" to turn around and see "'all whom ye have reverenced from youth'" for their "'righteousness, and prayerful aspirations.'" This night of their conversion, the children will learn of their spiritual leaders' "'secret deeds'":

> "how hoary-bearded elders of the church have whispered wanton words to the young maids of their households; how many a woman, eager for widows' weeds, has given her husband a drink at bedtime, and let him sleep his last sleep in her bosom; how beardless youths have made haste to inherit their fathers' wealth; and how fair damsels—blush not, sweet ones!—have dug little graves in the garden, and bidden me, the sole guest, to an infant's funeral."
>
> [P. 87]

These deeds are, broadly speaking, crimes of human sexuality. Clearly Brown's devil-preacher associates sin with sexuality.

The promised knowledge of the secret deeds will give the converts the ability to determine

> "all the places—whether in church, bed-chamber, street, field, or forest—where crime has been committed, and [they] shall exult to behold the whole earth one stain of guilt, one mighty blood-spot. Far more than this! It shall be [theirs] to penetrate, in every bosom, the deep mystery of sin, the fountain of all wicked arts, and which inexhaustibly supplies more evil impulses than human power . . . can make manifest in deeds."
>
> [P. 87]

The language of human sexuality is omnipresent: "one mighty blood-spot," "penetrate," "bosom," "fountain," and "deep mystery." Notice also the language of unification, of the "communion of [the] race," and the way in which the devil-preacher contradicts Brown's belief in separate spheres, especially his belief that only certain wicked people, usually men, have "evil" sexual longings (p. 86).

When Brown is finally face to face with his wife, just as the "Shape of Evil" prepares "to lay the mark of baptism upon their foreheads, that they might be partakers of the mystery of sin," he looks at his Faith and realizes what "polluted wretches would the next glance" mutually reveal them to be. He cries out to his wife to forego this baptism into adult sexuality and to "'[l]ook up to heaven, and resist the Wicked One'" (p. 88). Brown actually reverses roles here, now imagining himself leading Faith up to heaven. But it is all too late. The entire forest scene, including his wife, vanishes. He is alone because he has refused to acknowledge his wife's sexuality in this threshold experience, just as he had refused it in the doorway of his home. He has rejected the blurring of separate spheres that is the reality of adult life. Once peopled with an invisible multitude, the forest around him now is calm and quiet.

The reader is unsure what has happened to Brown, but Brown himself is quite certain that in his last words to Faith in the forest, he has resisted the devil; every inhabitant of Salem village he had formerly trusted, however, is in league with the devil or, at the very least, has secret sins of which each should be ashamed. Brown is quite right, of course, but his very lack of sin is a crime.[31] He returns to a community in which the blurring of the separate spheres is for the first time apparent to him, and he rejects it nonetheless. Deacon Gookin is inside his home now, but his words can be heard coming through his open window. Goody Cloyse, "that excellent old Christian," stands outside her house at the latticed gate "catechising a little girl." Brown's reaction—he snatches away the "child, as from the grasp of the fiend himself"—acknowledges his fears that the little girl could be deceived as he was—not by Goody Cloyse's catechizing, because Brown still believes in what he was taught, but by the old woman's failure to live what she preached. Approaching his home, he sees "the head of Faith, with the pink ribbons, gazing anxiously forth, and bursting into such joy at sight of him, that she skipt along the street, and almost kissed her husband before the whole village." But whatever attractions Brown had to human sexuality when he left the village— as, for example, when he turned back to kiss his wife in the doorway—are now banished by the events he witnessed in the forest. So convinced is he of her sinfulness that "Goodman Brown looked sternly and sadly into her face, and passed on without a greeting" (p. 89).

Goodman Brown becomes a "stern, a sad, a darkly meditative, a distrustful, if not a desperate man . . . from the night of that fearful dream" (p. 89). Whatever huffiness and silliness Brown possessed before leaving home has been tragically transformed by his forest refusal to recognize the blurring of spheres. Brown has "a goodly procession" of children and grandchildren, but clearly there was little joy in those sexual experiences (p. 90). The initiative was seldom his it seems: "Often, waking suddenly at midnight, he shrank from the bosom of Faith" (p. 89). And when he dies, "they carved no hopeful verse upon his tombstone, for his dying hour was gloom" (p. 90).

III

When we penetrate the oedipal and sexual anxieties of Hawthorne's early fiction, we tend to divorce them from the historical, and when we unearth the stories' historical concerns, we tend to separate them from the psychosexual and from Hawthorne's immediate social environment. In **"Young Goodman Brown,"** Hawthorne was not only asking his readers to imagine the synthesis of the historical and the psychosexual; he was investigating for them the relationship between Puritan anxieties about faith, morality, sexuality, and gender and his contemporaries' and his own anxieties about those subjects. A renewed interest during the 1830s in the Puritan experience and what it could offer the present probably led Hawthorne to believe that his ancestral line and his own research into Puritan history uniquely qualified him to contribute to the discourse that sought to construct a bridge between past and present New England.

In addition to recognizing Hawthorne's examination of the nexus of Puritan and contemporary experience in **"Young Goodman Brown,"** we must also consider the importance of contemporary gender issues. Nina Baym has argued that a sophisticated feminist criticism of Hawthorne's work "would be based on the presumption that the question of women is *the* determining motive in Hawthorne's works, driving [his female characters] as it drives Hawthorne's male characters."[32] Recent works by T. Walter Herbert and Gillian Brown have, while throwing men into the equation, largely heeded this call.[33] But when scholars turn their attention to issues of gender as well as other nineteenth-century contexts in Hawthorne, they tend to focus on the later works. This virtual neglect of the early material is repeated by David Leverenz, Joel Pfister, Richard H. Millington, and the above critics in their recent books focusing on Hawthorne as an observer of contemporary middle-class culture.[34] It appears, then, that adequately to give Hawthorne his due, we must focus on the whole question of gender—both masculine and feminine—in *all* of his works—early and late. Such a masterful critic of human nature deserves no less than a fully comprehensive view.

Notes

1. For a categorization of these readings, see D. M. McKeithan, "Hawthorne's 'Young Goodman Brown': An Interpretation," *Modern Language Notes* 67 (1952): 93.

2. Roy R. Male, *Hawthorne's Tragic Vision* (Austin: University of Texas Press, 1957), p. 77; Frederick C. Crews, *The Sins of the Fathers: Hawthorne's Psychological Themes* (New York: Oxford University Press, 1966), p. 102.

3. David Levin, "Shadows of Doubt: Specter Evidence in Hawthorne's 'Young Goodman Brown'" *American Literature* 34 (November 1962): 344-52; Michael J. Colacurcio, "Visible Sanctity and Specter Evidence: The Moral World of Hawthorne's 'Young Goodman Brown,'" *Essex Institute Historical Collections* 110 (1974): 259-99.

4. Frank Shuffleton, "Nathaniel Hawthorne and the Revival Movement," *American Transcendental Quarterly* 44 (Fall 1979): 321.

5. I have tried wherever possible to pinpoint developments to the decade or decades in which they occurred, but many changes experienced by the middle class in the late eighteenth and early nineteenth centuries continued into and only rose to hegemony in the middle of the nineteenth century. Hence, what is true for Hawthorne's family in his youth and for seacoast New England towns like Salem—where the absence of fathers away on work for long periods of time, for example, was a common phenomenon—may not yet be true of America in general until mid century or later. Hawthorne is writing, in part, about the world he knows and for a geographically limited, middleclass reading audience cognizant of these developments from other domestic literature.

6. Carl N. Degler, *At Odds: Women and the Family in America from the Revolution to the Present* (New York: Oxford University Press, 1980); Ellen Rothman, *Hands and Hearts: A History of Courtship in America* (New York: Basic Books, 1984); Karen Lystra, *Searching the Heart: Women, Men, and Romantic Love in Nineteenth-Century America* (New York: Oxford University Press, 1989). Nina Baym claims that woman's fiction "showed the home thoroughly penetrated at every point by the world, dominated by man" and that it held out the hope that perhaps "the direction of influence could be reversed so that home values dominated the world" (*Woman's Fiction: A Guide to Novels By and About Women in America, 1820-1870* [Ithaca: Cornell University Press, 1978], p. 48).

7. For example, Nancy F. Cott argues in *The Bonds of Womanhood: "Woman's Sphere" in New England, 1780-1835* (New Haven: Yale University Press, 1977), pp. 6 ff., that the 1830s "became a turning point in women's economic participation, public activities, and social visibility." Stephanie Coontz points out in *The Social Origins of Private Life: A History of American Families, 1600-1900* (London: Verso, 1988), p. 34, that "about the 1820s a new family system emerged"; and Joe L. Dubbert notes in *A Man's Place: Masculinity in Transition* (Englewood Cliffs, N.J.: Prentice Hall, 1979), p. 27, that "around 1830 the number of [guidebooks to male behavior] increased and their tone became more serious, especially in discussing sexual purity." See also Jack Larkin, *The Reshaping of Everyday Life, 1790-1840* (New York: Harper & Row, 1988), pp. 199-201; Lystra, *Searching the Heart*, pp. 28-32; Stephen Nissenbaum, *Sex, Diet and Debility in Jacksonian America: Sylvester Graham and Health Reform* (Westport, Conn.: Greenwood Press, 1980), pp. 4, 25-29; and Rothman, *Hands and Hearts*, pp. 51, 91.

8. Michael J. Colacurcio, *The Province of Piety: Moral History in Hawthorne's Early Tales* (Cambridge: Harvard University Press, 1984).

9. Nathaniel Hawthorne, "Young Goodman Brown," in *Mosses from an Old Manse*, vol. 10 of *The Centenary Edition of the Works of Nathaniel Hawthorne*, ed. William Charvat et al. (Columbus: Ohio State University Press, 1974), p. 74. All further references are to this edition and are identified parenthetically.

10. Levin and Colacurcio, in particular, have strengthened this sense by revealing the depth of Hawthorne's familiarity with Puritan sources. See also E. Arthur Robinson, "The Vision of Goodman Brown: A Source and Interpretation," *American Literature* 35 (May 1963): 218-25; B. Bernard Cohen, "Deodat Lawson's *Christ's Fidelity* and Hawthorne's 'Young Goodman Brown,'" *Essex Institute Historical Collections* 104 (1968): 349-70; James W. Clark, Jr., "Hawthorne's Use of Evidence in 'Young Goodman Brown,'" *Essex Institute Historical Collections* 111 (1975): 12-34; and Robert C. Grayson, "Young Goodman Hawthorne," *American Notes and Queries* 21 (March-April 1983); 103-6.

11. John Demos, *Past, Present and Personal: The Family and the Life Course in American History* (New York: Oxford University Press, 1986), p. 49.

12. Nancy F. Cott, "Passionlessness: An Interpretation of Victorian Sexual Ideology, 1790-1850," in *A Heritage of Her Own*, ed. Nancy F. Cott and Elizabeth H. Pleck (New York: Simon & Schuster, 1979), pp. 162-81; Nissenbaum, *Sex, Diet and Debility in Jacksonian America.*

13. Lois Banner, *American Beauty* (New York: Knopf, 1983), pp. 45, 46.

14. Cooper, quoted by Banner, in *American Beauty*, p. 46.

15. Banner, *American Beauty*, p. 53.

16. John Demos, *A Little Commonwealth: Family Life in Plymouth Colony* (New York: Oxford University Press, 1970), pp. 82-83.

17. Edmund S. Morgan, *The Puritan Family: Religion and Domestic Relations in Seventeenth-Century New England* (1944; revised ed., New York: Harper & Row, 1966), pp. 166-68; Cott, "Passionlessness," p. 167.

18. Carroll Smith-Rosenberg, "Domesticating 'Virtue': Coquettes and Revolutionaries in Young America," in *Literature and the Body: Essays on Populations and Persons*, ed. Elaine Scarry (Baltimore: Johns Hopkins University Press, 1988), p. 166.

19. On woman's work as social reproduction, see Coontz, *The Social Origins of Private Life.*

20. For a psychoanalytic reading of this opening passage as explicitly sexual, see Edward Jayne, "Pray Tarry with Me Young Goodman Brown," *Literature and Psychology* 29 (1979): 103-4.

21. See Lystra, *Searching the Heart*, pp. 57-58.

22. Perhaps Brown's insistence that Faith and her ribbons remain inside the public/private threshold is related also to the taboo that menstruation has a chaotic effect on social behavior. One best-selling

marriage manual of the 1830s declared that menstruating women were "'out of order'" and should be kept at home (see Charles Knowlton's *Fruits of Philosophy,* quoted in Joel Pfister's *The Production of Personal Life: Class, Gender, and the Psychological in Hawthorne's Fiction* [Stanford: Stanford University Press, 1991], p. 35). In addition, the repetition of "of all nights in the year" suggests that this particular night is important to both of them. Perhaps her ribbons are a sign that she is ovulating. It was generally held prior to the twentieth century that when a woman was menstruating she was also ovulating (see Thomas Laqueur, "Orgasm, Generation, and the Politics of Reproductive Biology," in *The Making of the Modern Body: Sexuality and Society in the Nineteenth Century,* ed. Catherine Gallagher and Thomas Laqueur [Berkeley: University of California Press, 1987], p. 3). Hence, Faith's omnipresent pink ribbons and sexual desire may be signs of her wish to pull her husband through yet another threshold into the joys of parenthood.

23. That many husbands, including Hawthorne, could, following the advice literature of the early decades of the nineteenth century, accept the moral superiority of their wives is clear from their letters and diaries. See Degler, *At Odds,* p. 30, and T. Walter Herbert, *Dearest Beloved: The Hawthornes and the Making of the Middle-Class Family* (Berkeley: University of California Press, 1993).

24. Herbert, *Dearest Beloved,* pp. 131-32; see also chaps. 8 and 10. In later decades, historian E. Anthony Rotundo proposes, a distinct "boy culture" grew up to counter the forces of "tender affection and moral suasion" each boy encountered when he crossed the threshold into his mother's home. This more "masculine" youth culture outside the home helped prepare boys for a manhood in which crossing the threshold between male and female worlds was more natural. In fact, some "of the most important lessons that a youngster learned from boy culture were those about living a life divided by a boundary between the two spheres." But in the early decades, such acculturation was quite limited. E. Anthony Rotundo, "Boy Culture: Middle-Class Boyhood in Nineteenth-Century America," in *Meanings for Manhood: Constructions of Masculinity in Victorian America,* ed. Mark C. Carnes and Clyde Griffen (Chicago: University of Chicago Press, 1990), pp. 16, 29.

25. Levin and Colacurcio read this story as, in part, concerned with the theological and epistemological problems the Puritans had with specter evidence, that Brown might mistake the specters in the forest for the people of the colony. Yet neither critic asks what specter evidence has to do with not recognizing that your companion is the "specter" of your father. Clearly the issue at this point in the story is not that Brown cannot tell a specter from a person or a saint from a sinner but that he does not recognize that someone looks like his father.

26. Carroll Smith-Rosenberg, "Beauty, the Beast and the Militant Woman: A Case Study in Sex Roles and Social Stress in Jacksonian America," *American Quarterly* 23 (1971): 575.

27. We might see this taunt as well as the serpentine phallus as challenges to Brown's manhood. The devil-father offers the competition and possible humiliation that a nineteenth-century son might find outside the home. David Leverenz argues that "any intensified ideology of manhood is a compensatory response to fears of humiliation" and that throughout his career Hawthorne "dramatizes manhood as demonic possession, often explicitly." But Leverenz virtually ignores "Young Goodman Brown," preferring to focus for the most part on one or two late stories and the novels. *Manhood and the American Renaissance* (Ithaca: Cornell University Press, 1989), pp. 4, 239.

28. On the possible sexual implications of Goody Cloyse being Brown's grandfather's gossip, see Daniel Hoffman, *Form and Fable in American Fiction* (New York: Oxford University Press, 1961), p. 163. For additional discussion of these sexually-laden paragraphs and the sexual aspects of the story, see Robinson, "The Vision of Goodman Brown," pp. 221-24; Jayne, "Pray Tarry with Me Young Goodman Brown," pp. 100-113; Male, *Hawthorne's Tragic Vision,* pp. 77-78; Crews, *Sins of the Fathers,* pp. 96-106; and Elizabeth Wright, "The New Psychoanalysis and Literary Criticism: A Reading of Melville and Hawthorne," *Poetics Today* 3 (Spring 1982): 89-105.

29. Ann Douglas, *The Feminization of American Culture* (New York: Knopf, 1977).

30. Gillian Brown, *Domestic Individualism: Imagining Self in Nineteenth-Century America* (Berkeley: University of California Press, 1990), p. 63.

31. That Brown is so confident that he is sin free leads to the possibility that he is pure of sexual "sin," that he left his wife and came to the forest still a virgin. This idea has been suggested to me by Professor Elizabeth Jane Hinds. Such a possibility would make Faith's pleas at the beginning of the tale all the more poignant, Brown's focus on stains and bloodspots covering the earth that much more vivid and significant, and his return to the village and his future life as the father of "a goodly procession" of children all that more personally tragic.

32. Nina Baym, "Thwarted Nature: Nathaniel Hawthorne as Feminist," in *American Novelists Revisited: Essays in Feminist Criticism,* ed. Fritz Fleischmann (Boston: G. K. Hall, 1982), p. 62.

33. Herbert, *Dearest Beloved,* and Gillian Brown, "Hawthorne, Inheritance, and Women's Property," *Studies in the Novel* 23 (1991): 107-18.

34. Leverenz, *Manhood and the American Renaissance*; Pfister, *The Production of Personal Life*; and Richard H. Millington, *Practicing Romance: Narrative Form*

and Cultural Engagement in Hawthorne's Fiction (Princeton: Princeton University Press, 1992). For some explanation of Pfister's preference for the later Hawthorne, see *Production of Personal Life*, p. 43.

Debra Johanyak (essay date 1999)

SOURCE: "Romanticism's Fallen Edens: The Malignant Contribution of Hawthorne's Literary Landscapes," in *College Language Association Journal*, Vol. 42, No. 3, 1999, pp. 353-63.

[*In the following essay, Johanyak explores Hawthorne's use of the forest in "Young Goodman Brown" and several of his other works, contending that Brown's sojourn in the forest serves to remind him that "we are everywhere surrounded by evil."*]

America's stern puritannical history provided nineteenth century writers with ideal plots and settings for the age-old conflict between good and evil. Edenic gardens and pastoral woodlands grace countless works of the Romantic era, wherein Adam- and Eve-like lovers succumb to temptation and find themselves not only cast out of their normative societies, but often torn from each other as well—whether spiritually, emotionally, or literally. Significantly, the forest settings of these tales contribute substantially and malignantly to the plot development of such stories.

None used the Edenic motif so pervasively as Nathaniel Hawthorne. His tales initially seem to draw our focus to a narrator who introduces characters and events. But Hawthorne's stories begin much earlier, in fact, commencing with landscape descriptions that set our goose bumps in motion. He accomplishes this in so artful a way that we are scarcely aware of it; hence we focus our mounting apprehension on a principal hero or heroine appearing signally in the narrative spotlight.

It is especially interesting that tales utilizing a contributory landscape are those emphasizing a Puritan backdrop against which a conflict-laced love story unfolds. Specifically, **"The Maypole of Merry Mount," "Young Goodman Brown,"** and *The Scarlet Letter* are Hawthorne's strongest revivals of the Edenic legend featuring Puritan protagonists. And although the couples remain bonded, legally or emotionally, until death's separation tears them asunder, a shared moral flaw or spiritual weakness blocks their enjoyment of a true or joyous marriage.

"Young Goodman Brown" (1835) places the protagonist in a haunted forest representing the hero's troubled state of mind as he secretly hurries toward a midnight rendezvous. Leaving his wife secure, as he believes, in the heart of their Puritan community, Goodman Brown begins a journey at dusk toward a universal temptation which dooms his relationship to Faith—his literal wife and metaphorical spirituality—when he is forced to face the all-pervasive weak and sinful nature of humanity. The wood-

land path parallels his morally dangerous purpose and enhances the tone—and moral—of Hawthorne's plot:

> He had taken a dreary road, darkened by all the gloomiest trees of the forest, which barely stood aside to let the narrow path creep through, and closed immediately behind. It was all as lonely as could be; and there is this peculiarity in such a solitude, that the traveller knows not who may be concealed by the innumerable trunks and the thick boughs overhead; so that with lonely footsteps he may yet be passing through an unseen multitude.[1]

The separation at sundown of Brown from his wife suggests the divisive nature of his temptation. Brown wrongly assumes that his is an isolated, one-time distraction to be easily rectified by returning to the Puritan fold the next morning. As Brown commences traveling, Hawthorne likens his forest path to the spiritual journey of a man questioning his religious faith. Rather than adhering to the superficial community standards of his Puritan counterparts, Brown moves alone down the woodland route to consummate a deep, secret longing—one that he little expects is universally shared. Allegorically—like much of Hawthorne's writing—the road depicts Brown's journey to the depths of his own soul as he questions his personal human nature and, later, that of his wife and surrounding community. Hawthorne describes the woodland setting in terms corresponding to Goodman Brown's desperate self-search. The Puritan's eagerness to reach his midnight goal parallels a dwindling moral reserve as his hopes, like the gloomy woodland path, become increasingly narrow, twisted, and obscure.

The haunted forest frames young Brown's spiritual wanderings, suggesting that human sinfulness is inextricably bound to Nature.[2] As the hero moves—at first hesitantly, but then quite purposefully—toward a seductive tryst in the heart of this wild woodland, it becomes apparent that he has exchanged his Puritan identity for pagan revelry. As Michael Bell notes, "[F]or Hawthorne nature itself is more a part of the European character than of the American. . . . '[N]ature' and the Old World are both comprehended, for Hawthorne, in the notion of the pagan."[3] Prefiguring Hester Prynne's escape plan to flee America for the Old World with Dimmesdale, Goodman Brown attempts to renounce his Puritan community, his Puritan faith, and his Puritan wife, in order to pursue Old World temptations embodied in the dark, mysterious depths of Nature. The woodland path, growing "wilder and drearier and more faintly traced," is enlivened by "frightful sounds" (62) which animate the otherwise-dead terrain, giving it human likeness. Into this eerie setting comes literal temptation, personified in an older gentleman who accompanies Brown through the wood where it is "deep dusk . . . and deepest in that part of it where these two were journeying" (55).

Thinking to escape his heritage, his marriage, and his humanity, Brown is instead lured along the forest path toward these restrictive elements in a shocking and irreparable recognition of all creation's spiritual degeneration.

His bridegroom's love for wifely Faith is assaulted by her metaphorical adultery with the Satanic mass when she betrays both faith and husband by participating in the group's devil worship. As Brown plods along the dreary route, his darkening path finally disappears, symbolizing the youth's complete lapse into spiritual depravity.

The journey climaxes when Brown arrives at the ritual in progress deep in the "heathen wilderness" (61), grimly portrayed by Hawthorne's lurid descriptions of the forest clearing:

> At one extremity of an open space, hemmed in by the dark wall of the forest, arose a rock, bearing some rude, natural resemblance either to an altar or a pulpit, and surrounded by four blazing pines, their tops aflame, their stems untouched, like candles at an evening meeting. The mass of foliage that had overgrown the summit of the rock was all on fire, blazing high into the night and fitfully illuminating the whole field. . . . As the red light arose and fell, a numerous congregation alternately shone forth, then disappeared in shadow, and again grew, as it were, out of the darkness, peopling the heart of the solitary woods at once.
>
> (63)

This devilish scene is heightened by a worship hymn, "not of human voices, but of all the sounds of the benighted wilderness pealing in awful harmony together" (63). Although the anguished husband cries out in despair, his voice blends in "unison with the cry of the desert" (63), and his unique lament of dissent is swallowed up by the encompassing evil about him, embodied as much in the wilderness setting as in the human celebrants. Eden's pathetic fallacy is inverted, like other biblical images, to conform to the Satan-worship of this story in honoring the "Prince of this World" and rejecting the heavenly Christ.

The climactical welcome chant to the lord of darkness is epitomized by cacophonic screams of "the roaring wind, the rushing streams, the howling beasts, and every other voice of the unconcerted wilderness . . . mingling and according with the voice of guilty man in homage to the prince of all" (65). Fallen Eden offers a grotesque parody of creation praise, as nature's wildest voices join and overtake the Puritans' lewd celebration.

Surrounded by humanity's and nature's evil, Goodman Brown is nearly powerless to resist Satan's draw. Somehow he finds strength to glance heavenward and urges his wife to do likewise. Ultimately he saves himself, unassisted by Faith, who remains an allegorical symbol of failed religious hope.

Unsure of whether his life is now a dream or reality, Brown abruptly faces a desolate future

> amid calm night and solitude, listening to a roar of the wind which died heavily away through the forest. He staggered against the rock, and felt it chill and damp; while a hanging twig, that had been all on fire, besprinkled his cheek with the coldest dew.
>
> (67)

Despite his harrowing escape, Brown's familiar world is scarcely more welcoming than the evil one of the previous night. Nature now appears dispassionate at best. The fire's midnight blaze is replaced by dawn's clammy cold; the warmth of his bed and comfort of his hope are as lost as his religious and wifely Faith.

Thus, it comes as no surprise that Young Goodman Brown's "dying hour was gloom" (68). The grave receives him devoid of "hopeful verse" (68), his happiness sacrificed in that one night's compromising journey. Although Hawthorne's young Puritan acknowledges his own and his wife's fleshly weaknesses, knowledge of the world's pervasive evil—represented in the personified forest—haunts him all his days. The woodland's midnight shades coupled with the town's gloomy daylight remind us that we are everywhere surrounded by evil; our only escape lies in this realization and in an attempt to find—and keep—a straight moral path. Hawthorne emphasizes in this tale, as in the others that follow, that the key to understanding and accepting humanity's natural depravity is a sense of balance between the values of head and heart;[4] thus Brown's lifelong gloom is as unhealthy as the Puritans' hypocritical double standards. . . .

Hawthorne marries Puritan themes to forest settings in ways that are often ambivalent; sometimes Nature projects celebration and joy, while at other times it depicts the evil characteristics and threatening gestures of menacing invaders. But like no other romancer, Hawthorne uses the native American soil to tremendous advantage in enhancing scenes, moods, and characters in stories featuring Puritan-based plots and conflict-challenged romances.

Notes

1. Nathaniel Hawthorne, "Young Goodman Brown," in *The Portable Hawthorne,* ed. Malcolm Crowley (New York: Penguin, 1948) 54. Hereafter cited parenthetically in the text.

2. Nancy Bunge, *Nathanial Hawthorne: A Study of the Short Fiction* (New York: Twayne, 1993) 13.

3. Michael Davitt Bell, *Hawthorn and the Historical Romance of New England* (Princeton: Princeton UP, 1971) 131.

4. J. Golden Taylor, *Hawthorne's Ambivalence Toward Puritanism* (Logan: Utah State UP, 1965) 28.

FURTHER READING

Bibliography

Stanton, Robert J. "Secondary Studies on Hawthorne's 'Young Goodman Brown,' 1845-1975: A Bibliography." *Bulletin of Bibliography and Magazine Notes* 33, No. 1 (January 1976): 32-44, 52.

    Comprehensive bibliography of criticism on the story from 1845 to 1975.

Criticism

Apseloff, Stanford and Marilyn. "'Young Goodman Brown': The Goodman." *American Notes and Queries* 21, No. 7 (March 1983): 103-06.
    Quoting sources of Scottish folklore, assert that the word Goodman was used to refer to the Devil, which gives a dual meaning to Hawthorne's tale.

Capps, Jack L. "Hawthorne's 'Young Goodman Brown.'" *Explicator* 40, No. 3 (Spring 1982): 25.
    Suggests that the third virtue of the Christian tryptich, charity—one not mentioned in the tale—is precisely what Brown is lacking to survive his experience with the Devil.

Christophersen, Bill. "'Young Goodman Brown' as Historical Allegory: A Lexical Link." *Studies in Short Fiction* 23, No. 2 (Spring 1986): 202-04.
    Discusses Hawthorne's ironic use of Exodus imagery in the tale.

Dickson, Wayne. "Hawthorne's 'Young Goodman Brown.'" *Explicator* 29, No. 5 (January 1971): item 44.
    Finds a reference to Corinthians in the tale, with the implication that Brown is lacking in charity.

Ensor, Allison. "'Whispers of the Bad Angel': A *Scarlet Letter* Passage as a Commentary on Hawthorne's 'Young Goodman Brown.'" *Studies in Short Fiction* 7, No. 3 (Summer 1970): 467-69.
    Refers to Chapter Five of *The Scarlet Letter* as a gloss on Hawthorne's attitude towards Brown in "Young Goodman Brown."

Ferguson, Jr., J. M. "Hawthorne's 'Young Goodman Brown.'" *Explicator* 28, No. 4 (December 1969): item 32.
    Asserts that Brown suffers from hubris, or pride, in "Young Goodman Brown."

Gallagher, Edward J. "The Concluding Paragraph of 'Young Goodman Brown.'" *Studies in Short Fiction* 12, No. 1 (Winter 1975): 29-30.
    Examines the last paragraph of "Young Goodman Brown," finding that Hawthorne offers neither a happy end nor a final peace to Brown.

Hardt, John S. "Doubts in the American Garden: Three Cases of Paradisal Skepticism." *Studies in Short Fiction* 25, No. 3 (Summer 1988): 249-59.
    Explores "Young Goodman Brown" along with Washington Irving's "Rip Van Winkle," and Edgar Allan Poe's "The Fall of the House of Usher" in terms of each author's negative use of natural settings.

Kurata, Marilyn. "'The Chimes': Dickens's Recasting of 'Young Goodman Brown.'" *American Notes and Queries* 22, No. 1 (September 1983): 10-12.
    Discusses parallels between Hawthorne's tale and Charles Dickens's short story "The Chimes."

Reynolds, Larry J. "Melville's Use of 'Young Goodman Brown.'" *American Transcendental Quarterly* 31 (Summer 1976): 12-14.
    Focuses on parallels between Hawthorne's tale and Herman Melville's *Moby-Dick*.

Shear, Walter. "Cultural Fate and Social Freedom in Three American Short Stories." *Studies in Short Fiction* 29, No. 4 (Fall 1992): 543-49.
    Compares "Young Goodman Brown," Washington Irving's "Rip Van Winkle," and Henry James's "The Jolly Corner," finding many structural similarities and asserting that all three tales treat "an asocial self within the social self."

Tepa, Barbara J. "Breakfast in 'Young Goodman Brown.'" *American Notes and Queries* 16, No. 8 (April 1978): 120-21.
    Suggests that the mention of breakfast in the tale contributes to its ambiguity since it leads to the conclusion that a communion has already taken place in the forest.

Wright, Elizabeth. "The New Psychoanalysis and Literary Criticism: A Reading of Hawthorne and Melville." *Poetics Today* 3, No. 2 (Spring 1982): 89-105.
    Uses Lacanian and Derridean literary theory to discuss patterns that undermine "the stable meaning" in "Young Goodman Brown" and Herman Melville's "Benito Cereno."

Zanger, Jules. "'Young Goodman Brown' and 'A White Heron': Correspondences and Illuminations." *Papers on Language and Literature* 26, No. 3 (Summer 1990): 346-57.
    Asserts that "Young Goodman Brown" and Sarah Orne Jewett's "A White Heron" comment thematically on each other.

Additional coverage Hawthorne's life and career is contained in the following sources published by the Gale Group: *Authors and Artists for Young Adults,* **Vol. 18;** *Concise Dictionary of American Literary Biography 1640–1865; Dictionary of Literary Biography,* **Vols. 1, 74, and 223;** *DISCovering Authors,* **Vol. 3;** *DISCovering Authors: British; DISCovering Authors: Canadian; DISCovering Authors Modules: Most Studied Authors,* **and** *Novelists; Short Story Criticism,* **Vols. 3, 29, and 39;** *World Literature Criticism, 1500 to the Present;* **and** *Yesterday's Authors of Books for Children,* **Vol. 2.**

Washington Irving
1783-1859

(Also wrote under the pseudonyms of Geoffrey Crayon, Diedrich Knickerbocker, Jonathan Oldstyle, and Launcelot Langstaff) American short story writer, essayist, historian, biographer, journalist, and editor. For additional information on Irving's life and works, see *NCLC,* Volume 2; for information on *The Sketch-Book of Geoffrey Crayon, Gent.,* see *NCLC,* Volume 19.

INTRODUCTION

Irving is considered both the first American man of letters and the creator of the American short story. Though best known for such tales of rural Americana as "Rip Van Winkle" and "The Legend of Sleepy Hollow," Irving later became a prolific and accomplished biographer as well as a distinguished statesman.

BIOGRAPHICAL INFORMATION

Born in New York in 1783, Irving was the youngest of eleven children. Though he studied the law and eventually worked at a law office, his legal studies were halfhearted; he much preferred writing for his brother Peter's journal, *The Morning Chronicle.* In 1802 Irving wrote a series of letters to the *Chronicle* under the pseudonym of Jonathan Oldstyle. These letters gently mocked New York society and brought Irving his first recognition as a writer. Failing health forced him to seek a change of climate, and he traveled to Europe. In 1806 he returned home and was admitted to the bar; however, his legal interest waned. Irving, his brother William, and brother-in-law James Kirke Paulding, along with some other friends, were known as the "Nine Worthies of Cockloft Hall," named after their favorite place for "conscientious drinking and good fun." They collaborated on the satirical journal *Salmagundi; or, The Whim-whams and Opinions of Launcelot Langstaff, Esq., and Others* (1807-1808), which included many essays by Irving that reflected his Federalist political attitudes and social stance. The venture proved unprofitable, however, and the young men were forced to abandon the publication. In 1809 Irving enjoyed a second literary success with the publication and favorable reception of the satirical *A History of New York, from the Beginning of the World to the End of the Dutch Dynasty.* His success, however, was overshadowed by the death of his fiancée, Matilda Hoffman, in 1809. Grief consumed Irving and his works were never again to be light-spirited. In an effort to forget his sorrow, Irving entered a period of fervid activity. He acted as his brother's law partner, helped in the family hardware

business, and edited a magazine, the *Analectic.* Irving eventually returned to England and worked in the Liverpool branch of his family's import-export firm for three years until it went bankrupt. After years of wavering indecisively between a legal, editorial, and mercantile career, he finally decided to make writing his livelihood. He began recording impressions, thoughts, and descriptions in a small notebook. These, polished and repolished in Irving's meticulous manner, eventually became *The Sketch Book of Geoffrey Crayon, Gent.* (1819-20). Irving's most enduring work, the collection ensured his reputation as a man of letters. Its timing proved opportune, as no one had yet produced a universally appealing piece of American literature. In 1826 Irving traveled as a member of the American diplomatic corps to Spain, where he wrote *A History of the Life and Voyages of Christopher Columbus* (1828). A subsequent tour of Spain produced *A Chronicle of the Conquest of Granada* (1829) and *The Alhambra* (1832). During the 1830s, Irving returned to America, taking part in a tour of the Oklahoma territory. His travels in the West were fodder for several of his subsequent books, including

The Crayon Miscellany (1835), *A Tour on the Prairies* (1835), *Astoria, or Anecdotes of an Enterprise Beyond the Rocky Mountains* (1836), and *The Adventures of Captain Bonneville* (1837). In 1842 Irving became minister to Spain. Though he enjoyed his role as a diplomat, he returned to the United States to further his career as a biographical writer. His biography of Oliver Goldsmith is considered a particularly fine example of Irving's concise, balanced style. His last years were spent at work on a biography of George Washington; though overly elaborate and lacking his former naturalness of tone, the work expresses Irving's belief in a glorious American past. Irving's funeral was attended by thousands of admirers who mourned the death of an author they loved.

MAJOR WORKS

Irving's initial forays into writing were essays that satirized the political, social, and cultural life of his native New York City. A number of these were published in the short-lived journal *Salmagundi*. Irving continued in this satirical vein with his first book, *A History of New York*. Narrated by the fictional Diedrich Knickerbocker, a fusty, colorful Dutch-American, the work provided a comical, deliberately inaccurate account of New York's past. Considered his most consistently optimistic work, Irving was able to expound on native themes with affection and candor; indeed, the name "Knickerbocker" has become synonymous with a period of early American culture. *The Sketch Book of Geoffrey Crayon, Gent.,* Irving's subsequent effort, is considered a landmark work in American fiction. The book not only introduced the modern short story form in the United States but was also the first work by an American author to gain recognition abroad. Noted chiefly today for the stories "Rip Van Winkle" and "The Legend of Sleepy Hollow," the collection was widely popular in both England and the United States. Purportedly the work of Geoffrey Crayon, a genteel, good-natured American wandering through Britain on his first trip abroad, *The Sketch Book* consists largely of his travel impressions. These sketches are picturesque, elegant, and lightly humorous in the tradition of the eighteenth-century essayists Richard Addison and Oliver Goldsmith, Irving's literary models. The most enduring pieces, however, are those in which Irving wove elements of legend, folklore, and drama into narratives of the New World. "Rip Van Winkle," the story of a lackadaisical Dutch-American who slumbers for twenty years, and "The Legend of Sleepy Hollow," which recounts Ichabod Crane's meeting with a headless horseman, have long been considered classics. Critics generally agree that these were the models for the modern American short story and that both tales introduced imagery and archetypes that enriched the national literature. Irving's later career is marked by his shift towards biography writing. While traveling through Europe in the 1820s, Irving was asked to translate some documents on Christopher Columbus. Instead, Irving decided to write a biography on the man central to the American identity. Critics praised *A History of the Life and Voyages of Christopher Columbus* as one of the greatest biographies ever written; the book earned Irving distinction both as a scholar and as a biographer. Irving employed his skills as a researcher again in his biographies on Oliver Goldsmith and George Washington. In addition, Irving's keen interest in the American character and identity led him to write several books about the American West. In his works *A Tour on the Prairies, Astoria,* and *Captain Bonneville,* Irving recounted the adventurous and sometimes brutal life of the frontiersman. He is credited with realistically portraying the pioneers' cruel treatment of Native Americans. However, he championed American enterprise and the courage of American men forging a future for the country.

CRITICAL RECEPTION

Contemporaneous reviews illustrate the level of approval Irving won in the nineteenth century. While many of these reviewers were aware of deficiencies in Irving's work, their praise is generally overwhelming. Not all subsequent critics have been so enthusiastic; critical reception of the author's work has been mixed over the past two centuries. However, most modern critics classify Irving as one of the greatest American writers, responsible for establishing an American style of writing, especially in the short story genre. He is well respected as a biographer and as a chronicler of American culture. His short stories "The Legend of Sleepy Hollow" and "Rip Van Winkle" are considered American masterpieces, their legacy so great that they have been infused into popular culture.

A handful of issues have dominated modern literary scholarship on Irving: questions about the author's views on gender, the relationship between his personal identity and the burgeoning national identity, and the fluctuations in the quality of his writing. One of the biggest debates to rage in Irving scholarship is over the issue of anti-feminism in his writing. In her 1997 essay, Marjorie Pryse explains the historical context for Irving's writing. She states that the United States underwent an identity crisis in the early 19th century, attempting to establish its own culture in the years following national independence. The need to maintain patriarchal power and concerns over the role of women in the new society were paramount. Against that backdrop, Pryse argues, Irving wrote stories that restored men's power. Jenifer S. Banks concurs, stating that *The Sketch Book* and *Bracebridge Hall* (1822) reflect Irving's personal conflict between responsibility, as represented by women characters such as Dame Van Winkle, and independence, which is reified in men like Rip Van Winkle. Banks posits that the tension is best seen in Irving's short stories "The Widow and Her Son" and "The Wife." Laura Plummer and Michael Nelson argue that, while gender ideology has been studied in "Rip Van Winkle," little attention has been focused upon "The Legend of Sleepy Hollow." They state that the story "reveals Irving's characteristic misogyny and the male fear of disempowerment played out again and again throughout the tale." Hugh J. Dawson disagrees; he argues that 19th century popular interpretations of "Rip Van Winkle" have confused and misled scholars into categorizing the tale anti-feminist. Redressing arguments made by critics Philip Young, Judith Fetterley, and Leslie A. Fiedler, Dawson writes that the story is a gothic tale which reaffirms the importance of marriage over the dark, destructive power of the forest in which Rip Van Winkle grows old.

Interwoven within these debates about gender ideology are the prevailing theories of the importance of national identity in Irving's writings. Pryse discusses Irving's need to establish an American hero, separate and unique from those in British literature. Walter Sondey contends that Irving was the first American writer to recognize the potential of American literature to form the identity of Americans. Brian Harding maintains that the connection between Irving's writings and his views on national identity are not so straightforward. Discussing the author's journey to the West, Harding states that while Irving did not attempt to repatriate himself with Americans after a long absence in Europe, *A Tour on the Prairies* is written in a European style, using stereotypes and foreign analogies. In his analysis of *Astoria* and *Captain Bonneville,* Harding posits that they demonstrate Irving's reservations about the American system as much as they celebrate the industry and skills of American frontiersmen. Laura J. Murray is skeptical of predominant arguments about American literary history; she questions the arguments of such critics as Jeffrey Rubin Dorsky, a noted Irving scholar, about the link between Irving's anxiety as a writer and the formation of a national character. In her analysis of *The Sketch Book* she dismisses the concept of anxiety, stating that Irving fashioned a book that would appeal both to the English with its exotic portrayals of "savages" and to Americans with reassuring depictions of England.

A third strain of arguments questions the overall quality of Irving's corpus. While most scholars agree that Irving was an exceptional writer, not all agree that all his works deserve praise. Alice Hiller states that while Irving's first works were promising, his conscious decision to appeal to the British in his writing of *The Sketch Book* lowered his quality in subsequent works. She maintains that, while he did reestablish himself with American writers with the publication of *A Tour on the Prairies,* he did not live up to the potential obvious in his first American works. Writing more than one hundred years earlier, critic Alexander Hill Everett concedes that Irving's work suffers from irregular language and concurs that in *The Sketch Book* Irving lost some of the "vivacity, freshness and power" that characterized his earlier works. However, Hill maintains that Irving was a master at history, praising *A History of the Life and Voyages of Christopher Columbus* as one of the greatest works of literature. The anonymous reviewer for the *Ladies' Repository* in 1848 echoes Hill, praising Irving's skill as an observer and researcher.

PRINCIPAL WORKS

Salmagundi; or, The Whim-whams and Opinions of Launcelot Langstaff, Esq., and Others [with William Irving and James Kirke Paulding] (satirical essays) 1807-1808

A History of New York, from the Beginning of the World to the End of the Dutch Dynasty [As Diedrich Knickerbocker] (historical parody) 1809

The Sketch Book of Geoffrey Crayon, Gent. [as Geoffrey Crayon] (short stories) 1819-20

Bracebridge Hall [as Geoffrey Crayon] (sketches) 1822

Tales of a Traveller [as Geoffrey Crayon] (travel sketches) 1824

A History of the Life and Voyages of Christopher Columbus (biography) 1828

A Chronicle of the Conquest of Granada (history) 1829

The Alhambra [as Geoffrey Crayon] (travel sketches) 1832

The Crayon Miscellany [as Geoffrey Crayon] (travel sketches) 1835

A Tour on the Prairies (travel sketches) 1835

Astoria, or Anecdotes of an Enterprize Beyond the Rocky Mountains (biography) 1836

The Adventures of Captain Bonneville (biography) 1837

Oliver Goldsmith (biography) 1849

The Life of George Washington (biography) 1855-59

CRITICISM

John Lambert (essay date 1811)

SOURCE: Introduction to *Salmagundi; or, The Whim-whams and Opinions of Launcelot Langstaff, Esq., and Others . . .* , L. M. Richardson, 1811, pp. v-liv.

[*In the following essay, Lambert explains the nature of the essays in* Salmagundi *and the particular qualities of American culture.*]

So little is really known of the United States of America, on this side of the Atlantic, that it is not a matter of much surprise to find the most absurd and ridiculous prejudices existing with regard to every thing belonging to that country. The unfortunate revolution, which terminated in the emancipation of our colonies, is certainly the ostensible cause of the jealousy which exists between the two nations; and, of the two, I think our prejudices against the Americans are stronger than their animosity towards us.—I believe it is more difficult for a parent to pardon the undutiful behaviour of a child than for a child to forget the ill-treatment of a parent. The same reasoning may, perhaps, apply to nations as well as to individuals; for the conduct of men, in their public capacity, is guided very often by the same feelings and passions as influence them in private life.

From what source, however, such antipathy may flow, it is, at all events, to be regretted, for it not only tends to prevent that friendship and cordiality which ought ever to exist between England and America, but will, if not timely checked, burst into a flame that may hereafter be difficult to quench. I do not here mean to cast any reflection on our government, who, it must be confessed, have exhibited, in repeated instances, a considerable degree of conciliation and forbearance. The Americans themselves are, in many respects, equally culpable; for, by their open encouragement of European traitors and emissaries, they have occasioned much of that rancour which has contributed both to retard the settlement of the differences between the two nations and to sow discord and enmity among themselves.

The animosity, however, of the Americans is chiefly of a political nature, whereas our prejudices extend to every thing American, whether it be the politics of the democrats, the manners of the people, or the ladies' teeth!—it is thus the Americans have the advantage of us. They are intemperate in politics, but their intemperance extends no farther; they are noisy and blustering, like ourselves, in their complaints of other nations; they are jealous of all encroachments on their liberties, and tenacious of their political opinions even to a fault.—But view them in private life; in their hours of relaxation; in the circle of friendship; and it will be found that they do not deserve the opprobrium that has been cast on their character. . . .

In introducing to the patronage of the British public a literary production of the United States, it is my first care to remove those prejudices which exist in the minds of too many of my countrymen against every thing of American origin; many, I dare say, already begin to prick up their ears at the very name of *American* literature, and, perhaps, suspect that I have an intention of palming upon them, for American genius, the sterling wit of some English author, driven to that country by his grinding creditors. Now, though I will not undertake to deny that many a poor author may really have made his escape to that land of freedom, yet I positively assure my *gentle,* as well as genteel, readers, that the **Salmagundi** is, bona fide, a *dish* of real American cookery; and, if they will only allow me first to disperse those little acrimonious crudities that prevent digestion, I will present them with such an excellent ragout of wit, humour, and genius, that they may feast on for ever without the least apprehension of a surfeit. A **Salmagundi** is, indeed, a dish that may at first alarm some of delicate appetites, especially those who have no great partiality to the country in which it was cooked; but if they can only be prevailed on to taste it, I promise them it will act like the stimulating curry of India, without which the poor half-stewed nabob would die for want of an appetite! But, metaphor apart, I am confident that, if these essays are favoured with an attentive perusal, and the mind of the reader divested of the prejudices in favour of our own

eminent writers in that department, they will not only find considerable amusement and instruction, but also be convinced that the contempt in which American literature is generally held in this country is both unjust and groundless. As it is my intention, in this introductory essay, to notice the most striking passages and characters in the **Salmagundi,** I shall, in order to prepare the reader for such observations, preface them with a hasty review of the origin of the American union, and of the present state of the manners, customs, and dispositions, of the people in that country. This will, I hope, serve both to elucidate a considerable portion of the work in question, and to remove many of those false impressions which now prejudice the minds of Englishmen; if I am instrumental, even in the smallest degree, to the removal of one such impression, I shall feel myself amply compensated for any feeble aid which I may have lent towards the attainment of so desirable an object. . . .

The distinguishing feature of the **Salmagundian Essays** is humourous satire, which runs through the whole work like veins of rich ore in the bowels of the earth. These essays partake more of the broad humour and satirical wit of Rabelais and Swift than the refined morality of Addison and Johnson; their chief aim is to raise a laugh at the expense of folly and absurdity, and to lash the vices of society with the rod of satire:—they do not pretend to improve mankind by a code of ethics and morals, and, therefore, should not be tried by the same critical laws as the British Essays. The American **Salmagundi** bears much the same relation to the *Spectator* and *Rambler* as Roderic Random does to Sir Charles Grandison and Pamela.—The authors, however, have, in several instances, proved that they can speak to the heart as well as the mind; it is only to be regretted that they have not oftener written in a style that seems by no means a stranger to their pen, and which might have contributed to give their work a more classical and instructive tone than it at present bears; nevertheless, it possesses a rich fund of information for those who are desirous of becoming acquainted with the manners of the American people; for, though it naturally partakes of caricature, yet the features of society are rather heightened than distorted. A very favourable trait in the character of this work, and of which few humourous productions can boast, is the chastity of idea as well as diction which pervades the whole. Though wit, humour, and satire, are its principal ingredients, yet the thoughts and language are clothed in the most chaste and modest habiliments. It is also as free from dulness, pedantry, and affectation, as it is from indecency and immorality; and the best proof of the good sense and abilities of its authors is, that they have avoided that quaint and ridiculous phraseology, so common among the generality of writers in their country. The **Salmagundi** has afforded much entertainment to the Americans, who have bestowed on it the utmost applause; and, as the whole of the Essays abound in applications to the manners, customs, and constitution, of England, it will therefore, I think, be read with almost as much interest by us as if it had been written expressly for this country. The characters are, for the most part, "representatives of their species," and apply equally to an Englishman as an American. It is thus that they become interesting to us in a double capacity;—First, in their general application to society at large, and, secondly, in the picture they present of American manners, hitherto so imperfectly known on this side of the Atlantic.

From an observation in No. 1, on the character of Anthony Evergreen, it appears that the hours for meals must have undergone as great a change in America as in Europe. "When the ladies paid tea visits at three in the afternoon"—they must have dined at eleven or twelve, breakfasted at six, and rose at four or five. It was then that that glorious luminary, the sun, was more honoured than the tallow-chandler: Now, the reverse is the case; and the votaries of pleasure and dissipation seem to dread the light of day, with as much horror as they dread the examination of their own hearts. How little we estimate the benefits we possess, and covet those beyond our reach, is strikingly exemplified in our disregard of one of the greatest enjoyments of this life,—*day-light. . . .*

Our dramatic authors and performers will, no doubt, agree with Launcelot Langstaff, that the critics, who so often unmercifully castigate their labours, "frequently create the fault they find, in order to yield an opening for their criticisms, and censure an actor for a gesture he never made, or an emphasis he never gave."—From the ire of Launcelot, against "neighbour Town," it would appear that New York can boast of as *sound* newspaper critics on the drama as London. As theatrical performances on the other side of the Atlantic are but of modern date, the Americans of course are acquainted only by name with the old English practice of pit-criticism, in vogue a century ago, consequently they cannot estimate the loss we have sustained, and the miserable exchange we have made from that open and manly decision on dramatic merits, to the anonymous criticism of concealed friends or foes. . . .

When we complain that the taste of the age, for dramatic spectacles, is vitiated and depraved, we may, in a great measure, attribute it to the change which has taken place in the mode of criticism, by which bad comedies, miserable farces, and despicable pantomimes, are puffed up, much oftener than good plays are written down. We are, now-a-days, so attentive to *costume* and *propriety,* that the more important parts of the drama are neglected; and the attention of the people diverted from the instructive lessons and delightful sentiments elicited in the many admirable dramatic pieces, of which our country can boast, to the gaudy display of pantomimical pageantry, and the exhibition of real dogs and horses. If former times were marked by errors in theatrical costume, they were, however, distinguished by a greater attention to the real worth and intrinsic merits of the drama. The sight of the critic in the pit was sufficient to check the least impropriety in the actor, and to rouse him to all the exertion of which he was master. The performer, a century ago, had the dread before him of having his talents investigated at "Button's," and other coffee-houses, by the first wits of the age;—and, if

he regarded his credit, he always took care how he passed through such an ordeal.

The observation of Will Wizard, that because he had "never seen Kemble in Macbeth, he was utterly at a loss to say whether Mr. Cooper performed well or ill," is an excellent piece of satire on those critics, whose only criterion of judgement is comparison; and who, being completely at a loss what to say respecting an actor's powers, are compelled to drag forward another, in order to *measure* the talents or defects of the one by the other. The suggestion that, if Lady Macbeth had stuck the candle in her night-cap, it would have had a greater effect than the setting it down on the table, or holding it in her hand, (as censured by other critics,) inasmuch as it would have marked more strongly the derangement of her mind, is highly ludicrous, as well as severe on those who are so apt to carp at trifles. So likewise are the observations on errors of costume, and not dipping the daggers so deep in blood by an inch or two, as formerly. The new reading of "*Sorry Sight,*" is no bad hint to the commentators on Shakespeare, and not inapplicable to Mr. Kemble's "*Aitches.*"

Frequent mention is made in these Essays of the word *Cockney.* This phrase is not meant merely for a Londoner, but is intended to designate those consequential gentlemen from England, who cross the Atlantic on the strength of a consignment from Birmingham or Liverpool. These gentry are too apt to estimate the genius of the Americans by the standard of their own intellects, and flatter themselves how much they will "astonish the natives" on their arrival. Disappointed, however, at not attracting that notice, and causing that degree of astonishment which they fondly expected, they speak with contempt of every thing that is American. The men are brutes;—the women have bad teeth;—the towns are paltry;—the plays are wretched;—the performers miserable;—in short, there is nothing in America as there is in England: and comparisons are hourly drawn between things which bear not the slightest resemblance to each other. Thus it is that the vender of hardware, and broad cloth becomes a critic out of mere spite: He dashes away while his consignment lasts, (too often indeed at the cost of his employers;) and, though he may fail to attract the notice of the *natives* by his merits, he generally contrives to appropriate to himself a tolerable share of their contempt. A most admirable portrait of a Birmingham hero is given in these Essays in the character of Tom Straddle: It abounds with comic touches, and displays a wit and humour, that would do honour to the productions of any of our essayists.

The allusions to the French people, in various passages of the *Salmagundian Essays,* prove that the writers entertained no very favourable opinion of those who have settled in the United States; and that they thought a little wholesome castigation from their pens might be of service to them. The numerous bands of Frenchmen, who have flocked to that country since the French revolution, have, by no means, tended to the improvement of American manners or morals, or the removal of any of those prejudices which existed between England and America; on the contrary, both domestic dissipation and foreign rancour have considerably increased. The lightness and frivolity of the French character is neatly touched off in several of the *Essays*; and the deleterious influence of their example on the grave disposition of the Americans successfully exposed. They have inundated America, as they have this country, and may well be said to "hop about the town in swarms, like little toads after a shower." It would have been happy for both parties, had their conduct been as exemplary as the reception they met with was liberal; but many are the melancholy instances to the contrary, both in the privacy of domestic retirement as well as in the public walk of politics. They have debauched the wives and daughters of their benefactors,—corrupted the manners of society,—and sowed dissention and rebellion throughout the country. Even their own countryman, the Duke de Rochefoucault Liancourt, in his travels through the United States, can find no excuse for them; and, unreservedly, consigns them to the merited execrations of the Americans. It would, however, be uncharitable to include all Frenchmen in this accusation; it is the dregs of the revolution only who have acted in this manner. There are many who have deserved the hospitality they met with; yet, I fear their number is not equal to those who have abused it.

In contrast to this feeling, with regard to the French, it must afford Englishmen much satisfaction to find the sentiments of a great portion of the American people highly favourable towards them, from a variety of causes. In various parts of these Essays, these favourable sentiments are repeatedly displayed,—particularly in the character of Christopher Cockloft—and the rest of his family. Their antipathy to the French,—partiality to every thing English,—Christopher's voyage to Halifax, to hear our king prayed for in church as he was before the revolution,—giving a dinner on the king's birth-day,—and a variety of other traits, which, though they may be nothing more than the eccentric features of a fictitious character, are, I think, intended as delineations of real traits existing among a considerable portion of the people. Several instances are also mentioned in these Essays of the attention and partiality displayed towards our countrymen arriving in the United States: even an insignificant fellow is represented as having worked himself into the good graces of the citizens, merely because he was an *Englishman*. The claim of consanguinity as well as individual interest is, no doubt, a strong motive of their attachment to Great Britain, which they often denominate *home,* especially those who once lived under the British government, and whose sentiments have been but little changed since the revolution. Others who were children when that event took place, have imbibed from their cradle, as it were, the true republican spirit. Hence though they may prefer British to French interests, are yet tenacious of their independence almost to a fault, and equally jealous of British usurpation as of French intrigue. As to those who are styled Democrats, Jacobins, and Tories, I look upon the violent among them more as a mixture of factious Europeans than real Americans. They have unfortunately from the nature of the government too much influence in political matters; but I think it extremely unfair to judge of the character of the Americans by the scum of the country.

The writers of *Salmagundi* have happily enough availed themselves of the opportunity which the Tripolitan prisoners gave them, to introduce a very humourous character into their work. *Mustapha Rub-a-dub Keli Khan* is one of the most diverting personages in the whole groupe; and his opinion of the Americans, formed on the prejudices of his own nation, open an extensive field for satire. This character has also the merit of being well supported, for he seldom exceeds the bounds of his supposed knowledge of American manners; and, where he has occasion to go farther, the information is generally conveyed to him through the medium of some acquaintance or bystander, by which means he is not a mere *American* observer, tricked out in a *shawl* and *turban*. He really possesses as much the semblance of a Mahomedan as it is possible for fiction to give. The Citizen of the World is more of an Englishman in a Chinese dress than Mustapha an American in masquerade. When a foreign character is brought forward for our amusement, he ought to reason as well as speak agreeable to his own ideas, formed on the manners, customs, and prejudices, of his nation; unless indeed we are to consider him as gifted with a cosmopolitan spirit, and general knowledge of the world,—a foundation on which Goldsmith most likely formed his Chinese Letters.
. . .

A considerable portion of *Salmagundi* is appropriated to the exposure and ridicule of certain travellers who have visited the United States; and whose illiberal aspersions and ridiculous prejudices have drawn upon them the censure of every candid and impartial person. Nor have others, who never crossed the Atlantic, altogether escaped the satirical lash of these witty writers, as the names of Carr and Kotzebue evidently prove. That the Irish knight should be so unfortunate as to excite the ridicule of the Americans as well as his own countrymen is rather singular; and if it had not been satisfactorily proved to the contrary, I should have condemned the "Stranger in New Jersey," as a plagiarism on "My Pocket Book!" That this was also the opinion of those American critics who endeavoured to write down the *Salmagundi* may be seen from the note attached to No. 13. From that declaration it however appears, that the "Stranger in New Jersey" is an original production, and made its appearance in these Essays at New York one month before "My Pocket Book" was published in London. This circumstance is peculiarly unfortunate for the knight's literary reputation, as it tends to confirm the opinion which the author of "My Pocket Book" had formed of his "Stranger in Ireland." He has also unluckily the double misfortune of suffering under American and English satire, as it were, of one accord, without the possibility of any previous understanding between the writers to that effect. Weld, Moore, Parkinson, and Priest, who have been particularly severe in their strictures on the American character, also come in for their share of the rod.—Indeed they merit it much more than poor Sir John, who was hardly a fair object of correction: but it might perhaps be done with a view to prevent his visiting the country, though from the general style of his writings I should conceive they would have found him perfectly harmless.

The Essay on Style may put in its claim for as large a portion of merit as any one in the whole work. The portrait which is there drawn of the manners of fashionable upstarts is an admirable picture from life, not only as it exists in New York, but also in London. How many families of "Giblets" have we seen in this metropolis, whose sudden elevation from the counter to the chariot has astonished the vulgar and alarmed the great. Never was style, as it is understood in fashionable language, better defined, nor its ridiculous absurdities better pourtrayed, than in that Essay. The humourous contrast of style as it is found in different countries, and the innovations which it occasions in domestic families, are agreeably depicted. But the preposterous whim of Bellbrazen, the Haytian beauty, and the sudden elevation of the Giblets, from the manners of their grub-worm father to the dashing career of fashionable folly, are most happily hit off, and display a rich fund of satirical wit and humour. Who is there that will not immediately recognize in the following passage the manners of our vulgar fashionables, and of those *ci-devant* citizens, who in their migration from Pudding-lane to Portman-square, have bewildered themselves with *style?*—

> Then commenced the hurry and bustle and mighty nothingness of fashionable life;—such rattling in coaches! such flaunting in the streets! such slamming of box-doors at the theatre! such a tempest of bustle and unmeaning noise wherever they appeared! the Giblets were seen here, there, and every where;—they visited every body they knew, and every body they did not know; and there was no getting along for the Giblets. Their plan at length succeeded: by dint of dinners, of feeding and frolicking the town, the Giblet family worked themselves into notice, and enjoyed the ineffable pleasure of being for ever pestered by visitors, who cared nothing about them; of being squeezed, and smothered, and par-boiled, at nightly balls and evening tea-parties. They were allowed the privilege of forgetting the few old friends they once possessed; they turned their noses up in the wind at every thing that was not genteel; and their superb manners and sublime affectation at length left it no longer a matter of doubt that the Giblets were perfectly in *style.*

Another admirable picture from life is presented to us in the character of "My good aunt Charity,"—a simple, curious, old maid, who unfortunately "died of a Frenchman!" This portrait is drawn with all that warmth of colouring which heightens without disfiguring the features; and though highly ludicrous, is yet a true delineation of human nature. Hogarth never painted with more animation and satirical truth than the authors of **Salmagundi** have written. Many an antiquated old maid, and many a female gossip, may contemplate the several features of their dispositions in that mirror of formality and curiosity. The buckram delicacy of "My aunt" in the hey-dey of youth,—and the religious turn she took when that period was past, are highly humorous; the latter is also an excellent satire on those who in their old age make up at "*love-feasts*" for the disappointments they have sustained in *real love*. The other peculiarities of aunt Charity's character are equally appropriate; and even that one, viz. *curiosity,* which unluckily caused her "to die of a Frenchman" was an innocent foible with her. It would be happy for society were it always so with others; but the invincible desire which some females at a certain age,—married as well as single,—widows as well as old maids,—have of knowing every body's character,—business,—and mode of living, and looking after every one's affairs but their own, is too frequently the offspring of pride, envy, and jealousy. There cannot be a more dangerous character in a small society than the *envious gossip,* who makes it her business to "get at the bottom of a thing," be it good or bad.—Under the specious mask of friendship and kindness a woman of this description will work herself into the favour of her unsuspecting acquaintance, and, when possessed of the information she sought for, will never fail to sow discord among them;—like poor aunt Charity, but with less innocent motives, "she will not sleep a wink all night" for fear another Mrs. Sipkins should get the start of her in the morning, and tell her story first. This endeavour "to give currency to the *good-natured* things said about every body" is not the only peculiarity of the *envious gossip,* for, so anxious does she pretend to be for the truth of what she asserts (as is the case with all notorious liars), that, if her word is doubted, her neighbours must be brought face to face; away, then, she hobbles from house to house, and never closes her eyes until she has set her little community together by the ears.

Women of this description are the pests of small towns and villages, and will, over their tea and cards, consign more reputations to infamy than even their tongues can repeat; for a shrug and a sneer are, if possible, more dangerous. By such arts married people have been made miserable, and friends and acquaintance been rendered implacable enemies. But what makes a character of this description the more detestable is, that every thing is done out of *pure loving kindness*; for instance, she shall be so mightily afraid lest you, or any of your family, should be contaminated, by acquainting with such and such a character, that she immediately discharges her whole budget of lies, scandal, and malignity, to the utter annihilation, perhaps, of the reputation of some worthy family or innocent girl; this is what she terms friendly advice, and a proof of the interest she takes in your welfare! Such is the true character of an *envious gossip,* whose impertinent interference in her neighbours' affairs, while it destroys their happiness, does but render herself miserable, and, sooner or later, makes her the object of universal hatred and disgust:—"Take warning, therefore, my fair country-women, and you, oh, ye excellent ladies! whether married or single, who pry into other people's affairs, and neglect those of your own household, who are so busily employed in observing the faults of others that you have no time to correct your own, remember the fate of my dear aunt Charity, and eschew the evil spirit of curiosity."

A considerable part of these essays are appropriated to the fair sex, and a tolerable portion of satirical correction and wholesome advice dealt out to them; their injurious experiments of tight-lacing, to render themselves fine figures, are frequently noticed, and some humourous animadversions passed thereon, which cannot, I should think, be unpalatable to them, even if they are not inclined to alter their proceedings. It is a pity that the American ladies, who are by nature elegantly made, should resort to experiments which injure their constitutions and put them in torture. The practice of tight-lacing, the eating of pickles and chalk, and the smoking of tobacco, are, I believe, no strangers to European females; but, whatever necessity the daughter of a Dutch burgomaster, or English farmer, might have for such arts to reduce their size, I do not think those who are naturally slim have any occasion to adopt them. . . .

Another subject of animadversion, on which the writers of **Salmagundi** have dwelt in some of their essays, is the folly of what is called style, and the present fashionable mode of "murdering time." Modern life is admirably displayed in the essay on style, and in some of the passages of Mustapha's letter on the assembly. After contemplating such scenes of folly, bustle, and dissipation, one cannot help being struck with the insensibility of the people who live in the vortex of fashionable life, and who pursue their career of daring extravagance and vapid nothingness to the very grave, without resting on their journey for one moment to contemplate the awfulness of their situation.—The old and the young are alike engaged in the same senseless routine of folly and absurdity. What man of sense, wishing to marry, would chuse a woman whose days and nights are engrossed with the preparations for, and participations in, continual routs, balls, and card-parties? What satisfaction can be derived from a woman thus educated? Surely such an incessant exposure of female youth and beauty to the gaiety and dissipation of public parties must be as detrimental to the morals as to the health. . . .

The observations which I have made in the course of these essays have arisen out of the various subjects contained therein, and if I have not done my authors all the justice they merit, it is because they have not had an editor of equal talent with themselves. I cannot do better than conclude this Introductory Essay in their own language, and hope my fair countrywomen will be as ready to comply with their request as the American ladies were:—"We recommend to all *mothers* to purchase our essays for their daughters, who will be taught the true line of propriety, and the most adviseable method of managing their beaux. We advise all *daughters* to purchase them for the sake of their mothers, who shall be initiated into the arcana of the bon ton, and cured of all those rusty old notions which they acquired during the last century.—Parents shall be taught how to govern their children; girls how to get husbands; and old maids how to do without them."

Alexander Hill Everett (essay date 1829)

SOURCE: Review of *Life and Voyages of Christopher Columbus,* in *North American Review,* Vol. 28, January, 1829, pp. 103-34.

[*In the following review, Everett compares* A History of the Life and Voyages of Christopher Columbus *to Irving's earlier works, describing his skill as a writer of humor, satire, and history.*]

This is one of those works, which are at the same time the delight of readers and the despair of critics. It is as nearly perfect in its kind, as any work well can be; and there is therefore little or nothing left for the reviewer, but to write at the bottom of every page, as Voltaire said he should be obliged to do, if he published a commentary on Racine, *Pulchrè! bene! optimè!* And as the reputation of the author is so well established, that he does not stand in need of our recommendation as a passport to the public favor, it may appear, and in fact is, almost superfluous to pretend to give a formal review of his book. Nevertheless, we cannot refuse ourselves the satisfaction of adding the mite of our poor applause to the ample and well deserved harvest of fame, that has already rewarded the labors of our ingenious, excellent, and amiable fellow citizen; nor would it, as we conceive, be proper to omit noticing in this journal a work, however well known to the public, which we consider as being, on the whole, more honorable to the literature of the country, than any one that has hitherto appeared among us. Before we proceed to give our opinion in detail of the **History of the Life and Voyages of Columbus** we shall offer a few remarks on the character and merit of Mr. Irving's other works, premising that we write under the influence of the feelings that naturally result from a good deal of friendly personal intercourse with this gentleman. If any reader shall suspect, that we judge Mr. Irving too favorably because we know him too well, he is quite at liberty to make any deductions from the sum total of our commendation, that he may on this account deem in candor to be necessary.

Mr. Irving shares, in some degree, the merit and the glory that belong to the illustrious hero of his present work, that of leading the way in a previously unexplored and untrodden path of intellectual labor. He is the first writer of purely Cisatlantic origin and education, who succeeded in establishing a high and undisputed reputation, founded entirely on literary talent and success. This was the opinion expressed by a very judicious and discerning writer in the Edinburgh Review, upon the first publication of the **Sketch Book**; and it is, as we conceive, a substantially correct one. In saying this, we are perfectly aware that there have been found among us, at every period during the two centuries of our history, individuals highly distinguished, both at home and abroad, by important and useful labors in various branches of art and science. We mean not to detract, in the least, from their well-earned fame, which we cherish, on the contrary, as the richest treasure that belongs to their posterity, and would do everything in our power to establish and enlarge. We say not that Mr. Irving is the first or the greatest man that ever handled a pen in the United States. . . .

In the rapid progress of our population, wealth, and literary advantages, the period arrived, when the calls of business no longer absorbed all the cultivated intellect existing in the country; when, after these were fully satisfied, there remained a portion of taste, zeal, and talent to be employed in purely literary and scientific pursuits; when the public mind was prepared to acknowledge and appreciate any really superior merit, that might present itself, in those departments; when in fact the nation, having been somewhat galled by the continual sneers of a set of heartless and senseless foreigners upon our want of literary talent, was rather anxious to possess some positive facts, which could be offered as evidence to the contrary, and was prepared of course to hail the appearance of a writer of undoubted talent, with a kind of patriotic enthusiasm; when finally, for all these reasons, the first example of success, that should be given in this way, would naturally be followed by an extensive development of the same sort of activity, throughout the country, in the persons of a host of literary aspirants, sometimes directly imitating their prototype, and always inspired and encouraged by his good fortune, who would make up together the front rank of what is commonly called a school of polite literature. To set this example was the brilliant part reserved, in the course of our literary history, for Mr. Washington Irving. His universal popularity among readers of all classes, on both sides of the Atlantic, resting exclusively on the purely literary merit of his productions, wholly independent of extraneous or interested motives, attested by repeated successes, in various forms of composition, and stamped by the concurrence and approbation of the most acute, judicious, and unsparing critics, justifies, beyond a shadow of doubt, his pretension to be viewed as the valorous knight, who was called, in the order of destiny, to break the spell, which appeared, at least to our good natured European brethren, to be thrown over us in this respect; to achieve the great and hitherto unaccomplished adventure of establishing a purely American literary reputation of the first order; and demonstrate the capacity of his countrymen to excel in the elegant, as they had before done in all the useful and solid branches of learning. To have done this is a singular title of honor, and will always remain such, whatever laurels of a different kind may hereafter be won by other pretenders. Thoroughly labored and highly finished as they all are, Mr. Irving's works will hardly be surpassed in their way. . . . it can never be disputed that the mild and beautiful genius of Mr. Irving was the Morning-Star, that led up the march of our heavenly host; and that he has a fair right, much fairer certainly than the great Mantuan, to assume the proud device, *Primus ego in patriam.* To have done this, we repeat, is a singular triumph, far higher than that of merely adding another name to a long list of illustrious predecessors, who flourished in the same country. It implies not merely taste and talent, but *originality,* the quality which forms the real distinction, if there be one, between what we call *genius* and every other degree of

intellectual power; the quality, in comparison with which, as Sir Walter Scott justly observes, all other literary accomplishments are as dust in the balance. It implies moreover the possession of high and honorable moral qualities; the bold and daring resolution, that plans with vigor and decision; the unyielding firmness of purpose, that never tires or falters in the task of execution. These qualities, which are obviously necessary to such success as that of Mr. Irving, have also, as exemplified in his writings, been carefully kept within bounds, and have not only been prevented from running into their kindred excesses, but, on the contrary, have been judiciously and gracefully veiled from the public eye, by the outward forms that rather belong to a character of an opposite cast; a modesty, that has never deserted him under all his popularity, and a scrupulous regard for decorum and propriety as well as the higher principles of morals, from which the dazzling success, that has unfortunately attended a different line of conduct in some contemporary writers, has never for a moment induced him to deviate. This combination of estimable and in some respects almost contradictory moral qualities, with a high intellectual power and fine taste, tends to render the influence of Mr. Irving's example not less favorable to the country, in a moral point of view, than it is in a purely literary one.

The great effect which it has produced, in this latter respect, is sufficiently evident already, in the number of good writers, in various forms of elegant literature, who have sprung up among us within the few years which have elapsed since the appearance of Mr. Irving, and who justify our preceding remark, that he may fairly be considered as the founder of a school. . . . We only intend to intimate, that he has the peculiar merit and fortune of having taken the lead, under the influence of these causes, in a course, in which he could not but be followed and sustained by numerous successors, who would of necessity be more or less affected by the form and character of his productions. The fact that several of the more distinguished writers, who have since appeared, are from his own state,—while it is partly accounted for by the vast extent, population, wealth, and generally thriving situation of that "empire in embryo," New York; circumstances which all tend very strongly to stimulate every form of intellectual activity,—must nevertheless be regarded in part, as a proof of the direct operation of the success of Mr. Irving.

Having thus noticed the circumstances, that attended the appearance of this writer in the literary career, we shall now offer a few observations on the character and value of his works. We trust that, in treating this subject somewhat fully, we shall not be considered, by our readers, as giving it a disproportionate importance. . . .

If we examine the works of Mr. Irving, with reference to the usual division of manner and substance, we may remark, in the first place, that his style is undoubtedly one of the most finished and agreeable forms, in which the English language has ever been presented. Lord Byron has somewhere spoken of him, as the second prose writer of the day, considering Sir Walter Scott as the first; but with due deference to his lordship's judgment, which was far from being infallible in criticism or anything else, we cannot but consider Mr. Irving, as respects mere style, decidedly superior to Sir Walter. The latter, no doubt, has exhibited a greater vigor and fertility of imagination, which, with his talent for versification, entitle him to a higher rank in the world of letters; but viewing him merely as a prose writer, his style, when not sustained by the interest of a connected narrative, will be found to possess no particular merit, and in some of his later writings is negligent and incorrect to an extent, that places it below mediocrity. That of Mr. Irving, on the contrary, is, in all his works, uniformly of the first order. Its peculiar characteristic is a continual and sustained elegance, the result of the union of a naturally fine taste, with conscientious and unwearied industry. His language is not remarkable for energy, nor have we often noticed in it any extraordinary happiness or brilliancy of mere expression. Though generally pure and correct, it is not uniformly so; and there are one or two unauthorized forms, which will be found by a nice observer to recur pretty often. Its attraction lies, as we have said, in the charm of finished elegance, which it never loses. The most harmonious and poetical words are carefully selected. Every period is measured and harmonized with nice precision. The length of the sentences is judiciously varied; and the *tout ensemble* produces on the ear an effect very little, if at all, inferior to that of the finest versification. Indeed such prose, while it is from the nature of the topics substantially poetry, does not appear to us, when viewed merely as a form of language, to differ essentially from verse. . . .

If the elegant prose of Mr. Irving be, as we think it is, but little inferior in beauty to the finest verse, and at all events one of the most finished forms of the English language, the character and the substance of his writings is also entirely and exclusively poetical. It is evident enough that "divine Philosophy" has no part nor lot in his affections. Shakespeare, though he was willing to "hang up philosophy," out of compliment to the charming Juliet, when he chose to take it down again, could put the Seven Sages of Greece to the blush. But such is not the taste of Mr. Irving. His aim is always to please; and never to instruct, at least by general truths. If he ever teaches, he confines himself to plain matter of fact. He even goes farther, and with the partiality of a true lover, who can see no beauty except in the eyes of his own mistress, he at times deals rather rudely with philosophy, and more than insinuates that she is a sort of prosing mad-cap, who babbles eternally without ever knowing what she is talking of. . . . But though we think Mr. Irving heretical on this head, we can hardly say that we like him the less for it, being always pleased to see a man put his heart and soul into his business, whatever it may be, even though he may, by so doing, (as often happens) generate in himself a sort of hatred and contempt for every other. Within the domain of poetry, taking this word in its large sense, to which he religiously confines himself, Mr. Irving's range is somewhat extensive. He does not attempt the sublime, but he is often successful in

the tender, and disports himself, at his ease, in the comic. Humor is obviously his *forte,* and his best touches of pathos are those, which are thrown in casually, to break the continuity of a train of melancholy thoughts, when they sparkle in part by the effect of contrast, like diamonds on a black mantle. But it is when employed on humorous subjects, that he puts forth the vigor of a really inventive genius, and proves himself substantially a poet. "Knickerbocker," for example, is a true original creation. His purely pathetic essays, though occasionally pleasing, are more generally somewhat tame and spiritless. As a writer of serious biography and history he possesses the merit of plain and elegant narrative, but does not aspire to the higher palm of just and deep thought in the investigation of causes and effects, that constitutes the distinction of the real historian, and supposes the taste for philosophical research, which, as we have said before, is foreign to the temper of our author.

Such, as we conceive, are the general characteristics of the style and substance of the works of Mr. Irving. We notice their deficiencies and beauties with equal freedom, for such is our duty as public critics, and we have too much respect for our friend to suppose, that his appetite for fame requires to be gratified by unqualified praise. This can never, in any case, be merited, and is therefore always worthless; while the favorable effect of just and candid criticism is heightened, by a discriminating notice of the weak points, that are of course to be found in all productions. We shall now proceed to offer a few more particular observations upon the separate works, dividing them, for this purpose, into the two classes of those that were written before and after the author's departure for Europe. Although the general characteristics, which we have pointed out, are common to both these classes, there are some differences of manner between them, that are worth attention. The **Life of Columbus,** again, varies materially from any of the preceding publications, and will naturally be considered by itself, as the immediate subject of this article.

The former class comprehends **Salmagundi** and the **History of New York,** besides some smaller and less important productions. These exhibit the talent of the author, in the full perfection of its power, developing itself with a freshness and freedom, that have not perhaps been surpassed, or even equalled, in any of his subsequent writings, but directed, on the other hand, by a somewhat less sure and cultivated taste. There is a good deal of inequality in **Salmagundi,** owing probably in part to a mixture of contributions by other hands; but the better pieces are written in Mr. Irving's best manner. Take it altogether, it was certainly a production of extraordinary merit, and was instantaneously and universally recognised as such by the public. It wants of course the graver merits of the modern British collections of Essays; but for spirit, effect, and actual literary value, we doubt whether any publication of the class since *The Spectator,* upon which it is directly modelled, can fairly be put in competition with it. We well remember the eagerness, with which the periodical return of the merry little yellow dwarf was anticipated by all classes of readers, and the hearty good will, with which he was welcomed. "Sport that wrinkled care derides, / And Laughter holding both his sides," uniformly followed in his train. So irresistibly attractive and amusing were the quips and cranks of the odd group of mummers that moved under his management, that our grave, business-loving, and somewhat disputatious citizens were taken, like Silence in the play, ere they were aware; and when the show was over, were surprised, and in some cases rather chagrined, to find that they had been diverted from their habitual meditations on the Orders in Council and the New England Platform, by the unprofitable fooleries of the Cockloft family and the Little Man in Black, the state of the Tunisian Ambassador's wardrobe, and the tragical fate of poor Aunt Charity, who died of a Frenchman. Mr. Irving appears to have had no other object in view, but that of making a sprightly book and laughing at everything laughable; but the work necessarily assumed, to a certain extent, the shape of a satire on the abuses of popular government; since the administration of the public affairs is the great scene of action, upon which the attention of the community is always fixed, and which must be treated, in jest or earnest, by all who mean to have an audience. The vices and follies, that most easily beset our practical statesmen, their endless prolixity in debate, their rage for the bloodless glory of heading the militia in a sham fight, their habitual waste of dollars in attempting to economize cents, are hit off in a very happy manner; but as the satire is always general, and the malice at bottom good-natured and harmless, nobody took offence and we all laughed honestly and heartily; each, as he supposed, at the expense of his neighbor. Nor are we to conclude that because Mr. Irving has made the abuses of popular government, and the weaknesses incident to those who administer such a system, the objects of his satire, that he is a political heretic and a secret foe to liberty. The best human institutions are of course imperfect, and there is quite as much advantage to be derived from a just and good-humored exposition of the weak points of our own government, as from a continued fulsome and exaggerated panegyric on its merits. Mr. Irving, we may add, was probably directed in the choice of the subjects on which to exercise his pleasantry, by the mere force of the circumstances under which he wrote, and not by any general views of the theory of government.

The decided success and universal popularity of his first attempt naturally encouraged him to repeat it, and *Salmagundi* was pretty soon followed by the *History of New York.* This we consider as equal to the best, and in some respects perhaps superior to any other of our author's productions. It is the one, which exhibits most distinctly the stamp of real inventive power, the true test, as we have hinted, of genius. The plan, though simple enough, and when hit upon sufficiently obvious, is entirely original. In most other works of the same general class of political satire, such as those of Rabelais and Swift, the object of the work is effected by presenting real events and characters of dignity and importance in low and ludicrous shapes. *Knickerbocker* reverses this plan, and produces effect by dressing up a mean and trifling fund of real history, in a garb of fictitious and burlesque gravity. The conception is akin, no doubt, to the general notion of the mock heroic, as exemplified, for instance, in Pope's *Rape of the Lock,* but the particular form, in which it is applied by the learned and ingenious Diedrich, is not only unusually happy, but wholly new; and the work possesses of course a character of complete originality, which does not belong to any of the others. *The Stout Gentleman* is a second application of the same principle, still more exquisitely wrought up and only inferior in the comparative smallness of the canvass. The execution of *Knickerbocker* corresponds in felicity with the merit of the plan. The graphic distinctness, with which the three Dutch governors, whom nobody ever heard of before, are made to pass before us, each endowed with his appropriate intellectual, moral, and personal habits and qualities, is quite admirable; and the political satire is conveyed with great effect, and at the same time in a very fine and delicate manner, through the medium of these remote characters of the old world. There are some ineffectual attempts at wit in particular passages, and here and there a little indelicacy, which is the more objectionable, as it is inconsistent with the plan of the mock heroic, and in place, if admitted at all, only in the *travestie.* There is also a somewhat uncouth display of commonplace historical learning in the first book, where the author, while in the act of ridiculing pedantry, as he supposes it to be exemplified in the person of the worthy "Diedrich," betrays, we fear, a slight shade of the same quality in himself. But notwithstanding these blemishes, which are indeed so trifling, that we are almost ashamed to have mentioned them, the execution of the *History of New York* is in the main completely successful. If we were called on to give a preference to any one of our author's productions over all the rest, we should with little hesitation assign the palm to this.

These, with some smaller pieces to which we shall briefly advert hereafter, are all the works, which were published by Mr. Irving before his departure for Europe, and which belong to what may be called his first manner. Soon after their appearance, he visited England, where, and in other parts of Europe, he has resided ever since; and we heard nothing of him for several years, until at length he brought out the *Sketch Book,* which first made him known to the literary world abroad. In the long interval which had elapsed, since the appearance of his former productions, a "change had come over the spirit of his dream." Advancing years had probably a little moderated the exuberant flow of his youthful spirits, and the natural effect of time had, we fear, been increased by other causes; if it be true, as we have reason to suppose, that our amiable countryman had in the interim taken some lessons in the school of that "rugged nurse of virtue," so beautifully celebrated by Gray, who has in all ages been but too much accustomed to extend the benefit of her tuition to the votaries of polite learning. Whether under the influence of these causes, aided perhaps by the wholesome terror, which an American candidate for European favor might be expected to feel of the iron rod of the ruling critics, or for whatever other reason, certain it is, that the genius of Mr. Irving appeared to be a little rebuked at this his second apparition, and spoke in a partially subdued tone. The characteristics of the **Sketch Book** are essentially the same with those of the preceding works; but, with somewhat more polish and elegance, it has somewhat less vivacity, freshness, and power. This difference constitutes the distinction between Mr. Irving's first and second manner, the latter of which is preserved in all his subsequent publications, excepting the one now immediately before us. Of these two manners the one or the other may perhaps be preferred by different readers, according to their different tastes. We incline ourselves to the former, conceiving that spirit and vigor are the highest qualities of style, and that the loss of any merit of this description is but poorly compensated by a little additional finish. The change would have been however of less importance, had it appeared only in the language, but it is also displayed in the substance of the second series of publications; and it is here particularly, that we discover what we deem the unpropitious influence of a residence abroad on our author's talent. Not only is his language less free and sparkling, but the reach of his inventive power seems to be reduced. The Crayons and Bracebridges, including Master Simon, are Sketches indeed, and in water colors, compared with the living roaring group of Cockloft Hall; and although we find occasional returns of the author's best manner in **"The Stout Gentleman,"** **"Rip Van Winkle," "Sleepy Hollow," "The Money-diggers,"** and so forth, the rich material employed in these pieces is not, as before, the staple of the work, but a passing refreshment, that serves excellently well to remind us of what we wanted, but from the smallness of its quantity rather awakens than satisfies the appetite.

As it is difficult or rather impossible to suppose any actual diminution of power in the author, we must take for granted, that the difference in question is owing to the change in the general character of his subject. Humor and satire are, as we said before, evidently his *forte* and these compose the substance of the preceding works. There is but little attempt at the pathos in **Salmagundi,** and none in **Knickerbocker.** The subjects of satire are principally the abuses of government and the follies of leading characters and classes; and hence these works, though light in form, have an elevated object, which gives them dignity and solid value. Looking at them in a literary point of view, the circumstance of writing upon subjects actually before his eyes gives his pictures the truth to nature, which is the chief element of all excellence in art. Had the author proceeded on the same plan in his latter publications, he would have taken for his subject the abuses of government and the follies of leading classes and characters, as exemplified in the old countries. This again would have opened a field for the exercise of his peculiar talent, still more rich and various than the former one. Into this, however, whether from a terror of criticism, a wish to conciliate all parties alike, a natural modesty, a want of acquaintance with foreign manners and institutions, or for whatever reason, he did not choose to enter. Indeed the task of satirizing the manners and institutions of a country, in which one is at the time residing as a guest, is so ungracious, that we

can neither wonder nor regret, that Mr. Irving should have shrunk from it with instinctive disgust. It is nevertheless certain, that the subjects alluded to are the best, indeed almost the only good ones, for lively and pungent satire; and that in voluntarily resigning them, our author was compelled to deprive himself almost wholly of the use of his favorite and most efficient instrument. He still, it is true, exercises it with no little skill and success, upon subjects afforded by the fund of vice and folly common to all nations, as in the story of the Lambs and the Trotters, but we think with less effect, than when following his original instinct, and laughing *con amore* at the peculiar foibles of his own dear countrymen. Conscious probably that the field for satire, which he felt himself at liberty to explore, was less rich and productive than he could have wished, he calls in the aid of the pathetic and sentimental; in which departments, though, as we have said before, occasionally successful, he is seldom eminently so,—seldom exhibits the bright, sharp, true expression of nature, which we see in his best comic pictures. In other portions of these works, such as the whole description of Bracebridge Hall, as it appears in the **Sketch Book,** and the work of that name, the tone wavers between the sentimental and the comic, and we hardly know whether the author meant to ridicule or eulogize the manners he describes; which, however, are in either case evidently manners of his own creation, having no prototype in this or any other period of English history. Bracebridge Hall with its Christmas sports and its Rookery, its antiquarian Squire, and its Master Simon, is as much a castle of fairy land, as the one in which the Fata Morgana held entranced for six hundred years the redoubtable champion of Denmark. The British country squire is now, as he ever was, and probably ever will be, either a fox-hunter or a politician. Western and Allworthy are the only two varieties of the species; and the squire of Mr. Irving, with his indifference to politics, and his taste for black-letter lore, is as completely a fancy-piece, as the Centaurs and Harpies of the ancient poets. These castles in Spain occupy a considerable portion of the second series of works; and we really cannot but wonder how Mr. Irving, generally so just and acute an observer of nature, should have failed so completely in seizing the true aspect of rural life in England, or why, if he saw it as it is, he should have given us an unreal mockery of it instead of a correct picture. It is refreshing and delightful to find how, under all the disadvantages of writing on domestic subjects in a foreign land, he recovers his wonted power, and disports himself with his pristine grace and sprightliness, the moment that he lays the scene of his fable at home. No sooner does he catch a glimpse of the venerable Kaatskill, lifting his shaggy head over his white ruff of ambient clouds, and frowning on the glorious Hudson as it rolls below; no sooner do the antique gable-roofed domes of the Manhattoes, and Albany, and the classic shades of Communipaw rise upon his fancy, than "his foot is on his native heath and his name is M'Gregor." When we think of this, although we rejoice that Mr. Irving has been able, as he might not otherwise have been, to levy a large and liberal golden contribution from the superfluity of the mother country, this being, as it were, a spoiling of the

Egyptians, we sometimes regret, for his own fame, that he ever left America. There was a fund of truth, as well as ill nature, in the remark of one of the paltry, scandal-mongering novelists of the day, that Mr. Irving would have done better to stay at home, and pass his life among the beavers.

We have stated above, that the sentiment, which probably induced Mr. Irving to refrain from exercising his satirical talent upon the institutions and public characters of Great Britain, was a natural and highly laudable one; but we cannot conscientiously speak with the same approbation of his apparent disposition to represent the British aristocracy under a favorable point of view, as compared with the other classes of the people. If this representation were true, we should not object to it, although the sort of complacency, with which it is put forward, would still, in a foreigner and a republican, be somewhat ungraceful. But the worst of it is, that it is obviously and notoriously the reverse of the truth. Let us take as an example the account given in the *Sketch Book* of the author's attendance on public worship at a village church, where he met with the family of a nobleman and that of a wealthy merchant. The former, especially the young men and women, were all attention, candor, simplicity, and true moral dignity; the latter all bad taste, affectation, and vulgarity. Now every one, who has seen anything of Europe, knows perfectly well, and Mr. Irving certainly by this time, whatever he may have done when he wrote the *Sketch Book,* better than any body, that if there be a class of persons in that part of the world, who as a class may be said to be more deficient than any other in simplicity, candor, and a correct notion of true moral dignity, it is precisely this very British aristocracy, especially in its younger branches, to which our author attributes these virtues. . . .

While we have felt it a duty to point out this error in the tone and spirit of Mr. Irving's later works, we must add, that we do not, as some have done, attribute it to any hankering in him after the aristocratic institutions and habits of Europe. We acquit him entirely, as we have said before, of political heresy; and without supposing him to be deeply versed in the theory of government, we have no doubt that he is strongly and sincerely attached to the republican institutions and forms established in his country. Neither do we believe, that he was influenced in making this representation, by an interested wish to conciliate the British aristocracy, for the purpose of obtaining their patronage as a writer, or admission into their circles as a gentleman. We have too high an opinion of Mr. Irving's independence, delicacy, and elevation of mind, to suspect him for a moment of such baseness. We think it probable, that he wrote the parts of his work to which we now allude, under the influence of an illusion, resulting naturally from his former situation and literary habits. Without having studied the subject of government very deeply in the abstract, or possessing probably any very precise general notions respecting it, he was led by the original bent of his mind and his local and social position, to employ himself, for several years, in ridiculing the abuses of popular institutions, and

the peculiar follies and weaknesses of republican statesman. Thus far he kept himself within the line of truth and nature; for popular governments, however valuable, certainly have their defects, and republican statesmen, like all other mortals, their besetting sins and characteristic foibles. Now, although it does by no means follow from this, that monarchy is a perfect system, or an established aristocracy *ex officio* a corps of Lord Orvilles and Sir Charles Grandisons, it was perhaps not unnatural, that Mr. Irving, habitually gathering his impressions more from impulse and feeling than argument, should, by constantly looking at the ridiculous features of one form, be led to take up a too flattering idea of the other. Some such mental operation as this appears to have been the source of the illusion under which, as we conceive, he was at one time laboring; and when he wrote the *Sketch Book,* where the error in question is most apparent, he probably had not had much opportunity to bring his ideal picture to the test of comparison with real life, for it was not, we believe, until he had acquired a high reputation in England, by the publication of this work, that he frequented very intimately the circles of the British aristocracy. We have reason to suppose that he has since reformed his theory on this subject, and we mention the fact with pleasure, as a proof that the opportunities he has had for actual observation, have not been lost upon his naturally acute and sagacious, as well as sensitive mind.

Having thus cleared our consciences (we trust without doing injustice to our author) by pointing out certain particulars, in which we consider his European manner inferior to his American one, we return with pleasure to the remark we made before, that the former has somewhat more of elegance and polish than the latter; that the characteristics of both are (with the deductions we have specified) substantially the same; that all his productions are among the most agreeable and attractive, as they certainly have been among the most popular of the time; that they do the highest honor to himself and through him to his country; and that he has already secured and will permanently maintain, in our literary annals, the brilliant position of the harbinger and founder of the American school of polite learning.

We come now to the *History of the Life and Voyages of Columbus,* which has furnished the immediate subject and occasion of the present article. This work differs essentially in manner, as we have already said, from any of the preceding. It exemplifies on a larger scale, and in a more complete and finished way, the plan of the short biographical sketches, which the author published before his departure for Europe, principally of contemporary officers of the navy. We shall first endeavor to ascertain the class of historical writing to which it belongs, and then make a few remarks upon the merit of the execution and the general value of the work.

The great division of this department of literature, is into the two classes of philosophical and purely narrative history. They are not, it is true, separated by a very strict line, but on the contrary run into each other, each possessing to a certain extent the peculiar characteristics of both; but the distinction is nevertheless real, and whenever a writer has talent enough to give his work a marked character, it is evident at once, to which of the two classes it belongs. The object of philosophical history is to set forth by a record of real events, the general principles, which regulate the march of political affairs; that of purely narrative history, to give a correct and lively picture of the same events, as they pass before the eye of the world, but with little or no reference to their causes or effects. . . .

Mr. Irving's present work, if technically classed according to the general principles just stated, belongs to the lower species of history, and is so described by himself in his preface. "In the execution of this work," he remarks, "I have avoided indulging in mere speculations or general reflections, excepting such as naturally arose out of the subject, preferring to give a minute and circumstantial narrative, omitting no particular that appeared characteristic of the persons, the events, or the times; and endeavoring to place every fact under such a point of view, that the reader might perceive its merits, and draw his own maxims and conclusions." The omission of all general speculation is indeed a good deal more complete than this preliminary declaration would have necessarily led us to suppose it, since the exception of "such reflections as naturally arise out of the subject" would admit almost any degree of latitude in this respect. In point of fact, there is no political speculation whatever, the very few reflections that are interspersed being on matters of ordinary private morality. In giving this color to his work, Mr. Irving doubtless followed instinctively the natural bent of his genius, which does not incline him, as we have repeatedly observed, to philosophical researches; but he has thereby produced a much more valuable literary monument, than with his peculiar taste and talent, he could have done in a different way. In estimating the positive worth of particular works, we must take into view the merit of the execution, as well as the dignity of the class to which they belong; and if the latter be, in the present instance, of a secondary order (though still secondary only as compared with the very highest and most glorious exercises of intellect), yet such have been the good taste and felicity of our author, in the selection of his subject; such his diligence, research, and perseverance in collecting and employing his materials; and such his care in giving the highest finish and perfection to the style; that he has been able to bring out a work, which will rank with the very best histories of any age or nation, which will take a permanent place in the classical literature of the language, which is, in fact, one of the most agreeable, instructive, and really valuable productions to be met with any where, and one that, as we remarked above, does, on the whole, more honor to the learning of our country, than any previous work written on this side of the Atlantic.

For the particular kind of historical writing, in which Mr. Irving is fitted to labor and to excel, the *Life of Columbus* is undoubtedly one of the best, perhaps we might say without the fear of mistake, the very best subject afforded by the annals of the world. While his discoveries possess the importance belonging to political events of the first magnitude, the generous elevation of his mind, the various fortunes that chequered his course, and the singularity, the *uniquity* rather, if we may be allowed to coin a word, of his achievements, throw a sort of poetical and romantic coloring over his adventures, and render him of all others the fittest hero for a work of this description; which, as we have shown above, is essentially a poem. The only objection, that could possibly be made to the choice of the subject, would be, that it was before exhausted; and this has in fact been said, by some of the newspaper critics of the mother country. The assertion is however quite groundless. Before the publication of the work before us, there was no satisfactory account of Columbus in any language. The one given by his son is, as is well known, merely a brief and imperfect sketch; and the portion of Robertson's *America* which is devoted to him, though as large as it could be with propriety, considering the author's plan, did not allow a detailed and accurate investigation of the events of his life. Into this and other general histories, Columbus enters partially as one of the leading personages of the age, and is treated in connexion with the rest; but the singular splendor and prodigious permanent importance of his actions, as well as the moral grandeur and sublimity of his character, entitled him fully to the honor of a separate and detailed biography. How much finer and loftier a subject is he, than his contemporary Charles the Fifth, who has yet furnished a theme for one of the best histories in the language! The materials, printed and manuscript, were ample, but not accessible in their full extent, excepting to a person resident, for the time, in the capital of Spain. We consider it therefore as a singularly fortunate circumstance, that Mr. Irving should have been led, in the course of his pilgrimage abroad, to visit this, on some accounts, unattractive part of Europe. Thus favorably situated, and possessed of all the talent and industry necessary for the purpose, he has at length filled up the void, that before existed, in this respect, in the literature of the world, and produced a work, which will fully satisfy the public, and supersede the necessity of any future labors in the same field. While we venture to predict that the adventures of Columbus will hereafter be read only in the work of Mr. Irving, we cannot but think it a beautiful coincidence, that the task of duly celebrating the achievements of the discoverer of our continent, should have been reserved for one of its inhabitants; and that the earliest professed author of first-rate talent, who appeared among us, should have devoted one of his most important and finished works to this pious purpose. "Such honor Ilion to her hero paid, / And peaceful slept the mighty Hector's shade."

In treating this happy and splendid subject, Mr. Irving has brought out the full force of his genius as far as a just regard for the principles of historical writing would admit. This kind of history, although it belongs essentially to the department of poetry, does not of course afford any room for the display of the creative power in the invention of facts or characters; but, in this case, the real facts and characters far surpass in brilliancy any possible creation of mere fancy, and in the other requisites of fine poetry, a judicious selection and disposition of the materials, a correct, striking, and discriminating picture of the different personages, a just and elevated tone of moral feeling, and above all, the charm of an elegant, perspicuous, and flowing style, Mr. Irving leaves us nothing to desire, and with all, who can look beyond mere forms and names into the substance of things, sustains his right, which he had before established, to the fame of a real poet. To say that this work is superior to any professed poem, that has yet been published, on the life of Columbus, would be giving it but poor praise; since the subject, although attempted by bards of no slight pretensions, has not yet been treated in verse with eminent success. We would go farther than this, and express the opinion, that Mr. Irving's production may be justly ranked with the fine narrative or epic poems of the highest reputation. A polished and civilized age may well be supposed to prefer, especially in a long composition, the delicate melody of flowing prose, setting forth a spirited and elegant picture of actual life, to the "specious wonders" of Olympus or fairy land, expressed in artificial measures, strains and subjects that seem more naturally adapted to a yet unformed, than to a mature and perfect taste. Hence a fine history and a fine novel may perhaps with propriety be viewed as the greater and lesser epic (to use the technical terms) of a cultivated period, when verse is better reserved for short poems accompanied by music. But however this may be, and with whatever class of compositions we may rank the work before us, its execution entirely corresponds, as we have said before, with the beauty of the subject, and leaves of course but little room for the labor of the critic. The interest of the narrative is completely sustained from the beginning to the conclusion, and is equal throughout, for any mature mind, to that of the best romance. Instinctively pursuing the bent of his genius, the author has everywhere brought out into full relief the most poetical features of the story. He dwells, for instance, with peculiar pleasure on the golden age of innocence and happiness, that reigned among the natives of Haiti before the arrival of the Spaniards. The careless and luxurious indulgence, in which they passed their peaceful hours beneath "the odorous shade of their boundless forests," under the amiable sway of a beautiful Queen, who is represented as charming their leisure with her own sweet poetry, seems to realize the notion of an earthly elysium; and if there be, as there probably is, some little exaggeration in the coloring of the picture, it must be viewed as a natural effect of the just indignation and horror, with which we contemplate the devilish malice which afterwards carried death and destruction through these bowers of simple bliss. The two leading personages are happily contrasted, not by labored parallels, but indirectly by the mere progress of the story. The towering sublimity and bold creative genius of the Admiral; the sagacity, activity, and dauntless courage of the Adelantado; the faithful and tender attachment with which they stood by each other, through a long life of labor, danger, and suffering; these are moral traits, that furnish out another picture, not less beautiful and even more edifying, than that of the Indian Paradise.

We are grateful to Mr. Irving, for bringing particularly into view the high religious feeling, which uniformly governed the mind of Columbus, which led him to consider himself as an agent, expressly selected by Providence for the accomplishment of great and glorious objects,—and how, but by a poor quibble upon words, can we refuse him that character?—which induced him finally to look forward to the recovery of the Holy Sepulchre, as the last labor of his life, to be undertaken after the complete accomplishment of all his projects in the New World. If there be any error in the passages, which treat of this particular, it consists in underrating the merit of this conception of Columbus, which appears to be viewed by Mr. Irving as the effect of an amiable, but somewhat visionary and mistaken enthusiasm. . . .

It would give us pleasure to expatiate at greater length upon the merit of the beautiful and valuable work before us; but we perceive that we have reached the proper limit of an article, and must here close our remarks. We cannot however refrain from expressing our satisfaction, at the very favorable manner with which Mr. Irving's *Life of Columbus* compares with one or two works of a similar kind, that were published about the same time by the best writers of the mother country. The *Life of Napoleon* by Sir Walter Scott, and the *Life of Sheridan* by Moore, particularly the former, resemble it so nearly in plan and form, that, coming out, as they all did, about the same time, they exhibit in a manner a trial of skill between three of the most elegant writers of the day. We feel a good deal of pride as Americans in adding, that our countryman appears to have retired from this dangerous contest with a very decided advantage, we think we might say a complete victory, over both his competitors. We mean not to deprive these illustrious transatlantic bards of any fame, to which they may be justly entitled, by the productions in question; nor do we mean to represent Mr. Irving's general reputation as at present superior or equal to theirs. We simply state the fact as it is, considering it to be one highly honorable to our countryman and our country. We shall even go farther, being in a patriotic vein, and while we freely admit that Mr. Irving's fame is and ought to be at present inferior to that of the two British poets abovementioned, we shall take the liberty of adding, that we are not quite sure whether it will always remain so. Moore and Scott have already done their best, and from the character of their productions for some years past, as compared with those of earlier date, it is evident that they will not hereafter excel or perhaps equal their past efforts. Mr. Irving's talent seems to us, on the contrary, to be in a state of progress; for although his second manner be, as we think, inferior, on the whole, to his first, the difference is not, as we have already expressly stated, owing to any decay of genius, but to an unfavorable change of scene and subject; and in this first specimen of a *third* series of publications, we recognise, though under a somewhat grayer form, a development of power superior to that which is displayed by any of the preceding ones, even should the *History of New York* as a bold original creation, be considered as belonging to a higher class of writings. We also recognise in the selection of the subject, the persevering industry with which the work has been executed, and the high tone of moral feeling that runs through the whole of it, the symptoms of a noble spirit, on which the intoxicating cup of public applause acts as a stimulant rather than an opiate. Mr. Irving is still in the vigor of life and health; and when we see him advancing in his course in this way, with renovated courage and redoubled talent at an age when too many hearts begin to wax prematurely faint, we are induced to anticipate the happiest results from his future labors; and are far from being certain, as we said above, that he may not in the end eclipse the most illustrious of his present contemporaries and rivals. We rejoice to find, from the selection of the subject of the work now before us, that though long a wanderer, his thoughts are still bent on the land of his birth. Although we wish not to hasten his return before the period when he shall himself deem it expedient, we indulge the hope that he will sooner or later fix his residence among us, and can assure him that whenever he may think proper to do so, he will be welcomed by his countrymen as a well deserving citizen and a public benefactor. When he shall be seated again upon his native soil, among his beavers, if Mr. D'Israeli pleases, when he shall again apply to those subjects of strictly native origin, in which his genius seems to take most delight, the force of his mature talent, and the lights of his long and varied experience, we think we may expect with reason a *fourth* series of publications, that shall surpass in value all the preceding ones, including even that, which he has now so honorably opened with the work before us.

Ladies' Repository (essay date 1848)

SOURCE: "Irving as a Writer," *Ladies' Repository,* Vol. 8, July, 1848, pp. 217-20.

[*In the following essay, the critic praises Irving as a writer of the highest quality, forever to be remembered and revered.*]

The name of Washington Irving will be for ever associated with American literature. He has attained the very highest eminence as a writer. Both in England and the United States his works have been universally read with pleasure. Perhaps they have been more generally admired, than the production of any living author on this side of the Atlantic. They are not confined to any class of readers. To nearly every mental condition, they have proved equally acceptable. Though dealing somewhat in fiction, it is evident that he employs it only as the garb in which he arrays real characters. He gives us lively sketches of human nature, concealing only dates, names, and places. But all these he doubtless has, with more or less distinctness, in his own view while writing. It is for this reason, principally, that the most serious minds have ever been in the habit of perusing even his more playful compositions.

Mr. Irving is not a novelist, as he is regarded by those not personally acquainted with his writings. He has not written a single novel. In this direction, he is merely a writer of stories, the facts for which are taken either from history, or from occurrences within the range of his own experience and observation. His first works were more nearly allied to fiction than his later ones. As his mind became more mature, and his moral feelings more settled, he turned his attention more exclusively to topics of serious import; and his success in sober composition is, after all, his best pledge of immortality.

Washington Irving is one of our very best historians. His *Life of Christopher Columbus* is equal to any thing of its kind ever written. It was never surpassed by the ablest writers of the classic ages. The celebrated *Lives of Plutarch* are worthy of no comparison, in my humble judgment, with this luminous biography. *The Agricola of Tacitus,* perhaps the most finished specimen of the species of composition, which we have received from antiquity, is, in many respects, meagre by the side of it. Large as is the work of Irving, few persons have ever taken it up, and laid it by again, for want of interest in its style and subject. No tasteful reader can lay it down, if he has leisure, without reading every page of it. So admirable is the tact, and so charming the style of the biographer, that, though at about midway of the work you perceive every thing that is coming, you read on with unabated pleasure. It is the only work I have ever seen, in which the notes, even to the last one of them, are equally captivating with the text they illustrate. In every respect, the *Life of Columbus* is a classical production, and, unless accidentally destroyed, will last as long as the English language.

Had Mr. Irving turned his attention more to historical subjects, he might have made himself a fame perhaps superior to that of Hume and Gibbon. Though not now so learned as the latter, nor so profound as the former, of these historians, in what he has attempted he has manifested equal capacity in every variety of talent. His *Conquest of Granada,* though evidently the work of his idle hours, and not more than a romantic history at best, exhibits fully enough his diligence in searching records and authorities, and his wonderful powers of historical description. His battle scenes are even more vivid than those of Julius Caesar. Let him have studied as laboriously as the author of the *Decline and Fall of the Roman Empire,* and he would probably have excelled him in any great work which he might have undertaken. His discrimination was not surpassed by that of the great infidel. His knowledge of human nature is decidedly more perfect. The simplicity of his diction forms a striking contrast to the grandiloquence of Gibbon. But more than all, his heart fits him, in every way, to excel that author in every species of composition. There is something peculiarly impressive in the moral character of Irving. No one need inquire what it is. It is found on almost every one of his pages. The great law of his being is human kindness. His large benevolence is ever conspicuous. He must be one of the most amiable men living. His very satire is merciful. He only shows you what he could do, were he not so unboundedly benevolent. He draws his bow upon you, and you acknowledge him a

skillful archer; but when the arrow hits you, you find he
was only playing. The point and the barb are nothing but a
feather. But the mercy of the satire makes you feel the
more humble. If you are really guilty, you have the uncomfortable consciousness of owing your life to his clem-
ency.

Mr. Irving is said to be a very quiet, contemplative man.
He spends much of his time in reading and meditation. It
is also reported of him, that he makes long rambles through
town and country, or did make them in his younger days,
for the only purpose of observing men and things, and repeating his thoughts by himself and at his leisure. This
love of solitude has given him a fine vein of sentiment.
His humanity is one of the most apparent of his mental
qualities; and it is derived from the same practice of reflection. Had he been exclusively a historian, he never
could have passed over, as others do, the bloody horrors
of a battle-field, by simply giving us a description of the
carnage. As the finishing stroke to every such bloody picture, he would have made you feel most sensibly "Man's
inhumanity to man." He would have forced conviction to
the most obdurate mind, that war is the foulest work of
mortals.

In his *Life of Columbus* he shows himself everywhere the
poor Indians' friend. When they are mercilessly butchered
by the Spaniard, with what pathos he pleads their cause!
When the reparminientos, or slavery system, was about to
be adopted, and the defenseless native turned loose to the
goading ambition of wicked men, with what sincerity and
spirit he rebukes the oppressors, though the heroes of his
work! But his humanity is equally evident in smaller
things. What reader of his can have forgotten the sensibility he manifested in the famous prairie hunting scene? His
company had been all day pursuing buffaloes on one of
the immense prairies of the west. The real sportsmen had
killed several in different parts of the field, while he had
been riding more to witness the sport of others, than to derive any for himself. But in the latter part of the day,
when, probably, his sensibilities had become rather blunted
by fatigue, he resolved to join in earnest in the chase. He
singled him out an object worthy of his aim. It was a
prime, large buffalo, and of the most perfect form. He put
spurs to his horse, and soon came within shooting distance
of his game. The fatal ball was fired, and lo! the noble
animal, in all his pride and glory, fell a dying victim at his
feet. Does the sportsman now swell, and bluster, and call
his companions to help him enjoy the glory of his deed?
Nay; but, standing there alone, he looks on him—he pities
him; and from his own account we might believe that he
suffers more pain, than the bleeding animal by his side.
When he had seen him breathe his last, he would have
given the whole prairies, had it been his property, could he
have revived the fallen monarch, and sent him bounding in
joyous life and liberty over his native plains.

They mistake the character of Mr. Irving as a writer, who
suppose him writing merely for the amusement of his
readers. This is not true of him even in his lighter articles.

His most comical pieces have always a serious end in
view. In these you will find him holding up to ridicule
some hurtful or good-for-nothing prejudice in the public
mind; he is weeding out the noxious plants, which have
been growing for centuries in the human heart. And he has
certainly been very successful in this business. But he
stops not there. He also sows good seed to supply the
place of what he has rooted out; and I must believe that he
sometimes, perhaps I should say frequently, feels a warm
delight, in the consciousness of having done much to im-
plant the principles of morality and virtue in a soil not so
likely to be cultivated by other hands. Where the mere
philosopher would not be welcome, where the moralist, or
even the devout Christian, would scarcely find entrance,
his fascinating style gives him joyful admittance; and he
rarely departs without leaving a good influence behind
him.

There are two peculiar effects of Mr. Irving's writings,
which ought to be particularly stated. The first is the pure
philanthropy he breathes into your feelings. His benevolence is really contagious. Wherever you read him, he perfectly imbues you with it. Sit down and read his productions a single hour, especially his pathetic pieces, and you
will not only rise up a better man, but think better of your
fellow creatures. You will compassionate the weak, sym-
pathize with the oppressed, and pity the sorrows of the
poor. The other trait in his works is not less happy in its
effects. It is the good tone he imparts to the domestic affections. Whenever he treats upon these subjects, he
touches, with almost a magic power, the family ties. Need
I name those inimitable pieces in the *Sketch Book,* **"the
Wife,"** and **"the Widow's Son"**? For the last fifteen years
I have never been able to read either of them, without
shedding such tears as do one good. It is hardly possible
for any person to peruse him frequently, without being a
more affectionate member of the domestic circle. Whether
a father, or mother, or brother, or sister, the reader acquires
a stronger, a purer, a holier attachment to family friends.
In this particular, Mr. Irving has spread the sweet influences of his good heart over all the families of the land.

The generosity of Mr. Irving is quite equal to his benevolence. Daily instances of this virtue are seen in his private
associations; but there are many, also, related of him in his
more public capacity. For a long time he had been intending to write a work on a topic connected with American
history. He had spent time and labor, and, doubtless,
money, in collecting books, manuscripts, and other sources
of information. Subsequently, learning that another gentleman—an unfortunate but gifted American author—had
chosen the same subject, Mr. Irving not only relinquished
his designs entirely to his competitor, but actually sent
him all the books and authorities he himself had collected
as a free-will offering of a good and noble heart to one
who needed and deserved the kindness.

So far as mere style is concerned, though comparatively a
minor consideration, Mr. Irving undeniably occupies the
very highest place. It has ever been a dispute among crit-

ics, whether he is not the best model of a writer now living. Some have placed him high above every writer in the English language. But it is difficult to compare him, in this respect, with most of his competitors. His diction is peculiar to himself, but only, perhaps, because other persons do not generally write quite so well. There is certainly nothing eccentric or affected in his compositions. He writes naturally, easily, smoothly along, as if it were no effort at all for him to compose. He is not so pompous as Gibbon, and writes less as if it were a trade. Burke is more pithy and sententious, but infinitely less beautiful and flowing. Burke sometimes fatigues his reader by gaudy and superfluous imagery. The sentences of Robert Hall are equally smooth and well turned; they are even more elevated and grand; but also more difficult, or rather less easy, to read. Mr. Hall's sentences are in general very lengthy, and slightly elaborate and complex, but never tangled or obscure. Mr. Irving writes with an easy, though not a readier, pen; and in his longest periods, you flow insensibly and without labor along the current of his thoughts, till he gives you liberty to pause.

Perhaps the best analogy lies between him and Mr. Addison as to style. They resemble each other more than any two writers in our language. Indeed, the question of superiority is, by many, reduced, in the final issue, to these two. It would be difficult for any person to decide which author, taken in all respects, he would prefer. So far as fancy, imagination, good taste, and graphic power are concerned, it would require a nice balance to determine which has the greater merit. There is one quality of a good writer, however, in which Mr. Irving, I think, clearly surpasses his great rival—a profound and critical knowledge of the etymology and definition of words. Mr. Addison has been accused, though I think unjustly, of writing as if he were doubtful precisely what word to employ. This is never so much as suspected in Mr. Irving. He always has the very word, generally the only word, capable of giving full expression to his thoughts, and yet glides along apparently without effort. There is another defect which critics have discovered in Mr. Addison's best works. He is said to have frequently added high-sounding but feeble expletives to his sentences, after the sense had been made complete, merely to give his period a round full close. If this be true, Mr. Irving is decidedly his superior, for I will venture to affirm that no such sentence can be found in the whole compass of his productions. Perhaps this may seem a bold expression of opinion; but I will offer no other amendment to it, than that I have, at different times, sought whole hours for an instance without success.

Thus far I have compared Mr. Irving as a writer only with those of the English school. It would be hazardous to attempt to find a man, on this side of the Atlantic, whose best friends would not readily acknowledge his inferior in the use of a beautiful and graphic pen. Dr. Channing surpassed him in the power of multiplying himself, if I may say so, in his readers; but it was evidently not so natural and easy for that distinguished author to compose. Daniel Webster has no superior in the purity, strength, and trans-

parency of his style; his thoughts are sometimes perfect thunderbolts, and scathe and blast every thing opposed to them, by the mere majesty of their power; but as a writer, the great defender of the Constitution must yield the palm to him, whose amiable humility has perhaps never cast a wish, or carried a reverie, to the height occupied by the statesman. What elevation Mr. Prescott would have reached, had Providence spared the continued use of his sight, no one can tell; but the Conquest of Mexico, notwithstanding it was composed by a man, who could not see well enough to correct his own proof, is, after all, the only American work worthy of contending with the *Life of Columbus* for the prize.

One of the chief sources of Mr. Irving's superiority is his perfect self-possession while he is writing. Unpracticed writers, and even men who have written much without having improved by their experience, frequently, perhaps I should say generally, manifest an uneasiness of spirit, as if they were not satisfied unless they were doing wonders all the while. They come to their task in a perfect frenzy. They continue to work themselves up to a most unnatural and disgusting excitement, and then pounce upon their paper, as if they would snatch it, like an eagle, to the clouds. They leap through their sentences, like the live thunder, from crag to crag. They gleam, and hiss, and roar, as if an Alpine tempest were about to break over your head. If they happen to think of any Greek or Latin author, while they are suffering under this chaos of passion, they will crowd a dozen classical allusions into a single paragraph, and quote twenty verses of Pagan poetry to a page. Fearful lest they have not done much in what they have already written, in order to redeem themselves in what remains, they dash, and foam, and thunder, more extravagantly as they proceed. Like ungifted speakers, from the beginning to the end of their performance, they never get fair possession of themselves; and, when all is over, they have only added another specimen to that already too numerous class of productions, whose single quality is their sound.

How differently from all this does Mr. Irving undertake his work! Without any effort, he writes his leading sentence. From this he proceeds naturally and smoothly along, as if it were the easiest thing in the world to write. As his subject grows in his own mind, he gives fuller and bolder expression to his thoughts. He seems to be in no hurry to strike his reader with any thing wonderful or new. He allows his theme to go on and make the development of itself. If it happen to touch on classical ground, it finds the writer perfectly at home. Without stopping to deluge you with quotations, he gives you one—but that one is a gem. If, in the progress of his work, an emotion is excited by any thing which his subject makes it necessary to say, he gives it a single stroke of his gifted pen, and it thrills to your very soul. He never quotes for the sake of quoting, nor to show off the extent and variety of his reading. Nor does he attempt to cover you up with roses; if a few flowers chance to be growing near his path, he weaves you a modest chaplet—but that blooms on your heart for ever. Nor is he incessantly making pictures, and pressing every ancient and modern dialect into service, in order to decorate them with all the gorgeousness of language. Dealing considerably in description, a variety of scenes must necessarily be crowded upon him on every page of his composition. But of these he is far from being prodigal. Instead of drawing out every one that occurs to him, he makes a choice selection. When one is chosen, wrought out, and finished, it throws its lustre all around him. His reader marks it with his pencil, or transfers it to his own imagination, to which it adds a splendor ever after.

But, on the other hand, Mr. Irving is not a timid, bashful, fastidious writer. He wears no straight-jacket on his intellectual faculties. With all his severity of taste, he is always free and easy. You see in him none of that finical nervousness, which trammels a writer's genius, and forbids his saying just what he thinks, and precisely as he thinks it. This is the natural consequence of his modesty. An ambitious writer, all the while goaded by the impulse of his ruling passion, is apt to be too careful—perhaps I should have said anxious—of the mere manner of his writing. As each sentence is written down, he looks back upon it to criticize its structure, when he ought to be pushing onward under the full and unchecked inspiration of his subject. Ambition, at least in a writer, is always weak and timid. The man loses his thoughts while he is looking after his periods. He ought to be himself lost, or nearly so, in the matter of which he is treating. His taste should be the only restraint upon him; and that should be reduced to such a habit, as to leave him quite unconscious of its influence. If, writing in this natural way, errors creep into his composition, they may be left for a future and critical recension.

There is a sort of sentimentalism, also, to which Mr. Irving is never subject. This consists, I suppose, in a writer's putting on more feeling than his ideas demand. To feel less than the truths advanced would justify, argues obduracy of mind; to feel more, whether in writing or in speaking, fanaticism, the concomitants of which are generally rant and bombast. When thought and feeling are exactly commensurate, when the one precisely tallies with the other, then you have words spoken fitly; and they are indeed "like apples of gold in pictures of silver." You rise from the perusal of a work thus written, neither hardened by contemplating great truths without emotion, nor softened to effeminacy by a continual conflict of boisterous and unmeaning passion. Sound thoughts have been passing down upon your soul, and they have left their own impression. You are a sounder, wiser, better, truer man yourself, by the influence of what you have been reading.

If the present age has produced the exact counterpart of our author, it is in the example of Mr. Dickens. In all this gentleman's productions, there is a constant tendency to over-drawing. His thoughts and feelings seem to be in a perpetual state of insurrection. Like a rake on the high road, he uses the lash too much; and his animal is in a continual perspiration. If his course happen to lie on a clean path, all goes merrily and smoothly onward; but whenever he falls into a rough passage, the dirt flies all around you. You are knocked, and thumped, and jerked, in this direction and in that, without the slightest mercy; and when the race is over, you need all the water he complained the want of in our taverns, not only to cleanse your person, but to cool your fever.

Such writers, to change the figure, seem to be somewhat suspicious of the bill of fare provided by them; and they are only shaking up their readers a little to favor their digestion. But it would be unjust to deny, that Mr. Dickens has written many pages which will forever form a part of the standard literature of our language; and, what is very much for any man's reputation as a writer, he has received the approbation—at least the qualified approbation—of Dr. Channing. But his style is generally too headlong to be commended.

In all respects Mr. Irving seems to stand first in this country as a writer. He has the singular merit of pleasing all classes equally. Those not prepared to admire the skill manifested in the select order of his language, and in the molding and turning of his periods, read him for the amusement gathered from the story. The fine flow of his sentences, his frequent and beautiful alliteration, the rich simplicity of his pictures, and the delightful splendor and genuineness of his emotions, charm other persons less captivated by his subjects. It seems to me that he surpasses all writers in one quality. His style evinces more real science, with less apparent labor, than that of any modern or ancient author.

Having given much merited praise, I will state almost my only objection to Mr. Irving. In nearly all that he has done, he has shown merely what he could do, had his subjects been better chosen. His *Sketch Book* and his *Columbus* are almost the only exceptions to this remark. In nearly all his other works, beautiful, charming, captivating as they are, a serious man feels all the while that he might have selected topics more worthy of his genius. It is true, there is next to nothing in all his writings to find fault with; his style is ever like its fountain, pure and splendid; he nowhere descends to vulgarity, even for a moment; and his morality is such as would become a minister at the altar. But, then, when we read such a man, the soul longs to see him soaring higher. We want to see him ranging in majesty through those fields, where such a spirit might meet with angels. We become almost anxious to witness the power of such a style as his on those sublime topics, which, in all ages, have formed the themes of those gifted minds, who have ever stood nearest to the bright purlieus of heaven. O, could the heart of Mr. Irving be touched by that live coal, which sanctified and hallowed the lips of the evangelical Isaiah, in what sweet and captivating splendor would Christianity appear on his classical and immortal pages!

But Mr. Irving is now advanced in years. The gray of age is sprinkled on the crown of his glory. He must soon descend from his lofty summit, and be buried in the dust with his fathers. Such a mind as his, so characterized by sense, so ripe in reflection, so just in perceptions on all other topics, has, undoubtedly, long since settled life's great question. When he goes, he will go with the blessings of his country upon him. Though his body may perish, and lie low in the sepulchre raised by his friends, his fame will survive; his sweet spirit, we trust, will ascend to its Author; and the sorrow of a nation, or rather of an age, will mingle its laments with the wail of the winds that sweep over his grave.

Jenifer S. Banks (essay date 1990)

SOURCE: "Washington Irving, the Nineteenth-Century American Bachelor" in *Critical Essays on Washington Irving,* edited by Ralph M. Aderman, G. K. Hall & Co., 1990, pp. 253-65.

[*In the following essay, Banks analyzes Irving's conflict between individual freedom and social responsibility as evidenced in his writings about women and his life.*]

The theme of growing up and accepting adult responsibility is central to a study of American literature; and relationships between men and women are a central element in this maturing, as such different critics as Leslie Fiedler and Judith Fetterley have shown. Washington Irving's **"Rip Van Winkle"** is often cited as a peculiarly American example of flight from this responsibility. Fetterley has noted that in fact Irving borrowed this story from German folklore and set it in an American scene; but among his most significant additions is the character of Dame Van Winkle, whom he presents as the cause of Rip Van Winkle's flight into the Catskill Mountains. She is an "obstacle to the achievement of the dream of pleasure. . . . Significantly, Irving's tale connects the image of woman with the birth of America as a nation and with the theme of growing up."[1] As the voice of duty and obligation, she most clearly exemplifies Irving's imaginative use of women as a focus of those elements in society he wished to escape. This image of the oppressive power of women and of men's flight from them—both literally and imaginatively—is just one manifestation of a larger and more pervasive issue concerning commitment present throughout Irving's life. Whether writing for publication or more personally in his correspondence, he reveals himself as a prototype of the American male struggling to reconcile the conflict between freedom and adult responsibility, independence and social obligation, fantasy and reality. Irving was clearly attracted to women; but whatever their surface appearance, most of his imaginative projections of women reflect some aspect of the repressiveness associated with Dame Van Winkle. Similarly, in real life, Irving's circumscribed relationships with women reflect his flight from commitment and adult responsibility. But if Irving was singularly ambivalent about women, his reactions to them also reflect many of the contradictions inherent in the attitudes dominating American society in the early nineteenth century. Through his images of women and his relationships with them, he reflects the contemporary struggle between the appeal of the old ordered and hierarchical society and the call of the new republican egalitarianism, between the security of established institutions and the independence of the new American Adam.

Irving's lifelong ambivalence toward women is manifested in both his personal letters and his published writings in an unresolved tension between fantasy and reality. There can be no doubt that Irving was a lady's man. Whether at nineteen boasting to his friend Amos Eaton that he could "never be in company with a fine girl half an hour without falling in love,"[2] or some forty years later in Madrid playing "the old beau to a young belle [Cuban singer Leocadia Zamora]," (6 December 1844, 3:843), or relishing the memory of how beautiful a certain lovely widow, Mrs. Ellis, had once appeared at a New York ball (10 February 1844, 2:679), he clearly enjoyed this concept of himself. He preferred, however, to remain an uncommitted observer, maintaining carefully circumscribed relationships with women—usually considerably younger than he or "safely" married. Irving's lifelong struggle between the appeal and the threat of women, between fantasy and his sense of reality, is reflected in his confidence to his close friend, Prince Dmitri Ivanovitch Dolgorouki, "Heavens! what power women would have over us if they knew how to Sustain the attractions which nature had bestowed upon them, and which we are so ready to assist by our imaginations" (22 January 1828, 2:265). The same ambivalence is implicit in his persona Geoffrey Crayon's observation in **"Wives"**: "It is appalling to those who have not adventured into the holy state, to see how soon the flame of romantic love burns out . . . in matrimony. . . . Men are always doomed to be duped, not so much by the arts of the sex, as by their own imaginations. They are always wooing goddesses, and marrying mortals."[3] Even as he grew fearful of being lonely in his old age, Irving's observations often included a wistfulness tinged with a certain cynicism. Reviewing his life in his late fifties, Irving confided to his niece Sarah Storrow, "God knows I have no great idea of bachelor hood, and am not one of the fraternity through choice—but providence has some how or other thwarted the warm wishes of my heart and the tendencies of my nature in those earlier seasons of life when tender and happy unions are made; and has protected me in those more advanced periods when matrimonial unions are apt to be unsuited or ungenial. . . ." (12 December 1842, 3:437).

Some have argued that at twenty-five he was permanently scarred by the tragic death of his first real love, Matilda Hoffman, and then kept running away from that pain. But, in a fifteen-year retrospective letter to Mrs. Amelia Foster, Irving revealed that his flight was based on more complex motives than grief alone. His relationship with her epitomizes the conflict between the ideals of social responsibility and individual freedom that influenced his relationships throughout his life. He described his possible child-bride, who was only seventeen when she died, as "a timid, shy, silent little being" with a "mantling modesty . . . intuitive rectitude of mind . . . native delicacy . . . exquisite propriety in thought, word & action" which he idolized. "I felt at times rebuked by her superior delicacy & purity and as if I were a coarse unworthy being in comparison" (April-May 1823, 1:738-39). However, if the idealized Matilda seemed unattainable as a paragon of virtue, the real-life Matilda forced him to face the harsh reality of the financial liability of a wife. In the same letter he explained that on his return from his European Grand Tour he had tried to devote himself to the study of law under Josiah Ogden Hoffman, who had promised him a partnership in his firm and his daughter in marriage if he could succeed in the profession. Irving had recognized that law "in America is the path to honour and preferment—to every thing that is distinguished in public life" (1:739), but he confessed that he had been unable to surmount his "insuperable repugnance" to it. "I had gone on blindly, like a boy in Love, but now I began to open my eyes and be miserable. I had nothing in purse nor in expectation. . . . I was in a wretched state of doubt and self distrust . . . [and] was secretly writing, hoping it would give me reputation and gain me Some public appointment" (1:739-40). Thus he faced apparently irreconcilable choices: marriage and the financial responsibilities of a dutiful husband, or freedom to write. Before he could "qualify" as a husband, Matilda died, and Irving described himself as drifting through New York society "without aim or object, at the mercy of every breeze; my heart wanted anchorage" (1:741). Because he could not escape from his own sense of unworthiness and inadequacy nor from the social pressure to succeed in some "useful and honourable application," Irving fled to England and Europe (1:742).

Irving spent almost half of his adult life in England and Europe, and his correspondence reveals that his long absences from home reflect his particular accommodations to the conflicting ideals in America of his day. His expatriation was determined in part by his pursuit of the middle-class dream of social advancement and financial security, in part by his more idiosyncratic pursuit of freedom, in part by his desire to serve as a literary and a political ambassador for America, and in part to avoid routine jobs. His decision to become a *professional* writer rather than to commit himself to a respected profession was a compromise he made with his society's materialistic definition of the self-made man and success.

Both the evolution and the content of *The Sketch Book* represent the coming together of fact and fiction in Irving's life, and they reflect his struggle with the conflicts among financial security, social status, and freedom. Irving initially submitted to family pressure and tried to help his brother Peter with the family business in Liverpool. He hated it; but because he was not immune to the value system that accorded a certain status to wealth and business acumen, he was devastated when they had to declare bankruptcy. "This was vile and sordid and humiliated me to the dust. . . . I felt cast down—abased—I had lost my *cast*— . . . I shut myself up from society—and would See no one." Feeling totally bereft of any social status, he then determined to avoid all financially secure but restrictive jobs by trying to "reinstate [himself] in the world's thoughts" through his writing. He therefore rejected both a lucrative clerkship in the navy that his brother William secured for him in America and an editorship that Walter Scott offered him in Edinburgh. In this way he produced *The Sketch Book* (April-May 1823, 1:742-43).

The popularity of both *The Sketch Book* and *Bracebridge Hall* confirms how successfully Irving catered to the dominant taste of his day. Through the persona of Crayon, a self-described wanderer and explorer since childhood, he appealed both to the American ideal of the individual who makes his own way alone and to the current interest in the romance of the past. But, even though Irving was writing for the market, the biographical facts reveal he was also pursuing his own conflicting ideals—a certain status in and freedom from society. Perhaps unintentionally Irving drew attention to the strong escapist dimension behind his apparently heroic decision to commit himself to being an author. In the "Preface" to the revised edition of *The Sketch Book* he recalled his real-life letter rejecting Scott's offer of the editorship: "My whole course of life has been desultory and I am unfitted for any periodically recurring task, or any stipulated labour of body or mind. . . . I shall occasionally shift my residence, and trust to the excitement of various scenes & objects to furnish me with materials" (20 November 1819, 1:570). In fiction he celebrated this free spirit in **"The Author's Account of Himself"** by immersing Crayon in the romance of the past and in "the charms of storied and poetical association" of Europe. He longed "to escape . . . from the commonplace realities of the present, and lose [himself] among the shadowy grandeurs of the past."[4] The autobiographical parallel with Rip Van Winkle becomes clearer.

In many ways Irving's life reflected that of the American male whom Fiedler described as "on the run—anywhere—to avoid 'civilization' which is to say the confrontation of a man and a woman which leads to the fall to sex, marriage and responsibility."[5] Irving's desire to escape civilization was based on a complex of related motives that incorporated but were larger than the fear of "confronting" a woman. She was an important part but only a part of the whole "civilization" that threatened him. He was often "on the run," ironically not like Huck Finn "lightin' out for the territory" but rather retreating into British and European society, and into history and myth. He thus avoided sustained involvement not only with American, British, and European women, but with American "civilization" and indeed with each "civilization" he visited. As Fetterley has argued, "'**Rip Van Winkle**' is the . . . inevitable consequence of the massive suppressions required by Franklin's code of success." Each work represents a different kind of American success story. "If Franklin's book is a testament to how lucky it is to be an American, '**Rip Van Winkle**' is perhaps the first registering of a disillusionment with America as idea and fact. . . ." (2).

But even thousands of miles away from home the free spirit is not totally free, and Irving, unlike Rip Van Winkle, was not able thus to "lose himself" in the past and slough off the influence of contemporary American thought and attitudes. His resistance to changes taking place in American thought is reflected in his conservative reaction to the contemporary reconsiderations of women's role in society. It is well-known that as a result of both the political and industrial revolutions in America, the role and status of women in the new republic came under considerable scrutiny in the late eighteenth and early nineteenth centuries. As Linda Kerber has argued, theoretically the republic depended on the virtue, intelligence, and responsibility of all of its citizens. Theoretically this was a step toward greater equality as the model republican woman became a figure of competence and independence, of self-confidence and rationality.[6] Irving seemed threatened by this movement toward women's independence and equality and the changes in the status quo that this philosophy implied. In his fiction as in his life, he reduced women to two basic and essentially adolescent classes: his positive category included figures of nurturing, sustaining supporters of men or figures of passive innocence and virtue; his negative category included the aggressor, the seductress and the albatross threatening or draining men. Despite their English subjects and their surface of sentimental fantasy, his essays on women in *The Sketch Book* and *Bracebridge Hall* reflect Irving's particular reactions to the changes and confusions in contemporary American thought and the cautionary tone of much contemporary American popular literature. Through Crayon, Irving explored several variations on the theme of women's latent power, and below the reassuring surface his images reveal his sense of inadequacy when faced with women's superior strength and powers of endurance.

The tension between Irving's idealized image of women and his sense of the reality of their power is evident in *The Sketch Book*. **"The Widow and Her Son"** presented an idealized version of the enduring strength of the republican mother. Since her husband died of grief at the young man's fate, only she survived to nurse her dying son. Crayon argued that she was sustained by a mother's love for her son which "transcends all other affections of the heart. It is neither to be chilled by selfishness—nor daunted by danger—nor weakened by worthlessness—nor stifled by ingratitude. . . . And if misfortune overtake him [her son] will be the dearer to her from misfortune" (87). Indeed, she was the only survivor since her husband had died of grief at their son's fatal illness. Ironically, in real life Irving dared not test his fantasy. When the family business in Liverpool went bankrupt, he expressed relief that his mother had died without learning of the financial disaster.

Similarly, **"The Wife"** reflects Irving's ambivalent feelings about the idealized republican wife. On the surface it romanticized the comfort a man can take from his supportive wife. Crayon assured Leslie, "Those disasters which break down the spirits of a man, and prostrate him in the dust, seem to call forth all the energies of the softer sex, and give such intrepidity and elevation to their character, that at times it approaches to sublimity" (22). The dominant images, however, are of Leslie's feelings of inadequacy as a provider and of Mary's towering resilience as she fulfills Crayon's promise. Their happiness depends on her strength of will. In real life Irving explained to Mrs. Foster that after the bankruptcy of the family business in Liverpool he felt he could not marry because he was "involved in ruin. It was not for a man broken down in the world to drag down any woman to his paltry circumstances, and I was too proud to tolerate the idea of ever mending my circumstances by matrimony" (April-May 1823, 1:737). But his motivation may have been influenced by more than financial concerns. If the idealized portraits of mothers and wives seem to offer appealing images of acceptance and support, they also project an awesome and inherently claustrophobic power. As Rip Van Winkle learned, to succumb to them is to submit to an ultimately stifling society.

Kerber has shown that to counter this threat of women's domination both radicals and conservatives used popular literature to warn women against trusting their own emotions and instinct (206, 235). Similarly, Joyce Warren has illustrated that whatever the theoretical base for the new republican society, the rising "cult of the individual" was male-dominated as women's sense of independence was subverted by pressure to establish their social status through marriage and their virtuous reputation through devotion to the well-being of the male. Despite the efforts of women's rights advocates such as Lucy Stone, Susan B. Anthony, and Elizabeth Cady Stanton, the "cult of the lady" emphasized "submissiveness, piety, purity and domesticity."[7]

Irving also imitated current didactic literature as he appealed to domestic responsibility, religion, and even nature to shore up the status quo. On the issue of women the tone of *Bracebridge Hall* is rather more dogmatic than the more sentimental *The Sketch Book*. The ultra-conservative Crayon presented his ideal couched in terms of female submission and self-control precluding any maturing or self-development. In **"Wives"** he argued that it is the woman's responsibility to sustain romantic love in a marriage by maintaining the girlish charms that originally made her so attractive—"the chariness of herself and her conduct," "the same niceness and reserve in her person and habits," "a freshness and virgin delicacy"; she must "protect herself from that dangerous familiarity, that thorough acquaintance with every weakness and imperfection incident to matrimony" (46-47). Just as Irving had seriously considered marriage only with Matilda Hoffman and Emily Foster, both considerably younger than he, so Crayon's image of marriage is far from a union of equals. The distinct roles of husband and wife are clear, sanctioned not only by tradition but also by the church. He closed his "musings" by citing Jeremy Taylor's sermon on the wedding ring: for the man love and duty, for the woman reverence and obedience. "He provides, and she dispenses; he gives commandments, and she rules by them; he rules her by authority, and she rules him by love; she ought by all means to please him, and he must by no means displease her" (47).

Conservatives were particularly opposed to romantic fiction which offered models of women who dared to trust their own feelings and instincts to break out of the traditional boundaries. Irving supported his advocacy of women's social submissiveness by focusing on the laws of nature to justify their present position. Through Crayon he countered his fear of women's hidden superior strength with more sentimental but evocative images of their vulnerability. In **"The Broken Heart"** he emphasized that while the conventions of society kept them economically dependent on men, the laws of nature held them emotionally dependent on men. A woman's *raison d'être* is the love of a man. This was her basic attraction. "Man is the creature of interest and ambition. His nature leads him forth into the struggle and bustle of the world. . . . But a woman's whole life is a history of the affections. The heart is her world . . . and if unhappy in her love, her heart is like some fortress that has been captured, and sacked, and abandoned, and left desolate." Without love "the great charm of existence is at an end" (56-57).

Irving wrote for a living, so his appeal to the majority through popular themes is to be expected, but his private life and correspondence reveal that he held to the conservative position for years after the publication of *The Sketch Book* and *Bracebridge Hall*. This is reflected within his own immediately personal circle in his reaction to Mary Shelley, the poet's widow. During the period 1823 to 1830 she showed sustained interest in Irving; he responded with disgust and determined evasion. This may have been because in general he resisted aggressive women or, as Ralph Aderman has suggested, "because he was unwilling to associate with someone whose unconventional behavior had provoked scandal and gossip."[8] Several years later Irving drew on the ladies of the Spanish court to vividly emphasize real-life warnings to the women of his family of the price women paid when they dared to venture beyond the natural, if proscriptive, roles of dutiful mother and wife. He particularly condemned the Infanta Luisa Carlota, the young queen's aunt, for participating in the public arena. Irving saw her as a woman of "strong passions and restless ambition" whose scheming nature and disappointment at her failure to marry her son to the queen first "mortified her pride and exasperated her temper" so that her looks began to fade and she suffered "a kind of fever of the mind" which "acting upon an extremely full, plethoric habit, hurried her out of existence" at thirty-nine. From Irving's perspective her arrogance was duly punished as she lay in state, "in a Gala dress, . . . the face livid and bloated with disease," reduced to the gaze and contempt of the "unmannered populace" (9 February 1844, 3:675). He had also condemned the Queen Regent for violating all natural laws because as a widow of the King she had abused her regal position and her woman's role by plotting both in Spain and in France to undermine the Spanish constitution. As a mother she indulged in even more unnatural behavior by establishing a "scandalous connexion" with one of the royal bodyguards and thus neglecting "her sacred duties to her legitimate children" (2 September 1842, 3:309). On her return Irving interpreted her aging physical appearance and her subdued spirit as signs of decline due to her unnatural behavior. While he explicitly used these women to moralize on royal grandeur and morality, he also exploited them to warn his women readers against any show of independence they might be contemplating.

Irving was often attacked as unpatriotic because of his lengthy absences abroad, and throughout his life he confessed that he longed for the "storied and poetical association" found in Britain and Europe but missing from America. However, as an expatriate author and politician he served his country as it strove to distinguish itself from its European and British heritage. His ambivalent reactions to the seduction of the old established European cultures and the appeal of the fresh young Republic are most often and vividly reflected in his contrasting portraits of European and American women. As a young man he responded most obviously to their sensuality and sexuality. At twenty-one Irving was clearly fascinated and repelled by the various forms of "immodesty" he saw in European women. In a representative letter to his friend Beebee his fascination emerges in his long and detailed descriptions, and his revulsion in the extravagance of his language. Every elaboration to his contemporaries on the sensual attractions in Europe is accompanied by refrain-like assurances of superior American morality and his attempts to keep his American morals "as untainted as possible from foreign profligacy." Delighted by the performance of French female dancers, he indulged in a detailed description of their "flesh colored habit that is fitted exactly to the shape and looks like the skin . . . their figures are perfectly visible" through the muslin dresses which, flying up, "discovers their whole person. . . ." But he assured Beebee, "my american notions of delicacy & propriety are not sufficiently conquerd for me to view this shameless exposure of their persons without sentiments bordering on disgust." His particular contempt was held for the married women who were "often *themselves the assailants*, . . . [throwing] out a lure with the most consummate address" (18 September 1804, 1:78-80).

As the more mature Irving recognized the conflict between his fantasies and the realities of Europe, he recorded the immorality he saw with resigned disappointment. He had once been deeply enough moved by a young bride in a tableau of Murillo's *Virgin of the Assumption* to describe it as "more like a vision of Something Spiritual and celestial than a representation of any thing merely mortal; or rather it was woman . . . approaching to the Angelic nature" (22 January 1828, 2:265). Fourteen years later he saw the same lady with her daughters, flaunting her younger lover at the theatre. Disappointed, he mused, "Time dispells charms and illusions. . . . She may have the customs of a depraved country and licentious state of society to excuse

her; but I can never think of her again in the halo of feminine purity and loveliness that surrounded the Virgin of
Murillo" (18 October 1842, 3:357).

While Irving was threatened by the open intrigue of the
Europeans, he felt secure, if bored, with the unworldly
American ladies who, in their apparent simplicity, seemed
harmless. Social bias, which ridiculed the **"Learned
Lady,"** and social practice, which limited female education, discouraged women from much public display of independent thought. As a petulant twenty-four-year-old,
Irving wrote from Richmond, Virginia, to Mary Fairlie
mocking the fashion for reading romances and complaining about the "novel-read damsels . . . [,] the tender
hearted fair ones [who] think you absolutely at their command—they conclude that you must of course be fond of
moonlight walks—and rides at day break and red hot
strolls in the middle of the day . . . and 'Melting hot—
hissing hot' tea parties—and what is worse they expect
you to talk sentiment. . . ." He had gone to Richmond to
observe the trial of Aaron Burr, and he praised the ladies
for their support of Burr, for their "compassion" which
"results from that merciful—that heavenly disposition im-
planted in the female bosom, which ever inclines in favour
of the accused & the unfortunate" (7 July 1807, 1:244-45).
Even while he joked that their unworldliness "exalted"
them ever higher in his estimation, he celebrated the laws
of nature that had made women all feeling and very little
thought and thus powerless.

Even in his maturity Irving rarely recognized women for
their intellect. In his descriptions of the American and European women he met in the social scene in Madrid, he repeated the same accolades, reflecting admiration for only
the most superficial qualities: affable, engaging, sensitive,
graceful, and conversable. His references to women's intellect were always brief, almost asides. He valued one of
his closest friends, Mrs. O'Shea, because she was "of
good understanding and the kindest and most amiable
manners" (12 March 1844, 3:692). When he first met Madame Calderón, he barely acknowledged her "lively" book,
Life in Mexico, emphasizing rather William H. Prescott's
Conquest of Mexico, in which he had been "deeply interested and highly pleased" (7 January 1844, 3:645). He
subsequently came to appreciate her as much for her "very
good humor" and "good spirits" as for her intelligence (13
April 1844, 3:720). In his letters to his sister and nieces
describing Spanish politics, he was equally condescending,
assuming their interests were restricted to the romance and
excitement of the events. He promised to pursue themes
from Spanish history for his sister Catharine Paris "as it
will be carrying on a living historical romance for her
gratification. . . ." (26 November 1842, 3:414). He was
patronizing even to his beloved niece, Sarah Storrow: "I
do not wonder that you are . . . disposed to think hardly
of Espartero for the measures he has taken to suppress the
insurrection: you would not have a womans feelings if you
did not. But you must not believe all that you read in the
newspapers. . . . I will endeavor in some future letter to
give you a key to the mysteries of Spanish politics. . . ."

(5 January 1843, 3:446). His highest praise went to those
women who exercised their abilities to maintain their
homes, their families, or Irving himself. He respected the
Duchess of Berwick primarily because she had been able
to restore her husband's "immense wealth" after his estates had been ruined by poor management (16 March
1844, 3:695). His dearest friend in Spain was his "fair
neighbor and countrywoman," Madame Albuquerque,
whose strongest appeal for him was that she acted "the
part of a niece towards" him (19 January 1844, 3:649).
She helped him organize his apartments, arrange official
dinner parties, and let him accompany her with her children on rides to the country.

Jeffrey Rubin-Dorsky has noted that during his earlier stay
in Spain the idea of an earthly paradise had become central in Irving's thinking and writing, but such an Eden had
eluded him until he found the Alhambra. Irving rejoiced,
"Behold for once a day-dream realized."[9] Never again did
he find what Rubin-Dorsky defined as a paradise "commensurate with his capacity for wonder," an ideal retreat
in a timeless place like this where historical fact, mystery,
and myth are accepted as equally valid and essentially in-
terchangeable by its inhabitants.[10] It was the ideal retreat
that demanded nothing from him. From the balcony of the
Hall of Ambassadors he used a pocket telescope to observe both nature and an alameda, or public walk, immediately below. Irving recalled, "It was a moving picture of
Spanish life and character, which I delighted to study. . . .
I was thus in a manner, an invisible observer, and, without
quitting my solitude, could throw myself in an instant into
the midst of society,—a rare advantage to one of somewhat shy and quiet habits, and fond, like myself, of observing the drama of life without becoming an actor in the
scene" (*Alhambra,* 71). Significantly, this is a paradise
with virtually no women, certainly none making any demands on him. He could fantasize about "the white arm of
some mysterious princess beckoning from the gallery, or
some dark eye sparkling through the lattice" (*Alhambra,*
32-33), or he could observe the colorful squatters like the
little old Cockle-queen. Mostly he allowed himself to be
attended by Tia Antonia, the custodian of the Alhambra,
and plump Dolores, his particular servant.

Only at Sunnyside did he reach anything like this domestic security. Having voluntarily undertaken the support of
several family members there, he had created a home for
himself and accepted the responsibilities of a family man
without the inconvenience of a wife. Sometimes he chafed
under the financial obligation of this arrangement, but
mostly he relished the idea of himself as *père de famille.*
Just as Rip Van Winkle returned from his dream, so did
Irving. Although he could never fully escape the social
and political pressures of the day, he could retreat to his
"little paradise on earth" (5 November 1842, 3:370). While
in Madrid, chafing to be at Sunnyside, he had come to appreciate that he had maintained a distanced posture which
had influenced most aspects of his life. He confided in Sarah Storrow, "Indeed I have been for so much of my life a
mere looker on in the game of society that it has become

habitual to me. . . ." He acknowledged that in his youth his "imagination was always in the advance, picturing out the future and building castles in the air, now memory comes in the place of imagination" to cast a soft light over the past (28 March 1845, 3:924). He ended his life at Sunnyside, absorbed by the past of his and America's mythic hero, George Washington, and "spoiled . . . by living continually in the bosom of a family surrounded by affectionate beings who cherished" him (29 May 1842, 3:303). Surely this was what he had been preparing himself for all of his life: surrounded by women, unwilling to let go totally of the public world and free to escape into the past whenever he chose.

Notes

1. Judith Fetterley, *The Resisting Reader: A Feminist Approach to American Fiction* (Bloomington: Indiana University Press, 1978), 3.

2. Washington Irving, *Letters*, ed. Ralph M. Aderman, Herbert L. Kleinfield, and Jenifer S. Banks (Boston: Twayne Publishers, vol. 1, 1978; vol. 2, 1979; vols. 3 and 4, 1982), 15 December 1802, 1:6. Subsequent references are given in the text with the date of each letter followed by the volume and page number.

3. Washington Irving, *Bracebridge Hall, or The Humourists: A Medley by Geoffrey Crayon, Gent.*, ed. Herbert F. Smith (Boston: Twayne Publishers, 1977), 43-44, 46.

4. Washington Irving, *The Sketch Book of Geoffrey Crayon, Gent.*, ed. Haskell Springer (Boston: Twayne Publishers, 1978), 9.

5. Leslie A. Fiedler, *Love and Death in the American Novel* (Cleveland: World Publishing Co., 1960), xx-xxi.

6. Linda K. Kerber, *Women of the Republic: Intellect and Ideology in Revolutionary America* (Chapel Hill: University of North Carolina Press, 1980), 189, 231.

7. Joyce M. Warren, *The American Narcissus* (New Brunswick: Rutgers University Press, 1984), 6-11.

8. Ralph M. Aderman, "Mary Shelley and Washington Irving Once More," *Keats-Shelley Journal*, 31 (1982), 24-28.

9. Washington Irving, *The Alhambra*, ed. William T. Lenehan and Andrew B. Myers (Boston: Twayne Publishers, 1983), 7.

10. Jeffrey Rubin-Dorsky, "*The Alhambra*: Washington Irving's House of Fiction," *Studies in American Fiction*, 2 (Autumn 1983), 179.

Laura Plummer and Michael Nelson (essay date 1993)

SOURCE: 'Girls can take care of themselves': Gender and Storytelling in Washington Irving's 'The Legend of Sleepy Hollow,'" *Studies in Short Fiction*, Vol. 30, No. 2, Spring, 1993, pp. 175-84.

[In the following essay, Plummer and Nelson explore gender ideology in "The Legend of Sleepy Hollow," arguing that the story reflects Irving's misogynist beliefs.]

Discussions of Washington Irving often concern gender and the artistic imagination, but these topics are usually mutually exclusive when associated with the two most enduring stories from the *Sketch Book of Geoffrey Crayon, Gent.* (1819-20): **"Rip Van Winkle"** and **"The Legend of Sleepy Hollow."** Many readings of the former focus on gender, while discussions of the latter most often explore its conception of the artist's role in American society.[1] **"The Legend of Sleepy Hollow"** does indeed address this second theme, but also complicates it by making art an issue of gender. Ichabod Crane is not only a representative of bustling, practical New England who threatens imaginatively fertile rural America with his prosaic acquisitiveness; he is also an intrusive male who threatens the stability of a decidedly female place. For Irving, the issue of art is sexually charged; in Sleepy Hollow, this tension finally becomes a conflict between male and female storytelling. A close look at the stories that circulate through the Dutch community shows that Ichabod's expulsion follows directly from women's cultivation of local folklore. Female-centered Sleepy Hollow, by means of tales revolving around the emasculated, headless "dominant spirit" of the region, figuratively neuters threatening masculine interlopers like Ichabod to ensure the continuance of the old Dutch domesticity, the Dutch wives' hearths, and their old wives' tales.

Although Irving often places the feminine in a pejorative light—the "feminine" in Ichabod is his unmanly, superstitious, trembling, and gullible side—he himself seems, in this tale, begrudgingly to acquiesce to the female sphere of Sleepy Hollow. And this sphere has none of the abrasiveness so blatant in **"Rip Van Winkle."** We have no shrewish wife, whose death in a "fit of passion" allows for Rip's carefree dotage upon his return to the village. Rather, we are left with a sense of relief at Ichabod's removal, at this snake's relegation to the mythology of the Hollow. Thus the tale presents a stark contrast to **"Rip Van Winkle."** In that story, women attempt and fail to confront men openly; in Sleepy Hollow, female behavior is much more subversive, and effective.

In **"The Legend of Sleepy Hollow,"** Irving's conservatism subverts itself, since conservation of the existing power structure means the continuance of a female (though certainly not feminist) hierarchy. Irving's tale is one of preservation, then, of maintenance of the feminine, and the landscape is the predominant female. Sleepy Hollow lies "in the bosom" of a cove lining the Hudson (*Sketch Book* 272), the valley is "embosomed in the great state of New York" (274), and the vegetating families of Sleepy Hollow are rooted in its "sheltered bosom" (274). Clearly the repose and security of the place rest in the maternal landscape—an assumption so pervasive that even our male narrator attests to it.[2] For as he observes, in this tale of a Dutch Eden even the adamic act of naming falls to women. "The good house-wives of the adjacent country, from the inveterate propensity of their husbands to linger about the village tavern on market days," have named the nearby "rural port" "Tarry Town" (272); the name and the power of naming thus operate as a gently sardonic means of reproaching unruly husbands and of preserving female dominance over the valley.

The narrator is not simply an idle observer, however. He comes to the Hollow to hunt:

> I recollect that when a stripling, my first exploit in squirrel shooting was in a grove of tall walnut trees that shades one side of the valley. I had wandered into it at noon time, when all nature is peculiarly quiet, and was startled by the roar of my own gun, as it broke the sabbath stillness around, and was prolonged and reverberated by the angry echoes. If ever I should wish for a retreat, whither I might steal from the world and its distractions, and dream quietly away the remnant of a troubled life, I know none more promising than this little valley.
>
> (272)

The tale thus begins with a paradigm of masculine experience in the maternal bosom of Sleepy Hollow: an acquisitive, intrusive male both perpetuates female influence over the region and also acquiesces to constraints on male behavior. As the narrator remarks, the Hollow is his choice for "retreat" and security. But although the return to Sleepy Hollow is therefore a return to the womb, unfortunately, he is no longer welcome there.[3]

For as he praises the soporific atmosphere of the Dutch valley, the narrator also admits it has repulsed him. It is clear that Mother Nature here produces a bower not to be disturbed by the masculine aggression of hunting, regardless of its tameness in the case of this "stripling." Hunting is not permitted, and trespassers will be startled into submission. Our gun-toting narrator is surprised not only by the roar of his own gun, his own masculine explosion into the place, but also by the sense that his behavior is inappropriate. This womb-like grove is for nurturing dream, not bloodsport; to be treated with respect due the sabbath, not rent asunder by blunderbuss ejaculations. Indeed, the "angry echoes" from the landscape suggest a rebellious reaction to such flagrant poaching. Indolent as the epigraph may make the place seem,[4] Sleepy Hollow does not take kindly to intruders; hence the narrator is properly awed into acquiescence.

The youthful exploit of this opening scene is echoed by the actions of Ichabod and the Headless Horseman. For like the narrator, both Ichabod and "the dominant spirit" of Sleepy Hollow—"the apparition of a figure on horseback without a head" (273)—are masculine, mercenary interlopers in this feminine place. The bony schoolmaster's desire to liquidate heiress Katrina Van Tassel's wealth, invest it "in immense tracts of wild land" (280), and take Katrina from the Hollow mirrors both the narrator's childhood intrusion and the former Hessian trooper's attempt to win Sleepy Hollow for Royalist forces "in some nameless battle during the revolutionary war" (273).[5] They embody the essence of masculine imperialism: war, fortune hunting, and even squirrel hunting are all expressions of the

same will to conquer. Gun, Hessian sword, or birch in hand, the narrator, the Horseman, and Ichabod all bear authority; and all three seek the spoils—political, material or sexual—of invading Sleepy Hollow.

Irving's bawdy imagery strongly suggests that all male intrusions in this female place are ultimately sexual.[6] Ichabod, for example, is described in insistently phallic terms:

> He had, however, a happy mixture of pliability and perseverance in his nature; he was in form and spirit like a supple jack—yielding, but tough; though he bent, he never broke; and though he bowed beneath the slightest pressure, yet, the moment it was away—jerk!—he was as erect, and carried his head as high as ever.
>
> (282)

The pedagogue's "pliability and perseverance"—Ichabod is elsewhere accredited with possessing "the dilating powers of an Anaconda" (275)—suggest that he will not be as easily scared or awed as the narrator. It will take more than just the roar of his gun to frighten this persistent "jack."

Storytelling is also a part of male imperialism. Of the numerous tales that circulate through Sleepy Hollow, those told by men concern their own fictionalized exploits. "The sager folks" at Van Tassel's farm sit "gossiping over former times, and drawling out long stories about the war"; "just sufficient time had elapsed to enable each storyteller to dress up his tale with a little becoming fiction, and in the indistinctness of his recollection, to make himself the hero of every exploit" (288). These stories are designed to increase the teller's status in the minds of his listeners by linking him to the heroic, historic, and masculine past.

True to this male practice of self-aggrandizing storytelling, Ichabod regales his female companions with scientific "speculations upon comets and shooting stars, and with the alarming fact that the world did absolutely turn round, and that they were half the time topsy-turvy!" (277). Though fantastic in themselves, these stories are to Ichabod the height of learning and scholarly achievement. Even his tales of the supernatural show him as "a perfect master of Cotton Mather's History of New England Witchcraft" (276). Ichabod's familiarity with the subject attests to his book learning and his reliance on the great masters of American thought, not to his understanding of folklore. Boastfully displaying his knowledge of worldly matters, this "travelling gazette" brings word of the "restless country" of "incessant change" outside Sleepy Hollow (276, 274). Part of the pioneer's repertoire, carried from town to town, his stories are meant to recommend him to each new audience by proving his erudition.

While male storytelling is a part of the will to compete and conquer, storytelling for the women of Sleepy Hollow moves beyond self-image to counter that male will. The "witching power" the narrator fails to define fully is a female influence that gently molds the inhabitants of Sleepy

Hollow through the folklore that emanates from that exclusively female, domestic province, the hearth (273):

> Another of [Ichabod's] sources of fearful pleasure was, to pass long winter evenings with the old Dutch wives, as they sat spinning by the fire, with a row of apples roasting and sputtering along the hearth, and listen to their marvellous tales of ghosts and goblins, and haunted fields and haunted brooks, and haunted bridges and haunted houses, and particularly of the headless horseman, or galloping Hessian of the Hollow, as they sometimes called him.
>
> (277)

Spinning, cooking, and spinning tales are simultaneous acts; the convergence of folklore and the domestic imbues everyday events with the supernatural.

The effectiveness of this domestication of the supernatural is clear from the extent to which folklore affects local inhabitants' behavior. At the tale's close, the bridge where the Horseman confronted Ichabod is no longer used, the schoolhouse is abandoned, and Ichabod's "magic books" have been burned in Hans Van Ripper's censorial flames (295); the community has accepted that the spirit world is larger than themselves, that despite their boasts and challenges, the lore of the place is still supreme and affects nearly every facet of their lives.

Perhaps the most convincing proof of the pervasiveness of female influence in Sleepy Hollow is that all the men have set themselves to challenging it. Accordingly, the narrator not only concedes the connection between women and spirits, but he also establishes women as the greatest source of fear for men:

> [Ichabod] would have passed a pleasant life of it, in despite of the Devil and all his works, if his path had not been crossed by a being that causes more perplexity to mortal man, than ghosts, goblins, and the whole race of witches put together, and that was—a woman.
>
> (278)

Although this passage is supposed to be humorous, it nonetheless reveals Irving's characteristic misogyny and the male fear of disempowerment played out again and again throughout the tale. In contrast to Rip Van Winkle, however, the Hollow men displace this fear from women to characters of folklore. It is a misunderstanding that, as in the case of Ichabod, ensures men's continued thralldom.

Given the misogynistic bent of **"The Legend of Sleepy Hollow,"** it is not surprising that despite the tale's narrative complexity, Irving suppresses actual female speech; in fact, the only narratives directly or indirectly related are spoken by men. This conspicuous absence of female narration underscores the way in which males both fear and resist the feminine. Thus, the narrator is at a loss to relate what Katrina says to Ichabod in their tête-à-tête after the frolic: "What passed at this interview I will not pretend to say, for in fact I do not know" (290). The war stories told at the Van Tassel frolic, like the narrative as a whole, are told by men. And it is Sleepy Hollow *men* who tell ghost stories at the frolic. Tales from the female sphere must be validated by male retelling.[7] That is, the story of the Headless Horseman originates in a tradition kept by women; storytelling sessions with women make Ichabod susceptible to local superstition; but men first reinforce, and then—as we shall see in the confrontation between Ichabod and Brom Bones—capitalize on the fears and superstitions engendered by women.

The ultimate irony concerning gender and storytelling, then, is that the very female stories males debunk influence their lives, often through their own telling of them. The men who continually joust fictionally with the Headless Horseman not only inflate their prowess, but also repeatedly confront in narrative the threatening world formed, unbeknownst to them, by the alliance of female and spirit. Fighting mock battles in which they defeat what they mistakenly consider their greatest adversary, men actually strengthen the female hold on the community by reinforcing and perpetuating the narratives through which women maintain order.

Indeed, Brom Bones and Ichabod provide an example of males literally enacting these stories. In his role as the Headless Horseman, by means of which he intends to humiliate his rival, Brom unwittingly serves as the means to achieve the goal of the female community: the removal of Ichabod and himself as threats to Sleepy Hollow's quietude. Posing as the Headless Horseman of legend, Brom plays upon Ichabod's superstition and credulity to eliminate his opponent. And it is Ichabod's association of legend and place, engendered in his mind by the female-controlled mythology, that proves his undoing. Riding home alone from the Van Tassel farm at "the very witching time of night," "all the stories of ghosts and goblins that he had heard in the afternoon, now came crowding upon his recollection;" "he was, moreover, approaching the very place where many of the scenes of the ghost stories had been laid" (291). Thus Brom Bones has at his disposal a carefully scripted and blocked drama with which to exploit Ichabod's credulity and superstitious fear.

The phallic language of this passage reiterates Ichabod's sexual threat and clearly indicates that the gullible pedagogue is essentially neutralized or neutered by figurative castration. Bones, masquerading as the Headless Horseman, appears as "something huge, misshapen, black and towering" "like some gigantic monster" (292), while Ichabod flees in terror from the apparition "stretch[ing] his long lank body away over his horse's head, in the eagerness of his flight" (293). Indeed, in this drama of competing masculinity, Ichabod's fear is of dismemberment. Ichabod, "unskilful rider that he was!" has trouble staying on his mount, slipping and bouncing from one side to the other "with a violence that he verily feared would cleave him asunder." Ichabod's fear is nearly realized when Brom hurls his pumpkin/head at the schoolmaster, "tumbl[ing] him] headlong into the dust" (294).

Brom Bones triumphs in this phallic contest of horsemanship and sexual potency—Ichabod is never seen in Sleepy Hollow again—but ironically this ejaculatory coup de grâce effects his own emasculation. His impersonation of the Horseman prefigures his domestication: donning the garb of the dismembered spirit, and ultimately throwing away his head, Brom insures that his days as a "roaring, roystering blade" are numbered (281).[8] The ultimate beneficiary of Brom's midnight prank is the Dutch community itself, the maintenance of whose dreamy repose and domestic harmony is the province of women.

The altercation between Brom and Ichabod and its inevitable outcome meet with tacit approval from the female sphere. Brom Bones, the "hero of the country round" with "more mischief than ill will in his composition" (281), appears not to share the schoolmaster's desire to take Katrina and her wealth out of the Dutch community. Since marriage is a most soporific state for the men of Sleepy Hollow, it is more than likely that Brom, who "had for some time singled out the blooming Katrina for the object of his uncouth gallantries" (282), will soon become as content and domesticated, and as plump and vegetable-like, as Katrina's father. Accordingly, there are no "angry echoes" to greet Brom's adventures; indeed, "the old dames" of the country, content with merely remarking "aye, there goes Brom Bones and his gang," indulge him in his revels and pranks (281). For Brom Bones would be a threat to Sleepy Hollow only if Ichabod should succeed in his suit, thus extending Brom's bachelorhood indefinitely (and enabling Ichabod to make off with the Van Tassel fortune).

Ichabod's expulsion from Sleepy Hollow, then, results from subtle manipulation of local folklore by women. **"The Legend of Sleepy Hollow"** thus provides a foil to the open male-female confrontation of **"Rip Van Winkle"**; the story is a darker, more paranoid vision of female power. Indeed, the narrative frame shows the lengths to which men go to find plausible alternatives to the female version of Ichabod's disappearance, which relegates him to the cosmos:

> The old country wives, however, who are the best judges of these matters, maintain to this day, that Ichabod was spirited away by supernatural means; and it is a favourite story often told about the neighborhood round the evening fire.
>
> (296)

The male account asserts that Ichabod

> had changed his quarters to a distant part of the country; had kept school and studied law at the same time; had been admitted to the bar, turned politician, electioneered, written for the newspapers, and finally had been made a Justice of the Ten Pound Court.
>
> (295-96)

This version translates the jerky young man into the self-reliant American jack-of-all-trades and self-made success.[9]

Yet this story is also an import; it arrives via "an old farmer, who had been down to New York on a visit several years after" (295). The ending is brought into Sleepy Hollow from New York, and by a man; it dismisses the supernatural perspective with a very plausible account of Ichabod's fear and mortification as impetus for his speedy removal, and places Ichabod in a respected occupation.

In similar fashion, Diedrich Knickerbocker attempts in the tale's postscript to lend credibility—a factual backbone—to his story, by placing it within a masculine sphere:

> The preceding Tale is given, almost in the precise words in which I heard it related at a corporation meeting of the ancient city of Manhattoes, at which were present many of its sagest and most illustrious burghers.
>
> (296)

These wise old men are intended to lend credence and authority to a story that operates on a plane beyond that of burghers and business meetings. And, as Knickerbocker relies upon the authority of "precise words," we are reminded of the narrator's having told us early in the narrative that his aim is to be "precise and authentic" (272). Something there is in these male storytellers that doesn't love a ghost.

The narrator's sardonic comment that "the old country wives . . . are the best judges of these matters" is clue enough to a rather disparaging attitude; resenting the authority of women is nothing new to Irving's fiction. Yet this remark does not alter the fact that the community listens to the women's stories. And this particular one is a favorite in Sleepy Hollow because it both warns and neutralizes threatening males. Ichabod becomes the community's most recent lesson by example, the shivering victim of his own acquisitive fantasies and proof positive of the truth of legend.

The postscript to the tale reiterates the gender conflict present in the story proper and the narrative frame. Diedrich Knickerbocker focuses on the confrontation between the narrator and a cynical listener that ends in the narrator's parodic syllogism and his ambiguous admission concerning his story that "I don't believe one half of it myself" (297). Their verbal jousting is reminiscent of Brom's and Ichabod's own rivalry. And Diedrich Knickerbocker's description of the narrator is most telling: he is "one whom I strongly suspected of being poor, he made such efforts to be entertaining" (296). This, too, allies the narrator with Ichabod and the men of the Dutch community; his performance stands as a final example of male self-aggrandizing storytelling. Indeed, the tale proper becomes the object of male desire and competition; it is the game our youthful narrator has waited the length of a "troubled life" to carry off. In turn, Diedrich Knickerbocker the antiquarian, and Geoffrey Crayon the sketch writer, extend this instance of storytelling as appropriation to fill the entire frame of the tale: its inclusion in *The Sketch Book*. The presence of gender as a central conflict is further buried under layers and layers of male acquisitiveness and competition.

But in **"The Legend of Sleepy Hollow,"** stories, like wealth and game, are not exportable. It is the association of lore and place, of supernatural and practical, that gives the legend of the Headless Horseman its power and efficacy in controlling males within the Dutch community; the very title of the sketch reinforces the primacy of place in storytelling. Like the Horseman himself, the tale is powerless outside a circumscribed area. The ability to tell it in New York, where its supernatural elements are so easily debunked, attests not to the power of the male storyteller who does the debunking—as the postscript would have us believe—but to the element of female storytelling in Sleepy Hollow that insures the success of the female order: its subtle, self-effacing nature. Diffused throughout the folklore and the practical, everyday world of a particular place, the source of power in the Hollow—women—is disguised, making belief in the supernatural a matter of course, not compulsion. When the tale is told outside this female-controlled landscape of the naturalized supernatural, the effectiveness of the story dissolves, leaving only a Hollow husk.

Notes

1. Leslie Fiedler and Judith Fetterley have provided the most influential readings of "Rip Van Winkle" that concentrate on gender: both see the tale as an instance of male flight from female influence and control. Lloyd M. Daigrepont summarizes and contributes to the extensive discussion of conflict in "The Legend of Sleepy Hollow" interpreted "in terms of the special concerns of the man of letters or the artist versus those of a practical-minded, progressive society" (68).

2. Several narratives make up "The Legend of Sleepy Hollow": antiquarian Diedrich Knickerbocker's manuscript recording the tale proper, related by an unnamed narrator to Knickerbocker and others at a meeting of burghers in New York; a postscript written by Knickerbocker explaining the setting in which the preceding tale was told, as well as its reception; and, within the unnamed narrator's story, numerous yarns told by the inhabitants of Sleepy Hollow and adjacent areas.

3. Annette Kolodny, one writer who does discuss gender in "The Legend of Sleepy Hollow," assesses both male escapism and the presence of a maternal landscape in "Rip Van Winkle" and "The Legend of Sleepy Hollow": "in escaping the traumas of history and progress, Rip Van Winkle and Brom Bones demonstrated the alternative commitment to a psychological adolescence through which, only, the ambience of the Mother might be maintained" (68). Our narrator shares this impulse.

4. The epigraph to the story is from James Thomson's "Castle of Indolence":

   A pleasing land of drowsy head it was
   Of dreams that wave before the half-shut eye;

And of gay castles in the clouds that pass,
Forever flushing round a summer sky.

(272)

5. As John Seelye observes, the presence of "Andre's Tree," and stories told by locals about this British major who conspired with Benedict Arnold to betray American forces, point to "still another alien intruder into the Hudson Valley" (420).

6. William P. Dawson notes that "In Irving's day, 'squirrel' was slang for harlot," and discusses the sexual suggestiveness of guns and hunting imagery in "Rip Van Winkle" (201).

7. In keeping with this dynamic, the narrator punctuates his opening enumeration of the female characteristics of Sleepy Hollow with the suggestion that the region's dreamy nature is the result of male actions: "Some say that the place was bewitched by a high German doctor during the early days of the settlement; others, that an old Indian chief, the prophet or wizard of his tribe, held his powows there . . ." (273).

8. Having lost his head to become a harmless spirit inhabitant of the region now governed by his former enemies, and trapped geographically and temporally—since he cannot venture beyond the Hollow and must return to his grave by sunup—the Horseman is an apt symbol of emasculated male potency.

9. Daniel Hoffman discusses Irving's use of character types drawn from American folklore.

Works Cited

Daigrepont, Lloyd M. "Ichabod Crane: Inglorious Man of Letters." *Early American Literature* 19 (1984): 68-81.

Dawson, William P. "'Rip Van Winkle' as Bawdy Satire." *ESQ* 27 (1981): 198-206.

Fetterley, Judith. *The Resisting Reader.* Bloomington: Indiana UP, 1978.

Fiedler, Leslie. *Love and Death in the American Novel.* Rev. ed. New York: Stein and Day, 1966.

Hoffman, Daniel. *Form and Fable in American Fiction.* New York: Oxford UP, 1961.

Irving, Washington. *The Sketch Book of Geoffrey Crayon.* Ed. Haskell Springer. Boston: Twayne, 1978.

Kolodny, Annette. *The Lay of the Land.* Chapel Hill: U of North Carolina P, 1975.

Seelye, John. "Root and Branch: Washington Irving and American Humor." *Nineteenth-Century Fiction* 38 (1984): 415-25.

Hugh J. Dawson (essay date 1994)

SOURCE: "Recovering 'Rip Van Winkle': A Corrective Reading," *ESQ: A Journal of the American Renaissance,* Vol. 40, No. 3, 1994, pp. 251-73.

[*In the following essay, Dawson contends that the forest scene in "Rip Van Winkle" is gothic rather than comic and that the story is not anti-feminist.*]

While compiling a notebook of reminiscences during his term as American minister to Spain, Washington Irving reflected upon the history behind a tale he had written a quarter century earlier. "The idea," he writes, "was taken from an old tradition" that he "picked up among the Harz Mountains." By using the New York Catskills as the background for **"Rip Van Winkle,"** he furthered his project of providing the young nation with a measure of the folk tradition dear to romanticism. He was astonished at his success: "When I first wrote the **'Legend of Rip van Winkle,'**" he records in his notebook,

> my thought had been for some time turned towards giving a colour of romance and tradition to interesting points of our national scenery which is so deficient generally in our country. My friends endeavored to dissuade me from it and I half doubted my own foresight when it was first published from the account of the small demand made for that number, but subsequent letters brought news of its success and of the lucky hit I had made.[1]

This essay attempts to advance understanding of **"Rip Van Winkle,"** first by revealing ways that Rip's experiences have been misunderstood and then by proceeding to find hitherto neglected meaning in the forest scene at the tale's center, arguing that, far from the comical interlude it is generally understood to be, the episode is pervasively gothic in character. The essay challenges ideological interpretations whereby Irving's story is read as a proof-text of American literary antifeminism and proposes that a proper appreciation of Irving's assignment of gender roles in the story requires consideration of its position in *The Sketch Book* and its meaning within that context.

1

Irving's story succeeded famously, possibly better than he expected. The fantasy of an individual's escape from time and social obligations that he appropriated from a German märchen was ages old,[2] but its appeal hardly promised to win the widespread popularity finally enjoyed by his localized tale. The story that initially appeared in *The Sketch Book,* at first a staple of schoolroom readers, gained broad acceptance as an indigenous American folktale; however, it was freely altered in consequent retellings. Within a decade of its original publication in 1819, **"Rip Van Winkle"** was adapted for the stage in the first of an assortment of dramatic versions that made Rip's travails familiar to nineteenth-century American and English theatergoers. Later adaptations, like Edmund Clarence Stedman's *Rip Van Winkle and His Wonderful Nap,* further popularized the legend of Rip's mountain stay. Meanwhile, the tale's fanciful episodes recommended themselves to a long line of popular illustrators, such as John Quidor and Felix O. C. Darley, whose sentimentalized scenes, often very different from Irving's originals, made Rip's adventures known to an even wider audience.[3] The tale remains one of the best known favorites of American popular culture, treasured even as it is unfailingly misremembered.

The influence of derivative versions may explain why the clear content of Irving's own telling is so regularly altered,

as when *The Oxford Companion to American Literature* tells of Rip's encounter with a "dwarf-like stranger" as he pauses for rest in the forest.[4] There is no warrant in Irving's text for the statement that Rip meets up with a deformed, gnome-like creature of the sort that Albert Gelpi takes to be "a little old man: an aged child, a homunculus of Rip, dwarfed and emasculated by his infantile regression."[5] In fact, the forest guide of *The Sketch Book* is very simply described as a figure of somewhat less than average height—"a short, square built old fellow, with thick bushy hair and a grizzled beard" (33).[6] The tale's central episode, Rip's encounter with the crew of Henry Hudson's *Half Moon,* is just as commonly altered. *The Cambridge Guide to English Literature,* for example, reports that an "amiable Dutch-American meets a strange dwarflike person[.] . . . joins him at a silent party of similar dwarfs[, and] . . . is given drink."[7]

Again and again the crew members are similarly misrepresented by various critics: they are described as "dwarfs," "dwarfish people," "little people," "little old boys," "little men," "a group of little old men," "aged children," "little boys[,] . . . aged little men," the "ghosts of certain jolly old Dutchmen[, and] . . . comic Netherlandish wraiths."[8] William L. Hedges finds Rip's low self-esteem reflected in what the critic characterizes as the lack of height and carefree mood of those in the group: "They are small and comical, one suspects, because they are in a sense mockheroic images of Rip himself; they represent his unconscious recognition of his lack of stature, and his willingness to put up with himself as he is even though he sees how little he amounts to."[9] No such party of happy gnomes is found in the text. The single seaman met laboring beneath a keg of gin is simply described as "short," and Rip finds nothing amusing in the conduct of the *Half Moon*'s complement (33). The impression that dwarfs or otherwise undersized figures exist in the tale can be traced to early dramatizations of "Rip," but no further. For instance, Rip meets a "grotesque dwarf" in Charles Burke's 1850 play, and well before Joseph Jefferson and Dion Boucicault's 1865 collaboration gave the theatricalized legend its classic form, the Dutch sailors' ghosts were fixed in a series of stage versions as "imps" and "demons," characters in the fashion of nineteenth-century low comedy who were endowed by playwrights with such extravagant, laughter-provoking names as "Swaggrino," "Gauderkin," and "Icken."[10]

The popularized accretions of Irving's tale repeatedly lead twentieth-century commentators into error. It is as mistaken to say that the bowlers Rip encounters "prove cordial, if silent," or that "they ply [Rip] with 'excellent Hollands'" as to speak of his warm reception into a "perfect communion of males."[11] In Irving's episode, not the slightest gesture of hospitality is made to welcome Rip. The *Half Moon* crew is, if not menacing, chillingly indifferent to this visitor from the world of the living. It is "with fear and trembling" that Rip submits to becoming their lackey, and only "when no eye [is] fixed upon him" does he dare steal a share of their beverage (34). One critic's error in describing this reunion of old sailors as an "eternal playtime in the hills" enjoyed in the "Happy Valley of natural ease and male camaraderie" is echoed in another's terming the morose Catskill glen "the ideal American territory," which "Irving invokes as playground."[12]

This tale of marital mismatch becomes for many critics an allegorical contest: "the conflict of Man and Woman," a tale in which "the opposition of Rip and Dame Van Winkle is extended to women and men in general."[13] But that dichotomy is not sustained even within the fictional hamlet where Rip is "a great favourite among all the good wives of the village, who . . . [take] his part in all family squabbles, and . . . lay all the blame on Dame Van Winkle" (30). Even before Leslie A. Fiedler propounded his imaginative readings of the tale, Philip Young discovered in it an exercise in "whimsical anti-feminism." Noting that the German legend from which the tale derives has no wife figure, Fiedler finds the sharp-tongued Dame Van Winkle symptomatic of Irving's double-barreled "attack on women and marriage," and Judith Fetterley warns that the sensitive female reader will find herself "summarized, explained, and dismissed through the convention of stereotypes as a 'termagant wife,' a shrew, a virago."[14] Such treatment of the tale disregards the narrator's explicit characterization of women as "the amiable sex" (30).[15]

Fetterley also argues that the very figure who is said to be a summary of American male vices and a despiser of women is a would-be female, claiming that "Rip rejects the conventional image of masculinity and the behavior traditionally expected of an adult male and identifies himself with characteristics and behaviors assumed to be feminine and assigned to women. Thus, the figure who 'presides over the birth of the American imagination' is in effect a female-identified woman-hater." In her reading, Rip the father proves as irresponsible as Rip the husband, so she employs critical sleight of hand to explain his offspring in terms of parthenogenetic fantasy: "Rip's children are difficult to account for; it would seem more likely that he sprung them magically from some part of himself in order to have playmates." Despite finding "the role [Irving] gives to women" to be "[c]entral" to the tale, Fetterley (like Fiedler) refuses to credit him with having transformed Rip's daughter, whose German counterpart had only a minor role, into the very incarnation of generosity.[16] Although Judith grows up without her father (but not without her mother's fierce denunciations of him), she is a paragon of filial love, welcoming to her hearth the old man she loyally memorialized by giving his name to her son. And she also accepts into her home her ne'er-do-well brother—the "urchin begotten in [Rip's] own likeness" who has grown to be his father's "ditto," carrying the old man's shiftless habits of life into another generation (31, 40).

Indeed, indolence is presented as the common trait of the Dutch husbands of Rip's acquaintance. Irving, perhaps responding to his readers' growing commitment to the young country's work ethic, may have meant his story to mock the socially sanctioned lethargy of the village's male popu-lation more than he intended the unique fury of Dame Van Winkle to stand as an indictment of American womanhood. Indeed, by focusing on negative patterns of men's conduct across several generations, Irving shows sons' failures to meet their fathers' expectations and their disavowal of the linear family more than he plays on men's disregard of women. Rip repudiates the military example of his forebears, "who figured so gallantly in the chivalrous days of Peter Stuyvesant, and accompanied him to the siege of Fort Christina" (29). He chooses instead to spend his time as a squirrel- and pigeon-hunter; he neglects his patrimonial estate, allowing it to sink into decay; and his irresponsible son disregards the confused and enfeebled Rip in his moment of greatest need. Finally, those who find the roots of American literary antifeminism in the story disregard the fact that the offensive traits of the Van Winkles descend only to the male. The father's faults seem genetically transmitted to a son who is both physically and temperamentally his clone, "a precise counterpart of himself, . . . apparently as lazy and certainly as ragged" (38).[17] Although the younger Rip has "an hereditary disposition to attend to any thing else but his business" (40), his sister Judith is conspicuously free of her mother's fierce temperament.

Critics who contend that Rip finds in the *Half Moon* crew's reunion every male's happy release from the imagined tyranny of womankind are again forced to rewrite Irving's text. Fetterley's explication of the tale's alleged bias includes an indictment of what she takes to be just such a celebration of masculine clannishness:

> [Rip gains] access to life in an all-male world, a world without women, the ideal American territory. Like Melville a half-century later, Irving invokes as playground a world which is perforce exclusively male— the world of men on ships exploring new territories. Rip encounters in the mountains the classic elements of American male culture: sport invested with utter seriousness; highly ritualized nonverbal communication; liquor as communion; and the mystique of male companionship. In an act of camaraderie, based on a sure and shared instinct as to the life-expectancy of termagants, the little men provide Rip with the opportunity and instrument of escape.[18]

Fetterley's pleonastic insistence upon "an all-male world, a world without women," is symptomatic of the misconstrued account that endows Hudson's crew with a gregariousness and an ability to intuit the years remaining to Dame Van Winkle that are without warrant in Irving's text. Clairvoyance and a gift for hexing, even at great distances, are frequently among the magical powers of elves met in fairy tales, but Irving's Dutch sailors are not to be confused with any such "little men."

Richard J. Zlogar also mischaracterizes the events in the forest when he relates the story's central episode of male overindulgence in drink to the moral content of a Dutch painting tradition. He argues that the old sailors' dissipation is to be read with reference to both the earlier account of the patriarchs of the colonial village assembled at Nicholaus Vedder's inn and the later scene of the early American elders gathered before Doolittle's hotel, and that the sequence of Irving's narrative panels imitates the moralistic *geselschapje* or "Merry Party" convention made popular by the Old Country painters.[19] However, this reading overlooks the unrelieved moroseness of Irving's old tars.

2

The events of the tale's central episode lack any carefree indulgence. Rip's experience is altogether different from the pattern of escape commonly set in the perpetual sunshine of the tropics rather than the nighttime of Catskill forest gloom, where the bacchanalian celebrants are lulled by sweet music rather than threatened by ominous thunder. In popular escapist fiction, the revelers' mood is brightened by the recovery of youth rather than burdened by the onset of old age. The fantasist imagines himself lord of all he surveys, not a lackey impressed into the duties of a scuttling taproom servant, and his dream world is peopled with compliant wahines rather than dominated by surly seadogs. In **"Rip Van Winkle,"** there is no Fayaway.

Rip's entry to the forest scene through a symbolic landscape that progressively darkens and his participation in a surreal scene that mingles ritual celebration and gothic terror more closely resembles the experiences of Hawthorne's Goodman Brown than those of male adventurers escaping to "new territories."[20] The narrator of "Young Goodman Brown" suggests (but does not verify) that Brown might have "fallen asleep in the forest and only dreamed a wild dream," and Irving leaves the same mystery unsolved in Rip's own case.[21] Beneath their shared gothic character, both stories possess a mythic quality in telling of nocturnal journeys that draw husbands away from the familiar reinforcements of society, initiate them into a threatening new awareness of life, and return them to their accustomed worlds transformed.[22]

Testimony to the scene's deeply disturbing psychological content is found in the sentimentalized theatrical versions of the ghostly confrontation, where the crew's profound alienation is transmuted into revelry and Rip's fear becomes the stuff of cheap comedy. Popular culture demanded that Rip's meeting with his mountain guide in the very beginning of the mountain episode be presented to theater audiences as a moment of comic surprise instead of heavy foreboding. In the tale, the Hudson River landscape, which Irving first describes in terms of an Arcadian *locus amoenus,* turns oddly ambiguous. "In this lonely and unfrequented place," the sudden calling of Rip's name stirs premonitions of danger. Immediately his dog "bristle[s] up his back," growls, "skulk[s] to his master's side," and looks "fearfully down into the glen." Rip feels a "vague apprehension stealing over him" as he looks "anxiously" to see who is summoning him. The sight of a "strange figure" in anachronistic dress clambering up the rocks is sufficiently unsettling to make the forest rambler

"distrustful," but he neither asks how his name is known nor inquires into the purposes of this curious "new acquaintance." The stranger's command that Rip render him assistance is conveyed in a mysterious sign language, but one so compelling that Rip responds "with his usual alacrity" (33). Although he wonders about the "object of carrying a keg of liquor up [the] wild mountain," he harbors no suspicions of smuggling; he asks no questions about the "stout keg that seem[s] full of liquor" (34, 33). Although Rip has arranged no forest rendezvous as did Goodman Brown, he shows the same lack of prudence in acceding to the stranger's insistence that he accompany him. Inevitably, like Salem's Puritan, he is drawn onward contrary to the dictates of good sense: for Rip as much as for Brown, "there [is] something strange and incomprehensible about the unknown, that inspire[s] awe and check[s] familiarity" (34).

When Rip and his guide arrive at the encampment of the ghost crew of the *Half Moon,* he discovers himself in the midst of a swarm of grotesques. Far from being attentive to any assigned duties or observing any command structure, the band of seamen, themselves oddly accoutred in two-centuries-old garb, have given themselves over to round after round of bowling and heavy drinking. Rip sees

> a company of odd looking personages playing at ninepins. They were dressed in a quaint outlandish fashion—some wore short doublets, others jerkins with long knives in their belts and most of them had enormous breeches of similar style with that of the guide's. Their visages too were peculiar. One had a large head, broad face and small piggish eyes. The face of another seemed to consist entirely of nose, and was surmounted by a white sugarloaf hat, set off with a little red cock's tail. They all had beards of various shapes and colours. (34)

Rip concludes that he has not arrived at any blessed domain of carefree spirits but has entered the world of the carnivalesque, where everyday expectations are suspended and the familiar conduct of life gives way to ritual. Language is abandoned in favor of gesture. Discipline and decorum disappear. Costume replaces dress. Most disconcerting of all are the mien and conduct of the not so "Merry Party." Their faces are grimly vacant and their inexplicable behavior, which at first seems reserved, turns vaguely threatening; "nothing interrupt[s] the stillness of the scene, but the noise of the balls," echoing "along the mountains like rumbling peals of thunder" (34).

As Rip and Wolf draw near, the "most melancholy party of pleasure" stops bowling and stares "with such fixed statue like gaze, and such strange uncouth, lack lustre countenances" that Rip's heart "turns" and "his knees sm[i]te together." When served their flagons of gin, the crewmen quaff them without a word and sullenly return to their dreary game. In such fantastic circumstances, the visitor finds it expedient to mask his terror with a becoming subservience, so when Rip is told to wait upon the party of morbid revelers, he obeys with "fear and trembling." Far from discovering the ease he has sought, Rip is pressed into performing as a servant (34).

The vicennial reunion of the ancient crew is essentially a conclave of transmogrified spirits. Their game of ninepins is an unending round of joylessness that Rip is never invited to join. Denied even the merest show of cordiality, he is never asked to share in the abundant drink but patiently endures a kind of studied humiliation. He bears with the crew's sullen rejection and bides his time for the moment "when no eye [is] fixed upon him, to taste the beverage" that permits his escape. Rip is never more than an interloper, at first fascinated but finally revolted by what he witnesses. He is especially disturbed by the spectacle of "the Commander," a "stout old gentleman, with a weatherbeaten countenance," wearing a "laced doublet, broad belt and hanger, high crowned hat and feather, red stockings and high heel'd shoes with roses in them" (34). This figure, made a mockery in popular versions, deserves respect and pity.

The full implication of the scene emerges only when Rip learns the identity of those before him: In 1611, two years after exploring New York's great river, many of Hudson's crew mutinied while searching for the Northwest Passage. The captain was stubborn and misguided, and the men, instead of murdering him, abandoned Hudson and his young son in a small boat on the waters of what would be named Hudson Bay. Rebaptized by Irving with the Dutch name Hendrick Hudson, this "first discoverer of the river and country," according to the legend as recounted by Peter Vanderdonk, returns every twenty years with his crew to "revisit the scenes of his enterprize and keep a guardian eye upon the river and the great city called by his name" (40). The fate of Hudson and his men recalls the curse of the *Flying Dutchman*. In the face of a heavy storm and against the protests of his passengers and crew, the *Dutchman*'s stubborn captain vowed to sail his ship around Africa's Cape of Good Hope or be damned in the attempt. According to European legend, he was condemned to pilot a phantom vessel manned by a "crew of dead men, who stand to their tasks unmoving, and will not answer questioning."[23]

3

In "Come Back to the Raft Ag'in, Huck Honey!" Fiedler proffers his conjecture that Americans' guilt concerning race and a repressive sexual history leads them to treat many classic romances as no more than "*boys'* books." At least in some respects, Rip's story seems to have had a similar fate. The appeal of his escape from time and societal demands—the "implacable nostalgia for the infantile"[24]—has had its response in a readiness to repopulate the central scene with little men amusing themselves at children's play. Rip's oneiric retreat brings him into an implausible, all-male society whose ambiguous sexuality is thinly veiled. Clear intimations of the zombified crew members' sterility—their lifelessness and absence of physicality, their advanced age, their silent tongues and loss of

voice—contrast strikingly with such conspicuous symbols of male genitalia as their prominently displayed knives, luxurious beards, and "peculiar" faces. One crewman is remarkable for his "piggish eyes" and another for his protruding nose and sugarloaf hat flamboyantly topped with a "little red cock's tail." The *Half Moon*'s demanding commander, Hudson, is impotent, reduced to posturing as a ridiculously caparisoned mannequin. His flaccid "hanger" contrasts with the "long knives" sported by his hostile crew (34).[25] He is no more than an irrelevant bit of stage property in an amphitheater of the absurd, where beings who are only ambiguously alive strive to overcome their essential loneliness in conduct so bizarre as to beggar the credulity of the townspeople to whom Rip returns.

Rip's experience, however, proves very different from those of the trio of American fictional male runaways—Natty Bumppo, Ishmael, and Huck Finn—in whom Fiedler discovers a pattern of sexual shyness.[26] None of the three are married, but Rip's marriage is the precipitant of his mountain adventure; he leaves behind a wife and at least two small children. The three "fugitives" discussed by Fiedler find boon companions whose masculine physicality, psychological integrity, and moral superiority are essential features of the liberation they incarnate. Rip's experience is quite the opposite. In a social setting of vexing sexual ambiguity, he meets not flesh-and-blood human beings but ghost-personages from the land of the living dead. These visitors display strangely discordant personalities, for even as they amuse themselves, they maintain "the gravest faces, the most mysterious silence." Their conflicted psyche is encapsulated in a series of oxymoronic phrases: this "most melancholy party of pleasure" survives in Rip's memory as a "woe begone party" and "grave roysters of the mountain" (34, 35).

Rip does not find an abiding comradeship; he recoils from those he meets; his curiosity turns to fear, then to uncanny suspicion, and finally to rejection. His suspicion that the men have "put a trick upon him, and . . . dosed him with liquor" is an attempt at self-deception (35). The long afternoons at the village inn that enable him to judge "the flavour of excellent hollands" have also taught him the release to be found in "a quieting draught" (34, 41). He escapes the mountain encampment by anesthetizing himself. When he awakens, he is "determined to revisit the scene" of his "gambol," but he has no desire to take up the ways of Hudson's men. His mood is confrontational: he wants to recover what he believes has been stolen from him; he resolves "to demand his dog and gun if he encounters them" (35). When he looks for the ravine that had given access to the mountain glen, his search has the character of an amateur topographer's land survey more than it seems an effort to regain access to a lost Shangri-la.

Popular dramatists mute the terrifying ambiguity of Rip's mountain visit with comedy, inverting the tale's testimony to the sad plight of growing old. It is to evade another bitter truth of Irving's story, its recognition that death forever diminishes one's familiar circle, that playwrights regularly arrange for Rip to have a tearful reunion with his still-living wife. Irving's grim recognition of the difficulty in coming to terms with an aging body, unreliable memory, and less adaptive personality is captured in the frenzy of Rip's identity crisis: "I'm not myself.—I'm somebody else—that's me yonder—no—that's somebody else got into my shoes—I was myself last night; but I fell asleep on the mountain—and they've changed my gun—and every thing's changed—and I'm changed—and I can't tell what's my name, or who I am!" (38-39). But in Rip's identity crisis, one recognizes an anxiety that runs deeper than do the worries of a person undergoing a social transition. There is a sense of existential loneliness, even of alienation from the self; it is as if Rip fears he is undergoing the same interior rupture he witnessed in those he met in the mountains. Rip is manifestly unequipped to understand the experience of entering his dotage overnight. He is, after all, "one of those happy mortals of foolish, well oiled dispositions, who take the world easy" and dismiss life's conflicts with a shrug (31).

Philip Young reads Rip's long sleep as symptomatic of the American need in the early national period to erase the traumatic memories either of complicity in the repudiation of a king or of an abstention from the movement for independence.[27] But like other political readings of the story, this interpretation focuses on the contrast between the casual ways of earlier village life and the commercial mania of the society to which Rip returns, reducing the tale to a reflection of the accidents of a historical moment. These readings disregard the critic's obligation to relate the particulars of the mountain episode to what precedes and follows it. Irving's story would lack unity if the events of its gothic central scenes were unrelated to the framing story. However much **"Rip Van Winkle"** resonates with the revolutionary experience of the colonies and with the lives of the Hudson River Valley communities that swelled with the post-war influx of New Englanders, the tale transcends the fortuities of history and the happenstance of a given region.

Political readings of **"Rip Van Winkle"** note that Rip's belated discovery of American independence has its analogue in his even more welcome liberation when he learns of his wife's death: "[T]here was one species of despotism under which he had long groaned and that was petticoat government. Happily that was at an end—he had got his neck out of the yoke of matrimony, and could go in and out whenever he pleased without dreading the tyranny of Dame Van Winkle" (40-41). But in the mountains, Rip did not find a happier life without her. As individuals, the strange creatures Rip meets are but the simulacra of men, Adamic isolatoes deprived of the Eves with whom they might have found fulfillment; collectively, they are a legion of lost, lonely souls ignorant of the cultural imperatives contemporary Western society made woman's special concern, "the values of work, responsibility, [and] adulthood."[28] Worse still, they live without woman's incarnation of the hope of progeny and the symbolic immortality rep-

resented by children. **"Rip Van Winkle"** is a gothic tale of a journey into a night world without pleasure. The primal scene from which Rip recoils is that Edenic condition of which it is said, "It is not good that . . . man should be alone."[29]

Loutish and drunk, caught up in a timeless round of repetition, Hudson's crew live in what Irving describes in **"The Wife"** as the perilous condition of the unmarried man, who is estranged even from himself, "apt to run to waste and self neglect[,] to fancy himself lonely and abandoned, and his heart to fall to ruin like some deserted mansion for want of an inhabitant."[30] Readers ready to laugh at the scene in which Rip recovers consciousness do not recognize that it is the remembrance of his wife's expectations that helps him regain his bearings. Without knowing his wife has died, he turns homeward expecting to resume married life.

Jeffrey Rubin-Dorsky notes that the cost of fame for **"Rip Van Winkle"** and **"The Legend of Sleepy Hollow"** has been that because they "have taken on a life of their own[,] . . . relatively few people are aware of the fact that they are part[s] of *The Sketch Book of Geoffrey Crayon, Gent.*, and therefore fully resonate only when read in that context."[31] The same warning was sounded earlier by Perry Miller, who counsels that the parts of *The Sketch Book* should not be read without regard for their relatedness:

> To excise is to spoil the unity of the work, a coherence which it does possess despite the piecemeal way in which Irving wrote and published the parts, despite the fact that **"Rip"** and **"Sleepy Hollow"** can stand by themselves and customarily are anthologized as "short stories." We must peruse the whole as a unit, observing the conscious alternation of moods—for example, the jolt intended by the shift from **"The Wife"** to **"Rip"**—in order to comprehend that Irving had every right to call the result a *book* and not a collection of random "sketches."[32]

The first lines of **"The Wife,"** which immediately precedes **"Rip Van Winkle"** in *The Sketch Book,* provide a sample of Irving's metaphoric celebration of women's contribution to marital happiness:

> As the vine which has long twined its graceful foliage about the oak, and been lifted by it to sunshine, will, when the hardy plant is rifted by the thunderbolt, cling round it with its caressing tendrils and bind up its shattered boughs; so is it beautifully ordered by providence, that woman, who is the mere dependent and ornament of man in his happier hours, should be his stay and solace when smitten with sudden calamity, winding herself into the rugged recesses of his nature; tenderly supporting the dropping head, and binding up the broken heart.[33]

In working its own variation of the ancient marriage topos of the elm and the vine, Irving's oversweet paean to domestic bliss is "sucked down into seas of tears and noble axioms."[34] The succeeding paragraphs, Rubin-Dorsky notes, are a rehearsal of "nineteenth-century platitudes about the mysterious way a woman overcomes her natural timidity in a crisis."[35] Here one seems to overhear Irving, morose amidst an accumulation of midlife uncertainties and nursing his decade-old sense of loss in the death of Matilda Hoffman, searching for some promise of meaning in his remaining years.[36] If a union based upon the assumed complementarity of husband and wife is not today's most widely shared vision of marriage, it was Irving's, and his paragraphs deserve to be read as an appreciation of marital fulfillment in the idiom of his day, when such indulgent prose was not considered tasteless. However cloying the manner Irving chooses to express his concept of wifely devotion, the position of **"The Wife"** immediately before the tale of **"Rip Van Winkle"** argues against reading the second tale as a categorical denigration of womankind.

Despite the differences between **"Rip Van Winkle"** and the story that precedes it, the similarity is significant. In **"The Wife,"** the fortunate husband, Charles Leslie, like Rip, makes the mistake of undervaluing the strengths of his devoted wife Mary. He learns his error in time to appreciate her for what she is. Rip, however, is beyond self-knowledge. He neglects his estate and ignores his wife. Unwilling to accept his lot and to acknowledge his own culpability, he flees to the forest, where he meets men who, eternally dispossessed of women, manifest a profound, inarticulate estrangement. He returns home unlikely to reform his ways even if his wife were not dead. He does not contemplate remarriage. Too dim to recognize a wife as helpmate or woman as social force, he lives out his days as a fond old man unable to come to terms with his encounter. He is content to be a small town celebrity endlessly revising his story for the happily uncomprehending young, auditors who are in many ways substitutes for Irving's many readers who are unable or unwilling to appreciate the deeper lessons of his text.

Nothing could be so wrong as to characterize Rip as a playboy of the Elysian fields reveling in a perpetual party, the envy of his layabout friends at the village tavern. Those in the company he meets linger on rather than live, serving out a Dantesque eternity. Alienated from one another, they experience only a parody of play in a realm beyond time where leisure loses its meaning. They wallow in swinishness, blankly staring at their visitor from beyond. They enjoy no satisfactions, knowing neither the rapport of friendship nor the cooperative achievement of crewing a ship. All that contemporary Western society had made the province of woman—the aspirations to higher culture, the moral formation of later generations, the maintenance of domestic order, the inculcation of such sanctioned folkways as the habit of saving, the deferral of gratifications, and the etiquette of common courtesies—all these are lost to them. Their commander is the epitome of sexual impotence. Customarily charged with maintaining discipline, he is instead a preening popinjay decked out in garb more appropriate for a transvestite masquerade party, a caricature of his former stern self whose claims to authority may now be ignored with impunity.

In exploring the sexual anxieties revealed in Irving's works, Rubin-Dorsky concentrates on those written after 1820. But this earlier story may be a revealing autobiographical reverie manifesting the same apprehension of marital inadequacy, since acceptance by his daughter provides Rip with a congenial substitute for remarriage. As a fiction about storytelling, it recalls the way Irving first related his tale in the warm family circle of his favorite sister, Sarah Van Wart.[37] In the story's closing picture of an old man living out his days entertaining the town's children, one recognizes the author's mid-life representation of himself as Hudson River Valley storyteller.

Despite its debts to traditions of gothic fantasy and folktale, Irving's story also plays on the twin fears that continued to trouble generations of American males as the frontier receded—the life without women that had been their past and the life in which women would be dominant that seemed their future. Three-quarters of a century later, the same insecurities attending the termination of male society's sloth, dissipation, and game playing provided the premise of "The Bride Comes to Yellow Sky."[38] The society that had not confidently accepted women—or racial minorities—oscillated between its polarized images of them. Rip's story and **"The Wife"** exemplify the frontier myth's simplism. If **"Rip Van Winkle"** does not portray marriage as the positive good enshrined in **"The Wife,"** it does acknowledge it as the cement of social conditions that is infinitely preferable to the communal breakdown and psychological ruin Rip experiences in the forest.

Notes

1. Washington Irving, first published by Barbara D. Simison as "Some Autobiographical Notes of Washington Irving," *Yale University Library Gazette* 38 (1963): 11.

2. Irving's indebtedness to the German story "Peter Klaus" is the subject of several studies. Henry A. Pochmann sets out the principal points of similarity in "Irving's German Sources in *The Sketch Book*," *Studies in Philology* 27 (1930): 477-94. The best summary of Irving's borrowings from German folktales is given by Walter A. Reichart, *Washington Irving and Germany* (Ann Arbor: Univ. of Michigan Press, 1957), 22-30.

3. For brief histories of early dramatizations of "Rip Van Winkle," see William Winter, *Life and Art of Joseph Jefferson* (New York: Macmillan, 1894), 175-83, 305-9; and Montrose J. Moses, ed., *Representative Plays by American Dramatists, 1856-1911* (New York: Dutton, 1921; New York: Benjamin Blom, 1964), 3:15-31. An extended treatment is found in Harold Brehm Obee's "A Prompt Script Study of Nineteenth-Century Legitimate Stage Versions of 'Rip Van Winkle,'" (Ph.D. diss., Ohio State Univ., 1961). An illustrated edition of Edmund Clarence Stedman's *Rip Van Winkle and His Wonderful Nap* was published in 1870 as part of the Uncle Sam Series for American Children (Boston: Ticknor and

Fields, 1870). For a history of painters' representations of the story, see George L. McKay, "Artists Who Have Illustrated Irving's Works," *American Collector* 16 (October 1947): 38-40. On John Quidor, see Bryan Jay Wolf, *Romantic Re-Vision: Culture and Consciousness in Nineteenth-Century American Painting and Literature* (Chicago: Univ. of Chicago Press, 1982), 152-73; and Christopher Kent Wilson, "John Quidor's *The Return of Rip Van Winkle* at the National Gallery of Art: The Interpretation of an American Myth," *American Art Journal* 19 (fall 1987): 23-45.

4. James D. Hart, *The Oxford Companion to American Literature,* 5th ed. (Oxford: Oxford Univ. Press, 1983), 641-42. This account also mistakenly says that Rip "is greeted by his old dog" after his twenty-year sleep. In fact, the larger dog breeds almost never live so long, and Irving writes only of a "half starved dog that look[s] like Wolf" (Washington Irving, "Rip Van Winkle," in *The Sketch Book of Geoffrey Crayon, Gent.,* ed. Haskell Springer, vol. 8 of *The Complete Works of Washington Irving* [Boston: Twayne, 1978], 36; hereafter cited parenthetically by page number).

5. Albert Gelpi, "White Light in the Wilderness: Landscape and Self in Nature's Nation," in *American Light: The Luminist Movement, 1850-1875,* ed. John Wilmerding (New York: Harper and Row, 1980), 296.

6. That is, the guide possesses the characteristics of neither of the two most nearly applicable dictionary definitions of a dwarf; he is not "a person whose bodily proportions are abnormal," nor is he "a small legendary manlike being who is . . . misshapen and ugly and skilled as an artificer" (*Merriam-Webster's Collegiate Dictionary,* 10th ed., s.v. "dwarf").

7. Michael Stapleton, *The Cambridge Guide to English Literature* (Cambridge: Cambridge Univ. Press, 1983), 814-15.

8. Philip Young, "Fallen from Time: The Mythic Rip Van Winkle," *Kenyon Review* 22 (1960): 556, 569; Jack Salzman, *The Cambridge Handbook of American Literature* (Cambridge: Cambridge Univ. Press, 1986), 209; Lewis Leary, *Soundings: Some Early American Writers* (Athens: Univ. of Georgia Press, 1975), 310; Judith Fetterley, *The Resisting Reader: A Feminist Approach to American Fiction* (Bloomington: Indiana Univ. Press, 1978), 7, 9, 191 n. 4; Mary Weatherspoon Bowden, *Washington Irving* (Boston: Twayne, 1981), 59; William L. Hedges, "Washington Irving: Nonsense, the Fat of the Land and the Dream of Indolence," in *The Chief Glory of Every People: Essays on Classic American Writers,* ed. Matthew J. Bruccoli (Carbondale: Southern Illinois Univ. Press, 1973), 152; William L. Hedges, "Irving, Hawthorne, and the Image of the Wife," in *Washington Irving Reconsidered: A Symposium,* ed. Ralph M. Aderman (Hartford: Transcendental Books, 1969), 25; Gelpi, "White Light," 296; and Leslie A. Fiedler, *The Return of the Vanishing American* (New York: Stein and Day, 1968), 59.

9. William L. Hedges, *Washington Irving: An American Study, 1802-1832* (Baltimore: Johns Hopkins Press, 1965), 138.

10. Charles Burke, *Rip Van Winkle: A Legend of the Catskills,* in Moses, *Representative Plays by American Dramatists,* 3:51; on the collaboration of Dion Boucicault and Joseph Jefferson, see Arthur Hobson Quinn, ed., "Rip Van Winkle from 1767 to the Present Day," in *Representative American Plays,* 7th ed. (New York: Appleton-Century-Crofts, 1953), 399-431. These three characters were "Spirits of the Catskills" in a 1763 version of "Rip Van Winkle" (Burke, *Rip Van Winkle,* 3:31).

11. Hedges, *Washington Irving,* 139; Fetterley, *Resisting Reader,* 7.

12. Leslie A. Fiedler, *Love and Death in the American Novel* (New York: Stein and Day, 1966), 341; Fetterley, *Resisting Reader,* 6.

13. Fiedler, *Return of the Vanishing American,* 52; Fetterley, *Resisting Reader,* 5. The same misreading is implicit in Jenifer S. Banks, "Washington Irving, the Nineteenth-Century Bachelor," in *Critical Essays on Washington Irving,* ed. Ralph M. Aderman (Boston: G. K. Hall, 1990), 253-65.

14. Leslie A. Fiedler, *What Was Literature? Class Culture and Mass Society* (New York: Simon and Schuster, 1982), 157; Young, "Fallen from Time," 572 n. 1; Fiedler, *Return of the Vanishing American,* 58; Fetterley, *Resisting Reader,* 9, 3.

15. Nina Baym distances herself from the misplaced emphasis critics have placed upon Rip's wife, finding that "the preeminent Dame Van Winkle is a creation of twentieth-century misogynist paranoia, the post-Wylie fear of 'mom'" (Letter, *New York Review of Books,* 13 May 1976, 48).

16. Fetterley, *Resisting Reader,* 5, 13, 3; quoting Fiedler's 1960 edition of *Love and Death,* xx.

17. Fetterley's treatment of the genetic transmission of personality traits is merely incest fantasy: "What is Judith really except her mother married to someone other than her father? Marry her to her brother and, sure enough, you would have a daughter as like the mother as the son is like the father." Fetterley concludes that Rip is a "woman-hater" (*Resisting Reader,* 10, 5). Although he fears and flees from his wife, nothing in the story suggests that he hates her or any other woman.

18. Fetterley, *Resisting Reader,* 6-7.

19. Richard J. Zlogar, "Accessories that Covertly Explain: Irving's Use of Dutch Genre Painting in 'Rip Van Winkle,'" *American Literature* 54 (1982): 44-62.

20. Fetterley, *Resisting Reader,* 6. Both Fetterley and Fiedler see similarities between Melville's sailors and Rip. Rip's puzzlement in the Catskills may have its true Melvillean analogue in the slow dawning awareness and mounting apprehension of Amasa Del-

ano moving among the alienated men of the *San Dominick* in "Benito Cereno," a crew like that of the *Half Moon,* who are sullen to the point of mutiny.

21. Nathaniel Hawthorne, "Young Goodman Brown," in *Mosses from an Old Manse,* ed. William Charvat et al., vol. 10 of the Centenary Edition of *The Works of Nathaniel Hawthorne* (Columbus: Ohio State Univ. Press, 1974), 89. Fiedler notes that Hawthorne considered rewriting Irving's story (*Return of the Vanishing American,* 55) and directs special attention to "Wakefield" (*Love and Death,* 341).

22. Rip's hibernation—his withdrawal up the narrow mountain defile, womb-like period of dormancy, and rebirth—follows the pattern noted by myth critics. During this cycle in the story, the national bird is born: the "wild, lonely, and shagged" mountain glen and dry ravine of the autumn landscape, above which the crow of death has circled, are found rejuvenated by a springtime mountain torrent "tumbling in a sheet of feathery foam," and while birds hop and twitter, "the eagle wheel[s] aloft and breast[s] the pure mountain breeze" (33, 35). Shortly thereafter, Rip learns of the Revolution, the birth of a new political society, the death of his wife, and the arrival of another generation.

23. Maria Leach, ed., *Funk and Wagnalls Standard Dictionary of Folklore, Mythology and Legend,* s.v. "Flying Dutchman." Irving returns to the *Flying Dutchman* legend in *Wolfert's Roost,* where "Rumbout Van Dam of graceless memory" is known in local lore as the "Flying Dutchman of the Tappan Sea, doomed to ply between Kakiat and Spiting Devil until the day of judgment" (*Wolfert's Roost,* ed. Roberta Rosenberg, vol. 27 of *The Complete Works of Washington Irving* [Boston: Twayne, 1979], 12).

24. Leslie A. Fiedler, "Come Back to the Raft Ag'in, Huck Honey!" in *The Collected Essays of Leslie Fiedler* (New York: Stein and Day, 1971), 1:144.

25. See also William P. Dawson, "'Rip Van Winkle' as Bawdy Satire: The Rascal and the Revolution," *ESQ: A Journal of the American Renaissance* 27 (1981): 198-206.

26. Fiedler, "Come Back," 144.

27. Young, "Fallen from Time," 547-73.

28. Fetterley, *Resisting Reader,* 3.

29. Gen. 2:8 Authorized Version.

30. Washington Irving, "The Wife," in *Sketch Book,* 23.

31. Jeffrey Rubin-Dorsky, *Adrift in the Old World: The Psychological Pilgrimage of Washington Irving* (Chicago: Univ. of Chicago Press, 1988), 100.

32. Perry Miller, afterword to *The Sketch Book of Geoffrey Crayon, Gent.,* by Washington Irving (New York: New American Library, 1961), 374. See also Albert J. von Frank, *The Sacred Game: Provincialism and Frontier Consciousness in American Literature, 1630-1860* (Cambridge: Cambridge Univ. Press, 1985), 74.

33. Irving, "The Wife," 22.

34. Stanley T. Williams, *The Life of Washington Irving* (New York: Oxford Univ. Press, 1935), 1:139. See also Peter Demetz, "The Elm and the Vine: Notes toward the History of a Marriage Topos," *PMLA* 73 (1958): 521-32.

35. Rubin-Dorsky, *Adrift in the Old World,* 50.

36. On the composition of "The Wife," see Washington Irving, *A Tour in Scotland, 1817, and Other Manuscript Notes,* ed. Stanley T. Williams (New Haven: Yale Univ. Press, 1927), 15-23.

37. Williams, *Life of Washington Irving,* 1:168-69.

38. Stephen Crane, "The Bride Comes to Yellow Sky," *McClure's Magazine,* February 1898, 377-84.

Brian Harding (essay date 1996)

SOURCE: "Washington Irving's Great Enterprise: Exploring American Values in the Western Writings" in *Making America/Making American Literature: Franklin to Cooper,* edited by A. Robert Lee and W. M. Verhoeven, Rodopi, 1996, pp. 199-220.

[*In the following essay, Harding probes Irving's complex relationship with Western expansion as evident in* A Tour on the Prairies, Astoria, *and* The Adventures of Captain Bonneville.]

When Irving returned to the United States in 1832, after an absence of seventeen years, he may have been shocked by the vulgarity of the "commonplace civilization" he found there[1] but he was certainly impressed by the immense vigor of the nation's economic life, particularly as that vigor manifested itself in westward expansion. To the man whose nightmare was of finding himself a lonely relic of a past age in his native city,[2] the America to which he returned was a country where everyone spoke of the future "with growing and confident anticipation"[3] and where the future lay in the West. The opportunity to make a tour on the prairies with Commissioner Henry Leavitt Ellsworth presented Irving with a chance to observe the process of growth in his country—to experience the future—though his own initial comments on the venture stressed the past. It would be, he wrote, an opportunity to see "those fine countries of the 'far west' while [they were] still in a state of pristine wilderness" and to see the remnants of the great Indian tribes that were, he believed, "about to disappear."[4]

The expedition left Independence, Missouri for Fort Gibson, on the Arkansas River, on September 27, 1832. In letters written on the tour, Irving stressed the wildness of the country through which he traveled and his excitement at being "completely launched in savage life."[5] Clearly, he got emotional gratification in imaging himself leading "a complete hunter's life,"[6] yet when Irving returned from Fort Gibson via Little Rock, Arkansas, the *Arkansas Gazette* claimed that the writer "acknowledges himself amazed at the fertility of the soil and the immense resources of the west."[7] Evidently, for public purposes at least, Irving was forward-looking; aware of the potential of the West. If we accept the theory that Irving was using the travel narrative as a means of repatriating himself intellectually after his long absence in Europe,[8] it is hardly surprising that he would stress his positive reaction to the West, but the text of *A Tour* problematizes his commitment to the American future as he glimpsed it on his tour.

A Tour on the Prairies was published as part of *A Crayon Miscellany* in March 1835 in London and in the following month in Philadelphia. It was welcomed with rapture by the reviews, among them the *Knickerbocker Review* and the *North American Review*.[9] Particular praise went to its depiction of western scenery. However, if *A Tour* is to be read as part of Irving's self-rehabilitation as an American writer, it is necessary to discount the obvious fact that he "dressed up" his material in literary trappings that belonged to European rather than American conventions. John Francis McDermott is not alone in believing that the journals Irving kept on the trip are more spontaneous and more powerful as literature than the published travelogue. In McDermott's view, Irving not only sacrificed realism by turning his fellow travelers into stock literary types; he also weakened the American significance of his scenes by importing European associations, imagining—for example—Moorish castles or the seats of country gentlemen in the wilderness.[10] To see the "western" landscape through a Claude glass, as Irving sometimes did (see, for example, 73), was no more appropriate a way to catch the distinctive features of the American scene than was Irving's tendency to find classical associations in the Amerindians (see 15). The disparity between manner and matter has led more than one reader to believe that Irving saw and described only the picturesque surfaces of the frontier and lacked any genuine interest in the significance of the frontier in American life.[11]

Aesthetic conventions apart, *A Tour* can be read as an authentic historical record of westward expansion partly in what it does *not* bring to explicit statement. An allusion to "the settlement of the Indian tribes migrating from the East to the West of the Mississippi" is a euphemistic reference to Indian Removal.[12] This reference is encoded in neutral terminology, but Irving's conscience was not always lulled to sleep by the mood of the times. In reporting a squatter's eagerness to whip a young Indian who brings him his lost horse *on the suspicion* of theft (20), Irving is unequivocal in his judgment on White injustice and cruelty. This is just one of many incidents that convince Irving that whites "are prone to treat the poor Indians as little better than brute animals" (27).[13]

A Tour does not engage directly with the theme of westward economic expansion because the expedition of which Irving was a member was not engaged in trade with the Indians. Yet—of course—Commissioner Ellsworth's mission was part of the process by which the wilderness was being tamed and opened up to economic exploitation.

Though Everett Emerson, the reviewer in the *North American Review* for July 1835 treated the work as "a sort of sentimental journey, a romantic excursion,"[14] it has also (and more recently) been read as "a kind of mock-heroic quest that quietly subverts the perennial American myth of westering."[15] In this reading, the West is seen waging a subtle war of attrition against the intruders and *winning* in its struggle against civilization. Certainly *A Tour* offers an eyewitness account of the destructive impact of White America on the wilderness as the young Americans who participate in the "adventure" lay waste to the land they traverse.

If we take *A Tour* seriously as a commentary on the frontier—if we reject the notion that Irving reacts as a literary tourist—then we may want to agree with Bruce Greenfield that the text explores "the basis upon which the individual American could assert a claim" to the Western lands, even though its author "appears disengaged from the ethos and institutions of American westering."[16] In other words, the Irving who wrote *A Tour* was genuinely concerned with the westering process as one of assimilating territory though he held aloof from it. More pointedly, Peter Antelyes argues that Irving used his "tourist's appraisal of the Western territories" as a means of expressing his doubts about the enterprise of economic expansion into those territories.[17] This reading makes *A Tour* a satire in which the popular imaginative form of the Indian adventure tale is used as a means of examining "the illusory and self-serving values of capitalist expansion." Whatever the motivation, *A Tour* remains a puzzling work. Perhaps one can account for the text's susceptibility to diverse and incompatible readings by recognizing that merely to write about his experience of the West was, for Irving, a step in the process of literary repatriation, even when his stance as a tourist allowed him to evade the semantic problems that were at the heart of national, as well as personal, self-definition. His next literary project would make the lexical detachment of *A Tour* impossible.

That project, a history of John Jacob Astor's fur trading venture in the Pacific Northwest, brought Irving into direct engagement with the dominant ideological values of his day. In undertaking to write the history of Astor's commercial enterprise, Irving was almost certainly not tempted, as Henry Rowe Schoolcraft supposed,[18] by bribe money paid to him by Astor. A much more likely explanation is that Irving was motivated, at least in part, by his Jacksonism, which was a matter of confidence in the nation's future in the West rather than an attachment to political personalities. In this view, each of his Western works was to some degree an expression of that confidence.[19] Recent commentary has put the case more forcefully. In Peter Antelyes' view *Astoria* is a celebration not only of Astor's commercial enterprise but of American business enterprise in general; it "does not question the identification of economic expansion with the American mission, nor does it locate the dangers to that mission in commercialism itself."[20] In this theory, Astor represented the entrepreneurial ideal for Irving. He seemed to fulfil the ideals of commercial culture and professional capitalism. Consequently, the aim of *Astoria* was the redefinition of American history as the history of the marketplace.

My own contention is that *Astoria* is an extremely important work precisely because, however strong Irving's identification of himself with entrepreneurial values, and with American national identity, the text problematizes those values. That is to say, there are in the narrative of the Astorians' adventures numerous sites of a semantic confusion and bewilderment at which the text deconstructs itself. By examining some of them closely, we can see that Irving was not able to carry out his avowed intention of celebrating Astor's—and his country's—values, in spite of the fact that he clearly identified his own literary "enterprise" with the merchant's commercial undertaking. Irving's statement—in August 1835—that he was "working away at the Astor enterprise"[21] surely suggests a total commitment to the values of his patron as well as to the literary project in which he was engaged. Yet the book he actually produced puts "business enterprize" and "the American mission" into question.

The story of the loss of the *Tonquin,* with the murder of its captain and of all its crew by the "perfidious" natives of Vancouver's Island, is told in chapter eleven of *Astoria.* It is the most vividly reported and the most shocking episode in a narrative that contains more than one example of cruelty and brutality. Moreover the incident has been given added literary significance by Poe's use of it in *The Narrative of Arthur Gordon Pym.* In Arthur Gordon Pym's account, the savages on the island of Tsalal prove themselves to be "among the most barbarous, subtle, and bloodthirsty wretches that ever contaminated the face of the globe." As Irving tells the story, the massacre of the white men is plotted by an Indian chief named Nookamis who is insulted by Captain Thorn, the commander of the *Tonquin,* as the two men are bargaining for an otter skin. The captain is described by Irving as "a plain, straight forward sailor, who never had two minds nor two prices in his dealings" and who was "deficient in patience and pliancy and totally wanting in the chicanery of traffic."[22] Thorn, we are told, "made what he considered a liberal offer for an otter skin" but Nookamis, who is described as a "wily old Indian" treated the white man with scorn and demanded more than double. Earlier we have been told that Captain Thorn had displayed his wares (blankets, cloths, knives, beads and fish hooks) to the natives, "expecting a prompt *and profitable* sale" (emphasis added). His expectations were disappointed because the Indians "were not so eager and simple as he had supposed." This is partly because they are guided by the "shrewd old chief" Nookamis.

As the tension mounts in the episode, Irving's language becomes patently biased. Nookamis is a "cunning old Indian" as he rejects Thorn's offered price and still "pesters" him to trade, jeering at Thorn for the mean prices he has offered. When Thorn loses his temper and assaults Nookamis, rubbing the otter skin in his face and pushing or kick-

ing him over the side of the ship, Irving treats the insult and the violence as comic: Thorn "dismissed him over the side of the ship with no very complimentary application to accelerate his exit" (74). Just before the violence occurs we learn that Thorn, who "had a vast deal of stern but honest pride in his nature" was not only short-tempered, and thus easily provoked, but "held the whole savage race in sovereign contempt" (73).

In summing up the disaster at the end of the account, Irving clearly holds Thorn responsible for it: "Had the deportment of Captain Thorn been properly regulated, the insult so wounding to Savage pride would never have been given" (78). Moreover, Thorn was guilty of ignoring Astor's repeated advice to treat "the Savages" courteously and kindly and to distrust them. But though the captain is blamed for lack of self-control, all the wickedness is clearly attributed to the natives. Irving intrudes into the narrative with a personal recollection of Thorn; "With all his faults and foibles we cannot but speak of him with esteem, and deplore his untimely fate," because he was a "frank, manly, soundhearted sailor" when on shore and among friends. On ship, as Irving has had to admit, Captain Thorn was an unbending disciplinarian and a tyrant. The essential moral issue, then, is here presented as a contrast between the honest, manly—if irascible—white officer and the treacherous, bloodthirsty savages. Thorn is hopelessly unsuitable for the delicate job of working with Astor's chosen men of business (he quarrels with the partners as soon as the voyage from New York begins), yet it is his frankness that puts him in jeopardy when attempting to bargain with the savages.

Irving's vocabulary, style, and tone constitute a bluff endorsement of Thorn's racial prejudices and in so doing serve to conceal an important ideological pattern in the text. As Wayne R. Kime has shown, Irving based his account of the disaster in part on Alfred Seton's journal, or the version of it that appeared in the *American Monthly Magazine* in 1835.[23] In Seton's version of the incident, Thorn's anger and violence (Seton specifies that Thorn rubbed the skin in the face of the chief) was caused by his frustration when unable to conclude a bargain. Another of Irving's sources—Ross Cox's *Adventures on the Columbia River* (1831)—states, in contrast, that Thorn had caught the chief pilfering.[24] In structuring the story in terms of the contrast between the frank, honest white man and the cunning savage, Irving overlays (conceals) his own understanding of the situation. Though the incident is attributed to Nookamis's frustrated "cunning" in bargaining, at the same time the narrator tells his reader that "The Indians . . . were not so eager and simple as he [Mr McKay] had supposed, *having learned the art of bargaining and the value of merchandize from the casual traders along the coast*" (73; emphasis added). What is more, Nookamis *"had grown gray in traffic with New England skippers and prided himself upon his acuteness"* (emphasis added). Clearly, then, the chief's offended dignity at Thorn's contemptuous treatment depends on what he has learned from *white* traders who have brought commercial ethics to the previously untutored savages. Nookamis, far from being the "simple" savage Thorn (and McKay) expect to profit from, getting otter skins for trifles, is sophisticated in the white man's ways; he and his tribe have learned commercial ethics; they drive a hard bargain, or, in realistic terms, they pitch their price at the trader's needs.

The point is not a minor one, for the story of Astoria is, as the reviewer in the *Westminster Review* so clearly saw, a story of commerce—of business.[25] Irving's history of Astor's enterprise in the Pacific Northwest is posited upon an orthodox estimate of the role played by commercial forces in "progress"—in the onward march of civilization. Consequently, Irving feels no need to apologize for the merchant's imperialistic motives. Astor's story is offered to the reader as essentially a tale of an attempt to advance civilized values into new areas. To recognise how orthodox this interpretation was we have only to turn to Alexander Ross's *Adventures of the First Settlers on the Oregon Or Columbia River* (1849). Ross, who had taken part in the adventures, announces in his first chapter that "the progress of discovery contributes not a little to the enlightenment of mankind."[26] To this true believer in "mercantile interests," there is no doubt that the "spirit of enterprise developed in the service of commercial speculation" is instrumental in the spread of civilisation. Whatever Irving's private and personal attitude towards business, and that was at least changeable, as historian of his patron's "great enterprise" he clearly planned to justify it on a high moral plane.

In the first chapter of *Astoria* Irving acknowledges that "the rich peltries of the north"—like the "precious metals of the south"—had provided the motive for daring enterprise in the Americas from the beginning of European involvement. Though the object was "commercial gain," the quests for furs and for gold "have thus in a manner been the pioneers and precursors of civilization" (5). Agriculture and colonization have followed in the paths opened by commerce, in Irving's formulation, but those paths have been discovered only because they are profitable. In the case of the fur trade, immense profits were made by the early French adventurers precisely because "the Indians, as yet unacquainted with the artificial value given to some descriptions of furs, in civilized life, brought quantities of the most precious kinds and bartered them away for European trinkets and cheap commodities."

Irving's introduction is personal; it tells his readers of his own fascination with the men of the North West Fur Company whom he met on visits to Canada as a young and impressionable man. In his words, "I was at an age when the imagination lends its coloring to every thing, and the stories of these Sindbads of the wilderness made the life of a trapper and fur trader perfect romance to me" (3). As Irving develops his theme, he stresses the dangers and the adventurousness of the fur trade, explaining the "charmed interest" in these terms. He will tell the story of his friend John Jacob Astor's attempt to carry the American fur trade to the shores of the Pacific because that story has romantic appeal to an author who not only has youthful memories of encounters with men who had "perilous adventures and hairbreadth escapes among the Indians," but has also recently returned from "a tour upon the prairies of the far west" and may be presumed, therefore, to be himself concerned to understand the experience of wilderness. Irving's obvious association of "adventure" and danger is a means of insisting that business enterprise is compatible with glamour, yet he insists equally on the dignity and cultural significance of Astor's attempt to make a success of his investment in the fur trade. This is done by repeatedly asserting that Astor's enterprise was patriotic—that he was motivated by a vision of American expansion into unsettled (by Whites) and disputed territories—and that Astor was indifferent to financial gain because he was already so rich that he could not seek to increase his fortune. In the explicit moral scheme of the narrative, John Jacob Astor is represented as the great man of vision who is able to transcend personal interests and consider the future greatness of his nation, as opposed to the politicians in Washington, who are stigmatized as petty and lacking in vision.[27] In this respect, as in much else, Irving's Astor is a nineteenth-century inheritor of the great explorer and visionary Irving had created in his ***Columbus***.[28]

From the beginning, however, the tale is necessarily concerned less with vision than with the details of Astor's business plans. We are told of the contacts he had with the Northwest Company before he set up his own Pacific Fur Company. As a shrewd businessman, Astor informed himself about the trade into which he entered. His venture was plainly not Quixotic; he calculated his chances carefully before venturing capital *and* he displayed the acumen of the successful businessman in the way he treated his rivals. Irving tells his readers that Astor deliberately employed men who had worked for the Northwest Company but were discontented, whether because of lack of advancement or dissatisfaction with the financial rewards.

In terms of the national theme, there are complications here, because the men in question were British nationals. In tempting them away from their fur company, Astor is recruiting foreigners to serve his "patriotic" purpose. Later, at the crisis caused by the War of 1812, Irving will accuse some of these men of treachery—of betraying Astor and selling out cheaply to the British. In doing so, Irving will take a high moral tone, by implication elevating his hero Astor above such baseness. Yet no reader can escape the impression that Astor has been hoist with his own petard. In suborning the Britons and attempting to use them to defeat his rival the North West Fur Company, Astor has made himself vulnerable to charges of cynicism. Put more bluntly, there is a suspicion of cant in *Irving's* moralising here. Having approved, or condoned, Astor's sharp practice in recruiting disaffected Northwesters to work against their fellow-countrymen, Irving sounds false when he takes the moral highground and judges those men when (or if) they are less than totally loyal to Astor's Pacific Fur Company.

This is not an isolated occurrence of the moral issue in the text; the ethics of business forms the constant subtext. Throughout, the reader is confronted with the central significance of trade. To trade successfully meant to persuade the Indians to exchange furs with a high value in white economic system for trinkets costing very little in that system. Ross Cox, for example, explains the Indians traded twenty beaver skins worth twenty-five pounds for guns which cost one pound, seven shillings wholesale. Two yards of cloth, worth twelve shillings, could purchase beaver skins worth eight to ten pounds. Cox adds, smugly, "but they were satisfied, and we had no cause to complain."[29] Rivalry became intense among the competing groups of white traders precisely because none expected to exchange goods of anything like equivalent value for the furs collected by the "children of nature" in the wilderness. In trade among "civilised" peoples, profit was always an ingredient and could be justified since, without it, there could hardly be adequate motivation for exchange, yet the standard moral justifications for commercial enterprise in the antebellum period included the caveat that profit should be moderate, that it should accumulate gradually, and that there should be no gambling. Irving would himself make an impressive application of these ideas in his 1840 *Knickerbocker* essay, **"A Time of Unexampled Prosperity."** In it "speculation" would be denounced as a form of "magic" or "enchantment" that tempted men with the dream of easy gain and brought the sober realities of trade, and the steady accumulation of profit, into contempt.[30] Yet the history of the fur trade was one of routine and ruthless exploitation of the native Americans by White traders intent on vast—and quick—profits.[31] Though the story Irving has to tell is of failure and loss for Astor and the men working for him, the unstated corollary is that his rivals made money and made it quickly and in large amounts, just as Astor intended to do.

In contrast to Antelyes, who believes that Irving expressed an unqualified approval of the dominant Jacksonian ideology of commercial enterprise in **Astoria,** speaking for Astor and endorsing his supposed values, Hugh Egan gives prominence to the negative elements of the story Irving tells. Egan attributes the undermining to the plots themselves. In this schema, Irving intends to celebrate entrepreneurial and commercial values by telling the story of Astor's (and later Captain Bonneville's) enterprise, but is frustrated by the story stuff itself: by the *fabula* in each case. This is to say that the stories resist the *discourse*. My own view is that there are numerous places or sites in Irving's Western narratives where contradictory values confront each other and clash irreconcilably. To what extent Irving was aware of these contradictions is less important than the fact that the *aporia* are crucial for the cultural discourse of the age. In a culture that based itself on the assumption that America was the land of enterprise, and that business enterprise was a *civilizing* force, a story in which that enterprise could be seen to be morally corrupting would necessarily be subversive of official values. At issue here was nothing less than the justification for territorial expansion and for American identity. If **Astoria** is,

as Wayne R. Kime believes, "historiographically orthodox," if it "sets forth its wide-ranging subject matter in a manner calculated to emphasize its national significance,"[32] then orthodoxy—I would submit—was compatible with confusion and significance was not always what was calculated. The incidental cruelties and brutalities practised by White Americans in the new lands at the expense of the children of nature could be assimilated into the grand narrative of the progress of civilization, but if the processes of commerce—if the market itself—appeared as morally deleterious (both on "civilized" Whites and on "savage" native Americans), then American national identity was put into question.

In his narratives, Irving more than once recounts incidents that feature conflicts between White traders and Indians who demand high prices for their furs, horses or whatever. Whereas the "simple" or "innocent" savage accepted gladly, or at least unresentfully, whatever the White man offered him in exchange for the desired possessions, some natives engaged in tough bargaining or even demanded "exorbitant" prices. Regularly, this behavior is attributed to their experience of White methods of trading—or their contamination by White values. Amerindians were not the only natives to learn from the Whites, of course. Before any contact is made with the native Americans, the Astorians under Thorn's captaincy encounter a native who is sharp in business: Tamaahmaah, King of Sandwich Islands. He drives a hard bargain, exploiting the needs of those who trade with him. In his encounter with the King, Captain Thorn starts to trade for hogs "in his plain, matter of fact way" but quickly learns that the native "had profited in more ways than one by his intercourse with white men. Above all other arts he had learnt the art of driving a bargain." (48) In this instance, Captain Thorn obviously controls his temper but seems to learn nothing about the psychology of "savages" who have acquired some "civilized" arts.

Truly innocent, unsophisticated, natives—those who have not learned the ethics of trade from white men—have no tradition of thus exploiting others' needs. When destitute or hungry Whites first encounter members of Western tribes who have the means of relieving their suffering, they find that the savages give generously, without calculation. To share and to give without calculating profit is, it seems, the *natural* pattern of behavior. But this innocence gives way to experience of White values and White exploitation as the innocent natives *fall* into economic sophistication, or—in other words—as they learn the system of trading for profit. They thus become *enterprising* natives; they are making the first steps towards becoming civilized and to becoming "Americans." Yet when they behave in this way they provoke the anger of the white Americans who have come to trade with (or exploit) them. The narrator, at such points, both acknowledges that the Indians' behavior is learned and—occasionally—represents their behavior as deplorable. Sometimes, indeed, the narrative condemns the "rascally" natives for their greed, seemingly unaware of the ironies implied in a text that indulges white sharp practice by normalising it.

The "savages" who murder Thorn and his crew are conforming to the prejudices that Thorn and other white traders bring with them when they engage in commercial transactions with the native Americans. When Indians fail to conform to another set of prejudices—those that portray them as "simple" children of nature with no sense of value in the white man's world—they are also condemned by the "civilized" whites who intend to take advantage of their supposed simplicity. A striking and parallel example comes late in the narrative (chap. 52), when one of the partners—Mr Clarke—encounters a village of Nez Perces on the confluence of the Lewis and Pavion rivers. Clarke intends to leave his boats here and travel the hundred and fifty miles to the Spokane tribe on horseback. When he tries to buy horses from the Nez Perces, however, "he had to contend with the sordid disposition of these people (311). The Indians are "sordid" in that "they asked high prices for their horses, and were so difficult to deal with that Mr. Clarke was detained seven days among them before he could procure a sufficient number." The "sordid" nature of the Indians is also evident in the pilfering they practise while the Clarke party is with them, but there is no doubt that Irving's narrative endorses the white trader's moral judgment: "savages" are sordid if they ask prices higher than the whites want to pay because the savages are exploiting the evident need of the whites. In other words, it is "sordid" if a "savage" uses the trading skills (and employs the trading ethics) regularly used by White men.

A more dramatic example is provided in Irving's account of the village of Wish-ram, the fishing mart on the Columbia (chap. 38). Its inhabitants live by trade, which has "sharpened their wits, though . . . not improved their honesty" in the opinion of Wilson Price Hunt (229), relayed without any distancing comment by Irving. Hunt finds these natives "shrewder and more intelligent than any Indians he had met with." Earlier, in chapter 10, Irving has described the village as "a solitary instance of an aboriginal trading mart, or emporium" (69). Since this is the market for fish from the mouth of the Columbia as well as horses and other commodities from the Rocky Mountains, there is a lively trade here before the fur traders make their entrance. Acting as middle men, the inhabitants of Wish-ram seem, to the first white explorers who meet them, "sleeker and fatter, but less hardy and active, than the tribes of the mountains and prairies." Irving then quotes "an honest trader" who describes them as "worthless dogs" (70). He adds a curious moral: "The habits of trade and the avidity of gain have their corrupting effects even in the wilderness, as may be instanced in the members of this aboriginal emporium" who, to the "honest trader" quoted above, are "'saucy, impudent rascals, who will, steal when they can, and pillage whenever a weak party falls in their power'" (70).

In contrast to these "sordid" savages, the members of a village of Arickaras visited by Hunt show him and his party "the hospitality of the Arab," entertaining the whites with kindness and generosity and sharing with them their food and tobacco. Generalizing, Irving states that "the In-

dian in his native state, before he has mingled much with white men, and acquired their sordid habits" always offers food to any stranger who enters his doors, "and never is the food thus furnished made a matter of traffic." (144) At this point in the text, "sordidness" is not only transferred from the savage to the civilized; it is also quite unambiguously associated with "trade" or "traffic."

Irving's narrative reveals how sordid the fur trade could be when he tells of the rivalry between the various companies competing for control of the supplies of peltries. On his overland journey to Astoria, Hunt discovers that his party is being pursued by Manuel Lisa of the Missouri Fur Company. Long before Hunt encounters Lisa, the reader is given information about him. A Spaniard by birth, Lisa is a man "of bold and enterprizing character" (92), who has established trading posts in Sioux country and among the Arickara and Mandan tribes in 1808. We are told this in a chapter dealing with Hunt's arrival in St. Louis on the start of his mission to Astoria. The appearance of a new fur company produced "a strong sensation among the Indian traders of the place, and awakened keen jealousy and opposition" from the Missouri Company (93). When Hunt gets to the Great Bend of the Missouri River (chapter 19), he is warned that his party is in danger from Sioux war parties, out for revenge on the whites for the casual killing of one of their warriors by Kit Carson. He is also warned that Lisa is not far behind him on the Missouri. Since Hunt has tried to out-maneuver Lisa and get to the trading grounds ahead of him, he is not at all pleased to find himself overtaken. The members of Hunt's party consider Lisa "artful and slippery" and "secretly anxious for the failure of their expedition" (133, 133-34). One of Hunt's companions, a Mr McLellan, threatens to shoot Lisa on sight because of an earlier "outrage" committed, he supposes, by the enterprising fur trader. Lisa, so his rivals believe, is determined to keep his monopoly of trade with the Indians, even to the extent of encouraging the Sioux in their hostility to his competitors.[33]

In terms of Irving's story, the encounter with Lisa is important only for what it reveals about the difficulties Hunt has to face in his heroic overland journey. In terms of our understanding of the fur trade, however, it is one of the most important episodes in the narrative. The rivalry between the two parties of white men almost leads to murder, when the leaders come face to face and insult each other. Bloodshed is narrowly avoided, and the whites smoke the pipe of peace with each other, but mutual mistrust and hostility is clearly not to be removed by protestations of common interest.

Though Irving was committed by his great literary enterprise to the belief that commerce was morally and culturally elevating, as the historian of the Astorian venture he had to tell a story of greed, jealousy, and unscrupulous exploitation of the Indians by whites who cared nothing for their present wellbeing or their future survival.[34] To be enterprising *always* meant to "drive a hard bargain" in the world of fur trading. Success was always measured by the disproportion between outlay and income.

While he was working on *Astoria,* Irving met Benjamin Bonneville, a friend of Astor's who had firsthand experience of the ferocious competition among fur traders in the Rocky Mountains and the Far West, having failed to break in to the trade dominated by the Hudson Bay Company.[35] Bonneville had spent three years, from April 30, 1832 to April 22, 1835, in apparently aimless and profitless wanderings west of Independence, Missouri, and wrote an account of his travels in the autumn and winter of the year of his return. The two men met at Astor's Hell Gate in mid September 1835, when Bonneville probably told Irving something of his adventures.[36] In a letter dated March 27, 1836, Irving tells of his agreement with Bonneville to work up the manuscript for publication. In fact, he paid Bonneville $1,000 for the manuscript and began working on it as soon as *Astoria* was published, that is in October 1836. Irving's enthusiasm for the project is clear from his comment that he had been interested and delighted with his materials "in their crude state" (in Bonneville's prose, presumably) and believed that they would "be very taking when properly dressed up." The story, he decided, was "full of adventure, discription [sic], and stirring incident; with occasional passages of humor."[37]

Irving wrote *The Rocky Mountains; Or, Scenes, Incidents, and Adventures in the Far West* (1837), later titled *The Adventures of Captain Bonneville,* rapidly. The English edition was published in May 1837; the American in June of that year. In his narrative Irving returns to his theme of "enterprise," imagining the Captain's feelings as he first sets eyes on the Rockies. Bonneville feels the emotions appropriate to the sublime—"awe and admiration" (31)—as he faces the magnificent prospect which will be "the vast and mountainous scene of his adventurous enterprise." Although Irving presents Bonneville as the inheritor of Astor's vision of American empire—the Captain plans to recapture the trade lost when Astoria collapsed (159)—the frequent emphasis on his romantic disposition makes Bonneville a man of sensibility rather than a businessman. American reviewers responded to Irving's emphasis on adventure and romance, contrasting the "heroic" nature of Bonneville's enterprise with the merely "commercial" connotations of "enterprise" as commonly understood (xxvi).

In his introduction Irving states that Bonneville inherited an excitable imagination from his unworldly and scholarly father. His interest in the West was stimulated by trappers' tales of the "vast and magnificent regions" through which they wandered (4). When he comes to such obvious opportunities for landscape description as the first sight of the Wind River Mountains (mentioned above), Irving decides that his hero "must have contemplated" them with awe and admiration (31). The implication clearly is that Irving has credited Bonneville with feelings *not* recorded in the manuscript the Captain sold him.

When Bonneville resolves to explore the Great Salt Lake (chapter 21), he does so because he intends to profit from it, but Irving puts the profit motive second to Bonneville's

imagination, which clothed the lake "with vague and ideal charms" (114). The strategy seems to be to clothe Bonneville's apparently pointless and unprofitable wanderings in romantic trappings. This is achieved by more passages devoted to landscape description than were found in *Astoria.* Even when not attributed to Bonneville, these reflections give an impression of sensibility that may be credited to him.

Another emphasis in *Bonneville* is on the adventurousness of the expedition and of the participants. Though the "wild freedom" that is to be contrasted with the "tame" life of the cities is essentially that of the American trapper rather than the career soldier, by association Bonneville shares in that exhilarating escape from the restrictions of civilized life.

In his opening chapter Irving pays tribute to the "courage, fortitude, and perseverance" of the pioneers of the fur trade (8). The role of honor includes Smith, Fitzpatrick, Bridger, Campbell and Sublette. Their "adventures and exploits partake of the wildest spirit of romance" (9). Clearly, Irving wishes to make these men heroes, for he describes them as "hardy, lithe, vigorous, and active . . . heedless of hardship, daring of danger; prodigal of the present, and thoughtless of the future" (11). They form the "wild chivalry" of the mountains (12), leading a "Robin Hood" sort of existence, but the air of boyish recklessness with which Irving endows them contrasts with the vicious meanness they display in the struggle to defeat their rivals. As Irving admits: "next to his own advantage, the study of the Indian trader is the disadvantage of his competitor" (11).

Irving cites one of his heroes, Fitzpatrick, on the evils of competition. (52) This experienced and brave trapper wants to put an end to the excesses of rivalry by dividing the fur trapping areas into zones of interest, but his plan is rejected by his competitors. When Bonneville meets his own hunting parties on the Green River in July 1833, he hears tales of their losses and misfortunes caused by competition with the Rocky Mountain Fur Company. These include broken traps, destroyed beaver lodges. Irving adds: "We forbear to detail these pitiful contentions" (108).

Irving's claim, in his first chapter, that the pioneers of the fur trade were men "whose adventures and exploits partake of the wildest spirit of romance" (9), clearly shows how he planned to give shape and significance to Bonneville's story. Essentially, *Captain Bonneville* was to be an adventure story celebrating the daring of the men who lived with boyish, uncalculating courage possible only beyond the bounds of civilization. We can observe this strategy most clearly in chapter 20, for in it Irving creates the life of the trappers at its most vividly carefree and picturesque. At the annual rendezvous, the trappers who have feuded with each other all through the hunting season mingle "on terms of perfect good fellowship" and engage in athletic and sporting contests—"running, jumping, wrestling, shooting with the rifle, and running horses" (111). Irving's prose captures the wild, saturnalian energies of the scene that, for him, demonstrates the uncalculating spirit of these wild men. In this scene of "wild prodigality" (112), men who have risked their lives collecting pelts in hazardous and severe circumstances squander their earnings in a few wild days of "revelry and extravagance." For Irving's readers, this must surely have provided the thrill of vicarious excitement. The West, it seemed, could breed men who were indifferent to all prudential, tame, civilized considerations.

Yet Irving's strategies are not only blatant; they are also self-defeating, for the story he tells is either pointless or moral in ways that threaten his program. Bonneville's supposed romantic sensibility makes no counterweight to the account of vicious, and sordid, competition among the men who are opening the West to American civilization. Moreover, Irving's honesty as an historian obliged him to include episodes of appalling brutality and cruelty on the part of the white trappers. The story of the malice and bitterness that characterized the rivalry between the Rocky Mountain Fur Company and its rivals, in chapter 19, is preceded by a shocking example of white savagery, in which Arickara hostages are burned to death by the whites when horses stolen by other members of their tribe are not all returned. The Battle of Pierre's Hole (chapter 6) is not an heroic episode but a sordid affair caused by the treachery of the half-breed Antoine Godin, one of Milton Sublette's trappers. His murder of a Blackfoot chief as the latter extended his hand in friendship is the signal for a general onslaught on the Blackfeet by rival Indian tribes and by the whites gathered at the annual rendezvous.

To argue, as Peter Antelyes does, that Irving's faith in the redemptive possibilities of adventurous enterprise (expressed unequivocally in *Astoria*) had become tenuous by the time he wrote *Bonneville,* and that the methods of the fur trade described in the later work constituted a frightening example of Jacksonian economic expansion, is to overlook the continuities between the two works and between both of them and Irving's *Columbus*.[38] The great visionary of the fifteen century imagined by Irving had a mind "elevated above selfish and mercenary views" (162; 434). Columbus was able to carry out his "grand enterprizes" in spite of all the difficulties presented by petty, jealous, avaricious rivals and patrons, because his ambition, unlike theirs, was "truly noble and lofty" and because in him the practical man of business was united with the spirit of poetry (565). The great benefit of his discovery of the New World was that it opened unbounded fields of "inquiry" and "enterprize" to Europeans (163). Columbus's imagination was always "sallying in advance and suggesting some splendid track of enterprize" (255). Yet his object in sailing west was to establish *commercial* relations with some opulent and civilized country of the east (111). When, instead, he arrived in Haiti, he found natives in an Edenic state, surrounded by natural blessings, living without toil in open undefended gardens, without laws, without artificial wants (119). On Hispaniola, when the Europeans arrived, the natives behaved "with remarkable frankness and generosity." They "had no idea of traffic,

but gave away everything with spontaneous liberality" (122). Irving later generalizes, noting that "the untutored savage, in almost every part of the world, scorns to make a traffic of hospitality" (218). Only when the white man has introduced the habits of trade, do the Indians learn "to profit by the necessities of the stranger" and demand a price for bread (348). The appalling transformation of an opulent and lovely island into a scene of desolation and misery is attributed by Irving to the "evil passions of the white men" (380). Regularly, the evil takes the form of that "avidity of gain" (540), that "avarice" and lust for gold regularly associated in Irving's text with the Spaniards and the Portuguese. Yet that text also—and unmistakably—presents the loss of innocence and the Fall from the golden age existence into the historical world of wickedness and exploitation as the introduction of artificial wants and the spirit of trade—of commercial enterprise in fact—into the Garden of Eden. If Irving's Astor is the nineteenth-century inheritor of the vision of Columbus, he is—in Irving's narrative of the West—also the businessman whose "great enterprise" put into question the very American values *Astoria* was meant to affirm.

Notes

1. Irving's words, in a letter to his niece, are quoted in Stanley T. Williams, *The Life of Washington Irving,* vol. 2 (New York: Oxford UP, 1935), 27.

2. Dahlia Kirby Terrell, ed., introduction, *The Crayon Miscellany,* by Washington Irving (Boston: Twayne, 1979), 7.

3. Irving's words, in a speech made on his return to New York city in April, 1832, are quoted in John Francis McDermott's introduction to his edition of *The Western Journals of Washington Irving* (Norman, OK: U of Oklahoma P, 1944), 4.

4. Irving, from a letter to Peter Irving (Dec. 12, 1832), quoted in McDermott, *Western Journals,* 10.

5. *The Life and Letters of Washington Irving,* ed. Pierre M. Irving, vol. 3 (London: Bentley, 1864), 23.

6. Ellsworth was more impressed by Irving's cultivation and refinement than by his "wild" qualities. He noted that the writer could not write unless washed and properly dressed. See Henry Leavitt Ellsworth, *Washington Irving on the Prairies; Or, A Narrative of a Tour of the Southwest in the Year 1832,* eds S. T. Williams and B. O. Simison (New York: American Book Company, 1937), 70.

7. Quoted in McDermott, *The Western Journals,* 38.

8. This is the thesis of Bruce Greenfield's *Narrating Discovery: The Romantic Explorer in American Literature, 1790-1855* (New York: Columbia UP, 1992). See, particularly, 113-22.

9. References to *A Tour* will be to *The Crayon Miscellany,* ed. Dahlia Kirby Terrell (1979) and will be included in parenthesis in my text. For the reviews, see Andrew B. Myers, "Washington Irving, Fur Trade Chronicler: An Analysis of *Astoria,* with Notes for a

Corrected Edition," diss., Columbia U, 1964, 33. See also, Martha Dula, "Audience Response to *A Tour on the Prairies* in 1835," *Western American Literature* 8 (1973), 67-74.

10. McDermott, *The Western Journals,* 43-44. See also Robert Edson Lee, *From West to East: Studies in the Literature of the American West* (Urbana and London: U of Illinois P, 1966) for an attack on Irving's literary methods in *A Tour.*

11. One of those who have judged *A Tour* in this way is Stanley T. Williams in his introduction to Henry Leavitt Ellsworth, *Washington Irving on the Prairies,* viii. In contrast, Wayne R. Kime argues persuasively that *A Tour* is the story of an Eastener's awakening to the significance of the West ("The Completeness of Washington Irving's *A Tour on the Prairies*," *Western American Literature* 8 [1973], 55-56).

12. See Terrell, ed., *Crayon Miscellany,* 10. As Dahlia Kirby Terrell's note points out, the Indian Removal Act was passed on June 30, 1830.

13. When he launched himself into his American themes, as Wayne R. Kime argues, Irving was at the height of his powers ("The Author As Professional: Washington Irving's 'Rambling Anecdotes' of the West," *Critical Essays on Washington Irving,* ed. Ralph M. Aderman [Boston: Hall, 1990], 237-53). In Kime's judgment, Irving never wrote so much and so well as in the years 1832 to 1836. In this view, Irving was already a mature and respected man of letters and a moralist of considerable sophistication when he wrote *A Tour.* Irving's sympathy for the Amerindian had been evidenced in his "Traits of Indian Character" and "Philip of Pockanockett" pieces in *The Sketch Book.*

14. Everett Emerson's review is quoted in *The Life and Letters,* ed. Pierre M. Irving, vol. 3, 46. In turn, Peter Antelyes, who also quotes from the review, treats it as an endorsement of Irving's literary exploitation of the West (*Tales of Adventurous Enterprise: Washington Irving and the Poetics of Western Expansion* [New York: Columbia UP, 1990], 93-95).

15. William Bedford Clark, "How the West Won; Irving's Comic Inversion of the Westering Myth in *A Tour on the Prairies,*" *American Literature* 50.3 (1978), 335-47. See, especially, 336.

16. Greenfield, *Narrating Discovery,* 132-33.

17. Antelyes, *Tales of Adventurous Enterprise,* 95. According to Antelyes, the deeper motivation of all Irving's Western writings can be understood in terms of his need to explore the self-justifying shape of the American commercial imagination at a time when Americans were powerfully influenced by tales of economic expansion in the Westward movement. See below for further discussion of this thesis.

18. Schoolcraft's charge that Astor paid Irving a huge sum (five thousand dollars) to write *Astoria* was refuted by Irving. See Williams, *Life of Washington Irving,* vol. 2, 75. See also Myers, "Washington Irving, Fur Trade Chronicler," 50.

19. The theory is that of Myers (see "Washington Irving, Fur Trade Chronicler," in particular 57).

20. Antelyes, *Tales of Adventurous Enterprise,* 149. See also 150-52.

21. *The Letters of Washington Irving,* vol. 2 (1823-38), ed. Ralph M. Aderman (Boston: Twayne, 1979), 839. Compare Irving's reference, in a letter dated Apr. 17, 1835, to Astor's "grand commercial . . . colonial enterprise" (818).

22. *Astoria; Or, Anecdotes of an Enterprize beyond the Rocky Mountains,* ed. Richard Dilworth Rust (Boston: Twayne, 1976), 73. References to this edition will be included parenthetically in the text.

23. Wayne R. Kime, "Alfred Seton's Journal; A Source for Irving's *Tonquin* Disaster Account," *Oregon Historical Quarterly* 71 (1970), 309-24. Kime states that Irving used Seton's anonymous account of the Astoria adventures in the May and July issues of the *American Monthly Magazine* and was familiar with Seton's journal. In Seton's words: "Captain Thorn could not agree with them [the natives] about the price" and, becoming enraged, rubbed the skin [about which they were haggling] in a chief's face" (Kime, "Alfred Seton's Journal," 314-15). In his "Washington Irving's Revision of the *Tonquin* Episode in *Astoria,*" Kime lists Irving's sources for the incident (*Western American Literature* 4 [1969], 51-59). In addition to Seton and Ross Cox (see below, note 24), these included Gabriel Franchère's *Relation d'un voyage* (Montreal, 1820). Franchère, like Seton, attributed the outbreak of violence to Thorn's frustration in bargaining for furs. Thorn struck a chief in the face with a fur, "having had trouble about the price" (see *Adventure at Astoria, 1810-1814* [*Relation d'un voyage*], trans. Hoyt C. Franchère [1820; Norman, OK: U of Oklahoma P, 1967], 80).

24. Ross Cox had taken part in the Astorian venture, arriving on the *Beaver* in 1811 and staying until 1813 (see Myers, "Washington Irving, Fur Trade Chronicler," 132). His account of the destruction of the *Tonquin* is given in chapter five. It includes a reference to Captain Thorn's detection of the chief's "petty theft."

25. In *The Westminster Review* 26 (1836-37), *Astoria* is described as "not a romance, but a plain . . . description of a mercantile speculation" (320). The review is quoted in I. S. McLaren's useful article "Washington Irving's Problems with History and Romance in *Astoria,*" *Canadian Review of American Studies* 21.1 (1990), 1-14. The reviewer also states that in Astor the "plain merchant" almost becomes the "founder of an empire" and the "aggrandizer of a nation" (320).

26. Alexander Ross, *Adventures of the First Settlers on the Oregon or Columbia River, Early Western Trav-*

els, 1748-1846, ed. Reuben Gold Thwaites, vol. 7 (1849; New York: AMS P, 1966), 34.

27. For a less flattering view of Astor's career, see Richard E. Oglesby, "John Jacob Astor . . . 'a better businessman than the best of them,'" *Journal of the West* 25 (1986), 8-14. As Sigmund Diamond demonstrates, some of Astor's obituaries in the American press treated his career as anything but exemplary, stressing the exploitative nature of his business enterprises (*The Reputation of the American Businessman* [Cambridge, MA: Harvard UP, 1955], chap. 2 ("John Jacob Astor").

28. The importance of the parallels between Irving's Astor and his Columbus has been clearly recognized by Antelyes (*Tales of Adventurous Enterprise,* 7-9) and Greenfield (*Narrating Discovery,* 148).

29. Ross Cox, *Adventures on the Columbia* (1831; San Francisco: California State Library [WPA Program], 1941), 79.

30. "A Time of Unexampled Prosperity," *Knickerbocker* 15 (1840), *Wolfert's Roost,* ed. Roberta Rosenberg (1855; Boston: Twayne, 1979), 95-119. See, especially, 96.

31. See Paul Chrisler Phillips, *The Fur Trade,* 2 vols (Norman, OK: U of Oklahoma P, 1961). In chapter 40, "The American Advance to the Pacific," he gives the example of the advance of 125% above cost paid by the Osages for goods supplied from St. Louis. The Indians paid skins and robes valued at 30,000 dollars for goods that had cost the white traders 20,000 dollars (vol. 2, 247). As Harold Hickerson points out in his "Fur Trade Colonisation and the North American Indians," from the beginning the Whites controlled supplies and set prices (*Journal of Ethnic Studies* 1 [1973], 24). Indian trappers became locked into a system organized by trading companies that were utterly indifferent to their needs and circumstances.

32. Kime, "The Author as Professional: Washington Irving's 'Rambling Anecdotes' of the West," *Critical Essays on Washington Irving,* ed. Aderman, 251.

33. For accounts of Lisa's trading enterprises, and his hopes of monopolising trade, see David J. Wishart, *The Fur Trade of the American West, 1807-1840* (Lincoln, NE: U of Nebraska P, 1979), 42ff. See also William H. Goetzmann, *New Lands, New Men: America and the Second Great Age of Discovery* (New York: Viking, 1986), 133ff. Lisa—a very successful fur trade entrepreneur—was so hated by his men that he dared not turn his back on them.

34. While explaining the rivalries between white fur traders and their companies, Irving devotes one paragraph to an account of the motivation of the Teton Sioux, first telling us that they were considered "a sort of pirates of the Missouri," who regarded the goods of American traders as fair game (116). These Indians trade with the British merchants, who are resolved to keep out all rivals. Moreover, the traders of the Northwest Company have supplied the Sioux with firearms and thus given them an immense superiority over tribes higher up the Missouri. Since the Teton Sioux had the only access to the white man's produce, they "made themselves also, in a manner, factors for the upper tribes, supplying them at second hand, and at greatly advanced prices, with goods derived from the white men" (116). If American traders were to reach the Upper Missouri, they would not only deprive the Teton Sioux of their lucrative role as middle men; they might also supply the other tribes with guns. Hence the determination of the Tetons to block the progress of the new traders, whether independent or belonging to new fur companies.

35. For an outline of Bonneville's career, see Edgeley W. Todd, "Benjamin L. E. Bonneville," *The Mountain Men and the Fur Trade of the Far West,* ed. LeRoy Hafen, vol. 5 (Glendale, CA: Clark, 1968), 45-63.

36. See John F. McDermott, "Washington Irving and the Journal of Captain Bonneville," *Mississippi Valley Historical Review* 43 (1956), 459-66.

37. Washington Irving, *The Adventures of Captain Bonville,* eds Robert A. Rees and Alan Sandy (1837; Boston: Twayne, 1977), introduction, xxiii. Hereafter cited parenthetically in the text.

38. Washington Irving, *History of the Life and Voyages of Christopher Columbus,* ed. John Harmon McElroy (1828; Boston: Twayne, 1981). Hereafter cited parenthetically in the text.

Laura J. Murray (essay date 1996)

SOURCE: "The Aesthetic of Dispossession: Washington Irving and Ideologies of (De)Colonization in the Early Republic," *American Literary History,* Vol. 8, No. 2, Summer, 1996, pp. 205-31.

[*In the following essay, Murray discusses early American views on identity and nationality through an analysis of the works of Irving and William Apess.*]

> We see that recognition of your alienation leads many of you to be empowered into the remarking of your culture, while we are paralyzed into a state of displacement with no place to go.
>
> María C. Lugones to Elizabeth V. Spelman, "Have We Got a Theory for You! Feminist Theory, Cultural Imperialism and the Demand for 'The Woman's Voice.'"

Insisting on the different positions of white women and women of color within society and within feminism, María Lugones points out in her dialogue with Elizabeth Spelman that white women's growing awareness of their disempowerment has in fact produced an empowerment that many white women are not comfortable to acknowledge.

Feminism, despite its rhetoric of universal sisterhood, has often excluded those women oppressed by not only gender but race, class, sexuality, or nationality; alternately, it has included them only at the expense of their particularity. Thus, increasingly, the limited nature of mainstream feminism's definition of the word *woman* has been questioned by women outside this definition, who have contributed to the theorization of new, plural, subjects of feminism. The world is not, as they have pointed out, divided only on gender lines, between men and women, but on many other material and ideological lines as well. White women, they assert, and women privileged in other ways, must be understood not only as victims of power, but also as agents possessing power.[1]

While the authors and issues I will discuss in this article are far removed from this late twentieth-century feminist debate, the thought generated by the (far from complete) renovation and complication of feminist practice and theory is, I think, methodologically suggestive for the work I will undertake. Let us consider the position of Americans of European descent, men and women, in the early years of American independence from Britain. Models that posit a binary relation of colonizer and colonized cannot be adequate to the multiplicities of this social and discursive context.[2] For while European Americans were actively engaged in appropriating the land of Native Americans, by treaty, war, or ruse, they also found themselves still enmeshed in ties of trade, ideology, and diplomacy with Great Britain, their former colonial center. They remained as well very much a cultural province of Britain. British reviewers routinely laughed at American cultural efforts, and against this background Americans with increasing fervor proclaimed projects of creating a national American culture. Such projects often involved Native American imagery or characters. Carved into icons mouthing immortal sentiments, Native Americans were valued in the symbolic economy of emerging nationalist discourse, but they were not valued as speaking subjects in elections or town squares. Native Americans, at least those within settled areas, were being assimilated by force into economic and cultural formations of European America, and yet by force they were kept on the margins of those formations.

Both the culture of the early republic and twentieth-century liberal feminism have included or desired Others—political legitimacy may even have depended on such inclusion—but the parameters of inclusion have been dictated largely from within the dominant discourse. Degrees or kinds of powerlessness have not been recognized; rather, the tendency has been toward rhetorical equations between kinds of oppression and marginality. Liberal feminists have said, "we're all women, we're all enslaved"; white Americans during the revolution likened themselves to slaves and dressed as Mohawks. Such assertions of identity across lines of race and history are often strategically effective, but their power derives from gross oversimplification of different institutions of suffering and patterns of culture.

What is needed in both these cases—that is, in forwarding feminism and in understanding early American nationalism—is a multidimensional approach to power, attentive to numerous spheres of conflict and contestation, that recognizes and articulates various kinds of experienced oppression and empowering action. It is not productive to argue over who is "more" oppressed or "as" oppressed as someone else; this is far too quantitative a model for deployment of power, and it is more important in any case to try to determine the relations between institutions and ideologies of oppression. I consider this essay to be a contribution to such a project, albeit a contribution based on one literary example. It is in order to clarify the interactions between sectors of colonialism in British North America and the US that I will discuss here an ideological phenomenon that muddied these interactions. Through what I call an aesthetic of dispossession, Euro-Americans cultivated their sense of vulnerability with respect to Britain, and in so doing rhetorically exculpated themselves from their colonizing role with respect to Native Americans.

1

It has finally become a commonplace to observe that from its earliest years, the study of American literature has been predominantly oriented towards defining the national traits of a national literature, and that this orientation has distorted our understanding of the diverse forms and functions of representation in American history. The Moses Coit Tyler to Sacvan Bercovitch sweep of scholarship on foundational Puritan thought patterns has encountered serious challenges (even from Bercovitch himself), and the transhistorical nature of myths of "the American Adam" or "the machine in the garden" has also been questioned. Proclaiming a nonnationalist, unteleological approach to literature of the 13 colonies or the early republic, many critics now emphasize the contingency or constructedness of American identity, the breaks and changes in the role of literature in American society, and the particular literary traits of particular periods and social groups in American history.

With respect to the literature of the early republic, this new work tends to emphasize not postrevolutionary ebullience and uniqueness, but instead the *fragility* of the nascent American nation as represented in its literature. The phenomenon of the "new" new republic could certainly not be identified as a unified school of research; rather, scholars coming from diverse theoretical directions, from biographical criticism through postcolonial theory and poststructuralism, have emphasized similar traits. Thus Jeffrey Rubin-Dorsky observes the "mirroring effect" between Washington Irving's "profound sense of homelessness and his acute longing for stability" and "the conflicts, anxieties, and needs of the new republic" (xv-xvi). In *Visionary Compacts,* claiming that authors of the American Renaissance sought social and imaginative security in prerevolutionary history, Donald Pease takes Edgar Allan Poe as an exemplar: "[B]y inventing the literary persona of a dispossessed aristocrat," he writes, "Poe found a way to experience life in the modern world as a terrifying loss" (159). Lawrence Buell brings the tools of postcolonial studies to American literature, discussing Herman Melville's *Billy Budd* as "an image of American postcolonial anxiety" ("Melville" 216), whereas Carroll Smith-Rosenberg's analysis of the divided European-American self in the writing of Charles Brockden Brown and Susanna Rowson evidently owes a great deal to poststructuralist theories of subjectivity. All of these projects, however diverse in methods and terminology, present an early republic fraught with anxiety, vulnerability, and fragmentation.

Such interpretations of the era often declare themselves to be critiques of previous overly monolithic portrayals of "the birth of the nation." Pease, for example, contrasts his emphasis on postrevolutionary longing for prerevolutionary communitarian values with the central place often accorded to the revolutionary mythos of the individual against the wilderness (9). Smith-Rosenberg asserts that whereas previous critics have considered *Edgar Huntly* (Charles Brockden Brown, 1799) and *Reuben and Rachel* (Susanna Rowson, 1798) to be "failures," critics aware of the "polyglot and socially fragmented world" of early America should hail these novels for their refusal to represent "closure and hierarchy" (504). Indeed, attention to the fitful and not-preordained transition from colonial culture to national culture is useful and timely—and it could be noted that I too have set up the opening of this section with the same polarized narrative of now and then, unified and fragmented, simple and complex. However, it would be wise to observe amidst the self-congratulation that there is a long-standing project *within* the nationalist tradition of American cultural history that attends to the *development* of national identity. Scholars such as Perry Miller, Fred Somkin, and many others have at times observed phenomena similar to those observed by more recent critics, even if they describe them as stages of development rather than moments of alternative possibility or textual rupture.

The recent work may not be straightforwardly distinct from earlier efforts; even accounts that fracture the notion of an instant or inherent American identity may be recuperated by the sheer narrative force that has accrued through and to the telling of American history over the years. Words like "young," "adolescence," "troubled," and "threatened" continue to appear frequently in writing about the early republic. These terms, and the narrative whose presence they announce, anthropomorphize the nation within a model of child/nation development. The "young" US is imagined as a childlike version of the late twentieth-century "mature" US; history is posited as natural continuum. Through this narrative of maturation, any moments of conflict or alternate possibilities in American history can be interpreted as, to borrow from the language of parentage, "just a phase," a temporary accident along the way of preordained development. Critics such as Smith-Rosenberg who eschew narrative models of subjectivity nonetheless may be slipped into them, with the caveat that they value as most telling or "natural" those mo-

ments of incoherence and confusion that to others may be best forgotten. This is not to say that there is not a profound difference between poststructuralist and developmental models of subjectivity, but rather that given the hegemony of the latter the former may have difficulty resisting narrativization.

Furthermore, I would claim that both the idea of the nation as anxious individual and the idea of the nation as decentered subject promote an exclusive or engulfing conception of American culture, always thought of as singular and continuous even if troubled within itself. Rubin-Dorsky and Smith-Rosenberg work from very different theoretical assumptions, but they both privilege texts manifesting anxiety and fragmentation as representative representations of early America. But if early America was so unstable and heteroglot, then surely it contained texts of bravado and clarity as well as texts of introspection and opacity. I would insist that anxiety is by no means the prominent trait in early American texts, especially if we consider women's writing, non-New England writing, writing by people of color, and non-canonical genres—and that when such writings *are* anxious, they are likely so for very different reasons. Smith-Rosenberg has pointed this out in her differentiation between Rowson's and Brown's social positions and representational strategies, although she ultimately identifies broadly identical traits in their writing, but Buell and Pease, among my examples, discuss only male canonical or elite writers. These writers, mostly middle-class and mostly from New England, had more to lose than many Americans and may have been correspondingly more concerned than others about America's turn away from the hierarchical society of England; furthermore, they tended to be more than commonly self-consciously involved in the nation-building project. Such caveats have to be made before their writing is held up as or implied to be representative.

Even within European-American writing, or more particularly within the canon, fracture and vulnerability are only one side of the story. It is certainly true that American leaders after the revolution found themselves unsure about what cultural and political models they should look to, and that this uncertainty is manifested in their writing. When Irving observed that American writers of his period were "exquisitely alive to the aspersions of England" (45), caught in a state of "mental vassalage" (47), he was not being disingenuous. However, to make a rather blunt historical point, anxiety existed alongside many other cultural characteristics and historical realities: the rise of industrial capitalism, territorial expansion, Indian removal and extermination, and republican ideals of true womanhood, individuality, and entrepreneurial spirit, for example. The US was hardly seriously incapacitated in its economic and cultural development; it would be a distortion to say so. This, I would suggest, poses a problem for Buell's grouping of Melville and late twentieth-century African writers Wole Soyinka and Ngugi wa Thiong'o: the "postcoloniality" in question in their respective cases is very different, however conscious they may all be about dual audiences and the inadequacies of language inherited from colonial powers. For one thing—to leave differences in historical moment aside—Euro-Americans were engaged in a colonizing project of their own at the same time as they disentangled themselves from their ties to England, and this second colonial relation in which European Americans had the position of cultural hegemony and military strength was equally defining for the new nation.[3]

As should be clear, then, I am not at all eager to make anxiety a foundational American characteristic. I am, however, interested in what it represents when it could be said to appear. Rather than dwelling on anxiety in isolation, I think it paramount that we examine the *relations between* symptoms of national insecurity and demands and actions for national security. That is, without denying that the early years of independence required complex political and ideological negotiation, we can examine how this negotiation worked, and in whose interests, identifying the US not only as an ex-colonized nation but as an expansionist and future imperial nation. This essay is an attempt to locate the "anxiety" identified with the early republic in a network of other traits and phenomena, beginning with examination of a work by the early republican writer most often described as anxious, Irving, and turning in closing to an author we might expect to be anxious but who simply is not, that is, William Apess, a Pequot Indian.

2

Although its style and charm have been admired on both sides of the Atlantic, Irving's *The Sketch Book of Geoffrey Crayon, Gent.* (1819-20) has long occupied the edges of the American national canon because of its preoccupation with England: during his seventeen years in Europe and since, Irving has been suspected of lack of devotion to his country or doubted as unrepresentative. His earlier writings, brash satires on American history, and his later writings, about the west, have been seen as more unequivocally American than *The Sketch Book.* On the grounds of subject matter, this judgment makes sense; *The Sketch Book,* like several other works of Irving's, is obsessed with the wonders of European history and culture. However, recent criticism of *The Sketch Book* defends its specifically American importance and literary value. Albert von Frank discusses Irving as an instance of the pervasive provincialism of antebellum American culture (61-78), and Joy Kasson compares Irving to other Europhilic Americans of his time (6-42). Rubin-Dorsky has recently authored a book-length study of Irving's writing between 1815 and 1832. He points out that *The Sketch Book*'s English preoccupations are not uncharacteristic of cultural production of the young US, when Americans, unsure about whether they wanted to reject all things English or to follow in England's footsteps, were drawn to explore their relation to England one way or another.

As valid as is his emphasis on the instability of American national identity represented in *The Sketch Book,* Rubin-Dorsky undermines his own claims by simultaneously re-

integrating Americanness in the person of Irving. From an observation that Irving was not atypical in his concerns, Rubin-Dorsky proceeds to make him into no less than an embodiment of the national spirit:

> Irving's most compelling subject as a writer—the displaced self adrift in a mutable world— . . . coincided with the uneasiness and uncertainty of the American people as they contemplated the fate of the nation in the early decades of the nineteenth century. The conflicts, anxieties, and needs of the new republic were reflected in Irving's profound sense of homelessness and his acute longing for stability; and it was, above all, the operation of this mirroring effect that subliminally captivated his audience. . . . Personal trauma paralleled national crisis. . . .
>
> (xv-xvi)

According to Rubin-Dorsky, the lack of cohesion of American identity can be represented metaphorically by one particular man's "real emotion" of instability, which Rubin-Dorsky perceives filtered through the frail device of the narrator (60). Such a reading not only presumes a very simple model of expressive writing, but reads anxiety as a temporary aberration from two fundamental unities, national and authorial identity, both of which I take to be problematic on historical and theoretical grounds.

Despite my reservations about Rubin-Dorsky's approach, it is clear that some of the traits he identifies in Irving's writing are indeed prominent there.[4] Seeking to contextualize Irving's much-noted anxiety, then, I will discuss here the workings of what I call the aesthetic of dispossession. I argue that this aesthetic, which operated through romanticization of the ideas of dispossession, homelessness, and loss, served to mask historical differences between settler colonialism and colonization of indigenous people. On the one hand, Irving nurtured a sense of dispossession from an English heritage, which became in his writing a poetic and poignant loss; on the other, he also dwelt with romantic fascination on the Native Americans' loss of land and life and lifeways, removing Native Americans from history and positioning them in the realm of romance. Romanticization of both England and of Native Americans is widespread in literature and art of this period, although they are rarely linked in critical discussions. But I would emphasize that the sense of loss so many critics attribute to the era actually *gained* those writers who emphasized it aesthetic value: writers preoccupied with their uncertain status produced poignant meditations that appealed to genteel readers in both England and America, and the destruction of Native American cultures and their incomprehensibility to white observers were well suited to literary exploitation as sublime or tragic. Irving's *The Sketch Book,* which crosses the ocean several times between chapters, indulges both American readers' fondness for "olde England" and English readers' interest in things exotic and savage.

The first two chapters of *The Sketch Book* clearly set the book up as a travel narrative, whose conventions would lead the reader to expect an orderly procession of impressions of English places and scenes, ending with a return home. Crayon has left the US, he says, in search of "the charms of storied and poetical association" (9); in Europe he has studied the "shifting scenes of life" with "the sauntering gaze with which humble lovers of the picturesque stroll from the window of one print shop to another" (9). And yet going to Europe, for Crayon, is in some respects the opposite of a pleasant exercise in nostalgia. In its narrative effect, the alarming chapter **"The Voyage"** is similar to Crayon's assessment of a sea crossing: "[I]t makes us conscious of being cast loose from the secure anchorage of settled life and sent adrift upon a doubtful world" (11). Larzer Ziff points out ("Questions" 94) that it almost seems as if Crayon were crossing the Atlantic in the other direction, as he describes the "thrilling cry of Land!" and the first view of "the land of promise" (14). Crayon's landfall is at once a coming home and a coming to a strange land, coming to an old world and coming to a new world. And although the emphatically European **"Roscoe"** chapter that follows seems to banish the potential reversal of new and old world, the two will be reversed and confused repeatedly throughout *The Sketch Book.*

In the fourth chapter, **"The Wife,"** and certainly by the fifth, **"Rip Van Winkle,"** *The Sketch Book*'s neatly launched travel narrative is quite thoroughly disrupted. Both these chapters are set in the US rather than England, and **"Rip Van Winkle"** particularly takes us completely away from the concerns of Geoffrey Crayon in England, back to a mythologized prerevolutionary Dutch America. The thematic continuities between **"Rip Van Winkle"** and the rest of *The Sketch Book* have been documented by Mary Witherspoon Bowden, Jane D. Eberwein, and Rubin-Dorsky, among others. But I am concerned here with the fact that in terms of narrative voice and continuity, this chapter marks a complete break. Although the English material soon resumes and continues, interrupted only for Irish, Dutch, and Swiss interludes, for 22 chapters, the early insistence on interpolating American material infuses the whole with a sense of underlying American concerns and destabilizes the pretense of travel narrative that structures the book. American themes are abruptly brought to the fore again following the sketch on **"Stratford-on-Avon,"** when the chapters **"Traits of Indian Character"** and **"Philip of Pokanoket"** intervene. Following more rambles in the English countryside with Crayon, the book concludes with two more American sketches before **"L'Envoy,"** the last chapter of the second volume.[5]

None of the American chapters of *The Sketch Book* are explicitly narrated by Crayon, which further unravels the premise of the book. **"Rip Van Winkle"** and **"The Legend of Sleepy Hollow"** are ostensibly from the pen of the fictional Dutch historian Diedrich Knickerbocker, and the two Indian sketches show no indication of any particular narrator at all.[6] It is strange that the narrator vanishes when the book is concerned with his native soil, but his absence indicates—I would here agree with Rubin-Dorsky—Irving's troubled attempt to make his book American

and acceptable to the English at the same time. Irving likely thought the American sketches would ground him in English readers' eyes as an American; the Indian sketches were not included in the first American edition, having been published previously in the *Analectic,* but they were published in the first British edition. Just as European explorers often invoked European culture and art while describing the American landscape, an American traveler in England would invoke Native American culture to locate himself as non-English by claiming a cultural and historical pedigree from another source. Even the Dutch stories could work this way, as a source for non-English identity. The American chapters of *The Sketch Book* interspersed with nostalgic English sketches can be seen to represent a compulsive composite of American discourses about England, on the one hand, and about clearly non-English Americans, on the other, through which the European American of the early republic becomes simultaneously visible and invisible.[7]

Another estranging effect in *The Sketch Book* is the historical setting: the American chapters are set far in the Puritan or Dutch colonial past, and the English chapters too focus on a mythologized Elizabethan England. One way Irving resolves tensions between diverse material is to cast over all of it a literary haze of time and sentiment. However, we can still discern such tensions, as an examination of a set of four consecutive chapters, **"Stratford-on-Avon," "Traits of Indian Character," "Philip of Pokanoket,"** and **"John Bull,"** will show. The Indian sketches have received very little critical attention, perhaps because they seem so conventional—they usually merit only a mention in discussions of the book[8]—and yet analysis of their juxtaposition with the English sketches will illustrate the workings of the dual aesthetic of dispossession I am discussing. It may also offer a way of breaking through the conventionality of Irving's sentimental discourse of noble savagery.

"Stratford-on-Avon" is vintage Crayon. Our genial narrator alternately mocks and defends his reverence toward the place of Shakespeare's birth and burial, as he visits all the standard shrines and conjures up some of his own. He listens to apocryphal tales with relish and spends a day at the Lucy estate imagining characters from Shakespeare plays behind every tree: "My mind had become so completely possessed by the imaginary scenes and characters connected with it, that I seemed to be actually living among them" (223). He goes on: "On returning to my inn, I could not but reflect on the singular gift of the poet; to be able thus to spread the magic of his mind over the very face of nature; to give to things and places a charm and character not their own, and to turn this 'working day world' into a perfect fairy land" (223). There are, of course, two poets "spreading magic" here, three if we count Irving as well as Crayon, and it is part of Crayon's romantic self-deprecating stance to ascribe all imaginative power to Shakespeare when it is in fact his own fertile fancy that pervades the Lucy estate that day. Likewise, we will see him emphasizing the inherently poetical qualities of Native American life rather than his own romantic interpretations of it: the agency of the European-American author and even his European-American narrator is masked, a crucial part of the aesthetic I am describing here, even as the role of the poet is being celebrated. Irving/Crayon recognizes the power of art to transform reality into romance, but he does not recognize this ability in himself.

The preoccupation with art and inspiration in **"Stratford-on-Avon"** is persistently interwoven with another of Crayon's concerns, that is, property and ownership, as announced in the very first lines of the chapter: "To a homeless man, who has no spot on this wide world which he can truly call his own, there is a momentary feeling of something like independence and territorial consequence, when, after a weary day's travel, he kicks off his boots, thrusts his feet into slippers, and stretches himself before an inn fire" (209). Crayon enjoys this kind of ownership because of its imaginary qualities and emphasizes his "homeless" situation in mock pathos—after all, tourists *seek* homelessness, as Crayon makes clear. Another passage on ownership in the Stratford chapter takes a similar approach, although its expansiveness is undercut by a story about Shakespeare that intervenes. Legend has it, we are told, that Shakespeare was ordered to leave Stratford for poaching, a punishment that initiated his theater career. Reminded that a man can be prosecuted for acting as if he owns another's property, we may be less enchanted than Crayon at the powers of the imagination touted in the following passage: "I delight in these hospitable estates, in which every one has a kind of property—at least as far as the footpath is concerned. It in some measure reconciles a poor man to his lot. . . . He breathes the pure air as freely, and lolls as luxuriously under the shade, as the lord of the soil; and if he has not the privilege of calling all that he sees his own, he has not, at the same time, the trouble of paying for it, and keeping it in order" (217). Extending this notion of ownership to Shakespeare, it would follow that Shakespeare obtained imaginative ownership of the Lucy estate, and indeed all of England, through being denied hunting rights, and more generally that the propertyless man, like Crayon himself, figuratively owns more than the propertied man. Irving, of course, made a career out of figurative possession and imaginative ownership, through artistic representation, of lands he did not belong to; in his various works, England, Spain, and the western territories are brought close to the reader through Irving's sublime communion with and alienation from them.

Immediately following **"Stratford-on-Avon,"** with no explanation or narrative premise provided, **"Traits of Indian Character"** and **"Philip of Pokanoket"** interrupt the mode of English pastoral that predominates in *The Sketch Book*. Setting and material notwithstanding, these chapters do share a certain Crayonesque sentimental style with the English chapters. Like **"Stratford-on-Avon,"** the Indian sketches are caught up in the romance of history: although the narrator (hardly distinguishable from Irving in these chapters) desperately laments the impossibility of having transparent access to the past, he also enjoys its inaccessi-

bility, which authorizes him to imaginatively recreate it. Thus, just as he chooses to write about Shakespeare rather than Sir Walter Scott, Irving focuses on King Philip's War of 1675 and excises the critique of the Creek War that framed the 1814 version of **"Traits of Indian Character."'** Whereas in the prejudiced accounts of Puritan historians, "Philip became a theme of universal apprehension" (241), Irving would rather he had been "rendered . . . the theme of the poet and the historian" (247). In *The Sketch Book* as in so many of its contemporary texts, the discourse of noble savagery smooths out the Native American path to extinction: Irving predicts that, "driven to madness and despair" (229), Indians will "vanish like a vapour from the face of the earth" (233). King Philip, Irving says, was one of a "band of native untaught heroes; who made the most generous struggle of which human nature is capable; fighting to the last gasp in the cause of their country, without a hope of victory or a thought of renown. Worthy of an age of poetry, and fit subjects for local story and romantic fiction, they have left scarcely any authentic traces on the page of history, but stalk, like gigantic shadows in the dim twilight of tradition" (235). While Irving laments the lack of historical record, this lack becomes an artistic opportunity, as this passage makes quite clear. Ziff has observed that "as political policy acknowledged the Indians' legal existence only after they surrendered their sovereignty . . . so literary representation acknowledged the Indians' culture only after they surrendered their history" (*Writing* 158-59); here, indeed, Irving deftly dismisses history and replaces it with "the dim twilight of tradition," all in generous admiration of Indian nobility.

The Indian chapters do challenge the idea that the English are only harmless and picturesque objects of touristic meditation. Irving does not flinch from depicting gross violence and dishonesty. The insistence on the violence of the English is carried further in **"Philip of Pokanoket"** by the clearly allegorical role of King Philip, "a patriot attached to his native soil" (246), fighting "to deliver his native land from the oppression of usurping strangers" (240). As an example of the "native growth of moral sentiment" (234), Philip becomes a model American as well as a noble Indian.

However, Philip also shares affinities with the English. He is a monarch, after all, and is treated by Irving with some of the same pathos as James I in the chapter **"A Royal Poet."** Crayon is nostalgic for aristocracy and admires it in both English and American settings. Furthermore, Philip and the Native Americans seem to share a kind of intellectual and aesthetic aristocracy with the Englishmen Crayon reveres. As the "wildness and irregularity" (215) of young Shakespeare's genius was nurtured by his environment, so that he became a "great poet of nature" (210), Native Americans too are represented as aesthetically formed by their wild and beautiful surroundings. And they too are poets. The epigraph to **"Traits of Indian Character"** is an excerpt from Chief Logan's celebrated speech, widely known among white Americans at the time as a specimen of superb Native American oratory, and Irving also cites at length the "beautifully simple and pathetic harangue" (228) of an anonymous Sachem lamenting the looting of his mother's tomb. The chapter ends with the words of an "old warrior": "We are driven back . . . our fires are nearly extinguished . . . we shall cease to exist!" (233).

Despite Irving's claims, of course, Logan, the nameless Sachem, and the nameless "old warrior" were moved to speak not immediately by natural beauty but by the violent behavior of white settlers. Not only did necessity impel and mold their actual speeches to white people (if these speeches are not entirely fictional to begin with), but European-American needs rather than Native American needs are served in the representation of these speeches in **The Sketch Book.** I would argue that Irving finds these speeches beautiful not only for their resonance from nature, but for the contradiction they represent, which becomes a sublime contradiction once translated from political to poetic discourse. The contradiction of forced utterance of spontaneous sentiment carries great aesthetic value for a white interpreter such as Irving, as it did for many whites in the early republic who indulged in the vogue for speeches of dying or surrendering Indians (Murray ch. 3) or tableaux of suicidal Indians (Sollors 102-30). Irving acknowledges white violence against Native Americans, but he isolates that knowledge from his understanding of their "natural" eloquence. The tension produced by this act of isolation actually intensifies the pleasure, in the way that, more recently, I would suggest, *Dances with Wolves*'s acknowledgment of injustice against native people intensifies its version of noble savage imagery, making it all the more poignant and only marginally more historical.

I will expand on the problem of white representation of Native American oratory, because it is a central component of the aesthetic of dispossession as I am defining it. Logan's speech, delivered in 1774, also appeared in newspapers all over America and England, was reprinted in McGuffey's Readers, was a central piece of evidence in Jefferson's argument for American potential, was reworked into set pieces in plays, and inspired a novel and many poems (see Seeber). The speech is an indictment of white treatment of the Native Americans; Logan asks "any white man to say, if he ever came to [Logan's] cabin hungry, and he gave him not meat" and he condemns the murder of his family in a random act of violence by white soldiers.[10] Jefferson compared Logan's eloquence to the oratorical art of Cicero and Demosthenes, and this assessment was shared and elaborated upon by many later commentators. It is interesting to note that the political content of the classical orators was also diffused by time so that they became dehistoricized symbols of universally powerful rhetoric. Like the documents of classical Greece and Rome, Native American oratory, once decontextualized, could be adapted to the political needs of the American nation. Consider this excerpt from the magazine *American Pioneer* of 1842: "[N]o piece of composition ever did more, if so much, as the speech of Logan, . . . to form the mind and develop the latent energies of the youthful

American orator. Its influence has extended even into the halls of Congress, and has been felt upon the bench and in the bar of this nation; nay more, the American pulpit has been graced by energies which that speech has, in its warm simplicity, called forth" (qtd. in Seeber 132). The passage assumes that Logan's speech is essentially mute and mutable. As Edward Seeber has noted, one of the strange things about the popularity of Logan's speech is that the speech itself is not really very remarkable; it is extremely short and to the point, with none of the metaphorical elaboration white commentators usually praised in Native American speeches (140). But perhaps this is why it served its symbolic purpose so well.

Arnold Krupat, commenting on the popularity of Native American autobiography in a later period, discusses the white need for Native American affirmation of white innocence and notes that "the production of an Indian's own statement of his inevitable disappearance required that the Indian be represented as speaking in his own voice" (35). This presence of the speaking Native American was thus both ideologically necessary and potentially destabilizing to the white text. However, David Murray delineates the process by which, in such quoting of Native American oratory, "the speakers are 'framed,' so that *what* they are saying is actually less important than the fact and manner of their saying it" (36). Sympathy with wronged Indians was "turned into an aesthetic, rather than a moral, sensation" (40), Murray notes. When their words were contained in the works of white authors, Native Americans could not claim figurative property or imaginative ownership as defined in Irving's **"Stratford-on-Avon"** chapter: neither poetic nor physical property was permitted them. Physical dispossession may have *produced* artistic possession for Irving and Crayon and Shakespeare, but it is causally linked in the Native Americans' case to *loss* of artistic possession: thus, "[the Indians] have been dispossessed of their hereditary possessions by mercenary and frequently wanton warfare," Irving writes, "and their characters have been traduced by bigoted and interested writers" (225). Both Native American political expression and artistic production were subsumed, when they came into contact with white writers, under the aesthetic of dispossession.

Putting this analysis of the aesthetic of Native American dispossession together with the aesthetic of dispossession applied to Crayon and Shakespeare, we see the mechanics of their interrelationship. By invoking a sense of loss even for the greatest English poet, the romantic discourse masks the historical differences between the losses incurred. Irving seems to be consoling himself that like Shakespeare, who was barred from hunting in the forest and forced into sublime artistic production, Native Americans can turn their loss of land and autonomy into aesthetic riches. If Native Americans are unfortunate in "becoming vagabonds in the land of their fathers" (237), they are perhaps fortunate that "the poetic temperament has naturally something in it of the vagabond" (215). But of course the youthful and probably apocryphal vagabondage of Shakespeare, the voluntary and gentlemanly vagabondage of Crayon and Irving, and the enforced vagabondage of Native Americans are hardly identical on any grounds outside of Irving's imagination.

"John Bull," an affectionate satire of English national character, follows **"Philip of Pokanoket"** and represents another variant on the theme of property in *The Sketch Book*. John Bull owns a huge crumbling manor house, metaphorical for England of course, which, while mortgaged to the hilt, will never be taken from him. And John Bull has "much less of poetry about him than rich prose. There is little of romance in his nature, but a vast deal of strong natural feeling" (249). As in the Christmas chapters or even **"The Legend of Sleepy Hollow,"** humor seems to be a mode more appropriate to the property owner than it is to the propertyless. In Crayon's aesthetic, propertied people are "down to earth" while propertyless people are visionary or tragic. Thus despite his many-winged house and multitudes of servants, John Bull's "virtues are all his own; all plain, homebred and unaffected" (256); Crayon divests John Bull of aristocracy as he invests Shakespeare and the Native Americans with it. The British, Crayon implies, lost their American colonies through incompetence, which makes them comical now; the Native Americans, on the other hand, were doomed to lose their land and are thus tragic. Crayon, in between John Bull and King Philip in terms of his grasp on history, identity, and land, is presented as alternately poignant and absurd.

As Irving elevated his own sense of loss and romanticized the Native Americans' historical loss such that both white Americans and Native Americans were represented as passive victims, he was not unique. This pattern can be found among other authors as well—particularly educated eastern Americans for whom England was an ideal and Native Americans distant enough to become mere ideals also. For example, in the Leatherstocking novels of James Fenimore Cooper, it is all Hawkeye can do to watch the demise of the Native Americans and step mournfully into their place. "In Hawkeye," Pease suggests, "Cooper invented a figure who was able to transform cultural dispossession—that of the Mohicans—into a form of self-possession. Cooper was also able to treat Hawkeye's act of taking possession of himself in the woods as a rationale for America's legal title to the frontier" (21). Smith-Rosenberg's reading of Edgar Huntly's somnambulism suggests a mystification of colonialism even more manifest than Irving's. We might also consider the pervasive trope in American culture of the white woman abducted by the Native American man. In this captivity narrative scenario, the colonizers, represented by the "weaker sex," represent the Native Americans as the aggressors and thus portray white actions as wholly innocent. The popularity of the captivity trope far outstrips the extent of the historical phenomenon and always decontextualizes it from provoking violence on the part of white settlers.

Another trend that I would connect to the "aesthetic of dispossession" in the period, not confined to literature but pervasive in policy and politics, was Americans' widespread insistence that they were not the instigators of the Revolution: England had thrust them from their filial relation to her by oppressing them and treating them like slaves, the story went, and they were forced to rebel. They then allowed themselves, as Irving did, to "cast back a look of regret, as [they wandered] farther and farther from the paternal roof, and lament the waywardness of the parent, that would repel the affections of the child" (47). In white Americans' parent-child conceptualization of their relations with Native Americans, however, it was the child who was represented as wayward, such that the parent (the white government) was reluctantly forced to chastise, constrain, or cast off the child (the Native American tribes; see Rogin ch. 4). White Americans often preferred to cast themselves in a passive role.[11]

Thus, white Americans who fostered and nurtured their unease at their independence masked their own colonizing position with respect to the Indians, whom they had dispossessed of their land. Crayon's famous humility and self-mockery can be seen as part of a constraining *and* useful discourse of ex-colonial vulnerability. For if "awe and reverence" for the English deprived Irving of "ease and confidence," as he claimed (299), he was nonetheless able to use his diffidence to artistic and, I have argued, ideological advantage.

3

I would like to turn next to the writing of William Apess, a Pequot Indian, who provides a rare challenge to the constraints and conventions of the aesthetic of dispossession and whose treatment of King Philip and Chief Logan can be directly compared to Irving's. I might note that Apess's effective exposure of the uses of romanticism and religion in obfuscating colonialism cannot be attributed simply to his being Native American. Other Native American writers, such as Charles Eastman and Pauline Johnson, have actively participated in the romanticization of Native American culture. It is, I think, Apess's clear-eyed and visceral understanding of Native American history, learned from books by white authors *and* from experience and Native American sources, that allows him to shatter the illusions of the aesthetic of dispossession. As I asserted earlier, there is little anxiety to be found in Apess's writing, even though his people had been systematically killed and dispossessed of their land, and those who survived lived precariously on the margins of the New England economy and culture. Rather than claiming the status of victim, Apess struggled to escape this status.

In preparing the second edition of his autobiography, *A Son of the Forest* (1831), Apess "somewhat abridged 'his life'" to make room for "some general observations on the origin and character of the Indians, as a Nation" (52). Apess does not privilege his own experience over a broader history, however difficult access to this broader history might be. His "general observations" are in fact largely selections from Elias Boudinot's *A Star in the West* (1816), itself a conglomeration of quotations from earlier authors in support of the thesis that the native people of North America are none other than the ten lost tribes of Israel. Apess makes the same claim, but his emphasis is on the sheer volume of wrongdoing against the Indians. Among the crowd of documents, Apess presents Irving's **"Traits of Indian Character"** with the sole comment that it "bear[s] testimony of the philanthropy of some of the white men" and that it "originally appeared in the Analectic Magazine, during the time that the United States was engaged in a war with the Creek Indians" (60). The text is from Boudinot, and thus Apess is working from the 1814 version of **"Traits of Indian Character,"** which unlike the version in *The Sketch Book* does refer to the Creek War. Despite his contextualization of the piece with respect to that war, Apess oddly excises Irving's direct criticism of the US Army's treatment of the Creeks, and includes some particularly racist material that Irving himself left out from later editions: "It has pleased heaven to give [Indians] but limited powers of mind," Apess ventriloquizes, "and feeble lights to guide their judgments: it becomes us who are blessed with higher intellects to think for them, and set them an example of humanity" (68). Apess's apparently haphazard borrowing (from Irving via Boudinot, alongside Boudinot's other borrowings borrowed again by Apess) plays havoc with any notion of authorial voice, with regard to either Apess, Boudinot, or Irving. But perhaps Apess's inattention to the content of Irving's sketch is similar to white authors' attitudes towards Chief Logan's speech. In an inversion of Irving's ventriloquism of un-named Indian chiefs, Apess, who may well not have known who wrote **"Traits of Indian Character,"** presents the sketch without naming its author. It is merely a demonstration that white people have the capacity for sympathy, despite their ignorance, just as Logan's speech served as a demonstration that native people could feel, despite their violence. Apess includes Logan's speech in his appendix also, another borrowing from Boudinot: rather than adjudicating among all these sources, Apess jumbles them together.

Apess's "Eulogy on King Philip," a speech delivered in Boston in 1836, speaks more directly to the substance of Irving's representation of Native Americans. While Apess had probably not read **"Philip of Pokanoket,"** he would have relied on some of the same sources as Irving and was thus conversant with the discourses of the history of King Philip's War. Unlike Irving and other chroniclers of King Philip, Apess refuses a tragic emplotment of Philip's life; he is reluctant to allow his audience the sentimental opportunity to "turn with horror" or "blush with indignation" (Irving 233). As in *A Son of the Forest*, Apess's approach here is to present "a mass of history and exposition" (289), complete with dates and places to a high degree of specificity. In addition to insisting on the concreteness of Native American history, Apess draws on the political discourse of republicanism to demand legal rights and protections for Native Americans. "Give the Indian his rights, and you may be assured war will cease" (307), he

proclaims; he also calls for the crimes of white Christians against native people to be judged by Christian standards (287).

Apess repeatedly invokes parallels between King Philip's War and the American Revolution, but he does so to an effect opposite that of Irving. While Irving makes Philip into a kind of forefather to white American revolutionaries, Apess insists that Philip was working toward his own revolution, "though unsuccessful, yet as glorious as the *American* Revolution" (277). In Apess's account, Philip was an even more worthy leader than the leaders of the later revolution: "[W]hen his men began to be in want of money, having a coat neatly wrought with mampampeag (i.e., Indian money), he cut it to pieces and distributed it among all his chiefs and warriors, it being better than the old continental money of the Revolution in Washington's day, as not one Indian soldier found fault with it, as we could ever learn; so that it cheered their hearts still to persevere to maintain their rights and expel their enemies" (297). Barry O'Connell proposes that in calling his speech a "eulogy," Apess makes a reference to Daniel Webster's patriotic speeches on the occasion, for example, of the deaths of Jefferson and Adams (xx–xxi). Indeed, Apess begins the speech by establishing a parallel between Philip and other famous leaders, and a contrast between his treatment at the hands of historians and theirs: "I do not arise to spread before you the fame of a noted warrior, whose natural abilities shone like those of the great and mighty Philip of Greece, or of Alexander the Great, or like those of Washington—whose virtues and patriotism are engraven on the hearts of my audience" (277). Instead, he plans to prove the "virtues and patriotism" of a man usually reviled as an enemy of the nation who was nonetheless, he claims, "the greatest man that was ever in America" (308).

What does it mean to demonstrate the *patriotism* of a Native American leader who was a declared enemy of the settlers? Philip, Apess says, is honored by his descendants; and "so will every patriot, especially in this enlightened age, respect the rude yet all-accomplished son of the forest, that died a martyr to his cause" (277). This use of the word "patriot" seems to mean American patriot (Apess's audience was mostly white), and thus he is asking white Americans to include in their notion of *patria* the idea that those who are harmed by the state have the right to armed insurrection. Philip is not "a patriot attached to his native soil" in Irving's metaphorical sense (246), but in a historical political sense. Philip is a patriot with respect to his own, Indian, nation, and also, Apess tries to persuade his audience, with respect to the American nation. Philip is here claimed as both native and American; he is a part of both histories and his life as told by Apess reveals the conflicts hidden by white American histories.

Apess's next manipulation of the conventions of pleas on behalf of Native Americans is quite spectacular. Rather than invoking a poetic Indian chief to speak about the inevitability of his disappearance, as did Irving and countless others, Apess forces the president to give an imaginary speech about the deliberate extermination of the Native Americans. The ventriloquized speech runs as follows:

> We want your land for our use to speculate upon; it aids us in paying off our national debt and supporting us in Congress to drive you off.
>
> You see, my red children, that our fathers carried on this scheme of getting your lands for our use, and we have now become rich and powerful; and we have a right to do with you just as we please; we claim to be your fathers. And we think we shall do you a great favor, my dear sons and daughters, to drive you out, to get you away out of the reach of our civilized people, who are cheating you, for we have no law to reach them, we cannot protect you although you be our children. So it is no use, you need not cry, you must go, even if the lions devour you, for we promised the land you have to somebody else long ago, perhaps twenty or thirty years; and we did it without your consent, it is true. But this has been the way our fathers first brought us up, and it is hard to depart from it; therefore, you shall have no protection from us.
>
> (307)

This "speech" describes in an extraordinarily succinct manner the ideological and economic connections between European Americans' relations to their colonial superiors and their own colonizing role with respect to Native Americans in the postrevolutionary US. "Our fathers," the president says, started the process of land stealing, and now "we claim to be your fathers." "This has been the way our fathers first brought us up," he says, "and it is hard to depart from it"; this is a more directly political example of the kind of masking of agency that I have claimed was common in the early republic. Apess perceptively observes that the father-child metaphor is not applied between the president and white citizens, even though this would be its most logical application; Apess has the president profess helplessness over those who elected him. Apess also comments with bitter sarcasm on the importance of having control over the telling of history: he has the president say "we promised the land you have to somebody else long ago, perhaps twenty or thirty years"—in the foreshortened historical vision of white Americans, "twenty or thirty years" can constitute a long time, time enough to recede into what Irving called "the dim twilight of tradition" (235) in which all manner of deeds can be justified.

Compared to this extended parody of a presidential speech, Apess's mention of Chief Logan in the "Eulogy" is fleeting. Apess brings up the speech in a somewhat ritualized way, as if recognizing its mandatory appearance in any discussion of wrongs done to Native Americans. "The speech of Logan, the white man's friend, is no doubt fresh in your memory" (309), he prompts his audience, and quickly rehearses the story of the murder of Logan's family with which he expects they are all familiar. But instead of quoting Logan, or elaborating on the horrors of his case, Apess passes by his case as "one in a thousand"

(309). He refuses to indulge his audience with the usual sentimental catharsis. By denying Logan specificity, I would argue, Apess denies the possibility of reducing Native Americans to one symbol, "Logan, the white man's friend," a symbol detached from historical structure or process and ritualistically invoked to allow emotional purging with no effect on that historical structure or process. In fact, I think we could see Apess's speech as a rewriting of Logan's, with many-pronged rhetoric and argument and historical evidence making it irreducible to a single aesthetic moment. Like Logan, Apess emphasizes Native Americans' kindness to whites and their betrayal by them. However, Apess does not lament, and he does not ask for pity.

4

Many postcolonial studies scholars have proclaimed the impossibility or at least the undesirability of comparing literatures of settler colonies and literatures developing out of colonization of indigenous people (see Shohat; McClintock; Brennan 35-36). Their reluctance to draw comparisons may come from a fear that if any party no matter how privileged can claim a "postcolonial" status, the term may lose its political and historical leverage. This could indeed be the effect of an exorbitation of the traits of anxiety, fragmentation, and vulnerability in the early American republic. The term *colonial* in American studies has for a long time referred largely to Puritans and planters, and the importation of colonial and postcolonial studies approaches into the field has only sporadically challenged this emphasis.

And yet I do not think the solution is to turn completely, as Anne McClintock might do, to the colonization of indigenous people as the only "real" colonialism in colonial America.[12] Instead, I am trying to develop a comparative method based on the principle of relation rather than likeness. In most colonies throughout history, settler colonialism and colonization of indigenous people developed simultaneously,[13] and to point out that European Americans were in different structural and cultural positions than Europeans hardly seems in itself a denial of difference between the positions of settler and indigenous colonized populations. I hope this essay has demonstrated that to "disqualify" settler colonialism from serious consideration would impede understanding of colonization of indigenous people, which took place in cultural, ideological, and economic relation with settler colonialism. In particular reference to my work in this essay, such disqualification would take away from analysis of writers like Apess, indigenous writers who self-consciously harnessed the anticolonial discourses of settler colonists in new and particular ways.

Perhaps I might return to my initial analogy to present-day feminism. Scholars in this field are doing an admirable job stepping through webs of historical, discursive, and emotional complexity; by identifying the "many varied tools of patriarchy" (Lorde 95), they are becoming better equipped to develop countertools. Tensions have not abated between different feminist communities, but neither should they, in a sense, since the interests and histories of these communities are often very different. There is even less likely to be one type of women's oppression than there is to be one type of colonialism. Intersection of different analyses and actions has been intermittent and difficult, but it has helped to show the inadequacies and inaccuracies of claims to victimhood as a political strategy, and the necessity of a more diversified conception of oppression. These are also tasks central to understanding the history of colonialism in British North America and the US. In comparisons of representational processes associated with the end of American settler colonialism and those associated with the continuing colonization of Native Americans, discussions within feminism can serve as a model and a reminder not to claim likeness or difference in terms too absolute.

Notes

1. For examples of such critiques, see hooks (ch. 4); Trinh (ch. 3); and Lorde. For examples of white women reflecting on their privilege, some 10 years after the Lugones and Spelman article, see Patai 139; Gallop, Hirsch, and Miller 354; and Childers's remarks in her article with hooks (62). I cannot attempt to do justice to all the nuances of terms and identities here; while Lugones speaks of the unacknowledged power of white, middle-class, educated, American women, feminists have more recently become concerned also with the privileges of region, language, sexuality, religion, age, and so on.

2. The bulk of colonial theory has remained concentrated on the two-sided colonial situation, from Albert Memmi's psychological model from the 1950s through Homi Bhabha's post-structuralist work of the 1980s.

3. See Kutzinski. Irving's reception in England certainly does invite comparison to the reception of present-day third-world writers. Brennan has observed that Salman Rushdie, Derek Walcott, Isabel Allende, and the rest of a coterie of "cosmopolitan" writers are well known in the metropole (which now includes New York as well as London) "not because they are necessarily 'better', but because they tell strange stories in familiar ways" (36). Such literary strategies have led to great success among these few authors: "[T]he metropolitan reader is surprised or delighted to find authors like Rushdie or Allende treating Third-World themes with 'sophistication,' and that surprise has everything to do with their current popularity" (38). Similarities with Irving and his context abound; *The Quarterly Review* (1819) found Irving's *Sketch Book* most charming, "written for the most part in a spirit of good sense and moderation which could scarcely be expected from an American" (qtd. in Rubin-Dorsky 40). Likewise the *Edinburgh Magazine and Literary Miscellany* (1819) observed with some surprise that *The Sketch Book* "proves to us distinctly that there is *mind* working in America, and that there are materials, too, for it to work upon, of a very singular and romantic kind" (qtd. in Rubin-Dorsky 40). Although the parallels appear strong, I would suggest another characterization of the relation between them: in a sense the condescension the twentieth-century postcolonial authors (and nonwhite American authors too) have faced is an *effect* of the condescension Irving and his contemporary European Americans faced. Americans built up a national culture in response to imperial condescension, and now protect its hegemonic aesthetic values in the way that the British defended theirs. The difference in time period is therefore significant.

4. Similar anxiety is also present in authors contemporary with Irving: Rubin-Dorsky names James Fenimore Cooper and Sarah J. Hale as examples of those nostalgic for a prerevolutionary world or worried about moral control in the new republic, and one might also consider Charles Brockden Brown's gothic experiments in psychological/national landscape, or the worry over republican female virtue in early American novels such as William Hill Brown's *The Power of Sympathy* or Hannah Foster's *The Coquette*. Again, I am not denying such traits but seeking to read them differently.

5. The Twayne edition of *The Sketch Book* follows the order of the 1848 American edition, although its copy texts derive from the first American edition (1819-20) and first English edition (1820).

6. "The Wife" may be set in the US, but its location bears no importance to the story; "The Angler" contains a reminiscence of the effect Izaak Walton's "Compleat Angler" had on a group of American boys (264), but the chapter is mainly set in Wales.

7. One might identify this same necessity in Margaret Fuller's travel sketches, *Summer on the Lakes,* in which chapters on Niagara and Indian villages are continually interspersed with romantic fables and meditations on German philosophers and Greek gods, or in Caroline Kirkland's *A New Home—Who'll Follow?* which, while discussing life in swampy half-settled Michigan, contains almost as many quotes from high European culture as does *The Sketch Book.*

8. Exceptions are Daniel Littlefield and Rubin-Dorsky, who read these sketches as examples of Irving's general fear of progress or sense of loss. But whereas these scholars seem unsurprised about the continuities between the Indian and English sketches, I found such continuities puzzling.

9. The 1814 "Traits of Indian Character" is overtly topical, and contains some three pages of criticism of the behavior of the US military in the Creek War: "In the present times," Irving begins, "when popular feeling is gradually becoming hardened by war, and selfish by the frequent jeopardy of life or property, it is certainly an inauspicious moment to speak in behalf of a race of beings, whose very existence has been pronounced detrimental to public security. But

it is good at all times to raise the voice of truth, however feeble" (145). By 1820, the Creek material would either have had to be revised or deleted; Irving chose the latter, making the tone uniformly nostalgic to fit in with the other sketches.

10. Jefferson's appendix attempts to pin down the circumstances under which the speech was given. Jefferson's treatment of the speech merits a separate discussion, but suffice it to say here that when challenged about the speech's authenticity, Jefferson amassed as much documentary corroboration as possible, and when that proved to be equivocal, he asserted that "whether Logan's or mine, [the speech] would still have been American" (230), a bold act of nationalist cultural appropriation if there ever was one.

11. Americans of relative privilege continue to have a fascination with victimhood, according to Wendy Kaminer. In her analysis of the American "recovery" or "self-help" movement of recent years, she observes that "[I]n recovery, whether or not you were housed, schooled, clothed, and fed in childhood, you can still claim to be metaphorically homeless. . . . At its worst, the recovery movement's cult of victimization mocks the notion of social justice by denying that there are degrees of injustice" (155).

12. McClintock's central point is a criticism of "how seldom the term [post-colonial] is used to denote *multiplicity*" (86), and yet she is nonetheless eager to make judgments about which nations "qualify" (87) as postcolonial and which do not. I am extremely wary of this exclusivist tendency.

13. The term colonization refers in its earliest definitions to plantations and satellite communities, that is, settler colonialism (see Finley); in North America, South America, the Caribbean, Australasia, South and East Africa, settler colonialism was part of the mechanism for colonization of indigenous people.

Works Cited

Apess, William. *On Our Own Ground: The Complete Writings of William Apess, A Pequot.* Ed. and introd. Barry O'Connell. Amherst: U of Massachusetts P, 1992.

Bhabha, Homi. "Interrogating Identity: The Postcolonial Prerogative." *Anatomy of Racism.* Ed. David Theo Goldberg. Minneapolis: U of Minnesota P, 1990. 183-209.

———. "Of Mimicry and Man: The Ambivalence of Colonial Discourse." *October* 28 (1984): 125-33.

Boudinot, Elias. *A Star in the West: Or, A Humble Attempt to Discover the Long Lost Ten Tribes of Israel.* Trenton, NJ, 1816.

Bowden, Mary Witherspoon. *Washington Irving.* Boston: Twayne, 1981.

Brennan, Timothy. *Salman Rushdie and the Third World: Myths of the Nation.* New York: St. Martin's, 1989.

Brown, William Hill. *The Power of Sympathy.* The Power of Sympathy *and* The Coquette. Ed. William S. Osborne. New Haven: College and University, 1970. 27-129.

Buell, Lawrence. "American Literary Emergence as a Postcolonial Phenomenon." *American Literary History* 4 (1992): 411-42.

———. "Melville and the Question of American Decolonization." *American Literature: A Journal of Literary History, Criticism, and Bibliography* 64 (1992): 215-37.

Childers, Mary, and bell hooks. "A Conversation about Race and Class." *Conflicts in Feminism.* Ed. Marianne Hirsch and Evelyn Fox Keller. New York: Routledge, 1990. 60-81.

Eastman, Charles A. *Indian Boyhood.* 1902. New York: Dover, 1971.

Eberwein, Jane D. "Transatlantic Contrasts in Irving's *Sketch Book.*" *College English* 15 (1988): 153-70.

Finley, M. I. "Colonies—An Attempt at a Typology." *Transactions of the Royal Historical Society* 5th ser. 26 (1976): 167-88.

Foster, Hannah. *The Coquette.* The Power of Sympathy *and* The Coquette. Ed. William S. Osborne. New Haven: College and University, 1970. 131-272.

Fuller, Margaret. *Summer on the Lakes.* 1844. New York: Haskell, 1970.

Gallop, Jane, Marianne Hirsch, and Nancy K. Miller. "Criticizing Feminist Criticism." *Conflicts in Feminism.* Ed. Marianne Hirsch and Evelyn Fox Keller. New York: Routledge, 1990. 349-69.

hooks, bell. *Talking Back: Thinking Feminist, Thinking Black.* Boston: South End, 1989.

Irving, Washington. *The Sketch Book of Geoffrey Crayon, Gent.* Ed. Haskell Springer. Boston: Twayne, 1978. Vol. 8 of *The Complete Works of Washington Irving.* 30 vols. 1969-89.

———. "Traits of Indian Character." *Analectic Magazine* 3 (1814): 145-56.

Jefferson, Thomas. *Notes on the State of Virginia.* Ed. William Peden. Chapel Hill: U of North Carolina P, 1955.

Johnson, E. Pauline. *Flint and Feather: The Complete Poems of Pauline Johnson.* Toronto: Musson, 1917.

Kaminer, Wendy. *I'm Dysfunctional, You're Dysfunctional: The Recovery Movement and Other Self-Help Fashions.* Reading: Addison-Wesley, 1992.

Kasson, Joy S. *Artistic Voyagers: Europe and the American Imagination in the Works of Irving, Allston, Cole, Cooper, and Hawthorne.* Westport: Greenwood, 1982.

Kirkland, Caroline. *A New Home—Who'll Follow?* Ed. William S. Osborne. New Haven: College and University, 1965.

Krupat, Arnold. *For Those Who Come After: A Study of Native American Autobiography.* Berkeley: U of California P, 1985.

Kutzinski, Vera M. "Commentary: American Literary History as Spatial Practice." *American Literary History* 4 (1992): 550-57.

Littlefield, Daniel. "Washington Irving and the American Indian." *American Indian Quarterly* 5 (1979): 135-54.

Lorde, Audre. "An Open Letter to Mary Daly." *This Bridge Called My Back: Writings by Radical Women of Color.* Ed. Cherrie Moraga and Gloria Anzaldúa. New York: Kitchen Table, 1983. 94-97.

Lugones, Maria C., and Elizabeth V. Spelman. "Have We Got a Theory for You! Feminist Theory, Cultural Imperialism and the Demand for 'The Woman's Voice.'" *Women's Studies International Forum* 6 (1983): 573-81.

McClintock, Anne. "The Angel of Progress: Pitfalls of the Term 'Post-Colonialism.'" *Social Text* 31-32 (1992): 84-98.

Memmi, Albert. *The Colonizer and the Colonized.* Trans. Howard Greenfield. New York: Orion, 1965.

Miller, Perry. *The New England Mind: From Colony to Province.* Cambridge: Harvard UP, 1953.

Murray, David. *Forked Tongues: Speech, Writing, and Representation in North American Indian Texts.* Bloomington: Indiana UP, 1991.

Patai, Daphne. "U.S. Academics and Third World Women: Is Ethical Research Possible?" *Women's Words: The Feminist Practice of Oral History.* Ed. Sherna Berger Gluck and Daphne Patai. New York: Routledge, 1991. 137-53.

Pease, Donald. *Visionary Compacts: American Renaissance Writings in Cultural Context.* Madison: U of Wisconsin P, 1987.

Rogin, Michael Paul. *Fathers and Children: Andrew Jackson and the Subjugation of the American Indian.* New York: Knopf, 1975.

Rubin-Dorsky, Jeffrey. *Adrift in the Old World: The Psychological Pilgrimage of Washington Irving.* Chicago: U of Chicago P, 1988.

Seeber, Edward D. "Critical Views on Logan's Speech." *Journal of American Folklore* 60 (1947): 130-46.

Shohat, Ella. "Notes on the 'Post-Colonial.'" *Social Text* 31-32 (1992): 99-113.

Smith-Rosenberg, Carroll. "Subject Female: Authorizing American Identity." *American Literary History* 5 (1993): 481-511.

Sollors, Werner. *Beyond Ethnicity: Consent and Descent in American Culture.* New York: Oxford UP, 1986.

Somkin, Fred. *Unquiet Eagle: Memory and Desire in the Idea of American Freedom, 1815-1860.* Ithaca: Cornell UP, 1967.

Trinh, T. Minh-ha. *Woman, Native, Other: Writing Postcoloniality and Feminism.* Bloomington: Indiana UP, 1989.

Tyler, Moses Coit. *A History of American Literature, 1607-1765.* 2 vols. New York, 1878.

von Frank, Albert J. *The Sacred Game: Provincialism and Frontier Consciousness in American Literature, 1630-1860.* Cambridge: Cambridge UP, 1985.

Ziff, Larzer. "Questions of Identity: Hawthorne and Emerson Visit England." *Forms and Functions of History in American Literature: Essays in Honor of Ursula Brumm.* Ed. Winfried Fluck, Jürgen Peper, and Willi Paul Adams. Berlin: Schmidt, 1981.

———. *Writing in the New Nation: Prose, Print, and Politics in the Early United States.* New Haven: Yale UP, 1991.

Alice Hiller (essay date 1997)

SOURCE: "'An Avenue to Some Degree of Profit and Reputation': *The Sketch Book* as Washington Irving's *entrée* and Undoing," *Journal of American Studies,* Vol. 31, No. 2, August, 1997, pp. 275-93.

[*In the following essay, Hiller traces the events which influenced* The Sketch Book of Geoffrey Grayon, Gent., *arguing that with this work, Irving lost his distinctive voice.*]

"I have," confided Washington Irving to his friend and effective literary agent Henry Brevoort, "by patient & persevering labour of my most uncertain pen, & by catching the gleams of sunshine in my cloudy mind, managed to open to myself an avenue to <a> some degree of profit & reputation."[1] The "avenue" in question was ***The Sketch Book of Geoffrey Crayon, Gent.***—America's first internationally acclaimed work of literature—which, by March 1821, had become a direct route to respectability and the British establishment, opening to Irving the world of stately homes and their real-life avenues, previously only glimpsed from afar. Pieced together after the collapse of his family business, the collection of sketches may have been a carefully engineered career move, but Irving avoided any suggestion of personal cost in catching only those "gleams of sunshine," and apparently censoring his cloudier, less amenable self. He continued: "I value it the more highly because it is entirely independent and self created; and I must use my best endeavours to turn it to account" (*LI*.614). In the context, "independent"—a charged word for his generation—is striking, given that ***The Sketch Book*** was anything but. While writing, Irving had appealed to Brevoort to let him know "what themes &c would be popular and striking in America" (*LI*.546), and his private papers reveal that the book's deferential, nostalgic, pastoralized view of Britain was in fact carefully tailored to what Irving believed were the tastes of his two markets, although not perhaps to those of the critics championing America's new spirit of literary nationalism and cultural independence.

Inspired by the successes of the war of 1812, their challenges and exhortations can be found in periodicals such as the newly founded *North American Review,* which, in 1815, attacked America's "literary delinquency," and her undue "dependence on English literature."[2] Meanwhile, *The Portico,* another new periodical, argued in the Advertisement to its first issue in 1816: "Dependence, whether literary or political, is a state of degradation fraught with disgrace; and to be dependent on a foreign mind for what we can ourselves produce, is to add to the crime of indolence, the weakness of stupidity."[3] Irving's earlier *History of New York* became a founding text for this movement, and his defection abroad and adoption of a more anodyne style of writing prompted accusations of betrayal, so that, after defining his avenue, Irving was obliged to respond to Brevoort's allegations that back home "many ask whether I mean to renounce my country" (*LI.*614). The charge was angrily denied—Irving claiming "Whatever I have written has been written with the feelings and published as the writing of an American," (*LI.*614). Yet a letter written the previous year to Sir Walter Scott reveals the complexity of his position, underlining both the pull of the Old World and the awe in which Irving apparently held its readers. Disdaining Knickerbocker's exuberant, experimental *History* as "local, crude and juvenile," (*LI.*590), Irving revealed of its successor: "I think I could have made it better, but I have been so new to the ground which I was treading, and so daunted by the idea of writing absolutely for a British public, that my powers, such as they are, have been almost paralyzed" (*LI.*590). If the insight intimates that the sketches were pitched deliberately at the British market, the reference to feelings of paralysis admits the cost of this manuvre, and anticipates difficulties of the sort which, I will argue, blocked Irving's subsequent writing and caused him to lose his way as an author thereafter. These problems were first intuited by the Massachusetts poet and essayist Richard Henry Dana in the *North American Review* of September 1819.

While generally admiring, when he reviewed *The Sketch Book,* after publication of the first numbers in America, Dana was forthright about his perception of its deficiencies, compared to Irving's earlier works: "He appears to have lost a little of that natural run of style, for which his lighter writings were so remarkable. He has given up something of his direct, simple manner, and plain phraseology for a more studied, periphrastical mode of expression" (*NAR.*7.348). In his epigraph, Irving had presented himself—citing Burton's *Anatomy of Melancholy*—as a deracinated observer and "mere spectator of other men's fortunes and adventures."[4] Dana takes up this point, implying that Irving had lost touch with his instinctive, "native" voice, but also reflects how complex an issue this remained for an American writing in 1819, particularly one born of a Scottish father and English mother: "He seems to have exchanged words and phrases, which were strong, distinct and definite, for a genteel sort of language, cool, less definite, and general. It is as if his mother English had been sent abroad to be improved, and in attempting to become accomplished, had lost too many of her home qualities"

(*NAR.*7.348). The wording of Dana's review effectively challenges Britain's cultural supremacy—deploying "mother English" to denote Irving's native American—but also implicitly registers the novelty of this enterprise, for which a vocabulary barely exists.

While agreeing with Dana's central contention—he argued "the manner perhaps throughout is more attended to than the matter"[5]—Francis Jeffrey interpreted Irving's approach very differently in the *Edinburgh Review* the following year, however. That January, Sydney Smith had famously used its pages to query "In the four quarters of the globe, who reads an American book? or goes to an American play? or looks at an American picture or stature?" (*ER.*33.79). Jeffrey then implied that it was partly Irving's "de-naturing" of his uvre that had allowed it to slip through the cultural barriers and appeal to more than just his fellow "natives," arguing: "Now, the most remarkable thing in a work so circumstanced certainly is, that it should be written throughout with the greatest care and accuracy, and worked up to great purity and beauty of diction, on the model of the most elegant and polished of our native writers." Hoping that "we may hail it as the harbinger of a purer and juster taste—the foundation of a chaster and better school, for the writers of that great and intelligent country" (*ER.*34.160), Jeffrey went on to compliment Irving's courtesy and conciliatoriness, though these were by no means always characteristic of his approach to Britain, as his private papers reveal.

Friendless and fearful, on his first visit in 1805, Irving had felt himself to be like "one of our savages when visiting a strange tribe. He courts their friendship tho he <distrusts their> eyes them with <caut> distrust [;] he holds out the calumet of peace but grasps his tomahawk in the other hand ready to defend himself."[6] Returning to Britain a decade later in 1815 on the visit which would result in *The Sketch Book,* and immediately after the end of the 1812-14 War (in which he had served although not seen action), Irving initially appeared less troubled. This may have been partly owing to the proximity of his brother, Peter, in Liverpool overseeing the British end of the family's import business, and his married sister, Sarah Van Wart. Irving himself disembarked in Liverpool on 1 July and three days later wrote to his mother from Sarah's house in Birmingham that the weather had been "uncommonly fine since my arrival, and the country is in all its verdure and beauty" (*LI.*395), adding "the journey from Liverpool to this place is through a perfect garden, so highly is the whole country cultivated" (*LI.*395). The letter makes no acknowledgement of the significance of the date—4 July—as if Irving wished to ignore any considerations which might separate him from the subjects of this "enchanting" (*LI.*398) country, where he told Henry Brevoort on 5 July that he had "experienced as yet nothing but kindness and civility" (*LI.*398).

Implicit in "as yet" is the inference that Irving somehow doubted this good will, or at least regarded it with a residual wariness, which would seem to have stemmed as much from his own complex feelings about Britain, as any overt British hostility. These feelings perhaps lie behind his sympathetic comments on Napoleon's plight following his defeat at Waterloo on 18 June, and subsequent surrender to the British at Plymouth on 24 July. The citizen of a nation *undefeated* by Britain, Irving wrote to Brevoort again on 16 July 1815 and, remembering *Macbeth,*[7] he compared Napoleon to an "eagle towering in his pride of place" beside the Prince Regent's "mousing owl" (*LI.*401). After Napoleon's capture, the resentment, longing, scorn, and excitement fermenting in his American breast were decanted into another letter of 27 July. Addressed to Jean Renwick, sister of Francis Jeffrey and mother of Irving's travelling companion that summer, it satirized the excesses of rampant John Bullism as they manifested themselves in a Birmingham church, with a reference to James Thomson's *The Castle of Indolence*—

> Here we found a "round sleek oily man of God" with a face that shone resplendent with roast beef & plumb pudding, holding forth on the late glorious battle of Waterloo & the surrender of Bonaparte. I was exceedingly amused with the awkward, goose like attempts of this full fed divine to get his imagination upon the wing. If you ever saw a gander, in a sudden fit of untoward volatility, endeavour to fly across a mill pond, <and> with his tail dragging in the water & his wings whipping the surface into froth and bubbles, you may form some idea of the soarings of this worthy preacher. There was a <comical> mixture of Poetry & prose, of figure & fact, of plain truth & slip shod heroics that was most delicately comic. The God of Battles, Lord Wellington, the destroying angel & several other military characters were jumbled to gether—& the <destroyer> tyrant was overthrown, the riegn[sic] of tyranny <averted> ended, the great fabric of delusion demolished and the standards of Waterloo brought express & laid at the feet of the prince regent, in the course of a single sentence. Such is a sample of the thousands of patriotic & triumphant sermons that are now droned forth, <ever> over velvet cushions, to honest fat headed hearers in every parish of this loyal little Kingdom.
>
> (*LI.*404)

Thomson had placed a "little, round, fat, oily man of God"[8] in amongst the pleasure seekers of the wizard's castle in Canto I of his poem, noting how he "shone all glittering with ungodly dew / If a tight damsel chanced to trippen by," (*CI.*lxix). Irving's use of the citation and allusion to the type of corrupt cleric which it involves recalls Dana's appropriation of the term "mother English," while also reflecting the extent to which this culture had indeed nurtured Irving, whose depiction of the war-like priest also seems to remember and subvert Chaucer's corrupt and slightly sinister Monk in the *Canterbury Tales.* The latter—"a lord ful fat and in good poynt"[9]—embodies the collusion between church and state which Irving satirizes, and also has a bald head "that shoon as any glas / And eek his face, as he hadde been enoynt" (*GP.*198-99), like Irving's gleaming cleric.

The echoing illustrates the necessity of the shared culture for deeper and more resonant writing, which was also admitted half involuntarily by Edward Tyrell Channing in his article "On Models in Literature," published in the *North American Review* the following July. Professor of Rhetoric and Oratory at Harvard, Channing prefaced his piece with a citation from Wordsworth's poem *The Excursion,* but went on to assert that a country must be "the former and finisher of its own genius" (*NAR.*3.207) before continuing in a way which underlined the near impossibility of creative and cultural independence for his generation of Americans. Confusingly, that self-same genius "has, or should have, nothing to do with strangers. They are not expected to feel the beauty of your old poetical language, depending as it does on early and tender associations; connecting the softer and ruder ages of the country, and inspiring an inward and inexplicable joy, like a tale of childhood" (*NAR.*3.207).

Channing's phrasing betrays the depth of his involvement with what can only be Britain's "old poetical language," in a year which also saw the *North American Review* featuring fifty pages of excerpts from the anonymous *Journal of a tour and residence in Great Britain during the years 1810 and 1811.* Originally published in England, it is considerably less artful than **The Sketch Book,** offering more of a survey, albeit a well written one, but reflects the hearty American appetite for details of the Old World. Irving would also cater to this curiosity, of course, although the same letter to Mrs Renwick also reveals the very real difficulties he had to overcome in order to find an acceptable way of conveying his experiences. If the writing manifests the force and nature of his attraction to this "loyal little Kingdom," it equally expresses his intermittent exasperated contempt for the "honest fat headed" subjects with their velvet cushions and droning preacher, even as the succulent, elaborately conceived imagery witnesses to the fertility and potential richness of British culture for his imagination. Though we see why, as a writer, Irving needed to return to Europe, we also feel the impossibility of his position once arrived. Much of what he had to say—at least continuing in the mode of inspired, demented satire pioneered in **Salmagundi** and **The History of New York**—would not, presumably, advance his career or win the acclaim he so ardently desired. How to find something else, without completely betraying his own voice, was in many ways the challenge of these early years in Britain.

Even on his first tour to Warwick, Kenilworth, and Stratford, on which he embarked immediately after writing, when he had been in England less than a month, Irving began casting around for a way of opening what he would later term his "avenue." Inspiration seems to have struck in the grounds of Charlecote Hall, which Irving visited "to see a old family mansion of the rign [*sic*] of Q Elzabet in fine preservation & certainly one which Shakspear in his boyhood must often have rambled about."[10] Remarkably, though his visit took place on 25 July, and he had previously only experienced England during the autumn and winter, Irving chose to describe the pleasure grounds amid the first stirrings of spring, writing in his journal: "The day was soft and balmy—The buds which had been retarded by lingering frosts were beginning to put forth—the snow drop the [ ] & other firstlings of the spring were seen under Lucy's Park Vast oak avenues deer fawns—rooks cawing—wind sounding among the branches—larks soaring up into the heaven" (*JII*.61-2). Henry James would document his own warm appreciation of Charlecote's "venerable verdure" in *English Hours*,[11] and the tone of Irving's entry suggests an awakening, or a belated thaw or coming to life. Whether he actually felt this sort of stirring within himself during his visit, or believed that the park *ought* to represent some sort of extraordinary experience, and was seeking a way of making this apparent, is not certain. Charlecote was undoubtedly a world apart, with the attractively decrepit Elizabethan hall rising out of an Arcadian landscape moulded by Capability Brown in the 1760s,[12] as numerous illustrations of the period testify.[13] Harping on "the majestic solemnity of these great <oaken> elm avenues—with the wind sounding among the branches & the rooks sailing & cawing above the tree tops" (*JII*.62), Irving's reverential approach to this idyll of the past could hardly be more different from his affectionately contemptuous satire of the preacher-goose and his middle-class parishioners' celebrations of contemporary British power.

This determinedly escapist vision of Britain was one which Irving would both promote in ***The Sketch Book*** and pursue again the following summer, after a winter largely spent struggling with the difficulties of the post-war economic climate, particularly as they affected his family business. Following Peter's over-purchasing, P. & E. Irving & Co. had embarked on the steady slide towards the bankruptcy which put them out of business on 4 March 1818. The experience was deeply distressing to Irving. But, rather than becoming more politicized or radical after seeing at first hand the harshness of the British system in this time of appalling hardship and suffering, like Mrs Trollope after her American tribulations, Irving sought only the more obstinately to deny its traumas, or at least to exclude them from his writing and correspondence, into which they almost never creep. The price of this repression was frequent silences. Writing to Brevoort in July 1816, he complained "my mind is in a sickly state and my imagination so blighted that it cannot put forth a blossom nor even a green leaf" (*LI*.449), although Irving then waxed eloquent about meeting a "Veteran angler of old Isaac Waltons school" (*LI*.450) by the River Dee, who had visited America in his youth. Subsequently immortalized in ***The Sketch Book***, this story-book character restored Irving's faith in human nature, and developed his vision of the Old World as the natural habitat of picturesque and unthreatening characters, who felt only goodwill towards America, unlike the bankers and merchants reluctant to help out the struggling Irving firm.[14] Or so Irving reassured Brevoort: "His whole conversation and deportment illustrated old Isaacs maxims as to the benign influences of angling over the human heart—I wished continually that you had been present, as I know you would have enjoyed with exquisite relish, this genuine Angler, & the characteristic scenes through which we rambled with him" (*LI*.451).

The same "amusing rencontre" (*LI*.451) inspired Irving and his brother Peter to spend their ten-day summer holiday that year in Izaak Walton's native Derbyshire. Interestingly, though, given what Irving had said about his depression and difficulties in writing, he did not write letters home about the excursion for several months, with the exception of two brief and factual notes to his mother, the first of which is dated 6 November. Addressed to Brevoort, it all but spells out the connections between Irving's material and creative lives, as he apologizes rather movingly:

> I am sensible my silence exposes me to many hard imputations, but I cannot help it—I can only say it is not for want of having you continually in my thoughts and near my heart, nor for want of the constant desire and frequent resolve to write. But some how or other there has been such a throng of worldly cares hurrying backward & forward through my mind for a long time past, that it is even as bare as a market place: and when I do take hold of my pen, I feel so poverty struck, such mental sterility, that I throw it down again in despair of writing any thing that should give you gratification.
>
> (*LI*.457)

Likening his mind to a bare "market place," overrun by anxieties, apparently triggers Irving's consciousness of its potential for productivity, however, he then goes on to recall his time in Buxton, caricaturing "the great tendency of the English to run into excrescences and bloat out into grotesque deformities" (*LI*.459) that he observed among those taking the waters. Singled out in particular is one General Trotter, whom, in an extension of Irving's satire on the preacher-goose, he terms a "toast & butter" soldier, left behind by "the hurry, the fierceness and dashing of the new system" (*LI*.460). No longer a threat, with his "broad hazy muffin face," "sleepy eye," and "full double chin," the general becomes grotesquely picturesque, a mutation on the theme of Bullish British overfeeding, and is seen as a degenerated, eroded landscape: "He had a deep ravine from each corner of his mouth, not occasioned by an irascible contraction of the muscles, but apparently the deep worn channels of two rivulets of gravy that oozed out from the huge mouthfuls that he masticated" (*LI*.460).

Toned down and rendered more tasteful, the general was the type of reassuring English man whom Irving would feature in ***The Sketch Book***, something like his characterization of John Bull. That the obsessive description of his eating addressed obliquely Irving's anxieties about the inequities of the British class system, and the suffering which it occasioned, emerges from another letter to Brevoort dated 9 December 1816. In what is his only explicit condemnation of the bitter suffering occasioned by the post-war slump, he laments:

> You have no idea of the distress and misery that prevails in this country: it is beyond the power of description: In America you have financial difficulties, the embarrassments of trade & the distress of merchants but here you have what is far worse, the distress of the poor—not merely mental sufferings—but the absolute miseries of nature—Hunger, nakedness, wretchedness

of all kinds that the labouring people in this country are liable to. In the best of times they do but subsist, but in adverse times they starve.

                                                        (*LI*.464)

Concluding abruptly "but I have some how or other rambled away into a theme which would neither edify nor amuse you, so we will not pursue it" (*LI*.465), however, Irving anticipates the almost total exclusion of such perspectives from **The Sketch Book,** unlike the *Journal of a tour and residence in Great Britain* in which he notes bitterly how "the poor are swept out of the way, as dust of the walks of the rich, in a heap out of their sight" (*NAR*.3.260). Characterizing his deviation as a "ramble," Irving associates it with Romantic notions of the involuntariness of thought and inspiration, from which he will subsequently endeavour to distance himself, as his writing becomes progressively more self-conscious and commercial.

The last letter relating to the Derbyshire excursion, dated 29 January 1819, seems to be a transitional one in this respect, dealing with a "ramble of curiosity" undertaken by the Irving brothers along Dovedale. A deep, narrow, craggy, wooded limestone valley, down which Walton's river cascaded spectacularly for two miles, skirted by a narrow footpath, Dovedale was deemed by Gilpin "one of the most pleasing pieces of scenery of the kind we any where met with."[15] Irving was keenly appreciative of these "scenes hallowed by the honest Walton's simple Muse" (*LI*.469), as he told Brevoort in a letter which reflects his ongoing interest in finding a way of covering British material from an American perspective, and indeed shaping his life experiences into commercial art. Venturing out, back in August, the brothers had met up by chance with their fellow hotel guests from Matlock—among them the three Miss Bathursts, whose presence prompted Irving to rechristen the gorge "Dove Dale" (*LI*.469). The Irvings were invited to tag along with the other party (complete with picnic and attendants)—and duly did. When he came to retell the story for Brevoort months later, Irving chose to focus on the company as much as the scenery, implying both were so delightful as barely to be credible, but leaving in his revisions as evidence of the difficulties he encountered in writing up his passage:

> If a man could not be happy with such a party in such a place, he may give up all hope of sublunary felicity. For my part I was in Elysium Nothing so soon banishes reserve and produces intimacy as a participation in difficulties. The path through the Dale was rugged and beset with petty hazards. We had to toil through thickets & Brambles—Sometimes to step cautiously from stone to stone in the margin of the little river where the precipitous hills over hung its current—We had to scramble up into caverns and to climb rocks— all these were calculated to place both parties in those relative situations which endear the Sexes. I had a <lovely> woman, lovely woman! clinging to me for assistance & protection—looking up with beseeching weakness & dependence in the midst of difficulties & Dangers—while I <with>in all the swelling

<spirit>pride of a lord of the Creation, looked upon my feeble companion with an eye of infinite benevolence & fostering care—braved every <danger>peril of land & water—and sustained a scratched hand or a wet foot with a fortitude that called forth the admiration of the softer sex!

<But then Brevoort>

But all these dangers past—when we had descended from the last precipice, and come to where the Dove flowed musically through a verdant meadow—then— fancy me—oh thou "Sweetest of Poets" wandering by the course of this romantic stream—a lovely <"object">girl <who felt "emotions with ten times the force of common ordinary mortals"> hanging on my arm—pointing the beauties of the surrounding scenery—and repeating in the most dulcet voice tracts of heaven born poetry! If a Strawberry Smotherd in cream has any consciousness of its delicious situation, it must feel as I felt at that moment.

                                                        (*LI*.468)

While the elaborate burlesquing, with its brambles, scratched hands, and wet feet, suggests Irving's inherent scepticism about something which he very obviously and simultaneously delights in; the extensive revisions attest to the self-consciousness of his reportage. Changing the phrasing of "lovely woman" to "woman, lovely woman," or substituting the more literary "peril" for plain "danger," or the more tender "girl" for "object," are the actions of a writer acutely alert to the tone of his text. In this context, to proclaim oneself "in Elysium" is no mean thing, but Irving substantiates his otherwise potentially bold claim by alluding to the physical pleasures of "those relative situations which endear the Sexes." Possibly punning on "relative," the phrase suggests closeness and intimacy—the reverse of the more habitual distance and reserve between England and America—although its emotional charge is complicated and undercut by the theatricality and seemingly staged nature of the description as a whole. Likewise, Irving's relentless and joyously savage mockery of romantic conventions—naming her "beseeching weakness," his "swelling pride," the "verdant meadow," and "musically" flowing Dove—suggests a resistance to buying into the sorts of values traditionally associated with these terms, assiduously promoted in sketches like **"The Wife"** or **"The Broken Heart."**

Moreover, alluding to his companion as a "woman, lovely woman," develops the intimations of illicit intimacy with reference to the somewhat less pure heroines of *The Vicar of Wakefield* and *The Story of Rimini*. In Goldsmith's novel, Olivia, the Vicar's daughter, sings, "When lovely woman stoops to folly / And finds too late that men betray," to her family as they breakfast together on the honeysuckle bank, after she has been seduced and abandoned by the dashing but dastardly Squire Thornhill.[16] In Leigh Hunt's poem, published on 19 January 1816 following his release from gaol, Paolo (originally from Dante's *Inferno*) finds "The two dearest things the world has got / A lovely woman in a rural spot"[17] when he is falling in love with his brother's wife Francesca. Like the "round sleek oily man of God" earlier, this phrase reflects how Irving saw Britain through a web of literature, but also shows that he wanted to write himself into the scenario, even at the expense of all but stifling his own voice in a welter of second-hand expressions.

The complexity of Irving's position during this "repast champêtre" seems to be registered in his closing comparison of himself to a "Strawberry Smotherd in cream." The image—which he had previously used in a letter written in America[18]—is misremembered from George Peele's *The Old Wives' Tale* where "Strawberries swimming in the cream / And schoolboys playing in the stream"[19] feature in a song about courtship and the pleasures of summer. Irving's switching of the verb from the active swimming to the passive smothering intensifies the image, but also adds a note of ambivalence, in that his strawberry is portrayed as immobilized and impotent—smothering leading to death—almost undone by the viscous extremes of pleasure to which it is subjected. Such an analysis chimes with Irving's subsequent admission to Scott of his "powers" having been "almost paralyzed" (*LI*.590) in Britain, and helps perhaps to explain his defensive use of burlesquing to defuse what would seem to be the powerful emotional charge of the memory.

Inevitably, very little, if any, of the writing in *The Sketch Book* would be so unguarded, experimental, or personally autobiographical, though. After returning from Dovedale, Irving had spent much of the autumn and winter of 1816-17 with his sister in Birmingham trying to write, and a letter to Washington Allston reflects clearly both his ambitions and his anxieties at the time: "It is infinitely preferable to stand foremost as one of the founders of a school of painting in an immense & growing country like America, in fact to be an object of national pride and affection, than to fall into the ranks in the crowded galleries of Europe; or perhaps be regarded with an eye of national prejudice, as the production of an American pencil is likely to be in England" (*LI*.478). Irving, however, was aiming to make it in Europe too. Having started work on his own sketches in early summer, by 11 July 1817 he was able to report somewhat pragmatically to Brevoort that he had "a plan which, with very little trouble, will yield me for the present a scanty but sufficient means of support, and leave me leisure to look round for something better" (*LI*.486). This was, of course, *The Sketch Book.* Although he was a little coy, Irving stressed the spirit of neediness in which he wrote: "I cannot at present explain to you what it is— you would probably consider it precarious, & inadequate to my subsistence—but a small matter will float a drowning man and I have dwelt so much of late on the prospect of being cast homeless & pennyless upon the world; that I feel relieved in having even a straw to catch at" (*LI*.486).

Motivated by desperation, Irving seems to have grasped his straw very adeptly. Later that summer he was assiduously cultivating literary contracts first in London, where he spent time with Campbell and Murray, then north of the border during a month-long tour of Scotland. Having met Francis Jeffrey and other Edinburgh luminaries, Irving moved on to Abbotsford. What started out as a courtesy call on Walter Scott became a three-day visit running from August 30 to September 3. Brevoort had earlier given Scott a copy of the *History of New York,* while Irving had reprinted Scott's poetry in the *Analectic Magazine.*[20] There would, however, seem to have been a measure of genuine affection on Scott's part for the younger writer, whom he would later help to launch *The Sketch Book* in England. To his brother Peter, Irving portrayed himself as being in heaven: "I have rambled about the hills with Scott; visited the haunts of Thomas the Rhymer—and other spots rendered classic by border tale and witching song—and have been in a kind of dream or delirium" (*LI*.501). This impression of a country rich in associations was something which Irving would endeavour to create in *The Sketch Book,* and he enthused further to Peter about his host in terms which would seem to value his professional attributes and the successes accruing from them alongside his personal qualities, reinforcing the feeling that he viewed Scott as a professional role model as well as exemplary friend and father figure—"As to Scott, I cannot express my delight at his character & manners—He is a sterling golden hearted old worthy—Full of the joyousness of youth, with an imagination continually furnishing forth picture—and a charming simplicity of manner that puts you at ease with him in a moment" (*LI*.501). Irving's feeling for Scott was undoubtedly very real—and yet his Scott is also a stock character, something like the Angler, to be wheeled out on future occasions and exploited. In this market-oriented vein, Irving would subsequently plan for his own "softly tinted style" of prose to possess "golden thread of thought camelion shades of beautiful imagination, Gems of thought" (*JII*.258). These ambitions tie in with describing Scott as a "sterling golden hearted old worthy," with a seeming pun on sterling, a phrase which at once sets him back in a tried and tested glorious historic past, but also connects him with the idea of something immensely lucrative.

Perhaps motivated by financial considerations, Irving took quite another view of what he saw as the less commendable interest in simplicity cultivated by Wordsworth and his followers, whose writing apparently manifested rather too much of that "natural run of style" admired by Dana. In his same Scottish journal, he deplored their "endeavour" (he had originally written "disposition") to introduce into poetry "all the common colloquial phrases and vulgar idioms." Irving maintained "in their rage for Simplicity they would be coarse and commonplace" (*JII*.104). Whilst "rage" may hint at a measure of unacknowledged sympathy for the energy and spirit of the Romantic project, Irving's disapproving allusion to less eloquent forms of expression reminds us of his new self-consciousness. Despite having previously played on Hunt's *Story of Rimini* in his Dovedale letter—whose "glittering and rancid obscenities" Blackwoods attacked—Irving also turned on his "heterogeneous taste" in the same poem. He claimed "a fondness for gorgeous material is mingled with an occasional proneness to the most grotesque—we fancy him a common stone mason with dirty apron & trowel in hand sometimes building with marble & sometimes with rubbish" (*JII.*104). Irving's conclusion indicated the way ahead: "Now the Language of poetry cannot be too pure and choice. Poems are like classical edifices, for which we seek the noblest materials—What should we think of the Arts of the architect who would build a Grecian temple of brick when he could get marble" (*JII.*104).

In contrast to Irving's earlier letter, when he wrote of his imagination being unable to put forth greenery, this comparison of writing to "classical edifices" is strikingly inorganic—as far away from Romantic nature poetry as possible. Additionally, the connections with planning and building emphasises those aspects of writing which are willed and deliberately constructed—against the spontaneous or haphazard movements of inspiration. That Irving should compare words with buildings, and particularly with buildings so explicitly associated with tradition and the ruling elite, would seem to reflect the determinedly pro-establishment nature of his literary undertaking. This ambition is evident in a further undated musing from the autumn of 1817, whose stiltedness and sense of an imposed agenda betrays the difficulty of this approach for Irving's writing, which more naturally turns towards American subjects. He notes, "England so richly dight with palaces—earth so studded & gemmed with castles & palaces—so embroiderd with parks & gardens So storied—so wrought up with pictures.—Let me wander along the streams of beautiful England & dream of my native rivers of my beautiful native country" (*JII.*182).

That Irving found Britain's accumulation of history—which had "studded & gemmed" its seemingly impenetrable surface—threatening emerges from a subsequent undated journal entry from the period. It presents the past as poised to crush those obliged to reside beneath it, while suggesting that the overwhelming weight is what gives it its value: "England the deposits of all English Antiquity, Usage &c. I should dread any revolution—I consider it as an old picturesque gothic building what may be very inconvenient to its inhabitants but I should dread to see it pulled down or even repaired—even a turret pulled down tho it threatened to fall on the heads of the inhabitants" (*JII.*287). In the context, "deposits" seems to have connotations both of banking and the accretions of time. Perhaps reflecting his own intentions of "trading" in this Old World merchandise, and in some manner confusing them with the difficulties experienced both by his brothers and American merchants since Independence, Irving continued "That it may not Eliminate the laws of fair & open commerce" (*JII.*287). This line of thought was developed in the letter he sent to Ebenezer Irving on 3 March 1819, accompanying the first number of *The Sketch Book,* which also looked forward to future issues. Deploying a term signifying both a piece of writing and an object for trade, he confided to his merchant brother his hopes of producing "articles from time to time that will be sufficient for my present support, and form a stock of copyright property, that may be a little capital for me hereafter" (*LI.*540).

Ebenezer had been encouraging his younger brother to return to America and take up regular employment. Irving concluded by indicating that he saw this as a last chance to establish himself as a writer, and make good his earlier career, saying "I feel myself completely committed in literary reputation by what I have already written; and I feel by no means satisfied to rest my reputation on my preceding writings" (*LI.*540). As if in some way denying his considerable American success to date, he presented *The Sketch Book* as a means of validating himself at home, telling Ebenezer that "it would repay me for a world of care and privation to be placed among the established authors of my country and to win the affections of my countrymen" (*LI.*541). Notwithstanding these hopes, in another letter, written on the same day to Henry Brevoort, Irving appeared to distance himself emotionally, as he had physically, from American culture and values, envisaging a role at once potentially independent of, and yet integral to, his nation's emerging cultural synthesis: "I seek only to blow a flute accompaniment in the national concert, and leave others to play the fiddle & frenchhorn" (*LI.*543).

In this delicately ambitious spirit, Irving wrote to Brevoort again, on 12 August 1819, that he wanted to cancel a sentence in the **"John Bull"** sketch which would have read: "He is like the man who would not have a wart taken off his nose because it had always been there & c & c" (*LI.*554). Witnessing his retreat from the gravy-drooling General Trotter, Irving decreed "I do not like the simile & question whether it is a good & pleasant one you had better run a pen through it and let the paragraph end with the word '*family abuses*'" (*LI.*554). This sensitivity to market values is reflected again in the same letter in his comment that their mutual friend James Paulding should not "write himself below his real value by hasty effusions" (*LI.*555). Irving's own position was spelt out that October, when he told Scott "the reverses of fortune I have experienced since I had the pleasure of Seeing You, make my literary success a matter of Serious importance to me" (*LI.*568), and asked him to sound out Constable regarding an English edition after Murray had turned *The Sketch Book* down. Scott responded very sympathetically, offering Irving the editorship of an anti-Jacobin magazine in Edinburgh with a salary of £500 a year, which he declined gratefully. He then asked Scott to press Constable for a decision, ending in a way that underscored the extent to which his mind turned to material considerations: "And now my dear Sir I will finish this egotistical scrawl by again expressing my heartfelt gratification at the interest you have taken in my concerns—and believe me I feel more joy and rejoicing in your good opinion than I should in all the Gold & Silver in friend Constables breeches pockets—albeit his pockets are none of the shallowest" (*LI.*570).

The construction of the sentence—reflecting an almost compulsive preoccupation with money—is a measure of the distance Irving had travelled during the gestation and composition of *The Sketch Book.* Together with his revision of the **"John Bull"** sketch, and desire only to play the flute in the national orchestra, it suggests the extent to which a conjunction of material and cultural pressures caused him to surrender or compromise both his creative autonomy and sense of national identity, notwithstanding his protestations to the contrary. Fenimore Cooper's first novel, *Precaution,* a genteel, English, comedy of manners published in 1820, was apparently similarly intimidated, but his second, *The Spy,* set during the War of Independence and published in 1821, embraced the American subject and was enthusiastically received. Indeed, after Irving had been recognized in England, no major American author would seem to have felt obliged to pander to the European market as he had done. While **The Sketch Book** probably gained as much as it lost from the compromises Irving forced upon himself—resulting as they did in the unique blend of European and American materials and perspectives—the same cannot be said of his subsequent output. None of the books which followed—**Bracebridge Hall, Tales of a Traveller,** his biography of Columbus, his **Chronicle of the Conquest of Granada,** or **The Alhambra**—lived up to his early promise or sparkle. By the early 1830s, John Murray would come to feel that Irving had written himself out, although he did subsequently find a new American lease of life in **A Tour on the Prairies.** While the tangle of reasons behind the change in his literary fortunes cannot fully be unravelled, in opening to himself his "avenue to some degree of profit and reputation," with all the compromises this entailed, Irving could of necessity have had little inkling where it might lead.

Notes

1. *Washington Irving Letters Volume I 1802-23* (Boston: Twayne Publishers, 1978), 614. Hereafter *LI*. Angled brackets are used in quotations in order to identify revisions made by Irving.

2. *North American Review,* I (Nov. 1815), 35. Hereafter *NAR.*

3. Cited in Benjamin Lease, *Anglo-American Encounters: England and the Rise of American Literature* (Cambridge University Press, 0000), 3.

4. *The Sketch Book of Geoffrey Crayon, Gent.* (Boston: Twayne Publishers, 1978), 1. Hereafter *SB.*

5. *Edinburgh Review,* 34 (Aug. 1820), 162. Hereafter *ER.*34.

6. *Washington Irving Journals and Notebooks,* Vol. 1 (University of Wisconsin Press, 1969), 456. Hereafter *JI.*

7. *Macbeth* II.iv.12.

8. *The Seasons and The Castle of Indolence* (Oxford: Clarendon Press, 1984) Canto 1, stanza LXIX. Hereafter *CI.*

9. *The Riverside Chaucer* (Oxford University Press, 1987), *The General Prologue,* Line 200. Hereafter *GP.*

10. *Washington Irving Journals and Notebooks,* Vol. II 1807-22 (Boston: Twayne Publishers, 1981), 61. Hereafter *JII.*

11. *English Hours* (London: William Heinemann, 1905), 201.

12. *Charlecote and the Lucys,* Alice Fairfax-Lucy (London, 1958), 224-27.

13. See illustrations.

14. *LI*.432.

15. *Observations Relating Chiefly to Picturesque Beauty* (London, 1772), 232.

16. *The Vicar of Wakefield* (London: Heron Books), 158.

17. *The Story of Rimini,* Canto III.257-58.

18. *LI*.353.

19. *The Old Wives' Tale,* 1595, George Peele (Manchester University Press 1980) lines 80-81.

20. This was a monthly collection of European periodical literature which Irving edited during the 1812-14 war.

Marjorie Pryse (essay date 1997)

SOURCE: "Origins of American Literary Regionalism: Gender in Irving, Stowe, and Longstreet" in *Breaking Boundaries: New Perspectives on Women's Regional Writing,* edited by Sherrie A. Inness and Diana Royer, University of Iowa Press, 1997, pp. 17-37.

[*In the following essay, Pryse explores the advent of regionalism by comparing Harriet Beecher Stowe's "Uncle Lot" to Irving's "The Legend of Sleepy Hollow" and "Rip Van Winkle."*]

Any attempt to construct a narrative of the origins of regionalism must begin by acknowledging the problematic status of such an attempt in a critical climate where both "origins" and "regionalism" are themselves contested terms. In a survey of this problem, Amy Kaplan builds her discussion of late-nineteenth-century regionalism on the post-Civil War cultural project of national reunification. For Kaplan, this project involved forgetting a past that included "a contested relation between national and racial identity" as well as "reimagining a distended industrial nation as an extended clan sharing a 'common inheritance' in its imagined rural origins" ("Nation" 242, 251). My own project in this essay takes up the concept of origins from an earlier historical point than does Kaplan. In her first published fiction, "A New England Sketch" (1834) (or "Uncle Lot," as she later retitled it when she included it in *The Mayflower* [1843]), Harriet Beecher Stowe associates regionalism with remembering that American literary culture emerged from a contested relation in which men were victorious, that, for Stowe, the values of women's sphere offered a moral ground for the construction of nation, and that any subsequent reinvention of national origins that did not take into account the contest over men's and women's "spheres" of influence would indeed serve as cultural "forgetting."

Philip Fisher complicates our understanding of the term "regionalism" by defining it as a series of "episodes" in American cultural history that have in common a politicized "struggle within representation," an ongoing cultural civil war that serves as "the counterelement to central myths within American studies" (243, 233). For the nineteenth century, sectional voices split along geographical lines; in the late nineteenth and early twentieth centuries, massive immigration between 1870 and 1914 produced "a regionalism of languages, folk customs, humor, music and beliefs" set against processes of Americanization; "the regionalism of our own times . . . is one of gender and race" (242-43). Suggesting that such a counterelement makes a critical move from myths (of a unified America) to rhetorics (as sites of cultural work), Fisher identifies Harriet Beecher Stowe as one of the "masters" of "collaborative and implicational relations between writer or speaker and culture" (237). For critics interested in how literature accomplishes what Jane Tompkins in *Sensational Designs* described as "cultural work," Stowe appears to have joined the late-twentieth-century conversation over the relationship between literature and culture.

Far from viewing Stowe herself and the particular form of regionalism she took for her fiction as a "diminished thing," a "subordinate order" (to cite James M. Cox's dismissive critical assessment of regionalism in *Columbia Literary History of the United States* [764-65]), we can view her work as engaged in a rhetoric of cultural dislocation, a project of inventing alternatives to national views on slavery, women's education, the profession of literature, and women's roles in nation building. Joan Hedrick observes in the preface to her recent biography of Stowe that the hostility to Stowe's writing that judged her work "to be amateur, unprofessional, and 'bad art'" emerged "in the 1860s between the dominant women writers and the rising literary establishment of men who were determined to displace them" (*Harriet Beecher Stowe* ix). As I shall demonstrate, although Stowe began writing before the Civil War and appears to equate regionalism with a geographical concept—and memory—of New England life in her first published work, she was from the beginning engaged in the kind of rhetorical contestation Philip Fisher associates with "new Americanist" concepts of regionalism. For Stowe, this cultural work involved gender and the role of women in the nation—a rhetorical struggle that remains unresolved.

In writing her first sketch Stowe discovers that the process of conversion, a distant forerunner of what feminists in the 1970s termed "consciousness raising," can provide the narrative intention for a work of fiction, thereby allowing ministers' daughters (both Stowe herself and Grace Griswold in the sketch) to imagine expanding their authority in literary and domestic spheres. My own understanding of conversion in Stowe is similar to that of Jane Tompkins, who writes in her analysis of *Uncle Tom's Cabin* that for Stowe, "historical change takes place only through religious conversion" but that such conversion for Stowe has "revolutionary potential" (133, 145). Tompkins argues that

Stowe pushes her beliefs "to an extreme and by insisting that they be applied universally, not just to one segregated corner of civil life, but to the conduct of all human affairs, Stowe means to effect a radical transformation of her society" (145). In "Uncle Lot," conversion becomes a model for narrative form as well as a transformative theme: Stowe is attempting to "convert" her (male) readers to the power of women's narrative authority.

In presenting conversion as both the source of action and the goal of fiction in "Uncle Lot," Stowe anticipates the empathic point of view characteristic of women regionalist writers and their narrators, thus originating the cultural and literary developmental line of the regionalist tradition. If for the Beechers conversion required a "private change of heart" (Sklar 27), the conversion of evolving American literary culture would require a cultural change of heart. And in this way, from her earliest published sketch, Stowe attempted to transform the direction of American fiction with the same passion that her sister Catharine addressed to the transformation of the profession of teaching; for both sisters, teaching and storytelling were forms of preaching, and women were suited to practice all three. By the time Harriet Beecher came to view herself as a writer, she already knew that American women wrote and published their work. Yet creating a legitimate arena within which American women might exert national influence would require for Stowe not the overt confrontation with paternal authority which had characterized her sister's experience of conversion, during which Catharine proved unable or unwilling to achieve conversion on her father, Lyman's, terms (Sklar 31-38), but the subtle, persuasive, affectional process of eliciting inner change. For women to achieve a position in American literary culture, Stowe's early work indicates, men, especially those men like Washington Irving who were already producing an "American" fiction, must also be "converted" to those same qualities that Catharine Beecher had argued "placed women closer to the source of moral authority and hence established their social centrality" (Sklar 83). Such an argument requires fuller elaboration and a more detailed and historicized reading than we have previously granted Stowe's first sketch and its rhetorical strategies. For while literary historians have recognized the contributions of humor of the Old Southwest, another "minor" literary tradition, to the development of American fiction, we have yet to acknowledge regionalism as either a narrative tradition in its own right or one that substantially influenced the direction of American literature.[1]

Although "Uncle Lot" has been ignored by literary historians, critics, and theorists alike, the sketch marks a significant moment in the development of American literature in the nineteenth century, and I read it in the context of this moment. Remaining within a critical regionalism that continues to define itself along the lines of Philip Fisher's "struggle within representation," I trace evidence of both conflict and influence that established Stowe from the beginning, even before the publication of *Uncle Tom's Cabin* in 1852, as a writer for whom civil war was as viable a cultural concept as it became an economic and political one by the 1860s.

"Uncle Lot" locates Stowe's early rhetorical position on the question of women's potential contribution to American authorship, and the position involves cultural battle lines and opposing sides. I suggest that we may view literary regionalism as the emergence of the "Ichabod Crane school" of American narrative, despite Crane's ignominious defeat at the hands of Brom Bones, and that we can identify Stowe's sketch as her attempt to "convert" American readers to the values of what Irving had termed, albeit disparagingly, the "female circle" and the "sleepy region." In the process Stowe creates the possibility of regionalism itself as a literary form capable of conferring literary authority on American women. What we might term the "Brom Bones school" emerges through the work of Augustus Baldwin Longstreet in *Georgia Scenes* (1835) and in the fiction of the Old Southwest humorists of the 1840s and 1850s, who respond to the question of gender either by relegating women characters to the source and object of sexual humor or by omitting women from their tales altogether. Stephen Railton's extensive discussion of southwestern humor and its "national audience of men" (91) makes a clear case for the gendered separation of early-nineteenth-century American fiction, suggesting that "gentlemen" themselves felt "excluded and powerless" in American society but "could find vicarious compensation in the rough world of the humorists, where it is women who do not matter, except as occasional objects of unfrustrated resentment" (103-04). The women writers of domestic and didactic scenes of American life, Catharine Sedgwick, Lydia Huntley Sigourney, and Stowe's sister Catharine Beecher, who influenced both Stowe and later writers in the regionalist tradition, occupied entirely different rhetorical and cultural territory from the humorists. Even the editors who published the works of these writers—William T. Porter and his *Spirit of the Times,* and James T. Hall and the *Western Monthly Magazine*—take up opposing or "separate" positions on the topic of women as cultural subjects. We can view the humor of the Old Southwest and early regionalism as manifestations of two possible but mutually exclusive gender-specific directions for the development of American fiction before the Civil War.

Although "Uncle Lot" announces a departure in American fiction from the sketches of Stowe's male predecessors and contemporaries, her own female successors would more fully delineate the features of regionalism and more explicitly link these features to women's lives in nineteenth-century America than Stowe herself did. Conversion based on "private change of heart" (Sklar 27) in Stowe reemerges as the "collaborative and implicational relations between writer or speaker and culture" (Fisher 237), to extend Fisher's formulation beyond Stowe herself, and becomes a feature of regionalist narrative. Later in the century, beginning with Alice Cary's *Clovernook* sketches of the early 1850s and including such writers as Rose Terry Cooke, Celia Thaxter, Sarah Orne Jewett, Mary

Wilkins Freeman, Zitkala-Sa, Grace King, Kate Chopin, Alice Dunbar-Nelson, Sui Sin Far, and Mary Austin, American women writers would refine regionalism as an approach to narrative that would develop parallel to but divergent from the techniques and forms of local color fiction. Judith Fetterley and I have made this argument in the introduction to *American Women Regionalists,* our collection of some of the central works in the regionalist tradition, and an analysis of the cultural moment in which "Uncle Lot" first appears provides early evidence that regionalism and "local color," though often conflated, do represent different articulations of and attitudes toward regional subjects.

Without Stowe's own later work, "Uncle Lot" would not assume the significance it does, but Stowe further elaborated the themes of "Uncle Lot" in her most important fiction. *Uncle Tom's Cabin,* as I have indicated, further develops the theme of conversion. *The Pearl of Orr's Island* (1862) establishes women's development and education as a contested site (see Fetterley, "Only a Story"). And in great late works, *Oldtown Folks* (1869) and *Sam Lawson's Oldtown Fireside Stories* (1872), Stowe continues to propose regionalism as a direction for American fiction. Sam Lawson, Stowe's narrator in these works, is a more successful and benign version of Rip Van Winkle. Stowe's persistence in developing these themes gives her first published sketch renewed significance in our own century, as we attempt to trace the origins of literary authority for American women writers and attempt, as well, to fairly assess their contribution to nineteenth-century American literature. Writing regional sketches in particular gave Stowe a way of educating her contemporaries. Stowe makes it possible for her readers to take a second look at characters others might find laughable or without literary value, such as Uncle Lot himself, or, later, in *The Pearl of Orr's Island,* Aunts Roxy and Ruey—rural, female, elderly, and otherwise disenfranchised persons. Reading "Uncle Lot" in its various contexts thus opens up, to use Stowe's own language in the sketch, a "chestnut burr" of genre in American fiction; the sketch kept alive for Stowe the possibility that her female successors might experience the authority of authorship, thereby "converting" her own readers to the idea that women's voices and women's values can influence her own postrevolutionary and our own postmodern American culture.

Two conclusions become possible from reexamining Stowe's first sketch within the context of early-nineteenth-century writers' responses to gender: first, that while some women began to make an issue of women's roles and rights after 1835,[2] the question of whether American fiction itself would follow lines confirmed by the cultural ideology of "separate spheres" remained as yet unanswered in the 1830s, so that ultimately our analysis of "Uncle Lot" presents a moment not unlike our own, in which gender as a cultural construct was much more fluid than it would be for at least the next century (or in our case, the previous century); and second, that the very consciousness of gender and its relation to narrative for early-nineteenth-century American writers created an opening for the development of "separate genres" or narrative traditions within which women writers might develop their authority as storytellers. Regionalism has its origins both in this as-yet-indeterminate relationship between gender and genre and at the same time in a consciousness of gender in Stowe's early work and the writing of her male and female contemporaries.

"Uncle Lot" makes for interesting reading in its own right: it is the first published sketch by an important American writer; it coincides with the influential Beecher family's move to Cincinnati and thus presents New England life and values to a western audience; and it is a work which has remained in the archives of American literary history.[3] But it becomes an even more interesting text read as the young Harriet Beecher's awareness of an emerging American fiction and her attempts to redirect that fiction by revising Washington Irving. An analysis of the significance of "Uncle Lot" as a cultural moment therefore begins with a discussion of **"Rip Van Winkle"** and **"The Legend of Sleepy Hollow."**

When Rip Van Winkle comes down from the mountain and finds his new place in his postrevolutionary village as a "chronicle of the old times 'before the war'" (40), Washington Irving creates a vocation for the American artist. At the beginning of the tale Rip has "an insuperable aversion to all kinds of profitable labour" (Irving 30), preferring instead to spend his time telling ghost stories to children, but he awakens from his twenty-year sleep to discover that the storyteller in the new republic has an important role to play. In **"Rip Van Winkle"** Irving avoids prescribing a form for the American story, but he does suggest that it will have a content different from English narrative; like the image of George Washington on the sign in front of the Union Hotel, American fiction may derive from English and European models but is also "singularly metamorphosed" (Irving 37). However, despite Rip's altered perception in the tale, Irving makes it clear that certain things have not changed. George is still a George, not a Dame; Irving allows Rip a "drop of comfort" when he discovers that he has survived two wars at once, the American Revolution and the tyranny of "petticoat government," for Dame Van Winkle is dead. And Irving spares Rip any complicity in her death; she has broken a blood vessel "in a fit of passion at a New-England pedlar" (Irving 39). Angry women do not survive to tell the story of the "old times 'before the war.'" Dame Van Winkle cannot be a candidate for the American artist; such would be a singular metamorphosis indeed.[4] For Irving the American storyteller, like the American hero, must be male.

By granting the postrevolutionary American artist a cultural role with secular rather than divine authority (George Washington replaces King George), Irving asserts the separation of literature from theology as the political ground for an American story. Irving's Knickerbocker tales reveal the gender anxiety that this shift created for early-nineteenth-century male American writers.[5] In their separation from Puritanism as a cultural base, turning away from the writing of sermons and toward the writing of fiction, Irving's male contemporaries split off that anxiety, which Irving figures as the psychocultural castration image of the headless horseman. They projected "headlessness" onto women writers and asserted masculinity itself as evidence of divine authority. Irving's narrator thus fiercely refuses to take women—the already "castrated"—seriously. And just in case his readers remain insufficiently convinced that Dame Van Winkle is dead and worry that she might return to haunt them or pose a threat to Rip's postrevolutionary authority, Irving resurrects her in a literary way as Ichabod Crane in **"The Legend of Sleepy Hollow,"** then frightens "her" out of town, not needing the Freudian and Lacanian theories of our own century to make the point that gender anxiety for men signifies the fear of absence, castration, headlessness.[6]

In **"The Legend of Sleepy Hollow,"** Irving removes the undesirable qualities that characterized Dame Van Winkle from his portraits of the Dutch wives and projects them instead onto the character of Ichabod Crane. During Ichabod's reign over his "little literary realm," the schoolroom, the pedagogue uses "a ferule, that sceptre of despotic power" and "the birch of justice reposed on three nails" to enforce his limited government (Irving 283). Like Dame Van Winkle, Ichabod Crane in the schoolroom becomes someone to escape, and Irving describes the scholars' early dismissal as "emancipation" (284). However, outside the schoolroom, Ichabod undergoes a transformation and becomes the embodiment of Rip rather than Dame. He has a "soft and foolish heart towards the [female] sex" like his counterpart in Irving's earlier tale. He becomes the playmate of his own charges and the congenial companion of their mothers: he would often "sit with a child on one knee, and rock a cradle with his foot, for whole hours together" (Irving 276). He seems initially content to become one of the region's "native inhabitants," deriving pleasure from visiting, "snugly cuddling in the chimney corner," filling the role of "travelling gazette," and expressing his desire for the "comforts of the cupboard" (Irving 273, 278, 276, 275). And within the "female circle," he enjoys the position of "man of letters" (Irving 276). Yet Irving does not grant him Rip's place as American artist; the extracts from Cotton Mather that Ichabod contributes to the storytelling at Van Tassel's castle do not appear to be successful in competing with the ghost stories Brom Bones tells.

Ichabod Crane will not serve as Irving's image of the American artist; neither will he provide a model for the American hero. For Irving reveals him to be a fraud—not a real contender for the love of Katrina Van Tassel but instead a glutton whose desire for Katrina derives from greed and gorging. Most startling of all, Ichabod turns out to be no settler after all but rather to have fantasies of sacking the "sleepy region" in order to invest "in immense tracts of wild land, and shingle palaces in the wilderness," toward which he would set off, Katrina and the children on top of a wagon and "himself bestriding a pacing mare" (Irving 280). Too much a member of the "female circle," as Irving defines women's culture, to bring off this quint-essentially masculine vision, Ichabod becomes by the end of the tale merely a debased version of it, an unsuccessful suitor, an "affrighted pedagogue," an "unskilful rider" (Irving 292, 294). Reminding us that women had produced "more than a third of the fiction published in America before 1820," Lloyd Daigrepont suggests that Irving "instilled in Ichabod Crane the characteristics of those writers who dominated the American literary scene" in the early days of the Republic—what he calls a "burgeoning popular taste for the excessive emotionalism of the sentimental tale, the novel of sensibility, and the Gothic romance"—and that in the conclusion of **"The Legend of Sleepy Hollow,"** Irving "symbolically portrayed their defeat" (69-70).

Irving creates Brom Bones instead as Crane's triumphant adversary and as an image of American manhood. "Brom Bones . . . was the hero of the scene," a man who has tamed Daredevil, a man "in fact noted for preferring vicious animals, . . . for he held a tractable well broken horse as unworthy of a lad of spirit" (Irving 287). As Daniel Hoffman observes, Brom Bones "is a Catskill Mike Fink, a Ring-Tailed Roarer from Kinderhook" (89). Brom Bones above all represents masculinity, a quality absent in Irving's characterizations of both Rip Van Winkle and Ichabod Crane, and this masculinity gives him authority over Ichabod. The "burley, roaring, roystering blade" has a "bluff, but not unpleasant countenance," "more mischief than ill-will in his composition," and "with all his overbearing roughness, there was a strong dash of waggish good humour at bottom" (Irving 737). The excesses of the "female circle" may threaten the cultural order with "petticoat government," but the excesses of masculinity merely contribute to our national health—we all have a good laugh at Ichabod Crane's cowardice, incompetence, and basic cultural impotence. **"The Legend of Sleepy Hollow"** turns the folktale into a tall tale: sobered by the seriousness of his own attempt to reflect American identity in the Republic's fiction, Irving rejects as "sleepy" any literary authority the Dutch wives might claim and establishes the "roaring blade" as the literary descendant of Rip Van Winkle.

Like many other writers in the 1830s, Stowe begins "Uncle Lot" by reworking Irving's **"The Legend of Sleepy Hollow."** Most of these writers, however, as Hennig Cohen and William B. Dillingham observe, imitated what they term the "ingredients of a typical sketch of Southwest humor: the physically awkward, ugly, and avaricious Ichabod; the good-natured but rowdy Brom Bones and his friends, who love a practical joke; the desirable plum, Katrina Van Tassel." Cohen and Dillingham report that "it would be difficult to estimate the number of Southern tales directly influenced by 'Sleepy Hollow,'" and they cite some examples: Joseph B. Cobb's "The Legend of Black Creek," William Tappan Thompson's "The Runaway Match" and "Adventures of a Sabbath-Breaker," and Francis James Robinson's "The Frightened Serenaders" (xii). Thus Stowe was not alone in modeling a work of fiction on **"The Legend of Sleepy Hollow."**[7] However, Stowe's text critiques Irving, thereby establishing the context for

regionalism, an approach to the representation of rural and regional people and values that involves respect and empathy and grants voice to regional characters in the work, an approach that differs markedly from that of the "humorists," who created such characters as objects of derision rather than subjects of their own agency.

Stowe's text specifically reveals similarities between her village of Newbury, "one of those out-of-the-way places where nobody ever came unless they came on purpose: a green little hollow" ("Uncle Lot" 2), and Irving's "little valley, or rather lap of land among high hills, which is one of the quietest places in the whole world," a "green, sheltered, fertile nook" (272, 279). Stowe notes the "unchangeability" of Newbury, particularly in its "manners, morals, arts, and sciences" ("Uncle Lot" 2); Irving describes the "population, manners, and customs" of his "sleepy region" as "fixed" (274). Both authors introduce their characters as representatives of the larger citizenry. Irving's Ichabod Crane "was a native of Connecticut, a state which supplies the Union with pioneers for the mind as well as for the forest" (274), and Stowe describes James Benton as "one of those whole-hearted, energetic Yankees" who possessed a "characteristic national trait" ("Uncle Lot" 3). Like Ichabod Crane, James Benton is a newcomer to the village of Newbury, he "figured as schoolmaster all the week, and as chorister on Sundays," he makes himself at home "in all the chimney-corners of the region," devouring "doughnuts and pumpkin pies with most flattering appetite," and he generally "kept the sunny side of the old ladies" ("Uncle Lot" 4, 6). James Benton holds what Stowe describes as "an uncommonly comfortable opinion of himself" ("Uncle Lot" 3); Irving characterizes as Ichabod's "vanity" his belief that in his performance as chorister "he completely carried away the palm from the parson" (276). Both tell stories, and both have, as Stowe writes of James Benton, "just the kindly heart that fell in love with everything in feminine shape" ("Uncle Lot" 6).

There is thus a great deal of evidence to suggest that Stowe begins "Uncle Lot" by invoking **"The Legend of Sleepy Hollow."** However, Stowe imitates in order to revise. For Stowe, there is no threat of castration, nothing to "lose"; what seems revolutionary about "Uncle Lot" is not its explicit content—since unlike Irving's tales, "Uncle Lot" reinforces the values of a theology based on inner feeling and a literature congruent with theology—but rather the demonstration of a woman's authority to be the writer of the tale.[8] Unlike Irving, Stowe identifies women's values not as debased but as central to the "private change of heart" that must precede cultural conversion, a conversion of domestic ideology that would acknowledge women's moral centrality and women's role in creating American culture, and she asserts the centrality of feeling in American culture by transforming Ichabod Crane into James Benton, a hero willing to acknowledge women's authority at least in the domestic sphere.[9] "Uncle Lot" thereby links place—Newbury as invocation and reinvention of Irving's "sleepy region"—with values of domestic ideology, conversion, and women's authority that together lay the foundation for her successors in the regionalist tradition. Regional "place" becomes more or less a feature of the fiction and a sign of preindustrial, even prepatriarchal authority for the women of faculty that move throughout Stowe's own work and the later herbalists, healers, and empathic visitors that populate sketches and stories by later women regionalist writers.

Stowe claims that her "main story" involves a romance between her hero, James Benton, and Uncle Lot Griswold's daughter, Grace. However, like Irving in his portrait of Katrina Van Tassel, Stowe gives her readers only an occasional glimpse of Grace; instead she focuses on the process by which male characters in the sketch become converted or transformed in various ways. Stowe places Uncle Lot at the thematic center of her sketch. She describes him as a "chestnut burr, abounding with briers without and with substantial goodness within" but "'the *settest* crittur in his way that ever you saw'" ("Uncle Lot" 7, 12). Initially Uncle Lot expresses an aversion to the young hero, James Benton, so in order to "win" Grace's favors, James must first elicit Uncle Lot's recognition of what James believes to be Uncle Lot's inner feelings. Thus the "conversion" of Uncle Lot's opinion of James replaces courtship as Stowe's organizing principle in the narrative; James tries to reach Uncle Lot behind the defenses he has created, the overlays of his "chestnut burr," and to convert him into a person capable of expressing feeling, that "substantial goodness within." In addition, James Benton achieves his own spiritual conversion, and conversion to the ministry, by falling in love with Grace's minister brother, George, then, upon young George's untimely death, replacing him within the family as Uncle Lot's "son." Marriage with Grace at the end of the sketch merely ritualizes this "son" relationship. Thus, despite Stowe's claim that Grace figures as her heroine, she pays very little attention to Grace herself.

However, unlike Irving's portrait of Katrina, what characterization Stowe does provide underscores Grace's intellectual capacity and moral superiority, features congruent generally with the ideology of domesticity and specifically with Stowe's sister Catharine's vision of women. Catharine appears to have believed that conversion was a much less strenuous task for women than for men, that women only needed to be educated in the schools she proposed, where they would "learn proper social, religious, and moral principles and then establish their own schools elsewhere on the same principles" (Sklar 95), and that women would then be in a position to assert their influence on the nation. As Katharine Kish Sklar writes, "Catharine Beecher not only wanted to 'save' the nation, she wanted women to save it" and engaged in a campaign to transform teaching from a men's profession to a profession "dominated by—indeed exclusively belonging to—women" (96, 97). Catharine Beecher herself took over much of the care of her younger siblings, including the then-four-year-old Harriet, after their mother, Roxana, died, and it was Catharine who supervised Harriet's education from the time she was about thirteen (Sklar 60).

Given her sister's powerful model, we can view Stowe's portrait of Grace Griswold as suggesting that her sketch does not need to convert Grace, who is the already-converted, and therefore does not need to focus on Grace's development as part of the sketch's "plot." Stowe describes Grace as follows:

> Like most Yankee damsels, she had a longing after the tree of knowledge, and, having exhausted the literary fountains of a district school, she fell to reading whatsoever came in her way. True, she had but little to read; but what she perused she had her own thoughts upon, so that a person of information, in talking with her, would feel a constant wondering pleasure to find that she had so much more to say of this, that, and the other thing than he expected.
>
> ("Uncle Lot" 9)

Grace already represents grace; she possesses the moral character to which the men in Stowe's sketch must aspire in order to demonstrate their own spiritual conversion, which becomes manifested for James in his success at winning over Uncle Lot, then winning a congregation and a wife, and for Uncle Lot in his ability to express his feeling for James Benton. The men in particular must experience that "private change of heart" which characterized conversion for Lyman Beecher (Sklar 27). Within the ideology that asserted women's moral centrality, it does not surprise readers that after speaking very little throughout the sketch, Grace asserts herself in the sketch's final scene, when she tells Uncle Lot, a visitor to her house following her marriage to James, "Come, come, father, I have authority in these days, so no disrespectful speeches" ("Uncle Lot" 31).[10]

Thus conversion, rather than the confrontation and defeat that characterize **"The Legend of Sleepy Hollow,"** gives Stowe's narrative its direction, and conversion figures as an aspect of plot as well as of theme. Stowe gives James Benton the task of trying to "convert" Uncle Lot; conversion, not seduction, becomes her hero's test. In the scene which depicts this "conversion," James Benton arrives for an unannounced visit to Uncle Lot's house with the ostensible goal of winning Uncle Lot's affection. Stowe writes:

> James also had one natural accomplishment, more courtier-like than all the diplomacy in Europe, and that was the gift of feeling a *real* interest for anybody in five minutes; so that, if he began to please in jest, he generally ended in earnest. With great simplicity of mind, he had a natural tact for seeing into others, and watched their motions with the same delight with which a child gazes at the wheels and springs of a watch, to "see what it will do."
>
> ("Uncle Lot" 16)

James wishes to open up the "chestnut burr" that characterizes Uncle Lot's defenses against feeling, and he uses powers of empathy—his "natural tact for seeing into others"—to help Uncle Lot recognize and reveal the "latent kindness" he holds within his "rough exterior" ("Uncle Lot" 16).

Stowe reverses Irving's condemnation of women, suggesting that instead of annihilating what Irving calls "petticoat government" at the end of **"Rip Van Winkle,"** American society might benefit from genuine government, at least in the domestic sphere, by women; and instead of frightening Ichabod Crane out of town, as Irving does in **"The Legend of Sleepy Hollow,"** she creates her own hero in Ichabod Crane's image, then "converts" him from his prankish boyishness into a man of deep feeling, into a man, in Catharine Beecher's sense, who becomes more like a woman as the sketch progresses and ends by submitting to Grace's authority.

In Stowe's world, Dame Van Winkle might exert genuine influence, might even speak, as does Stowe herself in assuming authorship; in "Uncle Lot," Stowe reinforces the nineteenth-century view of women's interest in feeling and moral character, while the masculine behaviors of Brom Bones disappear from the fiction. Thus Dame Van Winkle survives in the work of Harriet Beecher Stowe not as a shrill-voiced termagant but as a woman capable of using her verbal facility in order to assert, in Grace's closing lines, "authority in these days" ("Uncle Lot" 31). Irving has to justify the exclusion of women from the province of storytelling; Stowe wants not to exclude men but to include women in the profession of literature (even though, ironically, she never created a female narrator in her work). Nevertheless, the fact that "Uncle Lot" has remained unremarked for most of this century attests to the apparent victory of Irving's position. At least as literary history has recorded it, Brom Bones inspired an entire "school" of tall tale fiction by the Old Southwest humorists, whereas Ichabod Crane disappeared into the "sleepy region."

In reading "Uncle Lot" to the Semi-Colon Club, Stowe had the good fortune to attract the attention of editor James Hall of the *Western Monthly Magazine.* One of Stowe's biographers, in describing James Hall's influence, writes that he advocated "cheerfulness, morality, and regionalism" as a literary aesthetic, was "a chivalrous admirer of women writers," and encouraged payment for contributors to American periodicals (Adams, *Harriet Beecher Stowe* 35-36)[11] In awarding his fiction prize to Harriet Beecher's first New England sketch, he was also implicitly urging her to counter the portrait of American life that the frontier appeared to encourage—as he knew very well. In *Letters from the West,* Hall had recorded the telling of yarns by an old keelboatman named Pappy, whom he had encountered while traveling down the Ohio on a flatboat (W. Blair 70);[12] and as editor of *The Western Souvenir,* issued in Cincinnati in 1828, "the first of American gift books from beyond the Alleghenies" (Thompson 95-96), Hall achieved the distinction of having been the first editor to publish a lengthy account of the career of the legendary Mike Fink (W. Blair 81-82). Like Washington Irving, Hall appears to have been interested very early in the tall tale; but unlike Irving, he would choose, as editor of the *Western Monthly Magazine,* to encourage his contributors, especially women, to write about other regional material than the portraits of frontier life that would survive in American literary history as humor of the Old Southwest.[13]

Hall contrasts sharply with his contemporary, William T. Porter, whose sporting magazine, the *Spirit of the Times,* first published in 1831, provided gentlemen interested in the leisure pursuits of horse racing, hunting, and listening to tall tales with a way of gratifying their fantasies of upper-class superiority (since much of the humor Porter published derived from "the foibles and follies of the lower classes" [Yates 88]) and of ratifying their belief in masculine values and male dominance. Unlike Hall, whose interest in developing western material inspired his work, Porter was a commercialist, interested more in the culture of the sporting world than in literature. He initially catered "to the wealthy slaveholding sportsmen and their friends and allies, who 'ruled' racing" (Yates 17). With the decline of horse racing by the end of the 1830s, Porter began to include the early local color fiction literary historians term humor of the Old Southwest. As Norris W. Yates observes, "The bulk of [Porter's] later readers belong to a new and larger economic and social class—a class which may have shared the values and interests but not the economic resources of the old" (21). Thus the values and interests of the slave-holding sportsmen and their allies contrast decidedly with the values and interests of the audience for and contributors to Hall's *Western Monthly Magazine.* The readers who allowed the *Spirit of the Times* to flourish for more than thirty years may not have been able to prevent women from speaking out in public meetings, but by excluding morality from the province of humor they attempted to exclude the particular sphere of women's influence in nineteenth-century culture from fiction and effectively defined storytelling as a masculine occupation. The writers who contributed to William T. Porter's sporting magazine continued to develop American literature as a masculine enterprise. To the extent that humor of the Old Southwest establishes Brom Bones as the American hero, this particular literary genre describes a direction for fiction that women writers could not and did not follow.[14]

Augustus Baldwin Longstreet and his colleague on the Augusta *Sentinel,* William Tappan Thompson, both of whom published their sketches in the 1830s, were the only Old Southwest humorist writers who treated female characters in their fiction (W. Blair 74).[15] Of these two, Longstreet in *Georgia Scenes* (1835) had the greater influence.[16] *Georgia Scenes* is an important text to examine in establishing gender consciousness as a feature of early American fiction, for while it reaffirms Irving's perspective and establishes further precedent for the humorists' exclusion of women, it also suggests a lingering fluidity in the relationship between gender and genre in the 1830s. At the same time, *Georgia Scenes* suggests that Old Southwest humor evolved in part from suppressing the possibility of female literary authority. In Longstreet's preface to *Georgia Scenes* he tells us "that when he first wrote and published the sketches which went into the volume, he was 'extremely desirous' of concealing his authorship; and that in order to accomplish his purpose, he had used two pseudonyms. For sketches in which men are the principal actors, he says, he uses the name Hall; for those in which women are the most prominent, he writes under the name Baldwin" (Meriwether 358; Longstreet v).

James Meriwether writes that "the dominant figure of the book is Hall; . . . Baldwin simply serves as a foil to the ultimately much more masculine and successful Lyman Hall" (359). In Baldwin's sketches, the narrator becomes a moralist who stands back from the action, contrasting "country girls" with their urban counterparts and condemning women who become "charming" creatures and lead their husbands to early graves. By contrast, in Hall's sketches, Hall participates in the action, proves himself to be a crack shot, and establishes himself as a man's man. A third character who appears in the sketches, Ned Brace of "A Sage Conversation," establishes storytelling as one of many contests, like gander pulling, horse swapping, or horse racing, in which boys or men can prove their masculinity. Both Ned Brace and Lyman Hall achieve a less ambiguous masculinity than does Baldwin.

In suggesting Baldwin's ultimate ineffectuality, Longstreet, like Irving in his portrait of Ichabod Crane, links Baldwin to the world of women that he simultaneously mocks. The "country girls" of "The Dance" are so "wholly ignorant" of urban fashion that "consequently, they looked, for all the world, like human beings" (14); thus Longstreet manages to make fun of both country and urban "girls" in the same jest. In "The Song," piano player Miss Aurelia Emma Theodosia Augusta Crump has hands that engage in conflict at the keyboard, and "anyone, or rather no one, can imagine what kind of noises the piano gave forth" as a result (Longstreet 70). Longstreet's portraits of women characters, primarily in Baldwin's sketches, led his biographer Kimball King to remark, "It is hard to understand how a man who appears to have had close, satisfying relationships with his wife and daughters, all sensible, intelligent women who led exemplary lives, could portray their sex so unflatteringly, unless his bias were actually a pose, a part of his writer's mask" (80). However, the emerging gender consciousness of the 1830s makes this explicable; Longstreet, like Irving, associates storytelling with masculinity and political power, for Hall ends the volume, in "The Shooting-Match," by proving his marksmanship and thereby earning the potential votes of the country people. The people promise to support him if he "offers" for anything; "Longstreet makes it clear that the judgment of these people is to be respected and if Hall will accept such responsibilities he will be an able and successful public official" (Meriwether 361), such as Longstreet himself later became in his career as a judge, preacher, and college president. Baldwin, on the other hand, clearly lacks the shooting ability to qualify as either effective storyteller or political man; as he demonstrates in his failure to execute the humorous "double cross-hop" step of his first sketch in *Georgia Scenes,* he cannot even dance (Longstreet 21).

In Baldwin's most powerful sketch, "A Sage Conversation," the three aged matrons who relate anecdotes to each other prove Longstreet's point, for they seem unable to understand the meaning of the very anecdotes they are attempting to tell and thus do not succeed in the actively masculine pursuit of contriving and telling stories. Baldwin opens "A Sage Conversation" with the assertion, "I love the aged matrons of our land. As a class, they are the most pious, the most benevolent, the most useful, and the most harmless of the human family" (Longstreet 186). Nevertheless, the women cannot solve the riddle of Ned Brace's story concerning "two most excellent men, who became so attached to each other that they actually got married" (Longstreet 188), and although the women light their pipes and sit around the fire until late in the night, their talking never rises above the level of what one of them calls "an old woman's chat" (Longstreet 196). Although they may look like men, engaging in pipe smoking and late-night conversation, the women are innocents on the subject of cross-dressing, recalling women who "dress'd in men's clothes" and followed their true loves "to the wars," and one of them concludes that "men don't like to marry gals that take on that way" (Longstreet 191). They miss the humorous potential of their own material; they prove themselves incapable of sustaining the line of a narrative longer than a brief comment or two; they suggest that their only expertise lies in the realm of herbal remedies; and throughout, they demonstrate the general inability of women to be storytellers.

James M. Cox suggests, with irony, that in the final "showdown" between Stowe and the frontier humorists, Stowe "wins"; that in *Uncle Tom's Cabin,* she turns the bear hunt characteristic of much of southern and frontier humor into a man hunt; and that she "killed" the humorists by raising the question of serious moral culture. He claims that he does not wish to "put down Mrs. Stowe" but argues that it was ultimately Samuel Clemens who found the form of genius for the materials of native American humor ("Humor" 591-92). It is difficult to imagine how Stowe or any other woman writer of the 1830s and 1840s could have written the kind of American humor Cox refers to here, since in order to do so she would have had to achieve that humor at women's expense and ironically agree to take only masculine culture, with its sport, jests, frolics, and put-downs, seriously.[17] Cox views Clemens as the product of the implicit conflict between Stowe and the Old Southwest humorists, implying that the local color school of American fiction, including Bret Harte and Hamlin Garland, emerged from the same origins as Old Southwest humor.[18] For Cox, Stowe and Longstreet appear to sketch alternative directions in American fiction, and Hall's sketches in *Georgia Scenes* (if not Baldwin's) support this point. Hall's narratives create further variations on the theme of masculine dominance, serve to reify the distinctions between men and women characteristic of "separate spheres," and contribute to dividing early-nineteenth-century American fiction along the lines of humor at others' expense, exemplified by Old Southwest and local color "schools," and empathy for others, in the tradition of literary regionalism, primarily exemplified by women writers.[19]

With the publication of "A New England Sketch" or "Uncle Lot," Stowe joined an emerging group of women who had begun to publish in magazines—Lydia Maria Child, Catharine Sedgwick, Lydia Huntley Sigourney, among others—and who, by their very success as publishing authors, underscored the issue of gender in nineteenth-century literary culture. In her delineation of woman's fiction, however, Nina Baym suggests that Stowe's interests in slavery and religion were "issues transcending gender" and that they "set her apart from the other American women writing fiction in her day" (15). Stowe certainly knew Sedgwick's *A New England Tale* (1822), the novel Baym credits with inaugurating the genre of woman's fiction; Sklar notes that it had created controversy within the Beecher family and that Catharine in particular had attacked Sedgwick, a convert to Unitarianism, as having betrayed her social position and the Calvinist tradition (44-45). It was perhaps in recognition of Sedgwick as well as an attempt to distance herself from the controversy that led Stowe to change the title of "A New England Sketch" to "Uncle Lot." Yet if Stowe chooses not to model herself on Sedgwick, more is at stake than a defense of her family's social standing and theological allegiance; she also chooses not to write in the formal tradition of Sedgwick. Instead, she raises questions of region that Sedgwick, despite the regional flavor of her title, does not address.[20] Stowe's interests in "Uncle Lot" suggest that as early as 1834 there existed the possibility that women would create not a single major tradition but two—women's fiction and regionalism—that would develop independently of each other, yet share some common themes, concerns, and influences. Thus, while Stowe responds to Irving in "Uncle Lot," she also drew her inspiration from her female contemporaries. Critics have identified several works by women with the roots of the regional tradition in American fiction, in particular Lydia Huntley Sigourney, *Sketch of Connecticut: Forty Years Since* (1824), Sarah Josepha Hale, *Northwood: A Tale of New England* (1827), Eliza Buckminster Lee, *Sketches of a New-England Village in the Last Century* (1838), and Caroline Kirkland, *A New Home—Who'll Follow?; or, Glimpses of Western Life* (1839), in addition to Sedgwick's *A New England Tale.*[21]

Stowe herself, in *The Pearl of Orr's Island* (1862), would bring female characters and values into the center of a regional novel. In this book in particular, Stowe demonstrates the influence of Sigourney, who published the memoir *Sketch of Connecticut* in Hartford the same year thirteen-year-old Harriet Beecher moved there to become a student at her sister Catharine's Hartford Female Seminary.[22] In *Sketch of Connecticut,* Madam L. tells Farmer Larkin, a regional character who makes a brief appearance, that she doesn't recollect the names of his children. He replies, "It's no wonder that ye don't Ma'am, there's such a neest on 'em. They're as thick as hops round the fire this winter. There's Roxey and Reuey, they're next to Tim, and look like twins. They pick the wool, and card tow, and wind quills, and knit stockins and mittins for the fokes in the house; and I've brought some down with me to day, to see if they'll buy 'em to the marchants' shops, and let 'em have a couple o' leetle small shawls" (Sigourney 118). This passage provides evidence that

Stowe had read *Sketch of Connecticut* before she began *The Pearl of Orr's Island,* for she names her own characters Roxy and Ruey in that novel after the daughters of Farmer Larkin. The model Sigourney created in her New England farmer with his Connecticut speech rhythms also served to influence Stowe's own portrait of Uncle Lot, the one character in her first sketch who speaks in dialect. In her analysis of *Sketch of Connecticut,* Sandra A. Zagarell argues that Sigourney's writing "was quite directly concerned with the foundations and organization of public life," and that both she and Sedgwick (in *Hope Leslie* [1827]) "addressed a major political topic of the day, the nature of the American nation" ("Expanding" 225). Thus Sigourney becomes a model for Stowe in two ways: she offers regional characters for Stowe's later meditation and expansion in "Uncle Lot" and *The Pearl of Orr's Island,* and she also confirms for Stowe that women have an inalienable claim to an evolving American political and cultural vision. Sigourney explores, as Stowe would later do, the possibilities of literary authority for women.

"Uncle Lot," unlike *A New England Tale,* does not inaugurate a genre. Regionalism, in contrast to woman's fiction, begins inchoately, reflecting uncertainty on the part of both male and female writers in the 1830s concerning the ways in which the gender of the author might inscribe the formal concerns of the work. For by the 1830s the direction of critical judgment concerning women writers, though clearly forming, was not yet set. Stowe's vision of Uncle Lot as the "settest crittur you ever saw" and the challenge she sets her hero to convert Uncle Lot to the expression of feeling establishes her perspicacity in implicitly predicting that gender itself would remain a "chestnut burr" within American culture, that is, a briery issue difficult to open but yet containing its own reward. Genre is also a "chestnut burr" in the emerging world of "separate spheres."[23] What Stowe begins to explore in the regionalism of "Uncle Lot" is the possibility that the limits of genre can indeed be transformed or, to use a word more in keeping with the ideology of "woman's sphere," "converted" to the cultural work of developing a form for women's narrative voice.

Notes

1. Numerous scholars and critics are working to define the tradition of regionalism and to explicate its features and significance. Most scholars link regionalism with the development of the fictional sketch in nineteenth-century American literature. See Jeffrey Rubin-Dorsky for a discussion of Irving's development of the sketch form. See also Sandra Zagarell, "Narrative of Community: The Identification of a Genre," in which she identifies a "department of literature" she terms "narrative of community" and includes numerous American writers often described as regional in this "department." See also Josephine Donovan, *New England Local Color Literature: A Women's Tradition*; Perry D. Westbrook, *Acres of Flint: Writers of Rural New England, 1870-1900* and *The New England Town in Fact and Fiction*; and introductory essays on regional writers in Elizabeth

Ammons, ed., "Introduction"; Judith Fetterley, ed., "Introduction"; and Marjorie Pryse, ed., "Introduction," *Stories from the Country of Lost Borders*; see also critical essays on Cary, Cooke, and Stowe in Fetterley, ed., *Provisions: A Reader from 19th-Century American Women*; see also Pryse, "Introduction," *The Country of the Pointed Firs and Other Stories*; and Pryse, ed., *Selected Stories of Mary E. Wilkins Freeman.* Lawrence Buell notes some disagreement with the tendency of what he calls the "feminist revisionary scholarship" to identify the regionalist tradition as female. In his own work, he examines regional representation in American literature, arguably a broader survey but one which does not locate itself within the boundaries of prose fiction, although he does acknowledge that "the staple of regional prose, however, continued to be the short sketch or tale" (296). In Buell's survey of the field of regional representation, he finds that it "looks considerably more androgynous once we survey the whole panoply . . . So although I agree that the conception of social reality that underlay New England regional poetry and prose lent itself to feminist appropriation and became, in the postwar era, increasingly a woman's construct, . . . provincial literary iconography [is] a project in which writers of the two sexes participated together" (302-03). See Louis Renza for a discussion of the ways "minor literature" (such as regionalism) in Jewett demonstrates pressures to become "major literature," and see Richard Brodhead for "a different account of the regionalist genre from what feminist studies have proposed" (*Cultures* 144).

2. See Nancy Cott. She locates the origins of nineteenth-century American feminism within the decade of the 1830s and asserts that the development of feminism actually depended on the ideology of "woman's sphere."

3. Stowe herself collected "Uncle Lot," originally titled "A New England Sketch," in *The Mayflower, or Sketches of the Descendents of the Pilgrim* (1843), a work with a limited circulation and out of print by 1855. Following the success of *Uncle Tom's Cabin,* the collection was reissued, with additional sketches, and this collection then became part of the Riverside Edition of Stowe's works. However, the sketch has not appeared in anthologies of American literature and remains unknown except by Stowe scholars. John Adams included the sketch in his edition of Stowe's work (see Adams, ed., *Regional Sketches: New England and Florida*), and the sketch appears in Fetterley and Pryse, eds., *American Women Regionalists 1850-1910.*

4. For further explication of the significance of the silencing of Dame Van Winkle, see Fetterley, *The Resisting Reader* 1-11.

5. For a general discussion of gender unease in early-nineteenth-century American culture and the relationship between the minister and culture, see Ann Douglas, *The Feminization of American Culture,* although Douglas's work has been superseded by others. See in particular Jane Tompkins, *Sensational Designs: The Cultural Work of American Fiction 1790-1860.* For an argument that manhood produces its own anxiety for nineteenth-century writers, see David Leverenz, *Manhood and the American Renaissance.*

6. Railton discusses the "psychic underside" of early-nineteenth-century American men's public selves and suggests that "it reveals their instinctual doubts about the sacrifices that the role of gentleman in a democracy exacted of them" (102).

7. See also John Seelye, "Root and Branch: Washington Irving and American Humor." Buell notes that "probably the single most important American prose work in teaching native writers to exploit regional material for literary purposes was Washington Irving's *The Sketch-Book*" (294).

8. Biographical evidence suggests that Harriet Beecher was writing with her father as well as with Washington Irving in mind. Although she initially called her most interesting character in "A New England Sketch" Uncle Timothy Griswold, changing his name when the story reappeared as "Uncle Lot" in *The Mayflower,* there would have been no confusion in the Beecher family that "Uncle Tim" was based on Harriet's father Lyman's Uncle Lot Benton. Lyman Beecher's mother had died two days after his birth, he had been raised by a childless aunt and uncle instead of in his father's household, and he had apparently entertained his own children with numerous tales about his childhood with Uncle Lot (Rugoff 4, 219). Thus James Benton, who becomes the "adopted" son of Lot Griswold in the sketch, serves as Harriet's portrait of her father as a young man. By choosing to write a sketch based on her father's own tales from childhood, to become like Lyman Beecher a storyteller, Harriet implicitly expressed her desire to model herself on her father, but she carefully disclaimed the ambitiousness of this desire, describing her work, in a letter to her brother George, as "a little bit of a love sketch . . . , a contemptible little affair" (Boydston, Kelley, and Margolis 62). Thus we can see her hiding behind the "love sketch" as a story more suitable than others a woman might tell, even though her interest in conversion in the sketch clearly identifies her as the daughter of Lyman Beecher, the Congregational minister known in the early 1800s for his power as a revivalist and the man who produced seven sons, all of whom became ministers.

9. Although the senior Beecher had definite views about gender differences, often lamenting that Harriet, with her intelligence, had not been born a boy and therefore a potential minister, he appears to have made no distinctions between young men's and young women's potential for experiencing conversion, and Lyman Beecher taught both daughters and sons that conversion involved a "private change of heart"

10. In collecting "Uncle Lot" for *The Mayflower,* Stowe changed the original wording of Grace's closing lines. In "A New England Sketch," Grace tells her father, "I'm used to authority in these days" (191). The change, with its echo of biblical usage, serves to reinforce Grace's moral authority to speak.

11. Hall appears early in the history of the Beecher family's move to Cincinnati. Prior to the publication of "Uncle Lot," Hall's *Western Monthly Magazine* had published an essay titled "Modern Uses of Language," signed "B," and attributed to Catharine although written by Harriet (Boydston, Kelley, and Margolis 50-51). Sklar notes that Catharine viewed the *Western Monthly Magazine* as a potential outlet for her educational ideas, and that she included its editor James Hall among the trustees for the Western Female Institute, the school she opened in Cincinnati (110). Hall continued as a friend of the Beechers until he engaged in a defense of Roman Catholics in open conflict with Lyman Beecher's position on Catholicism, with the result that the *Western Monthly Magazine* lost its influential supporters and suffered financial failure, and Hall retired into banking (Flanagan 66-67).

12. Hall describes "Pappy" as a "humourist" who "would sit for hours scraping upon his violin, singing catches, or relating merry and marvellous tales" (182).

13. Ironically, in Flanagan's biography of James Hall, he writes that "Hall sketched women infrequently and on the whole rather badly" (143).

14. Caroline Kirkland may have been viewed as an exception; she was one of the few women, if not the only one, whom Porter published in *The Spirit of the Times*; Porter reprinted Kirkland, but she did not contribute original material (Yates 60).

15. William Tappan Thompson collected his Major Jones letters in 1843 as *Major Jones's Courtship,* the same year Stowe collected her own sketches in *The Mayflower.*

16. Alone among the major Southwest humorists, Longstreet did not publish his work in the *Spirit of the Times* (Blair 85).

17. See Blair's discussion of early American humor, especially 18-19.

18. Guttman terms "Sleepy Hollow" "a prefiguration of the tradition of Mark Twain and the frontier humorists" (171).

19. After Augustus Baldwin Longstreet graduated from Yale in 1813, he entered law school in Litchfield, Connecticut, where he attended sermons by the Reverend Lyman Beecher and visited in the Beecher home. "He also found time to visit Miss Pierce's School for Young Ladies, where he frequently regaled the young women with his droll accounts of rural Georgia in his 'country boy' pose. His first practice as a raconteur began during the Connecticut years" (King, *Augustus* 12), with women, and likely the Beecher family, as his audience. The young Harriet would not have directly benefited from hearing Longstreet's stories (she would have been hardly three years old), and yet it is one of the delightful coincidences of literary history that the two writers who would each begin to develop alternative possibilities for the treatment of American materials that Irving sets out in "The Legend of Sleepy Hollow"—Longstreet with his southern humor and male world of sporting stories, Stowe with the "sleepy" regionalism of "Uncle Lot"—would both have "met" in Litchfield, Connecticut.

20. Buell terms *A New-England Tale* "really more an expose than an exposition of provincial village culture, too heavily committed to a Cinderella plot . . . and anti-Calvinist satire . . . to accomplish much by way of regional mimesis" (295).

21. See discussions of Hale and Sedgwick in Nina Baym, *Woman's Fiction: A Guide to Novels by and about Women in America 1820-1870*; see discussions of Sigourney and Sedgwick in Sandra A. Zagarell, "Expanding 'America': Lydia Sigourney's *Sketch of Connecticut,* Catharine Sedgwick's *Hope Leslie.*"

22. John Adams in *Harriet Beecher Stowe* terms *Sketch* "a true forerunner of Mrs. Stowe's work" (31). As an adolescent, Harriet met, knew, and very likely read Sigourney, her sister's dear friend in Hartford.

23. Tompkins suggests that even Hawthorne, in some of his earliest sketches collected in *Twice-Told Tales* (1837) ("Little Annie's Ramble," "A Rill from the Town Pump," "Sunday at Home," and "Sights from a Steeple"), began as a "sentimental author" long before he would become the genius of the American romance and damn the "scribbling women" (10-18). Buell focuses on the iconographic representation of region rather than the relationship between regional representation and genre; he does observe that "the staple of regional prose, however, continued to be the short sketch or tale" (296).

Walter Sondey (essay date 1997)

SOURCE: "From Nation of Virtue to Virtual Nation: Washington Irving and American Nationalism" in *Narratives of Nostalgia, Gender and Nationalism,* edited by Jean Pickering and Suzanne Kehde, Macmillan Press, 1997, pp. 52-73.

[*In the following essay, Sondey demonstrates how Irving's use of nostalgia in* Salmagundi *and* The Sketch Book *promoted his views on conservatism and the national identity.*]

Washington Irving (1783-1859) began his literary career in the midst of the national identity crisis prompted by the transition from Federalist republicanism to Jeffersonian democracy. During the first decade of the nineteenth century Americans found themselves at odds over conflicting elitist and populist, public and private conceptions of the masculine persona representative of American nationality. On the one hand conservatives advocated an elitist conception of American character exemplified by the publicly virtuous legislator typical of classical republicanism. Democrats on the other hand advocated a popular conception of national character exemplified by the private liberal-democratic individual. The basic difference between these two personifications may be summed up as that between a corporatism that emphasizes duty to station and hierarchy over individual interests, and an individualism that emphasizes social mobility and self-interest over duty to social and political institutions. In *The Letters of the Republic* Michael Warner notes that the eventual ascendance of liberal democracy prompted the development of the bourgeois domestic character typical of modern American nationalism:

> Modern Nationalism is more at home. It constructs 'Americanness' as a distinctive but privately possessed trait. It allows you to be American in the way you tailor your coat, or the way you sing, or the way you read a book. It does not insist that you regard such activities as public, virtuous actions. I speak of a modern nationalist imaginary to emphasize that it requires your public self imagery to develop in a private sphere.
>
> (149)

My aim, insofar as this nationalist imaginary is of a literary nature, is to analyze how Irving taught his readers to experience national identity as a matter of reading a book. However in doing so I will argue that such a nationalism is more usefully discussed as a publicly developed representation that regulates the perception of self in a private sphere that consists of domestic life and individual taste or sensibility. More specifically I will argue that Irving was the first American author to realize that the productions of the literary press, particularly sentimental literature, constituted the primary means to regulate the nation's self-image. In other words his books demonstrate how the apparently moribund values of American conservatism might achieve a renewed influence over bourgeois individuals if distributed in a capillary fashion via the press and figured in terms of the domestic sentimentality associated with the private character of liberal democracy.

An examination of the changing role that nostalgia plays in two of Irving's earliest publications offers an unparalleled opportunity to trace the various purposes and circumstances that influenced the formation of the conservative or genteel strain of American nationalism that Irving pioneered. In *Salmagundi* (1807-8), a magazine of social and political satire, Irving employs nostalgia simultaneously to mourn and lampoon the decline of conservatism from a sociopolitical movement of national scope to a merely private disposition. There the public character of conservatism appears reduced to the nostalgic figure of an aging Federalist patriarch limited in power to the personal tastes

and authority he exercises within the confines of family life. It is not until the publication of *The Sketch Book* (1819), a collection of short stories, literary criticism and travel essays, that Irving demonstrates how nostalgia and patriarchal domesticity may be used to represent conservatism as a vital influence upon national character. In this case, rather than sponsoring mourning among conservatives for the lost public aspects of Federalist character, his work promotes a desire among liberal democrats to affiliate themselves with it on a private basis. The result is a literary mode of affiliation that links readers to a textual or virtual society whose substance is the commonly held desire for a genteel sensibility that appears as if it must be recovered from the past. In short, by showing how Irving learned to use nostalgia to create desire for a patriarchal representation of domesticity, I will demonstrate that his genteel nationalism provided American conservatism with the Trojan Horse it needed to carry its values into the bourgeois private sphere and regain there as a matter of cultural authority the influence it had lost in the public sphere.[1]

Like many conservatives during the Jefferson administration (1800-8), Irving believed that a hierarchical social order promoting class deference constituted the substance of republican national character and the essence of the public interest. Accordingly he believed that it was the personal duty of virtuous republican citizens and legislators to use national government to maintain that order and prevent the disorderly effects of the laissez-faire progressivism favoured by democrats. Indeed it was Irving's namesake, George Washington, who personified the paternalistic public character that conservatives hoped to institutionalize in the national government and from there impress upon society at large. However, the reelection of Jefferson in 1804 demonstrated that such political paternalism had poor prospects given the social and economic ambitions of the American electorate. Conservatives thus had little choice but to concede the hopelessness of promoting a 'republican' social and political character by means of national government.

In *Salmagundi* Irving attacks representative democracy for destroying the political aspects of republican character, namely the paternalistic rule of those elite few whose property, social standing and leisure allowed them the independence and education needed to serve the public good. He complains that in Jefferson's 'mobocracy' any virtuous candidate 'who possesses superior talents . . . will always be sacrificed to some creeping insect who will prostitute himself to familiarity with the lowest of mankind' (193). Such corrupt candidates, he continues, 'by administering to [the people's] passions, for the purposes of ambition' will ultimately 'convince them of their power' and thereby make government an instrument of popular interests (195). As the mixture of bestial, sexual and economic metaphors suggests, Irving assumes that democratic candidates have abandoned the cause of reason and morality: they have rejected the rational deliberation and paternalistic administration of the public good (political virtue) in order to give voice and power to the passing desires of an ignorant majority.

Other conservatives, however, trying to be less pessimistic about the prospects of preserving republican values, looked toward the voters for help. In an essay titled 'Phocion', Fisher Ames, a leading Federalist congressman during the Jefferson administration, raises the hope that the virtuous members of the electorate may yet remove the democrats from office. He bases this hope on the assumption that there still exists a sufficient number of voters who 'reverence' the transcendent good of social hierarchy, particularly those 'customs and institutions we derive from our English ancestors' (178). However, the affection among the national electorate for the elitist social institutions and deferential political relations found mainly on the long-settled east coast proved quite limited compared to that for representative democracy and laissez-faire liberalism.[2] Consequently Ames admits that a return to republicanism is in fact unlikely, a view to which he gives pointed expression in an 1805 essay titled 'The Dangers of Liberty'. There, after noting that the republican character of Rome resulted from a 'political virtue' of its people, he turns to the issue of American character: 'Is there any resemblance in [Roman virtue] to the habits and passions that predominate in America? Are not our people wholly engrossed by the pursuit of wealth and pleasure?' He then observes that 'Though grouped together into a society, the propensities of the individual still prevail; and if the nation discovers the rudiments of any character, they are yet to be developed' (*Works* 412-13). As a result, Ames concludes, the nation is 'descending from a supposed orderly and stable republican government into a licentious democracy, with a progress that baffles all means to resist' (429).

In *Salmagundi* Irving addresses the decline of conservative fortunes in his description of Christopher Cockloft, a nostalgic old Federalist whose disgust with liberal democracy drives him to retreat into his ancestral home, Cockloft Hall. There he indulges his 'propensity to save every thing that bears the stamp of family antiquity' (132-3) and attempts to create a refuge free from modern influence where he can preserve the 'little vivid spark of toryism which burns in a secret corner of his heart' (134). But even at home Cockloft must fend off the inroads of parvenu styles that threaten the English and colonial tastes that attest to the historical legitimacy of his character:

> The Miss Cocklofts have made several spirited attempts to introduce modern furniture into the hall, but with very indifferent success. Modern *style* has always been an object of great annoyance to honest Christopher, and is ever treated by him with sovereign contempt, as an upstart intruder. It is a common observation of his, that your old-fashioned substantial furniture bespeaks the respectability of one's ancestors, and indicates that the family has been used to hold up its head for more than the present generation; whereas the fragile appendages of modern style seemed to be emblems of mushroom gentility, and to this mind predicted that the family dig-

nity would moulder away and vanish with the finery thus put on of a sudden. The same whimwham made him averse to having his house surrounded with poplars, which he stigmatizes as mere upstarts, just fit to ornament the shingle palaces of modern gentry, and characteristick of the establishments they decorate.

(241)

Ironically, the use of domestic nostalgia to establish a standard of taste and to transform the illegitimacy of liberal-democratic character also highlights the historical failure of American conservatism. As Irving's satirical tone suggests, Cockloft's nostalgia is ridiculous insofar as it displaces criticism of liberal democracy on to taste and reduces what had been a momentous social and political struggle over national character to a contest of class sensibilities within the home. Thus his struggle to exorcize both liberal tastes and feminine influence from Cockloft Hall portrays a conservatism so socially and politically marginalized that it must retreat to the domestic scene and displace women from their traditional sphere of influence.

Nonetheless it would be incorrect to assume that Irving's satirical treatment of Cockloft implies a thorough detachment from the elitist values he represents. Prior to this passage Irving advises the reader to look kindly upon Cockloft's efforts to preserve in the privacy of his home those curious objects reflecting the values of his grandfather's generation: 'Let no one ridicule the whim-whams of [Cockloft's] grandfather:—If—and of this there is no doubt, for wise men have said it—if life is but a dream, happy is he who can make the most of the illusion' (239). As Irving's wistful comment suggests, nostalgia compensates to some degree for Federalist losses by constituting a private realm of sensibility where conservatives might enjoy an illusion of the paternalistic authority they had hoped to exercise in public.

Irving's use of the private sphere to figure larger social and political issues conforms to Eric Sundquist's observation regarding nineteenth-century American literature that metaphors of 'family or genealogy . . . act as surrogates for a more abstractly envisioned "past"' that 'stimulate the writer's *desire* to find in the family a model for the social and political constructs still so much in question for a recently conceived nation' (Sundquist xii). However, in Irving's case, this desire to find in the past familial models for contemporary social and political constructs was frustrated by conservatism's preemptive historical failure. The Cockloft family, rather than representing a private model for the character of the nation's public institutions, merely represents the private character of a class that had already lost its bid to define them. Moreover in telling the story of that loss, particularly its political consequences, Irving depicts a conservatism that also has lost all hope of reasserting any vital national influence.

Sundquist addresses the problem of preserving and distributing authority under revolutionary circumstances in terms derived from Freud's understanding of social genesis. He observes that the liberal-democratic victory over Federalist conservatism prompted the production of literature whose representation of paternal authority he likens to the ritual of celebration and atonement in Freud's account of the patricide that establishes fraternal authority and order. After noting how this guilt engenders a desire to recover the father's authority through cultural ritual, Sundquist comments that among American writers 'experiments in authorial desire must risk the possibility that they . . . will either become repetitive commemorations in the name of an overthrown authority, or else find themselves at a loss before the very absence of that authority' (xii). Ideally the resolution to this problem is the transfer of the overthrown paternal authority to the commemorative ritual. From there, it may then be distributed and made present among the sons as a means to assure the continuity and authority of the social order founded upon their revolt. However Irving's experiment in authorial desire constitutes a failure to transfer and distribute paternal authority. As a cultural ritual his nostalgia is merely a mournful commemoration of the destruction of such authority that leaves his audience at a loss as to how to compensate for its absence. Thus *Salmagundi*'s nostalgia merely serves to adumbrate the lost public dimension of Federalist ideology and reduce desire for the patriarchal family to a mournful reminder of conservatism's failure to impress its character upon the public institutions of the nation.

In *Salmagundi* Irving's nostalgia indicates that he had yet to realize the potential of the press as a means to form the national identity and preserve conservative authority. The disparaging comments he makes there regarding 'Logocracy', or rule by the printed word, indicate that he perceived the press (especially political publications) to be largely responsible for the partisan fighting that had undermined the Federalists' efforts to preserve republican character and public institutions. He notes that because of the political press many Americans 'are at a loss to determine the true nature and proper character of their government' which seems one moment to be a republican 'aristocracy' and another a democratic 'mobocracy'. But in fact the truth is 'a secret which is unknown to these people themselves, their government is a pure unadulterated LOGOCRACY or government of words' (142). Although Irving exaggerates to satirize, conservatives generally were frightened by the power of the press over the opinions of the people and policy of legislators. Ames makes clear the Federalist case against the press:

> The many, who before the art of printing never mistook in a case of oppression, because they complained from their actual sense of it, have become susceptible of every transient enthusiasm and of more than womanish fickleness of caprice. Publick affairs are now transacted on a *stage*, where all the interest and passions grow out of fiction, or are inspired by the art, and often controlled at the pleasure of the actors.
>
> (392)

Ironically Ames' complaint that political publications diminish the authority of experience, create a malleable

popular opinion and replace reasoned political deliberation with a popular sentimentalism elicited by fiction anticipates precisely Irving's use of the literary press in *The Sketch Book*. There Ames' bitter observation that many Americans 'learn only from newspapers that they are countrymen' (414) assumes a positive connotation and marks the difference between a republican national character based upon elitist social and political institutions and a modern nationalism founded upon popular participation in a textually propagated sensibility.[3]

In *The Sketch Book*'s first literary essay, **'English Writers on America,'** Irving states that 'Over no nation does the press hold a more absolute control than over the people of America; for the universal education of the poorest classes, makes every individual a reader' (74). He then addresses directly the role of the press in creating the 'public mind' that forms the substance of the national character when he warns his American readers not to let 'political hostility' arising from the press accounts of the recently concluded War of 1812 bias their attitude toward the English:

> Governed as we are entirely by public opinion, the utmost care should be taken to preserve the purity of the public mind. Knowledge is power, and truth is knowledge; whoever therefore knowingly propagates a prejudice, willfully saps the foundation of his country's strength.
>
> (77)

However the apparent opposition of rational judgment to sentiment (hostility), public interest to private prejudice, breaks down when Irving tries to explain his simple assertion that 'knowledge' governs the formation of the nation's collective 'mind'. On the one hand Irving objects to the use of the press to determine opinion for the public. He insists that its role in the democratic political process should be limited to providing the information that citizens need to make the individual rational judgments from which representative democracy derives popular will. Such citizens, he asserts, 'are individually portions of the sovereign mind and sovereign will, and should be enabled to come to all questions of national concern with calm and unbiassed judgments' (77). But on the other he claims that it is precisely the author's responsibility 'to make [the press] the medium of amiable and magnanimous feeling' (74) and invest the public mind with sentimental fictions that do bias it in matters of 'national concern'. It is in fact this latter approach that corresponds to Irving's use of sentimental literature to create a sensibility conducive to genteel nationalism.[4]

Gaining recognition for the press itself as a basis of modern society was only the beginning of Irving's struggle to promote genteel nationalism among American readers. Establishing the legitimacy and authority of the conservative sensibility he hoped to propagate there constituted his greatest challenge. To accomplish this required the use of English literary models whose patriarchal representations of domestic life sponsored the sort of sensibility from which Irving hoped to construct a genteel American nationalism.

The ongoing anxiety over the legitimacy of the American national character guaranteed Irving a ready audience for the account of his cultural 'pilgrimage' to England in 1815 that constitutes the majority of *The Sketch Book*.[5] There, in the guise of his authorial persona, Geoffrey Crayon, he attempts to elide the historical ruptures that had prevented Americans from looking toward England for models of private, if not social and political, character.[6] His nostalgic desire for English culture thus represents an effort to establish an affiliation with England that will allow that country to serve as 'a perpetual volume of reference . . . wherewith to strengthen and embellish [American] national character' (79). As his allusion to textuality and filiopiety implies, he proposes this affiliation in order to provide American literary culture with the genealogy and paternal character it needed to legitimize its own sentimental authority. Moreover in the course of doing so he also demonstrates the figural, narrative and associative techniques that give nostalgic discourse the ability to evoke desire among bourgeois readers for a conservative sensibility. For it is, he suggests, the study of these literary models and techniques, not the outright imitation of English social and political institutions, that will help Americans learn how to create their own nationalism.

In **'English Writers on America'** (*Sketch Book*) Irving clearly abandons the republican assumption that national identity depends primarily on its social and political institutions. Instead he emphasizes the spirit, thought, opinion and feeling typical of bourgeois sensibility as the bases of national character. Public institutions, he suggests, are merely the expression of a nation's private character, not vice versa. This change is particularly apparent when Irving advises his American readers not to resent the English for denigrating their character:

> We are a young people, necessarily an imitative one, and must take our examples and models, in a great degree, from the existing nations of Europe. There is no country more worthy of our study than England. The spirit of her constitution is most analogous to ours. The manners of her people,—their intellectual activity—their freedom of opinion—their habits of thinking on those subjects which concern the dearest interests and most sacred charities of private life, are all congenial to the American character; and in fact are all intrinsically excellent: for it is in the moral feeling of the people that the deep foundations of English prosperity are laid.
>
> (78)

Irving goes on to conclude that English social order itself, 'an edifice that so long has towered unshaken', owes its durability to 'foundations' in 'private life'. In particular he refers to those 'sacred charities' and 'moral feelings' that originate in the bourgeois family and bind the individual to the father as the source of the patrimony and legitimacy that guarantee social standing. Like Edmund Burke, who

claimed that 'We begin our public affections in our families' (315), Irving models the individual's relationship to the nation on patriarchal family life. Thus his domestically figured nationalism offers its readers membership in a virtual family that transforms their private lives into what Burke calls 'so many little images of the great country in which the heart [finds] something it [can] fill' (315). In this manner the modern nation substantiates itself in the mutual identification or recognition that bourgeois individuals realize through a shared desire for the cultural ideal represented by the patriarchal family.

In effect Irving proposes to synchronize and regulate American sentiments by establishing a paternalistic cultural authority modeled upon that of English domestic literature. To this end *The Sketch Book* engages its American readers in a nostalgic ritual meant to invoke the spirit of those days when they approached England 'with a hallowed feeling of tenderness and veneration as the land of our forefathers' and when after 'our own country there was none in whose glory we more delighted, . . . none toward which our hearts yearned with such throbbings of warm consanguinity' (75). Irving uses such filial and domestic sentiments to create the sense of impending patrimonial loss and genealogical discontinuity essential to the invocation of nostalgic desire, as is apparent when he reminds Americans who reject their English heritage for political reasons that

> there are feelings dearer than interest—closer to the heart than pride—that will still make us cast back a look of regret, as we wander farther and farther from the paternal roof, and lament the waywardness of the parent, that would repel the affections of the child.
>
> (75-6)

Of nearly a dozen literary essays, character sketches and short stories in *The Sketch Book* addressing questions of national identity, the character sketch **'John Bull'** offers the most pointed illustration of Irving's transformation of nostalgia. The sketch begins by examining how Bull, the personification of England in a series of political allegories by John Arbuthnot (1667-1735), contributed to the creation of modern English character. Irving observes that the wide-spread printing and sale of caricatures based on Arbuthnot's texts was a likely reason that Bull became the personification of 'common' or middle-class English character:

> Perhaps the continual contemplation of the character thus drawn of them, has contributed to fix it upon the nation; and thus to give reality to what at first may have been painted in a great measure from the imagination. Men are apt to acquire peculiarities that are continually ascribed to them. The common orders of the English seem wonderfully captivated with the *beau ideal* which they have formed of John Bull, and endeavour to act up to the broad caricature that is perpetually before their eyes.
>
> (379)

However, despite the focus of this passage on the pictorial aspect of Bull as an ego ideal, the main purpose of Irving's sketch is to elaborate a narrative context in which Bull may represent nostalgia as an effective conservative response to the conflict between tradition and progress. Toward this end, Irving sets Bull's story in the midst of a family crisis that poses his paternalism and reverence for tradition against his sons' democratic and progressive interests. But despite the apparent parallels between his story and Cockloft's, Bull's differs significantly in the positive effects it ascribes to nostalgia.

As a paternal figure 'who is given to indulge his veneration for family usages and family incumbrances, to a whimsical extent' (387), Bull maintains his home in a manner redolent of an English monarchism at odds with the progressive values held by his sons. Although he is inclined to listen to their counsel and slowly accommodate their modern tastes and interests, this 'wholesome advice has been completely defeated by the obstreperous conduct of one of his sons'. This impatient younger son sees little purpose in preserving the hierarchy and authoritarianism that characterize relationships among the inhabitants of Bull's estate and threatens to lead 'the poorest of his father's tenants' in revolt: 'No sooner does he hear any of his brothers mention reform or retrenchment, than he jumps up, takes the words out of their mouths, and roars out for an overturn.' Irving emphasizes the democratic or 'leveller' inclinations of the disobedient son by noting that he will not be satisfied until 'the whole family mansion shall be leveled with the ground, and a plain one of brick and mortar built in its place' (388). At this point Bull's story appears likely to be little more than a mournful recapitulation of Cockloft's. However its conclusion does not bear out such an assumption. Instead the older son sides with his father, helps preserve his rule and forestalls revolt 'against paternal authority'.

The story of Bull's relationship to his sons suggests an impending lower-class overthrow of upper-class paternalism much like that which American conservatives perceived in the rise of Jeffersonian democracy. However in this case the story concludes with the promise of reconciliation. The eldest son, though in favor of change, nonetheless seeks to preserve his patrimony and mitigate any outright destruction of paternal authority. As with Freud's account of the totem meal, Irving's story describes an attempt to balance the desire to assert independence from paternal authority with the desire to preserve that authority for the benefit of the sons. The ideal result, the story suggests, should be a 'wholesome' reformism or balance of the old and new.

Typically, Irving illustrates his conception of the proper manner in which to reform national character in terms of Bull's home and the tastes that it reflects:

> John had frequently been advised to have the old edifice thoroughly overhauled, and to have some of the useless parts pulled down, and the others strengthened with their materials; but the old gentleman always grows testy on this subject. . . . If you point out any part of the building as superfluous, he insists that it is material to the strength or decoration of the rest, and

> the harmony of the whole, and swears, that the parts are so built into each other, that if you pull down one, you run the risk of having the whole about your ears.

(385)

Again, like Burke, Irving subscribed to the belief that, compared to the simplicity of mere reaction or revolution, 'At once to preserve and reform is quite another thing' (Burke 80). Accordingly, Irving's architectural metaphor represents English nostalgia as an effective means supporting and preserving conservative interests. Bull's home represents the desired result of a communal narrative requiring that the old remain a vital part of the present and that the new not be added at the expense of those long-established interests 'built into' the extant order. Bull's home is thus an image of a patrilineal narrative that promises to confer power and authority (patrimony) upon those who seek at once to reform and to preserve its values rather than depose them through revolution. However, unlike England, the United States had no long-standing conservative social and political institutions to serve as foundations for a reformist narrative of this sort. As Irving's earlier effort to evoke nostalgia in *Salmagundi* indicates, any attempt to ask Americans to recall a desire for a 'traditional' social and political order they never had is ridiculous. Cockloft Hall is an illusory image of a past and a patrimony that American conservatives had merely wished for. It is not, however, ridiculous for Irving to offer his American readers a patrilineal cultural narrative featuring the 'traditional' values he would have them use to 'embellish' their liberal-democratic reality. In this case, it becomes entirely reasonable to suggest that Americans reform their liberal-democratic excesses in a manner consistent with the cultural patrimony represented by Bull and other figures drawn from English letters. It is in this case the 'traditional' sensibility exemplified by models of English private life that constitutes the substance of nostalgic desire. Consequently, the nostalgia and nationalism that Irving offers his American readers is more thoroughly virtual or cultural than that which he ascribes to the English, and the genteel reformism he promotes among Americans thus proceeds from the private realm of sensibility to the public realm via literature.

Irving offers a more personal example of how sensibility itself may constitute a basis for nationalism in his account of Geoffrey Crayon's literary pilgrimage to Stratford-on-Avon. Crayon, though an American, participates in English national community through the associations he has acquired from reading English books, particularly his tourist guide, the 'Stratford Guide Book,' and Shakespeare's plays.[7] Crayon announces that 'Indeed the whole country about here is poetic ground: every thing is associated with the idea of Shakespeare' (329). Irving represents the power of textual associations in the way that Crayon participates in English sensibility through his reading. Crayon exclaims at one point that 'My mind had become so completely possessed by the imaginary scenes and characters connected with [Stratford-on-Avon], that I seemed to be actually living among them.' Shakespeare, he goes on to note, 'is indeed the true enchanter, whose spell operates not upon the senses, but upon the imagination and the heart' (339). Despite his recognition that his participation in English society is merely a matter of textually propagated associations of questionable historical validity, he still defends the value of his experience: 'What is it to us whether these stories be true or false, so long as we can persuade ourselves into the belief of them, and enjoy all the charm of the reality?' (320). Unlike in *Salmagundi*, where Cockloft's sensibility constituted a barrier between the individual and community, the sensibility illustrated by Crayon reflects an understanding that a textually regulated sensibility provides a crucial means to link the individual to the larger community of those with similarly organized tastes.[8]

'The Legend of Sleepy Hollow' exemplifies how Irving applied these lessons of English nationalism to the United States. Narrated in the persona of the 'sentimental historian' Diedrich Knickerbocker, the story elaborates representations of prerevolutionary domestic life from vague hints of the Dutch colonial period in New York. As a little-studied group with few controversial historical or political associations, the Dutch offered Irving a relatively neutral set of figures upon which to inscribe the narrative and associations appropriate to a genteel nationalism. As might be expected, the narrative he uses is that of a contest between conservatism and progressivism. The Dutch are associated with the historical legitimacy that Irving ascribes to those who demonstrate a tasteful respect for paternalism, tradition and social hierarchy characteristic of members of the community of genteel sensibility. Their opponent, Ichabod Crane, the Yankee incarnation of modern America, exhibits the individualistic desires for economic gain and social mobility typically associated with liberal-democratic progressivism.[9]

'The Legend of Sleepy Hollow' satirizes these desires by subjecting Crane to Sleepy Hollow, an environment governed by the influence of the past.

> From the listless repose of the place, and the peculiar character of its inhabitants, who are descendants from the original Dutch settlers, this sequestered glen has long been known by the name of SLEEPY HOLLOW, and its rustic lads are called the Sleepy Hollow Boys throughout all the neighbouring country. A drowsy, dreamy influence seems to hang over the land, and to pervade the very atmosphere.
>
> (*Sketch Book* 417)

Unlike liberal-democratic society, with its fixation upon the future and social mobility, the Dutch village retains its conservative character in the midst of flux:

> it is in such little retired Dutch valleys . . . that population, manners, and customs remained fixed, while the great torrent of migration and improvement, which is making such incessant changes in other parts of this restless country, sweeps them by unobserved.
>
> (419)

Sleepy Hollow thus represents a nostalgic sensibility that shelters conservative values that no longer find acceptance in the liberal-democratic public sphere. There, ensconced in the privacy of the domestic scene and individual sensibility, they maintain their influence as matters of taste. In effect Irving's story represents a ritual space which permits the members of his audience to exorcize their unmitigated liberal-democratic progressivism through a literary act of sentimental bonding that affirms the paternal authority over the private sphere of a conservative sensibility ostensibly recovered from the past.

The story of Ichabod Crane's invasion of Sleepy Hollow centers upon his desire to marry Katrina Van Tassel and sell the land that forms her dowry to realize an investment scheme: Crane's 'heart yearned after the damsel who was to inherit these domains, and his imagination expanded with the idea, how they might be readily turned into cash, and the money invested in immense tracts of wild land, and shingle palaces in the wilderness' (428). Whereas the value of Katrina and her land to the villagers derives from their role as necessary means to reproduce their patriarchal family and communal values, their value to Crane is primarily economic. Consequently Crane's rival, the village hero, Brom, must defend the integrity of the village by asserting his claim (and that of the village) to Katrina and her land.

This confrontation between nostalgic and progressive modes of national ideology comes to a climax in the encounter between Brom (disguised as the Headless Horseman) and Crane. There the integrity of conservatism reasserts itself by subjecting the liberal-democratic desires that fire Crane's economic dreams to the conservative sensibility that they threaten. Ultimately, Crane's inability to understand Sleepy Hollow's legends as a virtual basis of the villagers' society causes his downfall. His literal belief in their 'marvellous' ghost stories and 'Mather's direful tales' provides them with a means to turn against him the sensibility that he represses.

Ironically, **'The Legend of Sleepy Hollow'** is a gothic ritual of exorcism in which the quotidian Crane represents the evil spirit and the Headless Horseman the figure of communal integrity. Thus the communal sensibility that Crane represses and threatens returns to haunt him and nearly trample underfoot the liberal ideology he represents:

> Ichabod cast a look behind him. . . . Just then he saw the goblin rising in his stirrups, and in the very act of hurling his head at him. Ichabod endeavoured to dodge the horrible missile, but . . . he was tumbled headlong into the dust, and . . . the goblin rider, passed like a whirlwind.
>
> (451-2)

Exiled from the community of genteel sensibility, Crane finds a more congenial home in the institutions of liberal-democratic public life. We are told that he

had changed his quarters to a distant part of the country; had kept school and studied law at the same time;
had been admitted to the bar, turned politician, elec-
tioneered, written for newspapers, and finally had been
made Justice.

(453-4)

This conclusion, however, may suggest an escapist fantasy
isolating conservative sensibility from a liberal democracy
that continues to gain power in the public institutions of
the nation, as Crane's subsequent career indicates. But insofar as sensibility replaces such institutional bases of national character (educational, legal and political and the
publishing system that supports them), their loss is not so
great a blow to conservatism. As the conclusion suggests,
Irving is willing to cede these institutions to democrats in
return for control of sentimental literature (the 'public
mind') that regulates the sensibility of American readers.

Although genteel nationalism may appear to be the conso-
lation prize for America's social and political losers, in reality it is a cultural institution of great importance. Irving
realized that being a modern American did not require participation in specific social or political institutions. What it
did require was participation in a desire organized by a
textually propagated sensibility whose tastes and manners
constituted the substance of the national character. In *The
Sketch Book* Irving defined the genteel aspect of the great
imaginary national family that has served for nearly two
centuries as the United States' principal cultural mechanism of ideological regulation. He was first among American writers to articulate clearly the narrative and associative strategies by which a culturally defined character
(sensibility) might mediate the social and political conflicts of a progressive nation. He was first, in other words,
clearly to articulate for Americans how the reading of domestic literature constitutes a socio-aesthetic ritual that
fuses elitist and populist, liberal and conservative elements
into an enduring basis for national community. However,
it is also this same cultural ritual, with its emphasis on genealogy, patrimony and paternal authority, that has promoted and legitimized the white, male and anti-democratic
character of American nationalism. In this context, Irving's abandonment of the myth of the republic for the genteel American Dream sets the terms for the subsequent development of the anglocentric and patriarchal culture that
continues to exercise a considerable, if not dominant, authority over the representation of American national character in academe and the popular media. And, as the current multicultural trend and conservative reaction to it
indicate, we have only recently begun to recognize the extent to which genteel nationalism has contributed to the
oppressive exclusions and divisions that characterize class,
gender and race relationships in the United States.

Notes

1. In *Salmagundi* Irving failed to recognize that the
United States was becoming a virtual nation founded
upon the printed page and that social and political institutions no longer constituted the principal means

of regulating its self-image. Not until the publication
of *The Sketch Book* does he finally employ a textually propagated desire for familial representations as
a public means to exercise cultural authority over the
private sphere. Kaja Silverman discusses this linkage
of desire to representation as the 'suture' or ideological bonding 'inherent in all the operations that constitute narrativity' (236). She goes on to note in reference to the work of Lacan and Jacques-Alain Miller
that 'Suture can be understood as the process
whereby the inadequacy of the subject's position is
exposed in order to facilitate (i.e. create the desire
for) new insertions into a cultural discourse which
promises to make good that lack' (231). Similarly,
Irving's nostalgia elicits a sense of lack that it subsequently fulfills.

2. As Isaac Kramnick notes, Jeffersonian America witnessed the ascendancy of the 'new liberal ideal' of 'a
society of achievement, a social order of competitive
individualism, in which social mobility was possible
and the rightful reward for ingenious people of talent
and hard work' (4). Although conservatives accepted
the 'improvement' of certain individuals of 'merit'
within a given social order, they condemned the self-
interest of competitive individualism as antithetical
to the character of a republic. From their perspective,
social hierarchy constituted the *raison d'être* of
American republicanism and the essence of the public good.

3. Irving's use of literature as a mode of community is
a variation on Benedict Anderson's account of how
newspapers helped create nationalism. In *Imagined
Communities* Anderson observes of newspaper reading that

the significance of this mass ceremony—Hegel
observed that newspapers serve modern man as a
substitute for morning prayers—is paradoxical. It
is performed in silent privacy, in the lair of the
skull. Yet each communicant is well aware that
the ceremony he performs is being replicated simultaneously by thousands (or millions) of others
of whose existence he is confident, yet of whose
identity he has not the slightest notion. Furthermore this ceremony is incessantly repeated at daily
or half-daily intervals throughout the calendar.
What more vivid figure for the secular,
historically-clocked, imagined community can be
envisioned . . . ? [This] remarkable confidence of
community in anonymity . . . is the hallmark of
modern nationalism.

(39-40)

It is precisely the synchronization and regulation that
Anderson ascribes to reading newspapers that Irving
employs in his attempt to reassert conservative authority by means of sentimental culture. Although *The
Sketch Book* does not qualify as a mass media production on the scale of newspapers, it nonetheless represented a prototype of popular prose fiction insofar as
it was aimed at an inclusive audience and written in a

sentimental style. Nonetheless Michael Gilmore notes in *The Columbia History of the American Novel* that the 5000 copies it sold made it a best-seller in its day (Elliot 58). He also comments that *The Last of the Mohicans* 'qualified as a best-seller in 1826 with 5750 copies in circulation' (54). See Jay Fliegelman's definitive study of metaphors of paternal authority in popular American publications of the late eighteenth century.

4. In a passage comparing the bourgeois individual to more traditional Anglo-American conceptions of the publicly active political subject, J. G. A. Pocock states that the bourgeois individual lived in an 'increasingly transactional universe of "commerce and the arts"' in which 'he was more than compensated for his loss of antique virtue by an indefinite and perhaps infinite enrichment of his personality, the product of multiplying relationships, with both things and persons, in which he became progressively involved. Since these new relationships were social and not political in character the capacities that they led the individual to develop were called not "virtues" but "manners"' (49). It is my contention that one of the most important manifestations of these manners is taste, which makes possible an affiliation to a class and, ultimately, a national community on the basis of sensibility.

5. Stanley T. Williams discusses Irving's life in England and Europe at great length in the first of his two-volume biography, *The Life of Washington Irving*. Irving's main residence from 1815 to 1832 was in England. Scott exercised an important influence upon him there prior to the publication of *The Sketch Book*. Both shared an enthusiasm for Edmund Burke's conservative reformism.

6. Irving's collaborator in *Salmagundi,* James Kirke Paulding, had entered into combat with the English in his 1812 satire *The Diverting History of John Bull and Brother Jonathan* (see Reynolds, *James Kirke Paulding,* 40-54). Works such as his contributed to the 'Paper War' between America and England that Irving hoped to dispel. This journalistic feud fueled considerable anger and insecurity among Americans regarding the historical legitimacy of their national character. Many, conservative and democrat alike, responded to English insults by arguing that the legitimacy of American character resulted from its radical newness and independence from the corrupt character of Europeans. Noah Webster takes this position in his *American Magazine* (1788) when he advises his readers to 'Unshackle your minds and act like independent beings. You have been children long enough, subject to the control and subservient to the interest of a haughty parent. You now have an interest of your own to augment and defend—and a national character to establish and extend by your wisdom and judgment' (Kohn 57). Nearly three decades later in 1815 periodical publisher Hezekiah Niles takes a similar stand when he declares that Americans have 'a National Character' whose virtues 'need no guarantee from the bloodstained and profligate princes and powers of *Europe*' (Kohn 59).

7. In *The Essay Concerning Human Understanding* (1700) Locke notes that it is the unconscious and habitual character of associationism that distinguishes it from rationally directed thought (with which he claimed it interfered):

> there is another connexion of ideas wholly owing to *chance or custom*: Ideas that in themselves are not at all of kin, come to be so united in some men's minds, that it is very hard to separate them; they always keep company, and the one no sooner at any time comes into the understanding, but its associate appears with it.
>
> (Kallich 32)

However, by the time Irving published *The Sketch Book* popular aesthetic works had established associationism as more than an impediment to clear rational thought. They had demonstrated that associations, when propagated and controlled by art, could be made to contribute significantly to the production of consensus and cohesion in modern society. Aesthetician Archibald Alison may be counted among the foremost proponents of the belief that associationism provides a basis for national community of sensibility or taste. For example in 1790 he noted associationism's contribution to national sensibility and sentiment in his remarks on music:

> There are other tunes of the same character, which, without any particular merit, yet always serve to please the people, whenever they are performed. The natives of any country, which possesses a national or characteristic music, need not be reminded, how strongly the performance of such airs brings back to them the imagery of their native land; and must often have had occasion to remark how inferior an emotion they excite in those who are strangers to such associations.
>
> (24)

In addition Alison notes how the sentiments associated with given cultural productions link the individual to that sense of cultural and communal genealogy essential to nationalism:

> There is no man in the least acquainted with the history of antiquity, who does not love to let his imagination loose on the prospect of its remains, and to whom they are not in some measure sacred, from the innumerable images they bring. Even the peasant, whose knowledge of former times extends but to a few generations, has yet in his village some monument of the deeds or virtues of his forefathers; and cherishes with a fond veneration the memorial of those good old times to which his imagination returns with delight, and of which he loves to recount the simple tales that tradition has brought him.
>
> (28)

So too modern literary culture creates the 'traditional' tales that link its readers to a past and make the 'virtues' of the forefathers the cultural patrimony of the modern nation.

8. In *Adrift in the Old World* Jeffrey Rubin-Dorsky argues that

> Irving was preoccupied with the loss of the nation-as-home, a loss that was not yet viewed as permanent. Following Irving to Europe . . . Americans sought along with him not only a release from the oppressive realities of a materialist culture but, as well, a source of continuity to replace the one that was fast becoming historically obsolete.

> He concludes that 'Irving's fictional world' was 'a substitute for the political order of George Washington's republican vision' (xviii-xix). Although I agree that Irving's vision of patriarchal domesticity indeed served as a substitute for a lost Federalist order, I do not see it as a 'release' or escape from the problems of liberal democratic society. In fact Irving's nostalgic vision employs the press in a positive manner that contests liberal-democratic progressivism and makes of sentimental literature a basis for a more conservative American society. It is in this sense that Irving indeed uses literature to create a sense of continuity and construct the nation-as-home on the pages of *The Sketch Book*.

9. Rubin-Dorsky asserts that the patriarchal ruler of the English country home, the squire or yeoman farmer, represents

> the principal stabilizing force in his society, with no aristocratic yearnings, liberal, sensible, and, above all, virtuous, [he] is Irving's English version of the yeoman farmer championed by Thomas Jefferson and reclaimed by Andrew Jackson as the source and strength of an American agrarian republic.

(141)

Although he observes that, 'like these agrarian idealists, [Irving] believed that virtue resided in the country' (147), he recognizes that such a vision was 'anachronistic' in Irving's time and fashioned to appeal 'to a nation uneasy with its own progress and changing self-image' (146). In effect Irving 'retreated' from liberal-democratic reality 'to his imagination' where he created from elements of the English and American past the agrarian home he desired. Whereas Rubin-Dorsky locates the main tension in Irving's work between Jeffersonian agrarianism and an ascendant liberalism, I argue that that tension resides mainly between liberal-democratic progressivism and conservatism. Although Irving had abandoned the Federalist persuasion as a viable social and political ideology for modern America, he only did so in order to revive it in a conservative sensibility, not in order to celebrate the egalitarian idyll of Jeffersonian agrarianism.

Works Cited

Alison, Archibald, *Essay on the Nature and Principles of Taste,* Edinburgh, 1790: repr. Hildesheim, Germany: Georg Olms Verslagbuchhandlung, 1968.

Ames, Fisher, *Works of Fisher Ames,* Boston: T. B. Wait, 1809.

Anderson, Benedict, *Imagined Communities,* London: Verso, 1983.

Burke, Edmund, *Reflections of the Revolution in France,* New York: Penguin, 1969.

Elliot, Emory (ed.), *The Columbia History of the American Novel,* New York: Columbia University Press, 1991.

Fliegelman, Jay, *Prodigals and Pilgrims: the American Revolution Against Patriarchal Authority, 1750-1800,* Cambridge: Cambridge University Press, 1982.

Irving, Washington, *Salmagundi* in *The Complete Works of Washington Irving,* vol. 6, Boston: Twayne, 1977.

———, *The Sketch Book,* New York: G. P. Putnam, 1859.

Kallich, Martin, *The Association of Ideas and Critical Theory in Eighteenth-Century England,* The Hague: Mouton, 1970.

Kohn, Hans, *American Nationalism,* New York: Collier Books, 1961.

Kramnick, Isaac, *Republicanism and Bourgeois Radicalism,* Ithaca, NY: Cornell University Press, 1990.

Pocock, J. G. A., *Virtue, Commerce and History,* Cambridge: Cambridge University Press, 1985.

Reynolds, Larry, *James Kirke Paulding,* Boston: Twayne, 1984.

Rubin-Dorsky, Jeffrey, *Adrift in the Old World,* Chicago: Chicago University Press, 1988.

Silverman, Kaja, *The Subject of Semiotics,* Oxford: Oxford University Press, 1983.

Sundquist, Eric, *Home as Found,* Baltimore: Johns Hopkins University Press, 1977.

Warner, Michael, *The Letters of the Republic,* Cambridge, MA: Harvard University Press, 1990.

Williams, Stanley T., *The Life of Washington Irving,* Oxford: Oxford University Press, 1935.

Susan M. Catalano (essay date 1998)

SOURCE: "Henpecked to Heroism: Placing Rip Van Winkle and Francis Macomber in the American Renegade Tradition," *Hemingway Review,* Vol. 17, No. 2, Spring, 1998, pp. 111-17.

[*In the following essay, Catalano compares "Rip Van Winkle" to Hemingway's "The Short Happy Life of Fran-*

cis Macomber," *arguing that both protagonists share a transformation against the powers of female authority.*]

As American citizens, both Washington Irving and Ernest Hemingway were aware of the "renegade spirit" distinguishing American culture from its confining European influences. As American artists, both authors were no less benefactors of this unique tradition than shapers of its modern form. Hemingway is especially known for extending the American renegade spirit beyond our borders to include safari hunters, matadors, and soldiers, yet undeniably "[Hemingway] is at home, too, with the Rip Van Winkle archetype, with . . . traditional evasions of domesticity and civil life" (Fiedler 305). Because "traditional" also constitutes "conventional," these "traditional evasions" may help explain how such "henpecked heroes" as Rip Van Winkle in Irving's **"Rip Van Winkle"** and Francis Macomber in Hemingway's "The Short Happy Life of Francis Macomber" manage to compel sympathy and survive this national iconoclastic tradition.

Even "reluctant renegades" must first confront the emasculating effects of spousal tyranny. Rip is rendered impotent as a provider; Francis is unable to satisfy his wife sexually and ultimately cuckolded. Because "Margot was too beautiful for Macomber to divorce her and Macomber had too much money for Margot ever to leave him" (*CSS* 18), Margot abates her disgust for Francis by kissing their safari guide Wilson full in the mouth. She later shares Wilson's double cot in what K. G. Johnston calls "her tribute to a man of courage" (46) in predictable allegiance to the American renegade tradition, and consistent with what Wilson names her "*American* female cruelty" (emphasis mine, *CSS* 9). All Francis holds is a healthy bankroll. He has achieved the masculine merit-badge of "provider," but lacks the confidence to wield this influence over his wife.

However, where Francis falters Rip proves himself, and vice versa. Rip has given his wife children; his lack of financial resolve is the issue. Rip's emasculation therefore takes the reverse form of Francis's, and because it is much more difficult for Dame Van Winkle to take financial revenge on Rip than for Margot to take sexual revenge on Francis, Rip's humiliation is limited to interminable tongue-lashings. Still, Rip is not lazy: he simply has an "insuperable aversion to all kinds of *profitable* labour," helping neighbors "in the roughest toil" and performing for other women "such little odd jobs as their less obliging husbands would not do for them" (emphasis mine, Irving 40). Oddly, Rip takes pleasure in helping his neighbors but simply doesn't want to toil for his family. While some may read this noncompliance as marital retaliation, I would suggest that Rip confirms his emasculation through an infantile rejection of responsibility.

Appropriately, Rip and Francis ultimately assert their masculinity through the hunt—the paradigm of masculine control. Rip finds virility in his shotgun's command over life and death. Hunting seemingly elevates him above his wife's reproach: "[Rip's] only alternative to escape from

the labour of the farm and the clamour of his wife, was to take gun in hand, and stroll away into the woods . . . [where] the still solitudes echoed and re-echoed with the reports of his gun" (42-3). While this "ability to dominate one's personal universe is what Rip had been seeking all along" (Plung 79), Rip's continual avoidance of his masculine responsibility leaves Dame Van Winkle little choice but to dominate the world outside Rip's "personal universe." In daily life, a mere archetypal hunt cannot achieve the heroic boon of success. Leslie Fiedler calls this "the American inversion of the traditional Yin-Yang symbols, an odd conversion of the male into a symbol of nature and the female into that of organized society" (335). Still, the success of such an inversion in the new American renegade tradition may be foretold by Rip's "shotgun," which only winds up rusted.

Links between the hunt and masculine potency abound throughout Hemingway's work, and Francis seeks remasculation through a safari he hopes will win him Wilson's respect and possibly a sexual "tribute" from Margot. Michelle Scalise Sugiyama explains that "the more successful a man is as a hunter, the more mates and offspring he is able to invest in" (20), so Francis's sexual prosperity is tied to this primal equation. Wilson's reply—"I have your big gun" (16)—is meant both literally and figuratively, as is his reaction to Francis's cowardice: "[He] suddenly felt as though he had opened the wrong door in a hotel and seen something shameful" (15). The seeming "nakedness" of Francis's fear emphasizes the cleft between his own sexual prowess and that of Wilson as the "experienced hunter," as does Wilson's professional discretion: when Francis asks if anyone will find out about his "misfire," Wilson responds, "No . . . I'm a professional hunter. We never talk about our clients. . . . It's supposed to be bad form to ask us not to talk though" (8). Lacking "good form" as well as other "essential knowledge" (Seydow 37), Francis snivels, "'I'm sorry,' . . . and looked at [Wilson] with his *American* face that would stay adolescent until it became middle-aged . . . 'I'm sorry I didn't realize that. There are lots of things I don't know'" (emphasis mine, *CSS* 8). Having a "face that would stay adolescent until it became middle-aged" (and having learned only "about sex in books . . . too many books" [18]) implies that Francis has missed his sexual peak, the height of his masculine powers, and possibly explains how Margot acquired such decisive marital control. In Hemingway's terms, "bagging a lion" or buffalo is analogous to "bagging" a woman, so Francis must "lose his virginity" through the hunt to achieve even a qualified heroism.

Notably, both characters' transitions into American antiheroism, while precipitated by the hunt, actually occur through a transgression of time. Both men temporarily exist in an accelerated state. For Rip, twenty years pass like an afternoon nap, although there are indications that his "dream" exceeds mere mental transportation: "Rip now felt a vague apprehension stealing over him. . . . He paused for an instant . . . there was something strange and incomprehensible about the unknown that inspired awe and checked familiarity" (43-4). David J. Kann calls this Rip's "little death" because of the vast change it effects on Rip's identity, and reiterates the necessity to "deal with the story as an abstraction rather than embedded in the linear movement of time" (194). While a "flock of idle crows . . . seemed to look down and scoff at the poor man's perplexities," "secure in their elevation" as part of the natural world that remains constant through time, Rip's village "was altered" by contrast: "Strange names were over the doors—strange faces at the windows—everything was strange. His mind now misgave him; he now began to doubt whether both he and the world around him were not bewitched" (46-7). Rip's identity is remade through time's effect on his village. Logically, then, Rip feels initially displaced once he is replaced into his usual rate of time.

Francis Macomber also achieves anti-heroism through temporal expediency. His "short, happy life" is a matter of minutes: at the peak of his buffalo hunt, Margot shoots her husband "about two inches up and a little to one side of the base of his skull" (28). Francis forgoes Rip's twenty-year transition and changes instantaneously from a "bloody coward" to a "ruddy fire-eater." Adhering to the Hemingway sex/hunt analogy, Wilson calls this "More of a change than any loss of virginity" (26). According to S. P. Jain, Francis's transformation is possible because "utter absorption in his insufferable situation naturally suspends 'the functioning of [his] imagination' (which, according to Hemingway, is the root-cause of all fear) and throws him 'completely in the very second of the present minute with no before and no after'" (129).

Francis describes a feeling "like a dam bursting" inside of himself, but the "wild, *unreasonable* happiness" that follows foreshadows his untimely end (emphasis mine, *CSS* 25). This speedy change disturbs Margot: "'You've gotten awfully brave, awfully suddenly,' his wife said contemptuously, but her contempt was not secure. She was very afraid of something. Macomber laughed, a very natural hearty laugh, 'You know I *have*,' he said. 'I really have'" (26). Because Margot can't thwart the transformation Jain calls "impregnated with a sense of inexorability" (129), she exercises the last control she retains over Francis, stopping him literally dead in his tracks.

Francis has his moment, and that is all the time he gets. But for Hemingway, this is all the time Francis needs to have *lived happily*—the story is, after all, not called "The Short Happy Day," "Hour," or "Moment" of Francis Macomber. Francis's achievement of true happiness, however brief, warrants Hemingway's choice of the word "Life." So Francis, too, achieves anti-heroism through his limited mastery over time.

As "henpecked heroes," Rip and Francis experience marital deliverance to achieve anti-heroism. While some might argue that Margot won the war of the Macombers with the help of her. 65mm Mannlicher (pronounced "manlicker"), the fact that such extremes were necessary to control Francis proves his victory. As Nina Baym explains, "whatever

she does, Margot is as 'buffaloed' as the buffalo," exercising a mere "illusion of power" which "rather than freeing her deliver[s] her from the power of one man to the power of another" (119). While Margot's infidelity and manslaughter only puts her at Wilson's disposal instead of Francis's, Francis's transformation makes him wholly independent. Wilson recognizes the signs of Margot's defeat: "she saw the change in Francis Macomber now. . . . She's worried about it already, he thought" (26), and becomes convinced of the change himself: "It had taken a strange chance of hunting, a sudden precipitation into action without opportunity for worrying beforehand, to bring this about with Macomber, but regardless of how it happened it had most certainly happened. Look at the beggar now. . . . Be a damn fire eater now" (25-6).

Francis's newfound happiness and emancipation, not his death, are meant to be the story's climax. His death, and especially the unresolved critical question of Margot's intention, is immaterial because Francis has heroically transcended his emasculating fear. Francis becomes an unequivocal hero, and Margot is purposely left to the reader's judgement. Joseph DeFalco recognizes that Francis "has severed the maternal-wife bond and achieved freedom from domination. The final shooting is anticlimactic, for it represents the woman's inability to recognize the freedom of the husband-son figure" (206). Wilson, too, notes this inability on Margot's part: "'That was a pretty thing to do,' he said in a toneless voice. 'He *would* have left you too. . . . Why didn't you just poison him?'" (28). Even after doling out the ultimate penalty for transgression, Margot cannot dilute Francis' fulfillment of a "short, *happy life.*"

Conversely, Rip survives his wife to become the undisputed victor of the war of the Van Winkles, so his anti-heroism differs as something that happens *to* him as a result of fortunate circumstances, rather than *within* him as a result of directly confronting his fears. Whereas Francis consciously feels the rush of his instantaneous transformation "like a dam bursting" (25), Rip is initially confused by his change: "He doubted his own identity, and whether he was himself or another man" (50). Although this problematizes our giving Rip credit for his transformation, the fact of his change remains.

When he emerges from his twenty-year nap having conquered the progression of time, Rip is no longer a henpecked loafer but an emancipated widower and ultimately, the village patriarch. Fittingly, Rip learns that Dame Van Winkle has precipitated her own demise by "[breaking] a blood vessel in a fit of passion at a New-England peddler" (51). Both justice *and* time are on his side. Rip feels unambiguously pleased about his new marital status and becomes the envy of the townsmen: "it is a common wish of all henpecked husbands in the neighborhood, when life hangs heavy on their hands, that they might have a quieting draft out of Rip Van Winkle's flagon" (53).

Rip's happiness differs from Francis's in being bound up with community: "In [Rip's] case context—chiefly the absence of critical viewpoints such as those of Dame Van Winkle—and the power of a past for a present that can perceive its relevance create the conditions for social happiness" (Shear 547). Rip's "social happiness" and patriarchal position are assured when Peter Vanderdonk, "a descendant of the historian of that name" who "was the most ancient inhabitant of the village, and well versed in all the wonderful events and traditions of the neighborhood," sanctions Rip's story about his time spent in the Kaatskills and "assured the company that it was a fact" (51-2). Thus, Vanderdonk validates Rip's place as American anti-hero.

Rip can now assume his "privileged rebirth into the 'storyteller'" (Rubin-Dorsky 399), reversing his patronage of those pseudo-pundits who had inhabited the inn. In fact, Rip finds his former cronies "all rather the worse for the wear and tear of time" and "preferred making friends among the rising generation, with whom he soon grew into great favour" (52). Still, Rip's newfound happiness is no less a product of his marital release than it is of his "being arrived at that happy age when a man can be idle with impunity" (52), so a twenty-year nap proves key to Rip's anti-heroic contentment.

Even modern veterans of the American literary tradition cannot dismiss Francis Macomber and Rip Van Winkle as casualties of the American renegade spirit that founded it. In spite of ourselves, we root for them. Both the hen and the henpecked can relate to their oppression. Everyone has at least felt the weight of parental control as children; hence the sympathy that Rip and Francis compel. Nevertheless, what constitutes "universal" also constitutes "ordinary," and the extraordinary step that Rip and Francis take to transcend their typical troubles makes them anti-heroes. In this sense, Washington Irving and Ernest Hemingway's "henpecked heroes" remain distinctly American despite their lack of adherence to the renegade spirit underlying our cultural and literary tradition.

Works Cited

Baym, Nina. "Actually, I Felt Sorry for the Lion." *New Critical Approaches to the Short Stories of Ernest Hemingway*. Ed. Jackson J. Benson. Durham: Duke UP, 1990. 112-120.

DeFalco, Joseph. *The Hero in Hemingway's Short Stories.* Pittsburgh: U of Pittsburgh P, 1963.

Fiedler, Leslie. *Love and Death in the American Novel.* New York: Criterion, 1960.

Hemingway, Ernest. "The Short Happy Life of Francis Macomber." *The Complete Short Stories of Ernest Hemingway: The Finca Vigía Edition.* New York: Macmillan, 1987. 5-28.

Irving, Washington. "Rip Van Winkle." *The Sketch Book.* 1819-20. New York: Signet Classic, 1961. 37-55.

Jain, S. P. *Hemingway: A Study of His Short Stories.* New Delhi: Heinemann, 1985.

Johnston, K. G. "In Defense of the Unhappy Margot Macomber." *The Hemingway Review* 2.2 (Fall 1983): 44-7.

Kann, David J. "'Rip Van Winkle': Wheels Within Wheels." *American Imago* 36 (1979): 178-96.

Plung, Daniel L. "'Rip Van Winkle': Metempsychosis and the Quest for Self-Reliance." *Rocky Mountain Review of Language and Literature* 31 (1977): 65-80.

Rubin-Dorsky, Jeffrey. "The Value of Storytelling: 'Rip Van Winkle' and 'The Legend of Sleepy Hollow' in the Context of *The Sketch Book*." *Modern Philology* (May 1985): 393-406.

Scalise Sugiyama, Michelle. "What's Love Got To Do With It? An Evolutionary Analysis of 'The Short Happy Life of Francis Macomber.'" *The Hemingway Review* 15.2 (Spring 1996): 15-32.

Seydow, John J. "Francis Macomber's Spurious Masculinity." *The Hemingway Review* 1.1 (Spring 1981): 33-41.

Shear, Walter. "Cultural Fate and Social Freedom in Three American Short Stories." *Studies in Short Fiction* 29.4 (1992): 543-9.

FURTHER READING

Criticism

Aderman, Ralph M. "Washington Irving as a Purveyor of Old and New World Romanticism." In *The Old and New World Romanticism of Washington Irving,* edited by Stanley Brodwin, pp. 13-25. New York: Greenwood Press, 1986.

> Considers the influence of European romanticism on Irving's writings, particularly in his later works.

Antelyes, Peter. *Tales of Adventurous Enterprise: Washington Irving and the Poetics of Western Expansion.* New York: Columbia University Press, 1990, 246p.

> Considers issues of Western expansion, literary imagination, and Irving's influence on the development of the "tale of adventurous enterprise" as a literary form.

Christensen, Peter. "Washington Irving and the Denial of the Fantastic." In *The Old and New World Romanticism of Washington Irving,* edited by Stanley Brodwin, pp. 51-60. New York: Greenwood Press, 1986.

> Provides an overview of Irving's treatment of the supernatural in his writings from 1819 to 1832.

Hagensick, Donna. "Irving: A Littérateur in Politics." In *Critical Essays on Washington Irving,* edited by Ralph M. Aderman, pp. 178-91. Boston: G. K. Hall & Co.

> Defends Irving's skills as a diplomat.

Haig, Judith G. "Washington Irving and the Romance of Travel: Is There an Itinerary in *Tales of a Traveler*?" In *The Old and New World Romanticism of Washington Irving,* edited by Stanley Brodwin, pp. 61-8. New York: Greenwood Press, 1986.

> Argues that the relationship between imagination and travel provides the key to interpreting *Tales of a Traveler.*

McElroy, John Harmon. "The Integrity of Irving's Columbus" In *Washington Irving: The Critical Reaction,* edited by James W. Tuttleton, pp. 126-36. New York: AMS Press, 1993.

> Examines the merit and critical reception of Irving's *History of the Life and Voyages of Christopher Columbus.*

McLamore, Richard V. "Postcolonial Columbus: Washington Irving and *The Conquest of Granada.*" In *Nineteenth-Century Literature* 48, No. 1 (June 1993): 26-43.

> Discusses the mocking tone of *The Chronicle of the Conquest of Granada.*

Pinsker, Sanford. "Uneasy Laughter: Sut Lovingood—Between Rip Van Winkle and Andrew Dice Clay." In *Sut Lovingood's Nat'ral Born Yarnspinner: Essays on George Washington Harris,* edited by James E. Caron and M. Thomas Inge, pp. 299-313. Tuscaloosa: University of Alabama Press, 1996.

> Comparison of the politically incorrect humor found in Irving's "Rip Van Winkle," George Washington Harris's Sut Lovingood stories, and the work of twentieth-century American comic Andrew Dice Clay.

Rubin-Dorsky, Jeffrey. "The Crisis Resolved(?): 'Rip Van Winkle' and 'The Legend of Sleepy Hollow.'" In *Adrift in the Old World: The Psychological Pilgrimage of Washington Irving,* pp. 100-22. Chicago: University of Chicago Press, 1988.

> Analyzes "Rip Van Winkle" and "The Legend of Sleepy Hollow" in the context of the collection *The Sketch Book of Geoffrey Crayon, Gent.*

West, Elsie Lee. "Washington Irving: Biographer." In *Washington Irving: The Critical Reaction,* edited by James W. Tuttleton, pp. 197-206. New York: AMS Press, 1993.

> Traces Irving's significance as a biographer.

Additional coverage of Irving's life and career is contained in the following sources published by the Gale Group: *Concise Dictionary of American Literary Biography; Dictionary of Literary Biography,* Vols. 3, 11, 30, 59, 73, 74, and 186; *DISCovering Authors; DISCovering Authors: British; DISCovering Authors: Canadian; DISCovering Authors Modules: Most-Studied Authors; Short Story Criticism,* Vols. 2 and 37; *World Literature Criticism, 1500 to the Present;* **and** *Yesterday's Authors of Books for Children.*

Thomas Percy
1729-1811

English poet, translator, and author.

INTRODUCTION

A well-known scholar and translator, Thomas Percy is best remembered for his three-volume collection of popular ballads titled *Reliques of Ancient English Poetry,* which he issued in 1765. The work was credited with the revival of English minstrel poetry in the eighteenth and nineteenth centuries and earned Percy both fame and respect as a pioneer in the field. Many of the individual pieces in *Reliques* were said to have inspired various Romantic poems.

BIOGRAPHICAL INFORMATION

Born in Shropshire, England, to Jane Nott and Arthur Lowe Percy, a grocer and tobacconist, Percy was encouraged in his early education by his father, who instilled in him an interest in books and reading. The young Percy did well in school and was eventually awarded a scholarship to Christ Church College, Oxford, where he graduated with a bachelor's degree in 1750. Percy was drawn to poetry as a young man, and he composed numerous poems and songs in these years, all dedicated to a woman named Flavia. Most of these pieces were not published during his lifetime and few have survived; however, those that are extant exhibit the influence of numerous early English balladeers as well as the work of such authors as John Milton, Alexander Pope, and Thomas Gray. Scholars also suggest that Percy's early efforts were influenced by a folio manuscript of ballads, romances, and lyric poems that he had acquired during his school years at the home of an old Shropshire friend, Humphrey Pitt. Percy was probably unaware of the value of this manuscript, and he asked for it only after he saw Pitt's maid using the pages to light the fire.

A second scholarship at Oxford helped Percy attain a master's degree in 1753, the same year he was ordained a priest. Percy was then appointed vicar of Easton Maudit, and acquired a second income as curate of Wilby three years later. The Earl of Wilby encouraged Percy's literary pursuits and also introduced him at court. It was while in London with Wilby that Percy met James Grainger and Samuel Johnson. His friendship with both writers lasted many years, and Grainger was especially influential in helping Percy develop his poetic and editorial talents. In 1759 Percy married Anne Gutteridge, with whom he had five daughters and one son. During these years, Percy con-

tinued to write poetry, and in 1758, a thirty-two line "Song" was published in Robert Dodsley's *Collection of Poems.* An imitation of a Scottish song, this short lyric was well received and frequently republished. Encouraged by Grainger, Percy then contributed several translations—including Tibullus's "Elegy I" and Ovid's "Elegy to Tibullus"—to Grainger's *Poetical Translations of the Elegies of Tibullus.* Yet, despite repeated entreaties from Johnson, Edward Lye, and other writers, Percy declined working on an edition of the ballads he had earlier acquired in Shropshire. Instead he continued to focus his energies on translating other works, including a seventeenth-century Chinese novel titled *Hau Kiou Choaan* (1761) and other related nonfiction titles. It was not until the early 1760s that Percy would turn his attention to the early manuscript of ballads and songs he had acquired, issuing it eventually as *Reliques of Ancient English Poetry,* the first of his publications to bear his name. The work was an immediate success, and Percy gained much fame following its issuance. He continued to publish other translations and collections of poetry while fulfilling his duties as a priest in the Church of England. Percy was eventually appointed Dean of Carlisle, and then promoted to Bishop of Dromore in 1782. He served in the latter position for over twenty years, achieving great success and respect for his leadership of the diocese and his devotion to the education of the young. Meanwhile, he continued to pursue his literary interests, even editing a fourth edition of the *Reliques,* which was never published. Percy died in 1811, five years after the death of his wife, Anne. Both were buried in the cathedral of Dromore.

MAJOR WORKS

Percy's first major translation was from a manuscript of a seventeenth-century Chinese novel titled *Hau Kiou Choaan.* He himself did not know Chinese, but used as his source a three-part translation into English by an earlier translator. The fourth part of the novel was in Portuguese, which Percy taught himself in order to complete the story, combining all four parts into a coherent whole. While both Percy and his publisher, Robert Dodsley, had expected success for the book, which was very similar in its storyline to such works as Samuel Richardson's *Pamela* and *Clarissa,* the book did not sell well. Contemporary reviewers were more impressed with Percy's annotations—which included a preface, a bibliography, a fifteen-page index and numerous notes ranging in length from short sentences to several long essays—than they were with the translation itself. It is believed that *Hau Kiou Choaan* may have been the first Chinese novel printed in England. Shortly thereafter, Percy issued a collection of seven essays on China by various authors, titled *Miscellaneous Pieces Relating to the Chinese.* In 1762, Percy published a collection of stories about widows who were false to their vows of fealty towards their dead husbands. Titled *The Matrons,* this was followed the next year by *Five Pieces of Runic Poetry* (1763), a slim volume of Icelandic poetry. Very little was known of Icelandic poetry in England prior to this translation. Percy himself was dependent on Latin versions of the works, and he had a great deal of difficulty capturing the spirit of the Nordic battle poems. His subsequent translation of *The Song of Solomon* (1764), for which he relied on the King James version, was much more readable, and he characterized this effort as an attempt to rescue "one of the most beautiful pastorals in the world."

In 1760, Percy had also begun work on a collection of ancient poems, selecting the best ballads from a folio manuscript of lyrics and poems he had acquired years earlier during his school days in Shropshire. He supplemented these songs with later poems, searching out ballads from other parts of Britain, particularly Scotland. Percy was aided by several of his friends in the selection effort. The resultant collection, *Reliques of Ancient English Poetry,* bearing a dedication by Samuel Johnson, was finally published by Robert Dodsley in 1765. The book was an instant success with readers and reviewers, and Percy himself was immediately appointed tutor to Algernon Percy, the younger son of the Earl of Northumberland. The Countess of Northumberland had supported Percy's work on the volume, and it is speculated that much of its initial success was due to her patronage as well as to Percy's adept citing of the several poets who had provided him assistance in its compilation. The list included such notables as Johnson, William Shenstone, and David Garrick. Regardless of the reasons for its initial success, the collection had been compiled with great care, quality being Percy's principal criteria for inclusion. Both Scottish and English ballads were included, and the poems were arranged chronologically. The three-volume collection also placed poems on similar subjects together and each group was preceded by an introduction or essays that were themselves noteworthy milestones in English literary history. Prior to Percy's interest, ballads had not been taken seriously and he was concerned that his efforts would be considered an inappropriate activity for a minister of the Church. Therefore, he took great pains to minimize the work and even went so far as to refer to it as "a strange collection of trash."

In addition to the *Reliques,* Percy had also begun work on numerous other translations; of these he completed work on only two, *A Key to the New Testament* (1766) and a translation of Paul Henri Mallet's *Introduction a l'Histoire de Dannemarc,* which was issued in 1770 as *Northern Antiquities. A Key to the New Testament* drew on several contemporary scholarly works for information and was written in clear and concise language. Although Percy modestly contended that the work had originally been written for the use of his parishioners, it found an enthusiastic audience with university students as well as clerical scholars, and at least six editions were published during Percy's lifetime. *Northern Antiquities* served a similar purpose to his earlier *Runic Poetry,* helping to familiarize his English readers with Scandinavian poetry and Nordic mythology and folklore. During Percy's service as Bishop of Dromore, he continued to edit several other works; his best-known work from this era is a long poem titled *The Hermit of Warkworth* (1771). neIn addition, Percy issued two more editions of his *Reliques,* and wrote several articles for the various literary magazines of the day.

CRITICAL RECEPTION

Prior to Percy's publication of the *Reliques,* ballads had not been considered a suitable subject for scholarly investigation. Because of this, and because of his position in English society as a church minister, Percy himself frequently minimized his efforts on this collection. Nonetheless, the *Reliques* have since been acknowledged as one of the most lasting and powerful influences in the revival of English minstrel poetry during the eighteenth and nineteenth centuries. A few years following the publication of the *Reliques,* Percy's editorial methods and accuracy came under attack by contemporary antiquarian, Joseph Ritson, who specifically focused on Percy's practice of altering the pieces in the collection without noting each change for the reader. This criticism led Percy to revise and reissue several new editions of his work during his lifetime. More recently, though, critics have come to Percy's defense, praising him as a highly-skilled scholar and editor. According to Cleanth Brooks, an assessment of Percy's talents must rest not only on his work with ballads but with several other pieces of pioneering work, including his translations of Nordic and Chinese literary texts. Similarly, in an essay appraising Percy's editing skills, Zinnia Knapman has noted that Percy's significance as a folklorist has been only grudgingly acknowledged. Knapman points out that most discussions of Percy's *Reliques* tend to focus on the influence this collection had on the Romantic poets or on the controversial nature of Percy's editorial methods. However, she believes that when examined from a historical perspective, Percy's work on this anthology can "only been seen as a sensible, creative, and positive force." Despite the controversy surrounding the editorial practices employed on the *Reliques*, Percy's achievement with the collection is now universally acknowledged, and the work is considered England's primary anthology of ballads and lyrics.

PRINCIPAL WORKS

Hau Kiou Choaan or The Pleasing History. A Translation from the Chinese Language. To Which Are Added, I. The Argument or Story of a Chinese Play, II. A Collection of Chinese Proverbs, and III. Fragments of Chinese Poetry. In Four Volumes. With Notes [editor and part translator] (novel) 1761

The Matrons. Six Short Histories [editor and part translator] (short stories) 1762

Five Pieces of Runic Poetry Translated from the Islandic Language [translator] (poetry) 1763

The Song of Solomon, Newly Translated from the Original Hebrew: With a Commentary and Annotations [translator] (poetry) 1764

Reliques of Ancient English Poetry: Consisting of Old Heroic Ballads, Songs, and other Pieces of our earlier Poets, (Chiefly of the lyric Kind.) Together with some few of later Date 3 vols. [editor] (poetry) 1765

A Key to the New Testament. Giving an Account of the several Books, their Contents, their Authors, And of the Times and Occasions, on which they were respectively written (nonfiction) 1766

Four Essays, as Improved and Enlarged in the Second Edition of the Reliques of Ancient English Poetry (essays) 1767

Northern Antiquities: Or, a Description of the Manners, Customs, Religion and Laws of the Ancient Danes, and other Northern Nations; Including those of Our own Saxon Ancestors. With a Translation of the Edda, or System of Runic Mythology, and Other Pieces, from the Ancient Islandic Tongue. In Two Volumes. Translated from Mons. Mallet's Introduction a l'Histoire de Dan-

nemarc, &.c. With Additional Notes by the English Translator, and Goranson's Latin Version of the Edda [translator] (poetry) 1770

The Hermit of Warksworth. A Northumberland Ballad. In Three Fits or Cantos (poetry) 1771

CRITICISM

Cleanth Brooks (essay date 1977)

SOURCE: "Introduction," in *The Percy Letters: The Correspondence of Thomas Percy & William Shenstone,* Yale University Press, 1977, pp. v-xxvii.

[*In the following essay, Brooks provides an overview of Percy's correspondence with author William Shenstone, focusing particularly on Shenstone's assistance in the compilation of Percy's* Reliques.]

I

The first extant letter of this correspondence is dated 24 November 1757. It is from Percy, and on it Shenstone has scribbled a note that reads: "Mr. Percy is domestic chaplain to the Earl of Sussex and has Genius and Learning, accompany'd with great Vivacity." The note suggests that the correspondence had just begun, for it is the sort of comment that one might jot down on an early letter but not on one received long after correspondence had begun. Percy himself is quite definite that the correspondence began in 1757. When his letters to Shenstone had been returned to him after Shenstone's death, he arranged them in sequence and wrote the following note on one of the early pages:[1] "A series of Letters, written to and from William Shenstone Esq of The Leasowes, begun in 1757, soon after our first acquaintance and continued down to the time of his death in 1763."

This note might be taken as decisive, but there is one piece of evidence, apparently contradictory, that has to be dealt with. Miss Marjorie Williams, in her *Letters of William Shenstone* (Oxford, Blackwell, 1939), conjectures that a certain letter, undated and without the name of the person to whom it was addressed, may have been written to Percy in 1753.[2] In this letter Shenstone refers to his correspondent's "polite Description of my Farm." Now, in a letter of 7 January 1760,[3] Shenstone observes that "Mʳ P.'s account of the Farm here must be a Little adjusted . . . ," and Percy has annotated this sentence as follows: "A Description of the Leasowes, which I had drawn up hastily in 1753."

One cannot, then, simply rule out the possibility that Percy and Shenstone were acquainted and were exchanging letters as early as 1753. Nevertheless, there are difficulties in the way of accepting this date. For example, if Percy had drawn up his account of The Leasowes in 1753, he was certainly behindhand in presenting it to Shenstone for his approval. Had Percy, in 1753, at the age of twenty-four, had the good fortune to meet Shenstone, that known *arbiter elegantiarum,* I find it hard to believe that he would not have followed up his advantage. Yet, if he did, where are the letters that passed between the two men in the four years between 1753 and 1757? Over fifty survive for the period between 1757 and 1763.

Internal evidence is also against 1753. None of the names that occur in the conjectural 1753 letter have any association with Percy. One of the people mentioned, Dr. Turton, does have a connection with an account of The Leasowes, but not with the one written by Percy. In this account, which is preserved in the James Marshall and Marie-Louise Osborn Collection in Yale University Library, the unidentified author quotes a passage about The Leasowes which is attributed to Turton. Evidently a number of people tried their hands at descriptions of Shenstone's estate.

Another such description is that printed in the second volume of Shenstone's *Works.* The ostensible author is Shenstone's publisher, Robert Dodsley. Percy, however, disputes Dodsley's authorship, and in a note in his own copy of the *Works* (now in the Bodleian Library) tells us that this description was a joint production in which he himself had a hand, but the date he assigns to its composition is 1762.[4] Internal evidence suggests that Percy's part was indeed considerable. Percy presumably incorporated his "account of the Farm" in the "Description" published in the *Works* in 1764.

Percy's note on Letter XV remains a puzzle. Was it a *lapsus pennae* or was Percy simply forgetful? I think that either of these possibilities is more likely than that Percy and Shenstone began to exchange letters in 1753.

Though we do not know through whom Percy first became acquainted with Shenstone, it is possible to make a plausible guess. The intermediary was probably one of Percy's Shropshire friends and neighbors. Percy found his celebrated Folio MS. "lying dirty on the floor under a Bureau in the Parlour" and begged it of its owner, whom he describes as "my worthy friend Humphrey Pitt, Esq., then living at Shifnal in Shropshire."[5] Pitt (d. 1769) was the uncle of the Reverend Robert Binnel (1716-63), rector of Shenton and Kemberton and minister of Newport, all Shropshire villages. Binnel's wife, Mary Congreve, was a distant relation of Percy's.

Pitt and Binnel are mentioned early in the Percy-Shenstone correspondence, and Shenstone had been acquainted with both men for many years. He refers to Pitt in a letter of 23 September 1741 (see Williams, p. 32) and to Binnel in a letter of 28 November 1745 (see Williams, p. 99). In Letter VI Shenstone makes direct reference not only to Pitt but to three other Shropshire gentlemen: to Charles Baldwyn, to Colonel John Cotes, and to a Mr. Slaney, who was probably either Robert (later Cotes's son-in-law) or Plowden (later Pitt's son-in-law).

Shenstone, then, was evidently well known in Percy's own county. He could indeed regard himself as a Salopian, for though his estate was only seven miles from Birmingham and was completely bounded by Warwickshire, his parish of Halesowen was a detached portion of Shropshire and legally a part of that county. The great landmark for all Shropshire men was the Wrekin. This hill, though thirty miles distant, was visible from The Leasowes, and at an appropriate viewpoint in his grounds, Shenstone placed "a seat, the back of which [was] so contrived as to form a table or pedestal for a bowl . . . thus inscribed—'To all friends round the Wrekin!'" So runs the account in Shenstone's *Works* (II, 348).

Of Percy's various Shropshire friends, Binnel was particularly close to Shenstone, not only in early associations, but in tastes and interests. He and Shenstone had long been acquainted, for they had been exact contemporaries at Pembroke College, Oxford. Binnel was a classicist and interested in *belles lettres.* Percy laments his death in a letter to Richard Farmer as "my great and irreparable Loss," and evidently regarded him as a man upon whom he could call for counsel in literary and scholarly matters. My guess is that it was to Binnel that Percy appealed for an introduction to Shenstone. But for another possibility see Letter XI, n. 16.

The very first letters that pass between Percy and Shenstone are filled with literary news of all sorts and not least with the discussion of folk ballads. Indeed, in his first letter, Percy informs his new friend that he is "possess'd of a very curious old MS. Collection of ancient Ballads," that "Mr Johnson" has seen it, and that Johnson hopes that Percy will publish it. Thus, by 1757 Percy was already at work in gathering materials for the *Reliques of Ancient English Poetry.*

Percy's next letter to Shenstone insists that it is only Johnson's "importunity" that has "extorted" from him a promise to publish his MS. But if Johnson is set forth as a main promoter of the enterprise and one who has made large promises of support, it soon becomes apparent, as we read on through the correspondence, that the other main promoter and supporter was Shenstone himself.

Confirmation of this is to be found in the tribute that Percy paid to Shenstone in the Preface to the *Reliques* and elsewhere. For example, writing to Richard Farmer of Shenstone's death, he calls Shenstone "one of the most elegant and amiable of men, and his tender writings were but the counterparts of his heart, which was one of the best that ever animated a human body."[6] In a letter of 30 August 1763 he tells Lord Hailes that he intends "to inscribe [to Shenstone's memory] the whole Collection [that is, the *Reliques*], as being un[der]taken at his request, and the plan of it formed under his elegant super-intendance."[7]

When the *Reliques* was published, a year and a half later, it was dedicated not to Shenstone but to the Countess of Northumberland; but in the Preface Percy states that it was

Shenstone, together with Samuel Johnson, who urged him to produce the work: "At length the importunity of his friends prevailed, and he could refuse nothing to such judges as the author of the RAMBLER and the late Mr. SHENSTONE."[8] On p. xii he specifies more precisely what he owed to Shenstone: "The plan of the work was settled in concert with the late elegant Mr. SHENSTONE, who was to have borne a joint share in it had not death unhappily prevented him: Most of the modern pieces were of his selection and arrangement, and the Editor hopes to be pardoned if he has retained some things out of partiality to the judgment of his friend."

In the Preface (p. xiii) the help of Johnson is also acknowledged: "To the friendship of Mr. Johnson [the Editor] owes many valuable hints for the conduct of the work." This is a judiciously accurate statement, for besides Johnson's initial encouragement to publish the Folio MS., Percy's testimony is that in spite of Johnson's promises to "assist [him] in selecting the most valuable pieces and in revising the Text of those he selected" and furnishing the work "with proper Notes," "This Promise he never executed: nor except a few slight hints delivered vivâ voce, did he furnish any contributions," etc.[9] Johnson was a very busy man during this period, attempting to complete his edition of Shakespeare, which was not issued until six months after the Reliques itself appeared. But Percy's acknowledgment in the Preface does not take into account a "council of War with Mr Johnson, [on the basis of which he had] at length come to the following resolutions.; Imprimis," etc.[10] There was also the very important matter of the graceful dedication which Johnson substantially wrote at Percy's request, though since Percy was the editor of the work it had of course to bear his own signature.

As his letters to Shenstone make abundantly clear, Percy relied heavily on Shenstone's taste, not merely in his choice of what poems to print, but with reference to the design and format of the book. Shenstone had evidently given his friend instruction in avoiding "busy" title pages, in the choice of typefaces, and in the selection of pleasing and appropriate illustrations. Shenstone, as his letters show, was concerned that Percy should provide a proper variety in choosing and arranging his texts. The reader, for instance, must not be wearied by a succession of long poems. The plan of dividing each volume of the Reliques into three series of poems was, by the way, suggested by Shenstone.

Percy took very seriously Shenstone's judgment of literature, especially his taste in songs, as Appendix I will show. Once the reader comes to realize that the Reliques is much more than a collection of folk ballads, that it was a songbook as well, and that Percy must be credited with bringing to the attention of the reading public of his day the importance of its heritage of English lyric poetry, he can better understand why Percy valued and relied greatly on Shenstone's judgment. He will also regard in a new light such matters as Shenstone's attempt to state the difference between a song and a ballad, his attempt to provide a defi-

nition of the ballad,[11] and the very considerable labor that he gave himself in sifting collections of songs for Percy's use in the Reliques.

This is not to say that Percy always followed his mentor's advice, but clearly he took it very seriously. One must not minimize, however, Shenstone's interest in the folk ballad. In his first letter to Percy he discusses ballads, remarking that "nothing gives me greater Pleasure than the simplicity of style and sentiment that is observable in old English ballads."[12] A modern reader may well question Shenstone's conception of what constituted "simplicity." To that matter we shall recur. But we might note that it was through the help of Shenstone that Percy actually obtained some of the finest ballads in the Reliques—"Sir Patrick Spence" and "Edward, Edward," are examples. (They do not occur in the Folio MS. but were sent from Scotland through Shenstone's helpful intervention.) If antiquarians like Richard Farmer, Thomas Warton, and Lord Hailes were Percy's great black-letter authorities, Shenstone, for better or worse, was his special authority on literary taste.

The pages of Shenstone's Miscellany[13] throw a good deal of light on his taste in poetry and therefore on the nature of Shenstone's influence on Percy during the period in which the Reliques was being prepared for publication. Shenstone's Miscellany is a collection of poems, most of them written by Shenstone's friends and neighbors. As Ian Gordon shows, the collection was more than a mere commonplace-book assemblage. Shenstone had evidently intended it for publication at the press of his near "neighbor Baskerville" though it did not, in fact, appear in print until nearly two centuries after Shenstone's death.

The notebook into which Shenstone had copied the poems that make up his Miscellany was sent to Percy a few months after Shenstone's death by Shenstone's neighbor and friend, John Scott Hylton (1726-93), of Lapal House, Halesowen, collector and dabbler in letters. Whether Shenstone had instructed Hylton to do so, we do not know. At any rate, though Percy apparently made no effort to publish the collection, he did annotate it with considerable care. After his death it passed through a succession of hands before it became part of the Alexander Turnbull Library at Wellington, New Zealand.

Percy is among the poets included, and is represented by no fewer than eight poems, one of them in two versions. The collection therefore provides some evidence of his taste in poetry as well as Shenstone's. Though the Miscellany includes seven old ballads, many epigrams, and some light satire, it is primarily a collection of songs. They range all the way from sentimental effusions to rather brittle vers de société. Seven of the poems included in the Miscellany came to be printed in the first edition of the Reliques.

The Percy whom we see reflected in Shenstone's Miscellany and who is even more directly expressed in his letters to Shenstone in the present volume is neither Percy the bishop-to-be nor the incompetent antiquary who signally failed to be the Ritson that Professor Furnivall thought he should have been. For two whole centuries it has been all but impossible to deliver from these two stereotypes the young man in his early thirties who actually edited the *Reliques*—the scholar who, in spite of his conventional neoclassical education, had become much interested in the older ballads of the folk and equally interested in the songs of Tudor and Elizabethan courtiers and playwrights. Percy would have been extraordinary indeed if, when it came to contemporary verse, he had escaped the prevailing taste of his own day. Percy, of course, did not know that he was somehow proving a traitor to the Romantic Revolt, for it had not yet occurred; nor did he think of himself as an austere and strait-laced antiquary. To him, antiquarianism was exciting. Besides, he was not interested in some of the older verse simply because it was old. He thought that there were better reasons for admiring it.

His letters to Shenstone breathe such a spirit. The writer is thoroughly human. He has enthusiasm. He has a sense of humor and high spirits. Though we may find in the tobacco-stopper plot[14] a schoolboy's prank rather than an exercise of genuine wit, it may be useful to be forced to associate the young Percy with a practical joke. Moreover, his list of preposterous curios[15] may serve to counterbalance the prevailing conception of him as always rather stiff, formal, and fearful of compromising his respectability.

II

PERCY'S METHOD OF EDITING THE FOLK BALLADS

One of the problems Percy faced in printing poems from his Folio MS. was the state of his texts. The Folio MS. ballads were often not only corrupt but imperfect and even fragmentary. What was to be done? To such questions as these, Shenstone had ready and positive answers. In his letter of 1 October 1760 he writes:

> As to alterations of a *word or two*, I do not esteem it a point of *Conscience* to *particularize them* on *this* occasion. Perhaps, where a whole *Line* or *More* is alter'd, it may be proper enough to give some Intimation of it. The Italick type may answer this purpose, if you do not employ it on other occasions. It will have the appearance of a modern *Toe* or *Finger,* which is *allowably* added to the best old *Status. . . .*[16]

Shenstone also warns his friend not to include too many poems of little literary merit simply because they have historical interest, and not to encumber his book with too many notes, historical or philological.[17] The material in the Folio MS. ought to be considered "as an hoard of gold, somewhat defac'd by Time; from which however you may be able to draw supplies upon occasion, and with which you may enrich the world hereafter under more *current* Impressions";[18] that is to say, the gold ought to be reminted where necessary.

Though there is no question Shenstone had a taste for the old ballads, he nevertheless insisted that they had to mea-

sure up to universal standards. We may not agree with Shenstone's conception of what those standards were—I, for one, do not—yet we ought to give Shenstone credit for not adopting a double standard—that of "good" poetry and another, applicable to merely quaint and historically interesting verse.

Percy was persuaded to add new toes and fingers to his antique treasures, and, on a few occasions, whole arms and legs. He also tried to clear up obscurities and infelicities. But, in doing so, he was to incur Joseph Ritson's righteous wrath some years later and even to be accused of deceit and forgery.

Sir Walter Scott's defense of Percy's honesty and scholarship scarcely availed to clear his reputation, and when in 1867-68 Hales and Furnivall published *Bishop Percy's Folio Manuscript,* the pummeling that Percy received was merciless. I believe that it is not unreasonable to say that to this day Percy's name has remained a byword for bad editing—even dishonest editing.

The reader of the letters in this volume will probably be inclined to lay most of the blame for this state of affairs on William Shenstone. Certainly, Shenstone did urge Percy to provide a readable and even elegant presentation of these texts "somewhat defac'd by Time." But one must concede that, presented with the problems set by the Folio MS., Percy might have been driven to adopt some such method had he never made Shenstone's acquaintance. Even if Samuel Johnson had had time to advise Percy—and we must not take it for granted that his counsel would have been to print selections from the Folio MS. *literatim*—it seems to me unlikely that the texts in the *Reliques* would have passed muster with Ritson.

The best defense that I know of the editorial method that Shenstone advised and Percy employed has been presented in Chapter 7 (entitled "Percy's **'Reliques'**") of Albert B. Friedman's *The Ballad Revival.*[19] The student interested in this problem should read this chapter in full. Yet it may be useful to indicate here, however briefly, the basic points that Professor Friedman makes, and even to give a few of his illustrations.

In the first place, Friedman indicates that the method Percy adopted was necessary. The texts of ballads like "The Marriage of Sir Gawaine," "The Child of Elle," and "Sir Cauline" were so defective that Percy's problem "was not whether to print them faithfully or to remodel them, but whether to remodel them or to leave them in MS unused." "The Marriage of Sir Gawaine," for example, has "six gaps of nine stanzas each—this in a ballad that was composed originally of about one hundred stanzas."[20]

Friedman points out furthermore that the method adopted by Percy worked. "Success justified Percy's attitude toward the letter of his ballads. As the saner critics from

Scott to Oliver Elton have always realized, 'the ballads would have been less read if [Percy] had been faithful to his texts.'"[21]

Percy should have indicated what he had done. But he fell back too trustfully on Shenstone's advice that he should "not esteem it a point of *Conscience* to *particularize*" such alterations as he made in the text, and as a result he has been consigned "to the special hell reserved for bad editors."[22]

In the third place, Friedman points out that sometimes, as in "The Heire of Lynne," Percy's "improvements are actually improvements, as Saintsbury, and even so inveterate an enemy of ballad-tampering as Child, grudgingly admit. . . . [In "Sir Aldingar"] Percy has dropped one or two characteristic folk touches and added a few incongruous elements, but by belletristic, if not by scholarly standards, his is the better version; and of course there can be no doubt that Percy's contemporaries would have considered it infinitely preferable to the text as given."[23]

The contrast that Friedman makes between scholarly standards and belletristic standards really fixes the point at issue. There seems no doubt that Percy would have said (with Shenstone's concurrence) that in presenting poems "defac'd by Time," his primary purpose was to preserve a sense of their literary qualities rather than to preserve the literal detail of the texts. Any first-year graduate student knows, of course, how unscholarly such a procedure is. But that is hardly the issue here. One grants that many of the ballads in the *Reliques* are presented in "bad" texts. Our concern here is with how it came about that Percy chose to use a method which scholarship has long condemned. (That Percy himself was acquainted with more scrupulous methods, we shall discuss on a later page.)

Finally,[24] Friedman points out that some of the greatest poets and critics of the succeeding generation cited ballads extensively reworked by Percy as representing what authentic ballads ought to be. What I have in mind here is more than a restatement of Friedman's contention that Percy's "improvements" are *really* improvements. Rather, what Friedman implies is that, on the testimony of the greater Romantic poets, Percy's remodeling of the ballads had been done in the spirit of the old ballad makers. Thus, Friedman points out that when Wordsworth acknowledges the great debt that he and his fellow poets owed to the *Reliques,* the only ballad that he names specifically is "Sir Cauline," which H. B. Wheatley cites as "the most flagrant example of Percy's manipulation." Furthermore, the three ballads which apparently had most influence on Coleridge's *Christabel* were all ballads reworked by Percy: "The Marriage of Sir Gawaine," "The Child of Elle," and "Sir Cauline."[25]

Most striking of all of Friedman's citations is a paragraph that he quotes from Wordsworth which sharply contrasts poems such as "The Hermit of Warkworth," written by Percy "in his own person and character as a poetical writer," and poems written by Percy "under a mask," that is, written after Percy had assumed the *persona* of the ancient ballad maker. In the former case, the diction of the poem is scarcely "distinguishable from the vague, the glossy, and unfeeling language of the day." But, writes Wordsworth, when "writing under a mask," Percy had not lacked the "resolution to follow his genius into the regions of true simplicity and genuine pathos (as is evinced by the exquisite ballad of Sir Cauline and by many other pieces. . . ."[26] A parallel case, I would suggest, is Chatterton's needing to assume the mask of Rowley, an imaginary monk of the fifteenth century, in order to find his own poetic voice. Other such examples from the eighteenth century could be cited if one cared to elaborate Wordsworth's point.

Though I believe that Friedman has clearly shown that one can make out a better case for Percy "than has ever yet been pleaded for him,"[27] nevertheless Friedman himself provides the best evidence of how indelibly Percy's character as a scholar has been blackened. For Friedman sometimes seems grudging in his concessions that Percy was actually right in what he did, and Friedman is often over-suspicious of Percy's motives.[28] Percy, to be sure, was thin-skinned, and increasingly concerned with what kind of figure he might cut in the public view. But he was not deceitful or devious. Friedman's occasional intimations that Percy kept closer to a *printed* text because his deviations from it might more easily be detected can be dismissed. So can the suspicion that he sat on MSS. and denied information to fellow scholars. He was happy to aid brother scholars, as is testified by the many notes he supplied for Warton's *History of English Literature* and by the notes he provided for several of the great eighteenth-century editions of Shakespeare.

Perhaps, however, the best testimony to Percy's competence as a textual editor and his scrupulous faithfulness even to the minute details of a text is to consider his edition of *Tottel's Miscellany,*[29] which was destroyed in a fire. This work contained poems that had not been "defac'd by Time," and in preparing his edition Percy used a proper method. He tried to locate the first edition to serve as his copy text and then sought to reproduce it in the original spelling as faithfully as possible. The first and second editions of *Tottel's Miscellany* were published in 1557, and the second edition is represented by two different settings of the text. Percy used for his copy text the second setting of the second edition, which Hyder Rollins designates C.[30]

I have compared 211 lines of Percy's edition with his copy text, Rollins' C. The lines collated fall into two blocks, the first composed of 137 consecutive lines (folios 10^v—12^r of C) and the second, of 74 consecutive lines (folios 85^v—86^r). Percy felt free to alter punctuation, adding or omitting commas, converting colons into full stops, etc., in order to bring the punctuation into some conformity with eighteenth-century standards.

Besides the changes in punctuation, I have counted twenty-three instances in which Percy's edition varies from C.

Nineteen of these variations involve minute changes in spelling, capitalization, or the consolidation or separation of word elements: iewell *for* iewel, driue *for* drive, Loue *for* loue, Whoso *for* Who so, Against *for* Agaynst, etc.

Two of his alterations of spelling seem to be not errors made by the typesetter but deliberate. Thus, Percy does not follow his copy text in reading "When in her grace thou held the most, she bare," etc. He alters "held the most" to "held thee most," lest the reader misinterpret—at least momentarily—the sense. Four lines further on, where the context makes it plain that "thee" is meant, Percy preserves C's spelling: *viz.*, "that promised was to the."

Another possible instance of such deliberate alteration is his substitution of "frinde" for the text's "frend." Surrey rhymes "frend" with "minde" and Percy's change of the spelling may have been calculated to alert the reader to the fact that a rhyme was intended.

Percy's alterations that have any substantive significance amount to corrections of the text. Thus, in changing "you ferse" to "your ferse," he removes an error in C and restores the reading found in the first edition (Rollins' A). So also (in line 7 of "A warning to the louer how he is abused by his loue") he brings the line back to metrical regularity by dropping a needless adverb ("well") first introduced by B and followed by C.

In "To the ladie that scorned her louer," Percy makes line 26 read "Me checke in your degre" rather than "Me checke in such degre," thus giving rhetorical point to the passage. But this alteration rests on more than Percy's subjective judgment: he here followed the reading of the third (D) and subsequent editions. (He himself owned a copy of D.)

Percy has gone out of his way to preserve Tottel's parentheses, line indentations, etc., and in general to give his reader some notion of how the sixteenth-century text looked on the page, though he has wisely substituted a roman typeface for Tottel's black-letter. In view of the pains that Percy obviously took to produce a *literatim* text, it is a pity that a more careful job of proofreading was not done. Even so, Percy shows himself to be a cautious and highly conservative editor, who respects his text and only rarely and for substantial reasons makes deliberate departures from it.

III

THE MANUSCRIPTS

The bulk of the Percy-Shenstone correspondence is preserved in the British Library as Additional Manuscript 28221. The following note in Percy's hand appears on f. 4^r of the MS.:

N. B.

Of my Correspondence with Mr Shenstone I have here preserved almost all his Letters and Billets, however inconsiderable: But of my Own (tho' all were returned me after his Death) I have kept only a few, chiefly such as tended to explain his Letters, or were some way or other referred to in them.

T. Percy. Easton Maud^t

April 24 1765

In a note on f. 1^r Percy has written, "26 Letters from Wm Shenstone to the Revd T. Percy—19 Letters from The Revd T. Percy to W. Shenstone Esq." In this volume, however, five additional letters from Shenstone to Percy are printed: one from the library of the Historical Society of Pennsylvania, one from the Bodleian Library, and three from the Pruden Collection of the Beinecke Library at Yale. Presumably, these letters—and perhaps still others—were never returned to Percy since, one assumes, all that were returned to him except those that he did not think worth preserving are now included in British Library Add. MS. 28221. The Table of Letters shows that at least six more letters from Shenstone have to be regarded as missing.

The "Billets" having to do with Shenstone's choice of songs for the *Reliques* constitute a special case. They apparently never were a part of Add. MS. 28221. They are now preserved in the Harvard College Library.

In the present volume there are twenty-one letters from Percy to Shenstone, not the nineteen specified in the note on f. 1^r. I assume that Percy twice took two letters to be one, or perhaps simply miscounted. In any case, he is speaking very loosely and inaccurately when he writes on f. 4^r that he preserved "only a few" of his own letters. Using his own count, he has preserved nearly as many of his own letters as he has of Shenstone's.

Percy clearly did attach a great deal of importance to his correspondence with Shenstone. One such indication is the fact that, so far as I know, this correspondence is the only one that he attempted to annotate with any thoroughness. In a preliminary note on f. 3^r he tells the reader that "Mr Shenstone died before the *Reliques* had only been printed to the beginning of Book III^d of what is now the III^d Volume but was then the 1st."[31] As the reader of this correspondence will see, he sets down from time to time various other explanatory notes.

His editing of the correspondence also involved excisions of parts of the letters. Some dozen of the Add. MS. 28221 letters lack a salutation and presumably the opening paragraphs as well, or they break off without a proper conclusion. I find nothing like this proportion of fragmented letters in the other Percy correspondences. Presumably the cuts were made by Percy after the letters had come back into his possession. But whoever it was that cut away sections of the letters, it was certainly Percy who was responsible for the heavy cross-outs and deletions.

There is no need to suspect that Percy's motive was the removal of scandalous matter. The reader's inspection of what I have been able to read under the heaviest inking will readily allay all but the most stubborn suspicions. I suspect that in making his cuts and deletions, Percy simply had in mind the thought of publication. The idea of publication would account for the excisions and deletions, just as it would account for Percy's supplying of notes. His motive would be to remove unimportant personal references and references to trivial matters generally, as well as to cut out references to living people who might resent certain frank comments on their lives and works. (See, for example, Letter XXVIII below.)

It is easy to suppose that Percy thought of submitting the correspondence for publication. Shenstone had already made a name as an elegant letter writer. In 1769 Dodsley was to publish a volume of his letters, and Thomas Hull was to publish a *Select Letters* in two volumes in 1778. One can easily imagine Percy's spending an afternoon in 1765 in putting his packet of letters into what he would have regarded as decent shape to show to a publisher, though, as it turned out, none of these letters was published before the twentieth century.

Yet, whatever the reason, Percy's editing of his correspondence indicates his special relation to Shenstone as a literary guide and as a friend. Only in his letters to Farmer does he unbend from his customary formality as he does in his letters to Shenstone. How concerned he was to preserve his friend's memory and to promote his literary reputation appears in the notes and comments he made in his copy of Shenstone's *Works* (see Appendix III). It is also seen in his efforts to preserve an earlier and, to his mind, more attractive version of Shenstone's "Pastoral Ballad" (see Appendix V).

·　·　·　·　·

Notes

1. See British Library, Add. MS., 28221, f. 3ʳ.

2. See pp. 390-91. This work is hereafter cited as Williams.

3. See Letter XV *infra.*

4. This note is quoted in full in Appendix III, marginal note II, 331. In 1764 Dodsley published two volumes of *The Works in Verse and Prose of William Shenstone, Esq.; Most of which were never before printed.* A third volume was added in 1769.

5. *Bishop Percy's Folio Manuscript,* ed. by John W. Hales and Frederick J. Furnivall, London, 1867-68, 3 vols., I, lxxiv; and see also Letter VI *infra.*

6. *The Correspondence of Thomas Percy and Richard Farmer,* ed. Cleanth Brooks, Baton Rouge, 1946, p. 37.

7. *The Correspondence of Thomas Percy and David Dalrymple, Lord Hailes,* ed. A. F. Falconer, Baton Rouge, 1954, p. 49.

8. Edition of 1765, p. ix.

9. See Letter III *infra.*

10. See Letter XXXV *infra.* The plan represented a final crystallization of ideas that had been in solution for

at least a year or more. The reader will recognize some of them as having emanated from Shenstone. Evidently Johnson's primary function had been to help Percy to clarify his ideas and organize them into a coherent editorial pattern.

11. See Letter XXXIV *infra.*

12. See Letter II *infra.*

13. Edited by Ian A. Gordon, Oxford, at the Clarendon Press, 1952.

14. See Appendix II.

15. See Letters X and XX *infra.*

16. See Letter XXV *infra.*

17. See Letter XXVII *infra.*

18. See Letter II *infra.*

19. Chicago, 1961.

20. Friedman, p. 208.

21. *Ibid.,* p. 204.

22. *Ibid.,* p. 205.

23. *Ibid.,* pp. 207-208.

24. I should make clear that I am responsible for setting up these four categories and the order in which I place them, not Professor Friedman.

25. *Ibid.,* p. 210.

26. *Ibid.,* p. 212.

27. *Ibid.,* p. 206.

28. See, for example, p. 206.

29. In his letters Percy usually refers to it as "Surrey's Poems." For a detailed account of this edition, see Percy-Farmer *Correspondence,* pp. 175-200.

30. *Tottel's Miscellany,* ed. by Hyder Edward Rollins, Harvard University Press, 1928-29, 2 vols., II, 7-36. If Percy knew of the unique copy of A in the Bodleian Library, which is also dated 1557, he presumably assumed that it was identical with C.

31. See L. F. Powell's "Percy's Reliques," *The Library,* Fourth Series, IX, 121.

Cleanth Brooks (essay date 1979)

SOURCE: "The Young Thomas Percy," in *Forum,* Vol. 17, No. 2, Spring, 1979.

[*In the following essay, Brooks offers an account of Percy's writings, noting that the preponderance of negative critical attention given to the* Reliques *diminishes Percy's reputation as a scholar.*]

Thomas Percy is usually remembered as a man of one book, the celebrated **Reliques of Ancient English Poetry,** the work that Wordsworth and Coleridge were to accord the highest praise; and the **Reliques** itself is all too often thought of as simply a collection of folk ballads. The result is that Percy has acquired a modest fame as a purveyor of folk ballads who, unwittingly and almost by accident, provided a stimulus to the Romantic poets and helped bring about a momentous shift in literary taste.

Yet such an account oversimplifies and distorts Percy's real accomplishments as a scholar. It even badly falsifies the nature of the *Reliques* itself, for though the ballad content of the book is large and very important, such an estimate fails to note how much of this anthology is devoted to a general recovery of sixteenth- and seventeenth-century English literature—and, more than that, some attempt to reclaim England's medieval heritage. Let me suggest something of the extent of Percy's range.

He was, for example, the first editor to publish one of Chaucer's short lyrics ("Youre two eyn will sle me sodenly"). He included in the *Reliques* a ten-page essay on **"The Metre of Pierce Plowman's Vision."** He sought out and published texts of sixteen songs that are partially quoted, or alluded to, in Shakespeare's plays. He included in the *Reliques* a ten-page essay on "The Origin of the English Stage." He took note of, and correctly adopted, Izaak Walton's ascription of "Come live with me, and be my love" to Christopher Marlowe, and the "Reply" to Sir Walter Raleigh. (All the editions current in Percy's time had given Marlowe's song to Shakespeare.) These several examples,—all of them taken from the first edition of the *Reliques*—may suggest the range and variety of matter contained in the three small volumes. They should also convey some sense of Percy's taste and responsible scholarship.

Percy's *Reliques* was published in 1765, yet it is only one item in a total of ten separate books that he published between 1761 and 1770. As the reader will observe, this tally amounts to a book every year. They are: *Hau Kiou Choaan,* the first Chinese novel to be translated into English, 1761; *Miscellaneous Pieces Relating to the Chinese,* 1762; *The Matrons,* six tales sharing a common plot and theme, gathered from six different cultures, 1762; *Five Pieces of Runic Poetry,* 1763; *The Song of Solomon, Newly Translated,* with an introduction and elaborate notes, 1764; the *Reliques* itself, 1765; and also in 1765 *A Description of the Ride to Hulne Abbey,* an early example of an account of a picturesque landscape; *A Key to the New Testament,* 1766; the *Household Book of the Earl of Northumberland in 1512,* 1768; and a translation of Henry Mallet's *Northern Antiquities,* a translation that opened up to English readers for the first time the treasures of the Elder Edda and Norse mythology generally, 1770.

There is variety here in God's plenty as well as several pieces of pioneering work of the first importance. Percy was clearly interested in not only the older British literature but in the literature of other cultures—the Chinese, the Norse, and the Hebrew. Only one of these books, his *Key to the New Testament,* is specifically ecclesiastical in nature. His new translation of *The Song of Solomon,* as

Percy tells us, was produced because of his interest in it as a fine example of ancient pastoral poetry and in its use of oriental imagery.[1]

Yet I have still not sketched fully the whole story of Percy's activities in this period. For during this same remarkable decade, he was at work on a collection of the writings of George Villiers, second Duke of Buckingham, the author of *The Rehearsal.* He was also hard at work on an edition of *Tottel's Miscellany.* Neither the *Tottel* nor the *Buckingham* ever achieved publication, even though they were printed off in great part during the 1760's. Their completion was delayed and delayed, and both finally perished in 1808 in a warehouse fire. One copy of the *Buckingham* escaped the flames and is now in the British Museum, or as it is now known, the British Library.[2] Of the *Tottel,* four copies are known to have survived.[3]

Tonson was originally to have been the publisher of the *Tottel.* But with Tonson's death in 1767, printing was suspended. Through the next forty years Percy continued to postpone completing it. Later on he was to discover that Wyatt and Surrey manuscripts were extant and so he delayed still further in order to perfect his text of the Wyatt and Surrey poems and to add further materials. Thus, again, may I point out, the editing of the British folk ballad proves to have been only one of Percy's multiform literary interests. If we are to come to any proper estimate of Percy's rank as a literary scholar and of the range of his literary interests, it is important not to tag him with the label "ballad man." He was much more. Small wonder that Dr. Johnson paid him his compliment on the width of his learning.[4]

Percy was early elected to the celebrated literary club. Johnson paid him a long summer visit at his country vicarage in 1764, and Percy is the source of some of the most charming anecdotes about Johnson's early life.[5] As a member of the Club, Percy was associated with Goldsmith and the Wartons, Burke, and Reynolds (who, by the way, painted his portrait), and the rest of the Johnson circle.

Percy also rose rapidly in the Church, in 1778 becoming Dean of Carlisle, and in 1782, a bishop. In fact, he is always referred to as "Bishop" Percy, a circumstance that I believe has not enhanced his standing as a scholar of the first rank. We don't—at least in America—expect our bishops to be scholars. I fear that they more closely resemble junior corporation executives—at least in the Episcopal Church that seems to be so.

Percy's scholarly reputation came under sharp attack in his own lifetime. Joseph Ritson, that rather splenetic lawyer and antiquary, viciously assailed Percy's handling of his ballads and even accused him of committing forgeries. The attack was overdrawn, as Sir Walter Scott was to insist.[6] But the stigma of having been guilty of unacceptable editorial practices has endured right on down to the present day.

In the Victorian period, Frederick J. Furnivall pressed the attack. For him, Percy was a conscienceless editor who

patched and mended and polished the texts of the old ballads that he collected and edited. He did so, in Furnivall's
judgement, under a wholly mistaken notion of what their
real merit was. Furnivall did not accuse Percy of forgery;
rather, he ridiculed him as a mealy-mouthed and over-
refined parson. Percy, Furnivall remarks, was foolish
enough to try to dress up the folk ballads in eighteenth-
century costume, complete with false hair, powder, and
pomatum.[7]

Furnivall did something else to Percy's reputation almost
as damaging: he portrayed Percy as a snob, insecure about
his own social position, eager to improve it, and fawning
on his noble patrons, the Duke and Duchess of Northumberland.

In the three-volume edition of **Bishop Percy's Folio Manuscript,** which Furnivall and John W. Hales brought out in
1867-68, Furnivall taunts Percy with having been the son
of a grocer. But he does not mention the matter once and
let it drop. He makes the point over and over in subsequent footnotes.[8]

Furnivall also makes much of the fact that Percy was to
alter the spelling of his wife's name from "Gutteridge" to
the more elegant "Goodriche," and that in his early years
he spelled his own surname "Piercy" rather than "Percy."
These shifts in spelling confirm Furnivall's estimate of
Percy as a social climber.[9] One may allow that in some
sense, Percy probably was. Most of us like to better our
position. Like a great many literary men in the eighteenth
century, he was grateful to find a patron, and like most of
the eighteenth-century clergy in the Church of England, he
certainly looked after his own interests in matters of ben-
efices and preferment. So much has to be conceded, though
we ought to take into account the accepted procedures of
the age.

Yet if Furnivall had known as much as most of us now
know about the state of spelling in the earlier centuries, he
might have paid less attention to the various ways in which
names were spelled and pronounced. Franklin Pierce of
New Hampshire, the fourteenth president of the United
States, in spite of his use of an "ie" spelling, apparently
pronounced his name "Purse." So at least says Robert
Frost, who ought to know. In his poem "New Hampshire,"
Frost writes of that state:

> She had one President (pronounce him Purse,
> And make the most of it for better or worse.
> He's your one chance to score against the state).

—But not because he spelled his name with an "ie."

Percy, by the way, demolished the fanciful etymology of
the name Percy which had been popularly derived from
the following circumstance. One of the chieftains of this
family had pierced the eye of a Scottish king in the course
of his defense of Alnwick Castle. Hence he came to be
known as "pierce-eye," which designation eventually became pronounced "purse-eye" though spelled "Percy."

Thomas Percy dismissed this bit of folk-etymology by
pointing out that the Percy family, who had come over
with William the Conqueror, brought with them a family
name derived from the Norman village from which they
came. Indeed, Percy located the village in question as the
chief of the three villages named Percy, the one "situate
near Villedieu, in the election of St. Lo."[10]

Percy actually set down in writing an account of when and
why he changed the spelling of his name. Among his genealogical papers occurs a note to the effect that his father
had always spelled the family name Piercy and that so had
he until 1756. In that year, however, he had discovered
that "in the old Registers of Worcester [the city from which
the family had originally come] it had been written Percy."
Consequently, in August, 1756, when the Earl of Sussex
presented him to the Rectory of Wilbye, he took care to
have his name written Percy in the "Instruments of [his]
Institution, Dispensation, etc."

When Percy wrote this note some years later he may have
already heard whispers about his motive for having done
so. For he points out in his note that long before, in 1756,
he had not had the "most distant hope of being ever known
to the Duke and Duchess (then Earl and Countess) of
Northumberland: The first time I had the honour to be introduced to either of them being November of 1764."[11]

Percy's father apparently was a grocer. But what of it?
The fact never seemed to trouble Dr. Johnson, the son of a
provincial bookseller, nor Oliver Goldsmith, the son of a
poor Irish clergyman, nor of such of Percy's friends as
were clearly gentry or of noble blood. It would seem that
it is Furnivall who is the snob, aghast that Thomas Percy
should dare to get above his breeding.

The fact is that Percy had no need to be ashamed of his
family. His great-grandfather had in 1662 been Mayor of
the city of Worcester. Percy had relatives of solid stock
scattered all over Worcestershire and Shropshire. Percy's
father was a burgess of his native city of Bridgnorth and
before he suffered severe financial losses, owned estates in
Bridgnorth and Worcester. The house in which our Thomas Percy was born is still standing, a rather elegant tim-
bered structure dating back to 1580.

In view of his talents and the really remarkable quality
and extent of his publications, Percy's rise in the world of
letters and in the Church is not in the least surprising. The
eighteenth-century Church of England was the great propa-
gator of historical and literary scholarship. Even those
who have chided the clergy of that rather tepid century for
the lack of fervent piety and for indifference to the state of
the poor, concede that the Church fostered and rewarded
scholarly accomplishment. Bishop William Warburton,
who edited Shakespeare and was Alexander Pope's literary
executor; Bishop Richard Hurd, author of *Letters on Chivalry and Romance*; Thomas Warton, whose *Observations
on the Faerie Queene* was a very significant work and
who wrote the first history of English poetry; Richard

Farmer, who wrote the seminal essay on Shakespeare's learning; and Edward Lye, who edited the *Etymologicum Anglicanum*—all of them were Church of England clergymen.

Yet, Furnivall's aspersions aside—his intimations that Percy was socially aggressive, self-seeking, and given to toadying to noblemen—it might be interesting to examine the specific steps by which Percy began his ecclesiastical and literary career. The examination may even provide some insight into the class system as it obtained in eighteenth-century England.

As a youth Percy had distinguished himself intellectually. He was elected from the Newport School to one of the newly-founded Careswell Exhibitions at Christ Church, Oxford. An "exhibition" provides less money and confers less honor than a scholarship proper; nevertheless, it was a meritorious achievement. At Oxford in 1747 Percy was elected to another exhibition, that founded by the redoubtable Dr. Fell. Percy took his A.B. in 1750; his M.A. in 1753; and was presented to a living in the disposition of Christ Church College. It was a modest preferment, the vicarage of Easton Mauduit in Northamptonshire. For some three years, however, Percy served as a curate nearer home, and did not take up residence at Easton Mauduit until 1756. The country seat of the Earl of Sussex happened to be in the village of Easton Mauduit, and Percy soon became acquainted with the Earl.

Easton Mauduit is, by the way, a pretty village with a charming fourteenth-century church. Now, in the twentieth century, the village is still very small, and it has obviously always been small. A nobleman who liked to spend at least part of the year in the country on his estates normally found it pleasant to have near at hand someone who was well-read, who would be almost invariably a graduate of one or the other of the two ancient universities, and a man who knew something of the great world outside the village. If this parish priest also happened to be of a lively mind and pleasant disposition, he could on occasion prove a welcome addition to a dinner party or useful in the nobleman's library or helpful in composing a document or drafting an important letter.

Percy's *Journal*[12] indicates that from the very beginning he saw a great deal of the Earl of Sussex. Witness such entries for the year 1756 as the following: May 22, "Ld Sussex treated me at Opera." May 20, "My Lord gave me a scarf"—signifying that Sussex had accepted him as his personal chaplain. On July 19, Percy notes that he was to dinner with the Earl and other guests and after tea "Walk'd with my Lord." On July 22, "My Lord and I went to Comb Abbey." In London, on August 2, "Found Capt Monson with my Lord—walk'd with my Lord." September 26, 'Din'd with [my Lord] . . . Evening with [him]."

Augustus, Yelverton, the second Earl of Sussex, was scarcely two years older than Percy. The two young men obviously hit it off well, for within a few weeks of Percy's taking up residence in Easton Mauduit, the Earl had presented Percy with the living of Wilbye. In 1758 the second Earl died suddenly and was succeeded by his brother Henry. Yet for Percy, Henry proved almost as good a friend and patron as had his elder brother. Percy, by the way, became well acquainted with the grandmother of the second and third Earls. She was Barbara, Viscountess de Longueville, who died, almost a hundred years old, in 1763. On her death, Percy remarked to a friend: "I have lost an excellent Chronicle and valuable friend."[13]

Granted the patronage system of the time, it was perfectly natural that Percy should have dedicated his translation of the Chinese novel to the Countess of Sussex, the third Earl's wife, and his ***Chinese Miscellanies*** to the Viscountess, the third Earl's grandmother.

There is no doubt that Percy felt genuine gratitude toward the Yelvertons, just as there is no reason to doubt that the young Earls of Sussex had from the first valued Percy and enjoyed his company. Furnivall notes that it was the Earl of Sussex who introduced Percy to the Earl of Northumberland and to his Countess,[14] the last descendant of the Northumberland Percys, to whom Percy dedicated his ***Reliques*** in 1765.

The fortunes of the Northumberlands were on the rise. The Earl soon became the Duke of Northumberland, and with the advocacy of this powerful friend at court to call attention to Percy's literary and scholarly achievements, Percy's road to ecclesiastical promotion became relatively easy. In 1778 he was made Dean of Carlisle and in 1782 consecrated Bishop of Dromore.

So much for how Percy became acquainted with his noble patrons. It is time to turn to what is a more interesting matter: namely, how he became acquainted with the literary scholars and distinguished men of letters of his time.

The greatest of these figures was, of course, Samuel Johnson, and Percy met him very early, indeed in 1756.[15] Percy was, we ought to remind ourselves, at that time a young man, only 26 or 27. Many years later he was to tell Robert Anderson how he had become acquainted with Johnson. "It was through his intimacy with Dr. Grainger [who was] a familiar visitant in Gough-square."[16] The late David Nichol Smith has dated Percy's meeting with James Grainger in September of 1756.[17] If the date is correct, Grainger had lost no time in introducing his new friend to Dr. Johnson.

In view of Johnson's subsequent laughter at some of Grainger's poetry and of his several disparaging remarks about Grainger's character,[18] Percy's statement that Grainger was in 1756 "a familiar visitant in Gough-square" is interesting. Johnson did not suffer fools gladly, and he had small patience with men of no principle, into which class Boswell records he once placed Grainger. I wish we knew more about the whole Johnson-Grainger relationship.

I also wish we knew more about Grainger himself. Grainger was a north countryman, a doctor of medicine, a translator of Tibullus, author of the familiar "Ode of Solitude," which appears in Dodsley's *Collection,* and of a curious didactic poem entitled "The Sugar Cane," a work that reflects the years that he spent in the sugar islands of the West Indies.

Percy valued Grainger as a man and as a poet. He seems to have entertained for Grainger a warm affection and mourned his early death at the age of forty-five.

Whatever his own literary and other merits, Grainger evidently had a wide acquaintance in literary London, for he introduced Percy not only to Johnson but to Goldsmith—on 21 February 1759, as Percy records in his *Journal.*

The date is worth noting, for it shows that Percy met Goldsmith over two years before Johnson met Goldsmith. In fact, it would seem to have been Percy who made the formal introduction of Goldsmith to Johnson. In the Memoir of Goldsmith, published in Volume I of the *Collected Works of Goldsmith,* 1801, nearly all of which was from Percy's own pen, Percy tells us of a supper that Goldsmith gave on 31 May 1761 to which Goldsmith had invited Johnson and other literary friends.[19]

He writes: "One of the company then invited [it was Percy himself], being intimate with our great Lexicographer, was desired to call upon him and take him with him. As they went together, the former [that is, Percy] was much struck with the studied neatness of Johnson's dress: he had on a new suit of cloaths, a new wig nicely powdered and every thing about him so perfectly dissimilar from his usual habits and appearance, that [he] could not help inquiring the cause of this singular transformation. 'Why sir,' said Johnson, 'I hear that Goldsmith, who is a very great sloven, justifies his disregard of cleanliness and decency, by quoting my practice, and I am desirous this night to show him a better example.'" In his *Journal* (for 31 May 1761) however, Percy was more laconic. He refers to the incident only as follows: "Evening at Goldsmith's with much company."[20]

The story of this memorable meeting is familiar to all Johnsonians, but I am concerned here to connect it with Percy. So also with another well-known story about Goldsmith having been found by a visitor lodged "in a wretched dirty room, in which there was but one chair, and when he, from civility, offered it to his visitant, himself was obliged to sit in the window."[21] Then follows, as many readers will remember, the entry into the room of "a poor ragged little girl of very decent behaviour . . . who, dropping a curtsie, said, 'My mamma sends her compliments, and begs the favour of you to lend her a chamber-pot full of coals." The visitant was Percy himself, and it is to his Memoir of Goldsmith that we owe the story.

If the young Percy was at this time of his life already on occasion dining at Lord Sussex's table, he evidently did not shrink from contact with the squalid life of Grub Street. What is left of his *Journal* for such years as 1756-7-8-9 shows that he was frequently with Johnson and Grainger. For one whose visits to London could be only occasional, he managed to see a great deal of both of them.

Johnson's encouragement was a powerful motive to Percy to undertake the *Reliques.* But it was William Shenstone who actually supplied much specific help in making the selection of songs and ballads and, as Percy acknowledges in his Preface, settling "the plan of the work." Shenstone indeed turned out to be for his younger friend both his good and his bad angel—his bad angel only in that he encouraged Percy to mend and patch the often mutilated ballad texts with which Percy was presented in his Folio Manuscript. Though Percy's love for the older literature was perfectly genuine, he nevertheless valued—I should say overvalued—both Shenstone's poetry and Shenstone's taste.

I think that there can be no doubt, however, that Shenstone also had a genuine love for the ballads as poetry, even though his own verse is too consciously elegant in the conventional eighteenth-century manner. For better or worse, then, Shenstone had much to do with both the virtues and the defects of the 1765 *Reliques.*

Percy seems to have become acquainted with Shenstone about a year after his first meeting with Johnson. The earliest letter in the Percy-Shenstone correspondence is dated 24 November 1757 and a note written on it by Shenstone reads: "Mr Percy is domestic Chaplain to the Earl of Sussex; and has Genius and Learning accompany'd with great vivacity."[22] This note suggests that their acquaintance had not been of any long standing.

It is worth inquiring into how Percy came to meet Shenstone, primarily because of Shenstone's powerful influence on the selection and arrangement of the separate songs and ballads which make up the *Reliques.* Had Percy not met with Shenstone just when he did, the *Reliques* might have become a rather different sort of book, both as to content and as to editorial method. But to trace the way in which Percy got to know his principal advisor yields a special dividend. It provides an insight into an aspect of eighteenth-century English life that modern Americans are likely to overlook. I refer to the extended family and the way in which any young man in the period would naturally, and quite without self-consciousness, make use of his widely ramified family connections and interconnections. Moreover, it will lead me back to where I began this paper: the matter of Thomas Percy's origins and his position in society. I make these secondary points because I think that it is highly likely that Percy's acquaintance with Shenstone came about through the perfectly natural channels provided by what the sociologists nowadays call "a kinship society."

Before returning to Percy's first letter to Shenstone, written in November 1757, I want to call attention to the early pages of Percy's *Journal,* especially for the years 1753-59—or rather, I should say, call attention to the extant entries for those years, for, I must repeat, the *Journal* has been heavily edited, not to say mutilated. No entries at all are preserved for some years and rarely more than a few weeks for any given year. Yet the fragmentary entries that remain provide eloquent testimony to the young Percy's close relations with such members of his family as had migrated from the counties of Shropshire and Worcestershire to London. But concrete examples will make my point much more vividly than any mere generalization can.

Sunday, 25 November 1753: "Breakfast at coffee house [;] at St. Clements—Mr Oldbrook Prayers, Mr Jones preach'd—All [Cousin] P[errin's] Family at Mr John Perins [.] At St. Clements Church Mr Oldbrook preach'd without Notes—Sup[per] and evening at Mr John Perin's."[23]

Now John Perrins was a London distiller. He married Mary Percy, the daughter of Thomas Percy's great-uncle. "Cuz Perrins," as Percy refers to him, was Frank Perrins, John Perrins's son. The Perrins family, it turns out, had originally come from Worchestershire, and when today we read the label on a bottle of Lea and Perrins Worchestershire Sauce, we probably receive an echo of that family name.

Next day, on Monday, November 26, Percy records that he dined at "Cuz Perrins" and found T. Woodington there, and thenceforward spent his nights at Woodington's until he left London on December 13. Now Thomas Woodington was another relative of Percy's. Both were descendants of Mary Taylor. By her first marriage to Dr. John Percy, she was Percy's great-great-grandmother; by her second marriage to a Mr. Meysey, she was Woodington's great-grandmother.[24]

The next day, November 27, Percy dined at Mr. Perrins's and treated his cousin, Frank Perrins, to the theater to see *The Beaux Stratagem.* Two days later, on Thursday, November 29, he called on Mr. Nott. This was Anthony Nott, the eldest son of Anthony Nott, a plumber and a glazier. The younger Nott was a first cousin of Percy's mother, Jane Nott Percy. Percy was to write of him in his "Account of the Percy Family" that he lived "at Boswell Court near Carey Street London" and that he had "a country seat and good Estate at Horsted in Sussex."[25]

Yet it ought to be noted that some others of Percy's kin had not been so successful. Nevertheless, though they had not been, Percy duly records their status. For example, he mentions one of his relatives, another Thomas Percy, as "a cabinet maker in London living in 1756 (still living in 1775)."[26] The last phrase indicates that Percy had evidently looked him up personally long after he had become chaplain to the Duke of Northumberland. He mentions another relative, Mary Percy Taylor, who "being left a widow with several children, kept a boarding School for young ladies: I remember to have been at her house in the year 1736 or 7."[27]

Percy mentions also another relative, one Edward Percy who died in 1735. Percy notes that this Edward was "a Clothier and latterly lived in London: but having been very unprosperous in his fortune retired a year or two before his death to his brother Arthur Percy at Bridgnorth [Percy's home town], who very cordially received him, and in whose house he died."[28]

These genealogical notes are by the same man who was proud that one of his great-grandfathers was the father of John Cleveland, the Cavalier poet, and who, to the shock and horror of Professor Funivall, dared to explore the possibility that the Worcestershire Percys, from whom he was descended, might have sprung from a cadet branch of the proud Northumberland Percys.

Yet, as I have just noted, in the elaborate genealogies that Thomas Percy worked out and on which I have been drawing for the matter of this paper, his obscure relatives appear, and Percy seems perfectly willing to record the circumstances of those who were "in trade" as clothiers, cabinet makers, and distillers. Though he destroyed perhaps eighty percent of his daily *Journal,* he did not destroy the genealogical tables he had searched out so carefully. Fie! For shame, Professor Funivall. It is you who have raised the issue of snobbery. The evidence would indicate that it recoils upon your own head.

Does not, however, the very existence of these elaborate genealogical charts indicate that Percy had an unhealthy interest in his family's antecedents? Not, I should say, in the context of times. A kinship society is always interested in these matters, even when they are not searched out and written down in detailed genealogical charts. It is clear that the young Percy in 1753, just twenty-three or twenty-four years old, knew very well, long before he had set down the exact birth and death dates and written down the family pedigrees, who his London relatives were—even those who were by our standards very remote cousins indeed. A kinship society has long memories and a lively oral tradition.

A quite incidental remark may be worth making here: it is interesting to note how many of Percy's relatives whose roots go back to Worcestershire or Shropshire had rather recently removed to London. I suspect that these represent only particular instances of a general movement from the provinces to the metropolis that was going on at this period.

In this paper I shall not try to note all Percy's relatives that are mentioned in his *Journal*—the Haslewoods and the Smiths and the Congreves, for example. In this matter of cousins, Percy, like Sir Joseph Porter in the Gilbert and Sullivan operetta, *H.M.S. Pinafore,* had enough cousins to number them by dozens. But it is high time to return to the matter I broached earlier: how Percy came to make his acquaintance with William Shenstone. I have already adumbrated the answer: through his relatives and his county connections.

I make mention of his "county connections" because they were important for Percy and it would appear that they were also important to Shenstone. Though living on the fringes of the great city of Birmingham, Shenstone considered himself to be a Salopian—a Shropshire man. And with good reason, for Halesowen, where he lived, was at this time still a detached portion of the County of Shropshire. There is plenty of evidence that Shenstone valued the Shropshire connection. The Wrekin, that great landmark for all Shropshire men—one recalls references to it in A. E. Housman's *A Shropshire Lad*—the Wrekin, though thirty miles distant, was clearly visible from The Leasowes, Shenstone's estate. Moreover, in his grounds Shenstone had placed a seat from which to view it. On the back of this seat, which was "so contrived as to form a table or pedestal for a bowl," he had inscribed the legend: "To all friends round the Wrekin."[29]

One need not, of course, take this gesture too seriously. Much more important for my argument is the fact that Shenstone had a large number of Shropshire friends, with whom he kept in touch. In one of his early letters to Percy, Shenstone mentions having recently had a visit from Charles Baldwyn, an M.P. for Shropshire, and Col. John Cotes of Woodcote in Shropshire. Later, in the same letter, he mentions having been recently visited by a Mr. Slaney, who was probably either Plowden or Robert Slaney, both of Hatton Grange, Shropshire.[30] Robert Slaney was later to marry the daughter of Col. Cotes. His brother Plowden was, in 1761, to marry Martha Pitt, the daughter and coheiress of Humphrey Pitt, of Shifnall, in Shropshire.[31]

In this same letter, Shenstone tells us that Slaney was accompanied by Humphrey Pitt who, Shenstone writes, "says he gave you those old Ballads." The collection referred to was, of course, the celebrated Folio MS. which Percy had found "lying dirty on the floor under a Bureau in the Parlour," the leaves of which were being used by the maids to light the fire.[32]

With this mention of Pitt's name we obviously get close to Thomas Percy himself. Pitt was, by the way, the uncle of the Rev. Robert Binnel, rector of Shenton and Kimberton, and minister of Newport, all Shropshire villages.[33] Binnel had been an exact contemporary of Shenstone's at Pembroke College, Oxford. Binnel's wife was, indeed, a distant relation of Percy. The Mary Taylor mentioned on an earlier page, was by her first marriage a great-great-grandmother of Thomas Percy, and by her second marriage, the great-grandmother of Mary Congreve, the wife of Robert Binnel.[34] The relation may seem remote to us; but not to Percy, who valued his relation to the Congreve family.

Since Binnel had been acquainted with Shenstone at Oxford, the two men had known each other for many years. Shenstone had also known Humphrey Pitt, Binnel's uncle and patron, for many years. One of Shenstone's letters to Pitt is dated as early as September 1741 and a letter of his to Binnel as early as 1745.

Thus, it was not Percy who introduced Pitt and Binnel to Shenstone. It must have been the other way around. Just which of these two friends of Shenstone actually made the introduction, I cannot say; but it seems plain that the young Percy probably met Shenstone through the mediation of one or the other of these two friends. In fact, the remarkable thing is that Percy and Shenstone had not been brought together earlier.

It was Percy, by the way, who introduced Grainger to Shenstone,[35] and it was Percy who tried very hard to introduce Shenstone to Johnson. Because of the natural inertia of both men and perhaps because of Shenstone's timidity, Percy did not succeed. This circumstance must have galled Percy when he read years later Johnson's rather grudging and unsympathetic life of Shenstone. Yet it is hard to believe that had the two men met, Johnson would have made a really different estimate of the master of *The Leasowes*.

In temperament and personality Johnson and Shenstone seem to represent polar extremes. Yet Percy genuinely admired both men, and that fact says something about Percy's own width of sympathies and his disposition to do a bit of hero-worshipping. Percy complained to Shenstone that Johnson never fulfilled his promises to help with the editing of the **Reliques,** though the dedication, as Percy confessed later, was largely Johnson's contribution. Shenstone, on the other hand, helped rather too much—at least according to modern editorial standards. But that is another story.

Notes

1. *The Correspondence of Thomas Percy and Richard Farmer,* ed. Cleanth Brooks (Baton Rouge: L.S.U. Press, 1946), pp. 40-41 and footnotes 9 and 11.

2. For a history of the Buckingham edition, see *The Correspondence of Thomas Percy and Thomas Warton,* ed. M. G. Robinson and Leah Dennis (Baton Rouge: L.S.U. Press, 1951), pp. 148-67.

3. For a history of the Tottel edition, see *The Percy-Farmer Correspondence,* pp. 175-200.

4. See Boswell's *Life of Samuel Johnson,* ed. G. B. Hill, rev. L. F. Powell, 6 vols. (Oxford: Clarendon, 1934-50), III, 278.

5. Robert Anderson, *The Life of Samuel Johnson,* 3rd ed. (Edinburgh, 1815), *passim.*

6. See his "Introductory Remarks on Popular Poetry" (1830) in *The Minstrelsy of the Scottish Border,* ed. T. F. Henderson, 4 vols. (Edinburgh, London, and New York, 1902), I, 1-54.

7. *Bishop Percy's Folio Manuscript,* ed. John W. Hales and Frederick J. Furnivall, 3 vols. (London: Trübner, 1867-68), I, xvi-xxiii.

8. *Percy's Folio MS,* I xx, xxvii and n. 2, xxix, n. 1, and lix and n. 1.

9. *Percy's Folio MS,* I, xxxii, n. 1 and xxvii, n. 1 and n. 2.

10. See Arthur Collins, *The Peerage of England,* 5th ed., 8 vols. (London, 1779), II, 280. In a letter to Edmond Malone, Percy wrote that he had "made innumerable corrections and additions to [the account] of the Northumb^d Family" as printed in Collins' fifth edition.

11. This note in Percy's hand is written on one of some dozen pages of genealogical (and other) notes associated (mistakenly, perhaps?) with British Library, Add. MS. 32, 336.

12. British Library, Add. MS. 32, 336-37. The quotations that follow in this article are all taken from Add. MS. 32, 336.

13. *Percy-Farmer Correspondence,* p. 33.

14. *Percy's Folio MS,* I, xxxix, n. 2.

15. Boswells' *Life of Johnson,* I, 48, n. 2.

16. Anderson, p. 285.

17. From a MS note by Nichol Smith, now in my possession.

18. *The Correspondence of James Boswell with Certain Members of the Club,* ed. Charles N. Fifer (New York: McGraw-Hill, 1976), pp. 327-31, and notes.

19. *The Collected Works of Goldsmith* was published in London in 4 vols. The quotation from it which follows occurs on pp. 62-63.

20. British Library, Add. MS. 32, 336: entry for 31 May 1761.

21. *Collected Works of Goldsmith,* I, 61.

22. *The Correspondence of Thomas Percy and William Shenstone,* ed. Cleanth Brooks (New Haven: Yale, 1977), p. 3, n. 14.

23. See Percy's "Account of the Private Family of Percy, formerly of Worcester, afterwards of Bridgnorth Shropshire," British Library, Add. MS. 32, 326, f. 9^v.

24. British Library, Add. MS. 32, 326, f. 12^v.

25. British Library, Add. MS. 32, 326, f. 19^v and f. 20^v.

26. British Library, Add. MS. 32, 326, f. 5^v, 6^v, and 7^r.

27. British Library, Add. MS. 32, 326, f. 8^r.

28. British Library, Add. MS. 32, 326, f. 9^r and 10^r.

29. *The Works of William Shenstone, Esq.,* 2 vols. (London: Dodsley, 1764, (a third volume was added in 1769), II, 348.

30. *Percy-Shenstone Correspondence,* pp. 17 and 19.

31. *Percy-Shenstone Correspondence,* p. 19, n. 18.

32. *Percy-Shenstone Correspondence,* I, lxxi^v.

33. *Percy-Shenstone Correspondence,* p. vii.

34. British Library, Add. MS. 32, 326, f. 25^v.

35. *Percy-Shenstone Correspondence,* p. 17.

Bertram H. Davis (essay date 1981)

SOURCE: "The *Reliques of Ancient English Poetry,*" in *Thomas Percy,* Twayne, 1981, pp. 72-108.

[*In the following excerpt, Davis examines Percy's* Reliques, *analyzing the text's sources and providing an overview of its contents and a brief survey of its various editions.*]

The eighteenth-century ballad revival has been so intimately associated with the ***Reliques of Ancient English Poetry*** that it has been easy to overlook the fact that Percy's compilation marks the end of an era of ballad interest as well as a beginning.[1] Most students of the period are familiar with Joseph Addison's 1711 *Spectator* papers, numbers 70 and 74, which dignified "Chevy Chase" with both high praise and serious critical analysis. Fewer are aware of the published volumes of verse that Percy, assisted by William Shenstone, turned over page by page in search of the gems that would help to distinguish his collection. Without them the ***Reliques*** would not merely have been different. It might never have come into existence at all.

I THE BACKGROUND OF THE *RELIQUES*

Of the 175 poems in the first edition of the ***Reliques,*** only about fifty can be traced directly to the folio manuscript which was the starting point of Percy's work. For the rest Percy had to seek elsewhere, and even for those in his own manuscript he welcomed the opportunity to collate and compare which the discovery of other versions permitted. Of the poems or alternate versions not yet known to him, some could be found only in manuscripts preserved in such archives as the Bodleian Library, the British Museum, and the library of Magdalene College at Cambridge, where Percy devoted eleven days in August, 1761, to transcribing ballads from the extraordinary Pepys collection of black-letter broadsides.[2] Others might be tucked away in published volumes of the late seventeenth and early eighteenth centuries which brought together songs, ancient ballads, and broadsides, at times in indiscriminate profusion, but always with the possibility that even the crudest mass might yield an occasional diamond. Three of the best-known ballads, "Johnnie Armstrong," "Little Musgrave," and "The Miller and the King's Daughter," had been published in *Wit Restor'd* as early as 1658 and reprinted in *Wit and Drollery* in 1682; and in Henry Bold's *Latine Songs* of 1685 a number of ballads, draped in the rich velvet of classical Latin, peered uncomfortably at their humbler English counterparts on facing pages. One ballad so transformed was "Chevy Chase"—"Ludus Chevinus" in its Latin finery—which, according to Bold, had been raised to its exalted state by order of the bishop of London![3] Thomas D'Urfey's *Pills to Purge Melancholy,* tapped by Percy for some half a dozen ballad texts, saw the old century out and the new century in with its five volumes published between 1698 and 1714, and in 1702 the publisher Jacob Tonson helped the eighteenth century off to a good start with one of his several *Poetical Miscellanies,* where

"Chevy Chase" in both native and Roman costumes rubbed shoulders with a number of songs from the seventeenth-century "drolleries" and "garlands." "Ludus Chevinus," surprisingly enough, was to be reprinted another three times before the end of the decade, and, as Albert Friedman notes, Bold's Latin translation may have inspired Addison to cite a number of classical parallels in his analysis of the English ballad.[4]

The primary object of Percy's quest was what has come to be known as the traditional or popular ballad. This was the type of early English or Scottish poem that Percy, born too soon to be schooled in folk-ballad theory, looked upon as the work of the minstrels, those "genuine successors of the ancient Bards who united the arts of Poetry and Music, and sung verses to the harp, of their own composing."[5] The quest was his major effort in the grandiose project of recovering the ancient poetry of various nations, and that fact accounts in part for his concern to date the ballads in the *Reliques* and to distinguish the minstrel ballads from the printed broadsides of a later date. The single-sheet broadsides had flourished as the art of printing developed and the English reading public increased, but their partisan political bent, their frequent bawdiness and scurrility, and their sheer numbers had brought the ballad into such disrepute in fashionable circles that Percy was never quite ready to admit that his work was anything but an idle amusement—"a relaxation from graver studies," as he described it in his 1765 preface (I, xiv).

The word "ballad" was often applied to poems that we would not consider ballads today, and Percy himself did not always discriminate. Anything that could be sung or that contained a narrative might be termed a ballad. In his *Dictionary* Johnson defined "ballad" as simply "A song" and quoted in illustration a deprecating comment of Isaac Watts: "*Ballad* once signified a solemn and sacred song, as well as trivial, when Solomon's Song was called the *ballad of ballads*; but now it is applied to nothing but trifling verse." In the cheaply printed seventeenth-century collections, poems of all kinds tended to be lumped together as ballads; and in volume 1 of the *Reliques* the book entitled "Ballads that illustrate Shakespeare" includes lyrics like "A Song to the Lute in Musicke" and "Take Those Lips Away." Nor could Percy always readily distinguish between the ballad of later invention—the broadside—and the minstrel ballad, since a number of the early ballads were printed in broadsides in the seventeenth and eighteenth centuries, and the origins of many were so obscure as to be quite indeterminate. Of "Chevy Chase" Percy published both a "minstrel" version printed by Thomas Hearne in 1719 from an Ashmole Library manuscript and the later broadside version praised by Addison in his *Spectator* papers (I, 1-17; 231-46).

In consultation with William Shenstone, Percy systematically leafed through such collections as Allan Ramsay's *Tea-Table Miscellany* (1723) and *The Evergreen* (1724), Elizabeth Cooper's *The Muses Library* (1737), Edward Capell's *Prolusions* (1760), and the anonymously compiled *The Hive* (1721) and *The Vocal Miscellany* (1734).[6] The anonymous *Collection of Old Ballads* (1723-1725) contained the texts of some twenty-five poems later published in the *Reliques,* although many of them had come to Percy's attention through other compilations as well. The format of the *Collection*—three volumes, with each containing early and late poems arranged in chronological order—was essentially the format that Percy adopted for the *Reliques,* although he gave it considerably more variety and interest by dividing each volume into three sections with separate chronological developments, and by grouping a number of poems with common themes or origins: Northumberland ballads, for example, mad songs, and ballads that illustrate Shakespeare. In the quality of its selections, the *Collection of Old Ballads,* which concentrated upon historical ballads, was in no way a match for the *Reliques.*[7]

Ballads, then, even if they lacked the stature of other kinds of poetry, were a commonplace of eighteenth-century English life long before Percy became aware of them; and, only a few years before the *Reliques,* James Macpherson's publication of the so-called Erse fragments had raised the interest in the poetry of ancient Britain to a new pitch. If Macpherson helped to direct Percy's attention to Scotland, from which he drew more than a dozen ballads for the *Reliques,* Percy's own alertness and curiosity, as well as a singular stroke of good luck, can be credited with arousing his interest in balladry in the first place. In a note which he inscribed on the flyleaf of his folio manuscript on November 7, 1769, Percy explained how the manuscript had come into his possession some years earlier:

> This very curious old Manuscript in its present mutilated state, but unbound and sadly torn &c., I rescued from destruction, and begged at the hands of my worthy friend Humphrey Pitt Esq., then living at Shiffnal in Shropshire, afterwards of Priorslee, near that town; who died very lately at Bath (viz. in Summer 1769). I saw it lying dirty on the floor under a Bureau in y⁰ Parlour: being used by the Maids to light the fires.[8]

Pitt was the uncle of the Reverend Robert Binnel, who had assisted Percy with the *Song of Solomon* and joined with him in contributing to Grainger's edition of Tibullus. Probably Percy came upon the manuscript sometime during his curacies of Astley abbots and Tasley, when he would have been in frequent company with his Shropshire friends; that is, between late 1751 and early 1756. Although he had had presence enough to shield the manuscript from the searing hands of Humphrey Pitt's maids, Percy confessed that he did not at first recognize its full value. As a result he had himself torn out one or two of its pages and sent the manuscript to a binder, who trimmed the top and bottom margins so closely that some parts of the text were cut away.[9] As for publication, it was Johnson who first impressed Percy with the manuscript's possibilities. In the opening letter of his correspondence with Shenstone, written on November 24, 1757, Percy noted that he had the manuscript in his possession and that Johnson had expressed a desire to see it printed.[10] On December 20 of that year he compiled a list of the manuscript's contents, and he began the actual work of editing the following summer.[11]

Once owned by Thomas Blount, author of the 1679 *Jocular Tenures,* the folio manuscript seems to have been compiled about 1650 by a Lancashire native of diverse tastes.[12] Its 500 pages included seventeen romances, twenty-four metrical histories, about a hundred miscellaneous songs, some broadside ballads, and forty-five which the great nineteenth-century ballad scholar Francis Child classified as popular ballads. Of these a number are incomplete: "The Marriage of Sir Gawaine," for example, had six gaps of nine stanzas each. Printing such a manuscript, or selections from it, might have afforded Percy a welcome challenge; an attempt to fill in the gaps, fruitless though it might at times have proved, would alone have required the kind of search in manuscript and printed sources that he delighted in. But in conference with Shenstone, Percy steadily worked out a plan to supplement selected ballads and songs from his own manuscript with others of similar merit, and to edit them in such a way as to make them acceptable to the general reading public. The book, originally projected in two volumes but later extended to three, was thus seen as an anthology of English poetry, with emphasis upon the early ballads of the minstrels and the lyrics of such sixteenth- and seventeenth-century poets as Shakespeare, Marlowe, Jonson, Suckling, Carew, and Crashaw. *Reliques of Ancient English Poetry: Consisting of Old Heroic Ballads, Songs, and Other Pieces of Our Earlier Poets, (Chiefly of the Lyric Kind.) Together with Some Few of Later Date*—such was its complete title. Because of their length, the romances of Percy's manuscript were to be excluded, as were the longest of the ballads and those which offended morality and decency. The restriction to English poetry was not so rigorously enforced as to exclude Scottish ballads or even Percy's own translations of the Spanish "Rio Verde, Rio Verde" and "Alcanzor and Zayda," the first of which was printed with its Spanish original.

Percy was in touch with Shenstone at just about every step of the way. Indeed, as more than one writer has noted, Percy always seemed happy to find someone to help him make decisions; and his reliance on Shenstone was so extensive that he tended to think of his friend as a partner rather than a consultant in his enterprise. He took very seriously the ratings which Shenstone assigned to each of the poems in the collections they perused, even though he did not always concur in them. From Shenstone came advice on the importance of alternating long and short poems, on organization, on the illustrations and the layout, and even on the desirability of an uncrowded title page.[13] Shenstone's continuing concern, however, was that the antiquarian in Percy not select poems only for their antiquity, and that the scholar not edit the collection in such a way as to discourage readers of taste.[14] Referring to the way in which corrupt and fragmentary texts might be handled, he wrote to Percy on October 1, 1760, as follows:

> I believe I shall *never* make any objection to such *Improvements* as you bestow upon them; unless you were

plainly to *contradict* Antiquity, which I am pretty sure will never be the Case.

> As to alterations of a *word or two,* I do not esteem it a point of *Conscience* to *particularize them* on *this* occasion. Perhaps, where a whole *Line* or *More* is alter'd, it may be proper enough to give some Intimation of it. The Italick type may answer this purpose, if you do not employ it on other occasions. It will have the appearance of a modern *Toe* or *Finger,* which is *allowably* added to the best old Statues: And I think I should always let the Publick imagine, that these were owing to *Gaps,* rather than to *faulty Passages.*

(72-73)

Percy, whose initial preference was for a minimally corrected text, was to go beyond the limits contemplated by Shenstone in this letter, with consequences which will be considered later in this chapter.

II PUBLISHING THE *RELIQUES*

With his preliminary work behind him, the indefatigable Percy set out in 1761 to secure the keys that would open the country's remaining ballad sources to him. On April 13, 1761, more than a month before signing a contract with Robert Dodsley—"Sold Dodsley my old Ballads," Percy recorded in his diary on May 22—he applied for admission to the Reading Room of the British Museum, where he was to find a dozen ballad texts he later made use of in the *Reliques.*[15] On May 28 he sent off a letter informing Thomas Warton at Oxford of his project and inquiring about materials in the Oxford libraries and the possibility of obtaining access to them. On July 21 he began a long correspondence with the Welsh scholar Evan Evans, and by May of 1762 he was exchanging friendly letters with Richard Farmer at Cambridge. On November 10, 1762, he introduced himself by letter to David Dalrymple in Edinburgh, Shenstone's efforts to gain the assistance of John McGowan having been largely unavailing, at least for the time being.[16] Evans understandably lent his best assistance with works like *Five Pieces of Runic Poetry* and *Northern Antiquities* rather than with the *Reliques,* but Warton and Farmer proved to be indispensable contacts at the two universities, and Dalrymple, in addition to other help, supplied such treasures from Scottish balladry that Percy dislodged a number of poems from his original contents in order to accommodate them.[17] At Cambridge Percy was also aided by Edward Blakeway of Magdalene College, where his eleven days in the Pepysian Library yielded some three dozen texts for his collection.

The death of Shenstone on February 11, 1763, was a heavy blow to Percy, and one of his first impulses was to dedicate the *Reliques* to Shenstone's memory.[18] But on March 10, 1764, as the work neared completion, he wrote to Elizabeth Percy, countess of Northumberland, to ask if she would accept the dedication.[19] The change was an understandable one. Whether or not the idea was Percy's own, one can imagine that he would have needed little encouragement to approach this colorful and influential Percy matriarch. She was a natural choice: descendant of ancient

Percys renowned in history, song, and ballad, and, Percy noted, "In her own right Baroness Percy, Lucy, Poynings, Fitz-Payne, Bryan, and Latimer." For Percy her acceptance of the dedication proved to be one of the happier strokes of fortune in a life generally subject to good fortune. It helped to assure his book, this parcel of old ballads that he never ceased to feel uneasy about, a ready passage into fashionable circles, and it marked the beginning of a long and intimate connection with the Northumberland family which brought an almost undreamed of fulfillment of Percy's literary, clerical, social, and financial aspirations. Percy was to retain his two Northamptonshire churches until he became bishop of Dromore in 1782, but in 1765 the modest vicarage at Easton Mauduit began the process of surrendering its occupant to Northumberland House and Alnwick Castle.

With the Northumberland stamp on his efforts assured, Percy felt impelled to revise his three volumes in order to give greater prominence to the Northumberland poems. Already in type, these were the major element of his third volume, and to accomplish his purpose he simply interchanged volumes 1 and 3. Thus the entire set of three volumes was aptly led off by "The Ancient Ballad of Chevy-Chase" and "The Battle of Otterbourne," with "An Elegy on Henry 4th Earl of Northumberland" closing the first book of volume 1, and "The More Modern Ballad of Chevy-Chase," "The Rising in the North," and "Northumberland Betrayed by Douglas" dominating the third. Among the longest and most notable poems in the collection, they record the deeds and misdeeds of the house of Percy and trumpet the relentless and at times impetuous valor of Harry Hotspur and his Northumberland followers.

Percy spent most of June, 1764, on the details of interchanging the first and third volumes, and on June 25 Samuel Johnson arrived at Easton Mauduit with Mrs. Anna Williams on a long-promised visit.[20] During Johnson's seven-week stay, Percy sought his assistance in explicating some of the more obscure words in the glossaries—one for each volume of the *Reliques*—which he finally had to send off to David Dalrymple in Edinburgh with a plea for help.[21] But Johnson's major assistance was in writing the dedication to the countess of Northumberland, a role which was not to be disclosed until 1791, when Boswell, having canceled at Percy's request a page of his *Life of Johnson* attributing the dedication to Johnson, neglected to delete the index reference to it.[22] The dedication, Percy later acknowledged, "owed its finest strokes" to Johnson's pen.[23] It may, in fact, be said to consist largely of fine strokes in the Johnson manner, and it has long been given a place in the canon of Johnson's works.[24]

On November 22, 1764, Percy waited on the countess of Northumberland and presented her with an advance copy of the three-volume set.[25] On February 11, 1765, copies were made available to the public at a cost, bound, of half a guinea.[26] Although the book was treated somewhat condescendingly in the April *Gentleman's Magazine,* it was reviewed favorably and at length in the February *Critical*

Review and the April *Monthly Review.*[27] But perhaps the best measure of the *Reliques*'s initial success is that James Dodsley, the sole proprietor of the publishing firm since his brother's death in 1764, contracted to pay Percy two hundred guineas, probably for a second edition, only a little more than a month after the book's publication.[28] "The *Reliques* sell far better than I could have expected," Percy wrote to David Dalrymple a week later on March 23, 1765. "Dodsley has already had 600 sets fetched away." And on July 2 Percy informed Thomas Warton that 1,100 copies of the total impression of 1,500 had been sold.[29]

III THE SUCCESS OF THE *RELIQUES*

The countess of Northumberland may have helped to introduce the *Reliques* into circles which might otherwise have neglected it, but it was out of her power to assure its success. For that, Percy had to depend largely on his own abilities, although his task was eased to no small extent by the changing tastes of the times. In its Gothic focus the *Reliques* bore a clear relationship to Macpherson's Ossian poems (1760), Hurd's *Letters on Chivalry and Romance* (1762), Walpole's *Castle of Otranto* (1764) and his mansion at Strawberry Hill, poems like Gray's "The Bard" (1757), and even Percy's modest runic translations; and, if such works as these had not already stimulated a general enthusiasm, they pointed clearly to that consuming public interest in the Gothic which was to characterize the following century.

The *Reliques* was itself disarmingly modest, at least in appearance. Its three volumes pressed lightly on the hand, and, attractively printed and illustrated as they were, they came close to being models of the bookmaker's art. To many of Percy's contemporaries, however, they must at first glance have seemed a mere collection of poems such as they were accustomed to finding occasionally in their bookstalls, with the obvious difference that these were mostly old and in language eccentric and at times obscure—"Ancient Songs and Ballads," as the running heads proclaimed across each double page. But if they read the poems, as of course many did, they discovered very quickly that the language was not quite so perplexing as it seemed, that it had in fact a charm of its own, and that it was conveying stories and songs of extraordinary variety and interest. For Percy, together with Shenstone, had taken infinite pains in the selection and placement of individual poems, with a view to holding the reader's attention both on the poem itself and on the collection as a whole.

It helped, of course, that the three volumes did not look forbiddingly crowded: individual poems and lines of verse were well spaced; the footnotes, mostly textual, were neither numerous nor long; the page margins were substantial. But, what was more important, the poems were both related to each other and constantly varied. The two long ballads which open the first book of volume 1, for example—"The Ancient Ballad of Chevy-Chase," thirteen pages in length exclusive of Percy's commentary, and

"The Battle of Otterbourne," ten and a half pages—are followed by "The Jew's Daughter" (2 pages), which, though allied with them in violence through its story of the Christian child murdered by the Jews, affords as striking a contrast with its predecessors in spirit as it does in length. The first book is then filled out with "Sir Cauline" (17 pages), "Edward, Edward" (2½ pages), "King Estmere" (12 pages), "Sir Patrick Spence" (2 pages), "Robin Hood and Guy of Gisborne" (10 pages), "The Tower of Doctrine" (3 pages), "The Child of Elle" (8½ pages), and "Edom o'Gordon" (6½ pages). In addition to its changing lengths and themes, the first book was given added variety by its lyric poems—Stephen Hawes' "The Tower of Doctrine" and John Skelton's "Elegy on Henry 4th Earl of Northumberland," which followed "Edom o'Gordon"—and by four ballads clearly designated as Scottish and interspersed among the six English ballads and the two lyrics.

The first book, moreover, in which the Northumberland Percys were dominant characters and valor and courage were recurring but not exclusive themes, was followed by a second book devoted to ballads that illustrate Shakespeare. Arranged in chronological order like those in the first book, the sixteen poems of book 2 begin with "Adam Bell, Clym of the Clough, and William of Cloudesly," at thirty-one pages the longest by far in the entire collection. They continue through familiar short lyrics like "Willow, Willow, Willow" and "The Passionate Shepherd to His Love" and less familiar ballads like "King Cophetua and the Beggar-Maid" and "The Frolicksome Duke, or the Tinker's Good Fortune," and they conclude with Percy's own **"The Friar of Orders Gray,"** a ballad fashioned out of some of the numerous snatches dispersed through Shakespeare's plays.

The third book resumes the Northumberland ballads, and, having opened it with "The More Modern Ballad of Chevy-Chase" of Elizabethan origin, Percy was constrained by his chronological pattern to confine the book to poems on the whole more recent than those of other books. "Chevy-Chase" is followed by James Shirley's "Death's Final Conquest," the Northumberland poems "The Rising in the North" and "Northumberland Betrayed by Douglas," the anonymous "My Mind to Me a Kingdom Is," and the Elizabethan William Warner's "The Patient Countess." A series of early seventeenth-century poems by such writers as Henry Wotton, Michael Drayton, Samuel Daniel, and Thomas Carew then concludes with the Scottish ballad "Gilderoy," probably dating from the mid-seventeenth century, and from there Percy leaps ahead to the 1726 "Winifreda" and thence to his own time and his own circle. Shenstone is represented by "Jemmy Dawson," "the ingenious Dr. *Harrington,* of Bath" by the 1756 "Witch of Wokey," and James Grainger by a West Indian ballad. Reserving the last word for himself, Percy closes the volume with his own translations from the Spanish, "Gentle River, Gentle River" and "Alcanzor and Zayda, a Moorish Tale."

The second volume consists largely of poems on historical and political subjects, among them "For the Victory at Agincourt," "On Thomas Lord Cromwell," "Queen Elizabeth's Verses, While Prisoner at Woodstock," and "The Murder of the King of Scots." The third, as Percy stated and many of the titles attest, is "chiefly devoted to romantic subjects": "The Boy and the Mantle," "The Knight, and Shepherd's Daughter," "Sweet William's Ghost," "The Children in the Wood," "The Dragon of Wantley." One of its sequences contains poems about "little foot-pages" and other young people; another focuses upon witches, hobgoblins, and fairies. Both the second and the third volumes follow the pattern of the first, with each of their three books developed chronologically, with constant variety in the themes and lengths of poems, and with lyrics spaced among the ballads and Scottish poems among the English. The third book of volume 2 contains a series of six "Mad Songs," madness being a subject, Percy observed, treated more frequently by the English than by their neighbors, although he declined to speculate whether the English were "more liable to this calamity than other nations" (II, 343).

The puffs given to himself and his friends through the insertion in the first volume of one poem each by Shenstone, Grainger, and himself and of two of his own translations were not repeated in subsequent volumes, although Percy's version of "Valentine and Ursine" was included in the third book of volume 3. Under Percy's initial plan, of course, the poems would have closed, not the first volume but the third, where they would have served as a kind of appendix, a relaxed self-indulgence, perhaps, as Percy rested after the labors of his three volumes. They can hardly be said to raise the poetic level of the *Reliques,* but they do help to give it some of its pleasant personal quality. Percy is like the director who cannot resist taking a part in his own production. But contemporary readers must have felt his presence constantly: he was at hand throughout to help them understand and enjoy what they were reading. Most poems have their own, usually brief, introductions and some have postscripts. And four widely separated essays help to unify parts of the collection and to illuminate them historically and critically: **"An Essay on the Ancient English Minstrels," "On the Origin of the English Stage," "On the [Alliterative] Metre of Pierce Plowman's Visions,"** and **"On the Ancient Metrical Romances."** Together these constitute a brief and selective history of early English poetry, but one much advanced for its time, and it is not surprising that James Dodsley gathered them into a single volume in 1767 and sold them apart from the *Reliques.*[30]

The **"Essay on the Ancient English Minstrels"** is the key essay as well as the first, for it sets the framework and the tone for much of what follows in the three volumes. The minstrels, as Percy perceives them, are romantic figures: poets, musicians, members of "a distinct order of men . . . [who] got their livelihood by singing verses to the harp, at the houses of the great." Their verses, of course, were not necessarily their own: "From the amazing variations, which occur in different copies of these old pieces, it is evident they made no scruple to alter each other's productions, and the reciter added or omitted whole stanzas, according to his own fancy or convenience" (I, xvi). In Anglo-Saxon times, Percy notes, the minstrel's admission to royal circles was accepted as a matter of course, and even as late as the reign of Henry VIII "the Reciters of verses, or moral speeches learnt by heart, intruded without ceremony into all companies; not only in taverns, but in the houses of the nobility themselves" (I, xix). By the end of Queen Elizabeth's reign, however, such men were included by statute among "rogues, vagabonds, and sturdy beggars" (I, xxi).

As long as the minstrels subsisted, Percy observed, "they seem never to have designed their rhymes for publication, and probably never committed them to writing themselves: what copies are preserved . . . were doubtless taken down from their mouths." Their ballads are "in the northern dialect, abound with antique words and phrases, are extremely incorrect, and run into the utmost licence of metre; they have also a romantic wildness, and are in the true spirit of chivalry" (I, xxii).

"I have no doubt," wrote Percy, "but most of the old heroic ballads in this collection were produced by this order of men" (I, xvi). The latest such poems he could discover were "The Rising in the North" and "Northumberland Betrayed by Douglas," both of the late sixteenth century. The "genuine old Minstrelsy," by then almost extinct, had gradually been replaced by "a new race of ballad-writers . . ., an inferior sort of minor poets, who wrote narrative songs meerly for the press." Their works, written in the southern dialect, are "in exacter measure, have a low or subordinate correctness, sometimes bordering on the insipid . . ., exhibit a more modern phraseology, and are commonly descriptive of more modern manners" (I, xxii-xxiii). Percy's preference for the older ballads was never in doubt.

"On the Origin of the English Stage" is the introductory essay for the "Ballads that Illustrate Shakespeare" in the second book of volume 1. In the essay Percy traces dramatic poetry from the solemn religious festivals of the Middle Ages through the mystery and morality plays and their sequels. Moralities like *Everyman,* he states, gave birth to modern tragedy, and moralities like *Hick-Scorner* to modern comedy. But "Moralities still kept their ground" and at length became the popular masques of the courts of James I and Charles I. Mysteries ceased to be acted after the Reformation, but seem to have given rise to historical plays, which the "old writers" considered distinct from tragedies and comedies (I, 118-28).

In the essay **"On the Metre of Pierce Plowman's Visions,"** which introduces the third book of volume 2, Percy describes the unrhymed alliterative verse of the Icelandic poets, gives the rules of Icelandic prosody as analyzed by Wormius in his *Literatura Runica* of 1636, and notes that *Pierce Plowman's Visions,* written, he says, by Robert Langland and published shortly after 1350, is "constructed

exactly" by those rules.[31] Langland, he observes, was neither the first nor the last English poet to use the alliterative verse; but after rhyme was superadded, it came at last to engross "the whole attention of the poet," with the result that "the internal imbellishment of alliteration was no longer studied," and the rules that Langland wrote by were forgotten. The cadences of alliterative verse, though not the alliteration, says Percy, may still be seen in French heroic verse (II, 260-70).

Percy's final volume opens with the last of his four essays, **"On the Ancient Metrical Romances,"** a subject particularly close to his heart. The romances, he asserts, may be traced back to the historical songs of the ancient Gothic scalds, who celebrated the chivalric ideas long before the Crusades or the adoption of chivalry as a military order. The earliest French romances of chivalry were metrical and date from the eleventh century, whereas the earliest English romance Percy had discovered, "Hornechild," dates from the twelfth. By the fourteenth century metrical romances had become so popular in England that Chaucer burlesqued them in his tale of "Sir Thopas," where he cited a number of romances still extant in manuscript in the eighteenth century. Many of these, Percy observes, illuminate the manners and opinions of their times and have substantial poetic merit; although they cannot be set in competition with Chaucer's works, "they are far more spirited and entertaining than the tedious allegories of Gower, or the dull and prolix legends of Lydgate." He concludes his account by summarizing the nine parts of "Libius Disconius," which he declares as "regular in its conduct, as any of the finest poems of classical antiquity" and worthy of being regarded as an epic (III, ii-xvi). He then appended to the essay a list of thirty metrical romances still extant, with the locations of manuscript and printed texts (III, xvii-xxiv).

In 1876, when Henry B. Wheatley published what continues to be the standard edition of the *Reliques,* he announced in the "Editor's Preface" that to treat the four essays as he had treated Percy's prefaces to individual poems—that is, by merely adding footnotes and terminal comments—"would necessitate so many notes and corrections as to cause confusion; and as the **"Essays on the English Stage,"** and the **"Metrical Romances,"** are necessarily out of date, the trouble expended would not have been repaid by the utility of the result." He had, accordingly, "thrown them to the end of their respective volumes, where they can be read exactly as Percy left them" (I, xi). In Percy's own day, however, almost no one was aware that the essays were in want of corrective or supplementary notes and comment, or that for such a want they would in time be "thrown" to the rear of their volumes, as accumulations of bric-a-brac are sometimes stuffed into inconspicuous closets. Percy—the first of his countrymen "to inspect actual English medieval romances" or "to demonstrate that alliteration was the principle of Anglo-Saxon and Germanic verse generally"[32]—had carried his readers about as far as was possible for any one person in 1765, and they had reason to be grateful for the sure hand with which he pointed out places of interest along the way. Like his essays, his introductions to the poems were written with whatever authority pioneer research would admit and, in spite of his disclaimer about a parcel of old ballads, with an infectious conviction that the poems in his collection were not simply curios but would repay serious attention with unusual delight. "This excellent old ballad," he says of "The Wandering Prince of Troy,"

> . . . is given from the editor's folio MS. collated with two different printed copies, both in black letter in the Pepys collection.

> The reader will smile to observe with what natural and affecting simplicity, our ancient ballad-maker has engrafted a Gothic conclusion on the classic story of Virgil, from whom, however, it is probable he had it not. Nor can it be denied, but he has dealt out his poetical justice with a more impartial hand, than that celebrated poet.

> (III, 192)

In discussing the ballads in the same breath with Chaucer, Spenser, Shakespeare, and, as in this passage, Virgil, Percy was according them a dignity they were seldom given; and in placing them side by side with poems of Ben Jonson, Richard Lovelace, Sir John Suckling, John Dryden, and others, he was providing his readers an opportunity to see that the older poems did not inevitably suffer by comparison and that the roots of the English literary genius struck as deep as English history. The *Reliques* was a work of national pride, and it is not surprising that a nation as proud as Britain took it to its heart.

Wheatley's relegation of the essays to the back pages tends to obscure an important aspect of the *Reliques.* The collection, to be sure, lacked the kind of tight organization which rendered all tampering with it dangerous. Percy spent countless hours putting together the pieces for the first edition, only to move a number of them for the second. More significantly, he found it expedient at the last moment to interchange the first and third volumes, and he accomplished this major structural change with minimum inconvenience and damage. The collection was, of course, an anthology, and like other anthologies it could be dipped into at practically any point. Inevitably that has been one of its attractions. But the *Reliques* also provides incentives for reading it through from beginning to end, and that is in fact the way in which it can be read most profitably. Unquestionably the **"Essay on the Ancient English Minstrels"** belonged at the head of the book, for it is a kind of Percy manifesto and its spirit pervades the entire work. The sections of each book are units, moreover, short enough and expertly enough selected and varied to be read without tedium in one sitting. They move ahead chronologically, have themes in common, and gain added coherence through the short introductions to separate poems. Even before starting a poem the reader may be invited to read on in the next: "This little moral sonnet," Percy says of James Shirley's "Victorious Men of Earth," "hath such a pointed application to the heroes of the foregoing and

following ballads, that I cannot help placing it here, tho' the date of its composition is of a much later period" (II, 222). The generally brief and unpedantic concern for dates, sources, backgrounds, and relationships gives the poems a special luster; Percy fusses over them just enough to make them seem wanted and important. They were largely dredged out of old books and manuscripts, for Percy preceded the era of the ballad hunter who recorded the words and music of rustic men and women singing at the plough or the spinning wheel. But his poems almost never come with the musty odor of old trunks or dank closets. Percy, moreover, although he knew little of music, was not oblivious to the possibilities of oral tradition, even if he did not pursue them assiduously. One is made aware from time to time that some of the best of the poems have been homely favorites of English and Scottish people; of "Gil Morrice," Percy tells us, two Scottish editions were printed from a copy collected "from the mouths of old women and nurses," and he himself is now inserting sixteen additional lines submitted in response to the Scottish editors' request for readers to help improve the text (III, 93).

Percy intrudes without being intrusive; he is informal, even chatty at times, a friend taking a friend into his confidence. He calls attention to another version of "Lord Thomas and Fair Ellinor" in the Pepys collection, an attempt at modernization by reducing the poem to a different measure: "A proof of it's popularity," he assures us (III, 82). He apologizes disarmingly for not placing "The Heir of Linne" earlier in volume 2: it was "owing to an oversight" (II, 309). Many of his introductions provide just enough information to whet his readers' appetites; he expects the poems to satisfy them. And taken all in all, there are not many among the songs and ballads of the *Reliques* that one would wish to replace. If Percy overlooked some of the best of the ballads, he also included many of the best: "Chevy-Chase," "The Battle of Otterbourne," "The Boy and the Mantle," "Sir Patrick Spence," "Edward, Edward," "Child Waters," "Barbara Allen's Cruelty," "The Children in the Wood," "The Bonny Earl of Murray"—the list is a long one, and it covers a broad range of human experience. No doubt it was this ability of Percy to recapture and not just to disinter the past that prompted Johnson's well known tribute to him: "Percy's attention to poetry has given grace and splendour to his studies of antiquity. A mere antiquarian is a rugged being."[33]

The difference for the *Reliques,* of course, was crucial, and Percy, who was well aware of it, articulated it with some feeling in one of the book's four essays. "It has happened unluckily," he wrote of the old metrical romances,

> that the antiquaries, who have revived the works of our ancient writers, have been for the most part men void of taste and genius, and therefore have always fastidiously rejected the old poetical Romances, because founded on fictitious or popular subjects, while they have been careful to grub up every petty fragment of the most dull and insipid rhimist, whose merit it was to deform morality, or obscure true history.

> (III, ix)

If compiling the **Reliques** did not require the genius of a Johnson, it did require taste and judgment, including an ability on the editor's part to put himself constantly in the reader's position, and these were precisely the qualities that Percy, with Shenstone's encouragement and assistance, was able to bring to his task.

IV THE SECOND AND THIRD EDITIONS

Percy's success with the first edition of the **Reliques** established him as England's leading ballad authority, and it did not take him long to follow up his success with a second edition. It was published by James Dodsley in 1767.[34] With so many excellent poems excluded from the first edition, and with his new-won fame bringing him ballad transcriptions and information from correspondents all over Britain, there must have been considerable temptation for Percy to revise the second edition extensively. He did not, however, perhaps because he hesitated to risk a proven success, and perhaps because he was reserving the best of his unused poems for other projects. Almost to the end of his life, for example, he nursed the idea of a fourth volume of the **Reliques,** a project he contemplated turning over to his son and then, following his son's death, to his nephew. At various times he drew up plans for special collections such as ballads on English history, English romances, and ancient English and Scottish poems.[35]

The changes in the second edition, in any event, seem minimal. Not a single poem in the first edition was deleted from the second, and only three were added. "Jephthah Judge of Israel," called to Percy's attention by George Steevens, was inserted among the "Ballads that Illustrate Shakespeare," where it remained through the third and fourth editions (2d ed., I, 176-79). The second addition was "Jealousy Tyrant of the Mind," identified in the second edition (and the third) as coming from "a Manuscript copy communicated to the Editor," and in the fourth edition as a song by Dryden from *Love Triumphant* (4th ed., III, 273). The third was a French translation of John Lyly's "Cupid and Campaspe" entitled "L'Amour et Glycere," which was written expressly for the **Reliques** by an unnamed friend and placed by Percy at the very end of volume 3. It seems strange that in revising his collection of "Ancient English" poetry Percy should have chosen to conclude it with a poem in modern French, but presumably friendship and the connection with "Cupid and Campaspe," printed earlier in volume 3, overcame any Percy doubts on that point, at least for the second and third editions. Percy omitted the poem in the fourth edition.

A total of eighteen poems were given new positions, although four of these were accounted for by two instances in which poems already adjacent to each other simply exchanged places. One change set up a circular chain reaction. When Percy discovered the printed text of "The Shepherd's Resolution" and thereby learned that George Wither was the author, he substituted the printed text for his fragmentary folio manuscript text and moved the poem from book 2 of volume 3 to the place occupied by "Dulcina" in book 3. "Dulcina" was moved forward seven positions to displace "The Auld Good Man," which in turn was moved forward to the place which had been occupied by "The Shepherd's Resolution." Percy must have gone through many such sequences when he was deciding upon the order of the poems for the first edition.

The other significant changes in the poems also resulted from Percy's use of texts previously unknown to him. The text of "My Mind to Me a Kingdom Is" was revised and the poem's last four stanzas were detached from the first seven and printed separately under the title "The Golden Mean," changes Percy based upon a 1588 publication of William Byrd's psalms, sonnets, and songs. "The Golden Mean" held its place in the third edition but was dropped from the fourth.[36] Punning commendatory verses attributed to King James I were replaced in the second edition by two sonnets of King James because someone had suggested to Percy that "the king only gave the quibbling commendations in prose, and that some obsequious court-rhymer put them into metre" (II, 303-4). Finally, "The Aspiring Shepherd," printed from the folio manuscript, was discovered to be George Wither's "The Stedfast Shepherd," and the entire seven stanzas, correctly titled, were printed in the second edition (III, 263-66) from *The Mistress of Philarete*, which was also Percy's source for the full text of "The Shepherd's Resolution."

Changes in the selections were even less numerous in the third edition, which was published in 1775. Two adjacent poems in the third volume, "Lucy and Colin" and "Margaret's Ghost," were transposed. In the same volume "The Wanton Wife of Bath," which, as Percy noted, Addison in the *Spectator* [No. 247] had pronounced an excellent ballad, was replaced by "The Bride's Burial." No doubt, in spite of Addison's assurance, the Wife of Bath, who at heaven's gate successively asserts her moral superiority to Adam, Jacob, Lot, Judith, David, Solomon, Jonas, Thomas, Mary Magdalen, Paul, and Peter, was a little *too* wanton for Percy's sustained comfort. The saintly virgin bride of "The Bride's Burial" could have posed no problems.

In the third edition Percy notes also that the texts of "Phillida and Corydon" and "The Shepherd's Address to His Muse," printed in volume 3 from a small Elizabethan quarto manuscript in his possession, have been improved by reference to printed copies in *England's Helicon*. The most significant change of this kind, however, occurred in "The Battle of Otterbourne," for which Percy substituted a text from a Cotton Library manuscript called to his attention by the Chaucer scholar Thomas Tyrwhitt.[37] The new text contained fifty-eight lines not found in the Harleian manuscript used by Percy in his first two editions.

In both the second and third editions, Percy occasionally added, deleted, or revised a note, and his changes in the introductions and postscripts to the poems were at times substantial, particularly when the discovery of a new text gave him a new view of the poem or its author. Among his more notable changes in the second edition are those in the annotations to the two "Chevy-Chase" ballads and "The Battle of Otterbourne," where his newly acquired intimacy with Northumberland and the Northumberland family is clearly reflected. He is no longer content, for example, to refer his readers to Fuller's *Worthies* and Crawfurd's *Peerage* (his first edition authorities) for information about the Scottish and Northumberland leaders slain in the bloody battle between Douglas and Hotspur:

> Thear was slayne with the lord Persè
>   Sir John of Agerstone,
> Sir Roger the hinde Hartly,
>   Sir Wyllyam the bold Hearone.
>
> Sir Jorg the worthè Lovele
>   A knyght of great renowen,
> Sir Raff the ryche Rugbè
>   With dyntes wear beaten dowene.
>
> (2d ed., I, 14)

Instead he provides, at the end of the second poem, a series of comments on each of the persons, or their families, whose names compose the rolls of honor in "The Ancient Ballad of Chevy-Chase" and "The Battle of Otterbourne": Lovele, for example, "*seems to be the ancient family of* Delaval, *of* Seaton Delaval, *in Northumberland*," and "*The family of* Haggerston *of* Haggerston, *near Berwick, has been seated there for many centuries, and still remains*" (2d ed., I, 32). A similar list follows "The More Modern Ballad of Chevy-Chase" (I, 266-68).[38]

Among the family treasures that the earl and countess of Northumberland brought out for Percy during the first months of their acquaintance was the manuscript of the ***Northumberland Houshold Book,*** which, as we have seen, Percy was to edit for a private printing in 1770. He began making use of the manuscript, however, in the second edition of the ***Reliques.*** A half-page extract from it is appended to "Gentle Herdsman, Tell to Me" to show the constant tribute paid to "Our Lady of Walsingham" (II, 399-400). Another, illustrating "the fondness of our ancestors" for miracle plays, constitutes about half of a five-page addition to the essay **"On the Origin of the English Stage"** (I, 367-69). Percy also finds support in the manuscript for his statement in the **"Essay on the Ancient English Minstrels"** that "Minstrels were retained in all great and noble families," and in a footnote to the text he observes with obvious pride that the house of Northumberland, which ages ago had three minstrels attending them in their Yorkshire castles, still retain three in their service in Northumberland (I, xxxiii; xxxv-xxxvi; lxxiii-lxxv).

Percy's changes in three of his essays are comparatively minor.[39] To the fourth, the **"Essay on the Ancient English Minstrels,"** he felt compelled to give major attention. In a paper read at a meeting of the Society of Antiquaries on May 29, 1766, the antiquarian Samuel Pegge expressed the view that Percy in his essay had given "a false, or at best, an ill-grounded idea" of the "rank and condition" of the minstrels in Saxon times.[40] Pegge argued that the cus-

toms of ancient Britons and Danes were too different from those of the Saxons to conclude, as Percy does, that, because the Britons and Danes accorded a high place to their bards and scalds, the Saxons would have done the same with their own minstrels. He went on to cast doubt upon two stories recounted by Percy to exemplify the Saxons's esteem for their minstrels, one of King Alfred assuming the dress and character of a minstrel in order to gain admittance to the Danish camp, and the other of the Danish King Anlaff employing the same ruse to gain admittance among the Saxons. The first he thought of doubtful authority, and the second probably adapted from it.

It is a revealing commentary upon Percy that his most extensive revision for the second edition should have been undertaken as a result of a paper read before a meeting of antiquarians and written by a man scarcely known outside of antiquarian circles. Percy was not present at the Society's May 29 meeting, but was sent a copy of Pegge's paper by Sir Joseph Ayloffe, and he was clearly annoyed that Pegge had not favored *him* with his objections rather than forcing him to rely upon a third person to convey them to him. As a result, he wrote to Pegge on July 13, 1767, he might have remained ignorant of them and thus incapable of retracting his errors.[41] Scholar that he was, Percy cared very much about his standing among fellow scholars.

Percy did not acknowledge his debt to Pegge's paper until the third edition of the ***Reliques*** in 1775, but readers of the second edition familiar with Pegge's comments could not have mistaken Percy's intentions. Percy, to be sure, does not confess to error, and when he finishes his revision for the 1767 edition his position is essentially what it was in 1765. But he is plainly acknowledging the justice of Pegge's assertion that he had given at best "an ill-grounded idea" of the rank and condition of the Saxon minstrels, for the whole intent of his effort is to establish his position on firmer ground.

The initial essay was nine pages long. The revised essay contains twenty pages. In 1765 the comments about the Anglo-Saxon minstrels, culminating in the stories of Alfred and Anlaff, fill the first three pages of the essay, with Percy stating categorically at the beginning that "Our Saxon ancestors . . . had been accustomed to hold men of this profession in the highest reverence" (I, xv). In 1767 he withholds any word about the Anglo-Saxons until he is midway into the second page, his introductory page and a half having been directed toward justifying a more cautious assertion: "As these honours were paid to Poetry and Song, from the earliest times, in those countries which our Anglo-Saxon ancestors inhabited before their removal into Britain, we may reasonably conclude, that they would not lay aside all their regard for men of this sort immediately on quitting their German forests" (I, xx). If, moreover, bards were revered in the countries inhabited by the Anglo-Saxons before they removed to Britain, and were "common and numerous" among descendants of the Anglo-Saxons in Britain after the Conquest, what, asks Percy, "could have become of them in the intermediate time?"

He sees no alternative to concluding that the minstrels still subsisted, "though perhaps with less splendour" than in Northern Europe. "and that there never was wanting a succession of them to hand down the art" (I, xxiii). He then repeats his stories of Alfred and Anlaff, adds a third story to them, defends his authorities, and insists upon the spirit of the stories if not the letter: "they are related by authors who lived too near the Saxon times, and had before them too many recent monuments of the Anglo-Saxon nation, not to know what was conformable to the genius and manners of that people" (I, xxiii-xxvi).

The revised account, in short, was fuller and more carefully reasoned than the original, and Percy also took the opportunity to inject into it some of the history of the minstrels between the Conquest and the reign of Edward II, a period he had ignored in the first edition. But the response to Pegge was still not finished when Percy had revised the text of the essay. The original had been footnoted unobtrusively, and the revised essay is footnoted with similar restraint, with the notes indicated by the customary asterisks, daggers, and crosses of the period. There is, however, a second system of reference marks in the revised essay which begins with *A* and proceeds through the alphabet and into a second alphabet to *Ff*. The letters are placed before the first words of paragraphs, and the notes to which they refer are printed at the end of the essay. The notes fill thirty-eight pages, almost twice as many, that is, as the revised essay itself. No such notes had been attached to the 1765 essay.

What Percy collects in these notes may be considered relevant to his essay, and much of it is interesting. He draws upon a wide variety of sources, including the Anglo-Saxon language, for such purposes as suggesting the likelihood that King Alfred excelled in music, describing the roles of the minstrels, demonstrating in response to a challenge by Pegge that the Anglo-Saxons had a word for minstrelsy, and above all supporting his thesis that they held both music and musicians in high regard. But what was relevant was not necessarily essential, and what was interesting in its parts was by no means interesting in the whole. Indeed, the conclusion is inescapable that in these thirty-eight pages Percy abandoned his chosen role as an editor seeking to please a general audience and was now the scholar addressing other scholars. What Shenstone feared and had counseled Percy against had happened. Readers who had enjoyed Percy's essay, and who would go on to delight in the songs and ballads that he spread before them, could only have turned with distaste from the "Notes and Illustrations Referred to in the Foregoing Essay." Its long, untranslated quotations in Latin, French, and Spanish stretched like roadblocks across a dozen and a half pages, while its five-page disquisition on the Anglo-Saxon language would have seemed better suited for a gathering at the Society of Antiquaries.

Percy's reaction to Pegge's criticism serves as a graphic reminder of his dilemma in editing the *Reliques,* as well as of Shenstone's influence in shaping the *Reliques* into

the landmark it became. The scholar in Percy impelled him to prop up his sagging essay with notes and references which would withstand further criticism. As for Shenstone, it is hard to imagine that he could have objected to the revised essay, which was clearly superior to the original; but surely if he had lived to see the thirty-eight pages of notes he would have thrown up his hands and urged Percy to communicate them to Pegge and the scholarly world in some other form. It would have been good advice, and it would probably have been taken.

In spite of their unpromising introduction, Percy and Pegge became good friends. In occasional letters Pegge answered Percy's inquiries on antiquarian matters, and Percy presented Pegge with copies of the *Ride to Hulne Abbey* and the *Northumberland Houshold Book.* Thus both seemed distressed in 1773 when the Society of Antiquaries published Pegge's 1766 observations in the second volume of *Archaeologia*; and Pegge wrote to Percy promptly to say that the Council of the Society was apparently unaware that Percy had responded to his objections in the 1767 *Reliques* and to state formally that Percy had removed his doubts "in a very satisfactory manner."[42] In the 1775 *Reliques* Percy announced that since the first edition the essay had been "very much enlarged and improved" as a result of Pegge's objections, which Pegge, "in the most liberal and candid manner," now acknowledged to have been removed (I, xviii).

V THE RITSON CONTROVERSY AND THE FOURTH EDITION

The controversy with Samuel Pegge, if it can be called a controversy, was settled amicably and fairly quickly, although not without Percy's going to an extraordinary effort to satisfy Pegge's objections. A controversy of a different sort, far from being settled quickly and amicably, was never settled at all, and it was much more serious in its implications and consequences.

It had its beginnings in a three-volume publication of 1783 entitled *A Select Collection of English Songs,* which was compiled by Joseph Ritson. Ritson, who became a solicitor of Gray's Inn, was an accomplished and brilliant scholar, but stormy and eccentric. His aggressive vegetarianism, along with his efforts to reform English spelling, provided considerable amusement for his contemporaries—a collection which he published in 1802 was entitled *Ancient Engleish Metrical Romanceës*—and his attacks upon other scholars resounded with an explosive mixture of irony, sarcasm, and invective that made him a feared and at times a hated controversialist. Alexander Chalmers, in a wry defense, noted that Ritson was "not absolutely incapable of civility."[43] He was to pursue Percy, with occasional lapses into civility, until his death in 1803 at the age of fifty-one.

In *A Select Collection of English Songs,* Ritson praised Percy's translation of "Rio Verde, Rio Verde" and printed "O Nancy, Wilt Thou Go with Me" among the large group of love songs in his first volume; a "most beautiful song," he called it.[44] But Ritson's attention, like Pegge's before him, was drawn primarily to Percy's **"Essay on the Ancient English Minstrels,"** which he considered in his own "Historical Essay on the Origin and Progress of National Song." While not attempting to controvert "the slightest fact laid down by the learned prelate," Ritson wrote, he thought that he might be permitted "to question the propriety of his inferences, and, indeed, his general hypothesis." It does not follow, he argues, that because the French honored the minstrels the English must have done so also; nor is there any proof that the English minstrels were "a respectable society" or that they deserved to be called a society at all:

> That there were men in those times, as there are in the present, who gained a livelihood by going about from place to place, singing and playing to the illiterate vulgar, is doubtless true; but that they were received into the castles of the nobility, sung at their tables, and were rewarded like the French minstrels, does not any where appear, nor is it at all credible.

(I, li-lii)

The reason, says Ritson, is evident. At least till the time of Henry VIII only the French language was spoken at court and in the households of the Norman barons, who despised the Saxon manners and language. Percy's essay should properly have been called an "Essay on the Ancient FRENCH Minstrels," for all that is known of the English is that by a law of Queen Elizabeth's time they were branded as "rogues, vagabonds, and sturdy beggars." Such characters could "sing and play; but it was none of their business to read or write"; thus their songs have perished along with them, and only "The Ancient Ballad of Chevy-Chase" and "The Battle of Otterbourne" can be ascribed with any plausibility to them (I, liii).

Ritson returned to this subject in *Ancient Songs, from the Time of King Henry the Third, to the Revolution,* which was published in 1790. In his 26-page "Observations on the Ancient English Minstrels," he attacks Percy's definition of the minstrel. This order of men who, he says (mocking Percy's words), "united the arts of poetry and music, and sung verses to the harp of their own composing," had in fact little more standing than the whores and lechers "for whose diversion . . . [they] were most miserably twanging and scraping in the booths of Chester fair" (vi-vii). Before Percy, he asserts, the word "minstrel" was never used by an English writer for anyone but an instrumental performer, "generally a fiddler, or such like base musician." No English minstrel "was ever famous for his composition or his performance; nor is the name of a single one preserved" (xiii, xvi).

Ritson then moved to his more significant attack upon Percy—one which he had begun in *A Select Collection of English Songs*—by noting that, of the black-letter ballads he had himself collated, not one had been printed faithfully or correctly by Percy. Percy's editorial practices now

became his essential focus, and he was to return to them again and again during the remaining years of his life.

He begins by doubting the very existence of Percy's folio manuscript: since the minstrels never committed their own rhymes to writing, it is extraordinary that this "multifarious collection" could have been compiled as late as 1650. And, to increase the manuscript's singularity, "no other writer has ever pretended to have seen [it]. The late Mr. Tyrwhitt . . . never saw it. . . . And it is remarkable, that scarcely any thing is published from it, not being to be found elsewhere, without our being told of the defects and mutilation of the MS" (xix). He then cites seven poems printed by Percy from the folio manuscript—"Sir Cauline," "Sir Aldingar," "Gentle Herdsman," "The Heir of Linne," "The Beggar's Daughter of Bednall-Green," "The Marriage of Sir Gawaine," and "King Arthur's Death"—in which Percy acknowledged his emendations largely in general terms, and he states that many "other instances might be noticed, where the learned collector has preferred his ingenuity to his fidelity, without the least intimation to the reader." It follows, asserts Ritson, that one can have no confidence in any of the *Reliques*'s "old Minstrel ballads" which cannot be found elsewhere (xx-xxi).

The minstrels, Ritson notes, lost favor to the ballad singers, who, without instruments, sung printed pieces to fine and simple melodies, possibly of their own invention," and whose verses, smoother in language than the minstrel poems and more accurate in measure and rhyme, were thought to be more poetical; and in fact (a view which Percy and later ballad scholars did not share with Ritson) they may "defy all the Minstrel songs extant, nay even those in the *Reliques of Ancient English Poetry,* for simplicity, nature, interest, and pathos." The minstrel songs are "curious and valuable," nonetheless, and if further light could be thrown on the people by or for whom they were "invented," a collection of all the available poems would be entertaining and interesting. But, he adds, with a final thrust at Percy, "if such a publication should ever appear, it is to be hoped that it will come from an Editor who prefers truth to hypothesis, and the genuine remains of the Minstrel Poets, however mutilated or rude, to the indulgence of his own poetical vein, however fluent or refined" (xxvi).

As early as the spring of 1784, James Dodsley inquired if Percy wished to supply copy for a fourth edition of the *Reliques*.[45] By then, of course, Percy was in Northern Ireland serving as bishop of Dromore, and, however he may have responded in 1784, he apparently wrote to Dodsley on November 19, 1785, to say that it was a matter of "perfect Indifference" to him whether the *Reliques* was ever republished or not. He would be glad to have it forgotten "among the other Levities & Vanities" of his youth, as he had concluded from an earlier Dodsley letter would be its fate. He was thus unprepared to send corrected copy immediately, and he left it to Dodsley either to consign the book to oblivion or to give him more time.[46]

As might have been expected, Dodsley chose the second of these alternatives, but no record of further negotiations remains. In its issue of July 8-10, 1794, the *St. James's Chronicle* announced that the fourth edition would "Speedily" be published, and though the three volumes bear the date 1794 a full year seems to have passed before they were actually made available to the public.[47] They were printed by Percy's friend and kinsman John Nichols and published by J. and C. Rivington rather than by Dodsley, who had retired from business.

In the "Advertisement" at the front of the fourth edition, which is signed by Percy's nephew Thomas Percy of St. John's College, Oxford, it is stated that the book would have remained unpublished had "the original Editor . . . not yielded to the importunity of his friends, and accepted the humble offer of an Editor in a Nephew" (I, ix). It is doubtful if anyone who has studied the *Reliques* has given much credence to that statement. Well paid though Percy's nephew was for whatever services he rendered,[48] his designation as editor of the fourth edition was almost certainly a polite fiction intended to mask the fact that the bishop of Dromore was publicly exposing the "Levities and Vanities" of his youth. Percy was later to take his nephew to task for revealing to George Steevens (of all people!) that he was only an "umbra" in the edition, a choice bit of news that the mischievous Steevens did not scruple to pass on to Ritson.[49] It seems a safe assumption also that Percy would not have entrusted the writing of a rather sensitive "Advertisement" to a nephew whose "Tastes & Persuits," as Percy wrote to his wife on September 17, 1799, "are so different from mine."[50] It is hard to think of anything else in the three volumes that might be claimed for the younger Thomas Percy.

Friends may have urged a new edition upon Percy, but in all likelihood the chief incentive for revising the third edition was to respond to Ritson's attack in *Ancient Songs* upon his integrity and method. Probably he could have passed over Ritson's strictures on the **"Essay on the Ancient English Minstrels"** in *A Select Collection of English Songs,* if only from the sheer weariness of having revised the essay once before. But Percy was not one to receive with equanimity the suggestion that his folio manuscript was a fabrication, like Chatterton's Rowley or Macpherson's Ossian poems. And one may suppose that, once he had decided upon the task of revision, the scholar in him would simply not permit him to ignore what Ritson had to say about the minstrels and leave his essay untouched. The result of this two-fold approach to the fourth edition was that the changes in it, if not numerous, were significant, and that nearly all of them can be traced to one or the other of the two Ritson works.

The opening "Advertisement" is itself a key part of Percy's response: "The appeal publicly made to Dr. JOHNSON . . . [in the 1765 preface], and never once contradicted by him during so large a portion of his life, ought to have precluded every doubt concerning the existence of the MS. in question." But because a doubt was expressed, the manuscript was left for a year at the home of John Nichols, where it was examined "by many Gentlemen of eminence

in literature" (I, x). Much of the rest of the "Advertisement" describes the manuscript, with emphasis upon its missing leaves and parts of leaves and its faulty transcriptions often made from defective copies, with the result that "a considerable portion of the song or narrative is sometimes omitted; and miserable trash or nonsense not unfrequently introduced into pieces of considerable merit" (I, xii). In a few paragraphs, in short, Ritson's intolerable implication is disposed of and a basis for Percy's editorial practice established.

The "Advertisement" was new to the fourth edition. Of the continuing parts of the text, Percy once again undertook a major revision of the **"Essay on the Ancient English Minstrels."** Already doubled in size to meet Samuel Pegge's objections, it was now increased by another two thirds, and its unsightly supplementary notes were swollen from thirty-eight pages to fifty-two. Percy's purpose is to make clear, first, that such a person as the *English* minstrel did in fact survive the Conquest and, second, that he was welcomed in the houses of leading English families. Drawing upon the histories of music published by Sir John Hawkins and Charles Burney in 1776, he progresses from the reign of Henry I to the reign of Elizabeth, filling in some of the gaps in the royal succession he had left in earlier editions and citing, when he can, both the names of minstrels and the honors accorded them. He acknowledges that "in the first ages after the Conquest no other songs would be listened to by the great nobility" than those composed in the Norman French (I, xxix-xxx). But the Anglo-Saxons, although they now occupied inferior positions, were not "extirpated," and they could understand only their own gleemen or minstrels—bards, harpers, even dancers and mimics—who were readily admitted into the households of the English gentry (I, xxx).

Thus, accepting Ritson's conclusions in part, Percy relegates the English minstrels to a position below that of the French but reputable nonetheless; and he follows the two lines of their histories as they are gradually drawn together while the French and English cultures in Britain blend into one. The result is both a fuller essay and a more discriminating one. It is not likely, of course, that Percy hoped to satisfy Ritson's doubts as he had satisfied Samuel Pegge's in 1767. Percy and Pegge were much closer in spirit, apostles of a politer form of scholarly controversy than Ritson ever pretended to. It was not impossible, on the other hand, that, satisfied or not, Ritson would call off his pursuit of Percy's essay. That he would cease his attacks upon Percy's editorial practices was hardly to be expected. Percy trusted Ritson so little, in fact, that he gave express orders that he was not to be shown the folio manuscript while it was on display at the home of John Nichols.[51] From other scholars Percy had reason to expect a sympathetic response. To grant Ritson access to the manuscript was to place a battery of cannon at his disposal with the likelihood that he would discharge it triumphantly in Percy's face at the first opportunity.

For Percy was well aware that editorially in the *Reliques* he and Ritson were in opposing and irreconcilable camps.

The difficulty of Percy's position was that, being a scholar himself, he could appreciate Ritson's concern for accurate texts of the poems, whereas he saw not the slightest chance that Ritson would appreciate his decision to subordinate textual accuracy to the desire to appeal to a broad spectrum of readers. It had been Shenstone's view that there were a good many encumbrances to the old poems which had to be shaken loose if the collection was to be a success, and Percy had agreed, although not without that lingering regret that scholars are likely to feel when they yield to the impulse to popularize. His hope, of course, was to have the best of both the scholarly and popular worlds. Scholars, including Ritson, were unfailingly impressed by the imagination and erudition that went into the *Reliques,* but in this instance Percy's sheer abilities had the consequence, at least with a fellow scholar of Ritson's caliber and temperament, of throwing his unscholarly editorial practices into sharp relief. A lesser man than Percy might have been ignored or at least more readily forgiven. If he was not, he might simply have charged Ritson with pedantry and counted upon his nonscholar readers to support him. But that course was not open to Percy. Ultimately the "improvements" that he subjected many of the poems to could be justified only on the ground of the book's success, and that was the ground that Percy chose.

The public, concludes the fourth edition "Advertisement" ostensibly written by Percy's nephew,

> may judge how much they are indebted to the composer of this collection; who, at an early period of life, with such materials and such subjects, formed a work which hath been admitted into the most elegant libraries; and with which the judicious Antiquary hath just reason to be satisfied, while refined entertainment hath been provided for every Reader of taste and genius.
>
> (I, xii)

Few of Percy's contemporaries would have thought the claim extravagant. The sale of three good-sized editions, the first and third of 1,500 copies[52] and probably the second also, was an achievement for a three-volume work of collected poetry in the late eighteenth century. For a collection largely of old ballads it was phenomenal, and until the publication of Walter Scott's *Minstrelsy of the Scottish Border* in 1802 no other collection began to approach the *Reliques* in popularity. Ritson's collections of accurately printed texts seem not to have captured the public's fancy at all.

A significant part of Percy's defense was the need to repair the damage suffered by many of the poems, some of which were missing whole sections. To have printed them as they were would have satisfied the desire for scholarly accuracy; but Shenstone and Percy were persuaded that it would turn away many of the very readers they were hoping to attract. The alternatives were not to print them at all or to print them with such interpolations or additions as Percy thought appropriate. He chose the second alternative.

Had he confined his efforts to those poems which, as he viewed them, could benefit from minor repairs, he would doubtless have been spared the full fury of later scholars when the folio manuscript was finally published by John W. Hales and Frederick J. Furnivall in 1867 and 1868. Smoothing the meter of the old verses and modifying the diction or the rhyme, along with such changes in punctuation, capitalization, and spelling as were commonplace among editors, might at times have been justified by the need to clarify the poems for eighteenth-century readers, whose knowledge of the old poetic vocabulary was minuscule. And even in a more extensively amended poem like "Gentle Herdsman, Tell to Me," Percy's additions were not likely to seem a serious disturbance, filling in conjecturally as they do a series of gaps in this unique copy of the poem. They appear in a sequence of thirteen lines toward the middle of the poem's sixty lines, with Percy's interpolations designated by his own italics:

> I am a woman, woe is me!
> *Born* to greeffe and irksome care.
>
> *For* my beloved, and well-beloved,
> *My wayward cruelty could kill:*
> *And though my teares will nought avail,*
> *Most dearely I bewail him* still.
>
> *He was the flower of n*oble wights,
> *None ever more sincere colde* bee;
> *Of comely mien and shape* he was,
> *And tenderlye he*e loved mee.
>
> *When thus I saw he lov*ed me well,
> *I grewe so proud his pai*ne to see,
> *That I, who did not* know myselfe,
> *Thought scorne* of *such a youth* as hee.
>
> (II, 73-74)

It cannot be said that Percy's invention rose to the challenge of these ragged verses. Most of his lines are banal at best, and *sincere* was an utter stranger to the ballad vocabulary. But Furnivall's comment in *Bishop Percy's Folio Manuscript* seems rather too harsh for the offense: "We are not quite sure that the hand of time was always more to be dreaded than the hand of the Bishop" (III, 526). Even Ritson did not object to Percy's practice with "Gentle Herdsman," although he was unable to resist commenting that the poem "has not the least appearance of being a Minstrel Song" (*Ancient Songs,* p. xx).

In the various prefaces to the poems cited by Ritson, Percy noted that his texts included "conjectural emendations" and even wholly rewritten or additional stanzas and sections. What he failed to do was to follow his practice in "Gentle Herdsman" and point out precisely the extent and location of his alterations. With "The Beggar's Daughter of Bednall-Green," for example, he stated that "the concluding stanzas, which contain the old Beggar's discovery of himself," are "a modern attempt to remove the absurdities and inconsistencies . . . of the song, as it stood before" (4th ed., II, 162), but that information still left the reader with some doubt as to which stanzas he had altered.

As for "The Marriage of Sir Gawaine," to cite another example from the seven poems, Percy had stated from the beginning that half of each manuscript leaf had been torn away and that he would in time print the truncated original text so that readers might compare it with his own interpolated version. With all these poems, of course, one could wish that Percy had found a convenient way to call attention both to his specific changes and to the originals, but it would be incorrect to conclude that he failed to inform his readers that he had taken liberties with his texts.

Considering the extent of Percy's changes, one can imagine the cry that Ritson would have sent up if he had been granted access to the folio manuscript. For some of Percy's "conjectural emendations" virtually obscured the manuscripts they were emendating. "The Child of Elle," for example, a mere thirty-nine lines in Percy's folio, grew to a strapping two hundred in the *Reliques,* while "Sir Cauline" nearly doubled its size from 201 to 392. "The Child of Elle" was an unprintable if unique fragment, however, without beginning or end but with enough apparent merit to stir the poet in Percy to "a strong desire to attempt a completion of the story" (I, 90). Indeed, Percy's only real offense in this instance was in not proving a better poet. With regard to "Sir Cauline" and some of the other poems, the controversy has been more substantial. Percy found his manuscript copy of "Sir Cauline" "so very defective and mutilated" that he added "several stanzas in the first part, and still more in the second, to connect and compleat the story in the manner which appeared to him most interesting and affecting" (4th ed., I, 41). Hales, letting Percy off comparatively lightly, remarked that Percy's version abounds in affectations and expressed a preference for the folio copy, "with all its roughness and imperfections."[53] Wheatley, less forgiving, saw "no necessity for this perversion of the original, because the story is . . . complete" (I, 62). Hales's indictment is of the poet; Wheatley's, of the editor. But sometimes with Percy the two roles merge, as they do in "Sir Cauline." If Percy found the temptation to experiment with his poems simply overwhelming at times, he also found support for that activity in one of his guiding principles: considerable license might be permitted an editor whose texts were not to be trusted—"copied from the faulty recitation of some illiterate minstrell," as he wrote of "Sir Cauline" in the fourth edition (I, 41).

This was not an easy position to carry in debate, however, and no doubt Percy was aware that he had stretched the principle pretty far in a few of the poems. Perhaps those facts account for his not replying to Ritson's criticisms with a detailed defense of specific alterations. On the other hand, he did not ignore them. He printed the folio manuscript fragment of "The Marriage of Sir Gawaine" at the end of the fourth edition and thus belatedly fulfilled a first edition promise (I, 11). He did not modify his texts of the seven poems cited by Ritson or provide any precise index of his revisions, but he placed three asterisks at the end of the forty-eight poems in which "any considerable liberties were taken with the old copies" (4th ed., I, xvii). Except

for the **"Essay on the Ancient English Minstrels,"** his changes in the fourth edition are, in fact, comparatively few, and, like those in the essay, most of them were obviously stimulated by Ritson's criticism. A good many relate to his use of the folio manuscript. They include a number of additional footnotes citing divergences from the manuscript, some additional introductory acknowledgments of Percy's changes in the poems, a reversion in the title of "The Wandering Prince of Troy" to the folio manuscript title "Queen Dido," and a note appended to "The Heir of Linne" indicating that "several ancient readings are restored from the folio MS." In the introduction to "Old Robin of Portingale," Percy announces that he is now dropping Robin's title of "Sir" because he is called only Robin in the manuscript; and in "A Lover of Late" he quietly corrects his only significant departure from the text by replacing "fond" in line seventeen with the manuscript's word "kind": "I was as kind as she was faire."[54]

Percy and Ritson were never reconciled either personally or professionally, and it cannot be said that their hostility brought out the best in either. In 1802 Ritson attacked Percy with particular fury in *Ancient Engleish Metrical Romanceës,* where he accused him of practicing "every kind of forgery and imposture" (cxliii, n.). As for Percy, he provided his friend Robert Nares with three paragraphs supplementary to Nares's review of *Ancient Engleish Metrical Romanceës* in the December, 1804, *British Critic,* of which Nares was editor, and Nares printed them separately in the January, 1805, issue as a "Supplemental Article" submitted by a "friend" of Percy.[55] Percy also secured an account of an incident shortly before Ritson's death in September, 1803, in which Ritson set fire to his manuscripts in his chambers in Gray's Inn and, when challenged respecting his behavior, replied that he was writing a pamphlet proving Christ to have been an impostor. Robert Anderson, to whom Percy sent a copy of the account, informed him in a letter of June 22, 1811, that it had been published in Cromek's *Select Scotish Songs.*[56]

If not already of that opinion, Percy—"the worthy and venerable Bishop of Dromore," as the *British Critic* called him—must have been convinced by the Gray's Inn incident that Ritson was quite insane, and perhaps it is not surprising that he took some pains to have the strange conduct of his severest critic made known. It would have been better, of course, for him to ignore Ritson's continuing attacks upon him. His reputation was secure, at least for his own time, and in his final edition of the *Reliques* he had put forth the best defense of his practices that he knew and had again shown himself ready to acknowledge criticism with careful self-examination. The excellent fourth edition of the *Reliques* was the high point of an extraordinary scholarly career, and it was itself the most persuasive argument in support of Percy's case.

Notes

1. The best discussion of the background of the *Reliques* is contained in Albert B. Friedman's *The Ballad Revival* (Chicago: University of Chicago Press, 1961), to which this chapter is much indebted.

2. Diary, August 19-30, 1761.

3. Henry Bold, *Latine Songs, with Their English: and Poems* (London, 1685), p. 80.

4. Friedman, p. 129. Addison also devoted number 85 of the *Spectator* to a discussion of "The Children in the Wood."

5. *Reliques of Ancient English Poetry* (London, 1765), I, xv.

6. [*The Correspondence of Thomas Percy and William Shenstone*, ed. Cleanth Brooks, VII of *The Percy Letters* (New Haven: Yale University Press, 1977)], 175-93.

7. Percy's use of the *Collection of Old Ballads* has been carefully analyzed by Stephen Vartin in *Thomas Percy's Reliques: Its Structure and Organization* (Ph.D diss., New York University, 1972).

8. The folio manuscript is British Library Add. MS. 27,879. It was edited in three volumes by John W. Hales and Frederick J. Furnivall and published as *Bishop Percy's Folio Manuscript* (London, 1867-1868); Percy's flyleaf inscription is printed at I, lxxiv, from which the extract is taken.

9. *Bishop Percy's Folio Manuscript*, I, lxxiv.

10. *Percy Letters*, VII, 3-4.

11. L. F. Powell, "Percy's Reliques," *The Library*, September, 1928, pp. 114-16.

12. *Bishop Percy's Folio Manuscript*, I, xiii.

13. *Percy Letters*, VII, 130, 134.

14. Ibid, p. 119.

15. British Library Add. MS. 45,867, A28, B40. Percy was granted admission to the Reading Room on April 24, 1761.

16. Like the Shenstone correspondence, all four of these correspondences have been published in separate volumes of *The Percy Letters*.

17. Percy's changes are discussed in Albert B. Friedman, "The First Draft of Percy's *Reliques*," *PMLA*, 69 (December, 1954), 1233-49; and *The Ballad Revival*, pp. 224-25. For discussions of Dalrymple's assistance see the introduction to the *Percy Letters* (vol. 4) and P. G. Thomas, "Bishop Percy and the Scottish Ballad," *TLS* [(London) *Times Literary Supplement*], July 4, 1929, p. 538. David C. Fowler argues persuasively that some of the best-known Scottish ballads ("Sir Patrick Spence" and "Edward, Edward" among them) were revised before they were sent to Percy (*A Literary History of the Popular Ballad* [Durham: Duke University Press, 1968], pp. 239-70).

18. *Percy Letters*, IV, 49.

19. British Library Add. MS. 32,334, f. 2.

20. Percy's diary entries related to Johnson's visit have been published in Boswell's *Life of Johnson*, I, 553-54.

21. *Percy Letters*, IV, 1.

22. Allen T. Hazen, *Samuel Johnson's Prefaces and Dedications* (New Haven: Yale University Press, 1937), pp. 161-62.

23. Robert Anderson, *The Life of Samuel Johnson, LL.D.*, 3d ed. (Edinburgh, 1815), p. 309.

24. Hazen, pp. 158-68.

25. Diary, November 22, 1764.

26. *Public Advertiser*, February 11, 1765.

27. *Critical Review*, February, 1765, pp. 119-30; *Monthly Review*, April, 1765, pp. 241-53; *Gentleman's Magazine*, April, 1765, pp. 179-83.

28. Diary, March 16, 1765.

29. *Percy Letters*, IV, 94; III, 119.

30. *Four Essays, as Improved and Enlarged in the Second Edition of the Reliques of Ancient English Poetry* (London, 1767). René Wellek said of the essays that they "represent, in many ways, the best and most learned collection of essays on older English literary history that appeared before Warton" (*The Rise of English Literary History* [Chapel Hill: University of North Carolina Press, 1941], p. 144).

31. The earliest manuscript of *Piers Plowman* is thought to date from about 1372. The attribution to William Langland, whom Percy mistakenly calls Robert, remains uncertain.

32. Wellek, *The Rise of English Literary History*, pp. 154, 158.

33. Boswell, *Life of Johnson*, III, 278.

34. The earliest advertisements I have found for the second edition are those in the *London Chronicle* and *London Evening-Post* for December 1-3, 1767. On June 25, 1767, however, Percy wrote to John Bowle to ask how he could convey a copy of the new edition to him, and on July 13 he wrote to express the hope that "the Books" had reached Bowle in accordance with his directions [University of Cape Town: BC 188, Bowle-Evans Collection, Correspondence between the Reverend Thomas Percy and the Reverend John Bowle, (4) and (5)].

35. Vincent H. Ogburn, "Thomas Percy's Unfinished Collection, Ancient English and Scottish Poems," *ELH*, 3 (1936), 183-89; E. K. A. Mackenzie, "Percy's Great Schemes," *Modern Language Review*, 43 (1948), 34-38.

36. In the first edition "My Mind to Me a Kingdom Is" is at I, 268-71 (11 stanzas). In the second edition it is at I, 292-94 (7 stanzas), and "The Golden Mean" is at I, 303-4 (4 stanzas).

37. Letter Thomas Tyrwhitt to Percy, August 30, 1768, Bodleian MS. Eng. Lett. d. 59, ff. 17-18.

38. In new footnotes to the Northumberland poems, Percy also writes familiarly of the county and the people. The "shyars thre" in line 14 of "The Ancient

Ballad of Chevy-Chase" he identifies in the second edition as the Northumberland districts of Islandshire, Norehamshire, and Bamboroughshire. He notes that "winn their haye" in line 2 of "The Battle of Otterbourne" is "the Northumberland phrase to this day" for "getting in their hay," and two stanzas later he identifies Ottercap Hill, Rodeliffe Cragge, and Green Leyton as "well-known places in Northumberland." In annotating "The More Modern Ballad of Chevy-Chase" he notes that "The Chiviot Hills and circumjacent Wastes are at present void both of Deer and Woods: but formerly they had enough of both to justify the Descriptions attempted here and in the Ancient Ballad" (I, 256).

39. It can be noted that Percy's continuing search permitted him to add seven items in the second edition to his list of thirty romances supplementary to the essay "On the Ancient Metrical Romances."

40. "Observations on Dr. Percy's Account of Minstrels among the Saxons," *Archaeologia* (London, 1773), II, 100-106.

41. Bodleian Mss. Percy c.11, f.17; Eng. Lett. d. 46, ff. 653-56.

42. *Lit. Illus.,* VIII, 164. The letter was published in *Archaeologia* (London, 1775), III, 310.

43. *The General Biographical Dictionary* (London, 1812-1816), "Joseph Ritson."

44. *A Select Collection of English Songs* (London, 1783), I, lxviii. Thomas Carter's music for Percy's song was printed in the third volume of the collection, pp. 219-20.

45. Bodleian MS. Percy c. 1, f. 122.

46. Harvard bMS Eng 891 (3), quoted by permission of the Houghton Library. Percy's letter of November 19, 1785, is unsigned and appears to be either a draft or a copy.

47. In his copy (at Yale-Beinecke), Joseph Haslewood tipped in a newspaper announcement of the edition ("This Day is published") marked in pen "July, 1795." This date is consistent with the first discussion of the edition in Percy's correspondence and elsewhere.

48. Percy recalled his nephew's receiving £160 for his part in the fourth edition (Bodleian MS. Percy c. 3, f. 200).

49. Ibid., f. 59; *Ancient Engleish Metrical Romanceës* (London, 1802), pp. cvii-cviii, n.

50. British Library Add. MS. 32,335, f. 197.

51. *Lit. Illus.,* VIII, 145; Bertrand H. Bronson, *Joseph Ritson Scholar-at-Arms* (Berkeley: University of California Press, 1938), I, 295.

52. *The Percy Letters,* III, 119; *Willis's Current Notes,* November, 1854, p. 91. In "Percy's Reliques" (p. 136), L. F. Powell cited a June 21, 1774, receipt signed by Percy for twenty guineas paid to him by James Dodsley "for correcting and improving the third edition . . . , which is to consist of a thousand Copies." *Willis's Current Notes,* however, cites a later agreement (March 7, 1775) whereby Dodsley, in consideration of being able to print 1500 copies, relinquished to Percy, as his future property, all the copperplates used in the *Reliques.* Dodsley also agreed to pay Percy forty guineas five years after the presswork on the third edition was completed, and Percy was not to republish the *Reliques* until all 1500 copies were sold.

53. *Bishop Percy's Folio Manuscript,* III, 2.

54. References in the paragraph are to the fourth edition: II, 137; III, 48, 178, 193.

55. *British Critic,* January, 1805, pp. 88-89. Nares had succeeded Percy as vicar of Easton Mauduit.

56. *Lit. Illus.,* VII, 215; Robert Burns, *Select Scotish Songs, Ancient and Modern,* ed. R. H. Cromek (London, 1810), I, 224-30.

Bertram H. Davis (essay date 1982)

SOURCE: "Thomas Percy: The Dilemma of a Scholar-Cleric," in *The Kentucky Review,* Vol. 3, No. 3, 1982, pp. 28-46.

[*In the following essay, Davis examines contemporary controversies surrounding Percy's* Reliques, *focusing specifically on Percy's accuracy and editorial practices.*]

"I bestow upon a few old poems," Thomas Percy wrote to David Dalrymple on 25 January 1763, "those idle moments, which some of my grave brethren pass away over a sober game at whist."[1] How Dalrymple reacted to Percy's analogy is not known, but the modern reader is likely to dismiss it as a facetious if not wholly insincere depreciation of Percy's own efforts, which were pointing toward the publication of England's most influential anthology, the three-volume *Reliques of Ancient English Poetry.* Percy's "idle moments" filled up much more than the odd hours and occasional evenings his comment would suggest: mornings and afternoons in the British Museum, for example; eleven days at Magdalene College, Cambridge, where Percy transcribed ballads from the Samuel Pepys collection of black letter broadsides; and important literary correspondences with poets and scholars like William Shenstone, Richard Farmer, Thomas Warton, Evan Evans, and David Dalrymple himself. Percy's course of reading and inquiry for the *Reliques* overshadowed not merely his numerous literary efforts of the decade, but his work as vicar of Easton Maudit in rural Northamptonshire and rector of nearby Wilby as well. Grave or frivolous, a clergyman with the devotion to whist that Percy displayed for old poems would have provided gossip not just for his immediate circle but for an entire diocese.

Percy's statement to Dalrymple antedated the publication of the *Reliques* by two years, and, as a stimulus for their ballad discussions, perhaps it had the appeal of disarming innocence. Percy was something of a novice in this field, and he was eager to benefit from the knowledge and taste of experienced and reputable scholars. As his great work took shape, however, one might expect that he would no longer have found reason to treat it so cavalierly. But Percy never changed in his self-assessment, even as he himself became the scholar of experience and reputation. Fifteen years later he employed an almost identical analogy in a letter to the young Scottish editor John Pinkerton: "I have commonly taken up these trifles, as other grave men have done cards, to unbend and amuse the mind when fatigued with graver studies."[2] Nor was "trifles" the worst of his disparagement. In 1765, when he sent an advance copy to Thomas Birch, he described the **Reliques** as a "strange collection of trash."[3] And in other private correspondence, he shrugged off his efforts variously as "the amusem[t] of idle hours," "the Sins and Follies of my Youth," and the "pleasurable amusements of my younger years."[4] In 1785, he informed his publisher, James Dodsley, who had inquired if Percy was contemplating a fourth edition, that he was quite "indifferent" about the prospects of further publication and would be glad to have the **Reliques** forgotten "among the other Levities & Vanities" of his youth.[5]

In print, Percy was no more generous in appraising the **Reliques.** He apologized in the Preface to the first edition for having "bestowed . . . attention on a parcel of OLD BALLADS," and observed that preparing the work for the press "has been the amusement of now and then a vacant hour amid the leisure and retirement of rural life, and hath only served as a relaxation from graver studies."[6] Nor did public approval of the **Reliques** move him to modify his apology, which remained unchanged through the revised editions of 1767, 1775, and 1795. Indeed, the only question that Percy is known to have raised about his apology was whether it had gone far enough. "Tell me if you think my apology at the end sufficient," he wrote to Richard Farmer in November 1764, when he enclosed a proof sheet of his Preface and dedication:

> Or shall I belabour the point more.—Tho' perhaps it may appear to you hardly true; for as my Letters to you have turned so much upon ballad-making, you will perhaps think the subject has taken up more of my time than it really has: yet I assure you, if you had been with me all the while you would have attested the truth of it.[7]

For all his professed indifference in 1785, Percy, stung by the sharp attacks of the scholar Joseph Ritson upon his accuracy, editorial practice, and integrity, authorized a fourth edition, which bears the date 1794 but was not published until July 1795. Such a change of heart, according to an "Advertisement" at the front of the fourth edition, resulted from the "importunity" of Percy's friends, "to which he at last yielded." But, the Advertisement implied, Percy had not himself returned in the role of editor. Instead, he had "accepted the humble offer of an Editor in a Nephew,"[8] whose name was also Thomas Percy.

It is impossible to take this last statement as it seems to have been intended. Percy's nephew, a precocious poet who had published *Verses on the Death of Dr. Samuel Johnson* when he was fifteen, was, to be sure, a fellow of St. John's College, Oxford, and after the death of Percy's son in 1783 he became Percy's announced candidate to edit a much talked about fourth volume of the **Reliques.** But he was an unsettled young man who barely escaped a suit by the parishioners of his first church, at Grays in Essex, and who chafed throughout the period he served as rector of Maralin in Percy's own diocese in Northern Ireland, where Percy had moved in 1783 following his appointment as Bishop of Dromore. Tom's "Tastes and Persuits," Percy wrote to his wife on 17 September 1797, "are so different from Mine."[9] The young man of such different tastes and pursuits seems to have been paid handsomely for whatever services he performed for the fourth edition, but we may be sure that they did not include editing this crucial response to the relentless attacks of Joseph Ritson. It was "most unfortunate," Percy wrote to his nephew on 20 February 1798, that the Shakespearean scholar George Steevens "got out of you, that you were only an Umbra" in the fourth edition.[10]

This was certainly an odd way for a scholar of Percy's stature to treat his major work, and it is not surprising that readers would question his sincerity in dismissing England's best loved and most influential anthology as a mere "parcel of OLD BALLADS" or, worse still, as a "strange collection of trash." Surely one is justified in asking if Percy's work of revision for the fourth edition does not demonstrate convincingly that his expression of indifference in 1785 was simply a pose, not intended to be taken seriously by his publisher. And could the pretended editorship of his nephew have been anything more than a device which permitted him to maintain the pose before the public, while he himself took up the challenge that Joseph Ritson had thrown out to him? Why in the first place was Percy so anxious to minimize, as in his letter to Farmer, an activity which his friends were not only aware of but stood ready to encourage and assist?

The answers to these and related questions are less obvious than they appear on the surface. They are buried deep in the history of the ballad in England and in the character and experience of Thomas Percy himself. Unlike later scholars, this Shropshire native had not been steeped from his youth in a tradition that honored the ballad as the genuine expression of the English and Scottish folk, a cultural phenomenon as distinctive in style as it often was in theme. Almost from the dawn of printing, English balladeers had seized the opportunity of quick publication to hawk their penny broadsides on London streets, where up-to-the-minute political satire, court intrigue, and gallows confession became part of the steady ballad fare. Drawn willy nilly into ballad scholarship by his chance discovery of the famous folio manuscript, Percy was quick to try to establish the line between the old and the new. The romantic figure of the minstrel, if not his own creation, embodied his conscious effort to distinguish the ancient "minstrel" ballads from these modern scurrilities, which had brought the very word "ballad" into disrepute. *"Ballad,"* wrote Isaac Watts, as cited in Johnson's *Dictionary of the English Language,* "once signified a solemn and sacred song, as well as trivial, when Solomon's Song was called the *ballad of ballads*; but now it is applied to nothing but trifling verse."

The distinction between the folk ballad and the broadside, obscured by the sheer mass of ballad literature, became further obscured as a number of the older poems were themselves published in sixteenth- and seventeenth-century broadsides, and as poems of all kinds were lumped together in hastily compiled collections like the 1658 *Wit Restor'd* and the 1682 *Wit and Drollery.* In the *Reliques* Percy printed both a "minstrel" and a later broadside version of "Chevy Chase," one of the most popular English ballads. He called attention also to a Latin translation of "Chevy Chase" published by Henry Bold in 1685 "By Order of the Bishop of London," a curious exercise in the laying on of episcopal hands.[11] In ordering its translation, Bishop Henry Compton may have invested "Chevy Chase" with a new dignity, but the effect of such preferment was to separate the poem still further from its humble origins in English border minstrelsy. Unlike "To drive the deere with hound and horne," "Cane, feras ut abigat" invoked no appealing image of Northumberland's Cheviot Hills. This Latin anomaly lingered on, nonetheless, through at least four reprintings in the first decade of the eighteenth century, until Joseph Addison thrust it into the shadows with his warm appraisal of the English broadside version in Numbers 70 and 74 of *The Spectator.*

Addison had kind words for other old ballads also, specifically "The Children in the Wood" and "The Wanton Wife of Bath,"[12] and partly through the impetus he had given it ancient English balladry enjoyed a modest revival in the 1720s and 1730s, most notably with the publication of the anonymously edited *A Collection of Old Ballads* from 1723 to 1725 and Elizabeth Cooper's *The Muses Library* in 1737. But the prejudice against the "vulgar" literature held its place among England's educated classes, and Percy had every reason to be mindful of it as he went about the task of preparing the *Reliques* for publication. The *Gentleman's Magazine* reviewer who greeted the book upon its appearance in 1765 no doubt expressed a common attitude: this collection, he wrote, "will please persons that have a taste for genuine poetry, chiefly as an object of curiosity. . . ."[13] The *Reliques,* in short, merited consideration as a museum piece rather than as a contribution to English letters.

One could wish that Percy, who clearly admired the poems he had brought together, could have held to his convictions whatever his concern for public reaction. Authors' apologies for their work are not always to be taken at face value. If Percy did indeed wish to dismiss the *Reliques* as a mere "parcel of OLD BALLADS," would he have intruded upon the public's patience to the extent of three volumes and some one thousand pages? One's immediate conclu-

sion is that the answer to the question has to be no. But Percy, one must acknowledge, was never quite certain of himself, and his motives as a result are not easy to determine. He looked constantly for advice and reassurance from the poet William Shenstone, who passed on his assessments of literally hundreds of poems in earlier collections and virtually guided Percy to a format for the *Reliques* which both of them hoped would appeal to readers of taste.

Percy's apology reflects his indecision. For whether or not he intended it, the apology was an instrument for blunting the expected criticism from an audience not partial and perhaps hostile to the ballad, and for encouraging the indulgence that modesty commonly draws to itself. If with this defense the book was still to be condemned, the apology at least freed Percy from a charge of harboring any serious pretensions for it.

II

What has been discussed so far deals primarily with one aspect of Percy's apology in one context: his disparagement of his ballad work in the light of contemporary ballad opinion. But Percy also observed in his Preface that the *Reliques* was "a relaxation from graver studies," with the unmistakeable implication that most of his time was devoted to pursuits of more consequence. Perhaps in 1765 such an observation was not wholly unjustified, even when one considers the extraordinary effort that Percy poured into the *Reliques.* Between 8 March 1759 and 23 March 1761, Percy contracted with the publisher Robert Dodsley for translations of a Chinese novel, *The Song of Solomon,* and a book of runic poetry; for a collection of stories called *The Matrons*; and for the two-volume *Miscellaneous Pieces Relating to the Chinese.*[14] And he actually completed and published each of these works before the *Reliques* appeared on 11 March 1765. In addition, he contracted with Jacob Tonson during the same period to edit the works of Buckingham, Surrey's poems, *The Guardian,* and *The Spectator.* In November 1763, he began the work of translating Henri Mallet's two-volume *L'Introduction à l'histoire de Dannemarc,* and by mid-1764 his *Key to the New Testament* was at the press.[15] All these, presumably, were intended fruits of his "graver studies," and all had one advantage in common over the ancient English ballads. They had never suffered in the public mind from association with the hawkers of disreputable broadsides.

Percy's diary leaves no room to doubt that, in addition to contracting for these numerous projects, he channeled enormous energies into them. On one day alone—18 May 1761—he read five plays, and by the spring of 1765 he had read more than 175 early Restoration plays in preparing a new key to *The Rehearsal* for his planned edition of Buckingham's works.[16] On 17 May 1764, a day stretched out from four in the morning until midnight, he translated twenty-two pages of Mallet's history, wrote ten letters, and took two rides. "I find you are indefatigable," wrote the Welsh scholar Evan Evans, caught up in the torrent of Percy's interests.[17] Percy's capacity for work, in fact, seems at times to have been almost superhuman, and the reader of his diary comes with relief upon the discovery that even Percy had to interrupt a twenty-hour day with two rides. One may wonder, to be sure, whether a regimen of 175 Restoration plays qualified as "graver" studies, but of course for *The Rehearsal* Percy would have focused upon the exploits afield of heroic characters like Almanzor and Pizarro rather than the close-quartered tilting of Dorimant, Horner, and their fellow rakes.

It is thus not at all impossible that Percy expressed a sincere conviction when he called his ballad work "a relaxation from graver studies." A few hours with "Sir Patrick Spence," "The Battle of Otterbourne," or "Sir Cauline" may well have proved restful after an extended engagement with Mallet's French or Drury Lane's heroics: needed diversions, like Percy's two rides on 17 May 1764. Nor is it necessary to assume that Percy intended a false picture of his activities when he assured Richard Farmer in November 1764, that the ballads pre-empted much less of his time than Farmer may have inferred from his letters. In writing to most scholars during this period, Percy alludes to such interests as his projected editions of *The Spectator* and Surrey's poems, but he seldom loses sight of the ballads; they move through the letters like soldiers in review, a virtual procession of title and quotation, text and variant, comment and question. For, far more than his other projects, the ballads required a close attention to detail. Dates, titles, language, word order, spelling—all had to be checked and checked again. And the ballads offered such scattered fields for exploration and study that Percy was compelled to rely upon his correspondences with learned friends in England, Scotland, and Wales if he was not to remain ignorant about much that he considered important. As a result, the letters—at least those of his major literary correspondences—provide a less reliable guide than his diary to the variety of his activities during the years that the *Reliques* was taking shape. The *Reliques* was a major, but by no means an exclusive, literary activity, and doubtless part of its attraction was that it provided Percy with constant new diversions when he grew weary of other work. Percy may have looked upon his "graver" projects as the proper business of a scholar, but the ballads were plainly his delight.

III

Percy's reluctance to give the impression that he took the ballads seriously may have been understandable in 1765, when the ballads were still awaiting general acceptance as literature of a high order, and when his own convictions might still have been shaken by an adverse reaction from readers of taste. But if the reputation of the ballads was the barrier to Percy's unabashed commitment to ballad study, one would expect him to have strengthened his convictions—and revised his Preface—when the barrier was lifted; that is, when the *Reliques* went into second, third, and fourth editions, and when it cleared the way for the ballad collections published between 1769 and 1791 by

David Herd, Thomas Evans, John Pinkerton, Joseph Ritson, and Charlotte Brooke. Yet, as has been noted, Percy left his Preface unchanged through the final edition of his lifetime in 1795, and he continued to disparage his ballad work privately as well as publicly. His tendency to dissociate himself from the *Reliques* seems, in fact, to have become increasingly pronounced as he rose in clerical dignity and stature. It was not Thomas Percy, Vicar of Easton Maudit—not even Thomas Percy, Dean of Carlisle—but Thomas Percy, Bishop of Dromore, who numbered the *Reliques* among the "Sins and Follies" and the "Levities & Vanities" of his youth. And it was the editor of only the fourth edition who invoked a nephew to mask his role in the revision. One wonders nonetheless if, even in his earlier years, Percy ever felt totally at ease in such an unclerical task as editing a parcel of old ballads.

In 1750, when Oxford awarded him the Bachelor's degree, Percy could hardly have seemed suited for the role of popularizer of the English and Scottish ballads, which had not been part of his Oxford studies. He was not even educated to be a scholar of the ballad, or, for that matter, of Chinese culture and literature, runic poetry, or the antiquities of Northern Europe. He was on his way to becoming a clergyman, and in time a prelate, of the Church of England. For, whatever the attraction of literary studies, Percy's commitment to the clerical life was to be wholehearted and unshakeable, an outgrowth perhaps from roots that were struck deep in his youth and are still visible.

Among the few remains of Percy's youthful writings is a sixteen-line **"Hymn by T.P. at school,"** which Percy himself apparently cared enough about to preserve for his children and grandchildren. In its opening lines the hymn, written sometime before Percy left for Oxford after turning seventeen, lays out in rudimentary fashion the moral course which was to guide him through the years ahead:

> Great God! Who rules the Earth & Sky,
> In whom all powers of goodness lie,
> O! if it be thy soveraign Will,
> Keep me from all o'erwhelming Ill,
> Teach me the paths of Sin to shun,
> From her deluding ways to run.
> O! let me not unthinking fall,
> But listen to Religion's call.[18]

One cannot, of course, make too much of such a poem. It was a juvenile effort, perhaps the kind of exercise that a schoolmaster might have set for any intelligent youth of Percy's age. But another Percy activity of this period bears a more individual stamp and may thus permit a keener insight into some of his youthful qualities. Before he matriculated at Oxford in July 1746, Percy had assembled and catalogued a library of some 265 books, and in a gesture of fraternal good will he appointed his younger brother Anthony librarian.[19] The library was more heavily weighted in classical and English literature than in religion, but, for a boy of seventeen, it was amazingly rich in all three. As one might expect of a conscientious mid-century schoolboy, the Latin poets, playwrights, and historians were represented in some profusion, along with such English greats as Shakespeare and Milton. But side by side with this traditional gathering stood a later English pantheon: Samuel Butler's *Hudibras,* the works of Abraham Cowley, and Gerard Langbaine's *Account of the English Dramatick Poets*; the plays of Dryden, Otway, Southerne, and Congreve; and Aphra Behn's novels, *Gulliver's Travels, Robinson Crusoe, Moll Flanders,* and *Pamela.* There were four untitled collections, two each of plays and poems. Germs of specific later interests can be seen in two volumes of "Antiquities," seven sets of Ovid's poems (Percy's choice for subsequent translation), and *The Seven Wise Maisters of Rome,* from which he was to take a story for **The Matrons** of 1762.

For all Percy's tender age, this was a young man's rather than a boy's library. Infrequent items like books of fairies, pirates, highwaymen, "Extraordinary Adventures," "Unparallel'd Varieties," and "Wonderful Prodigies" remained the sole clues to the boy from whom the young man had recently emerged. Clearly by the time he was seventeen Percy's literary tastes and interests had advanced far beyond those of most contemporaries, and it is not surprising that Christ Church, Oxford awarded him a scholarship when he was still "of the third Class from the top" at Newport School.[20] But the library, though it contained fewer religious than literary works, was no less remarkable for the intensity of its religious coloration. Such household texts as *The Whole Duty of Man* and *The Practice of Piety* were supplemented with *The New Whole Duty of Man, The Devout Soul's Exercise, The Practice of the Faithful,* and *A Guide to Heaven.* Perhaps these were simply additions to a young person's standard fare contributed by overzealous parents. But they were only the beginning. Half a dozen Bibles—in Greek, Latin, and English, the last in both black letter and modern print—suggest an aspiring cleric's rather than a schoolboy's interest, and other books would seem to reflect a curiosity transcending the need to strengthen one's moral and religious fiber through such everyday works as *The Whole Duty of Man* and *The Practice of Piety. The Companion to the Altar, A Persuasive to the Communion, Admonition against Swearing, Torments after Death, The Principles of Religion,* Burgess's sermons, and *A Reply to the Bishop of Exeter* point as surely to the later vicar, dean, and bishop as Percy's literary collection does to the poet and scholar.

The lines were not direct, of course. They took Percy through four years as an Oxford undergraduate and three as a candidate for the Master's degree, during the last two of which he served as a deacon at the Shropshire churches of Astley Abbots and Tasley, just outside his home town of Bridgnorth. The Dean and Chapter of Christ Church appointed him Vicar of Easton Maudit in October 1753, the year of his Master's degree and his ordination as a priest, but he continued as curate at Astley Abbots and Tasley until April 1756, when he began his long residence at Easton Maudit.

For Percy, these were years of intensive study. In addition to Latin and Greek, he acquired a sufficient knowledge of Hebrew to compose a number of short "dissertations" and, in 1764, to publish a translation of **The Song of Solomon.**[21] His Biblical studies culminated in the 1766 **Key to the New Testament,** a popular manual frequently reprinted and probably familiar to student and cleric alike.[22] His knowledge of French led to his translation of Mallet, published in 1770 in two volumes; his love of Spanish inspired him to attempt an edition of **Don Quixote,** relinquished in time to John Bowle, and to translate Spanish poetry, two examples of which he slipped into the first volume of the **Reliques.**[23] His library grew with him, from the 265 books recorded in 1746 to about 450 at the time of his move from Bridgnorth to Easton Maudit, when he sold or gave away just over half of them, presumably to ease the cost and effort of the move.[24] Percy's 1756 list, as could be expected, was richer than the 1746 list in both literature and religion. Three editions of Cervantes made their first appearance in it, along with Buckingham's works and sets of the *Tatler, Spectator,* and *Guardian.* All were to be Percy editorial projects within a few years. New religious works included a collection of eighteen sermons and Brian Hunt's *Parochial Pasturage.* Hunt's book was a gift, perhaps from a well-wisher as Percy embarked on his clerical career.

IV

Sometime before November 1757—and probably before his move to Easton Maudit in April 1756—occurred the event that was to transform Percy's life: his discovery of the now famous folio manuscript of ballads and romances in the home of his Shropshire friend Humphrey Pitt. "I saw it lying dirty on the floor under a Bureau in ye Parlour," Percy wrote, "being used by the Maids to light the fires."[25] Percy asked for the manuscript and was given it; and on 27 November 1757, he informed the poet William Shenstone, in the opening letter of their correspondence, that he had shown the manuscript to Samuel Johnson and that Johnson had expressed a desire to see it printed.[26] Shenstone himself responded enthusiastically, and he continued as Percy's chief advisor on the **Reliques** until his death on 11 February 1763, two years to the day before the **Reliques** was published.

For Percy, editing the **Reliques** required a radical shift in course, and he did not move quickly to turn Shenstone's enthusiasm to account. Perhaps he was simply enjoying Easton Maudit too much. Shortly after his arrival to take up his duties as vicar, he had been appointed chaplain to the young Earl of Sussex, who resided in the parish as lord of the manor. In less than four months the earl also appointed him rector of Wilby, about five miles distant from Easton Maudit. Percy found his work satisfying, but it was not so demanding that he did not have days on end when he was free to do almost exactly as he pleased. Both parishes were small, and the Earl of Sussex proved an easy taskmaster as well as a good friend. Except for a weekly sermon at each church, the calls upon Percy's time were infrequent and irregular: only about once in three weeks did a baptism, wedding, or burial interrupt his contemplation, reading, writing, or relaxation. In the decade between 1761 and 1771, he published ten books, for which much of the groundwork was laid during his Oxford period and the apprentice years of his priesthood.

No groundwork was laid in ancient balladry, however; in this his libraries of 1746 and 1756 were as deficient as the Oxford curriculum. Drawn though he was to writing poetry during his early manhood, his poetry had little in it of the drama and color of the ancient ballad. It consisted largely of songs and sonnets, many of them mere exercises in gallantry reflecting his pleasure in circles to which a handsome and lively bachelor was a welcome addition. "Flavia," "Delia," and "Mira" were much on his mind, at least until he met Anne Gutteridge, whom he married in April 1759. By contrast with such society verse, the ballads were street urchins, whose company Percy was not likely to seek out on his own initiative. Indeed, it must have been very difficult for him to contemplate, as his first major project, a publication so utterly foreign to the religious and literary studies that had been such an integral part of his existence since his youth.

Perhaps the prospect of trumpeting the deeds of the ancient Percys made it easier for him to yield to Samuel Johnson, who, as Percy wrote to Shenstone on 9 January 1758, "extorted a promise" that Percy would publish "the most valuable pieces" in his manuscript.[27] He took great pride in his Percy connection. In 1756 he changed the spelling of his name from Piercy to Percy, and in subsequent years he undertook to demonstrate that his family had descended from a great grandson of the second Earl of Northumberland who had migrated to Worcester in the early sixteenth century. Nonetheless, he must have had serious misgivings about fulfilling his promise to Johnson. "If I regarded only my own satisfaction," he informed Shenstone in the same letter, "I should by no means be eager to render my Collection cheap by publication." But surely Percy had other reasons for his reluctance to publish. No doubt he enjoyed the ownership of poems never before printed and perhaps unique in manuscript; but that was hardly a consideration which could lead logically to the apology of his 1765 Preface. A more likely sequel to it would have been an acknowledgment in the Preface that he felt an obligation to share such treasures with the public. But Percy never reached that point. As most of the manuscript poems, he wrote in the Preface,

> are of great simplicity, and seem to have been meerly written for the people, he was long in doubt, whether in the present state of improved literature, they could be deemed worthy the attention of the public. At length the importunity of his friends prevailed, and he could refuse nothing to such judges as the author of the RAMBLER, and the late Mr. SHENSTONE.[28]

Percy's real reservations grew out of his doubts about the poems and about the appropriateness of permitting his name to be associated with them, and it was not until the Countess of Northumberland consented to accept the dedication that he abandoned his plan to publish the *Reliques* anonymously.[29]

Such doubts seem strange to us today, but they were a natural consequence of the ballad's reputation in Percy's time and of his own experience and temperament. The word "ballad," as Isaac Watts noted, had come to suggest only "trifling verse," and Percy's description of the ballads as "trash" and "trifles" merely reflects a common attitude of his day. For his other pioneering efforts—his translations of a Chinese novel, for example, and of Icelandic and Spanish verse—he felt no need to apologize. For all the public knew, each might bring one to the edge of a promising unknown. But the ballad had been so discredited by constant use and abuse that any serious exploration of it could have been dismissed as misguided, if not quite foolhardy, and Percy was not prepared to run such a risk unprotected. the favorable judgments of Johnson, Shenstone, and others were the shield—or, to use Percy's word, amulet—that made his quest possible.[30]

As for Percy's judgment of the poems, one can hardly accept "trash" and "trifles" as representing a definitive view. Doubtless he expected some contemporaries to apply such words to the ballads, and he was never sufficiently sure of himself to state categorically that they would be wrong. His description of the *Reliques* as a "strange collection of trash" in his 1765 letter to Thomas Birch was probably a concession to the public view which he hoped would not be taken seriously, but perhaps he would not have been surprised if Birch had expressed agreement with it. It is unlikely, however, that Percy ever used such words to Johnson or Shenstone, whose support of his ballad efforts put all admirers of English poetry in their debt. Perhaps he confided to them as he did to poet and fellow antiquary Thomas Warton on 5 May 1765: "Ancient English Poetry will ever be my favorite subject."[31]

Under the circumstances, one cannot criticize Percy very severely for his indecision. He did not have the benefit of an earlier *Reliques,* as Herd, Ritson, and others did when they came to publish their collections. He only dimly perceived the value of his folio manuscript when he first discovered it, and for a time did little but scribble in its margins. Percy had to feel his way, and for him it was by no means an easy way. From his boyhood, literature and religion had captured his mind and heart. But the literature was not the ephemera of London streets. It was not even the folk strain of the ancient minstrel, the guiding spirit of Percy's work. It was the literature of Greece and Rome and of the latter-day English and continental greats; and this, of course, did not include the ballads, for which Percy found a place only as relaxations from his graver studies of literature and religion.

Ironically, the *Reliques,* more than anything else, was to be responsible for Percy's advancement in the church. Through his new patroness, the Countess of Northumberland, he became chaplain and secretary to the Earl of Northumberland in 1765. The Earl was made Duke of Northumberland the next year; and Percy moved ahead to become chaplain-in-ordinary to George III in 1767, Dean of Carlisle in 1778, and Bishop of Dromore in 1782. Even

Mrs. Percy was accorded an honor, though not a clerical one: in 1767 she was appointed wet nurse to the infant Prince Edward, who was to be the father of Queen Victoria. *Bishop* Percy might have been glad, as he stated in 1785, to have the *Reliques* forgotten "among the other Levities & Vanities of his youth," but it had gained him a reputation which he could not escape. On his way to the boat for Ireland in April 1798, for example, he stopped at the Welsh village of Llangollen, where he was introduced to Lady Eleanor Butler and Miss Sarah Ponsonby, who, as he wrote to his wife on 26 April

> have formed to themselves one of the most delightful Hermitages, that ever was . . . & they are more acquainted with all that is going on . . . than any Ladies I have seen in the *Beau Monde*. . . . There was none of the Nonsense I ever published, but what they had all by heart.—And in the most elegant & select Library I ever saw, I c^d. not but be flattered to see my GRAND WORKS. . . . In short I had great difficulty to tear myself away from these fair Inchantresses, whose magic spell w^d. have chained me there, to the end of time, if I had not broke thro' it with no little Violence to myself.[32]

The passage is a revealing one. In spite of his frequent dismissal of the *Reliques*—which in this letter is not singled out as his only "Nonsense"—he can still invoke the spirit of the young ballad editor sallying forth in search of adventure. He has been drawn to a hermitage, where "fair Inchantresses" have woven a spell with sweet words and a vision of his GRAND WORKS among the most elegant and select company he has ever seen. One can understand Percy's readiness to yield to such enchantment. But even as he recalls his pleasure in submission, he maintains the distance between the Bishop of Dromore and the young Vicar of Easton Maudit with his promise to Samuel Johnson and his countless publishers' contracts to fulfill. "Nonsense" is of a piece with his other terms of disparagement in his later years: "Sins," "Follies," "Levities," and "Vanities"; and it is significant that the word appears in a letter to his wife, whom he could not have deceived in such a matter. To appreciate Percy's meaning, perhaps one need only look back at his boyhood commitment to a religious life and at his forty-five-year ministry, with its overriding obligations, successively, to two parishes, a cathedral, and a diocese. Percy's chosen work was to serve God, and by contrast just about all of his other work must have seemed at times no better than "Nonsense," particularly after he achieved the eminence of a bishopric. Laetitia-Matilda Hawkins recalled his writing to her father "that he had infinitely more pleasure in his success in having obtained from the Government, money to build two churches in his diocese, than he could ever derive from the reception of his '**Reliques**.'"[33] At the same time, there can be no mistaking the note of satisfaction in his mock-heroic elevation of "Nonsense" to "GRAND WORKS." His delight in the praise and display of his books was genuine, and he was obviously pleased to be able to share it with his wife.

Percy was thus consistently of two minds about his ballad work, and what may seem like rank insincerity in his

apologies and his self-depreciation is generally no more than a reflection of his doubts. He constantly needed the support of men like Johnson and Shenstone, who, with Richard Farmer, Thomas Warton, David Dalrymple, Thomas Birch, and other men of "learning and character," were linked together in the 1765 Preface to form the "amulet" that would "guard him from every unfavourable censure, for having bestowed any attention on a parcel of OLD BALLADS."[34] He kept the amulet in place through all four editions of the *Reliques*. Perhaps also it was inevitable that his private strictures would become increasingly harsh in his later years, when the decorum of office, as he perceived it, required an almost total dissociation from the *Reliques*, if not from other early work as well. In August 1802, he rebuked Robert Nares, the editor of *The British Critic*, for citing his name in connection with the *Reliques*, and extracted an assurance that Nares would "take care in future to attend to . . . [his] wishes implicitly on the subject."[35]

This attitude helps to account for his expression of indifference to James Dodsley about the republishing of the *Reliques*, and for his use of his nephew as an "Umbra" when the fourth edition was actually published. There is no reason to think him insincere in his 1785 letter to Dodsley. It was understandable that the Bishop of Dromore would wish to discontinue his ballad activity and put the *Reliques* behind him. He had discharged his promise to Johnson in 1765 and had seen the *Reliques* through two corrected editions by 1775; and with his new position he wished to avoid even the appearance of a connection about which he had always had misgivings. His decision under the circumstances to undertake a still further revision can be accounted for only by the force of Joseph Ritson's attack upon him in the 1790 *Ancient Songs*, in which the very existence of Percy's folio manuscript was questioned.[36] But he might even then have held back had it not been for the "importunity" of his friends and the willingness of a nephew to permit the impression that he, rather than the Bishop of Dromore, was the editor of the new edition.[37]

The fourth edition, it is interesting to note, was not just the last but also the best of Percy's lifetime. The ballad editor, never totally submerged in the prelate, had gone to work once again with a will and had produced the edition on which scores of subsequent printings were to be based. The book came from the press, of course, still bearing its marks as "a parcel of OLD BALLADS" and "a relaxation from graver studies." For, whatever his fondness for the ballads, Percy never resolved the doubts that had beset him from the beginning.

Notes

1. *The Correspondence of Thomas Percy and David Dalrymple, Lord Hailes,* ed. A. F. Falconer, Vol. IV of *The Percy Letters* (Baton Rouge: Louisiana State University Press, 1954), p. 30.

2. *The Literary Correspondence of John Pinkerton,* ed. Dawson Turner (London, 1830), I, 10.

3. *Illustrations of the Literary History of the Eighteenth Century,* ed. John Bowyer Nichols (London, 1848; rpt. New York: Kraus, 1966), VII, 577.

4. Letter to J. C. Walker, 10 Sept. 1788 (Fitzwilliam Museum, Perceval K64); Letter to William Jessop, 6 April 1784 (Bodley MS. Percy c. 1, f. 122); Letter to Walter Scott, 10 Dec. 1800 (National Library of Scotland, MS. 3874, f. 87).

5. Harvard bMS Eng 891 (3). The letter to Dodsley is a draft or copy.

6. *Reliques of Ancient English Poetry* (London, 1765), I, xiv.

7. *The Correspondence of Thomas Percy and Richard Farmer,* ed. Cleanth Brooks, Vol. II of *The Percy Letters* (Baton Rouge: Louisiana State University Press, 1946), p. 80. Farmer's reply has not been preserved.

8. *Reliques,* 4th ed. (London, 1794), I, ix.

9. British Library Add. MS. 32, 333, f. 197.

10. Bodley MS. Percy c. 3, ff. 59, 200. Percy, who recalled that his nephew received £160 for his role in the fourth edition, was particularly distressed by the unauthorized disclosure because Steevens (known as "The Asp") promptly passed the information on to Percy's arch-critic Joseph Ritson.

11. Henry Bold, *Latine Songs* (London, 1685), p. 80. A full discussion of ballad history is contained in Albert B. Friedman, *The Ballad Revival* (Chicago: University of Chicago Press, 1961).

12. *The Spectator,* Nos. 85 and 247.

13. *Gentleman's Magazine,* 35, Pt. 1 (1765), p. 180.

14. British Library Add. MS. 32, 336 [Percy's Diary, Pt. 1], 8 March 1759; 21-23 March 1761.

15. *Illustrations of the Literary History of the Eighteenth Century,* ed. John Nichols (London, 1831), VI, 556-61; British Library Add. Mss. 38, 728 (ff. 167-73) and 32, 336 (21 Nov. 1763 and 16 July 1764). Shortly after the *Reliques* was published, Percy also contracted with Tonson to edit the *Tatler.*

16. Northamptonshire Record Office, Box X, 1079 E (S) 1218.

17. *The Correspondence of Thomas Percy and Evan Evans,* ed. Aneirin Lewis, Vol. V of *The Percy Letters* (Baton Rouge: Louisiana State University Press, 1957), p. 82.

18. I am indebted to Mr. Kenneth Balfour for permission to quote Percy's poem.

19. Bodley MS. Percy c. 9, ff. 33-42. Percy did not always provide exact titles in either this or the 1756 list, and I have not been able to identify all his books. Burgess's sermons, for example, would seem to be a loose collection of variously published sermons by Daniel Burgess, but I cannot be certain of that identification.

20. British Library Add. MS. 32, 326, f. 25. A useful article largely based on this autobiographical manuscript is J. F. A. Mason, "Bishop Percy's Account of His Own Education," *Notes and Queries,* New Series VI, No. 10 (Nov. 1959), pp. 404-08.

21. Percy offered his "dissertations" to Ralph Griffiths in 1761 for possible publication in *The Library* (Bodley MS. Add. c. 89, f. 310).

22. Percy revised it for publication in 1773, 1779, 1792, and 1805.

23. *Reliques* (1765), I, 317-29.

24. Bodley MS. Percy c. 9, ff 2-18.

25. *Bishop Percy's Folio Manuscript,* ed. John W. Hales and Frederick J. Furnivall (London: Trübner, 1867; rpt. Detroit: Singing Tree Press, 1968), I, xii.

26. *The Correspondence of Thomas Percy and William Shenstone,* ed. Cleanth Brooks, Vol. VII of *The Percy Letters* (New Haven: Yale University Press, 1977), pp. 3-4.

27. *Correspondence of Thomas Percy and William Shenstone,* p. 9.

28. *Reliques* (1765), I, ix.

29. *Correspondence of Thomas Percy and Evan Evans,* pp. 102-03.

30. *Reliques* (1765), I, xiv.

31. *The Correspondence of Thomas Percy and Thomas Warton,* ed. M. G. Robinson and Leah Dennis (Baton Rouge: Louisiana State University Press, 1951), p. 114.

32. British Library Add. MS. 32, 335, f. 5. Because of the mounting rebellion in Ireland, Mrs. Percy had stayed behind in London.

33. Laetitia-Matilda Hawkins, *Anecdotes, Biographical Sketches and Memoirs* (London, 1822), p. 314. Miss Hawkins's father was Sir John Hawkins, the historian of music and Johnson's executor and biographer.

34. *Reliques* (1765), I, xiii-xiv.

35. *Illustrations of the Literary History of the Eighteenth Century,* VII, 599.

36. Joseph Ritson, *Ancient Songs, from the Time of King Henry the Third, to the Revolution* (London, 1790), p. xix.

37. *Reliques,* 4th ed., I, ix.

Zinnia Knapman (essay date 1986)

SOURCE: "A Reappraisal of Percy's Editing," in *Folk Music Journal,* Vol. 5, No. 2, 1986, pp. 202-14.

[*In the following essay, Knapman discusses the critical evaluation, by both contemporaries and twentieth-century scholars, of Percy's editing practices in the* Reliques.]

In 1765, the year when George III's Stamp Act started the great 'No Taxation without Representation' row with the

American Colonies, Bishop Percy published a heavily edited and annotated anthology entitled ***Reliques of Ancient English Poetry.***[1] The collection, although a rich source of folk texts, has never been popular with folklorists and Percy's significance has only been grudgingly acknowledged. When writing of the ***Reliques,*** critics have either drawn attention to the influence the collection exerted on the Romantic Poets, or alternatively, and this is particularly true of folk scholars, they have bewailed Percy's editorial methods with vehement abuse. H. B. Wheatley complained of Percy's 'flagrant manipulation of his sources'[2] and Hales and Furnivall lamented that Percy had 'puffed out . . . pomatumed . . . and powdered' everything.[3] Percy's editing is still predominantly remembered as destructive although it is precisely due to his editing that the ***Reliques*** was able to have such considerable influence, not only upon the course of English literature but also upon the ballad and folksong revival. This essay sets out to look not so much at what Percy did, which has already been extensively researched,[4] but to use this information to see what he was trying to do. In historical perspective, Percy's editing can only be seen as a sensible, creative, and positive force.

The catalyst that sparked off the ***Reliques*** was Percy's discovery of what is now known as the Percy Folio Manuscript. Percy found it 'lying dirty on the floor, under a bureau in yᵉ parlour' in his friend Humphrey Pitt's residence at Shifnal in Shropshire, 'being used by the maids to light the fire'.[5] The manuscript, although somewhat mutilated, contained nearly two hundred texts: there are some seventeen romances, twenty-four metrical 'histories', forty-five Child ballads, and miscellaneous songs. The manuscript appears to have been compiled about 1650 from various sources, primarily written but also perhaps from memory and oral tradition. It is entitled 'curious old ballads wch. occasionally I have met with'. Percy, already a keen antiquary, seems to have at once been fascinated by the find. The manuscript was shown to Dr Samuel Johnson, the poet Shenstone, and other close friends of Percy. Although both Johnson and Shenstone agreed it should be published, there was some disagreement on how this might best be done. Shenstone advised against publishing the manuscript as it stood and against printing any pieces that had no other merit than age. He feared such a work would arouse little interest whereas 'All people of taste', he prophesied, would 'rejoice to see a correct and elegant collection of such pieces'.[6] There is less evidence to show exactly what Dr Johnson advised, although it is clear that he was not interested in ballads as literature, only as they related to and illustrated earlier authors. He was, however, a great lover of old romances and offered to annotate selected transcripts from the manuscript.[7] Presumably, Johnson would have liked to see the Folio in print as an antiquarian reference work; this is deducible from his contempt of the published ***Reliques,*** a literary collection with extensive 'improvements' and ballad imitations.

After some deliberation, it was Shenstone's proposals which Percy adopted, possibly having been lured by the more attractive role of poet/editor. Nevertheless, his decision was still both positive and calculated. How many people would have read such ballads and fragments so 'defective' as they were to Percy and his circle? Which of their contemporaries would have prefered the Folio 'Sir Gawaine' (III.3.19)[8] which has nine stanza gaps on every page, to the completed Reliques version? Although Hales and Furnivall complain that 'Percy puffed out the thirty-nine lines of the "Child of Elle" to two hundred', creating 'an objectionable mésalliance of true and false',[9] it is interesting to note that originally this was one of the most popular ballads in the collection. It was reprinted twice in fashionable magazines between the first and second editions of the ***Reliques.***[10] Similarly, 'Sir Cauline', which is considered to be far superior in the Folio manuscript, is the only ballad specifically praised by Wordsworth when acknowledging the great debt he and the new group of poets owed to the ***Reliques.***[11] It is clear that Percy was completely aware of what he was doing. In 1801, Percy sent Jamieson a copy of a piece from the Folio.[12] In the accompanying letter he writes:

> you will see the defective and incorrect state of the old text in the ancient folio MS., and the irresistible demand on the editor of the ***Reliques*** to attempt some of those conjectural emendations, which have been blamed by one or two rigid critics, BUT WITHOUT WHICH THE COLLECTION WOULD NOT HAVE DESERVED A MOMENT'S ATTENTION.[13]

Having completed his editing, Percy was still slightly apologetic about the ***Reliques*** and equally unsure of its reception. In the dedication he calls the contents 'the barbarous productions of unpolished ages'; they are to be viewed 'not as labours of art, but as effusions of nature'. It is hardly surprising that Percy worded his dedication with such restraint as the ballad had yet to become an accepted literary genre. Johnson's dictionary explains a ballad as 'a song', adding that the term 'is now applied to nothing but trifling verse'. As yet, there was no distinction between the broadside ballads that were still hawked in the streets and the older traditional ballads. A ballad was simply a ballad. Addison, in his famous 'ballad papers',[14] was in fact praising a broadside version of 'Chevy Chase' (I.3.1) rather than the finer older version which is first printed in the ***Reliques*** (I.1.1). Johnson's definition does not, however, give any idea of the increasing interest in the ballad that had been mounting during the century (unless we are to understand he included *all* ballad imitations under the term 'trifling verse'). The eighteenth-century cult of 'simplicity' made use of the ballad form in order to avoid use of complex metre. Tickell, for example, set out to write poetry that could be taken in at a glance. Settings were homely, recounting scenes of village life and events 'recent in the neighbourhood' (see Percy's introduction to ballads I.3.15, II.3.26 and III.3.17). Pre-Conquest Britain was a popular setting and the heroes and heroines were frequently Edgars, Harolds, Emilys, or Eleanors. Shenstone's 'Jeremy Dawson' (II.3.26) and Tickell's 'Lucy and Colin' (III.3.17) both belong to this body of writing. They were compounds of sweetness and marvellous coincidences; if one lover died under tragic circumstances, the other could be expected to die sympathetically. Ballad imitations were also popular. 'Gentle Herdsman, tell to me' (II.1.14) inspired Goldsmith's 'Edwin and Angelina'; the 'Not-Browne Mayd' (II.1.6) inspired Matthew Prior's 'Henry and Emma'. Perhaps the most influential of these ballads was Mallet's 'Margaret's Ghost' (III.3.16) which was first printed in the 1720s and continued to be popular throughout the century. It was extravagantly praised; Percy himself referred to it as 'one of the most beautiful ballads in our own or in any language'.[15]

When Percy began work on the *Reliques* the ballad was in no way forgotten or out of currency. Shenstone was right in predicting the time had come for 'a correct and elegant collection of such pieces'. The problem was to convert the literary élite: Warburton had sneered at Percy's earlier treatise on Chinese poetry;[16] Johnson, who seemed to take a peculiar delight in parodying ballad imitations, had mercilessly censured Percy's **'Hermit of Warkworth'**.[17]

Percy's editing was never directly aimed at the popular market; from the beginning it was the approval of the literary intelligentsia that Percy was seeking. In the *Reliques* he included examples of historical and etymological interest, ballads to illustrate Shakespeare, and other early literature, each one accompanied by a learned and instructive introduction. While preparing the collection Percy was in contact with such scholars and notables as Thomas Birch the historian, Edward Lye the etymologist, Richard Farmer the Shakespearean scholar, Thomas Warton then professor of poetry at Oxford, and many others. David Garrick lent Percy a number of rare old plays from his private collection. At its most basic level, Percy's editing sets out to make his poems and ballads fit for and acceptable to the literary public. The specimens he included were all to be of literary interest and value. When introducing the ballads illustrating Shakespeare, Percy apologizes for including pieces that lack such intrinsic merit. Everything was to be clear, complete, correct, and worthy of inclusion. As Hales and Furnivall complain:

> Percy looked upon his text as a young woman from the country with unkempt locks, whom he had to fit for fashionable society.[18]

Although later critics have called Percy's editing everything but clear, complete, and correct, it is not hard to understand why many of his contemporaries found it both pleasing and helpful. Older forms of English words and spelling were then far less common and acceptable to the reading public than they are today; words such as 'paramour', 'eke', 'dight', and 'thrall' were frequently glossed in the eighteenth century. The *Reliques* was in fact to play a significant role in the popularization of these words, many of which now have an established place in poetic diction. The following example from the Folio and *Relique* texts of 'Sir Andrew Barton' is a typical and seemingly trivial example of Percy's treatment of his older sources. However, when one recalls the outcry that fol-

lowed Coleridge's use of archaic language in 'The Ancient Mariner' Percy's changes become more understandable:

> goe ffeitch me downe my armour of prooffe
> for itt is guilded with gold soe cleere.

(Folio)

> Goe fetch me forth my armour of proofe;
> That gilded is with gold soe cleare.

(*Reliques*)

Percy does not consistently modernize his spelling; the *Reliques* contains both 'Scottified' ballads and conscious archaisms. In fact, throughout the work, Percy moves from one interpretation of language to another, and there is a clear tension between his love of the archaic and desire to conform to Augustan norms. It is as if he were searching for the ideal form in which to present his ballads. His employment of archaic and Scottish terms was often aimed at bringing his subject closer to a conjectured original, while in other examples, Percy chose to write completely in a modern idiom. What has been seen as 'flagrant manipulation', from the evidence in Percy's letters and the ballads themselves, seems to have been sincere experimentation by Percy. Much of what he was editing had never before been offered as serious literature; Percy had to search for the most acceptable medium if his collection was to be a success. It is one of the great strengths of the *Reliques* that it does offer its ballads in so many forms and idioms. One should not forget that alongside Percy's sentimental pieces are poems such as 'Richard of Almaigne' (II.1.1) and 'On the Death of King Edward the First' (II.1.2); both are printed with a fidelity to early text and language which was strikingly unconventional for the time.

If earlier authors and old ballads were to be appreciated, Percy and Shenstone saw it was essential that the collection should be 'correct and elegant'. This included pruning indelicacies of thought and language,[19] regularizing metre, and improving rhyme. Even when Percy printed from popular sources, he still subjected each poem to his exacting ideals. 'Sweet William's Ghost' (III.2.6), which appeared in Allan Ramsay's *Tea-Table Miscellany* (1725), and 'The Lady turned Servingman' (III.1.17) from *A Collection of Old Ballads* (1723)[20] were both 'corrected' by Percy. In Ramsay's fifth verse, given below, the a b c b rhyme lapses:

> Thy faith and troth thou's never get,
> Nor yet will I thee lend,
> Till that thou come within my bower
> And kiss my cheek and chin.

Percy prints

> Thy faith and troth thou'se nevir get,
> 'Of me shalt nevir win,'
> Till that thou come within my bower,
> And kiss my cheek and chin.

thus restoring the rhyme. Similarly, in 'The Lady turned Servingman' the a a b b metre is repaired. In the earlier copy the rhymes in the eighth verse run haire/attire, hat/neck: in Percy we are given haire/weare and band/land. *A Collection of Old Ballads* relates the tale in a confusion of the first and third persons, a practice frequently encountered in folksong; Percy uses the first person throughout.

'The Lady turned Servingman' also exhibits the kind of 'elegant improvements' that critics of the *Reliques* have found most objectionable. Everything is sentimentalized, intensified, and prettified. The heroine is no longer merely her 'father's chief and only Heir', but now becomes 'An ancient barons only heire'. In order to heighten the poetic portrait of Elise singing her sorrows to the lute, Percy first has her change out of her servingman's attire into suitable dress,

> With silken robes, and jewels rare,
> I deckt me, as a ladye faire.

Elise is a typical Percy heroine straight from the eighteenth-century romance tradition; she sighs, she trembles, and blushes for shame on discovery. Such 'improvements', which were very much in the style of the ballad imitations of Shenstone, Tickell, and Mallet, although no longer admired, were highly popular in Percy's day. What Percy did to his sources is not so deplorable when we consider that what Percy was actually doing, was presenting his ballads in the popular guise of the times. We can regret that Percy rejected the splendid opening of the Folio 'Sir Andrew Barton' (II.2.12) for the inferior lines of the Pepys's copy, (see also Percy's choice of opening lines to 'Valentine and Ursine' (III.3.12)) but we should not condemn his editing because his poetic taste is alien to our own. When H. B. Wheatley complains of Percy's 'flagrant manipulation' of his sources, along with Hales and Furnivall, he is condemning Percy for failing the editorial standards of later centuries.

As editor of the *Reliques,* Percy also included ballads which had been 'handled' by other poets. These throw some much needed light on the contemporary ideas concerning ballad editing and also upon the nature of the folk ballad. 'As ye came from the Holy Land' (II.1.16), according to Percy's introduction, 'was communicated to the editor by the late Mr. Shenstone as corrected by him from an ancient copy, and supplied with a concluding stanza'. As Wheatley points out, the 'ancient copy' was certainly from the Folio and Shenstone's ending is strikingly inferior to the original.[21] However, the important point which emerges is that Shenstone did not hesitate to admit that he had tampered with his source. To both Shenstone and Percy, such 'corrections' were often aimed at bringing the ballad nearer to a 'conjectured original', which in their opinion could only be more regular and complete than its 'corrupted' sources. *A Collection of Old Ballads,* from which Percy took twenty-three items for his *Reliques* claims to be 'corrected from the best and most ancient copies extant':[22] the works of Allan Ramsay, from which Percy also drew, are equally notorious.[23] Ramsay's main source for *The Ever Green* was the Bannatyne manuscript (1568) and a comparison of source and work clearly validates Ritson's opinion that all Ramsay's poems are 'altered, interpolated, forg'd and corrupted'.[24] Both Wheatley and Percy considered Ramsay's concluding stanzas of 'Sweet William's Ghost' (*The Tea-Table Miscellany* and *Reliques* III.2.6) to be modern. The last verse of Ramsay's version is given below. It is interesting to compare it with Percy's conclusion of 'Sir Cauline'; both are in the tradition of eighteenth-century romance.

> O stay, my only true love, stay,
> The constant Margaret cried:
> Wan grew her cheeks, she clos'd her een,
> Stretched her saft limbs, and died.

'Lady Anne Bothwell's Lament' (II.2.13) is another interesting example of Ramsay's editing and Percy's endorsement of it. The *Reliques* copy is given 'from a copy in the editor's folio MS corrected by another copy in Allan Ramsay's *Miscellany*'; needless to say, it is Ramsay's version which is the more corrupt. In the Folio and all sources that antedate Ramsay, 'Balowe' is an English song. Ramsay, working on a hint from Watson's *Comic and Serious Scots Poems* (1706-10) which suggested 'Balowe' was the lament of a Scottish noble lady, not only polished it in his usual manner but promptly scottified all the words. It is the scottified version which Percy follows in the *Reliques.*

'Edom o' Gordon' (I.1.12), 'Young Water' (II.2.18), and 'Gil Morrice' (III.1.18) were all published separately in Glasgow in 1755: 'Sir Patrick Spens' (I.1.7), 'Edward' (I.1.5), 'The Jew's Daughter' (I.1.3), and 'Lord Thomas and Fair Annet' (III.3.4) were received by Percy in a single package sent from Edinburgh by John MacGowan in August 1763. It is not known to what extent each of these ballads had been edited before they reached Percy, although from their style and content it is clear they had been substantially reworked. Percy tells us that 'Sir Patrick Spens' is given 'from *two* manuscript copies transmitted from Scotland': 'Lord Thomas and Fair Annet' is given '*with some corrections* from a manuscript copy transmitted from Scotland'. The latter, which Child was to call 'one of the most beautiful of our ballads and indeed, of all ballads', according to Percy, is probably a literary compound of 'Lord Thomas and Fair Ellinor' (III.1.15) and 'Fair Margaret and Sweet William' (III.2.4).

David Fowler examines each of these ballads in detail, but for the purposes of this essay his discussion of 'Edom o' Gordon' will provide excellent insight into literary recreation at work.[25] 'Edom o' Gordon', as it appeared in 1755, was edited by David Dalrymple, Lord Hailes, who later became Percy's Scottish expert during the preparation of the *Reliques.* He may also have been MacGowan's source for the Edinburgh ballads. I note that 'Edward', as it appears in the *Reliques,* was communicated by Dalrymple. The ending of the Glasgow text of 'Edom o' Gordon' differs from all earlier versions including that in the Folio manuscript. The Lord arrives at the burning castle before Gordon and his men have left. A battle ensues, after which the grief-stricken Lord throws himself into the flames.

And mony were the mudie men
Lay gasping on the grien,
And mony were the fair ladys
Lay lemanless at heme.

And round and round the waes he went,
Their ashes for to view;
At last into the flames he flew,
And bad the world adieu.

The ending is Dalrymple's. It was criticized in a letter from Percy to Dalrymple in 1764.[26] Percy felt the ending to be 'unnatural' and suggested the ballad would end very well at

And mony were the weiping dames
Lay lemanless at hame.

Percy had apparently suggested two stanzas which had in turn been rejected by Dalrymple. Percy now wished that some such line as

Ein wood wi' fel despair

might be inserted if the husband's catastrophe is retained. The revised ending contributed by Dalrymple survives in Percy's own copy of the *Reliques,* but Percy finally rejected it in favour of one of his own. This is based on the Folio version. The Lord tears his hair, wrings his hands, and rides off to avenge the death of his family.

And after the Gordon he is gane,
Sa fast as he might drie;
And soon i' the Gordon's foul hartis bluid,
He's wroken his dear ladie.

These examples of eighteenth century ballad editing put Percy's editing firmly into context. This is of particular importance to Percy treatment of what we now call 'folk' ballads. Although an invaluable source for early versions of folk ballads, Percy cannot be condemned for reworking texts which the world had not yet learned to revere. Percy was, in fact, the first to differentiate between the ballad types, referring to 'literary imitations', 'broadsides', and 'minstrel ballads'. His **'Essay on the Ancient Minstrels in England'**,[27] in which these terms are discussed, provided the foundation of the literature on the subject. Ironically, it was out of the interest inspired by the *Reliques* that both the concept of a folk ballad and the new standards of editing were born. The *Reliques* had to come before Ritson's criticism of Percy's methods. Before the *Reliques* no-one was sufficiently interested in ballads to care how they were edited. It is with this in mind that we should turn to the pieces for which Percy has been repeatedly condemned.

'Sir Cauline' (I.1.4), 'Sir Aldingar' (II.1.9), and 'The Child of Elle' (I.1.11) are all from the Folio manuscript. The Folio version of 'Sir Aldingar' is complete but, as with 'Sir Cauline', there are enough lost lines, defects, and ambiguities to validate Percy's opinion that 'without some corrections, this ['Sir Aldingar'] will not do for my *Reliques*'.[28]

What, for example, was one to make of lines 124-29 of the Folio 'Sir Cauline'?

ffirst he presented to the Kings daughter
    they hand, & then they sword.
'but a serrett buffett you haue him giuen
    the King & the crowne!' she sayd.
'I, but 34 stripes
    comen beside the rood.'

Or indeed, what was one to make of the 'Child of Elle' itself? In Percy's manuscript 'The Child of Elle' is a thirty-nine line fragment without beginning or end. 'Sir Cauline', 'Sir Aldingar', and 'The Child of Elle' all have incomplete verses. Lines 147-50 of the Folio 'Sir Aldingar' are to be found as follow;

with a Mu . . . [line cut Away]
a louelie child was hee:
when he came to that fier,
he light the Queene full nigh.

Five other verses in the same ballad consist of only two lines, while 'Sir Cauline' and 'The Child of Elle' both have the occasional six-line verses as well as the common a b c b ballad metre. Such features may be considered points of interest in a manuscript ballad, but as Percy fully appreciated, they would be seen as defects in a literary collection. He did, however, recognize the literary merit of these ballads and, as he tells us when introducing 'The Child of Elle', it was this that prompted him to work on them.

'The Child of Elle' Is given from a fragment in the Editor's folio MS. which tho' extremely defective and mutilated, appeared to have so much merit, that it excited a strong desire to attempt a completion of the story.

Percy then goes on to regret that the reader will be able to identify his supplementary stanzas by their inferiority. 'It is also significant that Percy asks for his additions to be considered in the light of how difficult it is to imitate 'the affecting simplicity and artless beauties of the original'. Had he, one wonders, tried to complete the 'Child of Elle' in the manner of the original, but found he was best suited to do this in his own poetic idiom? One may not appreciate Percy's sentimental style, but it cannot be denied that he was very good at producing this kind of poetry. It is possible that Percy would have liked to complete his ballads in verse of 'affecting simplicity and artless beauty', but knew only too well that this was not the kind of writing which came most naturally to him.

Percy's style has already been glanced at in 'The Lady turned Servingman', but it is in 'The Child of Elle' and 'Sir Cauline' that it is found at its most blatant. Rhyme and metre, as expected, are carefully corrected and the stories completed with such thoroughness that no motive is left unexplained. We are told explicitly why Sir Cauline cannot openly love Fair Christabelle and why Emmeline is betrayed by her serving-maid. The unnamed ballad ladies become 'Fair Christabelle' and 'Fair Emmeline', heroines who suffer intensely but delicately. In 'The Child of Elle' Emmeline continually 'sighs' and 'weeps', while in 'Sir Cauline' Christabelle expires sweetly and sentimentally:

> Then fayntinge in a deadly swoune,
> And with a deepe-fette sighe,
> That burst her gentle hearte in twayne
> Fayre Christabelle did dye.

It is amusing to note that in the Folio version, both Sir Cauline and his lady survive, the latter to bear fifteen sons;

> then he did marry this Kings daughter
> with gold & siluer bright,
> & 15 sonnes this Ladye beere
> to Sir Cawline the Knight.

The scene, however, is not that of the typical 'simplicity' ballad. Instead of the domestic tragedy of pre-Conquest Britain, we are offered a Gothic world of pageantry and nobility. To some extent, this may have been inspired by the medieval minstrel idiom of Percy's Folio manuscript, but reflections of the Gothic are to be found abundantly in the literature and architecture of the time. Percy's evocation of the medieval world in his *Reliques,* together with his focus on the minstrels, for some years after firmly established the ballad as a medieval phenomenon. This fusion of the ballad form and medieval setting can be seen reflected in the work of many of our major poets, Coleridge, for example, who was to use it to full effect in 'The Ancient Mariner'.

What therefore was taking place as Percy worked through his ballads, was completion or recreation in the editor's own idiom. His aim was to produce pleasing ballads of the highest possible literary merit and when working from fragmentary sources, Percy found the most effective way to achieve this was to rework them in his own style. We have already noticed Wordsworth's love of Percy's 'Sir Cauline'; other notable contemporaries such as Scott and Coleridge were equally appreciative. When the influence of the *Reliques* was studied on Coleridge's 'Christabel' by Lowes,[29] it was discovered that the three ballads which had been especially suggestive to Coleridge were 'The Marriage of Sir Gawaine' (III.1.2), 'The Child of Elle', and 'Sir Cauline', all of them ballads substantially reworked by Percy. Scott, recognizing Percy's hand in 'Sir Cauline', firmly believed that the ballad had derived all its beauties from 'Dr Percy's poetic powers'. Both Scott and Wheatley have drawn attention to the effectiveness of the following lines from the 'Child of Elle':

> The baron he stroakt his dark-brown cheeke,
> And turned his heade asyde
> To whipe awaye the starting teare,
> He proudly strave to hyde.

Nor can Percy's editing be dismissed lightly today; several of his ballad workings remain poetically among the best

or, indeed, are the best versions known. In 'Sir Aldingar', as Wheatley complains, Percy's rewriting contains 'much of the stock prettiness of the polite ballad-monger, some of the most vivid bits of the old ballad being passed over';[30] Percy's relating of the queen's dream, a feature found only in the Folio and *Reliques* versions, is certainly inferior to the earlier copy, but still Percy's 'Sir Aldingar' remains a notable ballad in its own right. A. B. Friedman, having considered the defective state of the original with its 'abruptnesses, loose ends, ineffective repetitions and lost line', realistically pronounced Percy's to be the better ballad.[31] Similarly, Percy's 'The Heir of Linne' (II.2.5), a collation of the Folio text with a broadside, is an improvement on both sources. Percy used the plot of the broadside (which is of no literary merit) to the full compliment of the other. As Professor Child said, 'Percy made a new ballad, and a very good one.'[32] This is high praise indeed, when one considers how unsympathetic Child was to most ballad reworkings. Child is also full of praise for Percy's 'King John and the Abbot of Canterbury' (II.3.6) which again is a collated version. Percy reworked the 'King John and Bishoppe' of the Folio with two black-letter broadsides, and as Child says 'thus making undeniably a very good ballad out of a very poor one'.[33] For once Percy refrained from sentimentalizing and, as he suggests in his introduction, reworked existing words and phrases into greater order and effect. In the *Reliques* there can be no doubt that Percy was offering a far better version of the ballad than had hitherto been known.

Percy's *Reliques,* above all else, was an experiment. It sought to offer the ballad as serious literature and this in turn necessitated an exploration of ballad language, form, and idiom. Percy's work was brilliant and blundering, inspiring both the interest and standards which were later to condemn it. It was, however, a noble experiment and one as remarkable for its failures as for its triumphs.

Notes

1. Thomas Percy, Bishop of Dromore *Reliques of Ancient English Poetry,* 3 vols (London: for J. Dodsley, 1765, 1767, 1775); (nominally) edited by his nephew T. Percy (really by Percy himself) (London: F. and C. Rivington, 1794, 1812); edited by Revd R. A. Willmott (London: Routledge's British Poets, 1857); edited by G. Gilfillan, 3 vols (Edinburgh: James Nichols, 1858); edited by Henry B. Wheatley, 3 vols (London: Bickers, 1876-77, 1891); edited by M. M. Arnold Schröer, 2 vols (Berlin: Felber, 1893); reprinted edition edited by Henry B. Wheatley (New York: Dover, 1966). Each edition published during Percy's lifetime contains revisions and alterations, but since the fourth edition of 1794 no substantial changes have been made. Willmott's edition cleared away Percy's essays and prefaces, and added shorter notes of his own.

2. Wheatley (1966), I, 62.

3. *Bishop Percy's Folio Manuscript: Ballads and Romances* edited by John W. Hales and Frederick Furnivall, 3 vols (London: Trübner, 1867-68), I, xvii.

4. Ibid.

5. Hales and Furnivall, I, lxiv.

6. *Percy and William Shenstone,* edited by Hans Hecht (Strasbourg: Karl J. Trübner, 1909), p. 46.

7. Hect, p. 53.

8. All examples from the *Reliques* are followed by their series, book, and ballad number. This will not restrict the reader to the use of any one edition.

9. Hales and Furnivall, I, 133.

10. *The London Chronicle,* 28 (1765), 405; *The Scots Magazine,* 27 (1765), 209-10.

11. William Wordsworth, *Poems Including Lyrical Ballads,* 2 vols (London: Longman, Hurst, Rees, Orme, and Brown, 1815), I, 361-62.

12. Robert Jamieson (1780?-1844), Scottish antiquary and ballad collector, a worthy preserver of oral tradition who annotated his work with scholarship and taste.

13. Wheatley, I, lxxxviii (my italics).

14. *The Spectator,* numbers 70, 74, and 85, 1711.

15. Wheatley, III, 309.

16. Wheatley, I, xc.

17. *The Works of Samuel Johnson,* Volume VI, *Poems* edited by E. L. McAdam, Jr, with George Milne (New Haven: Yale University Press 1964), p. 268.

18. Hales and Furnivall, I, xvi.

19. The Folio manuscript contained many bawdy songs which were passed over by Percy and only published a century later: *Loose and Humorous Songs from Bishop Percy's Folio Manuscript,* edited by F. J. Furnivall (London: 1868), reprinted edition (London: Jenkins, 1963). It is interesting to note that the other editors, Child and Hales, withdrew their names from the work when Furnivall refused to expurgate the songs.

20. Attributed to Ambrose Philips.

21. Wheatley, II, 102.

22. *A Collection of Old Ballads,* attributed to Ambrose Philips 3 vols (London: printed for F. or J. Roberts 1723-25), preface.

23. *The Ever Green,* edited by Allan Ramsay, 2 vols (Edinburgh: Thomas Ruddiman for the editor, 1724-27); *The Tea-Table Miscellany,* edited by Allan Ramsay, 4 vols (Edinburgh: Thomas Ruddiman for the editor, 1725-40).

24. A. B. Friedman, *The Ballad Revival* (Chicago: University of Chicago Press, 1961), p. 137.

25. David Fowler, *A Literary History of the Popular Ballad* (Durham, N.C.: Duke University Press, 1968).

26. *Percy-Hailes Correspondence,* edited by A. F. Falconer (Baton Rouge: Louisiana State University Press, 1954), Percy to Hailes, 28 February 1764.

27. Wheatley, I, appendix.

28. Hales and Furnivall, I, 165 note.

29. Friedman, p. 278.

30. Wheatley, II, 54.

31. Friedman, p. 207.

32. *The English and Scottish Popular Ballads,* edited by Francis James Child, 5 vols (Cambridge, Mass.: Houghton, Mifflin, and Company 1882-98), reprinted edition, 5 vols (New York: Dover, 1965), V, 12.

33. Child, I, 404.

Joseph M. P. Donatelli (essay date 1989)

SOURCE: "Old Barons in New Robes: Percy's Use of the Metrical Romances in the *Reliques of Ancient English Poetry,*" in *Hermeneutics and Medieval Culture,* edited by Patrick J. Gallacher and Helen Damico, State University of New York Press, 1989, pp. 225-35.

[*In the following essay, Donatelli analyzes the Folio manuscript that was the primary source for Percy's* Reliques, *and notes the influence of metrical romances on Percy's editorial selections for this work.*]

The publication of Thomas Percy's **Reliques of Ancient English Poetry** in 1765 changed the course of English literature. Wordsworth claimed that England's poetry "had been absolutely redeemed by it," and he acknowledged the debt which he and other Romantic poets, most notably Coleridge, owed to the **Reliques.**[1] In later life, Scott recounted how his happy discovery of Percy's anthology "beneath a large platanas tree in the ruins of an . . . old fashioned arbour" caused him to miss his dinner hour, "notwithstanding the sharp appetite of thirteen."[2] The **Reliques** went through four editions during Percy's lifetime, and the more than fifty editions of the work which have been published since Percy's death in 1811 attest to the continuing importance and stature of this collection of ballads, songs, and lyrics.

Even Dr. Johnson, an inveterate ballad-hater, had praised "the grace and splendour" which Percy had given to his studies of antiquity, while wryly observing that the "mere antiquarian is a rugged being."[3] Yet the very qualities that made Percy's work so attractive to a wide audience have been Percy's undoing among literary scholars. Because of his decision to alter his texts radically to cater to an eighteenth-century audience that had little taste for "unadulterated antiquity," Percy has been scorned as an unscrupulous editor and dismissed as a popularizer. One of Percy's contemporaries, Joseph Ritson, set the tone for the attack when he impugned Percy's judgment and morals, and viciously accused him of secretly suppressing original texts and substituting his own fabrications.[4]

I would like to continue the rehabilitation of Percy's reputation undertaken by more recent scholars, including

Walter Jackson Bate, Albert Friedman, and Cleanth Brooks,[5] by looking at the famous Folio manuscript (BL Add. 27879) which clearly sparked Percy's interest in early English poetry, and provided him with many of the "select remains of our ancient English bards and minstrels" which were published in the *Reliques.* I would suggest that this manuscript molded Percy's highly influential view of the close relationship between the ballad and the metrical romance, and that this view may explain, though perhaps not justify, the editorial procedures for which Percy has been so roundly condemned.

In what must be one of the most charming bibliographic discoveries, Percy rescued this "unbound and sadly torn" volume from the house of his friend, Sir Humphrey Pitt, where it lay under a bureau, being used by the maids to light the fire.[6] In this remarkable manuscript, Percy found late medieval versions of metrical romances, ballads, two alliterative poems (*Death and Liffe* and *Scottish Feilde*), and Tudor and Stuart lyrics and songs. The texts date from the late medieval period to the reign of Charles I. As we shall see, Percy believed this grand historical sweep to be even greater, and he put what he considered to be a survey of hitherto neglected medieval literary forms to good use, producing influential studies on the ballad and the role of the minstrel, the metrical romances, and alliterative poetry, all of which he included in the *Reliques.* Happily, this manuscript, which now bears his name, preserved unique copies of some of the best English ballads, yet the extraordinary corruption, in both sense and language, which characterizes these and other texts has led many a modern editor to wish that Percy had left the maids to their incendiary work.

The bulk of the Percy Folio manuscript is devoted to seventeen late versions of metrical romances. Although Percy did not include any romances in the *Reliques,* apparently because of their length, an essay on the metrical romances introduced the third volume of ballads on "romantic subjects," and it reveals the extent of Percy's scholarly knowledge.[7] Using the romances in his manuscript as a starting point, Percy published the first bibliography of Middle English romances in this essay. Percy had, in fact, transcribed twenty-six romances himself, and intended to publish a collection of them, although his plan was but one of many literary projects that the bishop never realized.[8] Percy also took up the apology for the genre begun by Bishop Hurd and Thomas Warton by providing a synopsis of the Folio manuscript version of *Libeaus Desconus* (entitled *Libius Disconius*) to demonstrate that a romance, despite its "barbarous unpolished language," could be "as regular in its conduct as any of the finest poems of antiquity."

The sheer volume of metrical romances largely determined Percy's assumptions about the entire contents of the manuscript, for he interpreted the discrete parts of his model, the ballads, against a background formed by a gestalt of romances, even though the romances themselves were strangely absent from the *Reliques.* The juxtaposition of ballads and romances in the Folio MS convinced Percy that the ballads were also medieval "reliques," closely related to the metrical romances. In an era with little first-hand knowledge of Middle English metrical romances, Percy believed that the ballads and romances in the manuscript describing heroes named in Chaucer's *Sir Thopas* (such as Guy of Warwick, Libeaus Desconus, and Sir Gawain) dated from before Chaucer's time. He concluded that Chaucer had borrowed the *Wife of Bath's Tale* from the ballad *The Marriage of Sir Gawaine,* and that Malory had only thrown together into a regular story "the Subject of a hundred Old Ballads."[9] Moreover, the highly corrupt and modernized state of the late romances in the Folio manuscript, which Derek Pearsall has described as half way to becoming ballads,[10] blurred the distinction between ballads and romances in Percy's mind, since there seemed to be little difference between the style and content of these works. His terminology is often tentative and uncertain: he calls *Libius Disconius* and *Sir Lambwell* ballads, while referring to *Sir Cauline* as a "romantic tale."[11]

Despite the wretched state of the Folio MS texts, Percy believed that both the ballads and romances were originally composed and recited by minstrels, to whom Percy accorded an exalted function comparable to that of a Homeric bard or skald. Percy's conception of the medieval minstrel as a companion of kings and nobles, "who got their livelihood by singing verses to the harp at the houses of the great," is a powerful, evocative image with a long history in Romantic poetry and subsequent medieval scholarship.[12] According to Percy, this order eventually became debased, transmitting and producing the inferior entertainment found in the Folio MS, as well as in the journalistic, hack efforts of ballad-mongers.

Percy's extensive reading in the metrical romances afforded him the opportunity to compare the Folio manuscript versions of romances with older witnesses. Upon comparing *Sir Lambwell* to *Sir Launfal* or *The Squier* to *The Squire of Low Degree,* for example, he realized how inferior his "mutilated, incorrect" texts were, and blamed latter-day minstrels for their "wretched readings," which in many places were nothing more than "unintelligible nonsense" (*Reliques,* I, 11). Percy inferred that the ballads had met a similar, if not a worse, fate. Although Percy was also able to compare versions of ballads, he seems to have used romance transmission as a model to explain how these poems, which he believed to have been originally composed for the court, had fallen so low. Percy could therefore envision a more perfect version of ballads, especially those on "romantic subjects," where in fact none existed, and he set about to "supplement," "correct," and "complete" these narratives by using the romances to restore something of their former splendor and glory. These efforts resulted in the introduction of poetry that was written by Percy, and his failure to report these alterations has consigned him to what Albert Friedman has termed "the special hell reserved for bad editors."

The blame for Percy's editorial decision has often been put on the shoulders of William Shenstone, who collaborated with Percy on the first edition of the *Reliques.*[13] As early as 1757, Percy had informed Shenstone of the Folio MS which had come into his possession. In his reply, Shenstone expressed concern that Percy would produce the letter, rather than the spirit of its contents. He advised Percy not to publish the contents of the MS, but rather to use its roughly hewn materials as a *materia informis* for his own poetic invention. In a sense, Shenstone counselled hermeneutic rather than editorial activity, for he recognized that Percy's success depended on his ability to mediate between a past that was something of an embarrassment and the fastidious taste of the present: the Folio MS, he argued, ought to be considered as a "hoard of gold, somewhat defac'd by Time" that could be restored "under more current Impressions."[14] Accordingly, these alterations could be compared to "a Modern Toe or Finger, which is allowably added to the best statues."[15]

Percy's revisions to many of the ballads included such "toes" and "fingers" typical of the "improving" editions and ballad *rifacimenti* fashionable during the period: he regularized the meter, corrected and improved rhymes, reworked the diction, and straightened syntax.[16] But these emendations are minor compared to the extensive interpolations and alterations introduced into ballads on "romantic subjects" in the *Reliques. Sir Cauline* and *The Marriage of Sir Gawaine* were swollen to twice their original length; *The Child of Elle,* a mere fragment of thirty-nine lines in the Folio MS, was amplified to 201 lines, while little of the original was left untouched. The term *reliques* was particularly apt for these ballads, for Percy seems to have conceived of them as mere vestiges of complete narratives, and as partial realizations of the promise inherent in his text. His headnote to *Sir Cauline* is instructive: "the whole appeared so far short of the perfection it seemed to deserve that the Editor was tempted to add several stanzas in the first part, and still more in the second, to connect and compleat the story in the manner which appeared to him most interesting and affecting" (*Reliques,* I, 61). Percy's conception of these ballads as fragmentary productions (or, as mere parts of a whole) seems to have depended upon his viewing them against a background of romance narratives, a perception which was prompted by their juxtaposition in his Folio manuscript.

In these ballads, Percy set about to reverse the process by which these works had become so threadbare, and the romances provided a ready, if not logical, source for his alterations, since he believed that the romances and ballads had been similarly composed, and that both had suffered by an oral transmission directed to a popular audience. Percy had grasped the conventional and episodic nature of romance narratives, and he applied this knowledge in his ballad restorations. As Percy read ballads that described romance commonplaces, he freely supplied plot incidents and details taken from the fuller expositions found in the romances to amplify and expand the terse, often fragmentary narrative of these ballads. In a sense, Percy composed in a manner similar to that of the medieval minstrels whom he so admired, for just as the composers and reciters of

such pieces "made no scruple" in altering each other's productions, Percy felt free to change and enrich these ballads by borrowing materials from the romances.

In his restoration of these ballads, Percy appropriated elements that were originally details of other texts, in other words, parts of different wholes. In his introductions to a few ballads, Percy uncovered his method and openly avowed his large debt to romance materials. In *Valentine and Ursine,* the ballad which he fashioned from a couplet version of *Valentine and Orson* in the Folio MS, Percy acknowledged not only that he had drawn details from the romance itself, but that he had gratuitously introduced a marvellous bridge (lined with bells) described in *Beues of Hampton* into the poem (*Reliques,* III, 265). This image had come to Percy's attention when he discovered that Richard Johnson had borrowed this bridge from *Beues* in his sixteenth-century romance, *The Seven Champions of Christendom,*[17] and he was so impressed with both the detail and his scholarly discovery of it in both texts (his headnote dwells on the latter) that he made use of it in this ballad. In a creative reworking of *King Arthur's Death,* Percy had relied upon a more congruous source, having turned to Malory for details concerning Arthur's death and the tossing of Excalibur into the water (*Reliques,* III, 27-8). But it is in his restoration of the ballad *The Legend of King Arthur* that Percy most closely approximates a modern editor, and his success in restoring this ballad testifies to his scholarly acumen. In his headnote to *The Legend* (*Reliques,* III, 39), Percy stated that he had relied upon the chronicles of Geoffrey of Monmouth and Caxton to correct corrupt forms of proper names and to transpose stanzas which were apparently misplaced. Charles Millican's discovery of the source for this ballad, an Elizabethan account of the Nine Worthies composed by Richard Lloyd, has shown that both of Percy's transpositions, as well as many of his emendations, were absolutely correct.[18] Percy knew the Arthurian tradition so well that he succeeded in reconstructing the exact continuity of the original text without ever seeing it.

The fifteenth-century ballad *The Marriage of Sir Gawaine* (*Reliques,* III, 13-24) provides a particularly interesting example of Percy's method. The *Marriage* is a loathly lady tale in which Arthur is charged with answering the question what women want most, and Gawain must marry the hag who provides the answer. Its narrative is most similar to the late romance *The Weddynge of Sir Gawen and Dame Ragnell.*[19] The unique text of the *Marriage* which survives in the Folio MS is indeed fragmentary since half of each folio on which the poem appears has been torn away.[20] The wretched physical state of this manuscript invited Percy to hermeneutic activity (see also Professor Robinson's essay, *supra,* pp. 193-200). Percy faced the task of bridging rather large narrative gaps, which he estimated to be nine stanzas in length, and he drew upon conventional romance episodes to replenish these lacunae.

The first few lines of the ballad describe a Christmas feast at Arthur's court at Carlisle; after the first gap, Arthur declines to fight a "bold baron" at Tarn Wadling, and is told that he must ransom himself by answering the question what it is that women want most. To get Arthur out of his court and to Tarn Wadling, Percy introduces a damsel who interrupts the feast and asks that Arthur avenge her since this bold baron has imprisoned her lover in his "bowre," and then "misused" her. From his reading in the Folio MS, Percy was familiar with the conventional opening of a romance at the king's court, and with the interruption of the feast by one who delivers a message or a challenge: *The Grene Knight* and *The Turke and Gowin* begin in precisely this way, and *The Boy and the Mantle,* yet another Arthurian ballad in the MS, begins with the court in residence at Carlisle.[21] But perhaps the closest episode is that found in the Folio MS version of *Libeaus Desconus,* in which Helen, a fair maiden, interrupts a feast, kneels before the king, and, according to Percy's synopsis, "comes to implore King Arthur's assistance to rescue a young princess . . . who is detained from her rights, and confined in prison."[22] Although the details of *Libeaus* do not correspond exactly, the underlying dramatic situation is similar to the one Percy introduces into the *Marriage,* and Percy may well have thought of *Libeaus* because it also tells a transformation story involving Gawain and his kin.

From his reading Percy had also concluded that Arthur's knights were characterized with certain attributes and manners: "thus *Gawaine* is always drawn courteous and gentle: *Kay* rugged and brutal: *Guenever* light and inconstant."[23] Although this observation seems only too obvious now, at the time Percy had excitedly communicated his discovery to a grateful and attentive Thomas Warton. In the *Marriage,* Arthur is unwilling to fight the "bold baron" and is discourteous to the loathly lady, a characterization which would have been unthinkable to a reader of romances and chronicles, let alone to a reader of Spenser.[24] Percy set about to alter the portrayal of a cowardly and rude Arthur in the ballad. The baron becomes a giant, who now lives in a castle built on "magicke ground" that saps Arthur of his strength when he sets foot upon it. The original detail of the baron carrying "a great club upon his back" may have first suggested Percy's transformation of this character into a giant, but the idea behind this scene may well have come from *The Faerie Queene,* for with the changing of a few details it is reminiscent of Red-Cross's defeat by the giant Orgoglio after the knight has drunk from a spring that has sapped him of his powers. Red-Cross is then imprisoned in Orgoglio's castle, and his release is only obtained when Una encounters Prince Arthur and begs his assistance (Book I.vii-viii).

Further, in Percy's version Arthur's silence upon meeting the hag is no longer interpreted as a sign of discourtesy; instead, Percy emphasizes how thunderstruck he is by her loathsome appearance. Percy also rejects Arthur's unprompted and unceremonious offer of Gawain as a husband. In his version, Arthur agrees to whatever the hag wishes, leaving Gawain an opportunity to exhibit his "old Courtesy" when he offers himself as a bridegroom in a subsequent interpolation: "Then bespake him Sir Gawaine, / That was ever a gentle knighte: / That lothly ladye I will wed; / Therefore be merry and lighte" (*MSG* [*Marriage of Sir Gawaine*] II.21-4).

Since Percy believed the *Marriage* to have been Chaucer's source for the *Wife of Bath's Tale,* it is hardly surprising that he went to the Wife's tale for a number of scenes. For example, the ballad omits a description of Arthur's fruitless search for an answer before he meets the hag. In Percy's version, Arthur rides everywhere in search of the answer immediately after being set the question, just as the knight does in the Wife's tale (*WBT* [*Wife of Bath's Tale,*] III.919-21).[25] Arthur receives answers which seem to be modernizations of the various responses given in Chaucer: Percy's "riches, pompe, or state," correspond to "richesse" and "honour"; "rayment fine and brighte" to "riche array"; "mirthe" and "flatterye" to "jolynesse" and "flaterye," and "a jolly knighte" may well represent a censored version of "lust abedde" (*MSG* I.81-4; *WBT* 925-34). The encounter with the loathly lady also contains hints of the *Wife of Bath's Tale.* Percy has Arthur offer the hag whatever she wishes in return for the answer, and he, just as the knight in Chaucer, must swear to keep his promise before learning what her request will be (*MSG* I.109-20; *WBT* 1008-13). Percy's reference to the answer as a "secrete" (*MSG* I.115) may owe something to Chaucer's image of the hag whispering it in the knight's ear (*WBT* 1021).

Much of the bedroom scene after the marriage of Gawain and the loathly lady is also missing from the ballad, although it is clear that the transformation of the hag into a beautiful woman takes place before the knight yields his sovereignty to the lady, as it does in the *Weddynge* as well as in Gower's *Tale of Florent.* The original states that the lady's enchantment is the work of a wicked stepmother; Percy adds that this "spelle" could not be lifted until "a young faire courtlye knight" married her, and agreed to be ruled by her. Percy may have inferred this explanation from the events described in the ballad, with the help of the clue provided by the *maistrie* won at the end of the *Wife of Bath's Tale;* however, the interpolation is sufficiently close to Gower's conclusion to make one wonder if Percy did not know the *Tale of Florent* as well. Yet Percy only mentions Gower in passing, and then merely to condemn his "tedious allegories" (**Reliques,** III, 354). On the other hand, Warton seems to have been one of the first scholars to have noticed the similarity between the loathly lady stories of Gower and Chaucer, and Percy may have benefited from this insight.[26]

It is possible to analyze *Sir Cauline* in a similar fashion. This ballad was cited by Henry Wheatley, who published what has become the standard edition of the **Reliques** in 1876, as Percy's "most flagrant violation of manuscript authority"; ironically, *Sir Cauline* was singled out for praise by Wordsworth, who judged it to be "an exquisite ballad," and Coleridge borrowed heavily from it in *Christabel.*[27] The numerous romance commonplaces in this ballad, notably a vassal's love for a king's daughter and the deeds of valor undertaken by Cauline to win the princess, were familiar to Percy from his reading of *King Horn, Guy of Warwick, The Squire of Low Degree,* and two Folio romances, *Sir Degree* and *Eglamore.*

Since Percy had not postulated a source for this ballad, he freely introduced and blended scenes and images from many of these romances in his version of *Sir Cauline.* From *Eglamore,* for example, he borrowed the name *Christabel,* with which he christened the unnamed lady of the ballad, and perhaps he modelled his reworking of Cauline's battle with a giant on Eglamore's defeat of the giant Marrocke and his brother. Imagery from *Eger and Grime,* which was also collected in the Folio manuscript, seems to have been introduced in Percy's handling of the relatively uncommon Eldridge king episode, for he seems to have observed parallels between Sir Gray-Steel and the Eldridge king which have not gone unnoticed by modern editors of these works.[28]

Yet Percy's rejection of the ending of the ballad, in which Cauline marries the princess and she bears him fifteen sons, reveals his willingness to sacrifice an authentic romance episode (confirmed by his reading in the *Earl of Toulouse*) if it did not cater to eighteenth-century sensibility. Having heeded Shenstone's advice, Percy is well aware that he is mediating between the past and an age that had little taste for "unadulterated antiquity." Percy seeks to bridge this historical distance by substituting a pathetic, tragic ending in which Cauline is mortally wounded and Christabel dies from sorrow. His reworking recalls the sentimental conclusions of ballad imitations, and demonstrates just how far Percy would stray from romance materials to create an "interesting and affecting" scene.

The theme of the present volume indicates perhaps that our modern critical sensibility is now prepared to acknowledge, though perhaps not to endorse, Percy's hermeneutic enterprise in the ***Reliques.*** Percy's extensive revisions and interpolations have received kinder assessments from more recent critics, who have called attention to the audience that this method won for previously neglected poetry, to the notoriously corrupt texts of the Folio MS, and to the superior poetry found in some of Percy's versions, which had impressed Scott, Wordsworth, and Coleridge. Undoubtedly, Percy's methods, if considered from the point of view of a modern scholarly editor, are absolutely indefensible. I would argue, however, that Percy never saw himself as an "editor" of these ballads in the modern sense of the word, but rather envisioned himself as a latter-day minstrel, trying to reshape the romance ballads of the Folio MS so that they might better please his eighteenth-century audience. In doing so, Percy was following in the steps of the antiquarian scribe who had compiled the Percy Folio MS in the preceding century, for he too had revived and remade forgotten poems and songs.

Shenstone had once remarked to Percy that his "improved" copies could still rank as old barons, however modern their robes might be.[29] But Percy had clothed these ballads according to his understanding of medieval minstrel activ-

ity, and he had woven his texts from romance materials that were originally medieval. It was this re-creation of minstrel activity in the eighteenth century, rather than the insipid and fussy emendations and modernizations suggested by Shenstone, that won Percy such a high place in English literature and captured the imagination of the Romantic poets.

Notes

1. *The Prose Works of William Wordsworth,* ed. W. J. B. Owen and Jane Worthington Smyser, 3 vols. (Oxford: Clarendon Press, 1974), 3:78.

2. *Scott on Himself,* ed. David Hewitt (Edinburgh: Scottish Academic Press, 1981), 28.

3. *Boswell's Life of Johnson,* ed. G. B. Hill, rev. L. F. Powell, 6 vols. (Oxford: Clarendon Press, 1934-50), 3:278. Despite this praise, Dr. Johnson's attitude towards Percy is not easily understood; Johnson's well-known parodies of Percy's ballad scholarship and compositions suggest a contempt for such projects. On this apparent contradiction, see Albert Friedman, *The Ballad Revival* (Chicago: University of Chicago Press, 1961), 188-94.

4. "To correct the obvious errors of an illiterate transcriber, to supply irremediable defects, and to make sense of nonsense, are certainly essential duties of an editor of ancient poetry, provided he act with integrity and publicity; but secretly to suppress the original text, and insert his own fabrications for the sake of providing more refined entertainment for readers of taste and genius, is no proof or either judgment, candour, or integrity," *Ancient English Metrical Romances,* ed. J. Ritson, rev. E. Goldsmid, 3 vols. (Edinburgh: E. and G. Goldsmid, 1884-86), 1:58. For an account of the Percy-Ritson feud, see Bertrand H. Bronson, *Joseph Ritson: Scholar-at-Arms,* 2 vols. (Berkeley: University of California Press, 1938), vol. 2, chap. 8.

5. Walter Jackson Bate, "Percy's Use of His Folio-Manuscript," *Journal of English and Germanic Philology* 43 (1944): 337-48; Friedman, *The Ballad Revival,* chap. 7; Cleanth Brooks, ed., *The Correspondence of Thomas Percy and William Shenstone,* vol. 7 of *The Percy Letters* (New Haven: Yale University Press, 1977), xv-xxiii.

6. Percy recorded the circumstances relating to this discovery in a note which appears on the inside cover of the Folio MS. The contents of the MS (including Percy's notes) have been edited by John W. Hales and Frederick J. Furnivall in *Bishop Percy's Folio Manuscript,* 3 vols. (London: N. Trübner and Co., 1867-68); a fourth volume, *Loose and Humorous Songs,* was edited and published by Furnivall in 1868. For the note in question, see Hales and Furnivall, 1: lxxiv. On the date of Percy's discovery, see Bertram H. Davis, *Thomas Percy* (Boston: Twayne Publishers, 1981), 75-6.

7. "On the Ancient Metrical Romances," in *Reliques of Ancient English Poetry,* ed. Henry B. Wheatley, 3

vols. (London: Swan Sonnenschein and Co., 1910), 3:339-76. Unless otherwise noted, all subsequent references to the *Reliques* are to Wheatley's edition.

8. "The favourable light in which Mr. Hurd and he [Warton] set the old Romances, I think will be an excellent preparative for such a collection of the old ones in metre as I think sometime or other to publish," *The Correspondence of Thomas Percy and Richard Farmer,* ed. Cleanth Brooks, vol. 2 of *The Percy Letters* (Baton Rouge: Louisiana State University Press, 1946), letter dated Sept. 9, 1762, p. 9; see also *The Correspondence of Thomas Percy and David Dalrymple, Lord Hailes,* ed. A. F. Falconer, vol. 4 of *The Percy Letters* (Baton Rouge: Louisiana State University Press, 1954), 55-6.

Arthur Johnston has discussed Percy's contribution to early romance scholarship in *Enchanted Ground: The Study of Medieval Romance in the Eighteenth Century* (London: Athlone Press, 1964), 75-99. See also Leah Dennis, "Percy's Essay 'On the Ancient Metrical Romances,'" *Publications of the Modern Language Association* 49 (1934): 81-97, and E. K. A. Mackenzie, "Thomas Percy's Great Schemes," *Modern Language Review* 43 (1948): 34-8.

9. *The Correspondence of Thomas Percy and Thomas Warton,* ed. M. G. Robinson and Leah Dennis, vol. 3 of *The Percy Letters* (Baton Rouge: Louisiana State University Press, 1951), 2.

10. *Old and Middle English Poetry* (London: Routledge and Kegan Paul, 1977), 260-4.

11. The relation between the ballad and medieval romance remains a vexed question; for a recent discussion, see H. O. Nygard, "Popular Ballad and Medieval Romance," in *Ballad Studies,* ed. E. B. Lyle (Cambridge: D. S. Brewer, 1976), 1-19.

12. Percy's famous views on the subject, which gave rise to considerable debate about the status of the medieval English minstrel, can be found in "An Essay on the Ancient Minstrels in England," *Reliques,* 1:345-430; Percy was willing to admit, however, that some of the longer romances may have been originally composed in writing (1:404-5).

13. Irving L. Churchill, "William Shenstone's Share in the Preparation of Percy's *Reliques,*" *Publications of the Modern Language Association* 51 (1936): 960-74; Leah Dennis, "Thomas Percy, Antiquarian *vs.* Man of Taste," *Publications of the Modern Language Association* 57 (1942): 140-54; and Cleanth Brooks's introduction to the Percy-Shenstone *Correspondence.*

14. Percy-Shenstone *Correspondence,* letter dated Nov. 24, 1757, 3-4.

15. Ibid., 73.

16. For a detailed account of these emendations, see Bate, 337-48; also Eileen Mackenzie, "Thomas Percy and Ballad 'Correctness,'" *Review of English Studies* 21 (1945): 58-60, and Friedman, 204ff.

17. Percy-Warton *Correspondence,* 38-42; Percy's bridge, in fact, has one hundred bells like Johnson's, not sixty as in *Beues.*

18. Charles Millican, "The Original of the Ballad 'Kinge: Arthurs Death' in the Percy Folio MS.," *Publications of the Modern Language Association* 46 (1931): 1020-24.

19. Laura Sumner, in her edition of *The Weddynge,* has argued that both works derive from the same source: see *Smith College Studies in Modern Languages,* vol. 5, no. 4. (Northampton, Mass., 1924): xx-xxvi.

20. For the Folio MS version of the *Marriage,* see Hales and Furnivall, 1:103-18; in response to Ritson's attacks, Percy produced a faithful transcription of the MS version in the fourth edition of the *Reliques* (published in 1794, and nominally edited by Percy's nephew) to demonstrate the extreme corruption of his MS texts.

21. Hales and Furnivall, 1:90-2; 2:58-62; 2:304-5; *The Marriage* follows *The Turke and Gowin* in the Folio MS.

22. Hales and Furnivall, 2:419-23, lines 109-77.

23. Percy-Warton *Correspondence,* 3.

24. In March, 1764, Evan Evans, an expert in Welsh poetry, had sent, at Percy's request, notes on the *Marriage,* in which he observed that "we never read of King Arthur's being ever worsted in any of his battles or single combats in any of our romances" (*The Correspondence of Thomas Percy and Evan Evans,* ed. Aneirin Lewis, vol. 5 of *The Percy Letters* [Baton Rouge: Louisiana State University Press, 1957], 70).

25. All references to Chaucer's poetry from *The Works of Geoffrey Chaucer,* ed. F. N. Robinson, 2nd ed. (Cambridge, Mass.: Houghton Mifflin, 1957).

26. Thomas Warton, *The History of English Poetry,* ed. W. Carew Hazlitt, 4 vols. (London: Reeves and Turner, 1871), 3:32.

27. On Coleridge's borrowings, see Donald Reuel Tuttle, "*Christabel* Sources in Percy's *Reliques* and the Gothic Romances," *Publications of the Modern Language Association* 53 (1938): 445-74.

28. See, for example, *Eger and Grime,* ed. James Ralston Caldwell (Cambridge, Mass.: Harvard University Press, 1933), 58-60; *The English and Scottish Popular Ballads,* ed. F. J. Child (1882-98; rpt., New York: The Folklore Press, 1957), 2:56-7.

29. Percy-Shenstone *Correspondence,* 137.

Gwendolyn A. Morgan (essay date 1995)

SOURCE: "Percy, the Antiquarians, the Ballad, and the Middle Ages," in *Studies in Medievalism,* Vol. 7, 1995, pp. 22-32.

[*In the following essay, Morgan assesses the literary status of ballads from medieval times to the present, specifically focusing on eighteenth-century perceptions of balladry via the works of Thomas Percy.*]

The eighteenth-century obsession with the Middle Ages in a search for a British national character brought with it the first examination of the traditional ballads. These, according to the antiquarians, evinced a primitive chivalry of thought and manners which indicated the essential nobility of the native English soul. Today, we still recognize in medieval balladry the voice and perceptions of the illiterate commoner, but our more demanding critical eye deems them debased forms or imperfect imitations of courtly writings, their literary merit negligible. Unfortunately, this persistent perception results, not from the songs themselves, but from the judgments of the Restoration and eighteenth-century *literati,* even such champions as Thomas Percy and Joseph Addison. Through their attempts to ennoble the medieval character through literature, the antiquarians in fact assured the scorn and neglect of the ballads—and, by extension, of the people who produced them—shaping our perceptions for some two hundred years.

Let me briefly recapitulate the status of medieval balladry in our studies. Despite their distinction as the primary literature produced by the largest segment of the medieval English population, they hold a peripheral position in medieval courses, usually as part of a sociological basis. The various medieval anthologies now in common use either ignore the ballads completely, or include perhaps half a dozen songs of which one is inevitably "Judas," not a popular composition at all but a clerical imitation. In research, the same holds true: we concentrate on source and linguistic studies. Of the fewer than thirty articles on ballads published in the last twenty-five years, perhaps one or two concentrate primarily on content or inherent literary qualities. Vastly more common are essays which address new manuscripts, historical sources, analogues, and occasionally some relationship between ballads and other literary forms. Only one monograph on medieval balladry has been written during the same period. Why?

Simply, we continue to insist that balladry represents an imitative impulse in the commoners' attempt to partake of the courtly ideology of their betters.[1] We ignore the ballads' subversive qualities as they satirize, belittle, scorn, and otherwise negate aristocratic chivalric mores, positing instead a world view based on pragmatism and the harsh realities of common life which of necessity rejects romanticism and idealism.[2] We forget that three of the only four surviving religious ballads were clerical compositions set to popular tunes in an attempt to rehabilitate a folk song tradition that the church found, in the main, offensive. In fact, between M. J. C. Hodgart's 1950 monograph and my own 1993 book, only Arthur Moore (in 1958) attempted any defense of the ballads *as literature,* and ultimately even he accepted consensus regarding the songs as flawed and imitative, disagreeing only by insisting that they had moments of artistry.[3] On the whole, Moore selected from among the usual adjectives applied to medieval balladry for three hundred years: rude, crude, rough, imitative, degenerate, unpolished, flawed, and so forth.

The eighteenth-century interest in Old and Middle English literature—part of a general preoccupation with national heritage—bred the first attempts to construct a literary history of England. A growing patriotism directed such efforts, combined with a "scientific" impulse toward the accumulation of knowledge and the era's obsession with definitions of refinement and propriety. Interestingly, social and political developments leading to a heightened awareness of popular opinion and its expression in popular song demanded that the long disregarded ballad be included as an object of study in all these areas.

Unfortunately, as it came to the antiquarians, the ballad was held in well established contempt, fruit of a long history of the form's appropriation as a vehicle for propaganda. A practice since medieval times, this nonetheless reached its height in the seventeenth and eighteenth centuries, when the resultant songs were often printed and publicly displayed, thereby earning the name of "broadsides" (see Friedman, 44). Obviously, broadsides caused the political elite no end of trouble and came to be viewed as an essential element in controlling public opinion. As early as 1703, Fletcher of Saltoun noted that "if a man were permitted to make all the ballads, he needed not care who should make the laws of the nation" (quoted in Friedman, 71), and shortly afterwards Daniel Defoe asserted that the ballads' primary function was "as a useful incentive to mischief."[4] Thus associated with rabble-rousing and civil disturbance, the idea arose that ballads could also be appropriated and used by the other side. Horace Walpole, for example, is known to have suggested the composition of ballads to ridicule the French Revolution and to support his own party. However, he was also aware that the genre was a two-edged sword which by its popular and derisive nature could increase social unrest, as his cautionary response to a colleague's idea of producing ballads to support the "cause of liberty" shows.[5] This association of balladry with riots continued throughout the century and proved a major problem for those who wished to raise the form to a position of literary importance.

Nonetheless, the *literati* met the challenge head on. In 1712, Sir Richard Steele observed that Elizabeth's minister of state had been in the habit of reviewing current ballads to determine the tide of public opinion and to manipulate it (*Spectator* Nos. 135, 502).[6] Some sixty years later, Thomas Warton noted in his *History of English Poetry* (1774) that a 1264 ballad against Henry III "proved very fatal to the interest of the king," and that a "ballad on Richard of Alemaigne probably occasioned a statute against libels in the year 1275." His conclusion that "political ballads . . . such as were the vehicles of political satire, prevailed much among our early ancestors" seems to have been shared by most of his contemporaries.[7] In consequence, in attempting the double task of validating the ballad as literature while establishing the nobility and gentility of early English character, and being elitist themselves, the antiquarians were forced to attempt a distinction between "good" and "bad" ballads. In the twentieth century, Albert B. Friedman, Vivian de Sola Pinto, and others managed to develop this distinction as that between broadsides and traditional ballads, but in the eighteenth century any criteria for defining the ballad as form had yet to be established.[8] Vaguely conceived as a popular song sung to a popular tune and containing certain standard mechanical devices, "ballad" referred equally well to both types.

It was for these very reasons that Bishop Thomas Percy, in his correspondence with his consultant and editor William Shenstone, expressed a concern that his *Reliques of Ancient English Poetry* (1765) might cause him to be known as "merely a Ballad-monger," and that his essentially antiquarian work might be misunderstood.[9] Likewise, Warton lamented the satirical, invective ballads but asserted that there were others which "in a much more ingenious strain . . . have transmitted to posterity the praises of knightly heroism, the marvels of romantic fiction, and the complaints of love" (59). Joseph Ritson, despite his disagreement with Warton on a number of basic issues, reached the same conclusion regarding the dual nature of ballad content in his *Dissertation on Romance and Minstrelsy* (1802).

Yet it was not only the propagandistic function of the broadside which caused problems for those defending the ancient ballads: even nonpropagandistic songs carried the stigma of vulgarity, of being unpolished products of the illiterate class. Both Percy and Ritson felt it necessary to apologize for the ballads included in their collections as important in their antiquity although unpolished and uncouth.[10] Warton too adopted this line in the Preface to his *History of English Poetry,* as he attempted to trace English literature from its "rude" beginnings to "its perfection in a polished age" (ii). The precedent was Dryden's *Of Dramatic Poesy* in the previous century (1668), which established the concept that the history of poetry was a linear progress.[11] Indeed, an essential part of Dryden's theory was that while plot and characterization may have been "pefected" by the time of Shakespeare, poetics of form, verse, and tasteful representation were the province of post-Restoration authors. Thus, the antiquarians could assert that the ballads were valuable as the first attempts of a primitive society to produce poetry, and consequently the seeds from which the artistic triumphs of the eighteenth-century authors had sprung. This compromise allowed Johnson, who on the whole saw no literary merit in the ballads and scorned the imitations of his contemporaries, at the same time to praise Percy's *Reliques* for their "attention to poetry" which bestowed "grace and splendor to his studies of antiquity."[12]

Johnson's comment elucidates another reason for the ballads' importance to the antiquarians: the belief that literature provided an accurate description of the society which produced it. Indeed, Percy justifies his selection of ballads in the Preface to his *Reliques* thus:

> Accordingly, such specimens of ancient poetry have been selected, as either show the gradation of our language, exhibit the progress of popular opinions, display the peculiar manners and customs of former ages, or throw light on our earlier classical poets.
>
> (8)

In 1790, Ritson followed Percy's lead, his "Advertisement" for his *Ancient Songs and Ballads* offering his collection to the public despite its lack of literary merit because the poems illustrate the "history, the poetry, the language, the manners, or the amusements of [our] ancestors." Indeed, all eighteenth-century ballad collections following the *Reliques* provide similar disclaimers, and so the antiquarians justified their examinations. Even Walpole, who dismissed all balladry as essentially broadside in nature, approved the publication of such collections as Percy's.

Despite forerunners such as Addison and Steele, it is indeed Percy who is credited not only with stimulating interest in medieval English literature on a large scale but with establishing the early ballads as legitimate objects of study. His *Reliques* is the first significant collection of early songs, and in it he established the selection principles and critical slant toward medieval popular song which dominate critical perspectives to the present day. Buying into the contemporary belief that literature had reached formal perfection in his own age, and sharing its concern with taste and decorum, Percy could not resist what Johnson called "enthusiastic improvement" (46) of the texts he found in his source manuscript. Indeed, Percy admitted doing so because "miserable trash or nonsense [was] not infrequently introduced into pieces of considerable merit" (Advertisement to the Fourth Edition, 6). In fact, however, he went far beyond this, succumbing to the temptation to eliminate what he interpreted as imperfect grammar, to exaggerate heroic effects, to emphasize medievalism, and to soften what may have been considered vulgarity by his readers' delicate tastes. A comparison between the version of "Chevy Chase" published in the *Reliques* and that found in Percy's Folio manuscript serves to illustrate the point.

Reliques

That ere my captaine fought on foote
And I stood looking on

91-2

Our English archers bent their bowes

105

O Christ! it was a griefe to see
And likewise for to heare,
The cries of men lying in their gore
And scattered here and there.

129–32

Who never spake more words than these

157

Did many thousands dye.

262

Folio MS

That ere my captain foughton foote
And I stand looking on

> 91–2

Our English archers bend their bowes

> 105

O Christ! it was great greave to see
How eche man chose his spere
And how the blood out of their brests
Did gush like water clere.

> 129–32

Who never sayd more words than these

> 157

Did many hundreds dye.

> 262

The Folio itself contains two versions of this ballad, and Percy clearly used the newer as his source. Many minor alterations, such as those in lines 92 and 105 and indeed frequently elsewhere in the text, simply correct tense shifts, where the narrative moves momentarily from past to present. These are instances, one supposes, of eighteenth-century "polish." Other alterations, however, are more interesting. Those made in lines 129-132 neither correct grammar or obscurity, nor do they change meter or rhyme. The difference, it seems, is one of taste, for the gory image presented in the manuscript of "how eche man chose his spere / and how the blood out of their brests / did gush like water clere" is much softened. Percy offers instead the delicate "and likewise for to heare / the cries of men lying in their gore / and scattered here and there." The impulse is the same as that which persuaded Dryden to move gore off the stage and allow for heroes' survival in his rewrites of Shakespeare, and therefore might be considered a concession to the decorum of the age. A third type of change is represented in line 157, where the word "said" is altered to "spake." One of many such, this is an instance of what Percy apparently thought was artistic "medievalizing" and formalizing of the poem's language. Finally, line 262 contains an example of his attempt to heighten the heroic nature of the event, and thereby of its participants: the "many hundreds" dying in the original version become with a stroke "many thousands" in Percy's emendation.

"Chevy Chase" is by no means the only ballad in the **Reliques** which underwent significant changes at the hand of the collector. While some alterations were indeed, as Percy noted in his Preface, intended to remove obscurity, most were similar to those just mentioned and apparently the result of deference to the sensibilities of the eighteenth-century reader. More importantly, Percy's changes set a precedent and legitimized a prejudice against medieval balladry regarding its language, imagery, and purpose. Consider Ritson, who disapproved of any alteration of original English "relics" and was noted for detecting bal-lad revisions and forgeries in published collections. Even he had intended to revise his version of "Chevy Chase" (which by then had become an accepted epitome of medieval heroic song) but died before he had completed the task.[13] What resulted was a sense that (1) ballads were crude and (2) they were intended to promote the same heroism as courtly literature. Both perceptions are wrong, yet they imbue modern critical consensus.

Depite the antiquarian nature of early interest in the ballads, the revival was not, as Friedman asserts, merely a translation of old songs into museum pieces (9) or an "antiquarian lark" (78). Respected men of letters discovered literary merit in the ballad in the early 1700s, and although the general condemnation of the form as vulgar and debased held ascendency, a heated debate over its literary status raged for almost a hundred years. Dissenters from the received view originally based their arguments on the classical idea of "Nature dressed in Art." Henry Felton, in his *Dissertation on Reading the Classics* (1709), observed that while Nature's "Dressers" should not "spoil her native Beauty," Nature herself was not enough, for "we are untaught by Nature, and the finest qualities will grow wild and degenerate" without proper ordering through wit and style. Moreover, he said, art must be blended with "a competent knowledge of the Nature and Decency of Things; in being acquainted with what . . . is *fit* to be spoken" (my emphasis).[14]

Despite the general opinions to which Felton gave voice, the veiled impulse toward simplicity contained in them became a primary concern of literary theoreticians of the eighteenth century. The rebellion against the artificiality of Neoclassicism gradually led to the cults of sensibility and found its roots in the concept that simplicity permitted the closest representations of the sublime. Addison's early defenses of the ballads as literature appeal to this. In his noted "Chevy Chase Papers" (*Spectator* Nos. 70 and 74), he asserts that "the sentiments in that ballad are extremely natural and poetical, and full of the majestic simplicity which we admire in the greatest of ancient poets," and that its rudeness is no excuse for "prejudice . . . against the greatness of the thought." Indeed, says Addison, "if this song had been written in the Gothic manner, which is the delight of all our little wits, whether writers or readers, it would not have hit the taste of so many ages, and have pleased so many readers of all ranks and conditions." He adds that the ballad also provides in its final stanza an "important precept of morality" which in his era was thought an essential quality of great poetry:

> The poet, to deter men from such unnatural contentions, desribes a bloody battle, and a dreadful scene of death. . . . That he designed this for the instruction of his poem, we may learn from the last four lines . . .

> God save the king, and bless the land
> In plenty, joy and peace;
> And grant henceforth that foul debate
> 'Twixt noblemen may cease.[15]

Ironically, Addison's admiration appears directed to a late seventeenth-century addition to the ballad, for while this last stanza forms part of the newer "Chevy Chase" in Percy's manuscript, it is absent from the older.[16]

Addison's defense of "Chevy Chase," for which, according to Johnson, he suffered much abuse from other eminent men of letters, began the long debate over balladry's literary status.[17] In spite of the jeering of such men as Dennis, Wagstaffe, and others, Addison shortly afterward offered an approving analysis of "Two Children in the Wood" (*Spectator* No. 85) as "a plain and simple copy of nature . . . able to move the mind of the most polite reader with inward meltings of humanity and compassion" (*Works* 397) and credited "The Wanton Wife of Bath" (*Spectator* No. 247) with significant merit. However, these later defenses of Addison's include significant stylistic critiques from which the songs do no emerge unscathed, such as accusations of a "despicable simplicity in the verse" and "mean" language.

Nonetheless, such defenses are rare in the debate. The only equal in praise of balladry is found in the 1715 tract *A Pill to Purge State-Melancholy,* which asserted that ballad poetics were at times developed and refined as modern poetry (Friedman, 148-49). Much more common were outright condemnations or highly tentative defenses. Consider, for example, that Pope qualified his praise of "A Pastoral Ballad" with his admission that polish of verse and style were missing.[18] The antiquarians of the mideighteenth century offer timid praise, like that of Warton in his *History,* or as is suggested by his inclusion of a number of ballad imitations in his *Odes on Various Occasions,* which, he insisted in his Advertisement, were "an attempt to bring Poetry back into its right channels" (quoted in Friedman, 84). Percy's position in the debate, however, is more decisive. In his Preface to the ***Reliques,*** he strikes what is clearly the common ground between the poles of decorum and sensibility:

> In a polished age like the present, I am sensible that many of these reliques of antiquity will require great allowances to be made for them. Yet they have, for the most part, a pleasing simplicity and many other artless graces which . . . if they do not dazzle the imagination, are frequently found to interest the heart.

(8)

As his editor, Shenstone also expressed a concern for literary merit in the ballads. The ordering and selection of the pieces included was governed by his desire to show a progressive improvement in English poetics over time. He did, moreover, believe that "throwing too many ballads together, that were irregular in point of Metre, or obscure in point of language" would reduce readability. He therefore suggested that it would be "safer to defer the publication of such old Pieces as have rather more merit in the Light of *Curiosity* than *Poetry*" (*Percy Letters* 8:120).

As always, Percy's attempts to elevate balladry's status backfired. Not only did Ritson's exposure (in his *Disserta-*

tion on Romance and Minstrelsy) of his modifications and omissions lead to the general opinion that ballads *needed* to be revised, but Percy's suggestion that ballads provided Shakespeare with plot ideas and dialogue drew from Ritson the response that medieval romances were sources for both the ballads and Shakespeare's dramas—an inaccurate opinion still current. Moreover, says Ritson in his Preface to *Ancient Songs and Ballads,* "it is remarkable that Shakespeare puts these shreds [of ballads] chiefly into the mouths of his fools and lunatics" and such examples as had any beauty or style were courtly imitations of the seventeenth century (lxxxii). Johnson closed the case against the ballad when he ridiculed the "Chevy Chase Papers" in his *Life of Addison* (*Lives,* 198) and defined the term "ballad" in his *Dictionary* as "applied to nothing but trifling verse."[19]

As unwittingly as Percy, the Romantics—especially Wordsworth and Coleridge with the publication of the *Lyrical Ballads*—condemned medieval balladry as simplistic and unpolished. In spite of his famous thesis outlined in the Preface to the publication regarding rustic subjects and simple language as the most sublime mode of poetry, Wordsworth too found it necessary to employ highly elevated language and classical imagery in his ballad imitations, and later Thomas Hardy's parodies reduced the form further with their misanthropic tone and occasionally off-color subject matter.

Subsequent theoreticians and critics have not only cited the early enemies of the form in their evaluations, but have noted repeatedly the "necessity" felt by Percy, Ritson, and the antiquarians—and by the Romantics and Victorians who professed to employ the form—to improve upon it. Even the once revered idea of simplicity and naturalism has contributed to the ballad's undoing in the twentieth century, for we continue to think it merely "simple." In short, we have inherited an ingrained disregard for medieval balladry established in the Restoration and eighteenth century. The ballad remains for the majority of scholars a debased form, not to be taken terribly seriously and certainly of no great import. If nothing else, the sense that the ballad's poor reputation is the result of uninformed prejudice and ill-advised attempts to defend it should encourage its re-examination.

Notes

This paper was originally delivered in a session on Makers of the Middle Ages sponsored by *Studies in Medievalism* at the Thirtieth International Congress on Medieval Studies, Western Michigan University, May 1995.

1. Consider the following: Vivian de Sola Pinto and Allan Edwin Roday, *The Common Muse* (London: Chatto and Windus, 1957); Louise Pound, *Poetic Origins of the Ballad* (New York: Russell & Russell, 1921); Thomas J. Garbaty, *Medieval English Literature* (Lexington, Mass.: Heath, 1984); M. J. C. Hodgart, *The Ballads,* 2nd ed. (London: Hutchinson, 1962); Albert B. Friedman, *The Ballad Revival* (Chicago: University of Chicago Press, 1961).

2. I have argued this at length in my book *Medieval Ballardy and the Courtly Tradition: Literature of Revolt and Assimilation* (New York: Peter Lang, 1993).

3. See Arthur K. Moore, "The Literary Status of the Popular Ballad," *Comparative Literature* 10 (1958): 1-20.

4. Daniel Defoe, "The Ballad Maker's Plea" (1722), in *Daniel Defoe: His Life and Recently Discovered Writings,* ed. William Lee, 3 vols. (New York: Franklin, 1969), 3:59.

5. *The Yale Edition of Horace Walpole's Correspondence,* ed. W. S. Lewis (New Haven: Yale University Press, 1947—), 15:232, 38:187, 15:63.

6. *The Spectator,* ed. George A. Aitken (New York: Longmans, Green, 1898); all further references are to this edition and indicated by issue numbers.

7. Thomas Warton, *History of English Poetry,* ed. René Wellek (1774; rpt. New York: Johnson Reprints, 1968), 43, 46, 57.

8. Today, broadsides are considered ballads only in that they mimic certain ballad meter and rhyme schemes, are popularly sung, and usually include an incremental repetition device; most essential characteristics of the folk ballad are missing. They lack the dramatic nature of "true" ballads, possess few traditional mechanical qualities such as question and answer, show a lack of descriptive detail and the usual tragic nature, and exhibit little artistic use of language or imagery. Broadsides, highly topical in nature, tend to lack the universality of traditional songs, and except for the printing press would unlikely have survived much beyond the circumstances they describe. Conversely, many songs found in the manuscripts of Percy, Ritson, and others have roots in the medieval period, and many (e. g., "Barbara Allen," "I Gave My Love a Cherry," "Sir Patrick Spens," and—in the form of "Billie McGee McGaw"—"The Three Ravens") continue to be sung in areas of Britain and America today.

9. *The Percy Letters,* ed. Cleanth Brooks and A. F. Falconer, 8 vols. (New Haven: Yale University Press, 1977), 7:165.

10. Thomas Percy, *Reliques of Ancient English Poetry,* ed. Henry B. Wheatley (London: Bickers, 1876), 1-2 (Dedication); Ritson, "Advertisement to the First Edition," *Ancient Songs and Ballads* (1790), ed. W. Carew Hazlitt (London: Reeves and Turner, 1877; rpt. Detroit: Singing Tree Press, 1968).

11. John Dryden, *"Of Dramatic Poesy" and Other Critical Essays,* ed. George Watson, 2 vols. (London: Dent, 1962), 85.

12. James Boswell, *Life of Johnson* (Oxford: Oxford University Press, 1980), 937.

13. Henry Alfred Burd, *Joseph Ritson: A Critical Biography* (Urbana: University of Illinois Press, 1916), 106.

14. Henry Felton, *A Dissertation on Reading the Classics* (New York: Garland, 1972), vii-viii, 7, 76.

15. *The Works of the Right Honourable Joseph Addison,* ed. Henry Bohn (London: Bohn, 1856), 2:384, 378.

16. Moreover, such explicit moralizing is uncharacteristic of the traditional ballad, though it is true that the more tragic or lyrical specimens may imply moral judgments.

17. Samuel Johnson, *Lives of the Poets,* 16 vols. (New York: Pafraets, 1903), 9:199.

18. *The Prose Works of Alexander Pope,* ed. Norman Ault, 2 vols. (Oxford: Shakespeare Head, 1936), 1:104-105.

19. Samuel Johnson, *A Dictionary of the English Language* (1755; rpt. New York: AMS, 1967).

Nick Groom (essay date 1996)

SOURCE: "Celts, Goths, and the Nature of the Literary Source," in *Tradition in Transition: Women Writers, Marginal Texts, and the Eighteenth-Century Canon,* edited by Alvaro Ribeiro, SJ and James G. Basker, Clarendon Press, 1996, pp. 275-96.

[*In the following essay, Groom examines the relevance of James Macpherson's* Ossian *to Percy's work on the* Reliques, *pointing to contemporary eighteenth-century controversies regarding the importance of textual histories and sources.*]

This chapter examines James Macpherson's sensational *Ossian* (1760-5)[1] and its relevance to Percy's *Reliques* (1765), arguing that Thomas Percy's work, which began as a straightforward response to the Scotsman, was actually predicated upon a crisis within the evolving canon of English literature. I will show that accounts of ancient cultures were determined by problems caused by the nature of the literary source, whether oral or literate. The rival claims of Macpherson and Percy on the literary establishment reveal that the presentation of the source was crucial to the reception of eighteenth-century antiquarian literature and its incorporation into the canon of English poetry: each writer employed an exclusive methodology, derived from opposed theories of British history, to validate his respective ancient poetry. The story of how Percy came to compile the *Reliques* is, therefore, full of significance for eighteenth-century poetic history, and the effects of his critical debate with Macpherson are clearly perceptible in how the literary canon henceforth evolved as a hierarchy of physical texts, distinct from the popular oral traditions which the next century codified as 'folklore'.

To redefine the relationship between *Ossian* and the *Reliques* I take an approach which is chronological and what I will term 'micro-bibliographical': explaining in detail how Percy read and used Macpherson, and how the context of the Ossianic controversy affected his own works.

Percy emphasized the written, indeed the physical, status of ancient English poetry—embodied by his folio manuscript and later the ***Reliques.*** He stated his theory most clearly in ***Five Pieces of Runic Poetry,*** and it is this work, written as an explicit rejoinder to Macpherson's *Fragments,* upon which I will concentrate. The first part of this chapter explains that the antiquarian background of *Ossian* was a series of competing interpretations of prehistoric Britain. I then describe the impact of *Fragments of Ancient Poetry* and *Fingal* upon Percy in his letters and in ***Runic Poetry.*** Finally, I will consider the effects of Richard Hurd's *Letters on Chivalry and Romance* (1762), Hugh Blair's *Critical Dissertation* (1763), and John Brown's *Dissertation on . . . Poetry and Music* (1763) on Percy's construction of the figure of the medieval minstrel as it appeared in the ***Reliques.*** The act of defining the nature of the literary source within the evolving canon was expressed as a series of attempts to assert a single nationalist ideology over the whole of Great Britain, but what this account shows is that the articulation of these ideologies was a haphazard and contradictory process, delegated to a tiny band of literary antiquarians, and critically influenced by their private whims.

The literary-antiquarian debates of the eighteenth century were all, to a degree, concerned with the ethnographical origins of culture and society: the invention of language, letters, and poetry. Among British antiquarians, these issues posed two related questions: who were the original inhabitants of Great Britain, and who were their descendants? Macpherson and Percy—who were working in the immediate wake of the 1759 'Year of Victories', at the height of the British Empire, and grappling with the definitions of national cultural identity that an emergent international power demanded—both tried to establish the pure racial origins of their material, but the ways in which they went about it were radically different. Each argument developed in a way that legitimated one poetic lineage and excluded the other.

The question concentrated on the Goths and the Celts. The word 'Gothic' is a semantic minefield in the eighteenth century.[2] The historical Goths were a particular tribe who crossed the Danube in AD 376 on their way to sack Rome. Following the sixth-century historian Jordanes, however, the term was used to describe the Germanic tribes in general, including the Angles, Saxons, and Jutes, who had landed with Hengist and Horsa in Kent and invaded England in AD 449. The Goths were reinvented and glorified in the sixteenth century as an aboriginal race originating in the *vagina gentium* ('womb of nations'), and therefore displaying in its purest form the instinctive love of liberty that had enabled them to overcome the tyranny of the Roman empire, and later assert the rights of Magna Carta over the Norman yoke. Consequently the word was used extensively by seventeenth-century Parliamentarians against the absolutist aspirations of the monarch, and subsequently by eighteenth-century Whigs to defend the peculiar advantages of the English constitution.

But the word also retained a strong pejorative sense which dated from the Renaissance. This usage deplored the fall of Rome to the Goths and the displacement of classical genius by a barbarism that had heralded the onset of the Dark Ages. Hence the Goths became gradually confused with the medieval, a time despised for its 'Gothic' taste. At the same time, the medieval pageantry of romantic Gothic was itself being revived: in architecture by Horace Walpole, who bought Strawberry Hill in 1748, and in literature by Thomas Warton. The latter's *Observations on the Faerie Queene of Spenser* (1754) was written with an antiquarian zeal that disclosed a conviction of the value of ancient native genius.

There did remain, however, a lingering popular distrust of the Gothic and even Thomas Percy retained a pejorative understanding of the term. On viewing the ruins of Melrose Abbey on the Tweed, he drafted a letter to Henry Revely on 9 August 1766 which gave his opinion of Gothic architecture: 'what I have generally ['ever' deleted] observed as faulty in our old Gothic Churches, has been for the most part a heavy clumsiness in the principal parts; and in the more minute, an injudicious load of fantastic and unnatural ['load' deleted] ornaments, crowded too thick together.'[3]

And there is perhaps one further dimension to the perplexed semantics of 'Gothic'. Lawrence Lipking suggests that the Walpole set 'enjoyed the iconoclastic feeling of daring that accompanied their praise of a word so weighted with derogatory connotations'.[4]

The definition of 'Celtic' is complicated in a different way. As Michael Hechter suggests, the Celts (the Irish, Scots, and Welsh) were imagined as a collection of peripheral peoples, excluded from the central core of power and resources by an English policy of internal colonialism. The Celts had resisted the Roman Invasion and enjoyed an indigenous geographic concentration; they had nurtured their own language, culture, and society, and had ambitions of political self-determination. They therefore had a profound sense of identity and locality which denied them the full integration afforded to the Picts, Frisians, Angles, Saxons, Danes, and Normans.[5]

The rhetoric of the Celtic fringe was also obscured by a rift between the Irish and the Scottish, who both claimed to be the original Celts. The Irish pedigree was the more respectable, originating in the fourteenth century with John of Fordun, and in the 1760s this argument was making itself felt through the work of the seventeenth-century historians Geoffry Keating and Roderic O'Flaherty. Central to the Irish claim was the evidence—indeed the very existence—of manuscript archives. Fordun's *Scotichronicon,* reprinted in 1759, relied on written records for its account: 'E Codicibus MSS. editum, cum notis et variantibus lectionibus'.[6] O'Flaherty, whose title-page likewise boasted materials 'Ex Pervetustis Monumentis fideliter inter se collatis eruta', argued that Ireland was nothing less than Homer's fabled island Ogygia, and entirely dismissed

Scottish history as 'no more than a fabulous modern production, founded on oral tradition, and fiction'.[7]

In response, the Scottish Celtic, devoid of physical records, was remodelled along the primitive lines of archaic Greek: a symbolic classical stand against the new eruption of the Gothic. It derived from the Aberdeen school of primitivism and in particular the Homeric criticism of Thomas Blackwell.[8] Savage societies bred poets: primitive language was constructed by metaphor, and those metaphors derived from natural images. Poets were nomadic prophets: gliding across social strata, reciting verses in company, and falling into frenzied extemporizations under the influence of the muse. Under these conditions, original poetic genius did not need to be confined to the Greek world, and the description provided an important basis for the development of a comparable Gaelic poet. Macpherson was to invoke Blackwell's Homer in a Scottish Celtic context as a way of actually celebrating his use of oral sources. Ironically, Blackwell also provided a useful model for Percy's ancient English minstrel.

These speculations and researches into racial origins were keenly contested. A great deal of national pride rested on their conclusions. And then on 14 June 1760, James Macpherson erupted on to the scene, with his anonymously published *Fragments of Ancient Poetry, collected in the Highlands of Scotland, and translated from the Galic or Erse Language*: a slim pamphlet containing fourteen prose pieces (fifteen in the second edition) which purported to be ancient Celtic translations. The *Fragments* immediately won fanatical popularity.

From 1756 James Macpherson had begun collecting old Gaelic poetry while working as a teacher in his native Ruthven, Speyside, forming a collection that included both transcriptions of local ballad-singers and manuscripts.[9] His poetic and nationalist aspirations were evident in his strongly partisan six-canto poem *The Highlander* (1758) and pieces which he had published in the *Scots Magazine*, before he turned his full attention to translating old Gaelic poetry.

Macpherson was put to the task of translating by John Home, a Scottish playwright whom he had met in Moffat in 1759. Home had a keen interest in Highland culture, but could not speak Gaelic himself, so he persuaded Macpherson to translate some pieces for him. Macpherson reluctantly did so, and Home excitedly carried them to Edinburgh, showing them to the Scottish literati: Alexander Carlyle, Hugh Blair (who was about to be appointed Professor of Rhetoric and Belles Lettres at Edinburgh University), William Robertson, Adam Ferguson, and Lord Elibank. Having spent a decade searching for ancient Highland verse, these Scottish intellectuals had their own cultural agenda, and Macpherson was rather overtaken by events.[10] Blair managed to persuade him to produce a few more translations, sent copies to Gray, Walpole, and Shenstone, and began making preparations for publication.

Macpherson attributed the poems to a Homerically blind third-century bard called Ossian, the son of Fingal, the last of the Celts. The Black-wellian conception of the bard—a prophetic ancient poet—had recently re-emerged in Thomas Gray's poem 'The Bard' in 1757, but bards were also part of Macpherson's Highland background. Fiona Stafford indicates that the bardic tradition had in some places survived the suppression following the Jacobite Rebellion of 1745, and clan chiefs were still sometimes attended by a bard 'who was responsible not only for the composition of poetry, but also for preserving the history of the Clan'.[11] In Ossian, Macpherson drew together the idealized product of antiquarian poetry with the living poets who recited Gaelic verse.

It should be stressed that *Ossian* was presented as an oral phenomenon. Macpherson made a crucial contribution to the antiquarian debates of racial origins and historiography by postulating that Celtic society was entirely illiterate: it was an oral culture. Macpherson's point was that this did not diminish the historical significance of the culture: on the contrary, it was an absolute proof of its antiquity. There was already a sense of the primal orality of language in mid-eighteenth-century thinkers as diverse as Johnson and Hume.[12] Macpherson capitalized on this feeling to stress the staggering age of his Celtic fragments and scotch the arguments of Irish antiquarians who relied on the documentary evidence of a later age. Furthermore, the Preface of Macpherson's *Fragments*, ghost-written by Hugh Blair, not only invoked the oral tradition of the Highlands; it actually resisted any indigenous literacy supposedly contemporary with the composition of the poems:

> In a fragment . . . which the translator has seen, a Culdee or Monk is represented as desirous to take down in writing from the mouth of Oscian, who is the principal personage in several of the following fragments, his warlike achievements and those of his family. But Oscian treats the monk and his religion with disdain, telling him, that the deeds of such great men were subjects too high to be recorded by him, or by any of his religion.[13]

It was claimed that the poems had survived only through bardic tradition. Gray, witnessing what appeared to be the incarnation of his 'Bard', was '*extasié*' with the *Fragments*' 'infinite beauty', believing Macpherson was 'the very Demon of Poetry, or he has lighted on a treasure hid for ages'.[14]

This bardic oral tradition defined *Ossian* on every level. The poems themselves constantly stressed their oracy. They were full of sound, several were dialogues, and 'voices' served as a metaphor for poetry, memory, the past, and the present. For example, 'Fragment VIII' ended with Ossian's lament: 'SUCH, Fingal! were thy words; but thy words I hear no more. Sightless I sit by thy tomb. I hear the wind in the wood: but no more I hear my friends. The cry of the hunter is over. The voice of war is ceased.'[15]

Stylistically, the poems were constructed out of accumulating resonances and repetitions, such as alliteration, concatenation, parallelism, and accumulation, which appeared to testify that they were primitive, exotic, and oral.[16] A sense of evanescent orality was also present in the structure of the *Fragments*: the collection was a shadow of something larger, a fragment of something complete. The whole work was finely structured through subtle allusion and shifting perspective, which gave the sense of another work struggling to find form: of a lost northern oral epic articulated as a printed pamphlet.

Thomas Percy's interest in literary antiquarianism was as deeply rooted, if differently directed, as Macpherson's. Percy was a country parson living at Easton Maudit in Northamptonshire, with a growing interest in old English poetry.[17] In the 1750s he had obtained a piece of Interregnum flotsam: a seventeenth-century handwritten miscellany of antique popular verse. This folio manuscript was to provide the impetus for his anthology *Reliques of Ancient English Poetry,* published in 1765. By 1760 he was actively cultivating contacts across the country and beyond to help him collect antique verse.

For over two years Percy had corresponded with the respected poet William Shenstone, a vogue leader of taste and incumbent of the Leasowes, who shared Percy's passion for antiquarian ballads. They had transcribed and revised a small number of ballad texts from the folio manuscript, intending that they would eventually publish some sort of selection. But in 1760, both were busy with other projects. It was not until the sudden appearance of Macpherson's *Fragments* that they were roused to begin serious work on what was to become the *Reliques.*

The story of how Macpherson provided the stimulus for Percy and Shenstone to begin the *Reliques* in earnest is important for explaining the accidents and local struggles that were to shape English literary history. On 21 June 1760 Shenstone was sent an early copy of the *Fragments* by John Macgowan, who accompanied the book with an evangelizing letter.[18] Shenstone excitedly informed Percy on 11 August: 'you *must instantly* procure the "antient Fragments" of Scotch Poetry' and Percy coincidentally visited Shenstone shortly afterwards and consulted the new work.[19] The unexpected arrival of Macpherson's *Fragments* at the Leasowes inspired and stimulated Percy, who had as yet done virtually nothing with the *Reliques,* to propose that he compile a comparable anthology of ancient English fragments, under the editorial guidance of Shenstone. Shenstone responded with the suggestion that they be included in a four-volume *Reliques.*

Percy's sudden and absorbing enthusiasm about the *Fragments,* and his proposal for a rival anthology, were not merely momentary excitements. His long-standing friendship with Edward Lye, for example, had already grounded him in the field of literary antiquarianism. Lye was an Anglo-Saxon scholar and the parson of Yardley Hastings, Bedfordshire, just a mile and a half away from Percy at Easton Maudit. He was a close and obliging neighbour—on 24 April 1759 he gave away Anne Gutteridge, Percy's bride. Bertram Davis notes that Lye 'seems to

have taken a fatherly interest' in Percy, and Percy's memoranda books from their first acquaintance in 1756 to Lye's death in 1767 show that the two antiquarian scholars frequently dined together.[20] In 1757 Lye offered help glossing the folio manuscript and in 1759 he taught Percy the Runic alphabet.[21]

This is why when Shenstone told Percy that he must '*instantly* procure' a copy of Macpherson's *Fragments,* Percy was able, after he had pored over the book at the Leasowes, to respond swiftly with fragments of his own: 'Inclosed I send you an ancient Celtic, (or rather Runic) Poem, translated from the Icelandic. I am making up a small Collection of Pieces of this kind for the Press, which will be about the Size of the Erse Fragments.'[22] Although Percy himself was at this early stage confusing the Celts with the Goths, the first Runic fragments he sent Shenstone in September 1760 were introduced with a scholarly note, the fruit of his dinners with Lye:

> It will be difficult to meet with many Celtic pieces so well preserved & so intire as, *the Epicedium of Haco*; or *the Incantation of Hervor* [in dryden's Misc.] [*sic*] because they are only to [be] met with inserted as Vouchers to Facts, in some of the Old Gothic Prose Histories. It will be more easy to meet with smaller fragments, which every where abound in those Histories.[23]

Percy transcribed two short fragments for Shenstone: six lines of 'Gandrode' and nine lines of the 'Death of King Guthlange' and wondered whether he should print the originals, 'which after all nobody will understand'.[24]

Shenstone thought that there was 'something good' in the 'Celtic [*sic*]' fragments, but advised not to over-annotate the poems, warning 'The absolute *Necessity* of Notes, will be the Rock that you may chance to split upon'. He suggested that Percy use either a preface, glossary, or endnotes, omit the originals and shorter pieces, and adopt 'a kind of *flowing* yet *pompous Prose*' in paragraphs.[25]

James Dodsley signed the contract for 'five pieces of *Runic Poetry translated from the Islandic Language*' (with *The Song of Solomon*) on 21 May 1761, the day before the *Reliques* deal was struck, and the next month 'The Incantation of Hervor' was published in the *Lady's Magazine.*[26] Although *Runic Poetry* was not published until April 1763, Percy never lost sight of his project as a response to Macpherson, because by June 1761, in the immediate wake of the *Fragments,* Percy had already decided on the title and the contents of *Runic Poetry,* and had edited at least one piece. Nevertheless, he spent the rest of the year hard at work on the *Reliques*: visiting Cambridge to transcribe ballads from the Pepysian Library, assembling his 'Alphabet Collection' of white-letter broadsides from Dicey's warehouse, engaging Thomas Astle, Thomas Warton, and Richard Farmer to aid him in his researches, and commencing printing early in 1762—but he confidently expected *Runic Poetry* to be published in the winter of 1761.[27] On 17 September 1761, Shenstone again wrote encouragingly: 'Let the Liberties taken by the Translator of the Erse-Fragments be a Precedent for *You.* Many old Pieces, *without* some alteration, will do nothing; and, *with your* amendments, will be striking.'[28] He was reminding Percy of Edward Young's *Conjectures on Original Composition,* published in 1759, a highly influential little tract. Indeed, Shenstone urged Percy to read Young: 'even tho' it shou'd dissuade you . . . from undertaking any more *translations.* I should not *murmur* at the *effect*; provided it stimulate you to write *Originals.*'[29]

Young roundly condemned imitations because, unlike colonizing originals, they sprang from over-considered words, books, and texts. Young offered the advice: 'Let us build our Compositions with the Spirit, and in the Taste, of the Antients; but not with their Materials'—precisely what Shenstone consistently told Percy to do.[30] This neatly illustrates the tensions of rival attitudes to the nature of the source: Shenstone had far more sympathy with Macpherson's technique of adaptation and remodelling than with Percy's scrupulous adherence to the text, and in the end the *Reliques* became a compromise between the two.

For reasons I have given elsewhere, *Five Pieces of Runic Poetry* was not published until 2 April 1763, but Percy still placed it in the context of Macpherson: 'It would be as vain to deny, as it is perhaps impolitic to mention, that this attempt is owing to the success of the *ERSE* fragments.'[31] Percy presented the work as a direct, if delayed, response to Macpherson. Like the *Fragments* it was a slim octavo containing short pieces of apparently ancient foreign verse translated into distinctive English prose. Percy, however, emphasized his use of documentary sources; in fact, the entire structure of *Runic Poetry* served as an authenticating mechanism. Its title-page was more elaborate than that of the *Fragments,* and displayed an engraving of a number of untranslated Runes, underlining the palpability of Percy's sources. Like the Chinese characters which adorned Percy's *Miscellaneous Pieces* (1762), these offered an opportunity to authenticate the work. The title-page of Macpherson's *Fingal* (1761) significantly portrayed a blind Ossian extemporizing his verses in the Celtic wilderness with no manuscript in sight.

Both the *Fragments* and *Runic Poetry* quoted Lucan as an epigraph, but there the physical similarities ended. *Runic Poetry* was printed on quality paper, was set more accurately, and the text was enlivened with frequent ornaments. It was not designed to be bound sympathetically with the *Fragments,* but to replace it. Percy's poems were not translated in the Ossianic idiom, and were prefaced with notes, clarified with footnotes, and concluded with endnotes. 'The Incantation of Hervor', for example, had a lengthy Preface 'To prevent as much as possible the interruption of notes', but there were still footnotes throughout the entire piece.[32] Macpherson's collection was lean by comparison: it simply had a brisk Preface contributed by Blair, and occasional, usually brief, explanatory footnotes.

Here Percy and Shenstone differed. Shenstone approved far more of the latter style, because it presented the pieces as poetry, and he disliked the antiquarian lumber which burdened Percy's poems. Percy in fact apologized for this in a letter to Shenstone: 'You will probably be disgusted to see it so incumbered with Notes; Yet some are unavoidable, as the Piece would be unintelligible without them.'[33] But Percy would not relinquish any critical apparatus which verified the physical existence of his Gothic poetry, and did not appreciate that it was the very unintelligibility that so appealed to Shenstone.

In *Runic Poetry* Percy outlined scholarly precedent, pleaded editorial integrity and verifiable sources, and listed appropriate references. In other words, he placed the work in a diagrammatic scholarly context: the literary establishment of books and writing, rather than the oral bardic tradition claimed by Macpherson. This is demonstrated most clearly in the Runic originals that were appended to the translations, of which he wrote: 'The Editor was in some doubt whether he should subjoin or suppress the originals. But as they lie within little compass, and as the books whence they are extracted are very scarce, he was tempted to add them as vouchers for the authenticity of his version.'[34] In fact, these originals were printed in roman, rather than Runic, characters, because they were themselves Swedish and Latin translations. They were included for the sake of form rather than to encourage scholarly precision: part of a grand textual conspiracy. Without authentic originals, Percy had no way of knowing whether his Gothic translations were more or less accurate than Macpherson's Celtic translations. But what is important about Percy's working of his textual machine is that it fixed the idea of extant manuscripts on to his work, a notion which he emphasized in his account of the Goths.

Percy's Goths were the ancient ancestors of the English, and had laid the foundations of national character, culture, and politics: 'It will be thought a paradox, that the same people, whose furious ravages destroyed the last poor remains of expiring genius among the Romans, should cherish it with all possible care among their own countrymen: yet so it was.'[35] They also invented rhyming verse, a claim Percy could 'prove' because they were inveterate scribblers, or rather carvers, of Runes. Just as the verbal clamour of Macpherson's Ossianic fragments stressed the oral culture of the Celts, so the prodigious textuality of *Five Pieces of Runic Poetry* underlined the literacy of the Goths. Percy demonstrated that his Goths differed from Macpherson's Celts in the crucial area of extant records, records which were keys to unlock 'the treasures of native genius' and settle the literary-antiquarian debates.[36] The confrontational Preface challenged Macpherson to publish his Ossianic originals: 'till the Translator of those poems thinks proper to produce his originals, it is impossible to say whether they do not owe their superiority, if not their whole existence entirely to himself. The Editor of these pieces had no such boundless field for licence.'[37]

While Percy had been trying to finish *Runic Poetry,* Macpherson published his first Ossianic epic, *Fingal, An Ancient Epic Poem, in Six Books,* on 1 December 1761.

Fingal was introduced with an account of Macpherson's manuscript-collecting expedition in the Highlands, undertaken in 1760 and sponsored by the Scottish literati, but it still renewed the *Fragments*' commitment to orality, and Macpherson's own account of the trip did not mention tangible manuscripts. Instead he claimed that it was 'in order to recover what remained of the works of the old bards'.[38] This was in spite of his haul of 'two Ponies laden with old Manuscripts'.[39] Macpherson persisted in marginalizing manuscripts from Ossian, and he described the Gaelic oral tradition by analogy with Tacitus' references to song in, ironically enough, the compendium of Gothic culture, *Germania*: 'This species of composition was not committed to writing, but delivered by oral tradition . . . This oral chronicle of the Germans was not forgot in the eighth century, and it probably would have remained to this day, had not learning, which thinks every thing, that is not committed to writing, fabulous, been introduced.'[40] Macpherson disputed the emphasis on written records in eighteenth-century accounts of ancient history, which he claimed had misrepresented the Celts. The literacy of classical nations was crucial to their ensuing historical renown: 'They trusted their fame to tradition and the songs of their bards, which, by the vicissitude of human affairs, are long since lost. Their ancient language is the only monument that remains of them.'[41]

The poem 'Fingal' itself was full of episodes from the *Fragments,* though not told with quite the same sound and fury. There was more emphasis on the singing of the bards as a universal metaphor than on the disembodied voices of the *Fragments.*

The orality of *Fingal* was most clearly demonstrated in Macpherson's use of episodes derived from the *Fragments,* episodes that were substantially changed. Macpherson indicated this in his voluminous footnotes—virtually every page of *Fingal* was annotated. Derick Thomson explains Macpherson's extreme footnoting as a contextual frame, but his annotation was also ideologically significant.[42] The fluctuation between versions demonstrated the inherent orality of the verses. Footnotes literally underwrote Macpherson's editing methods, not by positioning the text in the canon of antiquarian scholarship as Percy's did, but by exposing the evolution of the text and preventing closure. Macpherson was not simply pursuing the archetypal *Ossian,* but demonstrating by the constant fluctuation of each version the inadequacy of letters to communicate ancient Celtic poetry.

Neither the public, nor even Percy and Shenstone themselves, held simple or uniform views of Macpherson's project. 'What say you to Fingal—!' asked Shenstone, who had subscribed to the Scottish edition, 'What a treasure *these* for a modern Poet, before they were published?'[43] Percy's opinion was divided, noting 'too little simplicity of narration . . . affected and stiff . . . turgid and harsh . . . not what it is made to pass for', yet richly 'sublime and pathetic'.[44] Macpherson's work had a dramatic effect upon the world of letters. A storm of pro-test greeted *Fingal.* Irish nationalists, Wilkesites, and textual pedants forged an unlikely alliance against the Scottish literati, poets, and antiquarian cranks. There was a sudden demand for literary antiquarianism, and 1762 saw an explosion of books and pamphlets eager to turn a penny on *Ossian.* For Percy, in the middle of the ***Reliques,*** the most important of these was Richard Hurd's *Letters on Chivalry and Romance* (1762). This publication defined the place of ancient poetry in the popular imagination, marking the 'enchanted ground' on which Percy's Goths would fight Macpherson's Celts, and it consequently requires detailed consideration.[45]

Like Thomas Warton, Hurd was interested in the pervasive influence of the apparently low literature of Gothic Romance (which he had not read) on the great English poets, Spenser, Shakespeare, and Milton (whom he had). Hurd redefined the Gothic by paralleling the cultural and artistic fecundity of ancient Greece with medieval Europe, re-evaluating the medieval by redefining the Hellenic. The petty tyrannies, incessant warring, and feudal values of the Middle Ages were not unlike the martial politics of ancient Greece which had created the institutions of chivalry and bardism.

Hurd's strategy, however, was not simply to impose an anachronistic social and linguistic model on the classical canons of literature and taste, and he was not so naïve as to find classical beauties in Gothic art. Instead, he tried to demonstrate that, if the conditions and therefore execution of Gothic and classical art differed, their theories of composition coincided.

> When an architect examines a Gothic structure by Grecian rules, he finds nothing but deformity. But the Gothic architecture has it's own rules, by which when it comes to be examined, it is seen to have it's merit, as well as the Grecian. The question is not, which of the two is conducted in the simplest or truest taste: but, whether there be not sense and design in both, when scrutinized by the laws on which each is projected.[46]

Although he did not support Ossianic revivalism ('I would advise no modern poet to revive these faery tales in an epic poem') Hurd did propose an indigenous autonomy for Gothic art, rather than simply condemning it as mongrel degeneration.[47] In this way, Hurd's *Letters* helped to develop an English aesthetic by placing original genius in the Middle Ages and distinguishing it from the Franco-Scottish Celts.[48]

For a literary antiquarian like Percy, the work was a godsend. Hurd was effectively legitimating the medieval ballads Percy was editing from the folio manuscript for the ***Reliques*** by endowing them with native Gothic genius. ***Runic Poetry*** and the putative ***Reliques*** had an identical Gothic pedigree. The Goths were simultaneously being reinvented in two different ways: both as ancients and as medievals.

Yet even as Percy was developing an English answer to *Ossian,* Macpherson's publications found their defenders among the Scottish intelligentsia, for whom they formed the focus of a whole poetic and critical school. In 1763 Hugh Blair responded to Hurd's argument in his *Critical Dissertation,* which was designed to be bound into *Fingal*.[49] Blair argued that an archetypal genius was common to all nations at primitive stages of development. This original genius was the modernity of sentiment displayed by Ossian. He therefore attacked Percy's Gothic fragments for their barbaric and bloodthirsty images, which revealed them to be effete and worthless trash.

Blair further postulated that in early societies (for example, in Old Testament times) language was purely figurative. From this childlike state, 'Language advances from sterility to copiousness, and at the same time, from fervour and enthusiasm, to correctness and precesion. Style becomes more chaste; but less animated.'[50] Society progressed in a similar way: the four stages of hunters, gatherers, farmers, and capitalists. But although *Ossian* was nominally set in the primary moment of this Aristotelian social theory, it displayed all the artistry and enlightenment of later stages. Blair emphasized this social modernity in the language he used to compare Celtic with Gothic verse: 'When we turn from the poetry of Lodbrog to that of Ossian, it is like passing from a savage desart, into a fertile and cultivated country.'[51] The image was used advisedly. By demonstrating the Augustan sophistication of Ossian he could show that the ancient Celtic verse was both authentic and vastly superior to that of the Goths. 'In one remarkable passage, Ossian describes himself as living in a sort of classical age, enlightened by the memorials of former times, conveyed in the songs of bards; and points at a period of darkness and ignorance which lay beyond the reach of tradition.'[52] The pejorative shades of Gothic were reinscribed, once again merging the shadow of barbarism into the dark night of medieval ignorance: *Ossian* trod a fine, Homeric line between primitivism and enlightenment.

More importantly, Blair made a lengthy case against the Gothic fragments, retranslating the ubiquitous Nordic poem 'Regner Lodbrog'. The response of the Celtic *Ossian* supporters to 'Regner Lodbrog' was profoundly different from that of the Gothic revivalists, and clarifies how ancient poetry was being employed in new nationalist discourses. William Temple had translated this poem from Latin into English in 1690, but it had of course appeared most recently in Percy's versions in the *Lady's Magazine* and **Runic Poetry**.[53] Blair's version in his *Critical Dissertation* was certainly less florid than Percy's, but he emphasized its bloodthirsty images and formlessness. *Ossian* was completely different, combining 'the fire and the enthusiasm of the most early times . . . with an amazing degree of regularity and art'.[54] Blair discounted claims that the Goths invented rhyme, and characterized the style of Ossian as a 'measured prose' which exhibited all the native, ancient, and original genius of the works.[55]

Macpherson's second epic, *Temora, An Ancient Poem, in Eight Books,* which was also published in 1763, attempted to divide and rule the clamour of opposition that had risen against *Ossian.* As he wryly remarked, 'WHILE some doubt the authenticity of the poems of Ossian, others strenuously endeavour to appropriate them to the Irish nation.'[56]

Macpherson introduced *Temora* with an emphatic attack on the Irish claim to be the original Celts and thereby the composers of *Ossian.* He refuted the Irish in two ways: first, he derided their historians, and, secondly, he gave his own reading of the racial migrations of ancient Britain. Macpherson argued that John of Fordun's history was erroneous precisely because of the very paucity of records that were the hallmark of *Ossian*: 'Destitute of annals in Scotland, he had recourse to Ireland, which, according to the vulgar errors of the times, was reckoned the first habitation of the Scots.'[57] Keating and O'Flaherty were dismissed on the authority of Sir James Ware, whose *De Hibernia,* originally published in 1654, had been reprinted in 1739. Ware had argued for a more flexible approach to sources: 'it is Antiquity, and the Unfaithfulness of Oral Tradition that have created these Errors, and left nothing clear for Posterity to depend on'.[58] Macpherson's own attack lacked the tolerance of Ware: 'Credulous and puerile to the last degree, they have disgraced the antiquities they meant to establish.'[59]

Having combated the immediate threat of *Ossian* being hijacked by the Irish, Macpherson then delivered an Ossianic account of the racial composition of ancient Britain. The Romans invaded south Britain and drove the Caledonians into the north of the country, which remained unconquered. These Caledonians were the Celts or Gauls who had originally possessed Britain.

In distinguishing the Caledonians from the Romans, British, and Lowlanders, Macpherson rejected Ireland as well. The Irish were denied pure Celtic origins. Their country was initially colonized by the 'Firbolg', 'confessedly the Belgæ of Britain', before being invaded by the Caledonians, in support of which Temora was presented as proof.[60] *Ossian* was more than a cultural product: it was a confirmation of national identity.

Temora also placed the bards in a more contemporary light. Macpherson concentrated on their decline in status: they were expelled from clans for 'dull and trivial' compositions, took to 'satire and lampoon', and were accommodated by 'the vulgar'.[61] They began to invent incredible stories, interpolated the remains of *Ossian* with their 'futile performances', and subsequently created the romance.[62] Macpherson extended his Ossianic theory of the origin of poetry in the wake of Hurd's *Letters*: 'I firmly believe, there are more stories of giants, enchanted castles, dwarfs, and palfreys, in the Highlands, than in any country in Europe' in which, of course, 'the very language of the bards is still preserved'.[63] But Macpherson was actually retheorizing his material and belatedly considering *Ossian* manuscripts. The oral tradition was now defined by manuscripts, a new fidelity of the source:

> The reader will find some alterations in the style of this book. These are drawn from more correct copies of the

original which came to my hands, since the former publication. As the most part of the poem is delivered down by tradition, the style is sometimes various and interpolated. After comparing the different readings, I always made choice of that which agreed best with the spirit of the context.[64]

The context in fact overwhelmed the poetry. *Temora* was more fictional than earlier works, so Macpherson verified it historically. Fragments and poems that would have graced an earlier collection in their own right were literally reduced to footnotes in a larger argument, to prove the Gaelic language was purely and divinely harmonious. The integrity of Gaelic was its oracy. In other words, the language and style of the poem was not merely a source to settle the Celtic ancestry of the Scots over the Irish; it was the very object of their national quest, their true heritage. The original Celtic was imaginatively reconstructed: 'There is not a passage in all Temora, which loses so much in the translation as this. The first part of the speech is rapid and irregular, and is peculiarly calculated to animate the soul to war . . . The first is like torrents rushing over broken rocks; the second like the course of a full-flowing river, calm but majestic.'[65]

Macpherson claimed that the Gaelic language was universal and sentimental like music, rather than pictorial and abstract like hieroglyphs or runes: 'So well adapted are the sounds of the words to the sentiments, that, even without any knowledge of the language, they pierce and dissolve the heart.'[66] By arguing that the language was inherently musical, Macpherson was able to print an original text. Whether it was an original manuscript or dictated by oral tradition was irrelevant: the vocalic harmony of antique sounds was sufficient evidence for its authenticity. The document comprised twenty pages of what purported to be the ancient Gaelic: 'A SPECIMEN OF THE ORIGINAL OF TEMORA BOOK SEVENTH'. *Ossian,* for three years an oral phenomenon, at last sought the sanction of literacy.

The effect was disastrous. The introduction of manuscripts was not simply incongruous: it was lethal to the culture Macpherson and Blair had laboured to realize—the bardic oral tradition of the primigenial Highland Celts—because it dramatically increased the demand to see manuscript sources. The demand could not be met and, after an extended public controversy, *Ossian* was dismissed as a forgery.[67]

This belated literation and its attendant ruinous effect on Macpherson confirmed Percy's formulation of Gothic poetics, which he was rewriting for the **Reliques.** *Ossian* trespassed upon the written records of literate ancients like Percy's Goths, and paid the price. The source had become the deciding factor in the antiquarian canonization of literature. Percy's counterattack against Macpherson appeared in the **Reliques** in 1765 as the **'Essay on the Ancient English Minstrels'**, written during the summer of 1764—one of the last things he wrote before final publication. Percy considered the medium of literate poetry in a

new way. His thesis hinged on the representation and reputation of the ancient poets themselves.

Percy's immediate source was John 'Estimate' Brown's *Dissertation on the Rise, Union, and Power, the Progressions, Separations, and Corruptions, of Poetry and Music* (1763).[68] Brown asserted that poetry and music were naturally united, but had been gradually separated by civilized refinement. Uncultivated societies, such as the American Iroquois and Hurons, relied on bards for their history and ultimately for their cultural identity: 'The Profession of *Bard* or *Musician* would be held as very honourable, and of high Esteem. For he would be vested with a kind of *public Character*: and if not an original Legislator, yet still he would be regarded as a *subordinate* and *useful Servant* of the *State*.'[69] Emphasis was placed on the civic duties of the bard. At the cusp of literacy bards remodelled their traditional ancient songs as written verse, severed the connection with music, and broke with the past. The new literacy legitimated itself by rewriting history.

Brown agreed that 'the *Scythian* or *Runic* Songs' were the oldest extant literature in the North, and quoted Odin, who boasted that 'his Runic Poems were given him by the Gods'; but at the same time suggested that *Ossian* had been composed 'during the second Period of Music . . . when the Bard's Profession had separated from that of the Legislator, yet still retained its Power and Dignity in full Union'.[70] His conclusion, 'Of the possible Re-union of Poetry and Music', was strangely expectant, and so Percy's minstrel evolved from Brown's anticipation of cultural and national renewal. He devised a state role for the poet, and defined the relationship of the arts to the court by reviving patronage. For his models, Percy returned to **Runic Poetry** and the scalds.

Percy derived most of his information about ancient Scandinavia from Paul-Henri Mallet's *Introduction à l'histoire de Dannemarc* (1755-6). He had read Mallet by 1761 and, with the help of Lye, began translating it on 21 November 1763, devoting a whole week to the business.[71] According to Mallet, scalds were central to Scandinavian society. Their spiritual father was Odin, inventor of poetry and runes, and their runic poetry was both a divine gift and a social asset: 'Those that excelled in it, were distinguished by the first honours of the state: were constant attendants on their kings, and were often employed on the most important commissions.'[72]

From a draft of his proposal to the booksellers, it is clear that in **Northern Antiquities** Percy was writing a national myth by perfecting the word 'Gothic':

> Here he ['the English reader'] will see the seeds of our excellent Gothic constitution . . . many superstitions, opinions and prejudices . . . that the ideas of Chivalry were strongly rivetted in the minds of all the northern nations from the remotest ages . . . and . . . an ancient Islandic Romance that shews the original of that kind of writing which so long captivated all the nations of Europe.[73]

Percy warned the Welsh antiquarian Evan Evans that Mallet's biggest mistake was to compound the Goths with the Celts, 'a mistake which I shall endeavour to rectify in my translation'.[74] Percy worked hard to expunge all references to the Celts from Mallet's book. He produced a list of page references headed 'Notes concerning the Author's Confounding of Celtic & Gothic Antiquities' and methodically changed every Celt into a Goth.[75]

Thus the stage was set, as Percy sat down to begin his essay in August 1764, for a dramatic remodelling of the transmission of national literature. Percy was ready to draw together the threads of many arguments as he sought to reinvent the English poetic tradition, and it cannot be a coincidence that such an ambitious essay was begun under the eye of Johnson, who was staying at Easton Maudit with Percy at the time. Percy combined his sources: the folio manuscript and the Pepys and Dicey ballads, with his antiquarian research: the scalds and bards. The scalds became the Gothic forefathers of the ancient English minstrels and were disingenuously merged with the bards. He united the different senses of Gothic, attributing the invention of writing and poetry to the scalds, who became almost divine; dehistoricizing the bards by applying the term indiscriminately to scalds and minstrels; and making the medieval minstrels the inheritors of the Runic tradition. He invented a contemporary role, both cultural and ideological, for his English minstrels: they were the embodiment of the Gothic aesthetic.

The '**Essay on the Ancient English Minstrels**' began by picking up the thread of Brown's argument: 'THE MINSTRELS seem to have been the genuine successors of the ancient Bards, who united the arts of Poetry and Music, and sung verses to the harp, of their own composing. It is well known what respect was shown to their BARDS by the Britons: and no less was paid to the northern SCALDS by most of the nations of the Gothic race.'[76] Percy argued by analogy, claiming, in Hurd's style, that the bloody ferocity of scaldic society would have produced the institutions of chivalry. In his essay on metrical romances, the last to be finished for the *Reliques* on 1 November 1764, Percy concluded, 'That our old Romances of Chivalry are derived in a lineal descent from the ancient historical songs of the SCALDS is incontestible, because there are many of them still preserved in the North, which exhibit all the seeds of Chivalry, before it became a solemn institution.'[77]

Like the scald, Percy's minstrel was originally a 'privileged character' among the Anglo-Saxons and Danes: a historian, genealogist, poet, and harpist. Alfred and later Anlaff adopted minstrel disguises and were able to infiltrate their enemy's camps unchallenged.[78] By obscuring the role of the Welsh bards he was able to annex their court status, yet retain the marginal and indigent nature of the minstrels. The minstrels, moreover, were oral poets. Percy therefore argued that the Gothic literacy of the scalds generated an oral tradition, which was in turn absorbed into the ephemeral publishing of popular balladry and chapbook romance, and ultimately the inaccuracies of the folio manuscript. It is no surprise, considering Percy's absolute emphasis on written sources, that he imagined writing somehow came before speech. To distinguish his noble minstrels from the (usually female) hack ballad-singers who regaled passing Londoners with their wares in the 1760s, he adapted Brown and blended the oral ballads of the minstrels with the press-work of the ballad-singers:

> so long as the Minstrels subsisted, they seem never to have designed their rhymes for publication, and probably never committed them to writing themselves: what copies are preserved of them were doubtless taken down from their mouths. But as the old Minstrels gradually wore out, a new race of ballad-writers succeeded, an inferior sort of minor poets, who wrote narrative songs merely for the press.[79]

Percy's account of the decline of the minstrels exactly mirrored that of Macpherson's bards. They 'gave more and more into embellishment, and set off their recitals with such marvelous fictions, as were calculated to captivate gross and ignorant minds' and predictably created the romance.[80]

Percy's response to Macpherson's *Ossian* was to invent a Gothic tradition, and in the end he reinvented himself. He performed all the duties of a minstrel for his patrons the Northumberland Percys: acting as chaplain to the family and tutor to Algernon Percy, cataloguing the books at Syon House and writing a visitor's guide to the Alnwick estate, and ultimately composing a lengthy pastiche of a Northumbrian ballad, *The Hermit of Warkworth* (1771). Indeed, it could even be argued that this social toadying lay behind all of Percy's elaborate construction of state-Gothicism. But in doing so he fundamentally shifted the attention of scholars to the medium of literary remains, and all that that entailed: reading the interfaces of oral, manuscript, and print cultures, and the coefficient of transmission, in terms of national myths or the spatialization of culture. The effect of this endeavour was to confirm the limitations of the evolving canon and to confine it to physical rather than evanescent texts. This effect is also seen in other literature of the period, as diverse as *Tristram Shandy*, Boswell's *Life of Johnson*, and the Gothic novel, where the validity of different literary media (speech, manuscripts, and the press) is explored. Percy's *Reliques* stands not only as an example of the literary-antiquarian taste, an early attempt to assemble the nation's literary inheritance, and an influential anthology of popular verse, it is also a response to Macpherson's *Ossian*, a reinvention of the Gothic, and ultimately a manifesto for a new poetics of the source.

Notes

1. It is conventional to denote James Macpherson's four published Ossianic works (*Fragments of Ancient Poetry, collected in the Highlands of Scotland, and translated from the Galic or Erse Language* (Edinburgh, 1760); *Fingal, An Ancient Epic Poem, in Six Books: together with several other Poems, composed by Ossian the Son of Fingal* (London, 1761);

Temora, An Ancient Poem, in Eight Books: together with several other Poems, composed by Ossian, the Son of Fingal (London, 1763); *The Works of Ossian, the Son of Fingal* (2 vols.; London, 1765)) by the collective title *Ossian.*

2. For definitions of the 'Gothic', see Paul Frankl, *The Gothic: Literary Sources and Interpretations through Eight Centuries* (Princeton, NJ, 1960); Samuel Kliger, *The Goths in England: A Study in Seventeenth and Eighteenth Century Thought* (Cambridge, Mass., 1952); Hugh MacDougall, *Racial Myth in English History: Trojans, Teutons, and Anglo-Saxons* (Montreal, 1982); Michael Meehan, *Liberty and Poetics in Eighteenth Century England* (Beckenham, 1986).

3. BL [British Library] Add. MS 32335, fo. 12^v.

4. Lawrence Lipking, *The Ordering of the Arts in Eighteenth-Century England* (Princeton, NJ, 1970), 149.

5. Michael Hechter, *Internal Colonialism: The Celtic Fringe in British National Development, 1536-1966* (London, 1975).

6. Johannis De Fordun, *Scotichronicon* (Edinburgh, 1759), title-page (edited from manuscripts with notes and variant readings), 43.

7. Roderico O Flaherty, *Ogygia* (London, 1685), title-page (collected from antiquarian records faithfully compared with one another); Roderic O'Flaherty, *Ogygia, or, A Chronological Account of Irish Events,* trans. James Hely (Dublin, 1793), i. 226.

8. Thomas Blackwell, *An Enquiry into the Life and Writings of Homer* (London, 1735).

9. See Paul J. deGategno, *James Macpherson* (Boston, 1989); Richard B. Sher, *Church and University in the Scottish Enlightenment: The Moderate Literati of Edinburgh* (Edinburgh, 1985); Bailey Saunders, *The Life and Letters of James Macpherson* (London, 1894); Fiona Stafford, *The Sublime Savage: A Study of James Macpherson and the Poems of Ossian* (Edinburgh, 1988).

10. deGategno, *James Macpherson,* 24-6; Stafford, *The Sublime Savage,* 78-80.

11. Ibid. 13. René Wellek comments, 'The Tudor antiquarians, in their patriotic fervour for everything "British", had already raised the status of the bard, who slowly assumed heroic proportions long before Gray's poem and Macpherson's sentimentalized version' (*The Rise of English Literary History* (Chapel Hill, NC, 1941), 126).

12. Samuel Johnson, *A Dictionary of the English Language* (London, 1755), i. A2^r; David Hume, *Enquiries concerning Human Understanding and concerning the Principles of Morals,* ed. L. A. Selby-Bigge, rev. P. H. Nidditch (Oxford, 1975), 224, 241.

13. Macpherson, *Fragments,* pp. iv-v.

14. *The Correspondence of Thomas Gray,* ed. Paget Toynbee and Leonard Whibley (Oxford, 1935), ii. 680.

15. Macpherson, *Fragments,* 40.

16. Walther Drechsler, 'Der Stil des Macphersonschen Ossian', Ph.D. dissertation (Berlin, 1904); John Dwyer, 'The Melancholy Savage: Text and Context in the Poems of Ossian', in Howard Gaskill (ed.), *Ossian Revisited* (Edinburgh, 1991), 164-206; Robert P. Fitzgerald, 'The Style of Ossian', *Studies in Romanticism,* 6 (1966), 23, 29-31; Stafford, *The Sublime Savage,* 103-11; Janet Todd, *Sensibility: An Introduction* (London, 1986), 59-60.

17. See Bertram H. Davis, *Thomas Percy* (Boston, 1981), and *Thomas Percy: A Scholar-Cleric in the Age of Johnson* (Philadelphia, 1989).

18. Margaret M. Smith, 'Prepublication of Literary Texts: The Case of James Macpherson's Ossianic Verses', *Yale University Library Gazette,* 64 (1990), 132-57.

19. *The Percy Letters,* vii. *The Correspondence of Thomas Percy and William Shenstone,* ed. Cleanth Brooks (New Haven, Conn., 1977), 68.

20. BL Add. MS 32336, fos. 18-76.

21. The neglected research of Andrew Deacon ('The Use of Norse Mythology and Literature by some 18th and 19th Century Writers, with special reference to the work of Bishop Percy, Thomas Gray, Matthew Arnold and William Morris', B.Litt. thesis (Oxford, 1964)) describes the collaboration between Percy and Lye in the production of *Runic Poetry.* Percy certainly had some ability at Runes, but, like his tutor, was not a serious Runic scholar, and they both relied heavily on seventeenth-century critics. Deacon compares sources and establishes that Percy's texts were largely derived from Latin versions, and that Lye contributed more to the historical framework than the difficulties of translation.

22. *Percy Letters,* vii. 70.

23. Margaret M. Smith, 'Thomas Percy, William Shenstone, *Five Pieces of Runic Poetry,* and the *Reliques*', *Bodleian Library Record,* 12 (1988), 473; Bodl. MS Percy, c. 7, fo. 2^r.

24. *Percy Letters,* vii. 71. It is revealing that during this early and tentative work, Percy was inclined to regard poetry as a footnote to the text of history, for it implies that such fragments can be used to attack or defend interpretations of that history. His hints of a creative synthesis of fragments were realized three years later in the *Reliques,* in which his ballad 'The Friar of Orders Gray' was assembled from parts of ballads quoted by Shakespeare and, moreover, derived from Goldsmith's as yet unpublished 'Edwin and Angelina' (Thomas Percy, *Reliques of Ancient English Poetry* (3 vols.; London, 1765), i. 225-30; *The Poems of Gray, Collins, and Goldsmith,* ed. Roger Lonsdale (London, 1969), 596).

25. *Percy Letters,* vii. 74.

26. Bodl. MS Eng. lett. d. 59, fo. 8ʳ (this contract is one of the few omissions from *The Correspondence of Robert Dodsley 1733-1764,* ed. James E. Tierney (Cambridge, 1988), 563); *Lady's Magazine,* 2 (1761), 487-9.

27. *The Percy Letters,* iii. *The Correspondence of Thomas Percy and Thomas Warton,* ed. M. G. Robinson and Leah Dennis (Baton Rouge, La., 1951), 13; *The Percy Letters,* v. *The Correspondence of Thomas Percy and Evan Evans,* ed. Aneirin Lewis (Baton Rouge, La., 1957), 3.

28. *Percy Letters,* vii. 118.

29. Ibid. 26.

30. Edward Young, *Conjectures on Original Composition. In a Letter to the Author of Sir Charles Grandison* (London, 1759), 22. For Young, see Patricia Phillips, *The Adventurous Muse: Theories of Originality in English Poetics 1650-1760* (Uppsala, 1984), 95-110. Percy alluded to Young in his Advertisement to 'Fragments of Chinese Poetry' (*Hau Kiou Choaan or The Pleasing History* (4 vols.; London, 1761), iv. 199).

31. See my forthcoming article, 'Thomas Percy, Edward Lye, William Shenstone, and *Five Pieces of Runic Poetry*'; Thomas Percy, *Five Pieces of Runic Poetry translated from the Islandic Language* (London, 1763), A4ᵛ. Earlier (in 1761) Percy had placed his 'Fragments of Chinese Poetry' (*Hau Kiou Choaan,* iv. 197-254) in the context of Macpherson's *Fragments,* calling them 'striking and poetical' (iv. 200). This whole section of *Hau Kiou Choaan* was modelled on the layout of the Ossianic pamphlet and possibly was intended to be marketed separately.

32. Percy, *Runic Poetry,* 6.

33. *Percy Letters,* vii. 70.

34. Percy, *Runic Poetry,* A7ʳ.

35. Ibid. A2ᵛ.

36. Ibid. A8ʳ.

37. Ibid. A4ᵛ.

38. Macpherson, *Fingal,* a1ʳ.

39. Robert Lingel, 'The Ossianic Manuscripts: A Note by Gordon Gallie MacDonald', *Bulletin of the New York Public Library,* 34 (1930), 80.

40. Macpherson, *Fingal,* p. xiii.

41. Ibid., p. ii.

42. Derick S. Thomson, *The Gaelic Sources of Macpherson's 'Ossian'* (Aberdeen, 1952), 59. Macpherson's sources were probably medieval (1200-1600) oral ballads: see Donald E. Meek, 'The Gaelic Ballads of Scotland', in Gaskill (ed.), *Ossian Revisited,* 19-48.

43. *Percy Letters,* vii. 138, 125. Percy wrote to Evan Evans on 15 Oct. 1761 that 'hardly one reader in ten believes the specimens already produced to be genuine' (*Percy Letters,* v. 19).

44. *Percy Letters,* vii. 141-2.

45. Richard Hurd, *Letters on Chivalry and Romance* (London, 1762), 54. The neatest account of Hurd is Hoyt Trowbridge, 'Richard Hurd's *Letters on Chivalry and Romance*', in his *From Dryden to Jane Austen: Essays on English Critics and Writers* (Albuquerque, 1978), 175-184; see also Audley L. Smith, 'Richard Hurd's *Letters on Chivalry and Romance*', *English Literary History,* 6 (1939), 58-81. Percy borrowed a copy of Hurd's *Letters* from Farmer (*The Percy Letters,* ii. *The Correspondence of Thomas Percy and Richard Farmer,* ed. Cleanth Brooks (Baton Rouge, La., 1946), ii. 5). He had read it twice by 5 June 1762 and was encouraged that Hurd placed 'The Old Romances . . . in a very respectable light' (*Percy Letters,* ii. 7). Notwithstanding this, he wrote to Shenstone on the same subject twelve days later: 'Have you seen Hurd's new Letters on Chivalry? he is clever, but he is a Coxcomb' (*Percy Letters,* vii. 157).

46. Hurd, *Letters,* 61.

47. Ibid. 101.

48. Gerald Newman, *The Rise of English Nationalism: A Cultural History 1740-1830* (London, 1987), 110, 111; see also 117-18.

49. Hugh Blair, *A Critical Dissertation on the Poems of Ossian, the Son of Fingal* (London, 1763). A letter to Davies of Cadell and Davies (21 May 1782) shows that the *Dissertation* was based on a lecture Blair sold to Becket for 50 gns. (Historical Society of Pennsylvania, Gratz Collection, Case 10, Box 27). For Macpherson's hand in the published *Dissertation,* see R. W. Chapman, 'Blair on Ossian,' *Review of English Studies,* 7 (1931), 80-3: Macpherson effectively wrote the final paragraph. David Punter ('Blake: Social Relations of Poetic Form', *Literature and History,* 8 (1982), 182-205) reads the clash between Hurd and Blair as the antiquity of culture meeting its obverse, barbarism (p. 196). Steve Rizza develops this idea by examining Blair's use of the sublime ('A Bulky and Foolish Treatise? Hugh Blair's *Critical Dissertation* Reconsidered', in Gaskill (ed.), *Ossian Revisited,* 141-3).

50. Blair, *Critical Dissertation,* 3.

51. Ibid. 11.

52. Ibid. 15.

53. Frank Edgar Farley, *Scandinavian Influences in the English Romantic Movement* (Studies and Notes in Philology and Literature, 9; Cambridge, Mass., 1903), 59-69.

54. Blair, *Critical Dissertation,* 11.

55. Ibid. 53, 4 n.-6 n.

56. Macpherson, *Temora,* p. xx.

57. Ibid., p. iii.

58. *The Works of Sir James Ware concerning Ireland Revised and Improved,* rev. Walter Harris (3 vols.; Dublin, 1739), ii. 13.

59. *Temora,* p. xi.

60. Ibid., p. viii.

61. Ibid. 126 n.

62. Ibid. 184 n.; see also John Macpherson, *Critical Dissertations on the Origin, Antiquities, Language, Government, Manners, and Religion of the Ancient Caledonians, their Posterity the Picts, and the British and Irish Scots* (London, 1768), 204-6, 213-25, in which James had a hand (Stafford, *The Sublime Savage,* 152-3).

63. *Temora,* 184 n.

64. Ibid. 4 n.

65. Ibid. 50 n.

66. Ibid., p. xvii.

67. For the knotty problem of Macpherson's manuscripts, see Howard Gaskill, 'What did James Macpherson really Leave on Display at his Publisher's Shop in 1762?', *Scottish Gaelic Studies,* 16 (1990), 67-89 (summarized in Gaskill (ed.), *Ossian Revisited,* 6-16). The controversy blew up again in 1781: see Richard B. Sher, 'Percy, Shaw and the Ferguson "Cheat": National Prejudice in the Ossian Wars', in Gaskill (ed.), *Ossian Revisited,* 207-45; and Thomas M. Curley, 'Johnson's Last Word on Ossian: Ghostwriting for William Shaw', in Jennifer J. Carter and Joan H. Pittock (eds.), *Aberdeen and the Enlightenment* (Aberdeen, 1987), 375-431.

68. 'Estimate' Brown accompanied Thomas Percy and his charge Algernon Percy on their 1765 tour of Scotland (Davis, *Thomas Percy: A Scholar-Cleric,* 144-6).

69. John Brown, *A Dissertation on the Rise, Union, and Power, the Progressions, Separations, and Corruptions, of Poetry and Music* (London, 1763), 44.

70. Ibid. 51, 158-9.

71. *Percy Letters,* v. 16-17; BL Add. MS 32330, fo. 41^v-42^v.

72. *Runic Poetry,* A3^r.

73. *Percy Letters,* v. 84-5.

74. Ibid. 88.

75. Bodl. MS Percy, c. 7, fo. 42^r.

76. Percy, *Reliques,* i, p. xv.

77. Ibid. iii, p. iii.

78. Ibid. i, p. xvi.

79. Ibid. i, p. xxii.

80. Ibid. iii, p. iii.

FURTHER READING

Biographies

Anderson, W. E. K., ed. *The Correspondence of Thomas Percy & Robert Anderson.* New Haven: Yale University Press, 1988, 344 p.

A collection of Percy's correspondence with Robert Anderson, a friend during Percy's later years.

Brooks, Cleanth, ed. *The Correspondence of Thomas Percy & Richard Farmer.* Louisiana: Louisiana State University Press, 1946, 218 p.

A collection of letters between Percy and the scholar and antiquarian Richard Farmer.

Davis, Bertram H. *Thomas Percy: A Scholar-Cleric in the Age of Johnson.* Philadelphia: University of Pennsylvania Press, 1989, 361 p.

Book-length biography of Percy organized into chapters based on significant professional periods in Percy's life.

Falconer, A. F., ed. *The Correspondence of Thomas Percy & David Dalrymple, Lord Hailes.* Louisiana: Louisiana State University Press, 1954, 186 p.

The correspondence between Percy and Sir David Dalrymple, who assisted Percy in the collection of several Scottish poems which were included in the *Reliques.*

Falconer, A. F., ed. *The Correspondence of Thomas Percy & George Paton.* New Haven: Yale University Press, 1961, 198 p.

The correspondence between Percy and George Paton involving the collection of ballads and poems for a proposed fourth edition of *Reliques* and a separate publication on Scottish ballads—neither of which were published.

Lewis, Aneirin, ed. *The Correspondence of Thomas Percy & Evan Evans.* Louisiana: Louisiana State University Press, 1957, 213 p.

A collection of letters between Percy and Evan Evans that provides insight into the literary and antiquarian activities in England and Wales between 1761 and 1776.

Robinson, M. G. and Leah Dennis, eds. *The Correspondence of Thomas Percy & Thomas Warton.* Louisiana: Louisiana State University Press, 1951, 189 p.

The correspondence between Percy and poet and literary historian Thomas Warton.

Tillotson, Arthur, ed. *The Correspondence of Thomas Percy & Edmond Malone.* Louisiana: Louisiana State University Press, 1944, 302 p.

Selections from the thirty-year correspondence between Percy and Shakespearean scholar Edmond Malone.

Criticism

Beal, Peter. "Bishop Percy's Notes on *A Voyage to Abyssinia.*" In *Proceedings of the Leeds Philosophical and Literary Society* 16 (1975): 39-49.

Offers an account of Percy's annotations to Samuel Johnson's translation of Jeronymo Lobo's *Voyage to Abyssinia.*

Brooks, Cleanth. "Thomas Percy, *Don Quixote,* and Don Bowle." In *Evidence in Literary Scholarship: Essays in Memory of James Marshall Osborn,* edited by René Wellek and Alvaro Ribeiro. Oxford: Clarendon Press, 1979, pp. 247-61.

Presents an analysis of Percy's interest in Spanish language and literature, concentrating on his interest in translating a new edition of *Don Quixote.*

Davis, Bertram H. "Johnson's 1764 Visit to Percy." In *Johnson After Two Hundred Years,* edited by Paul J. Korshin. Philadelphia: University of Pennsylvania Press, 1986, pp. 25-41.

An account of Samuel Johnson's visit to Easton Maudit, Percy's vicarage; it is believed that Johnson wrote the preface to Percy's *Reliques* during this time.

Donatelli, Joseph M. P. "The Medieval Fictions of Thomas Warton and Thomas Percy." In *University of Toronto Quarterly* 60, No. 4 (Summer 1991): 435-51.

Compares Percy's *Reliques* with Warton's *History of English Poetry* as two preeminent works of scholarship that catered to an eighteenth-century preoccupation with the Middle Ages.

Groom, Nick. "*Fragments, Reliques,* & MSS: Chatterton and Percy." In *Thomas Chatterton and Romantic Culture,* edited by Groom. Houndmills: Macmillan Press, 1999, pp. 188-209.

Discusses the impact of Percy's *Reliques* on Thomas Chatterton and the controversy surrounding literary antiquarians in the eighteenth century.

Mahoney, John L. "Some Antiquarian and Literary Influences of Percy's *Reliques.*" In *College Language Association Journal* 7, No. 3 (1964): 240-46.

Offers an account of the affect of Percy's *Reliques* on the collection, preservation, and editing of English minstrelsy in the eighteenth and nineteenth centuries.

Ringler, Jr., William A. "Bishop Percy's Quarto Manuscript (British Museum MS Additional 34064) and Nicholas Breton." In *Philological Quarterly* 54, No. 1 (Winter 1975): 26-39.

A comparison of three poems Percy included in his *Reliques,* tracing their origins to an older manuscript of Elizabethan poetry.

Smith, Margaret M. "Thomas Percy, William Shenstone, *Five Pieces of Runic Poetry,* and the *Reliques.*" In *Bodleian Library Record* 12, No. 6 (April 1988): 471-77.

Brief outline of the correspondence between Percy and Shenstone that traces their collaboration on *Reliques* and *Five Pieces of Runic Poetry.*

Sutherland, Kathryn. "The Native Poet: The Influence of Percy's Minstrel from Beattie to Wordsworth." In *Review of English Studies* 33, No. 132 (November 1982): 414-33.

Examines the impact of Percy's presentation of the medieval minstrel as native poet and historian on scholars, antiquarians, and poets of his time.

Additional coverage of Percy's life and career is contained in the following source published by the Gale Group: *Dictionary of Literary Biography,* **Vol. 104.**

How to Use This Index

The main references

> **Calvino, Italo**
> 1923-1985 .... CLC 5, 8, 11, 22, 33, 39,
> 73; SSC 3

list all author entries in the following Gale Literary Criticism series:

BLC = *Black Literature Criticism*
CLC = *Contemporary Literary Criticism*
CLR = *Children's Literature Review*
CMLC = *Classical and Medieval Literature Criticism*
DA = *DISCovering Authors*
DAB = *DISCovering Authors: British*
DAC = *DISCovering Authors: Canadian*
DAM = *DISCovering Authors: Modules*
      DRAM: *Dramatists Module;* **MST:** *Most-Studied Authors Module;*
      MULT: *Multicultural Authors Module;* **NOV:** *Novelists Module;*
      POET: *Poets Module;* **POP:** *Popular Fiction and Genre Authors Module*
DC = *Drama Criticism*
HLC = *Hispanic Literature Criticism*
LC = *Literature Criticism from 1400 to 1800*
NCLC = *Nineteenth-Century Literature Criticism*
NNAL = *Native North American Literature*
PC = *Poetry Criticism*
SSC = *Short Story Criticism*
TCLC = *Twentieth-Century Literary Criticism*
WLC = *World Literature Criticism, 1500 to the Present*

The cross-references

> See also CANR 23; CA 85-88;
> obituary CA116

list all author entries in the following Gale biographical and literary sources:

AAYA = *Authors & Artists for Young Adults*
AITN = *Authors in the News*
BEST = *Bestsellers*
BW = *Black Writers*
CA = *Contemporary Authors*
CAAS = *Contemporary Authors Autobiography Series*
CABS = *Contemporary Authors Bibliographical Series*
CANR = *Contemporary Authors New Revision Series*
CAP = *Contemporary Authors Permanent Series*
CDALB = *Concise Dictionary of American Literary Biography*
CDBLB = *Concise Dictionary of British Literary Biography*
DLB = *Dictionary of Literary Biography*
DLBD = *Dictionary of Literary Biography Documentary Series*
DLBY = *Dictionary of Literary Biography Yearbook*
HW = *Hispanic Writers*
JRDA = *Junior DISCovering Authors*
MAICYA = *Major Authors and Illustrators for Children and Young Adults*
MTCW = *Major 20th-Century Writers*
SAAS = *Something about the Author Autobiography Series*
SATA = *Something about the Author*
YABC = *Yesterday's Authors of Books for Children*

Literary Criticism Series
Cumulative Author Index

Andersen, Hans Christian
1805-1875 .... **NCLC 7, 79; DA; DAB; DAC; DAM MST, POP; SSC 6; WLC**
See also CLR 6; DA3; MAICYA; SATA 100; YABC 1

Anderson, C. Farley
See Mencken, H(enry) L(ouis); Nathan, George Jean

Anderson, Jessica (Margaret) Queale
1916- .... **CLC 37**
See also CA 9-12R; CANR 4, 62

Anderson, Jon (Victor) 1940- . **CLC 9; DAM POET**
See also CA 25-28R; CANR 20

Anderson, Lindsay (Gordon)
1923-1994 .... **CLC 20**
See also CA 125; 128; 146; CANR 77

Anderson, Maxwell 1888-1959 .... **TCLC 2; DAM DRAM**
See also CA 105; 152; DLB 7, 228; MTCW 2

Anderson, Poul (William) 1926- .... **CLC 15**
See also AAYA 5, 34; CA 1-4R, 181; CAAE 181; CAAS 2; CANR 2, 15, 34, 64; CLR 58; DLB 8; INT CANR-15; MTCW 1, 2; SATA 90; SATA-Brief 39; SATA-Essay 106

Anderson, Robert (Woodruff)
1917- .... **CLC 23; DAM DRAM**
See also AITN 1; CA 21-24R; CANR 32; DLB 7

Anderson, Sherwood 1876-1941 ..... **TCLC 1, 10, 24; DA; DAB; DAC; DAM MST, NOV; SSC 1; WLC**
See also AAYA 30; CA 104; 121; CANR 61; CDALB 1917-1929; DA3; DLB 4, 9, 86; DLBD 1; MTCW 1, 2

Andier, Pierre
See Desnos, Robert

Andouard
See Giraudoux, (Hippolyte) Jean

Andrade, Carlos Drummond de CLC 18
See also Drummond de Andrade, Carlos

Andrade, Mario de 1893-1945 .... **TCLC 43**

Andreae, Johann V(alentin)
1586-1654 .... **LC 32**
See also DLB 164

Andreas-Salome, Lou 1861-1937 ... **TCLC 56**
See also CA 178; DLB 66

Andress, Lesley
See Sanders, Lawrence

Andrewes, Lancelot 1555-1626 .... **LC 5**
See also DLB 151, 172

Andrews, Cicily Fairfield
See West, Rebecca

Andrews, Elton V.
See Pohl, Frederik

Andreyev, Leonid (Nikolaevich)
1871-1919 .... **TCLC 3**
See also CA 104; 185

Andric, Ivo 1892-1975 .... **CLC 8; SSC 36**
See also CA 81-84; 57-60; CANR 43, 60; DLB 147; MTCW 1

Androvar
See Prado (Calvo), Pedro

Angelique, Pierre
See Bataille, Georges

Angell, Roger 1920- .... **CLC 26**
See also CA 57-60; CANR 13, 44, 70; DLB 171, 185

Angelou, Maya 1928- .... **CLC 12, 35, 64, 77; BLC 1; DA; DAB; DAC; DAM MST, MULT, POET, POP; PC 32; WLCS**
See also AAYA 7, 20; BW 2, 3; CA 65-68; CANR 19, 42, 65; CDALBS; CLR 53; DA3; DLB 38; MTCW 1, 2; SATA 49

Anna Comnena 1083-1153 .... **CMLC 25**

Annensky, Innokenty (Fyodorovich)
1856-1909 .... **TCLC 14**
See also CA 110; 155

Annunzio, Gabriele d'
See D'Annunzio, Gabriele

Anodos
See Coleridge, Mary E(lizabeth)

Anon, Charles Robert
See Pessoa, Fernando (Antonio Nogueira)

Anouilh, Jean (Marie Lucien Pierre)
1910-1987 .... **CLC 1, 3, 8, 13, 40, 50; DAM DRAM; DC 8**
See also CA 17-20R; 123; CANR 32; MTCW 1, 2

Anthony, Florence
See Ai

Anthony, John
See Ciardi, John (Anthony)

Anthony, Peter
See Shaffer, Anthony (Joshua); Shaffer, Peter (Levin)

Anthony, Piers 1934- .... **CLC 35; DAM POP**
See also AAYA 11; CA 21-24R; CANR 28, 56, 73; DLB 8; MTCW 1, 2; SAAS 22; SATA 84

Anthony, Susan B(rownell)
1916-1991 .... **TCLC 84**
See also CA 89-92; 134

Antoine, Marc
See Proust, (Valentin-Louis-George-Eugene-) Marcel

Antoninus, Brother
See Everson, William (Oliver)

Antonioni, Michelangelo 1912- .... **CLC 20**
See also CA 73-76; CANR 45, 77

Antschel, Paul 1920-1970
See Celan, Paul
See also CA 85-88; CANR 33, 61; MTCW 1

Anwar, Chairil 1922-1949 .... **TCLC 22**
See also CA 121

Anzaldua, Gloria (Evanjelina) 1942-
See also CA 175; DLB 122; HLCS 1

Apess, William 1798-1839(?) .... **NCLC 73; DAM MULT**
See also DLB 175; NNAL

Apollinaire, Guillaume 1880-1918 .. **TCLC 3, 8, 51; DAM POET; PC 7**
See also CA 152; MTCW 1

Appelfeld, Aharon 1932- ... **CLC 23, 47; SSC 42**
See also CA 112; 133; CANR 86

Apple, Max (Isaac) 1941- .... **CLC 9, 33**
See also CA 81-84; CANR 19, 54; DLB 130

Appleman, Philip (Dean) 1926- .... **CLC 51**
See also CA 13-16R; CAAS 18; CANR 6, 29, 56

Appleton, Lawrence
See Lovecraft, H(oward) P(hillips)

Apteryx
See Eliot, T(homas) S(tearns)

Apuleius, (Lucius Madaurensis)
125(?)-175(?) .... **CMLC 1**
See also DLB 211

Aquin, Hubert 1929-1977 .... **CLC 15**
See also CA 105; DLB 53

Aquinas, Thomas 1224(?)-1274 ..... **CMLC 33**
See also DLB 115

Aragon, Louis 1897-1982 .. **CLC 3, 22; DAM NOV, POET**
See also CA 69-72; 108; CANR 28, 71; DLB 72; MTCW 1, 2

Arany, Janos 1817-1882 .... **NCLC 34**

Aranyos, Kakay
See Mikszath, Kalman

Arbuthnot, John 1667-1735 .... **LC 1**
See also DLB 101

Archer, Herbert Winslow
See Mencken, H(enry) L(ouis)

Archer, Jeffrey (Howard) 1940- ...... **CLC 28; DAM POP**
See also AAYA 16; BEST 89:3; CA 77-80; CANR 22, 52; DA3; INT CANR-22

Archer, Jules 1915- .... **CLC 12**
See also CA 9-12R; CANR 6, 69; SAAS 5; SATA 4, 85

Archer, Lee
See Ellison, Harlan (Jay)

Archilochus c. 7th cent. B.C.- .... **CMLC 44**
See also DLB 176

Arden, John 1930- .... **CLC 6, 13, 15; DAM DRAM**
See also CA 13-16R; CAAS 4; CANR 31, 65, 67; DLB 13; MTCW 1

Arenas, Reinaldo 1943-1990 . **CLC 41; DAM MULT; HLC 1**
See also CA 124; 128; 133; CANR 73; DLB 145; HW 1; MTCW 1

Arendt, Hannah 1906-1975 .... **CLC 66, 98**
See also CA 17-20R; 61-64; CANR 26, 60; MTCW 1, 2

Aretino, Pietro 1492-1556 .... **LC 12**

Arghezi, Tudor 1880-1967 .... **CLC 80**
See also Theodorescu, Ion N.
See also CA 167; DLB 220

Arguedas, Jose Maria 1911-1969 .... **CLC 10, 18; HLCS 1**
See also CA 89-92; CANR 73; DLB 113; HW 1

Argueta, Manlio 1936- .... **CLC 31**
See also CA 131; CANR 73; DLB 145; HW 1

Arias, Ron(ald Francis) 1941-
See also CA 131; CANR 81; DAM MULT; DLB 82; HLC 1; HW 1, 2; MTCW 2

Ariosto, Ludovico 1474-1533 .... **LC 6**

Aristides
See Epstein, Joseph

Aristophanes 450B.C.-385B.C. .... **CMLC 4; DA; DAB; DAC; DAM DRAM, MST; DC 2; WLCS**
See also DA3; DLB 176

Aristotle 384B.C.-322B.C. .... **CMLC 31; DA; DAB; DAC; DAM MST; WLCS**
See also DA3; DLB 176

Arlt, Roberto (Godofredo Christophersen)
1900-1942 .... **TCLC 29; DAM MULT; HLC 1**
See also CA 123; 131; CANR 67; HW 1, 2

Armah, Ayi Kwei 1939- .... **CLC 5, 33, 136; BLC 1; DAM MULT, POET**
See also BW 1; CA 61-64; CANR 21, 64; DLB 117; MTCW 1

Armatrading, Joan 1950- .... **CLC 17**
See also CA 114; 186

Arnette, Robert
See Silverberg, Robert

Arnim, Achim von (Ludwig Joachim von Arnim) 1781-1831 ..... **NCLC 5; SSC 29**
See also DLB 90

Arnim, Bettina von 1785-1859 .... **NCLC 38**
See also DLB 90

Arnold, Matthew 1822-1888 ..... **NCLC 6, 29, 89; DA; DAB; DAC; DAM MST, POET; PC 5; WLC**
See also CDBLB 1832-1890; DLB 32, 57

Arnold, Thomas 1795-1842 .... **NCLC 18**
See also DLB 55

Arnow, Harriette (Louisa) Simpson
1908-1986 .... **CLC 2, 7, 18**
See also CA 9-12R; 118; CANR 14; DLB 6; MTCW 1, 2; SATA 42; SATA-Obit 47

Arouet, Francois-Marie
See Voltaire

Arp, Hans
See Arp, Jean

Arp, Jean 1887-1966 .... **CLC 5**
  See also CA 81-84; 25-28R; CANR 42, 77
Arrabal
  See Arrabal, Fernando
Arrabal, Fernando 1932- ... **CLC 2, 9, 18, 58**
  See also CA 9-12R; CANR 15
Arreola, Juan Jose 1918- .... **SSC 38; DAM MULT; HLC 1**
  See also CA 113; 131; CANR 81; DLB 113; HW 1, 2
Arrian c. 89(?)-c. 155(?) .... **CMLC 43**
  See also DLB 176
Arrick, Fran CLC 30
  See also Gaberman, Judie Angell
Artaud, Antonin (Marie Joseph)
  1896-1948 . **TCLC 3, 36; DAM DRAM; DC 14**
  See also CA 104; 149; DA3; MTCW 1
Arthur, Ruth M(abel) 1905-1979 ..... **CLC 12**
  See also CA 9-12R; 85-88; CANR 4; SATA 7, 26
Artsybashev, Mikhail (Petrovich)
  1878-1927 .... **TCLC 31**
  See also CA 170
Arundel, Honor (Morfydd)
  1919-1973 .... **CLC 17**
  See also CA 21-22; 41-44R; CAP 2; CLR 35; SATA 4; SATA-Obit 24
Arzner, Dorothy 1897-1979 .... **CLC 98**
Asch, Sholem 1880-1957 .... **TCLC 3**
  See also CA 105
Ash, Shalom
  See Asch, Sholem
Ashbery, John (Lawrence) 1927- .. **CLC 2, 3, 4, 6, 9, 13, 15, 25, 41, 77, 125; DAM POET; PC 26**
  See also CA 5-8R; CANR 9, 37, 66; DA3; DLB 5, 165; DLBY 81; INT CANR-9; MTCW 1, 2
Ashdown, Clifford
  See Freeman, R(ichard) Austin
Ashe, Gordon
  See Creasey, John
Ashton-Warner, Sylvia (Constance)
  1908-1984 .... **CLC 19**
  See also CA 69-72; 112; CANR 29; MTCW 1, 2
Asimov, Isaac 1920-1992 ..... **CLC 1, 3, 9, 19, 26, 76, 92; DAM POP**
  See also AAYA 13; BEST 90:2; CA 1-4R; 137; CANR 2, 19, 36, 60; CLR 12; DA3; DLB 8; DLBY 92; INT CANR-19; JRDA; MAICYA; MTCW 1, 2; SATA 1, 26, 74
Assis, Joaquim Maria Machado de
  See Machado de Assis, Joaquim Maria
Astley, Thea (Beatrice May) 1925- .. **CLC 41**
  See also CA 65-68; CANR 11, 43, 78
Aston, James
  See White, T(erence) H(anbury)
Asturias, Miguel Angel 1899-1974 .... **CLC 3, 8, 13; DAM MULT, NOV; HLC 1**
  See also CA 25-28; 49-52; CANR 32; CAP 2; DA3; DLB 113; HW 1; MTCW 1, 2
Atares, Carlos Saura
  See Saura (Atares), Carlos
Atheling, William
  See Pound, Ezra (Weston Loomis)
Atheling, William, Jr.
  See Blish, James (Benjamin)
Atherton, Gertrude (Franklin Horn)
  1857-1948 .... **TCLC 2**
  See also CA 104; 155; DLB 9, 78, 186
Atherton, Lucius
  See Masters, Edgar Lee
Atkins, Jack
  See Harris, Mark
Atkinson, Kate CLC 99
  See also CA 166

Attaway, William (Alexander)
  1911-1986 .... **CLC 92; BLC 1; DAM MULT**
  See also BW 2, 3; CA 143; CANR 82; DLB 76
Atticus
  See Fleming, Ian (Lancaster); Wilson, (Thomas) Woodrow
Atwood, Margaret (Eleanor) 1939- ... **CLC 2, 3, 4, 8, 13, 15, 25, 44, 84, 135; DA; DAB; DAC; DAM MST, NOV, POET; PC 8; SSC 2; WLC**
  See also AAYA 12; BEST 89:2; CA 49-52; CANR 3, 24, 33, 59; DA3; DLB 53; INT CANR-24; MTCW 1, 2; SATA 50
Aubigny, Pierre d'
  See Mencken, H(enry) L(ouis)
Aubin, Penelope 1685-1731(?) .... **LC 9**
  See also DLB 39
Auchincloss, Louis (Stanton) 1917- .. **CLC 4, 6, 9, 18, 45; DAM NOV; SSC 22**
  See also CA 1-4R; CANR 6, 29, 55, 87; DLB 2; DLBY 80; INT CANR-29; MTCW 1
Auden, W(ystan) H(ugh) 1907-1973 . **CLC 1, 2, 3, 4, 6, 9, 11, 14, 43, 123; DA; DAB; DAC; DAM DRAM, MST, POET; PC 1; WLC**
  See also AAYA 18; CA 9-12R; 45-48; CANR 5, 61; CDBLB 1914-1945; DA3; DLB 10, 20; MTCW 1, 2
Audiberti, Jacques 1900-1965 .... **CLC 38; DAM DRAM**
  See also CA 25-28R
Audubon, John James 1785-1851 . **NCLC 47**
Auel, Jean M(arie) 1936- .... **CLC 31, 107; DAM POP**
  See also AAYA 7; BEST 90:4; CA 103; CANR 21, 64; DA3; INT CANR-21; SATA 91
Auerbach, Erich 1892-1957 .... **TCLC 43**
  See also CA 118; 155
Augier, Emile 1820-1889 .... **NCLC 31**
  See also DLB 192
August, John
  See De Voto, Bernard (Augustine)
Augustine 354-430 .... **CMLC 6; DA; DAB; DAC; DAM MST; WLCS**
  See also DA3; DLB 115
Aurelius
  See Bourne, Randolph S(illiman)
Aurobindo, Sri
  See Ghose, Aurabinda
Austen, Jane 1775-1817 ...... **NCLC 1, 13, 19, 33, 51, 81, 95; DA; DAB; DAC; DAM MST, NOV; WLC**
  See also AAYA 19; CDBLB 1789-1832; DA3; DLB 116
Auster, Paul 1947- .... **CLC 47, 131**
  See also CA 69-72; CANR 23, 52, 75; DA3; DLB 227; MTCW 1
Austin, Frank
  See Faust, Frederick (Schiller)
Austin, Mary (Hunter) 1868-1934 . **TCLC 25**
  See also CA 109; 178; DLB 9, 78, 206, 221
Averroes 1126-1198 .... **CMLC 7**
  See also DLB 115
Avicenna 980-1037 .... **CMLC 16**
  See also DLB 115
Avison, Margaret 1918- .... **CLC 2, 4, 97; DAC; DAM POET**
  See also CA 17-20R; DLB 53; MTCW 1
Axton, David
  See Koontz, Dean R(ay)
Ayckbourn, Alan 1939- ...... **CLC 5, 8, 18, 33, 74; DAB; DAM DRAM; DC 13**
  See also CA 21-24R; CANR 31, 59; DLB 13; MTCW 1, 2

Aydy, Catherine
  See Tennant, Emma (Christina)
Ayme, Marcel (Andre) 1902-1967 ... **CLC 11; SSC 41**
  See also CA 89-92; CANR 67; CLR 25; DLB 72; SATA 91
Ayrton, Michael 1921-1975 .... **CLC 7**
  See also CA 5-8R; 61-64; CANR 9, 21
Azorin CLC 11
  See also Martinez Ruiz, Jose
Azuela, Mariano 1873-1952 . **TCLC 3; DAM MULT; HLC 1**
  See also CA 104; 131; CANR 81; HW 1, 2; MTCW 1, 2
Baastad, Babbis Friis
  See Friis-Baastad, Babbis Ellinor
Bab
  See Gilbert, W(illiam) S(chwenck)
Babbis, Eleanor
  See Friis-Baastad, Babbis Ellinor
Babel, Isaac
  See Babel, Isaak (Emmanuilovich)
Babel, Isaak (Emmanuilovich)
  1894-1941(?) .... **TCLC 2, 13; SSC 16**
  See also Babel, Isaac
  See also CA 104; 155; MTCW 1
Babits, Mihaly 1883-1941 .... **TCLC 14**
  See also CA 114
Babur 1483-1530 .... **LC 18**
Baca, Jimmy Santiago 1952-
  See also CA 131; CANR 81, 90; DAM MULT; DLB 122; HLC 1; HW 1, 2
Bacchelli, Riccardo 1891-1985 .... **CLC 19**
  See also CA 29-32R; 117
Bach, Richard (David) 1936- .... **CLC 14; DAM NOV, POP**
  See also AITN 1; BEST 89:2; CA 9-12R; CANR 18, 93; MTCW 1; SATA 13
Bachman, Richard
  See King, Stephen (Edwin)
Bachmann, Ingeborg 1926-1973 .... **CLC 69**
  See also CA 93-96; 45-48; CANR 69; DLB 85
Bacon, Francis 1561-1626 .... **LC 18, 32**
  See also CDBLB Before 1660; DLB 151, 236
Bacon, Roger 1214(?)-1292 .... **CMLC 14**
  See also DLB 115
Bacovia, George TCLC 24
  See also Bacovia, G.; Vasiliu, Gheorghe
  See also DLB 220
Badanes, Jerome 1937- .... **CLC 59**
Bagehot, Walter 1826-1877 .... **NCLC 10**
  See also DLB 55
Bagnold, Enid 1889-1981 ...... **CLC 25; DAM DRAM**
  See also CA 5-8R; 103; CANR 5, 40; DLB 13, 160, 191; MAICYA; SATA 1, 25
Bagritsky, Eduard 1895-1934 .... **TCLC 60**
Bagrjana, Elisaveta
  See Belcheva, Elisaveta
Bagryana, Elisaveta 1893-1991 .... **CLC 10**
  See also Belcheva, Elisaveta
  See also CA 178; DLB 147
Bailey, Paul 1937- .... **CLC 45**
  See also CA 21-24R; CANR 16, 62; DLB 14
Baillie, Joanna 1762-1851 .... **NCLC 71**
  See also DLB 93
Bainbridge, Beryl (Margaret) 1934- . **CLC 4, 5, 8, 10, 14, 18, 22, 62, 130; DAM NOV**
  See also CA 21-24R; CANR 24, 55, 75, 88; DLB 14, 231; MTCW 1, 2
Baker, Elliott 1922- .... **CLC 8**
  See also CA 45-48; CANR 2, 63
Baker, Jean H. TCLC 3, 10
  See also Russell, George William

Baker, Nicholson 1957- .... **CLC 61; DAM POP**
See also CA 135; CANR 63; DA3; DLB 227

Baker, Ray Stannard 1870-1946 .... **TCLC 47**
See also CA 118

Baker, Russell (Wayne) 1925- .... **CLC 31**
See also BEST 89:4; CA 57-60; CANR 11, 41, 59; MTCW 1, 2

Bakhtin, M.
See Bakhtin, Mikhail Mikhailovich

Bakhtin, M. M.
See Bakhtin, Mikhail Mikhailovich

Bakhtin, Mikhail
See Bakhtin, Mikhail Mikhailovich

Bakhtin, Mikhail Mikhailovich
1895-1975 .... **CLC 83**
See also CA 128; 113

Bakshi, Ralph 1938(?)- .... **CLC 26**
See also CA 112; 138

Bakunin, Mikhail (Alexandrovich)
1814-1876 .... **NCLC 25, 58**

Baldwin, James (Arthur) 1924-1987 . **CLC 1, 2, 3, 4, 5, 8, 13, 15, 17, 42, 50, 67, 90, 127; BLC 1; DA; DAB; DAC; DAM MST, MULT, NOV, POP; DC 1; SSC 10, 33; WLC**
See also AAYA 4, 34; BW 1; CA 1-4R; 124; CABS 1; CANR 3, 24; CDALB 1941-1968; DA3; DLB 2, 7, 33; DLBY 87; MTCW 1, 2; SATA 9; SATA-Obit 54

Bale, John 1495-1563 .... **LC 62**
See also DLB 132

Ball, Hugo 1886-1927 .... **TCLC 104**

Ballard, J(ames) G(raham) 1930- . **CLC 3, 6, 14, 36, 137; DAM NOV, POP; SSC 1**
See also AAYA 3; CA 5-8R; CANR 15, 39, 65; DA3; DLB 14, 207; MTCW 1, 2; SATA 93

Balmont, Konstantin (Dmitriyevich)
1867-1943 .... **TCLC 11**
See also CA 109; 155

Baltausis, Vincas
See Mikszath, Kalman

Balzac, Honore de 1799-1850 ... **NCLC 5, 35, 53; DA; DAB; DAC; DAM MST, NOV; SSC 5; WLC**
See also DA3; DLB 119

Bambara, Toni Cade 1939-1995 ...... **CLC 19, 88; BLC 1; DA; DAC; DAM MST, MULT; SSC 35; WLCS**
See also AAYA 5; BW 2, 3; CA 29-32R; 150; CANR 24, 49, 81; CDALBS; DA3; DLB 38; MTCW 1, 2; SATA 112

Bamdad, A.
See Shamlu, Ahmad

Banat, D. R.
See Bradbury, Ray (Douglas)

Bancroft, Laura
See Baum, L(yman) Frank

Banim, John 1798-1842 .... **NCLC 13**
See also DLB 116, 158, 159

Banim, Michael 1796-1874 .... **NCLC 13**
See also DLB 158, 159

Banjo, The
See Paterson, A(ndrew) B(arton)

Banks, Iain
See Banks, Iain M(enzies)

Banks, Iain M(enzies) 1954- .... **CLC 34**
See also CA 123; 128; CANR 61; DLB 194; INT 128

Banks, Lynne Reid CLC 23
See also Reid Banks, Lynne
See also AAYA 6

Banks, Russell 1940- .... **CLC 37, 72; SSC 42**
See also CA 65-68; CAAS 15; CANR 19, 52, 73; DLB 130

Banville, John 1945- .... **CLC 46, 118**
See also CA 117; 128; DLB 14; INT 128

Banville, Theodore (Faullain) de
1832-1891 .... **NCLC 9**

Baraka, Amiri 1934- . **CLC 1, 2, 3, 5, 10, 14, 33, 115; BLC 1; DA; DAC; DAM MST, MULT, POET, POP; DC 6; PC 4; WLCS**
See also Jones, LeRoi
See also BW 2, 3; CA 21-24R; CABS 3; CANR 27, 38, 61; CDALB 1941-1968; DA3; DLB 5, 7, 16, 38; DLBD 8; MTCW 1, 2

Barbauld, Anna Laetitia
1743-1825 .... **NCLC 50**
See also DLB 107, 109, 142, 158

Barbellion, W. N. P. TCLC 24
See also Cummings, Bruce F(rederick)

Barbera, Jack (Vincent) 1945- .... **CLC 44**
See also CA 110; CANR 45

Barbey d'Aurevilly, Jules Amedee
1808-1889 .... **NCLC 1; SSC 17**
See also DLB 119

Barbour, John c. 1316-1395 .... **CMLC 33**
See also DLB 146

Barbusse, Henri 1873-1935 .... **TCLC 5**
See also CA 105; 154; DLB 65

Barclay, Bill
See Moorcock, Michael (John)

Barclay, William Ewert
See Moorcock, Michael (John)

Barea, Arturo 1897-1957 .... **TCLC 14**
See also CA 111

Barfoot, Joan 1946- .... **CLC 18**
See also CA 105

Barham, Richard Harris
1788-1845 .... **NCLC 77**
See also DLB 159

Baring, Maurice 1874-1945 .... **TCLC 8**
See also CA 105; 168; DLB 34

Baring-Gould, Sabine 1834-1924 ... **TCLC 88**
See also DLB 156, 190

Barker, Clive 1952- ...... **CLC 52; DAM POP**
See also AAYA 10; BEST 90:3; CA 121; 129; CANR 71; DA3; INT 129; MTCW 1, 2

Barker, George Granville
1913-1991 .... **CLC 8, 48; DAM POET**
See also CA 9-12R; 135; CANR 7, 38; DLB 20; MTCW 1

Barker, Harley Granville
See Granville-Barker, Harley
See also DLB 10

Barker, Howard 1946- .... **CLC 37**
See also CA 102; DLB 13, 233

Barker, Jane 1652-1732 .... **LC 42**

Barker, Pat(ricia) 1943- .... **CLC 32, 94**
See also CA 117; 122; CANR 50; INT 122

Barlach, Ernst (Heinrich)
1870-1938 .... **TCLC 84**
See also CA 178; DLB 56, 118

Barlow, Joel 1754-1812 .... **NCLC 23**
See also DLB 37

Barnard, Mary (Ethel) 1909- .... **CLC 48**
See also CA 21-22; CAP 2

Barnes, Djuna 1892-1982 .... **CLC 3, 4, 8, 11, 29, 127; SSC 3**
See also CA 9-12R; 107; CANR 16, 55; DLB 4, 9, 45; MTCW 1, 2

Barnes, Julian (Patrick) 1946- .... **CLC 42; DAB**
See also CA 102; CANR 19, 54; DLB 194; DLBY 93; MTCW 1

Barnes, Peter 1931- .... **CLC 5, 56**
See also CA 65-68; CAAS 12; CANR 33, 34, 64; DLB 13, 233; MTCW 1

Barnes, William 1801-1886 .... **NCLC 75**
See also DLB 32

Baroja (y Nessi), Pio 1872-1956 ..... **TCLC 8; HLC 1**
See also CA 104

Baron, David
See Pinter, Harold

Baron Corvo
See Rolfe, Frederick (William Serafino Austin Lewis Mary)

Barondess, Sue K(aufman)
1926-1977 .... **CLC 8**
See also Kaufman, Sue
See also CA 1-4R; 69-72; CANR 1

Baron de Teive
See Pessoa, Fernando (Antonio Nogueira)

Baroness Von S.
See Zangwill, Israel

Barres, (Auguste-) Maurice
1862-1923 .... **TCLC 47**
See also CA 164; DLB 123

Barreto, Afonso Henrique de Lima
See Lima Barreto, Afonso Henrique de

Barrett, (Roger) Syd 1946- .... **CLC 35**

Barrett, William (Christopher)
1913-1992 .... **CLC 27**
See also CA 13-16R; 139; CANR 11, 67; INT CANR-11

Barrie, J(ames) M(atthew)
1860-1937 .... **TCLC 2; DAB; DAM DRAM**
See also CA 104; 136; CANR 77; CDBLB 1890-1914; CLR 16; DA3; DLB 10, 141, 156; MAICYA; MTCW 1; SATA 100; YABC 1

Barrington, Michael
See Moorcock, Michael (John)

Barrol, Grady
See Bograd, Larry

Barry, Mike
See Malzberg, Barry N(athaniel)

Barry, Philip 1896-1949 .... **TCLC 11**
See also CA 109; DLB 7, 228

Bart, Andre Schwarz
See Schwarz-Bart, Andre

Barth, John (Simmons) 1930- ... **CLC 1, 2, 3, 5, 7, 9, 10, 14, 27, 51, 89; DAM NOV; SSC 10**
See also AITN 1, 2; CA 1-4R; CABS 1; CANR 5, 23, 49, 64; DLB 2, 227; MTCW 1

Barthelme, Donald 1931-1989 ... **CLC 1, 2, 3, 5, 6, 8, 13, 23, 46, 59, 115; DAM NOV; SSC 2**
See also CA 21-24R; 129; CANR 20, 58; DA3; DLB 2, 234; DLBY 80, 89; MTCW 1, 2; SATA 7; SATA-Obit 62

Barthelme, Frederick 1943- ...... **CLC 36, 117**
See also CA 114; 122; CANR 77; DLBY 85; INT 122

Barthes, Roland (Gerard)
1915-1980 .... **CLC 24, 83**
See also CA 130; 97-100; CANR 66; MTCW 1, 2

Barzun, Jacques (Martin) 1907- ...... **CLC 51**
See also CA 61-64; CANR 22

Bashevis, Isaac
See Singer, Isaac Bashevis

Bashkirtseff, Marie 1859-1884 .... **NCLC 27**

Basho
See Matsuo Basho

Basil of Caesaria c. 330-379 .... **CMLC 35**

Bass, Kingsley B., Jr.
See Bullins, Ed

Bass, Rick 1958- .... **CLC 79**
See also CA 126; CANR 53, 93; DLB 212

Bassani, Giorgio 1916- .... **CLC 9**
See also CA 65-68; CANR 33, 177; MTCW 1

Bastos, Augusto (Antonio) Roa
See Roa Bastos, Augusto (Antonio)

Bataille, Georges 1897-1962 .... **CLC 29**
See also CA 101; 89-92

Bates, H(erbert) E(rnest)
1905-1974 . CLC 46; DAB; DAM POP;
SSC 10
See also CA 93-96; 45-48; CANR 34; DA3;
DLB 162, 191; MTCW 1, 2

Bauchart
See Camus, Albert

Baudelaire, Charles 1821-1867 . NCLC 6, 29,
55; DA; DAB; DAC; DAM MST,
POET; PC 1; SSC 18; WLC
See also DA3

Baudrillard, Jean 1929- .... CLC 60

Baum, L(yman) Frank 1856-1919 ... TCLC 7
See also CA 108; 133; CLR 15; DLB 22;
JRDA; MAICYA; MTCW 1, 2; SATA 18,
100

Baum, Louis F.
See Baum, L(yman) Frank

Baumbach, Jonathan 1933- .... CLC 6, 23
See also CA 13-16R; CAAS 5; CANR 12,
66; DLBY 80; INT CANR-12; MTCW 1

Bausch, Richard (Carl) 1945- .... CLC 51
See also CA 101; CAAS 14; CANR 43, 61,
87; DLB 130

Baxter, Charles (Morley) 1947- .... CLC 45,
78; DAM POP
See also CA 57-60; CANR 40, 64; DLB
130; MTCW 2

Baxter, George Owen
See Faust, Frederick (Schiller)

Baxter, James K(eir) 1926-1972 .... CLC 14
See also CA 77-80

Baxter, John
See Hunt, E(verette) Howard, (Jr.)

Bayer, Sylvia
See Glassco, John

Baynton, Barbara 1857-1929 .... TCLC 57
See also DLB 230

Beagle, Peter S(oyer) 1939- .... CLC 7, 104
See also CA 9-12R; CANR 4, 51, 73; DA3;
DLBY 80; INT CANR-4; MTCW 1;
SATA 60

Bean, Normal
See Burroughs, Edgar Rice

Beard, Charles A(ustin)
1874-1948 .... TCLC 15
See also CA 115; DLB 17; SATA 18

Beardsley, Aubrey 1872-1898 .... NCLC 6

Beattie, Ann 1947- ..... CLC 8, 13, 18, 40, 63;
DAM NOV, POP; SSC 11
See also BEST 90:2; CA 81-84; CANR 53,
73; DA3; DLBY 82; MTCW 1, 2

Beattie, James 1735-1803 .... NCLC 25
See also DLB 109

Beauchamp, Kathleen Mansfield 1888-1923
See Mansfield, Katherine
See also CA 104; 134; DA; DAC; DAM
MST; DA3; MTCW 2

Beaumarchais, Pierre-Augustin Caron de
1732-1799 . LC 61; DAM DRAM; DC 4

Beaumont, Francis 1584(?)-1616 .... LC 33;
DC 6
See also CDBLB Before 1660; DLB 58, 121

**Beauvoir, Simone (Lucie Ernestine Marie
Bertrand) de** 1908-1986 .... CLC 1, 2, 4,
8, 14, 31, 44, 50, 71, 124; DA; DAB;
DAC; DAM MST, NOV; WLC
See also CA 9-12R; 118; CANR 28, 61;
DA3; DLB 72; DLBY 86; MTCW 1, 2

Becker, Carl (Lotus) 1873-1945 ..... TCLC 63
See also CA 157; DLB 17

Becker, Jurek 1937-1997 .... CLC 7, 19
See also CA 85-88; 157; CANR 60; DLB
75

Becker, Walter 1950- .... CLC 26

Beckett, Samuel (Barclay)
1906-1989 .. CLC 1, 2, 3, 4, 6, 9, 10, 11,
14, 18, 29, 57, 59, 83; DA; DAB; DAC;
DAM DRAM, MST, NOV; SSC 16;
WLC
See also CA 5-8R; 130; CANR 33, 61; CD-
BLB 1945-1960; DA3; DLB 13, 15, 233;
DLBY 90; MTCW 1, 2

Beckford, William 1760-1844 .... NCLC 16
See also DLB 39

Beckman, Gunnel 1910- .... CLC 26
See also CA 33-36R; CANR 15; CLR 25;
MAICYA; SAAS 9; SATA 6

Becque, Henri 1837-1899 .... NCLC 3
See also DLB 192

Becquer, Gustavo Adolfo 1836-1870
See also DAM MULT; HLCS 1

Beddoes, Thomas Lovell
1803-1849 .... NCLC 3
See also DLB 96

Bede c. 673-735 .... CMLC 20
See also DLB 146

Bedford, Donald F.
See Fearing, Kenneth (Flexner)

Beecher, Catharine Esther
1800-1878 .... NCLC 30
See also DLB 1

Beecher, John 1904-1980 .... CLC 6
See also AITN 1; CA 5-8R; 105; CANR 8

Beer, Johann 1655-1700 .... LC 5
See also DLB 168

Beer, Patricia 1924- .... CLC 58
See also CA 61-64; 183; CANR 13, 46;
DLB 40

Beerbohm, Max -1956
See Beerbohm, (Henry) Max(imilian)

Beerbohm, (Henry) Max(imilian)
1872-1956 .... TCLC 1, 24
See also CA 104; 154; CANR 79; DLB 34,
100

Beer-Hofmann, Richard
1866-1945 .... TCLC 60
See also CA 160; DLB 81

Begiebing, Robert J(ohn) 1946- .... CLC 70
See also CA 122; CANR 40, 88

Behan, Brendan 1923-1964 ...... CLC 1, 8, 11,
15, 79; DAM DRAM
See also CA 73-76; CANR 33; CDBLB
1945-1960; DLB 13, 233; MTCW 1, 2

Behn, Aphra 1640(?)-1689 .... LC 1, 30, 42;
DA; DAB; DAC; DAM DRAM, MST,
NOV, POET; DC 4; PC 13; WLC
See also DA3; DLB 39, 80, 131

Behrman, S(amuel) N(athaniel)
1893-1973 .... CLC 40
See also CA 13-16; 45-48; CAP 1; DLB 7,
44

Belasco, David 1853-1931 .... TCLC 3
See also CA 104; 168; DLB 7

Belcheva, Elisaveta 1893- .... CLC 10
See also Bagryana, Elisaveta

Beldone, Phil "Cheech"
See Ellison, Harlan (Jay)

Beleno
See Azuela, Mariano

Belinski, Vissarion Grigoryevich
1811-1848 .... NCLC 5
See also DLB 198

Belitt, Ben 1911- .... CLC 22
See also CA 13-16R; CAAS 4; CANR 7,
77; DLB 5

Bell, Gertrude (Margaret Lowthian)
1868-1926 .... TCLC 67
See also CA 167; DLB 174

Bell, J. Freeman
See Zangwill, Israel

Bell, James Madison 1826-1902 ... TCLC 43;
BLC 1; DAM MULT
See also BW 1; CA 122; 124; DLB 50

Bell, Madison Smartt 1957- ...... CLC 41, 102
See also CA 111, 183; CAAE 183; CANR
28, 54, 73; MTCW 1

Bell, Marvin (Hartley) 1937- ...... CLC 8, 31;
DAM POET
See also CA 21-24R; CAAS 14; CANR 59;
DLB 5; MTCW 1

Bell, W. L. D.
See Mencken, H(enry) L(ouis)

Bellamy, Atwood C.
See Mencken, H(enry) L(ouis)

Bellamy, Edward 1850-1898 ...... NCLC 4, 86
See also DLB 12

Belli, Gioconda 1949-
See also CA 152; HLCS 1

Bellin, Edward J.
See Kuttner, Henry

**Belloc, (Joseph) Hilaire (Pierre Sebastien
Rene Swanton)** 1870-1953 ...... TCLC 7,
18; DAM POET; PC 24
See also CA 106; 152; DLB 19, 100, 141,
174; MTCW 1; SATA 112; YABC 1

Belloc, Joseph Peter Rene Hilaire
See Belloc, (Joseph) Hilaire (Pierre Sebastien Rene Swanton)

Belloc, Joseph Pierre Hilaire
See Belloc, (Joseph) Hilaire (Pierre Sebastien Rene Swanton)

Belloc, M. A.
See Lowndes, Marie Adelaide (Belloc)

Bellow, Saul 1915- . CLC 1, 2, 3, 6, 8, 10, 13,
15, 25, 33, 34, 63, 79; DA; DAB; DAC;
DAM MST, NOV, POP; SSC 14; WLC
See also AITN 2; BEST 89:3; CA 5-8R;
CABS 1; CANR 29, 53; CDALB 1941-
1968; DA3; DLB 2, 28; DLBD 3; DLBY
82; MTCW 1, 2

Belser, Reimond Karel Maria de 1929-
See Ruyslinck, Ward
See also CA 152

Bely, Andrey TCLC 7; PC 11
See also Bugayev, Boris Nikolayevich
See also MTCW 1

Belyi, Andrei
See Bugayev, Boris Nikolayevich

Benary, Margot
See Benary-Isbert, Margot

Benary-Isbert, Margot 1889-1979 .... CLC 12
See also CA 5-8R; 89-92; CANR 4, 72;
CLR 12; MAICYA; SATA 2; SATA-Obit
21

Benavente (y Martinez), Jacinto
1866-1954 .... TCLC 3; DAM DRAM,
MULT; HLCS 1
See also CA 106; 131; CANR 81; HW 1, 2;
MTCW 1, 2

Benchley, Peter (Bradford) 1940- . CLC 4, 8;
DAM NOV, POP
See also AAYA 14; AITN 2; CA 17-20R;
CANR 12, 35, 66; MTCW 1, 2; SATA 3,
89

Benchley, Robert (Charles)
1889-1945 .... TCLC 1, 55
See also CA 105; 153; DLB 11

Benda, Julien 1867-1956 .... TCLC 60
See also CA 120; 154

Benedict, Ruth (Fulton)
1887-1948 .... TCLC 60
See also CA 158

Benedict, Saint c. 480-c. 547 .... CMLC 29

Benedikt, Michael 1935- .... CLC 4, 14
See also CA 13-16R; CANR 7; DLB 5

Benet, Juan 1927- .... CLC 28
See also CA 143

Benet, Stephen Vincent 1898-1943 . TCLC 7;
DAM POET; SSC 10
See also CA 104; 152; DA3; DLB 4, 48,
102; DLBY 97; MTCW 1; YABC 1

Benet, William Rose 1886-1950 .... **TCLC 28; DAM POET**
See also CA 118; 152; DLB 45

Benford, Gregory (Albert) 1941- ..... **CLC 52**
See also CA 69-72; 175; CAAE 175; CAAS 27; CANR 12, 24, 49; DLBY 82

Bengtsson, Frans (Gunnar)
1894-1954 .... **TCLC 48**
See also CA 170

Benjamin, David
See Slavitt, David R(ytman)

Benjamin, Lois
See Gould, Lois

Benjamin, Walter 1892-1940 .... **TCLC 39**
See also CA 164

Benn, Gottfried 1886-1956 .... **TCLC 3**
See also CA 106; 153; DLB 56

Bennett, Alan 1934- .... **CLC 45, 77; DAB; DAM MST**
See also CA 103; CANR 35, 55; MTCW 1, 2

Bennett, (Enoch) Arnold
1867-1931 .... **TCLC 5, 20**
See also CA 106; 155; CDBLB 1890-1914; DLB 10, 34, 98, 135; MTCW 2

Bennett, Elizabeth
See Mitchell, Margaret (Munnerlyn)

Bennett, George Harold 1930-
See Bennett, Hal
See also BW 1; CA 97-100; CANR 87

Bennett, Hal CLC 5
See also Bennett, George Harold
See also DLB 33

Bennett, Jay 1912- .... **CLC 35**
See also AAYA 10; CA 69-72; CANR 11, 42, 79; JRDA; SAAS 4; SATA 41, 87; SATA-Brief 27

Bennett, Louise (Simone) 1919- ...... **CLC 28; BLC 1; DAM MULT**
See also BW 2, 3; CA 151; DLB 117

Benson, E(dward) F(rederic)
1867-1940 .... **TCLC 27**
See also CA 114; 157; DLB 135, 153

Benson, Jackson J. 1930- .... **CLC 34**
See also CA 25-28R; DLB 111

Benson, Sally 1900-1972 .... **CLC 17**
See also CA 19-20; 37-40R; CAP 1; SATA 1, 35; SATA-Obit 27

Benson, Stella 1892-1933 .... **TCLC 17**
See also CA 117; 155; DLB 36, 162

Bentham, Jeremy 1748-1832 .... **NCLC 38**
See also DLB 107, 158

Bentley, E(dmund) C(lerihew)
1875-1956 .... **TCLC 12**
See also CA 108; DLB 70

Bentley, Eric (Russell) 1916- .... **CLC 24**
See also CA 5-8R; CANR 6, 67; INT CANR-6

Beranger, Pierre Jean de
1780-1857 .... **NCLC 34**

Berdyaev, Nicolas
See Berdyaev, Nikolai (Aleksandrovich)

Berdyaev, Nikolai (Aleksandrovich)
1874-1948 .... **TCLC 67**
See also CA 120; 157

Berdyayev, Nikolai (Aleksandrovich)
See Berdyaev, Nikolai (Aleksandrovich)

Berendt, John (Lawrence) 1939- ...... **CLC 86**
See also CA 146; CANR 75, 93; DA3; MTCW 1

Beresford, J(ohn) D(avys)
1873-1947 .... **TCLC 81**
See also CA 112; 155; DLB 162, 178, 197

Bergelson, David 1884-1952 .... **TCLC 81**

Berger, Colonel
See Malraux, (Georges-)Andre

Berger, John (Peter) 1926- .... **CLC 2, 19**
See also CA 81-84; CANR 51, 78; DLB 14, 207

Berger, Melvin H. 1927- .... **CLC 12**
See also CA 5-8R; CANR 4; CLR 32; SAAS 2; SATA 5, 88

Berger, Thomas (Louis) 1924- .. **CLC 3, 5, 8, 11, 18, 38; DAM NOV**
See also CA 1-4R; CANR 5, 28, 51; DLB 2; DLBY 80; INT CANR-28; MTCW 1, 2

Bergman, (Ernst) Ingmar 1918- ...... **CLC 16, 72**
See also CA 81-84; CANR 33, 70; MTCW 2

Bergson, Henri(-Louis) 1859-1941 . **TCLC 32**
See also CA 164

Bergstein, Eleanor 1938- .... **CLC 4**
See also CA 53-56; CANR 5

Berkoff, Steven 1937- .... **CLC 56**
See also CA 104; CANR 72

Berlin, Isaiah 1909-1997 .... **TCLC 105**
See also CA 85-88; 162

Bermant, Chaim (Icyk) 1929- .... **CLC 40**
See also CA 57-60; CANR 6, 31, 57

Bern, Victoria
See Fisher, M(ary) F(rances) K(ennedy)

Bernanos, (Paul Louis) Georges
1888-1948 .... **TCLC 3**
See also CA 104; 130; CANR 94; DLB 72

Bernard, April 1956- .... **CLC 59**
See also CA 131

Berne, Victoria
See Fisher, M(ary) F(rances) K(ennedy)

Bernhard, Thomas 1931-1989 ..... **CLC 3, 32, 61; DC 14**
See also CA 85-88; 127; CANR 32, 57; DLB 85, 124; MTCW 1

Bernhardt, Sarah (Henriette Rosine)
1844-1923 .... **TCLC 75**
See also CA 157

Berriault, Gina 1926-1999 .... **CLC 54, 109; SSC 30**
See also CA 116; 129; 185; CANR 66; DLB 130

Berrigan, Daniel 1921- .... **CLC 4**
See also CA 33-36R; CAAE 187; CAAS 1; CANR 11, 43, 78; DLB 5

Berrigan, Edmund Joseph Michael, Jr.
1934-1983
See Berrigan, Ted
See also CA 61-64; 110; CANR 14

Berrigan, Ted CLC 37
See also Berrigan, Edmund Joseph Michael, Jr.
See also DLB 5, 169

Berry, Charles Edward Anderson 1931-
See Berry, Chuck
See also CA 115

Berry, Chuck CLC 17
See also Berry, Charles Edward Anderson

Berry, Jonas
See Ashbery, John (Lawrence)

Berry, Wendell (Erdman) 1934- ... **CLC 4, 6, 8, 27, 46; DAM POET; PC 28**
See also AITN 1; CA 73-76; CANR 50, 73; DLB 5, 6, 234; MTCW 1

Berryman, John 1914-1972 ... **CLC 1, 2, 3, 4, 6, 8, 10, 13, 25, 62**
See also CA 13-16; 33-36R; CABS 2; CANR 35; CAP 1; CDALB 1941-1968; DLB 48; MTCW 1, 2

Bertolucci, Bernardo 1940- .... **CLC 16**
See also CA 106

Berton, Pierre (Francis Demarigny)
1920- .... **CLC 104**
See also CA 1-4R; CANR 2, 56; DLB 68; SATA 99

Bertrand, Aloysius 1807-1841 .... **NCLC 31**

Bertran de Born c. 1140-1215 .... **CMLC 5**

Besant, Annie (Wood) 1847-1933 ..... **TCLC 9**
See also CA 105; 185

Bessie, Alvah 1904-1985 .... **CLC 23**
See also CA 5-8R; 116; CANR 2, 80; DLB 26

Bethlen, T. D.
See Silverberg, Robert

Beti, Mongo CLC 27; BLC 1; DAM MULT
See also Biyidi, Alexandre
See also CANR 79

Betjeman, John 1906-1984 ...... **CLC 2, 6, 10, 34, 43; DAB; DAM MST, POET**
See also CA 9-12R; 112; CANR 33, 56; CDBLB 1945-1960; DA3; DLB 20; DLBY 84; MTCW 1, 2

Bettelheim, Bruno 1903-1990 .... **CLC 79**
See also CA 81-84; 131; CANR 23, 61; DA3; MTCW 1, 2

Betti, Ugo 1892-1953 .... **TCLC 5**
See also CA 104; 155

Betts, Doris (Waugh) 1932- ...... **CLC 3, 6, 28**
See also CA 13-16R; CANR 9, 66, 77; DLBY 82; INT CANR-9

Bevan, Alistair
See Roberts, Keith (John Kingston)

Bey, Pilaff
See Douglas, (George) Norman

Bialik, Chaim Nachman
1873-1934 .... **TCLC 25**
See also CA 170

Bickerstaff, Isaac
See Swift, Jonathan

Bidart, Frank 1939- .... **CLC 33**
See also CA 140

Bienek, Horst 1930- .... **CLC 7, 11**
See also CA 73-76; DLB 75

Bierce, Ambrose (Gwinett)
1842-1914(?) .... **TCLC 1, 7, 44; DA; DAC; DAM MST; SSC 9; WLC**
See also CA 104; 139; CDALB 1865-1917; DA3; DLB 11, 12, 23, 71, 74, 186

Biggers, Earl Derr 1884-1933 .... **TCLC 65**
See also CA 108; 153

Billings, Josh
See Shaw, Henry Wheeler

Billington, (Lady) Rachel (Mary)
1942- .... **CLC 43**
See also AITN 2; CA 33-36R; CANR 44

Binyon, T(imothy) J(ohn) 1936- .... **CLC 34**
See also CA 111; CANR 28

Bion 335B.C.-245B.C. .... **CMLC 39**

Bioy Casares, Adolfo 1914-1999 ... **CLC 4, 8, 13, 88; DAM MULT; HLC 1; SSC 17**
See also CA 29-32R; 177; CANR 19, 43, 66; DLB 113; HW 1, 2; MTCW 1, 2

Bird, Cordwainer
See Ellison, Harlan (Jay)

Bird, Robert Montgomery
1806-1854 .... **NCLC 1**
See also DLB 202

Birkerts, Sven 1951- .... **CLC 116**
See also CA 128; 133; 176; CAAE 176; CAAS 29; INT 133

Birney, (Alfred) Earle 1904-1995 .. **CLC 1, 4, 6, 11; DAC; DAM MST, POET**
See also CA 1-4R; CANR 5, 20; DLB 88; MTCW 1

Biruni, al 973-1048(?) .... **CMLC 28**

Bishop, Elizabeth 1911-1979 ..... **CLC 1, 4, 9, 13, 15, 32; DA; DAC; DAM MST, POET; PC 3**
See also CA 5-8R; 89-92; CABS 2; CANR 26, 61; CDALB 1968-1988; DA3; DLB 5, 169; MTCW 1, 2; SATA-Obit 24

Bishop, John 1935- .... **CLC 10**
See also CA 105

Bishop, John Peale 1892-1944 ..... **TCLC 103**
See also CA 107; 155; DLB 4, 9, 45

Borrow, George (Henry)
1803-1881 .... **NCLC 9**
See also DLB 21, 55, 166

Bosch (Gavino), Juan 1909-
See also CA 151; DAM MST, MULT; DLB
145; HLCS 1; HW 1, 2

Bosman, Herman Charles
1905-1951 .... **TCLC 49**
See also Malan, Herman
See also CA 160; DLB 225

Bosschere, Jean de 1878(?)-1953 ... **TCLC 19**
See also CA 115; 186

Boswell, James 1740-1795 ...... **LC 4, 50; DA;**
DAB; DAC; DAM MST; WLC
See also CDBLB 1660-1789; DLB 104, 142

Bottoms, David 1949- .... **CLC 53**
See also CA 105; CANR 22; DLB 120;
DLBY 83

Boucicault, Dion 1820-1890 .... **NCLC 41**

Bourget, Paul (Charles Joseph)
1852-1935 .... **TCLC 12**
See also CA 107; DLB 123

Bourjaily, Vance (Nye) 1922- .... **CLC 8, 62**
See also CA 1-4R; CAAS 1; CANR 2, 72;
DLB 2, 143

Bourne, Randolph S(illiman)
1886-1918 .... **TCLC 16**
See also CA 117; 155; DLB 63

Bova, Ben(jamin William) 1932- ...... **CLC 45**
See also AAYA 16; CA 5-8R; CAAS 18;
CANR 11, 56, 94; CLR 3; DLBY 81; INT
CANR-11; MAICYA; MTCW 1; SATA 6,
68

Bowen, Elizabeth (Dorothea Cole)
1899-1973 . **CLC 1, 3, 6, 11, 15, 22, 118;**
DAM NOV; SSC 3, 28
See also CA 17-18; 41-44R; CANR 35;
CAP 2; CDBLB 1945-1960; DA3; DLB
15, 162; MTCW 1, 2

Bowering, George 1935- .... **CLC 15, 47**
See also CA 21-24R; CAAS 16; CANR 10;
DLB 53

Bowering, Marilyn R(uthe) 1949- .... **CLC 32**
See also CA 101; CANR 49

Bowers, Edgar 1924-2000 .... **CLC 9**
See also CA 5-8R; 188; CANR 24; DLB 5

Bowie, David CLC 17
See also Jones, David Robert

Bowles, Jane (Sydney) 1917-1973 ..... **CLC 3,**
68
See also CA 19-20; 41-44R; CAP 2

Bowles, Paul (Frederick) 1910-1999 . **CLC 1,**
2, 19, 53; SSC 3
See also CA 1-4R; 186; CAAS 1; CANR 1,
19, 50, 75; DA3; DLB 5, 6; MTCW 1, 2

Box, Edgar
See Vidal, Gore

Boyd, Nancy
See Millay, Edna St. Vincent

Boyd, William 1952- .... **CLC 28, 53, 70**
See also CA 114; 120; CANR 51, 71; DLB
231

Boyle, Kay 1902-1992 .... **CLC 1, 5, 19, 58,**
121; SSC 5
See also CA 13-16R; 140; CAAS 1; CANR
29, 61; DLB 4, 9, 48, 86; DLBY 93;
MTCW 1, 2

Boyle, Mark
See Kienzle, William X(avier)

Boyle, Patrick 1905-1982 .... **CLC 19**
See also CA 127

Boyle, T. C. 1948-
See Boyle, T(homas) Coraghessan

Boyle, T(homas) Coraghessan
1948- .... **CLC 36, 55, 90; DAM POP;**
SSC 16
See also BEST 90:4; CA 120; CANR 44,
76, 89; DA3; DLBY 86; MTCW 2

Boz
See Dickens, Charles (John Huffam)

Brackenridge, Hugh Henry
1748-1816 .... **NCLC 7**
See also DLB 11, 37

Bradbury, Edward P.
See Moorcock, Michael (John)
See also MTCW 2

Bradbury, Malcolm (Stanley)
1932- .... **CLC 32, 61; DAM NOV**
See also CA 1-4R; CANR 1, 33, 91; DA3;
DLB 14, 207; MTCW 1, 2

Bradbury, Ray (Douglas) 1920- .... **CLC 1, 3,**
10, 15, 42, 98; DA; DAB; DAC; DAM
MST, NOV, POP; SSC 29; WLC
See also AAYA 15; AITN 1, 2; CA 1-4R;
CANR 2, 30, 75; CDALB 1968-1988;
DA3; DLB 2, 8; MTCW 1, 2; SATA 11,
64

Bradford, Gamaliel 1863-1932 .... **TCLC 36**
See also CA 160; DLB 17

Bradford, William 1590-1657 .... **LC 64**
See also DLB 24, 30

Bradley, David (Henry), Jr. 1950- ... **CLC 23,**
118; BLC 1; DAM MULT
See also BW 1, 3; CA 104; CANR 26, 81;
DLB 33

Bradley, John Ed(mund, Jr.) 1958- . **CLC 55**
See also CA 139

Bradley, Marion Zimmer
1930-1999 .... **CLC 30; DAM POP**
See also AAYA 9; CA 57-60; 185; CAAS
10; CANR 7, 31, 51, 75; DLB 8;
MTCW 1, 2; SATA 90; SATA-Obit 116

Bradstreet, Anne 1612(?)-1672 ...... **LC 4, 30;**
DA; DAC; DAM MST, POET; PC 10
See also CDALB 1640-1865; DA3; DLB
24

Brady, Joan 1939- .... **CLC 86**
See also CA 141

Bragg, Melvyn 1939- .... **CLC 10**
See also BEST 89:3; CA 57-60; CANR 10,
48, 89; DLB 14

Brahe, Tycho 1546-1601 .... **LC 45**

Braine, John (Gerard) 1922-1986 . **CLC 1, 3,**
41
See also CA 1-4R; 120; CANR 1, 33; CD-
BLB 1945-1960; DLB 15; DLBY 86;
MTCW 1

Bramah, Ernest 1868-1942 .... **TCLC 72**
See also CA 156; DLB 70

Brammer, William 1930(?)-1978 ...... **CLC 31**
See also CA 77-80

Brancati, Vitaliano 1907-1954 .... **TCLC 12**
See also CA 109

Brancato, Robin F(idler) 1936- .... **CLC 35**
See also AAYA 9; CA 69-72; CANR 11,
45; CLR 32; JRDA; SAAS 9; SATA 97

Brand, Max
See Faust, Frederick (Schiller)

Brand, Millen 1906-1980 .... **CLC 7**
See also CA 21-24R; 97-100; CANR 72

Branden, Barbara CLC 44
See also CA 148

Brandes, Georg (Morris Cohen)
1842-1927 .... **TCLC 10**
See also CA 105

Brandys, Kazimierz 1916- .... **CLC 62**

Branley, Franklyn M(ansfield)
1915- .... **CLC 21**
See also CA 33-36R; CANR 14, 39; CLR
13; MAICYA; SAAS 16; SATA 4, 68

Brathwaite, Edward (Kamau)
1930- ...... **CLC 11; BLCS; DAM POET**
See also BW 2, 3; CA 25-28R; CANR 11,
26, 47; DLB 125

Brautigan, Richard (Gary)
1935-1984 .... **CLC 1, 3, 5, 9, 12, 34, 42;**
DAM NOV
See also CA 53-56; 113; CANR 34; DA3;
DLB 2, 5, 206; DLBY 80, 84; MTCW 1;
SATA 56

Brave Bird, Mary 1953-
See Crow Dog, Mary (Ellen)
See also NNAL

Braverman, Kate 1950- .... **CLC 67**
See also CA 89-92

Brecht, (Eugen) Bertolt (Friedrich)
1898-1956 .... **TCLC 1, 6, 13, 35; DA;**
DAB; DAC; DAM DRAM, MST; DC
3; WLC
See also CA 104; 133; CANR 62; DA3;
DLB 56, 124; MTCW 1, 2

Brecht, Eugen Berthold Friedrich
See Brecht, (Eugen) Bertolt (Friedrich)

Bremer, Fredrika 1801-1865 .... **NCLC 11**

Brennan, Christopher John
1870-1932 .... **TCLC 17**
See also CA 117; 188; DLB 230

Brennan, Maeve 1917-1993 .... **CLC 5**
See also CA 81-84; CANR 72

Brent, Linda
See Jacobs, Harriet A(nn)

Brentano, Clemens (Maria)
1778-1842 .... **NCLC 1**
See also DLB 90

Brent of Bin Bin
See Franklin, (Stella Maria Sarah) Miles
(Lampe)

Brenton, Howard 1942- .... **CLC 31**
See also CA 69-72; CANR 33, 67; DLB 13;
MTCW 1

Breslin, James 1930-
See Breslin, Jimmy
See also CA 73-76; CANR 31, 75; DAM
NOV; MTCW 1, 2

Breslin, Jimmy CLC 4, 43
See also Breslin, James
See also AITN 1; DLB 185; MTCW 2

Bresson, Robert 1901(?)-1999 .... **CLC 16**
See also CA 110; 187; CANR 49

Breton, Andre 1896-1966 .. **CLC 2, 9, 15, 54;**
PC 15
See also CA 19-20; 25-28R; CANR 40, 60;
CAP 2; DLB 65; MTCW 1, 2

Breytenbach, Breyten 1939(?)- .. **CLC 23, 37,**
126; DAM POET
See also CA 113; 129; CANR 61; DLB 225

Bridgers, Sue Ellen 1942- .... **CLC 26**
See also AAYA 8; CA 65-68; CANR 11,
36; CLR 18; DLB 52; JRDA; MAICYA;
SAAS 1; SATA 22, 90; SATA-Essay 109

Bridges, Robert (Seymour)
1844-1930 ... **TCLC 1; DAM POET; PC**
28
See also CA 104; 152; CDBLB 1890-1914;
DLB 19, 98

Bridie, James TCLC 3
See also Mavor, Osborne Henry
See also DLB 10

Brin, David 1950- .... **CLC 34**
See also AAYA 21; CA 102; CANR 24, 70;
INT CANR-24; SATA 65

Brink, Andre (Philippus) 1935- . **CLC 18, 36,**
106
See also CA 104; CANR 39, 62; DLB 225;
INT 103; MTCW 1, 2

Brinsmead, H(esba) F(ay) 1922- ...... **CLC 21**
See also CA 21-24R; CANR 10; CLR 47;
MAICYA; SAAS 5; SATA 18, 78

Brittain, Vera (Mary) 1893(?)-1970 . **CLC 23**
See also CA 13-16; 25-28R; CANR 58;
CAP 1; DLB 191; MTCW 1, 2

Broch, Hermann 1886-1951 .... **TCLC 20**
See also CA 117; DLB 85, 124

Castle, Robert
See Hamilton, Edmond
Castro (Ruz), Fidel 1926(?)-
See also CA 110; 129; CANR 81; DAM
MULT; HLC 1; HW 2
Castro, Guillen de 1569-1631 .... **LC 19**
Castro, Rosalia de 1837-1885 ... **NCLC 3, 78;
DAM MULT**
Cather, Willa -1947
See Cather, Willa Sibert
Cather, Willa Sibert 1873-1947 ...... **TCLC 1,
11, 31, 99; DA; DAB; DAC; DAM
MST, NOV; SSC 2; WLC**
See also Cather, Willa
See also AAYA 24; CA 104; 128; CDALB
1865-1917; DA3; DLB 9, 54, 78; DLBD
1; MTCW 1, 2; SATA 30
Catherine, Saint 1347-1380 .... **CMLC 27**
Cato, Marcus Porcius
234B.C.-149B.C. .... **CMLC 21**
See also DLB 211
Catton, (Charles) Bruce 1899-1978 . **CLC 35**
See also AITN 1; CA 5-8R; 81-84; CANR
7, 74; DLB 17; SATA 2; SATA-Obit 24
Catullus c. 84B.C.-c. 54B.C. .... **CMLC 18**
See also DLB 211
Cauldwell, Frank
See King, Francis (Henry)
Caunitz, William J. 1933-1996 .... **CLC 34**
See also BEST 89:3; CA 125; 130; 152;
CANR 73; INT 130
Causley, Charles (Stanley) 1917- .... **CLC 7**
See also CA 9-12R; CANR 5, 35, 94; CLR
30; DLB 27; MTCW 1; SATA 3, 66
Caute, (John) David 1936- .... **CLC 29; DAM
NOV**
See also CA 1-4R; CAAS 4; CANR 1, 33,
64; DLB 14, 231
Cavafy, C(onstantine) P(eter)
1863-1933 ...... **TCLC 2, 7; DAM POET**
See also Kavafis, Konstantinos Petrou
See also CA 148; DA3; MTCW 1
Cavallo, Evelyn
See Spark, Muriel (Sarah)
Cavanna, Betty **CLC 12**
See also Harrison, Elizabeth Cavanna
See also JRDA; MAICYA; SAAS 4; SATA
1, 30
Cavendish, Margaret Lucas
1623-1673 .... **LC 30**
See also DLB 131
Caxton, William 1421(?)-1491(?) .... **LC 17**
See also DLB 170
Cayer, D. M.
See Duffy, Maureen
Cayrol, Jean 1911- .... **CLC 11**
See also CA 89-92; DLB 83
Cela, Camilo Jose 1916- .... **CLC 4, 13, 59,
122; DAM MULT; HLC 1**
See also BEST 90:2; CA 21-24R; CAAS
10; CANR 21, 32, 76; DLBY 89; HW 1;
MTCW 1, 2
Celan, Paul **CLC 10, 19, 53, 82; PC 10**
See also Antschel, Paul
See also DLB 69
Celine, Louis-Ferdinand **CLC 1, 3, 4, 7, 9,
15, 47, 124**
See also Destouches, Louis-Ferdinand
See also DLB 72
Cellini, Benvenuto 1500-1571 .... **LC 7**
Cendrars, Blaise 1887-1961 ...... **CLC 18, 106**
See also Sauser-Hall, Frederic
Cernuda (y Bidon), Luis
1902-1963 .... **CLC 54; DAM POET**
See also CA 131; 89-92; DLB 134; HW 1
Cervantes, Lorna Dee 1954-
See also CA 131; CANR 80; DLB 82;
HLCS 1; HW 1

Cervantes (Saavedra), Miguel de
1547-1616 .. **LC 6, 23; DA; DAB; DAC;
DAM MST, NOV; SSC 12; WLC**
Cesaire, Aime (Fernand) 1913- . **CLC 19, 32,
112; BLC 1; DAM MULT, POET; PC
25**
See also BW 2, 3; CA 65-68; CANR 24,
43, 81; DA3; MTCW 1, 2
Chabon, Michael 1963- .... **CLC 55**
See also CA 139; CANR 57
Chabrol, Claude 1930- .... **CLC 16**
See also CA 110
Challans, Mary 1905-1983
See Renault, Mary
See also CA 81-84; 111; CANR 74; DA3;
MTCW 2; SATA 23; SATA-Obit 36
Challis, George
See Faust, Frederick (Schiller)
Chambers, Aidan 1934- .... **CLC 35**
See also AAYA 27; CA 25-28R; CANR 12,
31, 58; JRDA; MAICYA; SAAS 12;
SATA 1, 69, 108
Chambers, James 1948-
See Cliff, Jimmy
See also CA 124
Chambers, Jessie
See Lawrence, D(avid) H(erbert Richards)
Chambers, Robert W(illiam)
1865-1933 .... **TCLC 41**
See also CA 165; DLB 202; SATA 107
Chamisso, Adelbert von
1781-1838 .... **NCLC 82**
See also DLB 90
Chandler, Raymond (Thornton)
1888-1959 .... **TCLC 1, 7; SSC 23**
See also AAYA 25; CA 104; 129; CANR
60; CDALB 1929-1941; DA3; DLB 226;
DLBD 6; MTCW 1, 2
Chang, Eileen 1920-1995 .... **SSC 28**
See also CA 166
Chang, Jung 1952- .... **CLC 71**
See also CA 142
Chang Ai-Ling
See Chang, Eileen
Channing, William Ellery
1780-1842 .... **NCLC 17**
See also DLB 1, 59, 235
Chao, Patricia 1955- .... **CLC 119**
See also CA 163
Chaplin, Charles Spencer
1889-1977 .... **CLC 16**
See also Chaplin, Charlie
See also CA 81-84; 73-76
Chaplin, Charlie
See Chaplin, Charles Spencer
See also DLB 44
Chapman, George 1559(?)-1634 .... **LC 22;
DAM DRAM**
See also DLB 62, 121
Chapman, Graham 1941-1989 .... **CLC 21**
See also Monty Python
See also CA 116; 129; CANR 35
Chapman, John Jay 1862-1933 .... **TCLC 7**
See also CA 104
Chapman, Lee
See Bradley, Marion Zimmer
Chapman, Walker
See Silverberg, Robert
Chappell, Fred (Davis) 1936- ..... **CLC 40, 78**
See also CA 5-8R; CAAS 4; CANR 8, 33,
67; DLB 6, 105
Char, Rene(-Emile) 1907-1988 .... **CLC 9, 11,
14, 55; DAM POET**
See also CA 13-16R; 124; CANR 32;
MTCW 1, 2
Charby, Jay
See Ellison, Harlan (Jay)

Chardin, Pierre Teilhard de
See Teilhard de Chardin, (Marie Joseph)
Pierre
Charlemagne 742-814 .... **CMLC 37**
Charles I 1600-1649 .... **LC 13**
Charriere, Isabelle de 1740-1805 .. **NCLC 66**
Charyn, Jerome 1937- .... **CLC 5, 8, 18**
See also CA 5-8R; CAAS 1; CANR 7, 61;
DLBY 83; MTCW 1
Chase, Mary (Coyle) 1907-1981 .... **DC 1**
See also CA 77-80; 105; DLB 228; SATA
17; SATA-Obit 29
Chase, Mary Ellen 1887-1973 .... **CLC 2**
See also CA 13-16; 41-44R; CAP 1; SATA
10
Chase, Nicholas
See Hyde, Anthony
Chateaubriand, Francois Rene de
1768-1848 .... **NCLC 3**
See also DLB 119
Chatterje, Sarat Chandra 1876-1936(?)
See Chatterji, Saratchandra
See also CA 109
Chatterji, Bankim Chandra
1838-1894 .... **NCLC 19**
Chatterji, Saratchandra -1938 .... **TCLC 13**
See also Chatterje, Sarat Chandra
See also CA 186
Chatterton, Thomas 1752-1770 ..... **LC 3, 54;
DAM POET**
See also DLB 109
Chatwin, (Charles) Bruce
1940-1989 . **CLC 28, 57, 59; DAM POP**
See also AAYA 4; BEST 90:1; CA 85-88;
127; DLB 194, 204
Chaucer, Daniel -1939
See Ford, Ford Madox
Chaucer, Geoffrey 1340(?)-1400 .. **LC 17, 56;
DA; DAB; DAC; DAM MST, POET;
PC 19; WLCS**
See also CDBLB Before 1660; DA3; DLB
146
Chavez, Denise (Elia) 1948-
See also CA 131; CANR 56, 81; DAM
MULT; DLB 122; HLC 1; HW 1, 2;
MTCW 2
Chaviaras, Strates 1935-
See Haviaras, Stratis
See also CA 105
Chayefsky, Paddy **CLC 23**
See also Chayefsky, Sidney
See also DLB 7, 44; DLBY 81
Chayefsky, Sidney 1923-1981
See Chayefsky, Paddy
See also CA 9-12R; 104; CANR 18; DAM
DRAM
Chedid, Andree 1920- .... **CLC 47**
See also CA 145
Cheever, John 1912-1982 ..... **CLC 3, 7, 8, 11,
15, 25, 64; DA; DAB; DAC; DAM
MST, NOV, POP; SSC 1, 38; WLC**
See also CA 5-8R; 106; CABS 1; CANR 5,
27, 76; CDALB 1941-1968; DA3; DLB
2, 102, 227; DLBY 80, 82; INT CANR-5;
MTCW 1, 2
Cheever, Susan 1943- .... **CLC 18, 48**
See also CA 103; CANR 27, 51, 92; DLBY
82; INT CANR-27
Chekhonte, Antosha
See Chekhov, Anton (Pavlovich)
Chekhov, Anton (Pavlovich)
1860-1904 ...... **TCLC 3, 10, 31, 55, 96;
DA; DAB; DAC; DAM DRAM, MST;
DC 9; SSC 2, 28, 41; WLC**
See also CA 104; 124; DA3; SATA 90
Chernyshevsky, Nikolay Gavrilovich
1828-1889 .... **NCLC 1**

Crowley, John 1942- .... **CLC 57**
See also CA 61-64; CANR 43; DLBY 82;
SATA 65
Crud
See Crumb, R(obert)
Crumarums
See Crumb, R(obert)
Crumb, R(obert) 1943- .... **CLC 17**
See also CA 106
Crumbum
See Crumb, R(obert)
Crumski
See Crumb, R(obert)
Crum the Bum
See Crumb, R(obert)
Crunk
See Crumb, R(obert)
Crustt
See Crumb, R(obert)
Cruz, Victor Hernandez 1949-
See also BW 2; CA 65-68; CAAS 17;
CANR 14, 32, 74; DAM MULT, POET;
DLB 41; HLC 1; HW 1, 2; MTCW 1
Cryer, Gretchen (Kiger) 1935- .... **CLC 21**
See also CA 114; 123
Csath, Geza 1887-1919 .... **TCLC 13**
See also CA 111
Cudlip, David R(ockwell) 1933- .... **CLC 34**
See also CA 177
Cullen, Countee 1903-1946 .... **TCLC 4, 37;**
BLC 1; DA; DAC; DAM MST, MULT,
POET; PC 20; WLCS
See also BW 1; CA 108; 124; CDALB
1917-1929; DA3; DLB 4, 48, 51; MTCW
1, 2; SATA 18
Cum, R.
See Crumb, R(obert)
Cummings, Bruce F(rederick) 1889-1919
See Barbellion, W. N. P.
See also CA 123
Cummings, E(dward) E(stlin)
1894-1962 .... **CLC 1, 3, 8, 12, 15, 68;**
DA; DAB; DAC; DAM MST, POET;
PC 5; WLC
See also CA 73-76; CANR 31; CDALB
1929-1941; DA3; DLB 4, 48; MTCW 1,
2
Cunha, Euclides (Rodrigues Pimenta) da
1866-1909 .... **TCLC 24**
See also CA 123
Cunningham, E. V.
See Fast, Howard (Melvin)
Cunningham, J(ames) V(incent)
1911-1985 .... **CLC 3, 31**
See also CA 1-4R; 115; CANR 1, 72; DLB
5
Cunningham, Julia (Woolfolk)
1916- .... **CLC 12**
See also CA 9-12R; CANR 4, 19, 36;
JRDA; MAICYA; SAAS 2; SATA 1, 26
Cunningham, Michael 1952- .... **CLC 34**
See also CA 136
Cunninghame Graham, R. B.
See Cunninghame Graham, Robert
(Gallnigad) Bontine
Cunninghame Graham, Robert (Gallnigad)
Bontine 1852-1936 .... **TCLC 19**
See also Graham, R(obert) B(ontine) Cun-
ninghame
See also CA 119; 184; DLB 98
Currie, Ellen 19(?)- .... **CLC 44**
Curtin, Philip
See Lowndes, Marie Adelaide (Belloc)
Curtis, Price
See Ellison, Harlan (Jay)
Cutrate, Joe
See Spiegelman, Art
Cynewulf c. 770-c. 840 .... **CMLC 23**

Czaczkes, Shmuel Yosef
See Agnon, S(hmuel) Y(osef Halevi)
Dabrowska, Maria (Szumska)
1889-1965 .... **CLC 15**
See also CA 106
Dabydeen, David 1955- .... **CLC 34**
See also BW 1; CA 125; CANR 56, 92
Dacey, Philip 1939- .... **CLC 51**
See also CA 37-40R; CAAS 17; CANR 14,
32, 64; DLB 105
Dagerman, Stig (Halvard)
1923-1954 .... **TCLC 17**
See also CA 117; 155
Dahl, Roald 1916-1990 ...... **CLC 1, 6, 18, 79;**
DAB; DAC; DAM MST, NOV, POP
See also AAYA 15; CA 1-4R; 133; CANR
6, 32, 37, 62; CLR 1, 7, 41; DA3; DLB
139; JRDA; MAICYA; MTCW 1, 2;
SATA 1, 26, 73; SATA-Obit 65
Dahlberg, Edward 1900-1977 .. **CLC 1, 7, 14**
See also CA 9-12R; 69-72; CANR 31, 62;
DLB 48; MTCW 1
Daitch, Susan 1954- .... **CLC 103**
See also CA 161
Dale, Colin TCLC 18
See Lawrence, T(homas) E(dward)
Dale, George E.
See Asimov, Isaac
Dalton, Roque 1935-1975
See also HLCS 1; HW 2
Daly, Elizabeth 1878-1967 .... **CLC 52**
See also CA 23-24; 25-28R; CANR 60;
CAP 2
Daly, Maureen 1921-1983 .... **CLC 17**
See also AAYA 5; CANR 37, 83; JRDA;
MAICYA; SAAS 1; SATA 2
Damas, Leon-Gontran 1912-1978 .... **CLC 84**
See also BW 1; CA 125; 73-76
Dana, Richard Henry Sr.
1787-1879 .... **NCLC 53**
Daniel, Samuel 1562(?)-1619 .... **LC 24**
See also DLB 62
Daniels, Brett
See Adler, Renata
Dannay, Frederic 1905-1982 . **CLC 11; DAM**
POP
See also Queen, Ellery
See also CA 1-4R; 107; CANR 1, 39; DLB
137; MTCW 1
D'Annunzio, Gabriele 1863-1938 ... **TCLC 6,**
40
See also CA 104; 155
Danois, N. le
See Gourmont, Remy (-Marie-Charles) de
Dante 1265-1321 .... **CMLC 3, 18, 39; DA;**
DAB; DAC; DAM MST, POET; PC
21; WLCS
See also Alighieri, Dante
See also DA3
d'Antibes, Germain
See Simenon, Georges (Jacques Christian)
Danticat, Edwidge 1969- .... **CLC 94, 139**
See also AAYA 29; CA 152; CANR 73;
MTCW 1
Danvers, Dennis 1947- .... **CLC 70**
Danziger, Paula 1944- .... **CLC 21**
See also AAYA 4, 36; CA 112; 115; CANR
37; CLR 20; JRDA; MAICYA; SATA 36,
63, 102; SATA-Brief 30
Da Ponte, Lorenzo 1749-1838 .... **NCLC 50**
Dario, Ruben 1867-1916 .... **TCLC 4; DAM**
MULT; HLC 1; PC 15
See also CA 131; CANR 81; HW 1, 2;
MTCW 1, 2
Darley, George 1795-1846 .... **NCLC 2**
See also DLB 96
Darrow, Clarence (Seward)
1857-1938 .... **TCLC 81**
See also CA 164

Darwin, Charles 1809-1882 .... **NCLC 57**
See also DLB 57, 166
Daryush, Elizabeth 1887-1977 ...... **CLC 6, 19**
See also CA 49-52; CANR 3, 81; DLB 20
Dasgupta, Surendranath
1887-1952 .... **TCLC 81**
See also CA 157
Dashwood, Edmee Elizabeth Monica de la
Pasture 1890-1943
See Delafield, E. M.
See also CA 119; 154
Daudet, (Louis Marie) Alphonse
1840-(1897) .... **NCLC 1**
See also DLB 123
Daumal, Rene 1908-1944 .... **TCLC 14**
See also CA 114
Davenant, William 1606-1668 .... **LC 13**
See also DLB 58, 126
Davenport, Guy (Mattison, Jr.)
1927- .... **CLC 6, 14, 38; SSC 16**
See also CA 33-36R; CANR 23, 73; DLB
130
Davidson, Avram (James) 1923-1993
See Queen, Ellery
See also CA 101; 171; CANR 26; DLB 8
Davidson, Donald (Grady)
1893-1968 .... **CLC 2, 13, 19**
See also CA 5-8R; 25-28R; CANR 4, 84;
DLB 45
Davidson, Hugh
See Hamilton, Edmond
Davidson, John 1857-1909 .... **TCLC 24**
See also CA 118; DLB 19
Davidson, Sara 1943- .... **CLC 9**
See also CA 81-84; CANR 44, 68; DLB
185
Davie, Donald (Alfred) 1922-1995 .... **CLC 5,**
8, 10, 31; PC 29
See also CA 1-4R; 149; CAAS 3; CANR 1,
44; DLB 27; MTCW 1
Davies, Ray(mond Douglas) 1944- ... **CLC 21**
See also CA 116; 146; CANR 92
Davies, Rhys 1901-1978 .... **CLC 23**
See also CA 9-12R; 81-84; CANR 4; DLB
139, 191
Davies, (William) Robertson
1913-1995 .... **CLC 2, 7, 13, 25, 42, 75,**
91; DA; DAB; DAC; DAM MST, NOV,
POP; WLC
See also BEST 89:2; CA 33-36R; 150;
CANR 17, 42; DA3; DLB 68; INT
CANR-17; MTCW 1, 2
Davies, Walter C.
See Kornbluth, C(yril) M.
Davies, William Henry 1871-1940 ... **TCLC 5**
See also CA 104; 179; DLB 19, 174
Da Vinci, Leonardo 1452-1519 ..... **LC 12, 57,**
60
Davis, Angela (Yvonne) 1944- .... **CLC 77;**
DAM MULT
See also BW 2, 3; CA 57-60; CANR 10,
81; DA3
Davis, B. Lynch
See Bioy Casares, Adolfo; Borges, Jorge
Luis
Davis, B. Lynch
See Bioy Casares, Adolfo
Davis, Gordon
See Hunt, E(verette) Howard, (Jr.)
Davis, H(arold) L(enoir) 1894-1960 . **CLC 49**
See also CA 178; 89-92; DLB 9, 206; SATA
114
Davis, Rebecca (Blaine) Harding
1831-1910 .... **TCLC 6; SSC 38**
See also CA 104; 179; DLB 74
Davis, Richard Harding
1864-1916 .... **TCLC 24**
See also CA 114; 179; DLB 12, 23, 78, 79,
189; DLBD 13

Dunsany, Lord -1957 .... **TCLC 2, 59**
  See also Dunsany, Edward John Moreton
  Drax Plunkett
  See also DLB 77, 153, 156

du Perry, Jean
  See Simenon, Georges (Jacques Christian)

Durang, Christopher (Ferdinand)
  1949- .... **CLC 27, 38**
  See also CA 105; CANR 50, 76; MTCW 1

Duras, Marguerite 1914-1996 . **CLC 3, 6, 11,
  20, 34, 40, 68, 100; SSC 40**
  See also CA 25-28R; 151; CANR 50; DLB
  83; MTCW 1, 2

Durban, (Rosa) Pam 1947- .... **CLC 39**
  See also CA 123

Durcan, Paul 1944- .... **CLC 43, 70; DAM
  POET**
  See also CA 134

Durkheim, Emile 1858-1917 .... **TCLC 55**

Durrell, Lawrence (George)
  1912-1990 .... **CLC 1, 4, 6, 8, 13, 27, 41;
  DAM NOV**
  See also CA 9-12R; 132; CANR 40, 77;
  CDBLB 1945-1960; DLB 15, 27, 204;
  DLBY 90; MTCW 1, 2

Durrenmatt, Friedrich
  See Duerrenmatt, Friedrich

DuRrenmatt, Friedrich
  See Duerrenmatt, Friedrich

Dutt, Toru 1856-1877 .... **NCLC 29**

Dwight, Timothy 1752-1817 .... **NCLC 13**
  See also DLB 37

Dworkin, Andrea 1946- .... **CLC 43, 123**
  See also CA 77-80; CAAS 21; CANR 16,
  39, 76; INT CANR-16; MTCW 1, 2

Dwyer, Deanna
  See Koontz, Dean R(ay)

Dwyer, K. R.
  See Koontz, Dean R(ay)

Dwyer, Thomas A. 1923- .... **CLC 114**
  See also CA 115

Dybek, Stuart 1942- .... **CLC 114**
  See also CA 97-100; CANR 39; DLB 130

Dye, Richard
  See De Voto, Bernard (Augustine)

Dylan, Bob 1941- .... **CLC 3, 4, 6, 12, 77**
  See also CA 41-44R; DLB 16

E. V. L.
  See Lucas, E(dward) V(errall)

Eagleton, Terence (Francis) 1943- .. **CLC 63,
  132**
  See also CA 57-60; CANR 7, 23, 68;
  MTCW 1, 2

Eagleton, Terry
  See Eagleton, Terence (Francis)

Early, Jack
  See Scoppettone, Sandra

East, Michael
  See West, Morris L(anglo)

Eastaway, Edward
  See Thomas, (Philip) Edward

Eastlake, William (Derry)
  1917-1997 .... **CLC 8**
  See also CA 5-8R; 158; CAAS 1; CANR 5,
  63; DLB 6, 206; INT CANR-5

Eastman, Charles A(lexander)
  1858-1939 .... **TCLC 55; DAM MULT**
  See also CA 179; CANR 91; DLB 175;
  NNAL; YABC 1

Eberhart, Richard (Ghormley)
  1904- .. **CLC 3, 11, 19, 56; DAM POET**
  See also CA 1-4R; CANR 2; CDALB 1941-
  1968; DLB 48; MTCW 1

Eberstadt, Fernanda 1960- .... **CLC 39**
  See also CA 136; CANR 69

**Echegaray (y Eizaguirre), Jose (Maria
  Waldo)** 1832-1916 .... **TCLC 4; HLCS 1**
  See also CA 104; CANR 32; HW 1;
  MTCW 1

Echeverria, (Jose) Esteban (Antonino)
  1805-1851 .... **NCLC 18**

Echo
  See Proust, (Valentin-Louis-George-
  Eugene-) Marcel

Eckert, Allan W. 1931- .... **CLC 17**
  See also AAYA 18; CA 13-16R; CANR 14,
  45; INT CANR-14; SAAS 21; SATA 29,
  91; SATA-Brief 27

Eckhart, Meister 1260(?)-1328(?) ... **CMLC 9**
  See also DLB 115

Eckmar, F. R.
  See de Hartog, Jan

Eco, Umberto 1932- .... **CLC 28, 60; DAM
  NOV, POP**
  See also BEST 90:1; CA 77-80; CANR 12,
  33, 55; DA3; DLB 196; MTCW 1, 2

Eddison, E(ric) R(ucker)
  1882-1945 .... **TCLC 15**
  See also CA 109; 156

Eddy, Mary (Ann Morse) Baker
  1821-1910 .... **TCLC 71**
  See also CA 113; 174

Edel, (Joseph) Leon 1907-1997 .. **CLC 29, 34**
  See also CA 1-4R; 161; CANR 1, 22; DLB
  103; INT CANR-22

Eden, Emily 1797-1869 .... **NCLC 10**

Edgar, David 1948- .. **CLC 42; DAM DRAM**
  See also CA 57-60; CANR 12, 61; DLB 13,
  233; MTCW 1

Edgerton, Clyde (Carlyle) 1944- ...... **CLC 39**
  See also AAYA 17; CA 118; 134; CANR
  64; INT 134

Edgeworth, Maria 1768-1849 .... **NCLC 1, 51**
  See also DLB 116, 159, 163; SATA 21

Edmonds, Paul
  See Kuttner, Henry

Edmonds, Walter D(umaux)
  1903-1998 .... **CLC 35**
  See also CA 5-8R; CANR 2; DLB 9; MAI-
  CYA; SAAS 4; SATA 1, 27; SATA-Obit
  99

Edmondson, Wallace
  See Ellison, Harlan (Jay)

Edson, Russell **CLC 13**
  See also CA 33-36R

Edwards, Bronwen Elizabeth
  See Rose, Wendy

Edwards, G(erald) B(asil)
  1899-1976 .... **CLC 25**
  See also CA 110

Edwards, Gus 1939- .... **CLC 43**
  See also CA 108; INT 108

Edwards, Jonathan 1703-1758 .... **LC 7, 54;
  DA; DAC; DAM MST**
  See also DLB 24

Efron, Marina Ivanovna Tsvetaeva
  See Tsvetaeva (Efron), Marina (Ivanovna)

Ehle, John (Marsden, Jr.) 1925- ...... **CLC 27**
  See also CA 9-12R

Ehrenbourg, Ilya (Grigoryevich)
  See Ehrenburg, Ilya (Grigoryevich)

Ehrenburg, Ilya (Grigoryevich)
  1891-1967 .... **CLC 18, 34, 62**
  See also CA 102; 25-28R

Ehrenburg, Ilyo (Grigoryevich)
  See Ehrenburg, Ilya (Grigoryevich)

Ehrenreich, Barbara 1941- .... **CLC 110**
  See also BEST 90:4; CA 73-76; CANR 16,
  37, 62; MTCW 1, 2

Eich, Guenter 1907-1972 .... **CLC 15**
  See also CA 111; 93-96; DLB 69, 124

Eichendorff, Joseph Freiherr von
  1788-1857 .... **NCLC 8**
  See also DLB 90

Eigner, Larry **CLC 9**
  See also Eigner, Laurence (Joel)
  See also CAAS 23; DLB 5

Eigner, Laurence (Joel) 1927-1996
  See Eigner, Larry
  See also CA 9-12R; 151; CANR 6, 84; DLB
  193

Einstein, Albert 1879-1955 .... **TCLC 65**
  See also CA 121; 133; MTCW 1, 2

Eiseley, Loren Corey 1907-1977 .... **CLC 7**
  See also AAYA 5; CA 1-4R; 73-76; CANR
  6; DLBD 17

Eisenstadt, Jill 1963- .... **CLC 50**
  See also CA 140

Eisenstein, Sergei (Mikhailovich)
  1898-1948 .... **TCLC 57**
  See also CA 114; 149

Eisner, Simon
  See Kornbluth, C(yril) M.

Ekeloef, (Bengt) Gunnar
  1907-1968 ... **CLC 27; DAM POET; PC
  23**
  See also CA 123; 25-28R

Ekelof, (Bengt) Gunnar
  See Ekeloef, (Bengt) Gunnar

Ekelund, Vilhelm 1880-1949 .... **TCLC 75**

Ekwensi, C. O. D.
  See Ekwensi, Cyprian (Odiatu Duaka)

Ekwensi, Cyprian (Odiatu Duaka)
  1921- ...... **CLC 4; BLC 1; DAM MULT**
  See also BW 2, 3; CA 29-32R; CANR 18,
  42, 74; DLB 117; MTCW 1, 2; SATA 66

Elaine **TCLC 18**
  See also Leverson, Ada

El Crummo
  See Crumb, R(obert)

Elder, Lonne III 1931-1996 .... **DC 8**
  See also BLC 1; BW 1, 3; CA 81-84;
  CANR 25; DAM MULT; DLB 7, 38, 44

Eleanor of Aquitaine 1122-1204 ... **CMLC 39**

Elia
  See Lamb, Charles

Eliade, Mircea 1907-1986 .... **CLC 19**
  See also CA 65-68; 119; CANR 30, 62;
  DLB 220; MTCW 1

Eliot, A. D.
  See Jewett, (Theodora) Sarah Orne

Eliot, Alice
  See Jewett, (Theodora) Sarah Orne

Eliot, Dan
  See Silverberg, Robert

Eliot, George 1819- . **NCLC 4, 13, 23, 41, 49,
  89; DA; DAB; DAC; DAM MST, NOV;
  PC 20; WLC**
  See also CDBLB 1832-1890; DA3; DLB
  21, 35, 55

Eliot, John 1604-1690 .... **LC 5**
  See also DLB 24

Eliot, T(homas) S(tearns)
  1888-1965 ...... **CLC 1, 2, 3, 6, 9, 10, 13,
  15, 24, 34, 41, 55, 57, 113; DA; DAB;
  DAC; DAM DRAM, MST, POET; PC
  5, 31; WLC**
  See also AAYA 28; CA 5-8R; 25-28R;
  CANR 41; CDALB 1929-1941; DA3;
  DLB 7, 10, 45, 63; DLBY 88; MTCW 1,
  2

Elizabeth 1866-1941 .... **TCLC 41**

Elkin, Stanley L(awrence)
  1930-1995 .. **CLC 4, 6, 9, 14, 27, 51, 91;
  DAM NOV, POP; SSC 12**
  See also CA 9-12R; 148; CANR 8, 46; DLB
  2, 28; DLBY 80; INT CANR-8; MTCW
  1, 2

Elledge, Scott **CLC 34**

Elliot, Don
See Silverberg, Robert
Elliott, Don
See Silverberg, Robert
Elliott, George P(aul) 1918-1980 .... **CLC 2**
See also CA 1-4R; 97-100; CANR 2
Elliott, Janice 1931-1995 .... **CLC 47**
See also CA 13-16R; CANR 8, 29, 84; DLB 14; SATA 119
Elliott, Sumner Locke 1917-1991 ..... **CLC 38**
See also CA 5-8R; 134; CANR 2, 21
Elliott, William
See Bradbury, Ray (Douglas)
Ellis, A. E. CLC 7
Ellis, Alice Thomas CLC 40
See also Haycraft, Anna (Margaret)
See also DLB 194; MTCW 1
Ellis, Bret Easton 1964- ..... **CLC 39, 71, 117; DAM POP**
See also AAYA 2; CA 118; 123; CANR 51, 74; DA3; INT 123; MTCW 1
Ellis, (Henry) Havelock
1859-1939 .... **TCLC 14**
See also CA 109; 169; DLB 190
Ellis, Landon
See Ellison, Harlan (Jay)
Ellis, Trey 1962- .... **CLC 55**
See also CA 146; CANR 92
Ellison, Harlan (Jay) 1934- ... **CLC 1, 13, 42, 139; DAM POP; SSC 14**
See also AAYA 29; CA 5-8R; CANR 5, 46; DLB 8; INT CANR-5; MTCW 1, 2
Ellison, Ralph (Waldo) 1914-1994 .... **CLC 1, 3, 11, 54, 86, 114; BLC 1; DA; DAB; DAC; DAM MST, MULT, NOV; SSC 26; WLC**
See also AAYA 19; BW 1, 3; CA 9-12R; 145; CANR 24, 53; CDALB 1941-1968; DA3; DLB 2, 76, 227; DLBY 94; MTCW 1, 2
Ellmann, Lucy (Elizabeth) 1956- ..... **CLC 61**
See also CA 128
Ellmann, Richard (David)
1918-1987 .... **CLC 50**
See also BEST 89:2; CA 1-4R; 122; CANR 2, 28, 61; DLB 103; DLBY 87; MTCW 1, 2
Elman, Richard (Martin)
1934-1997 .... **CLC 19**
See also CA 17-20R; 163; CAAS 3; CANR 47
Elron
See Hubbard, L(afayette) Ron(ald)
Eluard, Paul TCLC 7, 41
See also Grindel, Eugene
Elyot, Sir Thomas 1490(?)-1546 .... **LC 11**
Elytis, Odysseus 1911-1996 .... **CLC 15, 49, 100; DAM POET; PC 21**
See also CA 102; 151; CANR 94; MTCW 1, 2
Emecheta, (Florence Onye) Buchi
1944- .. **CLC 14, 48, 128; BLC 2; DAM MULT**
See also BW 2, 3; CA 81-84; CANR 27, 81; DA3; DLB 117; MTCW 1, 2; SATA 66
Emerson, Mary Moody
1774-1863 .... **NCLC 66**
Emerson, Ralph Waldo 1803-1882 . **NCLC 1, 38; DA; DAB; DAC; DAM MST, POET; PC 18; WLC**
See also CDALB 1640-1865; DA3; DLB 1, 59, 73, 223
Eminescu, Mihail 1850-1889 .... **NCLC 33**
Empson, William 1906-1984 ... **CLC 3, 8, 19, 33, 34**
See also CA 17-20R; 112; CANR 31, 61; DLB 20; MTCW 1, 2

Enchi, Fumiko (Ueda) 1905-1986 ..... **CLC 31**
See also CA 129; 121; DLB 182
Ende, Michael (Andreas Helmuth)
1929-1995 .... **CLC 31**
See also CA 118; 124; 149; CANR 36; CLR 14; DLB 75; MAICYA; SATA 61; SATA-Brief 42; SATA-Obit 86
Endo, Shusaku 1923-1996 ..... **CLC 7, 14, 19, 54, 99; DAM NOV**
See also CA 29-32R; 153; CANR 21, 54; DA3; DLB 182; MTCW 1, 2
Engel, Marian 1933-1985 .... **CLC 36**
See also CA 25-28R; CANR 12; DLB 53; INT CANR-12
Engelhardt, Frederick
See Hubbard, L(afayette) Ron(ald)
Engels, Friedrich 1820-1895 .... **NCLC 85**
See also DLB 129
Enright, D(ennis) J(oseph) 1920- .. **CLC 4, 8, 31**
See also CA 1-4R; CANR 1, 42, 83; DLB 27; SATA 25
Enzensberger, Hans Magnus
1929- .... **CLC 43; PC 28**
See also CA 116; 119
Ephron, Nora 1941- .... **CLC 17, 31**
See also AAYA 35; AITN 2; CA 65-68; CANR 12, 39, 83
Epicurus 341B.C.-270B.C. .... **CMLC 21**
See also DLB 176
Epsilon
See Betjeman, John
Epstein, Daniel Mark 1948- .... **CLC 7**
See also CA 49-52; CANR 2, 53, 90
Epstein, Jacob 1956- .... **CLC 19**
See also CA 114
Epstein, Jean 1897-1953 .... **TCLC 92**
Epstein, Joseph 1937- .... **CLC 39**
See also CA 112; 119; CANR 50, 65
Epstein, Leslie 1938- .... **CLC 27**
See also CA 73-76; CAAS 12; CANR 23, 69
Equiano, Olaudah 1745(?)-1797 .... **LC 16; BLC 2; DAM MULT**
See also DLB 37, 50
ER TCLC 33
See also CA 160; DLB 85
Erasmus, Desiderius 1469(?)-1536 ...... **LC 16**
Erdman, Paul E(mil) 1932- .... **CLC 25**
See also AITN 1; CA 61-64; CANR 13, 43, 84
Erdrich, Louise 1954- .... **CLC 39, 54, 120; DAM MULT, NOV, POP**
See also AAYA 10; BEST 89:1; CA 114; CANR 41, 62; CDALBS; DA3; DLB 152, 175, 206; MTCW 1; NNAL; SATA 94
Erenburg, Ilya (Grigoryevich)
See Ehrenburg, Ilya (Grigoryevich)
Erickson, Stephen Michael 1950-
See Erickson, Steve
See also CA 129
Erickson, Steve 1950- .... **CLC 64**
See also Erickson, Stephen Michael
See also CANR 60, 68
Ericson, Walter
See Fast, Howard (Melvin)
Eriksson, Buntel
See Bergman, (Ernst) Ingmar
Ernaux, Annie 1940- .... **CLC 88**
See also CA 147; CANR 93
Erskine, John 1879-1951 .... **TCLC 84**
See also CA 112; 159; DLB 9, 102
Eschenbach, Wolfram von
See Wolfram von Eschenbach
Eseki, Bruno
See Mphahlele, Ezekiel

Esenin, Sergei (Alexandrovich)
1895-1925 .... **TCLC 4**
See also CA 104
Eshleman, Clayton 1935- .... **CLC 7**
See also CA 33-36R; CAAS 6; CANR 93; DLB 5
Espriella, Don Manuel Alvarez
See Southey, Robert
Espriu, Salvador 1913-1985 .... **CLC 9**
See also CA 154; 115; DLB 134
Espronceda, Jose de 1808-1842 ..... **NCLC 39**
Esquivel, Laura 1951(?)-
See also AAYA 29; CA 143; CANR 68; DA3; HLCS 1; MTCW 1
Esse, James
See Stephens, James
Esterbrook, Tom
See Hubbard, L(afayette) Ron(ald)
Estleman, Loren D. 1952- ..... **CLC 48; DAM NOV, POP**
See also AAYA 27; CA 85-88; CANR 27, 74; DA3; DLB 226; INT CANR-27; MTCW 1, 2
Euclid 306B.C.-283B.C. .... **CMLC 25**
Eugenides, Jeffrey 1960(?)- .... **CLC 81**
See also CA 144
Euripides c. 485B.C.-406B.C. .... **CMLC 23; DA; DAB; DAC; DAM DRAM, MST; DC 4; WLCS**
See also DA3; DLB 176
Evan, Evin
See Faust, Frederick (Schiller)
Evans, Caradoc 1878-1945 ... **TCLC 85; SSC 43**
Evans, Evan
See Faust, Frederick (Schiller)
Evans, Marian
See Eliot, George
Evans, Mary Ann
See Eliot, George
Evarts, Esther
See Benson, Sally
Everett, Percival 1956-
See Everett, Percival L.
Everett, Percival L. 1956- .... **CLC 57**
See also Everett, Percival
See also BW 2; CA 129; CANR 94
Everson, R(onald) G(ilmour) 1903- . **CLC 27**
See also CA 17-20R; DLB 88
Everson, William (Oliver)
1912-1994 .... **CLC 1, 5, 14**
See also CA 9-12R; 145; CANR 20; DLB 212; MTCW 1
Evtushenko, Evgenii Aleksandrovich
See Yevtushenko, Yevgeny (Alexandrovich)
Ewart, Gavin (Buchanan)
1916-1995 .... **CLC 13, 46**
See also CA 89-92; 150; CANR 17, 46; DLB 40; MTCW 1
Ewers, Hanns Heinz 1871-1943 ..... **TCLC 12**
See also CA 109; 149
Ewing, Frederick R.
See Sturgeon, Theodore (Hamilton)
Exley, Frederick (Earl) 1929-1992 .... **CLC 6, 11**
See also AITN 2; CA 81-84; 138; DLB 143; DLBY 81
Eynhardt, Guillermo
See Quiroga, Horacio (Sylvestre)
Ezekiel, Nissim 1924- .... **CLC 61**
See also CA 61-64
Ezekiel, Tish O'Dowd 1943- .... **CLC 34**
See also CA 129
Fadeyev, A.
See Bulgya, Alexander Alexandrovich
Fadeyev, Alexander TCLC 53
See also Bulgya, Alexander Alexandrovich
Fagen, Donald 1948- .... **CLC 26**

Fainzilberg, Ilya Arnoldovich 1897-1937
   See Ilf, Ilya
   See also CA 120; 165
Fair, Ronald L. 1932- .... **CLC 18**
   See also BW 1; CA 69-72; CANR 25; DLB
   33
Fairbairn, Roger
   See Carr, John Dickson
Fairbairns, Zoe (Ann) 1948- .... **CLC 32**
   See also CA 103; CANR 21, 85
Fairman, Paul W. 1916-1977
   See Queen, Ellery
   See also CA 114
Falco, Gian
   See Papini, Giovanni
Falconer, James
   See Kirkup, James
Falconer, Kenneth
   See Kornbluth, C(yril) M.
Falkland, Samuel
   See Heijermans, Herman
Fallaci, Oriana 1930- .... **CLC 11, 110**
   See also CA 77-80; CANR 15, 58; MTCW
   1
Faludi, Susan 1959- .... **CLC 140**
   See also CA 138; MTCW 1
Faludy, George 1913- .... **CLC 42**
   See also CA 21-24R
Faludy, Gyoergy
   See Faludy, George
Fanon, Frantz 1925-1961 ... **CLC 74; BLC 2;**
   DAM MULT
   See also BW 1; CA 116; 89-92
Fanshawe, Ann 1625-1680 .... **LC 11**
Fante, John (Thomas) 1911-1983 ..... **CLC 60**
   See also CA 69-72; 109; CANR 23; DLB
   130; DLBY 83
Farah, Nuruddin 1945- .. **CLC 53, 137; BLC**
   2; DAM MULT
   See also BW 2, 3; CA 106; CANR 81; DLB
   125
Fargue, Leon-Paul 1876(?)-1947 .... **TCLC 11**
   See also CA 109
Farigoule, Louis
   See Romains, Jules
Farina, Richard 1936(?)-1966 .... **CLC 9**
   See also CA 81-84; 25-28R
Farley, Walter (Lorimer)
   1915-1989 .... **CLC 17**
   See also CA 17-20R; CANR 8, 29, 84; DLB
   22; JRDA; MAICYA; SATA 2, 43
Farmer, Philip Jose 1918- .... **CLC 1, 19**
   See also AAYA 28; CA 1-4R; CANR 4, 35;
   DLB 8; MTCW 1; SATA 93
Farquhar, George 1677-1707 ... **LC 21; DAM**
   DRAM
   See also DLB 84
Farrell, J(ames) G(ordon)
   1935-1979 .... **CLC 6**
   See also CA 73-76; 89-92; CANR 36; DLB
   14; MTCW 1
Farrell, James T(homas) 1904-1979 . **CLC 1,**
   4, 8, 11, 66; SSC 28
   See also CA 5-8R; 89-92; CANR 9, 61;
   DLB 4, 9, 86; DLBD 2; MTCW 1, 2
Farren, Richard J.
   See Betjeman, John
Farren, Richard M.
   See Betjeman, John
Fassbinder, Rainer Werner
   1946-1982 .... **CLC 20**
   See also CA 93-96; 106; CANR 31
Fast, Howard (Melvin) 1914- .. **CLC 23, 131;**
   DAM NOV
   See also AAYA 16; CA 1-4R, 181; CAAE
   181; CAAS 18; CANR 1, 33, 54, 75; DLB
   9; INT CANR-33; MTCW 1; SATA 7;
   SATA-Essay 107

Faulcon, Robert
   See Holdstock, Robert P.
Faulkner, William (Cuthbert)
   1897-1962 .... **CLC 1, 3, 6, 8, 9, 11, 14,**
   18, 28, 52, 68; DA; DAB; DAC; DAM
   MST, NOV; SSC 1, 35, 42; WLC
   See also AAYA 7; CA 81-84; CANR 33;
   CDALB 1929-1941; DA3; DLB 9, 11, 44,
   102; DLBD 2; DLBY 86, 97; MTCW 1, 2
Fauset, Jessie Redmon
   1884(?)-1961 .... **CLC 19, 54; BLC 2;**
   DAM MULT
   See also BW 1; CA 109; CANR 83; DLB
   51
Faust, Frederick (Schiller)
   1892-1944(?) .... **TCLC 49; DAM POP**
   See also CA 108; 152
Faust, Irvin 1924- .... **CLC 8**
   See also CA 33-36R; CANR 28, 67; DLB
   2, 28; DLBY 80
Fawkes, Guy
   See Benchley, Robert (Charles)
Fearing, Kenneth (Flexner)
   1902-1961 .... **CLC 51**
   See also CA 93-96; CANR 59; DLB 9
Fecamps, Elise
   See Creasey, John
Federman, Raymond 1928- .... **CLC 6, 47**
   See also CA 17-20R; CAAS 8; CANR 10,
   43, 83; DLBY 80
Federspiel, J(uerg) F. 1931- .... **CLC 42**
   See also CA 146
Feiffer, Jules (Ralph) 1929- ..... **CLC 2, 8, 64;**
   DAM DRAM
   See also AAYA 3; CA 17-20R; CANR 30,
   59; DLB 7, 44; INT CANR-30; MTCW
   1; SATA 8, 61, 111
Feige, Hermann Albert Otto Maximilian
   See Traven, B.
Feinberg, David B. 1956-1994 .... **CLC 59**
   See also CA 135; 147
Feinstein, Elaine 1930- .... **CLC 36**
   See also CA 69-72; CAAS 1; CANR 31,
   68; DLB 14, 40; MTCW 1
Feldman, Irving (Mordecai) 1928- ..... **CLC 7**
   See also CA 1-4R; CANR 1; DLB 169
Felix-Tchicaya, Gerald
   See Tchicaya, Gerald Felix
Fellini, Federico 1920-1993 .... **CLC 16, 85**
   See also CA 65-68; 143; CANR 33
Felsen, Henry Gregor 1916-1995 ..... **CLC 17**
   See also CA 1-4R; 180; CANR 1; SAAS 2;
   SATA 1
Fenno, Jack
   See Calisher, Hortense
Fenollosa, Ernest (Francisco)
   1853-1908 .... **TCLC 91**
Fenton, James Martin 1949- .... **CLC 32**
   See also CA 102; DLB 40
Ferber, Edna 1887-1968 .... **CLC 18, 93**
   See also AITN 1; CA 5-8R; 25-28R; CANR
   68; DLB 9, 28, 86; MTCW 1, 2; SATA 7
Ferdowsi, Abu'l Qasem 940-1020 . **CMLC 43**
Ferguson, Helen
   See Kavan, Anna
Ferguson, Niall 1967- .... **CLC 134**
Ferguson, Samuel 1810-1886 .... **NCLC 33**
   See also DLB 32
Fergusson, Robert 1750-1774 .... **LC 29**
   See also DLB 109
Ferling, Lawrence
   See Ferlinghetti, Lawrence (Monsanto)
Ferlinghetti, Lawrence (Monsanto)
   1919(?)- .... **CLC 2, 6, 10, 27, 111; DAM**
   POET; PC 1
   See also CA 5-8R; CANR 3, 41, 73;
   CDALB 1941-1968; DA3; DLB 5, 16;
   MTCW 1, 2

Fern, Fanny 1811-1872
   See Parton, Sara Payson Willis
Fernandez, Vicente Garcia Huidobro
   See Huidobro Fernandez, Vicente Garcia
Ferre, Rosario 1942- ...... **CLC 139; HLCS 1;**
   SSC 36
   See also CA 131; CANR 55, 81; DLB 145;
   HW 1, 2; MTCW 1
Ferrer, Gabriel (Francisco Victor) Miro
   See Miro (Ferrer), Gabriel (Francisco
   Victor)
Ferrier, Susan (Edmonstone)
   1782-1854 .... **NCLC 8**
   See also DLB 116
Ferrigno, Robert 1948(?)- .... **CLC 65**
   See also CA 140
Ferron, Jacques 1921-1985 .... **CLC 94; DAC**
   See also CA 117; 129; DLB 60
Feuchtwanger, Lion 1884-1958 .... **TCLC 3**
   See also CA 104; 187; DLB 66
Feuillet, Octave 1821-1890 .... **NCLC 45**
   See also DLB 192
Feydeau, Georges (Leon Jules Marie)
   1862-1921 .... **TCLC 22; DAM DRAM**
   See also CA 113; 152; CANR 84; DLB 192
Fichte, Johann Gottlieb
   1762-1814 .... **NCLC 62**
   See also DLB 90
Ficino, Marsilio 1433-1499 .... **LC 12**
Fiedeler, Hans
   See Doeblin, Alfred
Fiedler, Leslie A(aron) 1917- .. **CLC 4, 13, 24**
   See also CA 9-12R; CANR 7, 63; DLB 28,
   67; MTCW 1, 2
Field, Andrew 1938- .... **CLC 44**
   See also CA 97-100; CANR 25
Field, Eugene 1850-1895 .... **NCLC 3**
   See also DLB 23, 42, 140; DLBD 13; MAI-
   CYA; SATA 16
Field, Gans T.
   See Wellman, Manly Wade
Field, Michael 1915-1971 .... **TCLC 43**
   See also CA 29-32R
Field, Peter
   See Hobson, Laura Z(ametkin)
Fielding, Henry 1707-1754 ..... **LC 1, 46; DA;**
   DAB; DAC; DAM DRAM, MST, NOV;
   WLC
   See also CDBLB 1660-1789; DA3; DLB
   39, 84, 101
Fielding, Sarah 1710-1768 .... **LC 1, 44**
   See also DLB 39
Fields, W. C. 1880-1946 .... **TCLC 80**
   See also DLB 44
Fierstein, Harvey (Forbes) 1954- .... **CLC 33;**
   DAM DRAM, POP
   See also CA 123; 129; DA3
Figes, Eva 1932- .... **CLC 31**
   See also CA 53-56; CANR 4, 44, 83; DLB
   14
Finch, Anne 1661-1720 .... **LC 3; PC 21**
   See also DLB 95
Finch, Robert (Duer Claydon)
   1900- .... **CLC 18**
   See also CA 57-60; CANR 9, 24, 49; DLB
   88
Findley, Timothy 1930- . **CLC 27, 102; DAC;**
   DAM MST
   See also CA 25-28R; CANR 12, 42, 69;
   DLB 53
Fink, William
   See Mencken, H(enry) L(ouis)
Firbank, Louis 1942-
   See Reed, Lou
   See also CA 117
Firbank, (Arthur Annesley) Ronald
   1886-1926 .... **TCLC 1**
   See also CA 104; 177; DLB 36

Fisher, Dorothy (Frances) Canfield
  1879-1958 .... **TCLC 87**
  See also CA 114; 136; CANR 80; DLB 9,
  102; MAICYA; YABC 1
Fisher, M(ary) F(rances) K(ennedy)
  1908-1992 .... **CLC 76, 87**
  See also CA 77-80; 138; CANR 44; MTCW
  1
Fisher, Roy 1930- .... **CLC 25**
  See also CA 81-84; CAAS 10; CANR 16;
  DLB 40
Fisher, Rudolph 1897-1934 .. **TCLC 11; BLC
  2; DAM MULT; SSC 25**
  See also BW 1, 3; CA 107; 124; CANR 80;
  DLB 51, 102
Fisher, Vardis (Alvero) 1895-1968 ...... **CLC 7**
  See also CA 5-8R; 25-28R; CANR 68; DLB
  9, 206
Fiske, Tarleton
  See Bloch, Robert (Albert)
Fitch, Clarke
  See Sinclair, Upton (Beall)
Fitch, John IV
  See Cormier, Robert (Edmund)
Fitzgerald, Captain Hugh
  See Baum, L(yman) Frank
FitzGerald, Edward 1809-1883 .... **NCLC 9**
  See also DLB 32
Fitzgerald, F(rancis) Scott (Key)
  1896-1940 .. **TCLC 1, 6, 14, 28, 55; DA;
  DAB; DAC; DAM MST, NOV; SSC 6,
  31; WLC**
  See also AAYA 24; AITN 1; CA 110; 123;
  CDALB 1917-1929; DA3; DLB 4, 9, 86;
  DLBD 1, 15, 16; DLBY 81, 96; MTCW
  1, 2
Fitzgerald, Penelope 1916- ... **CLC 19, 51, 61**
  See also CA 85-88; CAAS 10; CANR 56,
  86; DLB 14, 194; MTCW 2
Fitzgerald, Robert (Stuart)
  1910-1985 .... **CLC 39**
  See also CA 1-4R; 114; CANR 1; DLBY
  80
FitzGerald, Robert D(avid)
  1902-1987 .... **CLC 19**
  See also CA 17-20R
Fitzgerald, Zelda (Sayre)
  1900-1948 .... **TCLC 52**
  See also CA 117; 126; DLBY 84
Flanagan, Thomas (James Bonner)
  1923- .... **CLC 25, 52**
  See also CA 108; CANR 55; DLBY 80; INT
  108; MTCW 1
Flaubert, Gustave 1821-1880 .... **NCLC 2, 10,
  19, 62, 66; DA; DAB; DAC; DAM
  MST, NOV; SSC 11; WLC**
  See also DA3; DLB 119
Flecker, Herman Elroy
  See Flecker, (Herman) James Elroy
Flecker, (Herman) James Elroy
  1884-1915 .... **TCLC 43**
  See also CA 109; 150; DLB 10, 19
Fleming, Ian (Lancaster) 1908-1964 . **CLC 3,
  30; DAM POP**
  See also AAYA 26; CA 5-8R; CANR 59;
  CDBLB 1945-1960; DA3; DLB 87, 201;
  MTCW 1, 2; SATA 9
Fleming, Thomas (James) 1927- ...... **CLC 37**
  See also CA 5-8R; CANR 10; INT CANR-
  10; SATA 8
Fletcher, John 1579-1625 .... **LC 33; DC 6**
  See also CDBLB Before 1660; DLB 58
Fletcher, John Gould 1886-1950 .... **TCLC 35**
  See also CA 107; 167; DLB 4, 45
Fleur, Paul
  See Pohl, Frederik
Flooglebuckle, Al
  See Spiegelman, Art

Flora, Fletcher 1914-1969
  See Queen, Ellery
  See also CA 1-4R; CANR 3, 85
Flying Officer X
  See Bates, H(erbert) E(rnest)
Fo, Dario 1926- .... **CLC 32, 109; DAM
  DRAM; DC 10**
  See also CA 116; 128; CANR 68; DA3;
  DLBY 97; MTCW 1, 2
Fogarty, Jonathan Titulescu Esq.
  See Farrell, James T(homas)
Follett, Ken(neth Martin) 1949- ..... **CLC 18;
  DAM NOV, POP**
  See also AAYA 6; BEST 89:4; CA 81-84;
  CANR 13, 33, 54; DA3; DLB 87; DLBY
  81; INT CANR-33; MTCW 1
Fontane, Theodor 1819-1898 .... **NCLC 26**
  See also DLB 129
Foote, Horton 1916- .... **CLC 51, 91; DAM
  DRAM**
  See also CA 73-76; CANR 34, 51; DA3;
  DLB 26; INT CANR-34
Foote, Shelby 1916- ..... **CLC 75; DAM NOV,
  POP**
  See also CA 5-8R; CANR 3, 45, 74; DA3;
  DLB 2, 17; MTCW 2
Forbes, Esther 1891-1967 .... **CLC 12**
  See also AAYA 17; CA 13-14; 25-28R; CAP
  1; CLR 27; DLB 22; JRDA; MAICYA;
  SATA 2, 100
Forche, Carolyn (Louise) 1950- .... **CLC 25,
  83, 86; DAM POET; PC 10**
  See also CA 109; 117; CANR 50, 74; DA3;
  DLB 5, 193; INT 117; MTCW 1
Ford, Elbur
  See Hibbert, Eleanor Alice Burford
Ford, Ford Madox 1873-1939 ... **TCLC 1, 15,
  39, 57; DAM NOV**
  See also Chaucer, Daniel
  See also CA 104; 132; CANR 74; CDBLB
  1914-1945; DA3; DLB 162; MTCW 1, 2
Ford, Henry 1863-1947 .... **TCLC 73**
  See also CA 115; 148
Ford, John 1586-(?) .... **DC 8**
  See also CDBLB Before 1660; DAM
  DRAM; DA3; DLB 58
Ford, John 1895-1973 .... **CLC 16**
  See also CA 187; 45-48
Ford, Richard 1944- .... **CLC 46, 99**
  See also CA 69-72; CANR 11, 47, 86; DLB
  227; MTCW 1
Ford, Webster
  See Masters, Edgar Lee
Foreman, Richard 1937- .... **CLC 50**
  See also CA 65-68; CANR 32, 63
Forester, C(ecil) S(cott) 1899-1966 ... **CLC 35**
  See also CA 73-76; 25-28R; CANR 83;
  DLB 191; SATA 13
Forez
  See Mauriac, Francois (Charles)
Forman, James Douglas 1932- .... **CLC 21**
  See also AAYA 17; CA 9-12R; CANR 4,
  19, 42; JRDA; MAICYA; SATA 8, 70
Fornes, Maria Irene 1930- . **CLC 39, 61; DC
  10; HLCS 1**
  See also CA 25-28R; CANR 28, 81; DLB
  7; HW 1, 2; INT CANR-28; MTCW 1
Forrest, Leon (Richard) 1937-1997 .. **CLC 4;
  BLCS**
  See also BW 2; CA 89-92; 162; CAAS 7;
  CANR 25, 52, 87; DLB 33
Forster, E(dward) M(organ)
  1879-1970 ...... **CLC 1, 2, 3, 4, 9, 10, 13,
  15, 22, 45, 77; DA; DAB; DAC; DAM
  MST, NOV; SSC 27; WLC**
  See also AAYA 2, 37; CA 13-14; 25-28R;
  CANR 45; CAP 1; CDBLB 1914-1945;
  DA3; DLB 34, 98, 162, 178, 195; DLBD
  10; MTCW 1, 2; SATA 57

Forster, John 1812-1876 .... **NCLC 11**
  See also DLB 144, 184
Forsyth, Frederick 1938- .... **CLC 2, 5, 36;
  DAM NOV, POP**
  See also BEST 89:4; CA 85-88; CANR 38,
  62; DLB 87; MTCW 1, 2
Forten, Charlotte L. **TCLC 16; BLC 2**
  See also Grimke, Charlotte L(ottie) Forten
  See also DLB 50
Foscolo, Ugo 1778-1827 .... **NCLC 8**
Fosse, Bob **CLC 20**
  See also Fosse, Robert Louis
Fosse, Robert Louis 1927-1987
  See Fosse, Bob
  See also CA 110; 123
Foster, Stephen Collins
  1826-1864 .... **NCLC 26**
Foucault, Michel 1926-1984 . **CLC 31, 34, 69**
  See also CA 105; 113; CANR 34; MTCW
  1, 2
**Fouque, Friedrich (Heinrich Karl) de la
  Motte** 1777-1843 .... **NCLC 2**
  See also DLB 90
Fourier, Charles 1772-1837 .... **NCLC 51**
Fournier, Pierre 1916- .... **CLC 11**
  See also Gascar, Pierre
  See also CA 89-92; CANR 16, 40
Fowles, John (Philip) 1926- .. **CLC 1, 2, 3, 4,
  6, 9, 10, 15, 33, 87; DAB; DAC; DAM
  MST; SSC 33**
  See also CA 5-8R; CANR 25, 71; CDBLB
  1960 to Present; DA3; DLB 14, 139, 207;
  MTCW 1, 2; SATA 22
Fox, Paula 1923- .... **CLC 2, 8, 121**
  See also AAYA 3, 37; CA 73-76; CANR
  20, 36, 62; CLR 1, 44; DLB 52; JRDA;
  MAICYA; MTCW 1; SATA 17, 60, 120
Fox, William Price (Jr.) 1926- .... **CLC 22**
  See also CA 17-20R; CAAS 19; CANR 11;
  DLB 2; DLBY 81
Foxe, John 1516(?)-1587 .... **LC 14**
  See also DLB 132
Frame, Janet 1924- . **CLC 2, 3, 6, 22, 66, 96;
  SSC 29**
  See also Clutha, Janet Paterson Frame
France, Anatole **TCLC 9**
  See also Thibault, Jacques Anatole Francois
  See also DLB 123; MTCW 1
Francis, Claude 19(?)- .... **CLC 50**
Francis, Dick 1920- .... **CLC 2, 22, 42, 102;
  DAM POP**
  See also AAYA 5, 21; BEST 89:3; CA 5-8R;
  CANR 9, 42, 68; CDBLB 1960 to Present;
  DA3; DLB 87; INT CANR-9; MTCW 1,
  2
Francis, Robert (Churchill)
  1901-1987 .... **CLC 15**
  See also CA 1-4R; 123; CANR 1
Frank, Anne(lies Marie)
  1929-1945 . **TCLC 17; DA; DAB; DAC;
  DAM MST; WLC**
  See also AAYA 12; CA 113; 133; CANR
  68; DA3; MTCW 1, 2; SATA 87; SATA-
  Brief 42
Frank, Bruno 1887-1945 .... **TCLC 81**
  See also DLB 118
Frank, Elizabeth 1945- .... **CLC 39**
  See also CA 121; 126; CANR 78; INT 126
Frankl, Viktor E(mil) 1905-1997 ...... **CLC 93**
  See also CA 65-68; 161
Franklin, Benjamin
  See Hasek, Jaroslav (Matej Frantisek)
Franklin, Benjamin 1706-1790 .. **LC 25; DA;
  DAB; DAC; DAM MST; WLCS**
  See also CDALB 1640-1865; DA3; DLB
  24, 43, 73
**Franklin, (Stella Maria Sarah) Miles
  (Lampe)** 1879-1954 .... **TCLC 7**
  See also CA 104; 164; DLB 230; MTCW 2

Fraser, (Lady) Antonia (Pakenham)
1932- .... **CLC 32, 107**
See also CA 85-88; CANR 44, 65; MTCW
1, 2; SATA-Brief 32

Fraser, George MacDonald 1925- ...... **CLC 7**
See also CA 45-48, 180; CAAE 180; CANR
2, 48, 74; MTCW 1

Fraser, Sylvia 1935- .... **CLC 64**
See also CA 45-48; CANR 1, 16, 60

Frayn, Michael 1933- .... **CLC 3, 7, 31, 47;**
DAM DRAM, NOV
See also CA 5-8R; CANR 30, 69; DLB 13,
14, 194; MTCW 1, 2

Fraze, Candida (Merrill) 1945- .... **CLC 50**
See also CA 126

Frazer, J(ames) G(eorge)
1854-1941 .... **TCLC 32**
See also CA 118

Frazer, Robert Caine
See Creasey, John

Frazer, Sir James George
See Frazer, J(ames) G(eorge)

Frazier, Charles 1950- .... **CLC 109**
See also AAYA 34; CA 161

Frazier, Ian 1951- .... **CLC 46**
See also CA 130; CANR 54, 93

Frederic, Harold 1856-1898 .... **NCLC 10**
See also DLB 12, 23; DLBD 13

Frederick, John
See Faust, Frederick (Schiller)

Frederick the Great 1712-1786 .... **LC 14**

Fredro, Aleksander 1793-1876 .... **NCLC 8**

Freeling, Nicolas 1927- .... **CLC 38**
See also CA 49-52; CAAS 12; CANR 1,
17, 50, 84; DLB 87

Freeman, Douglas Southall
1886-1953 .... **TCLC 11**
See also CA 109; DLB 17; DLBD 17

Freeman, Judith 1946- .... **CLC 55**
See also CA 148

Freeman, Mary E(leanor) Wilkins
1852-1930 .... **TCLC 9; SSC 1**
See also CA 106; 177; DLB 12, 78, 221

Freeman, R(ichard) Austin
1862-1943 .... **TCLC 21**
See also CA 113; CANR 84; DLB 70

French, Albert 1943- .... **CLC 86**
See also BW 3; CA 167

French, Marilyn 1929- .... **CLC 10, 18, 60;**
DAM DRAM, NOV, POP
See also CA 69-72; CANR 3, 31; INT
CANR-31; MTCW 1, 2

French, Paul
See Asimov, Isaac

Freneau, Philip Morin 1752-1832 ... **NCLC 1**
See also DLB 37, 43

Freud, Sigmund 1856-1939 .... **TCLC 52**
See also CA 115; 133; CANR 69; MTCW
1, 2

Friedan, Betty (Naomi) 1921- .... **CLC 74**
See also CA 65-68; CANR 18, 45, 74;
MTCW 1, 2

Friedlander, Saul 1932- .... **CLC 90**
See also CA 117; 130; CANR 72

Friedman, B(ernard) H(arper)
1926- .... **CLC 7**
See also CA 1-4R; CANR 3, 48

Friedman, Bruce Jay 1930- ...... **CLC 3, 5, 56**
See also CA 9-12R; CANR 25, 52; DLB 2,
28; INT CANR-25

Friel, Brian 1929- .... **CLC 5, 42, 59, 115; DC
8**
See also CA 21-24R; CANR 33, 69; DLB
13; MTCW 1

Friis-Baastad, Babbis Ellinor
1921-1970 .... **CLC 12**
See also CA 17-20R; 134; SATA 7

Frisch, Max (Rudolf) 1911-1991 ... **CLC 3, 9,
14, 18, 32, 44; DAM DRAM, NOV**
See also CA 85-88; 134; CANR 32, 74;
DLB 69, 124; MTCW 1, 2

Fromentin, Eugene (Samuel Auguste)
1820-1876 .... **NCLC 10**
See also DLB 123

Frost, Frederick
See Faust, Frederick (Schiller)

Frost, Robert (Lee) 1874-1963 .. **CLC 1, 3, 4,
9, 10, 13, 15, 26, 34, 44; DA; DAB;
DAC; DAM MST, POET; PC 1; WLC**
See also AAYA 21; CA 89-92; CANR 33;
CDALB 1917-1929; CLR 67; DA3; DLB
54; DLBD 7; MTCW 1, 2; SATA 14

Froude, James Anthony
1818-1894 .... **NCLC 43**
See also DLB 18, 57, 144

Froy, Herald
See Waterhouse, Keith (Spencer)

Fry, Christopher 1907- .... **CLC 2, 10, 14;
DAM DRAM**
See also CA 17-20R; CAAS 23; CANR 9,
30, 74; DLB 13; MTCW 1, 2; SATA 66

Frye, (Herman) Northrop
1912-1991 .... **CLC 24, 70**
See also CA 5-8R; 133; CANR 8, 37; DLB
67, 68; MTCW 1, 2

Fuchs, Daniel 1909-1993 .... **CLC 8, 22**
See also CA 81-84; 142; CAAS 5; CANR
40; DLB 9, 26, 28; DLBY 93

Fuchs, Daniel 1934- .... **CLC 34**
See also CA 37-40R; CANR 14, 48

Fuentes, Carlos 1928- .. **CLC 3, 8, 10, 13, 22,
41, 60, 113; DA; DAB; DAC; DAM
MST, MULT, NOV; HLC 1; SSC 24;
WLC**
See also AAYA 4; AITN 2; CA 69-72;
CANR 10, 32, 68; DA3; DLB 113; HW
1, 2; MTCW 1, 2

Fuentes, Gregorio Lopez y
See Lopez y Fuentes, Gregorio

Fuertes, Gloria 1918- .... **PC 27**
See also CA 178, 180; DLB 108; HW 2;
SATA 115

Fugard, (Harold) Athol 1932- . **CLC 5, 9, 14,
25, 40, 80; DAM DRAM; DC 3**
See also AAYA 17; CA 85-88; CANR 32,
54; DLB 225; MTCW 1

Fugard, Sheila 1932- .... **CLC 48**
See also CA 125

Fukuyama, Francis 1952- .... **CLC 131**
See also CA 140; CANR 72

Fuller, Charles (H., Jr.) 1939- .... **CLC 25;
BLC 2; DAM DRAM, MULT; DC 1**
See also BW 2; CA 108; 112; CANR 87;
DLB 38; INT 112; MTCW 1

Fuller, Henry Blake 1857-1929 .... **TCLC 103**
See also CA 108; 177; DLB 12

Fuller, John (Leopold) 1937- .... **CLC 62**
See also CA 21-24R; CANR 9, 44; DLB 40

Fuller, Margaret
See Ossoli, Sarah Margaret (Fuller marchesa
d')

Fuller, Roy (Broadbent) 1912-1991 ... **CLC 4,
28**
See also CA 5-8R; 135; CAAS 10; CANR
53, 83; DLB 15, 20; SATA 87

Fuller, Sarah Margaret 1810-1850
See Ossoli, Sarah Margaret (Fuller marchesa
d')

Fulton, Alice 1952- .... **CLC 52**
See also CA 116; CANR 57, 88; DLB 193

Furphy, Joseph 1843-1912 .... **TCLC 25**
See also CA 163; DLB 230

Fussell, Paul 1924- .... **CLC 74**
See also BEST 90:1; CA 17-20R; CANR 8,
21, 35, 69; INT CANR-21; MTCW 1, 2

Futabatei, Shimei 1864-1909 .... **TCLC 44**
See also CA 162; DLB 180

Futrelle, Jacques 1875-1912 .... **TCLC 19**
See also CA 113; 155

Gaboriau, Emile 1835-1873 .... **NCLC 14**

Gadda, Carlo Emilio 1893-1973 .... **CLC 11**
See also CA 89-92; DLB 177

Gaddis, William 1922-1998 ... **CLC 1, 3, 6, 8,
10, 19, 43, 86**
See also CA 17-20R; 172; CANR 21, 48;
DLB 2; MTCW 1, 2

Gage, Walter
See Inge, William (Motter)

Gaines, Ernest J(ames) 1933- ...... **CLC 3, 11,
18, 86; BLC 2; DAM MULT**
See also AAYA 18; AITN 1; BW 2, 3; CA
9-12R; CANR 6, 24, 42, 75; CDALB
1968-1988; CLR 62; DA3; DLB 2, 33,
152; DLBY 80; MTCW 1, 2; SATA 86

Gaitskill, Mary 1954- .... **CLC 69**
See also CA 128; CANR 61

Galdos, Benito Perez
See Perez Galdos, Benito

Gale, Zona 1874-1938 .... **TCLC 7; DAM
DRAM**
See also CA 105; 153; CANR 84; DLB 9,
78, 228

Galeano, Eduardo (Hughes) 1940- . **CLC 72;
HLCS 1**
See also CA 29-32R; CANR 13, 32; HW 1

Galiano, Juan Valera y Alcala
See Valera y Alcala-Galiano, Juan

Galilei, Galileo 1546-1642 .... **LC 45**

Gallagher, Tess 1943- ...... **CLC 18, 63; DAM
POET; PC 9**
See also CA 106; DLB 212

Gallant, Mavis 1922- .. **CLC 7, 18, 38; DAC;
DAM MST; SSC 5**
See also CA 69-72; CANR 29, 69; DLB 53;
MTCW 1, 2

Gallant, Roy A(rthur) 1924- .... **CLC 17**
See also CA 5-8R; CANR 4, 29, 54; CLR
30; MAICYA; SATA 4, 68, 110

Gallico, Paul (William) 1897-1976 ..... **CLC 2**
See also AITN 1; CA 5-8R; 69-72; CANR
23; DLB 9, 171; MAICYA; SATA 13

Gallo, Max Louis 1932- .... **CLC 95**
See also CA 85-88

Gallois, Lucien
See Desnos, Robert

Gallup, Ralph
See Whitemore, Hugh (John)

Galsworthy, John 1867-1933 .... **TCLC 1, 45;
DA; DAB; DAC; DAM DRAM, MST,
NOV; SSC 22; WLC**
See also CA 104; 141; CANR 75; CDBLB
1890-1914; DA3; DLB 10, 34, 98, 162;
DLBD 16; MTCW 1

Galt, John 1779-1839 .... **NCLC 1**
See also DLB 99, 116, 159

Galvin, James 1951- .... **CLC 38**
See also CA 108; CANR 26

Gamboa, Federico 1864-1939 .... **TCLC 36**
See also CA 167; HW 2

Gandhi, M. K.
See Gandhi, Mohandas Karamchand

Gandhi, Mahatma
See Gandhi, Mohandas Karamchand

Gandhi, Mohandas Karamchand
1869-1948 .... **TCLC 59; DAM MULT**
See also CA 121; 132; DA3; MTCW 1, 2

Gann, Ernest Kellogg 1910-1991 ..... **CLC 23**
See also AITN 1; CA 1-4R; 136; CANR 1,
83

Garber, Eric 1943(?)-
See Holleran, Andrew
See also CANR 89

Gill, Eric 1882-1940 .... TCLC 85

Gill, Patrick
See Creasey, John

Gilliam, Terry (Vance) 1940- .... CLC 21
See also Monty Python
See also AAYA 19; CA 108; 113; CANR 35; INT 113

Gillian, Jerry
See Gilliam, Terry (Vance)

Gilliatt, Penelope (Ann Douglass) 1932-1993 .... CLC 2, 10, 13, 53
See also AITN 2; CA 13-16R; 141; CANR 49; DLB 14

Gilman, Charlotte (Anna) Perkins (Stetson) 1860-1935 .... TCLC 9, 37; SSC 13
See also CA 106; 150; DLB 221; MTCW 1

Gilmour, David 1949- .... CLC 35
See also CA 138, 147

Gilpin, William 1724-1804 .... NCLC 30

Gilray, J. D.
See Mencken, H(enry) L(ouis)

Gilroy, Frank D(aniel) 1925- .... CLC 2
See also CA 81-84; CANR 32, 64, 86; DLB 7

Gilstrap, John 1957(?)- .... CLC 99
See also CA 160

Ginsberg, Allen 1926-1997 .... CLC 1, 2, 3, 4, 6, 13, 36, 69, 109; DA; DAB; DAC; DAM MST, POET; PC 4; WLC
See also AAYA 33; AITN 1; CA 1-4R; 157; CANR 2, 41, 63; CDALB 1941-1968; DA3; DLB 5, 16, 169; MTCW 1, 2

Ginzburg, Natalia 1916-1991 .... CLC 5, 11, 54, 70
See also CA 85-88; 135; CANR 33; DLB 177; MTCW 1, 2

Giono, Jean 1895-1970 .... CLC 4, 11
See also CA 45-48; 29-32R; CANR 2, 35; DLB 72; MTCW 1

Giovanni, Nikki 1943- .... CLC 2, 4, 19, 64, 117; BLC 2; DA; DAB; DAC; DAM MST, MULT, POET; PC 19; WLCS
See also AAYA 22; AITN 1; BW 2, 3; CA 29-32R; CAAS 6; CANR 18, 41, 60, 91; CDALBS; CLR 6; DA3; DLB 5, 41; INT CANR-18; MAICYA; MTCW 1, 2; SATA 24, 107

Giovene, Andrea 1904- .... CLC 7
See also CA 85-88

Gippius, Zinaida (Nikolayevna) 1869-1945
See Hippius, Zinaida
See also CA 106

Giraudoux, (Hippolyte) Jean 1882-1944 .... TCLC 2, 7; DAM DRAM
See also CA 104; DLB 65

Gironella, Jose Maria 1917- .... CLC 11
See also CA 101

Gissing, George (Robert) 1857-1903 .... TCLC 3, 24, 47; SSC 37
See also CA 105; 167; DLB 18, 135, 184

Giurlani, Aldo
See Palazzeschi, Aldo

Gladkov, Fyodor (Vasilyevich) 1883-1958 .... TCLC 27
See also CA 170

Glanville, Brian (Lester) 1931- .... CLC 6
See also CA 5-8R; CAAS 9; CANR 3, 70; DLB 15, 139; SATA 42

Glasgow, Ellen (Anderson Gholson) 1873-1945 .... TCLC 2, 7; SSC 34
See also CA 104; 164; DLB 9, 12; MTCW 2

Glaspell, Susan 1882(?)-1948 . TCLC 55; DC 10; SSC 41
See also CA 110; 154; DLB 7, 9, 78, 228; YABC 2

Glassco, John 1909-1981 .... CLC 9
See also CA 13-16R; 102; CANR 15; DLB 68

Glasscock, Amnesia
See Steinbeck, John (Ernst)

Glasser, Ronald J. 1940(?)- .... CLC 37

Glassman, Joyce
See Johnson, Joyce

Glendinning, Victoria 1937- .... CLC 50
See also CA 120; 127; CANR 59, 89; DLB 155

Glissant, Edouard 1928- . CLC 10, 68; DAM MULT
See also CA 153

Gloag, Julian 1930- .... CLC 40
See also AITN 1; CA 65-68; CANR 10, 70

Glowacki, Aleksander
See Prus, Boleslaw

Gluck, Louise (Elisabeth) 1943- .. CLC 7, 22, 44, 81; DAM POET; PC 16
See also CA 33-36R; CANR 40, 69; DA3; DLB 5; MTCW 2

Glyn, Elinor 1864-1943 .... TCLC 72
See also DLB 153

Gobineau, Joseph Arthur (Comte) de 1816-1882 .... NCLC 17
See also DLB 123

Godard, Jean-Luc 1930- .... CLC 20
See also CA 93-96

Godden, (Margaret) Rumer 1907-1998 .... CLC 53
See also AAYA 6; CA 5-8R; 172; CANR 4, 27, 36, 55, 80; CLR 20; DLB 161; MAICYA; SAAS 12; SATA 3, 36; SATA-Obit 109

Godoy Alcayaga, Lucila 1889-1957 .... TCLC 2; DAM MULT; HLC 2; PC 32
See also BW 2; CA 104; 131; CANR 81; HW 1, 2; MTCW 1, 2

Godwin, Gail (Kathleen) 1937- ..... CLC 5, 8, 22, 31, 69, 125; DAM POP
See also CA 29-32R; CANR 15, 43, 69; DA3; DLB 6, 234; INT CANR-15; MTCW 1, 2

Godwin, William 1756-1836 .... NCLC 14
See also CDBLB 1789-1832; DLB 39, 104, 142, 158, 163

Goebbels, Josef
See Goebbels, (Paul) Joseph

Goebbels, (Paul) Joseph 1897-1945 .... TCLC 68
See also CA 115; 148

Goebbels, Joseph Paul
See Goebbels, (Paul) Joseph

Goethe, Johann Wolfgang von 1749-1832 ...... NCLC 4, 22, 34, 90; DA; DAB; DAC; DAM DRAM, MST, POET; PC 5; SSC 38; WLC
See also DA3; DLB 94

Gogarty, Oliver St. John 1878-1957 .... TCLC 15
See also CA 109; 150; DLB 15, 19

Gogol, Nikolai (Vasilyevich) 1809-1852 . NCLC 5, 15, 31; DA; DAB; DAC; DAM DRAM, MST; DC 1; SSC 4, 29; WLC
See also DLB 198

Goines, Donald 1937(?)-1974 . CLC 80; BLC 2; DAM MULT, POP
See also AITN 1; BW 1, 3; CA 124; 114; CANR 82; DA3; DLB 33

Gold, Herbert 1924- .... CLC 4, 7, 14, 42
See also CA 9-12R; CANR 17, 45; DLB 2; DLBY 81

Goldbarth, Albert 1948- .... CLC 5, 38
See also CA 53-56; CANR 6, 40; DLB 120

Goldberg, Anatol 1910-1982 .... CLC 34
See also CA 131; 117

Goldemberg, Isaac 1945- .... CLC 52
See also CA 69-72; CAAS 12; CANR 11, 32; HW 1

Golding, William (Gerald) 1911-1993 ..... CLC 1, 2, 3, 8, 10, 17, 27, 58, 81; DA; DAB; DAC; DAM MST, NOV; WLC
See also AAYA 5; CA 5-8R; 141; CANR 13, 33, 54; CDBLB 1945-1960; DA3; DLB 15, 100; MTCW 1, 2

Goldman, Emma 1869-1940 .... TCLC 13
See also CA 110; 150; DLB 221

Goldman, Francisco 1954- .... CLC 76
See also CA 162

Goldman, William (W.) 1931- ...... CLC 1, 48
See also CA 9-12R; CANR 29, 69; DLB 44

Goldmann, Lucien 1913-1970 .... CLC 24
See also CA 25-28; CAP 2

Goldoni, Carlo 1707-1793 .... LC 4; DAM DRAM

Goldsberry, Steven 1949- .... CLC 34
See also CA 131

Goldsmith, Oliver 1728-1774 . LC 2, 48; DA; DAB; DAC; DAM DRAM, MST, NOV, POET; DC 8; WLC
See also CDBLB 1660-1789; DLB 39, 89, 104, 109, 142; SATA 26

Goldsmith, Peter
See Priestley, J(ohn) B(oynton)

Gombrowicz, Witold 1904-1969 .... CLC 4, 7, 11, 49; DAM DRAM
See also CA 19-20; 25-28R; CAP 2

Gomez de la Serna, Ramon 1888-1963 .... CLC 9
See also CA 153; 116; CANR 79; HW 1, 2

Goncharov, Ivan Alexandrovich 1812-1891 .... NCLC 1, 63

Goncourt, Edmond (Louis Antoine Huot) de 1822-1896 .... NCLC 7
See also DLB 123

Goncourt, Jules (Alfred Huot) de 1830-1870 .... NCLC 7
See also DLB 123

Gontier, Fernande 19(?)- .... CLC 50

Gonzalez Martinez, Enrique 1871-1952 .... TCLC 72
See also CA 166; CANR 81; HW 1, 2

Goodman, Paul 1911-1972 ... CLC 1, 2, 4, 7
See also CA 19-20; 37-40R; CANR 34; CAP 2; DLB 130; MTCW 1

Gordimer, Nadine 1923- ...... CLC 3, 5, 7, 10, 18, 33, 51, 70, 123; DA; DAB; DAC; DAM MST, NOV; SSC 17; WLCS
See also CA 5-8R; CANR 3, 28, 56, 88; DA3; DLB 225; INT CANR-28; MTCW 1, 2

Gordon, Adam Lindsay 1833-1870 .... NCLC 21
See also DLB 230

Gordon, Caroline 1895-1981 . CLC 6, 13, 29, 83; SSC 15
See also CA 11-12; 103; CANR 36; CAP 1; DLB 4, 9, 102; DLBD 17; DLBY 81; MTCW 1, 2

Gordon, Charles William 1860-1937
See Connor, Ralph
See also CA 109

Gordon, Mary (Catherine) 1949- .... CLC 13, 22, 128
See also CA 102; CANR 44, 92; DLB 6; DLBY 81; INT 102; MTCW 1

Gordon, N. J.
See Bosman, Herman Charles

Gordon, Sol 1923- .... CLC 26
See also CA 53-56; CANR 4; SATA 11

Gordone, Charles 1925-1995 .... CLC 1, 4; DAM DRAM; DC 8
See also BW 1, 3; CA 93-96; 180; 150; CAAE 180; CANR 55; DLB 7; INT 93-96; MTCW 1

Gore, Catherine 1800-1861 .... NCLC 65
See also DLB 116

Griffith, D(avid Lewelyn) W(ark)
1875(?)-1948 .... **TCLC 68**
See also CA 119; 150; CANR 80
Griffith, Lawrence
See Griffith, D(avid Lewelyn) W(ark)
Griffiths, Trevor 1935- .... **CLC 13, 52**
See also CA 97-100; CANR 45; DLB 13
Griggs, Sutton (Elbert)
1872-1930 .... **TCLC 77**
See also CA 123; 186; DLB 50
Grigson, Geoffrey (Edward Harvey)
1905-1985 .... **CLC 7, 39**
See also CA 25-28R; 118; CANR 20, 33;
DLB 27; MTCW 1, 2
Grillparzer, Franz 1791-1872 .. **NCLC 1; DC
14; SSC 37**
See also DLB 133
Grimble, Reverend Charles James
See Eliot, T(homas) S(tearns)
Grimke, Charlotte L(ottie) Forten
1837(?)-1914
See Forten, Charlotte L.
See also BW 1; CA 117; 124; DAM MULT,
POET
Grimm, Jacob Ludwig Karl
1785-1863 .... **NCLC 3, 77; SSC 36**
See also DLB 90; MAICYA; SATA 22
Grimm, Wilhelm Karl 1786-1859 .. **NCLC 3,
77; SSC 36**
See also DLB 90; MAICYA; SATA 22
**Grimmelshausen, Johann Jakob Christoffel
von** 1621-1676 .... **LC 6**
See also DLB 168
Grindel, Eugene 1895-1952
See Eluard, Paul
See also CA 104
Grisham, John 1955- .... **CLC 84; DAM POP**
See also AAYA 14; CA 138; CANR 47, 69;
DA3; MTCW 2
Grossman, David 1954- .... **CLC 67**
See also CA 138
Grossman, Vasily (Semenovich)
1905-1964 .... **CLC 41**
See also CA 124; 130; MTCW 1
Grove, Frederick Philip TCLC 4
See also Greve, Felix Paul (Berthold
Friedrich)
See also DLB 92
Grubb
See Crumb, R(obert)
Grumbach, Doris (Isaac) 1918- . **CLC 13, 22,
64**
See also CA 5-8R; CAAS 2; CANR 9, 42,
70; INT CANR-9; MTCW 2
Grundtvig, Nicolai Frederik Severin
1783-1872 .... **NCLC 1**
Grunge
See Crumb, R(obert)
Grunwald, Lisa 1959- .... **CLC 44**
See also CA 120
Guare, John 1938- .... **CLC 8, 14, 29, 67;
DAM DRAM**
See also CA 73-76; CANR 21, 69; DLB 7;
MTCW 1, 2
Gudjonsson, Halldor Kiljan 1902-1998
See Laxness, Halldor
See also CA 103; 164
Guenter, Erich
See Eich, Guenter
Guest, Barbara 1920- .... **CLC 34**
See also CA 25-28R; CANR 11, 44, 84;
DLB 5, 193
Guest, Edgar A(lbert) 1881-1959 ... **TCLC 95**
See also CA 112; 168
Guest, Judith (Ann) 1936- .... **CLC 8, 30;
DAM NOV, POP**
See also AAYA 7; CA 77-80; CANR 15,
75; DA3; INT CANR-15; MTCW 1, 2

Guevara, Che CLC 87; HLC 1
See also Guevara (Serna), Ernesto
Guevara (Serna), Ernesto
1928-1967 .... **CLC 87; DAM MULT;
HLC 1**
See also Guevara, Che
See also CA 127; 111; CANR 56; HW 1
Guicciardini, Francesco 1483-1540 ..... **LC 49**
Guild, Nicholas M. 1944- .... **CLC 33**
See also CA 93-96
Guillemin, Jacques
See Sartre, Jean-Paul
Guillen, Jorge 1893-1984 .... **CLC 11; DAM
MULT, POET; HLCS 1**
See also CA 89-92; 112; DLB 108; HW 1
Guillen, Nicolas (Cristobal)
1902-1989 ... **CLC 48, 79; BLC 2; DAM
MST, MULT, POET; HLC 1; PC 23**
See also BW 2; CA 116; 125; 129; CANR
84; HW 1
Guillevic, (Eugene) 1907- .... **CLC 33**
See also CA 93-96
Guillois
See Desnos, Robert
Guillois, Valentin
See Desnos, Robert
Guimaraes Rosa, Joao 1908-1967
See also CA 175; HLCS 2
Guiney, Louise Imogen
1861-1920 .... **TCLC 41**
See also CA 160; DLB 54
Guiraldes, Ricardo (Guillermo)
1886-1927 .... **TCLC 39**
See also CA 131; HW 1; MTCW 1
Gumilev, Nikolai (Stepanovich)
1886-1921 .... **TCLC 60**
See also CA 165
Gunesekera, Romesh 1954- .... **CLC 91**
See also CA 159
Gunn, Bill CLC 5
See also Gunn, William Harrison
See also DLB 38
Gunn, Thom(son William) 1929- .. **CLC 3, 6,
18, 32, 81; DAM POET; PC 26**
See also CA 17-20R; CANR 9, 33; CDBLB
1960 to Present; DLB 27; INT CANR-33;
MTCW 1
Gunn, William Harrison 1934(?)-1989
See Gunn, Bill
See also AITN 1; BW 1, 3; CA 13-16R;
128; CANR 12, 25, 76
Gunnars, Kristjana 1948- .... **CLC 69**
See also CA 113; DLB 60
Gurdjieff, G(eorgei) I(vanovich)
1877(?)-1949 .... **TCLC 71**
See also CA 157
Gurganus, Allan 1947- . **CLC 70; DAM POP**
See also BEST 90:1; CA 135
Gurney, A(lbert) R(amsdell), Jr.
1930- ..... **CLC 32, 50, 54; DAM DRAM**
See also CA 77-80; CANR 32, 64
Gurney, Ivor (Bertie) 1890-1937 ... **TCLC 33**
See also CA 167
Gurney, Peter
See Gurney, A(lbert) R(amsdell), Jr.
Guro, Elena 1877-1913 .... **TCLC 56**
Gustafson, James M(oody) 1925- ... **CLC 100**
See also CA 25-28R; CANR 37
Gustafson, Ralph (Barker) 1909- ..... **CLC 36**
See also CA 21-24R; CANR 8, 45, 84; DLB
88
Gut, Gom
See Simenon, Georges (Jacques Christian)
Guterson, David 1956- .... **CLC 91**
See also CA 132; CANR 73; MTCW 2

Guthrie, A(lfred) B(ertram), Jr.
1901-1991 .... **CLC 23**
See also CA 57-60; 134; CANR 24; DLB
212; SATA 62; SATA-Obit 67
Guthrie, Isobel
See Grieve, C(hristopher) M(urray)
Guthrie, Woodrow Wilson 1912-1967
See Guthrie, Woody
See also CA 113; 93-96
Guthrie, Woody CLC 35
See also Guthrie, Woodrow Wilson
Gutierrez Najera, Manuel 1859-1895
See also HLCS 2
Guy, Rosa (Cuthbert) 1928- .... **CLC 26**
See also AAYA 4, 37; BW 2; CA 17-20R;
CANR 14, 34, 83; CLR 13; DLB 33;
JRDA; MAICYA; SATA 14, 62
Gwendolyn
See Bennett, (Enoch) Arnold
H. D. CLC 3, 8, 14, 31, 34, 73; PC 5
See also Doolittle, Hilda
H. de V.
See Buchan, John
Haavikko, Paavo Juhani 1931- .. **CLC 18, 34**
See also CA 106
Habbema, Koos
See Heijermans, Herman
Habermas, Juergen 1929- .... **CLC 104**
See also CA 109; CANR 85
Habermas, Jurgen
See Habermas, Juergen
Hacker, Marilyn 1942- ...... **CLC 5, 9, 23, 72,
91; DAM POET**
See also CA 77-80; CANR 68; DLB 120
Haeckel, Ernst Heinrich (Philipp August)
1834-1919 .... **TCLC 83**
See also CA 157
Hafiz c. 1326-1389 .... **CMLC 34**
Hafiz c. 1326-1389(?) .... **CMLC 34**
Haggard, H(enry) Rider
1856-1925 .... **TCLC 11**
See also CA 108; 148; DLB 70, 156, 174,
178; MTCW 2; SATA 16
Hagiosy, L.
See Larbaud, Valery (Nicolas)
Hagiwara Sakutaro 1886-1942 ..... **TCLC 60;
PC 18**
Haig, Fenil
See Ford, Ford Madox
Haig-Brown, Roderick (Langmere)
1908-1976 .... **CLC 21**
See also CA 5-8R; 69-72; CANR 4, 38, 83;
CLR 31; DLB 88; MAICYA; SATA 12
Hailey, Arthur 1920- ..... **CLC 5; DAM NOV,
POP**
See also AITN 2; BEST 90:3; CA 1-4R;
CANR 2, 36, 75; DLB 88; DLBY 82;
MTCW 1, 2
Hailey, Elizabeth Forsythe 1938- ..... **CLC 40**
See also CA 93-96; CAAS 1; CANR 15,
48; INT CANR-15
Haines, John (Meade) 1924- .... **CLC 58**
See also CA 17-20R; CANR 13, 34; DLB
212
Hakluyt, Richard 1552-1616 .... **LC 31**
Haldeman, Joe (William) 1943- .... **CLC 61**
See also Graham, Robert
See also CA 53-56, 179; CAAE 179; CAAS
25; CANR 6, 70, 72; DLB 8; INT
CANR-6
Hale, Sarah Josepha (Buell)
1788-1879 .... **NCLC 75**
See also DLB 1, 42, 73
Halévy, Elie 1870-1937 .... **TCLC 104**

Haley, Alex(ander Murray Palmer)
  1921-1992 . **CLC 8, 12, 76; BLC 2; DA;
  DAB; DAC; DAM MST, MULT, POP**
  See also AAYA 26; BW 2, 3; CA 77-80;
  136; CANR 61; CDALBS; DA3; DLB 38;
  MTCW 1, 2

Haliburton, Thomas Chandler
  1796-1865 .... **NCLC 15**
  See also DLB 11, 99

Hall, Donald (Andrew, Jr.) 1928- ...... **CLC 1,
  13, 37, 59; DAM POET**
  See also CA 5-8R; CAAS 7; CANR 2, 44,
  64; DLB 5; MTCW 1; SATA 23, 97

Hall, Frederic Sauser
  See Sauser-Hall, Frederic

Hall, James
  See Kuttner, Henry

Hall, James Norman 1887-1951 ..... **TCLC 23**
  See also CA 123; 173; SATA 21

Hall, Radclyffe -1943
  See Hall, (Marguerite) Radclyffe
  See also MTCW 2

Hall, (Marguerite) Radclyffe
  1886-1943 .... **TCLC 12**
  See also CA 110; 150; CANR 83; DLB 191

Hall, Rodney 1935- .... **CLC 51**
  See also CA 109; CANR 69

Halleck, Fitz-Greene 1790-1867 .... **NCLC 47**
  See also DLB 3

Halliday, Michael
  See Creasey, John

Halpern, Daniel 1945- .... **CLC 14**
  See also CA 33-36R; CANR 93

Hamburger, Michael (Peter Leopold)
  1924- .... **CLC 5, 14**
  See also CA 5-8R; CAAS 4; CANR 2, 47;
  DLB 27

Hamill, Pete 1935- .... **CLC 10**
  See also CA 25-28R; CANR 18, 71

Hamilton, Alexander
  1755(?)-1804 .... **NCLC 49**
  See also DLB 37

Hamilton, Clive
  See Lewis, C(live) S(taples)

Hamilton, Edmond 1904-1977 .... **CLC 1**
  See also CA 1-4R; CANR 3, 84; DLB 8;
  SATA 118

Hamilton, Eugene (Jacob) Lee
  See Lee-Hamilton, Eugene (Jacob)

Hamilton, Franklin
  See Silverberg, Robert

Hamilton, Gail
  See Corcoran, Barbara

Hamilton, Mollie
  See Kaye, M(ary) M(argaret)

Hamilton, (Anthony Walter) Patrick
  1904-1962 .... **CLC 51**
  See also CA 176; 113; DLB 191

Hamilton, Virginia 1936- ...... **CLC 26; DAM
  MULT**
  See also AAYA 2, 21; BW 2, 3; CA 25-28R;
  CANR 20, 37, 73; CLR 1, 11, 40; DLB
  33, 52; INT CANR-20; JRDA; MAICYA;
  MTCW 1, 2; SATA 4, 56, 79

Hammett, (Samuel) Dashiell
  1894-1961 .... **CLC 3, 5, 10, 19, 47; SSC
  17**
  See also AITN 1; CA 81-84; CANR 42;
  CDALB 1929-1941; DA3; DLB 226;
  DLBD 6; DLBY 96; MTCW 1, 2

Hammon, Jupiter 1711(?)-1800(?) . **NCLC 5;
  BLC 2; DAM MULT, POET; PC 16**
  See also DLB 31, 50

Hammond, Keith
  See Kuttner, Henry

Hamner, Earl (Henry), Jr. 1923- ...... **CLC 12**
  See also AITN 2; CA 73-76; DLB 6

Hampton, Christopher (James)
  1946- .... **CLC 4**
  See also CA 25-28R; DLB 13; MTCW 1

Hamsun, Knut **TCLC 2, 14, 49**
  See also Pedersen, Knut

Handke, Peter 1942- .... **CLC 5, 8, 10, 15, 38,
  134; DAM DRAM, NOV**
  See also CA 77-80; CANR 33, 75; DLB 85,
  124; MTCW 1, 2

Handy, W(illiam) C(hristopher)
  1873-1958 .... **TCLC 97**
  See also BW 3; CA 121; 167

Hanley, James 1901-1985 ..... **CLC 3, 5, 8, 13**
  See also CA 73-76; 117; CANR 36; DLB
  191; MTCW 1

Hannah, Barry 1942- .... **CLC 23, 38, 90**
  See also CA 108; 110; CANR 43, 68; DLB
  6, 234; INT 110; MTCW 1

Hannon, Ezra
  See Hunter, Evan

Hansberry, Lorraine (Vivian)
  1930-1965 ..... **CLC 17, 62; BLC 2; DA;
  DAB; DAC; DAM DRAM, MST,
  MULT; DC 2**
  See also AAYA 25; BW 1, 3; CA 109; 25-
  28R; CABS 3; CANR 58; CDALB 1941-
  1968; DA3; DLB 7, 38; MTCW 1, 2

Hansen, Joseph 1923- .... **CLC 38**
  See also CA 29-32R; CAAS 17; CANR 16,
  44, 66; DLB 226; INT CANR-16

Hansen, Martin A(lfred)
  1909-1955 .... **TCLC 32**
  See also CA 167; DLB 214

Hanson, Kenneth O(stlin) 1922- .... **CLC 13**
  See also CA 53-56; CANR 7

Hardwick, Elizabeth (Bruce)
  1916- .... **CLC 13; DAM NOV**
  See also CA 5-8R; CANR 3, 32, 70; DA3;
  DLB 6; MTCW 1, 2

Hardy, Thomas 1840-1928 .. **TCLC 4, 10, 18,
  32, 48, 53, 72; DA; DAB; DAC; DAM
  MST, NOV, POET; PC 8; SSC 2; WLC**
  See also CA 104; 123; CDBLB 1890-1914;
  DA3; DLB 18, 19, 135; MTCW 1, 2

Hare, David 1947- .... **CLC 29, 58, 136**
  See also CA 97-100; CANR 39, 91; DLB
  13; MTCW 1

Harewood, John
  See Van Druten, John (William)

Harford, Henry
  See Hudson, W(illiam) H(enry)

Hargrave, Leonie
  See Disch, Thomas M(ichael)

Harjo, Joy 1951- ...... **CLC 83; DAM MULT;
  PC 27**
  See also CA 114; CANR 35, 67, 91; DLB
  120, 175; MTCW 2; NNAL

Harlan, Louis R(udolph) 1922- .... **CLC 34**
  See also CA 21-24R; CANR 25, 55, 80

Harling, Robert 1951(?)- .... **CLC 53**
  See also CA 147

Harmon, William (Ruth) 1938- .... **CLC 38**
  See also CA 33-36R; CANR 14, 32, 35;
  SATA 65

Harper, F. E. W.
  See Harper, Frances Ellen Watkins

Harper, Frances E. W.
  See Harper, Frances Ellen Watkins

Harper, Frances E. Watkins
  See Harper, Frances Ellen Watkins

Harper, Frances Ellen
  See Harper, Frances Ellen Watkins

Harper, Frances Ellen Watkins
  1825-1911 ...... **TCLC 14; BLC 2; DAM
  MULT, POET; PC 21**
  See also BW 1, 3; CA 111; 125; CANR 79;
  DLB 50, 221

Harper, Michael S(teven) 1938- ... **CLC 7, 22**
  See also BW 1; CA 33-36R; CANR 24;
  DLB 41

Harper, Mrs. F. E. W.
  See Harper, Frances Ellen Watkins

Harris, Christie (Lucy) Irwin
  1907- .... **CLC 12**
  See also CA 5-8R; CANR 6, 83; CLR 47;
  DLB 88; JRDA; MAICYA; SAAS 10;
  SATA 6, 74; SATA-Essay 116

Harris, Frank 1856-1931 .... **TCLC 24**
  See also CA 109; 150; CANR 80; DLB 156,
  197

Harris, George Washington
  1814-1869 .... **NCLC 23**
  See also DLB 3, 11

Harris, Joel Chandler 1848-1908 ... **TCLC 2;
  SSC 19**
  See also CA 104; 137; CANR 80; CLR 49;
  DLB 11, 23, 42, 78, 91; MAICYA; SATA
  100; YABC 1

Harris, John (Wyndham Parkes Lucas)
  Beynon 1903-1969
  See Wyndham, John
  See also CA 102; 89-92; CANR 84; SATA
  118

Harris, MacDonald **CLC 9**
  See also Heiney, Donald (William)

Harris, Mark 1922- .... **CLC 19**
  See also CA 5-8R; CAAS 3; CANR 2, 55,
  83; DLB 2; DLBY 80

Harris, (Theodore) Wilson 1921- ..... **CLC 25**
  See also BW 2, 3; CA 65-68; CAAS 16;
  CANR 11, 27, 69; DLB 117; MTCW 1

Harrison, Elizabeth Cavanna 1909-
  See Cavanna, Betty
  See also CA 9-12R; CANR 6, 27, 85

Harrison, Harry (Max) 1925- .... **CLC 42**
  See also CA 1-4R; CANR 5, 21, 84; DLB
  8; SATA 4

Harrison, James (Thomas) 1937- ...... **CLC 6,
  14, 33, 66; SSC 19**
  See also CA 13-16R; CANR 8, 51, 79;
  DLBY 82; INT CANR-8

Harrison, Jim
  See Harrison, James (Thomas)

Harrison, Kathryn 1961- .... **CLC 70**
  See also CA 144; CANR 68

Harrison, Tony 1937- .... **CLC 43, 129**
  See also CA 65-68; CANR 44; DLB 40;
  MTCW 1

Harriss, Will(ard Irvin) 1922- .... **CLC 34**
  See also CA 111

Harson, Sley
  See Ellison, Harlan (Jay)

Hart, Ellis
  See Ellison, Harlan (Jay)

Hart, Josephine 1942(?)- .... **CLC 70; DAM
  POP**
  See also CA 138; CANR 70

Hart, Moss 1904-1961 .... **CLC 66; DAM
  DRAM**
  See also CA 109; 89-92; CANR 84; DLB 7

Harte, (Francis) Bret(t)
  1836(?)-1902 ... **TCLC 1, 25; DA; DAC;
  DAM MST; SSC 8; WLC**
  See also CA 104; 140; CANR 80; CDALB
  1865-1917; DA3; DLB 12, 64, 74, 79,
  186; SATA 26

Hartley, L(eslie) P(oles) 1895-1972 ... **CLC 2,
  22**
  See also CA 45-48; 37-40R; CANR 33;
  DLB 15, 139; MTCW 1, 2

Hartman, Geoffrey H. 1929- .... **CLC 27**
  See also CA 117; 125; CANR 79; DLB 67

Hartmann, Sadakichi 1867-1944 ... **TCLC 73**
  See also CA 157; DLB 54

Hartmann von Aue c. 1160-c.
  1205 .... **CMLC 15**
  See also DLB 138
Hartmann von Aue 1170-1210 ...... **CMLC 15**
Haruf, Kent 1943- .... **CLC 34**
  See also CA 149; CANR 91
Harwood, Ronald 1934- .... **CLC 32; DAM
  DRAM, MST**
  See also CA 1-4R; CANR 4, 55; DLB 13
Hasegawa Tatsunosuke
  See Futabatei, Shimei
Hasek, Jaroslav (Matej Frantisek)
  1883-1923 .... **TCLC 4**
  See also CA 104; 129; MTCW 1, 2
Hass, Robert 1941- ... **CLC 18, 39, 99; PC 16**
  See also CA 111; CANR 30, 50, 71; DLB
  105, 206; SATA 94
Hastings, Hudson
  See Kuttner, Henry
Hastings, Selina CLC 44
Hathorne, John 1641-1717 .... **LC 38**
Hatteras, Amelia
  See Mencken, H(enry) L(ouis)
Hatteras, Owen TCLC 18
  See also Mencken, H(enry) L(ouis); Nathan,
  George Jean
Hauptmann, Gerhart (Johann Robert)
  1862-1946 .... **TCLC 4; DAM DRAM;
  SSC 37**
  See also CA 104; 153; DLB 66, 118
Havel, Vaclav 1936- ..... **CLC 25, 58, 65, 123;
  DAM DRAM; DC 6**
  See also CA 104; CANR 36, 63; DA3; DLB
  232; MTCW 1, 2
Haviaras, Stratis CLC 33
  See also Chaviaras, Strates
Hawes, Stephen 1475(?)-1523(?) .... **LC 17**
  See also DLB 132
Hawkes, John (Clendennin Burne, Jr.)
  1925-1998 .. **CLC 1, 2, 3, 4, 7, 9, 14, 15,
  27, 49**
  See also CA 1-4R; 167; CANR 2, 47, 64;
  DLB 2, 7, 227; DLBY 80, 98; MTCW 1,
  2
Hawking, S. W.
  See Hawking, Stephen W(illiam)
Hawking, Stephen W(illiam) 1942- . **CLC 63,
  105**
  See also AAYA 13; BEST 89:1; CA 126;
  129; CANR 48; DA3; MTCW 2
Hawkins, Anthony Hope
  See Hope, Anthony
Hawthorne, Julian 1846-1934 .... **TCLC 25**
  See also CA 165
Hawthorne, Nathaniel 1804-1864 ... **NCLC 2,
  10, 17, 23, 39, 79, 95; DA; DAB; DAC;
  DAM MST, NOV; SSC 3, 29, 39; WLC**
  See also AAYA 18; CDALB 1640-1865;
  DA3; DLB 1, 74, 223; YABC 2
Haxton, Josephine Ayres 1921-
  See Douglas, Ellen
  See also CA 115; CANR 41, 83
Hayaseca y Eizaguirre, Jorge
  See Echegaray (y Eizaguirre), Jose (Maria
  Waldo)
Hayashi, Fumiko 1904-1951 .... **TCLC 27**
  See also CA 161; DLB 180
Haycraft, Anna (Margaret) 1932-
  See Ellis, Alice Thomas
  See also CA 122; CANR 85, 90; MTCW 2
Hayden, Robert E(arl) 1913-1980 . **CLC 5, 9,
  14, 37; BLC 2; DA; DAC; DAM MST,
  MULT, POET; PC 6**
  See also BW 1, 3; CA 69-72; 97-100; CABS
  2; CANR 24, 75, 82; CDALB 1941-1968;
  DLB 5, 76; MTCW 1, 2; SATA 19; SATA-
  Obit 26
Hayford, J(oseph) E(phraim) Casely
  See Casely-Hayford, J(oseph) E(phraim)

Hayman, Ronald 1932- .... **CLC 44**
  See also CA 25-28R; CANR 18, 50, 88;
  DLB 155
Hayne, Paul Hamilton 1830-1886 . **NCLC 94**
  See also DLB 3, 64, 79
Haywood, Eliza (Fowler)
  1693(?)-1756 .... **LC 1, 44**
  See also DLB 39
Hazlitt, William 1778-1830 ...... **NCLC 29, 82**
  See also DLB 110, 158
Hazzard, Shirley 1931- .... **CLC 18**
  See also CA 9-12R; CANR 4, 70; DLBY
  82; MTCW 1
Head, Bessie 1937-1986 .... **CLC 25, 67; BLC
  2; DAM MULT**
  See also BW 2, 3; CA 29-32R; 119; CANR
  25, 82; DA3; DLB 117, 225; MTCW 1, 2
Headon, (Nicky) Topper 1956(?)- ..... **CLC 30**
Heaney, Seamus (Justin) 1939- ..... **CLC 5, 7,
  14, 25, 37, 74, 91; DAB; DAM POET;
  PC 18; WLCS**
  See also CA 85-88; CANR 25, 48, 75, 91;
  CDBLB 1960 to Present; DA3; DLB 40;
  DLBY 95; MTCW 1, 2
Hearn, (Patricio) Lafcadio (Tessima Carlos)
  1850-1904 .... **TCLC 9**
  See also CA 105; 166; DLB 12, 78, 189
Hearne, Vicki 1946- .... **CLC 56**
  See also CA 139
Hearon, Shelby 1931- .... **CLC 63**
  See also AITN 2; CA 25-28R; CANR 18,
  48
Heat-Moon, William Least CLC 29
  See also Trogdon, William (Lewis)
  See also AAYA 9
Hebbel, Friedrich 1813-1863 .... **NCLC 43;
  DAM DRAM**
  See also DLB 129
Hebert, Anne 1916-2000 .... **CLC 4, 13, 29;
  DAC; DAM MST, POET**
  See also CA 85-88; 187; CANR 69; DA3;
  DLB 68; MTCW 1, 2
Hecht, Anthony (Evan) 1923- ...... **CLC 8, 13,
  19; DAM POET**
  See also CA 9-12R; CANR 6; DLB 5, 169
Hecht, Ben 1894-1964 .... **CLC 8**
  See also CA 85-88; DLB 7, 9, 25, 26, 28,
  86; TCLC 101
Hedayat, Sadeq 1903-1951 .... **TCLC 21**
  See also CA 120
Hegel, Georg Wilhelm Friedrich
  1770-1831 .... **NCLC 46**
  See also DLB 90
Heidegger, Martin 1889-1976 .... **CLC 24**
  See also CA 81-84; 65-68; CANR 34;
  MTCW 1, 2
Heidenstam, (Carl Gustaf) Verner von
  1859-1940 .... **TCLC 5**
  See also CA 104
Heifner, Jack 1946- .... **CLC 11**
  See also CA 105; CANR 47
Heijermans, Herman 1864-1924 .... **TCLC 24**
  See also CA 123
Heilbrun, Carolyn G(old) 1926- .... **CLC 25**
  See also CA 45-48; CANR 1, 28, 58, 94
Heine, Heinrich 1797-1856 .... **NCLC 4, 54;
  PC 25**
  See also DLB 90
Heinemann, Larry (Curtiss) 1944- .. **CLC 50**
  See also CA 110; CAAS 21; CANR 31, 81;
  DLBD 9; INT CANR-31
Heiney, Donald (William) 1921-1993
  See Harris, MacDonald
  See also CA 1-4R; 142; CANR 3, 58
Heinlein, Robert A(nson) 1907-1988 . **CLC 1,
  3, 8, 14, 26, 55; DAM POP**
  See also AAYA 17; CA 1-4R; 125; CANR
  1, 20, 53; DA3; DLB 8; JRDA; MAICYA;
  MTCW 1, 2; SATA 9, 69; SATA-Obit 56

Helforth, John
  See Doolittle, Hilda
Hellenhofferu, Vojtech Kapristian z
  See Hasek, Jaroslav (Matej Frantisek)
Heller, Joseph 1923-1999 . **CLC 1, 3, 5, 8, 11,
  36, 63; DA; DAB; DAC; DAM MST,
  NOV, POP; WLC**
  See also AAYA 24; AITN 1; CA 5-8R; 187;
  CABS 1; CANR 8, 42, 66; DA3; DLB 2,
  28, 227; DLBY 80; INT CANR-8; MTCW
  1, 2
Hellman, Lillian (Florence)
  1906-1984 .. **CLC 2, 4, 8, 14, 18, 34, 44,
  52; DAM DRAM; DC 1**
  See also AITN 1, 2; CA 13-16R; 112;
  CANR 33; DA3; DLB 7, 228; DLBY 84;
  MTCW 1, 2
Helprin, Mark 1947- .... **CLC 7, 10, 22, 32;
  DAM NOV, POP**
  See also CA 81-84; CANR 47, 64;
  CDALBS; DA3; DLBY 85; MTCW 1, 2
Helvetius, Claude-Adrien 1715-1771 .. **LC 26**
Helyar, Jane Penelope Josephine 1933-
  See Poole, Josephine
  See also CA 21-24R; CANR 10, 26; SATA
  82
Hemans, Felicia 1793-1835 ...... **NCLC 29, 71**
  See also DLB 96
Hemingway, Ernest (Miller)
  1899-1961 .... **CLC 1, 3, 6, 8, 10, 13, 19,
  30, 34, 39, 41, 44, 50, 61, 80; DA;
  DAB; DAC; DAM MST, NOV; SSC 1,
  25, 36, 40; WLC**
  See also AAYA 19; CA 77-80; CANR 34;
  CDALB 1917-1929; DA3; DLB 4, 9, 102,
  210; DLBD 1, 15, 16; DLBY 81, 87, 96,
  98; MTCW 1, 2
Hempel, Amy 1951- .... **CLC 39**
  See also CA 118; 137; CANR 70; DA3;
  MTCW 2
Henderson, F. C.
  See Mencken, H(enry) L(ouis)
Henderson, Sylvia
  See Ashton-Warner, Sylvia (Constance)
Henderson, Zenna (Chlarson)
  1917-1983 .... **SSC 29**
  See also CA 1-4R; 133; CANR 1, 84; DLB
  8; SATA 5
Henkin, Joshua CLC 119
  See also CA 161
Henley, Beth CLC 23; DC 6, 14
  See also Henley, Elizabeth Becker
  See also CABS 3; DLBY 86
Henley, Elizabeth Becker 1952-
  See Henley, Beth
  See also CA 107; CANR 32, 73; DAM
  DRAM, MST; DA3; MTCW 1, 2
Henley, William Ernest 1849-1903 .. **TCLC 8**
  See also CA 105; DLB 19
Hennissart, Martha
  See Lathen, Emma
  See also CA 85-88; CANR 64
Henry, O. TCLC 1, 19; SSC 5; WLC
  See also Porter, William Sydney
Henry, Patrick 1736-1799 .... **LC 25**
Henryson, Robert 1430(?)-1506(?) ...... **LC 20**
  See also DLB 146
Henry VIII 1491-1547 .... **LC 10**
  See also DLB 132
Henschke, Alfred
  See Klabund
Hentoff, Nat(han Irving) 1925- .... **CLC 26**
  See also AAYA 4; CA 1-4R; CAAS 6;
  CANR 5, 25, 77; CLR 1, 52; INT CANR-
  25; JRDA; MAICYA; SATA 42, 69;
  SATA-Brief 27
Heppenstall, (John) Rayner
  1911-1981 .... **CLC 10**
  See also CA 1-4R; 103; CANR 29

Heraclitus c. 540B.C.-c. 450B.C. ... **CMLC 22**
See also DLB 176

Herbert, Frank (Patrick)
1920-1986 .... **CLC 12, 23, 35, 44, 85;**
DAM POP
See also AAYA 21; CA 53-56; 118; CANR
5, 43; CDALBS; DLB 8; INT CANR-5;
MTCW 1, 2; SATA 9, 37; SATA-Obit 47

Herbert, George 1593-1633 ..... **LC 24; DAB;**
DAM POET; PC 4
See also CDBLB Before 1660; DLB 126

Herbert, Zbigniew 1924-1998 ..... **CLC 9, 43;**
DAM POET
See also CA 89-92; 169; CANR 36, 74;
DLB 232; MTCW 1

Herbst, Josephine (Frey)
1897-1969 .... **CLC 34**
See also CA 5-8R; 25-28R; DLB 9

Herder, Johann Gottfried von
1744-1803 .... **NCLC 8**
See also DLB 97

Heredia, Jose Maria 1803-1839
See also HLCS 2

Hergesheimer, Joseph 1880-1954 ... **TCLC 11**
See also CA 109; DLB 102, 9

Herlihy, James Leo 1927-1993 .... **CLC 6**
See also CA 1-4R; 143; CANR 2

Hermogenes fl. c. 175- .... **CMLC 6**

Hernandez, Jose 1834-1886 .... **NCLC 17**

Herodotus c. 484B.C.-429B.C. .... **CMLC 17**
See also DLB 176

Herrick, Robert 1591-1674 .... **LC 13; DA;**
DAB; DAC; DAM MST, POP; PC 9
See also DLB 126

Herring, Guilles
See Somerville, Edith

Herriot, James 1916-1995 ..... **CLC 12; DAM**
POP
See also Wight, James Alfred
See also AAYA 1; CA 148; CANR 40;
MTCW 2; SATA 86

Herris, Violet
See Hunt, Violet

Herrmann, Dorothy 1941- .... **CLC 44**
See also CA 107

Herrmann, Taffy
See Herrmann, Dorothy

Hersey, John (Richard) 1914-1993 .... **CLC 1,**
2, 7, 9, 40, 81, 97; DAM POP
See also AAYA 29; CA 17-20R; 140; CANR
33; CDALBS; DLB 6, 185; MTCW 1, 2;
SATA 25; SATA-Obit 76

Herzen, Aleksandr Ivanovich
1812-1870 .... **NCLC 10, 61**

Herzl, Theodor 1860-1904 .... **TCLC 36**
See also CA 168

Herzog, Werner 1942- .... **CLC 16**
See also CA 89-92

Hesiod c. 8th cent. B.C.- .... **CMLC 5**
See also DLB 176

Hesse, Hermann 1877-1962 ... **CLC 1, 2, 3, 6,**
11, 17, 25, 69; DA; DAB; DAC; DAM
MST, NOV; SSC 9; WLC
See also CA 17-18; CAP 2; DA3; DLB 66;
MTCW 1, 2; SATA 50

Hewes, Cady
See De Voto, Bernard (Augustine)

Heyen, William 1940- .... **CLC 13, 18**
See also CA 33-36R; CAAS 9; DLB 5

Heyerdahl, Thor 1914- .... **CLC 26**
See also CA 5-8R; CANR 5, 22, 66, 73;
MTCW 1, 2; SATA 2, 52

Heym, Georg (Theodor Franz Arthur)
1887-1912 .... **TCLC 9**
See also CA 106; 181

Heym, Stefan 1913- .... **CLC 41**
See also CA 9-12R; CANR 4; DLB 69

Heyse, Paul (Johann Ludwig von)
1830-1914 .... **TCLC 8**
See also CA 104; DLB 129

Heyward, (Edwin) DuBose
1885-1940 .... **TCLC 59**
See also CA 108; 157; DLB 7, 9, 45; SATA
21

Hibbert, Eleanor Alice Burford
1906-1993 .... **CLC 7; DAM POP**
See also BEST 90:4; CA 17-20R; 140;
CANR 9, 28, 59; MTCW 2; SATA 2;
SATA-Obit 74

Hichens, Robert (Smythe)
1864-1950 .... **TCLC 64**
See also CA 162; DLB 153

Higgins, George V(incent)
1939-1999 .... **CLC 4, 7, 10, 18**
See also CA 77-80; 186; CAAS 5; CANR
17, 51, 89; DLB 2; DLBY 81, 98; INT
CANR-17; MTCW 1

Higginson, Thomas Wentworth
1823-1911 .... **TCLC 36**
See also CA 162; DLB 1, 64

Highet, Helen
See MacInnes, Helen (Clark)

Highsmith, (Mary) Patricia
1921-1995 .... **CLC 2, 4, 14, 42, 102;**
DAM NOV, POP
See also CA 1-4R; 147; CANR 1, 20, 48,
62; DA3; MTCW 1, 2

Highwater, Jamake (Mamake)
1942(?)- .... **CLC 12**
See also AAYA 7; CA 65-68; CAAS 7;
CANR 10, 34, 84; CLR 17; DLB 52;
DLBY 85; JRDA; MAICYA; SATA 32,
69; SATA-Brief 30

Highway, Tomson 1951- .... **CLC 92; DAC;**
DAM MULT
See also CA 151; CANR 75; MTCW 2;
NNAL

Hijuelos, Oscar 1951- .... **CLC 65; DAM**
MULT, POP; HLC 1
See also AAYA 25; BEST 90:1; CA 123;
CANR 50, 75; DA3; DLB 145; HW 1, 2;
MTCW 2

Hikmet, Nazim 1902(?)-1963 .... **CLC 40**
See also CA 141; 93-96

Hildegard von Bingen 1098-1179 . **CMLC 20**
See also DLB 148

Hildesheimer, Wolfgang 1916-1991 .. **CLC 49**
See also CA 101; 135; DLB 69, 124

Hill, Geoffrey (William) 1932- ...... **CLC 5, 8,**
18, 45; DAM POET
See also CA 81-84; CANR 21, 89; CDBLB
1960 to Present; DLB 40; MTCW 1

Hill, George Roy 1921- .... **CLC 26**
See also CA 110; 122

Hill, John
See Koontz, Dean R(ay)

Hill, Susan (Elizabeth) 1942- .... **CLC 4, 113;**
DAB; DAM MST, NOV
See also CA 33-36R; CANR 29, 69; DLB
14, 139; MTCW 1

Hillerman, Tony 1925- . **CLC 62; DAM POP**
See also AAYA 6; BEST 89:1; CA 29-32R;
CANR 21, 42, 65; DA3; DLB 206; SATA
6

Hillesum, Etty 1914-1943 .... **TCLC 49**
See also CA 137

Hilliard, Noel (Harvey) 1929- .... **CLC 15**
See also CA 9-12R; CANR 7, 69

Hillis, Rick 1956- .... **CLC 66**
See also CA 134

Hilton, James 1900-1954 .... **TCLC 21**
See also CA 108; 169; DLB 34, 77;
SATA 34

Himes, Chester (Bomar) 1909-1984 .. **CLC 2,**
4, 7, 18, 58, 108; BLC 2; DAM MULT
See also BW 2; CA 25-28R; 114; CANR
22, 89; DLB 2, 76, 143, 226; MTCW 1, 2

Hinde, Thomas CLC 6, 11
See also Chitty, Thomas Willes

Hine, (William) Daryl 1936- .... **CLC 15**
See also CA 1-4R; CAAS 15; CANR 1, 20;
DLB 60

Hinkson, Katharine Tynan
See Tynan, Katharine

Hinojosa(-Smith), Rolando (R.) 1929-
See also CA 131; CAAS 16; CANR 62;
DAM MULT; DLB 82; HLC 1; HW 1, 2;
MTCW 2

Hinton, S(usan) E(loise) 1950- .... **CLC 30,**
111; DA; DAB; DAC; DAM MST,
NOV
See also AAYA 2, 33; CA 81-84; CANR
32, 62, 92; CDALBS; CLR 3, 23; DA3;
JRDA; MAICYA; MTCW 1, 2; SATA 19,
58, 115

Hippius, Zinaida TCLC 9
See also Gippius, Zinaida (Nikolayevna)

Hiraoka, Kimitake 1925-1970
See Mishima, Yukio
See also CA 97-100; 29-32R; DAM DRAM;
DA3; MTCW 1, 2

Hirsch, E(ric) D(onald), Jr. 1928- .... **CLC 79**
See also CA 25-28R; CANR 27, 51; DLB
67; INT CANR-27; MTCW 1

Hirsch, Edward 1950- .... **CLC 31, 50**
See also CA 104; CANR 20, 42; DLB 120

Hitchcock, Alfred (Joseph)
1899-1980 .... **CLC 16**
See also AAYA 22; CA 159; 97-100; SATA
27; SATA-Obit 24

Hitler, Adolf 1889-1945 .... **TCLC 53**
See also CA 117; 147

Hoagland, Edward 1932- .... **CLC 28**
See also CA 1-4R; CANR 2, 31, 57; DLB
6; SATA 51

Hoban, Russell (Conwell) 1925- . **CLC 7, 25;**
DAM NOV
See also CA 5-8R; CANR 23, 37, 66; CLR
3, 69; DLB 52; MAICYA; MTCW 1, 2;
SATA 1, 40, 78

Hobbes, Thomas 1588-1679 .... **LC 36**
See also DLB 151

Hobbs, Perry
See Blackmur, R(ichard) P(almer)

Hobson, Laura Z(ametkin)
1900-1986 .... **CLC 7, 25**
See also CA 17-20R; 118; CANR 55; DLB
28; SATA 52

Hoch, Edward D(entinger) 1930-
See Queen, Ellery
See also CA 29-32R; CANR 11, 27, 51

Hochhuth, Rolf 1931- .. **CLC 4, 11, 18; DAM**
DRAM
See also CA 5-8R; CANR 33, 75; DLB 124;
MTCW 1, 2

Hochman, Sandra 1936- .... **CLC 3, 8**
See also CA 5-8R; DLB 5

Hochwaelder, Fritz 1911-1986 .... **CLC 36;**
DAM DRAM
See also CA 29-32R; 120; CANR 42;
MTCW 1

Hochwalder, Fritz
See Hochwaelder, Fritz

Hocking, Mary (Eunice) 1921- .... **CLC 13**
See also CA 101; CANR 18, 40

Hodgins, Jack 1938- .... **CLC 23**
See also CA 93-96; DLB 60

Hodgson, William Hope
1877(?)-1918 .... **TCLC 13**
See also CA 111; 164; DLB 70, 153, 156,
178; MTCW 2

Kafka, Franz 1883-1924 . **TCLC 2, 6, 13, 29, 47, 53; DA; DAB; DAC; DAM MST, NOV; SSC 5, 29, 35; WLC**
See also AAYA 31; CA 105; 126; DA3; DLB 81; MTCW 1, 2

Kahanovitsch, Pinkhes
See Der Nister

Kahn, Roger 1927- .... **CLC 30**
See also CA 25-28R; CANR 44, 69; DLB 171; SATA 37

Kain, Saul
See Sassoon, Siegfried (Lorraine)

Kaiser, Georg 1878-1945 .... **TCLC 9**
See also CA 106; DLB 124

Kaletski, Alexander 1946- .... **CLC 39**
See also CA 118; 143

Kalidasa fl. c. 400- .... **CMLC 9; PC 22**

Kallman, Chester (Simon)
1921-1975 .... **CLC 2**
See also CA 45-48; 53-56; CANR 3

Kaminsky, Melvin 1926-
See Brooks, Mel
See also CA 65-68; CANR 16

Kaminsky, Stuart M(elvin) 1934- ..... **CLC 59**
See also CA 73-76; CANR 29, 53, 89

Kandinsky, Wassily 1866-1944 .... **TCLC 92**
See also CA 118; 155

Kane, Francis
See Robbins, Harold

Kane, Henry 1918-
See Queen, Ellery
See also CA 156

Kane, Paul
See Simon, Paul (Frederick)

Kanin, Garson 1912-1999 .... **CLC 22**
See also AITN 1; CA 5-8R; 177; CANR 7, 78; DLB 7

Kaniuk, Yoram 1930- .... **CLC 19**
See also CA 134

Kant, Immanuel 1724-1804 ..... **NCLC 27, 67**
See also DLB 94

Kantor, MacKinlay 1904-1977 .... **CLC 7**
See also CA 61-64; 73-76; CANR 60, 63; DLB 9, 102; MTCW 2

Kaplan, David Michael 1946- .... **CLC 50**
See also CA 187

Kaplan, James 1951- .... **CLC 59**
See also CA 135

Karageorge, Michael
See Anderson, Poul (William)

Karamzin, Nikolai Mikhailovich
1766-1826 .... **NCLC 3**
See also DLB 150

Karapanou, Margarita 1946- .... **CLC 13**
See also CA 101

Karinthy, Frigyes 1887-1938 .... **TCLC 47**
See also CA 170

Karl, Frederick R(obert) 1927- .... **CLC 34**
See also CA 5-8R; CANR 3, 44

Kastel, Warren
See Silverberg, Robert

Kataev, Evgeny Petrovich 1903-1942
See Petrov, Evgeny
See also CA 120

Kataphusin
See Ruskin, John

Katz, Steve 1935- .... **CLC 47**
See also CA 25-28R; CAAS 14, 64; CANR 12; DLBY 83

Kauffman, Janet 1945- .... **CLC 42**
See also CA 117; CANR 43, 84; DLBY 86

Kaufman, Bob (Garnell) 1925-1986 . **CLC 49**
See also BW 1; CA 41-44R; 118; CANR 22; DLB 16, 41

Kaufman, George S. 1889-1961 ...... **CLC 38; DAM DRAM**
See also CA 108; 93-96; DLB 7; INT 108; MTCW 2

Kaufman, Sue CLC 3, 8
See also Barondess, Sue K(aufman)

Kavafis, Konstantinos Petrou 1863-1933
See Cavafy, C(onstantine) P(eter)
See also CA 104

Kavan, Anna 1901-1968 .... **CLC 5, 13, 82**
See also CA 5-8R; CANR 6, 57; MTCW 1

Kavanagh, Dan
See Barnes, Julian (Patrick)

Kavanagh, Julie 1952- .... **CLC 119**
See also CA 163

Kavanagh, Patrick (Joseph)
1904-1967 .... **CLC 22; PC 33**
See also CA 123; 25-28R; DLB 15, 20; MTCW 1

Kawabata, Yasunari 1899-1972 ..... **CLC 2, 5, 9, 18, 107; DAM MULT; SSC 17**
See also CA 93-96; 33-36R; CANR 88; DLB 180; MTCW 2

Kaye, M(ary) M(argaret) 1909- .... **CLC 28**
See also CA 89-92; CANR 24, 60; MTCW 1, 2; SATA 62

Kaye, Mollie
See Kaye, M(ary) M(argaret)

Kaye-Smith, Sheila 1887-1956 .... **TCLC 20**
See also CA 118; DLB 36

Kaymor, Patrice Maguilene
See Senghor, Leopold Sedar

Kazakov, Yuri Pavlovich 1927-1982 . **SSC 43**
See also CA 5-8R; CANR 36; MTCW 1

Kazan, Elia 1909- .... **CLC 6, 16, 63**
See also CA 21-24R; CANR 32, 78

Kazantzakis, Nikos 1883(?)-1957 .... **TCLC 2, 5, 33**
See also CA 105; 132; DA3; MTCW 1, 2

Kazin, Alfred 1915-1998 ..... **CLC 34, 38, 119**
See also CA 1-4R; CAAS 7; CANR 1, 45, 79; DLB 67

Keane, Mary Nesta (Skrine) 1904-1996
See Keane, Molly
See also CA 108; 114; 151

Keane, Molly CLC 31
See also Keane, Mary Nesta (Skrine)
See also INT 114

Keates, Jonathan 1946(?)- .... **CLC 34**
See also CA 163

Keaton, Buster 1895-1966 .... **CLC 20**

Keats, John 1795-1821 ...... **NCLC 8, 73; DA; DAB; DAC; DAM MST, POET; PC 1; WLC**
See also CDBLB 1789-1832; DA3; DLB 96, 110

Keble, John 1792-1866 .... **NCLC 87**
See also DLB 32, 55

Keene, Donald 1922- .... **CLC 34**
See also CA 1-4R; CANR 5

Keillor, Garrison CLC 40, 115
See also Keillor, Gary (Edward)
See also AAYA 2; BEST 89:3; DLBY 87; SATA 58

Keillor, Gary (Edward) 1942-
See Keillor, Garrison
See also CA 111; 117; CANR 36, 59; DAM POP; DA3; MTCW 1, 2

Keith, Michael
See Hubbard, L(afayette) Ron(ald)

Keller, Gottfried 1819-1890 .... **NCLC 2; SSC 26**
See also DLB 129

Keller, Nora Okja 1965- .... **CLC 109**
See also CA 187

Kellerman, Jonathan 1949- .. **CLC 44; DAM POP**
See also AAYA 35; BEST 90:1; CA 106; CANR 29, 51; DA3; INT CANR-29

Kelley, William Melvin 1937- .... **CLC 22**
See also BW 1; CA 77-80; CANR 27, 83; DLB 33

Kellogg, Marjorie 1922- .... **CLC 2**
See also CA 81-84

Kellow, Kathleen
See Hibbert, Eleanor Alice Burford

Kelly, M(ilton) T(errence) 1947- ...... **CLC 55**
See also CA 97-100; CAAS 22; CANR 19, 43, 84

Kelman, James 1946- .... **CLC 58, 86**
See also CA 148; CANR 85; DLB 194

Kemal, Yashar 1923- .... **CLC 14, 29**
See also CA 89-92; CANR 44

Kemble, Fanny 1809-1893 .... **NCLC 18**
See also DLB 32

Kemelman, Harry 1908-1996 .... **CLC 2**
See also AITN 1; CA 9-12R; 155; CANR 6, 71; DLB 28

Kempe, Margery 1373(?)-1440(?) ... **LC 6, 56**
See also DLB 146

Kempis, Thomas a 1380-1471 .... **LC 11**

Kendall, Henry 1839-1882 .... **NCLC 12**
See also DLB 230

Keneally, Thomas (Michael) 1935- ... **CLC 5, 8, 10, 14, 19, 27, 43, 117; DAM NOV**
See also CA 85-88; CANR 10, 50, 74; DA3; MTCW 1, 2

Kennedy, Adrienne (Lita) 1931- ..... **CLC 66; BLC 2; DAM MULT; DC 5**
See also BW 2, 3; CA 103; CAAS 20; CABS 3; CANR 26, 53, 82; DLB 38

Kennedy, John Pendleton
1795-1870 .... **NCLC 2**
See also DLB 3

Kennedy, Joseph Charles 1929-
See Kennedy, X. J.
See also CA 1-4R; CANR 4, 30, 40; SATA 14, 86

Kennedy, William 1928- .. **CLC 6, 28, 34, 53; DAM NOV**
See also AAYA 1; CA 85-88; CANR 14, 31, 76; DA3; DLB 143; DLBY 85; INT CANR-31; MTCW 1, 2; SATA 57

Kennedy, X. J. CLC 8, 42
See also Kennedy, Joseph Charles
See also CAAS 9; CLR 27; DLB 5; SAAS 22

Kenny, Maurice (Francis) 1929- ..... **CLC 87; DAM MULT**
See also CA 144; CAAS 22; DLB 175; NNAL

Kent, Kelvin
See Kuttner, Henry

Kenton, Maxwell
See Southern, Terry

Kenyon, Robert O.
See Kuttner, Henry

Kepler, Johannes 1571-1630 .... **LC 45**

Kerouac, Jack CLC 1, 2, 3, 5, 14, 29, 61
See also Kerouac, Jean-Louis Lebris de
See also AAYA 25; CDALB 1941-1968; DLB 2, 16; DLBD 3; DLBY 95; MTCW 2

Kerouac, Jean-Louis Lebris de 1922-1969
See Kerouac, Jack
See also AITN 1; CA 5-8R; 25-28R; CANR 26, 54; DA; DAB; DAC; DAM MST, NOV, POET, POP; DA3; MTCW 1, 2; WLC

Kerr, Jean 1923- .... **CLC 22**
See also CA 5-8R; CANR 7; INT CANR-7

Kerr, M. E. CLC 12, 35
See also Meaker, Marijane (Agnes)
See also AAYA 2, 23; CLR 29; SAAS 1

Kerr, Robert CLC 55

Kerrigan, (Thomas) Anthony 1918- .. **CLC 4, 6**
See also CA 49-52; CAAS 11; CANR 4

Kerry, Lois
See Duncan, Lois

Kesey, Ken (Elton) 1935- ..... CLC 1, 3, 6, 11, 46, 64; DA; DAB; DAC; DAM MST, NOV, POP; WLC
See also AAYA 25; CA 1-4R; CANR 22, 38, 66; CDALB 1968-1988; DA3; DLB 2, 16, 206; MTCW 1, 2; SATA 66

Kesselring, Joseph (Otto) 1902-1967 .... CLC 45; DAM DRAM, MST
See also CA 150

Kessler, Jascha (Frederick) 1929- ...... CLC 4
See also CA 17-20R; CANR 8, 48

Kettelkamp, Larry (Dale) 1933- .... CLC 12
See also CA 29-32R; CANR 16; SAAS 3; SATA 2

Key, Ellen (Karolina Sofia) 1849-1926 .... TCLC 65

Keyber, Conny
See Fielding, Henry

Keyes, Daniel 1927- ..... CLC 80; DA; DAC; DAM MST, NOV
See also AAYA 23; CA 17-20R, 181; CAAE 181; CANR 10, 26, 54, 74; DA3; MTCW 2; SATA 37

Keynes, John Maynard 1883-1946 .... TCLC 64
See also CA 114; 162, 163; DLBD 10; MTCW 2

Khanshendel, Chiron
See Rose, Wendy

Khayyam, Omar 1048-1131 .... CMLC 11; DAM POET; PC 8
See also DA3

Kherdian, David 1931- .... CLC 6, 9
See also CA 21-24R; CAAS 2; CANR 39, 78; CLR 24; JRDA; MAICYA; SATA 16, 74

Khlebnikov, Velimir TCLC 20
See also Khlebnikov, Viktor Vladimirovich

Khlebnikov, Viktor Vladimirovich 1885-1922
See Khlebnikov, Velimir
See also CA 117

Khodasevich, Vladislav (Felitsianovich) 1886-1939 .... TCLC 15
See also CA 115

Kielland, Alexander Lange 1849-1906 .... TCLC 5
See also CA 104

Kiely, Benedict 1919- .... CLC 23, 43
See also CA 1-4R; CANR 2, 84; DLB 15

Kienzle, William X(avier) 1928- ..... CLC 25; DAM POP
See also CA 93-96; CAAS 1; CANR 9, 31, 59; DA3; INT CANR-31; MTCW 1, 2

Kierkegaard, Soren 1813-1855 ..... NCLC 34, 78

Kieslowski, Krzysztof 1941-1996 .... CLC 120
See also CA 147; 151

Killens, John Oliver 1916-1987 .... CLC 10
See also BW 2; CA 77-80; 123; CAAS 2; CANR 26; DLB 33

Killigrew, Anne 1660-1685 .... LC 4
See also DLB 131

Killigrew, Thomas 1612-1683 .... LC 57
See also DLB 58

Kim
See Simenon, Georges (Jacques Christian)

Kincaid, Jamaica 1949- ..... CLC 43, 68, 137; BLC 2; DAM MULT, NOV
See also AAYA 13; BW 2, 3; CA 125; CANR 47, 59; CDALBS; CLR 63; DA3; DLB 157, 227; MTCW 2

King, Francis (Henry) 1923- .... CLC 8, 53; DAM NOV
See also CA 1-4R; CANR 1, 33, 86; DLB 15, 139; MTCW 1

King, Kennedy
See Brown, George Douglas

King, Martin Luther, Jr. 1929-1968 .... CLC 83; BLC 2; DA; DAB; DAC; DAM MST, MULT; WLCS
See also BW 2, 3; CA 25-28; CANR 27, 44; CAP 2; DA3; MTCW 1, 2; SATA 14

King, Stephen (Edwin) 1947- .... CLC 12, 26, 37, 61, 113; DAM NOV, POP; SSC 17
See also AAYA 1, 17; BEST 90:1; CA 61-64; CANR 1, 30, 52, 76; DA3; DLB 143; DLBY 80; JRDA; MTCW 1, 2; SATA 9, 55

King, Steve
See King, Stephen (Edwin)

King, Thomas 1943- ... CLC 89; DAC; DAM MULT
See also CA 144; DLB 175; NNAL; SATA 96

Kingman, Lee CLC 17
See also Natti, (Mary) Lee
See also SAAS 3; SATA 1, 67

Kingsley, Charles 1819-1875 .... NCLC 35
See also DLB 21, 32, 163, 190; YABC 2

Kingsley, Sidney 1906-1995 .... CLC 44
See also CA 85-88; 147; DLB 7

Kingsolver, Barbara 1955- .... CLC 55, 81, 130; DAM POP
See also AAYA 15; CA 129; 134; CANR 60; CDALBS; DA3; DLB 206; INT 134; MTCW 2

Kingston, Maxine (Ting Ting) Hong 1940- .... CLC 12, 19, 58, 121; DAM MULT, NOV; WLCS
See also AAYA 8; CA 69-72; CANR 13, 38, 74, 87; CDALBS; DA3; DLB 173, 212; DLBY 80; INT CANR-13; MTCW 1, 2; SATA 53

Kinnell, Galway 1927- ..... CLC 1, 2, 3, 5, 13, 29, 129; PC 26
See also CA 9-12R; CANR 10, 34, 66; DLB 5; DLBY 87; INT CANR-34; MTCW 1, 2

Kinsella, Thomas 1928- .... CLC 4, 19, 138
See also CA 17-20R; CANR 15; DLB 27; MTCW 1, 2

Kinsella, W(illiam) P(atrick) 1935- . CLC 27, 43; DAC; DAM NOV, POP
See also AAYA 7; CA 97-100; CAAS 7; CANR 21, 35, 66, 75; INT CANR-21; MTCW 1, 2

Kinsey, Alfred C(harles) 1894-1956 .... TCLC 91
See also CA 115; 170; MTCW 2

Kipling, (Joseph) Rudyard 1865-1936 .... TCLC 8, 17; DA; DAB; DAC; DAM MST, POET; PC 3; SSC 5; WLC
See also AAYA 32; CA 105; 120; CANR 33; CDBLB 1890-1914; CLR 39, 65; DA3; DLB 19, 34, 141, 156; MAICYA; MTCW 1, 2; SATA 100; YABC 2

Kirkland, Caroline M. 1801-1864 . NCLC 85
See also DLB 3, 73, 74; DLBD 13

Kirkup, James 1918- .... CLC 1
See also CA 1-4R; CAAS 4; CANR 2; DLB 27; SATA 12

Kirkwood, James 1930(?)-1989 .... CLC 9
See also AITN 2; CA 1-4R; 128; CANR 6, 40

Kirshner, Sidney
See Kingsley, Sidney

Kis, Danilo 1935-1989 .... CLC 57
See also CA 109; 118; 129; CANR 61; DLB 181; MTCW 1

Kissinger, Henry A(lfred) 1923- ..... CLC 137
See also CA 1-4R; CANR 2, 33, 66; MTCW 1

Kivi, Aleksis 1834-1872 .... NCLC 30

Kizer, Carolyn (Ashley) 1925- ... CLC 15, 39, 80; DAM POET
See also CA 65-68; CAAS 5; CANR 24, 70; DLB 5, 169; MTCW 2

Klabund 1890-1928 .... TCLC 44
See also CA 162; DLB 66

Klappert, Peter 1942- .... CLC 57
See also CA 33-36R; DLB 5

Klein, A(braham) M(oses) 1909-1972 . CLC 19; DAB; DAC; DAM MST
See also CA 101; 37-40R; DLB 68

Klein, Norma 1938-1989 .... CLC 30
See also AAYA 2, 35; CA 41-44R; 128; CANR 15, 37; CLR 2, 19; INT CANR-15; JRDA; MAICYA; SAAS 1; SATA 7, 57

Klein, T(heodore) E(ibon) D(onald) 1947- .... CLC 34
See also CA 119; CANR 44, 75

Kleist, Heinrich von 1777-1811 ...... NCLC 2, 37; DAM DRAM; SSC 22
See also DLB 90

Klima, Ivan 1931- .... CLC 56; DAM NOV
See also CA 25-28R; CANR 17, 50, 91; DLB 232

Klimentov, Andrei Platonovich 1899-1951 .... TCLC 14; SSC 42
See also CA 108

Klinger, Friedrich Maximilian von 1752-1831 .... NCLC 1
See also DLB 94

Klingsor the Magician
See Hartmann, Sadakichi

Klopstock, Friedrich Gottlieb 1724-1803 .... NCLC 11
See also DLB 97

Knapp, Caroline 1959- .... CLC 99
See also CA 154

Knebel, Fletcher 1911-1993 .... CLC 14
See also AITN 1; CA 1-4R; 140; CAAS 3; CANR 1, 36; SATA 36; SATA-Obit 75

Knickerbocker, Diedrich
See Irving, Washington

Knight, Etheridge 1931-1991 . CLC 40; BLC 2; DAM POET; PC 14
See also BW 1, 3; CA 21-24R; 133; CANR 23, 82; DLB 41; MTCW 2

Knight, Sarah Kemble 1666-1727 .... LC 7
See also DLB 24, 200

Knister, Raymond 1899-1932 .... TCLC 56
See also CA 186; DLB 68

Knowles, John 1926- . CLC 1, 4, 10, 26; DA; DAC; DAM MST, NOV
See also AAYA 10; CA 17-20R; CANR 40, 74, 76; CDALB 1968-1988; DLB 6; MTCW 1, 2; SATA 8, 89

Knox, Calvin M.
See Silverberg, Robert

Knox, John c. 1505-1572 .... LC 37
See also DLB 132

Knye, Cassandra
See Disch, Thomas M(ichael)

Koch, C(hristopher) J(ohn) 1932- .... CLC 42
See also CA 127; CANR 84

Koch, Christopher
See Koch, C(hristopher) J(ohn)

Koch, Kenneth 1925- .... CLC 5, 8, 44; DAM POET
See also CA 1-4R; CANR 6, 36, 57; DLB 5; INT CANR-36; MTCW 2; SATA 65

Kochanowski, Jan 1530-1584 .... LC 10

Kock, Charles Paul de 1794-1871 . NCLC 16

Koda Rohan 1867-
See Koda Shigeyuki

Koda Shigeyuki 1867-1947 .... TCLC 22
See also CA 121; 183; DLB 180

Ledwidge, Francis 1887(?)-1917 .... **TCLC 23**
  See also CA 123; DLB 20
Lee, Andrea 1953- ... **CLC 36; BLC 2; DAM
  MULT**
  See also BW 1, 3; CA 125; CANR 82
Lee, Andrew
  See Auchincloss, Louis (Stanton)
Lee, Chang-rae 1965- .... **CLC 91**
  See also CA 148; CANR 89
Lee, Don L. CLC 2
  See also Madhubuti, Haki R.
Lee, George W(ashington)
  1894-1976 .... **CLC 52; BLC 2; DAM
  MULT**
  See also BW 1; CA 125; CANR 83; DLB
  51
Lee, (Nelle) Harper 1926- . **CLC 12, 60; DA;
  DAB; DAC; DAM MST, NOV; WLC**
  See also AAYA 13; CA 13-16R; CANR 51;
  CDALB 1941-1968; DA3; DLB 6;
  MTCW 1, 2; SATA 11
Lee, Helen Elaine 1959(?)- .... **CLC 86**
  See also CA 148
Lee, Julian
  See Latham, Jean Lee
Lee, Larry
  See Lee, Lawrence
Lee, Laurie 1914-1997 .... **CLC 90; DAB;
  DAM POP**
  See also CA 77-80; 158; CANR 33, 73;
  DLB 27; MTCW 1
Lee, Lawrence 1941-1990 .... **CLC 34**
  See also CA 131; CANR 43
Lee, Li-Young 1957- .... **PC 24**
  See also CA 153; DLB 165
Lee, Manfred B(ennington)
  1905-1971 .... **CLC 11**
  See also Queen, Ellery
  See also CA 1-4R; 29-32R; CANR 2; DLB
  137
Lee, Shelton Jackson 1957(?)- .... **CLC 105;
  BLCS; DAM MULT**
  See also Lee, Spike
  See also BW 2, 3; CA 125; CANR 42
Lee, Spike
  See Lee, Shelton Jackson
  See also AAYA 4, 29
Lee, Stan 1922- .... **CLC 17**
  See also AAYA 5; CA 108; 111; INT 111
Lee, Tanith 1947- .... **CLC 46**
  See also AAYA 15; CA 37-40R; CANR 53;
  SATA 8, 88
Lee, Vernon TCLC 5; SSC 33
  See also Paget, Violet
  See also DLB 57, 153, 156, 174, 178
Lee, William
  See Burroughs, William S(eward)
Lee, Willy
  See Burroughs, William S(eward)
Lee-Hamilton, Eugene (Jacob)
  1845-1907 .... **TCLC 22**
  See also CA 117
Leet, Judith 1935- .... **CLC 11**
  See also CA 187
Le Fanu, Joseph Sheridan
  1814-1873 ..... **NCLC 9, 58; DAM POP;
  SSC 14**
  See also DA3; DLB 21, 70, 159, 178
Leffland, Ella 1931- .... **CLC 19**
  See also CA 29-32R; CANR 35, 78, 82;
  DLBY 84; INT CANR-35; SATA 65
Leger, Alexis
  See Leger, (Marie-Rene Auguste) Alexis
  Saint-Leger
**Leger, (Marie-Rene Auguste) Alexis
  Saint-Leger** 1887-1975 .. **CLC 4, 11, 46;
  DAM POET; PC 23**
  See also CA 13-16R; 61-64; CANR 43;
  MTCW 1

Leger, Saintleger
  See Leger, (Marie-Rene Auguste) Alexis
  Saint-Leger
Le Guin, Ursula K(roeber) 1929- ..... **CLC 8,
  13, 22, 45, 71, 136; DAB; DAC; DAM
  MST, POP; SSC 12**
  See also AAYA 9, 27; AITN 1; CA 21-24R;
  CANR 9, 32, 52, 74; CDALB 1968-1988;
  CLR 3, 28; DA3; DLB 8, 52; INT CANR-
  32; JRDA; MAICYA; MTCW 1, 2; SATA
  4, 52, 99
Lehmann, Rosamond (Nina)
  1901-1990 .... **CLC 5**
  See also CA 77-80; 131; CANR 8, 73; DLB
  15; MTCW 2
Leiber, Fritz (Reuter, Jr.)
  1910-1992 .... **CLC 25**
  See also CA 45-48; 139; CANR 2, 40, 86;
  DLB 8; MTCW 1, 2; SATA 45; SATA-
  Obit 73
Leibniz, Gottfried Wilhelm von
  1646-1716 .... **LC 35**
  See also DLB 168
Leimbach, Martha 1963-
  See Leimbach, Marti
  See also CA 130
Leimbach, Marti CLC 65
  See also Leimbach, Martha
Leino, Eino TCLC 24
  See also Loennbohm, Armas Eino Leopold
Leiris, Michel (Julien) 1901-1990 ..... **CLC 61**
  See also CA 119; 128; 132
Leithauser, Brad 1953- .... **CLC 27**
  See also CA 107; CANR 27, 81; DLB 120
Lelchuk, Alan 1938- .... **CLC 5**
  See also CA 45-48; CAAS 20; CANR 1, 70
Lem, Stanislaw 1921- .... **CLC 8, 15, 40**
  See also CA 105; CAAS 1; CANR 32;
  MTCW 1
Lemann, Nancy 1956- .... **CLC 39**
  See also CA 118; 136
Lemonnier, (Antoine Louis) Camille
  1844-1913 .... **TCLC 22**
  See also CA 121
Lenau, Nikolaus 1802-1850 .... **NCLC 16**
L'Engle, Madeleine (Camp Franklin)
  1918- .... **CLC 12; DAM POP**
  See also AAYA 28; AITN 2; CA 1-4R;
  CANR 3, 21, 39, 66; CLR 1, 14, 57; DA3;
  DLB 52; JRDA; MAICYA; MTCW 1, 2;
  SAAS 15; SATA 1, 27, 75
Lengyel, Jozsef 1896-1975 .... **CLC 7**
  See also CA 85-88; 57-60; CANR 71
Lenin 1870-1924
  See Lenin, V. I.
  See also CA 121; 168
Lenin, V. I. TCLC 67
  See also Lenin
Lennon, John (Ono) 1940-1980 .. **CLC 12, 35**
  See also CA 102; SATA 114
Lennox, Charlotte Ramsay
  1729(?)-1804 .... **NCLC 23**
  See also DLB 39
Lentricchia, Frank (Jr.) 1940- .... **CLC 34**
  See also CA 25-28R; CANR 19
Lenz, Siegfried 1926- .... **CLC 27; SSC 33**
  See also CA 89-92; CANR 80; DLB 75
Leonard, Elmore (John, Jr.) 1925- . **CLC 28,
  34, 71, 120; DAM POP**
  See also AAYA 22; AITN 1; BEST 89:1,
  90:4; CA 81-84; CANR 12, 28, 53, 76;
  DA3; DLB 173, 226; INT CANR-28;
  MTCW 1, 2
Leonard, Hugh CLC 19
  See also Byrne, John Keyes
  See also DLB 13

Leonov, Leonid (Maximovich)
  1899-1994 .... **CLC 92; DAM NOV**
  See also CA 129; CANR 74, 76; MTCW 1,
  2
Leopardi, (Conte) Giacomo
  1798-1837 .... **NCLC 22**
Le Reveler
  See Artaud, Antonin (Marie Joseph)
Lerman, Eleanor 1952- .... **CLC 9**
  See also CA 85-88; CANR 69
Lerman, Rhoda 1936- .... **CLC 56**
  See also CA 49-52; CANR 70
Lermontov, Mikhail Yuryevich
  1814-1841 .... **NCLC 5, 47; PC 18**
  See also DLB 205
Leroux, Gaston 1868-1927 .... **TCLC 25**
  See also CA 108; 136; CANR 69; SATA 65
Lesage, Alain-Rene 1668-1747 .... **LC 2, 28**
Leskov, Nikolai (Semyonovich)
  1831-1895 .... **NCLC 25; SSC 34**
Lessing, Doris (May) 1919- ... **CLC 1, 2, 3, 6,
  10, 15, 22, 40, 94; DA; DAB; DAC;
  DAM MST, NOV; SSC 6; WLCS**
  See also CA 9-12R; CAAS 14; CANR 33,
  54, 76; CDBLB 1960 to Present; DA3;
  DLB 15, 139; DLBY 85; MTCW 1, 2
Lessing, Gotthold Ephraim 1729-1781 . **LC 8**
  See also DLB 97
Lester, Richard 1932- .... **CLC 20**
Lever, Charles (James)
  1806-1872 .... **NCLC 23**
  See also DLB 21
Leverson, Ada 1865(?)-1936(?) .... **TCLC 18**
  See also Elaine
  See also CA 117; DLB 153
Levertov, Denise 1923-1997 .. **CLC 1, 2, 3, 5,
  8, 15, 28, 66; DAM POET; PC 11**
  See also CA 1-4R, 178; 163; CAAE 178;
  CAAS 19; CANR 3, 29, 50; CDALBS;
  DLB 5, 165; INT CANR-29; MTCW 1, 2
Levi, Jonathan CLC 76
Levi, Peter (Chad Tigar)
  1931-2000 .... **CLC 41**
  See also CA 5-8R; 187; CANR 34, 80; DLB
  40
Levi, Primo 1919-1987 . **CLC 37, 50; SSC 12**
  See also CA 13-16R; 122; CANR 12, 33,
  61, 70; DLB 177; MTCW 1, 2
Levin, Ira 1929- .... **CLC 3, 6; DAM POP**
  See also CA 21-24R; CANR 17, 44, 74;
  DA3; MTCW 1, 2; SATA 66
Levin, Meyer 1905-1981 .... **CLC 7; DAM
  POP**
  See also AITN 1; CA 9-12R; 104; CANR
  15; DLB 9, 28; DLBY 81; SATA 21;
  SATA-Obit 27
Levine, Norman 1924- .... **CLC 54**
  See also CA 73-76; CAAS 23; CANR 14,
  70; DLB 88
Levine, Philip 1928- .. **CLC 2, 4, 5, 9, 14, 33,
  118; DAM POET; PC 22**
  See also CA 9-12R; CANR 9, 37, 52; DLB
  5
Levinson, Deirdre 1931- .... **CLC 49**
  See also CA 73-76; CANR 70
Levi-Strauss, Claude 1908- .... **CLC 38**
  See also CA 1-4R; CANR 6, 32, 57; MTCW
  1, 2
Levitin, Sonia (Wolff) 1934- .... **CLC 17**
  See also AAYA 13; CA 29-32R; CANR 14,
  32, 79; CLR 53; JRDA; MAICYA; SAAS
  2; SATA 4, 68, 119
Levon, O. U.
  See Kesey, Ken (Elton)
Levy, Amy 1861-1889 .... **NCLC 59**
  See also DLB 156
Lewes, George Henry 1817-1878 ... **NCLC 25**
  See also DLB 55, 144

Lord, Bette Bao 1938- .... **CLC 23**
See also BEST 90:3; CA 107; CANR 41,
79; INT 107; SATA 58
Lord Auch
See Bataille, Georges
Lord Byron
See Byron, George Gordon (Noel)
Lorde, Audre (Geraldine)
1934-1992 ... **CLC 18, 71; BLC 2; DAM
MULT, POET; PC 12**
See also BW 1, 3; CA 25-28R; 142; CANR
16, 26, 46, 82; DA3; DLB 41; MTCW 1,
2
Lord Houghton
See Milnes, Richard Monckton
Lord Jeffrey
See Jeffrey, Francis
Lorenzini, Carlo 1826-1890
See Collodi, Carlo
See also MAICYA; SATA 29, 100
Lorenzo, Heberto Padilla
See Padilla (Lorenzo), Heberto
Loris
See Hofmannsthal, Hugo von
Loti, Pierre TCLC 11
See also Viaud, (Louis Marie) Julien
See also DLB 123
Lou, Henri
See Andreas-Salome, Lou
Louie, David Wong 1954- .... **CLC 70**
See also CA 139
Louis, Father M.
See Merton, Thomas
Lovecraft, H(oward) P(hillips)
1890-1937 ...... **TCLC 4, 22; DAM POP;
SSC 3**
See also AAYA 14; CA 104; 133; DA3;
MTCW 1, 2
Lovelace, Earl 1935- .... **CLC 51**
See also BW 2; CA 77-80; CANR 41, 72;
DLB 125; MTCW 1
Lovelace, Richard 1618-1657 .... **LC 24**
See also DLB 131
Lowell, Amy 1874-1925 .... **TCLC 1, 8; DAM
POET; PC 13**
See also CA 104; 151; DLB 54, 140;
MTCW 2
Lowell, James Russell 1819-1891 ... **NCLC 2,
90**
See also CDALB 1640-1865; DLB 1, 11,
64, 79, 189, 235
Lowell, Robert (Traill Spence, Jr.)
1917-1977 .... **CLC 1, 2, 3, 4, 5, 8, 9, 11,
15, 37, 124; DA; DAB; DAC; DAM
MST, NOV; PC 3; WLC**
See also CA 9-12R; 73-76; CABS 2; CANR
26, 60; CDALBS; DA3; DLB 5, 169;
MTCW 1, 2
Lowenthal, Michael (Francis)
1969- .... **CLC 119**
See also CA 150
Lowndes, Marie Adelaide (Belloc)
1868-1947 .... **TCLC 12**
See also CA 107; DLB 70
Lowry, (Clarence) Malcolm
1909-1957 .... **TCLC 6, 40; SSC 31**
See also CA 105; 131; CANR 62; CDBLB
1945-1960; DLB 15; MTCW 1, 2
Lowry, Mina Gertrude 1882-1966
See Loy, Mina
See also CA 113
Loxsmith, John
See Brunner, John (Kilian Houston)
Loy, Mina CLC 28; DAM POET; PC 16
See also Lowry, Mina Gertrude
See also DLB 4, 54
Loyson-Bridet
See Schwob, Marcel (Mayer Andre)

Lucan 39-65 .... **CMLC 33**
See also DLB 211
Lucas, Craig 1951- .... **CLC 64**
See also CA 137; CANR 71
Lucas, E(dward) V(errall)
1868-1938 .... **TCLC 73**
See also CA 176; DLB 98, 149, 153; SATA
20
Lucas, George 1944- .... **CLC 16**
See also AAYA 1, 23; CA 77-80; CANR
30; SATA 56
Lucas, Hans
See Godard, Jean-Luc
Lucas, Victoria
See Plath, Sylvia
Lucian c. 120-c. 180 .... **CMLC 32**
See also DLB 176
Ludlam, Charles 1943-1987 .... **CLC 46, 50**
See also CA 85-88; 122; CANR 72, 86
Ludlum, Robert 1927-2001 .... **CLC 22, 43;
DAM NOV, POP**
See also AAYA 10; BEST 89:1, 90:3; CA
33-36R; CANR 25, 41, 68; DA3; DLBY
82; MTCW 1, 2
Ludwig, Ken CLC 60
Ludwig, Otto 1813-1865 .... **NCLC 4**
See also DLB 129
Lugones, Leopoldo 1874-1938 ...... **TCLC 15;
HLCS 2**
See also CA 116; 131; HW 1
Lu Hsun 1881-1936 .... **TCLC 3; SSC 20**
See also Shu-Jen, Chou
Lukacs, George CLC 24
See also Lukacs, Gyorgy (Szegeny von)
Lukacs, Gyorgy (Szegeny von) 1885-1971
See Lukacs, George
See also CA 101; 29-32R; CANR 62;
MTCW 2
Luke, Peter (Ambrose Cyprian)
1919-1995 .... **CLC 38**
See also CA 81-84; 147; CANR 72; DLB
13
Lunar, Dennis
See Mungo, Raymond
Lurie, Alison 1926- .... **CLC 4, 5, 18, 39**
See also CA 1-4R; CANR 2, 17, 50, 88;
DLB 2; MTCW 1; SATA 46, 112
Lustig, Arnost 1926- .... **CLC 56**
See also AAYA 3; CA 69-72; CANR 47;
DLB 232; SATA 56
Luther, Martin 1483-1546 .... **LC 9, 37**
See also DLB 179
Luxemburg, Rosa 1870(?)-1919 ..... **TCLC 63**
See also CA 118
Luzi, Mario 1914- .... **CLC 13**
See also CA 61-64; CANR 9, 70; DLB 128
Lyly, John 1554(?)-1606 .... **LC 41; DAM
DRAM; DC 7**
See also DLB 62, 167
L'Ymagier
See Gourmont, Remy (-Marie-Charles) de
Lynch, B. Suarez
See Bioy Casares, Adolfo; Borges, Jorge
Luis
Lynch, B. Suarez
See Bioy Casares, Adolfo
Lynch, David (K.) 1946- .... **CLC 66**
See also CA 124; 129
Lynch, James
See Andreyev, Leonid (Nikolaevich)
Lynch Davis, B.
See Bioy Casares, Adolfo; Borges, Jorge
Luis
Lyndsay, Sir David 1490-1555 .... **LC 20**
Lynn, Kenneth S(chuyler) 1923- ...... **CLC 50**
See also CA 1-4R; CANR 3, 27, 65
Lynx
See West, Rebecca

Lyons, Marcus
See Blish, James (Benjamin)
Lyotard, Jean-Francois
1924-1998 .... **TCLC 103**
Lyre, Pinchbeck
See Sassoon, Siegfried (Lorraine)
Lytle, Andrew (Nelson) 1902-1995 ... **CLC 22**
See also CA 9-12R; 150; CANR 70; DLB
6; DLBY 95
Lyttelton, George 1709-1773 .... **LC 10**
Maas, Peter 1929- .... **CLC 29**
See also CA 93-96; INT 93-96; MTCW 2
Macaulay, Catherine 1731-1791 .... **LC 64**
See also DLB 104
Macaulay, (Emilie) Rose
1881(?)-1958 .... **TCLC 7, 44**
See also CA 104; DLB 36
Macaulay, Thomas Babington
1800-1859 .... **NCLC 42**
See also CDBLB 1832-1890; DLB 32, 55
MacBeth, George (Mann)
1932-1992 .... **CLC 2, 5, 9**
See also CA 25-28R; 136; CANR 61, 66;
DLB 40; MTCW 1; SATA 4; SATA-Obit
70
MacCaig, Norman (Alexander)
1910- .... **CLC 36; DAB; DAM POET**
See also CA 9-12R; CANR 3, 34; DLB 27
MacCarthy, Sir(Charles Otto) Desmond
1877-1952 .... **TCLC 36**
See also CA 167
**MacDiarmid, Hugh CLC 2, 4, 11, 19, 63; PC
9**
See also Grieve, C(hristopher) M(urray)
See also CDBLB 1945-1960; DLB 20
MacDonald, Anson
See Heinlein, Robert A(nson)
Macdonald, Cynthia 1928- .... **CLC 13, 19**
See also CA 49-52; CANR 4, 44; DLB 105
MacDonald, George 1824-1905 .... **TCLC 9**
See also CA 106; 137; CANR 80; CLR 67;
DLB 18, 163, 178; MAICYA; SATA 33,
100
Macdonald, John
See Millar, Kenneth
MacDonald, John D(ann)
1916-1986 .. **CLC 3, 27, 44; DAM NOV,
POP**
See also CA 1-4R; 121; CANR 1, 19, 60;
DLB 8; DLBY 86; MTCW 1, 2
Macdonald, John Ross
See Millar, Kenneth
Macdonald, Ross CLC 1, 2, 3, 14, 34, 41
See also Millar, Kenneth
See also DLBD 6
MacDougal, John
See Blish, James (Benjamin)
MacDougal, John
See Blish, James (Benjamin)
MacEwen, Gwendolyn (Margaret)
1941-1987 .... **CLC 13, 55**
See also CA 9-12R; 124; CANR 7, 22; DLB
53; SATA 50; SATA-Obit 55
Macha, Karel Hynek 1810-1846 .... **NCLC 46**
Machado (y Ruiz), Antonio
1875-1939 .... **TCLC 3**
See also CA 104; 174; DLB 108; HW 2
Machado de Assis, Joaquim Maria
1839-1908 ..... **TCLC 10; BLC 2; HLCS
2; SSC 24**
See also CA 107; 153; CANR 91
Machen, Arthur TCLC 4; SSC 20
See also Jones, Arthur Llewellyn
See also CA 179; DLB 36, 156, 178
Machiavelli, Niccolo 1469-1527 ..... **LC 8, 36;
DA; DAB; DAC; DAM MST; WLCS**
MacInnes, Colin 1914-1976 .... **CLC 4, 23**
See also CA 69-72; 65-68; CANR 21; DLB
14; MTCW 1, 2

Man Without a Spleen, A
See Chekhov, Anton (Pavlovich)
Manzoni, Alessandro 1785-1873 .... **NCLC 29**
Map, Walter 1140-1209 .... **CMLC 32**
Mapu, Abraham (ben Jekutiel)
1808-1867 .... **NCLC 18**
Mara, Sally
See Queneau, Raymond
Marat, Jean Paul 1743-1793 .... **LC 10**
Marcel, Gabriel Honore 1889-1973 . **CLC 15**
See also CA 102; 45-48; MTCW 1, 2
March, William 1893-1954 .... **TCLC 96**
Marchbanks, Samuel
See Davies, (William) Robertson
Marchi, Giacomo
See Bassani, Giorgio
Margulies, Donald CLC 76
See also DLB 228
Marie de France c. 12th cent. - ..... **CMLC 8;
PC 22**
See also DLB 208
Marie de l'Incarnation 1599-1672 ...... **LC 10**
Marier, Captain Victor
See Griffith, D(avid Lewelyn) W(ark)
Mariner, Scott
See Pohl, Frederik
Marinetti, Filippo Tommaso
1876-1944 .... **TCLC 10**
See also CA 107; DLB 114
Marivaux, Pierre Carlet de Chamblain de
1688-1763 .... **LC 4; DC 7**
Markandaya, Kamala CLC 8, 38
See also Taylor, Kamala (Purnaiya)
Markfield, Wallace 1926- .... **CLC 8**
See also CA 69-72; CAAS 3; DLB 2, 28
Markham, Edwin 1852-1940 .... **TCLC 47**
See also CA 160; DLB 54, 186
Markham, Robert
See Amis, Kingsley (William)
Marks, J
See Highwater, Jamake (Mamake)
Marks-Highwater, J
See Highwater, Jamake (Mamake)
Markson, David M(errill) 1927- .... **CLC 67**
See also CA 49-52; CANR 1, 91
Marley, Bob CLC 17
See also Marley, Robert Nesta
Marley, Robert Nesta 1945-1981
See Marley, Bob
See also CA 107; 103
Marlowe, Christopher 1564-1593 ...... **LC 22,
47; DA; DAB; DAC; DAM DRAM,
MST; DC 1; WLC**
See also CDBLB Before 1660; DA3; DLB
62
Marlowe, Stephen 1928-
See Queen, Ellery
See also CA 13-16R; CANR 6, 55
Marmontel, Jean-Francois 1723-1799 .. **LC 2**
Marquand, John P(hillips)
1893-1960 .... **CLC 2, 10**
See also CA 85-88; CANR 73; DLB 9, 102;
MTCW 2
Marques, Rene 1919-1979 ..... **CLC 96; DAM
MULT; HLC 2**
See also CA 97-100; 85-88; CANR 78;
DLB 113; HW 1, 2
Marquez, Gabriel (Jose) Garcia
See Garcia Marquez, Gabriel (Jose)
Marquis, Don(ald Robert Perry)
1878-1937 .... **TCLC 7**
See also CA 104; 166; DLB 11, 25
Marric, J. J.
See Creasey, John
Marryat, Frederick 1792-1848 .... **NCLC 3**
See also DLB 21, 163
Marsden, James
See Creasey, John

Marsh, Edward 1872-1953 .... **TCLC 99**
Marsh, (Edith) Ngaio 1899-1982 .... **CLC 7,
53; DAM POP**
See also CA 9-12R; CANR 6, 58; DLB 77;
MTCW 1, 2
Marshall, Garry 1934- .... **CLC 17**
See also AAYA 3; CA 111; SATA 60
Marshall, Paule 1929- .. **CLC 27, 72; BLC 3;
DAM MULT; SSC 3**
See also BW 2, 3; CA 77-80; CANR 25,
73; DA3; DLB 33, 157, 227; MTCW 1, 2
Marshallik
See Zangwill, Israel
Marsten, Richard
See Hunter, Evan
Marston, John 1576-1634 .... **LC 33; DAM
DRAM**
See also DLB 58, 172
Martha, Henry
See Harris, Mark
Marti (y Perez), Jose (Julian)
1853-1895 ...... **NCLC 63; DAM MULT;
HLC 2**
See also HW 2
Martial c. 40-c. 104 .... **CMLC 35; PC 10**
See also DLB 211
Martin, Ken
See Hubbard, L(afayette) Ron(ald)
Martin, Richard
See Creasey, John
Martin, Steve 1945- .... **CLC 30**
See also CA 97-100; CANR 30; MTCW 1
Martin, Valerie 1948- .... **CLC 89**
See also BEST 90:2; CA 85-88; CANR 49,
89
Martin, Violet Florence
1862-1915 .... **TCLC 51**
Martin, Webber
See Silverberg, Robert
Martindale, Patrick Victor
See White, Patrick (Victor Martindale)
Martin du Gard, Roger
1881-1958 .... **TCLC 24**
See also CA 118; CANR 94; DLB 65
Martineau, Harriet 1802-1876 .... **NCLC 26**
See also DLB 21, 55, 159, 163, 166, 190;
YABC 2
Martines, Julia
See O'Faolain, Julia
Martinez, Enrique Gonzalez
See Gonzalez Martinez, Enrique
Martinez, Jacinto Benavente y
See Benavente (y Martinez), Jacinto
Martinez Ruiz, Jose 1873-1967
See Azorin; Ruiz, Jose Martinez
See also CA 93-96; HW 1
Martinez Sierra, Gregorio
1881-1947 .... **TCLC 6**
See also CA 115
Martinez Sierra, Maria (de la O'LeJarraga)
1874-1974 .... **TCLC 6**
See also CA 115
Martinsen, Martin
See Follett, Ken(neth Martin)
Martinson, Harry (Edmund)
1904-1978 .... **CLC 14**
See also CA 77-80; CANR 34
Marut, Ret
See Traven, B.
Marut, Robert
See Traven, B.
Marvell, Andrew 1621-1678 .. **LC 4, 43; DA;
DAB; DAC; DAM MST, POET; PC
10; WLC**
See also CDBLB 1660-1789; DLB 131
Marx, Karl (Heinrich) 1818-1883 . **NCLC 17**
See also DLB 129

Masaoka Shiki TCLC 18
See also Masaoka Tsunenori
Masaoka Tsunenori 1867-1902
See Masaoka Shiki
See also CA 117
Masefield, John (Edward)
1878-1967 ..... **CLC 11, 47; DAM POET**
See also CA 19-20; 25-28R; CANR 33;
CAP 2; CDBLB 1890-1914; DLB 10, 19,
153, 160; MTCW 1, 2; SATA 19
Maso, Carole 19(?)- .... **CLC 44**
See also CA 170
Mason, Bobbie Ann 1940- ... **CLC 28, 43, 82;
SSC 4**
See also AAYA 5; CA 53-56; CANR 11, 31,
58, 83; CDALBS; DA3; DLB 173; DLBY
87; INT CANR-31; MTCW 1, 2
Mason, Ernst
See Pohl, Frederik
Mason, Lee W.
See Malzberg, Barry N(athaniel)
Mason, Nick 1945- .... **CLC 35**
Mason, Tally
See Derleth, August (William)
Mass, William
See Gibson, William
Master Lao
See Lao Tzu
Masters, Edgar Lee 1868-1950 .... **TCLC 2,
25; DA; DAC; DAM MST, POET; PC
1; WLCS**
See also CA 104; 133; CDALB 1865-1917;
DLB 54; MTCW 1, 2
Masters, Hilary 1928- .... **CLC 48**
See also CA 25-28R; CANR 13, 47
Mastrosimone, William 19(?)- .... **CLC 36**
See also CA 186
Mathe, Albert
See Camus, Albert
Mather, Cotton 1663-1728 .... **LC 38**
See also CDALB 1640-1865; DLB 24, 30,
140
Mather, Increase 1639-1723 .... **LC 38**
See also DLB 24
Matheson, Richard Burton 1926- .... **CLC 37**
See also AAYA 31; CA 97-100; CANR 88;
DLB 8, 44; INT 97-100
Mathews, Harry 1930- .... **CLC 6, 52**
See also CA 21-24R; CAAS 6; CANR 18,
40
Mathews, John Joseph 1894-1979 .. **CLC 84;
DAM MULT**
See also CA 19-20; 142; CANR 45; CAP 2;
DLB 175; NNAL
Mathias, Roland (Glyn) 1915- .... **CLC 45**
See also CA 97-100; CANR 19, 41; DLB
27
Matsuo Basho 1644-1694 .... **LC 62; DAM
POET; PC 3**
Mattheson, Rodney
See Creasey, John
Matthews, (James) Brander
1852-1929 .... **TCLC 95**
See also DLB 71, 78; DLBD 13
Matthews, Greg 1949- .... **CLC 45**
See also CA 135
Matthews, William (Procter, III)
1942-1997 .... **CLC 40**
See also CA 29-32R; 162; CAAS 18; CANR
12, 57; DLB 5
Matthias, John (Edward) 1941- .... **CLC 9**
See also CA 33-36R; CANR 56
Matthiessen, F(rancis) O(tto)
1902-1950 .... **TCLC 100**
See also CA 185; DLB 63

Matthiessen, Peter 1927- ... **CLC 5, 7, 11, 32, 64; DAM NOV**
See also AAYA 6; BEST 90:4; CA 9-12R; CANR 21, 50, 73; DA3; DLB 6, 173; MTCW 1, 2; SATA 27

Maturin, Charles Robert 1780(?)-1824 .... **NCLC 6**
See also DLB 178

Matute (Ausejo), Ana Maria 1925- .. **CLC 11**
See also CA 89-92; MTCW 1

Maugham, W. S.
See Maugham, W(illiam) Somerset

Maugham, W(illiam) Somerset 1874-1965 ... **CLC 1, 11, 15, 67, 93; DA; DAB; DAC; DAM DRAM, MST, NOV; SSC 8; WLC**
See also CA 5-8R; 25-28R; CANR 40; CDBLB 1914-1945; DA3; DLB 10, 36, 77, 100, 162, 195; MTCW 1, 2; SATA 54

Maugham, William Somerset
See Maugham, W(illiam) Somerset

Maupassant, (Henri Rene Albert) Guy de 1850-1893 . **NCLC 1, 42, 83; DA; DAB; DAC; DAM MST; SSC 1; WLC**
See also DA3; DLB 123

Maupin, Armistead 1944- ..... **CLC 95; DAM POP**
See also CA 125; 130; CANR 58; DA3; INT 130; MTCW 2

Maurhut, Richard
See Traven, B.

Mauriac, Claude 1914-1996 .... **CLC 9**
See also CA 89-92; 152; DLB 83

Mauriac, Francois (Charles) 1885-1970 .... **CLC 4, 9, 56; SSC 24**
See also CA 25-28; CAP 2; DLB 65; MTCW 1, 2

Mavor, Osborne Henry 1888-1951
See Bridie, James
See also CA 104

Maxwell, William (Keepers, Jr.) 1908-2000 .... **CLC 19**
See also CA 93-96; CANR 54; DLBY 80; INT 93-96

May, Elaine 1932- .... **CLC 16**
See also CA 124; 142; DLB 44

Mayakovski, Vladimir (Vladimirovich) 1893-1930 .... **TCLC 4, 18**
See also CA 104; 158; MTCW 2

Mayhew, Henry 1812-1887 .... **NCLC 31**
See also DLB 18, 55, 190

Mayle, Peter 1939(?)- .... **CLC 89**
See also CA 139; CANR 64

Maynard, Joyce 1953- .... **CLC 23**
See also CA 111; 129; CANR 64

Mayne, William (James Carter) 1928- .... **CLC 12**
See also AAYA 20; CA 9-12R; CANR 37, 80; CLR 25; JRDA; MAICYA; SAAS 11; SATA 6, 68

Mayo, Jim
See L'Amour, Louis (Dearborn)

Maysles, Albert 1926- .... **CLC 16**
See also CA 29-32R

Maysles, David 1932- .... **CLC 16**

Mazer, Norma Fox 1931- .... **CLC 26**
See also AAYA 5, 36; CA 69-72; CANR 12, 32, 66; CLR 23; JRDA; MAICYA; SAAS 1; SATA 24, 67, 105

Mazzini, Guiseppe 1805-1872 .... **NCLC 34**

McAlmon, Robert (Menzies) 1895-1956 .... **TCLC 97**
See also CA 107; 168; DLB 4, 45; DLBD 15

McAuley, James Phillip 1917-1976 .. **CLC 45**
See also CA 97-100

McBain, Ed
See Hunter, Evan

McBrien, William (Augustine) 1930- .... **CLC 44**
See also CA 107; CANR 90

McCabe, Patrick 1955- .... **CLC 133**
See also CA 130; CANR 50, 90; DLB 194

McCaffrey, Anne (Inez) 1926- .... **CLC 17; DAM NOV, POP**
See also AAYA 6, 34; AITN 2; BEST 89:2; CA 25-28R; CANR 15, 35, 55; CLR 49; DA3; DLB 8; JRDA; MAICYA; MTCW 1, 2; SAAS 11; SATA 8, 70, 116

McCall, Nathan 1955(?)- .... **CLC 86**
See also BW 3; CA 146; CANR 88

McCann, Arthur
See Campbell, John W(ood, Jr.)

McCann, Edson
See Pohl, Frederik

McCarthy, Charles, Jr. 1933-
See McCarthy, Cormac
See also CANR 42, 69; DAM POP; DA3; MTCW 2

McCarthy, Cormac 1933- ...... **CLC 4, 57, 59, 101**
See also McCarthy, Charles, Jr.
See also DLB 6, 143; MTCW 2

McCarthy, Mary (Therese) 1912-1989 .. **CLC 1, 3, 5, 14, 24, 39, 59; SSC 24**
See also CA 5-8R; 129; CANR 16, 50, 64; DA3; DLB 2; DLBY 81; INT CANR-16; MTCW 1, 2

McCartney, (James) Paul 1942- . **CLC 12, 35**
See also CA 146

McCauley, Stephen (D.) 1955- .... **CLC 50**
See also CA 141

McClure, Michael (Thomas) 1932- ... **CLC 6, 10**
See also CA 21-24R; CANR 17, 46, 77; DLB 16

McCorkle, Jill (Collins) 1958- .... **CLC 51**
See also CA 121; DLB 234; DLBY 87

McCourt, Frank 1930- .... **CLC 109**
See also CA 157

McCourt, James 1941- .... **CLC 5**
See also CA 57-60

McCourt, Malachy 1932- .... **CLC 119**

McCoy, Horace (Stanley) 1897-1955 .... **TCLC 28**
See also CA 108; 155; DLB 9

McCrae, John 1872-1918 .... **TCLC 12**
See also CA 109; DLB 92

McCreigh, James
See Pohl, Frederik

McCullers, (Lula) Carson (Smith) 1917-1967 .... **CLC 1, 4, 10, 12, 48, 100; DA; DAB; DAC; DAM MST, NOV; SSC 9, 24; WLC**
See also AAYA 21; CA 5-8R; 25-28R; CABS 1, 3; CANR 18; CDALB 1941-1968; DA3; DLB 2, 7, 173, 228; MTCW 1, 2; SATA 27

McCulloch, John Tyler
See Burroughs, Edgar Rice

McCullough, Colleen 1938(?)- .... **CLC 27, 107; DAM NOV, POP**
See also AAYA 36; CA 81-84; CANR 17, 46, 67; DA3; MTCW 1, 2

McDermott, Alice 1953- .... **CLC 90**
See also CA 109; CANR 40, 90

McElroy, Joseph 1930- .... **CLC 5, 47**
See also CA 17-20R

McEwan, Ian (Russell) 1948- .... **CLC 13, 66; DAM NOV**
See also BEST 90:4; CA 61-64; CANR 14, 41, 69, 87; DLB 14, 194; MTCW 1, 2

McFadden, David 1940- .... **CLC 48**
See also CA 104; DLB 60; INT 104

McFarland, Dennis 1950- .... **CLC 65**
See also CA 165

McGahern, John 1934- ... **CLC 5, 9, 48; SSC 17**
See also CA 17-20R; CANR 29, 68; DLB 14, 231; MTCW 1

McGinley, Patrick (Anthony) 1937- . **CLC 41**
See also CA 120; 127; CANR 56; INT 127

McGinley, Phyllis 1905-1978 .... **CLC 14**
See also CA 9-12R; 77-80; CANR 19; DLB 11, 48; SATA 2, 44; SATA-Obit 24

McGinniss, Joe 1942- .... **CLC 32**
See also AITN 2; BEST 89:2; CA 25-28R; CANR 26, 70; DLB 185; INT CANR-26

McGivern, Maureen Daly
See Daly, Maureen

McGrath, Patrick 1950- .... **CLC 55**
See also CA 136; CANR 65; DLB 231

McGrath, Thomas (Matthew) 1916-1990 ..... **CLC 28, 59; DAM POET**
See also CA 9-12R; 132; CANR 6, 33; MTCW 1; SATA 41; SATA-Obit 66

McGuane, Thomas (Francis III) 1939- .... **CLC 3, 7, 18, 45, 127**
See also AITN 2; CA 49-52; CANR 5, 24, 49; DLB 2, 212; DLBY 80; INT CANR-24; MTCW 1

McGuckian, Medbh 1950- .... **CLC 48; DAM POET; PC 27**
See also CA 143; DLB 40

McHale, Tom 1942(?)-1982 .... **CLC 3, 5**
See also AITN 1; CA 77-80; 106

McIlvanney, William 1936- .... **CLC 42**
See also CA 25-28R; CANR 61; DLB 14, 207

McIlwraith, Maureen Mollie Hunter
See Hunter, Mollie
See also SATA 2

McInerney, Jay 1955- .... **CLC 34, 112; DAM POP**
See also AAYA 18; CA 116; 123; CANR 45, 68; DA3; INT 123; MTCW 2

McIntyre, Vonda N(eel) 1948- .... **CLC 18**
See also CA 81-84; CANR 17, 34, 69; MTCW 1

McKay, Claude **TCLC 7, 41; BLC 3; DAB; PC 2**
See also McKay, Festus Claudius
See also DLB 4, 45, 51, 117

McKay, Festus Claudius 1889-1948
See McKay, Claude
See also BW 1, 3; CA 104; 124; CANR 73; DA; DAC; DAM MST, MULT, NOV, POET; MTCW 1, 2; WLC

McKuen, Rod 1933- .... **CLC 1, 3**
See also AITN 1; CA 41-44R; CANR 40

McLoughlin, R. B.
See Mencken, H(enry) L(ouis)

McLuhan, (Herbert) Marshall 1911-1980 .... **CLC 37, 83**
See also CA 9-12R; 102; CANR 12, 34, 61; DLB 88; INT CANR-12; MTCW 1, 2

McMillan, Terry (L.) 1951- .... **CLC 50, 61, 112; BLCS; DAM MULT, NOV, POP**
See also AAYA 21; BW 2, 3; CA 140; CANR 60; DA3; MTCW 2

McMurtry, Larry (Jeff) 1936- .. **CLC 2, 3, 7, 11, 27, 44, 127; DAM NOV, POP**
See also AAYA 15; AITN 2; BEST 89:2; CA 5-8R; CANR 19, 43, 64; CDALB 1968-1988; DA3; DLB 2, 143; DLBY 80, 87; MTCW 1, 2

McNally, T. M. 1961- .... **CLC 82**

McNally, Terrence 1939- ... **CLC 4, 7, 41, 91; DAM DRAM**
See also CA 45-48; CANR 2, 56; DA3; DLB 7; MTCW 2

McNamer, Deirdre 1950- .... **CLC 70**

McNeal, Tom **CLC 119**

McNeile, Herman Cyril 1888-1937
See Sapper
See also CA 184; DLB 77
McNickle, (William) D'Arcy
1904-1977 .... **CLC 89; DAM MULT**
See also CA 9-12R; 85-88; CANR 5, 45;
DLB 175, 212; NNAL; SATA-Obit 22
McPhee, John (Angus) 1931- .... **CLC 36**
See also BEST 90:1; CA 65-68; CANR 20,
46, 64, 69; DLB 185; MTCW 1, 2
McPherson, James Alan 1943- .. **CLC 19, 77;**
BLCS
See also BW 1, 3; CA 25-28R; CAAS 17;
CANR 24, 74; DLB 38; MTCW 1, 2
McPherson, William (Alexander)
1933- .... **CLC 34**
See also CA 69-72; CANR 28; INT
CANR-28
McTaggart, J. McT. Ellis
See McTaggart, John McTaggart Ellis
McTaggart, John McTaggart Ellis
1866-1925 .... **TCLC 105**
See also CA 120
Mead, George Herbert 1873-1958 . **TCLC 89**
Mead, Margaret 1901-1978 .... **CLC 37**
See also AITN 1; CA 1-4R; 81-84; CANR
4; DA3; MTCW 1, 2; SATA-Obit 20
Meaker, Marijane (Agnes) 1927-
See Kerr, M. E.
See also CA 107; CANR 37, 63; INT 107;
JRDA; MAICYA; MTCW 1; SATA 20,
61, 99; SATA-Essay 111
Medoff, Mark (Howard) 1940- ... **CLC 6, 23;**
DAM DRAM
See also AITN 1; CA 53-56; CANR 5; DLB
7; INT CANR-5
Medvedev, P. N.
See Bakhtin, Mikhail Mikhailovich
Meged, Aharon
See Megged, Aharon
Meged, Aron
See Megged, Aharon
Megged, Aharon 1920- .... **CLC 9**
See also CA 49-52; CAAS 13; CANR 1
Mehta, Ved (Parkash) 1934- .... **CLC 37**
See also CA 1-4R; CANR 2, 23, 69; MTCW
1
Melanter
See Blackmore, R(ichard) D(oddridge)
Melies, Georges 1861-1938 .... **TCLC 81**
Melikow, Loris
See Hofmannsthal, Hugo von
Melmoth, Sebastian
See Wilde, Oscar (Fingal O'Flahertie Wills)
Meltzer, Milton 1915- .... **CLC 26**
See also AAYA 8; CA 13-16R; CANR 38,
92; CLR 13; DLB 61; JRDA; MAICYA;
SAAS 1; SATA 1, 50, 80
Melville, Herman 1819-1891 ... **NCLC 3, 12,**
29, 45, 49, 91, 93; DA; DAB; DAC;
DAM MST, NOV; SSC 1, 17; WLC
See also AAYA 25; CDALB 1640-1865;
DA3; DLB 3, 74; SATA 59
Menander c. 342B.C.-c. 292B.C. ... **CMLC 9;**
DAM DRAM; DC 3
See also DLB 176
Menchu, Rigoberta 1959-
See also CA 175; HLCS 2
Mencken, H(enry) L(ouis)
1880-1956 .... **TCLC 13**
See also CA 105; 125; CDALB 1917-1929;
DLB 11, 29, 63, 137, 222; MTCW 1, 2
Mendelsohn, Jane 1965- .... **CLC 99**
See also CA 154; CANR 94
Mercer, David 1928-1980 .... **CLC 5; DAM**
DRAM
See also CA 9-12R; 102; CANR 23; DLB
13; MTCW 1

Merchant, Paul
See Ellison, Harlan (Jay)
Meredith, George 1828-1909 .. **TCLC 17, 43;**
DAM POET
See also CA 117; 153; CANR 80; CDBLB
1832-1890; DLB 18, 35, 57, 159
Meredith, William (Morris) 1919- .... **CLC 4,**
13, 22, 55; DAM POET; PC 28
See also CA 9-12R; CAAS 14; CANR 6,
40; DLB 5
Merezhkovsky, Dmitry Sergeyevich
1865-1941 .... **TCLC 29**
See also CA 169
Merimee, Prosper 1803-1870 ... **NCLC 6, 65;**
SSC 7
See also DLB 119, 192
Merkin, Daphne 1954- .... **CLC 44**
See also CA 123
Merlin, Arthur
See Blish, James (Benjamin)
Merrill, James (Ingram) 1926-1995 .. **CLC 2,**
3, 6, 8, 13, 18, 34, 91; DAM POET; PC
28
See also CA 13-16R; 147; CANR 10, 49,
63; DA3; DLB 5, 165; DLBY 85; INT
CANR-10; MTCW 1, 2
Merriman, Alex
See Silverberg, Robert
Merriman, Brian 1747-1805 .... **NCLC 70**
Merritt, E. B.
See Waddington, Miriam
Merton, Thomas 1915-1968 ..... **CLC 1, 3, 11,**
34, 83; PC 10
See also CA 5-8R; 25-28R; CANR 22, 53;
DA3; DLB 48; DLBY 81; MTCW 1, 2
Merwin, W(illiam) S(tanley) 1927- ... **CLC 1,**
2, 3, 5, 8, 13, 18, 45, 88; DAM POET
See also CA 13-16R; CANR 15, 51; DA3;
DLB 5, 169; INT CANR-15; MTCW 1, 2
Metcalf, John 1938- .... **CLC 37; SSC 43**
See also CA 113; DLB 60
Metcalf, Suzanne
See Baum, L(yman) Frank
Mew, Charlotte (Mary) 1869-1928 .. **TCLC 8**
See also CA 105; DLB 19, 135
Mewshaw, Michael 1943- .... **CLC 9**
See also CA 53-56; CANR 7, 47; DLBY 80
Meyer, Conrad Ferdinand
1825-1905 .... **NCLC 81**
See also DLB 129
Meyer, June
See Jordan, June
Meyer, Lynn
See Slavitt, David R(ytman)
Meyer-Meyrink, Gustav 1868-1932
See Meyrink, Gustav
See also CA 117
Meyers, Jeffrey 1939- .... **CLC 39**
See also CA 73-76; CAAE 186; CANR 54;
DLB 111
Meynell, Alice (Christina Gertrude
Thompson) 1847-1922 .... **TCLC 6**
See also CA 104; 177; DLB 19, 98
Meyrink, Gustav **TCLC 21**
See also Meyer-Meyrink, Gustav
See also DLB 81
Michaels, Leonard 1933- .... **CLC 6, 25; SSC**
16
See also CA 61-64; CANR 21, 62; DLB
130; MTCW 1
Michaux, Henri 1899-1984 .... **CLC 8, 19**
See also CA 85-88; 114
Micheaux, Oscar (Devereaux)
1884-1951 .... **TCLC 76**
See also BW 3; CA 174; DLB 50
Michelangelo 1475-1564 .... **LC 12**
Michelet, Jules 1798-1874 .... **NCLC 31**
Michels, Robert 1876-1936 .... **TCLC 88**

Michener, James A(lbert)
1907(?)-1997 .... **CLC 1, 5, 11, 29, 60,**
109; DAM NOV, POP
See also AAYA 27; AITN 1; BEST 90:1;
CA 5-8R; 161; CANR 21, 45, 68; DA3;
DLB 6; MTCW 1, 2
Mickiewicz, Adam 1798-1855 .... **NCLC 3**
Middleton, Christopher 1926- .... **CLC 13**
See also CA 13-16R; CANR 29, 54; DLB
40
Middleton, Richard (Barham)
1882-1911 .... **TCLC 56**
See also CA 187; DLB 156
Middleton, Stanley 1919- .... **CLC 7, 38**
See also CA 25-28R; CAAS 23; CANR 21,
46, 81; DLB 14
Middleton, Thomas 1580-1627 .... **LC 33;**
DAM DRAM, MST; DC 5
See also DLB 58
Migueis, Jose Rodrigues 1901- .... **CLC 10**
Mikszath, Kalman 1847-1910 .... **TCLC 31**
See also CA 170
Miles, Jack CLC 100
Miles, Josephine (Louise)
1911-1985 .. **CLC 1, 2, 14, 34, 39; DAM**
POET
See also CA 1-4R; 116; CANR 2, 55; DLB
48
Militant
See Sandburg, Carl (August)
Mill, John Stuart 1806-1873 .... **NCLC 11, 58**
See also CDBLB 1832-1890; DLB 55, 190
Millar, Kenneth 1915-1983 ... **CLC 14; DAM**
POP
See also Macdonald, Ross
See also CA 9-12R; 110; CANR 16, 63;
DA3; DLB 2, 226; DLBD 6; DLBY 83;
MTCW 1, 2
Millay, E. Vincent
See Millay, Edna St. Vincent
Millay, Edna St. Vincent
1892-1950 .... **TCLC 4, 49; DA; DAB;**
DAC; DAM MST, POET; PC 6;
WLCS
See also CA 104; 130; CDALB 1917-1929;
DA3; DLB 45; MTCW 1, 2
Miller, Arthur 1915- ...... **CLC 1, 2, 6, 10, 15,**
26, 47, 78; DA; DAB; DAC; DAM
DRAM, MST; DC 1; WLC
See also AAYA 15; AITN 1; CA 1-4R;
CABS 3; CANR 2, 30, 54, 76; CDALB
1941-1968; DA3; DLB 7; MTCW 1, 2
Miller, Henry (Valentine)
1891-1980 .... **CLC 1, 2, 4, 9, 14, 43, 84;**
DA; DAB; DAC; DAM MST, NOV;
WLC
See also CA 9-12R; 97-100; CANR 33, 64;
CDALB 1929-1941; DA3; DLB 4, 9;
DLBY 80; MTCW 1, 2
Miller, Jason 1939(?)- .... **CLC 2**
See also AITN 1; CA 73-76; DLB 7
Miller, Sue 1943- .... **CLC 44; DAM POP**
See also BEST 90:3; CA 139; CANR 59,
91; DA3; DLB 143
Miller, Walter M(ichael, Jr.) 1923- ... **CLC 4,**
30
See also CA 85-88; DLB 8
Millett, Kate 1934- .... **CLC 67**
See also AITN 1; CA 73-76; CANR 32, 53,
76; DA3; MTCW 1, 2
Millhauser, Steven (Lewis) 1943- .... **CLC 21,**
54, 109
See also CA 110; 111; CANR 63; DA3;
DLB 2; INT 111; MTCW 2
Millin, Sarah Gertrude 1889-1968 ... **CLC 49**
See also CA 102; 93-96; DLB 225

Morante, Elsa 1918-1985 .... **CLC 8, 47**
See also CA 85-88; 117; CANR 35; DLB
177; MTCW 1, 2

Moravia, Alberto 1907-1990 .... **CLC 2, 7, 11, 27, 46; SSC 26**
See also Pincherle, Alberto
See also DLB 177; MTCW 2

More, Hannah 1745-1833 .... **NCLC 27**
See also DLB 107, 109, 116, 158

More, Henry 1614-1687 .... **LC 9**
See also DLB 126

More, Sir Thomas 1478-1535 .... **LC 10, 32**

Moreas, Jean TCLC 18
See also Papadiamantopoulos, Johannes

Morgan, Berry 1919- .... **CLC 6**
See also CA 49-52; DLB 6

Morgan, Claire
See Highsmith, (Mary) Patricia

Morgan, Edwin (George) 1920- .... **CLC 31**
See also CA 5-8R; CANR 3, 43, 90; DLB
27

Morgan, (George) Frederick 1922- .. **CLC 23**
See also CA 17-20R; CANR 21

Morgan, Harriet
See Mencken, H(enry) L(ouis)

Morgan, Jane
See Cooper, James Fenimore

Morgan, Janet 1945- .... **CLC 39**
See also CA 65-68

Morgan, Lady 1776(?)-1859 .... **NCLC 29**
See also DLB 116, 158

Morgan, Robin (Evonne) 1941- .... **CLC 2**
See also CA 69-72; CANR 29, 68; MTCW
1; SATA 80

Morgan, Scott
See Kuttner, Henry

Morgan, Seth 1949(?)-1990 .... **CLC 65**
See also CA 185; 132

Morgenstern, Christian 1871-1914 .. **TCLC 8**
See also CA 105

Morgenstern, S.
See Goldman, William (W.)

Moricz, Zsigmond 1879-1942 .... **TCLC 33**
See also CA 165

Morike, Eduard (Friedrich) 1804-1875 .... **NCLC 10**
See also DLB 133

Moritz, Karl Philipp 1756-1793 .... **LC 2**
See also DLB 94

Morland, Peter Henry
See Faust, Frederick (Schiller)

Morley, Christopher (Darlington) 1890-1957 .... **TCLC 87**
See also CA 112; DLB 9

Morren, Theophil
See Hofmannsthal, Hugo von

Morris, Bill 1952- .... **CLC 76**

Morris, Julian
See West, Morris L(anglo)

Morris, Steveland Judkins 1950(?)-
See Wonder, Stevie
See also CA 111

Morris, William 1834-1896 .... **NCLC 4**
See also CDBLB 1832-1890; DLB 18, 35,
57, 156, 178, 184

Morris, Wright 1910-1998 .. **CLC 1, 3, 7, 18, 37**
See also CA 9-12R; 167; CANR 21, 81;
DLB 2, 206; DLBY 81; MTCW 1, 2

Morrison, Arthur 1863-1945 .... **TCLC 72; SSC 40**
See also CA 120; 157; DLB 70, 135, 197

Morrison, Chloe Anthony Wofford
See Morrison, Toni

Morrison, James Douglas 1943-1971
See Morrison, Jim
See also CA 73-76; CANR 40

Morrison, Jim CLC 17
See also Morrison, James Douglas

Morrison, Toni 1931- . **CLC 4, 10, 22, 55, 81, 87; BLC 3; DA; DAB; DAC; DAM MST, MULT, NOV, POP**
See also AAYA 1, 22; BW 2, 3; CA 29-32R;
CANR 27, 42, 67; CDALB 1968-1988;
DA3; DLB 6, 33, 143; DLBY 81; MTCW
1, 2; SATA 57

Morrison, Van 1945- .... **CLC 21**
See also CA 116; 168

Morrissy, Mary 1958- .... **CLC 99**

Mortimer, John (Clifford) 1923- ..... **CLC 28, 43; DAM DRAM, POP**
See also CA 13-16R; CANR 21, 69; CD-
BLB 1960 to Present; DA3; DLB 13; INT
CANR-21; MTCW 1, 2

Mortimer, Penelope (Ruth) 1918-1999 .... **CLC 5**
See also CA 57-60; 187; CANR 45, 88

Morton, Anthony
See Creasey, John

Mosca, Gaetano 1858-1941 .... **TCLC 75**

Mosher, Howard Frank 1943- .... **CLC 62**
See also CA 139; CANR 65

Mosley, Nicholas 1923- .... **CLC 43, 70**
See also CA 69-72; CANR 41, 60; DLB 14,
207

Mosley, Walter 1952- .... **CLC 97; BLCS; DAM MULT, POP**
See also AAYA 17; BW 2; CA 142; CANR
57, 92; DA3; MTCW 2

Moss, Howard 1922-1987 ...... **CLC 7, 14, 45, 50; DAM POET**
See also CA 1-4R; 123; CANR 1, 44; DLB
5

Mossgiel, Rab
See Burns, Robert

Motion, Andrew (Peter) 1952- .... **CLC 47**
See also CA 146; CANR 90; DLB 40

Motley, Willard (Francis) 1909-1965 .... **CLC 18**
See also BW 1; CA 117; 106; CANR 88;
DLB 76, 143

Motoori, Norinaga 1730-1801 .... **NCLC 45**

Mott, Michael (Charles Alston) 1930- .... **CLC 15, 34**
See also CA 5-8R; CAAS 7; CANR 7, 29

Mountain Wolf Woman 1884-1960 .. **CLC 92**
See also CA 144; CANR 90; NNAL

Moure, Erin 1955- .... **CLC 88**
See also CA 113; DLB 60

Mowat, Farley (McGill) 1921- .... **CLC 26; DAC; DAM MST**
See also AAYA 1; CA 1-4R; CANR 4, 24,
42, 68; CLR 20; DLB 68; INT CANR-24;
JRDA; MAICYA; MTCW 1, 2; SATA 3,
55

Mowatt, Anna Cora 1819-1870 ..... **NCLC 74**

Moyers, Bill 1934- .... **CLC 74**
See also AITN 2; CA 61-64; CANR 31, 52

Mphahlele, Es'kia
See Mphahlele, Ezekiel
See also DLB 125, 225

Mphahlele, Ezekiel 1919- .... **CLC 25, 133; BLC 3; DAM MULT**
See also Mphahlele, Es'kia
See also BW 2, 3; CA 81-84; CANR 26,
76; DA3; DLB 225; MTCW 2; SATA 119

Mqhayi, S(amuel) E(dward) K(rune Loliwe) 1875-1945 ...... **TCLC 25; BLC 3; DAM MULT**
See also CA 153; CANR 87

Mrozek, Slawomir 1930- .... **CLC 3, 13**
See also CA 13-16R; CAAS 10; CANR 29;
DLB 232; MTCW 1

Mrs. Belloc-Lowndes
See Lowndes, Marie Adelaide (Belloc)

M'Taggart, John M'Taggart Ellis
See McTaggart, John McTaggart Ellis

Mtwa, Percy (?)- .... **CLC 47**

Mueller, Lisel 1924- .... **CLC 13, 51; PC 33**
See also CA 93-96; DLB 105

Muir, Edwin 1887-1959 .... **TCLC 2, 87**
See also CA 104; DLB 20, 100, 191

Muir, John 1838-1914 .... **TCLC 28**
See also CA 165; DLB 186

Mujica Lainez, Manuel 1910-1984 ... **CLC 31**
See also Lainez, Manuel Mujica
See also CA 81-84; 112; CANR 32; HW 1

Mukherjee, Bharati 1940- .... **CLC 53, 115; DAM NOV; SSC 38**
See also BEST 89:2; CA 107; CANR 45,
72; DLB 60; MTCW 1, 2

Muldoon, Paul 1951- .... **CLC 32, 72; DAM POET**
See also CA 113; 129; CANR 52, 91; DLB
40; INT 129

Mulisch, Harry 1927- .... **CLC 42**
See also CA 9-12R; CANR 6, 26, 56

Mull, Martin 1943- .... **CLC 17**
See also CA 105

Muller, Wilhelm NCLC 73

Mulock, Dinah Maria
See Craik, Dinah Maria (Mulock)

Munford, Robert 1737(?)-1783 .... **LC 5**
See also DLB 31

Mungo, Raymond 1946- .... **CLC 72**
See also CA 49-52; CANR 2

Munro, Alice 1931- .... **CLC 6, 10, 19, 50, 95; DAC; DAM MST, NOV; SSC 3; WLCS**
See also AITN 2; CA 33-36R; CANR 33,
53, 75; DA3; DLB 53; MTCW 1, 2; SATA
29

Munro, H(ector) H(ugh) 1870-1916
See Saki
See also CA 104; 130; CDBLB 1890-1914;
DA; DAB; DAC; DAM MST, NOV; DA3;
DLB 34, 162; MTCW 1, 2; WLC

Murdoch, (Jean) Iris 1919-1999 ... **CLC 1, 2, 3, 4, 6, 8, 11, 15, 22, 31, 51; DAB; DAC; DAM MST, NOV**
See also CA 13-16R; 179; CANR 8, 43, 68;
CDBLB 1960 to Present; DA3; DLB 14,
194, 233; INT CANR-8; MTCW 1, 2

Murfree, Mary Noailles 1850-1922 ... **SSC 22**
See also CA 122; 176; DLB 12, 74

Murnau, Friedrich Wilhelm
See Plumpe, Friedrich Wilhelm

Murphy, Richard 1927- .... **CLC 41**
See also CA 29-32R; DLB 40

Murphy, Sylvia 1937- .... **CLC 34**
See also CA 121

Murphy, Thomas (Bernard) 1935- ... **CLC 51**
See also CA 101

Murray, Albert L. 1916- .... **CLC 73**
See also BW 2; CA 49-52; CANR 26, 52,
78; DLB 38

Murray, Judith Sargent 1751-1820 .... **NCLC 63**
See also DLB 37, 200

Murray, Les(lie) A(llan) 1938- .... **CLC 40; DAM POET**
See also CA 21-24R; CANR 11, 27, 56

Murry, J. Middleton
See Murry, John Middleton

Murry, John Middleton 1889-1957 .... **TCLC 16**
See also CA 118; DLB 149

Musgrave, Susan 1951- .... **CLC 13, 54**
See also CA 69-72; CANR 45, 84

Musil, Robert (Edler von) 1880-1942 .... **TCLC 12, 68; SSC 18**
See also CA 109; CANR 55, 84; DLB 81,
124; MTCW 2

Norfolk, Lawrence 1963- .... **CLC 76**
See also CA 144; CANR 85
Norman, Marsha 1947- .... **CLC 28; DAM DRAM; DC 8**
See also CA 105; CABS 3; CANR 41; DLBY 84
Normyx
See Douglas, (George) Norman
Norris, Frank 1870-1902 .... **SSC 28**
See also Norris, (Benjamin) Frank(lin, Jr.)
See also CDALB 1865-1917; DLB 12, 71, 186
Norris, (Benjamin) Frank(lin, Jr.)
1870-1902 .... **TCLC 24**
See also Norris, Frank
See also CA 110; 160
Norris, Leslie 1921- .... **CLC 14**
See also CA 11-12; CANR 14; CAP 1; DLB 27
North, Andrew
See Norton, Andre
North, Anthony
See Koontz, Dean R(ay)
North, Captain George
See Stevenson, Robert Louis (Balfour)
North, Milou
See Erdrich, Louise
Northrup, B. A.
See Hubbard, L(afayette) Ron(ald)
North Staffs
See Hulme, T(homas) E(rnest)
Norton, Alice Mary
See Norton, Andre
See also MAICYA; SATA 1, 43
Norton, Andre 1912- .... **CLC 12**
See also Norton, Alice Mary
See also AAYA 14; CA 1-4R; CANR 68; CLR 50; DLB 8, 52; JRDA; MTCW 1; SATA 91
Norton, Caroline 1808-1877 .... **NCLC 47**
See also DLB 21, 159, 199
Norway, Nevil Shute 1899-1960
See Shute, Nevil
See also CA 102; 93-96; CANR 85; MTCW 2
Norwid, Cyprian Kamil
1821-1883 .... **NCLC 17**
Nosille, Nabrah
See Ellison, Harlan (Jay)
Nossack, Hans Erich 1901-1978 .... **CLC 6**
See also CA 93-96; 85-88; DLB 69
Nostradamus 1503-1566 .... **LC 27**
Nosu, Chuji
See Ozu, Yasujiro
Notenburg, Eleanora (Genrikhovna) von
See Guro, Elena
Nova, Craig 1945- .... **CLC 7, 31**
See also CA 45-48; CANR 2, 53
Novak, Joseph
See Kosinski, Jerzy (Nikodem)
Novalis 1772-1801 .... **NCLC 13**
See also DLB 90
Novis, Emile
See Weil, Simone (Adolphine)
Nowlan, Alden (Albert) 1933-1983 . **CLC 15; DAC; DAM MST**
See also CA 9-12R; CANR 5; DLB 53
Noyes, Alfred 1880-1958 ...... **TCLC 7; PC 27**
See also CA 104; DLB 20
Nunn, Kem **CLC 34**
See also CA 159
Nwapa, Flora 1931- .... **CLC 133; BLCS**
See also BW 2; CA 143; CANR 83; DLB 125
Nye, Robert 1939- . **CLC 13, 42; DAM NOV**
See also CA 33-36R; CANR 29, 67; DLB 14; MTCW 1; SATA 6
Nyro, Laura 1947- .... **CLC 17**

Oates, Joyce Carol 1938- .. **CLC 1, 2, 3, 6, 9, 11, 15, 19, 33, 52, 108, 134; DA; DAB; DAC; DAM MST, NOV, POP; SSC 6; WLC**
See also AAYA 15; AITN 1; BEST 89:2; CA 5-8R; CANR 25, 45, 74; CDALB 1968-1988; DA3; DLB 2, 5, 130; DLBY 81; INT CANR-25; MTCW 1, 2
O'Brien, Darcy 1939-1998 .... **CLC 11**
See also CA 21-24R; 167; CANR 8, 59
O'Brien, E. G.
See Clarke, Arthur C(harles)
O'Brien, Edna 1936- ..... **CLC 3, 5, 8, 13, 36, 65, 116; DAM NOV; SSC 10**
See also CA 1-4R; CANR 6, 41, 65; CD-BLB 1960 to Present; DA3; DLB 14, 231; MTCW 1, 2
O'Brien, Fitz-James 1828-1862 ..... **NCLC 21**
See also DLB 74
O'Brien, Flann **CLC 1, 4, 5, 7, 10, 47**
See also O Nuallain, Brian
See also DLB 231
O'Brien, Richard 1942- .... **CLC 17**
See also CA 124
O'Brien, (William) Tim(othy) 1946- . **CLC 7, 19, 40, 103; DAM POP**
See also AAYA 16; CA 85-88; CANR 40, 58; CDALBS; DA3; DLB 152; DLBD 9; DLBY 80; MTCW 2
Obstfelder, Sigbjoern 1866-1900 .... **TCLC 23**
See also CA 123
O'Casey, Sean 1880-1964 .... **CLC 1, 5, 9, 11, 15, 88; DAB; DAC; DAM DRAM, MST; DC 12; WLCS**
See also CA 89-92; CANR 62; CDBLB 1914-1945; DA3; DLB 10; MTCW 1, 2
O'Cathasaigh, Sean
See O'Casey, Sean
Occom, Samson 1723-1792 .... **LC 60**
See also DLB 175; NNAL
Ochs, Phil(ip David) 1940-1976 .... **CLC 17**
See also CA 185; 65-68
O'Connor, Edwin (Greene)
1918-1968 .... **CLC 14**
See also CA 93-96; 25-28R
O'Connor, (Mary) Flannery
1925-1964 .... **CLC 1, 2, 3, 6, 10, 13, 15, 21, 66, 104; DA; DAB; DAC; DAM MST, NOV; SSC 1, 23; WLC**
See also AAYA 7; CA 1-4R; CANR 3, 41; CDALB 1941-1968; DA3; DLB 2, 152; DLBD 12; DLBY 80; MTCW 1, 2
O'Connor, Frank **CLC 23; SSC 5**
See also O'Donovan, Michael John
See also DLB 162
O'Dell, Scott 1898-1989 .... **CLC 30**
See also AAYA 3; CA 61-64; 129; CANR 12, 30; CLR 1, 16; DLB 52; JRDA; MAICYA; SATA 12, 60
Odets, Clifford 1906-1963 ..... **CLC 2, 28, 98; DAM DRAM; DC 6**
See also CA 85-88; CANR 62; DLB 7, 26; MTCW 1, 2
O'Doherty, Brian 1934- .... **CLC 76**
See also CA 105
O'Donnell, K. M.
See Malzberg, Barry N(athaniel)
O'Donnell, Lawrence
See Kuttner, Henry
O'Donovan, Michael John
1903-1966 .... **CLC 14**
See also O'Connor, Frank
See also CA 93-96; CANR 84
Oe, Kenzaburo 1935- .... **CLC 10, 36, 86; DAM NOV; SSC 20**
See also CA 97-100; CANR 36, 50, 74; DA3; DLB 182; DLBY 94; MTCW 1, 2

O'Faolain, Julia 1932- .... **CLC 6, 19, 47, 108**
See also CA 81-84; CAAS 2; CANR 12, 61; DLB 14, 231; MTCW 1
O'Faolain, Sean 1900-1991 ...... **CLC 1, 7, 14, 32, 70; SSC 13**
See also CA 61-64; 134; CANR 12, 66; DLB 15, 162; MTCW 1, 2
O'Flaherty, Liam 1896-1984 .... **CLC 5, 34; SSC 6**
See also CA 101; 113; CANR 35; DLB 36, 162; DLBY 84; MTCW 1, 2
Ogilvy, Gavin
See Barrie, J(ames) M(atthew)
O'Grady, Standish (James)
1846-1928 .... **TCLC 5**
See also CA 104; 157
O'Grady, Timothy 1951- .... **CLC 59**
See also CA 138
O'Hara, Frank 1926-1966 .... **CLC 2, 5, 13, 78; DAM POET**
See also CA 9-12R; 25-28R; CANR 33; DA3; DLB 5, 16, 193; MTCW 1, 2
O'Hara, John (Henry) 1905-1970 . **CLC 1, 2, 3, 6, 11, 42; DAM NOV; SSC 15**
See also CA 5-8R; 25-28R; CANR 31, 60; CDALB 1929-1941; DLB 9, 86; DLBD 2; MTCW 1, 2
O Hehir, Diana 1922- .... **CLC 41**
See also CA 93-96
Ohiyesa
See Eastman, Charles A(lexander)
Okigbo, Christopher (Ifenayichukwu)
1932-1967 ... **CLC 25, 84; BLC 3; DAM MULT, POET; PC 7**
See also BW 1, 3; CA 77-80; CANR 74; DLB 125; MTCW 1, 2
Okri, Ben 1959- .... **CLC 87**
See also BW 2, 3; CA 130; 138; CANR 65; DLB 157, 231; INT 138; MTCW 2
Olds, Sharon 1942- ... **CLC 32, 39, 85; DAM POET; PC 22**
See also CA 101; CANR 18, 41, 66; DLB 120; MTCW 2
Oldstyle, Jonathan
See Irving, Washington
Olesha, Yuri (Karlovich) 1899-1960 .. **CLC 8**
See also CA 85-88
Oliphant, Laurence 1829(?)-1888 .. **NCLC 47**
See also DLB 18, 166
Oliphant, Margaret (Oliphant Wilson)
1828-1897 .... **NCLC 11, 61; SSC 25**
See also DLB 18, 159, 190
Oliver, Mary 1935- .... **CLC 19, 34, 98**
See also CA 21-24R; CANR 9, 43, 84, 92; DLB 5, 193
Olivier, Laurence (Kerr) 1907-1989 . **CLC 20**
See also CA 111; 150; 129
Olsen, Tillie 1912- .... **CLC 4, 13, 114; DA; DAB; DAC; DAM MST; SSC 11**
See also CA 1-4R; CANR 1, 43, 74; CDALBS; DA3; DLB 28, 206; DLBY 80; MTCW 1, 2
Olson, Charles (John) 1910-1970 .. **CLC 1, 2, 5, 6, 9, 11, 29; DAM POET; PC 19**
See also CA 13-16; 25-28R; CABS 2; CANR 35, 61; CAP 1; DLB 5, 16, 193; MTCW 1, 2
Olson, Toby 1937- .... **CLC 28**
See also CA 65-68; CANR 9, 31, 84
Olyesha, Yuri
See Olesha, Yuri (Karlovich)
Ondaatje, (Philip) Michael 1943- .... **CLC 14, 29, 51, 76; DAB; DAC; DAM MST; PC 28**
See also CA 77-80; CANR 42, 74; DA3; DLB 60; MTCW 2

Oneal, Elizabeth 1934-
See Oneal, Zibby
See also CA 106; CANR 28, 84; MAICYA;
SATA 30, 82
Oneal, Zibby CLC 30
See also Oneal, Elizabeth
See also AAYA 5; CLR 13; JRDA
O'Neill, Eugene (Gladstone)
1888-1953 .... **TCLC 1, 6, 27, 49; DA;
DAB; DAC; DAM DRAM, MST; WLC**
See also AITN 1; CA 110; 132; CDALB
1929-1941; DA3; DLB 7; MTCW 1, 2
Onetti, Juan Carlos 1909-1994 ... **CLC 7, 10;
DAM MULT, NOV; HLCS 2; SSC 23**
See also CA 85-88; 145; CANR 32, 63;
DLB 113; HW 1, 2; MTCW 1, 2
O Nuallain, Brian 1911-1966
See O'Brien, Flann
See also CA 21-22; 25-28R; CAP 2; DLB
231
Ophuls, Max 1902-1957 .... **TCLC 79**
See also CA 113
Opie, Amelia 1769-1853 .... **NCLC 65**
See also DLB 116, 159
Oppen, George 1908-1984 ...... **CLC 7, 13, 34**
See also CA 13-16R; 113; CANR 8, 82;
DLB 5, 165
Oppenheim, E(dward) Phillips
1866-1946 .... **TCLC 45**
See also CA 111; DLB 70
Opuls, Max
See Ophuls, Max
Origen c. 185-c. 254 .... **CMLC 19**
Orlovitz, Gil 1918-1973 .... **CLC 22**
See also CA 77-80; 45-48; DLB 2, 5
Orris
See Ingelow, Jean
Ortega y Gasset, Jose 1883-1955 ... **TCLC 9;
DAM MULT; HLC 2**
See also CA 106; 130; HW 1, 2; MTCW 1,
2
Ortese, Anna Maria 1914- .... **CLC 89**
See also DLB 177
Ortiz, Simon J(oseph) 1941- . **CLC 45; DAM
MULT, POET; PC 17**
See also CA 134; CANR 69; DLB 120, 175;
NNAL
Orton, Joe CLC 4, 13, 43; DC 3
See also Orton, John Kingsley
See also CDBLB 1960 to Present; DLB 13;
MTCW 2
Orton, John Kingsley 1933-1967
See Orton, Joe
See also CA 85-88; CANR 35, 66; DAM
DRAM; MTCW 1, 2
Orwell, George -1950 ...... **TCLC 2, 6, 15, 31,
51; DAB; WLC**
See also Blair, Eric (Arthur)
See also CDBLB 1945-1960; CLR 68; DLB
15, 98, 195
Osborne, David
See Silverberg, Robert
Osborne, George
See Silverberg, Robert
Osborne, John (James) 1929-1994 .... **CLC 1,
2, 5, 11, 45; DA; DAB; DAC; DAM
DRAM, MST; WLC**
See also CA 13-16R; 147; CANR 21, 56;
CDBLB 1945-1960; DLB 13; MTCW 1,
2
Osborne, Lawrence 1958- .... **CLC 50**
Osbourne, Lloyd 1868-1947 .... **TCLC 93**
Oshima, Nagisa 1932- .... **CLC 20**
See also CA 116; 121; CANR 78
Oskison, John Milton 1874-1947 .. **TCLC 35;
DAM MULT**
See also CA 144; CANR 84; DLB 175;
NNAL

Ossian c. 3rd cent. - .... **CMLC 28**
See also Macpherson, James
Ossoli, Sarah Margaret (Fuller marchesa d')
1810-1850 .... **NCLC 5, 50**
See also Fuller, Margaret; Fuller, Sarah
Margaret
See also CDALB 1640-1865; DLB 1, 59,
73, 183, 223; SATA 25
Ostriker, Alicia (Suskin) 1937- .... **CLC 132**
See also CA 25-28R; CAAS 24; CANR 10,
30, 62; DLB 120
Ostrovsky, Alexander 1823-1886 .. **NCLC 30,
57**
Otero, Blas de 1916-1979 .... **CLC 11**
See also CA 89-92; DLB 134
Otto, Rudolf 1869-1937 .... **TCLC 85**
Otto, Whitney 1955- .... **CLC 70**
See also CA 140
Ouida TCLC 43
See also De La Ramee, (Marie) Louise
See also DLB 18, 156
Ousmane, Sembene 1923- ... **CLC 66; BLC 3**
See also BW 1, 3; CA 117; 125; CANR 81;
MTCW 1
Ovid 43B.C.-17 . **CMLC 7; DAM POET; PC
2**
See also DA3; DLB 211
Owen, Hugh
See Faust, Frederick (Schiller)
Owen, Wilfred (Edward Salter)
1893-1918 .... **TCLC 5, 27; DA; DAB;
DAC; DAM MST, POET; PC 19; WLC**
See also CA 104; 141; CDBLB 1914-1945;
DLB 20; MTCW 2
Owens, Rochelle 1936- .... **CLC 8**
See also CA 17-20R; CAAS 2; CANR 39
Oz, Amos 1939- ...... **CLC 5, 8, 11, 27, 33, 54;
DAM NOV**
See also CA 53-56; CANR 27, 47, 65;
MTCW 1, 2
Ozick, Cynthia 1928- .... **CLC 3, 7, 28, 62;
DAM NOV, POP; SSC 15**
See also BEST 90:1; CA 17-20R; CANR
23, 58; DA3; DLB 28, 152; DLBY 82;
INT CANR-23; MTCW 1, 2
Ozu, Yasujiro 1903-1963 .... **CLC 16**
See also CA 112
Pacheco, C.
See Pessoa, Fernando (Antonio Nogueira)
Pacheco, Jose Emilio 1939-
See also CA 111; 131; CANR 65; DAM
MULT; HLC 2; HW 1, 2
Pa Chin CLC 18
See also Li Fei-kan
Pack, Robert 1929- .... **CLC 13**
See also CA 1-4R; CANR 3, 44, 82; DLB
5; SATA 118
Padgett, Lewis
See Kuttner, Henry
Padilla (Lorenzo), Heberto 1932- ..... **CLC 38**
See also AITN 1; CA 123; 131; HW 1
Page, Jimmy 1944- .... **CLC 12**
Page, Louise 1955- .... **CLC 40**
See also CA 140; CANR 76; DLB 233
Page, P(atricia) K(athleen) 1916- ...... **CLC 7,
18; DAC; DAM MST; PC 12**
See also CA 53-56; CANR 4, 22, 65; DLB
68; MTCW 1
Page, Stanton
See Fuller, Henry Blake
Page, Stanton
See Fuller, Henry Blake
Page, Thomas Nelson 1853-1922 .... **SSC 23**
See also CA 118; 177; DLB 12, 78; DLBD
13
Pagels, Elaine Hiesey 1943- .... **CLC 104**
See also CA 45-48; CANR 2, 24, 51

Paget, Violet 1856-1935
See Lee, Vernon
See also CA 104; 166
Paget-Lowe, Henry
See Lovecraft, H(oward) P(hillips)
Paglia, Camille (Anna) 1947- .... **CLC 68**
See also CA 140; CANR 72; MTCW 2
Paige, Richard
See Koontz, Dean R(ay)
Paine, Thomas 1737-1809 .... **NCLC 62**
See also CDALB 1640-1865; DLB 31, 43,
73, 158
Pakenham, Antonia
See Fraser, (Lady) Antonia (Pakenham)
Palamas, Kostes 1859-1943 .... **TCLC 5**
See also CA 105
Palazzeschi, Aldo 1885-1974 .... **CLC 11**
See also CA 89-92; 53-56; DLB 114
Pales Matos, Luis 1898-1959
See also HLCS 2; HW 1
Paley, Grace 1922- .... **CLC 4, 6, 37, 140;
DAM POP; SSC 8**
See also CA 25-28R; CANR 13, 46, 74;
DA3; DLB 28; INT CANR-13; MTCW 1,
2
Palin, Michael (Edward) 1943- .... **CLC 21**
See also Monty Python
See also CA 107; CANR 35; SATA 67
Palliser, Charles 1947- .... **CLC 65**
See also CA 136; CANR 76
Palma, Ricardo 1833-1919 .... **TCLC 29**
See also CA 168
Pancake, Breece Dexter 1952-1979
See Pancake, Breece D'J
See also CA 123; 109
Pancake, Breece D'J CLC 29
See also Pancake, Breece Dexter
See also DLB 130
Pankhurst, Emmeline (Goulden)
1858-1928 .... **TCLC 100**
See also CA 116
Panko, Rudy
See Gogol, Nikolai (Vasilyevich)
Papadiamantis, Alexandros
1851-1911 .... **TCLC 29**
See also CA 168
Papadiamantopoulos, Johannes 1856-1910
See Moreas, Jean
See also CA 117
Papini, Giovanni 1881-1956 .... **TCLC 22**
See also CA 121; 180
Paracelsus 1493-1541 .... **LC 14**
See also DLB 179
Parasol, Peter
See Stevens, Wallace
Pardo Bazan, Emilia 1851-1921 .... **SSC 30**
Pareto, Vilfredo 1848-1923 .... **TCLC 69**
See also CA 175
Paretsky, Sara 1947- .. **CLC 135; DAM POP**
See also AAYA 30; BEST 90:3; CA 125;
129; CANR 59; DA3; INT 129
Parfenie, Maria
See Codrescu, Andrei
Parini, Jay (Lee) 1948- .... **CLC 54, 133**
See also CA 97-100; CAAS 16; CANR 32,
87
Park, Jordan
See Kornbluth, C(yril) M.; Pohl, Frederik
Park, Robert E(zra) 1864-1944 ..... **TCLC 73**
See also CA 122; 165
Parker, Bert
See Ellison, Harlan (Jay)
Parker, Dorothy (Rothschild)
1893-1967 .... **CLC 15, 68; DAM POET;
PC 28; SSC 2**
See also CA 19-20; 25-28R; CAP 2; DA3;
DLB 11, 45, 86; MTCW 1, 2

Parker, Robert B(rown) 1932- .... **CLC 27; DAM NOV, POP**
See also AAYA 28; BEST 89:4; CA 49-52; CANR 1, 26, 52, 89; INT CANR-26; MTCW 1

Parkin, Frank 1940- .... **CLC 43**
See also CA 147

Parkman, Francis Jr., Jr. 1823-1893 .... **NCLC 12**
See also DLB 1, 30, 186, 235

Parks, Gordon (Alexander Buchanan) 1912- .... **CLC 1, 16; BLC 3; DAM MULT**
See also AAYA 36; AITN 2; BW 2, 3; CA 41-44R; CANR 26, 66; DA3; DLB 33; MTCW 2; SATA 8, 108

Parmenides c. 515B.C.-c. 450B.C. .... **CMLC 22**
See also DLB 176

Parnell, Thomas 1679-1718 .... **LC 3**
See also DLB 94

Parra, Nicanor 1914- ...... **CLC 2, 102; DAM MULT; HLC 2**
See also CA 85-88; CANR 32; HW 1; MTCW 1

Parra Sanojo, Ana Teresa de la 1890-1936
See also HLCS 2

Parrish, Mary Frances
See Fisher, M(ary) F(rances) K(ennedy)

Parson
See Coleridge, Samuel Taylor

Parson Lot
See Kingsley, Charles

Parton, Sara Payson Willis 1811-1872 .... **NCLC 86**
See also DLB 43, 74

Partridge, Anthony
See Oppenheim, E(dward) Phillips

Pascal, Blaise 1623-1662 .... **LC 35**

Pascoli, Giovanni 1855-1912 .... **TCLC 45**
See also CA 170

Pasolini, Pier Paolo 1922-1975 .. **CLC 20, 37, 106; PC 17**
See also CA 93-96; 61-64; CANR 63; DLB 128, 177; MTCW 1

Pasquini
See Silone, Ignazio

Pastan, Linda (Olenik) 1932- .... **CLC 27; DAM POET**
See also CA 61-64; CANR 18, 40, 61; DLB 5

Pasternak, Boris (Leonidovich) 1890-1960 .... **CLC 7, 10, 18, 63; DA; DAB; DAC; DAM MST, NOV, POET; PC 6; SSC 31; WLC**
See also CA 127; 116; DA3; MTCW 1, 2

Patchen, Kenneth 1911-1972 .. **CLC 1, 2, 18; DAM POET**
See also CA 1-4R; 33-36R; CANR 3, 35; DLB 16, 48; MTCW 1

Pater, Walter (Horatio) 1839-1894 . **NCLC 7, 90**
See also CDBLB 1832-1890; DLB 57, 156

Paterson, A(ndrew) B(arton) 1864-1941 .... **TCLC 32**
See also CA 155; DLB 230; SATA 97

Paterson, Katherine (Womeldorf) 1932- .... **CLC 12, 30**
See also AAYA 1, 31; CA 21-24R; CANR 28, 59; CLR 7, 50; DLB 52; JRDA; MAI-CYA; MTCW 1; SATA 13, 53, 92

Patmore, Coventry Kersey Dighton 1823-1896 .... **NCLC 9**
See also DLB 35, 98

Paton, Alan (Stewart) 1903-1988 ...... **CLC 4, 10, 25, 55, 106; DA; DAB; DAC; DAM MST, NOV; WLC**
See also AAYA 26; CA 13-16; 125; CANR 22; CAP 1; DA3; DLB 225; DLBD 17; MTCW 1, 2; SATA 11; SATA-Obit 56

Paton Walsh, Gillian 1937- .... **CLC 35**
See also Walsh, Jill Paton
See also AAYA 11; CANR 38, 83; CLR 2, 65; DLB 161; JRDA; MAICYA; SAAS 3; SATA 4, 72, 109

Paton Walsh, Jill
See Paton Walsh, Gillian

Patton, George S. 1885-1945 .... **TCLC 79**

Paulding, James Kirke 1778-1860 ... **NCLC 2**
See also DLB 3, 59, 74

Paulin, Thomas Neilson 1949-
See Paulin, Tom
See also CA 123; 128

Paulin, Tom CLC 37
See also Paulin, Thomas Neilson
See also DLB 40

Pausanias c. 1st cent. - .... **CMLC 36**

Paustovsky, Konstantin (Georgievich) 1892-1968 .... **CLC 40**
See also CA 93-96; 25-28R

Pavese, Cesare 1908-1950 .. **TCLC 3; PC 13; SSC 19**
See also CA 104; 169; DLB 128, 177

Pavic, Milorad 1929- .... **CLC 60**
See also CA 136; DLB 181

Pavlov, Ivan Petrovich 1849-1936 . **TCLC 91**
See also CA 118; 180

Payne, Alan
See Jakes, John (William)

Paz, Gil
See Lugones, Leopoldo

Paz, Octavio 1914-1998 . **CLC 3, 4, 6, 10, 19, 51, 65, 119; DA; DAB; DAC; DAM MST, MULT, POET; HLC 2; PC 1; WLC**
See also CA 73-76; 165; CANR 32, 65; DA3; DLBY 90, 98; HW 1, 2; MTCW 1, 2

p'Bitek, Okot 1931-1982 .... **CLC 96; BLC 3; DAM MULT**
See also BW 2, 3; CA 124; 107; CANR 82; DLB 125; MTCW 1, 2

Peacock, Molly 1947- .... **CLC 60**
See also CA 103; CAAS 21; CANR 52, 84; DLB 120

Peacock, Thomas Love 1785-1866 .... **NCLC 22**
See also DLB 96, 116

Peake, Mervyn 1911-1968 .... **CLC 7, 54**
See also CA 5-8R; 25-28R; CANR 3; DLB 15, 160; MTCW 1; SATA 23

Pearce, Philippa CLC 21
See also Christie, (Ann) Philippa
See also CLR 9; DLB 161; MAICYA; SATA 1, 67

Pearl, Eric
See Elman, Richard (Martin)

Pearson, T(homas) R(eid) 1956- .... **CLC 39**
See also CA 120; 130; INT 130

Peck, Dale 1967- .... **CLC 81**
See also CA 146; CANR 72

Peck, John 1941- .... **CLC 3**
See also CA 49-52; CANR 3

Peck, Richard (Wayne) 1934- .... **CLC 21**
See also AAYA 1, 24; CA 85-88; CANR 19, 38; CLR 15; INT CANR-19; JRDA; MAICYA; SAAS 2; SATA 18, 55, 97; SATA-Essay 110

Peck, Robert Newton 1928- .... **CLC 17; DA; DAC; DAM MST**
See also AAYA 3; CA 81-84, 182; CAAE 182; CANR 31, 63; CLR 45; JRDA; MAI-CYA; SAAS 1; SATA 21, 62, 111; SATA-Essay 108

Peckinpah, (David) Sam(uel) 1925-1984 .... **CLC 20**
See also CA 109; 114; CANR 82

Pedersen, Knut 1859-1952
See Hamsun, Knut
See also CA 104; 119; CANR 63; MTCW 1, 2

Peeslake, Gaffer
See Durrell, Lawrence (George)

Peguy, Charles Pierre 1873-1914 ... **TCLC 10**
See also CA 107

Peirce, Charles Sanders 1839-1914 .... **TCLC 81**

Pellicer, Carlos 1900(?)-1977
See also CA 153; 69-72; HLCS 2; HW 1

Pena, Ramon del Valle y
See Valle-Inclan, Ramon (Maria) del

Pendennis, Arthur Esquir
See Thackeray, William Makepeace

Penn, William 1644-1718 .... **LC 25**
See also DLB 24

PEPECE
See Prado (Calvo), Pedro

Pepys, Samuel 1633-1703 ..... **LC 11, 58; DA; DAB; DAC; DAM MST; WLC**
See also CDBLB 1660-1789; DA3; DLB 101

Percy, Thomas 1729-1811 .... **NCLC 95**
See also DLB 104

Percy, Walker 1916-1990 .... **CLC 2, 3, 6, 8, 14, 18, 47, 65; DAM NOV, POP**
See also CA 1-4R; 131; CANR 1, 23, 64; DA3; DLB 2; DLBY 80, 90; MTCW 1, 2

Percy, William Alexander 1885-1942 .... **TCLC 84**
See also CA 163; MTCW 2

Perec, Georges 1936-1982 .... **CLC 56, 116**
See also CA 141; DLB 83

Pereda (y Sanchez de Porrua), Jose Maria de 1833-1906 .... **TCLC 16**
See also CA 117

Pereda y Porrua, Jose Maria de
See Pereda (y Sanchez de Porrua), Jose Maria de

Peregoy, George Weems
See Mencken, H(enry) L(ouis)

Perelman, S(idney) J(oseph) 1904-1979 .. **CLC 3, 5, 9, 15, 23, 44, 49; DAM DRAM; SSC 32**
See also AITN 1, 2; CA 73-76; 89-92; CANR 18; DLB 11, 44; MTCW 1, 2

Peret, Benjamin 1899-1959 .... **TCLC 20; PC 33**
See also CA 117; 186

Peretz, Isaac Loeb 1851(?)-1915 ... **TCLC 16; SSC 26**
See also CA 109

Peretz, Yitzhok Leibush
See Peretz, Isaac Loeb

Perez Galdos, Benito 1843-1920 ... **TCLC 27; HLCS 2**
See also CA 125; 153; HW 1

Peri Rossi, Cristina 1941-
See also CA 131; CANR 59, 81; DLB 145; HLCS 2; HW 1, 2

Perlata
See Peret, Benjamin

Perloff, Marjorie G(abrielle) 1931- .... **CLC 137**
See also CA 57-60; CANR 7, 22, 49

Perrault, Charles 1628-1703 ... **LC 3, 52; DC 12**
See also MAICYA; SATA 25

Perry, Anne 1938- .... **CLC 126**
See also CA 101; CANR 22, 50, 84

Perry, Brighton
See Sherwood, Robert E(mmet)

Perse, St.-John
See Leger, (Marie-Rene Auguste) Alexis Saint-Leger

Perutz, Leo(pold) 1882-1957 .... **TCLC 60**
See also CA 147; DLB 81

Peseenz, Tulio F.
See Lopez y Fuentes, Gregorio

Pesetsky, Bette 1932- .... **CLC 28**
See also CA 133; DLB 130

Peshkov, Alexei Maximovich 1868-1936
See Gorky, Maxim
See also CA 105; 141; CANR 83; DA; DAC; DAM DRAM, MST, NOV; MTCW 2

Pessoa, Fernando (Antonio Nogueira)
1888-1935 .... **TCLC 27; DAM MULT; HLC 2; PC 20**
See also CA 125; 183

Peterkin, Julia Mood 1880-1961 ...... **CLC 31**
See also CA 102; DLB 9

Peters, Joan K(aren) 1945- .... **CLC 39**
See also CA 158

Peters, Robert L(ouis) 1924- .... **CLC 7**
See also CA 13-16R; CAAS 8; DLB 105

Petofi, Sandor 1823-1849 .... **NCLC 21**

Petrakis, Harry Mark 1923- .... **CLC 3**
See also CA 9-12R; CANR 4, 30, 85

Petrarch 1304-1374 .... **CMLC 20; DAM POET; PC 8**
See also DA3

Petronius c. 20-66 .... **CMLC 34**
See also DLB 211

Petrov, Evgeny **TCLC 21**
See also Kataev, Evgeny Petrovich

Petry, Ann (Lane) 1908-1997 ... **CLC 1, 7, 18**
See also BW 1, 3; CA 5-8R; 157; CAAS 6; CANR 4, 46; CLR 12; DLB 76; JRDA; MAICYA; MTCW 1; SATA 5; SATA-Obit 94

Petursson, Halligrimur 1614-1674 .... **LC 8**

Peychinovich
See Vazov, Ivan (Minchov)

Phaedrus c. 18B.C.-c. 50 .... **CMLC 25**
See also DLB 211

Philips, Katherine 1632-1664 .... **LC 30**
See also DLB 131

Philipson, Morris H. 1926- .... **CLC 53**
See also CA 1-4R; CANR 4

Phillips, Caryl 1958- . **CLC 96; BLCS; DAM MULT**
See also BW 2; CA 141; CANR 63; DA3; DLB 157; MTCW 2

Phillips, David Graham
1867-1911 .... **TCLC 44**
See also CA 108; 176; DLB 9, 12

Phillips, Jack
See Sandburg, Carl (August)

Phillips, Jayne Anne 1952- .... **CLC 15, 33, 139; SSC 16**
See also CA 101; CANR 24, 50; DLBY 80; INT CANR-24; MTCW 1, 2

Phillips, Richard
See Dick, Philip K(indred)

Phillips, Robert (Schaeffer) 1938- .... **CLC 28**
See also CA 17-20R; CAAS 13; CANR 8; DLB 105

Phillips, Ward
See Lovecraft, H(oward) P(hillips)

Piccolo, Lucio 1901-1969 .... **CLC 13**
See also CA 97-100; DLB 114

Pickthall, Marjorie L(owry) C(hristie)
1883-1922 .... **TCLC 21**
See also CA 107; DLB 92

Pico della Mirandola, Giovanni
1463-1494 .... **LC 15**

Piercy, Marge 1936- .... **CLC 3, 6, 14, 18, 27, 62, 128; PC 29**
See also CA 21-24R; CAAE 187; CAAS 1; CANR 13, 43, 66; DLB 120, 227; MTCW 1, 2

Piers, Robert
See Anthony, Piers

Pieyre de Mandiargues, Andre 1909-1991
See Mandiargues, Andre Pieyre de
See also CA 103; 136; CANR 22, 82

Pilnyak, Boris **TCLC 23**
See also Vogau, Boris Andreyevich

Pincherle, Alberto 1907-1990 .... **CLC 11, 18; DAM NOV**
See also Moravia, Alberto
See also CA 25-28R; 132; CANR 33, 63; MTCW 1

Pinckney, Darryl 1953- .... **CLC 76**
See also BW 2, 3; CA 143; CANR 79

Pindar 518B.C.-446B.C. .... **CMLC 12; PC 19**
See also DLB 176

Pineda, Cecile 1942- .... **CLC 39**
See also CA 118

Pinero, Arthur Wing 1855-1934 ... **TCLC 32; DAM DRAM**
See also CA 110; 153; DLB 10

Pinero, Miguel (Antonio Gomez)
1946-1988 .... **CLC 4, 55**
See also CA 61-64; 125; CANR 29, 90; HW 1

Pinget, Robert 1919-1997 .... **CLC 7, 13, 37**
See also CA 85-88; 160; DLB 83

Pink Floyd
See Barrett, (Roger) Syd; Gilmour, David; Mason, Nick; Waters, Roger; Wright, Rick

Pinkney, Edward 1802-1828 .... **NCLC 31**

Pinkwater, Daniel Manus 1941- .... **CLC 35**
See also Pinkwater, Manus
See also AAYA 1; CA 29-32R; CANR 12, 38, 89; CLR 4; JRDA; MAICYA; SAAS 3; SATA 46, 76, 114

Pinkwater, Manus
See Pinkwater, Daniel Manus
See also SATA 8

Pinsky, Robert 1940- .... **CLC 9, 19, 38, 94, 121; DAM POET; PC 27**
See also CA 29-32R; CAAS 4; CANR 58; DA3; DLBY 82, 98; MTCW 2

Pinta, Harold
See Pinter, Harold

Pinter, Harold 1930- .. **CLC 1, 3, 6, 9, 11, 15, 27, 58, 73; DA; DAB; DAC; DAM DRAM, MST; WLC**
See also CA 5-8R; CANR 33, 65; CDBLB 1960 to Present; DA3; DLB 13; MTCW 1, 2

Piozzi, Hester Lynch (Thrale)
1741-1821 .... **NCLC 57**
See also DLB 104, 142

Pirandello, Luigi 1867-1936 ...... **TCLC 4, 29; DA; DAB; DAC; DAM DRAM, MST; DC 5; SSC 22; WLC**
See also CA 104; 153; DA3; MTCW 2

Pirsig, Robert M(aynard) 1928- ... **CLC 4, 6, 73; DAM POP**
See also CA 53-56; CANR 42, 74; DA3; MTCW 1, 2; SATA 39

Pisarev, Dmitry Ivanovich
1840-1868 .... **NCLC 25**

Pix, Mary (Griffith) 1666-1709 .... **LC 8**
See also DLB 80

Pixerecourt, (Rene Charles) Guilbert de
1773-1844 .... **NCLC 39**
See also DLB 192

Plaatje, Sol(omon) T(shekisho)
1876-1932 .... **TCLC 73; BLCS**
See also BW 2, 3; CA 141; CANR 79; DLB 225

Plaidy, Jean
See Hibbert, Eleanor Alice Burford

Planche, James Robinson
1796-1880 .... **NCLC 42**

Plant, Robert 1948- .... **CLC 12**

Plante, David (Robert) 1940- ...... **CLC 7, 23, 38; DAM NOV**
See also CA 37-40R; CANR 12, 36, 58, 82; DLBY 83; INT CANR-12; MTCW 1

Plath, Sylvia 1932-1963 ..... **CLC 1, 2, 3, 5, 9, 11, 14, 17, 50, 51, 62, 111; DA; DAB; DAC; DAM MST, POET; PC 1; WLC**
See also AAYA 13; CA 19-20; CANR 34; CAP 2; CDALB 1941-1968; DA3; DLB 5, 6, 152; MTCW 1, 2; SATA 96

Plato 428(?)B.C.-348(?)B.C. ... **CMLC 8; DA; DAB; DAC; DAM MST; WLCS**
See also DA3; DLB 176

Platonov, Andrei
See Klimentov, Andrei Platonovich

Platt, Kin 1911- .... **CLC 26**
See also AAYA 11; CA 17-20R; CANR 11; JRDA; SAAS 17; SATA 21, 86

Plautus c. 251B.C.-184B.C. ... **CMLC 24; DC 6**
See also DLB 211

Plick et Plock
See Simenon, Georges (Jacques Christian)

Plieksans, Janis 1865-1929
See Rainis, Janis
See also CA 170; DLB 220

Plimpton, George (Ames) 1927- .... **CLC 36**
See also AITN 1; CA 21-24R; CANR 32, 70; DLB 185; MTCW 1, 2; SATA 10

Pliny the Elder c. 23-79 .... **CMLC 23**
See also DLB 211

Plomer, William Charles Franklin
1903-1973 .... **CLC 4, 8**
See also CA 21-22; CANR 34; CAP 2; DLB 20, 162, 191, 225; MTCW 1; SATA 24

Plowman, Piers
See Kavanagh, Patrick (Joseph)

Plum, J.
See Wodehouse, P(elham) G(renville)

Plumly, Stanley (Ross) 1939- .... **CLC 33**
See also CA 108; 110; DLB 5, 193; INT 110

Plumpe, Friedrich Wilhelm
1888-1931 .... **TCLC 53**
See also CA 112

Po Chu-i 772-846 .... **CMLC 24**

Poe, Edgar Allan 1809-1849 ..... **NCLC 1, 16, 55, 78, 94; DA; DAB; DAC; DAM MST, POET; PC 1; SSC 1, 22, 34, 35; WLC**
See also AAYA 14; CDALB 1640-1865; DA3; DLB 3, 59, 73, 74; SATA 23

Poet of Titchfield Street, The
See Pound, Ezra (Weston Loomis)

Pohl, Frederik 1919- .... **CLC 18; SSC 25**
See also AAYA 24; CA 61-64; CAAS 1; CANR 11, 37, 81; DLB 8; INT CANR-11; MTCW 1, 2; SATA 24

Poirier, Louis 1910-
See Gracq, Julien
See also CA 122; 126

Poitier, Sidney 1927- .... **CLC 26**
See also BW 1; CA 117; CANR 94

Polanski, Roman 1933- .... **CLC 16**
See also CA 77-80

Poliakoff, Stephen 1952- .... **CLC 38**
See also CA 106; DLB 13

Purdy, James (Amos) 1923- .... **CLC 2, 4, 10, 28, 52**
See also CA 33-36R; CAAS 1; CANR 19, 51; DLB 2; INT CANR-19; MTCW 1

Pure, Simon
See Swinnerton, Frank Arthur

Pushkin, Alexander (Sergeyevich) 1799-1837 . **NCLC 3, 27, 83; DA; DAB; DAC; DAM DRAM, MST, POET; PC 10; SSC 27; WLC**
See also DA3; DLB 205; SATA 61

P'u Sung-ling 1640-1715 .... **LC 49; SSC 31**

Putnam, Arthur Lee
See Alger, Horatio Jr., Jr.

Puzo, Mario 1920-1999 .... **CLC 1, 2, 6, 36, 107; DAM NOV, POP**
See also CA 65-68; 185; CANR 4, 42, 65; DA3; DLB 6; MTCW 1, 2

Pygge, Edward
See Barnes, Julian (Patrick)

Pyle, Ernest Taylor 1900-1945
See Pyle, Ernie
See also CA 115; 160

Pyle, Ernie 1900-1945 .... **TCLC 75**
See also Pyle, Ernest Taylor
See also DLB 29; MTCW 2

Pyle, Howard 1853-1911 .... **TCLC 81**
See also CA 109; 137; CLR 22; DLB 42, 188; DLBD 13; MAICYA; SATA 16, 100

Pym, Barbara (Mary Crampton) 1913-1980 .... **CLC 13, 19, 37, 111**
See also CA 13-14; 97-100; CANR 13, 34; CAP 1; DLB 14, 207; DLBY 87; MTCW 1, 2

Pynchon, Thomas (Ruggles, Jr.) 1937- ...... **CLC 2, 3, 6, 9, 11, 18, 33, 62, 72, 123; DA; DAB; DAC; DAM MST, NOV, POP; SSC 14; WLC**
See also BEST 90:2; CA 17-20R; CANR 22, 46, 73; DA3; DLB 2, 173; MTCW 1, 2

Pythagoras c. 570B.C.-c. 500B.C. . **CMLC 22**
See also DLB 176

Q
See Quiller-Couch, SirArthur (Thomas)

Qian Zhongshu
See Ch'ien Chung-shu

Qroll
See Dagerman, Stig (Halvard)

Quarrington, Paul (Lewis) 1953- ..... **CLC 65**
See also CA 129; CANR 62

Quasimodo, Salvatore 1901-1968 ..... **CLC 10**
See also CA 13-16; 25-28R; CAP 1; DLB 114; MTCW 1

Quay, Stephen 1947- .... **CLC 95**

Quay, Timothy 1947- .... **CLC 95**

Queen, Ellery CLC 3, 11
See also Deming, Richard; Dannay, Frederic; Davidson, Avram (James); Fairman, Paul W.; Flora, Fletcher; Hoch, Edward D(entinger); Kane, Henry; Lee, Manfred B(ennington); Marlowe, Stephen; Powell, Talmage; Sheldon, Walter J.; Sturgeon, Theodore (Hamilton); Tracy, Don(ald Fiske); Vance, John Holbrook

Queen, Ellery, Jr.
See Dannay, Frederic; Lee, Manfred B(ennington)

Queneau, Raymond 1903-1976 ..... **CLC 2, 5, 10, 42**
See also CA 77-80; 69-72; CANR 32; DLB 72; MTCW 1, 2

Quevedo, Francisco de 1580-1645 .... **LC 23**

Quiller-Couch, SirArthur (Thomas) 1863-1944 .... **TCLC 53**
See also CA 118; 166; DLB 135, 153, 190

Quin, Ann (Marie) 1936-1973 .... **CLC 6**
See also CA 9-12R; 45-48; DLB 14, 231

Quinn, Martin
See Smith, Martin Cruz

Quinn, Peter 1947- .... **CLC 91**

Quinn, Simon
See Smith, Martin Cruz

Quintana, Leroy V. 1944-
See also CA 131; CANR 65; DAM MULT; DLB 82; HLC 2; HW 1, 2

Quiroga, Horacio (Sylvestre) 1878-1937 .... **TCLC 20; DAM MULT; HLC 2**
See also CA 117; 131; HW 1; MTCW 1

Quoirez, Francoise 1935- .... **CLC 9**
See also Sagan, Francoise
See also CA 49-52; CANR 6, 39, 73; MTCW 1, 2

Raabe, Wilhelm (Karl) 1831-1910 . **TCLC 45**
See also CA 167; DLB 129

Rabe, David (William) 1940- .. **CLC 4, 8, 33; DAM DRAM**
See also CA 85-88; CABS 3; CANR 59; DLB 7, 228

Rabelais, Francois 1483-1553 .... **LC 5, 60; DA; DAB; DAC; DAM MST; WLC**

Rabinovitch, Sholem 1859-1916
See Aleichem, Sholom
See also CA 104

Rabinyan, Dorit 1972- .... **CLC 119**
See also CA 170

Rachilde
See Vallette, Marguerite Eymery

Racine, Jean 1639-1699 . **LC 28; DAB; DAM MST**
See also DA3

Radcliffe, Ann (Ward) 1764-1823 ... **NCLC 6, 55**
See also DLB 39, 178

Radiguet, Raymond 1903-1923 ...... **TCLC 29**
See also CA 162; DLB 65

Radnoti, Miklos 1909-1944 .... **TCLC 16**
See also CA 118

Rado, James 1939- .... **CLC 17**
See also CA 105

Radvanyi, Netty 1900-1983
See Seghers, Anna
See also CA 85-88; 110; CANR 82

Rae, Ben
See Griffiths, Trevor

Raeburn, John (Hay) 1941- .... **CLC 34**
See also CA 57-60

Ragni, Gerome 1942-1991 .... **CLC 17**
See also CA 105; 134

Rahv, Philip 1908-1973 .... **CLC 24**
See also Greenberg, Ivan
See also DLB 137

Raimund, Ferdinand Jakob 1790-1836 .... **NCLC 69**
See also DLB 90

Raine, Craig 1944- .... **CLC 32, 103**
See also CA 108; CANR 29, 51; DLB 40

Raine, Kathleen (Jessie) 1908- ..... **CLC 7, 45**
See also CA 85-88; CANR 46; DLB 20; MTCW 1

Rainis, Janis 1865-1929 .... **TCLC 29**
See also Plieksans, Janis
See also CA 170; DLB 220

Rakosi, Carl 1903- .... **CLC 47**
See also Rawley, Callman
See also CAAS 5; DLB 193

Ralegh, SirWalter 1554(?)-1618
See Raleigh, SirWalter

Raleigh, Richard
See Lovecraft, H(oward) P(hillips)

Raleigh, SirWalter 1554(?)-1618 .. **LC 31, 39; PC 31**
See also CDBLB Before 1660; DLB 172

Rallentando, H. P.
See Sayers, Dorothy L(eigh)

Ramal, Walter
See de la Mare, Walter (John)

Ramana Maharshi 1879-1950 .... **TCLC 84**

Ramoacn y Cajal, Santiago 1852-1934 .... **TCLC 93**

Ramon, Juan
See Jimenez (Mantecon), Juan Ramon

Ramos, Graciliano 1892-1953 .... **TCLC 32**
See also CA 167; HW 2

Rampersad, Arnold 1941- .... **CLC 44**
See also BW 2, 3; CA 127; 133; CANR 81; DLB 111; INT 133

Rampling, Anne
See Rice, Anne

Ramsay, Allan 1684(?)-1758 .... **LC 29**
See also DLB 95

Ramuz, Charles-Ferdinand 1878-1947 .... **TCLC 33**
See also CA 165

Rand, Ayn 1905-1982 ...... **CLC 3, 30, 44, 79; DA; DAC; DAM MST, NOV, POP; WLC**
See also AAYA 10; CA 13-16R; 105; CANR 27, 73; CDALBS; DA3; DLB 227; MTCW 1, 2

Randall, Dudley (Felker) 1914-2000 . **CLC 1, 135; BLC 3; DAM MULT**
See also BW 1, 3; CA 25-28R; CANR 23, 82; DLB 41

Randall, Robert
See Silverberg, Robert

Ranger, Ken
See Creasey, John

Ransom, John Crowe 1888-1974 .. **CLC 2, 4, 5, 11, 24; DAM POET**
See also CA 5-8R; 49-52; CANR 6, 34; CDALBS; DA3; DLB 45, 63; MTCW 1, 2

Rao, Raja 1909- ..... **CLC 25, 56; DAM NOV**
See also CA 73-76; CANR 51; MTCW 1, 2

Raphael, Frederic (Michael) 1931- ... **CLC 2, 14**
See also CA 1-4R; CANR 1, 86; DLB 14

Ratcliffe, James P.
See Mencken, H(enry) L(ouis)

Rathbone, Julian 1935- .... **CLC 41**
See also CA 101; CANR 34, 73

Rattigan, Terence (Mervyn) 1911-1977 .... **CLC 7; DAM DRAM**
See also CA 85-88; 73-76; CDBLB 1945-1960; DLB 13; MTCW 1, 2

Ratushinskaya, Irina 1954- .... **CLC 54**
See also CA 129; CANR 68

Raven, Simon (Arthur Noel) 1927- .. **CLC 14**
See also CA 81-84; CANR 86

Ravenna, Michael
See Welty, Eudora

Rawley, Callman 1903-
See Rakosi, Carl
See also CA 21-24R; CANR 12, 32, 91

Rawlings, Marjorie Kinnan 1896-1953 .... **TCLC 4**
See also AAYA 20; CA 104; 137; CANR 74; CLR 63; DLB 9, 22, 102; DLBD 17; JRDA; MAICYA; MTCW 2; SATA 100; YABC 1

Ray, Satyajit 1921-1992 .. **CLC 16, 76; DAM MULT**
See also CA 114; 137

Read, Herbert Edward 1893-1968 ..... **CLC 4**
See also CA 85-88; 25-28R; DLB 20, 149

Read, Piers Paul 1941- .... **CLC 4, 10, 25**
See also CA 21-24R; CANR 38, 86; DLB 14; SATA 21

Reade, Charles 1814-1884 .... **NCLC 2, 74**
See also DLB 21

Reade, Hamish
See Gray, Simon (James Holliday)

Rossetti, Christina (Georgina)
1830-1894 . NCLC 2, 50, 66; DA; DAB;
DAC; DAM MST, POET; PC 7; WLC
See also DA3; DLB 35, 163; MAICYA;
SATA 20

Rossetti, Dante Gabriel 1828-1882 . NCLC 4,
77; DA; DAB; DAC; DAM MST,
POET; WLC
See also CDBLB 1832-1890; DLB 35

Rossner, Judith (Perelman) 1935- . CLC 6, 9,
29
See also AITN 2; BEST 90:3; CA 17-20R;
CANR 18, 51, 73; DLB 6; INT CANR-
18; MTCW 1, 2

Rostand, Edmond (Eugene Alexis)
1868-1918 .... TCLC 6, 37; DA; DAB;
DAC; DAM DRAM, MST; DC 10
See also CA 104; 126; DA3; DLB 192;
MTCW 1

Roth, Henry 1906-1995 ..... CLC 2, 6, 11, 104
See also CA 11-12; 149; CANR 38, 63;
CAP 1; DA3; DLB 28; MTCW 1, 2

Roth, Philip (Milton) 1933- ... CLC 1, 2, 3, 4,
6, 9, 15, 22, 31, 47, 66, 86, 119; DA;
DAB; DAC; DAM MST, NOV, POP;
SSC 26; WLC
See also BEST 90:3; CA 1-4R; CANR 1,
22, 36, 55, 89; CDALB 1968-1988; DA3;
DLB 2, 28, 173; DLBY 82; MTCW 1, 2

Rothenberg, Jerome 1931- .... CLC 6, 57
See also CA 45-48; CANR 1; DLB 5, 193

Roumain, Jacques (Jean Baptiste)
1907-1944 ...... TCLC 19; BLC 3; DAM
MULT
See also BW 1; CA 117; 125

Rourke, Constance (Mayfield)
1885-1941 .... TCLC 12
See also CA 107; YABC 1

Rousseau, Jean-Baptiste 1671-1741 ...... LC 9

Rousseau, Jean-Jacques 1712-1778 .... LC 14,
36; DA; DAB; DAC; DAM MST; WLC
See also DA3

Roussel, Raymond 1877-1933 .... TCLC 20
See also CA 117

Rovit, Earl (Herbert) 1927- .... CLC 7
See also CA 5-8R; CANR 12

Rowe, Elizabeth Singer 1674-1737 ..... LC 44
See also DLB 39, 95

Rowe, Nicholas 1674-1718 .... LC 8
See also DLB 84

Rowley, Ames Dorrance
See Lovecraft, H(oward) P(hillips)

Rowling, J(oanne) K. 1966(?)- .... CLC 137
See also AAYA 34; CA 173; CLR 66; SATA
109

Rowson, Susanna Haswell
1762(?)-1824 .... NCLC 5, 69
See also DLB 37, 200

Roy, Arundhati 1960(?)- .... CLC 109
See also CA 163; CANR 90; DLBY 97

Roy, Gabrielle 1909-1983 .... CLC 10, 14;
DAB; DAC; DAM MST
See also CA 53-56; 110; CANR 5, 61; DLB
68; MTCW 1; SATA 104

Royko, Mike 1932-1997 .... CLC 109
See also CA 89-92; 157; CANR 26

Rozanov, Vassili 1856-1919 .... TCLC 104

Rozewicz, Tadeusz 1921- ..... CLC 9, 23, 139;
DAM POET
See also CA 108; CANR 36, 66; DA3; DLB
232; MTCW 1, 2

Ruark, Gibbons 1941- .... CLC 3
See also CA 33-36R; CAAS 23; CANR 14,
31, 57; DLB 120

Rubens, Bernice (Ruth) 1923- .... CLC 19, 31
See also CA 25-28R; CANR 33, 65; DLB
14, 207; MTCW 1

Rubin, Harold
See Robbins, Harold

Rudkin, (James) David 1936- .... CLC 14
See also CA 89-92; DLB 13

Rudnik, Raphael 1933- .... CLC 7
See also CA 29-32R

Ruffian, M.
See Hasek, Jaroslav (Matej Frantisek)

Ruiz, Jose Martinez CLC 11
See also Martinez Ruiz, Jose

Rukeyser, Muriel 1913-1980 . CLC 6, 10, 15,
27; DAM POET; PC 12
See also CA 5-8R; 93-96; CANR 26, 60;
DA3; DLB 48; MTCW 1, 2; SATA-Obit
22

Rule, Jane (Vance) 1931- .... CLC 27
See also CA 25-28R; CAAS 18; CANR 12,
87; DLB 60

Rulfo, Juan 1918-1986 ...... CLC 8, 80; DAM
MULT; HLC 2; SSC 25
See also CA 85-88; 118; CANR 26; DLB
113; HW 1, 2; MTCW 1, 2

Rumi, Jalal al-Din 1297-1373 .... CMLC 20

Runeberg, Johan 1804-1877 .... NCLC 41

Runyon, (Alfred) Damon
1884(?)-1946 .... TCLC 10
See also CA 107; 165; DLB 11, 86, 171;
MTCW 2

Rush, Norman 1933- .... CLC 44
See also CA 121; 126; INT 126

Rushdie, (Ahmed) Salman 1947- .... CLC 23,
31, 55, 100; DAB; DAC; DAM MST,
NOV, POP; WLCS
See also BEST 89:3; CA 108; 111; CANR
33, 56; DA3; DLB 194; INT 111; MTCW
1, 2

Rushforth, Peter (Scott) 1945- .... CLC 19
See also CA 101

Ruskin, John 1819-1900 .... TCLC 63
See also CA 114; 129; CDBLB 1832-1890;
DLB 55, 163, 190; SATA 24

Russ, Joanna 1937- .... CLC 15
See also CA 5-28R; CANR 11, 31, 65; DLB
8; MTCW 1

Russell, George William 1867-1935
See Baker, Jean H.
See also CA 104; 153; CDBLB 1890-1914;
DAM POET

Russell, (Henry) Ken(neth Alfred)
1927- .... CLC 16
See also CA 105

Russell, William Martin 1947- .... CLC 60
See also CA 164; DLB 233

Rutherford, Mark TCLC 25
See also White, William Hale
See also DLB 18

Ruyslinck, Ward 1929- .... CLC 14
See also Belser, Reimond Karel Maria de

Ryan, Cornelius (John) 1920-1974 ..... CLC 7
See also CA 69-72; 53-56; CANR 38

Ryan, Michael 1946- .... CLC 65
See also CA 49-52; DLBY 82

Ryan, Tim
See Dent, Lester

Rybakov, Anatoli (Naumovich)
1911-1998 .... CLC 23, 53
See also CA 126; 135; 172; SATA 79;
SATA-Obit 108

Ryder, Jonathan
See Ludlum, Robert

Ryga, George 1932-1987 .... CLC 14; DAC;
DAM MST
See also CA 101; 124; CANR 43, 90; DLB
60

S. H.
See Hartmann, Sadakichi

S. S.
See Sassoon, Siegfried (Lorraine)

Saba, Umberto 1883-1957 .... TCLC 33
See also CA 144; CANR 79; DLB 114

Sabatini, Rafael 1875-1950 .... TCLC 47
See also CA 162

Sabato, Ernesto (R.) 1911- .... CLC 10, 23;
DAM MULT; HLC 2
See also CA 97-100; CANR 32, 65; DLB
145; HW 1, 2; MTCW 1, 2

Sa-Carniero, Mario de 1890-1916 . TCLC 83

Sacastru, Martin
See Bioy Casares, Adolfo

Sacastru, Martin
See Bioy Casares, Adolfo

Sacher-Masoch, Leopold von
1836(?)-1895 .... NCLC 31

Sachs, Marilyn (Stickle) 1927- .... CLC 35
See also AAYA 2; CA 17-20R; CANR 13,
47; CLR 2; JRDA; MAICYA; SAAS 2;
SATA 3, 68; SATA-Essay 110

Sachs, Nelly 1891-1970 .... CLC 14, 98
See also CA 17-18; 25-28R; CANR 87;
CAP 2; MTCW 2

Sackler, Howard (Oliver)
1929-1982 .... CLC 14
See also CA 61-64; 108; CANR 30; DLB 7

Sacks, Oliver (Wolf) 1933- .... CLC 67
See also CA 53-56; CANR 28, 50, 76; DA3;
INT CANR-28; MTCW 1, 2

Sadakichi
See Hartmann, Sadakichi

**Sade, Donatien Alphonse Francois, Comte
de** 1740-1814 .... NCLC 3, 47

Sadoff, Ira 1945- .... CLC 9
See also CA 53-56; CANR 5, 21; DLB 120

Saetone
See Camus, Albert

Safire, William 1929- .... CLC 10
See also CA 17-20R; CANR 31, 54, 91

Sagan, Carl (Edward) 1934-1996 .... CLC 30,
112
See also AAYA 2; CA 25-28R; 155; CANR
11, 36, 74; DA3; MTCW 1, 2; SATA 58;
SATA-Obit 94

Sagan, Francoise CLC 3, 6, 9, 17, 36
See also Quoirez, Francoise
See also DLB 83; MTCW 2

Sahgal, Nayantara (Pandit) 1927- .... CLC 41
See also CA 9-12R; CANR 11, 88

Said, Edward W. 1935- .... CLC 123
See also CA 21-24R; CANR 45, 74; DLB
67; MTCW 2

Saint, H(arry) F. 1941- .... CLC 50
See also CA 127

St. Aubin de Teran, Lisa 1953-
See Teran, Lisa St. Aubin de
See also CA 118; 126; INT 126

Saint Birgitta of Sweden c.
1303-1373 .... CMLC 24

Sainte-Beuve, Charles Augustin
1804-1869 .... NCLC 5

**Saint-Exupery, Antoine (Jean Baptiste
Marie Roger) de** 1900-1944 .... TCLC 2,
56; DAM NOV; WLC
See also CA 108; 132; CLR 10; DA3; DLB
72; MAICYA; MTCW 1, 2; SATA 20

St. John, David
See Hunt, E(verette) Howard, (Jr.)

Saint-John Perse
See Leger, (Marie-Rene Auguste) Alexis
Saint-Leger

Saintsbury, George (Edward Bateman)
1845-1933 .... TCLC 31
See also CA 160; DLB 57, 149

Sait Faik TCLC 23
See also Abasiyanik, Sait Faik

Saki TCLC 3; SSC 12
See also Munro, H(ector) H(ugh)
See also MTCW 2

Sala, George Augustus NCLC 46

Saladin 1138-1193 .... CMLC 38

Schnitzler, Arthur 1862-1931 . **TCLC 4; SSC 15**
See also CA 104; DLB 81, 118
Schoenberg, Arnold Franz Walter
1874-1951 .... **TCLC 75**
See also CA 109
Schonberg, Arnold
See Schoenberg, Arnold Franz Walter
Schopenhauer, Arthur 1788-1860 .. **NCLC 51**
See also DLB 90
Schor, Sandra (M.) 1932(?)-1990 ..... **CLC 65**
See also CA 132
Schorer, Mark 1908-1977 .... **CLC 9**
See also CA 5-8R; 73-76; CANR 7; DLB 103
Schrader, Paul (Joseph) 1946- .... **CLC 26**
See also CA 37-40R; CANR 41; DLB 44
Schreiner, Olive (Emilie Albertina)
1855-1920 .... **TCLC 9**
See also CA 105; 154; DLB 18, 156, 190, 225
Schulberg, Budd (Wilson) 1914- .. **CLC 7, 48**
See also CA 25-28R; CANR 19, 87; DLB 6, 26, 28; DLBY 81
Schulz, Bruno 1892-1942 .. **TCLC 5, 51; SSC 13**
See also CA 115; 123; CANR 86; MTCW 2
Schulz, Charles M(onroe)
1922-2000 .... **CLC 12**
See also CA 9-12R; 187; CANR 6; INT CANR-6; SATA 10; SATA-Obit 118
Schumacher, E(rnst) F(riedrich)
1911-1977 .... **CLC 80**
See also CA 81-84; 73-76; CANR 34, 85
Schuyler, James Marcus 1923-1991 .. **CLC 5, 23; DAM POET**
See also CA 101; 134; DLB 5, 169; INT 101
Schwartz, Delmore (David)
1913-1966 ... **CLC 2, 4, 10, 45, 87; PC 8**
See also CA 17-18; 25-28R; CANR 35; CAP 2; DLB 28, 48; MTCW 1, 2
Schwartz, Ernst
See Ozu, Yasujiro
Schwartz, John Burnham 1965- .... **CLC 59**
See also CA 132
Schwartz, Lynne Sharon 1939- .... **CLC 31**
See also CA 103; CANR 44, 89; MTCW 2
Schwartz, Muriel A.
See Eliot, T(homas) S(tearns)
Schwarz-Bart, Andre 1928- .... **CLC 2, 4**
See also CA 89-92
Schwarz-Bart, Simone 1938- . **CLC 7; BLCS**
See also BW 2; CA 97-100
Schwitters, Kurt (Hermann Edward Karl Julius) 1887-1948 .... **TCLC 95**
See also CA 158
Schwob, Marcel (Mayer Andre)
1867-1905 .... **TCLC 20**
See also CA 117; 168; DLB 123
Sciascia, Leonardo 1921-1989 .. **CLC 8, 9, 41**
See also CA 85-88; 130; CANR 35; DLB 177; MTCW 1
Scoppettone, Sandra 1936- .... **CLC 26**
See also AAYA 11; CA 5-8R; CANR 41, 73; SATA 9, 92
Scorsese, Martin 1942- .... **CLC 20, 89**
See also CA 110; 114; CANR 46, 85
Scotland, Jay
See Jakes, John (William)
Scott, Duncan Campbell
1862-1947 .... **TCLC 6; DAC**
See also CA 104; 153; DLB 92
Scott, Evelyn 1893-1963 .... **CLC 43**
See also CA 104; 112; CANR 64; DLB 9, 48
Scott, F(rancis) R(eginald)
1899-1985 .... **CLC 22**
See also CA 101; 114; CANR 87; DLB 88; INT 101

Scott, Frank
See Scott, F(rancis) R(eginald)
Scott, Joanna 1960- .... **CLC 50**
See also CA 126; CANR 53, 92
Scott, Paul (Mark) 1920-1978 ...... **CLC 9, 60**
See also CA 81-84; 77-80; CANR 33; DLB 14, 207; MTCW 1
Scott, Sarah 1723-1795 .... **LC 44**
See also DLB 39
Scott, Walter 1771-1832 . **NCLC 15, 69; DA; DAB; DAC; DAM MST, NOV, POET; PC 13; SSC 32; WLC**
See also AAYA 22; CDBLB 1789-1832; DLB 93, 107, 116, 144, 159; YABC 2
Scribe, (Augustin) Eugene
1791-1861 ..... **NCLC 16; DAM DRAM; DC 5**
See also DLB 192
Scrum, R.
See Crumb, R(obert)
Scudery, Madeleine de 1607-1701 .. **LC 2, 58**
Scum
See Crumb, R(obert)
Scumbag, Little Bobby
See Crumb, R(obert)
Seabrook, John
See Hubbard, L(afayette) Ron(ald)
Sealy, I(rwin) Allan 1951- .... **CLC 55**
See also CA 136
Search, Alexander
See Pessoa, Fernando (Antonio Nogueira)
Sebastian, Lee
See Silverberg, Robert
Sebastian Owl
See Thompson, Hunter S(tockton)
Sebestyen, Ouida 1924- .... **CLC 30**
See also AAYA 8; CA 107; CANR 40; CLR 17; JRDA; MAICYA; SAAS 10; SATA 39
Secundus, H. Scriblerus
See Fielding, Henry
Sedges, John
See Buck, Pearl S(ydenstricker)
Sedgwick, Catharine Maria
1789-1867 .... **NCLC 19**
See also DLB 1, 74
Seelye, John (Douglas) 1931- .... **CLC 7**
See also CA 97-100; CANR 70; INT 97-100
Seferiades, Giorgos Stylianou 1900-1971
See Seferis, George
See also CA 5-8R; 33-36R; CANR 5, 36; MTCW 1
Seferis, George CLC 5, 11
See also Seferiades, Giorgos Stylianou
Segal, Erich (Wolf) 1937- . **CLC 3, 10; DAM POP**
See also BEST 89:1; CA 25-28R; CANR 20, 36, 65; DLBY 86; INT CANR-20; MTCW 1
Seger, Bob 1945- .... **CLC 35**
Seghers, Anna CLC 7
See also Radvanyi, Netty
See also DLB 69
Seidel, Frederick (Lewis) 1936- .... **CLC 18**
See also CA 13-16R; CANR 8; DLBY 84
Seifert, Jaroslav 1901-1986 .. **CLC 34, 44, 93**
See also CA 127; MTCW 1, 2
Sei Shonagon c. 966-1017(?) .... **CMLC 6**
Sejour, Victor 1817-1874 .... **DC 10**
See also DLB 50
Sejour Marcou et Ferrand, Juan Victor
See Sejour, Victor
Selby, Hubert, Jr. 1928- .... **CLC 1, 2, 4, 8; SSC 20**
See also CA 13-16R; CANR 33, 85; DLB 2, 227

Selzer, Richard 1928- .... **CLC 74**
See also CA 65-68; CANR 14
Sembene, Ousmane
See Ousmane, Sembene
Senancour, Etienne Pivert de
1770-1846 .... **NCLC 16**
See also DLB 119
Sender, Ramon (Jose) 1902-1982 ...... **CLC 8; DAM MULT; HLC 2**
See also CA 5-8R; 105; CANR 8; HW 1; MTCW 1
Seneca, Lucius Annaeus c. 1-c. 65 .... **CMLC 6; DAM DRAM; DC 5**
See also DLB 211
Senghor, Leopold Sedar 1906- .... **CLC 54, 130; BLC 3; DAM MULT, POET; PC 25**
See also BW 2; CA 116; 125; CANR 47, 74; MTCW 1, 2
Senna, Danzy 1970- .... **CLC 119**
See also CA 169
Serling, (Edward) Rod(man)
1924-1975 .... **CLC 30**
See also AAYA 14; AITN 1; CA 162; 57-60; DLB 26
Serna, Ramon Gomez de la
See Gomez de la Serna, Ramon
Serpieres
See Guillevic, (Eugene)
Service, Robert
See Service, Robert W(illiam)
See also DAB; DLB 92
Service, Robert W(illiam)
1874(?)-1958 .... **TCLC 15; DA; DAC; DAM MST, POET; WLC**
See also Service, Robert
See also CA 115; 140; CANR 84; SATA 20
Seth, Vikram 1952- .... **CLC 43, 90; DAM MULT**
See also CA 121; 127; CANR 50, 74; DA3; DLB 120; INT 127; MTCW 2
Seton, Cynthia Propper 1926-1982 .. **CLC 27**
See also CA 5-8R; 108; CANR 7
Seton, Ernest (Evan) Thompson
1860-1946 .... **TCLC 31**
See also CA 109; CLR 59; DLB 92; DLBD 13; JRDA; SATA 18
Seton-Thompson, Ernest
See Seton, Ernest (Evan) Thompson
Settle, Mary Lee 1918- .... **CLC 19, 61**
See also CA 89-92; CAAS 1; CANR 44, 87; DLB 6; INT 89-92
Seuphor, Michel
See Arp, Jean
Sevigne, Marie (de Rabutin-Chantal)
Marquise de 1626-1696 .... **LC 11**
Sewall, Samuel 1652-1730 .... **LC 38**
See also DLB 24
Sexton, Anne (Harvey) 1928-1974 ..... **CLC 2, 4, 6, 8, 10, 15, 53, 123; DA; DAB; DAC; DAM MST, POET; PC 2; WLC**
See also CA 1-4R; 53-56; CABS 2; CANR 3, 36; CDALB 1941-1968; DA3; DLB 5, 169; MTCW 1, 2; SATA 10
Shaara, Jeff 1952- .... **CLC 119**
See also CA 163
Shaara, Michael (Joseph, Jr.)
1929-1988 .... **CLC 15; DAM POP**
See also AITN 1; CA 102; 125; CANR 52, 85; DLBY 83
Shackleton, C. C.
See Aldiss, Brian W(ilson)
Shacochis, Bob CLC 39
See also Shacochis, Robert G.

Silverberg, Robert 1935- .... **CLC 7, 140;**
  DAM POP
  See also AAYA 24; CA 1-4R, 186; CAAE
  186; CAAS 3; CANR 1, 20, 36, 85; CLR
  59; DLB 8; INT CANR-20; MAICYA;
  MTCW 1, 2; SATA 13, 91; SATA-Essay
  104
Silverstein, Alvin 1933- .... **CLC 17**
  See also CA 49-52; CANR 2; CLR 25;
  JRDA; MAICYA; SATA 8, 69
Silverstein, Virginia B(arbara Opshelor)
  1937- .... **CLC 17**
  See also CA 49-52; CANR 2; CLR 25;
  JRDA; MAICYA; SATA 8, 69
Sim, Georges
  See Simenon, Georges (Jacques Christian)
Simak, Clifford D(onald) 1904-1988 . **CLC 1,**
  55
  See also CA 1-4R; 125; CANR 1, 35; DLB
  8; MTCW 1; SATA-Obit 56
Simenon, Georges (Jacques Christian)
  1903-1989 .... **CLC 1, 2, 3, 8, 18, 47;**
  DAM POP
  See also CA 85-88; 129; CANR 35; DA3;
  DLB 72; DLBY 89; MTCW 1, 2
Simic, Charles 1938- .... **CLC 6, 9, 22, 49, 68,**
  130; DAM POET
  See also CA 29-32R; CAAS 4; CANR 12,
  33, 52, 61; DA3; DLB 105; MTCW 2
Simmel, Georg 1858-1918 .... **TCLC 64**
  See also CA 157
Simmons, Charles (Paul) 1924- .... **CLC 57**
  See also CA 89-92; INT 89-92
Simmons, Dan 1948- .... **CLC 44; DAM POP**
  See also AAYA 16; CA 138; CANR 53, 81
Simmons, James (Stewart Alexander)
  1933- .... **CLC 43**
  See also CA 105; CAAS 21; DLB 40
Simms, William Gilmore
  1806-1870 .... **NCLC 3**
  See also DLB 3, 30, 59, 73
Simon, Carly 1945- .... **CLC 26**
  See also CA 105
Simon, Claude 1913- .... **CLC 4, 9, 15, 39;**
  DAM NOV
  See also CA 89-92; CANR 33; DLB 83;
  MTCW 1
Simon, (Marvin) Neil 1927- ... **CLC 6, 11, 31,**
  39, 70; DAM DRAM; DC 14
  See also AAYA 32; AITN 1; CA 21-24R;
  CANR 26, 54, 87; DA3; DLB 7; MTCW
  1, 2
Simon, Paul (Frederick) 1941(?)- ..... **CLC 17**
  See also CA 116; 153
Simonon, Paul 1956(?)- .... **CLC 30**
Simpson, Harriette
  See Arnow, Harriette (Louisa) Simpson
Simpson, Louis (Aston Marantz)
  1923- ...... **CLC 4, 7, 9, 32; DAM POET**
  See also CA 1-4R; CAAS 4; CANR 1, 61;
  DLB 5; MTCW 1, 2
Simpson, Mona (Elizabeth) 1957- .... **CLC 44**
  See also CA 122; 135; CANR 68
Simpson, N(orman) F(rederick)
  1919- .... **CLC 29**
  See also CA 13-16R; DLB 13
Sinclair, Andrew (Annandale) 1935- . **CLC 2,**
  14
  See also CA 9-12R; CAAS 5; CANR 14,
  38, 91; DLB 14; MTCW 1
Sinclair, Emil
  See Hesse, Hermann
Sinclair, Iain 1943- .... **CLC 76**
  See also CA 132; CANR 81
Sinclair, Iain MacGregor
  See Sinclair, Iain
Sinclair, Irene
  See Griffith, D(avid Lewelyn) W(ark)

Sinclair, Mary Amelia St. Clair 1865(?)-1946
  See Sinclair, May
  See also CA 104
Sinclair, May 1863-1946 .... **TCLC 3, 11**
  See also Sinclair, Mary Amelia St. Clair
  See also CA 166; DLB 36, 135
Sinclair, Roy
  See Griffith, D(avid Lewelyn) W(ark)
Sinclair, Upton (Beall) 1878-1968 ..... **CLC 1,**
  11, 15, 63; DA; DAB; DAC; DAM
  MST, NOV; WLC
  See also CA 5-8R; 25-28R; CANR 7;
  CDALB 1929-1941; DA3; DLB 9; INT
  CANR-7; MTCW 1, 2; SATA 9
Singer, Isaac
  See Singer, Isaac Bashevis
Singer, Isaac Bashevis 1904-1991 .. **CLC 1, 3,**
  6, 9, 11, 15, 23, 38, 69, 111; DA; DAB;
  DAC; DAM MST, NOV; SSC 3; WLC
  See also AAYA 32; AITN 1, 2; CA 1-4R;
  134; CANR 1, 39; CDALB 1941-1968;
  CLR 1; DA3; DLB 6, 28, 52; DLBY 91;
  JRDA; MAICYA; MTCW 1, 2; SATA 3,
  27; SATA-Obit 68
Singer, Israel Joshua 1893-1944 .... **TCLC 33**
  See also CA 169
Singh, Khushwant 1915- .... **CLC 11**
  See also CA 9-12R; CAAS 9; CANR 6, 84
Singleton, Ann
  See Benedict, Ruth (Fulton)
Sinjohn, John
  See Galsworthy, John
Sinyavsky, Andrei (Donatevich)
  1925-1997 .... **CLC 8**
  See also CA 85-88; 159
Sirin, V.
  See Nabokov, Vladimir (Vladimirovich)
Sissman, L(ouis) E(dward)
  1928-1976 .... **CLC 9, 18**
  See also CA 21-24R; 65-68; CANR 13;
  DLB 5
Sisson, C(harles) H(ubert) 1914- .... **CLC 8**
  See also CA 1-4R; CAAS 3; CANR 3, 48,
  84; DLB 27
Sitwell, Dame Edith 1887-1964 ..... **CLC 2, 9,**
  67; DAM POET; PC 3
  See also CA 9-12R; CANR 35; CDBLB
  1945-1960; DLB 20; MTCW 1, 2
Siwaarmill, H. P.
  See Sharp, William
Sjoewall, Maj 1935- .... **CLC 7**
  See also Sjowall, Maj
  See also CA 65-68; CANR 73
Sjowall, Maj
  See Sjoewall, Maj
Skelton, John 1463-1529 .... **PC 25**
Skelton, Robin 1925-1997 .... **CLC 13**
  See also AITN 2; CA 5-8R; 160; CAAS 5;
  CANR 28, 89; DLB 27, 53
Skolimowski, Jerzy 1938- .... **CLC 20**
  See also CA 128
Skram, Amalie (Bertha)
  1847-1905 .... **TCLC 25**
  See also CA 165
Skvorecky, Josef (Vaclav) 1924- ...... **CLC 15,**
  39, 69; DAC; DAM NOV
  See also CA 61-64; CAAS 1; CANR 10,
  34, 63; DA3; DLB 232; MTCW 1, 2
Slade, Bernard CLC 11, 46
  See also Newbound, Bernard Slade
  See also CAAS 9; DLB 53
Slaughter, Carolyn 1946- .... **CLC 56**
  See also CA 85-88; CANR 85
Slaughter, Frank G(ill) 1908- .... **CLC 29**
  See also AITN 2; CA 5-8R; CANR 5, 85;
  INT CANR-5
Slavitt, David R(ytman) 1935- ..... **CLC 5, 14**
  See also CA 21-24R; CAAS 3; CANR 41,
  83; DLB 5, 6

Slesinger, Tess 1905-1945 .... **TCLC 10**
  See also CA 107; DLB 102
Slessor, Kenneth 1901-1971 .... **CLC 14**
  See also CA 102; 89-92
Slowacki, Juliusz 1809-1849 .... **NCLC 15**
Smart, Christopher 1722-1771 .. **LC 3; DAM**
  POET; PC 13
  See also DLB 109
Smart, Elizabeth 1913-1986 .... **CLC 54**
  See also CA 81-84; 118; DLB 88
Smiley, Jane (Graves) 1949- ...... **CLC 53, 76;**
  DAM POP
  See also CA 104; CANR 30, 50, 74; DA3;
  DLB 227, 234; INT CANR-30
Smith, A(rthur) J(ames) M(arshall)
  1902-1980 .... **CLC 15; DAC**
  See also CA 1-4R; 102; CANR 4; DLB 88
Smith, Adam 1723-1790 .... **LC 36**
  See also DLB 104
Smith, Alexander 1829-1867 .... **NCLC 59**
  See also DLB 32, 55
Smith, Anna Deavere 1950- .... **CLC 86**
  See also CA 133
Smith, Betty (Wehner) 1896-1972 .... **CLC 19**
  See also CA 5-8R; 33-36R; DLBY 82;
  SATA 6
Smith, Charlotte (Turner)
  1749-1806 .... **NCLC 23**
  See also DLB 39, 109
Smith, Clark Ashton 1893-1961 .... **CLC 43**
  See also CA 143; CANR 81; MTCW 2
Smith, Dave CLC 22, 42
  See also Smith, David (Jeddie)
  See also CAAS 7; DLB 5
Smith, David (Jeddie) 1942-
  See Smith, Dave
  See also CA 49-52; CANR 1, 59; DAM
  POET
Smith, Florence Margaret 1902-1971
  See Smith, Stevie
  See also CA 17-18; 29-32R; CANR 35;
  CAP 2; DAM POET; MTCW 1, 2
Smith, Iain Crichton 1928-1998 .... **CLC 64**
  See also CA 21-24R; 171; DLB 40, 139
Smith, John 1580(?)-1631 .... **LC 9**
  See also DLB 24, 30
Smith, Johnston
  See Crane, Stephen (Townley)
Smith, Joseph, Jr. 1805-1844 .... **NCLC 53**
Smith, Lee 1944- .... **CLC 25, 73**
  See also CA 114; 119; CANR 46; DLB 143;
  DLBY 83; INT 119
Smith, Martin
  See Smith, Martin Cruz
Smith, Martin Cruz 1942- .... **CLC 25; DAM**
  MULT, POP
  See also BEST 89:4; CA 85-88; CANR 6,
  23, 43, 65; INT CANR-23; MTCW 2;
  NNAL
Smith, Mary-Ann Tirone 1944- .... **CLC 39**
  See also CA 118; 136
Smith, Patti 1946- .... **CLC 12**
  See also CA 93-96; CANR 63
Smith, Pauline (Urmson)
  1882-1959 .... **TCLC 25**
  See also DLB 225
Smith, Rosamond
  See Oates, Joyce Carol
Smith, Sheila Kaye
  See Kaye-Smith, Sheila
Smith, Stevie CLC 3, 8, 25, 44; PC 12
  See also Smith, Florence Margaret
  See also DLB 20; MTCW 2
Smith, Wilbur (Addison) 1933- .... **CLC 33**
  See also CA 13-16R; CANR 7, 46, 66;
  MTCW 1, 2

Smith, William Jay 1918- .... **CLC 6**
See also CA 5-8R; CANR 44; DLB 5; MAI-
CYA; SAAS 22; SATA 2, 68

Smith, Woodrow Wilson
See Kuttner, Henry

Smolenskin, Peretz 1842-1885 .... **NCLC 30**

Smollett, Tobias (George) 1721-1771 ... **LC 2, 46**
See also CDBLB 1660-1789; DLB 39, 104

Snodgrass, W(illiam) D(e Witt)
1926- .... **CLC 2, 6, 10, 18, 68; DAM POET**
See also CA 1-4R; CANR 6, 36, 65, 85;
DLB 5; MTCW 1, 2

Snow, C(harles) P(ercy) 1905-1980 ... **CLC 1, 4, 6, 9, 13, 19; DAM NOV**
See also CA 5-8R; 101; CANR 28; CDBLB
1945-1960; DLB 15, 77; DLBD 17;
MTCW 1, 2

Snow, Frances Compton
See Adams, Henry (Brooks)

Snyder, Gary (Sherman) 1930- . **CLC 1, 2, 5, 9, 32, 120; DAM POET; PC 21**
See also CA 17-20R; CANR 30, 60; DA3;
DLB 5, 16, 165, 212; MTCW 2

Snyder, Zilpha Keatley 1927- .... **CLC 17**
See also AAYA 15; CA 9-12R; CANR 38;
CLR 31; JRDA; MAICYA; SAAS 2;
SATA 1, 28, 75, 110; SATA-Essay 112

Soares, Bernardo
See Pessoa, Fernando (Antonio Nogueira)

Sobh, A.
See Shamlu, Ahmad

Sobol, Joshua CLC 60

Socrates 469B.C.-399B.C. .... **CMLC 27**

Soderberg, Hjalmar 1869-1941 ...... **TCLC 39**

Sodergran, Edith (Irene)
See Soedergran, Edith (Irene)

Soedergran, Edith (Irene)
1892-1923 .... **TCLC 31**

Softly, Edgar
See Lovecraft, H(oward) P(hillips)

Softly, Edward
See Lovecraft, H(oward) P(hillips)

Sokolov, Raymond 1941- .... **CLC 7**
See also CA 85-88

Solo, Jay
See Ellison, Harlan (Jay)

Sologub, Fyodor TCLC 9
See also Teternikov, Fyodor Kuzmich

Solomons, Ikey Esquir
See Thackeray, William Makepeace

Solomos, Dionysios 1798-1857 .... **NCLC 15**

Solwoska, Mara
See French, Marilyn

Solzhenitsyn, Aleksandr I(sayevich)
1918- .. **CLC 1, 2, 4, 7, 9, 10, 18, 26, 34, 78, 134; DA; DAB; DAC; DAM MST, NOV; SSC 32; WLC**
See also AITN 1; CA 69-72; CANR 40, 65;
DA3; MTCW 1, 2

Somers, Jane
See Lessing, Doris (May)

Somerville, Edith 1858-1949 .... **TCLC 51**
See also DLB 135

Somerville & Ross
See Martin, Violet Florence; Somerville,
Edith

Sommer, Scott 1951- .... **CLC 25**
See also CA 106

Sondheim, Stephen (Joshua) 1930- . **CLC 30, 39; DAM DRAM**
See also AAYA 11; CA 103; CANR 47, 67

Song, Cathy 1955- .... **PC 21**
See also CA 154; DLB 169

Sontag, Susan 1933- .... **CLC 1, 2, 10, 13, 31, 105; DAM POP**
See also CA 17-20R; CANR 25, 51, 74;
DA3; DLB 2, 67; MTCW 1, 2

Sophocles 496(?)B.C.-406(?)B.C. .... **CMLC 2; DA; DAB; DAC; DAM DRAM, MST; DC 1; WLCS**
See also DA3; DLB 176

Sordello 1189-1269 .... **CMLC 15**

Sorel, Georges 1847-1922 .... **TCLC 91**
See also CA 118

Sorel, Julia
See Drexler, Rosalyn

Sorrentino, Gilbert 1929- .. **CLC 3, 7, 14, 22, 40**
See also CA 77-80; CANR 14, 33; DLB 5,
173; DLBY 80; INT CANR-14

Soto, Gary 1952- .... **CLC 32, 80; DAM MULT; HLC 2; PC 28**
See also AAYA 10, 37; CA 119; 125; CANR
50, 74; CLR 38; DLB 82; HW 1, 2; INT
125; JRDA; MTCW 2; SATA 80, 120

Soupault, Philippe 1897-1990 .... **CLC 68**
See also CA 116; 147; 131

Souster, (Holmes) Raymond 1921- .... **CLC 5, 14; DAC; DAM POET**
See also CA 13-16R; CAAS 14; CANR 13,
29, 53; DA3; DLB 88; SATA 63

Southern, Terry 1924(?)-1995 .... **CLC 7**
See also CA 1-4R; 150; CANR 1, 55; DLB
2

Southey, Robert 1774-1843 .... **NCLC 8**
See also DLB 93, 107, 142; SATA 54

Southworth, Emma Dorothy Eliza Nevitte
1819-1899 .... **NCLC 26**

Souza, Ernest
See Scott, Evelyn

Soyinka, Wole 1934- .... **CLC 3, 5, 14, 36, 44; BLC 3; DA; DAB; DAC; DAM DRAM, MST, MULT; DC 2; WLC**
See also BW 2, 3; CA 13-16R; CANR 27,
39, 82; DA3; DLB 125; MTCW 1, 2

Spackman, W(illiam) M(ode)
1905-1990 .... **CLC 46**
See also CA 81-84; 132

Spacks, Barry (Bernard) 1931- .... **CLC 14**
See also CA 154; CANR 33; DLB 105

Spanidou, Irini 1946- .... **CLC 44**
See also CA 185

Spark, Muriel (Sarah) 1918- ..... **CLC 2, 3, 5, 8, 13, 18, 40, 94; DAB; DAC; DAM MST, NOV; SSC 10**
See also CA 5-8R; CANR 12, 36, 76, 89;
CDBLB 1945-1960; DA3; DLB 15, 139;
INT CANR-12; MTCW 1, 2

Spaulding, Douglas
See Bradbury, Ray (Douglas)

Spaulding, Leonard
See Bradbury, Ray (Douglas)

Spence, J. A. D.
See Eliot, T(homas) S(tearns)

Spencer, Elizabeth 1921- .... **CLC 22**
See also CA 13-16R; CANR 32, 65, 87;
DLB 6; MTCW 1; SATA 14

Spencer, Leonard G.
See Silverberg, Robert

Spencer, Scott 1945- .... **CLC 30**
See also CA 113; CANR 51; DLBY 86

Spender, Stephen (Harold)
1909-1995 .... **CLC 1, 2, 5, 10, 41, 91; DAM POET**
See also CA 9-12R; 149; CANR 31, 54;
CDBLB 1945-1960; DA3; DLB 20;
MTCW 1, 2

Spengler, Oswald (Arnold Gottfried)
1880-1936 .... **TCLC 25**
See also CA 118

Spenser, Edmund 1552(?)-1599 ..... **LC 5, 39; DA; DAB; DAC; DAM MST, POET; PC 8; WLC**
See also CDBLB Before 1660; DA3; DLB
167

Spicer, Jack 1925-1965 .... **CLC 8, 18, 72; DAM POET**
See also CA 85-88; DLB 5, 16, 193

Spiegelman, Art 1948- .... **CLC 76**
See also AAYA 10; CA 125; CANR 41, 55,
74; MTCW 2; SATA 109

Spielberg, Peter 1929- .... **CLC 6**
See also CA 5-8R; CANR 4, 48; DLBY 81

Spielberg, Steven 1947- .... **CLC 20**
See also AAYA 8, 24; CA 77-80; CANR
32; SATA 32

Spillane, Frank Morrison 1918-
See Spillane, Mickey
See also CA 25-28R; CANR 28, 63; DA3;
DLB 226; MTCW 1, 2; SATA 66

Spillane, Mickey CLC 3, 13
See also Spillane, Frank Morrison
See also DLB 226; MTCW 2

Spinoza, Benedictus de 1632-1677 .. **LC 9, 58**

Spinrad, Norman (Richard) 1940- ... **CLC 46**
See also CA 37-40R; CAAS 19; CANR 20,
91; DLB 8; INT CANR-20

Spitteler, Carl (Friedrich Georg)
1845-1924 .... **TCLC 12**
See also CA 109; DLB 129

Spivack, Kathleen (Romola Drucker)
1938- .... **CLC 6**
See also CA 49-52

Spoto, Donald 1941- .... **CLC 39**
See also CA 65-68; CANR 11, 57, 93

Springsteen, Bruce (F.) 1949- .... **CLC 17**
See also CA 111

Spurling, Hilary 1940- .... **CLC 34**
See also CA 104; CANR 25, 52, 94

Spyker, John Howland
See Elman, Richard (Martin)

Squires, (James) Radcliffe
1917-1993 .... **CLC 51**
See also CA 1-4R; 140; CANR 6, 21

Srivastava, Dhanpat Rai 1880(?)-1936
See Premchand
See also CA 118

Stacy, Donald
See Pohl, Frederik

Staël, Germaine de 1766-1817 .... **NCLC 91**
See also Staël-Holstein, Anne Louise Ger-
maine Necker, Baronne de
See also DLB 192

**Staël-Holstein, Anne Louise Germaine
Necker, Baronne de**
1766-1817 .... **NCLC 3**
See also Staël, Germaine de

Stafford, Jean 1915-1979 .. **CLC 4, 7, 19, 68; SSC 26**
See also CA 1-4R; 85-88; CANR 3, 65;
DLB 2, 173; MTCW 1, 2; SATA-Obit 22

Stafford, William (Edgar)
1914-1993 .. **CLC 4, 7, 29; DAM POET**
See also CA 5-8R; 142; CAAS 3; CANR 5,
22; DLB 5, 206; INT CANR-22

Stagnelius, Eric Johan 1793-1823 . **NCLC 61**

Staines, Trevor
See Brunner, John (Kilian Houston)

Stairs, Gordon
See Austin, Mary (Hunter)

Stairs, Gordon
See Austin, Mary (Hunter)

Stalin, Joseph 1879-1953 .... **TCLC 92**

Stannard, Martin 1947- .... **CLC 44**
See also CA 142; DLB 155

Stanton, Elizabeth Cady
1815-1902 .... **TCLC 73**
See also CA 171; DLB 79

Strindberg, (Johan) August
1849-1912 .... **TCLC 1, 8, 21, 47; DA; DAB; DAC; DAM DRAM, MST; WLC**
See also CA 104; 135; DA3; MTCW 2

Stringer, Arthur 1874-1950 .... **TCLC 37**
See also CA 161; DLB 92

Stringer, David
See Roberts, Keith (John Kingston)

Stroheim, Erich von 1885-1957 ..... **TCLC 71**

Strugatskii, Arkadii (Natanovich)
1925-1991 .... **CLC 27**
See also CA 106; 135

Strugatskii, Boris (Natanovich)
1933- .... **CLC 27**
See also CA 106

Strummer, Joe 1953(?)- .... **CLC 30**

Strunk, William, Jr. 1869-1946 ...... **TCLC 92**
See also CA 118; 164

Stryk, Lucien 1924- .... **PC 27**
See also CA 13-16R; CANR 10, 28, 55

Stuart, Don A.
See Campbell, John W(ood, Jr.)

Stuart, Ian
See MacLean, Alistair (Stuart)

Stuart, Jesse (Hilton) 1906-1984 ... **CLC 1, 8, 11, 14, 34; SSC 31**
See also CA 5-8R; 112; CANR 31; DLB 9, 48, 102; DLBY 84; SATA 2; SATA-Obit 36

Sturgeon, Theodore (Hamilton)
1918-1985 .... **CLC 22, 39**
See also Queen, Ellery
See also CA 81-84; 116; CANR 32; DLB 8; DLBY 85; MTCW 1, 2

Sturges, Preston 1898-1959 .... **TCLC 48**
See also CA 114; 149; DLB 26

Styron, William 1925- .... **CLC 1, 3, 5, 11, 15, 60; DAM NOV, POP; SSC 25**
See also BEST 90:4; CA 5-8R; CANR 6, 33, 74; CDALB 1968-1988; DA3; DLB 2, 143; DLBY 80; INT CANR-6; MTCW 1, 2

Su, Chien 1884-1918
See Su Man-shu
See also CA 123

Suarez Lynch, B.
See Bioy Casares, Adolfo; Borges, Jorge Luis

Suassuna, Ariano Vilar 1927-
See also CA 178; HLCS 1; HW 2

Suckling, John 1609-1641 .... **PC 30**
See also DAM POET; DLB 58, 126

Suckow, Ruth 1892-1960 .... **SSC 18**
See also CA 113; DLB 9, 102

Sudermann, Hermann 1857-1928 .. **TCLC 15**
See also CA 107; DLB 118

Sue, Eugene 1804-1857 .... **NCLC 1**
See also DLB 119

Sueskind, Patrick 1949- .... **CLC 44**
See also Suskind, Patrick

Sukenick, Ronald 1932- .... **CLC 3, 4, 6, 48**
See also CA 25-28R; CAAS 8; CANR 32, 89; DLB 173; DLBY 81

Suknaski, Andrew 1942- .... **CLC 19**
See also CA 101; DLB 53

Sullivan, Vernon
See Vian, Boris

Sully Prudhomme 1839-1907 .... **TCLC 31**

Su Man-shu **TCLC 24**
See also Su, Chien

Summerforest, Ivy B.
See Kirkup, James

Summers, Andrew James 1942- .... **CLC 26**

Summers, Andy
See Summers, Andrew James

Summers, Hollis (Spurgeon, Jr.)
1916- .... **CLC 10**
See also CA 5-8R; CANR 3; DLB 6

Summers, (Alphonsus Joseph-Mary Augustus) Montague
1880-1948 .... **TCLC 16**
See also CA 118; 163

Sumner, Gordon Matthew CLC 26
See also Sting

Surtees, Robert Smith 1803-1864 .. **NCLC 14**
See also DLB 21

Susann, Jacqueline 1921-1974 .... **CLC 3**
See also AITN 1; CA 65-68; 53-56; MTCW 1, 2

Su Shih 1036-1101 .... **CMLC 15**

Suskind, Patrick
See Sueskind, Patrick
See also CA 145

Sutcliff, Rosemary 1920-1992 .... **CLC 26; DAB; DAC; DAM MST, POP**
See also AAYA 10; CA 5-8R; 139; CANR 37; CLR 1, 37; JRDA; MAICYA; SATA 6, 44, 78; SATA-Obit 73

Sutro, Alfred 1863-1933 .... **TCLC 6**
See also CA 105; 185; DLB 10

Sutton, Henry
See Slavitt, David R(ytman)

Svevo, Italo 1861-1928 ...... **TCLC 2, 35; SSC 25**
See also Schmitz, Aron Hector

Swados, Elizabeth (A.) 1951- .... **CLC 12**
See also CA 97-100; CANR 49; INT 97-100

Swados, Harvey 1920-1972 .... **CLC 5**
See also CA 5-8R; 37-40R; CANR 6; DLB 2

Swan, Gladys 1934- .... **CLC 69**
See also CA 101; CANR 17, 39

Swanson, Logan
See Matheson, Richard Burton

Swarthout, Glendon (Fred)
1918-1992 .... **CLC 35**
See also CA 1-4R; 139; CANR 1, 47; SATA 26

Sweet, Sarah C.
See Jewett, (Theodora) Sarah Orne

Swenson, May 1919-1989 ...... **CLC 4, 14, 61, 106; DA; DAB; DAC; DAM MST, POET; PC 14**
See also CA 5-8R; 130; CANR 36, 61; DLB 5; MTCW 1, 2; SATA 15

Swift, Augustus
See Lovecraft, H(oward) P(hillips)

Swift, Graham (Colin) 1949- ...... **CLC 41, 88**
See also CA 117; 122; CANR 46, 71; DLB 194; MTCW 2

Swift, Jonathan 1667-1745 ..... **LC 1, 42; DA; DAB; DAC; DAM MST, NOV, POET; PC 9; WLC**
See also CDBLB 1660-1789; CLR 53; DA3; DLB 39, 95, 101; SATA 19

Swinburne, Algernon Charles
1837-1909 ...... **TCLC 8, 36; DA; DAB; DAC; DAM MST, POET; PC 24; WLC**
See also CA 105; 140; CDBLB 1832-1890; DA3; DLB 35, 57

Swinfen, Ann CLC 34

Swinnerton, Frank Arthur
1884-1982 .... **CLC 31**
See also CA 108; DLB 34

Swithen, John
See King, Stephen (Edwin)

Sylvia
See Ashton-Warner, Sylvia (Constance)

Symmes, Robert Edward
See Duncan, Robert (Edward)

Symonds, John Addington
1840-1893 .... **NCLC 34**
See also DLB 57, 144

Symons, Arthur 1865-1945 .... **TCLC 11**
See also CA 107; DLB 19, 57, 149

Symons, Julian (Gustave)
1912-1994 .... **CLC 2, 14, 32**
See also CA 49-52; 147; CAAS 3; CANR 3, 33, 59; DLB 87, 155; DLBY 92; MTCW 1

Synge, (Edmund) J(ohn) M(illington)
1871-1909 . **TCLC 6, 37; DAM DRAM; DC 2**
See also CA 104; 141; CDBLB 1890-1914; DLB 10, 19

Syruc, J.
See Milosz, Czeslaw

Szirtes, George 1948- .... **CLC 46**
See also CA 109; CANR 27, 61

Szymborska, Wislawa 1923- .... **CLC 99**
See also CA 154; CANR 91; DA3; DLB 232; DLBY 96; MTCW 2

T. O., Nik
See Annensky, Innokenty (Fyodorovich)

Tabori, George 1914- .... **CLC 19**
See also CA 49-52; CANR 4, 69

Tagore, Rabindranath 1861-1941 ... **TCLC 3, 53; DAM DRAM, POET; PC 8**
See also CA 104; 120; DA3; MTCW 1, 2

Taine, Hippolyte Adolphe
1828-1893 .... **NCLC 15**

Talese, Gay 1932- .... **CLC 37**
See also AITN 1; CA 1-4R; CANR 9, 58; DLB 185; INT CANR-9; MTCW 1, 2

Tallent, Elizabeth (Ann) 1954- .... **CLC 45**
See also CA 117; CANR 72; DLB 130

Tally, Ted 1952- .... **CLC 42**
See also CA 120; 124; INT 124

Talvik, Heiti 1904-1947 .... **TCLC 87**

Tamayo y Baus, Manuel
1829-1898 .... **NCLC 1**

Tammsaare, A(nton) H(ansen)
1878-1940 .... **TCLC 27**
See also CA 164; DLB 220

Tam'si, Tchicaya U
See Tchicaya, Gerald Felix

Tan, Amy (Ruth) 1952- . **CLC 59, 120; DAM MULT, NOV, POP**
See also AAYA 9; BEST 89:3; CA 136; CANR 54; CDALBS; DA3; DLB 173; MTCW 2; SATA 75

Tandem, Felix
See Spitteler, Carl (Friedrich Georg)

Tanizaki, Jun'ichiro 1886-1965 ... **CLC 8, 14, 28; SSC 21**
See also CA 93-96; 25-28R; DLB 180; MTCW 2

Tanner, William
See Amis, Kingsley (William)

Tao Lao
See Storni, Alfonsina

Tarantino, Quentin (Jerome)
1963- .... **CLC 125**
See also CA 171

Tarassoff, Lev
See Troyat, Henri

Tarbell, Ida M(inerva) 1857-1944 . **TCLC 40**
See also CA 122; 181; DLB 47

Tarkington, (Newton) Booth
1869-1946 .... **TCLC 9**
See also CA 110; 143; DLB 9, 102; MTCW 2; SATA 17

Tarkovsky, Andrei (Arsenyevich)
1932-1986 .... **CLC 75**
See also CA 127

Tartt, Donna 1964(?)- .... **CLC 76**
See also CA 142

Tasso, Torquato 1544-1595 .... **LC 5**

Tate, (John Orley) Allen 1899-1979 .. **CLC 2, 4, 6, 9, 11, 14, 24**
See also CA 5-8R; 85-88; CANR 32; DLB 4, 45, 63; DLBD 17; MTCW 1, 2

Tate, Ellalice
See Hibbert, Eleanor Alice Burford

Tate, James (Vincent) 1943- ..... **CLC 2, 6, 25**
See also CA 21-24R; CANR 29, 57; DLB
5, 169

Tauler, Johannes c. 1300-1361 ...... **CMLC 37**
See also DLB 179

Tavel, Ronald 1940- .... **CLC 6**
See also CA 21-24R; CANR 33

Taylor, Bayard 1825-1878 .... **NCLC 89**
See also DLB 3, 189

Taylor, C(ecil) P(hilip) 1929-1981 .... **CLC 27**
See also CA 25-28R; 105; CANR 47

Taylor, Edward 1642(?)-1729 ..... **LC 11; DA;
DAB; DAC; DAM MST, POET**
See also DLB 24

Taylor, Eleanor Ross 1920- .... **CLC 5**
See also CA 81-84; CANR 70

Taylor, Elizabeth 1912-1975 ..... **CLC 2, 4, 29**
See also CA 13-16R; CANR 9, 70; DLB
139; MTCW 1; SATA 13

Taylor, Frederick Winslow
1856-1915 .... **TCLC 76**

Taylor, Henry (Splawn) 1942- .... **CLC 44**
See also CA 33-36R; CAAS 7; CANR 31;
DLB 5

Taylor, Kamala (Purnaiya) 1924-
See Markandaya, Kamala
See also CA 77-80

Taylor, Mildred D. CLC 21
See also AAYA 10; BW 1; CA 85-88;
CANR 25; CLR 9, 59; DLB 52; JRDA;
MAICYA; SAAS 5; SATA 15, 70

Taylor, Peter (Hillsman) 1917-1994 .. **CLC 1,
4, 18, 37, 44, 50, 71; SSC 10**
See also CA 13-16R; 147; CANR 9, 50;
DLBY 81, 94; INT CANR-9; MTCW 1, 2

Taylor, Robert Lewis 1912-1998 .... **CLC 14**
See also CA 1-4R; 170; CANR 3, 64; SATA
10

Tchekhov, Anton
See Chekhov, Anton (Pavlovich)

Tchicaya, Gerald Felix 1931-1988 .. **CLC 101**
See also CA 129; 125; CANR 81

Tchicaya U Tam'si
See Tchicaya, Gerald Felix

Teasdale, Sara 1884-1933 .... **TCLC 4; PC 31**
See also CA 104; 163; DLB 45; SATA 32

Tegner, Esaias 1782-1846 .... **NCLC 2**

Teilhard de Chardin, (Marie Joseph) Pierre
1881-1955 .... **TCLC 9**
See also CA 105

Temple, Ann
See Mortimer, Penelope (Ruth)

Tennant, Emma (Christina) 1937- .. **CLC 13,
52**
See also CA 65-68; CAAS 9; CANR 10,
38, 59, 88; DLB 14

Tenneshaw, S. M.
See Silverberg, Robert

Tennyson, Alfred 1809-1892 ... **NCLC 30, 65;
DA; DAB; DAC; DAM MST, POET;
PC 6; WLC**
See also CDBLB 1832-1890; DA3; DLB
32

Teran, Lisa St. Aubin de CLC 36
See also St. Aubin de Teran, Lisa

Terence c. 184B.C.-c. 159B.C. ...... **CMLC 14;
DC 7**
See also DLB 211

Teresa de Jesus, St. 1515-1582 .... **LC 18**

Terkel, Louis 1912-
See Terkel, Studs
See also CA 57-60; CANR 18, 45, 67; DA3;
MTCW 1, 2

Terkel, Studs CLC 38
See also Terkel, Louis
See also AAYA 32; AITN 1; MTCW 2

Terry, C. V.
See Slaughter, Frank G(ill)

Terry, Megan 1932- .... **CLC 19; DC 13**
See also CA 77-80; CABS 3; CANR 43;
DLB 7

Tertullian c. 155-c. 245 .... **CMLC 29**

Tertz, Abram
See Sinyavsky, Andrei (Donatevich)

Tesich, Steve 1943(?)-1996 .... **CLC 40, 69**
See also CA 105; 152; DLBY 83

Tesla, Nikola 1856-1943 .... **TCLC 88**

Teternikov, Fyodor Kuzmich 1863-1927
See Sologub, Fyodor
See also CA 104

Tevis, Walter 1928-1984 .... **CLC 42**
See also CA 113

Tey, Josephine TCLC 14
See also Mackintosh, Elizabeth
See also DLB 77

Thackeray, William Makepeace
1811-1863 ...... **NCLC 5, 14, 22, 43; DA;
DAB; DAC; DAM MST, NOV; WLC**
See also CDBLB 1832-1890; DA3; DLB
21, 55, 159, 163; SATA 23

Thakura, Ravindranatha
See Tagore, Rabindranath

Tharoor, Shashi 1956- .... **CLC 70**
See also CA 141; CANR 91

Thelwell, Michael Miles 1939- .... **CLC 22**
See also BW 2; CA 101

Theobald, Lewis, Jr.
See Lovecraft, H(oward) P(hillips)

Theodorescu, Ion N. 1880-1967
See Arghezi, Tudor
See also CA 116; DLB 220

Theriault, Yves 1915-1983 .... **CLC 79; DAC;
DAM MST**
See also CA 102; DLB 88

Theroux, Alexander (Louis) 1939- .... **CLC 2,
25**
See also CA 85-88; CANR 20, 63

Theroux, Paul (Edward) 1941- ..... **CLC 5, 8,
11, 15, 28, 46; DAM POP**
See also AAYA 28; BEST 89:4; CA 33-36R;
CANR 20, 45, 74; CDALBS; DA3; DLB
2; MTCW 1, 2; SATA 44, 109

Thesen, Sharon 1946- .... **CLC 56**
See also CA 163

Thevenin, Denis
See Duhamel, Georges

Thibault, Jacques Anatole Francois
1844-1924
See France, Anatole
See also CA 106; 127; DAM NOV; DA3;
MTCW 1, 2

Thiele, Colin (Milton) 1920- .... **CLC 17**
See also CA 29-32R; CANR 12, 28, 53;
CLR 27; MAICYA; SAAS 2; SATA 14,
72

Thomas, Audrey (Callahan) 1935- .... **CLC 7,
13, 37, 107; SSC 20**
See also AITN 2; CA 21-24R; CAAS 19;
CANR 36, 58; DLB 60; MTCW 1

Thomas, Augustus 1857-1934 .... **TCLC 97**

Thomas, D(onald) M(ichael) 1935- . **CLC 13,
22, 31, 132**
See also CA 61-64; CAAS 11; CANR 17,
45, 75; CDBLB 1960 to Present; DA3;
DLB 40, 207; INT CANR-17; MTCW 1,
2

Thomas, Dylan (Marlais)
1914-1953 ...... **TCLC 1, 8, 45, 105; DA;
DAB; DAC; DAM DRAM, MST,
POET; PC 2; SSC 3; WLC**
See also CA 104; 120; CANR 65; CDBLB
1945-1960; DA3; DLB 13, 20, 139;
MTCW 1, 2; SATA 60

Thomas, (Philip) Edward
1878-1917 .... **TCLC 10; DAM POET**
See also CA 106; 153; DLB 98

Thomas, Joyce Carol 1938- .... **CLC 35**
See also AAYA 12; BW 2, 3; CA 113; 116;
CANR 48; CLR 19; DLB 33; INT 116;
JRDA; MAICYA; MTCW 1, 2; SAAS 7;
SATA 40, 78

Thomas, Lewis 1913-1993 .... **CLC 35**
See also CA 85-88; 143; CANR 38, 60;
MTCW 1, 2

Thomas, M. Carey 1857-1935 .... **TCLC 89**

Thomas, Paul
See Mann, (Paul) Thomas

Thomas, Piri 1928- .... **CLC 17; HLCS 2**
See also CA 73-76; HW 1

Thomas, R(onald) S(tuart) 1913- ...... **CLC 6,
13, 48; DAB; DAM POET**
See also CA 89-92; CAAS 4; CANR 30;
CDBLB 1960 to Present; DLB 27; MTCW
1

Thomas, Ross (Elmore) 1926-1995 .. **CLC 39**
See also CA 33-36R; 150; CANR 22, 63

Thompson, Francis Clegg
See Mencken, H(enry) L(ouis)

Thompson, Francis Joseph
1859-1907 .... **TCLC 4**
See also CA 104; CDBLB 1890-1914; DLB
19

Thompson, Hunter S(tockton)
1939- ... **CLC 9, 17, 40, 104; DAM POP**
See also BEST 89:1; CA 17-20R; CANR
23, 46, 74, 77; DA3; DLB 185; MTCW
1, 2

Thompson, James Myers
See Thompson, Jim (Myers)

Thompson, Jim (Myers)
1906-1977(?) .... **CLC 69**
See also CA 140; DLB 226

Thompson, Judith CLC 39

Thomson, James 1700-1748 ... **LC 16, 29, 40;
DAM POET**
See also DLB 95

Thomson, James 1834-1882 .... **NCLC 18;
DAM POET**
See also DLB 35

Thoreau, Henry David 1817-1862 .. **NCLC 7,
21, 61; DA; DAB; DAC; DAM MST;
PC 30; WLC**
See also CDALB 1640-1865; DA3; DLB 1,
223

Thornton, Hall
See Silverberg, Robert

Thucydides c. 455B.C.-399B.C. ..... **CMLC 17**
See also DLB 176

Thumboo, Edwin 1933- .... **PC 30**

Thurber, James (Grover)
1894-1961 .... **CLC 5, 11, 25, 125; DA;
DAB; DAC; DAM DRAM, MST, NOV;
SSC 1**
See also CA 73-76; CANR 17, 39; CDALB
1929-1941; DA3; DLB 4, 11, 22, 102;
MAICYA; MTCW 1, 2; SATA 13

Thurman, Wallace (Henry)
1902-1934 .... **TCLC 6; BLC 3; DAM
MULT**
See also BW 1, 3; CA 104; 124; CANR 81;
DLB 51

Tibullus, Albius c. 54B.C.-c.
19B.C. .... **CMLC 36**
See also DLB 211

Ticheburn, Cheviot
See Ainsworth, William Harrison

Tieck, (Johann) Ludwig
1773-1853 .... **NCLC 5, 46; SSC 31**
See also DLB 90

Tiger, Derry
See Ellison, Harlan (Jay)

Walker, Alice (Malsenior) 1944- ... CLC 5, 6,
9, 19, 27, 46, 58, 103; BLC 3; DA;
DAB; DAC; DAM MST, MULT, NOV,
POET, POP; PC 30; SSC 5; WLCS
See also AAYA 3, 33; BEST 89:4; BW 2, 3;
CA 37-40R; CANR 9, 27, 49, 66, 82;
CDALB 1968-1988; DA3; DLB 6, 33,
143; INT CANR-27; MTCW 1, 2; SATA
31

Walker, David Harry 1911-1992 ...... CLC 14
See also CA 1-4R; 137; CANR 1; SATA 8;
SATA-Obit 71

Walker, Edward Joseph 1934-
See Walker, Ted
See also CA 21-24R; CANR 12, 28, 53

Walker, George F. 1947- . CLC 44, 61; DAB;
DAC; DAM MST
See also CA 103; CANR 21, 43, 59; DLB
60

Walker, Joseph A. 1935- .... CLC 19; DAM
DRAM, MST
See also BW 1, 3; CA 89-92; CANR 26;
DLB 38

Walker, Margaret (Abigail)
1915-1998 .... CLC 1, 6; BLC; DAM
MULT; PC 20
See also BW 2, 3; CA 73-76; 172; CANR
26, 54, 76; DLB 76, 152; MTCW 1, 2

Walker, Ted CLC 13
See also Walker, Edward Joseph
See also DLB 40

Wallace, David Foster 1962- ..... CLC 50, 114
See also CA 132; CANR 59; DA3; MTCW
2

Wallace, Dexter
See Masters, Edgar Lee

Wallace, (Richard Horatio) Edgar
1875-1932 .... TCLC 57
See also CA 115; DLB 70

Wallace, Irving 1916-1990 .... CLC 7, 13;
DAM NOV, POP
See also AITN 1; CA 1-4R; 132; CAAS 1;
CANR 1, 27; INT CANR-27; MTCW 1,
2

Wallant, Edward Lewis 1926-1962 ... CLC 5,
10
See also CA 1-4R; CANR 22; DLB 2, 28,
143; MTCW 1, 2

Wallas, Graham 1858-1932 .... TCLC 91

Walley, Byron
See Card, Orson Scott

Walpole, Horace 1717-1797 .... LC 49
See also DLB 39, 104

Walpole, Hugh (Seymour)
1884-1941 .... TCLC 5
See also CA 104; 165; DLB 34; MTCW 2

Walser, Martin 1927- .... CLC 27
See also CA 57-60; CANR 8, 46; DLB 75,
124

Walser, Robert 1878-1956 .... TCLC 18; SSC
20
See also CA 118; 165; DLB 66

Walsh, Gillian Paton
See Paton Walsh, Gillian

Walsh, Jill Paton CLC 35
See also Paton Walsh, Gillian
See also CLR 2, 65

Walter, Villiam Christian
See Andersen, Hans Christian

Wambaugh, Joseph (Aloysius, Jr.)
1937- .... CLC 3, 18; DAM NOV, POP
See also AITN 1; BEST 89:3; CA 33-36R;
CANR 42, 65; DA3; DLB 6; DLBY 83;
MTCW 1, 2

Wang Wei 699(?)-761(?) .... PC 18

Ward, Arthur Henry Sarsfield 1883-1959
See Rohmer, Sax
See also CA 108; 173

Ward, Douglas Turner 1930- .... CLC 19
See also BW 1; CA 81-84; CANR 27; DLB
7, 38

Ward, E. D.
See Lucas, E(dward) V(errall)

Ward, Mary Augusta 1851-1920 ... TCLC 55
See also DLB 18

Ward, Peter
See Faust, Frederick (Schiller)

Warhol, Andy 1928(?)-1987 .... CLC 20
See also AAYA 12; BEST 89:4; CA 89-92;
121; CANR 34

Warner, Francis (Robert le Plastrier)
1937- .... CLC 14
See also CA 53-56; CANR 11

Warner, Marina 1946- .... CLC 59
See also CA 65-68; CANR 21, 55; DLB
194

Warner, Rex (Ernest) 1905-1986 ...... CLC 45
See also CA 89-92; 119; DLB 15

Warner, Susan (Bogert)
1819-1885 .... NCLC 31
See also DLB 3, 42

Warner, Sylvia (Constance) Ashton
See Ashton-Warner, Sylvia (Constance)

Warner, Sylvia Townsend
1893-1978 .... CLC 7, 19; SSC 23
See also CA 61-64; 77-80; CANR 16, 60;
DLB 34, 139; MTCW 1, 2

Warren, Mercy Otis 1728-1814 ..... NCLC 13
See also DLB 31, 200

Warren, Robert Penn 1905-1989 .. CLC 1, 4,
6, 8, 10, 13, 18, 39, 53, 59; DA; DAB;
DAC; DAM MST, NOV, POET; SSC 4;
WLC
See also AITN 1; CA 13-16R; 129; CANR
10, 47; CDALB 1968-1988; DA3; DLB
2, 48, 152; DLBY 80, 89; INT CANR-10;
MTCW 1, 2; SATA 46; SATA-Obit 63

Warshofsky, Isaac
See Singer, Isaac Bashevis

Warton, Thomas 1728-1790 ..... LC 15; DAM
POET
See also DLB 104, 109

Waruk, Kona
See Harris, (Theodore) Wilson

Warung, Price 1855-1911 .... TCLC 45
See also Astley, William

Warwick, Jarvis
See Garner, Hugh

Washington, Alex
See Harris, Mark

Washington, Booker T(aliaferro)
1856-1915 ...... TCLC 10; BLC 3; DAM
MULT
See also BW 1; CA 114; 125; DA3; SATA
28

Washington, George 1732-1799 .... LC 25
See also DLB 31

Wassermann, (Karl) Jakob
1873-1934 .... TCLC 6
See also CA 104; 163; DLB 66

Wasserstein, Wendy 1950- .. CLC 32, 59, 90;
DAM DRAM; DC 4
See also CA 121; 129; CABS 3; CANR 53,
75; DA3; DLB 228; INT 129; MTCW 2;
SATA 94

Waterhouse, Keith (Spencer) 1929- . CLC 47
See also CA 5-8R; CANR 38, 67; DLB 13,
15; MTCW 1, 2

Waters, Frank (Joseph) 1902-1995 .. CLC 88
See also CA 5-8R; 149; CAAS 13; CANR
3, 18, 63; DLB 212; DLBY 86

Waters, Roger 1944- .... CLC 35

Watkins, Frances Ellen
See Harper, Frances Ellen Watkins

Watkins, Gerrold
See Malzberg, Barry N(athaniel)

Watkins, Gloria Jean 1952(?)-
See hooks, bell
See also BW 2; CA 143; CANR 87; MTCW
2; SATA 115

Watkins, Paul 1964- .... CLC 55
See also CA 132; CANR 62

Watkins, Vernon Phillips
1906-1967 .... CLC 43
See also CA 9-10; 25-28R; CAP 1; DLB 20

Watson, Irving S.
See Mencken, H(enry) L(ouis)

Watson, John H.
See Farmer, Philip Jose

Watson, Richard F.
See Silverberg, Robert

Waugh, Auberon (Alexander) 1939- .. CLC 7
See also CA 45-48; CANR 6, 22, 92; DLB
14, 194

Waugh, Evelyn (Arthur St. John)
1903-1966 .. CLC 1, 3, 8, 13, 19, 27, 44,
107; DA; DAB; DAC; DAM MST,
NOV, POP; SSC 41; WLC
See also CA 85-88; 25-28R; CANR 22; CD-
BLB 1914-1945; DA3; DLB 15, 162, 195;
MTCW 1, 2

Waugh, Harriet 1944- .... CLC 6
See also CA 85-88; CANR 22

Ways, C. R.
See Blount, Roy (Alton), Jr.

Waystaff, Simon
See Swift, Jonathan

Webb, Beatrice (Martha Potter)
1858-1943 .... TCLC 22
See also CA 117; 162; DLB 190

Webb, Charles (Richard) 1939- .... CLC 7
See also CA 25-28R

Webb, James H(enry), Jr. 1946- ...... CLC 22
See also CA 81-84

Webb, Mary Gladys (Meredith)
1881-1927 .... TCLC 24
See also CA 182; 123; DLB 34

Webb, Mrs. Sidney
See Webb, Beatrice (Martha Potter)

Webb, Phyllis 1927- .... CLC 18
See also CA 104; CANR 23; DLB 53

Webb, Sidney (James) 1859-1947 .. TCLC 22
See also CA 117; 163; DLB 190

Webber, Andrew Lloyd CLC 21
See also Lloyd Webber, Andrew

Weber, Lenora Mattingly
1895-1971 .... CLC 12
See also CA 19-20; 29-32R; CAP 1; SATA
2; SATA-Obit 26

Weber, Max 1864-1920 .... TCLC 69
See also CA 109

Webster, John 1579(?)-1634(?) ... LC 33; DA;
DAB; DAC; DAM DRAM, MST; DC
2; WLC
See also CDBLB Before 1660; DLB 58

Webster, Noah 1758-1843 .... NCLC 30
See also DLB 1, 37, 42, 43, 73

Wedekind, (Benjamin) Frank(lin)
1864-1918 .... TCLC 7; DAM DRAM
See also CA 104; 153; DLB 118

Weidman, Jerome 1913-1998 .... CLC 7
See also AITN 2; CA 1-4R; 171; CANR 1;
DLB 28

Weil, Simone (Adolphine)
1909-1943 .... TCLC 23
See also CA 117; 159; MTCW 2

Weininger, Otto 1880-1903 .... TCLC 84

Weinstein, Nathan
See West, Nathanael

Weinstein, Nathan von Wallenstein
See West, Nathanael

Weir, Peter (Lindsay) 1944- .... CLC 20
See also CA 113; 123

Wicker, Tom CLC **7**
    See also Wicker, Thomas Grey
Wideman, John Edgar 1941- ...... CLC **5, 34, 36, 67, 122; BLC 3; DAM MULT**
    See also BW 2, 3; CA 85-88; CANR 14, 42, 67; DLB 33, 143; MTCW 2
Wiebe, Rudy (Henry) 1934- .. CLC **6, 11, 14, 138; DAC; DAM MST**
    See also CA 37-40R; CANR 42, 67; DLB 60
Wieland, Christoph Martin
    1733-1813 .... NCLC **17**
    See also DLB 97
Wiene, Robert 1881-1938 .... TCLC **56**
Wieners, John 1934- .... CLC **7**
    See also CA 13-16R; DLB 16
Wiesel, Elie(zer) 1928- .... CLC **3, 5, 11, 37; DA; DAB; DAC; DAM MST, NOV; WLCS**
    See also AAYA 7; AITN 1; CA 5-8R; CAAS 4; CANR 8, 40, 65; CDALBS; DA3; DLB 83; DLBY 87; INT CANR-8; MTCW 1, 2; SATA 56
Wiggins, Marianne 1947- .... CLC **57**
    See also BEST 89:3; CA 130; CANR 60
Wight, James Alfred 1916-1995
    See Herriot, James
    See also CA 77-80; SATA 55; SATA-Brief 44
Wilbur, Richard (Purdy) 1921- ..... CLC **3, 6, 9, 14, 53, 110; DA; DAB; DAC; DAM MST, POET**
    See also CA 1-4R; CABS 2; CANR 2, 29, 76, 93; CDALBS; DLB 5, 169; INT CANR-29; MTCW 1, 2; SATA 9, 108
Wild, Peter 1940- .... CLC **14**
    See also CA 37-40R; DLB 5
Wilde, Oscar (Fingal O'Flahertie Wills)
    1854(?)-1900 .... TCLC **1, 8, 23, 41; DA; DAB; DAC; DAM DRAM, MST, NOV; SSC 11; WLC**
    See also CA 104; 119; CDBLB 1890-1914; DA3; DLB 10, 19, 34, 57, 141, 156, 190; SATA 24
Wilder, Billy CLC **20**
    See also Wilder, Samuel
    See also DLB 26
Wilder, Samuel 1906-
    See Wilder, Billy
    See also CA 89-92
Wilder, Thornton (Niven)
    1897-1975 .. CLC **1, 5, 6, 10, 15, 35, 82; DA; DAB; DAC; DAM DRAM, MST, NOV; DC 1; WLC**
    See also AAYA 29; AITN 2; CA 13-16R; 61-64; CANR 40; CDALBS; DA3; DLB 4, 7, 9, 228; DLBY 97; MTCW 1, 2
Wilding, Michael 1942- .... CLC **73**
    See also CA 104; CANR 24, 49
Wiley, Richard 1944- .... CLC **44**
    See also CA 121; 129; CANR 71
Wilhelm, Kate CLC **7**
    See also Wilhelm, Katie (Gertrude)
    See also AAYA 20; CAAS 5; DLB 8; INT CANR-17
Wilhelm, Katie (Gertrude) 1928-
    See Wilhelm, Kate
    See also CA 37-40R; CANR 17, 36, 60, 94; MTCW 1
Wilkins, Mary
    See Freeman, Mary E(leanor) Wilkins
Willard, Nancy 1936- .... CLC **7, 37**
    See also CA 89-92; CANR 10, 39, 68; CLR 5; DLB 5, 52; MAICYA; MTCW 1; SATA 37, 71; SATA-Brief 30
William of Ockham 1285-1347 ..... CMLC **32**
Williams, Ben Ames 1889-1953 ..... TCLC **89**
    See also CA 183; DLB 102

Williams, C(harles) K(enneth)
    1936- .... CLC **33, 56; DAM POET**
    See also CA 37-40R; CAAS 26; CANR 57; DLB 5
Williams, Charles
    See Collier, James L(incoln)
Williams, Charles (Walter Stansby)
    1886-1945 .... TCLC **1, 11**
    See also CA 104; 163; DLB 100, 153
Williams, (George) Emlyn
    1905-1987 .... CLC **15; DAM DRAM**
    See also CA 104; 123; CANR 36; DLB 10, 77; MTCW 1
Williams, Hank 1923-1953 .... TCLC **81**
Williams, Hugo 1942- .... CLC **42**
    See also CA 17-20R; CANR 45; DLB 40
Williams, J. Walker
    See Wodehouse, P(elham) G(renville)
Williams, John A(lfred) 1925- ..... CLC **5, 13; BLC 3; DAM MULT**
    See also BW 2, 3; CA 53-56; CAAS 3; CANR 6, 26, 51; DLB 2, 33; INT CANR-6
Williams, Jonathan (Chamberlain)
    1929- .... CLC **13**
    See also CA 9-12R; CAAS 12; CANR 8; DLB 5
Williams, Joy 1944- .... CLC **31**
    See also CA 41-44R; CANR 22, 48
Williams, Norman 1952- .... CLC **39**
    See also CA 118
Williams, Sherley Anne 1944-1999 . CLC **89; BLC 3; DAM MULT, POET**
    See also BW 2, 3; CA 73-76; 185; CANR 25, 82; DLB 41; INT CANR-25; SATA 78; SATA-Obit 116
Williams, Shirley
    See Williams, Sherley Anne
Williams, Tennessee 1911-1983 . CLC **1, 2, 5, 7, 8, 11, 15, 19, 30, 39, 45, 71, 111; DA; DAB; DAC; DAM DRAM, MST; DC 4; WLC**
    See also AAYA 31; AITN 1, 2; CA 5-8R; 108; CABS 3; CANR 31; CDALB 1941-1968; DA3; DLB 7; DLBD 4; DLBY 83; MTCW 1, 2
Williams, Thomas (Alonzo)
    1926-1990 .... CLC **14**
    See also CA 1-4R; 132; CANR 2
Williams, William C.
    See Williams, William Carlos
Williams, William Carlos
    1883-1963 .... CLC **1, 2, 5, 9, 13, 22, 42, 67; DA; DAB; DAC; DAM MST, POET; PC 7; SSC 31**
    See also CA 89-92; CANR 34; CDALB 1917-1929; DA3; DLB 4, 16, 54, 86; MTCW 1, 2
Williamson, David (Keith) 1942- ..... CLC **56**
    See also CA 103; CANR 41
Williamson, Ellen Douglas 1905-1984
    See Douglas, Ellen
    See also CA 17-20R; 114; CANR 39
Williamson, Jack CLC **29**
    See also Williamson, John Stewart
    See also CAAS 8; DLB 8
Williamson, John Stewart 1908-
    See Williamson, Jack
    See also CA 17-20R; CANR 23, 70
Willie, Frederick
    See Lovecraft, H(oward) P(hillips)
Willingham, Calder (Baynard, Jr.)
    1922-1995 .... CLC **5, 51**
    See also CA 5-8R; 147; CANR 3; DLB 2, 44; MTCW 1
Willis, Charles
    See Clarke, Arthur C(harles)
Willy
    See Colette, (Sidonie-Gabrielle)

Willy, Colette
    See Colette, (Sidonie-Gabrielle)
Wilson, A(ndrew) N(orman) 1950- .. CLC **33**
    See also CA 112; 122; DLB 14, 155, 194; MTCW 2
Wilson, Angus (Frank Johnstone)
    1913-1991 . CLC **2, 3, 5, 25, 34; SSC 21**
    See also CA 5-8R; 134; CANR 21; DLB 15, 139, 155; MTCW 1, 2
Wilson, August 1945- ... CLC **39, 50, 63, 118; BLC 3; DA; DAB; DAC; DAM DRAM, MST, MULT; DC 2; WLCS**
    See also AAYA 16; BW 2, 3; CA 115; 122; CANR 42, 54, 76; DA3; DLB 228; MTCW 1, 2
Wilson, Brian 1942- .... CLC **12**
Wilson, Colin 1931- .... CLC **3, 14**
    See also CA 1-4R; CAAS 5; CANR 1, 22, 33, 77; DLB 14, 194; MTCW 1
Wilson, Dirk
    See Pohl, Frederik
Wilson, Edmund 1895-1972 .. CLC **1, 2, 3, 8, 24**
    See also CA 1-4R; 37-40R; CANR 1, 46; DLB 63; MTCW 1, 2
Wilson, Ethel Davis (Bryant)
    1888(?)-1980 .... CLC **13; DAC; DAM POET**
    See also CA 102; DLB 68; MTCW 1
Wilson, Harriet E. Adams
    1828(?)-1863(?) .... NCLC **78; BLC 3; DAM MULT**
    See also DLB 50
Wilson, John 1785-1854 .... NCLC **5**
Wilson, John (Anthony) Burgess 1917-1993
    See Burgess, Anthony
    See also CA 1-4R; 143; CANR 2, 46; DAC; DAM NOV; DA3; MTCW 1, 2
Wilson, Lanford 1937- .... CLC **7, 14, 36; DAM DRAM**
    See also CA 17-20R; CABS 3; CANR 45; DLB 7
Wilson, Robert M. 1944- .... CLC **7, 9**
    See also CA 49-52; CANR 2, 41; MTCW 1
Wilson, Robert McLiam 1964- .... CLC **59**
    See also CA 132
Wilson, Sloan 1920- .... CLC **32**
    See also CA 1-4R; CANR 1, 44
Wilson, Snoo 1948- .... CLC **33**
    See also CA 69-72
Wilson, William S(mith) 1932- .... CLC **49**
    See also CA 81-84
Wilson, (Thomas) Woodrow
    1856-1924 .... TCLC **79**
    See also CA 166; DLB 47
Winchilsea, Anne (Kingsmill) Finch Counte
    1661-1720
    See Finch, Anne
Windham, Basil
    See Wodehouse, P(elham) G(renville)
Wingrove, David (John) 1954- .... CLC **68**
    See also CA 133
Winnemucca, Sarah 1844-1891 ..... NCLC **79**
Winstanley, Gerrard 1609-1676 .... LC **52**
Wintergreen, Jane
    See Duncan, Sara Jeannette
Winters, Janet Lewis CLC **41**
    See also Lewis, Janet
    See also DLBY 87
Winters, (Arthur) Yvor 1900-1968 .... CLC **4, 8, 32**
    See also CA 11-12; 25-28R; CAP 1; DLB 48; MTCW 1
Winterson, Jeanette 1959- .... CLC **64; DAM POP**
    See also CA 136; CANR 58; DA3; DLB 207; MTCW 2
Winthrop, John 1588-1649 .... LC **31**
    See also DLB 24, 30

Yevtushenko, Yevgeny (Alexandrovich)
1933- .. **CLC 1, 3, 13, 26, 51, 126; DAM POET**
See also CA 81-84; CANR 33, 54; MTCW 1

Yezierska, Anzia 1885(?)-1970 .... **CLC 46**
See also CA 126; 89-92; DLB 28, 221; MTCW 1

Yglesias, Helen 1915- .... **CLC 7, 22**
See also CA 37-40R; CAAS 20; CANR 15, 65; INT CANR-15; MTCW 1

Yokomitsu, Riichi 1898-1947 .... **TCLC 47**
See also CA 170

Yonge, Charlotte (Mary)
1823-1901 .... **TCLC 48**
See also CA 109; 163; DLB 18, 163; SATA 17

York, Jeremy
See Creasey, John

York, Simon
See Heinlein, Robert A(nson)

Yorke, Henry Vincent 1905-1974 ..... **CLC 13**
See also Green, Henry
See also CA 85-88; 49-52

Yosano Akiko 1878-1942 .... **TCLC 59; PC 11**
See also CA 161

Yoshimoto, Banana CLC 84
See also Yoshimoto, Mahoko

Yoshimoto, Mahoko 1964-
See Yoshimoto, Banana
See also CA 144

Young, Al(bert James) 1939- . **CLC 19; BLC 3; DAM MULT**
See also BW 2, 3; CA 29-32R; CANR 26, 65; DLB 33

Young, Andrew (John) 1885-1971 ...... **CLC 5**
See also CA 5-8R; CANR 7, 29

Young, Collier
See Bloch, Robert (Albert)

Young, Edward 1683-1765 .... **LC 3, 40**
See also DLB 95

Young, Marguerite (Vivian)
1909-1995 .... **CLC 82**
See also CA 13-16; 150; CAP 1

Young, Neil 1945- .... **CLC 17**
See also CA 110

Young Bear, Ray A. 1950- ..... **CLC 94; DAM MULT**
See also CA 146; DLB 175; NNAL

Yourcenar, Marguerite 1903-1987 ... **CLC 19, 38, 50, 87; DAM NOV**
See also CA 69-72; CANR 23, 60, 93; DLB 72; DLBY 88; MTCW 1, 2

Yuan, Chu 340(?)B.C.-278(?)B.C. . **CMLC 36**

Yurick, Sol 1925- .... **CLC 6**
See also CA 13-16R; CANR 25

Zabolotsky, Nikolai Alekseevich
1903-1958 .... **TCLC 52**
See also CA 116; 164

Zagajewski, Adam 1945- .... **PC 27**
See also CA 186; DLB 232

Zamiatin, Yevgenii
See Zamyatin, Evgeny Ivanovich

Zamora, Bernice (B. Ortiz) 1938- .. **CLC 89; DAM MULT; HLC 2**
See also CA 151; CANR 80; DLB 82; HW 1, 2

Zamyatin, Evgeny Ivanovich
1884-1937 .... **TCLC 8, 37**
See also CA 105; 166

Zangwill, Israel 1864-1926 .... **TCLC 16**
See also CA 109; 167; DLB 10, 135, 197

Zappa, Francis Vincent, Jr. 1940-1993
See Zappa, Frank
See also CA 108; 143; CANR 57

Zappa, Frank CLC 17
See also Zappa, Francis Vincent, Jr.

Zaturenska, Marya 1902-1982 ..... **CLC 6, 11**
See also CA 13-16R; 105; CANR 22

Zeami 1363-1443 .... **DC 7**

Zelazny, Roger (Joseph) 1937-1995 . **CLC 21**
See also AAYA 7; CA 21-24R; 148; CANR 26, 60; DLB 8; MTCW 1, 2; SATA 57; SATA-Brief 39

Zhdanov, Andrei Alexandrovich
1896-1948 .... **TCLC 18**
See also CA 117; 167

Zhukovsky, Vasily (Andreevich)
1783-1852 .... **NCLC 35**
See also DLB 205

Ziegenhagen, Eric CLC 55

Zimmer, Jill Schary
See Robinson, Jill

Zimmerman, Robert
See Dylan, Bob

Zindel, Paul 1936- ..... **CLC 6, 26; DA; DAB; DAC; DAM DRAM, MST, NOV; DC 5**
See also AAYA 2, 37; CA 73-76; CANR 31, 65; CDALBS; CLR 3, 45; DA3; DLB 7, 52; JRDA; MAICYA; MTCW 1, 2; SATA 16, 58, 102

Zinov'Ev, A. A.
See Zinoviev, Alexander (Aleksandrovich)

Zinoviev, Alexander (Aleksandrovich)
1922- .... **CLC 19**
See also CA 116; 133; CAAS 10

Zoilus
See Lovecraft, H(oward) P(hillips)

Zola, Emile (Edouard Charles Antoine)
1840-1902 .... **TCLC 1, 6, 21, 41; DA; DAB; DAC; DAM MST, NOV; WLC**
See also CA 104; 138; DA3; DLB 123

Zoline, Pamela 1941- .... **CLC 62**
See also CA 161

Zoroaster 628(?)B.C.-551(?)B.C. ... **CMLC 40**

Zorrilla y Moral, Jose 1817-1893 .... **NCLC 6**

Zoshchenko, Mikhail (Mikhailovich)
1895-1958 .... **TCLC 15; SSC 15**
See also CA 115; 160

Zuckmayer, Carl 1896-1977 .... **CLC 18**
See also CA 69-72; DLB 56, 124

Zuk, Georges
See Skelton, Robin

Zukofsky, Louis 1904-1978 ... **CLC 1, 2, 4, 7, 11, 18; DAM POET; PC 11**
See also CA 9-12R; 77-80; CANR 39; DLB 5, 165; MTCW 1

Zweig, Paul 1935-1984 .... **CLC 34, 42**
See also CA 85-88; 113

Zweig, Stefan 1881-1942 .... **TCLC 17**
See also CA 112; 170; DLB 81, 118

Zwingli, Huldreich 1484-1531 .... **LC 37**
See also DLB 179

Literary Criticism Series
Cumulative Topic Index

This index lists all topic entries in Gale's *Classical and Medieval Literature Criticism, Contemporary Literary Criticism, Literature Criticism from 1400 to 1800, Nineteenth-Century Literature Criticism,* and *Twentieth-Century Literary Criticism.*

the influence of science and occultism, 254-66

supernatural fiction and society, 266-86

Supernatural Fiction, Modern TCLC 30: 59-116

evolution and varieties, 60-74

"decline" of the ghost story, 74-86

as a literary genre, 86-92

technique, 92-101

nature and appeal, 101-15

Surrealism TCLC 30: 334-406

history and formative influences, 335-43

manifestos, 343-54

philosophic, aesthetic, and political principles, 354-75

poetry, 375-81

novel, 381-6

drama, 386-92

film, 392-8

painting and sculpture, 398-403

achievement, 403-5

Symbolism, Russian TCLC 30: 266-333

doctrines and major figures, 267-92

theories, 293-8

and French Symbolism, 298-310

themes in poetry, 310-4

theater, 314-20

and the fine arts, 320-32

Symbolist Movement, French NCLC 20: 169-249

background and characteristics, 170-86

principles, 186-91

attacked and defended, 191-7

influences and predecessors, 197-211

and Decadence, 211-6

theater, 216-26

prose, 226-33

decline and influence, 233-47

Television and Literature TCLC 78: 283-426

television and literacy, 283-98

reading vs. watching, 298-341

adaptations, 341-62

literary genres and television, 362-90

television genres and literature, 390-410

children's literature/children's television, 410-25

Theater of the Absurd TCLC 38: 339-415

"The Theater of the Absurd," 340-7

major plays and playwrights, 347-58

and the concept of the absurd, 358-86

theatrical techniques, 386-94

predecessors of, 394-402

influence of, 402-13

Tin Pan Alley See American Popular Song, Golden Age of

Tobacco Culture LC 55: 299-366

social and economic attitudes toward tobacco, 299-344

tobacco trade between the old world and the new world, 344-55

tobacco smuggling in Great Britain, 355-66

Transcendentalism, American NCLC 24: 1-99

overviews, 3-23

contemporary documents, 23-41

theological aspects of, 42-52

and social issues, 52-74

literature of, 74-96

Travel Writing in the Nineteenth Century NCLC 44: 274-392

the European grand tour, 275-303

the Orient, 303-47

North America, 347-91

Travel Writing in the Twentieth Century TCLC 30: 407-56

conventions and traditions, 407-27

and fiction writing, 427-43

comparative essays on travel writers, 443-54

Tristan and Isolde Legend CMLC 42: 311-404

True-Crime Literature CLC 99: 333-433

history and analysis, 334-407

reviews of true-crime publications, 407-23

writing instruction, 424-29

author profiles, 429-33

***Ulysses* and the Process of Textual Reconstruction** TCLC 26:386-416

evaluations of the new *Ulysses,* 386-94

editorial principles and procedures, 394-401

theoretical issues, 401-16

Utilitarianism NCLC 84: 272-340

J. S. Mill's Utilitarianism: liberty, equality, justice, 273-313

Jeremy Bentham's Utilitarianism: the science of happiness, 313-39

Utopianism NCLC 88: 238-346

overviews: Utopian literature, 239-59

Utopianism in American literature, 259-99

Utopianism in British literature, 299-311

Utopianism and Feminism, 311-45

Utopian Literature, Nineteenth-Century NCLC 24: 353-473

definitions, 354-74

overviews, 374-88

theory, 388-408

communities, 409-26

fiction, 426-53

women and fiction, 454-71

Utopian Literature, Renaissance LC 32: 1-63

overviews, 2-25

classical background, 25-33

utopia and the social contract, 33-9

origins in mythology, 39-48

utopia and the Renaissance country house, 48-52

influence of millenarianism, 52-62

Vampire in Literature TCLC 46: 391-454

origins and evolution, 392-412

social and psychological perspectives, 413-44

vampire fiction and science fiction, 445-53

Victorian Autobiography NCLC 40: 277-363

development and major characteristics, 278-88

themes and techniques, 289-313

the autobiographical tendency in Victorian prose and poetry, 313-47

Victorian women's autobiographies, 347-62

Victorian Fantasy Literature NCLC 60: 246-384

overviews, 247-91

major figures, 292-366

women in Victorian fantasy literature, 366-83

Victorian Hellenism NCLC 68: 251-376

overviews, 252-78

the meanings of Hellenism, 278-335

the literary influence, 335-75

Victorian Novel NCLC 32: 288-454

development and major characteristics, 290-310

themes and techniques, 310-58

social criticism in the Victorian novel, 359-97

urban and rural life in the Victorian novel, 397-406

women in the Victorian novel, 406-25

Mudie's Circulating Library, 425-34

the late-Victorian novel, 434-51

Vietnamese Literature TCLC 102: 322-386

Vietnam War in Literature and Film CLC 91: 383-437

overview, 384-8

prose, 388-412

film and drama, 412-24

poetry, 424-35

Violence in Literature TCLC 98: 235-358

overviews and general studies, 236-74

violence in the works of modern authors, 274-358

Vorticism TCLC 62: 330-426

Wyndham Lewis and Vorticism, 330-8

characteristics and principles of Vorticism, 338-65

Lewis and Pound, 365-82

Vorticist writing, 382-416

Vorticist painting, 416-26

Well-Made Play, The NCLC 80: 331-370

overviews, 332-45

Scribe's style, 345-56

the influence of the well-made play, 356-69

Women's Autobiography, Nineteenth Century NCLC 76: 285-368

overviews, 287-300

autobiographies concerned with religious and political issues, 300-15

autobiographies by women of color, 315-38

autobiographies by women pioneers, 338-51

autobiographies by women of letters, 351-68

Women's Diaries, Nineteenth-Century NCLC 48: 308-54

overview, 308-13

diary as history, 314-25

sociology of diaries, 325-34

diaries as psychological scholarship, 334-43

diary as autobiography, 343-8

diary as literature, 348-53

Women in Modern Literature TCLC 94: 262-425

overviews, 263-86

American literature, 286-304

other national literatures, 304-33

fiction, 333-94

poetry, 394-407

drama, 407-24

Women Writers, Seventeenth-Century LC 30: 2-58

overview, 2-15

women and education, 15-9

women and autobiography, 19-31

women's diaries, 31-9

early feminists, 39-58

World War I Literature TCLC 34: 392-486

overview, 393-403

English, 403-27

German, 427-50

American, 450-66

French, 466-74

and modern history, 474-82

Yellow Journalism NCLC 36: 383-456

overviews, 384-96

major figures, 396-413

Young Playwrights Festival

1988 CLC 55: 376-81

1989 CLC 59: 398-403

1990 CLC 65: 444-8

NCLC Cumulative Nationality Index

AMERICAN

Alcott, Amos Bronson **1**
Alcott, Louisa May **6, 58, 83**
Alger, Horatio Jr. Jr. **8, 83**
Allston, Washington **2**
Apess, William **73**
Audubon, John James **47**
Barlow, Joel **23**
Beecher, Catharine Esther **30**
Bellamy, Edward **4, 86**
Bird, Robert Montgomery **1**
Brackenridge, Hugh Henry **7**
Brentano, Clemens (Maria) **1**
Brown, Charles Brockden **22, 74**
Brown, William Wells **2, 89**
Brownson, Orestes Augustus **50**
Bryant, William Cullen **6, 46**
Burney, Fanny **12, 54**
Calhoun, John Caldwell **15**
Channing, William Ellery **17**
Child, Lydia Maria **6, 73**
Chivers, Thomas Holley **49**
Cooke, John Esten **5**
Cooper, James Fenimore **1, 27, 54**
Crockett, David **8**
Dana, Richard Henry Sr. **53**
Delany, Martin Robinson **93**
Dickinson, Emily (Elizabeth) **21, 77**
Douglass, Frederick **7, 55**
Dunlap, William **2**
Dwight, Timothy **13**
Emerson, Mary Moody **66**
Emerson, Ralph Waldo **1, 38**
Field, Eugene **3**
Foster, Stephen Collins **26**
Frederic, Harold **10**
Freneau, Philip Morin **1**
Hale, Sarah Josepha (Buell) **75**
Halleck, Fitz-Greene **47**
Hamilton, Alexander **49**
Hammon, Jupiter **5**
Harris, George Washington **23**
Hawthorne, Nathaniel **2, 10, 17, 23, 39, 79, 95**
Hayne, Paul Hamilton **94**
Holmes, Oliver Wendell **14, 81**
Horton, George Moses **87**
Irving, Washington **2, 19, 95**
Jackson, Helen Hunt **90**
Jacobs, Harriet A(nn) **67**
James, Henry Sr. **53**
Jefferson, Thomas **11**
Kennedy, John Pendleton **2**
Kirkland, Caroline M. **85**
Lanier, Sidney **6**
Lazarus, Emma **8**
Lincoln, Abraham **18**
Longfellow, Henry Wadsworth **2, 45**
Lowell, James Russell **2, 90**
Melville, Herman **3, 12, 29, 45, 49, 91, 93**
Mowatt, Anna Cora **74**
Murray, Judith Sargent **63**

Parkman, Francis Jr. Jr. **12**
Parton, Sara Payson Willis **86**
Paulding, James Kirke **2**
Pinkney, Edward **31**
Poe, Edgar Allan **1, 16, 55, 78, 94**
Rowson, Susanna Haswell **5, 69**
Sedgwick, Catharine Maria **19**
Shaw, Henry Wheeler **15**
Sheridan, Richard Brinsley **5, 91**
Sigourney, Lydia Howard (Huntley) **21, 87**
Simms, William Gilmore **3**
Smith, Joseph Jr. **53**
Southworth, Emma Dorothy Eliza
 Nevitte **26**
Stowe, Harriet (Elizabeth) Beecher **3, 50**
Taylor, Bayard **89**
Thoreau, Henry David **7, 21, 61**
Timrod, Henry **25**
Trumbull, John **30**
Truth, Sojourner **94**
Tyler, Royall **3**
Very, Jones **9**
Warner, Susan (Bogert) **31**
Warren, Mercy Otis **13**
Webster, Noah **30**
Whitman, Sarah Helen (Power) **19**
Whitman, Walt(er) **4, 31, 81**
Whittier, John Greenleaf **8, 59**
Wilson, Harriet E. Adams **78**
Winnemucca, Sarah **79**

ARGENTINIAN

Echeverria, (Jose) Esteban (Antonino) **18**
Hernandez, Jose **17**

AUSTRALIAN

Adams, Francis **33**
Clarke, Marcus (Andrew Hislop) **19**
Gordon, Adam Lindsay **21**
Kendall, Henry **12**

AUSTRIAN

Grillparzer, Franz **1**
Lenau, Nikolaus **16**
Nestroy, Johann **42**
Raimund, Ferdinand Jakob **69**
Sacher-Masoch, Leopold von **31**
Stifter, Adalbert **41**

CANADIAN

Crawford, Isabella Valancy **12**
Haliburton, Thomas Chandler **15**
Lampman, Archibald **25**
Moodie, Susanna (Strickland) **14**
Richardson, John **55**
Traill, Catharine Parr **31**

COLOMBIAN

Isaacs, Jorge Ricardo **70**

CUBAN

Marti (y Perez), Jose (Julian) **63**

CZECH

Macha, Karel Hynek **46**

DANISH

Andersen, Hans Christian **7, 79**
Grundtvig, Nicolai Frederik Severin **1**
Jacobsen, Jens Peter **34**
Kierkegaard, Soren **34, 78**

ENGLISH

Ainsworth, William Harrison **13**
Arnold, Matthew **6, 29, 89**
Arnold, Thomas **18**
Austen, Jane **1, 13, 19, 33, 51, 81, 95**
Bagehot, Walter **10**
Barbauld, Anna Laetitia **50**
Barham, Richard Harris **77**
Barnes, William **75**
Beardsley, Aubrey **6**
Beckford, William **16**
Beddoes, Thomas Lovell **3**
Bentham, Jeremy **38**
Blake, William **13, 37, 57**
Borrow, George (Henry) **9**
Bronte, Anne **4, 71**
Bronte, Charlotte **3, 8, 33, 58**
Bronte, Emily (Jane) **16, 35**
Browning, Elizabeth Barrett **1, 16, 61, 66**
Browning, Robert **19, 79**
Bulwer-Lytton, Edward (George Earle Lytton) **1, 45**
Burton, Richard F(rancis) **42**
Byron, George Gordon (Noel) **2, 12**
Carlyle, Thomas **22, 70**
Carroll, Lewis **2, 53**
Clare, John **9, 86**
Clough, Arthur Hugh **27**
Cobbett, William **49**
Coleridge, Hartley **90**
Coleridge, Samuel Taylor **9, 54**
Coleridge, Sara **31**
Collins, (William) Wilkie **1, 18, 93**
Cowper, William **8, 94**
Crabbe, George **26**
Craik, Dinah Maria (Mulock) **38**
Darwin, Charles **57**
De Quincey, Thomas **4, 87**
Dickens, Charles (John Huffam) **3, 8, 18, 26, 37, 50, 86**
Disraeli, Benjamin **2, 39, 79**
Dobell, Sydney Thompson **43**
Du Maurier, George **86**
Eden, Emily **10**
Eliot, George **4, 13, 23, 41, 49, 89**
FitzGerald, Edward **9**
Forster, John **11**
Froude, James Anthony **43**
Gaskell, Elizabeth Cleghorn **5, 70**

Mazzini, Guiseppe **34**
Nievo, Ippolito **22**

JAPANESE

Ichiyo, Higuchi **49**
Motoori, Norinaga **45**

LITHUANIAN

Mapu, Abraham (ben Jekutiel) **18**

MEXICAN

Lizardi, Jose Joaquin Fernandez de **30**

NORWEGIAN

Collett, (Jacobine) Camilla (Wergeland) **22**
Wergeland, Henrik Arnold **5**

POLISH

Fredro, Aleksander **8**
Krasicki, Ignacy **8**
Krasinski, Zygmunt **4**
Mickiewicz, Adam **3**
Norwid, Cyprian Kamil **17**
Slowacki, Juliusz **15**

ROMANIAN

Eminescu, Mihail **33**

RUSSIAN

Aksakov, Sergei Timofeyvich **2**
Bakunin, Mikhail (Alexandrovich) **25, 58**
Bashkirtseff, Marie **27**

Belinski, Vissarion Grigoryevich **5**
Chernyshevsky, Nikolay Gavrilovich **1**
Dobrolyubov, Nikolai Alexandrovich **5**
Dostoevsky, Fedor Mikhailovich **2, 7, 21, 33, 43**
Gogol, Nikolai (Vasilyevich) **5, 15, 31**
Goncharov, Ivan Alexandrovich **1, 63**
Granovsky, Timofei Nikolaevich **75**
Herzen, Aleksandr Ivanovich **10, 61**
Karamzin, Nikolai Mikhailovich **3**
Krylov, Ivan Andreevich **1**
Lermontov, Mikhail Yuryevich **5, 47**
Leskov, Nikolai (Semyonovich) **25**
Nekrasov, Nikolai Alekseevich **11**
Ostrovsky, Alexander **30, 57**
Pisarev, Dmitry Ivanovich **25**
Pushkin, Alexander (Sergeyevich) **3, 27, 83**
Saltykov, Mikhail Evgrafovich **16**
Smolenskin, Peretz **30**
Turgenev, Ivan **21, 37**
Tyutchev, Fyodor **34**
Zhukovsky, Vasily (Andreevich) **35**

SCOTTISH

Baillie, Joanna **2**
Beattie, James **25**
Blair, Hugh **75**
Campbell, Thomas **19**
Carlyle, Thomas **22, 70**
Ferrier, Susan (Edmonstone) **8**
Galt, John **1**
Hogg, James **4**
Jeffrey, Francis **33**
Lockhart, John Gibson **6**

Mackenzie, Henry **41**
Oliphant, Margaret (Oliphant Wilson) **11, 61**
Scott, Walter **15, 69**
Stevenson, Robert Louis (Balfour) **5, 14, 63**
Thomson, James **18**
Wilson, John **5**
Wright, Frances **74**

SPANISH

Alarcon, Pedro Antonio de **1**
Caballero, Fernan **10**
Castro, Rosalia de **3, 78**
Espronceda, Jose de **39**
Larra (y Sanchez de Castro), Mariano Jose de **17**
Tamayo y Baus, Manuel **1**
Zorrilla y Moral, Jose **6**

SWEDISH

Almqvist, Carl Jonas Love **42**
Bremer, Fredrika **11**
Stagnelius, Eric Johan **61**
Tegner, Esaias **2**

SWISS

Amiel, Henri Frederic **4**
Burckhardt, Jacob (Christoph) **49**
Charriere, Isabelle de **66**
Keller, Gottfried **2**
Meyer, Conrad Ferdinand **81**
Wyss, Johann David Von **10**

UKRAINIAN

Shevchenko, Taras **54**

NCLC-95 Title Index

ISBN 0-7876-4550-8

FOR REFERENCE

Do not take from this room

LINCC